BRIEF CONTENTS

CONTENTS

1.00 INTRODUCTION TO SPORT LAW

2.00 NEGLIGENCE LAW

3.00 INTENTIONAL TORTS AND CRIMINAL ACTS

4.00 RISK MANAGEMENT

PREFACE

In this Sixth Edition, John, Doyice, and the contributing authors have worked hard to provide:

1. **An easy-to-read, user-friendly text** of accurate legal information appropriate for recreation majors, sport management majors, and recreation and sport managers in the field.

2. A recreation and sport law text that contains information that is **current and up-to-date.** Every chapter is updated in each edition and the book is revised every three years. We are able to do this only because we have 38 contributing authors who do considerable research and are serious about keeping the text fresh and accurate.

3. A text that can be effective with both **undergraduate and graduate students**. We try to use language that can be understood by the undergraduate in his or her first recreation or sport law class, and at the same time provide in-depth material appropriate for a graduate student.

4. A **wide range of topics** so that the professor can select the chapters and topics he or she feels are most important for his or her students. This book is the only book in the field that provides in-depth study in tort law, risk management, contract law, constitutional law, and sport-related legislation. This edition has 56 chapters from which to select.

5. **A reference book** for future use by the professor and student.

Change in the law is constant and the same is true for *Law for Recreation and Sport Managers*. In this edition, in addition to several new authors, we have **two major changes**.

1. **All chapters have been updated**. In this edition (1) some chapters had minor changes (updates, changes to add clarity, and/or new sections added); (2) some had major changes (usually due to substantial changes in the case law); (3) some chapters have been totally rewritten by new authors, updating the material and providing a fresh approach; and (4) almost all chapters have 5 relevant cases on the Supplemental Web Site—a total of about 275 sport and recreation related cases readily available to the professor and student.

2. **Two chapters address totally new topics.** In the Negligence Law section, Chapter 2.13 *Liability of Sports Participants, Sports Instructors, and Sports Officials* addresses the issue of under what circumstances these parties are liable for their own negligence. In the Constitutional Law section, Chapter 6.16 *First Amendment* examines the rights of Freedom of Speech; Freedom of the Press; and Freedom of Religion guaranteed under the United States Constitution.

OUR HOPE!

It is our hope that professors adopting the text and students using the text will find it even more helpful than previous editions. We welcome any comments or suggestions that would make the text more useful to you.

— Doyice and John

ACKNOWLEDGMENTS

Many persons deserve credit for the success of this 6th edition of **Law for Recreation and Sport Managers.**

First, thanks go to the diligent efforts of the chapter authors and co-authors. Their writing and research are major factors in making this the most widely-used text in the area of sport and recreation law. Special thanks to Kristi Schoepfer Bochicchio who bailed us out by accepting and writing an excellent chapter at the last minute.

We would also like to thank the following Syracuse University Sport Management students: Danielle Berman, Michael Botwinick, Danielle Czysz, Christine Davis, Charma Harris, Joshua Nightingale for providing some much needed assistance during the project.

An often unrecognized contributor to a book is the user—the professors who adopt the text and the students who use it. We would like to thank you for your loyalty and especially thank those of you who have written in with suggestions for improvement. This text is always changing (just like the law) and we try to address as many of your recommendations as possible. While some suggestions do not fit with the goals of the text, you will see many changes in the book. In the 5th edition, we added the Supplemental Web Site containing three cases relating to most chapters. In this edition, we have increased the number to five per chapter in most cases. Users will also note a few new topics have been added. Keep the suggestions coming!

Thanks go to Kendall Hunt's Lynne Rogers who is a model of efficiency and with whom it is always a pleasure to work. Also, thanks to the many behind-the-scenes professionals at Kendall Hunt Publishing who helped to make this edition successful.

And finally, thanks to our wives and families: to Doyice's wife, Mary, for her support and invaluable assistance in the editing process; and to John's wife and family, Nicole, J.T. and Katie, for their love and support.

— Doyice & John

ABOUT THE AUTHORS

DOYICE J. COTTEN

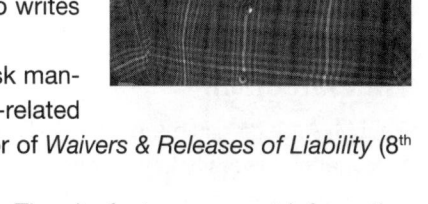

Doyice J. Cotten is an emeritus professor of sport management at Georgia Southern University where he taught graduate and undergraduate courses in sport law and risk management. He manages his own writing and risk management consulting business, Sport Risk Consulting.

Dr. Cotten's major area of interest is liability waivers. He speaks on waivers at conferences such as the Athletic Business Conference, the American College of Sports Medicine (ACSM), and the National Equine Law Conference. He also writes waivers for all types of sport and recreation businesses.

Dr. Cotten has published more than 150 articles on legal liability and risk management. He has collected and analyzed over 1,000 sport- and recreation-related waiver cases and has coauthored two books on the subject. He is co-author of *Waivers & Releases of Liability* (8th ed.) based on over 1200 sport and recreation waiver cases.

Readers are invited to visit Dr. Cotten's website, www.sportwaiver.com. The site features current information regarding both risk management and liability waivers and contains more than 150 articles by Dr. Cotten and many other authorities in the field.

JOHN T. WOLOHAN

Attorney John Wolohan is a professor of Sports Law and Graduate Director of the Sport Venue and Event Management Program in the Department of Sport Management in the David B. Falk College of Sport and Human Dynamics at Syracuse University.

As well as being the author of the "Sports Law Report" a monthly article that appears in *Athletic Business*, Professor Wolohan has also published numerous articles and book chapters in the areas of athlete's rights, intellectual property and antitrust issues in sport in such Journals as the *Marquette Sports Law Journal*, *Seton Hall Journal of Sports Law, Villanova Sports & Entertainment Law Journal, University of Missouri-Kansas City Law Review, Educational Law Reporter, International Sports Law Journal, Journal of the Legal Aspects of Sport and the Journal of Sport Management*. In addition, Professor Wolohan has made numerous presentations in the area of sports law to such organizations as the American Bar Association, International Sports Lawyers Association, Athletic Business, US Sport Congress, US Indoor Sports Association, the Sport and Recreation Law Association, the North American Society of Sport Management, the European Association for Sport Management and the Asser Sports Law Institute.

Professor Wolohan, who is a member of the Massachusetts Bar Associations, received his B.A. from the University of Massachusetts-Amherst, and his J.D. from Western New England University, School of Law.

CONTRIBUTING AUTHORS

Robin Ammon Jr.

Robin Ammon, Jr. is an Associate Professor and Sport Management Program Coordinator at the University of South Dakota. He received his B.S. degree from the University of Colorado in Physical Education, his M.S. degree from Louisiana State University in Exercises Science and his doctorate from the University of Northern Colorado in Sport Administration. Dr. Ammon currently teaches classes in Sport Law and in Facility and Event Management at both the undergraduate and graduate levels. His areas of research include: legal liabilities in sport, risk management in sport athletics, and premises liability. He is a co-author of four textbooks, plus he has authored chapters in many other edited texts. In addition, Dr. Ammon has 33 years of practical experience working with crowd and event management as a consultant and manager.

Paul Anderson

Paul M. Anderson is the Associate Director of the National Sports Law Institute and an Adjunct Professor of Law at Marquette University Law School. Professor Anderson teaches the advanced legal research—sports law, legal and business issues in collegiate athletics, legal issues in youth, high school and recreational sports, selected topics in sports law, entertainment law, and sections of sports venues, economics of sports, and athlete agent courses. He coordinates all events, internships, and the Sports Law Certificate program within Marquette's Sports Law program, the nation's most comprehensive sports law program. He also coordinates all events, publications, and activities of the National Sports Law Institute. He is the author or editor of several books and numerous chapters and articles. Professor Anderson is former Editor-in-Chief and current faculty co-advisor to the Marquette Sports Law Review, and former Editor of the Journal of Legal Aspects of Sport, and former Managing Editor of the Journal of Sport and Social Issues. A member of the Case-law Committee of the International Association of Sports Law, he is also Chair of the numerous national and international organizations including the Sports Lawyers Association and the ABA's Forum on Entertainment and Sports Industries. He earned his B.A. in economics and philosophy, cum laude and Phi Beta Kappa, and his J.D. from Marquette University where he also was the first recipient of the Joseph E. O'Neill scholarship for sports ethics.

Thomas A. Baker, III

Dr. Baker is an Assistant Professor at the Sport Management and Policy program at the University of Georgia. He conducts research in sport management that primarily focuses on the application of the law to sport. Within that focus he specializes in how commercial laws influence and affect the sport industry. Additionally, he conducts risk management research focused on: (a) preventing sexual abuse in youth sports, and (b) terrorism management at sports facilities. Dr. Baker received his Ph.D. from the University of Florida in Sport Management where he was a Dr. Charles W. LaPradd Ph.D. Fellow, earned the Clifford A. Boyd Graduate Scholarship Award, and the Norma M. Leavitt Scholarship. He earned his J.D. from Loyola University New Orleans School of Law where he graduated in the top 10% of his class (cum laude) earning the distinction of William L. Crowe, Cr. Scholar.

Paul Batista

Paul J. Batista, J.D., is an Associate Professor, Chair of the Sport Management Division, and Associate Department Head in the Department of Health and Kinesiology at Texas A&M University. He received his law degree from Baylor University Law School in 1976, and his B. S. in Business Administration from Trinity University in 1973. He is admitted to practice before the United States Supreme Court, is licensed to appear in all Texas courts, is a certified Mediator and Arbitrator, and is a former Judge in Burleson County, Texas. Prof. Batista has taught graduate and undergraduate courses involving the legal aspects of sport in the Sport Management program at Texas A & M since 1991. He has received the Association of Former Students Distinguished Achievement Award in Teaching, the Student Lead Award for Teaching Excellence, and has been named a Montague Center for Teaching Excellence Scholar. He is a member and Past President of the Sport and Recreation Law Association, which has named him a Research Fellow. His primary research interest is sports related liability issues in school settings, with particular emphasis on First Amendment religion and free speech issues. He has delivered research presentations at numerous conferences throughout the United States, as well as in Canada, China, Germany, Slovenia and South Korea.

Kristi Schoepfer Bochicchio

Kristi L. Schoepfer Bochicchio is an Associate Professor in the Department of Physical Education, Sport and Human Performance at Winthrop University in Rock Hill, South Carolina. She currently serves as Program Director for the undergraduate Sport Management Program and teaches Legal Issues in Sport courses at the undergraduate and graduate level. Additionally, she teaches Sport Marketing, Sport Public Relations and Introduction to Sport Management at the undergraduate level. She received a B.S. in Secondary Education from the University of Dayton and a J.D. from Marquette University. Additionally, she earned a certificate in Sport Law from the National Sport Law Institute. Prior to assuming her current position, she taught for five years at the University of Wisconsin-Parkside in Kenosha, Wisconsin.

Linda Jean Carpenter

Linda Jean Carpenter, Ph.D., J.D., Professor Emerita of Physical Education and Exercise Science at Brooklyn College of the City University of New York, is also a member of the New York State and United States Supreme Court Bars. She has published numerous books and articles as well as speaking at many national and international professional meetings. Her research, including the national longitudinal study on the status of women in sport, coauthored with Vivian Acosta and now in its 35th year, is frequently cited in scholarly writing as well as the lay press and has been used often in Senate and Congressional hearings on Title IX and equity in sport. She holds the B.S. and M.S. from Brigham Young University, the Ph.D. from the University of Southern California and the J.D. from Fordham Law School.

Rodney L. Caughron

Rod Caughron, Ph.D., is an Associate Professor in the KNPE/Sport Management Department at Northern Illinois University, and serves as Director of Graduate Studies in Sport Management. He received both his B.A. in Political Science and M.S. in Exercise Physiology from Iowa State University and his Ph.D. from The University of Iowa in Athletic Administration. Previous to his current position, Caughron served as Coordinator of Fitness for the Saudi Air Force and worked in the Student Services and ticket office at The University of Iowa. Professor Caughron currently teaches graduate courses in sport law and sport management and leadership.

Margaret Ciccolella

Margaret E. Ciccolella is a Professor in the Department of Health, Exercise, and Sport Sciences at the University of the Pacific. She received her doctorate in exercise physiology from Brigham Young University and her law degree from Humphreys College. Dr. Ciccolella's research focuses on the integration of law and science, and in recent years has published primarily in the area of disability law. At the University of the Pacific, she teaches graduate and undergraduate courses in sports law and higher education law.

Colleen Colles

Colleen Colles is a Professor in the Sport Industry Operations program at Metropolitan State College of Denver. She received her bachelor's degree in Health and Fitness Management from Northern Michigan University, her master's degree in Physical Education from Eastern Kentucky University and her doctorate in Sport Administration from the University of Northern Colorado. She has experience as a collegiate volleyball coach, event manager and employee wellness director. She is an active member of SRLA and NASSM and currently serves on the COSMA Board of Commissioners. Her primary research interests include gender equity in sport and sport management pedagogy.

Dan Connaughton

Dan Connaughton is a Professor in the Sport Management program in the Department of Tourism, Recreation & Sport Management at the University of Florida (UF). He received a B.S. in Exercise and Sport Sciences and a M.S. in Recreation from the UF, a M.S. in Physical Education (Administration) from Bridgewater State College, and an EdD. in Sport Administration from the Florida State University. Dr. Connaughton has held management positions in campus and public recreation departments, aquatic facilities, and health/fitness programs. At the UF, Connaughton teaches and conducts research in the areas of sport law and risk management. An author/co-author of three textbooks and several journal articles, he is a Research Fellow with the Sport and Recreation Law Association and with the Research Consortium of the AAHPERD.

Anne DeMartini

Anne L. DeMartini is an Assistant Professor of Sport Management at Flagler College where she teaches Sport Law, Sport Ethics, Sport Sociology and Introduction to Sport Management. She received her undergraduate degree in political science and physical education and exercise science from the University of North Carolina—Chapel Hill. She received a Master's degree in sports studies and juris doctorate from the University of Georgia. Her research interests include transgender participation in sport and college and university liability for non-traditional sports. She is an active member in the Sport and Recreation Law Association and a certified Level 1 Crossfit Trainer.

Mark Dodds

Mark Dodds is an Associate Professor teaching sport law and sport marketing at the State University of New York, College at Cortland. He holds a J.D. from Marquette University Law School, a M.B.A. with a sport management concentration from Robert Morris University and a B.S. in marketing management from Syracuse University. While at MULS, he earned a Sport Law Certificate from the National Sport Law Institute. His research area is focused on legal issues of sport, the use of sport in civic engagement, sponsorship activation and sport brand equity creation. He was an editor for The Encyclopedia of Sport Management and Marketing, and has published articles in journals such as: Marquette Sports Law Review, The Journal of Physical Education, Recreation, and Dance, Journal of Sponsorship, International Journal of Sport Management and Marketing and College Athletics and the Law.

JoAnn Eickhoff-Shemek

JoAnn Eickhoff-Shemek is a Professor and the Coordinator of the Exercise Science program at the University of South Florida in Tampa. Her teaching and research focus on legal liability and risk management issues in the health/fitness field. She is the lead author of a comprehensive textbook entitled *Risk Management for Health/Fitness Professionals: Legal Issues and Strategies*. Dr. Eickhoff-Shemek served as an associate editor and the legal columnist for *ACSM's Health & Fitness Journal* from 2001–2010. She is an ACSM certified Health/Fitness Director and Exercise Test Technologist and a Fellow of ACSM and AWHP. Dr. Eickhoff-Shemek received her Ph.D. from the University of Nebraska-Lincoln in 1995.

Sarah K. Fields

Sarah K. Fields is an Associate professor in the sport humanities program at the Ohio State University where she teaches, among others, courses on Sports Law. She received her undergraduate degree from Yale University, her juris doctorate from Washington University in St. Louis, her master's degree from Washington State University, and her doctorate in American Studies from the University of Iowa. She is the author of *Female Gladiators: Gender, Law, and Contact Sport in America* (2005) as well as articles in scholarly journals including the *Journal of Sport History*, the *Journal of College and University Law*, the *American Journal of Sports Medicine*, and *Pediatrics*.

Lynne P. Gaskin

Lynne Gaskin is the Associate Dean of the College of Education and Professor Emerita of Physical Education at the University of West Georgia. She received her B.S. degree from Wesleyan College and her M.S. and Ed.D. degrees from the University of North Carolina at Greensboro. Dr. Gaskin has written and spoken extensively at the national and international levels in the area of sport law. She received the Ethel Martus Lawther Award and the Research Excellence Award from the University of North Carolina at Greensboro; the Honor Award from the North Carolina Alliance for Health, Physical Education, Recreation and Dance; the Service Award from Phi Delta Kappa; the Presidential Citation for Meritorious Service from the Georgia Association of Health, Physical Education, Recreation and Dance; and the Honor Award for Meritorious Service Award from the Sport and Recreation Law Association. Dr. Gaskin teaches graduate and undergraduate courses in sport law, marketing, and facility management.

John Grady

John Grady is an Associate Professor in the Department of Sport & Entertainment Management at the University of South Carolina. He received a B.S. in Management with Honors in Finance from Penn State University. Both his law degree and Ph.D. are from Florida State University. Dr. Grady's research interests focus primarily on the legal aspects of the business of sport. This includes concentrations in the implementation of the Americans with Disabilities Act by the sport venue industry as well as intellectual property protection by professional and collegiate sport properties. At the University of South Carolina, he teaches graduate and undergraduate courses in the areas of sport law and risk management.

Curt Hamakawa

Curt Hamakawa is an Associate Professor of Sport Management at Western New England University where he teaches courses in sport management, sport law, and international sport policy. Mr. Hamakawa is the founding director of the Center for International Sport Business, a forum for the study of the business of sport in the global arena. Prior to joining academia, Mr. Hamakawa worked for the United States Olympic Committee in successive capacities as its associated general counsel, athlete services director, and international relations director, and previously worked for the National Collegiate Athletic Association in its compliance and enforcement department. A law graduate of Western New England University, Mr. Hamakawa holds a master's degree from Springfield College and a bachelor's degree from the University of Hawaii.

Mary A. Hums

Mary A. Hums, PhD, is a Professor of Sport Administration at the University of Louisville. In addition to being the 2009 NASSM Earle F. Zeigler Lecturer and a 2008 Erasmus Mundus Fellow in Belgium, Hums is a past President of SSLASPA. She was a co-contributor to the United Nations Convention on the Rights of Persons with Disabilities, and has co-authored or co-edited five sport management textbooks. She is a member of the International Olympic Academy Participants Association as well as NASSM, SRLA, and AAHPERD, and has worked at four Paralympic Games. She is also a member of the Indiana ASA Softball Hall of Fame.

Terry MacDonald

Terry MacDonald is an Internship Placement Coordinator for the Department of Sport Management in the David B. Falk College of Sport and Human Dynamics at Syracuse University. MacDonald earned her Master's degree in learning disabilities and Ph.D. in special education from Syracuse University. Previous to her current position, she was an Assistant Professor of Special Education at Utica College and has served as the Assistant Director/

Learning Specialist for athletic/academic support services in the Department of Intercollegiate Athletics at Syracuse University. MacDonald's research focus is in the areas of athletes with disabilities, women in sport, and intercollegiate athletics.

Jim Masteralexis

Jim Masteralexis is an Assistant Professor of Sport Law at Western New England College in Springfield, Massachusetts. His research focuses on professional baseball, and labor and employment issues in sport. He is a graduate of the University of New Hampshire and Suffolk University Law School and is a partner in a professional athlete management firm.

Lisa Pike Masteralexis

Lisa P. Masteralexis is the Department Head and an Associate Professor in the Mark H. McCormack Department of Sport Management at the University of Massachusetts, Amherst. She earned a J.D. at Suffolk University School of Law and a B.S. in Sport Management at the University of Massachusetts. Professor Masteralexis' research interests are in sport law and labor relations in sport. In addition to her academic articles, Professor Masteralexis is co-editor of *Principles and Practice of Sport Management*. A member of the Massachusetts and U.S. Supreme Court Bars, she co-authored an amicus brief to the U.S. Supreme Court on behalf of professional golfer Casey Martin. She is a certified agent with the Major League Baseball Players Association. Professor Masteralexis is currently on the Board of the Sports Law Institute at the University of Vermont after stints on the Boards of the Women's Sports Foundation and the National Sports Law Institute.

John D. McMillen

John McMillen is a Professor at Fresno State University in California. He is the undergraduate and graduate Sport Administration Program Director. Dr. McMillen received his law degree from Drake University and his B.A., M.Ed., and Ph.D. from the University of Nebraska-Lincoln. His primary research area is equity and justice in sport.

Bill Miller

Bill Miller is an Associate Professor and Chairperson for the Health, Exercise Science and Sport Management Department at the University of Wisconsin-Parkside. He received his B.A. from Ripon College and a J.D. from Marquette University Law School. Prior to joining UWP, Miller spent seven years as a consultant to numerous major and minor league franchises, private entities and governmental bodies on a variety of sports business issues. He has authored or co-authored multiple books and articles related to sports facility development and leases, naming rights, sports ownership and assorted sports law issues. Miller is also a former Chair of the Entertainment and Sports Law Section of the State Bar of Wisconsin.

Merry Moiseichik

Merry Moiseichik is currently a Full Professor at the University of Arkansas in Recreation and Sport Management. She received her doctorate from Indiana University in Recreation Administration and Bachelors and Masters from SUNY Cortland in Recreation, and a Juris Doctorate from the University of Arkansas. Dr. Moiseichik has worked in recreation administration in central New York, Her research interests are in community development and legal aspects both as they affect recreation and sport. She teaches courses in Legal Aspects of Sport and Recreation Services, Sport and Recreation Risk Management as well as other recreation and sport administration courses.

Anita M. Moorman

Anita M. Moorman, J.D. is a Professor of Sport Administration at the University of Louisville where she teaches Sport Law and Legal Aspects of Sport. She joined the faculty at the University of Louisville in 1996. Professor Moorman has a law degree from Southern Methodist University and also holds an M.S. in Sport Management from the University of Oklahoma, and a B.S. in Political Science from Oklahoma State University.

Professor Moorman is the co-author of a highly reviewed textbook—"Sport Law: A Managerial Approach" published by Holcomb Hathaway, now in its second edition. Professor Moorman has served or is currently serving on the Editorial Boards of the *Journal of Sport Management*, *Journal of Legal Aspects of Sport*, and the *Sport Marketing Quarterly*. She has published more than 35 articles in academic journals/proceedings including the *Journal of Sport Management*, *Sport Management Review*, *Sport Marketing Quarterly*, *Journal of Legal Aspects of Sport*, *JOPERD*, *Leisure Science*, *International Sport Journal*, *Journal of Sport and Social Issues; Journal of the Academy of Marketing Science; and ACSM's Health and Fitness Journal* and contributed more than a dozen book chapters in sport management texts.

Rebecca J. Mowrey

Rebecca Mowrey is Director of Graduate Sport Management programs and Professor of Sport Management at Millersville University of Pennsylvania. Her teaching includes graduate and undergraduate sport law and risk management. Dr. Mowrey is Past-President of the Sport and Recreation Law Association (SRLA), Past-President of the Sport Management Council of the National Association for Sport and Physical Education (NASPE), and President of the Safety and Risk Management Council of the American Association for Physical Activity and Recreation (AAPAR). Her professional contributions include serving as a member of the editorial boards of the Journal of Legal Aspects of Sport, the Recreational Sports Journal, and the Sport Management Education Journal.

Bridget Niland

Bridget Niland is an Associate Professor of Business Administration at Daemen College in Amherst, New York. She currently serves as Coordinator of the Sport Management Specialization and teaches courses in Sport Law, Sport Management, Labor Relations and Business Law. She earned a B.S. in History, Political Science and Legal Studies and an M.Ed. in Higher Education Administration from the State University of New York at Buffalo, and a J.D. from the University of Buffalo School of Law. Prior to joining the Daemen faculty, she served as a trial attorney for the United States Department of Justice in Washington, D.C. and was an Associate Director of Legislative Services at the National Collegiate Athletic Association. Her research focuses on legal issues in inter-collegiate athletics.

Barbara Osborne

Barbara Osborne is an Associate Professor in Exercise and Sport Science, and an adjunct professor in Law at the University of North Carolina at Chapel Hill. She has earned degrees in Communications (University of Wisconsin-Parkside), Sport Management (Boston University) and Law (Boston College Law School) and worked for 14 years as an administrator in intercollegiate athletics. She practiced law at Ice Miller LLP in the Collegiate Sports practice group, and has also had experience as a coach, public relations coordinator, television sports commentator, publisher and sports information director. Barbara is licensed to practice law in North Carolina and Massachusetts, and serves as general Counsel for the National Association for Collegiate Women Athletics Administrators (NACWAA). Her current academic research focuses on legal issues in intercollegiate athletics, Title IX, and women's issues in sport.

Gina Pauline

Gina Pauline is an Assistant Professor of Sport Management in the David B. Falk College of Sport and Human Dynamics at Syracuse University. Pauline has an undergraduate degree in psychology from Binghamton University, a master's degree in sport management from West Virginia University, and a doctoral degree from Ball State University. Pauline's research focus is in the areas of event management, experiential pedagogy, and gender equity. She teaches courses within the areas of sport event management and sport marketing.

Gary Rushing

Garold Rushing, Full Professor, received his Ed.D. from the University of Northern Colorado, his B.S. and M.S. from the University of Arizona. Currently he is the Human Performance Department Chair at Minnesota State University, Mankato. His research and teaching areas include a variety of sport management courses such as Sport Law and Facility Design and Management. He has published in several law reporters and coaching journals and has over twenty-five years of experience in athletics as a coach and administrator.

Todd L. Seidler

Todd Seidler is currently Professor and Chair of the Department of Health, Exercise, and Sports Sciences at the University of New Mexico. He is also a member of the faculty of the Sport Administration Program, one of only a few programs that offer both the Master's and Doctorate in Sport Administration. Dr. Seidler received his Bachelor's degree in Physical Education from San Diego State University and then taught and coached in high school. He then went on to graduate school and earned his Master's and Ph.D. in Sports Administration from the University of New Mexico. Prior to returning to U.N.M., Dr. Seidler spent six years as the coordinator of the graduate Sports Administration Program at Wayne State University and then was the coordinator of the undergraduate Sport Management Program at Guilford College in North Carolina. Dr. Seidler is currently Executive Director and a former President of the Sport and Recreation Law Association, a professional organization for those interested in teaching Sport Law and Risk Management. He has also served on the Executive Board and as Chair of both the Sport Management Council and the Council on Facilities and Equipment within the American Alliance for Health, Physical Education, Recreation and Dance (AAHPERD) and is an active member of the North American Society for Sport Management (NASSM). Dr. Seidler is also a Certified Strength and Conditioning Specialist (C.S.C.S., 1987) through the National Strength and Conditioning Association (N.S.C.A.).

Dr. Seidler's primary areas of interest include risk management and legal issues in sport and in planning and managing sports facilities. He is active as a consultant on facility planning and risk management for sport and recreation and frequently presents, publishes, and teaches classes such as Risk Management in Sport, Sport Facility Planning and Design, Facility and Event Management, and Legal Aspects of Sport.

David Snyder

David Snyder is a Professor of Sport Management Emeritus at the State University of New York at Cortland. He continues to teach at Tompkins Cortland Community College as a part-time, tenure-track full professor in the sport management program.

Professor Snyder received his J.D. from the University of Tennessee and has been licensed to practice law in New York since 1986. Prior to accepting his position at SUNY Cortland, he served as president of an international sports marketing company headquartered in Tokyo, Japan. He is currently pursuing his doctoral degree in sports management at the Deutsche Sporthochsule Köln in Germany. His doctoral thesis is a cross-cultural comparative analysis of labor relations in Major League Baseball and the Nippon Professional Baseball (NPB) league in Japan.

He has been a long-time member of many sport law and sport management related organizations including the Sports Lawyers Association (SLA) and the Sport Marketing Association (SMA), among others. Professor Snyder is former chair of the Asian Baseball Committee for the Society for American Baseball Research (SABR) and he served a three-year term as a program reviewer for the Sport Management Program Review Council (SMPRC).

He has served on the editorial boards of several journals including the *International Journal of Sports Marketing and Sponsorship (IJSM&S)* and the *Journal for the Legal Aspects of Sport (JLAS)*. He previously was the Editor-in-Chief of *Asian Baseball Journal (ABJ)* for the Society of American Baseball Research (SABR), and currently is the Interviews Editor for *IJSM&S*.

He has authored or co-authored number of articles that have appeared in such journals as *The DePaul Journal of Sport Law and Contemporary Problems, The Marquette Sports Law Review, The Sports Marketing Quarterly, The Journal of Physical Education, Recreation & Dance (JOPERD)*, and *Albany Government Law Review*, among others. In addition to writing chapters for previous editions of this book, Professor Snyder co-authored chapters in two textbooks, the third edition of *Contemporary Sport Management* and *International Sport Management*, published by Human Kinetics.

Ellen Staurowsky

Dr. Staurowsky is a full professor in the Department of Sport Management at Drexel University. She is internationally recognized as an expert on social justice issues in sport which include gender equity and Title IX, pay equity and equal employment opportunity, the exploitation of athletes, the faculty role in reforming college sport, representation of women in sport media, and the misappropriation of American Indian imagery in sport. She is co-author of the book, *College Athletes for Hire: The Evolution and Legacy of the NCAA Amateur Myth*. In addition to publications in scholarly journals such as the *Harvard Journal of Law and Gender, Journal of Sport and Social Issues, Sociology of Sport Journal, Quest, Journal of Sport Management*, the *International Journal of Sport Sociology*, the *Marquette Sports Law Review*, the *Journal of Legal Aspects of Sport*, and the *International Journal of Sport History*, her critiques and analyses on a variety of issues have appeared in *The Chronicle of Higher Education, Street &Smith's SportsBusiness Journal, The NCAA News, The New York Times, The Atlantic, Athletic Management Magazine*, and *News From Indian Country*. She serves on the executive boards of the College Sport Research Institute and the NCAA Scholarly Colloquium. She also serves as a member at large on the executive committee of the North American Society for Sport Management.

Stephanie Tryce

Stephanie A. Tryce, Esq. holds a Juris Doctorate from Temple University School of Law, a Bachelor of Science in Business Administration from Drexel University and is a Masters Candidate in Sport Management at the University of Massachusetts-Amherst. Recently, Ms. Tryce resigned her position as an Assistant City Solicitor in the Major Tax Enforcement Unit of the City of Philadelphia's Law Department to return to teaching in the fall of 2012, as an Assistant Professor of Sport Marketing at St. Joseph's University.

Besides practicing law, Ms. Tryce taught Introduction to Sport Law, and two upper-level electives titled *Amateur Sport and the Law* and *Professional Sport and the Law* in the Sport Management Department of the University of Massachusetts-Amherst. Upon returning to her native Philadelphia, Ms. Tryce was affiliated faculty in the Legal Studies and Business Ethics Department of the Wharton School of the University of Pennsylvania, where she taught *Introduction to Law and Legal Process* and *The Business of Sport*. Ms. Tryce also served as the Internship Supervisor to sport management seniors at the University of Delaware.

Ms. Tryce has presented at the annual conferences of the North American Society for the Sociology of Sport and the Sport and Recreation Law Association. She has participated in research activities at the intersection of race, gender and sports, assisted in editing the 3rd edition of the *Essentials of Sport Law*, co-authored a book chapter in *Sport Law for Sport Managers* titled "Employment Law and Sport: Title VII of the Civil Rights Act of 1964" and co-authored an article in the Special Issue of the Journal for the Study of Sports and Athletics in Education.

Nita Unruh

Nita Unruh is currently a Professor, the Department Chair of HPERLS and Degree Coordinator for the Sports Management program in the Health, Physical Education, Recreation and Leisure Studies Department at the University of Nebraska Kearney. She received her Ed.D. from the University of Arkansas, an M.S. from Florida State University and her B.S. from Henderson State University. She enjoys helping students become familiar with and become interested in the areas of Risk Management and Legal Issues in Sport and Recreation.

Jo Williams

Jo Williams is an Associate Professor at the University of Southern Maine. She received her bachelor's degree from West London Institute of Higher Education (Brunel University) and her master's degree and doctorate from Springfield College, MA. Her research interests include sport marketing, particularly the use of digital media, and collegiate athletics. Additional interests focus on curricula innovation and student engagement. Williams teaches sport management and marketing courses and has previous experience as an event director in professional golf. She is an active member of NASSM and COSMA.

Sara J. Young

Sarah J. Young is an Associate Professor with the Department of Recreation, Park & Tourism Studies at Indiana University—Bloomington. She earned her B.S. degree in Recreation and Park Administration from Illinois State University, and earned both her Ph.D. in Leisure Behavior with a minor in Law, and her M.S. in Recreational Sport Administration from Indiana University. Sarah also worked as an Assistant Director of Intramural Sports for nine years with the Division of Recreational Sports at Indiana University. Sandwiched between her IU experiences, Sarah was as Assistant Professor with the Leisure Studies program in the College of Hotel Administration at University of Nevada, Las Vegas for four years. Sarah is an active member of NIRSA, NRPA, and SRLA, and teaches legal aspects of sport and recreation management courses.

INTRODUCTION TO SPORT LAW

1.00

In today's litigious society, it is important that sport and recreation administrators have a sound understanding of the law. The following *Introduction to Sport Law* section consists of three chapters covering a wide range of legal areas intended to provide administrators with a basic introduction to legal principles as they apply to the sport and recreation industry.

This sixth edition features a completely new Chapter 1.10 *The Legal System.* The chapter, written by a different author, presents a totally new approach to the subject. This first chapter is intended to help the reader understand how the legal system functions and prepare the reader for effectively using this book.

The second chapter, Chapter 1.20 *Legal Research*, introduces the reader to the tools that are available for conducting legal research. Additionally, the author provides guidance to the reader regarding the basic steps to be used in conducting legal research.

The third chapter, Chapter 1.30 *Business Structure and Legal Authority*, provides an overview of the business structures available to the recreation and sport manager. Guidance is given regarding the type of protection provided by a number of popular business structures.

1.10

THE LEGAL SYSTEM
Kristi L. Schoepfer Bochicchio | Winthrop University

The United States has become an increasingly litigious society; annually, millions of lawsuits are filed by citizens seeking legal remedy to problems they have encountered in the course of their personal or professional lives. As such, recreation and sport managers are likely to encounter legal issues related to the administration of their organizations and programs. Specifically, legal concerns are present in recreation and sport in many different areas, such as negligence (tort law), risk management, contract law, constitutional law, and federal legislation regarding gender equity, employment discrimination and intellectual property. However, before these and other specific legal concerns can be presented, recreation and sport managers must understand the basic components of the complex United States legal system, including origins of the law, the legal system, and the legal process.

FUNDAMENTAL CONCEPTS

Origins of the Law

The **law** is a collection of rules and regulations that govern the affairs of a community and are enforced by a legal authority. There are multiple sources of law including Constitutional law and laws enacted, enforced, and interpreted by the three branches of government.

A **constitution** is a document that sets forth the basic principles of government, including limits on government power. The federal government, as well as all 50 states, has a constitution; each constitution provides citizens many protections. Additionally, the federal and state governments each have three branches that exist as a source of law: the legislative branch, which is responsible for enacting new laws and amending existing laws through federal or state legislatures; the executive branch, which enforces existing laws through elected officials or administrative agencies; and, the judicial branch which interprets constitutions or other existing laws through the federal and state court systems. At both the federal and state level, constitutions and all three branches of government have a specific and important role in establishing the law.

Legislative Branch

A Congress (or legislature), either state or federal, is the legislative branch of the government, comprised of elected officials in the Senate and in the House of Representatives.[1] This legislative branch of government is responsible for enacting and amending statutory laws. Statutory laws, or **statutes**, are written laws adopted by legislatures at all levels including federal, state, city, county and municipal (statutes at the local level are typically called ordinances). Statutes are only valid in the area governed by the authoring legislature; in other words, South Carolina statutes are only valid in South Carolina. Any individual in South Carolina, either a South Carolina citizen or visitor, must abide by South Carolina statutes; however, South Carolina statutes do not have any legal significance in any other state.

For example, the South Carolina legislature has enacted statutory law that both defines bungee jumping and prohibits certain acts related to bungee jumping. Specifically, South Carolina statute §52-19-20 reads:

> "For purposes of this chapter, the term "bungee jumping" includes and refers to the sport, activity, or practice of jumping, stepping out, dropping, or otherwise being released into the air while attached or fastened to a cord made of rubber, latex, or other elastic type material, whether natural or synthetic, whereby the cord, stops the fall, lengthens and shortens, allows the person to bounce up and down, and is intended to finally bring the person to a stop at a point above the surface."

---

[1]Every state has a bicameral legislature that consists of two houses except for Nebraska; the Nebraska Legislature is unicameral. Additionally, states use varying names to identify the two legislative branches of government within the state.

Further, South Carolina statute §52-19-30 reads:

(A) The practice of bungee jumping from a device other than a fixed platform is prohibited in this State.
(B) The practice of bungee jumping using an ankle harness is prohibited in this State.
(C) The practice of pre stretching and releasing bungee cords for the purpose of catapulting jumpers is prohibited in this State.
(D) The practice of bungee jumping over water, sand, or any surface other than a safety air bag is prohibited in this State.
(E) The practice of tandem or multiple bungee jumping is prohibited in this State.
(F) The practice of sandbagging is prohibited in this State. For purposes of this chapter, "sandbagging" means the practice of holding onto any object (including another person) while bungee jumping, for the purpose of exerting more force on the bungee cord in order to stretch it further, and then releasing the object during the jump causing the jumper to rebound with more force than could be created by the jumper's weight alone.
(G) The use of any mechanical lifting device in conjunction with bungee jumping is prohibited.

This statute may be subject to interpretation if it were ever part of a lawsuit (see subsequent section on the Judicial branch); however, by writing this statute the South Carolina legislature has provided the law in the state regarding bungee jumping. That is the function of statutes; to create the law within a particular area.

Executive Branch
Often times, statutes require further explanation to be applied to real-life scenarios. This guidance typically comes in the form of regulations created by the executive branch, or an administrative agency created by the executive branch. **Regulations** are "rules and administrative codes issued by governmental agencies at all levels, municipal, county, state and federal. Although they are not laws, regulations have the force of law, since they are adopted under authority granted by statutes, and often include penalties for violations." For example, the National Labor Relations Act is federal statutory law. While the law itself is guiding, many of the provisions have been further interpreted through regulations enacted by the National Labor Relations Board ("NLRB"), a federal agency given this charge. Although the NLRB provisions are not laws, they have the force of law; thus, the executive branch plays a role in creating law.

Judicial Branch
Whether the source of law is a constitution, a statute, or a regulation, the judicial branch is charged with interpreting and applying the law by adjudicating legal claims. When a court makes a decision in a legal case, and authors a written opinion, the decision is referred to as **case law**; the collective body of case law is called **common law**.

The collective body of common law is exceptionally important because it establishes precedent for future cases. **Precedent** exists when a prior reported opinion of an appeals court establishes the legal rule for future cases involving the same legal question. Further, there are two types of precedent: Binding precedent and persuasive precedent. **Binding precedent** exists within a specific court system and must be followed by all courts within that system at the same or lower level. For example, if the Wisconsin Supreme Court decides a case on a particular legal issue, all future cases on that same issue in the Wisconsin court system will be bound by the decision (meaning the courts must follow the precedent and make the same decision). In contrast, **persuasive precedent** can come from any court system. For example, if the Idaho Court of Appeals makes a decision that supports a legal claim in Texas, the lawyer arguing the case in Texas can present the Idaho decision as persuasive precedent. The court in Texas may choose to allow the Idaho decision to influence its own decision, but the Texas court is not required to do so; thus, any precedential value the Idaho case may have is only persuasive. When you are reading the Significant Cases in each chapter of the textbook, you will frequently encounter precedent, both binding and persuasive.

The Legal System
Once laws are created, they must be interpreted and applied to particular circumstances; as discussed above, this interpretation/application occurs in the judiciary, or court systems. A **court system** is a structured collection of individual courts, each court being an "organized body with defined powers, meeting at certain times

and places for the hearing and decision of causes and other matters brought before it" (Black's, 1990). There are multiple court systems that can apply the laws; three primary court systems must be discussed, as well as how an individual decides which court system is appropriate in any given case.

Federal Court System

The federal court system uses a hierarchal approach, meaning that cases originate in lower courts, and when appropriate, may be appealed to higher level courts (see Figure 1.10.1). The lowest tier in the federal hierarchy is the District Court level; **District Courts** are the courts of origin in the federal court system. If a lawsuit is filed in the federal court system, a District Court will be the first to hear the case. There are 94 District Courts in the United States. Each state has at least one federal District Court within its boundaries (although these courts are not part of the state court system), and some larger states, such as California, have multiple District Courts. An individual or corporation wishing to use the federal court system for its lawsuit will access a federal District Court within its state.

If a party to the lawsuit does not feel the law was properly interpreted or applied in the District Court, he or she may **appeal** the case on the basis of legal error; in other words, ask a higher level court to review the case for mistakes of law. The middle tier in the federal hierarchy is known as the **Circuit Courts**. This appellate level is divided into 11 geographic circuits, and a separate circuit for the District of Columbia (see Figure 1.10.2).[2] The geographic location of the original district court determines which of the 12 appellate circuits will hear the case on appeal.

Lastly, a party may choose to again appeal his or her case to the highest tier in the federal court system, the **United States Supreme Court** (USSC). To appeal a case to this highest level, the party must request **certiorari** by filing a petition asking the USSC to hear the case; the USSC will either grant or deny this request.[3] The USSC is very selective about the cases it chooses to hear; each year, the USSC accepts less than 5% of the certiorari requests.

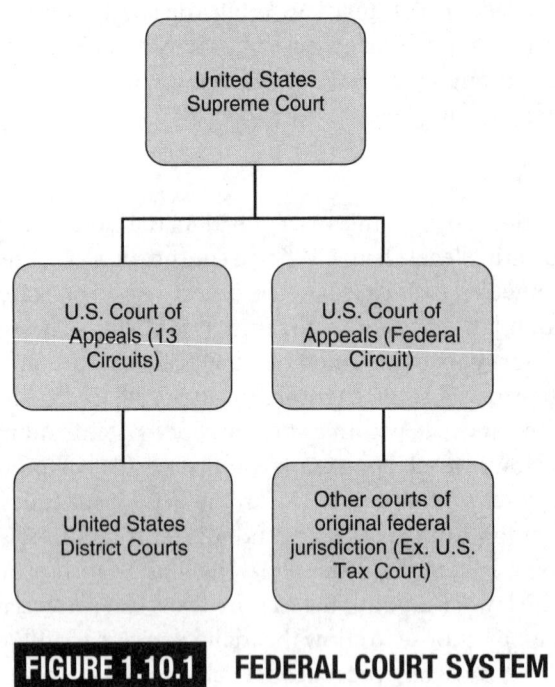

FIGURE 1.10.1 **FEDERAL COURT SYSTEM**

---

[2]There is also an additional federal appellate court called the United States Court of Appeals for the Federal Circuit. This court hears appeals from all district courts in patent law cases, as well as appeals from the U.S. Court of Federal Claims and the Court of International Trade.

[3]Certiorari is "an order of a higher court to a lower court to send all the documents in a case to it so the higher court can review the lower court's decision." If the USSC grants certiorari, they are accepting the case for review.

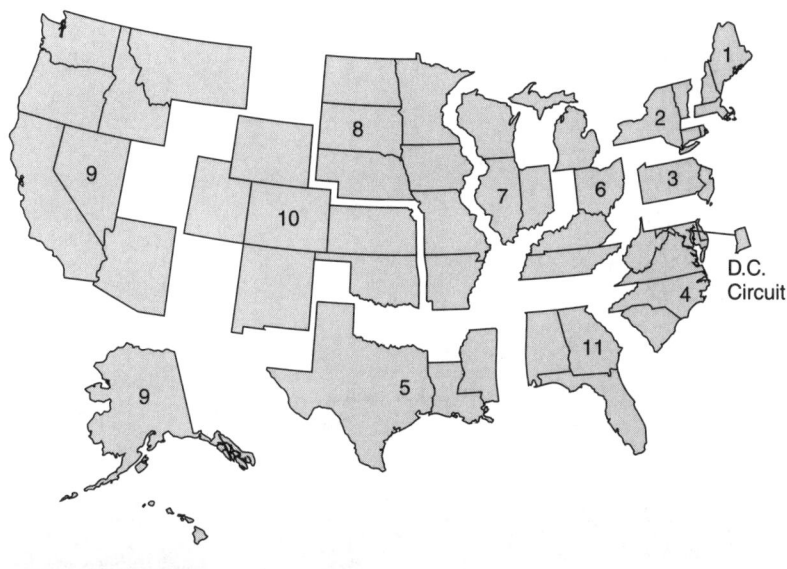

FIGURE 1.10.2 **FEDERAL CIRCUIT COURTS**

Source: www.thehrspecialist.com

State Court System

Each state has its own court system. Similar to the federal court system, most states also use the hierarchal approach, separating the courts into three levels. Most states have *trial courts* of either limited or general jurisdiction (see subsequent discussion on jurisdiction), *appellate courts,* and a *supreme court.* However, there are many variances among state court systems; not all states use the same court names or structure.

For example, in Colorado the trial court level is divided into separate courts (see Figure 1.10.2). The County Courts hear a variety of cases, including those with alleged damages under $15,000; the District Courts hear civil cases in any amount (and uniquely, serve as an appellate court for the County Courts). The Colorado Court of Appeals is the appellate court for the District Courts and also reviews state administrative agencies. The Colorado Supreme Court, the state's highest court, hears appeals from the Court of Appeals.

In Maryland, the hierarchal approach is similar, but the trial courts and appellate courts use different names (see Figure 1.10.3). There are two types of courts classified as trial courts, District Courts and Circuit Courts. District Courts do not have juries; rather, trials are by judges only and cover civil claims up to $30,000, as well as other civil and criminal matters. The Circuit Courts handle major civil cases, along with more serious criminal matters, and do allow for trial by jury. In the appellate courts, the Court of Special Appeals serves as the intermediate appellate court, reviewing cases from the trial courts; the Court of Appeals (commonly called the Supreme Court in other states) is the highest court in the state and hears cases almost exclusively based on certiorari.

Some states, Montana for instance, have only trial courts and a supreme court with no intermediate appellate review (see Figure 1.10.3). Regarding court names, the New York court system is vastly different from most other states using the name Supreme Court to identify its trial courts (see Figure 1.10.3). The intermediate appellate courts are called Appellate Divisions of the Supreme Court and the Court of Appeals is the highest court of the state.

These examples demonstrate that while state court systems are similar in their hierarchal approach, the similarities end there. All 50 states have their own unique variances that impact the progression of a case through the respective state court system.

Administrative Court System

The vast majority of recreation and sport lawsuits are filed in state or federal courts; however, the administrative court system is still noteworthy. As discussed, the executive branch of government includes administrative agencies that create regulations, or rules to operationalize statutes created by legislatures. Administrative courts

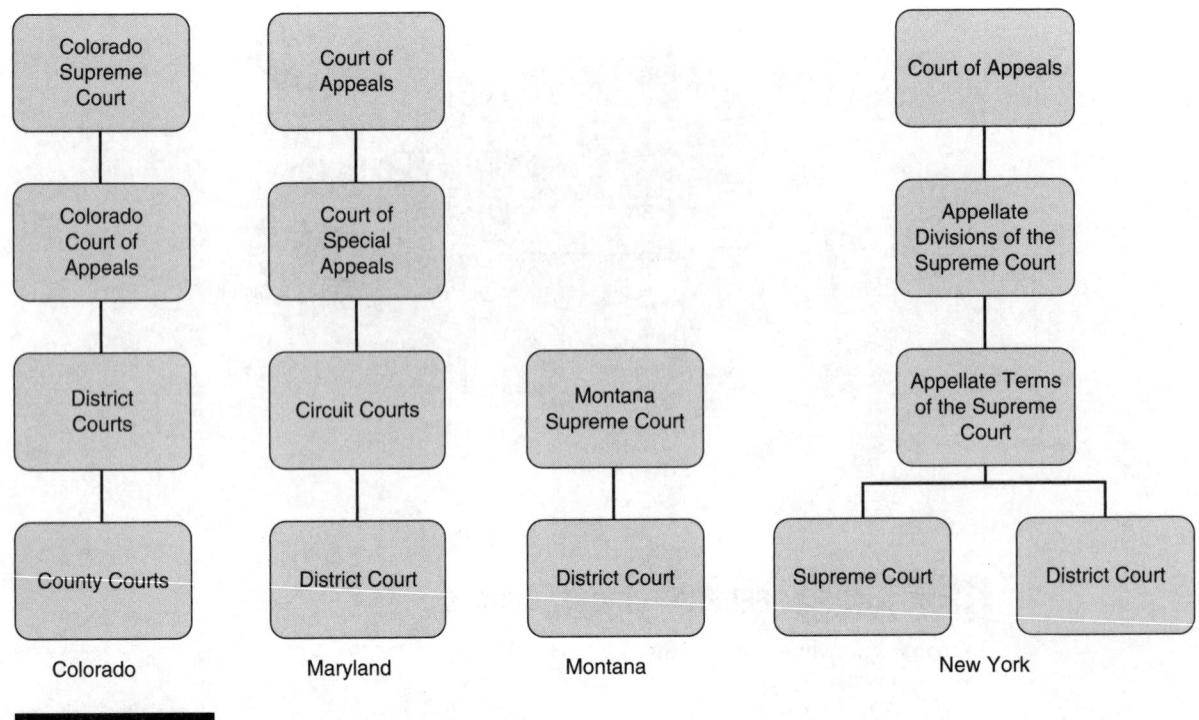

FIGURE 1.10.3 STATE COURT SYSTEMS

sit as fact-finding bodies that apply these regulations. When disputes arise regarding the implementation of the regulations, evidence is presented to an administrative law judge, who will make a decision.

At the state level, administrative court procedures again vary by state. For example, in Montana, all workers' compensation claims are heard in Workers' Compensation Court, which has the limited ability to review only that type claim. In this administrative court, there are no jury trials; rather, the judge decides how the regulations should be applied in each individual case. When federal regulations are in question, a federal administrative law judge will render a decision; any appeal of the administrative law judge's findings will go to the federal appellate level, or Circuit Courts. Although these appeals can be heard in any circuit, most appeals from federal agencies are heard in the District of Columbia Circuit.

Jurisdiction

Given that more than one court system exists, it is necessary to understand when it is appropriate to use each one. Selecting the proper court system requires a determination of which court has **jurisdiction**; a court's ability to hear a case and provide remedy. A court must have both **personal jurisdiction**, which is power over the parties in the case, and **subject matter jurisdiction**, the power to hear the type of case (see Figure 1.10.4). When filing a lawsuit, a party must be certain that jurisdiction is correct, or the case may be dismissed.

In the federal court system, a District Court determines whether personal jurisdiction exists by using the procedural rules of the state in which it is located. For example, a federal district court located in Michigan will follow Michigan procedural rules governing personal jurisdiction. To determine if personal jurisdiction exists, the court will consider such factors as location of the parties, location of property or consent to personal jurisdiction by the defendant. To obtain federal subject matter jurisdiction, one of the following criteria must be met: (1) the claim must arise from federal statutes or the U.S. Constitution (**federal question jurisdiction**); (2) the claim must be filed by (or against) the federal government; or (3) the amount in controversy exceeds $75,000, and all opposing parties live in different states (**diversity of citizenship jurisdiction**). Federal courts also have exclusive subject matter jurisdiction over lawsuits between states, federal criminal cases, bankruptcy

State Courts	Federal Courts	State or Federal Courts
Crimes under state legislation.	Crimes under statutes enacted by congress.	Crimes punishable under both federal and state law.
State constitutional issues and cases involving state laws or regulations.	Most cases involving federal laws or regulations (for example: tax, Social Security, broadcasting, civil rights)	Federal constitutional issues.
Family law issues.	Matters involving interstate and international commerce, including airline and railroad regulation.	Certain civil rights claims.
Real property issues.	Cases involving securities and commodities regulation, including takeover of publicly held corporations.	"Class action" cases.
Most private contract disputes (except those resolved under bankruptcy law).	Admiralty cases.	Environmental regulations.
Most issues involving the regulation of trades and professions.	International trade law matters.	Certain disputes involving federal law.
Most professional malpractice issues.	Patent, copyright, and other intellectual property issues.	
Most issues involving the internal governance of business associations such as partnerships and corporations.	Cases involving rights under treaties, foreign states, and foreign nationals.	
Most personal injury lawsuits.	State law disputes when "diversity of citizenship" exists.	
Most workers' injury claims.	Bankruptcy matters.	
Probate and inheritance matters.	Disputes between states.	
Most traffic violations and registration of motor vehicles.	Habeas corpus actions.	
	Traffic violations and other misdemeanors occurring on certain federal property.	

FIGURE 1.10.4   **SUBJECT MATTER JURISDICTION OF FEDERAL AND/OR STATE COURTS**

Source: http://www.uscourts.gov/EducationalResources/FederalCourtBasics/CourtStructure/JurisdictionOfStateAndFederalCourts.aspx

cases, patent, trademark and copyright cases, antitrust cases, maritime cases, and cases arising out of federal statutes.

In the state court systems, a court has personal jurisdiction over parties that reside in the state, conduct business in the state, consent to jurisdiction (typically through court appearance) or have sufficient "minimum contact" with the state (a court determines if a party has enough contact with the state to make jurisdiction appropriate). Subject matter jurisdiction exists for any event or activity that occurred within the state. Within the state trial courts, some courts have limited subject matter jurisdiction, and can only hear specific claims; areas of limited subject matter jurisdiction may include family law, probate law, juvenile court, etc. Other trial level courts have general subject matter jurisdiction and can hear claims related to any area of law, so long as the case involves an event or activity that occurred within the state.

Finally, **concurrent jurisdiction** must be addressed; that is when one case qualifies for both federal and state jurisdiction. For example, if a Minnesota Vikings fan, who is a Minnesota resident, attends a Green Bay Packers game in Green Bay, WI, and accidentally injures a local Packers fan, the Packers fan (plaintiff, see Trial Phase later) will need to decide where to file the claim. The plaintiff may file the lawsuit in federal or state court based on his or her preference; the case may be filed in the jurisdiction where the defendant lives or the jurisdiction where the cause of action arose. The plaintiff can chose a court system based on preference regarding procedure, choice of law, or other factors related to legal procedure. However, if the case is filed in state court, the defendant may opt to have the case removed to federal court (changing from state jurisdiction to federal jurisdiction based on diversity of citizenship).

State courts also have concurrent jurisdiction regarding federal questions; any state court may interpret the U.S. Constitution or a federal statute if the applicable provision has a direct bearing on a case brought in state court under a state law.

The Legal Process

Cases must be filed in accordance with a well established legal process. There are many steps involved in this process, often referred to as civil procedure (or criminal procedure for criminal cases; this chapter only addresses civil law). The following discussion is not intended to cover completely all procedural elements of a legal case; rather, the selected elements are highlighted to help you understand subsequent Significant Cases in the textbook. Each element will be discussed and, when appropriate, you will find a definition, an example from an actual case, and an explanation of the example that highlights the particular element. Also, the discussion is separated into two separate phases: the trial phase, which is the where a case originates, and the appellate phase, which only occurs if a party to the case appeals the original decision based on legal error.

Trial Phase

Standing. The legal right to file a lawsuit is called **standing.** To establish standing, a plaintiff (see next section) must establish that he or she sustained a harm, that the court has the power to provide a remedy, and that the plaintiff has an interest in the outcome of a case. Typically, the issue of standing is raised by the defendant (see next section); the plaintiff does not need to prove that standing exists unless it is challenged.

Parties to the Lawsuit. The **plaintiff(s)** is the party filing the lawsuit; this is the individual or group that has allegedly suffered harm and seeks legal remedy from the court. The **defendant(s)** is the party against whom the claim is filed. In many cases, there are multiple defendants; often, more than one person or group may have been responsible for a harm occurring. Also, some cases are filed as **class action** lawsuits, meaning that a large group of people are filing a lawsuit collectively against a defendant.

Case Example #1: This case demonstrates that parties to a case can vary in number; multiple plaintiffs and defendants are common.

IAIN FRASER; STEVE TRITTSCHUH; SEAN BOWERS; MARK SEMIOLI; RHETT HARTY; DAVID SCOTT VAUDREUIL; MARK DODD; and MARK DOUGHERTY, Plaintiffs v. MAJOR LEAGUE SOCCER, L.L.C.; KRAFT SOCCER, L.P.; ANSCHUTZ SOCCER, INC.; ANSCHUTZ CHICAGO SOCCER, INC.; SOUTH FLORIDA SOCCER, L.L.C., TEAM COLUMBUS SOCCER, L.L.C.; TEAM KANSAS CITY SOCCER, L.L.C.; LOS ANGELES SOCCER PARTNERS, L.P.; EMPIRE SOCCER CLUB, L.P.; WASHINGTON SOCCER, L.P.; and UNITED STATES SOCCER FEDERATION, INC., Defendants
2000 U.S. Dist. LEXIS 5434

MEMORANDUM AND ORDER
April 19, 2000

The individual **plaintiffs** are the representatives of the **certified class** of professional soccer players who are or who have been employed by the **defendant** Major League Soccer, L.L.C. ("MLS"). MLS is a limited liability company ("LLC") organized under Delaware law. The **defendant** United States Soccer Federation, Inc. ("USSF") is the national governing body for professional and amateur soccer in the United States. **All the other defendants** are investors in MLS, each a capital-contributing member of MLS that has contracted with MLS to operate one or more of MLS's teams.

Explanation

Often times, the plaintiff(s) and defendant(s) can be determined from looking at the case name; however, most court opinions also offer further explanation of the parties in the first paragraph. In this case, the named plaintiffs represent a larger group who has filed a class action lawsuit against the defendants. Major League Soccer, the respective MLS teams, and the United States Soccer Federation are the defendants in this case.

Jurisdiction. The preceding section of this chapter presents a complete discussion of jurisdiction; however, Case Example #2 further clarifies the importance of identifying the appropriate jurisdiction before filing a lawsuit.

Filing the Complaint. After the plaintiff has identified the appropriate jurisdiction to file the lawsuit, he or she will formally commence the legal process by filing a complaint. A **complaint** is a formal pleading to the court that must state both the factual and legal basis for the claim. Also, a complaint must follow specific statutory requirements regarding form. For example, a complaint must follow a specific format, name both the party making the claim and all defendants, and state what result (damages or performance, see subsequent discussion) the plaintiff is requesting. When a complaint is filed, the court will issue a **summons**, which gives the name and file number of the lawsuit and instructs the defendant to file an answer or other response. A copy of the complaint and the summons must be served on a defendant before a response is required.

Prior to filing a complaint, a plaintiff must be aware of the statute of limitations in the selected jurisdiction regarding the claim. A **statute of limitations** is the maximum amount of time a potential plaintiff can wait before filing a legal claim; these statutes vary by court system, both state and federal, jurisdiction, and subject matter. For example, in Connecticut, "no action founded upon a tort shall be brought but within three years from the date of the act or omission complained of" (Conn. Gen. Stat. § 52-577 (2012)). In other words, plaintiff wishing to file a personal injury lawsuit based on tort law must do so within three years of the cause of action occurring. Alternatively, in Minnesota, a plaintiff has six years to file a personal injury claim (Minn. Stat. § 541.01 (2012). In most states, the statute of limitations will differ for cases filed under contract law, tort law (personal injury) or property law (see Chapter 2.21, *Defenses against Negligence*).

Filing the Answer. After a complaint is filed, and summons issued, a defendant has a specific period of time, typically 30 or 60 days, in which to file an answer with the court. An **answer** is a pleading to the court, filed by a defendant, which responds to each allegation in the complaint. A defendant may deny the claims, admit the claims, or do either in part. The answer may also include affirmative defenses, such as comparative negligence (see Chapter 2.21 *Defenses against Negligence*), allegations which contradict the complaint, or allegations which are intended to derail the claims in the complaint. Similar to the complaint, the format of the answer must follow specific rules established within each jurisdiction.

Discovery and Motions. After the defendant files an answer, both parties to the lawsuit enter the discovery and motions phase. **Discovery** is the period of time during which both parties gather facts and information to be used as evidence in a trial. Discovery includes requests for documents, requests to admit facts into evidence (declarations), and depositions (statements given by parties to the case under oath). Opposing counsel has the right to discover any material reasonably related to the case.

Motions are formal requests made to the court seeking a specific action or decision. Various motions are common in the legal process; they can be made both before and after discovery. Some common motions include: (1) a **motion for judgment on the pleadings**, which asserts that no cause of action exists even if everything in the complaint were true; (2) a **motion to dismiss**, often based on expiration of the statute of limitations or filing in the wrong jurisdiction; and (3) a **motion for summary judgment**, which is filed when one party believes that no questions of fact are present in the case, and the legal issue can be decided as a matter of law. Both parties ascertain the facts of the case during discovery; if either party feels that the facts are not in dispute, and do not need to be substantiated by a fact-finding body (a jury), they will file a motion for summary judgment. A motion for summary judgment is very common in the legal process; these motions eliminate the need for a jury to determine the facts based on evidence, since the facts are not in question. The party moving for summary judgment must initially establish that there is no genuine issue of material fact and that he or she is entitled to judgment as a matter of law. Therefore, when a motion for summary judgment is filed, if the facts of the case are not in dispute, the judge will consider the facts, apply the law in question to those facts, and render a judgment. Generally, a motion for summary judgment is not made until all discovery has been completed (see Case Example #3).

Case Example #2: This case incorporates many examples from the previous sections; specifically, the issue in the case is jurisdiction, but the court also discusses matters related to the complaint, motions, and discovery.

MARLON BRANDO ROMAN, a Minor, etc., Plaintiff and Appellant, v. LIBERTY UNIVERSITY, INC., et al., Defendants and Respondents.

2008 Cal. App. LEXIS 636

A. Plaintiff's Complaint: **Plaintiff . . . filed an action for personal injury damages against defendants in the Superior Court of the State of California, County of San Bernardino.**

The **complaint** alleged that Liberty's recruiting coordinator had come to Rialto, California, before June 5, 2003, to recruit plaintiff to play football for Liberty in Virginia . . . Plaintiff executed Liberty's 2003–2004 Athletic Scholarship/Grant-in-Aid Agreement at his home in Rialto on June 8, 2003, and executed a revised agreement in Rialto on July 19, 2003. Thereafter, plaintiff attended Liberty and played first string defensive back for its football team.

The **complaint** alleged that, while at Liberty, plaintiff's roommate, Lancaster [(also a defendant and also from Virginia)], played football for Liberty's team. Plaintiff and Lancaster had a history of leaving campus to consume alcohol after curfew . . . On April 21, 2004, plaintiff and Lancaster went out drinking. During the evening, Lancaster physically assaulted plaintiff. Plaintiff started to walk back to campus and fell from a train trestle. He sustained catastrophic brain injuries.

B. Liberty's Motion: **Liberty filed a motion to quash service of summons for lack of personal jurisdiction.**

Jerry Falwell, Jr., the vice chancellor and general counsel for Liberty, **provided a declaration** . . . stating that Liberty is incorporated in Virginia and maintains its principal place of business in Virginia. Liberty has no employees in California, does not have an office or mailing address in California, does not own or lease any real property in California, is not registered or otherwise qualified to do business in California, and does not have an agent for service of process in California. Liberty does not pay any income, property, or use taxes to the state of California. Liberty does not manufacture any product that could find its way through the stream of commerce into California. **Falwell's declaration further states** that coach Pete Sundheim, who had direct personal contact with plaintiff, lives and works in Virginia. Coach Ed Gomes, the director of spiritual development for Liberty's football team, also had personal contact with plaintiff and also lives and works in Virginia.

The Court of Appeal affirmed the trial court's orders. The court concluded that the **trial court properly granted the university's motion to quash for lack of personal jurisdiction.** The university did not purposely avail itself of the benefits of doing business in California such that it could expect to be subject to the jurisdiction of California courts. The only conduct plaintiff established was that the university's recruiting coordinator visited him in California to recruit him to play football for the university, and thereafter, the university mailed plaintiff a scholarship agreement and amended scholarship agreement that plaintiff executed in California. The nexus between the university's activities in California and the injury plaintiff suffered in Virginia was so attenuated as to be virtually nonexistent.

Explanation

The legal issue in this case is whether the California state court system has personal jurisdiction over Liberty University. The court's opinion sets forth the arguments the plaintiff used in attempt to substantiate minimum contacts with California, as well as arguments made by Liberty University to defeat a finding a personal jurisdiction. The court concludes that the California court system does not have personal jurisdiction over Liberty University, and thus the California state court system lacks jurisdiction to hear the case.

Case Example #3: This case focuses primarily on a motion for summary judgment. This case is on appeal, meaning it is a review of the trial court decision. The discussion of the legal issues has been omitted, but the appellate court concludes that the motion for summary judgment is appropriate, meaning the case has reached its conclusion.

JOSH SANDERS, Plaintiff-Appellant, v. KUNA JOINT SCHOOL DISTRICT and MR. "JOHN DOE" EMERY, Defendants-Respondents.

876 P.2d 154 (1994)

FACTS AND PROCEDURE

The underlying facts of this lawsuit are generally agreed upon by all of the parties. On May 15, 1990, Josh Sanders, a student at Kuna High School, attempted to slide into first base during a softball game and broke his ankle. Sanders had been enrolled in a specialized physical education class which provided instruction in weight lifting. On the date of the incident, the instructor, respondent Ron Emry[4], decided to have the class play softball outside instead of weight lifting. The students were not informed of this decision until after they appeared in the school's weight room. According to Sanders, on that particular day he was wearing a pair of "Saucony Shadows," a shoe designed specifically for running. Once on the softball field, Emry did not give instruction in the game of softball and supervised the game from behind a backstop. During one particular sequence of play, Sanders attempted to slide into first base in order to avoid being tagged out. During the slide, Sanders broke his ankle.

Following proper notice as required by I.C. §§ 6-901 et seq., Sanders filed suit against Emry and the school district as Emry's employer. Sanders claimed that Emry had been negligent by requiring the students to play softball, by failing to adequately supervise the students, including inspecting their footwear, and by failing to properly instruct the students on how to play softball.

After initial discovery was completed, the respondents filed a motion for summary judgment on grounds that, accepting the truth of Sanders' evidence, it did not prove a claim of negligence as a matter of fact. The district court granted the respondents' motion. Sanders now appeals to this Court, claiming that the district court improperly granted the summary judgment.

* * * *

CONCLUSION

The respondents in this case properly carried their burden on their motion for summary judgment by showing that Sanders was unable to present sufficient evidence on the causal connection between the alleged negligence and the injury. The burden then shifted to Sanders to show that a genuine issue did exist. Sanders failed to meet this burden and therefore the **summary judgment was properly granted.**

Explanation

As noted by the court, the facts of this case were not disputed by either party; thus the defendants filed a motion for summary judgment. The defendants argued that the facts presented by the plaintiff were insufficient to establish the claim; because the facts were agreed upon by both parties, and no additional facts would be determined by a jury, the judge in the case should decide the case as a matter of law. After consideration of the facts presented, the court concluded that summary judgment was appropriate.

Settlement, Alternative Dispute Resolution, or Trial. After the motion and discovery phase is complete, the parties in the case will proceed towards a final resolution, which can be reached in many ways. First, the parties may settle the case; this occurs as a result of negotiations between the parties to reach a result that both sides agree with. A **settlement** is carried out using formal contractual agreements that are filed with the court;

---

[4]The court spelled defendant Emery's name incorrectly throughout the case.

often times, settlement agreements are not made public and only the parties to the case know the final result. Another option is to seek resolution using a form of **alternative dispute resolution** ("ADR") such as **arbitration** or **mediation.** These formalized resolution processes are intended to reach an outcome, yet avoid litigation. Both arbitration and mediation are discussed completely in Chapter 5.30, *Alternative Dispute Resolution.* Lastly, the parties may opt not to settle or use ADR and proceed to trial seeking adjudication. A trial is a part of the legal process that has its own specific rules and procedure which will not be discussed; however, in a civil case, a trial will most often result in a either a finding of liability on behalf of the defendant (victory for the plaintiff) or a finding of non-liability (victory for the defendant). This is a generalized way of discussing the potential outcome, because shared liability is possible as well; for a full discussion, see Chapter 2.21, *Defenses against Negligence.*

Damages. If the defendant is found liable, damages will likely be awarded to the plaintiff (although this is not always the case). As discussed in Chapter 2.11, *Negligence,* **damages** is the monetary compensation awarded as a remedy for defendant liability. Damages can be compensatory (intended to compensate for harm) or punitive (intended to punish the wrongdoer and deter similar future acts), and vary based on the specific claim and individual outcome of each trial.

Appellate Phase

After a trial court adjudicates a claim, either party has the opportunity to file a **notice of appeal**, requesting that the appropriate appellate court review the case. As noted earlier, appeals are requested based on legal error; a misinterpretation or misapplication of the law. Neither party has the right to appeal simply because they disagree with the trial court outcome; the appeals process is intended to correct legal error, not give the parties a second chance at their claim. All 50 states and the federal court system have very specific rules regarding appellate procedure; they are as complex, if not more so, than the trial process. While the full appellate process will not be discussed in this chapter, it is important to discuss the role of an appellate court generally.

On appeal, the reviewing court will use the facts of the case established at the trial court level; the appellate court is not a fact-finding court. Using those facts, the appellate court will determine whether the decision reached by the trial court was correct in totality (**affirmed**), correct in part (**affirmed in part**), incorrect in totality (**reversed**), or incorrect in part (**reversed in part**). Often times, when the appellate court affirms or reverses a decision in part, it will also **remand** the case back to the trial court for further proceedings consistent with the appellate decision, which means the appellate court will ask the court of origin to hear parts of the case a second time.

Most of the Significant Cases you will read in this textbook are authored by appellate courts; thus, the opinion you read will likely summarize the finding and decisions at the trial court level, and then proceed with the appellate review. Any precedential value that the case has (binding or persuasive, see earlier discussion) will come from the appellate court decision.

Case Example #4: This case highlights a majority of the procedural elements discussed in the Legal Process section. Note that the Factual and Procedural Background section is a summary of the trial court level case, written by the appellate court (who authored this opinion). The discussion of the legal issues at the appellate level is omitted; however, the appellate court's disposition (decision) is included.

MARIO SOLIS et al., Plaintiffs and Appellants, v. KIRKWOOD RESORT COMPANY,
Defendant and Respondent.
114 Cal. Rptr. 2d 265 (2001)

OPINION
Mario (**plaintiff**) and Janelle Solis sued Kirkwood Resort Company (**defendant**, the true name of which is Kirkwood Mountain Resort, LLC), after a ski accident. The **trial** court granted defendant's motion for summary judgment, finding plaintiff signed a release of negligence liability which embraced this accident, and that defendant owed no duty to plaintiff under the primary assumption of the risk rule. **Plaintiff filed a timely notice of appeal from the ensuing judgment.**

(Continued)

We conclude plaintiff established an ambiguity in the release and a jury could find it was not intended to cover this accident. Moreover, there is a critical factual question regarding whether defendant increased the risk of harm to skiers beyond that inherent in the sport. **We reverse**.

STANDARD OF REVIEW

Summary judgment is properly granted to a defendant who shows without refutation that a plaintiff cannot establish an essential element of his cause of action or that there is an affirmative defense which bars recovery: Our review is de novo.

FACTUAL AND PROCEDURAL BACKGROUND

The **complaint** alleges Mario Solis was skiing at defendant's resort when, without warning, he entered an area of the resort that had recently been altered to accommodate a ski race. This area now consisted of hazardous man-made jumps, which increased the risk of harm to skiers and caused him to fall down. **The complaint raised theories of negligence and premises liability, with a pendent loss of consortium claim for plaintiff's wife, Janelle.**

The answer generally denied the allegations and asserted a number of defenses, including a release of liability signed by plaintiff, and primary assumption of the risk.

The undisputed facts show the accident occurred on Sunday, March 28, 1999. Earlier that ski season, plaintiff bought a midweek season pass from defendant, entitled "Season Pass & Liability Release Agreement." This allowed him to use defendant's facilities Monday through Friday for the entire season, except for designated holiday dates. Part of the application for the season pass consists of a release of liability form, the terms of which will be recited in a moment. The entire application is reproduced as an appendix to this opinion. Although a checked box indicates plaintiff bought a "Midweek Plus Season Pass," the parties agree he paid for and obtained the "Midweek Season Pass." In part this states "Pass is only valid Monday through Friday," with certain exceptions not relevant to this case. Because his season pass did not allow weekend usage, in order to ski the Sunday of the accident, plaintiff had to buy a day pass. Defendant does not require purchasers of day passes to sign a release or at least did not require plaintiff to do so.

Defendant produced declarations of two ski patrollers who helped plaintiff after the accident, and supporting documentation including photographs and reports prepared by the ski patrol. The gist of this evidence was that plaintiff, through inattention or for a thrill, skied past a line of crossed bamboo poles, which closed the jumps off from the run plaintiff was using. Defendant acknowledged that that part of the mountain had been turned into a racing start for a special event scheduled for later that day. **Defendant also produced portions of plaintiff's deposition, where he described himself as an expert skier.** Plaintiff had claimed a mound or "berm" of snow "kicked me into the air."

Plaintiff argued defendant "created a temporary hazard that caused the injury." **According to declarations submitted by plaintiff and by his skiing partner that day**, the bamboo warning poles were not erected until after the accident. Plaintiff argued the release contained in his season pass application was temporally delimited by the scope of the pass itself, that is, the release was operative only Monday through Friday.

The trial court granted summary judgment, as follows: "Kirkwood's evidence establishes that plaintiff Mario Solis executed a valid, binding, and enforceable contract when he signed the 'Season Pass & Liability Release Agreement.' The court finds that the contract is clear and unambiguous on it[s] face, and specifically finds that the Liability Release contained within the contract is not limited by the type of pass that a skier purchases. The clear intent of the contract is that the Liability Release bars all claims by all season pass holders, regardless of the type of pass purchased.

(*Continued*)

"Plaintiffs do not dispute that the Release is inherently valid and enforceable; instead **plaintiff argues that because the accident occurred on a day on which his particular pass was not valid, the Release was also not valid. The Court finds this argument unpersuasive**. The Release is not a part of, subordinate to, or governed by the season pass; both are encompassed by the 'Season Pass & Liability Release Agreement.' The obvious intent of that document is that one release shall bind all claims by all pass holders.

"The agreement is devoid of language which suggests that the Release's applicability is dependent upon the type of pass. Nor does the language support an interpretation that the Release is only valid on days when the pass is also valid. Such a conclusion contradicts the simple and clear language on the face of the document. The court finds that plaintiff entered the contract without mistake of fact.

"The court finds that plaintiffs' claims are also barred by the doctrine of primary assumption of risk. Plaintiff's descriptions of the terrain feature on which he lost control are inconsistent. Based upon the evidence presented, the court is unable to rule whether the terrain feature is [natural] or man-made. **In either event, plaintiffs' evidence does not establish that the terrain feature on which plaintiff lost control increased the risks inherent in the sport**. Whether the object was natural or man-made, the evidence supports a finding that it posed a risk inherent in the sport of skiing. **Plaintiff's deposition testimony establishes that he was familiar with such risks, and understood that skiers assume the dangers posed thereby**. The plaintiffs' claims are, therefore, also barred under the doctrine of primary assumption of risk."

A judgment was entered accordingly and plaintiff filed a timely notice of appeal therefrom.

DISCUSSION: Omitted

DISPOSITION:
The **trial court judgment is reversed with directions to vacate the order granting summary judgment and enter an order denying the motion**. Defendant is to pay plaintiff's costs of this appeal.

Explanation

*This case demonstrates the complexity of the legal process, highlighting many of the important steps along the way. The plaintiff initiated the case by filing a complaint with the appropriate trial court in the California state court system; the defendant then filed an answer. Both parties conducted discovery, obtaining declarations and depositions. After discovery, the defendant filed a motion for summary judgment, which was granted by the trial court. The plaintiff appealed that finding to the Court of Appeal of California, who reversed the decision and entered judgment for the plaintiff denying the motion for summary judgment. **It is important to note** what this means procedurally; this does not mean that the plaintiff has won the case or will receive damages; rather, this means that the plaintiff can proceed with the original complaint in trial court and continue to a trial if he so desires. Other options for the plaintiff include settlement or ADR.*

QUESTIONS YOU SHOULD BE ABLE TO ANSWER

1. What is the difference between common law and statutory law?

2. What is precedent? How is it created? What forms of precedent exist?

3. Describe the difference between the federal and state court systems.

4. What is a motion for summary judgment? When/Why is it typically filed?

5. What is the role of the appellate courts in the legal process?

REFERENCES
Cases
Fraser v. Major League Soccer, 2000 U.S. Dist. LEXIS 5434
Roman v. Liberty University, et. al., 2008 Cal. App. LEXIS 636
Sanders v. Kuna Joint School District, 876 P.2d 154 (1994)
Solis v. Kirkwood Resort Company, 114 Cal. Rptr. 2d 265 (2001)

Publications
Black, H. C. (1990). Black's Law Dictionary, (6th Ed.) St. Paul: West Publishing Co.
Colorado State Court System. Available at: http://www.courts.state.co.us/Courts/Index.cfm
Hill, G.and Hill, K. Online Legal Dictionary. Available at: http://dictionary.law.com/
Maryland's Judicial System. Available at: http://www.courts.state.md.us/overview.html
Montana Judicial System. Available at http://home.mcn.net/~montanabw/judsys.html
New York State Unified Court System. Available at http://www.courts.state.ny.us/courts/structure.shtml

Legislation
Conn. Gen. Stat. § 52-577 (2012)
Minn. Stat. § 541.01 (2012)
S.C. Code Ann. §52-19-20 (2011)

1.20   LEGAL RESEARCH

Anita M. Moorman | University of Louisville

Many sport organizations have legal counsel on staff or have ready access to outside legal counsel who can certainly assist as legal issues arise. However, recreation and sport managers should also have the ability to perform and analyze legal research for themselves either in an effort to proactively anticipate legal issues or to respond to a legal issue once it has arisen. In addition, the ability to conduct legal research will allow the recreation and sport manager to obtain information about current and emerging legal developments. A meaningful understanding of current legal developments is as critical to the recreation and sport manager as is a firm understanding of current developments in communication, marketing, finance, sponsorship, ethics, and many other areas. This chapter will introduce future recreation and sport managers to the variety of legal resources available in the traditional law library as well as from electronic and Internet sources.

Locating legal information is much easier if the researcher has a comfortable understanding of how the legal system works. Thus, it is imperative for the recreation and sport manager to understand that the U.S. judicial system is divided into distinctly separate federal and state systems. Thus, legal information is also separated based on whether a legal issue involved a state law or a federal law. For example, the court decision in *Brady v. National Football League* (2011) which permitted the league to continue to lockout the players was made by a federal court because it involved a question of federal law related to federal labor law. The "law" can mean different things to different people, but for the purposes of conducting legal research "the law" refers to a source that actually establishes a legal standard, principle, or mandate. For example, to govern a democratic society such as the United States, that society typically will create a governing document that will define how it will govern itself. Typically, this governing document is called a Constitution and it will define the powers and authority of the various branches of the government as well as limitations on governmental powers and authority. Thus both the United States Constitution and the various state constitutions are examples of primary sources of law. Another example of the law can be found in legislation or statutes. Legislation or statutes are enacted by the state and federal legislatures which in turn rely on state and federal agencies to enforce the statutes. Thus administrative agencies tend to be primarily responsible for writing or promulgating rules and regulations to enforce the statutes. Lastly, the courts must interpret the statutes or rules and fill any gaps left by the legislatures or administrative agencies. Thus, **Constitutions**, **Statutes**, **Administrative Regulations/Rules**, and **Court Decisions** make up the four primary sources of law. All the activities described above are recorded, cataloged, stored, indexed, and housed in thousands of volumes. And while the sheer volume of this legal information can appear daunting to a beginning researcher, because it is cataloged and indexed so thoroughly, a well-planned research project can be managed effectively.

The purpose of this chapter is to help the reader understand legal research. First, we will look at the legal resources available to the researcher. These include the four **primary sources** listed above (the actual law), **secondary sources** (explanations/definitions/summaries of the law), and certain **research tools** (digests, electronic databases, computerized legal research). Then we will look at two important techniques to use in conducting legal research. These are **Developing the Research Plan** and **Summarizing Cases**.

LEGAL RESOURCES

Primary Legal Resouces

Primary legal sources include constitutions, statutes, rules and regulations, and court decisions. Primary legal sources represent the actual law, whether it is a decision of the U.S. Supreme Court or a state statute enacted by the State of Oklahoma. *Regardless of the type of legal research being conducted, ultimately only primary legal sources can be relied on in determining what the law is and what the law requires.*

Constitutions/Statutes/Rules/Regulations

The U.S. Constitution is the supreme law of the land. It both authorizes and restricts conduct of the federal and state governments, as well as conduct of private citizens. Each of the fifty states will similarly have a state constitution governing conduct of the state government and citizens of that state. The U.S. Congress and fifty state legislatures enact laws known as statutes addressing issues ranging from the enforceability of contracts, to sport lotteries, to registration of trademarks. The federal statutes are codified (or published) in a series of volumes known as the *United States Code* (U.S.C.). Each of the fifty states also codifies its state statutes, which are often called civil codes, public laws, session laws, or revised statutes. Both the *United States Code* and the state statutes are published in both print and electronic formats. Many of the codes also contain **annotations** that categorize court decisions, law review articles, and legal treatises interpreting the statute in question. These annotations are similar to an index and will assist the researcher in locating specific court decisions and understanding how the statute has been interpreted and applied by the courts. For example, if you were trying to determine whether a federal district court in your state had ruled in a case involving the *Olympic and Amateur Sports Act* (this is the act that created and empowered the U.S. Olympic Committee), you could use the annotations to locate specific cases decided by courts in your state.

Congress and the state legislatures also create regulatory bodies such as the Federal Aviation Administration, Environmental Protection Agency, Equal Employment Opportunity Commission, and many others. These regulatory bodies often are required to create rules and regulations to fulfill their assigned purpose. These rules and regulations for federal agencies are codified in the *Code of Federal Regulations* (C.F.R.) and can be a useful resource for research related to a particular agency's activities. Most state and federal agencies also maintain up to date information concerning rules, regulations, and policies on the Internet to permit easy access to this information. A partial list of constitutional and statutory resources is as follows:

U.S. Constitution	State Constitutions
Treaties	Federal Statutes (the *U.S. Code* [U.S.C.])
State Statutes	Municipal Ordinances
Rules of Court	Executive Orders and Promulgations
Rules/Regulations of Federal Administrative Agencies (C.F.R.)	
Rules/Regulations of State Administrative Agencies	
Attorney General Opinions—federal and state	

Court Decisions

A court decision results from a jury verdict or court order that resolves a case or an issue in a case. For example, suppose Tim Tebow sued John Brown Company based on the company's unauthorized use of Tim Tebow's name in an advertisement. Tebow's lawsuit or case will probably include several different legal claims such as trademark infringement, violation of the right of publicity, and misappropriation of goodwill. It is possible that John Brown would file a motion for summary judgment (remember this was discussed in the previous chapter) asking the court to dismiss Tebow's trademark infringement claim. When the court either grants or denies the motion for summary judgment, it will enter an order to that effect. This order represents a court decision. Ultimately, if the case goes to trial, another court decision will be entered reflecting the outcome of the trial. Either or both of these court decisions may be published. Thus, if we want to be able to find and read this decision, we must understand when and where these court decisions are published.

Understanding the court system (which was covered in the previous chapter) aids us in locating these decisions. You may recall that court systems are hierarchical in structure, that is, that some courts are superior to others. The highest court is usually a supreme or superior court, followed by an intermediate appellate court, and ending with a district or trial court at the bottom. Most cases will originate at the trial or district court level and work their way *up* through the court system. This process can take years for a case to move through all levels of the court system. Any number of court decisions may be entered in a case as it winds its way through the court system to its ultimate conclusion, so to find court decisions, you need to understand how those decisions are reported. First, we will explore the federal court system and then the state court system.

Federal Courts

In the federal court system, the vast majority of federal cases originate in the U.S. District Court. The U.S. District Court is the federal trial court and the first level within the federal court system. Any appeal from a U.S. District Court decision would be made to the appropriate U.S. Court of Appeals. Any party to the district court action may appeal to the U.S. Court of Appeals. The U.S. Courts of Appeals represent the second level or the intermediate appellate level in the federal court system. As explained in the previous chapter, the court of appeals only exercises appellate jurisdiction. That means cases do not originate in the court of appeals; instead, a case would only reach the court of appeals after a decision has been made in a lower court (such as the district court) and a party appeals from that decision. That appeal requests the appellate court to review a portion of the lower court's decision to determine whether the lower court made a mistake. After the U.S. Court of Appeals renders its decision, a party can still request another appellate review by the U.S. Supreme Court. However, the U.S. Supreme Court is not required to hear these appeals. The appellate jurisdiction of the U.S. Supreme Court is considered discretionary and, as such, requests for appeal (known as petitions for *certiorari*) are rarely granted. The U.S. Supreme Court is the highest court in the land, and its decisions are considered the supreme law of the land, which must be followed by all lower federal and state courts. As the federal courts make these decisions regarding cases, they are published or reported in the reporters listed following.

U.S. District Courts. Federal Supplement and *Federal Supplement Second Series* (cited F. Supp., or F. Supp. 2d). (Note: These reporters are a continuing series of cases reported by the U.S. District Courts from 1932 to the present date. This reporter is in its second series or edition now).

Sample Citation: *Hoopla Sports and Entertainment, Inc. v. Nike, Inc.*, 947 F. Supp. 347 (N.D. Ill. 1996). This citation tells us that this court decision can be located in volume 947 at page 347 in the Federal Supplement. It further tells us that the decision was made by the U.S. District Court for the Northern District of Illinois in 1996.

U.S. Courts of Appeals. Federal Reporter, Federal Reporter Second Series, Federal Reporter Third Series (cited F., F.2d, or F.3d). (Note: These reporters are a continuing series of cases reported by the U.S. Courts of Appeals from 1880 to the present date. This reporter is in its third series or edition now).

Sample Citation: *National Basketball Association v. Motorola, Inc.*, 105 F.3d 841 (2nd Cir. 1997). This citation tells us that this court decision can be found in volume 105 at page 841 in the Federal Reporter Third Series. It further tells us that the decision was made by the U.S. Court of Appeals for the Second Circuit in 1997.

U.S. Supreme Court. U.S. Supreme Court Reports (cited U.S.); Supreme Court Reporter (cited S. Ct.); Lawyer's Edition (cited L.Ed.2d). (Note: These three reporters all report the same Supreme Court cases. *U.S. Supreme Court Reports* is the official Supreme Court reporter, but *Supreme Court Reporter* is most commonly used and user friendly).

Sample Citation: *PGA Tour, Inc. v. Martin*, 532 U.S. 661, 121 S. Ct. 1879, 149 L. Ed. 2d 904 (2001). You will often see all three reporters cited, this is called a string cite. The first part of the string is the citation to the U.S. Supreme Court Reports (532 U.S. 661), followed by the citation to the Supreme Court Reporter (121 S. Ct. 1879), and ending with the citation to the Lawyer's Edition (149 L. Ed. 2d 904). You may also see a Supreme Court case cited with only one of these three possible citations, such as *PGA Tour, Inc. v. Martin*, 121 S. Ct. 1879 (2001). This citation tells us that this decision can be found at volume 121 at page 1879 in the Supreme Court Reporter. It further tells us that this decision of the U.S. Supreme Court was made in 2001.

State Courts

The state court systems are organized in a similar fashion to the federal courts. Most states will have several trial or district courts located in the various counties in the state. Most cases will originate in the trial or district courts and then follow a similar path as federal cases with appeals going to an intermediate appellate court or directly to the state supreme court. Typically, only decisions made by a state's Supreme Court are selected for publication in the **state reporters.** These decisions, once published, are organized in a reporter system in two different ways. Each state's decisions can be found in its separate state reporter such as the *California Reporter.* However, many law libraries only carry the individual state reporter for the state in which they are located. For all other states' court decisions, the library will likely have the **regional reporter** that publishes the same state court decisions but grouped together in a specific region. The regional reporters are broken down following.

>**Atlantic Reporter** (cited A. and A.2d)
>>[Pennsylvania, Vermont, New Hampshire, Maine, Rhode Island, Connecticut, New Jersey, Delaware, and Maryland]
>**North Eastern Reporter** (cited N.E. and N.E.2d)
>>[New York, Massachusetts, Ohio, Indiana, and Illinois]
>**North Western Reporter** (cited N.W. and N.W.2d)
>>[North Dakota, South Dakota, Minnesota, Wisconsin, Michigan, Nebraska, and Iowa]
>**Pacific Reporter** (cited P. and P.2d)
>>[Kansas, Oklahoma, New Mexico, Colorado, Wyoming, Montana, Arizona, Utah, Idaho, Nevada, Washington, Oregon, California, Hawaii, and Alaska]
>**South Eastern Reporter** (cited S.E. and S.E.2d)
>>[West Virginia, Virginia, North Carolina, South Carolina, and Georgia]
>**Southern Reporter** (cited So. and So.2d)
>>[Louisiana, Mississippi, Alabama, and Florida]
>**South Western Reporter** (cited S.W. and S.W.2d)
>>[Kentucky, Tennessee, Missouri, Arkansas, and Texas]

The following sample citations to state reporters follow a similar format to those we examined in the federal courts:

Maisonave v. Newark Bears Professional Baseball Club, 881 A.2d 700 (N.J. 2005). This case can be found in volume 881 at page 700 in the Atlantic Reporter, Second Series. This is a 2005 decision of the New Jersey Supreme Court.

Rowe v. Pinellas Sports Auth., 461 So. 2d 72 (Fla. 1984). This case can be found in volume 461 at page 72 in the Southern Reporter, Second Series and is a 1984 decision of the Florida Supreme Court.

Kelly v. Marylanders for Sports Sanity, Inc. 530 A.2d 245 (Md. Ct. App. 1987). This case can be found in volume 530 at page 245 of the Atlantic Reporter, Second Series; however, notice that it is a 1987 decision of the Maryland Court of Appeals. This is one of those instances where an intermediate appellate court decision was published and the use of the term "App." or "Ct. App." in the parenthesis with the date is how you can distinguish between decisions of the court of appeals and those of the various state supreme courts. If the citation does not contain "App" or "Ct. App," but instead just the state abbreviation as in the first two sample citations, that means the decision was made by the state's highest court (either a supreme court or superior court).

Secondary Resources

Secondary resources include articles, journals, papers, and other written sources that summarize, explain, interpret, or analyze certain issues or topics of the law. In addition to making a scholarly contribution to the understanding of legal issues and topics, they provide the sport or recreation manager with an overview or insight into a particular area. Secondary resources also can be a valuable source for locating additional or related primary sources; however, only primary resources represent the actual law. *Thus, secondary resources should never be solely relied on as legal authority.* Following is a listing of several secondary resources by type and description.

>**Legal Dictionaries:** *Black's Law Dictionary* provides definitions of legal terms. It is a must for studying and researching law. Many paperback, condensed versions are available.
>**Lawyer Directories:** Martindale-Hubbell is useful for locating attorneys in any state in the United States.
>**Annotated Law Reports (A.L.R.):** A.L.R. contains commentary and summary on areas of law. It covers both state and federal courts. The annotation usually includes a case summary together with commentary about the case and how it may or does affect other cases or the current status of the law. A.L.R. is very useful if you have a specific case for which you wish to study the impact it has had on the law.

Legal Encyclopedias: *Corpus Juris Secundum* and *American Jurisprudence* (Am. Jur.). A legal encyclopedia functions like a standard encyclopedia and includes topical summaries of numerous legal issues. The summary will also include supporting references to cases, statutes, and other primary and secondary resources. This is a good place to start if you know little or nothing about a topic and want a jumping-off point. These will not provide much analysis and may not contain the latest developments.

Restatement of Law (Torts, contracts, etc.): Restatements are comprehensive surveys of a specific and major category of law. For example, the **Restatement of Contracts** summarizes the origin, development, and current application of contract law in the United States noting differences among individual states, majority positions, and the general rule of law for all issues related to contracts. These can be useful to develop a better understanding of the principle and theory of law if the reader has some familiarity with the law already.

Treatises (Textbooks, Casebooks, and Hornbooks): Treatises are written by scholars and experts on a particular legal issue or topic. These resources are usually very comprehensive and provide an in-depth examination of the issue or topic. Note, however, that a treatise represents the author's interpretation of the law—a treatise is not the actual law. Treatises can provide the reader with substantial references and resources on a specific topic. Most law libraries have extensive collections of treatises. The preeminent publication in the field is the three-volume set by Betty van der Smissen entitled *Legal Liability and Risk Management for Public and Private Entities*. Some sport law treatises include: *Torts and Sports: Legal Liability in Professional and Amateur Athletics* by Raymond L. Yasser; *Sports and Law: Contemporary Issues* by Herb Appenzeller.

Shepard's Citations: Shepard's Citations is a publication that allows the researcher to track a court decision or statute through a citation index. The citation index lists court decisions that have cited previous court decisions and court decisions interpreting specific statutory sections. This resource is useful to locate additional cases once the research has located a major or dispositive case. But more importantly, this index tracks any "treatment" of a particular case. Thus, the index identifies if a case the researcher is relying on has been questioned, criticized, followed, reversed, or otherwise interpreted by later court decisions. This is extremely important to ensure that court decisions relied on are indeed still representative of the current legal standard.

Legal Indexes (*Index to Legal Periodicals* (ILP)): The ILP allows the researcher to locate law review articles by topic and/or author. The ILP is available both in the traditional book form and electronically. The researcher can conduct a topical electronic search and will be provided with citation and location information for law review articles on that topic.

Law Review Articles: Published primarily by law schools or professional law associations throughout the United States. To date there are numerous law reviews/journals regularly addressing sport law issues. Some of these include: *Marquette Sports Law Review*; *Villanova Sports & Entertainment Law Journal*; *Univ. Miami Entertainment & Sports Law Review*; *Seton Hall Journal of Sport Law*; *American Bar Association Entertainment & Sports Lawyer*; and *Sports Lawyers Journal*.

Academic Legal Journals: Several academic associations publish journals focused on legal issues. In sport, the Sport and Recreation Law Association publishes the *Journal of Legal Aspects of Sport* containing scholarly papers related to legal issues in sport and recreation. Other scholarly publications include *From the Gym to the Jury*; *Sports in the Courts*; *Sports, Parks and Recreation Law Reporter*; and *The Exercise, Sports and Sports Medicine Standards & Malpractice Reporter*.

Business or Academic Journals: Many current legal issues related to sport may be covered in business and academic journals. Many academic business journals also contain special sections for legal developments. For example, the *Sport Marketing Quarterly* has a column entitled Marketing and the Law featured in each issue. *Journal of Marketing & Public Policy* also has a similar feature.

Business Magazines and Newspapers: The sport industry is often the subject of articles in business magazines and daily newspapers. Often current developments in the sport industry have a legal impact. For example, the filing of a case will often be reported in major newspapers both in their print and electronic versions. Street and Smith's *SportsBusiness Journal* and *Athletic Business* often report on recent legal developments and issues. These articles can help sport and recreation managers identify the issues and stay current with legal developments in the sport and recreation industries.

Additional Research Tools

The preceding secondary sources are especially helpful in locating topical and/or general information. However, ultimately the researcher must locate primary legal resources. Although the secondary sources will normally identify many useful primary resources, often the primary resources identified are not exhaustive or the most current. At this point several additional research tools are available, including printed digests and a number of electronic databases.

Digests

Digests are particularly useful for locating court decisions on a particular topic. **Digests** are basically subject indexes to the federal and state reporters described earlier. For each state reporter there is a corresponding digest and for federal cases there is a *Federal Practice Digest* as well as several general digests that contain state and federal cases grouped by year. To make it even easier, remember the fifty states are grouped by region, so those court decisions that were published together in a regional state reporter also have a corresponding regional digest (for example, the Atlantic Reporter has a corresponding Atlantic Digest).

For example, if the researcher does not know the citation for a specific case but would like to find cases pertaining to a promoter's liability for an injury to a spectator during a wrestling match in the state of Vermont, the researcher could locate the Vermont or Atlantic Digest and topically search for key words such as "spectator," "wrestling," and "assumption of the risk." The digest will contain a listing of all cases in Vermont or the Atlantic region related to that topic. Now this sounds a bit easier than it actually is, because the law is not always indexed in the manner that an ordinary person may think. Consider the injured spectator example: the actual key word used by the digest to index these cases is "theatres and shows." The digests have **indexes** to help find the appropriate key word, but the researcher will have to explore many variations and be persistent in his or her search. Nevertheless, the digests provide a great wealth of information once the appropriate key word is found.

Electronic and Web-based Research

Electronic Search Engines and Databases. The availability and efficiency of electronic and Web-based research tools has enabled almost all legal research to be conducted via computer. Many law schools provide students with access to electronic databases known as **WESTLAW** and **LEXIS**, which allow the researcher to search topically or for a specific case or statute. Some law libraries restrict access to these databases to law students. In that case, **LexisNexis Academic Universe**, available through most college and university libraries, is also a valuable research tool and provides for searching top news; general news topics; company, industry, and market news; legal news; company financial information; law reviews; federal case law; *U.S. Code*; and state legal research. In the event that your library does not have or allow access to any of these resources, there are several additional Web-based research sites.

In addition to using electronic databases, we also have many electronic subscription services available to keep us abreast of current legal developments specific to the sport industry. Many of these services are free, such as the *FindLaw* Website, which offers a free subscription to a weekly e-mail listing current developments in sport law. An excellent paid subscription is available from *Sports Litigation Alerts*. Students are offered reduced subscription rates and will receive a bi-weekly, detailed summary of recent sport law developments. A listing and description of several other excellent electronic resources is contained at the end of the chapter.

Legal Blogs and Internet Searches. Thanks to Google and Yahoo and other Internet-based search engines, legal information often times can be accessed with just a click of the mouse. For example, if you enter the search term "sport law" into Google, Google's search engine will return more than 230,000 results from your search if you happened to put "sport law" in parenthesis to limit the number of hits. If you didn't put "sport law" in parentheses, Google will actually return more than 199,000,000 hits in just a few seconds. This capability can be both a benefit and a detriment. The speed and ease of such a search is a great benefit, but obviously, it could take days or even weeks to sort through 230,000 results, and tackling almost two hundred million results is nearly impossible. So for maximum effectiveness, our searches need to be as specific and detailed as possible.

Google and other search engines can also be used very effectively to locate current relevant developments in sport law. For example, assume you are a sport or recreation manager and have been following a pending lawsuit. In the past, it could take days or even weeks after a final decision was made in that pending case for you to be able to learn of the decision and access a copy of the court's order or opinion. Today, often times the notification of the final decision is made almost simultaneously with the decision itself and the actual written decision or order is available within just a few minutes or hours. Almost every major news outlet delivers the news via the Internet and enables you to receive instant notifications of breaking news stories. A good example of just how useful these services are to a sport or recreation manager can be found related to Bobby Petrino's termination as the University of Arkansas head football coach in April, 2012. This case was being watched with great interest by most college athletic administrators since, in addition to the obvious contract law issues associated with terminating a coach, this situation also raised questions of potential sexual harassment claims and employment discrimination claims. If you had been following this situation, and subscribed to one of the many daily email news updates available today, you would have been notified immediately when the University of Arkansas decided to fire Coach Petrino. In addition, within just a few hours a great deal of legal commentary was also accessible interpreting and analyzing the university's decision. This kind of immediate information concerning legal developments can be very useful to a sport or recreation manager.

In addition to the search engines and news alerts, a number of legal blogs also exist that can be a valuable resource for practitioners. **Blogs** (which is short for weblogs) originally began as websites where individuals posted commentary or personal diaries. In the past, a blog was not a very useful research source, particularly for legal research because it primarily represented the personal opinion of the blogger and contained anonymous and/or random comments by the blog's readers. It was very difficult to discern whether the blogger possessed any particular expertise or knowledge and whether the blogger's posts were credible and reliable. Thus, the web made it possible for any person who has an opinion or knowledge about anything, to post that opinion or share that knowledge on the Internet. Like Google searches, not every post on a blog is credible, particularly when one is conducting legal research. Legal research must lead to verifiable and credible conclusions. For example, a post by a blogger that Coach Petrino should be fired may be interesting conversation, but is not useful or reliable when trying to understand the legal repercussions of the University of Arkansas' decision or the legal impact of the decision going forward. Thus, while blogs generally should still be viewed with some skepticism when conducting legal research, a number of "credible legal authorities" provide their opinions, commentary, and legal analysis via weblogs. These legal blogs, such as the Sports Law Blog are a useful legal resource for tracking current legal developments, reviewing credible commentary concerning legal issues, and linking to additional resources related to legal developments. The researcher still should exercise caution when citing to these sources unless he or she is able to satisfy himself or herself that the information is credible and reasonable to rely upon to support his or her conclusions. And if the researcher is going to rely upon these sources, he or she needs to take care to cite the sources properly to assure that the reader understands that a particular statement or conclusion is based upon a *secondary source* (not a primary source) and represents the opinion or analysis of an another, not necessarily the opinion or analysis of a court or legal expert or authority. If used cautiously and properly though, legal blogs are quite effective research tools.

Electronic and Internet Resources. Provided below are a number of Websites, search engines, electronic resources, and sport and recreation law blogs that should help you rapidly locate current developments in sport law as well as conduct more in-depth research.

General Legal Research: Searchable databases that cover a broad range of topics including general federal and state law information, federal and state court decisions:

FindLaw Search Database: www.findlaw.com/
Internet Reference Desk Website: www.refdesk.com
Law Library Resource Xchange: www.llrx.com
Law Journal EXTRA! Federal Courts: http://lawonline.ljx.com/federal/
Where to Find Court Opinions: www.legalonline.com/courts.htm
National Center for State Courts: www.ncsc.dni.us/
Law Crawler-Legal Search: www.lawcrawler.com/

The 'Lectric Law Lexicon: www.lectlaw.com//ref.html
American Law Source On-Line: www.lawsource.com/also/

Government Research Sources: Websites, some searchable, that provide information about government agencies, governmental functions, Congress, and general information:

United States Patent and Trademark Office: http://trademarks.uspto.gov/
United States Geological Survey: http://mapping.usgs.gov/www.gnis
State and Local Government on the Net: www.piperinfo.com/state/states.html
United States Federal Trade Commission: www.ftc.gov
United States Department of Labor: www.dol.gov.
United States Congress: www.congress.org.
United States Library of Congress: http://thomas.loc.gov/
United States Supreme Court: http://www.supremecourtus.gov/

University Sponsored Research Sites: Searchable databases and links that include general research of state and federal court decisions, the Constitution, and state and federal statutes as well as Websites focused on a single topic, such as Title IX and hazing:

The Legal Information Institute of Cornell Law School: www.law.cornell.edu
University of Iowa Gender Equity in Sports Project: http://bailiwick.lib.uiowa.edu/ge/
Alfred University Hazing Study: www.alfred.edu/news/html/hazing_study.html
The Legal Education Network at the University of Pittsburgh: http://jurist.law.pitt.edu/
Indiana State University Sport Law Links: http://library.indstate.edu/level1.dir/lio.dir/sportslaw.htm#Sports

Law Journals and Associations Sites: Websites with sport law links and general information about sport law studies and research:

Emory Law School: www.law.emory.edu/FEDCTS/
Marquette Law School: www.marquette.edu/law/sports/links.html
National Sport Law Institute publications: http://law.marquette.edu/cgi-bin/site.pl?2130&pageID=463#YMTC
https://law.marquette.edu/national-sports-law-institute/recent-developments-sports-law-formerly-you-make-call
Sport and Recreation Law Association: www.srlaweb.org

Miscellaneous Private Sites: Dozens of individuals and companies offer sport law information and links:

Mark's Sports Law News: www.sportslawnews.com/
Insurance Information Website: www.insure.com
Waiver/Risk Management Website: www.sportwaiver.com
Court TV Glossary of Legal Terms: www.courttv.com/legalterms/glossary.html
Sport Law Blogs
http://www.sportslawblog.com
http://thesportslawprofessor.blogspot.com/
http://blog.willamette.edu/wucl/journals/sportslaw/
http://abajournal.com/blawgs/entertainment+sports+law
http://ctsportslaw.com/
http://athleteagent.blogspot.com/
http://www.sportsagentblog.com/
http://rec-law.blogspot.com/
www. http://defendingsportsblog.com/

RESEARCH TECHNIQUES

Developing the Research Plan

Once the researcher is comfortable with the court system and how legal information is codified and reported, it is time to begin the actual research. Having a clearly defined research plan is vital to locating legal information efficiently. Otherwise, the researcher could spend countless hours in the law library with little to show for it. The following six steps represent a good approach to conducting legal research.

Step One: Identify the Problem or Issue

Step One is by far the most important step in the research process. If the issue or problem is not clearly identified, it will be impossible to narrow your search enough to produce meaningful results. A clearly defined issue will also help to discover key words, phrases, and terms that may facilitate the research. However, before you can identify the legal issue involved, you must search current business and professional literature to stay on top of industry activities. For example, when the State of Maryland passed legislation exempting fantasy sports from state gambling prohibitions, interest increased regarding which other states either already permitted fee-based fantasy sports contests or where such contests may be legally permissible (Rosenwald, 2012). Under the new exemption, individuals who participate in fee-based fantasy sports leagues in Maryland can legally collect the prize money that comes along with winning a fantasy sports league. A number of legal scholars commented on this development and published law review articles on the subject which could be easily located by sport industry professionals to help them understand the legislation as well as its implications for the gaming industry (Edelman, 2012). Even though no lawsuit had been filed, the actual legal issues which would be raised in such a case may have implications that extend beyond the State of Maryland and could impact various sport industry segments.

Several good sources of recent developments in the sport industry are available. The *Chronicle of Higher Education* has sections on college athletics, which report recent educational, administrative, business, and legal developments. Several industry publications such as Street and Smith's *SportsBusiness Journal* also will report emerging business and legal issues. In addition, any current news source will be a good place to locate current trends and issues. Once the general issue has been identified, it then becomes easier to identify the legal issues. However, if instead of a specific recent development, a familiar topic or subject in the sport industry is to be the focus of our research, such as Title IX (Gender Equity), then the *Index to Legal Periodicals* and **LexisNexis Academic Universe** are helpful to track down previous law review articles on the subject. Also, remember electronic sources such as **www.findlaw.com** and **www.law.com** have subject sections available with links to numerous other information sources.

Step Two: Consult an Encyclopedia or Treatise

Once the issue is identified, legal encyclopedias, treatises, and digests will help the researcher gain familiarity with the general area of the law implicated by the current problem or issue. For example, consider the situation where you are interested in researching whether coaches can be terminated from their jobs for violent behavior. Determine what area of law is implicated: labor relations, assault and battery, teacher rights, or some other area. **Encyclopedias** and **treatises** will help to sift through the information to narrow the search to what ultimately may be a simple question of either contract law (Does the coach have a contract, and if so, what does it say about termination?), or employer/employee relations (Is the coach an employee at will, or must the school demonstrate just cause to terminate?). **Digests** will provide references to court decisions related to your issue or subject. If you have discovered that your issue relates to a specific state or federal statute, most statutes contain **Annotations** that identify other related statutes, legislative history, law review articles, and court decisions relating to that specific statutory provision. Step Two will also help to refine the problem or issue defined in Step One as more information becomes available to the researcher.

Step Three: Read and Summarize Cases

Cases identified in Step Two need to be read thoroughly and then summarized according to their importance and relevance to the issue. A sample summary for a key case is provided at the end of this chapter. Any relevant literature such as law review articles, business journal articles, or other literature must be summarized to help frame the importance of the issue to the sport industry.

Step Four: Locate Additional Cases and Shepardize

Once a few key cases are located, locating more recent or relevant cases is fairly simple. For this task the **West's Key Number System** together with the **digests** is critical. Each case published in the West's Reporter System will contain several short summaries indexed by topic and key number throughout the West's Digest System. Basically, once you have found a major case relevant to your problem, finding other similar cases from the same jurisdiction or from other states or federal cases is easy to accomplish using the West's Digest. **Shepard's Citations** is the most available updating service. Shepard's Citations will also help to locate additional cases and verify whether the cases the researcher is relying on are still good law. This process is usually referred to as "Shepardizing." If the cases you are relying on have been reversed, overruled, or somehow disregarded by later courts, your position can be severely weakened. Although the service is a bit cumbersome to use, it is important to make the effort. Most law librarians will demonstrate how to use the service once you have a particular case citation that you would like to update.

Step Five: Determine Any Constitutional or Statutory Connections

Not every problem or issue requires an examination of constitutional and statutory law; however, if a particular article of a constitution or a statute, state or federal, is implicated, it needs to be located and thoroughly read and updated. It is not uncommon for Congress or state legislatures to frequently amend and modify existing statutory laws; thus, the researcher must find the most current version of any statutory provisions. Always be sure to consult the "pocket part" of any statutory volume for the latest amendments or modifications.

Step Six: Organize Your Information

Organizing all the general information, cases, and statutes can be a daunting task, but it is critical to effectively answer your question or problem identified in Step One. It is recommended that you summarize every case, define and redefine your issue as you gain a better understanding of the issue, search other jurisdictions for similar or dissimilar cases, and then locate any relevant statutory laws. After that, you will be able to integrate all the information together. For example, if your issue deals with gender equity in sports, you will soon learn that not only is there a specific federal statute to consider (Title IX), but numerous court decisions have also been published that help to interpret and understand the statute. Also, you will find that some rules or regulations issued by the Office of Civil Rights help in understanding the scope and impact of Title IX. In addition, scholars are frequently writing treatises and law review articles on this subject. A researcher could literally find hundreds of pages of information about Title IX.

So how does a researcher organize hundreds of pages of information? Simple, look back to the original problem or question. Limit or narrow the inquiry to only those bits of information that actually provide an answer to the original problem or question. Once that is completed, it is recommended that you then organize the information as follows:

Statement of Facts: Identify the facts or circumstances that created the need to study the problem.

Statement of the Issue/Problem: State the actual issue, question, or problem that will be answered.

Identification of the Relevant Law: Identify the cases, statutes, or other information needed to understand this issue. This should include a brief summary of relevant cases, relevant statutory language, and other information needed to understand the law.

Application of the Law: This section should include a detailed analysis of the law identified in the *Identification of the Relevant Law* section and how it applies to the *Statement of Facts* section to answer the question identified in the *Statement of the Issue/Problem* section.

Conclusion: Discuss the anticipated effect of your analysis in the *Application of the Law* section. How are recreation and sport managers or the industry affected by this legal issue?

SUMMARIZING CASES

As mentioned earlier, planning and organization are critical to the research plan. Court decisions must be read, summarized, and applied to answer the original research question. Following is an excerpt of a tort case involving an injury received by a fan at a wrestling match.

Illustrative Case

This case presents a good opportunity to demonstrate how to condense a case into its most important elements: citation, key facts, issues to be decided, decision of the court, and reasoning of the court. If every important case revealed during your research is summarized in this fashion, you will be able to quickly and efficiently incorporate this information into any report or written findings.

Dusckiewicz v. Jack Carter, d/b/a/, Jack Carter Enterprises

Supreme Court of Vermont
52 A.2d 788 (1947)

This is a tort action. The complaint is based upon the alleged negligence of the defendant in conducting a wrestling match, resulting in injury to the plaintiff, a spectator at that contest. The plaintiff had a verdict and judgment below in the sum of $150. . . .

* * *

We first consider the defendant's motion for a directed verdict. Material to this issue the jury could reasonably find the following facts from the evidence, viewed in the light most favorable to the plaintiff.

The defendant does business under the name "Jack Carter Enterprises". As one of his enterprises, Carter put on a show at the armory in Rutland on the evening of June 6, 1945. The principal feature of his show was a wrestling match. Through a booking office in Montreal, Carter engaged as contestants in this match two men skilled in the art of wrestling, one by the name of Savoli and the other's name is Ryan. Ryan had performed for Carter three times previous to this engagement and Savoli, once. At some time before June 6, 1945, Carter went to Rutland and made the necessary arrangements for putting on this show. Compensation for each wrestler, as arranged by Carter through the booking office, was a guaranty that each should receive a certain flat sum with a percentage option. That is, if the agreed percentage of the gate receipts amounted to more than the sum guaranteed then the wrestler concerned could elect to receive such percentage in lieu of the flat sum named in the guaranty. Compensation paid by Carter did not include payment of hotel bills or other expenses, in addition to payment as above stated.

On the evening of the show Carter saw the wrestlers, made sure that they were ready for the contest but gave them no instructions as to the manner of their behavior during the contest. Savoli then weighed about 230 lbs. and Ryan about 225 lbs. A "ring" was erected in the armory as the arena where the contest was staged. This arena platform was at an elevation of about four feet from the floor and was enclosed by three ropes extending around the outsides of it. Carter inspected this "ring" after it had been set up. Folding chairs fastened together in sets of three or four were provided as seats for spectators. The four or five rows nearest the "ring" were called "ring side seats" and sold for $1.50 each and the others were general admission seats and were cheaper. The chairs were not fastened to the floor.

The plaintiff resides in West Rutland and at the time in question was running a barbershop there. The owner of this shop was in service of the United States armed forces and it was agreed between him and the plaintiff that when the owner returned he was to take over this shop. The owner returned sometime in October or December of 1945 and then took over that business. The plaintiff made about seventy-five dollars per week from his barbering business and he also got about $20 per week as his part of the proceeds of a licensed pin ball machine then in the shop. As stated by the plaintiff in cross examination, he was "a wrestling fan". He invited two of his friends to attend this match with him and at the armory entrance he purchased three tickets for ring-side seats. These seats were in the front row nearest the ring. A person in the employ of the defendant ushered them to their seats which were numbered to correspond with numbers on their tickets. The plaintiff paid $1.50 each for the seats. After the match had been going on for some time, one of the wrestlers threw the other through the ropes in the direction where the plaintiff was seated. When the plaintiff saw the wrestler coming he put up his right hand to protect himself from the oncoming wrestler landing on him and as a result he received a sprained hand and wrist. It is for this injury and resulting alleged damages that the plaintiff seeks to recover.

The defendant based his motion for a directed verdict on grounds which may be briefly stated as follows. The plaintiff assumed the risk of the danger which resulted in his alleged injury; the wrestlers were independent contractors and not employees of the defendant and the evidence does not show any negligence on the part of the defendant.

As to the question of assumption of risks, the evidence shows that the plaintiff was a business visitor of the defendant at the time and place in question. He had paid $1.50 for his seat and was occupying it for the purpose as intended by the defendant. * * * An invitee at a place of amusement ordinarily assumes the risk of an obvious danger or of one that is a matter of common knowledge; conversely, such a person does not assume the risk of a hidden or undisclosed danger, not of common knowledge, in the absence of warning or personal knowledge. * * * That the danger which resulted in the plaintiff's injury was not an obvious danger is self-evident. However, the defendant contends that the plaintiff must be taken to have assumed the risks of the danger which resulted in his injury, because he had personal knowledge of it and also because such danger is a matter of common knowledge, and he cites several baseball cases in support of this contention. These cases hold that an invitee, familiar with the game of baseball, buying a seat in a part of the stands not protected by screens, who is hit by a batted ball during the progress of a ball game proceeding in a normal manner, can not recover, because it is a matter of common knowledge that chance is an important factor in determining the direction a batted ball may take as it leaves the bat. Such spectator assumes the risks of dangers of which he has personal knowledge and also he assumes the risks of those dangers which are matters of common knowledge.

The defendant in his brief makes the following statement. "The intent and purpose of a baseball game is to hit the ball as far as possible, and apparently one of the purposes of a wrestling match is to throw a wrestler as far as possible." It is to be noted that while the defendant makes a positive assertion as to the purpose and object of baseball, he is less positive and more cautious in speaking of the purposes and objects of wrestling. If it is true that one of the objects of wrestling is to throw a wrestler as far as possible from the ring, such purpose can not be said to be a matter of common knowledge, and we so hold. The number of people who know how a wrestling match is conducted and what may reasonably be expected to happen there is small when compared with the great number who know what may reasonably be expected to happen at a baseball game played in the normal manner.

While the record shows that the plaintiff stated in cross examination that he is a "wrestling fan", there is nothing therein showing the rules under which this contest was conducted nor whether such rules permit one wrestler to throw the other from the ring and neither does it appear that the plaintiff had ever seen that done previous to the occasion in question. From what has been hereinbefore stated, it follows that it can not be held as a matter of law that the plaintiff assumed the risks of the danger which resulted in his injury.

Whether the wrestlers were employees of the defendant or were independent contractors is not important in determining the questions before us. The defendant was putting on a show and as a feature of this he engaged these wrestlers to put on this match. It was his business to know the kind and type of performance that he was exhibiting and to use reasonable care as to location of seats and all other matters connected with this enterprise, for the reasonable protection of his invitees. Whether he performed this duty was, under the circumstances, a jury question.

* * *

Judgment reversed. Plaintiff's motion for a new trial on all issues raised by the pleadings is granted, and cause remanded.

Illustrative Case Summary

Dusckiewicz v. Jack Carter

d/b/a/, Jack Carter Enterprises, 52 A.2d 788 (Vt. 1947).

Key Facts

Teaching Note: In this section, you should select only those facts that directly relate to the court's final decision. Which facts were relevant to the court in reaching its conclusion?

The Plaintiff, a spectator at a wrestling match, sued Jack Carter *dba* Jack Carter Enterprises for negligence in his presentation of the wrestling match. The Plaintiff purchased ringside seats to watch a professional wrestling match being presented by Carter. Carter selected which wrestlers would be featured and hired two men who were considered skilled in the art of wrestling. Both men had performed for Carter previously. The ring was elevated four feet from the floor and was enclosed by three ropes around the entire ring. During the course of the match one wrestler threw the other through the ropes toward the Plaintiff's seat. The Plaintiff used his right hand to protect himself from the airborne wrestler. The Plaintiff received a sprained hand and wrist.

Issues to Be Decided

Teaching Note: In this section, you should identify the specific legal question that the court is being asked to decide. It should be stated in the form of a question and should incorporate enough of the facts involved in the case so that it is distinctive. This question will be answered in the next section.

1. Whether a spectator at a professional wrestling match has assumed the risk of injury associated with the likelihood that one of the contestants will be thrown from the ring?
2. Whether the risks associated with throwing a wrestler as far as possible from the ring is a matter of common knowledge to ordinary spectators of wrestling events?

Decision of the Court

Teaching Note: In this section, you should simply answer the question posed in the previous section. Your answer should be an affirmative or negative restatement of the question posed above.

1. A spectator at a wrestling match does not assume the risk of injury associated with the likelihood that one of the contestants will be thrown from the ring absent evidence of personal knowledge on the part of the spectator of such risks.
2. Risks associated with throwing a wrestler as far as possible from the ring during a wrestling match are not a matter of common knowledge to ordinary spectators.

Reasoning of the Court

Teaching Note: This section summarized the reasoning or rationale of the court. It answers the "why" question. Why did the court answer the legal question in the way that it did? This section is critical to being able to apply the decision of case to future cases and vital to an in-depth understanding of the legal question and outcome.

With regard to whether *Dusckiewicz had assumed the risk of being injured by a thrown wrestler,* the court initially observed that *Dusckiewicz* was a business visitor of Carter Enterprises during the match. As such, an invitee at a place of amusement only assumes the risk of an **obvious danger** or of dangers that are a **matter of common knowledge**. Dangers that are hidden or undisclosed are not assumed unless there is evidence of warning or personal knowledge on the part of the injured party. In concluding that the risk of being injured by a thrown wrestler was not a matter of common knowledge, the court rejected Carter Enterprises reliance on several baseball cases. Carter argued that the risk of a wrestler being thrown as far as possible from the ring is as common to wrestling as the risk of having a baseball being hit as far as possible from the baseball field. The court rejected the Defendant's comparison because Carter was not able to demonstrate that throwing a wrestler as far as possible from the ring is a purpose associated with wrestling. Further, the court concluded that even if it had been shown that such purpose was associated with wrestling, it was still not reasonable to expect that many spectators would have known such purpose. Even though the Plaintiff identified himself as a wrestling fan, there was no evidence that he was aware of any such purpose. The Defendant's other arguments concerning whether the wrestlers were independent contractors were rejected as unimportant to the court's decision.

QUESTIONS YOU SHOULD BE ABLE TO ANSWER

1. Explain the difference between primary legal sources and secondary legal sources.

2. Identify and provide an example of each of the four primary legal sources.

3. Summarize the steps in the research process.

4. Why should researchers exercise caution when relying on secondary legal sources especially Internet-based sources or blogs?

5. What is the legal "issue" and "rationale of the court" in a court decision and why is it important to be able to properly identify the legal issue and the court's reasoning in a court decision?

REFERENCES

Cases

Brady v. National Football League, 644 F.3d 661 (8th Cir. 2011).

Sources

Edelman, M. (2012, January). A short treatise on fantasy sports and the law: How America regulates its new national pastime. *Harvard Journal of Sports & Entertainment Law, 3*, 1–53. Retrieved at: http://papers.ssrn.com/sol3/papers.cfm?abstract_id=1907272&download=yes

Larsen, S., & Bourdeau, J. (1997). *Legal research for beginners.* Hauppauge, NY: Barron's Educational Series, Inc.

Rosenwald, M.S. (2012, April 10). Md. Legislature in chaos, but it did legalize fantasy football. *The Washington Post.* Retrieved at: http://www.washingtonpost.com/blogs/rosenwald-md/post/md-legislature-in-chaos-but-it-did-legalize-fantasy-football/2012/04/10/gIQAmwKE8S_blog.html

West Publishing Co. (1991). *Sample pages* (3rd ed.). St. Paul, MN: West Publishing Co.

Useful Books on Legal Research

Delaney, S. (2002). *Electronic legal research: An integrated approach.* Albany, NY: West/Thomson Learning.

Elias, S., & Levinkind, S. (2002). *Legal research: How to find and understand the law.* Berkeley, CA: Nolo.

Journal of International Law & Economics. (2002). *Guide to international legal research.* Newark, NJ: LexisNexis/Matthew Bender.

Manz, W. H. (2002). *Guide to state legislative and administrative materials.* Buffalo, NY: William S. Hein.

Redfield, S. E. (2002). *Thinking like a lawyer: An educator's guide to legal analysis and research.* Durham, NC: Carolina Academic Press.

BUSINESS STRUCTURE AND LEGAL AUTHORITY

1.30

John T. Wolohan | Syracuse University

One of the first, and perhaps most important, decisions a sport or recreation business owner must make is how to organize or structure the new business. For example, the owner of the new sport and recreation organization must decide whether to use one of the traditional common business structures, such as a sole proprietorship, partnership, or corporation or a newer one, like a limited liability corporation (LLC). Although each business structure has some distinct advantages and disadvantages, such as federal, state, and local taxes, as well as the limited legal liability of the business owners, the type of structure a new sport and recreation organization chooses should depend in large part on the nature of the business. This section examines the legal issues surrounding new businesses, and identifies some of the advantages and disadvantages of the different business structures used in the sport and recreation industry.

FUNDAMENTAL CONCEPTS

Three of the most common business structures in sport and recreation include sole proprietorships, partnerships, and corporations. In selecting the business structure or form that is appropriate for your business, sport and recreation administrators should be aware of the following factors: limited legal liability; federal, state, and local tax laws; flexibility; access to capital; cost and ease of formation; and transferability of ownership in the business (Hamilton, 2001).

Sole Proprietorships

The most common business structure in the United States, and the easiest one for an individual to start and maintain, is the sole proprietorship. A **sole proprietorship** is an unincorporated business, owned by one individual, which has no legal existence apart from the owner (Eisenberg, 2005). The courts will automatically view the business as a sole proprietorship, unless the individual starting the business files articles of incorporation with the secretary of state in the state in which the business is located.

The sole proprietorship is one of the most popular business structures in the sport and recreation industry because of the low costs and ease involved in its formation. The cost of formation is low because there are no legal papers to file, thus eliminating legal expenses. In addition, because the income and expenses of the business are attributed to the owner, there are no business or corporate taxes to be paid or additional tax forms to file.

The sole proprietorship does have some disadvantages over other business forms. First, because the business has no legal existence apart from the owner, the owner has unlimited personal liability for all the financial and legal risks of the business. Other disadvantages are that the life of the business is limited to the life of the owner; when he or she dies, the business ends. In addition, the business's ability to raise large amounts of capital is limited to the owner's assets or borrowing power (Miller, 1997).

Partnerships

Another common form of business in the sport and recreation industry is the general partnership. A **partnership** is created when two or more people, each contributing one or more of: money, property, labor, or skill, enter into a business with the expectation that each will share proportionally in the profits and losses (*Crane & Bromberg*, 1968). Because a partnership is basically a creation of contract law, no formal written agreement is necessary to create a valid partnership. However, like any good contract, to help avoid future disagreements, it is important that there be a formal written partnership agreement so that all partners understand their rights and obligations, and how profits and losses will be shared (Hamilton, 2001). For example, unless otherwise stated in a partnership agreement, the partners will share in the profits and losses of the business equally.

Partnerships enjoy many of the same benefits of the sole proprietorship, such as low costs, ease of formation, and single taxation. Partnerships have conduit or pass-through taxation, in that income or loss of the partnership is passed on to personal income taxes of the partners. While the IRS requires the partnership to file an annual informational tax return to document profits and losses among the partners, the partnership pays no tax (Crane & Bromberg, 1968).

The major disadvantage of the partnership over other forms of business is that each partner has a fiduciary duty toward the other partners, through which they are legally bound by each other's actions. As a result of this fiduciary duty, each of the partners has unlimited joint and several liability for the acts of each of the other general partners, regardless of whether the partner consented or had notice of such acts (Miller, 1997). Therefore, it is essential that partners trust each other and are aware of each other's activities. Another disadvantage of the partnership is that, because it is created by contract, partners are prohibited from selling or transferring their share in the partnership, even with the consent of the other partners. In order for one to sell or transfer their share in the partnership, the partners must dissolve the first partnership and create a second separate partnership (Miller, 1997).

Limited Partnerships

The only real difference between a limited partnership and a general partnership is that the limited partner(s) enjoys limited legal and financial liability for the debts and legal obligations of the partnership. To receive limited liability, however, the limited partner must not have any involvement in the day-to-day operations of the business (Hamilton, 2001). Once a limited partner becomes involved in the management of the business, he or she forfeits their status as a limited partner and becomes a general partner, assuming unlimited joint and several liability for the acts of the partnership (Crane & Bromberg, 1968).

Corporations

Although there are a number of different types of corporations, all corporations share some basic characteristics. First, to do business as a corporation, the business must file "Articles of Incorporation" with the secretary of state in the state of incorporation. The state of incorporation is usually the state in which the business is located. A business, however, can incorporate in any state it chooses. Once the Articles of Incorporation are filed, the laws of the state of incorporation govern the corporation. Second, all corporations are treated as separate legal entities, with many of the same legal rights as an individual. For example, corporations can sue or be sued, carry on business activities, enter into contracts, and own property and other tangible and intangible assets (Eisenberg, 2005). Third, because a corporation is a separate legal entity, the business can be sold or transferred through the sale of stock, making changes in ownership simple. Fourth, the life of a corporation is unlimited. Because a corporation is a separate legal entity, the life of the business extends beyond the illness or death of the owners, individual officers, managers, or shareholders. Finally, and most importantly, all corporations provide the owner or shareholders with limited liability for corporate obligations. In other words, because corporations are treated as individual entities, separate from the owner or shareholders, the only legal and financial liability of the owner or shareholder is the money they invested into the company (Eisenberg, 2005).

In addition to the preceding benefits of corporations, there are a number of disadvantages involved in incorporating; these include the cost, the formal legal requirements, state and federal rules and regulations, and double taxation. First, because to form a corporation, an individual must file articles of incorporation with the secretary of state, a corporation requires more paperwork and record-keeping than other business forms. Also, unlike other forms of business, corporations must pay taxes on the income of the business, rather than passing it through to the owner's personal income tax (Hamilton, 2001). In addition, individual shareholders must also pay taxes on any dividends the corporation distributes. As a result, the corporation's profits are taxed twice, once at the corporate rate and again at the individual shareholder's rate (Hamilton, 2001). Finally, because an attorney is needed to help file all the necessary forms and meet all the requirements and formalities, there is a higher cost associated with the formation of a corporation.

Due to the inherent physical risks associated with most sports and recreation activities, it might seem that the advantages of limited liability are so great that all businesses in the sports and recreation industry should be conducted as corporations (Hamilton, 2001). However, the nature of the business is only one factor that a new business should consider when selecting a business form. For example, you should also consider the tax consequences, cost of formation, the formal requirements, flexibility, and simplicity.

Although all corporations share some of the same characteristics; Congress has created certain tax benefits or other advantages that distinguish different corporations. The following section examines some of the differences among corporate forms.

Limited Liability Company (LLC)

Another unincorporated business structure is the Limited Liability Company (LLC). The LLC structure is attractive to businesses because it provides greater flexibility in management of the business and has less-restrictive ownership requirements. It combines the best aspects of both the partnership and the corporation forms (Soderquist, 2005). For example, like a partnership, the LLC usually qualifies for pass-through taxation. In other words, the LLC's profits pass through to the company's members, who report their share of the profits on their personal federal tax returns. The company itself does not pay a federal tax before the money is distributed to the members, as in the case of C corporations (see the following section). However, as a separate legal entity, like a corporation, the LLC provides all the members with limited liability protection from business debts (Callison & Sullivan, 2008).

Another advantage of the LLC is that, unlike S corporations (see below), there can be an unlimited number of members, and membership is not limited to individuals, but may include partnerships, corporations, other LLCs and foreign entities. Most states also permit "single member" LLCs, those having only one owner. Finally, because it is designed as a single entity, the LLC also provides the business with important protection from federal antitrust law. (For more information on single entities and antitrust law see Section 7.31, *Antitrust Law: Professional Applications*). In fact, the LLC is so attractive as a new business form that Major League Soccer established themselves as an LLC.

The sport or recreation business may be managed either by its members or by a designated group of managers, who may or may not be members of the company. If the members, as in a partnership, manage the business, each of the members has the same ability as a partnership to bind the entire business through their acts. However, as mentioned earlier, the LLC provides each member limited liability. If a designated group, as in a corporation, manages the business, members do not have the ability to bind the entire business unless they are in the designated group managing the business (Soderquist, 2005).

C Corporations

C corporations are the most common form of corporation. C corporations get their name because the tax rate these corporations use is found in subchapter C of the Internal Revenue Code. C corporations may have an unlimited number of shareholders, and may issue more than one class of stock (Hamilton, 2001). In deciding whether to form a new business as a C corporation, it is important to understand that all corporate income that is distributed to shareholders under C corporations is subject to double taxation. For example, as indicated previously, if at the end of the year the business has taxable income, the corporation must pay a corporate income tax. If any income is distributed to the shareholders, each individual shareholder must declare the income on his or her individual tax return and pay a second tax on the same money.

S Corporations

Instead of electing to be taxed under subchapter C of the Internal Revenue Code, a corporation can elect to be taxed under subchapter S; therefore, the choice is more of a tax election. Corporations making this selection are called S corporations. To be eligible for S corporation status, corporations must have fewer than seventy-five (75) shareholders, may not have shareholders who are nonresident aliens, and may only issue one class of stock (Hamilton, 2001). Although S corporations have the same basic features as C corporations, S corporations have the benefit of allowing shareholders to elect to be taxed under a conduit or pass-through taxation approach that is similar to a partnership or proprietorship (Lind, Schwarz, Lathrope & Rosenberg, 2008).

Publicly Traded Corporations

The main reason for "going public" with your business is financial. For example, in 1998, the Cleveland Indians raised $55 million by selling four million shares of stock in the team. However, besides the financial benefit, there are a number of other issues to consider. First, the organization must comply with all Security and Exchange Commission (SEC) rules and regulations. Second, the corporation must make full financial disclosures concerning profits and losses. Third, because common shareholders are owners of the corporation, they have certain rights, such as voting on the makeup of the board of directors and attending annual meetings. Therefore, there are more legal formalities, and organizations have less control. Finally, there are the added costs to the organization. The corporation must have annual board of directors meetings, create and mail annual financial reports, assign staff for investor relations, and incur added legal costs (Eisenberg, 2005).

Nonprofit Corporations

Some organizations, due to their special nature or mission, are nonprofit corporations. The major difference between a nonprofit and a regular for-profit corporation is that, unlike regular corporations, nonprofit corporations do not have shareholders or owners of any kind (Soderquist, 2005). Instead, nonprofit corporations are run by the members of the organization or people in the community (van der Smissen, 1999). No matter who is running the nonprofit corporation, the members or the people in the community, none of the income or property generated by the nonprofit can be distributed as a dividend (Soderquist, 2005). It should be noted, however, that this does not mean that nonprofit corporations cannot make a profit. It only means that none of the profits can be distributed to the members.

An example of a nonprofit, publicly owned corporation is the Green Bay Packers. Incorporated and publicly owned since August 18, 1923, the Packers have sold over 5 million shares, to about 380,000 stockholders none of whom receives any dividend on the initial investment. In 2011, the Green Bay Packers sold more than 268,000 shares in their fifth stock offering in team history, raising $67 million (Tkach, March 2, 2012). The corporation is governed by a board of directors and a seven member executive committee. To protect against someone taking control of the team, the articles of incorporation prohibit any person from owning more than 200,000 shares.

There are generally two types of nonprofit corporations: **eleemosynary** (or charitable) and **mutual benefit**. In distinguishing the two types, the courts look at whether the purpose of the corporation is to benefit its members or to benefit some other group (Soderquist, 2005). Private schools and universities are generally classified as eleemosynary, whereas private clubs would generally be considered mutual benefit nonprofit corporations. The trustees to the eleemosynary corporation are analogous to directors and stockholders in a business corporation in that their duty is the administration of the charitable trust or corporation (*Gilbert v. McLeod Infirmary*, 1951).

No matter which type of nonprofit corporation (eleemosynary or mutual benefit), because nonprofit corporations serve a public purpose, they receive a number of benefits or privileges not available to other types of corporations. Some of these benefits include being exempt from most federal and state taxes, special postage rates, and exemption from certain labor law requirements (van der Smissen, 1999). At the federal level, nonprofit corporations are known as having 501 (c)(3) tax status. Even if a corporation is nonprofit, however, it is also important to note that any profits that arise from essentially commercial activities will be taxable in the same manner they would be in a business corporation (Soderquist, 2005).

For a business to be recognized as a nonprofit corporation, it must file the required forms and meet the established legal requirements. Currently every state has legislation establishing nonprofit corporations, and the incorporation process usually follows the same procedure as business corporations.

Public Corporations

Another type of corporation that is involved in providing sports and recreational activities is a public corporation. Public corporations are usually municipalities such as cities, towns, and villages (Soderquist, 2005). In addition to municipalities, public corporations are sometimes formed by special legislative acts to perform some special purpose. For example, the National Park Service was formed by Congress and has administrative control over all national parks and forests. In forming a public corporation, like the National Park Service, Congress hopes to take the organization, operation, and finances of the organization from the governmental sphere of influence and place them in a more businesslike structure (Soderquist, 2005).

SIGNIFICANT CASE

The following case examines the decision of Major League Soccer to organize as a limited liability company and whether the league is a single entity for antitrust purposes.

FRASER V. MAJOR LEAGUE SOCCER

United States District Court for the District of Massachusetts
97 F. Supp. 130 (2000)

Memorandum and Order

The individual plaintiffs are the representatives of the certified class of professional soccer players who are or who have been employed by the defendant Major League Soccer, L.L.C. ("MLS"). MLS is a limited liability company ("LLC") organized under Delaware law. The defendant United States Soccer Federation, Inc. ("USSF") is the national governing body for professional and amateur soccer in the United States.

The plaintiffs assert a number of antitrust claims. In Count I, they allege that MLS and several of its investors who operate MLS teams (hereafter "operator-investors" or "operators") have unlawfully combined to restrain trade or commerce in violation to § 1 of the Sherman Anti-Trust Act, 15 U.S.C. § 1, by contracting for player services centrally through MLS, effectively eliminating the competition for those services that would take place if each MLS team were free to bid for and sign players directly. . . . Count III alleges that all defendants have jointly exercised monopoly power in violation of § 2 of the Sherman Act, 15 U.S.C. § 2. In Count IV, the plaintiffs allege that the transaction which brought MLS into existence violated § 7 of the Clayton Act, 15 U.S.C. § 18.

* * *

The plaintiffs have moved for summary judgment as to the defendants' so-called "single entity" defense. The gist of their argument is that although MLS appears to be a single business entity, so that its method of hiring players centrally can be characterized as the act of a single economic actor for antitrust purposes, the organizational form is really just a sham that should be considered ineffective to insulate from condemnation what are in substance illegal horizontal restraints on the hiring of players resulting from the unlawful concerted behavior of the several MLS team operators. . . .

I. Relevant Facts

At the time MLS was formed, no "Division I" or "premiere" professional outdoor soccer league operated in the United States. The last premiere soccer league to operate in this country had been the North American Soccer League ("NASL"), which led a turbulent existence from 1968 until the mid-1980s, when it collapsed. In 1988, Federation Internationale de Football Association ("FIFA") awarded to the United States the right to host the 1994 World Cup, soccer's illustrious international competition. In consideration for that award, the organizers of the event promised to resurrect premiere professional soccer in the United States.

In the early 1990s, Alan Rothenberg, the President of USSF and of World Cup USA 1994, with assistance from others began developing plans for a Division I professional outdoor soccer league in the United States. Rothenberg and others at the USSF consulted extensively with potential investors in an effort to understand what type of league structure and business plan they might find attractive. He also consulted antitrust counsel in the hope of avoiding the antitrust problems that which other sports leagues such as the National Football League ("NFL") had encountered. Eventually the planners settled on the concept of organizing a limited liability company to run the league, and in 1995 MLS was formed.

The structure and mode of operation of MLS is governed by its Limited Liability Company Agreement ("MLS Agreement" or "Agreement"). The MLS Agreement establishes a Management Committee consisting of representatives of each of the investors. The Management Committee has authority to manage the business and affairs of MLS. Several of the investors have signed Operating Agreements with MLS which, subject to certain conditions and obligations, give them the right to operate specific MLS teams. There are also passive investors in MLS who do not operate teams. None of the passive investors is a defendant here.

Operator-investors do not hire players for their respective teams directly. Rather, players are hired by MLS as employees of the league itself and then are assigned to the various teams. Each player's employment contract is between the player and MLS, not between the player and the operator of the team to which the player is assigned.

MLS centrally establishes and administers rules for the acquisition, assignment, and drafting of players, and all player assignments are subject to guidelines set by the Management Committee. Among other things, the guidelines limit the aggregate salaries that the league may pay its players.

Under applicable player assignment policies, MLS centrally allocates the top or "marquee" players among the teams, aiming to prevent talent imbalances and assure a degree of comparability of team strength in order to promote competitive soccer matches. These assignments are effective unless disapproved by a two-thirds vote of a subcommittee of the Management Committee. Most of the rest of the players—the non-"marquee" players—are selected for teams by the individual operator-investors through player drafts and the like. The league allows player trades between teams, but MLS's central league office must approve (and routinely does approve) such trades. Team operators are not permitted to trade players in exchange for cash compensation.

MLS distributes profits (and losses) to its investors in a manner consistent with its charter as a limited liability company, not unlike the distribution of dividends to shareholders in a corporation. Revenues generated by league operations belong directly to MLS. MLS owns and controls all trademarks, copyrights, and other intellectual property rights that relate in any way either to the league or to any of its teams. MLS owns all tickets to MLS games and receives the revenues from ticket sales. There are central league regulations regarding ticket policies, even including limits on the number of complimentary tickets any team may give away. Team operators do retain the ability to negotiate some purely local matters, including local sponsorship agreements with respect to a limited array of products and services and local broadcast agreements, but they do so as agents of MLS.

Under the Operating Agreement, each team operator receives from MLS a management fee. As of the time this action was filed, the management fee consisted of (a) 100% of the first $1.24 million, and 30% of the excess over $1.24 million, of local television broadcast and sponsorship revenues, the latter percentage subject to some specified annual increase; (b) 50% of ticket revenues from home games, increasing to 55% in year six of the league's operation; and (c) 50% of stadium revenues from concessions and other sources.

Expenses are allocated in a way similar to the allocation of revenues. MLS is responsible for most expenses associated with league operations. For example, MLS pays all player acquisition costs, player salaries, and player benefits. It also pays the salaries of all league personnel (including referees), game-related travel expenses for each team, workers' compensation insurance, fees and expenses of foreign teams playing in exhibition games promoted by MLS within the U.S., league-wide marketing expenses, and 50% of each individual team's stadium rental expense.

The team operators are responsible for the other half of their stadium rents, costs of approved local marketing, licensing, and promotion, and general team administration, including salaries of the team's management and coaching staff.

Passive investors do not pay any team operating expenses or receive any management fee. They share in the general distribution of profits (and losses) resulting from league operations.

Team operators cannot transfer their MLS interests or operational rights without the consent of the Management Committee. That consent may be withheld without cause, but the league is required to repurchase the team operator's interest at its fair market value if approval is withheld. Team operators derive whatever rights they may have exclusively from MLS, and the league may terminate these rights if a team operator violates these provisions or fails to act in the best interest of the league.

* * *

III. The Operation of MLS

Section 1 of the Sherman Act forbids contracts, combinations, and conspiracies in restraint of trade or commerce. See 15 U.S.C. § 1. Agreements between separate economic actors that have the effect of substantially and unreasonably reducing competition in a particular market violate § 1. The plaintiffs argue that MLS player policies constitute an unlawful agreement among the various team operators to limit or eliminate competition in the market for players' services.

Though the language of § 1 is sweeping, there are some limits to its reach. One critical limitation for the purposes of this case is that the statute does not prohibit single economic entities from acting unilaterally in ways that may, in some manner, decrease competition. . . . Because it is directed against contracts, combinations or conspiracies, § 1 only prohibits collective activity by plural economic actors, which unreasonably restrains competition. See *Copperweld Corp. v. Independence Tube Corp.*, 467 U.S. 752 (1984). The MLS defendants contend that MLS is a "single entity" and that even if its policies and practices have the effect of substantially reducing competition for players' salaries, they do not—*cannot* as a matter of law—violate § 1.

MLS is a limited liability company organized under Delaware law. An LLC is a form of statutory business organization that combines some of the advantages of a partnership with some of the advantages of a corporation. Under Delaware law, an LLC is a separate legal entity distinct from its members. Del. Code Ann. tit. 6, § 18-201(b). As in a corporation, investors (shareholders in a corporation, members in an LLC) have limited liability (*Id.*, § 18-303), own undivided interests in the company's property (§ 18-701), are bound by the terms of their Agreement (like the corporate Articles), and share in the overall profits and losses ratably according to their investment or as otherwise provided by the organizing Agreement (§ 18-503). The Federal Trade Commission has treated LLCs like corporations. . . . In the present context, there is little reason to treat an LLC such as MLS differently from a corporation.

MLS's operations should therefore be analyzed as the operations of a single corporation would be, with its operator-investors treated essentially as officers and shareholders. There can be no § 1 claim based on concerted action among a corporation and its officers, nor among officers themselves, so long as the officers are not acting to promote an interest, from which they would directly benefit, that is independent from the corporation's success. . . . If an LLC should be considered like a corporation for these purposes, as I conclude it should, then there can be no § 1 violation by reason of concerted action between the LLC as an entity and its members, or between the individual members themselves, unless the members are acting not in the interest of the entity, but rather in their own separate self-interest. The "independent personal stake" exception has not yet been squarely addressed in this Circuit; recognizing the risk that this exception, if left unchecked, might swallow the rule, courts that employ it have done so conservatively.

* * *

The plaintiffs argue that even if MLS is deemed a single entity, the divergent self-interests of the operator-investors provides sufficient cause to invoke the independent personal stake exception. The plaintiffs base this argument largely on their assertion that the operator-investors do not truly share in MLS's profits and losses. Instead of owning undivided interests in the league that are not attached to the operation of any given team, they pay certain operating expenses individually and receive management fees from MLS that are calculated in large part according to their local team-generated revenues. Also, they are able to harvest the value of the particular teams they operate by selling their operational rights or, if the Management Committee vetoes the sale, by requiring the league to pay them the fair market value of their investment.

The management fee arrangement exists in addition to, not in place of, the overall profit and loss sharing specified in the Agreement. Indeed, the fact that there are passive investors in MLS is strong evidence that the payment of management fees and assignment of local expenses do not account for all economic risks and benefits associated with the league's operation.

Furthermore, successful local operation of a team benefits the entire league. The league's net revenues, not just the local operator's management fees, increase when more local revenues are generated.

A similar effect is foreseeable in the market for operator-investor shares. Admittedly, unlike undifferentiated shares of stock, the market value of a team operator's investment will not simply reflect an aliquot share of the whole enterprise, but will also reflect in certain respects the success of the local operation. Nonetheless, unlike competition in most markets, where the value of an enterprise would usually be enhanced if its

competitors grew weaker, the value of the right to operate an MLS team would be diminished, not enhanced, by the weaknesses of other teams, their operators, and the league as a whole. Management fees and operational rights notwithstanding, every operator-investor has a strong incentive to make the league—and the other operator-investors—as robust as possible. Each operator-investor's personal stake is not independent of the success of MLS as a whole enterprise.

The plaintiffs point to other ways in which the operator-investors compete on and off the field. That teams (and, by extension, their operators) compete playing soccer, and that operators directly hire certain staff, such as coaches, to make teams more capable of on-field heroics, does nothing to assist the plaintiffs. Exciting on-field competition between teams is what makes MLS games worth watching. *Chicago Prof 'l Sports*, 95 F.3d at 598-99 ("a league with one team would be like one hand clapping"). Game competition, without doubt, is part of the league's entertainment product, not an indicator of divergent economic interests among operators.

On balance, the business organization of MLS is quite centralized. The league owns the teams themselves; disgruntled operators may not simply "take their ball and go home" by withdrawing the teams they operate and forming or joining a rival league. MLS also owns all intellectual property related to the teams. It contracts for local-level services through its operators, who act on its behalf as agents. Operators risk losing their rights to operate their teams if they breach the governing Agreement. The Management Committee exercises supervisory authority over most of the league's activities. It may reject, without cause, any operator's individual attempt to assign the rights to operate a team.

It is true that MLS is run by a Management Committee that can be controlled by the operator-investors, who constitute the majority of the members of the Committee. It is not remarkable that principal investors can collectively control the governing board of an LLC (or of a corporation). That fact hardly proves that the investors are pursuing economic interests separate from the interests of the firm. The notion that the members of the Management Committee of a single firm violate the antitrust laws when they vote together to maximize the price or minimize the cost of the firm's product is easily rejected.

As a factual matter, therefore, there is insufficient basis in the record for concluding that operators have divergent economic interests within MLS's structure. Even if one draws the most favorable inference on the plaintiffs' behalf, there is no reasonable basis for imposing § 1 liability.

MLS's player policies, in particular, do not call for application of the independent personal stake exception. The operator-investors benefit from those policies because centralized contracting for player services results in lower salaries. However, that benefit is, in the

MLS structure, a derivative one. No operator has an individual player payroll to worry about; the league pays the salaries. Moreover, the MLS investor gets the lower-cost benefit in exchange for having surrendered the degree of autonomy that team owners in "plural entity" leagues typically enjoy. The reason an individual team owner in one of those other leagues is willing to bid up players' salaries to get the particular players it wants is because by paying high salaries to get desirable players, the owner can achieve other substantial benefits, such as increased sales of tickets and promotional goods, media revenues, and the like. The MLS operator-investors have largely yielded that opportunity to the central league office. Plainly, there are trade-offs in the different approaches. The MLS members have calculated that the surrender of autonomy, together with the attendant benefit of lower and more controlled player payrolls and greater parity in talent among teams, will help MLS to succeed where others, notably NASL, failed. That is a calculation made on behalf of the entity, and it does not serve only the ulterior interests of the individual investors standing on their own. It is not an occasion for application of the independent personal stake exception to the general single-entity rule described in *Copperweld*.

The plaintiffs also argue that the structure of MLS is a sham designed to allow what is actually an illegal combination of plural actors to masquerade as the business conduct of a single entity. The plaintiffs do not argue that the structure of MLS as established by the its organizing Agreement is legally defective so that it should not be recognized as a lawful entity under Delaware law. Rather, they say that even if MLS is a legitimate LLC—a legitimate single entity for state law purposes—a court should disregard that legal form in evaluating under antitrust principles whether the operator—investors are engaged in a horizontal restraint in the market for players' services. To make the argument, the plaintiffs put a reverse spin on the *Copperweld* holding.

Copperweld held that a corporation could not conspire with its wholly owned subsidiary in violation of § 1 because, though the parent and subsidiary were distinct legal entities, the economic reality was that they functioned as a single business enterprise. Cases following *Copperweld* have mainly addressed the question whether to disregard formal distinctions among entities in order to find economic singularity for the purposes of § 1. See, e.g., *Sullivan v. NFL*, 34 F.3d 1091, 1099 (1st Cir. 1994) (NFL, composed of separately owned clubs, not a single entity in the market for ownership of teams); *Chicago Prof 'l Sports Ltd. Partnership v. NBA*, 95 F.3d 593, 597-600 (7th Cir. 1996) (characterizing NBA, composed of separately owned clubs, as a single entity for the purpose of league-wide limitations on locally televising games through "superstations," though expressly withholding judgment as to whether NBA was single entity in other markets, such as player contracting). . . .

The plaintiffs propose that the "economic reality" test should be applied not only to *ignore* formal legal distinctions between separate corporations as the court did in *Copperweld*, but conversely to *envision* distinctions in what is formally a single legal entity when doing so would accurately describe how the business of the entity actually operates. The argument may have some superficial appeal, but on close examination it appears that it rests on a misconception of the scope of the *Copperweld* principle.

It was noted above that the courts have not given the sweeping language of § 1 its broadest possible effect. The "rule of reason" is an obvious example of a limitation on the literal scope of the statutory language. . . .

The *Copperweld* rule similarly limits the reach of the statute's broad language. While concerted action between two separate corporations, one the parent and the other a subsidiary, could literally be described as a "combination" that restrains trade, the Supreme Court concluded that it was not the kind of combination that § 1 was intended to forbid. Like the coordination between a corporation and its unincorporated division, an agreement between a parent and its subsidiary did not represent "a sudden joining of two independent sources of economic power previously pursuing separate interests." *Copperweld*, 467 U.S. at 770. The plaintiffs are correct that the Court was looking to substance, not merely form.

But that does not mean that form is irrelevant. Copperweld does not support the proposition that a business organized as a single legal entity should have its form ignored, or its "veil" pierced, so that courts could examine whether participants in the firm have conducted concerted activity that would violate § 1. Merely posing that proposition suggests how troublesome it would be as a practical matter. It would permit the atomization of firms into their constituent parts, then to have the relationships of those parts examined to see if they produced anticompetitive effects that, had they been brought about by independent economic actors, would have violated § 1. The number of companies that could be vulnerable to examination of internal business decisions under such an approach would be mind-boggling. No case has suggested that it would be appropriate to deconstruct a corporate entity in that way.

Practical objections aside, the theory is also fundamentally incompatible with the axiom the *Copperweld* Court's analysis started with—that coordination of business activities within a single firm is not subject to scrutiny under § 1. *Copperweld* cannot be understood to authorize an "economic reality" analysis that would require rejection of the very premise the holding of the case depended on. Moreover, the plaintiffs' proposition would plainly interfere with the objective of the antitrust laws. "Subjecting a single firm's every action to judicial scrutiny for reasonableness would threaten to discourage the competitive enthusiasm that the antitrust laws seek to promote." *Copperweld*, 467 U.S. at 775.

In sum, the plaintiffs' deconstruction efforts are unavailing. MLS is what it is. As a single entity, it cannot conspire or combine with its investors in violation of § 1, and its investors do not combine or conspire with each other in pursuing the economic interests of the entity. MLS's policy of contracting centrally for player services is unilateral activity of a single firm. Since § 1 does not apply to unilateral activity—even unilateral activity that tends to restrain trade—the claim set forth in Count I cannot succeed as a matter of law.

IV. The Formation of MLS

In addition to the claim that the player policies of MLS are an unlawful horizontal restraint of trade, the plaintiffs also claim that the very formation of MLS in the first place violated § 7 of the Clayton Act, which prohibits acquisitions or mergers the effect of which "may be substantially to lessen competition, or to tend to create a monopoly" in any line of commerce or activity affecting commerce, 15 U.S.C. § 18, as well as § 1 of the Sherman Act. The two theories are related.

* * *

2. Existing Market

. . . There can be no § 7 liability because the formation of MLS did not involve the acquisition or merger of existing business enterprises, but rather the formation of an entirely new entity which itself represented the creation of an entirely new market. The relevant test under § 7 looks to whether competition in *existing* markets has been reduced. . . . Where there is no existing market, there can be no reduction in the level of competition. There are no negative numbers in this math; there is nothing lower than zero. Competition that does not exist cannot be decreased. The creation of MLS did not reduce competition in an existing market because when the company was formed there was no active market for Division I professional soccer in the United States.

B. The Sherman Act Claim

In addition to the Clayton Act theory, the plaintiffs urge that the formation of MLS, by which multiple operator-investors combined to create the single entity, also violated the Sherman Act's prohibition of contracts, combinations or conspiracies in restraint of trade.

It is generally held that a coming together that does not violate § 7 of the Clayton Act does not violate § 1 of the Sherman Act either. See *White Consol. Indus. v. Whirlpool Corp.*, 781 F.2d 1224, 1228 (6th Cir. 1986) (failure to show Clayton § 7 violation precluded Sherman § 1 violation for same conduct). A merger of market participants that does not lessen competition and thus does not offend § 7 ordinarily would not constitute a combination in restraint of trade in violation of § 1. Though the statutory provisions present slightly different modes of analysis, when those modes are applied to the same constellation of facts, the answer will ordinarily be the same.

Here, the pertinent facts are that the founding investors of MLS created both a new company and simultaneously a new market, in effect increasing the number of competitors from zero to one. As explained above, that did not represent a lessening of actual or potential competition in an existing market. Similarly, it did not represent a "sudden joining of . . . independent sources of economic power previously pursuing separate interests," see *Copperweld*, 467 U.S. at 770, which is what is forbidden by § 1.

V. Conclusion and Order

For all the reasons set forth above, the defendants' motion for summary judgment in their favor under Counts I and IV of the Amended Complaint is GRANTED. It follows that the plaintiffs' motion for summary judgment on the defendants' "single entity" defense is DENIED.

It is so ordered.

QUESTIONS YOU SHOULD BE ABLE TO ANSWER

1. What are the advantages of forming a corporation rather than a partnership?

2. What are the disadvantages of forming a corporation rather than a partnership?

3. What happens when a limited partner becomes active in managing the business?

4. For sport organizations, what are some of the major benefits of a LLC?

5. Since publicly traded businesses are able to generate additional revenue by selling stock, why are there not more publicly traded sports organizations?

REFERENCES

Cases
Fraser v. Major League Soccer, 97 F. Supp. 130 (2000).
Gilbert v. McLeod Infirmary, 219 S.C. 174 (S.C. 1951).

Publications
Callison, J. W., & Sullivan, M. A. (2008). *Limited Liability Companies: A State-By-State Guide to Law and Practice.* Eagan, MN: Thomson/West Publishing.

Crane, J. A., & Bromberg, A. R. (1968). *Law of Partnership.* St. Paul, MN: West Publishing.

Eisenberg, M. A. (2005). *Corporations and other Business Organizations* (9th ed.). New York, NY: Foundation Press.

Hamilton, R. W. (2001). *Corporations: Including partnerships and limited partnerships* (7th ed.). St. Paul, MN: West Publishing.

Lind, S. A., Schwarz, S., Lathrope, D. J., & Rosenberg, J. D. (2008). *Fundamentals of Corporate Taxation* (7th ed.). New York, NY: Foundation Press.

Miller, L. K. (1997). *Sport business management.* Gaithersburg, MD: Aspen Publishers.

Soderquist, L. B. et al. (2005). *Corporations and other business organizations* (6th ed.). Newark, NJ: LexisNexis Publishing Group.

John Tkach, F1's Barrichello to race in IndyCar, USA TODAY, March 2, 2012, at 9C.

Van der Smissen, B. et al. (1999) *Management of park and recreation agencies.* Ashburn, VA: National Recreation and Park Association.

NEGLIGENCE LAW

2.00

Negligence law is that law which deals with unintentional torts committed by individuals or organizations. *Negligence* is an unintentional tort that injures an individual in person, property, or reputation. Negligence Law is divided into three sections. The first section, 2.10 *Negligence Theory* examines both the elements of negligence and which parties are liable. New to this section is a third chapter which addresses the liability of sports participants, sports instructors, and sports officials. This section serves as a foundation for each of the two succeeding sections.

It is important that the recreation or sport manager understand that being sued for negligence does not necessarily mean that one will lose that suit. Section 2.20 *Defenses* addresses many of the defenses available to recreation and sport providers. Some of these defenses are based in common law, some in contract law, and some in statutory law.

Section 2.30 *Recreation and Sport Management Applications* addresses some of the many recreation and sport management applications of negligence theory. This section includes seven comprehensive chapters illustrating the application of negligence theory in various settings.

* * *

The reader is cautioned, however, regarding a limitation of this or any other text. **Negligence law is primarily state law and, as such, will vary considerably from state to state. It is impossible to cover all of the quirks and variations in the various laws and court rulings for each state. It is, therefore, necessary to utilize generalizations or "general rules" when discussing most topics. The reader must understand that these generalizations are not necessarily true in every state and that certain exceptions may exist.**

NEGLIGENCE THEORY

2.11 NEGLIGENCE[1]

2.10

Doyice J. Cotten | Sport Risk Consulting

In every state, case law is replete with legal actions against sport, recreation, and fitness service providers. Defendants include a diversity of providers such as universities, public schools, professional sports teams, recreation departments, state and national parks, vehicle racing providers, ski resorts, country clubs, equine activity providers, adventure outfitters, bowling alleys, personal trainers, and health clubs.

The majority of these lawsuits involve injuries to a participant (plaintiff) who alleges negligence on the part of the service provider (defendant). **Negligence** is an unintentional tort that causes injury to a person in the form of physical injury, property loss, or reputation. In negligence, there is no intent to cause injury or harm. Negligence may be in the form of an **act of omission** (something one should have done, but did not do) or in the form of an **act of commission** (something that one did, but should not have done).

Authorities have defined negligence in many ways. *Black's Law Dictionary* (1990) offers the following definitions that help one understand the concept:

- Negligence is the failure to use such care as a reasonably prudent and careful person would use under similar circumstances; it is the doing of some act which a person of ordinary prudence would not have done under similar circumstances or failure to do what a person of ordinary prudence would have done under similar circumstances.
- Conduct which falls below the standard established by law for the protection of others against unreasonable risk of harm.
- The term refers only to that legal delinquency which results whenever a man fails to exhibit the care which he ought to exhibit, whether it be slight, ordinary, or great. (p. 1032)

There are four elements of negligence. To prove negligence against the service provider, the plaintiff must show that all four of the elements are present. *If all four of the elements are present, there is negligence—and subsequent liability. If any one of the elements is not met, there is no negligence* and the service provider is not liable. The elements are:

1. **Duty.** The service provider must owe a duty (created by a special relationship between the service provider and the participant) to protect the participant from unreasonable risk of harm.
2. **Breach of Duty.** The service provider must breach its duty to protect the participant from unreasonable risk of harm.
3. **Damage or Injury.** The participant must suffer physical damage to person or property, or emotional damage.
4. **Proximate Cause.** The breach of duty must have been the proximate cause (reason) the injury occurred.

FUNDAMENTAL CONCEPTS

Duty

The first requirement for liability is that one must have owed the plaintiff a legal duty of care. According to van der Smissen (1990, Part A, pp. 2-3), **duty** (as an element of negligence) refers to a responsibility toward others (arising from a relationship between parties) **to protect them from unreasonable risk of injury.**

---

[1]Special thanks to Lynne Gaskin for valuable input regarding this chapter.

van der Smissen frequently distinguished between the term *duty* (the first element of negligence) and what she often referred to as **obligations** to parties to whom a duty is owed. These obligations are the means by which one fulfills the duty to protect them from unreasonable risk of injury. In fact, she frequently stressed that calling these obligations "duties" (e.g., duty to warn, duty to inspect, duty to supervise) is a misnomer; they should be referred to as "obligation" to warn, "obligation" to inspect, and "obligation" to supervise. Additionally, van der Smissen pointed out that there is no duty to inspect, duty to warn, or duty to supervise unless one first has a duty based on a status or special relationship to others (1990, Part A, pp. 2-3).

Courts traditionally have imposed certain obligations (often referred to as duties) on those who have a duty to protect others from unreasonable risk of injury. The particular obligations required in any specific situation vary depending upon such factors as the nature of the activity, nature of the participants, nature of the facility, and location of the activity. Examples of obligations include:

Obligation to warn	Obligation to inspect facilities and equipment
Obligation to supervise	Obligation to provide a safe environment
Obligation to instruct	Obligation to provide safe vehicles
Obligation to match competitors	Obligation to provide safety equipment
Obligation to hire qualified staff	Obligation to provide first aid & emergency care
Obligation to provide "fit" staff	Obligation to evaluate for injury or incapacity

For any specific situation, a service provider might have additional obligations not listed here; conversely, many of these obligations might not apply in some situations. For example, a health club might have no obligation to match competitors or to provide safe vehicles, but it might have an obligation to screen participants for certain health problems. *It is important to remember that if the provider has no duty to protect participants from unreasonable risk of injury, the provider has no obligations.*

> To illustrate, suppose Happy Holiday Stables rents a horse to a novice rider for a trail ride. Due to their relationship of equine provider and client, Happy Holiday has the duty to protect the rider from unreasonable risk of injury. To fulfill this duty, the stable has many obligations to the novice rider. Some obligations required to fulfill the provider's duty to protect might include providing a properly trained horse, matching the rider to the appropriate horse, providing proper tack, correctly saddling the horse, warning the rider of the inherent risks, providing basic instruction if needed, and providing a competent, qualified employee to supervise and lead the ride. If the stable met all of its obligations and the client fell from the horse and broke a leg when the horse was startled by a nearby lightning strike (an inherent risk of a trail ride), Happy Holiday would not be liable because (1) it fulfilled its duty to protect the rider from the unreasonable risk of injury and (2) the stable is not required to protect the rider from the inherent risks of the activity.

Sources of Duty

There are three sources or origins of *duty as an element of negligence.* They are (1) from a relationship inherent in the situation, (2) from the voluntary assumption of a duty, and (3) from duties mandated by statutes.

Inherent Relationship. A duty arises when one has an inherent relationship with another party. Examples of such a relationship include that of a parent and child, coach and athlete, health club and patrons, school and students, scoutmaster and scouts, bus driver and passengers, and service provider and users. The general duty owed is to protect others from exposure to unreasonable risks that may cause injury; however, the specific duties (or obligations) owed depend upon many factors (van der Smissen, 2007).

For example, a vacationer casually walking down the beach has no *legal* duty to rescue a stranger in the water who is shouting for help because there is no special relationship between them. On the other hand, the lifeguard on duty at the time does have a legal duty to do all that he or she can to rescue the drowning party because of the lifeguard-swimmer relationship.

Voluntary Assumption. There are occasions when one has no duty, but voluntarily assumes such a duty. When one voluntarily assumes a duty, a special relationship is established, bestowing an obligation to perform the act with the appropriate standard of care. For example, if the vacationer walking on the beach, hears the shouts for help from the swimmer in distress, rushes into the water, swims out, and tries to rescue the swimmer, he or she voluntarily assumes the duty of rescue and an obligation to do all that he or she can to rescue the drowning party.

Voluntary assumption of a duty often is associated with a decision to aid one in need (e.g., a passerby administering CPR, rescuing a swimmer in difficulty, or assisting at an automobile accident). In such cases, there might be a moral duty to rescue or assist, but there is generally no legal duty. A few states have very limited "duty to rescue" statutes, but they often carry insignificant penalties and are seldom enforced.

The voluntary assumption of a duty is not limited to one administering emergency care. A parent who volunteers to serve as a little league coach creates a relationship with the team members and assumes the duty to protect them from unreasonable risk of injury. As the coach, he then has the responsibility to act as a reasonable, prudent coach and perform the obligations of such a coach (e.g., to instruct, supervise, inspect, warn, etc.). Other examples of individuals who voluntarily assume a duty include one who volunteers to direct traffic before a game, a physician who volunteers to be the team doctor, a teacher who volunteers to sponsor a club, and a sport management major who volunteers time to work with a professional team.

Statutes. Statutes or laws often specify duties of one party to another. If the state legislature passes a statute requiring that an ambulance and a physician are present at every high school football game, an athletic director failing to provide both might be found to have breached his statutory duty. West Virginia has a statute that specifies that whitewater guides and ski operators owe their patrons a duty of ordinary care (W.Va.C. 20-38-1 to 8). Since this duty is a statutory duty, operators may not shield themselves from liability for negligent conduct by using a liability waiver.

Violations of statutes and ordinances frequently are associated with negligence *per se*. **Negligence *per se*** has been described as negligence attached to acts that are deemed negligent without having to prove negligence or investigate the reasonableness of the conduct (van der Smissen, 1990). The act is so opposed to common prudence that it is obvious that no reasonable person would have done it. However, violation of a statute or ordinance does not always constitute negligence *per se*. The law varies greatly among states but, generally, one must show that a statute was broken, that it was a safety statute, and that the violation of the statute was the actual proximate cause of the injury. According to Prosser (Keeton, 1984, p. 227), a defendant may become liable in some cases simply by violating a statute; and neither ignorance nor any excuse will avoid liability. In these cases, the statute falls under strict liability, yet often is referred to as negligence *per se*.

Foreseeability

Foreseeability involves one's ability to predict what will occur as a result of his or her action (commission) or inaction (omission). Since no conduct can be considered to be unreasonable when there is no foreseeable risk, the scope of liability is governed by whether the risk of injury is foreseeable. The question then becomes "what is foreseeable?" Foreseeability is established by showing that a person of ordinary intelligence and circumspection reasonably should have been able to predict the consequences of an action or a failure to act. van der Smissen (1990) concluded that when negative results of an act cannot be reasonably anticipated by reasonable people, it cannot be said that the result was foreseeable; therefore, there is no duty to protect against it. It is important, then, to understand that although one has a special relationship and owes a duty to protect, there is no liability for an injury caused by an unforeseeable risk.

Another situation where no proactive action to protect is necessary in spite of a duty created by a special relationship is when there is an "open and obvious" environmental hazard. Since the hazard is open and obvious, it generally is not foreseeable that an individual would ignore the hazard and continue the activity. So, in spite of the special relationship, one generally has no duty to protect (van der Smissen, 2007).

The key to foreseeability is foresight and the reasonable, prudent professional must be able to anticipate or foresee dangers or risks faced by the participant. *One is not required to be able to foresee the exact nature of the accident or of the injury—one need only to foresee that injury is likely.* Of course, reasonable people can disagree as to what is, or should have been, foreseeable. When reasonable people disagree, it is the job of the jury to resolve the question.

Breach of Duty

The second requirement for liability is that the defendant must have breached his duty to the plaintiff. Black (1990) described breach of duty as "any violation or omission of a legal or moral duty. More particularly, [it is] the neglect or failure to fulfill in a just and proper manner the duties of an office or fiduciary employment" (p. 189).

> In the Happy Holiday Stables illustration, the business relationship between Happy Holidays and the novice rider imposes the duty to protect the rider from unreasonable risk of injury. Two obligations of the stable include the provision of good tack and proper saddling of the horse. If the novice rider falls and breaks a leg because worn and faulty tack breaks or because the Happy Holiday employee failed to tighten the saddle adequately resulting in the saddle slipping, Happy Holiday could be liable for negligence because the stable failed to meet its obligations and breached its duty to protect the rider from unreasonable risk of injury.

There are three components used to determine if the duty has been breached. These three components may be addressed by asking the questions: What are the types of risk? What is reasonable care? Was the risk foreseeable?

What Are the Types of Risks?

The first question asked to determine whether there is a breach of duty is "What type of risk caused the injury?" Risks may be placed into three categories. They are risks arising from (1) inherent risks, (2) ordinary negligence, and (3) aggravated negligence (extreme behavior that goes beyond ordinary negligence [e.g., gross negligence, reckless misconduct, and willful and wanton misconduct]). Generally, the service provider has no duty to protect one from the inherent risks of an activity. The provider does have a duty, however, to protect participants from unreasonable risks of injury that include risks created by both negligent behavior and aggravated negligence.

Risks Arising from Inherent Risks

Inherent risks are those risks that are integral to the activity; risks that if removed would essentially alter the nature of the sport or activity (van der Smissen, 2007). *The provider of an activity generally has no duty to protect one from the inherent risks of the activity.* Examples of inherent risks include a softball player pulling a hamstring while running the bases, a college football player suffering an ACL injury when tackled, a raft striking a rock and capsizing during a whitewater rafting expedition, a hiker in the mountains encountering a dangerous animal, and one's horse being spooked by thunder or lightning while on a trail ride. These risks are inherent to the activity and cannot be eliminated. In fact, if whitewater rafting were done on a stream with no rocks or rapids, it is no longer "whitewater" rafting and loses much of its excitement and appeal.

Under the doctrine of primary assumption of risk (see Chapter 2.21 *Defenses Against Negligence*), a participant generally assumes the inherent risks of the activity. Thus, *"[T]here is no liability for injury that occurs due to inherent risks of which the injured participant is knowledgeable or should have been knowledgeable"* (van der Smissen, 2007, p. 38). In *Harting v. Dayton Dragons Professional Baseball Club, LLC (2007)*, Roxane Harting was struck in the head by a foul ball and knocked unconscious while she was distracted by the San Diego Chicken. She argued that the mascot was not an inherent risk of a baseball game, but the court ruled that it was perfectly reasonable for a spectator at a baseball game to observe mascots, such as the Chicken, during the course of the game.

van der Smissen (2007) emphasized the importance of a participant being knowledgeable of inherent risks to which he or she is exposed. Therefore, in the whitewater rafting example above, it is important that the provider adequately warn the participant of the inherent risks of whitewater rafting or the provider may be found liable for injury resulting from inherent risks unknown to the participant. One may inform participants of the risks through (1) oral instructions; (2) detailed risk information in documents such as applications, assumption of risk agreements, or liability waivers; and (3) detailed printed risk information in brochures, handouts, and signs. The information regarding the inherent risks must provide the participant with adequate information so that he or she will know, understand, and appreciate the inherent risks of the activity (van der Smissen, personal communication, March 6, 1996).

Risks Arising from Ordinary Negligence

Negligent acts fall below the required standard of care and constitute a breach of the duty to protect others from unreasonable risk of injury. The California Supreme Court stated, "[A]lthough defendants generally have no legal duty to eliminate (or protect a plaintiff against) risks inherent in the sport itself, it is well established that defendants generally *do have a duty to use due care not to increase the risks to a participant over and above those inherent in the sport*" (*Knight v. Jewett*, 1992, p. 14). When a provider increases the risks by negligent actions, these risks are not assumed by the participant and the provider can be found liable for any resulting injuries.

Two cases illustrate acts of ordinary negligence. A girl suffered injury when she collided with an unpadded metal pole that supported a basketball backboard. The school district was found negligent because the school increased the risk by allowing students to play basketball around poles that they knew were dangerous (*Gill v. Tamalpais Union High School District, 2008*). In *Sisino v. Island Motocross of N.Y., Inc. (2007)*, motorcyclist Sisino was injured when his motorcycle was struck by an all-terrain vehicle (ATV). The court said that the owners were negligent by allowing ATV riders to use the track at the same time as motorcyclists since they increased the risk of injury beyond those risks inherent in the sport.

Risks Arising from Aggravated Negligence

There are at least two schools of thought regarding negligence and aggravated negligence. One school holds that there are no degrees of negligence (Keeton, 1984). Those who hold this view suggest **that the standard of care required for reasonable conduct** must vary with the apparent risk faced in the activity—accordingly, as the danger increases, the caution or care required of the provider increases commensurately. The level of care required for the conduct of a very dangerous activity is very high and the threshold for negligence is low (e.g., when operating a bungee jump, where the danger is great, even slight faults or mistakes might be considered unreasonable, and thereby, constitute negligence due to the potential consequences of a mistake). However, the level of care required for reasonable conduct of a relatively safe, low-risk activity is less and the threshold for negligence is higher (e.g., when operating a water slide, where the risk of serious injury is slight, faults that might result in minor injuries might be considered reasonable and not trigger negligence). In other words, the standard of care for reasonable conduct varies depending upon the risk of the activity. Consequently, according to this school of thought, the creation of degrees of negligence is not necessary. Jurisdictions adopting this approach recognize only reasonable care (no negligence) and negligence.

Another school of thought regarding degrees of negligence advocates that there are distinct degrees of negligence (Keeton, 1984). Supporters of this approach propose that there are both small and large departures from reasonable care or conduct—these departures are most commonly identified as ordinary negligence, gross negligence, reckless misconduct, and willful and wanton misconduct. Gross negligence, reckless misconduct, and willful and wanton misconduct are considered more extreme departures from reasonable care than ordinary negligence and are sometimes referred to as **aggravated negligence**.

Those who attempt to distinguish among the degrees of aggravated negligence encounter a number of problems. First, one finds that defining the concepts that commonly constitute aggravated negligence is problematic. For instance, when Black's definitions of gross negligence, reckless misconduct, and willful and wanton misconduct are examined carefully, there appears to be considerably more similarities than differences among the concepts.[2] Second, the situation is complicated further by the fact that jurisdictions using the same term frequently define the term differently. Therefore, when one encounters the terms *gross negligence, reckless misconduct, and willful and wanton conduct*, he or she should be aware that while the same

---

[2]Black (1990, p. 1033) defined **gross negligence** as "The intentional failure to perform a manifest duty in reckless disregard of the consequences as affecting the life or property of another." He defined **reckless misconduct** as a situation in which ". . . the actor intentionally does an act or fails to do an act which it is his duty to another to do, knowing or having reason to know of facts which would lead a reasonable man to conclude such conduct creates an unreasonable risk of bodily harm . . ." (p. 1271). He defined **willful and wanton misconduct** as "Conduct which is either intentional or committed under the circumstances exhibiting a reckless disregard for the safety of others . . ." (p. 1600).

term might be used, the actual definition of the term will vary from jurisdiction to jurisdiction.[3] Third, one finds that while courts in most jurisdictions are consistent in employing the term "ordinary negligence," terms used to describe degrees of aggravated negligence vary greatly among jurisdictions.[4] And finally, one finds that, in light of the lack of a common, discriminating definition and consistent application of the terms in all jurisdictions, it is impossible to draw clear lines of demarcation among the recognized degrees of aggravated negligence.

While distinguishing among the three degrees of aggravated negligence may seem futile, legislatures (in statutes) and courts (in case law) in most jurisdictions have endeavored to define and recognize one or more degrees of aggravated negligence. Generally gross negligence is considered the least outrageous of the three and is considered to be less extreme than willful and wanton misconduct. In fact, there appears to be an unofficial hierarchy from gross negligence to reckless misconduct to willful and wanton misconduct.

In light of these critical variations in state law, *it is essential that the recreation and sport manager ascertain both the degrees of aggravated negligence recognized in his or her state and how each is defined by the courts in that particular state.*

Importance of Distinguishing among the Degrees of Negligence. In spite of the problems associated with degrees of negligence, it is necessary to address them. Distinguishing among the degrees of departure from reasonable care is important for at least five reasons.

First, the **immunity** provided by legislation (e.g., governmental immunity, state tort claims acts, recreational user statutes, Good Samaritan statutes, AED statutes, volunteer statutes, and sport immunity statutes) depends upon compliance with the standard of care required in the statute. Some statutes protect when the service provider is grossly negligent, some when the service provider is negligent, and some only when the injury was the result of an inherent risk of the activity. Few, if any, apply when the service provider has committed reckless or willful and wanton acts (see Chapter 2.21 *Defenses Against Negligence* and Chapter 2.22 *Immunity*).

Second, while **liability waivers** protect providers from liability for ordinary negligence in most states, they protect against liability resulting from gross negligence or reckless misconduct in only six states. Further, no waivers in any state have been found that protect against liability for willful and wanton actions or intentional acts (see Chapter 2.23 *Waivers and Releases*).

Third, although the law regarding **exemplary** or **punitive damages** varies by state, generally such damages are not awarded for injury unless gross negligence, reckless conduct, or willful and wanton actions are involved. The degree required for such awards varies with state law (see the Damage section later in this chapter).

Fourth, the general rule in most jurisdictions is that a **participant** is not liable for injuries to a **co-participant** that result from ordinary negligence. Participants generally are liable if the act is reckless or willful and wanton, but usually are not liable for ordinary negligence except in a few jurisdictions and under select circumstances (*Pfister v. Shusta* [Ill. 1995]; see also Chapter 2.13 *Liability of Sports Participants, Sports Instructors, and Sports Officials*). In some states, courts have ruled that a sports instructor or coach is not liable for ordinary negligence in certain circumstances. In *Kahn v. East Side Union School District* (2003), the California Supreme Court

---

[3]For example, California courts defined *gross negligence* as "a want of even scant care" or "an extreme departure from the ordinary standard of conduct" (*City of Santa Barbara v. Superior Court*, 2007 p. 6), while the Wisconsin Jury Instruction 1006 defined *gross negligence* as conduct "which shows either a willful intent to injury or reckless and wanton disregard of the rights [or] safety" of another person. Similarly, a Michigan court defined both *reckless misconduct* and *willful and wanton conduct* as conduct by a person who may have no intent to harm, but who intentionally acts while knowing harm is highly probable (*Lamp v. Reynolds*, 2002). A California court defined reckless misconduct as an act where one is aware that one's conduct is likely to cause injury, yet proceeds to act heedlessly, willfully, and wantonly (*City of Santa Barbara v. Superior Court*, 2007, p. 6).

[4]Some jurisdictions use only one of these terms to describe aggravated negligence, in effect, establishing two degrees of negligence (e.g., ordinary and gross; ordinary and reckless; or ordinary and willful/wanton). Other jurisdictions employ two or more terms to distinguish among degrees of aggravated negligence (e.g., ordinary, gross, and reckless; ordinary, gross, reckless, and willful/wanton), thereby, establishing three or more degrees of negligence. The terms utilized and their definitions are employed in the jurisdiction's statutory law and case law.

stated that in a case alleging that a sports instructor required an athlete to perform beyond his capacity, the plaintiff must show

> that the instructor acted with intent to cause a student's injury or that the instructor acted recklessly in the sense that the instructor's conduct was "totally outside the range of the ordinary activity" involved in teaching or coaching the sport. (p. 43)

Fifth, the degree of negligence can affect the liability of the service provider for the actions of its employees. The doctrine of *respondeat superior* (vicarious liability) holds that the negligence of the employee is imputed to the corporate entity if the employee is acting within the scope of the employee's responsibility and authority, and if the act is not grossly negligent, willful/wanton, and does not involve malfeasance (van der Smissen, 1990). Therefore, if the act is aggravated negligence, the employee generally stands alone and the employer is often not liable.

What Is Reasonable Care?

The second component of breach of duty can be evaluated only after determining what constitutes reasonable care. The **standard of care** is determined by the reasonable and prudent person concept (*i.e.*, one is required to act as a reasonable and prudent person would act under the circumstances). *One should note, however, that when an individual is a professional in a field (e.g., sport management, coaching, recreation, athletic training), it is not enough to act as the imaginary reasonable and prudent "person;" but as a **reasonable and prudent "professional"** would act under the given circumstances* (van der Smissen, 1990).

A service provider is not required to be an insurer of the safety of its patrons, but is expected to provide reasonably safe premises and conditions for the activity. In a Maine case involving the standard of care required of an athletic trainer, the court held that the defendant trainer "has the duty to conform to the standard of care required of an ordinary, careful trainer" (*Searles v. Trustees of St. Joseph College*, 1997). Likewise, in *Cerny v. Cedar Bluffs Junior/Senior High* (2004), the Nebraska Supreme Court ruled that a football coach allowing a football player to participate after an injury is held to the standard of conduct of a reasonably prudent person holding a Nebraska teaching certificate with a coaching endorsement.

A Single Standard of Care

Since the required standard of care is that of a reasonable and prudent professional, an inexperienced physical educator, sport manager, or park ranger is held to the same standard of care required of an experienced, reasonable, and prudent physical educator, sport manager, or park ranger. In other words, there is only one standard of care for a given situation. van der Smissen (1990) stressed that "*the standard is not that of a person with the actual qualification of the individual, but of a person competent for the position for which the individual holds oneself to be qualified*" (Part A, p. 43).

Was the Risk Foreseeable?

The third component of breach of duty is to determine whether the risk was foreseeable by a reasonable and prudent professional. As discussed in the Duty section of this chapter, there is liability only if the risk was foreseeable. The reasonable and prudent professional needs only to have foreseen that an injury was likely and need not have been able to foresee the exact nature of the incident or of the injury.

Proximate Cause

The fact that a duty exists and is breached does not necessarily mean that there is liability. The injured party must show that the breach of duty was the cause-in-fact of the injury (*i.e.*, the proximate cause). Black [1990] defined **proximate cause** or **cause-in-fact** as "[T]hat particular cause which produces an event and without which the event would not have occurred" (p. 221). In other words, proximate cause refers to an act from which an injury is the natural, direct, and uninterrupted consequence.

> Returning to the Happy Holiday Stables illustration, one of the obligations of the stable is to consider the ability and experience of the rider when assigning a horse. If the stable employee fails to assign a

disciplined, easy-to-handle horse to a novice rider, the undisciplined horse is too headstrong for the novice rider to control, and the novice falls from the horse breaking a leg, Happy Holiday may be liable for negligence. On the other hand, suppose the employee fails to match the horse to the rider properly and the horse bolts when struck by a snake, causing the rider to be thrown and break a leg, Happy Holiday would not be liable because the breach of duty had nothing to do with the injury because even a properly matched horse would have bolted under the circumstances. Happy Holiday would not be liable because the breach of duty was not the proximate cause of the injury.

Southwest Key Program, Inc. v. Gil-Perez (2000) illustrates an instance in which a negligent act was the proximate cause of the injury (see the Supplemental Web Site). Gil-Perez was injured when employees of the Southwest Key Program allowed the boys to play tackle football without pads, instruction, or supervision. On the other hand, *Rutecki v. CSX Hotels* (2007) is a case in which the negligent act was not determined to be the proximate cause of injury. In *Rutecki*, the resort operator conducted a horseback ride and violated a statute by failing to determine the riding skill of the plaintiff. During the ride, the guide's horse misbehaved and fell, startling the plaintiff's horse, and causing the plaintiff to fall. The court ruled that the violation of the statute was not causally related to the injury and ruled for the defendant.

Many states use the **probable consequences rule** that holds the defendant liable for injuries that are the natural and probable consequences of one's negligent act. A Texas court stated that the elements of proximate cause may be inferred from the circumstances of the event and that the jury should be allowed latitude in determining proximate cause. Other jurisdictions have adopted the **substantial factor test**. Under this theory, the law does not require that a negligent act be the only causal factor, but may be a substantial factor among several factors that cause the injury. In a Kentucky case (*Figure World v. Farley*, 1984), a bar sold alcohol to six minors in violation of a state statute. The boys drank most of the alcohol, went swimming in a pond, and one of the boys drowned. The court ruled that a jury could find that injury was foreseeable and that the sale of the alcohol to the minors was a substantial factor in the death and remanded the case for trial.

Many plaintiffs name **failure to supervise** as the proximate cause of an injury. Most jurisdictions, however, require that supervision must be the actual proximate cause (i.e., show that the injury was a consequence of the lack of supervision and would not have occurred had there been adequate supervision.)

When two parties commit two separate negligent acts prior to an injury, the court must determine which of the acts constituted the proximate cause. *Cirillo v. City of Milwaukee* (1967) illustrates such a situation. When a teacher left an unsupervised physical education class of 49 adolescent boys shooting baskets, the boys (including the plaintiff) soon began participating in roughhousing and rowdy behavior. After 25 minutes, Cirillo was injured and his parents subsequently sued alleging negligence on the part of the teacher. In this case, both the action of the teacher and the rowdy behavior of the plaintiff were instrumental in causing the injury. The question was which act constituted the proximate cause of the injury—the failure to supervise, which allowed the roughhousing, or the intervening act of roughhousing indulged in by the student.

When a negligent act is followed by a second unforeseeable and independent negligent act by another party, the second negligent act can be deemed the proximate cause—thereby intervening and averting liability from the doer of the first negligent act. Such an act is called an **intervening act** or **intervening cause**. The intervening act must be independent of the original act, must be capable in itself of creating the injury, and must not have been foreseeable by the party committing the first act.

Damage

The fourth element of negligence is damage. If there is no damage, then there is no negligence and, therefore, no compensation. **Damage** is "injury, loss, or deterioration caused by the negligence, design, or accident of one person to another in respect to the latter's person or property" (Black, 1996, p. 389). Although the damage that is compensable varies from state to state, it commonly includes (1) economic losses, (2) physical pain and suffering, (3) emotional distress, and (4) physical impairment (van der Smissen, 1990).

Economic loss may include medical expenses, lost wages, rehabilitation expenses, custodial care, and much more. The court determines the economic loss based upon actual expenses and projected expenses by expert witnesses. Monetary award for **pain and suffering** is determined by the jury. The amount of such awards depends on many factors such as the credibility of witnesses, whether the plaintiff's actions are consistent with one in pain, pre-existing injuries, whether the plaintiff can do what he or she could do in everyday life, the plaintiff's pain tolerance, the plaintiff's occupation, whether the plaintiff makes a sympathetic witness, and the skill of the attorney (http://injury-law.freeadvice.com). **Emotional distress** is not always compensable in negligence cases. In states that allow awards for emotional distress, the distress generally is in the form of fright, anxiety, humiliation, and loss of being able to enjoy a normal life. **Physical impairments** may constitute damage and may be considered in lieu of emotional distress. The award may be given for temporary and permanent impairments as well as for partial or total impairments (van der Smissen, 1990).

Damages

Damage and damages are sometimes confused. Whereas damage is the actual element of negligence (injury or loss), **damages** is the monetary compensation sought or awarded as a remedy for a tortious act. There are two major types of damages—compensatory and punitive. **Compensatory damages** denote a monetary award intended to compensate the injured party for injury or loss caused by the wrong. The award is intended to restore the injured party to his or her position prior to the injury. **Punitive** or **exemplary damages** entail an award beyond the compensatory damages, generally where the action involves violence, oppression, malice, fraud, or wanton conduct by the defendant. This award is intended (1) to punish the wrongdoer for outrageous conduct and (2) to deter such acts in the future.

Punitive or exemplary damages vary greatly from state to state. Some states do not permit them, while others limit the amount of the award. Generally, these awards are made only when the negligent party acts from a wrongful motive or knowing indifference for the safety and rights of others. Thus, these awards generally are available when the act is gross negligence (rarely), reckless misconduct, or willful and wanton acts (varying by state), and usually are at the discretion of the jury (van der Smissen, 1990).

In *Borne v. Haverhill Golf and Country Club, Inc.* (2003), Borne and eight other women sued the club alleging that the club, a place of public accommodation, discriminated unfairly against them on the basis of their sex. The trial judge instructed the jury that punitive damages could be awarded only if there had been extraordinary misconduct by the defendant—". . . for malicious, wanton or oppressive conduct done in reckless disregard of the plaintiff's rights or in callous indifference to the plaintiff" (p. 28). After a 22-day trial, the court ruled in favor of the plaintiffs and awarded $1,967,400 in damages including $1,430,000 in punitive damages. The appellate court affirmed the trial court verdict.

Finally, in the Happy Holiday Stables illustration, the novice rider suffered a broken leg due to the fall from the horse. A physical injury such as this constitutes damage and creates the possibility of monetary recovery if a negligent act by the Happy Holidays was the proximate cause of the injury. In the event of negligence, the court can award compensatory damages—*e.g.*, medical expenses, pain and suffering, and lost wages (in the case of a working adult). The plaintiff would not be eligible for punitive damages because the conduct of the stables was ordinary negligence and involved no outrageous conduct. If the injury resulted from an inherent risk of horseback riding (e.g., horse bolting because of a snake or nearby lightning strike), Happy Holidays would not be liable and there would be no damages awarded.

SIGNIFICANT CASE

This is a case that illustrates the necessity that all four elements of negligence be present in order to show negligence. Each of the three allegations—negligent supervision, negligent instruction, and negligence in failing to inspect the plaintiff's shoes prior to play—fails because the plaintiff did not provide evidence showing that negligence in any of the three areas was a causative factor in producing the injury.

SANDERS V. KUNA JOINT SCHOOL DISTRICT

Court of Appeals of Idaho
125 Idaho 872; 876 P.2d 154; 1994 Ida. App. LEXIS 77
June 16, 1994, Filed

Opinion: Perry, J.

Josh Sanders appeals from a district court order granting summary judgment in favor of the respondents, Kuna Joint School District and Ron Emry. For the reasons stated below, we affirm the judgment.

Facts and Procedure

The underlying facts of this lawsuit are generally agreed upon by all of the parties. On May 15, 1990, Josh Sanders, a student at Kuna High School, attempted to slide into first base during a softball game and broke his ankle. Sanders had been enrolled in a specialized physical education class which provided instruction in weight lifting. On the date of the incident, the instructor, respondent Ron Emry, decided to have the class play softball outside instead of weight lifting. The students were not informed of this decision until after they appeared in the school's weight room. According to Sanders, on that particular day he was wearing a pair of "Saucony Shadows," a shoe designed specifically for running. Once on the softball field, Emry did not give instruction in the game of softball and supervised the game from behind a backstop. During one particular sequence of play, Sanders attempted to slide into first base in order to avoid being tagged out. During the slide, Sanders broke his ankle.

Following proper notice as required by I.C. @@ 6-901 et seq., Sanders filed suit against Emry and the school district as Emry's employer. Sanders claimed that Emry had been negligent by requiring the students to play softball, by failing to adequately supervise the students, including inspecting their footwear, and by failing to properly instruct the students on how to play softball.

After initial discovery was completed, the respondents filed a motion for summary judgment on grounds that, accepting the truth of Sanders' evidence, it did not prove a claim of negligence as a matter of fact. The district court granted the respondents' motion. Sanders now appeals to this Court, claiming that the district court improperly granted the summary judgment.

Analysis

In this case, Sanders would bear the burden of proof at trial to establish the elements of negligence. In Idaho, a cause of action in negligence requires proof of the following: (1) the existence of a duty, recognized by law, requiring the defendant to conform to a certain standard of conduct; (2) a breach of that duty; (3) a causal connection between the defendant's conduct and the resulting injury; and (4) actual loss or damage. Black Canyon Racquetball Club, Inc. v. Idaho First Nat'l Bank, N.A., 119 Idaho 171, 175–76, 804 P.2d 900, 904–05 (1991).

The respondents contended in their summary judgment motion that Sanders had failed to offer sufficient proof of causation. In order to properly analyze the evidence of causation, we must look separately at the negligent instruction and negligent supervision claims.

As to the negligent instruction claim, we agree with the district court that the record reveals a lack of evidence as to causation. Sanders simply claims that Emry failed to instruct the students in the game of softball and that such a failure caused the injury. Sanders does not, however, offer any evidence as to what the instructions should have been, how such instructions would have prevented the injury, or how Sanders improperly slid. We agree with the conclusion of the district court that a rational jury could not find a causal connection between the failure to instruct and the resulting injury on the evidence presented. Therefore, the district court did not err in granting summary judgment as to Emry's alleged negligent instruction.

With respect to the negligent supervision claim, there are two separate issues we must consider—the actual supervision of the game as it was being played and the failure to inspect the footwear of the students. Again, as with the negligent instruction claim, Sanders' allegation of negligent supervision during the actual game must fail for lack of proof of causation. Sanders alleges that Emry failed to supervise the game and that such a failure caused the injury. Sanders does not offer any evidence, however, as to what the supervision of the game should have entailed, how that supervision was related to sliding or how such supervision would have prevented the injury. The only causal connection offered is the naked inference that if Emry had been standing on the field giving instruction to each student as the class played, this injury would not have occurred. Such an implausible inference does not rise to the level of evidence, however. In short, Sanders has failed to offer sufficient evidence of the causal connection between Emry's alleged negligent supervision and the injury. The district court's conclusion that no reasonable jury, on this evidence, could find a causal connection between the two was correct and, therefore, the summary judgment was properly granted as to this issue.

As to the issue of whether Emry was negligent in failing to inspect Sanders' shoes and should have prevented Sanders from playing in them, there is a mere scintilla of evidence presented. Sanders offered his own deposition testimony that he was playing in shoes that were designed for running. In response to the summary judgment motion, Sanders submitted the affidavit of the owner/manager of an athletic shoe store. The witness states that, "from a safety standpoint I would not recommend the use of the Saucony Shadow Shoe for use as a baseball or softball shoe." No evidence was offered, however, beyond the post hoc inference that because this was a running shoe with a wide sole, it must have caused the injury. Further, there was no evidence how a different shoe would have prevented the injury. Offering the mere coincidence that Sanders was injured and that he was wearing running shoes at the time is not sufficient to establish a causal connection. There must be some evidence that the shoe caused the injury. The evidence offered, the testimony of Sanders and the owner/manager of the shoe store, is not a sufficient basis upon which a jury could base a verdict for Sanders.

Jurors may draw inferences of causation where such inferences are within the common experience of the average person. In this case, however, we do not believe that the common experience of the average person includes knowledge of the properties of specialized running shoes versus other types of footware. Nor do we think the average person possesses knowledge in the mechanics of sliding or injuries from sliding. Without sufficient evidence on the differences in design, purpose, and function of the shoes worn by Sanders and other shoes, no reasonable jury could infer causation under the facts as presented in this case. Likewise, with no evidence as to the actual mechanics of this injury, a jury should not be left to speculate as what might have been the cause. Sanders has simply failed to offer any competent evidence as to the cause of this injury. Alleging temporally coincidental events is not a sufficient basis upon which a jury could find or infer causation. Therefore, the district court did not err by granting the summary judgment.

As an alternative basis for its summary judgment argument, the respondents asserted that Sanders had failed to offer sufficient evidence as to the existence of a duty. Having decided that the summary judgment was proper on the issue of causation, we need not consider this issue here.

Conclusion

The respondents in this case properly carried their burden on their motion for summary judgment by showing that Sanders was unable to present sufficient evidence on the causal connection between the alleged negligence and the injury. The burden then shifted to Sanders to show that a genuine issue did exist. Sanders failed to meet this burden and therefore the summary judgment was properly granted.

Costs on this appeal are awarded to respondents; no attorney fees are awarded.

WALTERS, C.J., and LANSING, J., concur.

CASES ON THE SUPPLEMENTAL WEB SITE

Craig v. Amateur Softball Association of America, 2008 PA Super 123; 951 A.2d 372; 2008 Pa. Super. LEXIS 1108. The primary issue in this case is whether or not a duty was owed.

Spotlite Skating Rink, Inc. v. Barnes, 988 So. 2d 364; 2008 Miss. LEXIS 322. This case illustrates the need for the plaintiff to show a duty, a breach of duty, and causation. Notice that there is conflicting testimony regarding the facts of the case so the court must judge who is telling the truth.

Southwest Key Program v. Gil-Perez, 2000 Tex. App. LEXIS 7851; 79 S.W.3d 571. The court established that a duty was owed to the plaintiff, that the duty was breached, and that the breach was the proximate cause of injury. Further, they found that the injury was foreseeable.

Howard v. Missouri Bone and Joint Center, Inc., 2010 U.S. App. LEXIS 16699. The major point to focus on in this case is causation.

Zavras v. Capeway Rovers Motorcycle Club, Inc., 1997 Mass. App. LEXIS 248. This case has an interesting discussion distinguishing between gross and ordinary negligence. The court also discusses gross negligence in relation to negligent hire and gross negligence by an employee.

QUESTIONS YOU SHOULD BE ABLE TO ANSWER

1. What is the difference in duty *as an element of negligence* and duty *as a requirement of actions*?

2. Compare the duty of a person who has an inherent relationship (e.g., a teacher to his or her student) to the duty of a person who volunteers to perform a task (e.g., coach a little league team or administer first aid).

3. What are three reasons why the distinction between ordinary negligence and gross negligence is important?

4. Compare the standard of care owed by a first year coach, a coach with 10 years of experience, and a coach with 30 years of experience.

5. Explain proximate cause and the effect of an intervening act. Give a clear example.

REFERENCES
Cases
Barnes v. New Hampshire Karting Association, 1991 La. App. LEXIS 158.
Borne v. Haverhill Golf and Country Club, 2003 Mass App. LEXIS 642.
Cerny v. Cedar Blff's Junior/Senior Public School, 679 N.W.2d. 198 (Neb. 2004).
Cirillo v. City of Milwaukee, 1967 Wisc. LEXIS 1123.
City of Santa Barbara v. Superior Court, 2007 Cal. LEXIS 7603.
Durrell v. Parachutes Are Fun,1987 Del. Super. LEXIS 1321.
Figure World v. Farley, 680 S.W.2d 33 (Tex. App. 1984).
Gill v. Tamalpais Union High School District, 2008 Cal. App. Unpub. LEXIS 3928.
Gouger v. Hardtke, 1992 Wisc. LEXIS 183.
Cincinnati Ins. Co. v. Oancea, 2004 Ohio App. LEXIS 3891.
Harting v. Dayton Dragons Professional Baseball Club, LLC, 2007 Ohio App LEXIS 1956.
Hatch v. V.P. Fair Foundation, Inc., 990 S.W.2d 126 (Mo. App. 1999).
Hawkins v. Peart, 2001 Utah LEXIS 177.
Kahn v. East Side Union High School District, 2003 Cal. LEXIS 6373.
Knight v. Jewett, 3 Cal.4th 296; 834 P.2d 696 (1992).
Lamp v. Reynolds, 2002 Mich. App. LEXIS 123.
Milne v. USA Cycling Inc., 2007 U.S. Dist. LEXIS 42579.
Pfister v. Shusta, 1995 Ill. LEXIS 201.
Rodriguez v. City of Moses Lake, 2010 Wash. App. LEXIS 2682.
Rutecki v. CSX Hotels, Inc., 2007 U.S. Dist. LEXIS 3181.
Searles v. Trustees of St. Joseph College, 695 A2d. 1206 (Me 1997).
Sisino v. Island Motocross of N.Y., Inc., 2007 WL 1629958 (N.Y. App. Div. June 5, 2007).
Southwest Key Program v. Gil-Perez, 2000 Tex. App. LEXIS 7851; 79 S.W.3d 571.
Sparks v. Starks, 2006 Ill. App. LEXIS 881.
Wagner v. SFX Motor Sports, Inc., 2006 U.S. Dist. LEXIS 79099.
Wolfgang v. Mid-America Sports, Inc., 1997 U.S. App. LEXIS 8817.
Zavras v. Capeway Rovers Motorcycle Club, Inc., 1997Mass. App. LEXIS 248.

Publications
Black, H.C. (1990). Black's Law Dictionary, (6th Ed.) St. Paul: West Publishing Co.
Keeton, W.P. (1984). *Prosser and Keeton on the law of torts* (5th ed.). St. Paul, MN: West Publishing Co.
van der Smissen, B. (2007). Elements of Negligence. In Cotten, D.J. and Wolohan. J.T. Law for recreation and Sport Managers (4th Ed.) Dubuque, Iowa: Kendall/Hunt Publishing Co.
van der Smissen, B. (1996) .Tort Liability and Risk Management. In Parkhouse, B.L. The Management of Sport (2nd Ed.) C.V.Mosby Company: St. Louis.
van der Smissen, B. (1990). Legal Liability and Risk Management for Public and Private Entities. Cincinnati: Anderson Publishing Company.

Websites
http://injury-law.freeadvice.com/injury-law/pain_and_suffering_factors.htm

Legislation
W.Va.C. 20-38-1 to 8.

2.12   WHICH PARTIES ARE LIABLE?

Doyice J. Cotten | Sport Risk Consulting

Recreation and sport law students often ask, "Why did they sue the school system or the recreation department when it was the teacher or the employee who was negligent?" or "If I am the supervisor, will I be liable if someone in my charge is negligent?" These questions represent just two of the many issues to be considered in answering the question of which parties may be liable when an injury occurs. Where in the past, the party sued was usually the corporate entity or the "deep pocket," today the trend is to sue everyone associated with the incident leading to the injury. For instance, suppose an aerobics instructor employed by a health club conducts an aerobics class in a room where speakers have been placed very near the participants. A participant loses his or her balance, falls into the speaker, and suffers injury. The participant might well name as individual defendants not only the aerobics instructor, but the manager of the health club, the program director, the person responsible for room setup and maintenance, the owner of the health club, as well as the health club corporate entity.

The question to be addressed in this chapter is: Who is liable when a negligent act results in an injury? The reader should remember, however, that since the laws regarding liability in such situations differ somewhat from state to state, the discussion will be general in nature. State law in any one state may differ somewhat from these general concepts.

FUNDAMENTAL CONCEPTS

There are three categories of parties that may be liable in any given situation. The first category consists of the **employee** or **service personnel** involved. This is usually the person who committed the negligent act. This category includes persons who generally have actual contact with the participants (e.g., teacher, coach, weight room attendant, referee, aerobics instructor, scout master). Also included in this category are the maintenance personnel or custodians who are often in direct contact with the participant.

The second category is the **administrative or supervisory personnel**. These are generally individuals who have some sort of administrative or supervisory authority over the service personnel. Examples include a director of recreation and intramurals, city recreation director, a principal, a head coach, a school superintendent, a manager of a health club, or a general manager of a professional baseball club. It is important to remember, however, that the classification of this individual can vary with the act being performed. For instance, the department head would be categorized as service personnel when teaching a class, but as administrative when performing scheduling duties.

The third category is the **corporate entity**. This category includes the governing body of the organization. Examples include the county school board, the municipal recreation board, the university board of regents, the corporation board of directors, the owner of a business, or the local health club corporation.

Who Is Liable?

The liability of three categories or groups is addressed here—employees or service personnel, administrative/supervisory personnel, and the corporate entity. In general, both employees and administrative/supervisory personnel are liable for their own negligence. In addition, under the doctrine of *respondeat superior*, the employer or corporate entity is liable for injury to person or property when the injury results from the negligent acts of the employee—so long as the injury occurs while the employee is acting within the scope of his or her authority. While each can be liable under certain circumstances, state immunity statutes (intended to help protect providers and employees from liability in certain situations) affect that liability.

Immunity. Sovereign or governmental immunity, still in effect in some states, generally protects the public corporate entity but not its employees. However, officials of public bodies are generally immune from liability for discretionary acts performed within the scope of their authority (see Chapter 2.21 *Defenses against Negligence* and Chapter 2.22 *Immunity*) and a few states do provide the employee with immunity from liability for any act as long as it is in performance of the employee's duties and is not willful and wanton (van der Smissen, 1990). In addition, many states have passed limited liability statutes that provide immunity to certain individuals under selected circumstances. These statutes include recreational use statutes (landowners), Good Samaritan statutes (those who come to the aid of the injured), various sport volunteer statutes (volunteer coaches and officials), and assumption of risk statutes for specific activities, for general activities, and for hazardous recreational activities (providers of recreational activities and sports). Most states also have passed laws which allow either for the indemnification of a public employee or for liability insurance coverage of the employee (see Chapter 2.21 *Defenses against Negligence* and Chapter 4.25 *Managing Risk Through Insurance*).

Employees/Service Personnel

In the absence of immunity, *employees are individually liable for their own negligent conduct.* The employee who performed the negligent act is generally the person in close contact with the participant (e.g., a teacher, a lifeguard, a camp counselor, an assistant coach, an athletic trainer, or a maintenance person). If the employee has a duty, breaches that duty by failing to meet the required standard of care, and that breach is the proximate cause of injury to the plaintiff, the employee is negligent and may be legally liable. Sometimes employees think they are not liable because they have insurance coverage. Insurance does not prevent or bar liability; however, it may pay the damages in the event of an award.

The aerobics instructor in the example at the beginning of this chapter would fall into the employee/service personnel category. If the instructor breaches a duty to the aerobics class by allowing participation too close to a hazard (the speaker), and that breach is shown to be the proximate cause of the injury, then the instructor is negligent and may be legally liable for damages.

Administrative/Supervisory Personnel

Whereas the question regarding liability of service personnel is relatively simple, the question of liability of the administrative or supervisory personnel for the negligence of subordinates is much more complex. *When there is no immunity, the general rule is that administrative/supervisory personnel are individually liable for their own negligent conduct, but are not liable for the negligence of subordinates. The administrator/supervisor is liable, however, if the administrator owes a duty and acts (or omissions) of the administrator enhanced the likelihood of injury* (van der Smissen, 1990).

Administrative duties fall into five categories (van der Smissen, 1990). These duties are to:

1. Employ competent personnel and discharge those unfit;
2. Provide proper supervision and to have a supervisory plan;
3. Direct the services or program in a proper manner;
4. Establish safety rules and regulations and to comply with policy and statutory requirements;
5. Remedy dangerous conditions and defective equipment or to warn users of dangers involved.

In the example involving the aerobics instructor, the health club manager would fall into the administrative/supervisory personnel category. Normally the manager is not liable for the negligence of the aerobics instructor unless the manager did something that enhanced the likelihood of injury. The health club manager hired a qualified, certified instructor, supervised the program adequately, and the aerobics program was conducted according to standards suggested by a national association. The manager may have breached an administrative/supervisory duty, however, by failing to establish or enforce safety rules regarding hazards on the floor or minimal clear space requirements, or by failing to identify and remedy or warn of dangerous conditions. On the other hand, if the presence of the speaker on the floor was a one-time occurrence and the manager had safety rules regarding hazards and space and regularly enforced them, then the manager would likely not be liable since the manager breached no duty and did not increase the likelihood of injury.

However, the administrative or supervisory personnel can be liable for human resources law violations (see *Respondeat Superior* in Human Resources Law later in this chapter). Human resources law includes three major areas of concern: (1) The employment process (including recruitment, selection, hiring, and firing of employees); (2) The workplace environment (including hostile work environment, sexual harassment, and employee protection laws; and (3) Employee behaviors (addressing employment process negligence, negligent supervision, negligent hire, and negligent retention) (van der Smissen, 2007).

The Corporate Entity

The next question regards the liability of the business or corporate entity for the negligence of an employee, whether that employee is classified as service personnel or administrative/supervisory personnel. The answer to this question is governed by the **doctrine of *respondeat superior*** (also referred to as **vicarious liability**) which states that *the negligence of an employee is imputed to the corporate entity if the employee was acting within the scope of the employee's responsibility and authority and if the act was not grossly negligent, willful/wanton, and did not involve malfeasance* (van der Smissen, 1990). So, according to this doctrine, if an employee commits ordinary negligence while engaged in the furtherance of the employer's enterprise, the employer as well as the employee can be liable.

In the foregoing example, the aerobics instructor instructing the class was acting within the scope of responsibility and authority and was engaged in the furtherance of the employer's enterprise. If it is shown that allowing activity too near the speakers constituted negligence, then not only is the instructor liable, but liability is also imputed to the health club corporate entity.

***Ultra Vires* Acts.** Acts that are beyond the scope of responsibility and authority of the employee are considered ***ultra vires* acts** and, generally, such an act relieves the corporate entity of liability via *respondeat superior*. The city in *Myricks v. Lynnwood Unified School District* (1999) was not liable for an accident transporting a team since the trip was not within the scope of the driver's responsibility. Exceptions to this rule occur when the corporate entity benefited from, had notice of, or condoned the act.

Respondeat Superior* in Human Resources Law.** When employment torts are concerned, the corporate entity is liable for the intentional torts and criminal acts of its employees. Traditionally, under the doctrine of *respondeat superior*, an employer is liable for injuries to the person or property of third persons resulting from actions by an employee that were within the scope of employment, but the employer carried no liability for unauthorized acts by employees including willful acts to injure another. In recent years, however, many jurisdictions have extended the **doctrine of *respondeat superior to include workplace torts (i.e., the wrongdoing of those in positions of authority), sexual assaults, sexual harassment, and abuse by a party in a position of authority over children (Carter, 1995; van der Smissen, 1996; *Williams v. Butler*, 1991). The concept of "acting within the scope of authority" continues to apply, but is more broadly interpreted to mean any activities which carry out the objectives of the employer (van der Smissen, 1996) and those during which the employer was or could have been exercising control of the activities of the employee (*Longin v. Kelly*, 1995).

The employer may also be held liable for acts of the employee in cases of **employment process negligence** (i.e., when the employer in the employment process negligently allows the assignment of an unfit employee or fails to use reasonable care to discover the unfitness of an employee). Liability of the employer can result from negligent hiring, negligent supervision, negligent training, negligent retention, and negligent referral of an employee that is unfit (van der Smissen, 1996; Carter, 1995).

Board Members. *Board members are not individually liable for the actions of the board or for the negligence of employees of the organization.* Board members are, however, individually liable for (1) collective acts of the board or individual acts that are outside the scope of authority; (2) breaches of statutory duty or violation of participant/employee Constitutional rights; and (3) intentional torts (e.g., assault and battery, slander, libel) (Kaiser & Robinson, 1999).

Intentional Torts or Willful Acts by an Employee. Many employers believe that they are not liable for intentional acts committed by their employees. This commonly held belief is not always true. In fact, courts generally look at whether there is social justification for holding the employer liable rather than at whether the conduct of the employee was intentional or negligent. So whether the employer is vicariously liable for an intentional act by the employee depends upon whether the action was (1) within the scope of employment (required by or was incidental to employment) or (2) reasonably foreseeable by the employer. If either prong of the test is met, the employer can be held liable even if the employee's act was willful or malicious.

Three cases in which an employee assaulted a patron while on duty resulted in rulings in favor of the victim (*Glucksman v. Walters*, 1995; *Rogers v. Fred R. Hiller Company of GA., Inc.*, 1994; *Pelletier v. Bilbiles*, 1967). Each court stated that a master is liable for the willful torts of his servant if the tort was committed within the scope of the servant's employment and in furtherance of his master's business. The *Glucksman* court further stated that the fact that the specific method employed to accomplish the master's orders is not authorized does not relieve the master of liability. One fact that employers should remember is that the court determines what falls "within the scope of employment" and there is little consistency among courts.

Furthermore, employers can be found liable in some cases even when the employee's action was not within the scope of employment if the employer ratifies the employee's action. Ratification may be either express or implied and can include such factors as failing to investigate the complaint, failing to redress the harm done, and failing to discharge the employee.

So there is no simple rule of thumb that the employer is not liable for intentional or willful acts of an employee. Each case is different and the result will turn on the facts of the particular case.

Volunteers, Trainees, and Interns. The question often arises as to whether the acts of a **volunteer**, a **trainee**, or an **intern** fall under the doctrine of *respondeat superior*. In general, volunteers, trainees, and interns are liable individually for their own negligence. If they were under the control of the corporate entity and were acting within the scope of "employment," authority, and responsibility, the corporate entity is liable under the doctrine of *respondeat superior*. Volunteers of public or nonprofit organizations are immune from liability for their own negligence if they qualify under the federal Volunteer Protection Act of 1997 or a state volunteer immunity statute (see Chapter 2.21 *Defenses against Negligence* and Chapter 2.22 *Immunity*). In those instances, the corporate entity is usually still liable for the negligence of the volunteer (van der Smissen, 1990; Manley, 1995). It is worth noting that the volunteer, trainee, or intern *is held to the same standard of care as that of an experienced, competent professional.*

University Athletes. An issue that sometimes arises is whether a university is liable under *respondeat superior* for the negligent acts of a university varsity athlete (*Townsend v. The State of California*, 1987; *Hanson v. Kynast*, 1986; *Brown v. Day*, 1990). Courts have ruled the applicability of the doctrine requires an individualized determination of whether a master-servant relationship exists between the tortfeasor and the university. The *Townsend* court concluded that whether on scholarship or not, the athlete is not an employee and the university is not vicariously liable for the athlete's negligent acts.

Joint and Several Liability and Uniform Contribution Among Joint Tortfeasors. The **joint and several liability doctrine** holds that one defendant can be held liable for the total damages even though other defendants were also at fault. If more than one party is found liable, the court does not limit the injured party's recovery against each to a proportionate share of fault. A classic example of this can be found in *Walt Disney World Co. v. Wood* (1987) where Disney was found 1 percent at fault, plaintiff was 14 percent at fault, and other defendants were 85 percent at fault. Under joint and several liability, Disney was ordered to pay the entire 86 percent of damages. In the 1980s, however, most states enacted statutes that provide for **uniform contribution among joint tortfeasors** in equitable portions, but not necessarily equal portions. When one tortfeasor has paid a disproportionate share of damages, that tortfeasor can file suit against the other tortfeasor in a separate action.

In *Universal Gym Equipment, Inc. v. Vic Tanny International, Inc.* (1994), the plaintiff was injured while working on a Universal machine. She had signed a waiver that protected Tanny from litigation, so she sued Universal and obtained a settlement of $225,000. Universal then commenced action against Tanny alleging failure to maintain safe premises and that Tanny had an obligation to indemnify or contribute to any settlement between the injured plaintiff and Universal. Michigan law allowed Tanny to use any defense that would have been valid against liability for the injury to exonerate it from liability for contribution. Thus, the waiver signed by the injured party protected Tanny from liability for contribution to Universal. The court remanded the case to determine if Tanny was grossly negligent—in which case, the waiver would not protect Tanny from liability for the injury, nor from liability for the contribution.

Limiting Corporate Liability by Contract

Corporate entities frequently limit their liability through the use of various types of contractual arrangements. The following are four methods in common use.

Leasing Facilities

The use of sport and recreational facilities by another group or organization is a common practice. The details of these transactions can range from free use by oral agreement to a formal lease with a rental charge. In any case, the question is: What is the liability of the owner of the premises when an injury occurs on the premises while being used by another organization? To determine such liability, one must first determine whether the injury was premise-related (resulting from unsafe premises) or activity-related (resulting from the conduct of the activity) (van der Smissen, 1990). Unless specified in the contract, the owner generally remains liable for premise-related injuries. Second, if the injury is activity-related, one must determine if the owner retained *control* over the activity or the use of the premises. Essentially, the liability for activity-related injury generally lies with the party that had control over the activity. Thus, if a university leases an arena to a promoter of an ice skating event and retains no control over how the activity is conducted, the university would not be liable for activity-related injuries, but might be liable if the injury resulted from an unsafe facility.

Facility owners generally require that the leasing party provide a certificate of insurance showing adequate liability insurance for the event. Many require that the owners be named as a co-insured on the policy (see Chapter 2.21 *Defenses against Negligence* and Chapter 2.31 *Premises Liability*).

Independent Contractors

An **independent contractor** is an individual or a company that contracts to perform a particular task using his own methods and is subject to the employer's control only as to end product or final result of his work (Black's Law Dictionary, 1990). Examples of persons that are often classified as independent contractors include referees for a contest, an aerobics specialist at a health club, a team physician, or a diving business that teaches scuba diving for a municipal recreation department.

A major reason that corporations use independent contractors is to reduce the amount of liability faced by the service provider. *The general rule is that if an injury results from the negligence of the independent contractor, the liability for negligence is shifted from the corporate entity to the independent contractor* (see Table 1 in Chapter 2.21 *Defenses Against Negligence*). Thus, the *corporate entity* avoids much of the potential liability posed by offering the activity. However, the *corporate entity* does retain some responsibilities. The *corporate entity* is responsible (1) for using reasonable care in selecting a competent independent contractor and for inspection after completion; (2) for keeping the premises reasonably safe for invitees and employees; and (3) for "inherently dangerous activities" (e.g., activities presenting substantial harm unless precautions are taken such as fireworks displays, keeping of dangerous animals, ultra hazardous activities).

In *Hatch v. V.P. Fair Foundation, Inc.* (1999), a patron was injured when an independent contractor at a fair failed to attach the bungee cord to the platform prior to the jump. The court ruled that a landowner who hires an independent contractor to perform an "inherently dangerous activity" has a non-delegable duty to take special precautions to prevent injury from the activity. The landowner remains liable for the torts of the contractor even though the landowner was not negligent.

Often, whether one is an employee or an independent contractor is at issue. Courts generally rule that one is an **employee** if one is hired, paid a set wage or salary, is often trained by the employer, works on an ongoing basis, must perform the work as directed by the employer, and is paid by the hour, week, or month. An **independent contractor** is one who is generally engaged for a specific project, usually for a set sum, often paid at the end of the project, may do the job in one's own way, often furnishes one's own equipment, is subject to minimal restrictions, and is responsible only for the satisfactory completion of the job (*Jaeger v. Western Rivers Fly Fisher*, 1994). The distinction is important from a financial standpoint because the classification can affect the amount owed for (1) unemployment contributions, (2) workers' compensation, (3) FICA, and (4) federal and state income tax withholding. The IRS and other relevant agencies can levy heavy fines for failure to pay sufficient taxes or fees when companies have been improperly classified as independent contractors.

Unfortunately, there is no specific number of these conditions that must be met and no magic formula for weighting these conditions to determine if, indeed, one is an independent contractor. A review board or court may determine that failure, to some degree, to meet any one of the conditions is sufficient to invalidate the claim for independent contractor status. The difficulty in determining whether the person is properly classified as an employee or an independent contractor is illustrated in a recent case dealing with fitness instructors. Fitness Plus provided fitness classes for corporate clients on the premises of the client (*In the Matter of Fitness Plus, Inc.*, 2002). Fitness Plus would assess the needs of the client, contact one of about 30 instructors, negotiate a fee, bill the client, pay the instructor regardless of profit or loss, pay the instructor every two weeks, and report their income on a 1099 form. Most of these procedures fit the conditions for an independent contractor. In selecting the instructors, Fitness Plus conducted interviews, checked background, training, certification, and experience, and usually observed them in a class—seemingly meeting the requirement that they select qualified contractors. Instructors worked generally one to six hours weekly and signed an agreement that their status was that of an independent contractor. The court determined that there was sufficient evidence that Fitness Plus exercised sufficient direction and control over the services of the instructors to support the Unemployment Insurance Appeal Board ruling that they were employees.

Indemnification

An **indemnification agreement** is an agreement by which one party agrees to indemnify, reimburse, or restore a loss of another upon the occurrence of an anticipated loss. They are sometimes referred to as **hold harmless agreements** or **save harmless agreements**. Indemnification agreements can be very effective when one business indemnifies another business against loss; however, they are not always enforceable when used as a waiver of liability in which the user of the service must agree to indemnify the service provider for loss resulting from the negligence of the provider (see also Chapter 2.21 *Defenses Against Negligence*).

A perfect example of a business entity requiring that another associated business entity indemnify it from liability is illustrated in *Southwick v. City of Rutland* (2011). In this case (included on the Supplemental Web Site), the City of Rutland required the Vermont Swim Association (VSA) to indemnify the city for any loss the city might incur as a result of VSA holding a swim meet on city facilities. A child was injured on the adjoining city playground and sued the city. VSA claimed that the agreement did not cover injury resulting from the negligence of the city. The appellate court ruled that the indemnification agreement signed by VSA was clear and unambiguous. The court upheld the lower court award to the city.

For more information on indemnification, see Chapter 2.21 *Defenses against Negligence* and Chapter 2.23 *Waivers and Releases*.

Waivers

The corporate entity may protect itself and its employees from liability by use of waivers of liability in which the participant or service user contractually releases the business from liability for negligence by the corporate entity or its employees (see also Chapter 2.23 *Waivers and Releases*).

Corporate Liability in Other Situations

Financial Sponsorship

Many organizations provide financial sponsorship for recreational activities or teams. **Financial sponsorship** exists when the sponsoring organization provides financial support, but exercises no control over the activity. An example of this type of sponsorship would be civic clubs or private businesses sponsoring recreation department softball teams. Financial sponsorship of this sort generally carries with it no liability. Whether the sponsoring organization is liable for injuries that occur due to negligence depends upon several things: (1) was the person in charge an agent of the organization?; (2) did the organization have control over the activity?; and (3) was a duty owed to the participant? (van der Smissen, 1990).

In *Wilson v. United States of America* (1993), the issue was whether an agency relationship existed between the Boy Scouts of America and adult volunteers of a troop so as to provide for vicarious liability for the negligence of the adult troop leaders. The court stated that liability based upon *respondeat superior* requires evidence of a master-servant relationship. In this case, there was no liability since the national organization exerts no direct control over the leaders or the activities of individual troops. In an older case, Boy Scouts of America was found liable for the negligence of an adult volunteer at a Scout-o-Rama controlled by the regional council. The key difference was control (*Riker v. Boy Scouts of America*, 1959). In *Fazzinga v. Westchester Track Club* (2008), PepsiCo was named in a negligence suit involving a death in a 5K run. The court ruled that PepsiCo was not liable because it did not supervise or control the event and was a "mere sponsor" of the race. By way of contrast, in *Williams v. City of Albany* (2000) the defendant Capital District Flag Football, Inc. claimed to be only a sponsor of a flag football game in which Williams was injured. The court rejected this contention because the organization organized the league in question, arranged for the use of six fields, provided referees for league play, and acquired insurance for its protection.

Program Sponsorship and Joint Programming

Program sponsorship exists when an organization or entity organizes an event or maintains control over an event. An example would be when a recreation department organizes and conducts a Fourth of July slate of special activities. **Joint programming** is when more than one entity is involved in program sponsorship. Examples of such sponsorship or programming include an NCAA championship event, a high school game under the auspices of the state high school athletic association, and an event sponsored and conducted by the University of Georgia and the Southeastern Conference.

When leagues or athletic associations exert control over the conduct of the game and the eligibility of the participants, duties are created and liability for negligence emerges. When two organizations are involved in joint programming or joint sponsorship of an activity, each is responsible and liable for injuries resulting from negligence.

Governing Organization Sponsorship

Governing organizations of sports or other activities often sponsor events or lend their name to such events. If the organization has no hand in the actual conduct of the event, it owes no duty to the participants. Of course, there is no liability when there is no duty.

In *Lautieri v. Bai v. USA Triathlon, Inc.* (2003), the liability of a governing organization was at issue. The governing organization was USA Triathlon, Inc. (USAT), the program sponsor was William Fiske d/b/a Fiske Independent Race Management. Fiske was found to be grossly negligent, however, the court held that for USAT to be liable, it must be established that USAT owed a duty of care to the plaintiff. To accomplish this, the plaintiff would have to show that such a duty has a source (1) existing in social values and customs or that (2) USAT voluntarily, or for consideration, assumed a duty of care to the plaintiff. Evidence indicated that USAT's only involvement was its approval of the application of the organizer of the event. There was no evidence to indicate that USAT was obligated to or was expected to participate in the planning, operation, or supervision of the race.

Joint Ventures

A **joint venture** is "an agreement between two or more persons, ordinarily, but not necessarily limited to a single transaction for the purpose of making a profit" (*Jaeger v. Western Rivers Fly Fisher*, 1994, p. 1224). Some essential elements for a joint venture include combining of property, money, efforts, skill, labor, knowledge, and a sharing of losses and profits. A group of college students who wanted to go whitewater rafting, put up notices informing other students of the proposed trip, met, planned the trip, shared resources, and went on the trip would form a joint venture. It would not be a joint venture if the campus recreation department conceived the idea of the trip, publicized the proposed trip, helped them plan the trip, and supplied equipment for the trip. In the latter case, the university would be a sponsor of the activity and would be liable in the event of negligence. In a true joint venture, there is no group sponsorship and, hence, no liability for the corporation.

Apparent Authority

Apparent authority is a legal doctrine that describes a situation in which the principal (a person or organization) treats a second party in such as way as to lead a third party to think that the second party is an agent of the principal or has the authority to bind the principal. Under agency law, the principal is responsible for or liable for the acts of a second party that the principal allows to appear to have authority. Those in the recreation and tourism industries, in particular, need to take steps to insure that the relationship between the organization and independent contractors creates no confusion that might cause the client to rely on the appearance of an agency relationship between the principal and the apparent agent.

In a 2004 case (*Cash v. Six Continents Hotels*), two tourists were injured while climbing Dunn's River Falls in Jamaica. While the tour was provided by Harmony Tours (which had a desk in the hotel lobby), the plaintiffs had booked the tour through their hotel. They claimed the hotel was liable for Harmony Tours' negligence under the doctrine of apparent authority since the hotel allowed it to appear that the company was an agent of the hotel. The court found for the hotel since the hotel did not make representations of an affiliation, had a large sign stating "Harmony Tours" near the desk, and included a statement on the ticket informing that the company was an independent contractor and that the hotel was not responsible.

SIGNIFICANT CASE

This significant case was chosen because it addresses the duties and liability of several categories of defendants—vicarious liability of the team sponsor of the player who committed the act resulting in injury, the other financial (or team) sponsor, the softball league hosting the tournament, a national softball association that sponsors the league, the owner of the property, and the insurer of some of the defendants. Also included is a discussion of assumption of risk and participant responsibilities.

ALLEN V. DOVER CO-RECREATIONAL SOFTBALL LEAGUE

The Supreme Court of New Hampshire
2002 N.H. LEXIS 145
Opinion Issued: September 30, 2002

duggan, J. * * *

The plaintiffs allege the following facts. On September 13, 1998, Carol Allen was injured while participating in a recreational softball game when an errantly thrown softball struck her in the head as she ran to first base. The game was part of an adult, co-recreational, slow-pitch softball tournament.

The defendants are all organizations associated with the softball tournament. The teams playing in the tournament were part of defendant Dover Co-Recreational Softball League (league), which is sponsored by defendant Amateur Softball Association, Inc. (ASA). The ASA promulgates rules that govern the play of its member leagues. The teams playing in this particular game were sponsored by defendant Daniel's Sports Bar and Grill (Daniel's) and defendant Thompson Imports (Thompson). Team sponsors provided t-shirts for the players. The game was played on a field owned by defendant Martel-Roberge American Legion Post #47 (American Legion). Defendant Bollinger Fowler Company (Bollinger)

provided liability insurance coverage for the league, ASA, the American Legion, the Daniel's team and the Thompson team.

On the day the plaintiff was injured, she was playing for the Daniel's team in a one-pitch tournament. As set forth in ASA official rules, the softball used when women batted was smaller than the softball used when men batted. This use of different balls is intended to allow the women to hit more competitively with the men. The defendants did not recommend, require or provide helmets for players. Although a slow-pitch game under the ASA official rules is played with five men and five women for each team, the game on September 13 was played with seven men and three women on each team.

When batting for the first time on September 13, Carol Allen hit a ball toward shortstop. A male player for the Thompson team fielded the ball and threw it toward first base. His throw, however, was inaccurate and struck Carol Allen in the head. * * *

The plaintiffs subsequently filed a writ alleging several counts of negligence. First, the plaintiffs allege that **the league** and **Daniel's** acted negligently when they conducted the softball game "without utilizing all reasonable safety precautions including but not limited to recommending, requiring, or providing batting helmets for the players, using less dangerous softballs, and maintaining proper male/female player ratios." The plaintiffs further allege that **ASA** breached its duty to promulgate and enforce rules that required batting helmets to be worn in softball games, use of a less dangerous softball and each team to play with five men and five women, and to otherwise minimize the risk of injury to participants in co-recreational softball games. The plaintiffs also allege that ASA "had a duty to warn, advise, inform and instruct its members regarding the risk of injury to participants in co-recreational softball games and the manner in which such risks could be minimized." As for the **American Legion**, the plaintiffs claim that as the owner of the softball field, it "had a duty to require that softball games played on its field were played pursuant to rules and in a manner which minimized the risk of injury to participants." The plaintiffs further allege that **Thompson** "is vicariously liable for the negligence of its shortstop in errantly throwing the softball." Finally, the plaintiffs allege that because Bollinger provided risk management services to its insureds—the league, ASA, the American Legion, the Daniel's team and the Thompson team—"**Bollinger** had a duty to warn, advise, inform, and instruct its insureds regarding the risk of injury to participants in co-recreational softball games and the manner in which such risks could be minimized." (bold added)

All of the defendants moved to dismiss the case arguing, among other things, that they owed no duty to protect Carol Allen from the inherent risks of injury that arose out of her participation in the softball game. * * *

* * * The court ruled that participants do not owe a duty to other participants to refrain from "injury-causing events which are known, apparent or reasonably foreseeable consequences of the participation" but rather participants "in recreational sporting events owe a duty to other participants to refrain from reckless or intentional conduct [that may injure the other participants]." Because the plaintiffs alleged that Thompson's shortstop acted negligently, not recklessly or intentionally, when he errantly threw the ball, the court concluded, "Thompson Imports cannot be held vicariously liable under the circumstances of this case."

* * * The court ruled that the league, ASA, Daniel's, and Thompson, as sponsors, and the American Legion, as owner of the field, owed the plaintiffs "a duty to refrain from reckless[ly] or intentional[ly causing injury to a participant]." Rather than acting recklessly or intentionally to create a risk of injury, the court observed that the defendants' alleged conduct involved the ordinary risks of injury inherent in playing recreational softball. * * * Accordingly, the trial court dismissed all counts of the plaintiffs' writ.

On appeal, the plaintiffs argue that the trial court erred by applying the doctrine of assumption of the risk. Applying the doctrine, the plaintiffs contend, was error because under New Hampshire common law, the doctrine was historically applied only to employer-employee relationships and supplanted altogether when the legislature enacted the comparative fault statute. See RSA 507:7-d (1997).

* * *

The comparative fault statute does not apply in this case because the defendants do not claim that Carol Allen acted negligently in causing her own injury; rather, they argue that they owed no duty to protect her against the risk that she would be injured by an errantly thrown softball.

Assumption of the Risk

We next determine the applicability of the doctrine of assumption of the risk. The defendants and the plaintiffs disagree on what the term "assumption of the risk" means and how it should be applied in this case. To resolve this issue, we must examine the history and various uses of the term "assumption of the risk."

The term "assumption of the risk" has been used to express distinct common law theories, derived from different sources, which apply when a plaintiff has knowingly exposed herself to particular risks. The three distinct legal concepts encompassed by the term are: (1) a plaintiff's consent in exposing herself to a defendant's negligence; (2) a defendant's negligence together with a plaintiff's negligence which causes the plaintiff injury; and (3) a plaintiff's voluntary participation in a reasonable activity with known risks such that a defendant owes no duty to the plaintiff to protect against harm arising from those risks.

* * *

The third theory, the doctrine of primary implied assumption of the risk, applies when a plaintiff voluntarily and reasonably enters into some relation with a defendant, which the plaintiff reasonably knows involves certain obvious risks such that a defendant has no duty to protect the plaintiff against injury caused by those risks. * * * This primary implied assumption of risk doctrine, the defendants argue, applies to this case. The plaintiffs, however, contend that this doctrine applies only where there is an employer-employee relationship.

* * *

When, however, a defendant owes no duty to a plaintiff in light of a particular risk, the defendant cannot be held accountable to a plaintiff who is injured upon the plaintiff's voluntary encounter with that risk. * * * In other words, a defendant who has no duty cannot be negligent. Moreover, contrary to the plaintiffs' contention, the comparative fault statute does not supplant this common-law doctrine because a plaintiff's fault is irrelevant in determining whether a defendant has a duty. It is this third theory that is applicable here.

Defendants' Duty

Under this theory, we must determine what duty if any the defendants owed to Carol Allen to protect her against the risk that she would be injured when she participated in the softball game. The defendants argue that they owed no duty to protect her against the risk that she might be injured when a softball struck her head because that was an ordinary risk of playing co-recreational softball, a reasonable activity in which she voluntarily participated. We conclude that when Carol Allen voluntarily played softball—a reasonable activity that she knew involved obvious risks—the defendants had no duty to protect her against injury caused by those risks.

However, even if there is no duty to protect a plaintiff against ordinary risks, we must address the standard of care that co-participants, sponsors and organizers owe to participants in recreational sports activities when extraordinary risks are alleged. Generally, "persons owe a duty of care only to those who are foreseeably endangered by their conduct and only with respect to those risks or hazards whose likelihood made the conduct unreasonably dangerous."

* * *

"We believe that the negligence standard, properly understood and applied, is suitable for recreational athletic activities because the conduct of a participant, sponsor or organizer is measured against the conduct that a reasonable participant, sponsor or organizer would engage in under the circumstances. See Lestina v. West Bend Mut. Ins. Co., 501 N.W.2d 28, 33 (Wis. 1993); * * * When one creates an unreasonable risk under the circumstances, however, he has breached the standard of care. Crawn, 630 A.2d at 373

To determine the appropriate standard of care to be applied to participants, sponsors and organizers of recreational athletics, we consider: (1) the nature of the sport involved; (2) the type of contest, i.e., amateur, high school, little league, pick-up, etc.; (3) the ages, physical characteristics and skills of the participants; (4) the type of equipment involved; and (5) the rules, customs and practices of the sport, including the types of contact and the level of violence generally accepted. See Lestina, at 33. "A defendant may be held liable to the plaintiff for [unreasonably] creating or countenancing risks other than risks inherent in the sport, or for increasing inherent risks, and in any event will be held liable for reckless] or intentional injurious conduct totally outside the range of ordinary activity involved in the sport, but liability should not place unreasonable burdens on the free and vigorous participation in the sport." A defendant, however, may not be held liable for negligent, or even reckless or intentional injurious conduct that is not outside the range of ordinary activity involved in the sport.

In this case, we first consider the nature of the sport of softball. The sport of softball is a reasonable activity, commonly played by men, women and children of varying skill levels. Consistent with this wide variety of players, a wide variety of rules are applied. Whether played by men, women or children, skilled or unskilled, participation in a softball game generally gives rise to the risk that a player may be struck by a ball that has been hit by a batter or thrown by a fielder.

* * *

Under the circumstances of this game, the only duty the defendants had was not to act in an unreasonable manner that would increase or create a risk of injury outside the range of risks that flow from participation in an adult co-recreational softball game. The plaintiffs argue the defendants' duty specifically included taking the following actions: (1) participants had a duty to not make errant throws when fielding the ball; (2) the league, Daniel's and Thompson had a duty to utilize all reasonable safety precautions in their conduct of the games; (3) the American Legion and ASA had a duty to promulgate or enforce rules that would minimize the risk of injury; and (4) ASA and Bollinger had a duty to warn, advise, inform and instruct the league regarding the risk of injury to participants and the manner in which such risks could be minimized. We examine each act the plaintiffs contend was required of the defendants in turn.

The plaintiffs first argue that the shortstop had a duty to not make an errant throw when fielding the ball. Participants in an adult co-recreational slow-pitch softball game have a duty to not create an unreasonable risk of injury. When fielding the ball, therefore, a fielder has a duty to not act unreasonably. In other words, the fielder has a duty to not act in a manner outside the range of the ordinary activity involved in playing softball. A fielder, however, does not have a duty to make only accurate throws. Because reasonable fielders commonly make errant throws, being injured by an errant throw is a common risk inherent in and arising out of a softball game. A fielder therefore cannot be held liable for errant throws that reasonably flow from participation. * * * Accordingly, the plaintiffs' claim based upon the shortstop's errant throw does not constitute a legal basis for relief.

The plaintiffs next argue that the league, Daniel's and Thompson had a duty to utilize all reasonable safety precautions in their conduct of the games. * * * Because we assume the facts as pled by the plaintiffs are true, we will assume that Daniel's and Thompson as team sponsors, in fact, conducted the game. To the extent a team sponsor conducts a game, it has a duty to conduct the game in a manner that does not unreasonably increase the risks that flow from the ordinary play of the game. See Hacking, 143 N.H. at 553.

The plaintiffs' complaint alleges that the team sponsors had a duty to conduct this game using certain equipment, specifically batting helmets and "less dangerous softballs." While the plaintiffs allege that batting helmets should have been used when conducting this game, they do not allege that batting helmets are ordinarily worn by players in adult co-recreational slow-pitch softball games. The ASA rules the plaintiffs allege applied to this game do not require batting helmets to be worn. Further, the plaintiffs do not allege that reasonable teams use batting helmets when playing in adult co-recreational softball games. They have thus failed to make an allegation that gives rise to a duty for these team sponsors to recommend, require or provide helmets when conducting an adult co-recreational softball game. Thus, under the circumstances of this game, not recommending, requiring or providing batting helmets did not unreasonably increase or create a new risk outside of the range of ordinary activity.

The plaintiffs further allege that the softball manufactured for use when adult men play softball is less dangerous than the softball manufactured for use when children and women play softball. * * * Because the risk that a player may suffer an injury upon being struck by a ball is an ordinary risk incident to playing softball, using the smaller softball manufactured for use by women to allow the women in a co-ed game to hit more competitively with men did not unreasonably increase the ordinary risks inherent in the game. Therefore, the team sponsors' duty to Carol Allen did not include using the least "dangerous" softball available when conducting an adult co-recreational softball game. * * *

Finally, the plaintiffs allege that the defendants had a duty to adhere to a strict five-male to five-female ratio * * *. Being struck by a ball thrown by a male player is an ordinary risk inherent in co-ed softball. The ratio rule did not unreasonably increase or conceal the risk that Carol Allen would be struck by a ball thrown by a male player * * *. Thus, by not using a strict five-female to five-male ratio the defendants did not unreasonably increase her risk of injury or create a new risk outside the range of risks that ordinarily flow from participation in an adult co-recreational softball game. Therefore the defendants did not owe a duty to Carol Allen to adhere to the five-male to five-female ratio.

* * *

The plaintiffs' writ also alleges that defendants American Legion, as owner of the softball field, and ASA, as sponsor of the league, had a duty to promulgate or enforce rules that would minimize the risk of injury. * * *. The defendants thus have a duty to promulgate or enforce rules that minimize the risk of injury, if without those rules the game is otherwise unreasonably dangerous. While the plaintiffs allege that promulgating and enforcing rules that required batting helmets, a larger, softer softball, or a certain male-female ratio would make the game safer, they do not allege that failing to promulgate and enforce such rules created risks outside the risks ordinarily involved in softball and made the game unreasonably dangerous. Consequently, the plaintiffs' writ does not allege facts that, if true, would show that the defendants breached the duty they owed to Carol Allen to promulgate and enforce rules that were necessary to minimize injury in an otherwise unreasonably dangerous sport. Therefore, it does not allege a basis for legal relief.

Finally, the plaintiffs allege ASA and Bollinger had a duty to warn, advise, inform and instruct the league regarding the risk of injury to participants and the manner in which such risks could be minimized. As we have previously stated, the defendants may not be held liable to the plaintiffs for creating or countenancing those risks inherent in the sport of softball. * * * Thus, the defendants may be held liable if the plaintiffs allege that a reasonable person would customarily warn, advise, inform and instruct the league regarding the risk of injury to participants and the manner in which such risks could be minimized and their failure to do so caused the plaintiff's injuries. The plaintiffs, however, do not allege that reasonable sponsors and insurers customarily warn or instruct leagues regarding the risk of injury to participants. Therefore the defendants, in this case, had no duty to warn and instruct the league regarding the risk of injury.

In sum, the plaintiffs' writ does not allege any facts from which one could reasonably infer that the standard of care required the defendants to recommend, require or provide helmets, use a less dangerous softball or maintain a ratio of five men and five women on each team, and therefore, the writ does not allege sufficient facts that the defendants unreasonably created a new risk outside the ordinary risks or unreasonably increased the inherent risk that Carol Allen would be injured when struck by a softball while participating in an adult co-recreational softball game. * * * Because the plaintiffs' allegations do not constitute a legal basis for relief, the trial court properly dismissed the case.

Affirmed.

BROCK, C.J., and DALIANIS, J., concurred.

CASES ON THE SUPPLEMENTAL WEB SITE

Rostai v. Neste Enterprises, 2006 Cal. App. LEXIS 476. In this case, both the club and the independent contractor personal trainer were sued for the alleged negligence of the trainer.

Avenoso v. Mangan, 2006 Conn. Super. LEXIS 489. Under agency theory, the agency (the soccer club) is not liable if the agent (the coach) is not negligent. Why, then, didn't the court rule that the soccer club was not liable?

Eastman v. Yutzy, 2001 Mass. Super. LEXIS 157. Note the number of defendants, their positions in the camp, and what the court says about their duties.

B.R. v. Little League Baseball, Inc., 2009 Cal. App. Unpub. LEXIS 7652. Little League Baseball was sued because a minor was molested by a registered sex offender employed by a local little league organization. Discover why Little League Baseball, Inc. was not liable.

Southwick v. City of Rutland, 2011 Vt. LEXIS 51. This case clearly illustrates how liability can be shifted from one business entity to another by an indemnification agreement.

QUESTIONS YOU SHOULD BE ABLE TO ANSWER

1. Under what circumstances is the administrator or supervisor liable for the negligence of employees whom they supervise?

2. When is the corporate entity liable for willful acts by employees?

3. Why is it necessary to determine if a party is an independent contractor or an employee?

4. When an injury results from negligence at an event, who is most likely to be held liable, a financial sponsor, the program sponsor, or a national governing organization? Why?

5. When a teacher is negligent, who is liable, the teacher or the school district? Explain.

REFERENCES
Cases
Cash v. Six Continents Hotels (Need Reference completed)
Doe v. Taylor Independent School District, 15 F.3d 443 (Texas 1994).
Glucksman v. Walters, 659 A.2d 1217 (Conn. 1995).
Hanson v. Kynast, 494 N.E.2d 1091 (Ohio 1986).
Hatch v. U.P. Fair Foundation, Inc., 1999 MO. App. LEXIS 315.
In the Matter of Fitness Plus, Inc., 2002 N.Y. App. Div. LEXIS 3830.
Jaeger v. Western Rivers Fly Fisher, 855 F. Supp. 1217 (Utah 1994).
Lautieri v. Bai v. USA Triathlon, Inc., 2003 Mass. Super. LEXIS 290.
Longin v. Kelly, 875 F. Supp. 196 (NY 1995).
Myricks v. Lynnwood Unified School District, 87 Cal. Rptr. 2d 734 (Cal. App. 2 Dist. 1999).
Pelletier v. Bilbiles, 227 A.2d 251 (Conn. 1967).
Riker v. Boy Scouts of America, 183 N.Y.S.2d 484 (1959).
Rogers v. Fred R. Hiller Company of Georgia, Inc., 448 S.E.2d 46 (Ga. 1994).
Southwick v. City of Rutland, 2011 Vt. LEXIS 51.
Townsend v. The State of California, 237 Cal. Rptr. 146 (Cal. 1987).
Universal Gym Equipment, Inc. v. Vic Tanny International, Inc., 526 N.W.2d 5 (Mich. 1994).
Walt Disney World Co. v. Wood, 489 So.2d 61 (1986); 515 So.2d 198 (Fla. 1987).
Williams v. Butler, 577 So.2d 1113 (La. App. 1 Cir. 1991).
Wilson v. United States of America, 989 F.2d 953 (Mo. 1993)

Publications
Carter, P. (1995). Employer's Liability for Assault, Theft, or Similar Intentional Wrong Committed by Employee at Home or Business of Customer, 13 A.L.R.5th 217.
Creason, J. and Dunlap L. Evaluating Employers' Liability for Intentional Torts of Employees. http://www.creasonandaarvig.com/CM/Articles/Articles2.asp
Kaiser, R., & Robinson, K. (1999). Risk Management. In van der Smissen, B., Moiseichik, M., Hartenburg, V., & Twardgik, L. (Eds.). *Management of park and recreation agencies* (pp. 713–741). Ashuba, VA: National Recreation and Parks Association.
Manley, A. (1995). Liability of Charitable Organization Under *Respondeat Superior* Doctrine for Tort of Unpaid Volunteer, 82 A.L.R. 3d 1213.
van der Smissen, B. (1990). *Legal liability and risk management for public and private entities.* Cincinnati: Anderson Publishing Co.
van der Smissen, B. (1996). *Legal liability and risk management for public and private entities.* Cincinnati: Anderson Publishing Co. (Prepublication supplement)
van der Smissen, B. (2007). Human Resources Law in Cotten, D. and Wolohan, J. (Eds.) *Law for Recreation and Sport Managers* (4th ed.) Dubuque, Iowa: Kendall-Hunt Publishing Company.

2.13 LIABILITY OF SPORTS PARTICIPANTS, SPORTS INSTRUCTORS, AND SPORTS OFFICIALS[1]

Doyice J. Cotten | Sport Risk Consulting

Under tort law, when a person is injured due to the negligence or carelessness of another person, the injured party may file a claim for compensation for the injury. If a person slips and falls because of a puddle inside a grocery store, the business may be found liable for damages. If a driver drives carelessly and causes an accident and injury, the driver may be found liable. In other words, under tort law, one may be found liable for one's harmful behavior (see Chapter 2.11 *Negligence*).

In sports activities, however, actions that would be found to be unlawful in daily life may be perfectly acceptable. Examples are abundant in sport—ranging from throwing a baseball at a batter or a base runner colliding with the catcher to dislodge the ball to hitting the quarterback long after he has thrown the football. Sometimes the actions (e.g., colliding with the catcher to dislodge the ball) are within the rules or are considered part of the game (*Avila v. Citrus Community College District*, 2006). On the other hand, the action is sometimes a violation of the rules and a penalty is prescribed by the rules of the sport. (e.g., hitting the quarterback late incurs a 15 yard penalty).

When the actions of sports participants, sports instructors, and sports officials result in an injury to a sport participant, legal action is sometimes taken by the injured party. Whether the actor is liable for the injury depends upon several factors—the circumstances, the nature of the activity, and the issue to be examined in this chapter, the standard of care the participant, instructor, or official owes the injured party. These parties are held to either the negligence standard or the recklessness standard, depending upon state law.

The recreation and sport manager should understand that this chapter examines state law and that not only does the required standard of care vary by state, but that within many states the required standard varies by sport or type of activity.[2] The states and cases discussed and listed here provide an explanation of the concepts and how the law differs in different jurisdictions; however, complete examination of the standards and law in each state is beyond the scope of this chapter. Therefore, it is important that the recreation and sport manager learn the required standard of care for sports participants, sports instructors, and sports officials in his or her particular state.

FUNDAMENTAL CONCEPTS

Standards of Care

The most common standards of care that determine liability in sports situations are the negligence standard and the recklessness standard. It is important that the recreation and sport manager understand the difference between these two standards.

The **negligence standard** is the standard of care described in Chapter 2.11. This standard requires that the actor (i.e., sports participant, sports instructor, or sports official) protect the participant from unreasonable risk of harm. Under this standard, the actor is held liable for actions reaching the level of ordinary negligence.

---

[1]Special thanks to John Wolohan and Kristi L. Schoepfer Bochicchio for valuable input regarding this chapter.

[2]This variation in state law is illustrated best in the case of golf. In several states, when a golf participant is injured due to the negligence of a co-participant, courts hold the co-participant liable for the injury. However, in a number of other states, the co-participant is not held liable unless the injury resulted from grossly negligent, reckless, or wanton and willful actions of the co-participant. More details regarding liability involving golf participants will be discussed later in this chapter.

This concept is exemplified in an Illinois case (*Novak v. Virene*, 1991) in which a skier struck and injured another skier. The court found that 1) Virene owed his fellow skier a duty of reasonable care; 2) Virene breached that duty by failing to control his momentum while skiing; 3) Novak suffered injury in the collision; and 4) the breach of duty was the cause of the injury. The court ruled that there is no reason to exempt downhill skiers from liability if they negligently collide with other skiers. The court went on to say that many activities in life are fraught with danger, and absent a specific assumption of risk, one may obtain damages when injured by another's negligence.

The other standard of care is the **recklessness standard**. This standard maintains that the actor (i.e., sports participant, sports instructor, or sports official) is not liable for injuries resulting from his or her negligent actions, but is liable only if the injury results from actions that go beyond the scope of ordinary negligence—hence, the term recklessness standard. Note that while this concept is commonly referred to as the "recklessness standard" in the literature and case law, it would be more accurate to say that the act must exceed ordinary negligence (i.e., gross negligence, recklessness, willful-wanton actions or intentional acts). Refer to the discussion of *Aggravated Negligence* in Chapter 2.11 *Negligence*.

This standard is illustrated in *Mark v. Moser* (2001), an Indiana triathlon case in which Mr. Moser maneuvered his bicycle carelessly and caused a collision of bicycles. Ms. Mark was seriously injured, but was unable to recover damages because the court ruled sports participants assume the risks and recover only if the other participant either intentionally caused the injury or his conduct was so reckless as to be totally outside the range of ordinary activity associated with the sport.

Participants and Co-Participants

Incidental harm to a participant is a common occurrence in any recreation or sport activity. However not all participants have claims when injured. Under the theory of primary assumption of risk (see Chapter 2.21 *Defenses against Negligence*), a voluntary participant in a sport or recreational activity assumes the risks inherent in the particular activity and, generally, may not recover damages from injuries resulting from those risks. However, when the injury results from risks other than the inherent risks [ordinary negligence or aggravated negligence (recklessness)] by a co-participant, liability may attach—depending upon the standard of care required in that jurisdiction.

Recklessness Standard

Most jurisdictions have adopted the **recklessness standard** which means that a participant is not liable to a co-participant unless he or she was reckless or intended to cause injury. This standard was first established in Illinois in a case in which a young soccer player recklessly kicked another player in the head (*Nabozny v. Barnhill*, 1975) (see the Significant Case). That court stated that a player is liable if his conduct is either deliberate, willful, or demonstrates a reckless disregard for the safety of a co-participant. The theory that sports participants in contact sports (e.g., football, hockey, softball, basketball) are not liable for acts of ordinary negligence against co-participants came to be called the **contact sports exception** and was accepted in many states. In time, a number of states have extended the exception to include some **informal recreational activities** and some **individual sports and non-contact sports**.

Contact Sports Exception

After *Nabozny*, other Illinois courts as well as courts in other jurisdictions (*Oswald v. Township High School District No. 214*, 1980) followed the lead of *Nabozny* believing participants in bodily contact games willingly assume greater risks that do participants in non-physical contact sports, thus justifying a different standard of care for the two types of activities. Illinois courts have subsequently expanded the contact sports exception to include team practices (*Savino v. Robertson*, 1995) and to unorganized, informal, and sometimes spontaneous sports-related activities such as kick-the-can and killerball (*Pfister v. Shusta*, 1995; *Azzano v. Catholic Bishop of Chicago*, 1999).

Other courts have referred to **contact sports and competitive sports** as a category, suggesting that the recklessness standard is appropriate for both. Contact sports (e.g., football, basketball, softball, soccer, and hockey) are classified as such due to the high intensity and the heightened risk. While bodily contact is not the intent in some competitive sports (e.g., bicycle racing, foot races, horseracing), contact is common in the heat of competition. Because of a normal desire to win and the natural competitiveness of many participants, rules violations and injuries will occur in sports (particularly contact sports). For these reasons, the rules of the sport often provide for common rule infractions by penalties such as ejection from the game, yardage penalties, foul shots, free kicks, yellow cards, and penalty boxes.

Since *Nabozny*, courts in other jurisdictions have adopted the recklessness standard. The California Supreme Court (*Knight v. Jewett*, 1992) examined a case in which a number of acquaintances at a Super Bowl party played an informal game of touch football at halftime. A young woman was injured when a man jumped for a ball and came down on her causing injury. The court stated that participants have "a duty to use due care not to increase the risks to a participant over and above those inherent in the sport." The court went on to say that *careless conduct of others is sometimes treated as an inherent risk of the activity* and bars recovery (p. 315–316). In other words, some negligent actions by participants in sports and recreational activities can be considered an inherent risk—resulting in no participant liability. The court ruled in favor of the defendant stating that a participant in an active sport breaches his or her duty to co-participants only if the participant intentionally injures the co-participant or engages in reckless conduct that is outside the range of the ordinary activity of the sport. Further, the ruling in a West Virginia horse-racing case clearly illustrates participant error can be an inherent risk of activity (*Santiago v. Clark*, 1978). Santiago cut his horse in front of Clark's horse causing a fall. The court stated that horseracing is a perilous sport marked by a 100 pound jockey attempting to maneuver a 1000 pound horse through traffic at full speed. The court went on to say that jockey error is commonplace and is an inherent risk in the sport, ruling that there can be no recovery for "jockey error" and "careless riding" in horseracing.

Some other jurisdictions applying the recklessness standard include: courts in Louisiana, Missouri, Idaho, Rhode Island, and Virginia, to softball (*Picou v. Hartford Ins. Co*, 1990; *Ross v. Clouser*, 1982; *Galloway v. Walker*, 2004: *Kiley v. Patterson*, 2000; *Stephenson v. Redd*, 1990); an Illinois court, to a horserace (*Lang v. Silva*, 1999); a California court, to touch football (*Knight*, 1992); a Nebraska court, to a pick-up basketball game (*Dotzler v. Tuttle*, 1990); a Texas court, to a polo match (*Connell v. Payne*, 1991); a Connecticut court, to a coed indoor soccer game (*Jaworski v. Kiernan*, 1997); and, a Michigan court, to a hockey fight (*Overall v. Kadella*, 1984).

In a 1993 Wisconsin Supreme Court case involving soccer, the court ruled that the ordinary negligence standard provides a sufficiently flexible and acceptable standard in personal injury actions resulting from sports activities. (*Lestina v. West Bend Mutual Insurance Co*, 1993) Shortly thereafter, however, the Wisconsin Legislature passed a statute (**W.S. 895.525, 4(m)(a)**) which states that participants in all recreational activities that include physical contact between persons in a sport involving amateur teams may be held liable if the act was committed recklessly or with intent to cause injury. This statute was applied in a cheerleader case in 2008 (*Noffke v Bakke*). It is unclear which standard applies to informal recreational activity.

Informal Recreational Activities. Like Illinois, many jurisdictions have extended the contact sports exception to include not only traditional and team sports, but also **informal recreational activities.** The New Jersey Supreme Court held that recreational players owe the recklessness standard of care to one another in recreational sporting contexts (*Schick v. Ferolito*, 2001). The recklessness standard was also applied in a horseback riding case under Wyoming law (*Cooperman v. David*, 2000). Cooperman was injured and sued alleging wrangler error (ordinary negligence) in failing to tighten the cinch. The court relied on the Wyoming Sport Safety Act **W.S.A 1-1-123(b)** which provides that a loose cinch is an inherent risk of horseback riding because cinching a horse is a matter of judgment and the horse will sometimes be cinched incorrectly (negligently). Thus, liability did not hinge on whether the wrangler was negligent, but on whether there was a duty to eliminate an inherent risk. There might have been liability had the action of the wrangler been grossly negligent, reckless, or willful and wanton. Additionally, the Iowa Supreme Court extended the contact sports exception, applying the reckless standard to paintball (*Leonard v. Behrens*, 1999). Similarly, two Oklahoma courts and one

Texas court applied the recklessness standard in cases involving paintball and BB guns (*Taylor v. Hesser*, 1998; *Reddell v. Johnson*, 1997; *Moore v. Phi Delta Theta Co.*, 1998).

Individual Sports and Non-Contact Sports
Some jurisdictions distinguish among contact sports, individual sports, and non-contact sports. For instance, some jurisdictions have applied the recklessness standard to **individual sports**. Some examples include: a Michigan court, to ice skating (*Ritchie-Gamester v. City of Berkley*, 1999); a New Jersey court, to karate and roller skating (*Rosania v. Carmona*, 1998; *Calhanas v. South Amboy Roller Rink*, 1996). While these activities are individual sports, one can see that contact often occurs. Due to the likelihood of physical contact (including that caused by negligence or recklessness of co-participants), courts seem to feel that imposing liability for ordinary negligence might have a curbing effect on participation.

The Ohio Supreme Court was one of the first to apply the recklessness standard to a **non-contact sport**—golf (*Thompson v. McNeill*, 1990). Since then other states, including California (*Dilger v. Moyles*, 1997), Texas (*Allen v. Donath*, 1994); Indiana (*Gyuriak v. Millice*, 2002); and Massachusetts (*Mangone v. Pickering*, 1997) have also applied the recklessness standard to golf. The Kentucky Supreme Court ruled that the recklessness standard is appropriate for tennis (*Hoke v. Cullinan*, 1995), as did California courts for sailing and figure skating (*Stimson v. Carlson*, 1992; *Staten v. Superior Court*, 1996).

Although New Mexico courts have applied the recklessness standard to organized team sports and to pick-up football games (*Kabella v. Bouschelle*, 1983), they declined to extend the recklessness standard to a case involving teenager roughhousing and horseplay. The New Mexico court stated that horseplay participants owe co-participants a duty of ordinary care (*Yount v. Johnson*, 1996).

Rationale
Several reasons have been given in support of the recklessness standard of care. Some of them include the belief that: (1) the negligence standard would have a chilling effect on participation; (2) the courts may not have the ability to discern what constitutes reasonable conduct in informal sports activity; (3) the negligence standard would spur litigation; and (4) the recklessness standard recognizes a commonsense distinction between excessive conduct and the normal rough and tumble activity inherent in sport. Regardless of the seemingly reasonable arguments for the recklessness standard, the fact is that it leaves the injured participant unable to recover for the negligent or careless actions of a co-participant.

Negligence Standard for Participants
While the recklessness standard has been adopted in most states, the negligence standard has been supported to some extent in a number of jurisdictions. Four states seem to apply the standard to all participants of sports and recreation activities, while a number of jurisdictions apply the negligence standard to one or more sports.

Negligence Standard for all Activities
The Nevada Supreme Court, in a case in which the defendant's horse kicked and injured the plaintiff, established the negligence standard for all recreational injury cases stating:

> The negligence standard is sufficiently flexible to accommodate liability issues underlying all recreational injury cases. There is no reduction in the defendant's standard of care (e.g., reckless or intentional), nor is there any fictitious undertaking that the defendant does not owe a duty to the plaintiff (*Auckenthaler v. Grundmeyer*, 1994, p. 16).

The court stated that "Within the factual climate of recreational activities or even sporting events, the question posed is whether the defendant participated in a reasonable manner and within the rules of the game or in accordance with the ordinary scope of the activity." (p. 16)

A Tennessee appellate court (*Becksfort v. Jackson*, 1996) examined the issue of the required standard of care that a participant owed a co-participant in a tennis case. The court disagreed with the reasoning in *Knight* that use of the negligence standard would stifle competition and result in more lawsuits. The court thought that the public would recognize that the reasonableness of one's conduct will be measured differently on the playing field than in non-sport situations. The court further stated that a different standard of care for each sport is not needed because Tennessee courts will recognize that the reasonable conduct standard of care should be determined in context with the sport.

An Arizona appellate court (*Estes v. Tripson*, 1997) declined to vary from the general negligence standard. The case involved a softball baserunner stepping on the leg of a catcher. The court held that the baserunner did not breach a duty to the catcher and was not negligent.

Likewise, the Supreme Court of New Hampshire (*Allen v. Dover*, 2002) refused to adopt the recklessness standard in a coed slow-pitch softball case. The court applied the negligence standard stating "We believe that the negligence standard, properly understood and applied, is suitable for recreational athletic activities because" participant conduct is measured against the conduct of a reasonable participant, under similar circumstances. (p. 21)

Negligence Standard for Non-competitive, Non-contact Recreational Activities

Courts in some jurisdictions have held that the recklessness standard should not apply to some **non-competitive, non-contact recreational activities** (e.g., skiing, badminton, fishing, bowling), reasoning that the assumed risks in those activities are not created by participant negligence, but by the nature of the activity. In this type of activity, the possibility of a lawsuit for participant negligence would not place a damper on participation (*Cruz v. Gloss*, 2002).

The following is a sample of states that have adopted the negligence standard for a selected activity or activities. In a Colorado case, the U.S. Court of Appeals applied the negligence standard when the activity was skiing (*LaVine v. Clear Creek Skiing Corp*, 1977). In addition, the Colorado Ski Safety Act 33-44-109(2) provides that the skier has a duty to avoid collisions and collisions with other skiers is not an inherent or assumed risk. Negligence was also the standard in skiing cases in New York, Illinois, and Utah (*Duncan v. Kelly*, 1998; *Novak v. Virene*, 1991; *Ricci v. Schoultz*, 1998). Likewise, courts in Illinois, Massachusetts, and New York applied the negligence standard in golf cases (*Zurla v. Hydel*, 1997; *Orth v. Novelli*, 1997; *Jackson v. Livingston Country Club, Inc.*, 1977). Also regarding golf, the Virginia Supreme Court held that "the basic rule of law applicable to golfers is that a player upon a golf course must exercise reasonable care in playing the game to prevent injury to others" (*Thurston Metals & Supply Co. v. Taylor*, 1986, p. 3).

A Missouri court (*Gamble v. Bost*, 1995) applied the negligence standard in a bowling case, stating that a negligence standard would impose no burden on bowling establishments. In a Michigan case (*Williams v. Wood*, 1932), the negligence standard was applied to fishing. In the *Davis v. LeCuyer* case (2006), the Indiana court ruled that the recklessness standard might only apply to organized sports. It suggested that jet skiing was recreation and not a sport.

Sports Instructors and Sports Officials

Injuries to sports participants sometimes result from actions of sports instructors or actions by the sports officials handling the contest. Sports instructors (e.g., coaches, teachers, personal trainers, aerobics instructors, tennis pros, trip leader) and sports officials (e.g., referees, umpires) generally owe a duty of reasonable care to those whom they teach, coach, or officiate. Sports instructors and officials have a number of duties or obligations to the participant (e.g., supervision, provide safety equipment, to provide a relatively safe environment) (see Chapter 2.34 *Supervision* and Chapter 2.31 *Premises Liability*). Both the sports instructor and the sports official can be legally liable if he or she breaches a duty and that breach results in an injury. For example, a gymnastics coach can be unfocused and fail to adequately spot an athlete; or a fist fight resulting in injury may occur when an instructor leaves the class unsupervised. Either might be found liable in the event of a lawsuit.

In *Everett v. Warren*, (1978), the coach supplied a player with a defective helmet. In 1997, a school and its coaches were sued when a pole vaulter was injured in an unsafe pit while using a pole that was too light for his weight (*Moose v. Massachusetts Institute of Technology*). In *Lautieri v. Bae* (2003), triathlon organizers were sued alleging negligent course layout, signage, and supervision. In each of these cases, the negligence standard was applied and the coaches and schools were held liable. A New York appellate court case (*Parisi v. Harpursville Central School District*, 1990) illustrates coach liability for failure to provide reasonable care. The coach, with two catcher's masks available, failed to suggest or require a second baseman to wear a mask when she volunteered to catch a pitcher considered to be an expert in high-velocity pitching. A handbook issued by the State Public High School Athletic Association governing interscholastic modified sports programs required that any player warming up a pitcher, on or off the fields, wear protective equipment. Plaintiff sued alleging negligence by the coach in failing to use reasonable care in supervision and in failing to provide protective equipment. The court upheld the lower court ruling denying summary judgment and remanded the case for trial to determine negligence.

The law is quite clear and consistent among states regarding sports instructor and sports official liability when he or she has breached a duty or obligation. However, the law regarding the liability of sports instructors and sports officials varies from state to state when the situation involves errors in judgment by the instructor or official. At issue is whether the instructor or official should be held to the negligence standard or to the recklessness standard.

Recklessness Standard

In the course of instructing, leading a group, coaching, or officiating, sports instructors (and coaches) and sports officials sometimes make errors in judgment. They can misjudge the environmental conditions, the fitness of the participant, or the capability of a participant and urge or "push" a participant to exert greater effort to improve performance or continue the activity, resulting in injury to the participant. In some jurisdictions, these actions might be construed as ordinary negligence on the part of the instructor or coach and result in a negligence action. In other jurisdictions, these same acts are considered inherent risks of the activity and the instructor or coach is not liable. In the latter jurisdictions, the recklessness standard is being extended to liability suits against sports instructors and officials.

California courts were the ground-breakers in defining actions involving errors in judgment by sports instructors and officials as an inherent risk. The California Supreme Court in *Knight* (1992) said that one typically has a duty to use due care to avoid injury to others, but that in sport, actions that would usually be deemed as dangerous are often an integral part of the sport itself. Hence, *Knight* says it is important to consider the nature of the sport when defining the duty of care owed. *Knight* states that defendants generally have no duty to eliminate risks inherent in the sport, but *do have a duty to not increase the risks above those inherent in the sport.* Since instructor or official misjudgment of conditions or capacity of the participant is considered an inherent risk of some activities—and the instructor or coach has no duty to eliminate inherent risks—no liability is incurred by the instructor or coach in those activities.

In *Bushnell v. Japanese-American Religious and Cultural Center* (1996), the court stated that sport instruction often involves challenging or "pushing" the athlete to attempt new and more difficult tasks. It went on to say *that the athlete's failure to meet the challenge is an inherent risk in learning a sport and to impose a duty to mitigate the inherent risks could have a chilling effect on teaching a sport.* The court held that liability should not be imposed on the coach or instructor when hindsight shows the task was beyond the ability of the athlete, absent recklessness or other risk-increasing conduct by the coach or instructor.

Subsequently, in a California case involving ski instruction (*Kane v. National Ski Patrol System, Inc.*, 2001), a California appellate court held that *instructor errors, whether judging skill level or difficulty of conditions, are within the range of ordinary activity involved in a sport.* To reach egregiousness sufficient for liability, one must show the instructor conduct took the skier beyond the risks inherent in attempting to improve the skills of a skier already considered to be an expert.

In *Kahn v. East Side Union High School Dist.* (2003), the California Supreme court expanded its prior ruling in *Knight* stating that

> . . . *the risks associated with learning a sport may themselves be inherent risks of the sport,* and that an instructor or coach generally does not increase the risk of harm inherent in learning the sport simply by urging the student to strive to excel or to reach a new level of competence. (p.115)[Emphasis added]

This thinking places an important limitation on the duty of a sports instructor, saying, in effect, that "... *a sports instructor may be found to have breached a duty of care to a student or athlete only if the instructor intentionally injures the student or engages in conduct that is reckless in the sense that it is 'totally outside the range of the ordinary activity' involved in teaching or coaching the sport.*" (p.107) [emphasis added] A number of California decisions illustrate the impact of this approach on the liability of sports instructors and coaches. A tae kwon do drill necessarily involved risk of injury from being kicked (*Rodrigo v. Koryo Martial Arts*, 2002); a coach continued baseball practice at twilight and failed to remove a wild pitcher (*Balthazor v. Little League Baseball, Inc.*, 1988); and a coach/instructor urged aggressive play in football practice (*Fortier v. Los Rios Community College Dist.*, 1996). In each case the court ruled for the instructor or coach, holding that he did not recklessly increase the risk inherent in the sport.

California courts are not alone in this approach to liability of instructors and coaches. Other states have elected to hold to the recklessness standard when participant injury is caused by sports instructor negligence. In Michigan, a football coach was angry at an injured player during practice and struck him with a blocking shield (*Barry v. Ishpeming-Nice Community Schools*, 2005). The appellate court remanded the case for determination of gross negligence (recklessness standard). The Maryland Court of Special Appeals (*Kelly v. McCarrick*, 2004) ruled that the same principles applicable to negligent play should also apply to negligent coaching claims. The court supported the recklessness standard in saying "... it would not be appropriate to recognize a duty of care when to do so would require that an integral part of the sport be abandoned, or would discourage vigorous participation in sporting events" (p. 32).

The *Geiersbach v. Frieje* (2004) court, in an Indiana case involving a baseball injury, cited language used in *Mark v. Moser* (2001) regarding participant to co-participant injuries which stated:

> ... voluntary participants in sports activities assume the inherent and foreseeable dangers of the activity and cannot recover for injury unless it can be established that the other participant either intentionally caused injury or engaged in conduct so reckless as to be totally outside the range of ordinary activity involved in the sport.

The *Geiersbach* court then expanded the statement to define *"participant" to include all participants in the sporting event or practice, including players, coaches, and players who are on the bench* [emphasis added]. The court went on to say that the participant should not be able to recover from the player, team, or stadium without proving recklessness or intent. So "participant" would include coaches, and probably officials as well. In determining the law in your state, it would be important to first determine how the courts define "participant" in a sport activity. It may well be that many more states classify sports instructors and sports officials as participants.

In Ohio (*Kline v. OID Assocs., Inc.*, 1992), a soccer referee was sued following an injury caused by one player kicking another. The plaintiff alleged negligent and reckless supervision. The appellate court used the recklessness standard in ruling for the defendant citing Ohio Supreme Court which stated:

> Traditional tort concepts place the emphasis on the conduct or actions of the tort-feasor. Thus, we ... require that before a party may proceed with a cause of action involving injury resulting from a recreational or sports activity, reckless or intentional conduct must exist. (*Marchetti v. Kalish*, 1990, p. 99–100)

Immunity Statutes. Another factor that affects the required standard of care is state immunity statutes. For instance, almost every state legislature has enacted legislation to help protect selected recreation and sport providers from liability for injuries resulting from the inherent risks and/or the ordinary negligence of the provider and/or its employees. Many of these raise the standard of care to recklessness. Statutes relating to equestrian activities, skating, and skiing are the most common, but some states have statutes relating to activities such as motor sports, fishing, outfitters, sport shooting, and snowmobiling (See Chapter 2.22 *Immunity*).

In addition, more than 20 state legislatures have enacted volunteer immunity statutes specifically for coaches and sports officials in amateur sports (See Chapter 2.22 *Immunity*). While these statutes vary somewhat, they generally provide protection from liability for ordinary negligence—thus, in effect, adopting the recklessness standard. States with these statutes include: Arkansas, Colorado, Delaware, Georgia, Hawaii, Indiana, Illinois, Kansas, Louisiana, Maryland, Massachusetts, Minnesota, Mississippi, Nevada, New Hampshire, New Jersey, New Mexico, North Dakota, Oklahoma, Pennsylvania, Rhode Island, Tennessee, and Texas.

It is important to note that these statutes vary in wording, effectiveness, and in which parties are protected, but most do provide some protection for the coach and official in amateur sport. For instance, in a Rhode Island case involving a cheerleading injury (*Schultz v. Foster-Glocester Regional School District*, 2000), the court applied the volunteer immunity statute, **R.I.G.L 9-1-48,** which stated "...no person who renders services as a manager, coach, instructor . . . shall be liable . . . unless the acts or omissions were committed in willful, wanton, or reckless disregard for the safety of the participants in the interscholastic or intramural sports program." The coach was deemed to be immune from liability.

Negligence Standard

While California and a number of other jurisdictions hold sports instructors and sports officials to the recklessness standard in certain circumstances, other states continue to apply the negligence standard—holding instructors and officials liable for injuries to sports participants resulting from any instructor or official negligence.

In *Hearon v. May* (1995), the Nebraska Supreme Court examined an injury that occurred when a participant was injured while wrestling with a referee who was coaching the plaintiff in a wrestling move. The court affirmed the recklessness standard for participant to co-participant injuries, but held that

> . . . instructors, teachers, and coaches are liable for injuries sustained by an instructee if such injuries are received by the instructee while the instructor, teacher, or coach engages in physical contact with the instructee and the instructee's injuries are the proximate result of the ordinary negligence of the instructor, teacher, or coach. p. 15

The court held ordinary negligence to be the proper cause of action when negligent supervision or negligent instruction is involved in a sporting activity. In a subsequent case involving actions taken following an injury, the Nebraska Supreme Court stated that the standard of care required of coaches is that of the reasonably prudent person holding a Nebraska teaching certificate with a coaching endorsement (*Cerny v. Cedar Bluffs Junior/Senior Public School*, 2001).

The New Hampshire Supreme Court failed to grant coaches and referees discretionary immunity on decisions made during a contest (*Hacking v. Town of Belmont*, 1999). The court stated that forcing an individual to bear the loss caused by the negligence of a municipal employee is against the basic principles of equality and ordinary justice. Both coaches and referees were held to the negligence standard.

New York's highest court, The Court of Appeals, ruled that the board of education and its employees (which would include coaches and referees) must exercise ordinary reasonable care to protect student athletes in extracurricular activities "from unassumed, concealed, or unreasonably increased risks" (*Benitez v. New York City Board of Education*, 1989).

Carabba v. Anacortes School District, No. 103 (1967), in Washington State, involved a case in which a serious injury occurred while the wrestling referee was momentarily distracted. The appellate court adhered to the negligence standard.

Those advocating the negligence standard hold that the sports instructor or official has a duty to participants to act reasonably; and if a failure to do so results in injury, he/she should be held liable. In the case of a charge of negligence against the instructor or official, the law will determine if the instructor or official acted as a reasonable and prudent person would have acted in similar circumstances.

SIGNIFICANT CASE

This is the seminal case relating to participant-co-participant liability. A child playing soccer was kicked in the head in a reckless or willful act and the trial court granted summary judgment in favor of the defendant. The appellate court overturned that decision establishing the precedent that a participant is liable for injury in a tort action if his conduct is such that it is either deliberate, willful or with a reckless disregard for the safety of the other player.

NABOZNY V. BARNHILL

Appellate Court of Illinois, First District, Fourth Division
334 N.E.2d 258; 1975 Ill. App. LEXIS 2772
July 23, 1975, Filed

Opinion

Plaintiff, Julian Claudio Nabozny, a minor, by Edward J. Nabozny, his father, commenced this action to recover damages for personal injuries allegedly caused by the negligence of defendant, David Barnhill. Trial was before a jury. At the close of plaintiff's case on motion of defendant, the trial court directed a verdict in favor of the defendant. Plaintiff appeals from the order granting the motion.

Plaintiff contends on appeal that the trial judge erred in granting defendant's motion for a directed verdict and that plaintiff's actions as a participant do not prohibit the establishment of a prima facie case of negligence. Defendant argues in support of the trial court's ruling that defendant was free from negligence as a matter of law (lacking a duty to plaintiff) and that plaintiff was contributorily negligent as a matter of law.

In light of Pedrick v. Peoria & Eastern R.R. Co. (1967), 37 Ill.2d 494, 229 N.E.2d 504, our statement of facts reflects an examination of all of the evidence viewed in its aspect most favorable to plaintiff.

A soccer match began between two amateur teams at Duke Child's Field in Winnetka, Illinois. Plaintiff was playing the position of goalkeeper for the Hansa team. Defendant was playing the position of forward for the Winnetka team. Members of both teams were of high-school age. Approximately 20 minutes after play had begun, a Winnetka player kicked the ball over the midfield line. Two players, Jim Gallos (for Hansa) and the defendant (for Winnetka) chased the free ball. Gallos reached the ball first. Since he was closely pursued by the defendant, Gallos passed the ball to the plaintiff, the Hansa goalkeeper. Gallos then turned away and prepared to receive a pass from the plaintiff. The plaintiff, in the meantime, went down on his left knee, received the pass, and pulled the ball to his chest. The defendant did not turn away when Gallos did, but continued to run in the direction of the plaintiff and kicked the left side of plaintiff's head causing plaintiff severe injuries.

All of the occurrence witnesses agreed that the defendant had time to avoid contact with plaintiff and that the plaintiff remained at all times within the "penalty area," a rectangular area between the 18th yard line and the goal. Four witnesses testified that they saw plaintiff in a crouched position on his left knee inside the penalty zone. Plaintiff testified that he actually had possession of the ball when he was struck by defendant. One witness, Marie Shekem, stated that plaintiff had the ball when he was kicked. All other occurrence witnesses stated that they thought plaintiff was in possession of the ball.

Plaintiff called three expert witnesses. Julius Roth, coach of the Hansa team, testified that the game in question was being played under "F.I.F.A." rules. The three experts agreed that those rules prohibited all players from making contact with the goalkeeper when he is in possession of the ball in the penalty area. Possession is defined in the Chicago area as referring to the goalkeeper having his hands on the ball. Under "F.I.F.A." rules, any contact with a goalkeeper in possession in the penalty area is an infraction of the rules, even if such contact is unintentional. The goalkeeper is the only member of a team who is allowed to touch a ball in play so long as he remains in the penalty area. The only legal contact permitted in soccer is shoulder to shoulder contact between players going for a ball within playing distance. The three experts agreed that the contact in question in this case should not have occurred. Additionally, goalkeeper head injuries are extremely rare in soccer. As a result of being struck, plaintiff suffered permanent damage to his skull and brain.

The initial question presented by this appeal is whether, under the facts in evidence, such a relationship existed between the parties that the court will impose a legal duty upon one for the benefit of the other. "[M]re simply, whether the interest of the plaintiff which has suffered invasion was entitled to legal protection at the hands of the defendant." Prosser, Law of Torts § 37, at 206 (4th ed. 1971).

There is a dearth of case law involving organized athletic competition wherein one of the participants is charged with negligence. There are no such Illinois cases. A number of other jurisdictions prohibit recovery generally for reasons of public policy. (Eg., Gaspard v. Grain Dealers Mutual Insurance Co. (La. App. 1961), 131 So. 2d 831.) We can find no American cases dealing with the game of soccer.

This court believes that the law should not place unreasonable burdens on the free and vigorous participation in sports by our youth. However, we also believe that organized, athletic competition does not exist in a vacuum. Rather, some of the restraints of civilization must accompany every athlete on to the playing field. One of the educational benefits of organized athletic competition to our youth is the development of discipline and self-control.

Individual sports are advanced and competition enhanced by a comprehensive set of rules. Some rules secure the better playing of the game as a test of skill. Other rules are primarily designed to protect participants from serious injury. Restatement (Second) of Torts § 50, comment b (4th ed. 1971).

For these reasons, this court believes that when athletes are engaged in an athletic competition; all teams involved are trained and coached by knowledgeable personnel; a recognized set of rules governs the conduct of the competition; and a safety rule is contained therein which is primarily designed to protect players from serious injury, a player is then charged with a legal duty to every other player on the field to refrain from conduct proscribed by a safety rule. A reckless disregard for the safety of other players cannot be excused. To engage in such conduct is to create an intolerable and unreasonable risk of serious injury to other participants. We have carefully drawn the rule announced herein in order to control a new field of personal injury litigation. Under the facts presented in the case at bar, we find such a duty clearly arose. Plaintiff was entitled to legal protection at the hands of the defendant. The defendant contends he is immune from tort action for any injury to another player

that happens during the course of a game, to which theory we do not subscribe.

It is our opinion that a player is liable for injury in a tort action if his conduct is such that it is either deliberate, wilful or with a reckless disregard for the safety of the other player so as to cause injury to that player, the same being a question of fact to be decided by a jury.

Defendant also asserts that plaintiff was contributorily negligent as a matter of law, and, therefore, the trial court's direction of a verdict in defendant's favor was correct. We do not agree. The evidence presented tended to show that plaintiff was in the exercise of ordinary care for his own safety. While playing his position, he remained in the penalty area and took possession of the ball in a proper manner. Plaintiff had no reason to know of the danger created by defendant. Without this knowledge, [it cannot be said that plaintiff unreasonably exposed himself to such danger or failed to discover or appreciate the risk. The facts in evidence revealed that the play in question was of a kind commonly executed in this sport. Frank Longo, one of plaintiff's expert witnesses, testified that once the goalkeeper gets possession of the ball in the penalty area, "the instinct should be there [in an opposing player pursuing the ball] through training and knowledge of the rules to avoid contact [with the goalkeeper]." All of plaintiff's expert witnesses agreed that a player charging an opposition goaltender, under circumstances similar to those which existed during the play in question, should be able to avoid all contact. Furthermore, it is a violation of the rules for a player simply to kick at the ball when a goalkeeper has possession in the penalty area even if no contact is made with the goalkeeper.

Using the standard set out in Pedrick v. Peoria & Eastern R.R. Co., 37 Ill.2d 494, 229 N.E.2d 504, for determining both freedom from negligence and contributory negligence as matters of law, we conclude that the trial court erred in directing a verdict in favor of defendant. It is a fact question for the jury.

This cause, therefore, is reversed and remanded to the Circuit Court of Cook County for a new trial consistent with the views expressed in this opinion.

Reversed and remanded.

CASES ON THE SUPPLEMENTAL WEB SITE

Karas v. Strevell, 2008 Ill.LEXIS 284. The Illinois Supreme Court applied the contact sports exception in a recent ice hockey contest.

Kahn v. East Side Union High School District, 2003 Cal. LEXIS 6373. Look particularly at the duty of the sports instructor and under what circumstance the instructor is liable for injuries to students.

Thompson v. McNeill, 1990 Ohio LEXIS 341. In this case, the Ohio Supreme Court expresses reasoning to justify the application of the recklessness standard to a non-contact sport.

Auckenthaler v. Grundmeyer, 1994 Nev. LEXIS 87. The Nevada Supreme Court adopted the negligence standard in this ruling stating that the negligence standard is sufficiently flexible to accommodate liability issues underlying all recreational injury cases.

Kline v. OID Associates, Inc., 1992 Ohio App. LEXIS 2371. The Ohio court ruled that participant liability is possible only if there is reckless or intentional misconduct; and applied this rule to non-participants involved in the game (coaches, officials).

QUESTIONS YOU SHOULD BE ABLE TO ANSWER

1. What is meant by the term "negligence standard?"

2. What is meant by the term "recklessness standard?"

3. What is meant by the term "contact sports exception?"

4. What is the rationale for having a different standard for contact sports and non-contact sports?

5. Under what circumstances might a coach not be liable for his or her ordinary negligence?

REFERENCES

Cases

Allen v. Donath, 1994 Tex. App. LEXIS 816.
Allen v. Dover, 2002 N.H. LEXIS 145.
Auckenthaler v. Grundmeyer, 1994 Nev. LEXIS 87.
Azzano v. Catholic Bishop of Chicago, 1999 Ill. App. LEXIS 195.
Balthazor v. Little League Baseball, Inc., 1998 Cal. App. LEXIS 194.
Barry v. Ishpeming-Nice Community Schools, 2005 Mich. App. LEXIS 2818.
Becksfort v. Jackson, 1996 Tenn. App. LEXIS 257.
Benitez v. New York City Board of Education, 1989 N.Y. LEXIS 662.
Bushnell v. Japanese-American Religious and Cultural Center, 1996 Cal. App. LEXIS 216.
Calhanas v. South Amboy Roller Rink, 1996 N.J. Super. LEXIS 306.
Carabba v. Anacortes School District, 1967 Wash. LEXIS 880.
Cerney v. Cedar Bluffs Junior/Senior Public School, 2004 Neb. LEXIS 80.
Connell v. Payne, 1991 Tex. App. LEXIS 2347.
Cruz v. Gloss, 2002 Pa. Dist. & Cnty. Dec. LEXIS 140.
Davis v. LeCuyer, 2006 Ind. App. LEXIS 1203.
Dilger v. Moyles, 1997 Cal. App. LEXIS 380.
Dotzler v. Tuttle, 1990 Neb. LEXIS 1.
Duncan v. Kelly, 1998 N.Y. App. Div. LEXIS 4515.
Estes v. Tripson, 1997 Ariz. App. LEXIS 24.
Everett v. Warren, 1978 Mass. LEXIS 1123.
Fortier v. Los Rios Community College Dist., 1996 Cal. App. LEXIS 441.
Galloway v. Walker, 2004 Ida. App. LEXIS 89.
Gamble v. Bost, 1995 Mo. App. LEXIS 789.
Geiersbach v. Frieje, 2004 Ind. App. LEXIS 757.
Gyuriak v. Millice, 2002 Ind. App. LEXIS 1586.
Hacking v. Town of Belmont, 1999 N.H. LEXIS 42.
Hearon v. May, 1995 Neb. LEXIS 229.
Hoke v. Cullinan, 1995 Ky. LEXIS 140.
Jackson v. Livingston Country Club, Inc., 1977 N.Y. App. Div. LEXIS 10401.
Jaworski v. Kiernan, 1997 Conn. LEXIS 182.
Kabella v. Bouschelle, 1983 N.M. App. LEXIS 791.
Kahn v. East Side Union High School Dist., 2003 Cal. LEXIS 6373.
Kane v. National Ski Patrol System, 2001 Cal. App. LEXIS 254.
Kelly v. McCarrick, 2004 Md. App. LEXIS 13.
Kiley v. Patterson, 2000 R.I. LEXIS 246.
Kline v. OID Assocs., Inc., 1992 Ohio App. LEXIS 2371.
Knight v. Jewett, 1992 Cal. LEXIS 3969.

Lang v. Silva, 1999 Ill. App. LEXIS 543.

Lautieri v. Bae, 2003 Mass. Super. LEXIS 290.

Leonard v. Behrens, 1999 Iowa Sup. LEXIS 255.

Lestina v. West Bend Mutual Insurance Co., 1993 Wisc. LEXIS 532.

LaVine v. Clear Creek Skiing Corp., 1977 U.S. App. LEXIS 12808.

Mangone v. Pickering, 1997 Mass. Super. LEXIS 458.

Marchetti v. Kalish, 1990 Ohio LEXIS 342.

Mark v. Moser, 2001 Ind. App. LEXIS 671.

Moore v. Phi DeltaTheta Co., 1998 Tex. App. LEXIS 2676.

Moose v. Massachusetts Institute of Technology, 1997 Mass. App. LEXIS 189.

Nabozny v. Barnhill, 1975 Ill. App. LEXIS 2772.

Noffke v. Bakke, 2009 Wisc. LEXIS 5.

Novak v. Virene, 1991 Ill. App. LEXIS 2194.

Orth v. Novelli, 1997 Mass. Super. LEXIS 119.

Oswald v. Township, 1980 Ill. App. LEXIS 2962.

Overall v. Kadella, 1984 Mich. App. LEXIS 3019.

Parisi v. Harpursville Central School District, 1990 N.Y. App. Div. LEXIS 3756.

Pfister v. Shusta, 1995 Ill. LEXIS 201.

Picou v. Hartford Ins. Co., 1990 La. App. LEXIS 663.

Reddell v. Johnson, 1997 Okla. LEXIS 82.

Ritchie-Gamester v. City of Berkley, 1999 Mich. LEXIS 2060

Rodrigo v. Koryo Martial Arts, 2002 Cal. App. LEXIS 4462.

Rosania v. Carmona, 1998 N.J. Super. LEXIS 93.

Ross v. Clouser, 1982 Mo. LEXIS 403.

Santiago v. Clark, 1978 U.S. Dist. LEXIS 20322.

Savino v. Robertson, 1995 Ill. App. LEXIS 480.

Stephenson v. Redd, 1990 Va. Cir. LEXIS 466.

Staten v. Superior Court, 1996 Cal. App. LEXIS 498.

Taylor v. Hesser, 1998 Okla. Civ. App. LEXIS 120.

Thompson v. McNeill, 1990 Ohio LEXIS 341.

Thurston Metals & Supply Co. v. Taylor, 1986 Va. LEXIS 149.

Williams v. Woods, 1932 Mich. LEXIS 1121.

Yount v. Johnson, 1996 N.M. App. LEXIS 23.

Zurla v. Hydel, 1997 Ill. App. LEXIS 387.

DEFENSES

2.20

2.21 DEFENSES AGAINST NEGLIGENCE

Doyice J. Cotten | Sport Risk Consulting

In today's litigious society, lawsuits against recreation and sport businesses are common. The fact that a recreation or sport business is sued, however, does not necessarily mean that loss of the suit is inevitable. There are many effective defenses that may be used by the defendant. The most common defenses are described in this and the three subsequent chapters (see Chapter 2.22 *Immunity*, Chapter 2.23 *Waivers and Releases*, and Chapter 2.24 *Agreements Related to the Inherent Risks*)

But one should not wait until one is sued to consider defenses! One must plan ahead. Through effective risk management, potential and existing risks can be identified. Once identified, positioning oneself to ameliorate or transfer liability by allocation of risk can prepare one to defend against the risks (see Chapter 4.11 *Risk Management Process*). Knowing the type of risks one anticipates or which have previously resulted in injury is critical in selecting an appropriate defense.

There are essentially two types of risk—inherent risks and negligence risks. The **inherent risks** are those that are a normal, integral part of the activity—risks that cannot normally be eliminated without changing the nature of the activity itself. Such injuries as an athlete pulling a hamstring while running wind sprints, a hiker spraining an ankle while hiking over rough terrain, or a football player breaking his collarbone while throwing a block exemplify the inherent risks of the activity. On the other hand, some injuries result from the **negligence** of the service provider or its employees. The following are some examples where the injury might have been due to negligence: a baseball player injuring a knee when he steps in one of many outfield holes while running for a fly ball; a tumbler injured doing a handspring when no spotter is provided; or a player suffering additional injury when the coach fails to secure proper medical treatment for an injury (see Chapter 2.11 *Elements of Negligence*).

FUNDAMENTAL CONCEPTS

The allocation of risk to other parties may be accomplished by recreation and sport businesses through the utilization of several defenses. All of these defenses come from one of three sources—common law, contract law, and statutory law. **Common law** is that body of principles and rules of action that derive their authority solely from the prior judgments and decrees of the courts. It is the body of law that develops and derives through judicial decisions—as distinguished from legislative enactments. **Contract law** is that body of law that governs the rules regarding binding agreements between parties. Several means by which risk can be allocated derive from this body of law. **Statutory law** is that body of law that is created by acts of a legislative body. Such law requiring or prohibiting specific acts or actions may apply to individuals, public recreation and sport entities, or private recreation and sport entities—depending upon the intent and wording of the legislation. *The reader is cautioned that there is significant disparity among states and that the defenses discussed in this chapter do not apply in all states.*

The reader is directed to Table 2.21.1, which outlines the allocation of risk in terms of (1) to whom the risk is allocated, (2) who is eligible for the defense, (3) which risks are allocated, (4) the effect upon the standard of care required, and (5) the impact on the liability of the service provider. To use the table effectively, one must consider the facts of any given situation. By way of illustration, suppose a skateboarder is injured in a skateboard competition. Applying this situation to the table, one of the defenses available to the business conducting the competition would be primary assumption of risk. If the player consented to the activity, participated voluntarily, and understood the risks of the activity, the risk would be allocated to the player rather than the recreation or sport business. From the table, one can see that this defense could protect the business from liability for the inherent risks of the activity, but does not affect the required standard of care; the business would still be liable for its own ordinary negligence. If the business was negligent, but could show that fault-related conduct by the skateboarder contributed to the injury, then the defense of secondary assumption of risk would apply. Additionally, under comparative-fault statutes, this secondary assumption of risk would ameliorate the financial liability by barring or reducing any monetary award to the skateboarder.

However, suppose management had required that the skateboarder sign a waiver of liability prior to the event, releasing the recreation or sport business from liability for its own negligence. From Table 2.21.1, one can see that if the participant is of majority age, the waiver allocates the risk of ordinary negligence from the business to the participant skateboarder.

Defenses Based on Common Law

Elements of Ordinary Negligence Not Proven

Perhaps the best defense against a claim of negligence is that one or more of the elements required for negligence is not present. As discussed in Chapter 2.11 *Negligence*, to be liable, one must have a legal duty to the plaintiff, must breach that duty, and the breach of duty must be the proximate cause of an injury to the plaintiff. If one of these elements is missing (duty, breach, proximate cause, or injury), then no other defense is necessary—no negligence, no liability.

Primary Assumption of Risk[1]

Primary assumption of risk is a legal theory by which a plaintiff may not recover for an injury received when the plaintiff voluntarily exposes himself or herself to a known and appreciated danger. In other words, when one knows the inherent dangers involved and voluntarily participates, one assumes those risks inherent in the activity (but not risks of negligence) and the service provider is not liable for injuries resulting from those inherent risks. In *Daigle v. West Mountain* (2001), the court held that while participants assume those risks that are known, apparent, or reasonably foreseeable, they do not assume risks that are unique and result in dangerous conditions over and above the usual dangers inherent in the activity.

Primary assumption of risk is presumed when an individual has voluntarily participated in an activity that involves inherent or well-known risks. One is held to have consented, by virtue of one's voluntary participation, to those injury-causing events that are known and reasonably foreseeable (*Truett v. Fell*). Primary assumption of risk acts as a defense in that it relieves the defendant of a duty that might otherwise be owed to the plaintiff. The organizer of an event has a duty to produce a reasonably safe event and is required to use ordinary care not to increase the risk beyond what is inherent in the activity.[2] For example, if a man attends a YMCA, knows and appreciates the risks involved in weight lifting, chooses to lift weights, and injures his back, the YMCA has no duty and bears no responsibility, absent negligence on its part, because of primary assumption of risk (or more specifically, implied assumption of risk [see below]).

---

[1]The author must re-emphasize to the recreation or sport manager that these defenses differ significantly from state to state. This is particularly important when examining primary assumption of risk because its availability and effectiveness have changed greatly over the years. Most states have abolished contributory negligence and gone to a form of comparative fault (discussed later in the chapter). With the adoption of comparative fault, many states have eliminated primary assumption of risk as a complete defense and treat it as a factor that may reduce any recovery due the plaintiff.

[2]However, a California court (*Saffro v. Elite Racing, Inc.*, 2002) held that the organizer of a marathon has a duty to "take reasonable steps to minimize the risks without altering the nature of the sport, including the provision of sufficient water and electrolyte replacement drinks" at 1.

TABLE 2.21.1   ALLOCATION OF RISK[1][2]

Authority and Defenses	To Whom Risk is Allocated	Eligibility for Defense	Which Risks Are Allocated	Effect on Standard of Care Owed	Impact on Liability of Provider
COMMON LAW					
Elements of Ordinary Negligence Not Proven	participant	any service provider	injuries not due to provider negligence	none	provider not liable
Primary Assumption of Risk	participant	consent/voluntary; inherent risks; know, understand, & appreciate risks	inherent risks	none	provider not liable for inherent risks
Secondary Assumption of Risk	participant	fault-related conduct; understands dangers; usually age 6 or older	participant fault that enhances chance of injury	none	bars or reduces award
Sovereign & Gov't. Immunity (See Statutory Codification)	participant	public entity only	all risks related to governmental function	reduces duty to wilful/wanton	bars provider from liability for ordinary or gross negligence.
Ultra Vires Acts	employee	action outside scope of responsibility or authority	ordinary negligence	none	liability shifts from employer to employee alone
CONTRACT LAW					
Waivers	participant	participant of majority age	ordinary negligence	reduces duty to gross negligence	not liable for ordinary negligence
Inherent Risk Agreements Informed Consent (ADA, rehab, research, fitness regimen, therapy)	participant or subject	adequately informed of treatment risk; majority age or parental signature	treatment risks	none	stronger primary & secondary assumption of risk defenses
Agreement to Participate (Including Assumption of Risk Agreement)	participant	adequately informed of activity risks and behavioral expectations	inherent risks	none	stronger primary & secondary assumption of risk defenses
Facility Lease Agreements	lessee	authorization for lease by corporate entity; lessee of majority age	activity risks to lessee; facility risks to lessee & lessor	none	not liable for activity risks; leesee & provider share facility risk as per contract
Equipment Rental Agreements	user (renter)	user of majority age	inherent risks; risks from equipment misuse or user misconduct; provider retains risk of equipment failure; may include waiver	none	not liable for inherent risks or risks from misuse or misconduct

[1]Table was adapted with the permission and assistance of Dr. Betty van der Smissen from a chart on allocation of risk in a handout entitled "How to Defend Yourself and Your Program," SSLASPA, 1997.

[2]The reader is cautioned that a table is simply an outline of the subject and that it is impossible to include all elements of the subject or all exceptions. This table is meant as an overview of Allocation of Risk and the reader is directed to this chapter as well as Chapter 2.22 *Immunity*, Chapter 2.23 *Waivers and Releases*, and Chapter 2.24 *Inherent Risk-Related Defenses* for more detail regarding the subject.

(Continued)

Authority and Defenses	To Whom Risk is Allocated	Eligibility for Defense	Which Risks Are Allocated	Effect on Standard of Care Owed	Impact on Liability of Provider
Indemnity Agreements	indemnitor	appropriate relationship	financial loss of indemnitee	none	indemnitee losses pass to indemnitor
Independent Contract for Services	independent contractors	authorization of entity; check contractor credentials	all risks of provider except for "inherently dangerous" activities	none	all liability transfers to indep. contractor (except "inherently dangerous" activities)
STATUTORY LAW					
Comparative Fault	shared with participant based on % fault	fault-related conduct; participant usually age 6 or older; all providers eligible	risk shared for damages allocation based on % of fault	none	reduces damages by % participant at fault
Legislation-Based Immunity Charitable Immunity	participant	charitable, educational, and religious organizations	ordinary negligence	reduces duty to gross negligence	not liable for ordinary negligence
Tort Claims Acts	participant	public entities qualified by specific state statutes	discretionary acts; negligence except dangerous physical conditions usually	reduced to w/w; retain duty for dangerous physical conditions	provider liable for dangerous physical conditions and for wilful/wanton acts
Recreational User Immunity	user	owners of natural, undeveloped area; no fee for use of land; specified by state statute	open & obvious premise risks & all activity risks; retain ultra hazardous environmental risks	only duty: to warn of ultra-hazardous & of known, hidden hazards	no liability except for ultra-hazardous; retains liability for wilful/malicious (sometimes gross)
Volunteer Immunity (State)	participant	charitable & educational organization volunteers; safety training in some states	ordinary negligence in most states	volunteer to gross negligence	no effect on liability of provider
Federal Volunteer Protection Act	participant	volunteers of public and non-profit organizations within scope of responsibility who hold appropriate certifications	ordinary negligence	volunteer to gross negligence	no effect on liability of provider
Good Samaritan (First Aid) Immunity	injured party	In good faith; gratuitous	usually ordinary negligence	caregiver to gross negligence	not available to provider
Good Samaritan (AED) Immunity	injured party	in good faith, gratuitous aid; training in some states	usually ordinary negligence	caregiver to gross negligence	immunity in many states
Rec & Sport Provider Immunity Specific Activity Statutes (Equine, Ski, skating, & other specified activities)	inherent to participant, sometimes negligence	usually all providers & participants in specified activities	inherent activity risk to participant; provider retains operational, facility & premise risks	participant assumes inherent risks; sometimes reduces to gross	not liable for inherent activity-related risks; sometimes not liable for negligence

(Continued)

TABLE 2.21.1   **ALLOCATION OF RISK**[1][2]   **(CONTINUED)**

Authority and Defenses	To Whom Risk is Allocated	Eligibility for Defense	Which Risks Are Allocated	Effect on Standard of Care Owed	Impact on Liability of Provider
General Rec & Sport Statutes (Applies to numerous sports & activities in one statute)	inherent to participant	all providers & participants in specified activities	inherent activity risk to participant; provider retains operational, facility & premise risks	none; participant assumes inherent risks	not liable for inherent activity-related risks; liable for negligence
Hazardous Recreational Activity (Applies to numerous activities in one statute)	participant	public entities & employees w/o fee for activity	inherent activity risks & secondary assumption of risk to participant; provider must warn of dangerous conditions and maintain premises	reduces activity duty to gross; no effect on duty to warn, construct/ maintain facility/ equipment	not liable for inherent risk or activity-related negligence; liable for operational, facility, & premise risks & failure to warn
Procedural Noncompliance Statute of Limitations	participant	all providers	all risks	none	limits the time during which suit can be filed
Notice of Claim (Tort Claims Act)	participant	only public entities	all risks	none	limits time during which notice of intent to sue must be given

The doctrine of primary assumption of risk embodies the legal conclusion that the defendant has "no duty" to protect the plaintiff from a particular risk. In sport-related cases, however, the issue of whether a duty is owed depends upon (1) the nature of the activity or sport involved and (2) the relationship of the defendant and the plaintiff (*Knight v. Jewett*, 1992). The service provider generally has no duty to protect the client against the inherent risks of the sport; however, sometimes the relationship between provider and client creates a *duty to not increase the risks* inherent in the activity. For instance, in *El-Halees v. Chaucer* (2002), the court found Chaucer liable for injury to a six-year-old client due to a fall from a gymnastic apparatus because Chaucer left the child unattended on the uneven parallel bars—thereby violating the duty to not increase the risk of injury.

Courts have ruled that three elements must exist for a successful primary assumption of risk defense. They are: *(1) the risk must be inherent to the sport or activity; (2) the participant must voluntarily consent to be exposed to the risk; and (3) the participant must know, understand, and appreciate the inherent risks of the activity.* However, this varies somewhat from state to state (e.g., under Missouri law, a skier assumes the inherent risks of or incidental to skiing, regardless of his or her subjective knowledge of those risks [*Bennett v. Hidden Valley Golf and Ski, Inc.*, 2003]).

It is important that the recreation or sport manager understand that the participant assumes only the risks that are **inherent** to the sport or activity. Examples of inherent risks might include falling while skiing, falling from a horse while horseback riding, or pulling a muscle while putting the shot. The participant does not normally assume risks incurred as a result of the negligence of the service provider. Examples of negligence risks might include being struck by a bat with an untaped handle when it slipped from the batter's hand during a swing; being struck in the face by an elbow in an excessively rough basketball game when the officials failed to control the game; or a football player suffering a facial injury when supplied with a helmet with no face guard.

A person who is playing recreation league softball, a person in a pickup basketball game, or a person on the varsity football team is participating by choice and thus meets the second requirement for primary assumption of risk—**voluntary consent**. Voluntary consent is sometimes at issue in cases regarding injuries in required physical education classes. If the plaintiff is a student in a required class where gymnastics is a required activity and is injured performing a mandatory back handspring, the voluntary consent requirement would be difficult to meet. On the other hand, if the student elected from among several choices to take gymnastics to meet the physical education requirement, there might be a degree of voluntary participation.

Thirdly, one cannot assume a risk of which one has no **knowledge, understanding, or appreciation**. Courts have ruled that one must not only know of the facts creating the danger, but also must comprehend and appreciate the nature of the danger to be confronted. Whether one is held to know, understand, and appreciate the risks usually depends upon the plaintiff's age, experience, and opportunity to become aware of the risks. Courts have held that it is not necessary that the injured plaintiff foresee the exact manner in which his or her injury occurred (*Tremblay v. West Experience Inc.*, 2002). In some jurisdictions, however, knowledge and appreciation are measured by an objective test and can be determined by law when "any person of normal intelligence in [the plaintiff's] position must have understood the danger" (*Leakas v. Columbia Country Club*, 1993).

One way to strengthen the primary assumption of risk defense is to ensure that participants know, understand, and appreciate the risks of the activity. An effective way to accomplish this is through the use of participant agreements (see Chapter 2.23 *Waivers and Releases*), informed consent agreements, and agreements to participate (see Chapter 2.24 *Agreements Related to Inherent Risks*). Use of these documents provides documentation that the participant was aware of the risks.

Implied Primary Assumption of Risk and Express Assumption of Risk

There are two types of primary assumption of risk—implied primary assumption of risk and express assumption of risk. **Implied primary assumption of risk** is that form of primary assumption of risk where it is evident by the conduct or actions (i.e., participation) of the individual that the participant has voluntarily taken part in an activity that involves inherent or well-known risks. The participant has signed no document by which he or she assumes the risk.

Express assumption of risk is that form of primary assumption of risk in which the participant sets forth in words (either verbally or in writing) that he or she assumes the *inherent risks* of the activity. Participant agreements (see Chapter 2.23), informed consent agreements, and agreements to participate (see Chapter 2.24) are instruments that can be used to obtain this type of assumption of risk. In these agreements, the participant explicitly agrees to assume the *inherent risks (or the treatment risks)* of the activity.

Understanding of the concept of express assumption of risk is complicated by the fact that courts vary as to its definition. In some jurisdictions, express assumption of risk refers specifically to contractual agreements (i.e., waivers of liability) in which the participant releases the provider from liability for negligence rather than the inherent risks of the activity.

Secondary Assumption of Risk

Secondary assumption of risk (formerly called contributory negligence and contributory fault) involves the voluntary choice or conduct of the participant to encounter a known or obvious risk created by the negligent conduct of the service provider, or to fail to follow rules or heed warnings set down by the provider (*Riddle v. Universal Sport Camp*, 1990).

There are three types of situations in which secondary assumption of risk may occur. In the first, the participant voluntarily participates when there is a substantial risk that the defendant will act in a negligent manner (e.g., going up in a plane with someone who has a reputation for wild or careless acts). The second is when the service provider has already been negligent and the participant takes part anyway (e.g., playing softball in an outfield that has obvious rocks and holes scattered about). The third is when the participant fails to follow rules or heed warnings (e. g. refuses to wear safety equipment). In each case, the conduct of the participant (electing to participate) falls below the standard to which one is required to conform for one's own protection (see Comparative Fault below).

Sovereign and Governmental Immunity

Sovereign and governmental immunity are judicial doctrines that prevent one from filing suit against the government and its political subdivisions without their consent (see Chapter 2.22 *Immunity*).

Ultra Vires Act

A defense that can be very helpful to the corporate entity is the defense that the act by the employee was an *ultra vires* act—one that is not within the authority or scope of responsibility of the employee. Normally under the doctrine of *respondeat superior*, the employer is liable for the negligent acts of the employee (see Chapter 2.12 *Which Parties Are Liable?*). A major exception to this rule, however, is when the employee had no authority or responsibility to perform the act in question. In such a case, generally only the employee is liable for the negligent act.

If a coach injured a youngster while administering corporal punishment when the school had a strict rule prohibiting corporal punishment, the act would be outside the authority of the coach and the school system would probably escape liability. The coach would still be liable for the act. Note, however, that if the school is aware of the fact that the coach uses corporal punishment and has failed to act upon this knowledge, the school will also be liable for the action. In essence, by not taking action after knowing of the coach's behavior, the school is in fact condoning the act and may be liable.

Defenses Based on Contract Law

Waivers

A **waiver** is a contract in which the participant or user of a service agrees to relieve the provider of the duty of ordinary care. The signer relinquishes the right to pursue legal action against the service provider in the event that the *negligence* of the provider results in an injury to the participant (see Chapter 2.23 *Waivers and Releases*).

Informed Consent

An **informed consent agreement** is a formal contract used to protect the provider from liability for the informed treatment risks of a treatment or program to which the signer is subjected. The agreement is designed to provide full disclosure to the individual regarding both the known risks and the anticipated outcome or benefits of the treatment, thereby enabling the participant to make an informed decision regarding acceptance of the treatment. *By signing the agreement, the signer is agreeing to assume the treatment risks of which he or she is informed. The signer is not agreeing to relieve the entity from liability for injury resulting from negligent acts of the entity or its employees* (see Chapter 2.24 *Agreements Related to the Inherent Risks*).

Agreement to Participate

The **agreement to participate,** while technically not a contractual agreement, is a document which helps to protect by informing participants in recreation, sport, or educational activities of (1) the nature of the activity, (2) the risks to be encountered through participation in the activity, and (3) the behaviors expected of the participant. It is designed to help protect the provider from liability for injuries resulting from the inherent risks of the activity, but is informative rather than contractual in nature. An assumption of risk agreement is usually included within the agreement to participate. The **assumption of risk agreement** is a statement whereby the signer (1) explicitly asserts that the signer knows the nature of the activity, understands the physical and skill demands of the activity, and appreciates the types of injuries that may result from participation; (2) asserts that participation is voluntary; and (3) agrees to assume those risks that are inherent to the activity (see Chapter 2.24 *Agreements Related to the Inherent Risks*).

Facility Lease Agreements

Owners of facilities often permit groups or other businesses to make use of their facilities. A recreational softball team might sign up for a field to conduct a team practice; a facility owner might lease an arena to a promoter for a concert; or a facility owner might lease the entire facility or a part of the facility for a matter of months or years (e. g. a university might lease its dressing facilities and practice fields to a professional football team for several months for preseason practice). When an injury occurs at the facility, it is not unlikely that the facility owner will be named as a defendant in a lawsuit regarding the injury. A defense against such litigation may be provided to owners of property/lessors by virtue of their status as lessors or by contractual provisions.

To determine the extent of the liability of the facility owner, one must determine if the injury was **activity-related** or **premise-related**. Generally, injuries that are activity-related are the responsibility of the lessee. When injuries are premise-related, liability may rest on both the entity conducting the activity and the facility owner. Generally, the facility owner is responsible for structural type problems and the entity conducting the activity is often responsible for maintenance type problems. In the instance of the softball team using the field, the facility owner would retain liability. In the case of the football team leasing the facility for preseason practice, the responsibility would probably be shared by lessor and lessee depending on the nature of the hazard unless the lease contract includes provisions that assign sole responsibility for certain types of hazards to the lessee football team (see Chapter 2.31 *Premises Liability*).

It is common practice for lessors of property to include an indemnification clause within the lease agreement (see the Indemnification Agreements section below).

Equipment Rental Agreements

When individuals rent equipment, rental agreements are often used to help protect the lessor or renter (owner of equipment or property). Rental agreements often include a waiver of liability signed by the lessee (user or party acquiring the use of equipment) of the equipment as well as an indemnification agreement. By including a waiver in the rental agreement, the provider is passing the liability for a negligence-related injury on to the lessee. An indemnification agreement is usually included to have the lessee agree to repay the provider for loss of or damage to equipment and loss due to litigation resulting from accidents to the lessee or to a third party (see the next section).

Rental agreements can also function much like an agreement to participate (see also Chapter 2.24 *Agreements Related to Inherent Risks*) in that they can inform the lessee of behavior expected and his/her responsibility for third-party injuries, and gain affirmation that the lessee is knowledgeable regarding the use of the equipment. The renter then passes along much of the responsibility for injury to the lessee and enhances the position of the renter when comparative negligence is determined. The renter, however, usually retains liability for injury relating to defective equipment.

Indemnification Agreements

An **indemnification agreement** is an agreement by which one party agrees to indemnify or reimburse another upon the occurrence of an anticipated loss. The agreement creates a contractual right under which the loss is generally shifted from a tortfeasor (e.g., facility lessor) who is passively at fault to one that is actively responsible (e.g., facility lessee). Indemnification agreements are commonly included in facility leases to protect the property owner from loss resulting from litigation by the lessee or by a third party patron naming the owner as a defendant. For instance, a municipality leasing an arena to a wrestling promoter for an event would generally include within the lease a provision by which the promoter agrees to indemnify or reimburse the municipality for any loss resulting from the event. Then if an injury occurs to a spectator or a wrestler and the municipality is named as a co-defendant, the promoter is responsible for the municipality's legal fees, any award, and any other related expenses. In *Auburn School District No. 408 v. King County* (1999), the school district agreed to indemnify the county for loss due to the district's use of the county swimming pool. A student injured in the pool sued both the county and the school district. The school district was ordered to reimburse the county for its financial loss. This defense is summarized in Table 2.21.1 (see also Chapter 2.23 *Waivers and Releases* and Chapter 2.12 *Which Parties Are Liable?*).

The law regarding the enforcement of indemnification agreements is more exacting in some states than in others. For instance, in Georgia the public policy is reluctant to cast the burden for negligent actions upon one who is not actually at fault. Unless a contract for indemnification explicitly and expressly states that the negligence of the indemnitee is covered, courts will not enforce the contract against the indemnitor. In *Pride Park Atlanta v. City of Atlanta* (2000), the agreement was not enforced because the agreement said ". . . agrees to protect and hold harmless . . . from any and all claims . . ." and did not explicitly refer to negligence by the indemnitee.

While most indemnity agreements involve two corporate entities, some involve a corporate entity and an individual. Some courts have held that indemnification agreements used with consumers and intended to perform much like a waiver are not enforceable, but indemnification law varies from state to state. A rafting company (*Madsen v. Wyoming River Trips, Inc.*, 1999) required that a father agree to indemnify the company on behalf of himself and his family. When the wife was injured due to negligence of the rafting company, the Wyoming court refused to enforce the agreement stating that such contracts are enforced when the indemnitor is assuming liability for an act that was no fault of the indemnitee. The court ruled that the agreement, which sought to hold an innocent party liable for the negligence of the indemnitee, was void as against public policy.

In *Yang v. Voyagaire Houseboats, Inc.* (2005), Voyagaire had rented a houseboat to Yang and required that Yang sign an indemnity agreement. After six members of Yang's party suffered injury from carbon monoxide poisoning, Yang and others filed suit against Voyagaire; however, Voyagaire claimed protection by the waiver and indemnity agreement signed by Yang. The Supreme Court of Minnesota ruled that the waiver and indemnity agreement were against public policy since Voyagaire was, in effect, a resort providing a public service by furnishing sleeping accommodations to the public. It also stated that the indemnity clause was unenforceable because it did not contain language that (1) specifically refers to negligence, (2) expressly state that the renter will indemnify Voyagaire for Voyagaire's negligence, or (3) clearly indicate that the renter would indemnify Voyagaire for negligence occurring before the renter took possession of the houseboat. This ruling suggests that parties relying on indemnity agreements take care to clearly state the intent of the clause.

On the other hand, courts in some states have upheld such agreements (*Beaver v. Foamcraft, Inc.*, 2002). In a 2005 Wisconsin case, a man was injured during a tractor pull contest after signing a waiver and indemnification agreement. The waiver protected against the plaintiff's claims, but did not protect against a loss of consortium claim by the wife. The indemnity language within the document stated clearly and without ambiguity that the plaintiff agreed to indemnify the provider for all claims—thus the indemnity agreement protected the provider from the loss of consortium claim (*Walsh v. Luedtke*, 2005).

In several cases, corporate entities (in an effort to bypass the law in some states that disallows liability waivers signed by parents on behalf of minors) have attempted to gain liability protection by having parents sign indemnity agreements in order for the child to be able to participate in an activity. Some courts have said that such agreements are enforceable because they involve a contract between two adults (*Eastman v. Yutzy*, 2001). Other courts have ruled such an agreement invalid as against public policy since it is inconsistent with the parent's duty to the child (*Hawkins v. Peart*, 2001; *Cooper v. The Aspen Skiing Company*, 2002).

Independent Contract for Services

An independent contract for services involves an agreement between the corporate entity and an individual or a company that contracts to perform a service for the corporate entity (see Chapter 2.12 *Which Parties Are Liable?*). When one contracts with an independent contractor, the corporate entity generally avoids liability for injuries resulting from the negligence of the independent contractor. However, the employer retains the responsibility: (1) to use reasonable care in selecting a competent independent contractor and to inspect after completion of the project; (2) to keep the premises reasonably safe for invitees and employees; and (3) for "inherently dangerous activities" (e.g., fireworks displays, keeping of dangerous animals, and ultra hazardous activities) (see Chapter 2.12 *Which Parties Are Liable?*).

Defenses Based on Statutory Law

Comparative Fault

Comparative fault is not a true defense against liability for negligence. More precisely, **comparative fault** is a method for apportioning damages awarded based on the fault or blame or the relative degree of responsibility for the injury. The jury compares the fault of each party (i.e., the plaintiff and the defendant) and generally allocates the fault by percentage.[3] Any fault allotted to the plaintiff reduces the award to the plaintiff based upon the percentage of fault resulting from the plaintiff's own negligence.

Comparative fault was enacted to ameliorate the harsh effect of contributory negligence where the plaintiff receives no award if the plaintiff's actions contribute at all to the injury, regardless of how little it contributes. Comparative fault has two forms, pure and modified. **Pure comparative fault** has been adopted by a number of states. In this form, the award to the plaintiff is reduced by the percentage of fault assigned to the plaintiff. For

---

[3]**Contributory fault** (formerly called contributory negligence) exists when the conduct of the plaintiff in any way helps to cause or aggravate the plaintiff's injury. In the past, this was a major defense against negligence claims because in states adhering to the contributory fault doctrine, any contributory fault by the plaintiff, regardless of how slight, served as a complete bar to recovery. Now, however, only four states (Alabama, Maryland, North Carolina, and Virginia) and the District of Columbia hold to this doctrine. In **comparative fault** states, contributory fault serves to reduce the award to the plaintiff by the proportion of fault allotted to the plaintiff. Even under the comparative fault theory, however, most states bar recovery if the fault of the plaintiff is 50 percent or greater.

Regarding age, the general rule has been that children over the age of fourteen are capable of negligence and children under seven are incapable of negligence. Those between seven and fourteen are judged capable of negligence in certain circumstances. These lines of demarcation seem to be weakening in recent years as cases in various jurisdictions have begun to allocate contributory fault to children six years of age and under (*Grace v. Kumalaa*, 1963; *Lash v. Cutts*, 1991; *Robertson v. Travis*, 1980).

example, suppose the award is $100,000 and the fault is apportioned 75 percent to the plaintiff and 25 percent to the defendant. Since the plaintiff is 75 percent to blame, the plaintiff's award would be reduced by 75 percent and the plaintiff would receive $25,000. **Modified comparative fault** operates on the theory that the plaintiff is not entitled to recovery if the plaintiff is substantially at fault. State statutes vary—but, in essence, if the fault of the plaintiff is 50 percent or more, the plaintiff is barred from recovery and receives no award. Under this system, if the award is $100,000 and the plaintiff is 40 percent to blame, the plaintiff would receive $60,000. However, if the plaintiff is 51 percent to blame, there would be a complete bar to recovery and the plaintiff would receive nothing.

Legislation-based Immunity

There are several forms of legislation-based immunity that affect recreation and sport managers as well as the business entity. **Charitable immunity** is a doctrine that relieves or immunizes charitable organizations from liability for tort. Most states have abolished this defense; however it is still strong in a few states. **Federal** and **state tort claims acts** rescinded sovereign/governmental immunity and enumerated the areas or acts for which immunity was retained. **Recreational user immunity** was passed to protect certain landowners who gratuitously allow others to use their property for recreational purposes. **Volunteer immunity** was enacted to aid in the recruitment of volunteers for public, charitable, and nonprofit entities. **AED statutes** and **Good Samaritan statutes** protect those utilizing AEDs and rendering aid to victims in cases of medical emergency. **Shared responsibility and statutory assumption of risk statutes** are intended to help protect providers of recreation and sport activities from liability for injuries resulting from the inherent risks (and negligence in some statutes) of the activity or sport. These are discussed in detail in Chapter 2.22 *Immunity*.

Procedural Noncompliance

A **statute of limitations** is a restriction on the length of time an injured party has in which to file suit. The law differs from state to state and also with the nature of the claim. In tort claims, states allow one to four years in which to file suit with most allowing two or three years. When minors are involved, the statute of limitations does not begin running until the minor has reached the age of majority. So, if a child is injured at age 11 due to the negligence of an employee at a recreation department, the youngster would have one to four years (the length of the statute of limitations in that state) after reaching the age of 18 (in most states) in which to file suit.

Notice of claim statutes relate usually to tort claim statutes and provide that the plaintiff must provide the defendant *public entity* with a notice of intent to file suit. This notice must be filed within a period of time (ranging from 90 days to 2 years, depending on the state) following the accident or the right to sue is lost. In essence, the notice of claim is a form of statute of limitations with a similar effect. In a 2010 Arizona case (*Little v. State of Arizona*), failure to file a notice of claim within the 180 day time limit was at issue. A member of the University of Arizona's women's basketball team died as a result of medical misconduct; however, the claim was dismissed because plaintiff failed to comply with the notice of claim requirement. Not all states have a notice of claim provision in their tort law statutes and the notice of claim requirements apply only when the defendant is a public entity.

SIGNIFICANT CASE

In this case, the defendant claims that the school district is not liable because of recreational user immunity and because of implied primary assumption of risk. The opinion presents an enlightening discussion of each of the defenses

HOME V. NORTH KITSAP SCHOOL DISTRICT
2 Wn. App. 709; 965 P.2d 1112; 1998 Wash. App. LEXIS 1405
October 2, 1998, Filed

In 1993, Home was a teacher in the Central Kitsap School District, an organization not related to the North Kitsap School District. He taught at Central Kitsap Junior High, where he was also a part-time assistant football coach. Ken Anderson was the head football coach.

On November 3, 1993, Home's Central Kitsap team played an away game on the football field at North Kitsap Junior High. * * * The football field is a permanent facility with football goal posts at each end and a track around the perimeter. It is available for public use when not being used for school events or activities. On November 3, it was being used exclusively for the North Kitsap-Central Kitsap football game, a school-sponsored event to which parents and other spectators were admitted without charge.

When Home and Anderson arrived at the North Kitsap field, they saw a curb "raised several inches above ground level," separating the football area from the track area. The curb ran along the outside of the football field's sideline area, not far from the sideline itself. Home and Anderson thought it was a hazard to any player who might be propelled out of bounds by momentum or by another player. After discussing several courses of action, they decided that Home would station himself in front of the curb, so he could stop any player who might be heading for it. Later, during the game, Home was standing in front of the curb when the Central Kitsap team ran a "sweep" play toward his side of the field. As he testified later: I saw the kid coming to the sideline, I saw the tackler coming and saw imminent collision.

* * * My kid was a full stride out of bounds and starting a second stride when he was impacted. He was going into the cement. And using both hands, I took him to the ground. And the North Kitsap player with most of his weight came across my left thigh. Home was injured, he alleges, as a result of this impact.

In July 1996, Home sued the North Kitsap School District for negligence. North Kitsap moved for summary judgment, contending (1) that it was immune under RCW 4.24.210, the recreational land use statute; (2) that Home was a licensee who could not prove a breach of the duty owed to licensees; and (3) that Home knowingly and voluntarily assumed the risk that culminated in the accident. The trial court granted the motion, and this appeal followed.

I.

North Kitsap argues that RCW 4.24.210 renders it immune from liability to Home. * * * The purpose of RCW 4.24.210(1) is "to encourage owners or others in lawful possession and control of land and water areas or channels to make them available to the public for recreational purposes." RCW 4.24.210(1) provides in pertinent part:

> *Any public or private landowners or others in lawful possession and control of any lands whether designated resource, rural, or urban, or water areas or channels and lands adjacent to such areas or channels, who allow members of the public to use them for the purposes of outdoor recreation, which term includes, but is not limited to, the cutting, gathering, and removing of firewood by private persons for their personal use without purchasing the firewood from the landowner, hunting, fishing, camping, picnicking, swimming, hiking, bicycling, * * * boating, nature study, winter or water sports, viewing or enjoying historical, archaeological, scenic, or scientific sites, without charging a fee of any kind therefor, shall not be liable for unintentional injuries to such users.*

According to Division One, the proper approach when applying this statute is to analyze the purpose for which the landowner was using the land, as opposed to the purpose for which the plaintiff was using the land. We agree, although we observe that a landowner may use the land for different purposes at different times. Here, then, it is necessary to focus on the nature of the landowner's use at the time of the accident being litigated.

* * *

Turning to this case, a North Kitsap school administrator testified that the North Kitsap field, "including the area used for football games, is available for public use when school is not in session and when it is not being used for a scheduled sport, such as a junior high school football game." Thus, it is undisputed that North Kitsap was not holding the football field open for use by members of the public when Home was injured, and North Kitsap is not immune by virtue of RCW 4.24.210.

II.

We next consider whether Home was an invitee or licensee. As we explained in Thompson v. Katzer, "An invitee is either a public invitee or a business visitor." "A public invitee is a person who is invited to enter or remain on land as a member of the public for a purpose for which the land is held open to the public." "A business visitor is a person who is invited to enter or remain on land for a purpose directly or indirectly connected with business dealings with the possessor of the land." In contrast, a "licensee" enters the occupier's premises with the occupier's permission or tolerance, either (a) without an invitation or (b) with an invitation but for a purpose unrelated to any business dealings between the two. * * *

Here, Home was an assistant football coach invited to North Kitsap's field so that a school-sponsored football game could be played. His presence was related to North Kitsap's business of running its schools, and he was an invitee as a matter of law.

III.

North Kitsap claims that Home assumed the specific risk that culminated in the accident. Home disagrees, arguing primarily that he had no reasonable alternative course of action. Traditionally, the doctrine of assumption of risk has four facets: (1) express assumption of risk; (2) implied primary assumption of risk; (3) implied reasonable assumption of risk; and (4) implied unreasonable assumption of risk. The third and fourth facets, implied reasonable and implied unreasonable assumption of risk, are nothing but alternative names for contributory negligence, and neither is pertinent here. The first and second facets, express assumption of risk and implied primary assumption of risk, raise the same question: Did the plaintiff consent, before the accident or injury, to the negation of a duty that the defendant would otherwise have owed to the plaintiff? If the answer is yes, "the defendant does not have the duty, there can be no breach and hence no negligence." Thus, when either facet applies, it bars any recovery based on the duty that was negated. Although the first and second facets involve the same idea—the plaintiff's consent to negate a duty the defendant would otherwise have owed to the plaintiff—they differ with respect to the way in which the plaintiff manifests consent. With express assumption of risk, the plaintiff states in so many words that he or she consents to relieve the defendant of a duty the defendant would otherwise have. With implied primary assumption of risk, the plaintiff engages in other kinds of conduct, from which consent is then implied. Here, we focus on implied consent, which we alternatively refer to as assumption of risk.

To invoke assumption of risk, a defendant must show that the plaintiff knowingly and voluntarily chose to encounter the risk. Thus, "the evidence must show the plaintiff (1) had full subjective understanding (2) of the presence and nature of the specific risk, and (3) voluntarily chose to encounter the risk." Put another way, the plaintiff "must have knowledge of the risk, appreciate and understand its nature, and voluntarily choose to incur it." Knowledge and voluntariness are questions of fact for the jury, except when reasonable minds could not differ. Whether a plaintiff decides knowingly to encounter a risk turns on whether he or she, at the time of decision, actually and subjectively knew all facts that a reasonable person in the defendant's shoes would know and disclose, or, concomitantly, all facts that a reasonable person in the plaintiff's shoes would want to know and consider. Thus, "The test is a subjective one: Whether the plaintiff

in fact understood the risk; not whether the reasonable person of ordinary prudence would comprehend the risk." The plaintiff must "be aware of more than just the generalized risk of [his or her] activities; there must be proof [he or she] knew of and appreciated the specific hazard which caused the injury." And a plaintiff "appreciates the specific hazard" or risk only if he or she actually and subjectively knows all facts that a reasonable person in the defendant's shoes would know and disclose, or, concomitantly, all facts that a reasonable person in the plaintiff's shoes would want to know and consider when making the decision at issue. Whether a plaintiff decides voluntarily to encounter a risk depends on whether he or she elects to encounter it despite knowing of a reasonable alternative course of action. Thus, Division One has said that in order for assumption of risk to bar recovery, the plaintiff "must have had a reasonable opportunity to act differently or proceed on an alternate course that would have avoided the danger." The Restatement comments:

> Since the basis of assumption of risk is the plaintiff's willingness to accept the risk, take his chances, and look out for himself, his choice in doing so must be a voluntary one. If the plaintiff's words or conduct make it clear that he refuses to accept the risk, he does not assume it. The plaintiff's mere protest against the risk and demand for its removal or for protection against it will not necessarily and conclusively prevent his subsequent acceptance of the risk, if he then proceeds voluntarily into a situation which exposes him to it. Such conduct normally indicates that he does not stand on his objection, and has in fact consented, although reluctantly, to accept the danger and look for himself.

* * *

In this case, Home does not seriously dispute that he knew all the facts that a reasonable person would have wanted to know and consider when deciding whether to position himself or herself as Home did. He does contend, however, that a rational trier of fact could find that once he actually and subjectively discovered the hazard that later culminated in the accident, he had no reasonable alternative but to stand in front of it and protect his students. Taking the evidence and inferences in the light most favorable to Home, we think that a rational trier could so find. Accordingly, we conclude that whether Home voluntarily assumed the risk is a question of fact for the jury, and that summary judgment should not have been granted.

Reversed and remanded for further proceedings.

CASES ON THE SUPPLEMENTAL WEB SITE

Knight v. Jewett, (3 Cal.4th 296 [1992]). This is the seminal case concerning the doctrine of assumption of risk, in which the California Supreme Court considered the application of assumption of risk in light of the adoption of comparative fault principles. Note the distinction made between "primary assumption of risk" and "secondary assumption of risk."

Ribaudo v. La Salle Institute, (2007 NY Slip Op 8431; 45 A.D.3d 556; 2007 N.Y. App. Div. LEXIS 11249). The court emphasized that the doctrine of primary assumption of the risk will not serve as a bar to liability if the risk is unassumed, concealed, or unreasonably increased.

Cicconi v. Bedford Central School District, 2005 N.Y. App. Div. LEXIS 8484. Note the reasoning why the court ruled that the doctrine of assumption of risk protected the school district.

Bartell v. Mesa Soccer Club, Inc., 2010 Ariz. App. Unpub. LEXIS 882. The issue of whether a volunteer is an agent of the club or is an independent contractor is addressed. Liability of the club rides on the issue.

Cohen v. Five Brooks Stable, 2008 Cal. App. LEXIS 222. The defendants claim assumption of risk and waiver of risks as defenses.

QUESTIONS YOU SHOULD BE ABLE TO ANSWER

1. What is meant by an inherent risk? Give an example.

2. Explain the concept of primary assumption of risk

3. What is secondary assumption of risk? Give an example

4. What is meant by comparative fault?

5. Explain the role of an indemnification agreement in a facility lease agreement.

REFERENCES

Cases

Auburn School District No. 408 v. King County, 1999 Wash. App. LEXIS 1748.
Beaver v. Foamcraft, Inc., 2002 U.S. Dist. LEXIS 4651.
Bennett v. Hidden Valley Golf and Ski, Inc., 2003 U.S. App. LEXIS 1658.
Cooper v. The Aspen Skiing Company, 2002 Colo. LEXIS 528.
Daigle v. West Mountain 2001 N.Y. App. Div. LEXIS 12326
Eastman v. Yutzy, 2001 Mass. Super. LEXIS 157.
El-Halees v. Chauser, 2002 Cal. App. Unpub. LEXIS 8124.
Grace v. Kumalaa, 387 P.2d 872 (Hawaii 1963).
Hawkins v. Peart, 2001 Utah LEXIS 177.
Home v. North Kitsap School District, 965 P.2d 1112; 1998 Wash. App. LEXIS 1405.
Knight v. Jewett, 3 Cal.4th 296; 11 Cal. Rptr. 2d, 834 P.2d 696 (1992).
Leakas v. Columbia Country Club, 831 F. Supp. 1231 (Md. 1993).
Little v. State of Arizona, 2010 Ariz. App. LEXIS 158.
Madsen v. Wyoming River Trips, Inc., 1999 U.S. Dist. LEXIS 77.
Pride Park Atlanta v. City of Atlanta, 2000 Ga. App. LEXIS 1330.
Riddle v. Universal Sport Camp, 786 P.2d 641 (Kan. 1990).
Robertson v. Travis, 393 So.2d 304 (La. 1980).
Saffro v. Elite Racing, Inc., 2002 Cal. App. LEXIS 2076 at 1
Tremblay v. West Experience Inc., 2002 N.Y. App. Div. LEXIS 7591.
Truett v. Fell, 68 N.Y.2d 432.
Walsh v. Luedtke, 2005 Wisc. App. LEXIS 744.
Yang v. Voyagaire Houseboats, Inc., 2005 Minn. LEXIS 465.

Publications and Presentations

Gregg, C.R. (2000). "Inherent Risks," SSLASPA Conference, Albuquerque.
van der Smissen, B. (1990). *Legal liability and risk management for public and private entities.* Cincinnati: Anderson Publishing Co.
van der Smissen, B. (1997) How to Defend Yourself and Your Program. Unpublished handout at an SSLASPA Conference.
Volunteer Protection Act of 1997, PL 105-19 (S543) June 18, 1997.

2.22 IMMUNITY

Doyice J. Cotten | Sport Risk Consulting

A major category of defense for individuals and service providers in the fields of recreation and sport management is immunity from liability. **Immunity** is the state of being exempt from or protected against civil liability under certain circumstances. In this chapter, several types of immunity that apply to recreation and sport managers will be presented—ranging from sovereign immunity to sport-related statutes pertaining to the recreational user, sport volunteers, Good Samaritan acts, statutory assumption of risk, and shared responsibility. Since it is not possible to spell out the law in each state regarding each type of immunity, the reader is encouraged to use Table 2.22.1 to research the law in his or her state. Moreover, the reader should consult Table 2.21.1 in Chapter 2.21 *Defenses against Negligence* for a summary of each of these defenses.

Many types of immunity are available to those in the fields of recreation and sport. Each has been designed to provide shelter from liability to one or more protected classes of people or entities. Statutes are aimed at providing protection for public entity service providers (tort claims acts, sovereign immunity, hazardous recreation statutes), private service providers (shared responsibility statutes, statutory assumption of risk statutes), nonprofit and charitable providers (charitable immunity), and property owners (recreational user statutes). Volunteer statutes are enacted to encourage volunteers (Volunteer Protection Act, state volunteer statutes), sport volunteers (sport volunteer statutes), and medical emergency volunteers (Good Samaritan statutes, AED Good Samaritan statutes). There is also immunity designed to protect public employees (hazardous recreation statutes, tort claims acts, discretionary act immunity) and private employees (AED Good Samaritan statutes).

FUNDAMENTAL CONCEPTS

Sovereign/Governmental Immunity

Sovereign immunity refers to "the immunity of the state and its agencies, departments, boards, institutions, et al." (van der Smissen, 1990, p. 148). **Governmental immunity**, on the other hand, "is the protection afforded local governing entities, such as municipalities (cities, towns, villages) and schools." (van der Smissen, 1990, p. 148). It is important to understand that while many states distinguish between the two concepts, the terms sovereign immunity and governmental immunity are often used interchangeably. In this chapter, the term "sovereign/governmental immunity" will be used to refer to both concepts.

There are two major limitations to sovereign/governmental immunity. First, *it applies only to governmental entities* and second, *it does not extend to the officers, agents, or employees of the governing entity* (except when the statute specifically provides for it). This doctrine of sovereign/governmental immunity was the commanding approach to immunity until the 1950s. However, during the last half of the twentieth century most states abolished or significantly weakened and restricted this immunity so that it no longer has the dominant impact that it once did. The rationale for the change was that the immunity was unfair to the innocent victim of negligent actions by the governmental entity or its employees. Common law regarding immunity has been collected and arranged more systematically, or codified, in the tort claims acts. These acts, to be discussed below, extend immunity to government officers, agents, and employees in many states.

Tort Claims Acts

In 1946, Congress passed the **Federal Tort Claims Act** (28 U.S.C. 2671–2680 [1976]) with the intent of waiving sovereign/governmental immunity, thereby allowing liability exposure for the federal government comparable to that of the private sector. The statute removed the power of the federal government to claim immunity from a lawsuit for damages due to negligent or intentional injury by a federal employee in the scope of his/her work for the government. While the Federal Tort Claims Act allows suit of the government in certain instances, unlike sovereign/governmental immunity, *it provides immunity for federal officials performing discretionary acts within the scope of their responsibilities.*

Individual states began to follow suit, passing their own **state tort claims acts** to enable individuals harmed by torts, including negligence, to file suit under certain conditions. *In essence, what these acts did was (1) to rescind sovereign/governmental immunity at the state level in those states and (2) to enumerate those areas or acts for which immunity was retained.*

Discretionary/Ministerial Function

One major change at this time was movement from that of governmental/proprietary function to the discretionary/ministerial doctrine. The **governmental/proprietary doctrine** classified the functions of public entities as either a fundamental **governmental function** (e.g., police, fire, and education), for which immunity was granted, or as a **proprietary function** (e.g., water works, electrical power, selling game refreshments, and other for-profit activities), for which no immunity was granted. The **discretionary/ministerial doctrine** grants immunity for discretionary acts, but, for the most part, not for ministerial acts.

Discretionary acts are those that involve deliberation, planning, decision making, policy making, and most often involve managerial level personnel such as the athletic director or head of the recreation department. **Ministerial acts** are more likely to involve operational acts, obedience of orders, performance of a duty, implementation of decisions or policies, and lower echelon employees such as assistant coaches and aerobics instructors. Under this doctrine, the classification is not based upon who performed the act, but upon the nature of the act. The rationale behind this immunity is to free the governing body charged with making policy decisions regarding public welfare from suits that might restrain them from performing their duties. Distinction between discretionary and ministerial acts is difficult at best. It has been growing increasingly so as the courts in some states have persisted in blurring the lines of distinction, often interpreting even trivial decisions as discretionary. Classifying most acts as discretionary, in effect, strengthens the immunity of the employee and the entity.

The governmental/proprietary doctrine provided immunity based upon the nature of the function provided by the governmental entity. Immunity was provided if the action was a "public good" function of the entity (an inspection of the recreation facility), but not for proprietary or money-making functions of the entity (operation of a soft-drink machine). The discretionary/ministerial doctrine provides immunity based on the act of the employee—not the function. Thus an employee might be immune for actions deemed discretionary (policy-related planning for a 5K Run) but not immune for actions ruled ministerial (carrying out the policies for a 5K Run).

In *Feagins v. Waddy* (2007), a girl on the track team suffered injury when she was assigned to compete in the high jump in a meet without prior instruction. The court held that the coach had immunity as a state agent because the selection of participants for events involves an exercise of judgment and is, therefore, a discretionary duty.

Charitable Immunity

During the first half of the twentieth century, charitable immunity provided substantial liability protection to charitable, educational, and religious organizations. **Charitable immunity** is a doctrine that relieves or immunizes charitable organizations from liability for tort. The doctrine is based upon four premises: (1) public policy encourages charitable organizations since they benefit the public; (2) money possessed by such organizations was donated for other purposes and is held in trust; (3) since the recipient of the charity receives benefits, he or she, in turn, accepts the risks of negligence; and (4) there is no *respondeat superior* since the charity does not benefit from the actions of employees.

Charitable immunity, which focused on the protection of the agency or institution, has been repealed in most states. In most of the few states that retain some semblance of charitable immunity, the immunity has been emasculated to the point where its effectiveness is very limited.[1] Today volunteer protection acts do

---

[1]Charitable immunity is still strong in New Jersey (*Gilbert v. Seton Hall University*, 2003) and Virginia (*Chrisman v. Brown*, 2007; *Kuykendall v. Young Life*, 2006).

provide protection for the nonprofit or charitable institution volunteer. In addition, a few states still protect those gratuitously serving such institutions as a member, director, trustee, or board member.

Recreational User Statutes[2]

In order to encourage private owners of natural, rural areas to allow others to use their property for recreational purposes, state legislatures began passing recreational user statutes in the 1960s. The **recreational user statute** is a law designed to provide protection for the private property-owner against lawsuits by parties injured while on the landowner's property for recreational purposes. Originally, the immunity laws applied when four conditions were met: (1) private landowners; (2) no fee charged; (3) unimproved, undeveloped land for recreational use; and (4) owner fulfilled his or her obligation to provide a warning for any known, concealed danger that would not be apparent to the recreational user.

Today, all states have enacted some type of recreational user statute. While differences exist among the statutes, they were enacted with comparable intent. Statutes generally (1) are intended to encourage landowners to make their property available to the public for recreational use; (2) stipulate that no fee is charged for the use of the land; (3) declare that the owner owes no duty of care to keep the land safe for use for recreational purpose nor to warn of a dangerous condition; (4) state that the landowner extends no assurance that the land is safe for any purpose and does not confer on the user the legal status of invitee or licensee; and (5) say that the landowner does not assume responsibility for or incur liability for any injury, death, or loss to any person or property caused by an act or omission of the landowner.

Resultant of the immunity provided by most such statutes, the provider's only duty is to warn of ultra hazardous situations and of known hidden hazards. In most states, the provider has no liability except for willful or malicious acts and for ultra hazardous situations. The immunity generally applies to all activity risks and all open and obvious premise risks.

While most recreational user statutes were adopted for the same purpose (encouraging property owners to open their land for recreational use), courts in some states have significantly broadened their application. Courts in those states have expanded the immunity provided by the statutes by interpreting them liberally (e.g., by applying the statutes in cases where the injury occurred on a tennis court or when a fee was paid). The reader is encouraged to read an excellent presentation on the subject in Chapter 2.32 *Property Law*. The specific statutes for each state may be found in Table 2.22.1 of this chapter and a summary of recreational user immunity may be found in Table 2.21.1 in Chapter 2.21 *Defenses against Negligence*.

Volunteer Immunity Statutes

Prior to the decade of the 1980s, lawsuits against volunteers in recreation and sport activities were rare. In that decade, insurance coverage became both expensive and difficult to obtain, some coverage was unavailable, more exclusions were included in policies, many agencies discontinued or reduced insurance coverage, volunteer lawsuits began to increase in frequency, and volunteer recruitment became more difficult. This predicament prompted a number of states to pass legislation aimed at protecting certain volunteers in recreational and sport activities (see Table 2.22.1 in this chapter).

State Volunteer Immunity Statutes

In the late 1980s, state legislatures were encouraged to pass a model act designed to protect volunteers working with certain nonprofit organizations and governmental entities from liability for injuries resulting from the ordinary or gross negligence of the volunteers. The Model State Act called for immunity from civil liability for any act or omission of the volunteer that resulted in damage or injury if the volunteer was acting in good faith and within the scope of duty for a nonprofit organization or governmental entity—so long as the injury was not caused by wanton and willful misconduct and did not involve the operation of a motor vehicle. The model act, however, intended no protection for the nonprofit or governmental agency for which the volunteer worked.

---

[2]Convenient access to the complete recreational user statutes in every state is available on the internet thanks to the work of Holly Rudolph, J.D. All statutes and an informative article by Ms. Rudoph are available at http://www.sportwaiver.com/landowner-liability-under-equine-and-recreational-use-statutes/. They may also be found at http://elcr.org/ss2.htm.

Subsequently, all states now have either (1) a general volunteer liability statute (often modeled after the Model State Act) designed to provide protection for volunteers, or (2) a statute intended to protect certain volunteers in recreation and sports activities (*e.g.*, coaches, referees), or (3) both types of statutes. The general volunteer statutes vary greatly from state to state. Many of the states protect only directors or officers in the organization and all have exceptions to immunity. Common exceptions include the motor vehicle exception, action based on federal law, action that constitutes gross negligence, willful and wanton acts, and, in a few states, ordinary negligence. Many of these general state statutes are worded such that they should provide immunity for recreation and sport volunteers. Additionally, in 1997 the volunteer was provided with even more protection when Congress enacted the Volunteer Protection Act (discussed in detail below).

Recreation and Sport Volunteer Immunity Statutes

Twenty states have passed some type of volunteer statute for volunteer sport coaches and officials.[3] In addition, a Hawaii statute protects volunteers at public skateboard parks and youth sport volunteers are specifically mentioned in the Oklahoma and Texas general volunteer immunity statutes.

There are ten points that are frequently addressed in recreation and sport volunteer immunity statutes.

1. The volunteer must be **unpaid**. Some statutes specify that officials (e.g., referees, umpires) may receive a small stipend and retain their immunity.
2. The volunteer must act in **good faith**.
3. The volunteer must act within the **scope** of his or her duties.
4. **Protected parties** are usually specified and may include any or all of athletic coach, assistant coach, manager, assistant manager, instructor, official, referee, umpire, leader, league official, athletic trainer, and physician or other healthcare provider. The law in Arkansas, Kansas, and Mississippi restricts eligibility for immunity to sports officials who officiate at any level of competition.
5. Additionally, most statutes define the **type organization** (e.g., nonprofit, charitable, educational) whose volunteers qualify.
6. Some states stipulate that protected parties must undergo an approved **training program**, usually relating to safety or first aid.
7. Some states specify that immunity does not protect when activities are **unsupervised**.
8. Most, but not all, exclude public and private **school coaches** from immunity.
9. It is the **nature of the act** that is protected. Most include immunity for ordinary negligence, but several include gross negligence, excluding only wanton and willful acts or intentional acts. Pennsylvania and New Mexico statutes specify immunity unless the conduct is substantially below the generally accepted level.
10. Almost all exclude negligence in the operation of a **motor vehicle** from immunity.

Heard v. City of Villa Rica (2010) illustrates the function of these statutes. A boy was injured when training for the long jump under the instruction of a volunteer coach. The coach claimed immunity while the plaintiff claimed immunity did not apply when the coach was grossly negligent. The court held that there was no gross negligence and held that the defendant was immune under the statute.

Volunteer Protection Act (VPA)

The **Volunteer Protection Act** (VPA) was signed into law in 1997 (Public Law 105-19). This federal statute preempts state laws (except for those that provide for more volunteer protection than the VPA) and is intended to provide broad protection to volunteers nationwide under the following conditions:

- The volunteer was acting within the scope of the volunteer's responsibilities in the nonprofit organization or governmental entity at the time of the act or omission;
- If appropriate or required, the volunteer was properly licensed, certified or authorized by the appropriate authorities for the activities or practice in the state;

[3]Arkansas, Colorado, Delaware, Georgia, Illinois, Indiana, Kansas, Louisiana, Maryland, Massachusetts, Minnesota, Mississippi, Nevada, New Hampshire, New Jersey, New Mexico, North Dakota, Pennsylvania, Tennessee, and Rhode Island. Volunteer recreation and sport statutes may be found in Table 2.22.1 in this chapter.

TABLE 2.22.1 STATE RECREATION- AND SPORT-RELATED IMMUNITY LEGISLATION

State	Recreational User Statutes	Rec/Sport Volunteer Statutes	Good Samaritan Statutes	AED Good Samaritan Statutes	Equine Immunity Statutes	Ski Operator Immunity Statutes	Skating Immunity Statutes	Other Sport & Recreation Statutes	General Sport & Recreation Statutes	Hazardous Recreational Activity Statutes
U.S.		PL. 105-19 42 U.S.C.S. 14,501-14,505		P.L. 107-188 42 U.S.C.S. 238q						
AL	AC 35-15- (1-28)		AC 6-5-332	AC 6-5-332	AC 6-5-337		AC 6-5-342 Skateboard Parks			
AK	AS 09.65.200 AS 34.17.055		AS 09-65-090	AS 09.65.090	None	AS 05.45.010 to .210			AS 09.65. 290 (2009)	
AZ	ARS 33-1551		ARS 32-1471 ARS 32-1472 ARS 36.21.1	ARS 36-2261-2264	ARS 12-553	ARS 5-705 (1)		ARS 12-554 Baseball ARS 12-556 Motor Sports		
AR	ARS 18-11- 301 to 307	ARS 16-120-102	ARS 17-95-101	ARS 20-13-1305 ARS 20-13-1306	ARS 16-120-201 to 202					
CA	CCC 846, 846.1		CCHSC 1799.102	ACC 1714.21 HSC 1797.190 SB 911 of 1999	None	5 county ordinances	CGC 831.7 (Hazardous Rec. Act. Statute)			CGC 831.7
CO	CRS 33-41- 101 to106	CRS 13-21-116	CRS 13-21-15.5	CRS 13-21-108.1	CRS 13-21-119	CRS 33-44-101 to 114		CRS 13-21-111.8(1) and 25-12-109 Sport Shooting CRS 13-21-120 Baseball CRS 12-55-103 to 118 Outfitters & Guides		
CT	CGSA 52-557f-k		CGSA 52-557B	CGSA 52-57b	CGSA 52-557p	CGSA 29- 201 to 214				
DE	7 DCA 5901-5907	16 DCA 6835 16 DCA 6836	16 DCA 6801	DCA 6801	10 DCA 8140					
FL	FS 375.251		FS 768.13	FS 768.1325	FS 773.01 to .05		FS 316.0085 Skateboard Parks Inline skating	549.09 Motorsports 316.0085 Mountain or off-road biking, paintball 790.333 and 823.16 Sport Shooting		FS 316.0085
GA	OCGA 51-3-20 to 26; OCGA 27-3-1	OCGA 51-1-20.1	OCGA 51-1-230 OCGA 768.135	OCGA 31-11-53.1 OCGA 51-1-29.3	OCGA 4-12-1 to 5		OCGA51-1-43 Roller Skating	OCGA 27-4-280 to 283 Fishing		

(Continued)

TABLE 2.22.1 STATE RECREATION- AND SPORT-RELATED IMMUNITY LEGISLATION (CONTINUED)

State	Recreational User Statutes	Rec/Sport Volunteer Statutes	Good Samaritan Statutes	AED Good Samaritan Statutes	Equine Immunity Statutes	Ski Operator Immunity Statutes	Skating Immunity Statutes	Other Sport & Recreation Statutes	General Sport & Recreation Statutes	Hazardous Recreational Activity Statutes
HI	HRS 520-1 to 8	HRS 662D - 4	HI 663-1.5	HRS 663-1.5	HRS 663B-1 to 2		HRS 662-19, HRS 46-72.5, HRS 662D-4 Skateboarding		HRS 663-1.54	
ID	IC 36-1604		IC 5-330	IC 5-337	IC 6-1801 to 1802	IC 6-1101-1109		IC 6-1201 to 1206 Outfitters & Guides IC 6-2701 to 2702 Sport Shooting		
IL	745 ILCS 65/1 to 7	745 ILCS 80/1	745 ILCS 49/12	410 ILCS 4/30 745 ILCS 49/12	745 ILCS 47/1 to 47/999		745 ILCS 72/1 to 30 Roller Skating	745 ILCS 52/1 to /99 Hockey Facilities		745 ILCS 10/3-109
IN	ICA 14-22-10-2 to 2.5	ICA 34-30-4-2 ICA 34-30-19-3 to 4	ICA 34-30-12-1	ICA 16-31-6.2 ICA 34-30-12-1	ICA 34-6-2-40 to 43, 69, 95, 103; ICA 34-31-5-1 to 5		ICA 34-31-6-1 to 4 Roller Skating			
IA	ICA 461C.1 to .7		ICA 115.3 ICA 915.3	ICA 147A.10	ICA 673.1 to 4		ICA 670.4 Skateboard Parks			
KS	KSA 58-3201 to 3207	KSA 60-3607	KSA 65-2891	KSA 65-6149a	KSA 60-4001 to 4004					
KY	KRS 150.645 KRS 411.190		KRS 411.148 KRS 411.150	KRS 311.668	KRS 247.401 to 4029					
LA	LRS 9:2791, 2795	LRS 9:2798	LRS 9:2793	LRS 40:1236. 11 to .14 LRS 9:2793	LRS 9: 2795.1					
ME	14 MRSA 159- A		14 MRSA 164	22 MRSA 2150-C	7 MRSA 4101-4104A	26 MRSA 471 -490-G 32 MRSA 15201 to 15227	8 MRSA 23-601-608 Roller Skating 8 MRSA 24-621- 626 Ice Skating	8 MRSA 801-806 Amuse Rides; 32 MRSA 15219 Hang Gliding		
MD	MCA 5-1101 to1109	MCA 5-607 MCA 5-802	MCA 5-603	MCA 13-517	None					
MA	21 MGL 17C	231 MGL 85V	71 ALM 55A 111C ALM 20	112 ALM 12V1/2	128 MGL 2D	143 MGL 71H to 71S				

(Continued)

State	Recreational User Statutes	Rec/Sport Volunteer Statutes	Good Samaritan Statutes	AED Good Samaritan Statutes	Equine Immunity Statutes	Ski Operator Immunity Statutes	Skating Immunity Statutes	Other Sport & Recreation Statutes	General Sport & Recreation Statutes	Hazardous Recreational Activity Statutes
MI	MCLA 324.73301		MCLA 691.1501 MCLA 691.1507 MCLA 333.20965	MCLA 333.20965	MCLA 691.1661 to 1667	MCLA 408.321 to .344 or MSA 13A.82126	MCLA 445.1721 to .1726 Roller Skating	MCLA 681. 1541 to .1544 MCLA 691.1544 Sport Shooting; MCLA 342.82126 Snow Mobiling		
MN	MSA 604A.20 to 27	MSA 604A.11	MSA 604A.01	MSA 604A.01	MSA 604A.12					
MS	MCA 89-2- 1 to 27	MCA 95-9-3	MCA 63-3-405 MCA 73-25-37	MCA 41-60-33	MCA 95-11-1 to 7					
MO	MAS 537.345 to .348		RSM 537.037	RSM 190.092	MAS 537.325			RSMO 537.327 Outfitters, Paddlesports (canoe, raft, kayak, tubing)		
MT	MCA 70-16-301 to 302		MCA 27-1-714	MCA 50-6-505	MCA 27-1-725 to 728	MCA 23-2-732 to -736		MCA 23-2-651 to 656 Snowmobiling MCA 27-1-733 Rodeos		
NE	NRS 37-729 to 736		NRS 25-21, 186	NRS 71-51, 102	NRS 25-21.249 to .253		NRS 13-910 (2009) Skateparks, inline skating, Skateboarding, Bicycle Moto-cross Parks, Bicycling,	NRS 13-910 (2009) Bicycle Motocross Parks, Bicycling,		
NV	NRS 41.510	NRS 41.630	NRS 41.5000	NRS 41.500	None	NRS 455A.010 to -.190	NRS 455B.200 to 300 Skateboard Parks	NRS 455B.010 to 455B.100 Amuse Rides		
NH	NHSA 212:34, NHSA 231-A:1 to 8	NHSA 508.17	RSA 508:12	RSA 153-A:31	NHSA 508:19	NHSA 225-A:1 to :26	NHSA 507 - B:11 Skateboard Parks			NHSA 507 B-11
NJ	NJS 13:1B-15. 134 to 142 NJS 2A:42A-2 to 10	NJS 2A:62A-6	NJS 2A:62A-1 NJS 26:2K-29	NJS 2A:62A-25	NJ S 5:15-1 to 12	NJS 34:4A-1; NJS 5:13-1 to 11	NJS 5:14-1 to 7 Roller Skating			
NM	NMSA 17-4-7	NMSA 41-12-1 NMSA 41-12-2	NMSA 24-10-3	NMSA 34-10B-4	NMSA 42-13-2 to 5	NMSA 24-15- 1-14				

(*Continued*)

TABLE 2.22.1 STATE RECREATION- AND SPORT-RELATED IMMUNITY LEGISLATION (CONTINUED)

State	Recreational User Statutes	Rec/Sport Volunteer Statutes	Good Samaritan Statutes	AED Good Samaritan Statutes	Equine Immunity Statutes	Ski Operator Immunity Statutes	Skating Immunity Statutes	Other Sport & Recreation Statutes	General Sport & Recreation Statutes	Hazardous Recreational Activity Statutes
NY	NY GOL 9-103		NYCLSPH 3000-a	NYCLSPH 3000-a NYCLSPH 3000-b	None	NY GOL 18-101 to -108 NYLL 865 to 868				
NC	NCGS 38A-1 to 4		NCGS 20-166 NCGS 90-21.14	NCGS 90-21.15	NCGS 99E-1 to 3	NCGS 99C-1 to 5	NCGS 99E-10 to 14 Roller Skating	NCGS 14-409.46 Sport Shooting		NCGS Art 99E – 21-25
ND	NDCC 53-08- 01 to 06	NDCC 32-3-46	NDCC 32-03.1-02	NDCC 32-03.1-02.3	NDCC 53-10- 01 to 02	NDCC 53-09-01 to 11				
OH	ORCA 1533.18 ORCA 1533.181		ORCA 2305.23	ORCA 2305.235	ORCA 2305.321	ORCA 4169.01 to .99	ORCA 4171.01 to .10 Roller Skating			
OK	2 OS 1301-315 76 OS 5, 11 OS 76-10 to 15	76 OS 31	OS 76.5	76 OS 5A	OS 76 50.1 to -4					
OR	ORS 105.670 to .700		ORS 30.800 ORS 433.830	ORS 30.802	ORS 30.687 -.697	ORS 30.970 to .990				
PA	68 PCSA 477-1 to 7	42 PCSA 8332.1	42 PCSA 8332	42 PCSA 8331.2	None	42 PCSA 7102 or 40 PCSA 2051				
RI	RIGL 32-6-1 to 7	RIGL 9-1-48	RIGL 9-1-27.1 RIGL 9-1-34	RIGL 9-1-34	RIGL 4-21-1 to 4	RIGL 41-8-1 to 4		RIGL 9-20-5 Snow Mobiles & ATVs		
SC	SCCA 27-3-10 to 70		SCCA 15-1-310	SCCA 4-76-40	SCCA 47-9-710 to 730		SCCA 52-21-10 to 60 Ice Skating and Roller Skating			
SD	SDCLA 20-9-12 to 18		SDCLA 32034-3 SDCLA 20-9-3	SDCLA 20-9-4.1	SDCLA 42-11-1 to 5			SDCLA 32-20A-21to 22 Snow Mobiling	SDCLA 20-9-12 to 18 More than 25 out-door sports	
TN	TCA 11-10-101 to 105 TCA 70-7-101 to 105	TCA 62-50-201-203	TCA 63-6-218	TCA 63-6-218	TCA 44-20-101 to 105	TCA 68-114-102 to 107		TCA 70-7-201-204 Whitewater rafting		

(Continued)

State	Recreational User Statutes	Rec/Sport Volunteer Statutes	Good Samaritan Statutes	AED Good Samaritan Statutes	Equine Immunity Statutes	Ski Operator Immunity Statutes	Skating Immunity Statutes	Other Sport & Recreation Statutes	General Sport & Recreation Statutes	Hazardous Recreational Activity Statutes
TX	TCPRC 4-75.001 to .004	TCPRC 84.0001 to 008	VTCA 74.001-/003	TCPRC 74.001	TCPRC 87.001 to .005		759.001 to .005 Roller Skating 760.001 to .006 Ice Skating	TCPRC 4-75.001 Hockey, hunting, fishing, water skiing, more.		
UT	UCA 57-14-1 to 7		UCA 78-11-22	UCA 28-8-7.5 or 75	UCA 78-27b-101 to 103	UCA 78-27-51 to 54	See Gen Rec & Sport Statutes for Skateboard Parks	UCA 47-3-1 to 3 Sport Shooting; UCA 78-27-61 Amuse Rides; UCA 78-27-62 Hockey Facil	UCA 78-27-63	
VT	12 VSA 5791-5795		12 VSA 519	18 VSA 907	12 VSA 1039	12 VSA 1036 to 1038	See Genl Rec & Sport Statutes for Skateboard Parks	10 VSA 5227 Sport Shooting	12 VSA 1037	
VA	VCA 29.1-.509		VCA 8.00-225	VCA 8.01-225	VCA 3.1-796.130 to .133					
WA	RCW 4.24.200 to 210		RCW 4.24.300	RCW 70.54.310	RCW 4.24.530 to .540	RCW 70.117.010 to .040; RCW 79A.45.010 to .060	RCW 4.24.210 Skateboarding (among others)		RCW 4.24.210 More than 20 activities	
WV	WVC 19-25-1 to 7		WVC 55-7-15	WVC 16-4D-3 to 4	WVC 20-4-1 to 7	WVC 20-3A-1 to 8		WVC 20-3B-1 to 5 Outfitters & Guides		
WI	WSA 895.52 to .525)		WSA 895.48	WSA 895.48	WSA 895.481-895.481 3 (e)	WSA 895.525	See Gen Rec & Sport Statutes for Skateboard Parks	WSA 875.527 Sport Shooting	WSA 895.525	
WY	WYO STAT 34-19-101 to 106		WYO STAT 1-1-120	WYO STAT 35-26-102 to 103	WYO STAT 1-1-121 to 123	WYO.STAT. 1-1-121 to 123		WYO.STAT. 1-1-118 Rodeos 23-2-401 to 418 Outfitters and Guides	WYO STAT 1-1-121 to 123	

- The harm was not caused by willful or criminal misconduct, gross negligence, reckless misconduct, or a conscious, flagrant indifference to the rights or safety of the individual harmed by the volunteer;
- The harm was not caused by the volunteer operating a motor vehicle . . . for which the State requires . . . an operator's license; or . . . insurance.

Of particular interest is the second condition—that the immunity applies only if the volunteer is licensed, certified or authorized when such empowerments are relevant. *It is important to note that the act does not affect the liability of any nonprofit or governmental entity—but rather protects only individuals from liability.* In *Avenoso v. Mangan* (2006), Mangan, a volunteer soccer coach, caused injury to Avenoso when he ran too close to him. The court granted summary judgment on the basis of the VPA, but ruled that the co-defendant soccer club did not qualify for immunity under the act.

Acts that are not encompassed by the statute include (1) crimes of violence or terrorism, (2) hate crimes, (3) sexual offense convictions, (4) violation of federal or state civil rights law, and (5) those committed while under the influence of drugs or alcohol. Punitive damages can be awarded only if the volunteer's actions constituted willful or criminal misconduct or a conscious flagrant indifference to the rights and safety of the injured party. For losses due to physical or emotional pain, the volunteer will be liable only to the extent of his or her percentage of responsibility.

First Aid Statutes (Good Samaritan)

Every state has some form of Good Samaritan statute which is intended to provide immunity from liability for certain parties who voluntarily and gratuitously come to the aid of injured persons. Good Samaritan laws were developed to encourage both physicians and laymen to help others in emergency situations.

There is no general legal duty to assist or rescue injured parties in most states. An exception is Vermont, which requires a person who knows that another is exposed to grave physical harm to give reasonable assistance to the exposed person if he can do so without danger or peril to himself. Penalty for violation, however, is only $100. Mississippi, North Carolina, and South Dakota require that the driver of a vehicle involved in an accident assist injured parties if needed if assisting presents no danger to the one assisting. Most then provide immunity for the driver. Georgia has a duty to assist and rescue in the event of watercraft accidents.

There are six elements that are common to most Good Samaritan statutes. The first is the stipulation of **who is protected** by the statute. The most common designation is any person who comes to the aid of another in an emergency situation. More than 40 states offer protection for any individual who assists in an emergency situation. Some states, however, restrict the immunity to healthcare personnel (physicians, surgeons, nurses, EMS personnel, physical therapists, and/or others) or those with first aid training. Many states exclude healthcare professionals from protection if the action is within the scope of the duty of the healthcare professional.

The second and third elements are that the parties must act in **good faith** and without expectation of **remuneration**. Almost every state specifies one or the other and most list both. Fourth, almost all of the statutes specify that the action must occur in an **emergency situation** away from a medical facility. There are also many states that have statutes specific to assisting those choking on food in restaurants. A few statutes limit coverage to more specific situations (e.g., choking, crime victims, cardiopulmonary rescues, life-threatening situations, athletic events) and some apply to volunteer team physicians. Fifth, the statutes almost always stipulate that the care must be done **at the scene** of the accident. A number also add protection during transport to the hospital.

Finally, virtually all of the statutes specify a **standard of care required.** Unfortunately, that standard varies by state. A few states, including Arkansas, Florida, and Mississippi require that the acts of the volunteer be those of a reasonable and prudent person. In these states, and possibly a few others, the "Good Samaritan" is **not** protected against liability for negligence. Most states protect the volunteer from liability when the act is negligent, but not if it is grossly negligent, reckless, or willful and wanton. Statutes in a few states specify that there is immunity unless there is reckless or willful and wanton conduct.

While "Good Samaritan" laws differ considerably among states, the typical statute asserts that *any person who, in good faith, gratuitously renders emergency care at the scene of an accident cannot be held liable for injury resulting from acts and omissions unless the conduct constitutes gross negligence or willful/wanton conduct.* It is, however, prudent for one to know the law in one's own state. Good Samaritan legislation in each state may be found in Table 2.22.1 in this chapter and is summarized in Table 2.21.1 in Chapter 2.21 *Defenses against Negligence*.

In a recent California Supreme Court ruling (*Van Horn v. Watson*, 2008), the court held that the California Good Samaritan statute applied only to the rendering of care at the scene of a medical emergency and did not encompass rescue or extrication. Injuries incurred during a rescue or while transporting the injured party to medical aid (e.g., after an accident in a wilderness area) may subject the rescuer/transporter to civil liability. Californians are not the only ones who may be affected by this situation since a number of other states have similar provisions in their statute.

AED Statutes

The development of the automated external defibrillator (AED) in the 1990s provided a major technological advance in the fight against sudden cardiac arrest deaths in the United States. The **AED** is a medical device which (1) recognizes the presence or absence of ventricular fibrillation; (2) is capable of determining if defibrillation should be performed; (3) can automatically charge and request delivery of an electrical impulse; and (4) can deliver an appropriate impulse upon action by the operator. While it has been estimated that more than half of the 250,000 plus deaths annually in the nation could be prevented by timely use of an AED, its widespread use has been hampered by the lack of laws enabling its use by non-medical personnel.

With the intent of encouraging the extensive use of the AED, some states began passing Good Samaritan legislation specifically aimed at AED usage while others added the AED to existing Good Samaritan statutes. While all states have now passed some type of AED legislation, that legislation differs significantly from state to state in terms of (1) who is protected, (2) requirements for immunity, and (3) what acts are immunized. AED legislation in each state may be found in Table 2.22.1 in this chapter and the immunity is summarized in Table 2.21.1 in Chapter 2.21 *Defenses against Negligence*.

Parties protected may include any or all of the following, varying by state: (1) trained users, (2) any user in a perceived emergency, (3) the entity that acquires the device, (4) the prescribing physician, (5) parties who train others to use the AED, or (6) certified healthcare professionals. A major difference involves the requirements for immunity. Many states offer immunity for **any user** who acts gratuitously and in good faith in a perceived medical emergency to render emergency care. Many other states provide the same immunity, but only to **trained users**. The definition of trained also differs considerably. Some states require that expected users (or employees) be trained, but that a "Good Samaritan" passerby is immune regardless of training. Legislation in a few states seems to legalize the use of the device, but provides no immunity.

There is also great variance in what acts are immunized by the law. At least one provides immunity only where the user acted as an ordinary reasonably prudent person would have acted—seemingly providing no immunity from negligence. Most specify no immunity protection for grossly negligent actions or willful or wanton misconduct—thereby providing immunity for negligence. Several exclude only willful and wanton actions from immunity—thus apparently creating immunity for grossly negligent acts. Several also seem to provide blanket immunity, specifying no restrictions on the immunity of an AED user.

AED Requirement. A number of states (Arkansas, California, Illinois, Indiana, Louisiana, Massachusetts, Michigan, New Jersey, New York, Oregon, Rhode Island, and Washington D.C.) have passed statutes requiring AED availability in health clubs. A number of states now require or encourage AEDs in schools. Colorado, Florida, Georgia, Illinois, Iowa, Maryland, Michigan, Nevada, New York, Ohio, Pennsylvania, South Carolina, Virginia and Wisconsin require devices in at least some schools; however, the degree of implementation varies. Tennessee and California encourage their use.

Requiring availability of AEDs, however, does not always insure that available AEDs will be utilized. In a New York case (*Deguilio v. Gran, Inc.*, 2009), a client collapsed in a health club. An AED was available, but was not used because employees thought it was locked up. After the client died, suit was filed alleging negligence in failing to make the AED easily accessible and/or failing to advise its employees that the cabinet housing it was unlocked. The court ruled that the club had no duty to use a defibrillator because the client had assumed the risk of cardiac arrest by walking on the treadmill. The club was not found liable because it complied with the statute to maintain an accessible defibrillator on the premises. See Chapter 2.33 *Emergency Care* for more information regarding AEDs.

Cardiac Arrest Survival Act (CASA)

In an effort to further combat sudden cardiac arrest deaths, Congress passed the **Cardiac Arrest Survival Act** (2002) (42 *USCS* 238q[2002]). The legislation, like the state legislation preceding it, is designed to accelerate the widespread use of automated external defibrillators by providing Good Samaritan immunity in those states not having such protection. The legislation was intended to augment existing state "Good Samaritan" laws by providing federal liability protection for both users and purchasers of AEDs.

The law specifies that "**any person who uses** or attempts to use an AED device on a victim of a perceived medical emergency is immune from civil liability for any harm resulting from the use or attempted use of such device," including healthcare professionals outside the scope of their license or certification. This immunity to the Good Samaritan user applies regardless of training and protects the user from liability for ordinary negligence. **Any person who acquires the device** is also immune from such liability provided the harm was not due to failure of the acquirer to notify appropriate local entities of the placement of the device, to properly maintain and test the device, or to provide appropriate training to employees using the device.

CASA preempts state law only where the state statute does not provide protection for a user or acquirer. Thus, CASA fills in the immunity gaps left by some state legislation since all users and acquirers are covered by state law (if state statute provides immunity) or by federal law (if immunity is not provided for by state law). When state law fails to protect either the user or the acquirer, CASA provides that protection.

Immunity is not provided by CASA: (1) for willful or criminal misconduct, gross negligence, reckless misconduct or a conscious, flagrant indifference to the rights or safety of the victim who was harmed; (2) for licensed health professionals operating within the scope of their employment; or (3) for certain healthcare providers or lessors of AEDs.

There are also some exclusions that would not normally be relevant to providers of health, fitness, recreation, and sport activities. These are (1) when the person using the device is a licensed or certified health professional acting within the scope of his or her duties; (2) a hospital, clinic or other entity with the purpose of providing health care; or (3) when the acquirer leased the AED to a healthcare entity and an employee caused harm while acting within the scope of the entity.

Shared Responsibility and Statutory Assumption of Risk Statutes

Legislation has been enacted in most states to help protect selected recreation and sport providers from liability for injuries resulting from the inherent risks of particular activities, or in many cases, from certain types of ordinary negligence by the provider. Some of these acts are in the form of shared responsibility statutes while others are more accurately designated as statutory assumption of risk statutes. These acts, originally called **sport safety acts,** usually seek to provide some liability protections for recreation and sport businesses that make certain activities available to the public.

Shared responsibility statutes generally have four distinguishing features. They enumerate the **duties of the recreation or sport provider**. Failure to satisfy these duties constitutes negligence and makes the statute inapplicable. Duties enumerated in such statutes have been deemed to establish a statutory standard of care. The second earmark of these statutes is that they specify **duties of the participant**. Common duties listed include the responsibility to read and obey signs and to stay within the limits of his or her ability. Failure to perform the required participant duties could constitute secondary assumption of risk. Secondary assumption of risk (formerly called contributory negligence) would serve to decrease situations in which recovery for participants is possible and may, at the same time, increase liability of the participant to other participants. Shared responsibility statutes usually contain certain **provisions that preclude recovery**. Most specify that recovery is not permitted when the injury resulted from inherent risks. Many statutes specifically define the inherent risks of the activity or sport, prompting many courts to grant summary judgment based upon the statute. The final feature of these statutes is that **some type of immunity is provided**—or perhaps, more accurately, they reassert that there is *no liability* for injuries resulting from the inherent risks. Some, however, provide that there is no liability unless the provider failed to comply with the specified duties; others provide immunity from liability for certain types of negligence.

Some statutes are more accurately classified as **statutory assumption of risk statutes** since the major provision of the statute is to make clear that the participant is assuming the inherent risks of the activity. These statutes usually do not include duties of the participant. Notwithstanding the differences between these two types of statutes, the characteristic they have in common is that they usually are intended to protect the service provider from liability for injury resulting from the inherent risks of the activity, and in many cases, from liability for injuries resulting from ordinary negligence.

These two types of statutes have been grouped into six categories: (1) equine liability statutes; (2) skiing statutes; (3) skating statutes [*i.e.*, roller skating, ice skating, skateboarding, in-line skating, skate parks]; (4) statutes pertaining to other activities; (5) general recreation and sport statutes; and (6) hazardous recreational activity statutes.

Equine Liability Statutes[4]

State legislatures have enacted equine liability statutes in 44 states. Equine acts usually include horses, ponies, donkeys, mules, hinnies, and in some states, llamas. The laws are designed to protect owners, sponsors, and organizers of named equine activities from liability for equine-related accidents resulting from the inherent risks of the activity, and in many cases from ordinary negligence. Most may be closer to statutory assumption of risk statutes than to shared responsibility statutes since they generally do not specify responsibilities or duties of the participant. While the statutes differ somewhat from state to state, most equine statutes *immunize equine owners from liability for injuries resulting from the inherent risks of equine activities except when the provider*

1. provided faulty equipment or tack that caused the injury;
2. failed to make reasonable and prudent efforts to determine the ability of the participant to engage safely in the activity or determine the ability of the participant to safely manage the particular equine;
3. failed to post warning of known dangerous latent conditions on the facilities; or
4. commits an act or omission that is below the required level of care. The minimum level described varies by state, but includes ordinary negligence, gross negligence, reckless conduct, and willful and wanton conduct.

In general, these statutes do not provide the same protection as that provided by the immunity statutes described in previous sections of this chapter since under most equine statutes the provider remains liable for injuries resulting from some or all negligent acts. Statutes generally define the equine activities covered by the law, the categories of providers protected, the immunity provided, the exceptions, signage requirements, and the inherent risks of equine activities. Usually included in the inherent risks are (1) equine behavior propensities, (2) unpredictability of animal reactions, (3) hazards such as surface and subsurface conditions, (4) collisions with other equines and objects, and (5) the potential of a participant to act in a negligent manner that may cause injury. Equine legislation in each state may be found in Table 2.22.1 in this chapter.

Ski Operator Immunity Statutes

Ski operator statutes were among the first shared-responsibility statutes—*intended to clarify the duties of the ski operator and the skier and to reduce litigation arising from injuries due to the inherent risks of skiing*. At least 27 state legislatures have enacted some type of shared responsibility ski statute. While these statutes differ considerably, they generally include duties of the ski operator, duties of the skier, a listing of the inherent risks of skiing, and the affirmation that the skier assumes the inherent risks of the activity and that the ski operator is not liable for injuries resulting from the inherent risks. Lists of operator and skier duties are generally extensive. These acts generally include no immunity for ordinary negligence, however, in some states, negligence is limited to the failure to perform specified duties.

States approach inherent risks in various ways. Some states (e.g., Tennessee, New Mexico, and Idaho) express that any injury not caused by a violation of the ski operator duties is an inherent risk of the activity and that subsequent legal action is barred. Colorado, North Carolina, and Alaska statutes specify that a violation of the statute by either operator or skier constitutes negligence. Other states require a jury to determine if the risk was inherent. Ski legislation in each state may be found in Table 2.22.1 in this chapter.

---

[4]Convenient access to the complete **equine liability statute** in each state is available on the internet thanks to the work of Holly Rudolph, J.D. All statutes and an informative article by Ms. Rudoph are available at http://www.sportwaiver.com/landowner-liability-under-equine-and-recreational-use-statutes/ and at http://elcr.org/ss2.htm.

Skating Statutes

About twenty states have enacted roller-skating, ice skating, inline skating, and/or skateboarding statutes of some kind. These statutes generally contain four critical sections: (1) duties of the operator—usually including posting of notices regarding duties of skaters and inherent risks of skating; (2) duties of the skater—usually including skating within the range of one's ability, maintaining control of the skater's speed and course at all times, and heeding safety warnings; (3) some of the inherent dangers of skating; and (4) a declaration that the skater assumes the inherent risks and a statement that a skater or operator who violates duties set forth is liable to an injured person in a civil action. Skating legislation in each state may be found in Table 2.22.1 in this chapter. In addition, a number of states have adopted omnibus legislation (discussed later) or recreational user statutes that provide some liability protection for providers of certain types of skating.

Skateboard Parks. Popular types of skating emerging in recent years have included skateboarding, roller-blading, roller skiing, and in-line skating. Several state legislatures have passed legislation protecting providers of facilities for such activities as well as for stunt or freestyle biking.

The Nevada legislature passed a shared-responsibility statute that provides limited protection for an agency or political subdivision of the state that provides skateboard parks for public use. Iowa passed an assumption of risk statute that immunizes municipalities and their employees from liability for injuries resulting from the inherent risks of skateboarding or in-line skating on public property. The injured person must have known or reasonably should have known that the activity created a substantial risk of injury. Likewise, the Utah and Vermont legislatures established statutory assumption of risk statutes providing protection from liability for inherent risks of skating and skateboard-type activities. The Vermont statute encompassed all providers of all sports and the Utah statute included county and municipalities providing facilities for bike riding, biking, skateboarding, roller skating, and in-line skating (see *General Recreation and Sport Immunity Statutes* below). *These statutes have granted protection to governmental providers (except Vermont which included all sport providers) and their employees from liability for injuries resulting from the* **inherent risks** *of the activities.*

California, Florida, and New Hampshire have enacted hazardous recreational activity legislation that includes skateboard parks (see *Hazardous Recreational Activity Immunity Statutes* below). *This legislation grants protection from liability for some types of* ordinary negligence *to governmental entities (and employees) that provide these activities.*

Statutes Pertaining to Other Activities

Immunity statutes affecting other recreation and sport activities have also been enacted. Statutes were found in eight states for sport shooting, five states for outfitters and guides, and four states for snow-mobile operators. Acts for these sports vary significantly by activity and by state. For instance, **sport shooting** statutes designate that the participant (and spectator in Colorado) assumes the inherent risks of the activity. In Utah, the statute names the risks and specifies that the risks that are obvious and inherent are assumed. Utah and Michigan statutes declare that operators are generally not civilly or criminally liable for noise and limit claims of nuisance. However, the Idaho statute protects the operator for liability for injuries incurred because of operator ordinary negligence. **Outfitter and Guide** statutes, usually true shared-responsibility statutes, designate duties of both operators and participants and limit the liability of the outfitter to those specified duties. They usually specify that operators are liable only in the event of negligence. **Snowmobile statutes** usually announce that the operator is not liable for the inherent risks. In some states the immunity is extended to ordinary negligence. They, like the other statutes included in this paragraph, are shared-responsibility statutes as they prescribe duties of participants and operators. Interestingly, in South Dakota, providers renting snowmobiles are liable only if they are grossly negligent.

Statutes found less frequently include **amusement rides, baseball, bicycling, hockey, paddle sports, rodeo, fishing,** and **hang gliding**.

These statutes are as varied as the activities to which they relate. Some are true shared-responsibility statutes, while others are more accurately labeled statutory assumption of risk statutes as they simply declare that the participant assumes the inherent risks. However, regardless of the differences among these statutes, *the common link is that they are all intended to protect the provider from liability for injuries resulting from the inherent risks (and in some cases, ordinary negligence) of the activity.* Legislation relating to these activities may be found in Table 2.22.1 in this chapter.

General Recreation and Sport Immunity Statutes

Six states have enacted laws sometimes referred to as **omnibus legislation** (Spengler & Burket, 2001) that is intended to encompass a large number of activities and sports rather than one or two. The intent is to enact one law that will give immunity from liability for injuries resulting from the inherent risks to the service providers of a number of different sports. These states are Alaska, Hawaii, Utah, Vermont, Wisconsin, and Wyoming. The Vermont statute is the most inclusive, including all sports and all providers and the Utah statute is the least inclusive—protecting only counties and municipalities from liability for rodeo, bike riding, biking, equestrian, skateboarding, roller skating, and in-line skating. Wisconsin and Wyoming protect all providers of more than 20 recreational and sport activities while Alaska lists more than 30 activities. *In each of these states, providers are immune from liability for inherent risks, but retain liability for the negligence of the entity or its employees.* Some of these statutes prescribe duties of the participant and the provider, and thus, could be classified as shared responsibility statutes. In addition, the recreational user statutes in both South Dakota and Washington list more than 25 outdoor activities and serve essentially the same function as the omnibus statutes (see Table 2.22.1 for the statutes).

Hazardous Recreational Activity Immunity Statutes

Legislatures in two states, California and Illinois, have passed statutes similar to the omnibus legislation just mentioned—except for two major differences. First, *the laws protect only public entities and their employees.* Secondly, the statutes protect the service provider and its employees from liability *for at least some types of ordinary negligence.* Protection is not provided (1) for failure to guard or warn of a known dangerous condition, (2) when a fee is charged for participation in the activity (a fee may be charged for entrance into the park), (3) for failure to properly construct or maintain recreational equipment or machinery, (4) when the entity recklessly or with gross negligence promoted the participation, or (5) when the injury resulted from gross negligence or reckless conduct of the entity or its employees. Thus, the entity and its employees are not liable for ordinary negligence except for failure to guard or warn of a dangerous condition and for failure to properly construct or maintain recreational equipment and machinery. In each state, more than 30 sports and activities are included within the protection. California has passed subsequent legislation specifically listing skateboarding as a hazardous recreational activity.

Three other states, Florida, New Hampshire, and North Carolina, have passed similar legislation affecting fewer activities. The Florida and North Carolina statutes protect governmental entities and their employees from liability for ordinary negligence (except the failure to warn of dangerous conditions of which the participant cannot reasonably expect to have notice) for three hazardous activities—skateboarding, in-line skating, and freestyle bicycling. New Hampshire provides immunity from liability for ordinary negligence for municipalities and school districts that without charge provide facilities for skateboarding, rollerblading stunt biking, or roller skiing (see Table 2.22.1 for the statutes).

CASES ON THE SUPPLEMENTAL WEB SITE

Fowler v. Tyler Independent School District, (2007 Tex. App. LEXIS 6433,*;232 S.W.3d 335). Because it is a governmental unit, a school district is immune from suit under the doctrine of sovereign/governmental immunity. Here, the Fowlers claim that since TISD was renting its stadium to the two high schools, TISD was acting in a proprietary capacity at the time of Bridget Fowler's

injury, and therefore was not protected by sovereign/ governmental immunity from suit.

Mounts v. Van Beeste, (2004 Mich. App. LEXIS 2062). This is a case in which the court addresses the issue of whether the equine immunity statute applies.

Thompson v. Rochester Community Schools, (2006 Mich. App. LEXIS 3233). This is an interesting case involving sovereign/governmental immunity of a school, a number of employees, and the lack of emergency care administered to an unconscious student. There is a very informative discussion of gross negligence and proximate cause.

Vaughn v. Barton, 2010 Ill. App. LEXIS 694. In this youth baseball case, coach immunity is claimed based on

the Recreational User Statute and the Sport Volunteer Immunity Act.

Yeater v. Board of Education, Labrae School District, 2010 Ohio App. LEXIS 3139. An injury to a student results in a suit alleging negligence by a student, a teacher, and the school district. Read carefully to learn why the immunity defense failed.

QUESTIONS YOU SHOULD BE ABLE TO ANSWER

1. Explain the intended function of the Federal Tort Claims Act and the state tort claims acts.

2. Give an example that illustrates how a school can lose immunity because of a proprietary act.

3. What are the restrictions placed on qualification for Good Samaritan immunity?

4. What are the main differences between the shared responsibility acts and the statutory assumption of risk laws?

5. Regarding the recreation and sport volunteer immunity statutes, describe the immunity granted to the volunteer and the immunity granted to the organization.

REFERENCES

Cases
Avenoso v. Mangan, 2006 Conn. Super. LEXIS 489.
Chrisman v. Brown, 2007 Tex. App. LEXIS 7745.
Deguilio v. Gran, Inc., 2009 N.Y. Misc. LEXIS 2962.
Feagins v. Waddy, 978 So.2d 712 (Ala. 2007).
Gilbert v. Seton Hall University, 2003 U.S. App. LEXIS 11722.
Heard v. City of Villa Rica, 2010 Ga. App. LEXIS 924.
Kuykendall v. Young Life, 2006 U.S.Dist. LEXIS 81380.
Ola v. YMCA, 2005Va. LEXIS 93.
Van Horn v. Watson, 2008 Cal. LEXIS 14589.

Publications
Brown, J. (1997). Legislators strike out: Volunteer little league coaches should not be immune from tort liability. *Seton Hall J. Sports L., 7*, 559.
Carter-Yamauchi, C.A. (1996). Volunteerism—A risky business? Honolulu: Legislative Reference Bureau.
Centner, T. J. (2000). Tort liability for sports and recreational activities: Expanding statutory immunity for protected classes and activities. *J. Legis, 26*, 1.
Centner, T. J. (2001). Simplifying sports liability law through a shared responsibility chapter. 1 *Va. Sports & Ent. L. J., 1*, 54.
Chalat, J. H. (2000). Survey of ski law in the United States. Vail, CO: CLE International Ski Liability Conference.
Dawson, R. O. (1999). Equine activity statutes: Part I—IV. Online, Internet. www.law.utexas.edu/dawson/horselaw/update1.htm
Jordan, B. (2001). What is the Good Samaritan law? Online, Internet. http://pa.essortment.com/goodsamaritanl_redg.htm
Ridolfi, K. M. (2000). Law, ethics, and the Good Samaritan: Should there be a duty to rescue? *Santa Clara L. Rev., 40*, 957.
Runquist, L. A., & Zybach, J. F. (1997). Volunteer Protection Act of 1997—an imperfect solution. Online, Internet. www.runquist.com/article_vol_protect.htm
Slank, N. L. (1999). A symposium on tort and sport: Leveling the playing field. *Washburn L. J., 38*, 847.
Spengler, J. O., & Burket, B. P. (2001). Sport safety statutes and inherent risk: A comparison study of sport specific legislation. *Journal of Legal Aspects of Sport, 11*(2), 135.
van der Smissen, B. (1990). *Legal liability and risk management for public and private entities*. Cincinnati: Anderson Publishing Company.

2.23 WAIVERS AND RELEASES

Doyice J. Cotten | Sport Risk Consulting

Much has been written regarding waivers and how to write them. Many judges have made suggestions, but the judge in *Cohen v. Five Brooks Stable* (2008) gave what may be the most thought- provoking and insightful statement yet.

> While it is true, as we have seen, that California courts hold releases of liability to a high standard of clarity, it does not in our view require Olympian efforts to meet the standard. **An effective release is hard to draft only if the party for whom it is prepared desires to hide the ball, which is what the law is designed to prevent.** A release that forthrightly makes clear to a person untrained in the law that the releasor gives up any claim against the releasee for the latter's own negligence . . . or that the releasee cannot be held liable for *any and all risks* the releasor encounters while on the former's premises or using its facilities . . . , ordinarily passes muster (*Cohen v. Five Brooks Stable*, 2008, pp. 27–28).

A **waiver** or **release of liability** in the recreation or sport setting is a contract in which the participant or user of a service agrees to relinquish the right to pursue legal action against the service provider in the event that the ordinary negligence of the provider results in an injury to the participant. Injuries in sport and recreation result from one of three causes—(1) inherent risks of the activity (common accidents), (2) negligence by the service provider or its employees, and (3) more extreme or aggravated acts by the service provider or its employees (i.e., gross negligence, reckless conduct, or willful/wanton conduct) (see Chapter 2.11 *Negligence*).

It is important to understand that *the waiver is usually meant to protect the service provider from liability for the ordinary negligence of the service provider or its employees.* It will not generally protect the service provider from liability for degrees of negligence.[5] Although providers are not generally liable for injuries resulting from the inherent risks of the activity, the document can include language that will help protect the provider from liability for injuries resulting from inherent risks (see Participant Agreements later in this chapter). The waiver is an important tool in the risk management arsenal of the service provider.

Although waivers are commonly used by more recreation- and sport-related businesses than ever before, many service providers are still under the erroneous impression that waivers are worthless and offer no protection to the service provider. The validity of a waiver, however, is determined by the law in each state and subsequently, the validity of a waiver will vary depending upon the state.

Cotten and Cotten (2012) have placed each state, some territories, and Washington, D.C. into one of five categories depending upon the degree of rigor required for a valid waiver by the courts in that state. Figure 2.23.1 presents an updated classification of each state, Washington, D.C., Virgin Islands, and Puerto Rico. The first category (Lenient) includes the Virgin Islands and 12 states that not only allow waivers, but also have very lenient requirements for their enforcement. The second category (Moderate) includes 19 states as well as D.C. and Puerto Rico in which waivers are allowed and the requirements for enforcement are moderate in nature. The third category (Strict) includes 14 states that allow waivers, but maintain very rigorous requirements for a waiver to be upheld. The fourth category (Strict or Not Enforced) consists of four states in which the impact of their constitution, legislation, or Supreme Court decisions is unclear. At the very least, waivers will have to pass rigorous standards for enforcement, and at the most, waivers will not protect the service provider from liability for negligence. The final category (Not Enforced) consists of three states in which waivers have been declared unenforceable either by statute or by the state Supreme Court. *Thus, in at least 43 states, D.C., Puerto Rico, and*

---

[5]Waivers in four states (Florida, Illinois, Kentucky, and North Carolina) may be able to protect the service provider from liability for gross negligence. Courts in two states, West Virginia (*Murphy v. North American River Runners, Inc.*, 1991) and Pennsylvania (*Scott v. Altoona Bicycle Club*, 2010) have stated that one may contract to relieve a party of the liability for reckless conduct.

Lenient	Moderate	Strict	Strict Or Not Enforced	Not Enforced
Alabama	Colorado	Alaska	Arizona	Louisiana
Arkansas	*D.C.*	California	Connecticut	Montana
Georgia	Florida	Delaware	Hawaii	Virginia
Kansas	Idaho	Indiana	Wisconsin	
Maryland	Illinois	Maine		
Massachusetts	Iowa	Mississippi		
Michigan	Kentucky	Missouri		
Nebraska	Minnesota	Nevada		
North Dakota	New Mexico	New Hampshire		
Ohio	North Carolina	New Jersey		
South Carolina	Oklahoma	New York		
Tennessee	Oregon	Pennsylvania		
Virgin Islands	Pennsylvania	Utah		
	Puerto Rico	Vermont		
	Rhode Island			
	South Carolina			
	South Dakota			
	Texas			
	Washington			
	West Virginia			
	Wyoming			

FIGURE 2.23.1   **CLASSIFICATION OF STATES, D.C., AND TERRITORIES AS TO THE RIGOR REQUIRED FOR ENFORCEABLE WAIVERS[2]**

the Virgin Islands a well-written, properly administered waiver, voluntarily signed by an adult, can be used to protect the recreation or sport business from liability for ordinary negligence by the business or its employees.

Providers must understand, however, that not all waivers are upheld in lenient states and that many well-written waivers are upheld in strict states. The category simply indicates the degree of rigor or specific requirements that must be met in the state for a waiver to be enforceable. Providers should also be aware that the law is never static so requirements are always subject to change. Providers should also keep in mind that this categorization is based upon the subjective judgment of the authors and will change as state requirements change.

FUNDAMENTAL CONCEPTS

There are a number of terms that are often confused by both students and professionals in recreation and sport. It is important that recreation and sport managers understand the meaning of each term. A **waiver** is a contract by which the participant releases the provider from liability for injuries resulting from provider negligence. A **release** is a term often used synonymously with waiver; however, it can be confusing because *release* also refers to a settlement agreement signed after the injury. An **exculpatory agreement** and **covenant not to sue** are also generally used synonymously with waivers. A **disclaimer** is a statement by which the provider proclaims that the provider is not liable for injury. It is often found on a ticket or on a sign, is not signed by the

---

[2]Cotten, D.J. and Cotten, M.B., 2012.

patron, and is usually ineffective. An **informed consent** is a contract by which a provider informs the signer of the risks and benefits of a treatment or training program. Many erroneously use the term synonymously with waiver; however, it provides no protection from liability for negligence. A **parental permission form** grants permission for the youngster to participate, but it, too, provides no protection from liability for negligence.

Requirements for a Valid Waiver

A waiver is a legal contract and, as such, must adhere to the basic requirements of contract law. Some contract requirements are presented here, but the reader should refer to Chapter 5.10 *Contract Essentials* for more information regarding contracts.

Public Policy

A contract or waiver is not valid if it is against **public policy**—sometimes defined as that principle of law under which freedom of contract or private dealings is restricted for the good of the community (*Merten v. Nathan*, quoting *Higgins v. McFarland*, 1955). A waiver is generally against public policy if (1) it pertains to a service important to the public (*e.g.* medical care, electric power), (2) if the parties are not of equal bargaining power (e.g., employer-employee), (3) the agreement is unconscionable (e.g., grossly unfair to one party), or (4) it attempts to preclude liability for aggravated degrees of conduct such as gross negligence, reckless misconduct, or willful and wanton conduct. *The general rule in most states is that recreation- or sport-related waivers are not against public policy.*

Consideration

A valid contract requires that something of value be exchanged between parties. The courts have held that the opportunity to participate constitutes consideration on the part of the service provider. Waivers usually include language such as "In consideration for being allowed to participate, I hereby waive. . . ."

Parties to the Contract

Three important points relate to the parties involved in a waiver. They are parties relinquishing their rights to redress, parties protected by the contract, and whether parties have the capacity to contract (See also Chapter 5.10 *Contract Essentials*).

Parties Relinquishing Rights. When signing a waiver, the signer is obviously relinquishing the rights of the signer to hold the service provider liable in the event of injury. However, the spouse or heirs often file suit against the service provider when the signer is seriously injured or killed. A phrase by which the signer relinquishes the right of others to recover for injury or death is usually included in the waiver (e.g., on behalf of self, spouse, heirs, estate, and assigns). Providers should be aware, however, that such phrases are not enforceable in all states because some states hold that **loss of consortium**[6] and **wrongful death**[7] claims are independent causes of action and are not derivative upon whether the signer has or would have had a valid claim.

Parties Protected by the Waiver. The waiver must specify the parties protected by the agreement. Parties for which protection is often sought (e.g., corporation, management, employees, sponsors, volunteers) should be listed. One is safer to list all protected parties, at least by category, than to rely on some inclusive phrase such as ". . . and all others who are involved."

Parties Who Do Not Have Capacity to Contract. The third point of importance regards the capacity of the individual to contract. Contract law specifies that certain classes of individuals are not generally bound by contracts. Among those classes are persons lacking mental capacity, those unduly influenced by drugs or alcohol, and persons who have not reached the age of majority (see the following Waivers and Minors section).

---

[6]**Loss of Consortium** is the loss of material services and intangibles such as companionship and sexual relations. The non-signing spouse of a participant suffering serious injury often seeks damages for loss of consortium.
[7]The non-signing spouse or others often seek damages through **wrongful death** actions when the cause of death was a negligent or willful act of another.

Waivers and Minors

The general rule has long been *that a waiver is a contract and that a minor cannot be bound by a contract that is signed only by the minor.* Consequently, while the service provider contracting with a minor is bound by the contract, the minor is not. Thus the waiver will not prevent the minor from taking legal action against a negligent service provider. This general rule is well-supported. In *Dilallo v. Riding Safely Inc.* (1997), a 14-year-old Florida girl signed a waiver absolving a stable of liability. The court held that "a minor child injured because of a defendant's negligence is not bound by her contractual waiver of her right to file a lawsuit." In a Pennsylvania case (*Emerick v. Fox Raceway,* 2004), the court did not enforce a waiver signed by a 16-year-old boy who misrepresented his age in order to enter a motocross race.

Since waivers signed solely by the minor are ineffective, providers have used three strategies in attempting to gain protection. They have (1) required that the parent or guardian sign the waiver on behalf of the minor client (**parental waiver**); (2) required the parent to indemnify the provider [agree to repay the provider for any loss suffered due to the participation of the minor, e.g., monetary award by the court] (**parental indemnity agreement**); and (3) most recently, by requiring the parent to sign a mediation/arbitration agreement by which the parent agrees to submit any claim to mediation and/or arbitration rather than filing a lawsuit (**parental arbitration agreement**). See Chapter 5.30 *Alternative Dispute Resolution* for more information on mediation and arbitration.

Parental Waivers. In the past, parental waivers have not been effective. For example, a 10-year-old girl was injured when another child jumped into a swimming pool on top of her. The girl's mother signed a post-injury release in exchange for a $3275 settlement. Eight years after the accident, upon reaching the age of majority, the girl filed suit against the YMCA. The court stated that "It is well settled in Michigan that, as a general rule, a parent has no authority, merely by virtue of being a parent, to waive, release, or compromise claims by or against the parent's child" and ruled that the YMCA was not protected by the release signed by the mother (*Smith v. YMCA of Benton Harbor/St. Joseph,* 1996). The Michigan Supreme Court reinforced this ruling in *Woodman v. Kera* in 2010.

In recent years, however, courts in some states have begun to enforce waivers and indemnity agreements signed by parents on behalf of their minor children (see Figure 2.23.2). California courts were the first to enforce parental waivers. In 1990, *Hohe v. San Diego Unified Sch. Dist.* made it clear that while minors are free to disaffirm contracts signed by the minor, they cannot disaffirm contracts made by the parent or guardian of the minor. Since that time, numerous California courts have ruled similarly. The Supreme Court of Ohio also ruled waivers signed by parents in favor of non-profit, public service providers are enforceable against the minor child (*Zivich v. Mentor Soccer Club,* 1998). Courts in a number of other states have enforced parental waivers (See Figure 2.23.2). From the figure, one can see that courts in some states have enforced parental waivers only when the defendant is a non-profit entity; others, when a commercial entity was the provider. Five states have enforced parental waivers regardless of the status of the provider.

Trumping a Colorado Supreme Court ruling prohibiting parental waivers, the Colorado Legislature passed a statute allowing such waivers. The Alaska legislature has subsequently passed a statute allowing parental waivers. So, parental waivers are now enforceable in at least nine to twelve states.[5]

Parental Indemnity Agreements and Parental Arbitration Agreements. Courts in two states, Connecticut and Massachusetts, have upheld parental indemnity agreements. Courts in California, Hawaii, Ohio, Louisiana, New Jersey, and Florida have upheld agreements by which parents agreed to submit any claims of the minor to arbitration. Alternatively, courts in Idaho, Pennsylvania, and Texas have ruled that minors are not bound by parental arbitration agreements.

It is also important to understand that the enforceability of parental waivers, indemnity agreements, and arbitration agreements has not been addressed by the courts in most states; for this reason, they may be enforced in a number of those states as well. Consequently, providers in all states might consider the use of such agreements when dealing with minor participants. However, in doing so, the provider should remember two things: (1) always have the parents sign the document and (2) use liability protection in addition to the waiver and/or indemnity agreement.

---

[5]Refer to footnotes in Figure 2.23.2.

Insufficient Information to Predict			Do Not Enforce			Enforces Waivers for		
						School & Community Recreation Waivers	Commercial Recreation Entity Waivers	Both
GA	ID	KS	AL	AR	FL[2]	CT[3]	AZ[4]	AK
KY	MO	MS	HI	IA	IL	FL[5]	IN[6]	CA
NC	NE	NV	LA	MD	ME	ND	MN	CO
NH	NM	NY	MI	MT	NJ	IN	WI[7]	MA
OK	OR	RI	PA	TN	TX		DE	OH
SC	SD	VT	UT	VA	WA			
WY			WV					

FIGURE 2.23.2   LIKELIHOOD OF ENFORCEMENT OF PARENTAL WAIVERS[1]

Format of the Waiver

Waivers are generally found in one of four formats. The first is as a **stand-alone document**—one in which the only function of the document is to provide liability protection for the service provider. The patron is asked to sign a sheet of paper containing only a waiver and related exculpatory material. The second format is the **waiver within another document** such as a membership agreement, an entry form, or a rental agreement (see the example in the Significant Case). The third format is a **group waiver**—which generally includes a waiver at the top of a sheet on which several parties sign (e.g., a team roster, a sign-in sheet at a health club). Both the waiver within another document and the group waiver can be effective when carefully worded and properly administered; however, many courts, and this author, have encouraged providers to use the stand-alone waiver since it reduces the likelihood of ambiguity and can provide much more protection than the shorter agreements. The fourth format is the **disclaimer** of liability, often found on the back on tickets and sometimes in the form of a posted sign. A disclaimer is a statement asserting that the provider is not responsible for injuries. The disclaimer is not signed, provides no evidence that the participant agreed to it, and, with a few exceptions, is ineffective. There is no harm in including such disclaimers on the back of a ticket, but they will only be enforced if the provider has conclusive evidence that the party was aware of the disclaimer. Such evidence is difficult to obtain without a signature by the party. Consequently, the service provider should operate on the assumption that the statement will not effectively protect the business.

Participant Agreement

Since many courts recommend the use of a stand-alone document, that format will be emphasized in this chapter. In fact, the most comprehensive stand-alone document recommended is sometimes called a participant agreement. The **participant agreement** is a relatively new concept in liability protection and is much more than a simple waiver. While the participant agreement includes a basic waiver, it differs in that it (1) is designed to improve the rapport and understanding between the provider and the participant; (2) increases the understanding of the rewards and activity risks of the participant, (3) prepares them psychologically for any

---

[6]Cotten, D.J. and Cotten, M.B., 2012.

[7]A 2008 **Florida** Supreme Court ruling declared parental waivers by commercial entities unenforceable.

[8]Recent Supreme Court rulings in **Connecticut** and **Wisconsin** seem to indicate that any sport- or recreation-related waivers may be unenforceable in those states. At present, the status of parental waivers is uncertain.

[9]A.R.S 12–553 A.2 equine statute allows owners to use parental waivers for liability protection; however, the Supreme Court has interpreted the **Arizona** Constitution to mean that all assumption of risk questions are a matter for the jury and not to be decided by summary judgment. Presumably, the waiver could still be used during the trial.

[10]Parental waivers for school- or community-based activities are still enforced by appellate courts in some Florida jurisdictions.

[11]I.C. 34-28-3 Partial Emancipation for Minors to Participate in Automobile and Motorcycle Racing Act allows waivers and indemnity agreements by certain minors and their parents for participation in professional automobile and motorcycle racing events in **Indiana**.

[12]See the Connecticut footnote above.

discomforts, making legal action less likely; (4) allows participants to make more informed decisions as to participation; and (5) provides a much broader range of protection. The mere existence of a waiver or participant agreement can often deter a party from filing a claim. If a claim is filed, both the waiver and the participant agreement provide the potential for early dismissal.

Content of the Participant Agreement. The participant agreement is much broader in scope than a simple waiver clause or even a broad stand-alone waiver. The contents of the document are meant to provide protections for the provider and to serve as an exchange of information (providing information about the activity to the participant and collecting information about the participant). Suggested content of the participant agreement is listed below.

1. Material meant to inform the participant of the **nature of the activity** and to help them understand and appreciate the risks involved;
2. An **assumption of inherent risks** to protect against liability for the inherent risks;
3. A **waiver** of liability as protection against ordinary negligence. Most states do not require the use of the term "**ordinary negligence**" in the exculpatory language; however any waiver is stronger when this term is used.
4. An **indemnification agreement** to provide further protection against both the risks of ordinary negligence and the inherent risks;
5. Five selected clauses calling for **severability** (provides that if any part of the document is void, the rest remains in effect), for **mediation and/or arbitration** (provides that any resultant claims will be submitted to mediation and binding arbitration rather than entering the court system) [see Chapter 5.30 *Alternative Dispute Resolution*], **venue and jurisdiction** (specifies where legal action must occur and which court has legal authority), **covenant not to sue** (a contract not to sue to enforce a right of action), and an **integration clause** which asserts that this is the entire agreement and supersedes any previous oral or written agreements.
6. Authorizations, assertions, and agreements regarding **health status**, **emergency care**, and **rules and safety** (information that allows the provider to better meet the needs of the participant and provide a safer activity environment); and
7. A **final acknowledgement of release and assumption of risk** prior to the signatures. Space should be provided for signatures by both the participant and the parents or guardians if the participant is a minor.

The scope of this book does not allow the presentation of further detail. For a complete discussion of waivers and participant agreements, including the waiver law in each state and more than 50 guidelines for writing and preparing waivers and participant agreements, the reader is referred to Cotten and Cotten, 2012.

Administering the Waiver

Many waivers fail to protect the provider from liability because of flaws in the administration process. Some administration guidelines that will help to ensure the enforcement of a waiver are:

1. Be straightforward in explaining what the waiver is and what it is intended to do. Do not claim it is just an unimportant insurance requirement or any other false claim. Educate your staff regarding administration and see that they make no false claims.
2. Allow the signer enough time to read the document and provide conditions conducive to reading (e.g., adequate lighting).
3. If the waiver is a group waiver, have an employee explain the waiver to the group if possible. If not, explain it to the group member who will be administering the waiver and stress that he/she communicates the importance to the signers.
4. Do not allow signers to cross out parts of the waiver. Require that all participants (without exception) sign before participating.
5. If clients had to pay a fee in advance and refuse to sign when presented with the waiver, the fee should be refunded. Always inform clients in advance that a waiver will be required.
6. Store your waivers on CDs and retain waivers forever. A discarded waiver offers little protection.

SIGNIFICANT CASE

Stokes v. Bally's Pacwest, Inc. provides an excellent, straightforward example of the value of liability waivers in protecting against liability for negligence in the recreation or sport setting. The case illustrates very clearly the need to make sure the waiver is conspicuous and that the document plainly provides for protection against liability for negligence. When read carefully, one can see that Stokes specifically releases Bally's from liability for Bally's negligence. While the recommended waiver format is the stand-alone waiver, this waiver within another document is better than average and provided effective liability protection to Bally. Observe, also, that the fact Stokes did not read the waiver is irrelevant.

STOKES V. BALLY'S PACWEST, INC.
COURT OF APPEALS OF WASHINGTON, DIVISION ONE
113 Wn. App. 442; 54 P.3d 161; 2002 Wash. App. LEXIS 2233
September 16, 2002, Filed

Opinion: Cox, A.C.J. –

Persons may expressly agree in advance of an accident that one has no duty of care to the other, and shall not be liable for ordinary negligence (Chauvlier v. Booth Creek Ski Holdings, Inc., 109 Wn. App. 334, 339, 35 P.3d 383 (2001)). Such exculpatory agreements are generally enforceable, subject to three exceptions. Because the "waiver and release" language at issue here was conspicuously stated in the agreement that Michael Stokes signed, we reverse both summary judgment orders and direct entry of summary judgment in favor of Bally's Pacwest Total Fitness Center on remand.

Stokes joined Bally's, a health club. He signed a retail installment contract that evidenced the terms and conditions of membership. The contract contained the waiver and release provisions at issue in this appeal. Several months after signing the agreement, Stokes slipped on a round metallic plate placed in a wooden floor at the club while playing basketball. He injured his knee and shoulder. Stokes sued Bally's, alleging that the health club's negligence caused him serious, painful, and permanent injuries. Bally's moved for summary judgment, which the trial court denied. According to the trial court, there were "material questions of fact whether the 'Waiver and Release' provisions set forth in the Retail Installment Contract [that Stokes signed], were sufficiently conspicuous or knowingly consented to by [him]."

We granted discretionary review of that decision. Pursuant to RAP 7.2, we also granted Bally's permission to renew its summary judgment motion in the trial court in order to allow that court to consider this court's then recent decision in Chauvlier. Following Bally's renewed motion, the trial court again denied summary judgment for the same reason that it did before.

* * *

We now focus our attention on the two orders before us. To prevail on his ordinary negligence claim against Bally's, Stokes must establish that the health club owed him a duty. Whether such a duty exists is a question of law. As we recently noted in Chauvlier, our Supreme Court has recognized the right of parties, subject to certain exceptions, to expressly agree in advance that one party is under no obligation of care to the other, and shall not be held liable for ordinary negligence.

The general rule in Washington is that such exculpatory clauses are enforceable unless (1) they violate public policy; (2) the negligent act falls greatly below the standard established by law for protection of others; or (3) they are inconspicuous (Scott v. Pacific West Mountain Resort, 119 Wn.2d 484, 492, 834 P.2d 6 (1992). Neither of the first two of these exceptions is at issue here. The trial court expressly relied on only the third exception in making its rulings, denying summary judgment on the ground that a genuine issue of material fact existed whether the waiver and release clause was inconspicuous.

This court will not uphold an exculpatory agreement if "the releasing language is so inconspicuous that reasonable persons could reach different conclusions as to whether the document was unwittingly signed" (Chauvlier, at 341). Conversely, where reasonable persons could only reach the conclusion that the release language is conspicuous, there is no question of the document having been unwittingly signed. Whether Stokes subjectively unwittingly signed the form is not at issue. Rather, the question is whether, objectively, the waiver provision was so inconspicuous that it is unenforceable.

As we stated in Chauvlier, a person who signs an agreement without reading it is generally bound by its terms as long as there was ample opportunity to examine the contract and the person failed to do so for personal reasons. Here, Stokes admitted that he did not remember reading the waiver and release provision of the contract. But this admission does not end our review. We must still determine whether the waiver and release language is inconspicuous so as to invalidate Stokes' release of Bally's from any duty to him for its alleged ordinary negligence.

We most recently considered whether a release was inconspicuous and unwittingly signed in Chauvlier. The release in that case was printed on a ski pass application. Comparing the release to those considered in Baker and Hewitt v. Miller, n16 we held that the release was sufficiently conspicuous to be enforceable. We noted that the release was not hidden within part of a larger agreement, and that it was clearly entitled "LIABILITY RELEASE & PROMISE NOT TO SUE. PLEASE READ CAREFULLY!." We also noted that the words "RELEASE" and "HOLD HARMLESS AND INDEMNIFY" were set off in capital letters throughout the agreement, and that the release contained the language, just above the signature line, "Please Read and Sign: I have read, understood, and accepted the conditions of the Liability Release printed above."

At the other end of the spectrum of reported cases is Baker (Baker, 79 Wn.2d at 202). There, our Supreme Court held that a disclaimer in a golf cart rental agreement, consisting of several lines of release language printed in the middle of a paragraph discussing other information, was so inconspicuous that enforcement of the release would be unconscionable.

In McCorkle, another division of this court held that a trial court erred in granting summary judgment on McCorkle's negligence claims against a fitness club. The holding was that there were genuine issues of material fact whether a liability statement contained in a membership application McCorkle signed was sufficiently conspicuous.

The provision at issue in that case had as a heading "LIABILITY STATEMENT." In the first few sentences, the provision declared that the member accepted liability for damages that the member or the member's guests caused. The last sentence of the provision stated that the member waived any claim for damages as a result of any act of a Club employee or agent. And nothing in the document alerted the reader to the shift in the liability discussion from liability of the member to waiver of liability for claims against the Club.

The parties now before us cite to other cases, Hewitt and Conradt v. Four Star Promotions (Hewitt, 11 Wn. App. at 78-80; Conradt, 45 Wn. App. at 850). Both are factually distinguishable. In each of those cases, the waiver and release form was in a separate document, not a separate provision in one document

Here, the release is more like that in Chauvlier and unlike that in Baker or McCorkle. In our view, reasonable minds could not differ regarding whether the waiver and release provisions in this retail installment sales contract

were so inconspicuous that it was unwittingly signed. The language is conspicuous, as a matter of law, and it was not unwittingly signed.

The release provision in this retail installment contract, which Stokes signed, must be read in context. Several lines above Stokes' signature is a section in bold type, which states:

NOTICE TO BUYER: (a) Do not sign this Contract before you read it or if any of the spaces intended for the agreed terms, except as to unavailable information, are blank. . . .

THIS IS A RETAIL INSTALLMENT CONTRACT, THE RECEIPT OF AN EXECUTED COPY OF WHICH, AS WELL AS A COPY OF THE CLUB RULES AND REGULATIONS AND A WRITTEN DESCRIPTION OF THE SERVICES AND EQUIPMENT TO BE PROVIDED, IS HEREBY ACKNOWLEDGED BY THE BUYER.

Immediately following Stokes' signature is a line, starting in bold and capital letters, stating: "WAIVER AND RELEASE: This contract contains a WAIVER AND RELEASE in Paragraph 10 to which you will be bound."

Paragraph 10, which is expressly referenced in the line directly below Stokes' signature, is entitled "WAIVER AND RELEASE." It states as follows:

You (Buyer, each Member and all guests) agree that if you engage in any physical exercise or activity or use any club facility on the premises, you do so at your own risk. This includes, without limitation, your use of the locker room, pool, whirlpool, sauna, steamroom, parking area, sidewalk or any equipment in the health club and your participation in any activity, class, program or instruction. You agree that you are voluntarily participating in these activities and using these facilities and premises and assume all risk of injury to you or the contraction of any illness or medical condition that might result, or any damage, loss or theft of any personal property. You agree on behalf of yourself (and your personal representatives, heirs, executors, administrators, agents and assigns) to release and discharge us (and our affiliates, employees, agents, representatives, successors and assigns) from any and all claims or causes of action (known or unknown) arising out of our negligence. This Waiver and Release of liability includes, without limitation, injuries which may occur as a result of (a) your use of any exercise equipment or facilities which may malfunction or break, (b) our improper maintenance of any exercise equipment or facilities,

(c) our negligent instruction or supervision, and (d) you slipping and falling while in the health club or on the premises. You acknowledge that you have carefully read this Waiver and Release and fully understand that it is a release of liability. You are waiving any right that you may have to bring a legal action to assert a claim against us for our negligence.

Unlike the waiver provisions in Baker and McCorkle, this paragraph discusses only Stokes' agreement to release Bally's from liability for its negligence. Stokes' argument that he believed that the paragraph somehow related to release from liability for his financial obligations under the retail installment sale agreement is wholly unpersuasive. As our Supreme Court stated in National Bank, it "would be impossible for a person of ordinary intelligence, much less a person of the intelligence and ability of appellant, to have misunderstood the contents of this instrument upon a casual reading thereof . . ." The same principle applies here. Reasonable persons could not disagree that the content of paragraph 10 is quite clearly a waiver and release of liability for negligence, not financial obligations. Likewise, reasonable persons could not disagree that the waiver and release provisions of the paragraph are conspicuously displayed within the larger document.

Stokes also argues that an exculpatory provision may be placed in a document separate from the retail installment sales agreement, but concedes that this is not required. Bally's counters that RCW 63.14.020 and other laws require that the exculpatory clauses and financial terms and conditions between a health club and its members all must be within one document.

We need not decide in this case whether Bally's' argument is correct. It is sufficient to state that no authority supports the proposition that an exculpatory clause must be contained in a separate document to be enforceable. Rather, what is required is that the release language in a document be conspicuous.

The language at issue in this case is conspicuous and enforceable. Bally's owes no duty to Stokes for his injuries. Summary judgment in favor of Bally's is required.

We reverse both summary judgment orders, and direct entry of summary judgment in favor of Bally's on remand.

WE CONCUR.

CASES ON THE SUPPLEMENTAL WEB SITE

Kirton v. Fields, 2008 Fla. LEXIS 2378. This is the latest state Supreme Court ruling on the issue of parental waivers. Compare the two rationales. Also notice that this ruling applies only to waivers used by commercial businesses.

Moore v. Waller (2007 D.C. App. LEXIS 476). Examine the discussion regarding unequal bargaining power and adhesion contracts. Also of interest is the section regarding the necessity of using the word "negligence." Finally, read and evaluate the waiver used in this case.

Cohen v. Five Brooks Stable (2008 Cal. App. LEXIS 222). Study carefully the court's discussion regarding ambiguity and the use of the term "negligence."

Bailey v. Palladino, 2006 N.J. Super. Unpub. LEXIS 1774. The most interesting points in this waiver case involving a martial arts student are the lack of supervision and the fact that the martial arts business was not named as a protected party in the waiver.

Johnson v. Ubar, LLC., 2009 Wash. App. LEXIS 710. In this case, a lady is injured while working with a personal trainer in a health club. The waiver, found within the membership contract, was not enforced, in part because it was inconspicuous.

QUESTIONS YOU SHOULD BE ABLE TO ANSWER

1. Explain what is meant by the term *public policy* and explain why recreation- and sport-related waivers are generally not against public policy.

2. Contrast the rationale for enforcing parental waivers with that against such enforcement.

3. Other than the waiver of negligence section of the participant agreement, what is the most important component? Defend your answer.

4. In *Stokes v. Bally's Pacwest*, how was the waiver made conspicuous? Why was it important that it be conspicuous?

5. Some people feel that a waiver is "bad" or unethical. Defend their use by a recreation- or sport-related business.

REFERENCES

Cases

Atkins v. Swimwest Family Fitness Center, 2005 Wisc. LEXIS 2.

Bothell v. Two Point Acres, Inc., 1998 Ariz.App. LEXIS 32.

Cohen v. Five Brooks Stable, 2008 Cal. App. LEXIS 222.

Coughlin v. T.M.H. International Attractions, Inc., 1995 U.S. Dist. LEXIS 12499 (Ky).

Craig v. Lakeshore Athletic Club, Inc., 1997 Wash. App. LEXIS 907.

Davis v. Sun Valley Ski Education Foundation, Inc., 1997 Ida. LEXIS 82.

Dilallo v. Riding Safely Inc., 687 S o.2d 353 [Fla. 4th Dist. 1997].

Hanks v. Powder Ridge Restaurant Corporation, 2005 Conn. LEXIS 500.

Hohe v. San Diego Unified Sch. Dist., 274 Cal.Rptr. 647 (1990).

Hong v. Hockessin Athletic Club, 2012 Del. Super. LEXIS 340.

Huffman v. Monroe County Community School, 564 N.E.2d 961 (Ind., 1991).

Lantz v. Iron Horse Saloon, Inc., 717 So.2d 590 [Fla. 5th Dist. 1998].

Kirton v. Fields , 2008 Fla. LEXIS 2378.

Mahoney v. USA Hockey, Inc., 1999 U.S. Dist. LEXIS 19359.

Maurer v. Cerkvenik-Anderson Travel, Inc., 165 Ariz. Adv. Rep. 51 (1994).

Merten v. Nathan, 321 N.W.2d 173, quoting *Higgins v. McFarland*, 86 S.E.2d 168 at 172 (Va., 1955).

Murphy v. North American River Runners, Inc., 412 S.E.2d. 504 (1991).

Pena v, The Rolladium, 2002 Cal. App. Unpub. LEXIS 1466.

Phelps v. Firebird Raceway, Inc., 2005 Ariz. LEXIS 53.

Quinn v. Mississippi State University, 1998 Miss. LEXIS 328 59.

Reardon v. Windswept Farm LLC., 2006 Conn. LEXIS 330.

Rosen v. BJ's Wholesale Club, Inc., 2012 Md. App. LEXIS 100.

Smith v. YMCA of Benton Harbor/St. Joseph, 550 N.W.2d 262 [Mich. 1996].

Swierkosz v. Starved Rock Stables, 607 N.E. 2d 280 (Ill., 1993).

Wabash County YMCA v. Thompson, 2012 Ind. App. LEXIS 428.

Woodman v. Kera, Mich. LEXIS 1125.

Zivich v. Mentor Soccer Club, 1997 Ohio App. LEXIS 1577.

Publications

Cotten, D. J. and Cotten, M. B. (1997). *Legal aspects of waivers and releases in sport, recreation and fitness activities.* Canton, OH: PRC Publishing, Inc.

Cotten, D. J. and Cotten, M. B. (2012). *Waivers & Releases of Liability.* 8th ed. Sport Risk Consulting: www.createspace.com.

van der Smissen, B. (1990). *Legal liability and risk management for public and private entities.* Cincinnati: Anderson Publishing Co.

2.24 AGREEMENTS RELATED TO THE INHERENT RISKS

Doyice J. Cotten I Sport Risk Consulting

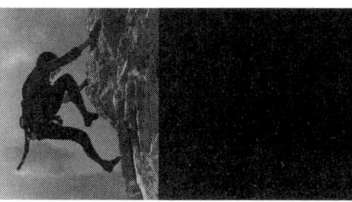

This chapter presents three additional documents that can strengthen defenses for the service provider—the informed consent agreement, the agreement to participate, and the assumption of risk agreement. Each addresses the inherent risks of the activity, training program, or treatment and helps to produce a stronger assumption of risk defense.

INFORMED CONSENT AGREEMENTS

The **informed consent** agreement is a document used to protect the provider from liability for the informed, treatment risks of a treatment, program, or regimen to which the signer is subjected. The factor that makes the informed consent unique is that **something is done to the participant** by another party with the consent of the participant. It may be in the form of medical treatment, rehabilitation, therapy, fitness testing, or a training program (e.g., when one is to be treated for an injury by an athletic trainer, when a participant is to undergo a training program developed by a personal trainer). The document informs the signer of the risks, thereby enabling the signer to make an educated, informed decision. The informed consent is based in contract law, thus the signing parties must be of age. The informed consent offers little or no protection against liability for injuries resulting from negligence.

The doctrine of informed consent derives from two principles: (1) a person's inherent right to control what happens to his or her body and (2) the physician's fiduciary duty to the patient—to warn the patient of risks and make certain the patient knows enough to make an informed decision regarding his or her care. It is an ethical, moral, and legal concept that is ingrained in American culture.

There are two separate, but related, components of informed consent—**disclosure** and **consent** (Nolan-Haley, 1999). The doctrine requires that those who consent be competent (i.e., of legal age, intellectually capable of consent), sufficiently informed about the treatment to enable an educated decision, and consent voluntarily with no duress (Koeberle & Herbert, 1998).

Medicine

Informed consents originated with and have been primarily used in conjunction with the medical profession. The first cases defining informed consent appeared in the late 1950s and were based on the tort of **battery**—the intentional, unpermitted, unprivileged, and offensive touching (physical contact) of the person of one individual by another. Today most medical cases are based on **negligence** since consent is obtained and the issue is whether the consent was adequately "informed." Informed consent is more than simply getting a patient to sign a written consent form—it is a communication process by which the physician provides relevant information to enable the patient to make an educated, informed decision (American Medical Association, 1998). While state law regarding informed consent varies from state to state, generally physicians are required to inform regarding the nature of the proposed treatment, foreseeable risk and discomforts, anticipated benefits, alternative procedures, and instructions regarding food, drink, or lifestyles.

Human Subject Research

A major application of the informed consent has been in the area of human subject research. The American College of Sports Medicine (1999) stated that:

By law, any experimental subject or clinical patient who is exposed to possible physical, psychological, or social injury must give informed consent prior to participating in a proposed project. (p. vi)

The Office of Human Subjects Research of the National Institutes of Health outlines requirements for such research. The consent should (1) be obtained in writing, (2) be understandable, (3) be obtained in non-coercive circumstances, and (4) contain no language suggesting a relinquishment of rights.

Some of the elements that should be included in the consent are: (1) purpose and duration of the research, (2) description of the procedures, risks, and discomforts involved, (3) benefits and compensation to the subject, (4) alternative procedures, (5) confidentiality policies, (6) compensation and treatment available in the event of injury, 7) whom to contact for questions, and (8) a statement of voluntary participation. They specify that the document should be written at a level below that of a high school graduate—making liberal use of sub-heads, avoiding multi-syllable words when possible, and keeping sentences short and understandable (Office of Human Subjects Research, 2000).

Sport and Fitness

In recent years, informed consents have been used more frequently in sport and fitness. Service providers are becoming more aware of the necessity of utilizing informed consents for participants in certain types of programs. Injury rehabilitation programs, fitness testing, and fitness regimens directed by personal trainers are three examples of situations in which the use of informed consents is standard practice.

Koeberle and Herbert (1998) describe the informed consent in the fitness setting as "a voluntary agreement from a client who has been informed of, appreciates, and understands the material and relevant risks associated with participation in the activity or range of activities involved in exercise testing and activity provided through prescription" (p. 52). Since having a client undergo an exercise prescription or fitness test can be construed as either **actual** or **constructive contact**, they stress that an informed consent is necessary to gain the client's permission for contact. Without the informed consent, the fitness professional is risking action for civil or criminal battery. Koeberle and Herbert suggest that informed consents in personal fitness settings do not require consent forms in the same detail as those required of physicians. The trainer is not held to a standard as high as that of the physician since activity programs contain a very low incidence of risk when compared to even the safest medical procedures.

The following guidelines for the content and administration of the informed consent for sport, recreation, and fitness activities are drawn from four sources (Herbert & Herbert, 2002[8]; Independent Review Consulting, Inc., 2000; Koeberle & Herbert, 1998; Oliver & Oliver, 2001).

Content

The content of the informed consent for the recreation, sport, and fitness setting should:

- Be in writing on a preprinted form;
- Be written in plain, understandable language;
- State the purpose of the exercise program, test, or prescribed action;
- Include a general description of the exercise program, test, or prescribed action;
- List any likely discomforts that might be associated with the program, test, or activity;
- List the potential risks and potential benefits of the exercise program, test, or activity;
- Be worded to allow all staff members to have physical contact or interact with the participant;
- Have participant acknowledge voluntary participation;
- Have participant acknowledge that consent was not signed under duress;
- Have participant acknowledge an opportunity to ask questions and have them answered to his or her satisfaction;
- Have participant acknowledge that the participant read and understood the informed consent document.

---

[8]Consult this publication for an in-depth look at the concept of the informed consent.

Administration

The administrative procedures relating to the obtaining and handling of the informed consent can make a difference in the effectiveness of the agreement.

- A separate form should be used for each type of activity (e.g., exercise program, test, rehabilitation, fitness activity).
- The professional should explain the content of the informed consent and give the participant an opportunity to ask and have his or her questions answered satisfactorily.
- The consent form should be signed by the participant and professional, and dated.
- A copy of the consent should be provided to the participant.
- The signed and dated consent should be placed in the participant's file.

If the participant is a **minor**:

- It is imperative that one or both parents sign the agreement;
- The provider should use an informed consent form written specifically for parents of minors;
- The consent should contain language directed to the parent by which the parent gives permission for the activity, acknowledges an understanding of the risks, and signs the agreement.

An illustrative informed consent for personal trainers is presented in Figure 2.24.1. This form is for illustrative purposes only and the reader is cautioned to consult a competent attorney for legal advice regarding such a form.

It is important that the recreation or sport manager understand that the informed consent is important in avoiding liability for injuries resulting from the inherent risks of the activity. It is equally important that the recreation or sport manager remember two things about the informed consent: (1) that the informed consent is contractual in nature, thus requiring the signature of a parent or guardian when the client is a minor, and (2) that the consent provides no protection against liability for injuries resulting from the negligence of the service provider, its employees, or its agents. For such protection, a waiver should be utilized (see Chapter 2.23 *Waivers and Releases*).

Documentation

Herbert and Herbert (2002) stress the importance of documentation and record-keeping when working with individuals who have consented to programs. Just as physicians now must keep detailed notes on patient visits (e.g., complaints, treatments, responses to treatment, instructions), personal trainers, therapists, and other providers utilizing informed consents should do the same. While the extent of documentation required might not be the same, all documentation and notes can serve as evidence and can help the provider recollect the facts if called upon to testify in the event of litigation—sometimes years later. Development and use of a standardized form that includes spaces for the date, signature, and notes is suggested.

AGREEMENTS TO PARTICIPATE

The **agreement to participate** (not to be confused with the participant agreement in Chapter 2.23) is a document intended to strengthen the defenses against liability for injuries resulting from the inherent risks of the activity. The agreement to participate is an agreement by which the signer is (1) made aware of and acknowledges knowledge of the inherent risks of the activity and (2) is informed of the rules of the activity and behavioral expectations and agrees to abide by them (van der Smissen, 1990). The agreement to participate is often used when persons are about to participate in an activity, sport, or class (e.g., extreme sport participants, physical education class members, participants in intramural or recreational programs). The agreement is based in tort law and does not constitute a formal contract; therefore it is an ideal instrument for dealing with minor participants. The agreement differs from the informed consent in that it is not a contract and nothing is *done to* the participant. Rather, the participant is **seeking to participate**.

The agreement to participate, unlike the informed consent, is not a contract. It is simply an agreement by which the participant is informed of the inherent risks and behavioral expectations of participants and affirms

PERSONAL FITNESS TRAINING PROGRAM INFORMED CONSENT

Program Objectives

I understand that my physical fitness program is individually tailored to meet the goals and objectives agreed upon by my personal trainer and myself.

Description of the Exercise Program

I understand that my exercise program can involve participation in a number of types of fitness activities. These activities will vary depending upon the objectives that my personal trainer and I establish, but can include: (1) aerobic activities including, but not limited to, the use of treadmills, stationary bicycles, step machines, rowing machines, and running track; (2) muscular endurance and strength building exercises including, but not limited to, the use of free weights, weight machines, calisthenics, and exercise apparatus; (3) nutrition and weight control activities; and (4) selected physical fitness and body composition tests, including but not limited to strength tests, cardiovascular fitness tests, and body composition tests.

Description of Potential Risks

I understand that my personal trainer cannot guarantee my personal safety because all exercise programs have inherent risks regardless of the care taken by a personal trainer. **I will initial the types of activities (including their risks) that my trainer and I have selected for my program to acknowledge that I understand the potential risks of my training program.**

_____ **Aerobic Activities:** I realize that participation in any cardiovascular activity may involve sustained, vigorous exertion which places stress on the muscles, joints, and cardiovascular system, sometimes resulting in injuries ranging from minor injuries (e.g., muscle soreness, pulled muscles, and musculoskeletal strains and sprains) to the infrequent serious injury (e.g., torn ligaments, heart attack, and stroke) to the rare catastrophic incident (e.g., death, paralysis).

_____ **Muscular Endurance & Strength:** I realize that participation in muscular endurance and strength building activities involves repetitive exertions and maximal exertions which can result in stress-related injuries ranging from minor injuries (e.g., muscle soreness, muscle strains, and ligament injuries) to the infrequent serious injury (e.g., torn rotator cuffs, herniated disks or other back injuries, crushed fingers, and heart attack) to the rare catastrophic incident (e.g., death, paralysis).

_____ **Nutrition and Weight Control:** I realize that the nutrition and weight control program may involve a dietary change, selected nutritional supplements, and regular exercise. I also understand that no nutrition and weight control program is without risk and that some of the risks range from minor concerns (e.g., failure to achieve my goals, muscle soreness, and strains) to the infrequent serious injury (e.g., physical reaction to food supplements or nutrition products, adverse body reaction to weight loss, or heart attack) to the rare catastrophic incident (e.g., death, paralysis).

_____ **Fitness and Body Composition Tests:** I realize that participation in tests can result in injuries ranging from minor injuries (e.g., muscle soreness, pulled muscles, and sprains) to the infrequent serious injury (e.g., torn ligaments, back injuries, and heart attack) to the rare catastrophic incident (e.g., death, paralysis).

Description of Potential Benefits

I understand that a regular exercise program has been shown to have definite benefits to general health and well-being. **I will initial the types of activities (including their benefits) that my trainer and I have selected for my program to acknowledge that I understand the potential benefits of my training program.**

FIGURE 2.24.1 ILLUSTRATIVE INFORMED CONSENT FOR PERSONAL TRAINERS

_____ **Aerobic Activities:** loss of weight, reduction of body fat, improvement of blood lipids, lowering of blood pressure, improvement in cardiovascular function, reduction in risk of heart disease, increased muscular endurance, improved posture, and improved flexibility.

_____ **Muscular Endurance & Strength:** loss of weight, reduction of body fat, increased muscle mass, improvement of blood lipids, lowering of blood pressure, improved strength and muscular endurance, improved posture.

_____ **Nutrition and Weight Control:** loss of weight, reduction of body fat, improvement of blood lipids, lowering of blood pressure, improvement in cardiovascular function, reduction in risk of heart disease.

_____ **Fitness and Body Composition Tests:** learn current status and gain information regarding areas needing improvement.

Participant Responsibilities

I understand that it is my responsibility to (1) fully disclose any health issues or medications that are relevant to participation in a strenuous exercise program; (2) cease exercise and report promptly any unusual feelings (e.g., chest discomfort, nausea, difficulty breathing, apparent injury) during the exercise program; and (3) clear my participation with my physician.

Participant Acknowledgments

In agreeing to this exercise program:

- I acknowledge that my participation is completely voluntary.
- I understand the potential physical risks and believe that the potential benefits outweigh those risks.
- I give consent to certain physical touching that may be necessary to ensure proper technique and body alignment.
- I understand that the achievement of health or fitness goals cannot be guaranteed.
- I have had a voice in planning and approving the activities selected for my exercise program.
- I have been able to ask questions regarding any concerns, and have had those questions answered to my satisfaction.
- I am in good physical condition, have no disability that might prevent my participation in such activities, and have been advised to consult a physician prior to beginning this program.
- I have been advised to cease exercise immediately if I experience unusual discomfort and feel the need to stop.

I have read and understand the above agreement; I have been able to ask questions regarding any concerns I might have; I have had those questions answered to my satisfaction; and I am freely signing this agreement.

_____   _____   _____   _____   _____
Signature of Participant   Name of Participant (Print)   Date   Signature of Trainer   Date

_____   _____   _____
Signature of Parent/Guardian   Name of Parent/Guardian (Print)   Date
(If Participant is a Minor)

_____   _____   _____
Signature of Parent/Guardian   Name of Parent/Guardian (Print)   Date
(If Participant is a Minor)

FIGURE 2.24.1 **ILLUSTRATIVE INFORMED CONSENT FOR PERSONAL TRAINERS (CONTINUED)**

his or her assumption of the inherent risks of participation in the activity. However, like the informed consent, the signer (1) must have knowledge of the nature of the activity, (2) must understand the activity in terms of his or her own condition and skill, and (3) must appreciate the type of injuries that may occur. It is important to the provider that the participant understands these inherent risks and the provider should take steps (e.g., the agreement to participate) to insure this understanding. Since the agreement is merely informative in nature, it can be used when the participant or client is a minor. The signature of a parent is desirable from a public relations standpoint, but is not mandated.

The agreement provides protection in two ways. First, it helps to establish the primary assumption of risk defense by providing evidence that participation was voluntary and that the participant was aware of and assumed the inherent risks of the activity. Second, it strengthens the secondary assumption of risk defense (sometimes referred to as contributory fault) by showing that the participant knew the expected participant behaviors and agreed to adhere to them. By establishing that the participant was aware of the conduct expected, any conduct contrary to expected participant behaviors might be a factor in causing the injury to the participant. For instance, suppose a member of a racquetball class, after instruction prohibiting more than four players on a court at the same time, is injured while playing with five players on the court. His negligent act could be considered a contributing factor to the injury, thereby preventing recovery in contributory negligence states and reducing recovery in comparative negligence states. This, in effect, would either eliminate or reduce any liability by the teacher or provider.

Contents

There are no "magic phrases" that are either legally required or even universally useful in the construction of agreements to participate. There also is no ironclad format that is required. However, certain information should be in any agreement to participate and the following would serve as a logical order for inclusion (Cotten & Cotten, 2012).

Nature of the Activity

It is important that the activity be described in some detail. The description should be specific to the activity and not generic in nature. It should include a description of what the activity is like, remembering that the less familiar the participant is with the activity, the more detail required in the description. Include negative or unpleasant aspects that the participant should expect, how much physical stress is involved, and the intensity level of the activity. Each section of the agreement to participate is illustrated in Figure 2.24.2.

Possible Consequences of Injury

Two areas should be covered in this section. First, the participant should be made aware of the types of accidents that may occur in the specific sport involved. Here one should list some insignificant accidents that are common to the sport (being struck by the ball in racquetball), as well as some serious accidents that occur occasionally (falling and striking one's head on the floor in racquetball). Second, include some of the injuries that can occur in the sport. List some minor injuries that are common to the sport (e.g., bruises, strains, sprains in racquetball), some more serious injuries (e.g., loss of vision, broken bones, concussions), as well as catastrophic injuries (e.g., paralysis and death). Use phrases such as "some of the . . . ," "injuries such as . . . ," and "including, but not limited to . . ." in listing both accidents and injuries.

Behavioral Expectations of the Participant

The major purpose of this section is to transfer some of the responsibility for the participant's safety from the recreation or sport business to the participant. One might list several very important rules to which the participant is expected to adhere. An example in racquetball might be that participants are required to wear eye protection at all times. If there are few rules, they might be listed on the front of the agreement. If there are numerous rules, the participant might be referred to the back of the sheet where they are listed. In either case, giving the participant a copy of these rules would be desirable. Once again, one should not attempt to make the list all-inclusive.

AGREEMENT TO PARTICIPATE AND LIABILITY WAIVER FOR MINORS PARTICIPATING IN THE *ANNUAL 5K FUN RUN*

All physical activities involve certain inherent risks making it impossible to ensure the safety of all participants. The *5K Fun Run* is a vigorous, cardiovascular activity requiring *sustained running endurance, coordination, and running skill.* While the *Club* is using care in conducting the event, it is unable to eliminate all risk from the activity.

It is possible for *runners* to suffer common injuries such as *cramps, muscle strains, and sprains.* More serious, but less frequent, injuries such as *broken bones, cuts, concussions, heart attacks, strokes, paralysis, and death* may also occur. These injuries, and others, may result from such incidents as (but not limited to) *slips and falls, tripping, colliding with another runner, imperfections in the street surfaces, heat-related illnesses, and stress placed on the cardiovascular system.*

All *runners* are expected to follow these safety guidelines:

1. *Wear proper footwear.*
2. *Be alert for unanticipated hazards on the course.*
3. *Do not crowd other runners.*
4. *Consume adequate liquids during the run.*
5. *Follow all announced or posted rules.*

I agree to follow the preceding safety rules, all posted safety rules, and all rules common to *running.* Further, I agree to report any unsafe practices, conditions, or equipment to the *race* management.

I certify that (1) I possess a sufficient degree of physical fitness to safely participate in *the 5K Fun Run,* (2) I understand that I am to discontinue *running* at any time I feel undue discomfort or stress, and (3) I will indicate below any health-related conditions that might affect my ability to safely *complete the run* and I will verbally inform activity management immediately.

Circle: Diabetes   Heart Problems   Seizures   Asthma   Other _____

I have read the preceding information and my questions have been answered. **I know, understand, and appreciate the risks associated with *distance runs* and I am voluntarily participating in the activity. In doing so, I am assuming all of the inherent risks of the sport.** I further understand that in the event of a medical emergency, *management will call EMS to render assistance and that I will be financially responsible for any expenses involved.*

Signature of Participant	Date	Name of Participant (Please Print)
Signature of Parent	Date	Name of Parent (Please Print)
Signature of Parent	Date	Name of Parent (Please Print)

Waiver of Liability: In consideration of being permitted to run in the *5K Fun Run,* on behalf of myself, my family, my heirs, and my assigns, **the undersigned Participant and Parent or Guardian hereby release the club from liability for injury, loss, or death** to the minor, while *participating in the run or while in any way associated with participating in the event now or in the future,* **resulting from the ordinary negligence of the club, its agents, or employees.**

Signature of Participant	Date	Name of Participant (Please Print)
Signature of Parent	Date	Name of Parent (Please Print)
Signature of Parent	Date	Name of Parent (Please Print)

FIGURE 2.24.2   ILLUSTRATIVE AGREEMENT TO PARTICIPATE FOR MINORS

Condition of the Participant

The participant should affirm that he or she possesses the physical condition and required competencies to participate in the activity safely. The required level, which will vary with the activity, should be described in Section I of the agreement. The participant will also affirm that the participant has no physical conditions that would preclude participation in the activity and will identify any conditions of which the recreation or sport business should be aware (e.g., heart problems, seizures, asthma). Particularly for vigorous activities, a statement that the participant should discontinue the activity if undue discomfort or stress occurs should be included. Participant affirmation of condition is generally adequate for activities such as 5K runs, health club memberships, and between-inning promotions at baseball games. Other situations might require more confirmation of condition. For example, residential camps usually require health histories and schools generally demand pre-participatory physical exams prior to varsity competition.

Concluding Statement

This concluding section should contain six items. They are: (1) a statement by which the participant affirms knowledge, understanding, and appreciation of the inherent risks of the activity; (2) affirmation that participation is voluntary, if that is the case; (3) an assumption of risk statement; (4) notice of the procedures to be followed in the event of an emergency and the financial responsibility of the participant for emergency actions; (5) insurance requirements; and (6) a space for the signature of the participant (and the parent if the participant is a minor) at the bottom of the agreement. The critical signature is that of the minor; however, the parent's signature is important for public relations purposes.

Optional Sections

Waiver. This is an optional section that may be used with agreements to participate (see Chapter 2.23 *Waivers and Releases*). This section should follow the signature section of the agreement to participate and provide space for a second signature by the participant (and parent, if the participant is a minor) relating specifically to the exculpatory clause (an illustrative agreement to participate including the critical information is given in Figure 2.24.2).

   Parental Permission Form. This optional section merely gives permission for a minor to participate in the activity—strengthening neither the primary nor secondary assumption of risk defense. Contrary to widespread belief, neither the parent nor child is giving up the right to file suit in the event of injury due to negligence. The form has some public relations value in informing the parent of the activity in which the child will be participating and can be used to gain permission for emergency medical treatment, to assign financial responsibility for such treatment, and to obtain permission for the use of the participant's name and photograph. It may be convenient to include it as a component of the agreement to participate when the participant is a minor.

Using the Agreement to Participate

Some guidelines regarding the use of the agreement to participate can help to insure the effectiveness of the agreement in strengthening the assumption of risk and the contributory negligence defenses. First, presentation of the agreement should be accompanied by a verbal explanation of the risks participants will encounter through participation and of their responsibility for their own safety. Second, it is important to provide an opportunity for the signer to ask questions and gain clarification. Third, stress the participants' duty to inform you of any dangerous practices, hazardous conditions, or faulty equipment of which they may become aware while participating. This, however, in no way reduces or relieves the recreation or sport business of its duty to inspect the facility, examine the equipment, or supervise the activity. In addition, the language used in both the agreement and the verbal explanation should be appropriate to the age and maturity of the participant.

   Finally, keep in mind that the agreement to participate can serve as important evidence in the event of a lawsuit. These records should be safely stored so that they may be retrieved when needed. The time during which a person may file a timely suit varies from one to four years after the injury, depending upon the state. However, keep in mind that a minor who is injured can generally file a suit until one to four years after reaching the age of majority. So in the event of an injury, it would be helpful to make and carefully store a file on that individual which would include the agreement to participate along with all other pertinent documentation (e.g., accident report, written statements by witnesses, parental permission slips).

ASSUMPTION OF RISK AGREEMENTS

The **assumption of risk agreement** is quite similar to the agreement to participate. They both are intended to have the participant acknowledge the assumption of the inherent risks of the activity. Though they may differ in format and length, the assumption of risk agreement is a pact by which the participant or client is informed of the inherent risks of the activity and attests that he or she assumes the inherent risks of the activity. The participant or client further confirms that he or she (1) has been informed of the nature of the activity and its inherent risks, (2) understands the activity in terms of its demands on the participant's own physical condition and skill level, and (3) appreciates the type of injuries that may occur and the consequences of such injuries. Finally, the participant or client should verify that his or her participation is voluntary. The agreement can be used prior to participation in recreation and sport activities, prior to internships, or in almost any situation in which the service provider wants documentation that the participant understood and assumed the inherent risks of the activity. The assumption of risk agreement can be a stand-alone document, but is often (and should be) included as part of a liability waiver. *Regardless of its form, the assumption of risk agreement applies to assumption of the inherent risks and offers no protection against liability for provider negligence.*

As with the informed consent and the agreement to participate, the assumption of risk agreement may contain a written characterization of the nature of the activity and a listing of the inherent risks involved. The listing of the risks should not attempt to be all-inclusive, but should include the likely minor injuries, the unlikely major injuries, and the highly unlikely catastrophic injuries or death. One should not shy away from presenting the possibility of serious injuries.

The assumption of risk agreement used in conjunction with a liability waiver helps to provide more protection for the service provider. The waiver protects against liability for negligence while the assumption of risk statement helps to protect against liability for injuries resulting from the inherent risks of the activity. An assumption of risk agreement used with a waiver is presented in Figure 2.23.1, Chapter 2.23 *Waivers and Releases* and an agreement used without a waiver can be seen in the *Fairchild v. Amundson* Significant Case below.

The importance of an up-to-date assumption of risk statement was made evident in a recent waiver case (*Niedbala v. SL—Your Partners in Health*, 2002). The Connecticut court failed to uphold a waiver when a health club client was injured while lifting weights since the club had no weight lifting equipment when Niedbala signed the waiver. Waiver language included:

> "I understand and am aware that strength, flexibility and aerobic exercise, including the use of equipment, is a potentially hazardous activity. I also understand that fitness activities involve a risk of injury and even death and that I am voluntarily participating in these activities and using equipment and machinery with knowledge of the dangers involved. I hereby agree to expressly assume and accept all risks of injury or death."

The plaintiff argued that at the time he signed the waiver, he was not fully aware of the risks he was assuming because the facility did not contain the equipment he was using. The court stated that it was difficult to see how Niedbala could have foreseen the risk of using equipment that was not even on site at the time of signing and noted that he was inexperienced in the use of weights. The court asserted that the procurement of a new agreement when substantially different equipment is added does not create too great a burden for a sports facility.

King v. University of Indianapolis (2002) illustrates one of the limitations of an assumption of risk agreement. King signed an agreement prior to his death while practicing for varsity football. The agreement would have protected the university from liability had his death been due to the inherent risks, but offered no protection against the allegation of negligence. The case was remanded for trial. On the other hand, the court in *Stowers v. Clinton Central School Corporation* (2006) admitted an acknowledgement and release form into evidence which neither contained the word "negligence" nor relieved the defendant of liability for negligence.

The court said the form was relevant to the defense of incurred risk since it provided evidence that the plaintiff knew and appreciated the risks involved and voluntarily accepted those risks.

Interestingly, some service providers use an assumption of risk clause while under the impression that it is a waiver of liability for negligence. In a health club case in California (*Zipusch v. LA Workout*, 2007), LA Workout included an assumption of risk agreement within its membership agreement. At the end of the assumption of risk, the club included the sentence "The member or guest will defend and indemnify LA Workout for any negligence EXCEPT the sole negligence of the club" p. 3. The club learned that the agreement offered no protection against its negligence.

SIGNIFICANT CASE

This case illustrates perfectly the value of the assumption of risk agreement. Observe in reading the case four different facts that help to establish that Fairchild was aware of the inherent risks of whitewater rafting. It is also important to understand that the assumption of risk document protects Amundson from liability for an injury resulting from the inherent risks of the activity as contrasted with the waiver case in Chapter 2.23 in which the waiver protects the provider from liability for negligence. Note that in this case, negligence was not at issue before the trial court and was, therefore, not considered by the appellate court.

FAIRCHILD V. AMUNDSON

Court of Appeals of Washington, Division One
2001 Wash. App. LEXIS 149
January 29, 2001, Filed

Opinion By: Ronald E. Cox

At issue is whether Wild Water River Tours owed a duty to its customer, Thomas Fairchild, for injuries that he suffered during a rafting trip on the Toutle River. Because the doctrine of implied primary assumption of risk bars Fairchild's claim, we affirm the summary dismissal of this action.

In April 1995, Tom Fairchild participated in a whitewater rafting trip on the Toutle River. Rodney Amundson, d/b/a Wild Water River Tours (WWRT), guided the commercial rafting trip. Fairchild had been on whitewater rafting trips before, and knew that one of the dangers inherent in rafting was the possibility that rafters would fall out into the water. He also read brochures of WWRT that described certain dangers of river rafting.

On the day of the rafting trip, Fairchild and his church group assembled near the river under the supervision of WWRT. Fairchild donned a wetsuit, helmet, and life vest issued by WWRT. The rafters all signed an "Acknowledgement of Risk" form. WWRT guides then instructed them on paddling techniques and safety measures. The safety measures included instructions on maneuvering the raft near logs, rocks, and reversals.

They also included instructions on swimming in the event rafters are in the water, pulling a swimmer back into the raft, and escaping from underneath a capsized raft.

River rapids are classified on a scale from class I (easiest) to class VI (most difficult). The Toutle River has two class IV rapids, one of which is known as Hollywood Gorge (Gorge). The Gorge also contains a "reversal," a point in the river subject to strong downward pressure that may cause a raft to overturn.

As they approached the Gorge, all the rafts stopped, and Amundson and other WWRT guides got out of the rafts and scouted the Gorge. After everyone returned to their rafts and re-entered the river, Amundson's raft successfully navigated through the Gorge to an eddy just beyond the reversal. Amundson then waited for the other rafts.

As Fairchild's raft entered the Gorge, it was sucked into a reversal, and all the occupants were thrown into the water. Amundson observed this from his raft and immediately paddled out of the eddy and into the river's current to retrieve Fairchild. Amundson and others administered CPR to Fairchild, who had been floating face down in the river, and resuscitated him. Thereafter, Fairchild went to a hospital, where he was treated and released the next day.

Fairchild sued. The trial court granted WWRT's motion for summary judgment.

Fairchild appeals.

Implied Assumption of Risk

Fairchild argues that material factual issues exist as to whether the doctrine of implied primary assumption of risk bars his recovery. We disagree.

We may affirm an order granting summary judgment if there are no genuine issues of material fact and the moving party is entitled to judgment as a matter of law. We consider all facts and reasonable inferences in the light most favorable to the nonmoving party. We review questions of law de novo.

The moving party bears the initial burden of showing the absence of a genuine issue of material fact. Once that burden is met, the burden shifts to the party with the burden of proof at trial to make a showing sufficient to establish the existence of an element essential to that party's case. If the claimant fails to meet that burden, the trial court should grant the motion because there can be no genuine issue of material fact given that a complete failure of proof concerning an essential element of the nonmoving party's case necessarily renders all other facts immaterial.

WWRT asserts that the doctrine of assumption of risk bars recovery. That doctrine has four facets: (1) express assumption of risk, (2) implied primary assumption of risk, (3) implied reasonable assumption of risk, and (4) implied unreasonable assumption of risk. Implied primary assumption of risk is at issue here. It occurs where the plaintiff impliedly has consented to relieve the defendant of an obligation or duty to act. With implied primary assumption of risk, the plaintiff engages in conduct from which consent is then implied. If implied primary assumption of risk is established, it bars any recovery.

At summary judgment, WWRT was required to show that (a) Fairchild had full subjective understanding of the nature and presence of a specific risk, and (b) he voluntarily chose to encounter the risk. Knowledge of and appreciation of the specific risk of danger, and voluntariness are questions of fact for the jury, except when reasonable minds could not differ.

Here, WWRT established both elements of implied primary assumption of risk. First, the evidence shows that Fairchild subjectively knew and understood the specific risk of falling into the water and drowning. Prior to the rafting trip, Fairchild read WWRT's brochures describing whitewater rafting on the Toutle River. The brochures listed the Toutle River as a class IV river and described rafting on that river as "fast & furious" and "[y]ou'll never know when you're going to hit crushing waves and bottomless holes." Fairchild testified in his deposition that he had been rafting on a slower river before and wanted a more exciting whitewater rafting trip when he signed up with WWRT. Prior to boarding the rafts, WWRT outfitted Fairchild with a wetsuit, helmet, and vest. It also instructed him on swimming techniques. Moreover, Fairchild admitted in his deposition that getting thrown from the raft into a rushing river was a danger inherent to whitewater rafting on the Toutle River. Reasonable minds could not differ in deciding that Fairchild knew of and appreciated the specific risk of falling into the water and possibly drowning. Likewise, reasonable minds could not differ that Fairchild was aware of the above specific risks when he signed the "acknowledgment of risk" form which states that:

> I am aware that participating in this raft trip arranged by Wildwater River Tours, its agents or associates, that I face certain risks, dangers, and personal property damage. This may include but not be limited to the hazards of traveling down rivers in inflatable rafts, accident or illness in remote places without medical facilities, forces of nature and travel by automobile or other conveyance. In consideration of, and as part payment for the right to participate in this trip and the services and food arranged for me by Wildwater River Tours, and its agents or associates, I do hereby acknowledge all of the above risks. The terms hereof shall serve as my acknowledgment of risk for my heirs, executors and administrators and for all members of my family . . . I have carefully read this agreement and fully understand its contents. (Italics ours)

The above facts all establish that Fairchild knew of the nature and presence of the specific risk of falling into the river and possibly drowning. It also shows that he voluntarily assumed those risks.

Fairchild attempts to establish that a genuine issue of material fact exists as to his subjective knowledge or understanding of the risk of being thrown into the water. We reject this argument.

"When a party has given clear answers to unambiguous [deposition] questions which negate the existence of any genuine issue of material fact, that party cannot thereafter create such an issue with an affidavit that merely contradicts, without explanation, previously given clear testimony." In his declaration, Fairchild stated that he was not aware of the risk of being thrown into the water at the time he signed the "acknowledgment of risk" form. But this contradicts, without explanation, Fairchild's prior deposition testimony in which he admitted that he knew of that specific risk. Thus, Fairchild has failed to establish a genuine issue of material fact on the issue of whether he subjectively knew the presence and nature of the risk of being thrown into the water.

Fairchild also attempts to show that a genuine issue of material fact exists as to whether he voluntarily chose to encounter the risk of being thrown into the water. He contends that because there were no reasonable alternatives available to him to assuming the inherent risks of river rafting, he did not voluntarily choose to assume those risks. We disagree.

Whether a plaintiff decides voluntarily to encounter a risk depends on whether he or she elects to encounter it despite knowing of a reasonable alternative course of action. In other words, the plaintiff must have had a reasonable opportunity to act differently or proceed on an alternate course that would have avoided the danger in order for assumption of risk to bar recovery.

Here, Fairchild chose to encounter the risk of being thrown into the water despite having numerous reasonable alternatives. He could have chosen to take a slower rafting trip. He could have elected to forego whitewater rafting altogether. He could have chosen not to continue with the trip once he reached the starting point or gotten out when his raft stopped and WRRT guides walked on the bank to scout the Gorge. In sum, Fairchild fails to establish a genuine issue of fact as to whether he voluntarily encountered the risk.

Fairchild also argues that he did not assume the risk of WWRT's alleged negligence in operating the raft because he knew that he might fall out of the raft and into the river. This was not an argument that Fairchild made below. Thus, we need not consider it for the first time on appeal. In any event, there is nothing in this record that establishes that any action or omission of WWRT was outside the scope of the risks that are inherent in the sport of river rafting.

We need not address Fairchild's contention that by signing the "acknowledgment of risk" form, he did not expressly assume the risk of falling into the water. WWRT does not argue that express assumption of risk applies to bar Fairchild's recovery. Rather, the issue is whether implied assumption of risk applies. We hold that it does.

Fairchild also asserts that the trial court improperly placed the burden of proof on him "to show that there was negligence rather than [placing] the burden on [WWRT] to show that no reasonable jury could find negligence from the material facts submitted in the record." There was no improper shifting of burden here. WWRT moved for summary judgment based on implied primary assumption of risk. It was then Fairchild's burden to show whether a genuine issue of material fact exists as to the doctrine. He simply failed to do so.

We affirm the order granting defendants' motion for summary judgment.

CASES ON THE SUPPLEMENTAL WEB SITE

McDermott v. Carie (2005 MT 293; 329 Mont. 295; 124 P.3d 168; 2005 Mont. LEXIS 480). No cases involving agreements to participate have been found, however, this case illustrates the value of listing a selection of inherent risks on a waiver. In this Montana case (where waivers are not enforced) the document was admitted with the waiver language redacted to show the plaintiff understood the inherent risks.

Vaughan v. Nielson (2008 Tex. App. LEXIS 6608). This case illustrates failure to obtain an informed consent in a medical situation.

King v. CJM Country Stables (2004 U.S. Dist. LEXIS 7511). This case includes the Hawaii statute which says waivers are enforceable to protect against liability for inherent risks providing there is full disclosure of the inherent risks associated with the activity.

Crase v. Kent State University, 2009 Ohio App. LEXIS 5785. The cheerleader, who was injured by a fall from a pyramid, sued. The defendant university sought protection from an informed consent agreement, but that agreement protected against informed activity risks, not negligence.

King v. University of Indianapolis, 2002 U.S. Dist. LEXIS 19070. A college football player signed an assumption of risk agreement prior to participation and subsequently died in football practice. The university sought protection from the assumption of risk agreement, but it provided no protection from liability for negligence.

QUESTIONS YOU SHOULD BE ABLE TO ANSWER

1. What is the primary difference between an informed consent agreement and an agreement to participate?

2. Which of the three agreements in this chapter requires the signature of a parent? Why?

3. Explain what is meant by "disclosure" and "consent" when writing an informed consent agreement.

4. Explain how an agreement to participate might reduce or eliminate a service provider's liability for negligence.

5. What role did the Wild Water River Tours brochures and their "acknowledgement of risk" form play in the court's verdict in the Significant Case?

REFERENCES

Cases

Fairchild v. Amundson, 2001 Wash. App. LEXIS 149.
King v. University of Indianapolis, 2002 U.S. Dist LEXIS 19070.
Niedbala v. SL—Your Partners in Health, 2002 Conn. Super. LEXIS 2835.
Stokes v. Bally's Pacwest, Inc., 54 P.3d 161 (2002).
Stowers v. Clinton Central School Corporation, 2006 Ind. App. LEXIS 2151.
Zipusch v. LA Workout, 2007 Cal. App. LEXIS 1652.

Publications

American College of Sports Medicine. (1999). Policy statement regarding the use of human subjects and informed consent. *Medicine and Science in Sports and Exercise, 31* (7), vi.

American Medical Association. (1998). *Informed consent*. Online, Internet. www.ama-assn.org/ama/pub/category/4608.html.

Cotten, Doyice J. and Cotten, Mary B. (2012). *Waivers & Releases of Liability*. 8th ed. Sport Risk Consulting: www.createsspace.com.

Herbert, D. L., & Herbert, W. G. *Legal aspects of preventive, rehabilitative and recreational exercise programs.* (4th ed.). Canton, OH: PRC Publishing, Inc.

Independent Review Consulting, Inc. (2000). *Post-approval requirements: informed consent*. Corte Madera, CA.

Koeberle, B. E., & Herbert, D. L. (1998). *Legal aspects of personal fitness training*, (2nd ed.). Canton, OH: PRC Publishing, Inc.

Nolan-Haley, J. M. (1999). Informed consent in mediation: A guiding principle for truly educated decision making. *Notre Dame L. Rev.* , 74, 775.

Office of Human Subjects Research (OHSR) National Institutes of Health. (2000). *Guidelines for writing informed-consent documents*. Online, Internet. http://ohsr.od.nih.gov/info_6.php3

Olivier, S. & Olivier, A. (2001). Informed consent in sport science. *Sportscience*. Online, Internet. www.sportsci.org/jour/0101/so.htm

van der Smissen, B. (1990). *Legal liability and risk management for public and private entities*. Cincinnati, OH: Anderson Publishing.

RECREATION AND SPORT MANAGEMENT APPLICATIONS

2.30

2.31 PREMISES LIABILITY

John Grady | University of South Carolina

"[T]he operator of a commercial recreational [or sport] facility, like the operator of any other business, has a general duty to exercise reasonable care for the safety of its patrons" (*Schneider v. American Hockey and Ice Skating Center, Inc.*, 2001, p. 534).

Premises liability is the body of law which makes the person who is in possession of land or premises responsible for certain injuries suffered by persons who are present on the premises (American Lawyer Directory, n.d.). Black's Law Dictionary (2009) defines premises liability as "a landowner's or landholder's tort liability for conditions or activities on the premises" (p. 1300). It is expected that the owner or operator of a sport or recreation business will provide a reasonably safe environment for all who enter the premises (Seidler, 2005).

FUNDAMENTAL CONCEPTS

Duty of Care

A landowner "owes a duty of reasonable care to guard against any dangerous conditions on his or her property that the owner either knows about or should have discovered" (Restatement (Second) of Torts § 343 (1969)). The specific legal duties owed by the sport or recreation business to its patrons arise not only because the patrons provide the business with an economic benefit and should, therefore, be entitled to protection from harm while on the premises but also because "the operator is in the best position to know of risks, or to discover risks, that threaten customers" (Maloy & Higgins, 2000, p. 35).

The legal duty that a landowner owes to individuals entering his or her premises depends upon the status of the entrant (62 AM. JUR. 2D Premises Liability § 68 [2012]). Persons entering the land are classified into three groups, each of which incurs a different level of care depending on the entrant's relationship with the landowner. The landowner's duty to the entrant varies depending on whether the entrant was an invitee, licensee, or trespasser.

Invitee

"An invitee is a person who has an express or implied invitation to enter or use another's premise," such as a customer to a store (Black's Law Dictionary, 2009, p. 904). *Invitees are owed the greatest level of protection. The landowner is required to maintain his or her premises in a reasonably safe condition under the circumstances. The duty owed to an invitee also extends to warning about known dangers, inspecting the land for hidden dangers, and not exposing the invitee to an unreasonable risk.*

Patrons of sport and recreation businesses would typically be classified as **business invitees** because they are expressly invited onto the land and their presence also provides the business with some economic benefit. For example, spectators at a sporting event or participants in a commercial white water rafting trip would be classified as business invitees. Where the land is open to the public, such as a community park, the visitor would be classified as a **public invitee** since the visitor is invited to enter and remain on the property for a purpose for which the property is held open to the public (Black's Law Dictionary, 2009). A public invitee is owed the same legal obligations by the premise owner as a business invitee.

In *Creely v. Corpus Christi Football Team, Inc.* (2007), Creely was the owner of a cheerleading gym. Pursuant to a contract with the local football team, the Hammerheads, Creely became an official sponsor of the Hammerheads

Cheerleaders and Shark Attack Rowdy Squad. In exchange for various types of advertising, she agreed to organize half-time performances by the cheerleading and tumbling camp participants. During a football game, Creely was getting ready for a half-time performance and was standing 25 to 30 feet into what she describes as a "tunnel," located at the end of the stadium next to the stage. A football from the field flew into the tunnel and hit her, injuring her left thumb. The injury required surgery.

Creely sued the Hammerheads for failing to exercise reasonable care in ensuring her safety during the football event. Creely attached a copy of the agreement she entered into with the Hammerheads. The court found that, by virtue of the agreement, Creely was an invitee on the premises. *The general rule is that an owner or occupier of land has a duty to use reasonable care to keep the premises under his control in a safe condition and to use reasonable care to protect an invitee from reasonably foreseeable injuries.* As the duty of reasonable care applies to stadium owners, the court found that the evidence was sufficient to establish that the Hammerheads owed her a duty of reasonable care.

Licensee

A **licensee** is "one who has permission to enter or use another's premises, but only for one's own purposes and not for the occupier's benefit" (Black's Law Dictionary, 2009, p. 1004). *Social guests of the landowner are often classified as licensees.* For example, a landowner inviting neighbors over to swim in a private swimming pool in the landowner's backyard would be a licensee situation. Licensees are owed the same duties as invitees with one exception, *the licensee is to be warned or protected only from harms of which the possessor of the land is aware; there is no duty to inspect the land for hidden dangers.* When compared to the duty owed to invitees, the lower standard of care owed to licensees is justified if one compares the social guest to a member of the landowner's family. "The guest understands when he comes that he is to be placed on the same footing as one of the family, and must take the premises as the occupier himself uses them, without any preparations made for his safety . . ." (Prosser, 1942, p. 604).

Trespasser

A **trespasser** is one "one who intentionally and without consent or privilege enters another's property" (Black's Law Dictionary, 2009, p. 1643). *Trespassers are owed the least amount of protection, sometimes referred to as "zero duty."* In cases involving a trespasser, the landowner is only required to avoid **willful and wanton misconduct** (See Chapter 2.11 *Negligence*) and to refrain from making the premises more dangerous than the trespasser would ordinarily expect. For example, the landowner could not set a trap whereby the trespasser would be injured upon entering the land.

Attractive nuisance is an exception to the general liability standard for trespassers. Attractive nuisance is defined as "a dangerous condition that may attract children onto land, thereby causing a risk to their safety" (Black's Law Dictionary, 2009, p. 1171). The landowner can be held responsible for creating the dangerous condition because the landowner is obliged to realize that the condition is sufficient to lure persons, particularly children, onto the land. Attractive nuisance can also be applied where the person injured was a trespasser because the landowner should realize that the situation present on his/her land would be both attractive and dangerous. A frequently occurring risk that many landowners may not even think about, but which definitely could give rise to an attractive nuisance claim, is an unguarded trampoline in a homeowner's backyard. The probability of a trampoline luring neighborhood children onto the land is high and this type of recreational equipment can cause serious bodily injury if used improperly, particularly when used at night. Sport and recreation managers must also be vigilant about safeguarding active construction areas on their premises due to the potential for children to be lured into the construction area and become injured by climbing onto heavy-duty construction equipment or a pile of sand or gravel. *Attractive nuisance may also apply to adults if the injury or death was the result of an attempt to rescue the child from danger on the land.* In the recreation context, it is important to recognize that a body of standing water, such as a lake or pond or flowing water, such as a creek, would not be considered an attractive nuisance in the absence of hidden inherent dangers because the danger of drowning is an apparent open danger (*City of Mangum v. Powell*, 1946).

Recreational User

A recreational user is someone who enters upon land for the purpose of engaging in a recreational activity covered under their state's recreational user statute and is recreating on land suitable for the activity and covered under the statute. For example, Arkansas's recreational user statute defines recreational purposes to include hunting, fishing, swimming, boating, camping, picnicking, and hiking, among others (A.C.A. § 18-11-302). Recreational user statutes, in effect, serve as an affirmative defense to claims of negligence by those engaged in recreational activities on the landowner's property (Clark, 1998).

Currently, all 50 states have a type of tort immunity legislation commonly referred to as recreational user statutes (Spengler, Carroll, Connaughton, & Evenson, 2010). "The basic intent of these statutes is to limit landowner liability when allowing people to utilize their land for recreational purposes" (Carroll, Connaughton, & Spengler, 2007). The court in *Conant v. Stroup* (2002), interpreting Oregon's recreational user statute (Or. Rev. Stat. § 105.682), stated the statute's purpose as follows: If landowners "will make their lands available to the general public for recreational purposes, the state will 'trade' that public access for immunity from liability that might result from the use of the property" (p. 275–276). (For additional discussion of the legal benefits that recreational user statutes can offer the recreation or sport provider, see Chapter 2.32 *Property Law* and Chapter 2.22 *Immunity*).

Trend toward the Reasonable Care Standard

The extent of the duty owed by landowners depends upon state law and varies from state to state. While the status of the visitor is still retained in most states, the legislatures or courts in many states have adopted a different standard of care for property owners. Eight states (Alaska, California, Hawaii, Louisiana, Montana, Nevada, New York, and Tennessee) have abolished the distinctions of invitee, licensee, and trespasser for purposes of premises liability (Daller, 2010). They now state that a *landowner owes a duty to act as a reasonable person in maintaining his property in a reasonably safe condition under the circumstances.*

Fifteen states (Delaware, Illinois, Iowa, Kansas, Maine, Massachusetts, Michigan, Nebraska, New Mexico, North Carolina, North Dakota, Rhode Island, West Virginia, Wisconsin, and Wyoming) and the District of Columbia have abolished the distinction between invitee and licensee and have determined that *owners and occupiers of land owe a duty to exercise reasonable care under the circumstances to any person that is lawfully on his or her property* (Daller, 2010). New Hampshire law is less clear. While in the past, the traditional three-pronged classification of entrants on land was in effect for determining the obligations of landowners, landowners now must use reasonable care in the maintenance or operation of their property. However, the court has ruled that the character of and circumstances surrounding the entry is relevant and important in determining the standard of care owed to the entrant (*Ouellette v. Blanchard*, 1976).

Given the variations in state law, it is important for landowners to recognize whether their state retains the legal distinctions for entrants of invitee, licensee, and trespasser. As a practical matter, however, a landowner who maintains a duty of reasonable care, the highest standard of care owed to invitees, should, in theory, always be protected from liability regardless of the status of the entrant.

Factors Affecting Liability

Foreseeability

Premises liability law imposes a duty upon landowners to only protect invitees from foreseeable dangers. In *McPherson v. Tennessee Football Incorporated* (2007), New Orleans Saints player Adrian McPherson participated in a preseason football game between the Saints and the Tennessee Titans in Nashville. Before the start of the second half, McPherson alleges that he was catching punts from the Saints' punter and that while doing so, T-Rac, the Titans' mascot, drove a golf cart in his area and struck and injured him. The court found that Tennessee law imposes a duty upon owners and operators of business premises to protect its customers from probable or foreseeable dangers and noted that this duty has been extended to supervision of athletic events. In another case, *Sall vs. Smiley's Golf Complex* (2006), a golf patron who was struck by lightning and suffered permanent injuries sued the golf course for failing to warn him about the risks of lightning while playing golf. The court found the golf course had no duty to protect or warn patrons of lightning because a lightning strike is not foreseeable.

Actual v. Constructive Notice

While the landowner has a duty to protect invitees from foreseeable dangers, the landowner (or invitor) is not the insurer of the invitee's safety (*Hammond v. Allegretti*, 1974). Before liability may be imposed, the premise owner must have actual or constructive notice of the danger. **Actual notice** refers to situations when the premise owner becomes aware of a problem or defect on the land. For example, an arena manager may discover that a pipe is leaking by discovering water on the floor during a periodic inspection of the restroom. There are a number of other ways for the premise owner to obtain actual notice of a danger. These include being told about it by an employee or patron or, in the worst case, discovering the problem when someone is injured as a result of it.

Constructive notice, on the other hand, arises in situations where the facility manager should have discovered the danger during the course of prudent facility management, including routine facility inspections. If the facility manager would have been aware of the condition by being reasonably attentive, the manager has constructive notice (*Sall vs. Smiley's Golf Complex*, 2006). Establishing that the facility manager had constructive notice may require the use of an expert witness to establish the legal standard of care and to detail what a reasonably prudent facility manager would have done under similar circumstances. For example, in evaluating what is a reasonable time for repair of a broken stadium seat, the expert witness's testimony could establish the reasonableness of the facility manager's actions and whether what was done complied with industry standards. "The determination of what constitutes a reasonable time period between inspections will necessarily vary according to the particular circumstances" (*Zipusch v. LA Workout*, 2007, p. 1293).

In *Stadt v. United Center Joint Venture* (2005), Gary Stadt was injured when he slipped and fell on a puddle of water in the "Standing Room Only" section of the United Center which was hosting a Chicago Black Hawks hockey game. Upon further inspection of the area where Stadt fell, a beer cup was discovered next to the puddle. Stadt sued for negligence asserting that the defendants, including the facility, the team, and the facility maintenance company, were negligent for failing to maintain the premises in a reasonably safe condition. The defendants argued that they did not know of the spilled liquid on which the Stadt allegedly slipped and therefore could not be held liable for his injuries.

Stadt did not argue that the defendants actually knew about the liquid, so the issue before the court was whether the facility had constructive notice of liquid on the floor. "Constructive notice can be established under two alternative theories: (1) the dangerous condition existed for a sufficient amount of time so that it would have been discovered by the exercise of ordinary care, or (2) the dangerous condition was part of a pattern of conduct or a recurring incident" (*Culli v. Marathon Petroleum Co.*, 1988, p. 123). Because Stadt could not show when the spill occurred, he had to rely upon the **recurring incident theory**. Applying this theory, the court found that the spilling of liquids may be characterized as recurring incidents since patrons oftentimes spill drinks in the stadium, including the standing room only section where plaintiff fell. The court held that a dangerous condition that frequently occurs may establish constructive notice because the recurrence of the condition provides opportunities to take measures and rectify or prevent the condition.

"Open and Obvious" Dangers

A premises owner's duty to protect the invitee from an unreasonable risk of harm caused by a dangerous condition on the land generally does not encompass a duty to protect an invitee from **"open and obvious" dangers** (Marks, 2005). For example, a pothole in a stadium parking lot, snow and ice accumulating on an outdoor surface, or a puddle of water on a rainy day would all be considered "open and obvious" dangers because the conditions themselves serve as adequate notice of the danger.

In *Miller v. Dunham's Discount Sports* (2011), plaintiff Marcia Miller broke her foot when she fell while attempting to get off an elliptical machine at defendant Dunham's Discount Sports. There was evidence that the elliptical machine was in a row of machines with only a narrow space of only about three to four inches between each machine. The court of appeals agreed with the trial court that the "close proximity of the machines was an open and obvious danger" (p. 3). Nothing prevented plaintiff from seeing the machines side-by-side in close proximity. Miller even indicated that she noticed their close proximity before getting on the elliptical. The machines' close proximity significantly reduced the available amount of level flooring to get on or off the machine. The court found that "an average person of ordinary intelligence would be aware of the risk of tripping or falling when attempting to get on and off an exercise machine that has been placed three inches away from another machine" (p. 3). The court further explained, "The standard is whether the reasonable person would have gotten on the elliptical, seeing the danger, and whether a reasonable person would have looked before getting off the elliptical" (p. 3).

However, if there are "special aspects" of a condition that make even an "open and obvious" danger "unreasonably dangerous," the landowner still is obligated to undertake reasonable precautions to protect invitees from the danger. In *Mann v. Shusteric Enterprises* (2004), a case involving an intoxicated bar patron who slipped and fell on ice and snow that had accumulated in the bar's parking lot during a blizzard, the court stated that "special aspects" are defined by whether an otherwise "open and obvious" danger is "effectively unavoidable" or "impose[s] an unreasonably high risk of severe harm" to the invitee (*Mann*, 2004, p. 579). Moreover, the court noted that the fact-finder must consider the condition of the premises, not the condition of the plaintiff, effectively minimizing the significance of the plaintiff's intoxication when he fell. A typical open and obvious danger, such as a pothole, would not give rise to these "special aspects" because the condition does not involve an especially high likelihood of injury, a reasonable person would typically be able to see the pothole and avoid it, and there is little risk of severe harm.

While premise owners have a duty to protect invitees from *unreasonable* risks of harm, *they are not absolute insurers of the safety of their invitees. Therefore, where a danger is "open and obvious," the premise owner cannot be held liable for a failure to warn the invitee of the danger.* However, practically speaking, this should not discourage premise owners from warning participants and patrons of any dangerous conditions, including dangers that might not presently exist but frequently occur (Carroll & Baker, 2006, p. 9).

There is one well-known exception to the duty to warn about "open and obvious" dangers. The **distraction exception** applies where the person would be distracted from noticing the "open and obvious" danger and, because of the distraction, fail to take reasonable precautions to avoid the risk of danger. In *Menough v. Woodfield Gardens* (1998), a young man was injured while playing a pick-up game of basketball at the apartment complex owned by the defendant. The basketball court at the complex consisted of a single pole anchored inside a concrete-filled tire. During the course of play, the plaintiff made a "lay-up shot" at the net. When his foot came down, it landed on the tire, snapping plaintiff's ankle. The plaintiff testified that he had not played on the basketball court at the Woodfield Gardens apartment complex prior to the date he was injured. He stated that he first became aware of the tire under the basketball net when he fell on it.

The apartment complex argued that the risk of harm posed by a tire which anchored the pole holding a backboard and net was open and obvious and therefore it owed no duty to remedy that condition. The court found the distraction theory to be applicable in this case because it was reasonably foreseeable that he would have been distracted and fail to see the tire. Therefore, the apartment complex owed a duty of reasonable care to warn the ball player about the presence of the tire.

Limited Duty Rule

An exception to general negligence principles which applies to sport and recreation facilities, notably baseball stadiums and hockey arenas, is the **limited duty rule**. A sports facility operator's limited duty of care has two components: first, the operator must provide protected seating sufficient for those spectators who may be reasonably anticipated to desire protected seats on an ordinary occasion, and second, the operator must provide protection for spectators in the most dangerous section of the stands (*Akins v. Glens Falls City Sch. Dist., 1981*). The second component of this limited duty ordinarily may be satisfied by the operator providing screened seats behind home plate in baseball and behind the goals in hockey (*Akins v. Glens Falls City Sch. Dist.*, 1981).

Edward C. v. City of Albuquerque (2010) illustrates the application of the limited duty rule. In the case, a child was injured by a baseball during pre-game batting practice at Isotopes stadium in Albuquerque, New Mexico. The child was seated in the picnic area beyond the left field wall when, without warning, pre-game batting practice began and a batted baseball went over the wall, struck him, and fractured his skull. On appeal, the New Mexico Supreme Court had to consider what duty owner/occupants of commercial baseball stadiums have to protect spectators from projectiles leaving the field of play. The court also had to decide whether New Mexico should recognize a limited duty for owner/occupants of commercial baseball stadiums. The court held that an owner and/or occupant of a commercial baseball stadium owed a duty that was symmetrical to the duty of the spectator. Spectators had to exercise ordinary care to protect them from the inherent risk of being hit by a projectile that leaves the field of play and the owner/occupant was required to exercise ordinary care not to increase that inherent risk. Factually significant, the court acknowledged that it was alleged that the injured child was not in an area dedicated solely to viewing the game, but was in the picnic area with tables positioned perpendicular to the field of play, described as a multi-purpose area. Given the scope of the duty outlined by the court, summary judgment for defendants based on the limited duty rule was not appropriate and the case was remanded for further proceedings.

Legal Obligations of Sport and Recreation Facility Managers

The sport or recreation manager's duty to use reasonable care to keep the premises under his/her control in a safe condition can be further delineated in terms of five obligations (Seidler, 2005).

Keep the Premises in Safe Repair

Routine maintenance by the facility management and staff is necessary to keep patrons safe while they are engaged in sport or recreation, either as a participant or spectator. For example, a fitness center would have an obligation to re-surface a swimming pool deck where the slip-resistant surface had worn off and an obligation to maintain exercise equipment used by patrons. In *Zipusch v. LA Workout* (2007), a health club member alleged that the club negligently maintained its exercise equipment. This resulted in a sticky substance remaining on a treadmill, causing Zipusch to lose her balance when her foot became stuck to it. In considering whether the health club kept the exercise equipment in working order, the court stated that, "unlike those who run outside on cracked sidewalks speckled with gum, [the plaintiff] and other health club members pay dues in exchange for access to a safe and well-maintained exercise environment" (p. 1292).

Inspect the Premises to Discover Obvious and Hidden Hazards

Periodic inspections are a necessary and expected obligation of facility managers. Through the use of inspection checklists, the facility is able to document that they have taken reasonable steps to discover hazards on the premises and remedy them. In addition to the claims for negligent maintenance, the court in *Zipusch v. LA Workout* (2007), discussed above, also considered whether LA Workout negligently failed to inspect the equipment. The court held that the health club had an obligation to inspect and maintain the equipment. Based on Zipusch's own observations, no staff member inspected or cleaned the equipment in the 85 minute time period prior to the accident. Because of the fact that numerous individuals are engaging in vigorous physical activity at the health club, a reasonable argument could be made that inspection of the premises was especially important, and that the time period between inspections was unreasonably long (*Zipusch*, 2007). Evidence that the facility manager failed to periodically inspect the premises before an accident is normally sufficient to infer that the risk existed long enough for the property owner, in the exercise of due care, to have discovered and removed it (*Ortega v. Kmart Corp.*, 2001).

Remove the Hazards or Warn Others of Their Presence

Once a dangerous condition is discovered on the premises, the facility manager has the obligation to either remove it or warn patrons of its presence. For example, consider college basketball patrons bringing wet umbrellas into an arena and causing the floor to be slippery. This would be a typical situation where the facility manager has an obligation to try to keep the floor dry. In addition, the facility manager would have an obligation to use "Wet Floor" signs near the entrance to warn patrons about the dangerous condition in the entry way. Other commonly occurring hazards in sport or recreation facilities include uneven surfaces or deteriorated materials or equipment.

In *Goldman v. Young Israel of Woodmere* (2010), ten year old Zachary Goldman was injured when he ran into a gymnasium door after running through home plate during a game of indoor kickball. Goldman argued that the owner/operator of the gym was negligent in the placing of home plate too close (two to three feet) to unpadded gym doors. The plaintiff's expert, relying upon alleged violation of guidelines promulgated by the World Adult Kickball Association and the American Society for Testing and Materials Standard (as to padding on the walls and doors), stated that a space of 10 feet from home plate (i.e., a "buffer zone") is needed to allow a base runner to run through the bases. The expert stated that Young Israel should have provided more staff and warnings. The court found that the guidelines and standards relied upon by the expert were neither mandatory nor intended to be the exclusive standards for indoor children's kickball game. Therefore, the court ruled for the defendants, finding that the plaintiffs' expert failed to identify the violation of any specific safety standard which was applicable to a children's kickball game at night in a gym.

For a hazard that cannot be removed, such as the threat of lightning on a golf course, the premise owner still has the obligation to warn participants about the danger that is present. While the golf course in the *Salls* (2006) case obviously could not remove the threat of lightning or other weather-related risks, the golf course's warning procedure was to blow an air horn as a signal to return to the clubhouse in the event of dangerous weather. The golf course's policies or procedures for inclement weather also called for the manager on duty to monitor the local television stations, radar images on the Internet, and visually inspect the weather by stepping outside and to monitor conditions using a weather radio.

Anticipate Foreseeable Uses and Take Reasonable Precautions to Protect

This obligation of the facility owner/operator to **anticipate foreseeable uses and activities by invitees and take reasonable precautions to protect the invitees from foreseeable dangers** takes into consideration the normal uses of the facility and frequently occurring incidents or activities by patrons (e.g., tailgating prior to a football game). In *Hayden v. University of Notre Dame* (1999), a season ticket holder at a Notre Dame football game was injured when, after the football was kicked into the stands, several people from the crowd lunged for the ball in an effort to retrieve it. Hayden claimed that Notre Dame was negligent in failing to protect her. Notre Dame argued that it owed no duty to protect her from a third party's criminal act (arguably a battery). Notre Dame contended that the third party's action was unforeseeable, and that it therefore owed no duty to anticipate it and protect her. Given evidence that there were many prior incidents of people being jostled or injured by efforts of fans to retrieve the ball, the court found that the totality of the circumstances established that Notre Dame should have foreseen that injury would likely result from the actions of a third party. As a result, it owed a duty to Hayden to protect her from such injury.

In the context of premises liability, the **"totality of the circumstances" test** "requires landowners to take reasonable precautions to prevent foreseeable criminal actions against invitees" (*Delta Tau Delta v. Johnson*, 1999, p. 973). "Under the totality of the circumstances test, a court considers all of the circumstances surrounding an event, including the nature, condition, and location of the land, as well as prior similar incidents, to determine whether a criminal act was foreseeable" (p. 972). "A substantial factor in the determination is the number, nature, and location of prior similar incidents, but the lack of prior similar incidents will not preclude a claim where the landowner knew or should have known that the criminal act was foreseeable" (p. 973).

In *Pfenning v. Lineman* (2010), a sixteen year old volunteer was driving a beverage cart during a golf tournament when she was struck in the mouth by an errant ball. The beverage cart did not contain a canopy or a windshield to provide her with some measure of protection from being struck by a flying golf ball. Pfenning contends that the sponsor of the tournament (Whitey's, a local bar) and the Elks, as the owner/operator of the golf course, breached a duty of reasonable care owed to her under the theory of premises liability. She argued that the court should have looked to the "totality of the circumstances" to determine if the defendants breached a duty of care owed to her under the theory of premises liability law. Applying this test, the court ruled that "Pfenning does not assert that a third party's criminal act caused her injury; that the act was foreseeable; or that there had been similar prior incidents" (p. 56). Thus, the Elks and Whitey's did not have a duty to protect her from the danger of an errant golf ball while operating a beverage cart.

Perhaps more instructive to sport and recreation managers who rely on volunteers to staff their events, the court in *Pfenning* found unpersuasive the plaintiff's arguments that, because she was not a participant in the golf tournament, the Elks and Whitey's owed a duty to protect her from harm. The court ruled that, if not for the golf scramble, the volunteer would not have been on the golf course the day of the incident. Although not a player herself, she clearly was "part of the sporting event involved" (p. 52). Therefore, Pfenning, as a volunteer, was deemed to be a participant in the golf scramble and defendants did not owe a duty to prevent her injury.

Conduct operations on the premises with reasonable care for the safety of all. No matter if the sport or recreation business consists of providing amusement at a water park or proving recreational opportunities on intramural fields, the facility manager must conduct operations on the premises in such a way that provides that anyone who comes onto the land will be safe. The golf lightning cases illustrate the point that when a golf course has taken steps to protect golfers from lightning strikes, it owes them a duty of reasonable care to implement its safety precautions properly (*Maussner v. Atlantic City Country Club, Inc.*, 1997). If a golf course builds shelters on the course for golfers who get stranded on the course during inclement weather, it must build lightning-proof shelters (*Maussner*, 1997). Similarly, if a golf course has an evacuation plan, the evacuation plan must be reasonable and must be posted (*Maussner*, 1997). Depending on the industry, there may be an industry standard or customary practice for how best to protect patrons from specific dangers common to that industry, such as lightning strikes on golf courses or how to protect skiers from colliding into snow making equipment on ski slopes.

SIGNIFICANT CASE

The case below illustrates several of the concepts in the chapter, including obligation to provide a reasonably safe environment, obligation to warn of a dangerous condition, and obligation to conduct a reasonable inspection. Specifically, the case discusses negligence claims for failure to provide a safe playing surface due to inadequate maintenance performed by a janitorial staff member. The full case also contains issues related to apportioning economic and non-economic damages in premises liability cases which have been edited here for space reasons. All are commonly raised issues in sport and recreation premise liability actions.

RENEE RODRIGUEZ V. L.A. FITNESS INTERNATIONAL, LLC ET AL.

SUPERIOR COURT OF CONNECTICUT, JUDICIAL DISTRICT OF STAMFORD-NORWALK AT STAMFORD
2011 Conn. Super. LEXIS 3139 (2011)

Opinion

Memorandum of Decision on Defendant L.A. Fitness International LLC's: Motion to Set Aside Verdict (No. 160), Motion for Remittitur (No. 161), and Motion for Judgment Notwithstanding the Verdict (No. 165).

In his Amended Complaint Pursuant to [Conn Gen. Stat. §]52-102b the plaintiff alleged that on March 10, 2008 he was a business invitee at the health club located at 52 Sixth Street, Stamford, Connecticut owned and controlled by the apportionment defendant UB Stamford LP ("UB Stamford"), leased to and controlled by the defendant L.A. Fitness International, LLC ("L.A. Fitness"). He claims that about 7:40 AM on that date was playing basketball with another club member in gym or basketball court of the club when he slipped and fell as the result of water on the gymnasium floor caused by a leak in the premises, sustaining right leg distal and fibular fractures requiring hospitalization and surgical intervention with internal placement of plate and screws, and a second surgical intervention for the removal of hardware and causing a shock to his nervous system and emotional upset and distress all of which prevent him from enjoyment of life as he is entitled. He further alleges that he incurred medical bills and expenses and may continue to do so in the future. He alleges that his fall and resulting injuries were caused by the negligence of the defendants in that they, or their agents or servants allowed or permitted the floor of the gymnasium to be and remain in a slippery, unsafe,

and dangerous condition, failed to warn the plaintiff of that dangerous condition, failed to remedy or repair said conditions when the same was reasonably necessary under the conditions, and failed to make proper and reasonable inspection of the floor area when a reasonable inspection would have disclosed the dangerous condition. The defendants denied any liability for plaintiff's injuries.

Following a five-day trial in June of 2011 the jury awarded the plaintiff $400,000 in economic damages and $4,000,000 in non-economic damages apportioned 65% to the defendant L.A. Fitness and 35% to the defendant UB Stamford. Now before the court are the post-trial motions of the defendant LA Fitness[1] asking the court to set aside the verdict both as to liability and/or as to damages, to order a remittitur as to both economic and non-economic damages awarded by the jury, and to enter judgment in its favor notwithstanding the verdict. The court will discuss these motions together, addressing separately the issues of liability and damages.

* * *

Discussion

A. Liability Issues

Defendant's motion to set aside the verdict and its motion for judgment notwithstanding the verdict are based on the same argument that there was insufficient evidence that defendant had notice of the specific defect that caused plaintiff's fall and injury and can therefore be discussed together. Plaintiff and his basketball companion Robert Velasqez both testified that at approximately

7:40 AM, after they had been playing basketball for approximately five or ten minutes, plaintiff fell while chasing the basketball which had rebounded off the rim when his left foot slipped on an accumulation of water on the court, causing him to fall backward onto his right leg and ankle. Mr. Velasquez described the puddle of water as "about the size of a personal pizza" or 6 to eight inches in diameter. Both the plaintiff and Mr. Velasquez observed one or two drops of water coming down from the ceiling above the spot where plaintiff fell as he was lying on the court awaiting removal to the hospital. Mr. Velasquez took a photograph of the water (which had been covered with paper towels), which picture is an exhibit in the case.

Defendant argues that plaintiff failed to present evidence that L.A. Fitness had legal notice of the defect (the accumulation of water). Citing Pollack v. Gampel, 163 Conn. 462, 468, 313 A.2d 73 (1972), defendant argues that plaintiff presented no evidence that LA Fitness had actual knowledge of the defect or that they were chargeable with constructive notice of it, because, had they exercised a reasonable inspection of the premises they would have discovered it. They further argue under Monahan v. Montgomery, 153 Conn. 386, 216 A.2d 824 (1966), that "notice, whether actual or constructive, must be notice of the very defect which occasioned the injury and not merely of conditions naturally productive of that defect even though subsequently in fact producing it."

***

Viewing the evidence most favorably to the plaintiff, the court concludes that there was evidence from which the jury could reasonably conclude that defendant L.A. Fitness had constructive notice of the accumulation of water on the basketball court which caused the plaintiff's fall, and that it failed to inspect the court within a reasonable time to discover and remove that defect, or take other appropriate safeguards.

Both the plaintiff and Mr. Velasquez testified that they observed water dripping very slowly from the ceiling area above the court (only two drops observed over a period of about thirty minutes after the fall) from which the jury could reasonably have concluded that the accumulation of water had started to occur before approximately 6 AM (about 100 minutes before the plaintiff's fall). Defendant relies heavily on the testimony of Fernando Collazzo, the janitor at the premises, that every weekday[2] his routine was to come in at 4 AM and clean the men's bathroom and locker room and then dry-mop the entire floor of the basketball court finishing at approximately 6 AM. He could not recall specifically if he mopped the court on March 10, 2008, but he testified that he followed the foregoing routine every Monday through Friday morning. But there was testimony that he was not consistent in dry-mopping the basketball court every day. Daniel Boyd, who came to work as a "crisis manager" at the Stamford Club shortly after Mr. Rodriguez' accident testified that when he arrived at the club, Mr. Collazzo's performance of that duty was inconsistent, and that "you would be lucky if it was done twice a week." Cindy Melendez

who was Mr. Collazzo's supervisor at the time, testified that during February and March of 2008 she "had to go after" Mr. Collazzo for not mopping the floor and cleaning glass. The jury had an adequate basis to conclude that Mr. Collazzo did not dry mop or inspect the basketball court on the morning of March 10, 2008 and that, had he done so, he would have discovered water accumulating slowly on the floor in the area where the plaintiff was to fall, and could have prevented this accident from happening. Mr. Collazzo testified that no cleaning was done on weekends, and that the last inspection prior to Monday March 10, 2008 would have occurred the previous Friday afternoon during a "walk-through" just before he went home. The jury also was well within their discretion to conclude that an inspection two and a half days earlier was not reasonable. "The greater likelihood of danger, the greater is the amount of care required in making an inspection of the premises to meet the standard of due care." DeSantis v. New England Furniture Company, 132 Conn. 134, 138, 42 A.2d 792 (1945). It is common knowledge that persons playing basketball will be keeping their eyes mostly on the ball, the basket, and each other, and not looking at the floor they are playing on. It is also common knowledge that, as part of the game, they will run, jump, swerve, and stop suddenly, making themselves prone to falling on any slippery or foreign substance [*9] on the court. With this knowledge, the jury could reasonably have concluded that an inspection on the morning of March 10, before opening the court to play by members, was required in the exercise of due care, and was not performed. This conclusion is further justified by the circumstantial evidence of other accumulations of water observed in this same area both before and after March 10. Most notably Max Jean-Quillaume, a personal trainer at the club, testified that about two weeks prior to March 10, 2008 his nephew was playing basketball on the court and slipped and fell on a accumulation of dripping water in the same spot, fortunately without serious injury. The witness testified that he reported that fall to the front desk of L.A. Fitness. Evidence of prior similar conditions is admissible, and "would often be relevant to prove the existence of the defect relied upon, its nature, and the time when it should have been observed..." Ormsby v. Frankel, 54 Conn.App. 98, 103, 734 A.2d 575 (1999), quoting from Pajor v. Wallingford, 47 Conn.App. 365, 372 n.3, 704 A.2d 247 (1997), cert. denied, 244 Conn. 917, 714 A.2d 7 (1998).

***

Order

For the foregoing reasons, the Defendant L.A. Fitness International LLC's Motion to Set Aside Verdict (No. 160), and Motion for Judgment Notwithstanding the Verdict (No. 165), are denied and Plaintiff's objections thereto are sustained. [*20]

***

Alfred J. Jennings, Jr.
Judge Trial Referee

CASES ON THE SUPPLEMENTAL WEB SITE

Bearman v. Notre Dame, 453 N.E.2d 1196 (Ind. Ct. App. 1983). Pay particular attention to the discussion of duty owed and the foreseeability of harm given prior similar tailgating incidents.

Sciarrotta v. Global Spectrum, 944 A.2d 630 (N.J. 2008). Notice how the court's decision expands the limited duty rule to apply to all activities on the field of play, including pre-game warm-ups as well as clarifies the facility manager's duty to warn spectators in respect of objects leaving the field of play.

Maheshwari v. City of New York, 810 N.E.2d 894 (N.Y. App. 2004). Focus on what factors the court analyzed in determining whether the landowner had a duty to protect the plaintiff from the criminal acts of third parties.

Young v. New Southgate Lanes, et al., 2007 Ohio App. LEXIS 2700 (Ohio Ct. Appeals 2007). What evidence was the plaintiff able to use to try to establish that a negligent act or omission on the part of the business caused her to slip and fall?

Hopkins v. Connecticut Sports Plex, LLC, 2006 Conn. Super. LEXIS 1710 (Conn. Sup. Ct. 2006). Focus specifically on the negligence claims for failure to provide adequate security as well as the alcohol liability issues.

QUESTIONS YOU SHOULD BE ABLE TO ANSWER

1. From a policy perspective, why are business invitees owed the highest duty of care?

2. How and why does the court's willingness to expand the application of recreational user statutes provide additional protection from liability for sport and recreation businesses?

3. If a danger is "open and obvious," how does this fact alter the premise owner's duty to warn?

4. In applying the "totality of the circumstances" test to determine the foreseeability of criminal acts by third parties in a case for negligent security at a sport or recreation facility, what factors might be dispositive?

5. How does the limited duty rule differ from the business invitee rule in terms of the sport facility's duty to protect patrons from the risk of flying objects?

REFERENCES

Cases

Akins v. Glens Falls City Sch. Dist, 424 N.E.2d 531 (Ct. App. N.Y. 1981).

City of Mangum v. Powell, 165 P.2d 136 (Okla. 1946).

Conant v. Stroup, 51 P.3d 1263 (Ct. App. OR 2002).

Creely v. Corpus Christ Football Team, Inc. d/b/a Corpus Christi Hammerheads, 2007 Tex. App. LEXIS 6769 (Ct. App. T.X., Thirteenth Dist. 2007).

Culli v. Marathon Petroleum Co., 862 F.2d 119 (7th Cir. 1988).

Delta Tau Delta v. Johnson, 712 N.E.2d 968 (Ind. 1999)

Edward C. v. City of Albuquerque, 241 P.3d 1086 (N.M. 2010).

Goldman v. Young Israel, 2010 N.Y. Misc. LEXIS 5365 (N.Y. Sup. Ct. 2010).

Hammond v. Allegretti, 311 N.E.2d 821 (Ind. 1974).

Hayden v. University of Notre Dame, 716 N.E.2d 603 (Ind. Ct. App. 1999).

Mann v. Shusteric Enters., 683 N.W.2d 573 (Mich. 2004).

Maussner v. Atlantic City Country Club, Inc., 691 A.2d 826 (N.J. App.Div. 1997).

McPherson v. Tennessee Football Incorporated, 2007 U.S. Dist. LEXIS 39595 (M.D. Tenn. 2007).

Miller v. Dunham's Discount Sports, 2010 Mich. App. LEXIS 2424 (Mich. Ct. App. 2010).

Menough v. Woodfield Gardens, 694 N.E.2d 1038 (Ill. Ct. App. 1998).

Ortega v. Kmart Corp., 36 P.3d 11 (Cal. 2001).

Ouellette v. Blanchard, 364 A.2d 631 (N.H. 1976).

Pfenning v. Lineman, et al, 922 N.E.2d 45 (Ind. Ct. App. 2010).

Saffro v. Elite Racing, Inc. 98 Cal.App.4th 173 (Cal. App. 4th Dist. 2002)).
Sall vs. Smiley's Golf Complex, (136 P.3d 471 (Kan. 2006).
Schneider v. American Hockey and Ice Skating Center, 777 A.2d 380 (N.J. App.Div. 2001)).
Stadt v. United Center Joint Venture, 2005 U.S. Dist. LEXIS 9580 (N.D. Ill. 2005)
Zipusch v. LA Workout, Inc., 155 Cal.App.4th 1281 (Cal. Ct. App. 2007).

Publications

62 Am. Jur. 2d Premises Liability § 68 (2012).
American Lawyer Directory. (n.d.). Premise liability. Retrieved February1, 2012 from http://www.statelawyers.com/Practice/ Practice_Detail.cfm/PracticeTypeID:77
Carroll, M.S. & Baker, T.A. (2006). The use of constructive notice in slip and fall cases in sport facilities. *JOPERD, 77*(8), 8–9.
Carroll, M.S., Connaughton, D.P, & Spengler, J.O. (2007). Recreational user statutes and landowner immunity: a comparison study of state legislation, *Journal of Legal Aspects of Sport, 17*(2), 163–182.
Clark, P.F. (1998). Into the wild: A review of the recreational use statute. *New York State Bar Journal, 70*(5), 22–26.
Connolly, M.J., Black, H.C., Nolan-Haley, J.M., & Nolan, J.R. (2009). *Black's law dictionary,* 9th ed. St. Paul, Minn: West Publ.
Daller, M.F. (2010) Tort Law Desk Reference. New York: Aspen Publishers.
Lewis, J. (1991). Recreational use Statutes: Ambiguous laws yield conflicting results, 27 *Trial , 27,* 68.
Maloy & Higgins. (2000). *No Excuses Risk Management.* Carmel, IN: Cooper Publishing Group.
Marks, J.H. (2005). The limit to premises liability for harms caused by "known or obvious" dangers: Will it trip and fall over the duty-breach framework emerging in the Restatement (Third) of Torts? *Texas Tech Law Review, 38,* 1–71.
Prosser, W.L. (1942). Business visitors and invitees, *Minnesota Law Review, 26,* 573.
Restatement (Second) of Torts (1969).
Seidler, T. (2005). Conducting a facility risk review. In H. Appenzeller, *Risk management in sport: Issues and Strategies* (2nd ed.), 317–328. Durham, NC: Carolina Academic Press.
Spengler, J.O., Carroll, M.S., Connaughton, D.P., & Evenson, K.R. (2010). Policies to promote the community use of schools. *American Journal of Preventive Medicine, 39,* 81–88.

Legislation

Ark. Code Ann.§18-11-302 (2012).
Or. Rev. Stat. § 105.682 (2009).

2.32 PROPERTY LAW

Sarah J. Young | Indiana University

It is important that recreation and sport managers possess a basic understanding of property law because they are responsible for land areas containing sport facilities, parks, and natural attractions, such as lakes, rivers, cliffs, and hiking trails. This chapter will examine property law as it pertains to recreation and sport management with specific focus on real property, recreational use statutes, and nuisance actions.

FUNDAMENTAL CONCEPTS

Real Property

Real property is land and generally any structure that is affixed to, erected on, or growing on the land. Sport facilities are constructed and maintained on real property. It is essential that the recreation or sport manager possess a sound understanding of the legal aspects of acquisition and control of property.

Rights of Real Property

To gain a basic understanding of property law as it relates to recreation and sport, it is important to first identify the rights an organization has under different modes of acquisition. There are basically two types of rights in real property: fee simple absolute and less than fee simple. **Fee simple absolute** is the term used to describe a landowner who has complete control of the property. Swanson, Arnold and Rasmussen (2005) described fee simple absolute as a control that includes "the right to exclude others, to sell or contract away one or more rights, and to make any use of the property not restricted by law" (p. 207). A fee simple title means that the legal holder of the title has the authority to do whatever he desires to the property within the limits of the law.

Less than fee simple describes the use of property that is generally based on a contract. Examples of less than fee simple titles include easements, leases, use permits, and joint use or cooperative agreements (Swanson et al., 2005). The existence of less than fee simple titles is common in recreation, sport, and leisure services. For example, a community sports program conducted by a private association on a school-owned sports complex illustrates a joint use agreement. Additionally, pedestrian access strips across private oceanfront property enabling public access to the beach are easements and examples of less than fee simple rights in real property. It is essential that rights to the easement are clearly articulated in property deeds as illustrated by *Konneker v. Romano* (2010). In a dispute over whether plaintiffs' easement granted riparian rights (i.e., access to waterway or body of water), the court ruled the language of the deed containing the easement was ambiguous.

Modes of Acquisition

A number of modes of property acquisition are available to the recreation or sport manager. The most common one is **purchase** of a parcel of land or a facility. Acquisition of property through purchasing falls under the fee simple absolute category of rights. Typically, when one purchases a piece of property, total control of that land would be assumed. The purchase of property is usually based on a fair market value on which both the buyer and seller agree. However, there are a number of variations that both the buyer and seller may use to make the deal better from each of their perspectives. Buyers may choose to enter into an option to buy with the seller, thereby purchasing the right to buy the property with no other competition until a mutually agreed on date. Sellers may add restrictive covenants into the purchase that dictate how the property may be used. For example, a private off-road club may desire to purchase an open parcel of land from a municipality to be used for dirt bike and ATV trails. However, before purchasing, the buyer notices a noise restriction contained in the purchase agreement. This type of restrictive covenant would be detrimental to the purpose for which the land was to be used by the off-road club. As a result, buyers must be particularly aware of any restrictions in the title.

Gifts are another type of acquisition under the fee simple rights of real property that many recreation, sport, and leisure services agencies can use to their advantage. Property gifts can be made outright by the donor, as part of an annuity plan, or as the result of an individual's will. Although a gift of property is usually considered an asset to an organization, the manager should be aware of possible restrictions or requirements of the gift agreement. This is especially true if the title is not given in fee simple. For example, if a parcel of land is given to an entity, yet the gift is contingent on the performance of some function or service by the recipient, then the entity may want to carefully consider whether the gift is feasible to accept.

Dedication of land is yet another mode of acquisition in real property. This type of acquisition typically corresponds with the fee simple absolute rights. Mandatory or statutory, dedication of land requires land developers to set aside a portion of their development for public use purposes. Because development generally decreases open space, it increases the demand on remaining open spaces or existing park and recreation facilities. This provides the rationale for this type of acquisition (Swanson et al., 2005). Dedication of property can also be a voluntary act whereby a landowner dedicates land for public use. Typically two elements are necessary for a complete dedication: (1) the intention of the owner to dedicate, and (2) acceptance by the public. An example of a voluntary act of dedication is found in a Washington case where in 1899 a private landowner allowed the city to build a road across his property to the beach. The landowner dedicated the right-of-way to the city of Bainbridge Island. In the more than 100 years since this transaction, the property had been subdivided and developed into lots, with several lot owners challenging the public's use of the right-of-way to gain access to the beach area. In an attempt to prevent public access, several lot owners erected a fence and a locked gate barring passage on the road. The court ruled that although the exact property boundary was not known, the intent of the original landowner had been to dedicate the road on his property to the city, the public had accepted the dedication, and the current lot owners were on notice as to the public nature of the area when they purchased their properties (*City of Bainbridge Island v. Brennan*, 2005).

When the owner of property is unwilling to sell his or her land, another mode of acquisition that can be implemented is known as **eminent domain** or **condemnation**. Under the U.S. Constitution, the taking of private property for public use cannot occur without just and fair compensation to the owner. Eminent domain is the power of the government to take private property, whereas condemnation is the vehicle through which this power is generally exercised. Condemnation of private property is appropriate only when the use of the property will be public, the public interests require it, and the property being condemned is necessary to accomplish a public purpose. In recent years a number of states have supported the use of eminent domain and condemnation for the construction of professional sport venues (Hubbard, 2008). This phenomenon is illustrated in *Goldstein v. Pataki* (2008) where a group of Brooklyn, New York property owners challenged an eminent domain taking for the purpose of building a new multi-use urban arena for the New Jersey Nets to be relocated and renamed the Brooklyn Nets. Plaintiffs in the case argued that taking of their homes and businesses for a basketball arena did not meet the U. S. Constitution public use requirement. Further, plaintiffs claimed that behind the project's public benefits façade, the private developer of the project and owner of the Nets would stand to profit most from the project's completion. The court ruled in favor of defendant developers holding that the development of Atlantic Yards would not only provide a stadium for the Nets, but would also provide public open space, creation of affordable housing units and "redevelopment of an area in downtown Brooklyn afflicted for decades with substantial blight" (p. 52).

Related to the taking of property is **adverse possession**—the transfer of property ownership over time in an actual, hostile, open, continuous, and exclusive manner. Dating back to ancient English common law, adverse possession has been used to clarify title to land as well as to discourage property owners from "sleeping on their rights" by neglecting to take the appropriate legal steps to maintain their property. One who claims title by adverse possession cannot simply stretch "one's boundaries to include property beyond one's deed" (*Moore v. Stills*, 2010, p. 72), but must provide clear evidence of actual, continuous, exclusive, visible, and distinct possession usually over a specified period of time. For example in the State of Pennsylvania, the time period for possession is 21 years (*Recreation Land Corp. v. Hartzfeld*, 2008). An example of adverse possession is found in *Hillsmere Shores Improvement Association v. Singleton* (2008), where several residents of a subdivision sought declaration for gaining title by adverse possession of a community beach situated between their lots and a river. For over 20 years, the residents maintained the property, built bulkheads along the waterfront, and were even assessed taxes on the property. The court ruled the residents had fully demonstrated to have acquired title to the property through adverse possession.

Modes of acquisition falling under the less than fee simple rights of real property include easements, leases, and cooperative agreements. These modes of acquisition most often correspond with less than fee simple rights and refer to acquiring the use of property rather than ownership. An **easement** is defined as extending to certain individuals the right to use the land of another for a specific purpose. Affirmative and negative easements are most commonly recognized. An **affirmative easement** allows the right of use over the property of another such as allowing the public access to a road over the private property of a church camp to gain access to their own private lots (*Lyons v. Baptist School of Christian Training*, 2002). A **negative easement**, on the other hand, restricts use in a particular manner. For example, a scenic easement may restrict the construction of facilities to protect a beautiful vista (Swanson et al., 2005). **Leases** are used extensively in sport and recreation situations and are considered a common method of acquiring the use of land or buildings for a specified length of time. Finally, **cooperative agreements** are frequently used to allow two organizations to share the same facilities.

Land Use Controls

In addition to the acquisition of property, the recreation or sport manager must have a basic knowledge of the legal aspects of controlling the use of land under their supervision. A common law device of controlling land use is the public trust doctrine. **The public trust doctrine** provides that submerged and submersible lands are preserved for public use in navigation, fishing, and recreation. "Historically, the doctrine was applied primarily to water and submerged lands under navigable waters" (van der Smissen, 1990, p. 75); however, the doctrine has evolved to apply to dry lands as well. The main purpose of the public trust doctrine is the idea that certain natural resources belong to the public and should be preserved for the good of society. Management and control over the property held in trust cannot be relinquished by transfer of property (Garcia & Baltodano, 2005). Further, it is the responsibility of public agencies to control the use of these natural resources and areas so they can be enjoyed by current and future generations. A New Jersey case concerning whether the public has a right to use the area of the beach above the mean high water mark of ocean front property illustrates the application of the public trust doctrine. Defendant landowners attempted to prevent plaintiff from sitting on their private beach. Yet, the court ruled the property line of an owner of oceanfront property only extends to the high water mark with all property below that line considered as public. The public had a right to use oceanfront property held in trust for recreational activities such as sunbathing and swimming (*Bubis v. Kassin*, 2008).

Another type of land use control commonly implemented in recreation is **zoning**, defined as dividing "a municipality into geographical districts or zones and then regulating the nature and use of land in the various zones" (van der Smissen, 1990, p. 78). The regulation extends not only to the development of the land, but also to the structures on the land and the activities conducted thereon. Further, van der Smissen explained "zoning is primarily a legislative function of the municipality and represents judgment of the elected governing body as to how land should be utilized within its jurisdiction" (p. 79). In California, a private nonprofit water ski club purchased an island designated as open space and zoned as agricultural. The county's zoning ordinances allowed no more than one single-family residence per five-acre parcel of land. Over 35 years, however, the water ski club built 28 residential units and docks on the five-acre island. Because the water ski club had knowingly violated the county's zoning ordinance and land use requirement, the court ruled in favor of the county demolishing all but one structure on the island (*Golden Gate Water Ski Club v. County of Contra Costa*, 2008).

The **control of activities** and the use of property are central to the issue of zoning. Zoning regulations generally correspond with a governmental agency's comprehensive plan to avoid claims of arbitrary or unreasonable zoning ordinances. This also ensures the proper use and development of property for current and future public needs. In Michigan, a township government was successful in permanently enjoining a private landowner from using his property as a hunting and gun club. The appellate court ruled the township was within its statutory authority to enact zoning ordinances and regulate the use of the land. In order to continue to engage in various shooting activities on his property, the landowner was required to seek special land use permits allowing for those activities (*Smolarz v. Colon Township*, 2005).

Recreational User Statutes

Recreational user statutes are legislative acts that are established in all states for the purpose of protecting land-owners from liability if they permit the public to use their property for recreation at no cost to the user (see Chapter 2.22, *Immunity*). In 1965, the Council of State Governments addressed a growing need in the United States for more recreational land by recommending that states pass an act known as the Model Act encouraging private landowners to open their property to the public for recreational enjoyment and use. Legislation of this type was eventually adopted by all 50 states but with a great deal of variation by state. As a result, one should be familiar with the aspects of the statute for a specific state. Yet, the overall essence of the statute is that land-owners owe no duty to recreational users of their property (*Matheny v. United States*, 2006) creating a defense against ordinary negligence claims, but not claims for willful and wanton conduct (*Webb v. City of Richland*, 2011). A listing by state, a link to each entire statute, and summary of each state recreational user statute is provided by Holly Rudolph in one convenient location (Rudolph, 2010)[9].

General Characteristics

Although each state has its own variation of the recreational user statute and interpretations through case law, there are several characteristics of the statute common to most states. These common denominators are discussed following.

The first of these characteristics is that the statute only applies to the **owner of the land**. In some states, the immunity protection provided by the statute is targeted toward private landowners, whereas in other states owners of public lands (i.e., local, state, and federal government agencies) are also afforded immunity. The original intent of the Model Act was to encourage private landowners to open their property to the public for recreational use. For example, a private landowner attempted to use the Illinois recreational use statute as a defense to a negligence claim of a woman injured on a luge-like sled run built in his backyard. The Illinois Supreme Court ruled that defendant was not shielded from liability by the state's recreational use statute because his sled run was not open to the public, but only to invited guests (*Hall v. Henn*, 2003). A number of states have broadened their interpretation from the private landowner to any property owner, lessees, tenants, occupants, or persons controlling the premises. As a result, many public agencies now look to recreational use statutes as an alternative source of immunity. For example in *Yagle v. United States* (2009) plaintiff was operating his ATV at Steele Peak in California on property owned by the federal government through the Bureau of Land Management (BLM). While riding his ATV, plaintiff fell into an abandoned mineshaft and was injured. To reach the mineshaft, plaintiff had traveled off-road, uphill, and off designated trails. There were signs in the area advising riders to stay on trails and to not climb the hills as the terrain was uneven and covered in heavy vegetation. Plaintiff sued for the extent of his injuries he alleged were negligently caused by BLM. Under the California recreational use statute, plaintiff's claim was barred because landowners are not liable for negligence to individuals using their lands for recreational purposes. In another case, a municipality in Montana was protected by the state's recreational use statute after plaintiff fell through a damaged plank on a city-owned dock where he was fishing (*Jobe v. City of Polson*, 2004).

The broad interpretation of qualified property owners by many states has led to the practice of school districts also seeking protection under recreational user statutes. In *Auman v. School District of Stanley-Boyd* (2001), the Wisconsin court specifically addressed the issue of whether a school district could seek protection under the statute. Although the recreational user statute did not apply in the *Auman* case, a number of school districts have successfully defended themselves from liability for negligence using their state's statute (*Fritts v. Clover Park School District*, 2003; *Poston v. Unified School District No. 387*, 2008).

A second characteristic of the recreational user statute is that the landowner **cannot charge a fee** for individuals to use the premises. Although most state statutes have provided that immunity will not apply if a fee is charged, there is some variation among the states as to how "fee" is interpreted. Most courts have maintained

---

[9]Convenient access to the complete recreational user statutes in every state is available on the internet thanks to the work of Holly Rudolph, J.D. All statutes and an informative article by Ms. Rudoph are available at http://www.sportwaiver.com/landowner-liability-under-equine-and-recreational-use-statutes/. They may also be found at http://elcr.org/ss2.htm.

immunity for landowners except where an actual fee has been charged for entry onto the land. This type of charge is a narrow interpretation of the law, which requires an explicit quid pro quo arrangement of payment in exchange for admission onto the premises. For example, in *Albertson v. Fremont County* (2011) plaintiff was killed when his snowmobile trail located on national forest lands intersected with a state highway and he was struck by a vehicle. In the negligence suit that followed, plaintiff's family argued that warning signs or traffic control signals should have been placed at the intersection to warn both snowmobile operators and motorists. The National Forest Service argued immunity under the Idaho Recreational Use statute even though plaintiff had been required to pay a $31 fee to register his snowmobile prior to using the trails. While plaintiffs argued this constituted a fee, the court ruled the fee was not charged for entry onto the public land, thereby allowing defendant immunity under the Idaho state statute. Illustrating another perspective of the quid pro quo arrangement, the Oregon Supreme Court ruled the recreational use statute did not apply to a state park where plaintiff was injured while riding his bike. The state park had charged plaintiff a fee to camp at the park, and as campers, plaintiff and his wife were entitled to use all park facilities including the bike trails. The court ruled that when the fee was charged for permission to use the land, even if plaintiff was not engaged in camping, he was engaged in a recreational pursuit, and defendant forfeited its immunity (*Coleman v. Oregon Parks & Recreation Dept.*, 2009).

A third characteristic of the recreational user statute is that land is being used for a **recreational purpose**. The interpretation of this characteristic varies widely from state to state with a number of states applying the statute to developed recreational facilities such as ball fields, playgrounds, and swimming pools. For example, in California, a court ruled that the statute provided defendant immunity after plaintiff fell while exploring unguarded mine shafts in the Dumont Dunes area of the southern part of the state (*Schafer v. United States of America*, 2011). In *Scott v. United States* (2011) plaintiff was attending a private party in the Officer's Club at the Naval Station in Newport, Rhode Island when she slipped and fell on wet stairs. Partying and social events fell within the broad definition of recreational activity resulting in defendant successfully seeking immunity under the state's recreational use statute.

A final general characteristic of the recreational user statute involves **obligations of the landowner**. The owner's only obligation under the statute is to provide a warning for any known concealed danger that would not be apparent to the recreational user. Owners have no duty to warn of open and obvious hazards, nor do they have a duty to warn of conditions that are unknown to them. A Kentucky case involving a skate park illustrates this characteristic. An 11-year-old boy was seriously injured when he inadvertently rode his bike from the beginner's section of a municipal skate park into the advanced section of the park, which contained an 11-foot bowl with nearly vertical walls. Because there had been two similar accidents a couple of months earlier, the city had consulted the park designer, who recommended a soft barrier be situated between the beginners' section and the 11-foot bowl. This barrier had not yet been installed when the accident leading to this case occurred. Although the trial court ruled defendants immune from liability under the recreational user statute, the appellate court was called on to determine whether the city had failed to guard or warn users of the risk. The court found there was evidence to raise a material fact that the city had failed to guard users from concealed hazards and failed to warn users of potential dangers (*Woods v. Louisville/Jefferson County Metro Government*, 2005). Another case illustrating the obligations of landowners involved a cyclist riding a bike trail through a city park. While crossing a bridge at a moderate speed, plaintiff encountered two protruding wooden planks on the far side of the arched bridge. Attempting to jump his bike over the planks, plaintiff was thrown from his bike. In his negligence claim against the city, the court ruled the planks were clearly obvious to anyone using the bridge and the city had no notice of the hazard because it was created by heavy rains over the weekend. As a result, the state's recreational use statute protected the city from liability (*City of Dallas v. Hughes*, 2011)

A Two-Pronged Analysis of Applicability

Many states use a two-pronged analysis to determine whether the recreational user statute applies and the defendant is entitled to immunity. The first analysis is whether the activity is a recreational activity. The determination of what constitutes a recreational activity has been the focus of a number of cases. In *Parent v. State of Tennessee* (1999), the Supreme Court of Tennessee ruled that an all-inclusive list explicitly enumerating every single activity that is recreational in nature would be extremely cumbersome. A majority of states use the phrase "included, but not limited to" (van der Smissen, 1990, p. 213) in providing a list of recreational activities. In an Ohio case, being a participant/spectator of the discus throw at a junior high school track meet was considered a recreational activity. The plaintiff who was hit in the face with a discus thrown by a teammate was not able to collect for damages because the school district was entitled to immunity under the recreational user statute (*Mason v. Bristol*, 2006). Conversely, an Illinois court ruled even though plaintiff was participating in a summer football camp on school property, defendant could not produce evidence showing the camp was being used for recreational purposes (*Peters v. Herrin Comm. School Dist.*, 2010).

The second prong of the analysis is whether the plaintiff is recreating on land suitable for the activity. In *McCarthy v. New York State Canal Corp.* (1998) the court ruled that a concrete seawall on the Mohawk River was an area suitable for the recreational activity of fishing. Once again, there is some variation in the manner in which each state interprets the suitability of the land for recreational activity. In Hawaii, the proper focus is on the landowner's intent (*Howard v. United States of America*, 1999). In other words, if a landowner has opened up lands for recreational use without a fee, then it is not significant that a person coming onto the property may have a non-recreational or commercial purpose in mind. In a California case, the court determined recreational use through "consideration of the totality of facts and circumstances" (*Armstrong v. United States*, 2008, p. 8). Plaintiff argued the recreational use statute did not apply to the Golden Gate National Recreation Area because he was riding his bicycle in a parking lot rather than on the bike trail. The court ruled that although he was in a parking lot when he hit a pothole causing him to fall, he was riding for a recreational purpose allowing defendant to prevail under the statute.

Nuisance Law

Nuisance is an area of property law dealing with activity or use of one's property that produces material annoyance, inconvenience, and discomfort for those around the property. The law of nuisance is fairly comprehensive and includes that which endangers life and health, gives offense to the senses, violates laws of decency, or obstructs reasonable use of property. Nuisances are typically classified as public or private. **Public nuisances** are acts that obstruct the enjoyment or use of common property or cause inconvenience or damage to the public. For example, plaintiff homeowners around the New Britain, Connecticut minor league baseball stadium sued defendants alleging the fireworks show coordinated with music constituted an offensive disruption to their lives on Friday nights throughout the spring and summer. The reverberations from the fireworks caused plaintiffs' houses to tremble and the smoke from the fireworks would linger for hours. The court acknowledged that while the fireworks generated revenue for the baseball team and the city, the burden of fireworks every Friday night home game was simply too much for residents to bear. The permanent injunctive relief reduced the number of fireworks shows to one time per month along with damages of $100 per plaintiff (*Esposito v. New Britain Baseball Club, Inc.*, 2005).

Private nuisance is defined as a non trespassory invasion of another's interest in the use or enjoyment of one's own property. In a private nuisance claim courts are usually expecting plaintiffs to present evidence showing an injury specific to the use and enjoyment of his or her land (*Tally Bissell Neighbors, Inc. v. Eyrie Shotgun Ranch, LLC*, 2010). The primary factors to be considered in a private nuisance claim are the gravity of the harm to the plaintiff, the value of the defendant's activity to the community, the burden that will be placed on the defendant if a particular remedy is granted, and whether the defendant's activity was in progress when the plaintiff arrived at the locality. *Hot Rod Hill Motor Park v. Triolo* (2008) provides a good example of a private nuisance. Plaintiff claimed racing activities on defendant landowner's track was deafening, loud, excessive, and disturbing. The noise from race cars would cause neighbors' windows and light fixtures to shake, and prevent them from sleeping, watching television, or spending time outdoors during the evenings when the track was operating. The court ruled that while defendant had taken steps to reduce the noise, the track was a private nuisance that seriously interfered with his neighbors use and enjoyment of their property.

Attractive nuisance is another dimension of nuisance law that is focused on children entering property because they are attracted by a unique, artificial condition such as a swimming pool (*Bennett v. Stanley*, 2001), paintball activity (*Goldhirsch v. Taylor*, 2000), or a trampoline (*Kopczynski v. Barger, 2008*). For the doctrine of attractive nuisance to apply, the landowner of the artificial condition should know or have reason to know that children are likely to trespass the premises. Additionally, the landowner should know or have reason to know that the condition will involve an unreasonable risk to trespassing children, and the children, because of their youth and inexperience, will not realize this danger. Finally, the burden of eliminating the condition is minimal to the landowner, yet, he or she fails to protect children from the condition. Attractive nuisance was the claim in *Butler v. Newark Country Club* (2005), when plaintiff's 8-year-old son fell through the ice and drowned in a pond located on a golf course while on his way to the local community center. The boy was accompanied by his 11-year-old sister and 13-year-old cousin, who had tested the ice by stomping on it prior to them playing on the pond. Although the pond was artificial in that it was man-made and contained a large spillway pipe, it was determined that was not the quality that had attracted the children to it. The court ruled that attractive nuisance doctrine did not apply because it was the natural properties (i.e., the frozen pond) that lured the children to venture onto the ice. Generally, park, recreation, and sport facilities are not nuisances, but may become such if not properly planned, located, or managed according to recognized standards.

SIGNIFICANT CASE

This case from the Connecticut state court system provides a great illustration of the general characteristics of recreational use statutes discussed in the chapter.

THOMAS ALEXSON, JR. V. WHITE MEMORIAL FOUNDATION, INC.

Superior Court of Connecticut, Judicial District of Litchfield at Litchfield
2008 Conn. Super. LEXIS 567
March 5, 2008, Decided
March 5, 2008, Filed

Opinion By: Judge Richard M. Marano

On June 6, 2007 the plaintiff, Thomas Alexson, Jr., commenced this action by service of process against the defendant, White Memorial Foundation. The plaintiff filed a single-count complaint in which he alleges the following facts. At some time prior to July 24, 2006, workmen for the defendant were notified that a tree had fallen across a roadway on the defendant's property. The workmen subsequently attended to the obstruction and began to cut up fallen tree, but failed to complete the task prior to the date on which the defendant collided with the obstruction. On July 24, 2006, the plaintiff was riding his bicycle on the defendant's property and, after seeing the portion of the tree which still blocked the roadway, decided that he could push the obstruction aside as he passed. The plaintiff alleges that the collision with the branch while on his bicycle resulted in serious injury to his person. The plaintiff alleges that the defendant was careless and negligent in only partially removing the branch from a portion of roadway on the defendant's property and that

the failure of the defendant to warn or guard against the obstruction was wilful and intentional.

The defendant filed a motion for summary judgment on December 12, 2007 and simultaneously filed a memorandum of law in support. The plaintiff filed a memorandum in opposition on January 9, 2008.

Discussion

* * *

The defendant moves for summary judgment on the ground that there are no genuine issues of material fact and it is entitled to judgment as a matter of law because the defendant is immune from liability pursuant to General Statutes §52-557g(a) otherwise known as the Recreational Use Act. The defendant argues that it is undisputed that the defendant is: (1) the owner of the land in question; (2) that the defendant made all or part of the land where the plaintiff was injured available for use to the public free of charge; and (3) that the plaintiff, at the time that he was injured, was using the land for a recreational purpose.

In support of its motion for summary judgment, the defendant submits the following evidence: (1) the signed and sworn affidavit of Keith Cudworth, executive director of the White Memorial Foundation; (2) the deposition testimony of the plaintiff; and (3) the deposition of the plaintiff's companion, Ray Messenger, who witnessed the plaintiff's injuries.

The plaintiff argues that there is a genuine issue of material fact as to whether the defendant made the land available to the public free of charge, as required by §52-557g. In addition, the plaintiff argues that there is a genuine issue of material fact as to whether the exception to the recreational land use immunity statute, codified in §52-557h, applies to the defendant because, as alleged by the plaintiff, the defendant wilfully and maliciously failed to warn against a dangerous and defective condition.

In support of his memorandum in opposition the plaintiff submits the following evidence: (1) a printed version of information from the defendant's website, indicating the services that the defendant provides; (2) the signed, sworn affidavit of Thomas Alexson, Jr.; and (3) the signed, sworn affidavit of Stephen Alexson, the plaintiff's uncle who witnessed the accident.

In order to fall within the purview of §52-557g(a), the defendant . . . must establish only that it is the possessor of the fee interest in land available to the public without charge for recreational purposes. In essence, three separate prongs must be proven in order for a defendant to qualify for immunity under §52-557g(a); the defendant must: (1) qualify as an owner; and (2) all or part of the land must be available to the public free of charge; and (3) the land must be available for recreational purposes.

The first prong of the statute requires the defendant to be the owner of the land in question. Pursuant to §52-557f(3), "owner" means, *inter alia,* the possessor of a fee interest . . . or [a] person in control of the premises. In the present case, it is undisputed that the defendant was the owner of the land in question. Therefore, the defendant satisfies the first prong of the statute.

The second prong of the statute requires that the defendant make all or part of the land where the plaintiff was injured, available for use by the public, free of charge. Pursuant to §52-557f(1), "[c]harge" means the admission price or fee asked in return for invitation or permission to enter or go upon the land. The defendant has submitted the affidavit of Keith Cudworth, the executive director of the White Memorial Foundation, wherein he states that the land on which the plaintiff was injured was always available for recreational use to the public, without charge. The plaintiff does not dispute that on the day he was injured, he was not charged by the defendant. In addition, the plaintiff indicates, in his deposition testimony, that the only time he has been charged a fee was when he was admitted into the museum. The plaintiff admits he was never charged to ride his bicycle on the land surrounding the museum. There is no genuine issue

of material fact as to the defendant making the land upon which the plaintiff was injured available, free of charge, to the public. Thus, the defendant satisfies the second prong of the test.

The last prong of the statute requires that the land be available for recreational purposes. Section 52-557f(4) provides: 'recreational purpose' includes, but is not limited to, any of the following, or any combination thereof: Hunting, fishing, swimming, boating, camping, picnicking, hiking, pleasure driving, nature study, water skiing, snow skiing, ice skating, sledding, hang gliding, sport parachuting, hot air ballooning and viewing or enjoying historical, archaeological, scenic or scientific sites. It is noted, however, that, this statute clearly states that [r]ecreational purpose includes, but is *not limited to,* any of the following . . . It is evident that the enumerated activities set forth in the statute are not exclusive. Riding a bicycle falls within the penumbra of activities that are considered "recreational" for the purpose of §52-557g(a). Therefore the defendant satisfies the third prong of the statute. Thus, the defendant is entitled to statutory immunity, unless the exception in General Statutes §52-557h applies.

Section 52-557h states Nothing in sections 52-557f to 52-557i, inclusive, limits in any way the liability of any owner of land which otherwise exists: (1) For wilful or malicious failure to guard or warn against a dangerous condition, use, structure or activity; (2) for injury suffered in any case where the owner of land charges the person or persons who enter or go on the land for the recreational use thereof, except that, in the case of land leased to the state or a subdivision thereof, any consideration received by the owner for the lease shall not be deemed a charge within the meaning of this section.

The courts have not yet interpreted 'wilful or malicious' failure to warn with respect to §52-557h. However, the phrase 'wilful or malicious,' has been interpreted under a companion recreational immunity statute, §52-557j, to mean conduct which 'must encompass both the physical act proscribed by the statute and its injurious consequences.' . . . Additionally, Connecticut law is replete with interpretations of the phrase 'wilful misconduct' in other contexts . . . Wilful misconduct has been defined as intentional conduct designed to injure for which there is no just cause or excuse. Its characteristic element is the design to injure either actually entertained or to be implied from the conduct and circumstances. Not only the action producing the injury but the resulting injury also must be intentional.

A party's conclusory statements, in the affidavit and elsewhere . . . do not constitute evidence sufficient to establish the existence of disputed material facts. In the present case, the plaintiff alleges that on or about July 24, 2006, the workmen of the defendant began cutting a tree; failed to complete the job; and left the tree in the road without any warning. The plaintiff argues that this constitutes a wilful failure to guard or warn against a danger sufficient to fall within the purview of 52-557h.

The plaintiff's conclusory statements in his complaint, coupled with the conclusory statements in the affidavit of Stephen Alexson (the admissibility of which are dubious at best) do not raise a genuine issue of material fact. The complaint is bereft of the factual predicate necessary to lead a reasonable person to infer that the workmen intended to injure passers by, and this plaintiff in particular, by their actions.

Conclusion

For the foregoing reasons, the evidence submitted by both parties shows that there is no genuine issue of material fact and that the defendant is entitled to statutory immunity under §52-557g(a). Therefore the defendant's motion for summary judgment is GRANTED.

CASES ON THE SUPPLEMENTAL WEB SITE

Goldstein v. Pataki (516 F.3d 50, 2008). The reader should note the court's opinion that once a valid public use has been discerned, it makes no difference that the property will be transferred to private developers. Also of interest is to identify at what point is the public use requirement satisfied?

Klein v. United States of America (235 P.3d 42, 2010). The reader should note how the recreational use statute did not shield the defendant landowner from negligent liability against a cyclist as a result of negligent driving of landowner's employee.

McAfee MX v. Foster (2008 Tex. App. LEXIS 968). The reader should note the discussion of balancing the equities that courts must consider in determining an appropriate remedy for a nuisance claim.

Webb v. City of Richland (2011 U.S. Dist. LEXIS 71857). This case illustrates how the Washington recreational use statute did not provide defendant immunity because there was a question of wanton misconduct.

Tally Bissell Neighbors, Inc. v. Eyrie Shotgun Ranch, LLC (228 P.3d 1134, 2010). The reader should note this case involves claims of public, private and attractive nuisance all involving the defendant's shooting range.

QUESTIONS YOU SHOULD BE ABLE TO ANSWER

1. Explain the difference between fee simple absolute and less than fee simple absolute types of real property. What are examples of each?

2. What are the pros and cons of taking private property for professional sport venues?

3. What is the primary purpose of the recreational use statute? Identify the characteristics common to recreational use statutes.

4. Explain the two-prong analysis used by courts to determine whether the recreational use statute might apply to a situation.

5. What are the factors the court will consider in determining whether property contains an attractive nuisance?

REFERENCES

Cases

Albertson v. Fremont County, Idaho, 2011 U.S. Dist. LEXIS 139645
Alexson v. White Memorial Foundation, Inc., 2008 Conn. Super. LEXIS 567
Armstrong v. United States of America, 2008 U.S. Dist. LEXIS 95578
Auman v. School District of Stanley-Boyd, 635 N.W. 2d 762 (2001).
Bennett v. Stanley, 748 N.E.2d 41 (2001).
Bubis v. Kassin, 960 A.2d 779 (2008).
Butler v. Newark Country Club, 2005 Del. Super. LEXIS 301 (2005).

City of Bainbridge Island v. Brennan, 2005 Wash. App. LEXIS 1744 (2005).
City of Dallas v. Hughes, 344 S.W.3d 549 (2011).
Coleman v. Oregon Parks & Recreation Department, 217 P.3d 61 (2009).
Esposito v. New Britain Baseball Club, Inc., 895 A.2d 291 (2005).
Fritts v. Clover Park School District No. 400, 2003 Wash. App. LEXIS 2895 (2003).
Golden Gate Water Ski Club v. County of Contra Costa, 165 Cal. App. 4th 249 (2008).
Goldhirsch v. Taylor, 87 F. Supp.2d 272 (2000).
Goldstein v. Pataki, 516 F.3d 50 (2008).
Hall v. Henn, 802 N.E.2d 797, (2003).
Hillsmere Shores Improvement Association v. Singleton, 959 A.2d 130 (2008).
Howard v. United States of America, 181 F.3d 1064 (1999).
Hot Rod Hill Motor Park v. Triolo, 2008 Tex. App. LEXIS 9040 (2008).
Jobe v. City of Polson, 157 P.3d 743 (2004).
Klein v. United States of America, 235 P.3d 42 (2010).
Konneker v. Romano, 785 N.W.2d 432 (2010).
Kopczynski v. Barger, 887 N.E.2d 928 (2008).
Lyons v. Baptist School of Christian Training, 804 A.2d 364 (2002).
Mason v. Bristol, 2006 Ohio App. LEXIS 5126 (2006)
Matheny v. United States of America, 469 F.3d 1093 (2006).
McAfee v. Foster, 2008 Tex. App. LEXIS 968 (2008).
McCarthy v. New York State Canal Corp., 244 A.D.2d 57 (1998).
Moore v. Stills, 307 S.W.3d 71 (2010).
Parent v. State of Tennessee, 991 S.W.2d 240 (1999).
Peters v. Herrin Community School District No. 4, 928 N.E.2d 1258 (2010).
Poston v. Unified School District No. 387, 189 P.3d 517 (2008).
Recreation Land Corporation v. Hartzfeld, 947 A.2d 771 (2008).
Reed v. National Council of the Boy Scouts of America, Inc., 706 F.Supp. 2d 180 (2010).
Schafer v. United States of America, 2011 U.S. Dist. LEXIS 83748
Scott v. United States of America, 2011 U.S. Dist. LEXIS 135695
Smolarz v. Colon Township, 2005 Mich. App. LEXIS 997 (2005).
Tally Bissell Neighbors, Inc. v. Eyrie Shotgun Ranch, LLC, 228 P.3d 1134 (2010).
Webb v. City of Richland, 2011 U.S. Dist. LEXIS 71857
Woods v. Louisville/Jefferson County Metro Government, 2005 Ky. App. LEXIS 106 (2005).
Yagle v. United States of America, 2009 U.S. Dist. LEXIS 75783

Publications

Garcia, R., & Baltodano, E. F. (2005). Free the beach! Public access, equal justice, and the California coast. *Stanford Journal of Civil Rights and Civil Liberties,* 2, 143–208.
Hubbard, T. E. (2008). For the public's use? Eminent domain in stadium construction. *Sports Lawyers Journal,* 15, 173–193.
Rudolph, Holly C. (2010). Landowner liability under equine and recreational use statutes. http://www.sportwaiver.com/landowner-liability-under-equine-and-recreational-use-statutes/. Also, http://elcr.org/ss2.htm.
Swanson, T., Arnold, R. C., Rasmussen, G. A. (2005). Physical resource planning. In B. van der Smissen, M. Moiseichik, & V. J. Hartenburg (Eds.), *Management of park and recreation agencies* (2nd ed., pp. 205–242). Ashburn, VA: National Recreation and Park Association.
van der Smissen, B. (1990). *Legal liability and risk management for public and private entities* (Vol. I & II). Cincinnati, OH: Anderson Publishing Company.

2.33 EMERGENCY CARE

Kristi L. Schoepfer Bochicchio | Winthrop University

According to the Centers for Disease Control Injury Center (CDC), more than 10,000 people are treated in emergency departments each day for injuries sustained in sport, recreation, and exercise activities. In recent years, Americans made an estimated 1.5 million emergency department visits for injuries sustained while playing basketball, baseball, softball, football, or soccer. Further, approximately 715,000 sports and recreation injuries occur each year in school settings alone (CDC, 2006). Due to the heightened risk of injury in recreation and sport activities, ranging from minor to catastrophic harms, recreation and sport managers must understand the responsibility to plan for and provide emergency care. **Emergency care** can be defined as the provision of medical assistance to an injured person in an urgent, immediate, or unexpected circumstance. When injuries occur, recreation and sport managers (or staff) have a duty to provide competent medical assistance or summon such assistance in a timely manner. Also, emergency care includes planning for the various emergencies that are likely to occur in a recreation or sport setting.

FUNDAMENTAL CONCEPTS

Origins of the Duty

The responsibility to plan for and provide emergency care stems from a special relationship that exists between recreation and/or sport business and its participants/patrons. As defined in Chapter 2.11 *Negligence*, this special relationship creates a duty that gives rise to an obligation to protect the individual from an unreasonable risk of harm. Previous chapters have outlined the various origins of this relationship, including inherent relationships, voluntary assumption, and relationships created by statute (*see* Chapter 2.11 *Negligence*). Further, Chapter 2.31 *Premises Liability* outlined relationships that exist between premise owners/operators and visitors.

Inherent Relationship

An inherent relationship is one that is obvious or inseparable; it is essential to the activity. Such a relationship exists in many recreation and sport contexts, such as an activity director/participant or coach/player (see Chapter 2.11 *Negligence*). Regarding emergency care, an inherent relationship gives rise to the duty to plan for and provide emergency care. A participant or patron in the recreation or sport setting with an inherent relationship to the provider must be able to rely upon that provider for emergency care. For example, in the Significant Case (*Kleinknecht v. Gettysburg College*, 1993), the court provides a lengthy discussion of the relationship that existed between the college and the student athlete. This relationship, in addition to other considerations, resulted in a finding that the college had a duty to provide emergency care.

Voluntary Assumption

A duty is voluntarily assumed when an individual chooses to engage in an activity that creates a special relationship. For example, if an individual volunteers to coach a youth soccer team, he or she has voluntarily created a special relationship between himself or herself and the players on the team. In this situation, the voluntary relationship results in a duty to provide emergency care (among others).

Individuals may assume a relationship by voluntarily rendering aid in an emergency circumstance. When volunteers provide emergency care, they have a duty to act as the reasonable person would in the same or similar circumstance; however, absent gross negligence or willful and wanton conduct, an individual who voluntarily renders aid may be covered by a Good Samaritan statute should a harm occur (see Chapter 2.22 *Immunity*).

Statute

A statute is a law passed by a legislative body that mandates or regulates conduct. Many states have statutes that require specific emergency equipment, services, or responsibilities. For example, 11 states require health and fitness facilities to have automatic external defibrillators (AEDs) on site (this topic will be discussed later in this chapter). Other examples include the following. In North Carolina, the Gfeller-Waller Concussion Awareness Act requires public schools offering interscholastic sports to create an emergency action plan specific to head injuries (2011 N.C. ALS 147). A city ordinance in Fairfield, Alabama, requires an ambulance to be on site at all varsity high school games and college games in the city (Norris, 2011). In Texas, each athletic coach must participate in AED instruction, and maintain certification from the American Red Cross or American Heart Association [Tex. Educ. Code § 22.902 (2012)].

Premises Liability

As discussed in Chapter 2.31 *Premises Liability*, premise owners and operators owe a duty to invitees to keep a facility reasonably safe. This includes an obligation to respond to medical emergencies in a prompt and competent manner. Regardless of whether an individual is an activity participant or a spectator, those persons classified as invitees have a reasonable expectation of emergency care.

Elements of Emergency Care

Recreation and sport managers that have a duty to provide adequate emergency care must carefully consider four distinct elements. These include: (1) Emergency planning; (2) Appropriate personnel/injury assessment; (3) Adequate equipment/certifications; and (4) Implementation of emergency procedures. All four elements are essential to adequately fulfill the duty to provide emergency care.

Emergency Planning

Once a duty to provide emergency care is established, recreation and sport organizations must participate in emergency planning in order to adequately prepare for future emergencies. While no emergency can be anticipated with absolute certainty, many emergency circumstances in recreation and sport are reasonably foreseeable (see Chapter 2.11 *Negligence*). Emergency planning includes reviewing each foreseeable emergency separately, and developing an **Emergency Response Plan** (ERP) according to the needs of individual emergency situations. According to the Risk Management Manual published by the National Intramural-Recreational Sports Association (NIRSA), an **ERP** is a "predetermined plan to deal with an emergency in an organized and efficient manner." General planning is not adequate; rather, specific emergencies must be planned for.[10]

In planning for specific emergencies, sport and recreation managers should be aware of research relating to possible injuries. For example, recent data and research demonstrate that head injuries are foreseeable within sport and recreation. Specifically, estimates indicate that in the United States, 3.8 million sport and recreation related concussions occur each year (Majerske, 2008); further, the CDC projects that a minimum of 96,000 youth, aged 5–18, experience sports-related concussions annually (Diehl, 2010). In contrast to the decline of other serious injuries over the past ten years, the incidence of concussions has doubled (Diehl, 2010). Given the foreseeability of such occurrences, all sport and recreation service providers should specifically plan for head injury response and management. Further, in some states, this planning is mandated by state law. Currently, 35 states have passed youth concussion laws, also referred to as **Lystedt laws**[11] (Toporek, 2012). While these laws vary by jurisdiction, most prescribe head injury protocols and contain specific "return to play" requirements.

---

[10]Many organizations offer activity specific guides to emergency planning on their respective websites. See American College of Sports Medicine (www.acsm.org); U.S. Department of Education (www.ed.gov); American Heart Association (www.americanheart.org); American Red Cross (www.redcross.org); and National Athletic Trainers Association (www.nata.org).

[11]These laws are named for Zachary Lystedt, a middle school football player who suffered a brain injury after returning to a football game with a concussion. His parents, physicians, and community partners lobbied the Washington state legislature to pass a youth concussion law to protect young athletes. Since passage of the Lystedt law in 2009, the NFL and NCAA have successfully lobbied other states to pass similar laws (NFL Health and Safety, 2012).

The importance of emergency planning for head injuries is further substantiated through case law. In recent years, there have been many lawsuits filed where plaintiffs claimed that response to a sustained head injury was inadequate. For example, in 2012, Three Forks High School in Montana was sued by the parents of a football player who sustained repeated concussions during football practice. The parents alleged that their son was allowed to return to practice prematurely, where he sustained additional concussions. Further, the lawsuit alleged that "despite being knocked unconscious and receiving an obvious second concussion, the coaches did not call 911, did not contact the school nurse and did not contact [the students] parents. Instead, they merely sat him on the sidelines and sent him home after practice." This case, however, is only one of many similar examples (See *Pinson v. State of Tennessee,* 1995; *Plevretes v. La Salle University,* PA 2005 [settlement for $7.5M]; *Dougherty v. Montclair High School, NJ* 2008 [case pending]; *Lystedt v. Tahoma School District, WA* 2009 [settlement for $14.6M]; *Gault v. Sequin School District* [case pending]; *Frith v. Lafayette County School District, MO* 2009 [settlement for $3M]; *Sellers v. Rudert, et al,* 918 N.E.2d 586 [2009]).

Beyond head injuries, emergency planning must consider other types of emergencies which are foreseeable in sport and recreation such as over-exertion, heat related illness, cardiac arrest, or other medical situations. According to the NIRSA Manual, the primary concern for medical emergencies is "dealing with the ill/injured person by ensuring that the plan covers immediate attention to the medical condition, coupled with an effective system to get professional assistance." Lastly, emergency planning should also encompass non-medical foreseeable emergencies, such as those related to a fire or chemical spill.

Appropriate Personnel/Injury Assessment

A well-written ERP will designate appropriate personnel to respond in a given emergency. These designations must be based on which staff members are best suited to respond quickly and competently in an emergency situation.

In determining staff roles and responsibilities, a recreation or sport manager must consider staff assignments; specifically, are there enough personnel available at any given time? Does each staff member know his or her role during a medical emergency? Is there a clear chain of command in place? According to the NIRSA Manual, there are three clear roles during an emergency: (1) the **Charge person**, who assumes the overall responsibility and has specific training; (2) the **Call person**, who calls and meets summoned emergency personnel; and (3) the **Control person**, who is responsible for keeping people away from the scene. Recreation and sport managers must designate appropriate personnel to fill these roles.

In addition, when designating which staff members will respond in an emergency, and which roles they will play, a recreation or sport manager must consider each staff member's ability to assess injury. Injuries must be assessed immediately so that proper treatment can be administered. In *Ashburn v. Bowling Green State Univ.* (2011), a Bowling Green University football player died at his first football practice from a full-blown sickle cell anemia episode that resulted in cardiac arrest. During the practice, the player complained of leg cramps; his cramps intensified so severely that he discontinued practice. Assuming he was faking injury, a coach ordered him off the field, sending only a student athletic trainer to monitor him. Shortly thereafter, the cramping impacted his whole body, at which point 911 was called. The player stopped breathing after 911 was summoned, and was not resuscitated. In finding for the University, the court relied on expert medical testimony to determine that the player died from a unique set of metabolic abnormalities, and that faster emergency medical care would not have changed the outcome. However, the facts of this case demonstrate that timely access to injury assessment should be part of an ERP. Minimally, key personnel in the recreation and sport industry should be certified in first aid and should be competent to assess various injury types. However, the staff member with highest level of certification, and most knowledge regarding injury assessment, should generally be designated in the *Charge* role discussed earlier.

Adequate Certifications/Equipment

Recreation and sport managers must ensure that staff members have both the necessary certifications and medical equipment to respond in a medical emergency. While many emergencies require the prompt attention of professional emergency medical technicians, recreation and sport staff may need to care for the injured individual until professional care arrives. Requiring personnel to maintain appropriate certifications and having proper equipment in place will facilitate this interim care.

Mandatory certifications can vary depending on factors such as the specific activity involved, and the age of the participants. There are many professional organizations that provide published standards of practice to guide management decisions in recreation and sport. Examples of such organizations are listed in Chapter 4.21 *Standards of Practice*. While specific mandates vary depending on the activity, most published standards indicate that all personnel should maintain certifications in basic first aid, cardio pulmonary resuscitation (CPR) and automated external defibrillation.

Regarding adequate medical equipment, all recreation and sport organizations should minimally be equipped with a first aid kit including items such as adhesive bandages, Save-A-Tooth, slings, finger splints, and ace wraps. These medical devices are often required to treat minor or moderate injuries. However, in a catastrophic situation such as sudden cardiac arrest, an **automated external defibrillator** (AED) is desirable. An **AED** is a portable electronic device that can be used by non-medical personnel to treat a person in cardiac arrest. Per the American Heart Association (AHA), more than 294,000 Americans experience sudden cardiac arrest (SCA) outside of a hospital each year. While only 7.9 % of SCA victims survive, on average, CPR and early defibrillation with an AED more than double a victim's chance of survival.

Automated External Defibrillators (AED). There are two primary legal issues surrounding the use of AEDs. First, which facilities are required by law to have AEDs? Second, is immunity granted to those individuals using an AED in a medical emergency?

AED Required by Law. There is currently no legal mandate requiring AEDs in all facilities offering recreation and/or sport services. However, several states have adopted legislation that mandates AEDs in certain facilities, such as school buildings, health/fitness clubs, state parks and state buildings.

In Alabama, Arkansas, Colorado, Florida, Georgia, Illinois, Louisiana, Maine, Maryland, Nevada, New Hampshire, New Mexico, New York, North Dakota, Ohio, Oklahoma, Oregon, Pennsylvania, Rhode Island, South Carolina, Tennessee, Texas, and West Virginia AEDs are required or encouraged in some schools, although the extent varies. For example, in Maryland, each school board is required to develop an AED program to ensure an AED is present at every school site; further, the statute requires that a person trained in the operation and use of an AED is present at every high-school sponsored athletic event [Md. Educ. Code Ann. § 7-425 (2011)]. Similarly, in Florida, "each public school that is a member of the Florida High School Athletic Association must have an operational automated external defibrillator on the school grounds" [Fla. Stat. §1006.165 (2012)]. In Nevada, the Board of Regents of the University of Nevada must ensure that at least two automated external defibrillators are placed in central locations at each of: (1) The largest indoor sporting arena or events center controlled by the University in a county whose population is 100,000 or more but less than 700,000; and (2) The largest indoor sporting arena or events center controlled by the University in a county whose population is 700,000 or more. [Nev. Rev. Stat. Ann. § 450B.600 (2011)]. However, some states only "encourage" AEDs. For example, New Hampshire encourages "all schools to obtain and maintain automated external defibrillators at appropriate school locations for the safety and protection of students and others participating in or attending school athletic and related activities" [RSA 195-I:1 (2012)]. In Tennessee, schools "are encouraged, within existing budgetary limits, to place automated external defibrillator (AED) devices in schools" [Tenn. Code Ann. § 49-2-122 (2011)].

For health and fitness facilities, Arkansas, California, Illinois, Indiana, Louisiana, Massachusetts, Michigan, New Jersey, New York, Oregon, Rhode Island and Washington D.C. require AEDs. In addition to requiring the presence of an AED, some statutes also dictate proper use requirements. For example, the Arkansas statute states specific requirements for the number, placement and use of AEDs in both staffed and unstaffed situations.

A recent trend is statutes mandating AEDs in state buildings or state parks. For example, Florida now encourages AEDs in state parks, along with proper training for park employees and registration of the AED with the appropriate medical emergency services director [Fla. Stat. § 258.0165 (2012)]. Also, Arizona, California, and New Jersey make this distinction, requiring AEDs in all state owned, operated, or constructed facilities.

However, it is important to note that not all states have statutory requirements; and in these states, case law does not support a duty to maintain an AED. In *Rutnik v. Colonie Center Club, Inc.* (1998), *Atcovitz v. Gulph Mills Tennis Club, Inc.* (2002) and *Salte v. YMCA* (2004) defendants were found not to have a duty to defibrillate patrons who suffered cardiac arrest. Further, even when facilities do have an AED on site, the duty to notify patrons of the AED's location may be questioned. In *Rotolo v. San Jose Sport and Entertainment, LLC* (2007), parents of the deceased alleged that the defendant owner/operator of an ice skating rink had a duty to notify users of the existence and location of an AED at the facility. In affirming the trial court's holding, the California Court of Appeals disagreed stating "the duty the parents sought to impose was not supported by the statutes or the principles developed in California common law."

Immunity for AED Use. All states and the U.S. federal government have enacted legislation that provides some form of immunity to AED users. Most provide protection to those non-medical persons who use an AED in a medical emergency. See Chapter 2.22, *Immunity*. Without these statutes, some recreation and sport managers might be hesitant to purchase and utilize AEDs due to the risk of alleged negligence for AED misuse. AED immunity statutes seemingly allow recreation and sport managers to create ERPs that include the use of AEDs in an emergency without fear of increased liability.

Most important to note is that the extent of the immunity provided, and to whom it applies, varies in each state. Prior to creating an ERP that includes an AED, a recreation or sport manager should thoroughly investigate the laws in the individual state, making certain to comply with any necessary training, maintenance, or supervisory provisions. Operating an AED outside of these legislative provisions may disqualify an individual from the immunity protection.

Implementation of Emergency Procedures

Even after the above considerations are made, recreation and sport managers must properly train staff and personnel regarding implementation of the ERP. A manager can never assume that personnel will be able to execute the plan in a given emergency situation.

Consider the facts in *Carter v. City of Cleveland*, (1998). Carter, a twelve year old boy, nearly drowned at the Alexander Hamilton indoor swimming pool. When Carter's body was discovered in the pool, emergency care was not summoned promptly. As a consequence of the near drowning, he developed acute bronchial pneumonia and was declared brain dead four days later. Lifeguards had not been instructed on the use of 911 nor told that it was necessary to first dial a nine to get an outside line. When asked about the lack of training, the pool manager testified that he just assumed that the guards had been briefed how to get an outside line to dial 911. The court stated, "the city, in its admitted failure to train its employees on the use of 911, left them without the knowledge necessary to handle the emergency as it arose." This case clearly illustrates the need to train all recreation and sport staff on how to implement the Emergency Response Plan to ensure actual execution of proper emergency procedures.

Specific Sport and Recreation Applications

As noted, the duty to provide emergency care requires recreation and sport mangers to address the specific concerns present in varying participation and spectator opportunities. The following analysis is intended to identify some of the legal obligations that recreation and sport providers have in meeting the duty to provide emergency care to clients in various sport and recreation settings.

Sport Participation

School-based Sport. Emergency care for student athletes must be an important consideration in any school setting. Athletic administrators, coaches, and athletic trainers have a responsibility to ensure that student athletes with injuries or symptoms of medical distress (e.g., head injury, heat-related illness, diabetic coma, etc.) receive prompt and competent emergency care.

There is ample case law to support this fact. First, in *Kleinknecht v. Gettysburg College* (1993), the U.S. Court of Appeals for the Third Circuit found that a college owes a duty of emergency care to student athletes that are recruited by the university (see the Significant Case). Also, in *Mogabgab v. Orleans Parish School Board* (1970) the Louisiana Court of Appeals found that sport coaches owe participants a legal duty to recognize when emergency care is needed and promptly summon competent medical attention. Further, the court held that attempted first aid procedures should stabilize the situation until emergency medical personnel arrive; and, any attempted first aid should not take the place of prompt medical care (see the Supplemental Web Site for Chapter 4.23). Also, in *Pinson v. State* (1995) and *Halper v. Vayo* (1991) the courts found that coaches or activity instructors must employ proper post-injury procedures so as to not aggravate the injury.

However, case law does not confirm a duty to provide emergency care in every situation. In *Kennedy v. Syracuse University* (1995), the court found that failure to have an athletic trainer present to render first aid was not the cause of an injured gymnast's injury, nor did it exacerbate the injury. In *Yatsko v. Berezwick* (2008), a female basketball player with a head injury was intentionally kept from trainers so she could remain in the game; she consequently suffered severe brain injuries. The court found that the coaches' actions did not "shock the conscience" and dismissed the claims. Lastly, in *Avila v. Citrus Cmty. Coll. Dist.,* (2006) a baseball player was hit in the head with a pitch and suffered serious injuries. Avila claimed the college was negligent when it failed to provide medical care; however, the court found that the college was not liable because it was protected by the assumption of risk doctrine.

Youth Sport Programs. Similar to school-based programs, emergency care must be carefully considered in youth sport programs. This can be particularly challenging given the nature of youth sport and the prevalence of volunteer staff. While many programs are organized and offered through organizations such as the YMCA or community recreation centers, coaches and other supervisory staff are often volunteers. This poses a problem relative to the four considerations regarding emergency care. While organizations may be able to conduct emergency planning, it may not always be possible to identify adequate personnel with appropriate certifications. Depending on the local situation, volunteer coaches and others assisting may or may not be required to maintain certifications such as First Aid and CPR. Further, having appropriate emergency equipment available at all youth sport events is unlikely given the varied facilities in which youth sport take place. Lastly, properly communicating and actually implementing an ERP may be difficult for youth sport organizations who use volunteers. In spite of the logistical challenges regarding emergency care, youth sport organizations still must undertake emergency care planning.

The Estate of Deshaun Newton, et al. v. Wes Grandstaff, et. al (2011) provides a recent example of why youth sport organizations must carefully consider emergency care planning prior to hosting events. In 2008, Newton was participating in a 128 team basketball tournament at a YMCA facility in Dallas, Texas. The tournament was sponsored by Grandstaff as owner of Next Level Ballers, a youth basketball organization. After playing in the first half of a game, Newton was seated on the bench when he suddenly went into cardiac arrest. The coach attempted CPR, but no one else came to his aid. Emergency medical personnel were ultimately dispatched, but could not enter the facility quickly; no professional care was available for 30 minutes. The Estate claimed that Grandstaff failed to "hire or arrange for any medical personnel, or trainers certified in administering CPR, to provide first aid to injured players in need of medical attention; provide for any emergency medical equipment, such as a defibrillator to be available in the event of a medical emergency; and provide effective ingress and egress to the facility that would have allowed emergency medical personnel to access quickly the premises and render immediate and necessary medical aid." To date, the court has only ruled on defendants motion to dismiss; however, in doing so they have clearly articulated that under Texas law, using multiple theories, the Estate has "plausibly asserted that defendants owed Newton a legal duty," thus denying defendants motion (see Supplemental Web Site).

Other case law exists that further demonstrates the difficulties present in emergency care planning in youth sport. In *Lasseigne v. American Legion, Nicholson Post #38* (1990), a youth baseball player was hit on the head with a ball thrown by a team member. Although a fill-in coach examined the player and ordered him to sit down, the player resumed play shortly thereafter; he required head surgery 24 hours later. The family filed a lawsuit alleging that the fill-in coach "did not render such aid and assistance as would be expected from ordinary prudent persons in a like position." The court held for the defendants, finding that the coach "acted reasonably under the circumstances." In *Kelly, et al. vs. The Catholic Archdiocese of Washington D.C. et al.* (2004) a seventh grade CYO softball player severely injured her ankle (see the Supplemental Web Site). Her parents sued alleging, among other claims, that the defendants failed to ensure coaches and volunteers were trained to handle emergencies involving injuries. Specifically, the parents contended that transporting the injured off the field and into her mother's care was improper. The parents stated she should have been left on the field until emergency technicians arrived. The court held that there was no delay in treatment attributable to the manner in which she left the field, nor was there a lack of emergency care training. Also, in *Myers v. Friends of Shenendehowa Crew, Inc.* (2006) a 14 year old, who trained in rowing with defendant at a YMCA, fainted during practice. The supervisor took the child to the YMCA front desk and asked for a nurse; however, the child was left unattended after the request was made. The child subsequently fainted, hit her head, and had multiple seizures.

In denying the defendants motion for summary judgment, the court held that a question of fact existed as to whether leaving the child unattended after an injury was negligent.

Recreation/Fitness Participants

Campus Recreation Centers. Participation rates in intramural and other recreational collegiate activities have increased significantly in recent decades. Along with this growth comes a rise in the number of accidents and injuries that occur in the campus recreational setting (Steir and Kampf, 2008).

With such a variety of intramural activities now offered, including non-traditional sports such as rock climbing, water polo, kayaking, skiing, and boxing, the emergency care planning process has become a more significant undertaking. Best practice requires campus recreation managers to create an ERP for each individual activity, carefully considering personnel, equipment and implementation. In *Spiegler v. State of Arizona* (1996) a female student working out in the campus weight room at the University of Arizona suffered a cardiac arrest. The ERP in place required the supervising student staff member to administer CPR as necessary; however, this was not done. The supervising student employee did call 911, but the impaired student suffered permanent brain damage. The jury found for the plaintiff stating that she had not been given the standard of care required by the campus policies for emergency care. Additional examples are found in *Lemoine v. Cornell University* (2003) where a student was injured when she fell from a rock climbing wall during a rock climbing class and *Kyriazis v. University of West Virginia* (1994) where a male rugby participant was injured while playing intramural rugby.

Aquatics. Recreation and sport facilities with aquatic components such as swimming pools or lakes must carefully consider emergency care. All states have specific regulatory codes that dictate what aquatic facilities must maintain regarding safety equipment, personnel, and certifications. However, even though many of the required elements of an ERP are mandated in an aquatics facility, managers of these areas still must carefully consider additional elements of emergency planning.

Cases that have considered emergency care in aquatics facilities also often consider whether supervision was adequate (see Chapter 2.34 *Supervision*). In *Robinson v. Chicago Park District* (2001), a swimmer at a county pool was spotted at the bottom of the deep end. Lifeguards on duty were alleged to have hesitated in retrieving the deceased, thus causing a delay in emergency care. Even though allegations existed that the deceased should have been resuscitated much sooner, the defendants were not liable pursuant to the Illinois Tort Immunity Act. Similarly, in *Trotter v. School District* (2000) a member of a freshman swim class died after struggling, and subsequently drowning, in the deep end of the school pool. The instructor hired to teach the freshman swimming class did not have water safety or lifeguarding certifications; also, there were problems accessing emergency lifesaving equipment. Although the Illinois Appellate court granted the school district's motion for summary judgment regarding immunity, the case was remanded to consider the question of whether the instructor was adequately skilled to provide supervision and/or first aid to a swim class. Lastly, in *Walker v. Daniels* (1991), a student at Fort Valley State College drowned during a recreational swim session that did not have the approval of campus administration. The lifeguards present were alleged to be inattentive; further, medical evidence demonstrated that the student had been underwater for at least four to six minutes before he was discovered, and additional time elapsed before emergency care was administered. The college was assessed damages of 1.5 million dollars based on these breaches of duty.

Health Clubs and Spas. Fitness facilities and health clubs are highly susceptible to claims of negligence regarding inadequate emergency care. Failure to provide First Aid/CPR (*Lewin v. Fitworks of Cincinnati, LLC*, 2005); failure to summon emergency medical services (*Chai v. Sport and Fitness Clubs of America*, 2005); failure to do more than summon emergency medical services (*Brown v. Atlas-Kona Kai*, 2009); and, in some states failure to have and/or use an AED are all potential areas of risk for health/fitness facility operators (*Rotolo v. San Jose Sports and Entertainment, LLC*, 2007). In *L.A. Fitness International v. Mayer* (2008), the daughter of Alessio Tringali filed a wrongful death action against the club after her father died as a result of cardiac arrest suffered while using a step machine. Among other claims, Mayer asserted that L.A. Fitness failed to administer CPR; failed to have an AED on its premises; and failed to train its employees and agents to handle medical emergencies. Noting that the issue of the duty owed by a health club owner to an injured patron was one of first impression in Florida, the Florida Court of Appeals held that L.A. Fitness satisfied its duty to render assistance when it summoned emergency medical assistance. Further, the court held that in Florida, there is no common law or statutory duty for a health club to have an AED on its premises (see the Supplemental Web Site).

In contrast, the court in *Miglino v. Bally Total Fitness of Greater New York* (2011), held that under New York law, fitness facilities are not only required to have an AED on premise, but also have an inherent duty to make use of the AED. In that case, decedent Miglino collapsed while playing racquetball at defendants facility; a gym employee assessed the situation and called 911; however, the employee did not use the available AED. In reviewing NY General Business Law § 627-a, which mandates health clubs provide both an AED and someone trained in its use, the court "imposed an affirmative duty of care upon the facility so as to give rise to a cognizable statutory cause of action in negligence for failure to use the device" (see Supplemental Web Site).

Additionally, many fitness and health clubs require patrons to sign a waiver and/or release of liability (see Chapter 2.23 *Waivers and Releases*). However, a waiver may not be enforceable regarding the failure to provide emergency care. In *Brown v. Bally Total Fitness Corporation* (2003), a patron experienced heart problems while on the treadmill. The plaintiff alleged "that defendant's employees failed to check decedent's pulse, failed to administer cardio-pulmonary resuscitation (CPR) and prevented a good Samaritan, off-duty police officer, from attempting lifesaving procedures. In addition, plaintiffs alleged that defendant knew or should have known that its employees were not qualified, nor able, to provide emergency medical services, including CPR." After careful analysis of the waiver, the court reversed summary judgment for Bally's indicating that the waiver of liability did not apply to negligence in rendering emergency care.

Other Participant Activities. Court cases provide examples of other recreation and sport activities where emergency care was an issue.

Skating Rinks. In *Spotlite Skating Rink Inc. v. Barnes* (2008), a 10 year-old died after falling and hitting her head on the ice rink operated by the defendant. The Supreme Court of Mississippi held that the skate rink had a duty to provide appropriate medical treatment to the patron, and that there was sufficient evidence to support a finding that the rink breached its duty of care to render aid (see the Supplemental Web Site).

Road Races/Fitness Challenges. In *Gehling v. St. George's University School of Medicine* (1989), a medical student participated in a 2.5 mile road race sponsored by the University. After completing the race, Earl Gehling collapsed, suffering from heat stroke, and died a short time later. After reviewing the emergency care measures in place such as water on the course, trained medical staff, and a person trailing the race to aid injured runners, the Court found in favor of the defendant.

Adult Recreation/Sport Activities. In *Colon v. Chelsea Piers Mgmt.* (2006), the decedent suffered cardiac arrest and died while playing in an adult basketball league at Chelsea Piers. The plaintiff alleged that the defendant had a duty to provide staff adequately trained in medical care, as well as maintain emergency equipment, such as a resuscitation device, on the premises. The court held that the operator of the basketball league did not have this duty and granted summary judgment for the defendant. Also, in *Carter v. Baldwin*, (2009), an off-road racer suffered injuries in a collision with another car and claimed the injuries were exacerbated due to a lack of adequate emergency medical care at the track. On appeal of the trial court's decision to dismiss the gross negligence claim, the court affirmed, holding the promoters did not breach any duty they owed to Carter because he assumed the risk of injury from the risks inherent in the sport. While the court noted that the alleged lack of proper medical care may have increased the severity of the injury, the court did not address whether the promoters had a duty to provide reasonable medical care on the premises.

Golf. Although no case law was found specifically addressing the duty to provide emergency care on a golf course, injuries in golf are common and range from moderate, such as a ball strike (*Yoneda v. Tom*, 2006; *Sullivan-Coughlin v. Palos Country Club, Inc.*, 2004) to severe, such as a lightning strike (*Hames v. State*, 1991; *Maussner v. Atlantic City Country Club*, 1997). Further, according to the American Heart Association, golf courses rank in the top five most common public places for sudden cardiac arrest to occur. As such, golf course owner operators should have an ERP that adequately considers these common golf injuries, as well as the necessity for and availability of an AED.

Professional Sport Teams. All athletes risk injury, even professional ones. Take, for example, Korey Stringer of the Minnesota Vikings who died from heat stroke during football practice (*Stringer v. Minnesota Vikings Football Club, L.L.C.*, 2004); or take Carl Phelps, a professional racecar driver who suffered severe burns at Firebird Raceway when his car erupted into flames. (*Phelps v. Firebird Raceway, Inc.*, 2005). Allegations of inadequate medical care after the injury were made in both of these cases, however the *Stringer* Court ruled that the plaintiff received emergency care. In *Phelps*, the appellate court did not specifically address the issue of emergency care since the primary issue was the validity of a waiver. However, both cases demonstrate the importance of emergency care in professional sport.

Sport Spectators

Stadia. While the duty to provide emergency care is clearly a concern regarding participant injuries, sport spectators are also entitled to emergency care. Based on premises liability law, and the classification of sport patrons as invitees, stadium owners have a duty to provide a reasonably safe premise for spectators at sporting events. Sport and recreation facility managers must be concerned with the safety of attendees, spectators and patrons (Madden, 1998). Specific considerations regarding emergency care for spectators and patrons are discussed in Chapter 4.22 *Audits in Risk Management*; Chapter 4.23 *Crisis Management*; and Chapter 4.24 *Crowd Management*.

SIGNIFICANT CASE

The following case is one of the most significant regarding the duty to provide emergency care. The court provides a clear and thorough discussion of the origin of the duty; most notably, the court discusses the special relationship between the college and the athlete, as well as the foreseeability of the harm. When reading this case, take note of these two discussions, as well as the facts leading up to the allegation of negligence. This case clearly supports a need for emergency care planning, identification of appropriate personnel, equipment and certifications, as well as implementation of the ERP.

KLEINKNECHT V. GETTYSBURG COLLEGE

United States Court Of Appeals For The Third Circuit
989 F.2d 1360 (1993)

II. Factual History

In September 1988, Drew Kleinknecht was a sophomore student at the College, which had recruited him for its Division III intercollegiate lacrosse team. The College is a private, four-year liberal arts school. In 1988, it * * * * supported twenty-one intercollegiate sports teams involving approximately 525 male and female athletes. * * *

Lacrosse players can typically suffer a variety of injuries. * * * * Before Drew died, however, no athlete at the College had experienced cardiac arrest while playing lacrosse or any other sport.

In September 1988, the College employed two full-time athletic trainers, Joseph Donolli and Gareth Biser. Both men were certified by the National Athletic Trainers Association, which requires, *inter alia*, current certification in both cardio-pulmonary resuscitation ("CPR") and standard first aid. In addition, twelve student trainers participated in the College's sports program. * * *

Because lacrosse is a spring sport, daily practices were held during the spring semester in order to prepare for competition. Student trainers were assigned to cover both spring practices and games. Fall practice was held only for the players to learn "skills and drills," and

to become acquainted with the other team members. No student trainers were assigned to the fall practices.

Drew participated in a fall lacrosse practice on the afternoon of September 16, 1988. Coaches Janczyk and Anderson attended and supervised this practice. It was held on the softball fields outside Musselman Stadium. No trainers or student trainers were present. Neither coach had certification in CPR. Neither coach had a radio on the practice field. The nearest telephone was inside the training room at Musselman Stadium, roughly 200–250 yards away. The shortest route to this telephone required scaling an eight-foot high cyclone fence surrounding the stadium. According to Coach Janczyk, he and Coach Anderson had never discussed how they would handle an emergency during fall lacrosse practice.

[At] the September 16, 1988 practice * * * * Drew was a defenseman and was participating in one of the drills when he suffered a cardiac arrest. According to a teammate, Drew simply stepped away from the play and dropped to the ground. Another teammate stated that no person or object struck Drew prior to his collapse.

After Drew fell, his teammates and Coach Janczyk ran to his side. Coach Janczyk and some of the players noticed that Drew was lying so that his head appeared to be in an awkward position. No one knew precisely what had happened at that time, and at least some of those present suspected a spinal injury. Team captain Daniel Polizzotti testified that he heard a continuous "funny" "gurgling" noise coming from Drew, and knew from what he observed that something "major" was wrong. Other teammates testified that Drew's skin began quickly to change colors. One team member testified that by the time the coaches had arrived, "[Drew] was really blue."

According to the College, Coach Janczyk acted in accordance with the school's emergency plan by first assessing Drew's condition, then dispatching players to get a trainer and call for an ambulance. Coach Janczyk himself then began to run toward Musselman Stadium to summon help.

The Kleinknechts dispute the College's version of the facts. They note that although Coach Janczyk claims to have told two players to run to Apple Hall, a nearby dormitory, for help, Coach Anderson did not recall Coach Janczyk's sending anyone for help. Even if Coach Janczyk did send the two players to Apple Hall, the Kleinknechts maintain, his action was inappropriate because Apple Hall was not the location of the nearest telephone. It is undisputed that two other team members ran for help, but the Kleinknechts contend that the team members did this on their own accord, without instruction from either coach.

The parties do not dispute that Polizzotti, the team captain, ran toward the stadium, where he knew a training room was located and a student trainer could be found. In doing so, Polizzotti scaled a chain link fence that surrounded the stadium and ran across the field, encountering student trainer Traci Moore outside the door to the training room. He told her that a lacrosse player was down and needed help. She ran toward the football stadium's main gate, managed to squeeze through a gap between one side of the locked gate and the brick pillar forming its support, and continued on to the practice field by foot until flagging a ride from a passing car. In the meantime, Polizzotti continued into the training room where he told the student trainers there what had happened. One of them phoned Plank Gymnasium and told Head Trainer Donolli about the emergency.

Contemporaneously with Polizzotti's dash to the stadium, Dave Kerney, another team member, ran toward the stadium for assistance. Upon seeing that Polizzotti was going to beat him there, Kerney concluded that it was pointless for both of them to arrive at the same destination and changed his course toward the College Union Building. He told the student at the front desk of the emergency on the practice field. The student called his supervisor on duty in the building, and she immediately telephoned for an ambulance.

Student trainer Moore was first to reach Drew. She saw Drew's breathing was labored, and the color of his complexion changed as she watched. Because Drew was breathing, she did not attempt CPR or any other first aid technique, but only monitored his condition, observing no visible bruises or lacerations.

By this time, Coach Janczyk had entered the stadium training room and learned that Donolli had been notified and an ambulance called. Coach Janczyk returned to the practice field at the same time Donolli arrived in a golf cart. Donolli saw that Drew was not breathing, and turned him on his back to begin CPR with the help of a student band member who was certified as an emergency medical technician and had by chance arrived on the scene. The two of them performed CPR until two ambulances arrived at approximately 4:15 p.m. Drew was defibrillated and drugs were administered to strengthen his heart. He was placed in an ambulance and taken to the hospital, but despite repeated resuscitation efforts, Drew could not be revived. He was pronounced dead at 4:58 p.m.

As the district court observed, the parties vigorously dispute the amount of time that elapsed in connection with the events following Drew's collapse. The College maintains that "Coach Janczyk immediately ran to Drew's side, followed closely by assistant coach, Anderson. Team captain Polizzotti estimated that it took him no more than thirty seconds to get from the practice field to the training room. The College contends that it took Moore no more than two minutes to get from the training room to Drew's side. In fact, the College maintains, the lacrosse team was practicing on this particular field because of its close proximity to the training room and the student trainers. The College estimates that an ambulance was present within eight to ten minutes after Drew's collapse.

The Kleinknechts, on the other hand, assert that as much as a minute to a minute and a half passed before Coach Janczyk arrived at Drew's side. * * * * They estimate that it took Polizzotti a minute and a half to arrive at the stadium training room from the practice field, advise someone on duty, and have that person notify Donolli. The Kleinknechts also estimate that it took Kerney two minutes and thirteen seconds to arrive at the College Union Building, speak to the student at the desk, and then have the secretary telephone for an ambulance. They point to Donolli's deposition testimony indicating that it took him approximately three minutes and fifteen seconds to arrive at the scene. The Kleinknechts further maintain, and the College does not dispute, that at least five minutes elapsed from the time that Drew was first observed on the ground until Head Trainer Donolli began administering CPR. Thus, the Kleinknechts contend that * * * * as long as twelve minutes elapsed before CPR was administered. They also estimate that roughly ten more minutes passed before the first ambulance arrived on the scene.

Prior to his collapse, Drew had no medical history of heart problems. * * * * In January 1988, a College physician had examined Drew to determine his fitness to participate in sports and found him to be in excellent health. The Kleinknecht's family physician had also examined Drew in August 1987 and found him healthy and able to participate in physical activity.

Medical evidence indicated Drew died of cardiac arrest after a fatal attack of cardiac arrhythmia.

* * * *

The Kleinknechts present three general issues on appeal: (1) the district court erred in determining that the College had no legal duty to implement preventive measures assuring prompt assistance and treatment in the event one of its student athletes suffered cardiac arrest while engaged in school-supervised intercollegiate athletic activity; (2) the district court erred in determining that the actions of school employees following Drew's collapse were reasonable and that the College therefore did not breach any duty of care; and (3) the district court erred in determining that both Traci Moore and the College were entitled to immunity under the Pennsylvania Good Samaritan Act. [discussion omitted]

IV. Analysis

1. The Duty of Care Issue

Whether a defendant owes a duty of care to a plaintiff is a question of law . . . In order to prevail on a cause of action in negligence under Pennsylvania law, a plaintiff must establish: (1) a duty or obligation recognized by the law, requiring the actor to conform to a certain standard of conduct; (2) a failure to conform to the standard required; (3) a causal connection between the conduct and the resulting injury; and (4) actual loss or damage resulting to the interests of another. . .

The Kleinknechts assert three different theories upon which they predicate the College's duty to establish preventive measures capable of providing treatment to student athletes in the event of a medical emergency such as Drew's cardiac arrest: (1) existence of a special relationship between the College and its student athletes; (2) foreseeability that a student athlete may suffer cardiac arrest while engaged in athletic activity; and (3) public policy [discussion omitted].

* * * *

a. Special Relationship

The Kleinknechts argue that the College had a duty of care to Drew by virtue of his status as a member of an intercollegiate athletic team. The Supreme Court of Pennsylvania has stated that "duty, in any given situation, is predicated on the relationship existing between the parties at the relevant time . . . ." *Morena*, 462 A.2d at 684. The Kleinknechts argue that although the Supreme Court has not addressed this precise issue, it would conclude that a college or university owes a duty to its intercollegiate athletes to provide preventive measures in the event of a medical emergency.

In support of their argument, the Kleinknechts cite the case of *Hanson v. Kynast*, No. CA-828 (Ohio Ct. App. June 3, 1985), *rev'd on other grounds*, 494 N.E.2d. 1091 (Ohio 1986). In *Hanson* an intercollegiate, recruited lacrosse player was seriously injured while playing in a lacrosse game against another college. The plaintiff alleged that his university breached its legal duty to have an ambulance present during the lacrosse game. The trial court granted the defendant's motion for summary judgment based on its holding, *inter alia*, that

> There is no duty as a matter of law for the Defendant College or other sponsor of athletic events to have ambulances, emergency vehicles, trained help or doctors present during the playing of a lacrosse game or other athletic events, and the failure to do so does not constitute negligence as a matter of law.

The court of appeals reversed, concluding, "It is a question of fact for the jury to determine whether or not appellee University acted reasonably in failing to have an ambulance present at the field or to provide quick access to the field in the event of an emergency." *Id.* at 6. By directing the trial court to submit the case to a jury, the court of appeals implicitly held that the university owed a duty of care to the plaintiff.

Although the *Hanson* court did not specify the theory on which it predicated this duty, we think it reached the correct result, and we predict that the Supreme Court of Pennsylvania would conclude that a similar a duty exists on the facts of this case. Like the lacrosse student in *Hanson*, Drew chose to attend Gettysburg College because he was persuaded it had a good lacrosse program, a sport in which he wanted to participate at the intercollegiate level. Head Trainer Donolli actively recruited Drew to play lacrosse at the College. At the time he was stricken, Drew was not engaged in his own private affairs as a student at Gettysburg College. Instead, he was participating in a scheduled athletic practice for an intercollegiate team sponsored by the College under the supervision of College employees. On these facts we believe that the Supreme Court of Pennsylvania would hold that a special relationship existed between the College and Drew that was sufficient to impose a duty of reasonable care on the College.

* * * *

Drew was not acting in his capacity as a private student when he collapsed. Indeed, the Kleinknechts concede that if he had been, they would have no recourse against the College. There is a distinction between a student injured while participating as an intercollegiate athlete in a sport for which he was recruited and a student injured at a college while pursuing his private interests, scholastic or otherwise. This distinction serves to limit the class of students to whom a college owes the duty of care that arises here. Had Drew been participating in a fraternity football game, for example, the College might not have owed him the same duty or perhaps any duty at all. There is, however, no need for us to reach or decide the duty question either in that context or in the context of whether a college would owe a duty towards students participating in intramural sports. On the other hand, the fact that Drew's cardiac arrest occurred during an athletic event involving an intercollegiate team of which he was a member does impose a duty of due care on a college that actively sought his participation in that sport. We cannot help but think that the College recruited Drew for its own benefit, probably thinking that his skill at lacrosse would bring favorable attention and so aid the College in attracting other students.

* * * *

In conclusion, we predict that the Supreme Court of Pennsylvania would hold that the College owed Drew a duty of care in his capacity as an intercollegiate athlete engaged in school-sponsored intercollegiate athletic activity for which he had been recruited.

b. Foreseeability

This does not end our inquiry, however. The determination that the College owes a duty of care to its intercollegiate athletes could merely define the class of persons to whom the duty extends, without determining the nature of the duty or demands it makes on the College. Because it is foreseeable that student athletes may sustain severe and even life-threatening injuries while engaged in athletic activity, the Kleinknechts argue that the College's duty of care required it to be ready to respond swiftly and adequately to a medical emergency. . . .

* * * *

The type of foreseeability that determines a duty of care, as opposed to proximate cause, is not dependent on the foreseeability of a specific event . . . Instead, in the context of duty, "the concept of foreseeability means the likelihood of the occurrence of a general type of risk rather than the likelihood of the occurrence of the precise chain of events leading to the injury." *Suchomajcz v. Hummel Chem. Co.*, 524 F.2d 19, 28 n.8 (3d Cir. 1975) (citing Harper & James, The Law of Torts § 18.2, at 1026, § 20.5, at 1147-49 (1956)). . . . Only when even the general likelihood of some broadly definable class of events, of which the particular event that caused the plaintiff's injury is a subclass, is unforeseeable can a court hold as a matter of law that the defendant did not have a duty to the plaintiff to guard against that broad general class of risks within which the particular harm the plaintiff suffered befell. . . .

* * * *

Although the district court correctly determined that the Kleinknechts had presented evidence establishing that the occurrence of severe and life-threatening injuries

is not out of the ordinary during contact sports, it held that the College had no duty because the cardiac arrest suffered by Drew, a twenty-year old athlete with no history of any severe medical problems, was not reasonably foreseeable. Its definition of foreseeability is too narrow. Although it is true that a defendant is not required to guard against every possible risk, he must take reasonable steps to guard against hazards which are generally foreseeable. . . Though the specific risk that a person like Drew would suffer a cardiac arrest may be unforeseeable, the Kleinknechts produced ample evidence that a life-threatening injury occurring during participation in an athletic event like lacrosse was reasonably foreseeable. In addition to the testimony of numerous medical and athletic experts, Coach Janczyk, Head Trainer Donolli, and student trainer Moore all testified that they were aware of instances in which athletes had died during athletic competitions. The foreseeability of a life-threatening injury to Drew was not hidden from the College's view. Therefore, the College did owe Drew a duty to take reasonable precautions against the risk of death while Drew was taking part in the College's intercollegiate lacrosse program.

* * * *

Our holding is narrow. It predicts only that a court applying Pennsylvania law would conclude that the College had a duty to provide prompt and adequate emergency medical services to Drew, one of its intercollegiate athletes, while he was engaged in a school-sponsored athletic activity for which he had been recruited. Whether the College breached that duty is a question of fact. . . .

* * *

2. The Reasonableness of the College's Actions

On the duty question, it remains only for us to address the district court's second holding that the conduct of the College's agents in providing Drew with medical assistance and treatment following his cardiac arrest was reasonable. . . . The question of breach must be reconsidered on remand in light of this Court's holding that the College did owe Drew a duty of care to provide prompt and adequate emergency medical assistance to Drew while participating as one of its intercollegiate athletes in a school-sponsored athletic activity.

* * *

V. Conclusion

The district court's holding that the College's duty of care to Drew as an intercollegiate athlete did not include, prior to his collapse, a duty to provide prompt emergency medical service while he was engaged in school-sponsored athletic activity will be reversed. . . .We will remand this matter to the district court for further proceedings consistent with this opinion. . . .

CASES ON THE SUPPLEMENTAL WEB SITE

Estate of Newton v. Grandstaff, (2011 U.S. Dist. LEXIS 73897). The reader should note the courts implied finding that youth sport organizations have a duty to provide emergency care to participants.

L.A. Fitness International v. Mayer (2008 Fla. App. LEXIS 5893). The reader should note the court's holding that summoning professional emergency assistance satisfies the duty to provide emergency care.

Miglino v. Bally Total Fitness of Greater New York (2011 N.Y. App. Div. LEXIS 9478). The reader should note the court's holding that fitness facilities are not only required

to have an AED on premise, but also have an inherent duty to make use of the AED.

Mogabgab v. Orleans Parish School Board (1970 La. LEXIS 3455). This classic case illustrates the duty owed by sport coaches to recognize when emergency care is needed and summon prompt medical attention.

Spotlite Skating Rink, Inc. v. Barnes (2008 Miss. LEXIS 322). The reader should note the court's interpretation of the duty to provide emergency care, and consider possible implications for service providers.

QUESTIONS YOU SHOULD BE ABLE TO ANSWER

1. Describe the four elements of emergency care.

2. As a manager of a health/fitness facility, should you advocate purchasing an AED? Why or why not?

3. What certifications should be held by all staff employed in recreation and sport?

4. How would you best communicate an ERP to your staff? How would you insure they read and understand the requirements?

5. Select a facility or activity at your school. What do you need to consider regarding the four elements of emergency care?

REFERENCES

Cases
Ashburn v. Bowling Green State Univ., No. 10AP-716, 2011 Ohio App. LEXIS 1297
Atcovitz v. Gulph Mills Tennis Club, Inc., 812 A.2d 1218 (2002)
Avila v. Citrus Cmty. Coll. Dist., 131 P.3d 383 (2006)
Brown v. Atlas-Kona Kai, 2009 Cal. App. Unpub. LEXIS 2108
Brown v. Bally Total Fitness, 2003 Cal. App. Unpub. LEXIS 8245
Carter v. Baldwin, 2009 Cal. App. Unpub. LEXIS 529
Carter v. City of Cleveland, 83 Ohio St. 3d (1998)
Chai v. Sport and Fitness Clubs of America (2005)
Colon v. Chelsea Piers Mgmt., 2006 N.Y. Misc. LEXIS 2831
Estate of Newton v. Grandstaff, 2011 U.S. Dist. LEXIS 73897
Gehling v. St. George's University School of Medicine, Ltd., 705 F.Supp 761 (E.D.N.Y. 1989)
Halper v. Vayo, 568 N.E.2d 914 (1991)
Hames v. State, 1990 Tenn. App. LEXIS 53
Kelly et al. vs. Catholic Archdiocese of Washington D.C. et al., 841 A.2d 869 (2004)
Kennedy v. Syracuse University, 1995 U.S. Dist. LEXIS 13539
Kleinknecht v. Gettysburg College, 989 F.2d 1360 (1993)
Kyriazis v. University of West Virginia, 450 S.E.2d 649 (1994)
L.A. Fitness International v. Mayer, 980 So.2d 550 (2008)
Lasseigne v. American Legion, 588 So.2d 614 (1990)
Lemoine v. Cornell University, 2003 N.Y. App. LEXIS 13209
Lewin v. Fitworks of Cincinnati (2005)
Maussner v. Atlantic City Country Club, Inc., 691 A.2d 826 (1997)
Miglino v. Bally Total Fitness of Greater New York, 2011 N.Y. App. Div. LEXIS 9478

Mogabgab v. Orleans Parish School Board, 239 So.2d 456 (1970)

Myers v. Friends of Shenendehowa Crew, Inc., 31 A.D.3d 853 (2006)

Phelps v. Firebird Raceway, 83 P.3d 1090 (2004)

Pinson v. State, 1995 Tenn. App. LEXIS 807

Robinson v. Chicago Park Dist., 757 N.E.2d 565 (2001)

Rotolo v. San Jose Sports and Entertainment, 2007 Cal. App. LEXIS 843

Rutnik v. Colonie Center Club, Inc., 672 N.Y.S.2d 451 (1998)

Salte v. YMCA of Metroploitan Chicago Foundation, 814 N.E.2d 610 (2004)

Sellers v. Rudert, et al, 918 N.E.2d 586 (2009)

Spiegler v. State of Arizona, Maricopa County Supreme Ct., Case No. CV92-13608

Spotlite Skating Rink, Inc., v. Barnes, 988 So. 2d 364 (2008)

Stringer v. Minnesota Vikings Football Club, L.L.C., 686 N.W.2d 545 (2004)

Sullivan-Coughlin v. Palos Country Club, Inc., 812 N.E.2d 496 (2004)

Trotter v. School Dist., 733 N.E.2d 363 (2000)

Walker v. Daniels, 407 S.E.2d 70 (1991)

Yatsko v. Berezwick, 2008 U.S. Dist. LEXIS 47280

Yoneda v. Tom, 133 P.3d 796 (2006)

Publications

American Heart Association. *Heart Disease and Stroke Statistics–2009 Update. Circulation*; 2008. Available at: http://circ.ahajournals.org/cgi/reprint/CIRCULATIONAHA.108.191261.

Carrabis, A.B. (2011). *Head hunters: The rise of neurological concussions in American football and its legal implications.* 2 Harvard Journal of Sport & Ent. Law 371.

Center for Disease Control, *Injury Research Agenda.* Available at http://www.cdc.gov/ncipc/pub-res/research_agenda/05_sports.htm

Connaughton, D.P, Spengler, J.O. & Zhang, J.J. (2007). *An analysis of automated defibrillator implementation and related risk management practices in health/fitness clubs.* 17 Legal Aspects of Sport, 81–106.

Diehl, E.A. (2010). *Note: What's all the headache?; Reform needed to cope with the effects of concussions in football.* 23 J.L. & Health 83.

Dworkin, G.M. (1993). *The standard of care in lifeguarding,* in *American lifeguard magazine.* Available at http://www.lifesaving.com/issues/articles/standard_of_care.html

Eickhoff-Shemek, J.M., Herbert, D.L., & Connaughton, D.P. (2009). *Risk management for health/fitness professionals: legal issues and strategies.* Baltimore, MD: Lippincott, Williams & Wilkins.

Glassman, S.J. & Holt, B.D. (2011). *Concussions and student athletes: Medical-legal issues in concussion care and physician and school system risks.* 52 N.H.B.J. 26.

Hausen, J. (2012). Former Three Forks football player suing school for head injuries. Available at: http://www.bozemandailychronicle.com/news/crime/article_5152ae26-881c-11e1-a1c0-001a4bcf887a.html

Madden, T. D. (1998). *Risk management and facility insurance.* In T. D. Madden (Ed.), Public assembly facility law (pp. 199–230). Irving, TX: International Association of Assembly Managers.

Majerske, C. W. et al. (2008). *Concussion is sports: Postconcussive activity levels, symptoms, and neurocognitive performance.* 43 Journal of Athletic Training 265, 265.

McGregor, I., MacDonald, J. (1990). *Risk management manual for sport and recreation organizations.* Corvallis, OR: NIRSA

NFL Health and Safety: Lystedt Law Overview. Available at http://nflhealthandsafety.com/zackery-lystedt-law/lystedt-law-overview/

Norris, T. (2011). *New Fairfield ordinance requires ambulances on site for high school, college games in the city.* Available at http://blog.al.com/birmingham-news-stories/2011/10/new_fairfield_ordinance_requir.html

Prentice, W.E. (2006). *Athletic training: an introduction to professional practice.* New York, NY: McGraw Hill.

Shamberg, J.E. et. al (2009). *Football Concussion Results in $3 Million Settlement with High School Coaches and Administrators in Brain Injury Case,* Available at http://www.sjblaw.com/CM/Newsletters/2009-spring.pdf.

Spengler, J.O., Connaughton, D.P., & Pittman, A.T. (2006). *Risk management in sport and recreation.* Champaign, IL: Human Kinetics.

Steir, W.F, Schneider, R.C., Kampf, S. et. al (2008). *Selected risk management policies, practices, and procedures for intramural activities at NIRSA institutions,* in Recreational Sport Journal, 32, 28–44.

Toporek, B. (2012). Schools expanding reach of concussion policies for students. Available at http://blogs.edweek.org/edweek/schooled_in_sports/2012/01/schools_expanding_reach_of_concussion_policies_for_students.html

Weisfeldt, M.L., Kerber, R.E., McGoldrick, R.P. et al. (1995) *A statement for healthcare professionals from the American Heart Association task force on automatic external defibrillation.*

Wood, S. (2009). *La Salle to Pay Brain Injured Footballer $7.5 Million.* Available at *http://articles.philly.com/2009-11-30/news/24988280_1_second-impact-syndrome-braininjuries-concussion.*

Young, S.J., Fields, S.K. & Powell, G.M. (2007). *Risk perceptions versus legal realities in campus recreational sport programs,* in Recreational Sports Journal, 31, 131–145.

Legislation

Code of Ala. § 16-1-45 (2011)
A.C.A. § 6-10-122 (2012)
A.C.A. § 20-13-1306 (2012)
A.R.S. § 34-401 (2011)
Cal Health & Saf Code § 104113 (2012)
C.R.S. 22-1-125 (2011)
Fla. Stat. § 258.0165 (2012)
Fla. Stat. § 1006.165 (2012)
O.C.G.A. § 20-2-775 (2011)
105 ILCS 110/3 (2012)
210 ILCS 74/15 (2012)
Burns Ind. Code Ann. § 24-4-15-5 (2011)
La. R.S. 40:1236.11 (2012)
La. R.S. 40:1236.13 (2012)
20-A M.R.S. § 6304 (2011)
MCLS § 333.26312 (2012)
Md. Educ.Code Ann. § 7-425 (2011)
Nev. Rev. Stat. Ann. § 450B.600 (2011)
RSA 195-I:1 (2012)
N.M. Stat. Ann. § 24-10C-1 (2011)
NY CLS Gen Bus § 627-a (2011)
NY CLS Educ. § 917 (2011)
N.J. Stat. § 2A:62A-31 (2012)
2011 N.C. ALS 147
N.D. Cent. Code, § 15.1-07-31 (2011)
ORS § 327.365 (2009)
ORS § 431.680 (2009)
70 Okl. St. § 1210.200 (2012)
ORC Ann. 3313.717 (2012)
24 P.S. § 14-1423 (2011)
R.I. Gen. Laws § 5-50-12 (2012)
R.I. Gen. Laws § 23-6.2-2 (2012)
S.C. Code Ann. § 59-17-155 (2011)
Tex. Educ. Code § 22.902 (2012)
Tex. Educ. Code § 38.017 (2012)
W. Va. Code § 16-4D-1 (2011)

2.34 SUPERVISION

Paul J. Batista | Texas A & M University

Lynne P. Gaskin | University of West Georgia

Most lawsuits filed against recreation and sport organizations for injuries sustained during activities allege not only negligence, but include the more specific complaint regarding inadequate supervision. In fact, van der Smissen (1990) estimated that approximately 80 percent of cases involving programmatic situations allege **lack of supervision** or **improper supervision**.

Supervision is a broad term denoting responsibility for an area and for the activities that take place in that area (Kaiser, 1986) and includes coordinating, directing, overseeing, implementing, managing, superintending, and regulating (*Longfellow v. Corey*, 1997). The courts have provided direction in defining non-negligent supervision.

For example, in *Toller v. Plainfield School District 202* (1991), the court determined that a teacher used reasonable care by teaching the rules of wrestling; demonstrating wrestling maneuvers; matching students according to height, weight, and size; and closely supervising them. Similarly, when learning an activity, students should receive proper instruction and preparation including basic rules and procedures, suggestions for proper performance, and identification of risks (*Scott v. Rapides Parish School Board*, 1999). In addition to an instructor's explaining how to use athletic equipment and demonstrating proper techniques, the importance of observing the participant's use of the equipment also has been emphasized (*David v. County of Suffolk*, 2003). The significant case in the chapter *Kahn v. East Side Union High School District* (2003) emphasizes the importance of providing consistent, progressive instruction concerning safe performance of a skill and not coercing participants through threats.

FUNDAMENTAL CONCEPTS

Duty to Supervise

According to van der Smissen (1990), the **duty to supervise** arises from three sources: (a) a duty inherent in the situation, (b) a voluntary assumption of a duty, or (c) a duty mandated by law (see Chapter 2.11, *Elements of Negligence*). "The basis of the duty is whether or not there is a special relationship between plaintiff and defendant which requires that the defendant take affirmative action to provide a reasonably safe environment" (van der Smissen, 1990, p. 164).

When sponsoring an activity, certain organizational relationships such as school/students, fitness club/clients, and recreation department/participants, constitute **special relationships** and require the defendant organization to exercise reasonable care for the protection of participants under its supervision. Individual supervisors also have a duty to supervise that arises from the relationships inherent in the situation. These may include teacher/student, coach/player, recreation leader/participant, and supervisor/facility user. Negligence on the part of these individuals may result in both individual liability and liability for the organization (see Chapter 2.12, *Which Parties Are Liable?*).

In certain situations, there may be no duty to supervise, such as the immunity provided in numerous **recreational user statutes** (see Chapter 2.22, *Immunity*). Other examples include playgrounds at a recreation center, school grounds after hours, public beaches, and a nature trail in a public park (for a listing of individual state statutes, see Table 2.22.1 in Chapter 2.22, *Immunity*). However, the owner of the land, recreation department, school, or other sport or recreation organization can **voluntarily assume** a duty to supervise. If the decision is made to provide supervision (e.g., by having lifeguards supervise a beach and adjacent ocean at an unimproved city beach), such supervision must be non-negligent or the organization will be liable (*Fleuhr v. City of Cape May*, 1999).

In many cases, state legislatures impose a **statutory duty** to supervise various activities. For example, an Indiana statute requires roller-skating rink operators to have at least one floor supervisor for each 175 skaters, maintain the skating surface in proper and reasonably safe condition, clean and inspect the skating surface before each skating session, and maintain the rental skates in good mechanical conditions, among other duties. (Ind. Code § 34-31-6, *et seq.*, 2009). In *St. Margaret Mercy Healthcare Centers, Inc. v. Poland* (2005), the plaintiff was injured while skating when she was knocked to the floor by a skater who was skating very fast and aggressively in violation of the statute. Although the defendant asserted that the plaintiff had assumed the inherent risks of skating (see Chapter 2.21 *Defenses against Negligence*), including being knocked down by another skater, the court held the operator liable for not supervising properly according to the requirements imposed by the statute.

When a duty to supervise exists, the individual in the supervisory role also has a duty not to increase the risks inherent in learning, practicing, or participating in the activity or sport (*Lilley v. Elk Grove Unified School Dist.*, 1998).

Foreseeability and Causation Factors

When filing suit alleging improper supervision, plaintiffs must establish both that the injury was **reasonably foreseeable** under the circumstances, and that the defendant's negligent behavior was the **proximate cause** of the injury. Although supervisors are expected to be on site and in reasonable proximity to the activity they are supervising, failure to be present when an injury occurs does not necessarily mean that the supervisor is automatically liable. The plaintiff still must show that the failure to supervise was the proximate cause of the injury. In other words, no liability exists if the injury would have occurred notwithstanding the supervisor's absence (see Chapter 2.11, *Negligence*).

When the plaintiff alleges that the supervisor's absence was the proximate cause of the injury, the plaintiff must prove that the supervisor's presence would have prevented the injury. A number of cases, however, demonstrate that there are situations in which no amount of supervision would have prevented an injury. For example, a roller skater being struck by another skater (*Blashka v. South Shore Skating, Inc.*, 1993), basketball players bumping heads while jumping for the ball (*Kaufman v. City of New York*, 1961), a player running head first and colliding with a catcher who was blocking home plate (*Passantino v. Board of Educ.*, 1976), and a child falling down at a day care center while running in a grassy area of the playground (*Ward v. Mount Calvary Lutheran Church*, 1994).

Non-negligent supervision entails supervisors taking action to prevent reasonably foreseeable injuries to participants. For example, an injured plaintiff prevailed in a case in which he alleged negligent supervision since it was reasonably foreseeable that a catcher chasing a foul ball would trip over spectators who were allowed to congregate close to the base line. The supervisors had stopped the game twice prior to the injury to move the spectators back away from the third-base line and against the fence. The court found the defendants negligent for failing to control the crowd and found that the plaintiff was not guilty of contributory negligence (*Domino v. Mercurio*, 1963). In *Sheehan v. St. Peter's Catholic School* (1971), the court held that it was reasonably foreseeable that unattended students would throw rocks at each other, resulting in blindness in one of the children. Similarly, in *Dailey v. Los Angeles Unified School District* (1970), a boy died as a result of a head injury incurred during a slap-boxing incident. The person on duty at the time was in his office eating lunch rather than supervising the students. Because the injury to the boy was foreseeable and proper supervision would have prevented the injury, the court found that Dailey was liable for negligent supervision. Although *Ferguson v. DeSoto Parish School Board* (1985) involved an incident at a school, the principles established by the court should apply to all sport and recreation organizations:

> School teachers charged with the duty of superintending children in the school must exercise reasonable supervision over them, commensurate with the age of the children and the attendant circumstances. A greater degree of care must be exercised if the student is required to use or to come in contact with an inherently dangerous object, or to engage in an activity where it is reasonably foreseeable that an accident or injury may occur. The teacher is not liable in damages unless it is shown that he or she, by exercising the degree of supervision required by the circumstances, might have prevented the act which caused the damage, and did not do so. It also is essential to recovery that there be proof of

negligence in failing to provide the required supervision and proof of a causal connection between that lack of supervision and the accident.

In summary, if the potential for injury is foreseeable and the presence of the supervisor would have prevented the injury, there is a likelihood the defendant will be found liable. If, however, the injury was not reasonably foreseeable or would have occurred even if the supervisor had been there, there can be no liability. Supervisors cannot ensure the safety of participants and cannot be expected to prevent all injuries that might occur during the course of normal play or sporting activities.

Types of Supervision

Supervision, which may be general, specific, or transitional, should be predicated on the age, skill, experience, judgment, and physical condition of participants and the activity involved. **General supervision** is overseeing individuals or groups involved in an activity that does not require constant, unremitting scrutiny of the activity or facility. General supervision should be used to observe participants and activities on the playground, in the gymnasium, in the weight room, on a baseball field, or in the swimming pool, when the supervisor is not expected to have every individual under constant supervision (*Fagan v. Summers*, 1972; *Herring v. Bossier Parish School Board*, 1994; *Partin v. Vernon Parish School Board*, 1977; *Stevens v. Chesteen*, 1990). General supervision includes knowing what and how to observe, where to stand, how to move around the area, when to respond, and what action to take if a problem occurs.

Specific supervision is constant and continuous, the type of supervision that is more appropriate for individuals or small groups receiving instruction, involved in high-risk activities, or using areas that have the potential for serious injury. For example, participants who are learning an activity or skill need specific, direct supervision. Similarly, participants who are not able to perform a skill adequately need specific supervision. Specific supervision also is mandated when participants behave, or would be expected to behave, in ways that may injure themselves or others. Specific supervision also implies proximity; that is, how close the supervisor needs to be to the participants or activity to be effective. The more dangerous the activity, the more closely it should be supervised.

According to van der Smissen (1990), supervision cannot be categorized simply as general or specific, but is frequently **transitional** in nature. For example, supervision may change from specific, to general, then back to specific, depending on such factors as the participants' need for instruction, their ability to perform certain activities, their use of equipment, their involvement with others, and their use of the facility. As the potential for harm increases, the degree of supervision should increase proportionally. Specific supervision is appropriate when the supervisor perceives a situation as dangerous. Whether involved in general or specific supervision, or moving from one to the other, supervisors are expected to identify dangerous activities and intervene to stop the activity or facilitate its continuing safely.

Attributes of Proper Supervision

Qualifications of Supervisors

Organizations should hire only supervisors who have exhibited competence in properly supervising the participants involved, activities conducted, and facilities utilized. Whenever possible, supervisors should be regular, full-time employees who have appropriate qualifications and undergo regular staff development to improve their skill and knowledge. Requiring that employees hold all mandated qualifications and certifications can help protect the organization in the event of employee negligence. However, possession of required certifications and qualifications by the supervisor does not protect the supervisor from liability for his or her negligence. For example, if a supervisor is negligent (e.g., failure to enforce a "no diving" rule in the shallow end of the pool results in injury), the supervisor having certificates and qualifications helps to protect the organization from liability, but does not provide protection for the supervisor.

Individuals in supervisory positions should have the appropriate qualifications, certification, experience, and training necessary for the job. An example of standards regarding qualifications in the health and fitness industry is found in the benchmarks developed by the American College of Sports Medicine (ACSM). Notably, one of the six standards explicitly addresses supervision of youth services and programs, and another addresses competencies of those responsible for program supervision (American College of Sports Medicine, 1997). The standard of care imposed on a supervisor is not dependent on his or her qualifications, but is the degree of care that a person of ordinary prudence, charged with comparable duties, would exercise under the same circumstances.

In a joint endeavor with the American Heart Association, ACSM advocated more stringent standards and guidelines for health and fitness facilities for cardiovascular screening, staffing (supervision), and emergency policies and procedures (ACSM & American Heart Association [AHA], 1998). Both of these efforts have been recognized for their importance in assisting health and fitness facilities with standard of care issues (Herbert, 1997, 1998). Supervisors will be measured against these guidelines in determining whether they acted as reasonably prudent health and fitness practitioners.

Number of Supervisors

The number of persons required to provide reasonable supervision depends on the participants and the nature of the activity. Moreover, when plaintiffs allege negligence due to an insufficient number of supervisors, they must show that inadequate supervision was the proximate cause of the injury and that additional supervisors would have prevented the injury (*Kaczmarcsyk v. City & County of Honolulu*, 1982). Except for swimming pool and school playground cases, however, the courts generally have not imposed liability when there has been at least one supervisor present (Gaskin, 2003). Instead of focusing on the number of supervisors, the courts generally have examined whether the supervision was reasonable in light of the age, maturity, and experience of the participants and the circumstances that existed at the time of the accident. As the court said in *Glankler v. Rapides Parish School Board* (1993), "in considering a defendant's duty to a particular person, consideration should be given to the person's age, maturity, experience, familiarity with the premises and its dangers, and other factors which might increase or decrease the risk of harm to that person."

Not only must supervisors warn of dangers, they also must make sure the participants comply with the warnings and expected behavior. In *Rollins v. Concordia Parish School Board* (1985), a teacher warned very young students to slow down a merry-go-round because it was going too fast. When a dispute over a basketball arose between other students, her attention was drawn away from the children on the merry-go-round, and one of the children was hurt. The teacher and school were held liable for injuries to the student based on failure to supervise properly. Another teacher was available to be on the playground at the time, but instead she was allowed to take a break during the period rather than help supervise.

Established Standards of Conduct

To properly organize and manage an event, a supervisor must be familiar with any standards of conduct or practice that establish criteria for proper handling of the event. *Black's Law Dictionary* (Garner, 2004) defines a **standard** as "a model accepted as correct by custom, consent, or authority" and "a criterion for measuring acceptability, quality, or accuracy." Failure to adhere to recognized standards of practice can leave the supervisor subject to liability (see Chapter 4.21, *Standards of Practice*).

Primary Duties of Supervision

Although there are numerous legal duties associated with proper supervision of recreation and sporting activities, authors differ on the number and description of those duties (McCaskey & Biedzynski, 1996; Nygaard & Boone, 1985). These commonly recognized duties can be condensed to six primary general duties, each requiring that the prudent supervisor undertake various specific actions. The six duties are (1) effective planning, (2) proper instruction, (3) warning of risks, (4) providing a safe environment, (5) evaluating the physical and mental condition of participants, and (6) providing emergency care.

Effective Planning

Effective planning is the first, and most important, element of proper supervision. Just as successful coaches prepare game plans for upcoming games, the prudent recreation or sport manager will organize every activity or event in advance by taking into account all foreseeable dangers or risks of potential injury to the participants.

Recreation and sport managers need to develop, implement, and evaluate a supervision plan for facilities, activities and individuals on the premises. Although many of the elements of proper supervision overlap, effective planning precedes all of them. Regardless of the situation, a systematic procedure should be developed to document specifically each component to be addressed in supervision: **who, what, when, where, how,** and **why.** There should be both a master plan (including all the facilities, when they will be used, by whom, for what, and who will be supervising) and a detailed supervision plan for each area and activity. The prudent supervisor will ask, "What is the worst thing that could happen here, and how do we avoid it?"

Several cases support the necessity of having adequate supervision plans. In *Dailey v. Los Angeles Unified School Dist.* (1970), negligent supervision was at issue when the supervision plan did not provide for a formal supervision schedule, and allowed too much discretion on the part of subordinates. In *Broward County School Board v. Ruiz* (1986), the supervision plan failed to provide for supervision in an after-school waiting area. Due to inadequate supervision plans, negligence was found in each of these cases. Other cases where supervisors have created liability for themselves or their organizations include failure to prepare a plan (*Landers v. School District No. 203*, 1978), deviating from an approved plan (*Keesee v. Board of Education of the City of New York*, 1962), failing to follow an approved plan (*Brahatcek v. Millard School District No. 17*, 1979), and creating a hazardous plan (*DeGooyer v. Harkness*, 1944).

An effective supervision plan requires detailed planning, development, implementation, evaluation, and revision. Everyone involved in the activity should be involved in developing supervision plans, evaluating them, and revising them with primary emphasis on maintaining the safety of participants in a safe environment. Although the framework for a supervision plan may vary, the plan should be in writing, be specific, and be evaluated on a regular schedule to assess its effectiveness.

Proper Instruction

The standard of care imposed on supervisors is the degree of care that persons of ordinary prudence, charged with comparable duties, would exercise under the same circumstances (*Dailey v. Los Angeles Unified School District*, 1970). In *Green v. Orleans Parish School Board (1978)*, a 16-year-old male was permanently paralyzed by injuries sustained while performing a wrestling drill in a required physical education class. While addressing the issue of whether the teacher's method of conducting the class was so substandard as to create an unreasonable risk of injury to students, the court described some of the attributes of **proper instruction**. The court included the following factors: an explanation of basic rules and procedures, suggestions for proper performance (of wrestling moves), identification of risks (including the extent of physical conditioning), the difficulty and inherent dangerousness of the activity, and the age and experience of the students. In *Scott v. Rapides Parish School Board* (1999), an 18-year-old student successfully sued for a knee injury sustained when the track coach gave him a tryout for the long jump without instructions on proper technique.

Proper instruction includes the requirement that participants be trained in the proper use of the premises and equipment involved in the activity. Supervisors and all staff members should make sure that all participants are instructed in the safe use of equipment and facilities; are observed to ensure that they are using the equipment and facility properly; and are informed of the risks and possible injuries associated with the equipment, facility, and activity (*Corrigan v. Musclemakers, Inc.*, 1999). In *Thomas v. Sport City, Inc.* (1999), a health club member was injured after he did not properly secure a squat machine that he had used. The court confirmed that the health and fitness facility owed a duty of reasonable care to protect members from injury while they are on the premises, and that the duty includes insuring that the members know how to use the exercise equipment properly.

Proper instruction also should be clear, age appropriate, in logical sequence, repeated as many times as necessary for the participants to understand the activity, and include sufficient time for feedback (including questions and answers) for the instructor to be satisfied that the participants have grasped the directions.

Warnings of Risks

Supervisors of activities have a **duty to warn** of all inherent risks associated with the activity. **Inherent risks** are those that are foreseeable and customary risks of the sport or recreational activity (*Barakat v. Pordash*, 2005). Although most courts have concluded that participants assume the inherent risks of the activities in competitive sporting events, the rule may be different for other activities. When dangerous conditions exist or when there is an **elevated risk** of injury in conducting the activity, courts have found activity supervisors liable for failure to adequately warn of the risks or dangers involved. In *Corrigan v. Musclemakers, Inc.* (1999), despite the fact that the 49-year-old health club patron had never used a treadmill, her personal trainer placed her on the treadmill, left her unattended, and failed to instruct her how to adjust the speed, stop the belt, or operate the control panel. The court rejected the defendant's argument that plaintiff had assumed the risk, finding that the risks were not obvious to an untrained patron. The prudent supervisor will warn of all risks associated with any activity, assuming that the courts will scrutinize whether or not the participant was aware of all the risks, both inherent and otherwise.

Many states have passed various **immunity statutes** requiring that written warnings be posted for the proprietor or operator to benefit from limited liability. An example of such statutes is the equine statutes passed in virtually every state. These statutes generally require that the operator post a sign advising participants that taking part in the activity subjects them to assumption of all inherent risks of the activity, thereby relieving the operator from any liability for injury caused by such risks. *St. Margaret Mercy Healthcare Centers, Inc. v. Poland* (2005) discusses a similar statute for roller-skating (see Chapter 2.22, Immunity [especially Table 2.22.1], Chapter 2.21, *Defenses against Negligence*, and Chapter 3.10, *Property Law*).

Providing a Safe Environment

Courts often declare that supervisors are not **guarantors** that participants will not be hurt or injured. Stated another way, supervisors are not charged with a legal duty to protect participants from the inherent risks of the activity, or to eliminate all risks of taking part in the activity (*Kahn v. East Side Union High School District*, 2003; *Kelly v. McCarrick*, 2002). However, supervisors have a duty not to increase the risk of harm beyond that which is inherent in the activity or to expose participants to risks that are concealed (*Benitez v. New York City Board of Education*, 1989).

Courts have established different standards for compulsory participation (such as required school physical education courses) and purely voluntary activities (such as extracurricular interscholastic school sports). In the latter, courts consistently hold that the participant assumes the inherent risks of the activity provided the participant is aware of the risks. Hurst and Knight (2003) summarized the difficulty in establishing liability against the coach and school in such cases by indicating that a successful plaintiff must prove "serious misconduct" amounting to "serious inattention, ignorance and indifference." In the compulsory participation circumstance, the defense of assumption of risk may not be a protection from liability when the injured party is compelled to participate by a superior (*Benitez v. New York City Board of Education*, 1989). The court's rationale is that participation and assumption of the risks are no longer voluntarily undertaken by the participant.

Providing a safe environment includes the obligation to provide **safe facilities** for participants by properly maintaining equipment, buildings, playgrounds, and other facilities. Although this duty is charged to the owner or operator, supervisors who work for the owners or operators continually must inspect the facility, repair or eliminate dangerous conditions, and warn users of concealed or hidden hazards (see Chapter 2.31, *Premises Liability*).

Another aspect of a safe environment is the proper use of equipment, particularly safety equipment. Courts discussed liability relating to equipment use in the following cases: failure to require that a previously injured football player wear a neck roll according to doctor's instructions (*Harvey v. Ouachita Parish School Board*, 1996); reversal of a summary judgment for the school when a football player was injured after running into a blocking sled that was stored on the sidelines of the practice field (*Cruz v. City of New York*, 2001); reversal and remand of a case in which the school was held not liable for failing to furnish eye goggles that were necessary for the safety of the player (*Palmer v. Mount Vernon Township High School District 201*, 1995); and furnishing a football uniform, but not furnishing a knee brace to a recently injured player (*Lowe v. Texas Tech University*, 1975).

Evaluating the Physical and Mental Condition of Participants

The responsibility to supervise varies with the age and experience of participants, their mental condition, and the nature of the activity in which they are engaged.

Young Children. Supervisors observing young children have a heightened duty of care (*Ferguson v. DeSoto Parish School Bd.*, 1985). Ordinarily, it is necessary to exercise greater caution for the protection and safety of a young child than for an adult who possesses normal physical and mental faculties. A supervisor dealing with children must anticipate the ordinary behavior of children. Children usually do not use the same degree of caution for their own safety as adults do, and they often are thoughtless and impulsive. It is precisely this lack of mature judgment that necessitates a higher degree of supervision. (*Calandri v. Ione Unified School Dist.*, 1963).

Youth. Even older high school volleyball players who are left unsupervised may engage in horseplay and incur debilitating injuries (*Barretto v. City of New York*, 1997). However, at least one court rejected the theory that a lower standard of care is warranted when supervising high school (as opposed to elementary school) students (*Beckett v. Clinton Prairie School Corp.*, 1987).

Adults. In comparison with children, adults participating in activity generally require less supervision. Just as when dealing with children, however, supervisors must be alert to adults who may be involved in horseplay and be prepared to intervene as necessary.

Novices. The reasonableness of supervision is also related to the abilities of participants. Novice participants (adult or children) require close supervision because it is foreseeable that they may be injured primarily because they are unfamiliar with, and inexperienced in, the activity (*Brahatcek v. Millard School District*, 1979).

Disabled Participants. Generally, greater caution is required for participants with disabling conditions, and the courts have provided sound direction for supervising children with disabling conditions. For example, in *Foster v. Houston General Insurance Co.* (1982), when a Special Olympics team was walking three blocks from campus to a gymnasium to practice basketball, a developmentally disabled child unexpectedly ran into the street and was run over, resulting in his death. The court noted that the teachers' duty was to protect the child from his own impulsive acts, and held that the teachers were negligent for failing to provide an adequate number of supervisory personnel, and for failing to select the safest route for the walk, particularly given the mental abilities of the students.

Dangerous Activities. Participants involved in dangerous activities mandate a higher degree of supervision than others do. If an activity is dangerous or has the potential to be dangerous, it is essential that supervisors provide participants with detailed instructions, familiarize them with basic rules and procedures necessary for executing skills, and warn them of reasonably foreseeable dangers before they attempt the skill or engage in the activity. Both *Green v. Orleans Parish School Board* (1978) and *Carabba v. Anacortes School District No. 103* (1967) involved wrestling. Both courts held that continuous and constant supervision is required.

Mismatching. Mismatching is a situation in which a smaller, younger, less-skillful, and/or less-experienced participant is injured while participating with a larger, older, more skillful, and/or more experienced participant. Many mismatching cases involve a situation where one participant is an inexperienced, smaller member of a junior varsity team who is pitted against a larger, advanced skill-level player (*Tepper v. City of New Rochelle School District*, 1988). Allegations of mismatching also have been made where the defendant supervisor (teacher, coach, or leader) breached the standard of care by failing to fulfill his or her duties to provide non-negligent supervision by becoming a participant in the activity. Some courts have found the defendant supervisor at fault while others have ruled that participating while supervising did not constitute a breach of duty. Examples include a wrestling case in which the referee-instructor injured a high school wrestler while attempting to show him the fireman's carry (*Hearon v. May*, 1995), a tag game in an after-school child care program in which the adult-leader participated (*Longfellow v. Corey*, 1997), a touch football game in which the teacher participated during lunch recess (*Hamill v. Town of Southampton*, 1999), and an after-school Big Buddy Program in which a child was injured in a basketball game in which the coach participated (*Prejean v. East Baton Rouge Sch. Brd.*, 1999).

Although supervision often includes directing, teaching, and demonstrating techniques, it does not encompass prolonged, active participation that rises to the level of intense one-on-one competition that has a winner and a loser. Under such circumstances, the teacher, coach, or leader may be abandoning the role of supervisor and becoming an equal competitor with the participant(s).

Supervisors who use **coercion** or **threats** to induce participants to perform some activity raise the potential of liability in the event the participant is injured. It is not unusual for participants to make excuses why they should not perform the activity assigned by the supervisor. At that point, the supervisor is placed in the position of both doctor and psychiatrist, trying to determine whether the reluctance is legitimate or not. Caution should be used before coercing participants to continue with the activity. In *Kahn v. East Side Union High School District* (2003), this chapter's significant case, the inexperienced swimmer had "a deep-seated fear that she would suffer a traumatic head injury from diving into shallow water" and had so informed her coaches. They ignored her fear and required her to dive, resulting in a broken neck. Although the court in this case did not find the coach responsible for negligent supervision, it did remand the case to the trial court for such a determination. In *Koch v. Billings School Dist. No. 2* (1992), a junior high student was encouraged by his teacher to squat-press 360 pounds against the plaintiff's protests. The plaintiff sustained significant injuries when he could not sustain the weight. Although the case was decided on sovereign immunity issues, the court remanded the case to determine whether the teacher was negligent in pushing the student to lift the weight. Supervisors must be very cautious to find the delicate balance between appropriately pushing participants to a higher level of performance, and coercing or threatening them unreasonably, thereby increasing the risk of injury.

Providing Emergency Care

In the event that a participant is injured during the conduct of the activity, a supervisor has a duty to provide adequate emergency care (see Chapter 2.33, *Emergency Care*).

Adhering to Policies or Standards in Manuals

Knowledge of and adherence to policies in staff manuals have become increasingly important in helping supervisors demonstrate that they know what is expected of them and that they have followed these policies or standards in carrying out their responsibilities. In *Kahn v. East Side Union High School District* (2003), the Red Cross manual for swimming coaches, which the coach indicated that he followed, contained specific recommendations about the progression coaches should use in helping swimmers learn a racing dive. The coach failed to instruct the plaintiff how to perform a shallow-water racing dive before she was asked to do so in a competitive swim meet, resulting in her injury. Failure to follow the Red Cross standard was one of the pivotal factors in the court's decision to reverse and remand the case for further proceedings.

If the defendant fails to follow policies or standards in a manual that have been adopted, developed, and shared by the organization, association, or program, the individual may be accused of negligent supervision. Although having a policy manual demonstrates that there are standards employees are expected to follow, it is equally important that these policies are shared, discussed, and practiced. When policies are clear, well-understood, and valued, employees have a sense of confidence in being up-to-date in adhering to standards of practice that reflect strong professional competency (see Chapter 5.21, *Standards of Practice*).

SIGNIFICANT CASE

The California Supreme Court case of Kahn v. East Side Union High School District is a treasure-trove of legal principles that includes discussion of many of the subjects covered in this and other chapters. Among the issues discussed in this case are proper supervision, proximate cause, primary assumption of risk, inherent risks, duty not to increase the risks inherent in the activity, coercion to perform by an authority figure (coach), effect of applicable standards or guidelines established by professional associations, and use or nonuse of safety training manuals. The case was reversed and remanded for trial to determine whether the coach's actions in teaching and coaching the plaintiff were reckless, and were the proximate cause of plaintiff's injuries. The case presented here has been significantly condensed to save space. The full opinion also includes discussions of premises liability, summary judgment review, proximate cause and intervening acts, and the weight to be given to expert witness testimony.

KAHN V. EAST SIDE UNION HIGH SCHOOL DISTRICT

Supreme Court of California
49 P.3d 349 (2003)

This case presents a question concerning the proper application of the doctrine of primary assumption of risk. At the time of her injury, plaintiff was a 14-year-old novice member of defendant school district's junior varsity [high school] swim team. She was participating in a competitive swim meet when she executed a practice dive into a shallow racing pool that was located on defendant school district's property and broke her neck. She alleged that the injury was caused in part by the failure of her coach, a district employee, to provide her with any instruction in how to safely dive into a shallow racing pool. She also alleged lack of adequate supervision and further that the coach breached the duty of care owed to her by insisting that she dive at the swim meet despite her objections, her lack of expertise, her fear of diving, and the coach's previous promise to exempt her from diving.

* * * In the present case, we recognize that the relationship of a sports instructor or coach to a student or athlete is different from the relationship between coparticipants in a sport. But because a significant part of an instructor's or coach's role is to challenge or "push" a student or athlete to advance in his or her skill level and to undertake more difficult tasks, and because the fulfillment of such a role could be improperly chilled by too stringent a standard of potential legal liability, we conclude that the same general standard should apply in cases in which an instructor's alleged liability rests primarily on a claim that he or she challenged the player to perform beyond his or her capacity or failed to provide adequate instruction or supervision before directing or permitting a student to perform a particular maneuver that has resulted in injury to the student. A sports instructor may be found to have breached a duty of care to a student or athlete only if the instructor intentionally injures the student or engages in conduct that is reckless in the sense that it is "totally outside the range of the ordinary activity" involved in teaching or coaching the sport.

Applying this standard to the present case, we conclude that, on the basis of the declarations and deposition testimony filed in support of and in opposition to defendants' motion for summary judgment, the Court of Appeal majority erred in determining that the doctrine of primary assumption of risk warranted entry of summary judgment in defendants' favor. We conclude that the totality of the circumstances precludes the grant of defendants' motion for summary judgment. Specifically, we refer to evidence of defendant coach's failure to provide plaintiff with training in shallow-water diving, his awareness of plaintiff's intense fear of diving into shallow water, his conduct in lulling plaintiff into a false sense of security by promising that she would not be required to dive at competitions, his last-minute breach of this promise in the heat of a competition, and his threat to remove her from competition or at least from the meet if she refused to dive. Plaintiff's evidence supports the conclusion that the maneuver of diving into a shallow racing pool, if not done correctly, poses a significant risk of extremely serious injury, and that there is a well-established mode of instruction for teaching a student to perform this maneuver safely. The declarations before the trial court raise a disputed issue of fact as to whether defendant coach provided any instruction at all to plaintiff with regard to the safe performance of such a maneuver, as well as to the existence and nature of the coach's promises and threats. Under these circumstances, the question whether the coach's conduct was reckless in that it fell totally outside the range of ordinary activity involved in teaching or coaching this sport cannot properly be resolved on summary judgment. Accordingly, the judgment of the Court of Appeal is reversed.

* * *

Plaintiff did not have prior experience as a competitive swimmer, but she was a competent swimmer and had executed dives into deep water on a recreational basis. She recalled that during a team practice session, Coach McKay directed other team members to help her practice diving off the deck of the diving pool into deep water. Coach Chiaramonte-Tracy observed her dives, plaintiff asserted, and stated that plaintiff needed more practice. Teammates remarked that plaintiff had gone in too deep. Plaintiff had a deep-seated fear that she would suffer a traumatic head injury from diving into shallow water, and had so informed the two coaches when she joined the team in September. She alleged that during the few weeks between the commencement of the swim season and the accident, the coaches failed to offer her any instruction or training in shallow-water racing diving, nor, prior to the date of her accident, did she receive such instruction from her teammates. McKay assured her that, although three out of the four team members who participate in a relay must dive into the pool, plaintiff would not be required to dive at meets. Rather, she would be the team member who started from inside the pool. At the two or three meets that preceded the occasion on which plaintiff was injured, McKay directed plaintiff to execute the first leg of the relay race, which caused her to start in the water rather than from the deck of the pool.

Plaintiff asserted that McKay informed her, minutes before the meet was to begin * * * that this time he would not permit her to start her relay from inside the pool. She panicked and begged him to change the rotation so she could start in the water. She reiterated that she was afraid to dive into the shallow pool, that she did not know how to perform a racing dive, and that she never had performed one. McKay, she claimed, informed her that unless she dove off the starting block, he would not permit her to participate. (She could not recall whether he said she could not participate in the meet or could not be on the team.) She claimed that he did not give her the option of diving from the deck of the pool. Two teammates offered to show plaintiff how to perform the racing dive, and without any coach's supervision she began to practice diving from the starting block into the shallow racing pool. Plaintiff asserted that the coaches had not directed her to refrain from practicing unless they were present. Plaintiff could see coach McKay in her peripheral vision. On her third practice dive, she broke her neck.

In support of her opposition to defendants' motion for summary judgment, plaintiff offered a Red Cross safety training manual for swim coaches, a manual whose recommendations McKay stated that he followed. The manual notes that diving into water less than five feet deep is dangerous and that 95 percent of swimming injuries occur in water five feet deep or less. The manual states: "Even an experienced diver can be seriously injured by diving improperly . . . or diving from starting blocks without proper training and supervision." The manual also states that "[i]t is important that swim coaches take all reasonable precautions to prevent accidents in shallow water entries." Coaches should require persons learning the racing dive to perform adequate shallow dives from the deck into the deep pool on a consistent basis, then require students to perform a shallow dive from a starting block into the deep pool. This is important, the manual declares, "because of the increased velocity the swimmer achieves from entering the water from an increased height." Then, "[w]hen the swimmer's skill level has been consistently established from the starting block in deep water and the swimmer is able to maintain his or her racing start depth at two to two and a half feet, the swimmer may proceed to the shallow end. The coach then takes the swimmer through the same steps, beginning with shallow dives from the deck and then moving up to the block."

Plaintiff's expert, Stanley Shulman, had been a certified water safety instructor for 40 years, had coached junior and senior high school swimming for 17 years, and had published a number of studies of swimming injuries. He stated that diving into three and a half feet of water from the deck of a pool or from a starting block is extremely dangerous, and is ultrahazardous if done by a swimmer without adequate training. The sequence of instruction laid out in the Red Cross manual should be strictly followed, he declared, and "[b]efore an inexperienced diver attempts a racing dive into a shallow pool, [he or she] should perfect the same dive off starting blocks in the deep pool. [¶] The dive should be consistently done in the deep pool at a depth not exceeding two to two and a half feet before attempting it in shallow water."

On January 14, 2000, the trial court granted summary judgment in favor of defendants. It found that, under the doctrine of primary assumption of risk, defendants could not be liable unless they had elevated the risks inherent in competitive swimming or had behaved recklessly. Viewing the evidence in the light most favorable to plaintiff, the trial court determined that defendants were entitled to judgment as a matter of law and entered judgment in their favor. Plaintiff's motion for new trial was denied, and she appealed.

In February 2002, the Court of Appeal affirmed the grant of summary judgment on the theory that the doctrine of primary assumption of risk barred plaintiff's claim. In a split decision, the court concluded that shallow-water diving is a fundamental part of competitive swimming and that such diving presents a danger that is an inherent risk of the sport.

In reaching its decision, the court considered whether defendants should be liable for plaintiff's injury because they "pushed plaintiff beyond her capabilities or because they increased her risk in some other way." The majority determined that, assuming coach McKay required plaintiff to compete at a level beyond her existing skill level, coaches who merely challenge their students to move beyond their current level of performance have not breached a duty of care.

* * *

Although persons generally owe a duty of due care not to cause an unreasonable risk of harm to others (Civ. Code, § 1714, subd. (a)), some activities—and, specifically, many sports—are inherently dangerous. Imposing a duty to mitigate those inherent dangers could alter the nature of the activity or inhibit vigorous participation. In a game of touch football, for example, there is an inherent risk that players will collide; to impose a general duty on coparticipants to avoid the risk of harm arising from a collision would work a basic alteration—or cause abandonment—of the sport.

* * *

But the question of duty depends not only on the nature of the sport, but also on the "role of the defendant whose conduct is at issue in a given case." [Knight v. Jewett (1992) 3 Cal.4th 296] Duties with respect to the same risk may vary according to the role played by particular defendants involved in the sport.

* * *

We had occasion to comment in passing on an instructor's duty * * * Citing Court of Appeal cases that had been decided subsequent to our decision in Knight, * * * we explained that "there are circumstances in which the relationship between defendant and plaintiff gives rise to a duty on the part of the defendant to use due care not to increase the risks inherent in the plaintiff's activity. For example, a purveyor of recreational activities owes a duty to a patron not to increase the risks inherent in the activity in which the patron has paid to engage. [Citations.] Likewise, *a coach or sport instructor owes a duty to a student not to increase the risks inherent in the learning process undertaken by the student.* * * *

The general proposition that a sports instructor or coach owes a duty of due care not to increase the risk of harm inherent in learning an active sport is consistent with a growing line of Court of Appeal opinions that have applied the *Knight* analysis to claims against such defendants. In these cases, the reviewing courts examined the particular circumstances of the sport, its inherent risks, and the relationship of the parties to the sport and to each other. Most also examined the question whether imposing broader liability on coaches and instructors would harm the sport or cause it to be changed or abandoned. In each instance, the Courts of Appeal have agreed that although the coach or athletic instructor did not have a duty to eliminate the risks presented by a sport, he or she did have a duty to the student not to increase the risk inherent in learning, practicing, or performing in the sport. * * *

Subsequent decisions have clarified that the risks associated with *learning* a sport may themselves be inherent risks of the sport, and that an instructor or coach generally does not increase the risk of harm inherent in learning the sport simply by urging the student to strive to excel or to reach a new level of competence. This line of cases analyzes and articulates an important and appropriate limitation on the duty of a sports instructor. The cases point out that instruction in a sport frequently entails challenging or "pushing" a student to attempt new or more difficult feats, and that "liability should not be imposed simply because an instructor asked the student to take action beyond what, with hindsight, is found to have been the student's abilities." * * * As a general matter, although the nature of the sport and the relationship of the parties to it and to each other remain relevant, a student's inability to meet an instructor's legitimate challenge is a risk that is inherent in learning a sport. To impose a duty to mitigate the inherent risks of learning a sport by refraining from challenging a student, as these cases explain, could have a chilling effect on the enterprise of teaching and learning skills that are necessary to the sport. At a competitive level, especially, this chilling effect is undesirable.

* * *

We agree that the object to be served by the doctrine of primary assumption of risk in the sports setting is to avoid recognizing a duty of care when to do so would tend to alter the nature of an active sport or chill vigorous participation in the activity. This concern applies to the process of learning to become competent or competitive in such a sport. Novices and children need instruction if they are to participate and compete, and we agree with the many Court of Appeal decisions that have refused to define a duty of care in terms that would inhibit adequate instruction and learning or eventually alter the nature of the sport. Accordingly, we believe that the standard set forth in *Knight*, * * * as it applies to coparticipants, generally should apply to sports instructors, keeping in mind, of course, that different facts are of significance in each

setting. In order to support a cause of action in cases in which it is alleged that a sports instructor has required a student to perform beyond the student's capacity or without providing adequate instruction, it must be alleged and proved that the instructor acted with intent to cause a student's injury or that the instructor acted recklessly in the sense that the instructor's conduct was "totally outside the range of the ordinary activity" (*Knight, supra,* 3 Cal.4th at p. 318,) involved in teaching or coaching the sport.

The Court of Appeal majority in the present case concluded that in light of plaintiff's allegations and supporting evidence, coach McKay merely challenged her to go beyond her current level of competence. We believe that this takes an unduly narrow view of plaintiff's claim and her evidence, which went far beyond a claim that the coach made an ordinary error of judgment in determining that she was ready to perform the shallow-water dive.

As noted above, the Red Cross teaching manual submitted by plaintiff acknowledged that the principal danger faced by persons learning to compete in swimming is the shallow-water dive. The risk presented is not simply that the swimmer might suffer bruises or even break an arm; the risk is that the student may sustain serious head and spinal cord injuries by striking the bottom of the pool. Plaintiff presented evidence, both documentary and expert, that a settled progression of instruction in the dive is considered essential to a student's safety. Her own declaration and deposition testimony was that she had not received any instruction at all from her coaches or teammates on the performance of the shallow-water dive. She also claimed that she had expressed a mortal fear of performing the shallow-water dive and that she had been assured by the coach that she would not be required to perform it. Her evidence was that the coach made a last-minute demand that she take a position in the relay race that would require her to dive, threatening that if she did not comply, either she would be dropped from the team or she would not be permitted to compete that day.

Defendant McKay did not challenge the sequence of instruction prescribed by the Red Cross manual, but said in his declaration and deposition testimony that he generally followed it.

* * *

We agree that the following factors indicated a triable issue with respect to whether the coach's behavior was reckless: the lack of training in the shallow-water dive disclosed by plaintiff's evidence, especially in the face of the sequenced training recommended in the Red Cross manual submitted by plaintiff; the coach's awareness of plaintiff's deep-seated fear of such diving; his conduct in lulling her into a false sense of security through a promise that she would not be required to dive, thereby eliminating any motivation on her part to learn to dive safely; his last-minute breach of that promise under the pressure of a competitive meet; and his threat to remove her from the team or at least the meet if she refused to dive.

Clearly, a disputed issue of fact exists as to whether the coach provided any instruction at all on shallow-water diving, and the nature of the coach's promises and threats to plaintiff also are in dispute. If a jury were to find that defendant coach directed plaintiff (a novice on the swim team) to perform a shallow racing dive in competition without providing any instruction, that he ignored her overwhelming fears and made a last-minute demand that she dive during competition, in breach of a previous promise that she would not be required to dive, we believe the trier of fact properly could determine that such conduct was reckless in that it was totally outside the range of the ordinary activity involved in teaching or coaching the sport of competitive swimming. Accordingly, on this record, we conclude that the trial court erred in granting summary judgment in favor of defendants and that the Court of Appeal erred in affirming that determination.

* * *

Keeping in mind that ultimately it will be plaintiff's obligation to establish the elements of her cause of action before the trier of fact by a preponderance of the evidence, we believe that triable issues of material fact exist regarding the question whether coach McKay breached a duty of care owed to plaintiff, thereby causing her injury, by engaging in conduct that was reckless in that it was totally outside the range of ordinary activity involved in teaching or coaching the sport of competitive swimming.

For the foregoing reasons, the judgment of the Court of Appeal is reversed and the matter is remanded for further proceedings consistent with this opinion.

CASES ON THE SUPPLEMENTAL WEB SITE

Brahatcek v. Millard School Dist., 202 Neb. 86, 273 N.W.2d 680 (Neb. 1979). Plaintiff alleged lack of supervision as the proximate cause of the 14-year-old student's death when he was struck by a golf club in a physical education class. The court discussed heightened supervision required for a young and inexperienced student.

Green v. Orleans Parish School Bd., 365 So.2d 834 (La. App., 1978). A 16-year- old student was injured while wrestling in a required physical education class. The court recognized that the teacher had the legal duty to conduct classes in such a way that students were not exposed to an unreasonable risk of injury. The court also acknowledged that students should receive proper instruction, basic rules, suggestions for proper performance, and recognition of risks involved.

Mirand v. City of New York, 84 N.Y.2d 44 (N.Y. 1994). Even though this case does not involve sport or recreation, it is instructive on the requirements for proper supervision of students who might injure other students. When the school is aware of potential danger and reasonably could have anticipated one student injuring another, failure to adequately supervise students could make the school liable. The court in this case acknowledged that while schools are not the insurer of students' safety, they are charged with providing adequate supervision.

St. Margaret Mercy Healthcare Centers, Inc. v. Poland, 828 N.E.2d 396 (Ind. Ct. App. 2005). An injured roller skater alleged that the roller rink operator was guilty of negligent supervision. Indiana has a statute that places a legal duty on rink operators to ". . . use reasonable care in supervising roller skaters." The court reviewed the facts of the case to determine whether the rink had discharged its obligations under the statute. The court analyzed the four elements of negligence in resolving the negligent supervision issue. The court also discussed the application of assumption of risk as a complete defense, and comparative fault in order to apportion damages.

Zipusch v. LA Workout, Inc., 155 Cal. App. 4th 1281, 66 Cal. Rptr. 3d 704 (Cal. App. 2 Dist., 2007). Plaintiff alleged the health club was negligent for failing to inspect and maintain its exercise equipment when a sticky substance on a treadmill caused her fall, resulting in an injury.

QUESTIONS YOU SHOULD BE ABLE TO ANSWER

1. Identify the three sources from which the duty to supervise arises and briefly discuss the important aspects of each.

2. A participant is injured and alleges negligence on the part of the supervisor. Describe how the concepts of foreseeability and causation apply, specifically, concerning the presence or absence of the supervisor.

3. Identify and briefly describe the appropriateness of the three types of supervision as they relate to the age, skill, experience, judgment, and physical condition of participants and the activity involved.

4. When teaching or coaching, what are the most important concepts for one to consider in planning, instructing, and warning of risks involved in the activity?

5. What are the major concerns one should consider when supervising young children, high school students, adults, and individuals with varying abilities?

REFERENCES
Cases

Barakat v. Pordash, 842 N.E.2d 120, 2005 WL 3074729 (Ohio App. 8 Dist., 2005).
Barretto v. City of New York, 229 A.D.2d 214; 655 N.Y.S.2d 484 (1997).
Beckett v. Clinton Prairie School. Corp., 504 N.E.2d 552 (Ind. 1987).
Benitez v. New York City Board of Education, 541 N.E.2d 29 (NY 1989).
Blashka v. South Shore Skating, Inc., 598 N.Y.S.2d 74 (App. Div. 2d Dept. 1993).
Brahatcek v. Millard School Dist., 202 Neb. 86, 273 N.W.2d 680 (Neb. 1979).
Broward County School Board v. Ruiz, 493 So.2d 474 (Fla. App. 1986).
Calandri v. Ione Unified School Dist., 219 Cal. App.2d 542, 33 Cal.Rptr. 333 (1963).
Carabba v. Anacortes School District No. 103, 72 Wash.2d 939, 435 P.2d 936 (Wash. 1967).
Corrigan v. Musclemakers, Inc., 258 A.D.2d 861, 686 N.Y.S.2d 143 (1999).
Cruz v. City of New York, 288 A.D.2d 250 (N. Y. App. Div. 2001).
David v. County of Suffolk, 1 N.Y. 3d 525 (2003).
Dailey v. Los Angeles Unified School District, 470 P.2d 360 (Cal. 1970).
DeGooyer v. Harkness, 13 N.W. 2d 815 (SD, 1944).
Domino v. Mercurio, 17 A.D.2d 342, 234 N.Y.S.2d 1011 (1962), *aff'd*, 13 N.Y.S.2d 922, 193 N.E.2d 893, 244 N.Y.S.2d 69 (1963).
Fagan v. Summers, 498 P.2d 1227 (Wyo. 1972).
Ferguson v. DeSoto Parish School Bd., 467 So.2d 1257 (La. 1985).
Fluehr v. City of Cape May, 732 A.2d 1035 (N.J. 1999).
Foster v. Houston General Insurance Co., 407 So.2d 759 (La. Ct. App. 1982).
Glankler v. Rapides Parish School Board, 610 So.2d 1020 (La. App. 1993).
Green v. Orleans Parish School Board, 365 So.2d 834 (La. Ct. App. 1978).
Hamill v. Town of Southampton, 261 A.D.2d 361, 689 N.Y.S.2d 196 (App. Div. 1999).
Harvey v. Ouachita Parish School Board, 674 So.2d 372 (La. App. 2 Cir. 1996).
Hearon v. May, 248 Neb. 887, 540 N.W.2d 124 (1995).
Herring v. Bossier Parish School Board, 632 So.2d 920 (La. Ct. App. 1994).
Kaczmarcsyk v. City & County of Honolulu, 63 Hawaii 612, 656 P.2d 89 (Hawaii 1982).
Kahn v. East Side Union High School District, 75 P. 3d 30 (Cal. 2003).
Kaufman v. City of New York, 30 Misc.2d 285, 214 N.Y.S.2d 767 (1961).
Keesee v. Board of Education of the City of New York, 235 N.Y.S. 2d 300 (N. Y. Sup. Ct. 1962).
Kelly v. McCarrick, 841 A.2d 869 (Md. Ct. Spec. App. 2002).
Landers v. School District No. 203, O'Fallon, 383 N.E.2d 645 (Ill. App. Ct.—5th Dist. 1978).
Lilley v. Elk Grove Unified School Dist., 68 Cal. App.4th 939, 80 Cal. Rptr.2d 638 (1998).
Longfellow v. Corey, 286 Ill. App.3d 366, 368, 675 N.E.2d 1386 (1997).
Lowe v. Texas Tech University, 540 S.W.2d 297 (Tex. 1976).
Mirand v. City of New York, 84 N.Y.2d 44 (N.Y. 1994).
Palmer v. Mount Vernon Township High School District 201, 647 N.E.2d 1043 (Ill. App. Ct. 1995).
Partin v. Vernon Parish School Board, 343 So.2d 417 (La. App. 1977).
Prejean v. East Baton Rouge Sch. Brd., 729 So.2d 686 (La. 1999).
Rollins v. Concordia Parish School Board, 465 So.2d 213 (La. App. 1985).
Scott v. Rapides Parish School Board, 732 So.2d 749 (La. App. 1999).
Sheehan v. St. Peter's Catholic School, 29 Minn. 1, 188 N.W.2d 868 (1971).
Stevens v. Chesteen, 561 So.2d 1100 (Ala. 1990).
St. Margaret Mercy Healthcare Centers, Inc. v. Poland, 828 N.E.2d 396 (Ind. Ct. App. 2005).
Tepper v. City of New Rochelle School District, 531 N.Y.S.2d 367 (N. Y. Sup. Ct. 1988).
Thomas v. Sport City, Inc., 738 So.2d 1153 (La. App. 2nd Cir. 1999).
Toller v. Plainfield School District 202, 582 N.E.2d 237 (Ill. App. 1991).
Zipusch v. LA Workout, Inc., 155 Cal. App. 4th 1281, 66 Cal. Rptr. 3d 704 (Cal. App. 2 Dist., 2007).

Publications

American College of Sports Medicine. (1997). *ACSM's health/fitness facility standards & guidelines* (2nd ed.). Champaign, IL: Human Kinetics.

American College of Sports Medicine & American Heart Association. (1998). Recommendations for cardiovascular screening, staffing, and emergency policies at health/fitness facilities. *Medicine & Science in Sports & Exercise, 30*(6), 1009–1018.

Gaskin, L. P. (2003). Supervision of Participants. In D. J. Cotten & J. T. Wolohan (Eds.), *Law for recreation and sport managers* (pp. 138–148). Dubuque, IA: Kendall/Hunt.

Garner, B. A. (Ed.). (2004). *Black's law dictionary* (8th ed.). St. Paul, MN: Thomson/West.

Herbert, D. L. (1997). A review of ACSM's standards & guidelines for health & fitness facilities. *The Sports, Parks & Recreation Law Reporter, 11*(2), 23–24.

Herbert, D. L. (1998). New standards for health and fitness facilities from the American Heart Association (AHA) and the American College of Sports Medicine (ACSM). *The Sports, Parks & Recreation Law Reporter,* 12(2), 30–31.

Hurst, T. R., & Knight, J. M. (2003). Coaches' liability for athletes' injuries and deaths. *Seton Hall Journal of Sport Law, 13,* 27–51.

Kaiser, R. A. (1986). *Liability and law in recreation, parks, and sports.* Englewood Cliffs, NJ: Prentice Hall.

McCaskey, A. S., & Biedzynski, K. W. (1996). A guide to the legal liability of coaches for a sports participant's injuries. *Seton Hall Journal of Sport Law, 6,* 7–125.

Nygaard, G., & Boone, T. H. (1985). *Coaches guide to sport law.* Champaign, IL: Human Kinetics.

van der Smissen, B. (1990). *Legal liability and risk management for public and private entities.* Cincinnati, OH: Anderson.

Legislation

Limited Liability for Operators of Roller Skating Rinks, Ind. Code Ann. § 34-31-6, et seq. (2009).

Volunteer Protection Act of 1997, 42 U. S. C. § 14501, et. seq. (2009).

2.35 TRANSPORTATION

Paul J. Batista | Texas A&M University

Participants' safety and welfare should be the primary concern for those organizations that transport participants involved in recreation or sport activities. Both public and private entities, as well as individuals, must be aware of the duty of care required by law when providing transportation. The potential for liability extends not only to transporting them to and from events, but also to the use of vehicles in completing special tasks associated with the event (such as transporting injured persons to a hospital), and to supervisory concerns before, during, and after transport (see Chapter 2.34 *Supervision*).

FUNDAMENTAL CONCEPTS

Duty to Provide Transportation

As a general rule, organizations are under no legal duty to provide transportation to and from events or activities. However, in the event that an organization elects to provide transportation, the organization assumes the legal duty to use ordinary care, and act as a reasonably prudent person.

If the organization chooses to provide transportation, then it must be provided in a safe manner regardless of the mode of travel. The duty to provide transportation usually begins at the point of departure and continues until those using the transportation have been returned to the original departure point. Liability exists regardless of whether the participants meet at the designated place and are then assigned a particular vehicle, or they are picked up by the driver at their homes or elsewhere. It may be possible to avoid liability by establishing a policy that no transportation will be provided for anyone for a particular event. In that case, participants are instructed to convene at the site of the event. However, this policy may not be practical if the event is located far away, large numbers of people are involved, or participants do not have access to an alternative form of transportation. The organization must also establish a policy governing the conditions under which a participant may leave an event by transportation other than that provided by the organization. For minors, parental permission should be required, with each child being "signed out" by the responsible parent or guardian. The supervisor should create a specific policy, and insure that everyone involved in transportation is aware of, and conforms to, the policy. Do not allow any exceptions to the policy. Allowing a parent or participant to avoid the policy requirement by making exceptions will increase the potential for liability.

Duty of Care

When an organization provides transportation, it owes a duty of care with respect to such transportation. Generally, reasonable and ordinary care under the circumstances is the appropriate standard of care. However, there is authority that indicates that the operators of school buses are in the same general position as common carriers, requiring the highest degree of care consistent with the practical operation of the bus. The standard of care required of the drivers is determined by the particular circumstances. Some factors that may be considered in determining the standard of care include the age, knowledge, judgment, and experience of both the driver and passengers.

In a situation where a driver or organization has violated a specific statute enacted for the protection of the passengers, and that violation is the proximate cause of an injury, the standard of care is irrelevant. In that instance, the organization would be held absolutely liable.

Jurisdictions differ as to the duty required concerning supervision. In some jurisdictions the duty of care includes a duty to provide a location where participants can wait for the transportation with reasonable safety, and a duty to select a discharge point that does not needlessly expose them to any unreasonable or significant safety hazards. The duty to provide a reasonably safe location may also impose a duty upon the organization to provide proper supervision (see Chapter 2.34 *Supervision*). In contrast, courts in other jurisdictions have ruled that the duty of an organization toward participants under its control applies only during the period they are transported to and from the event, beginning when the participant enters the vehicle and continuing until they have been safely discharged. Likewise, absent the existence of a special duty, this duty may not extend to situations where the participant is no longer under the organization's authority or is no longer under its physical custody. In order to decrease the potential of liability and insure the safety of participants, the best policy in every state would include providing appropriate supervision from the time the participant arrives at the pick-up point at the beginning of the trip until the participant leaves the discharge point at the end of the excursion.

Transportation Options

The transportation of participants to and from recreation or sport events and activities can be accomplished in one of three ways: (a) through an independent contractor, (b) by using an organization-owned vehicle, or (c) by privately owned vehicles (owned either by the employee or by a non-employee third person, such as a participant's parent). The potential for liability varies from situation to situation with the least potential for liability existing where independent contractors are used, and the greatest potential where private vehicles are used. The risk of liability is not as high when an organization uses an independent contractor because most of the risk is transferred to the contractor. The risk of liability is greatest when non-employee vehicles are used because the organization has the least control. The keys to the determination of liability are the ownership of the vehicle and the relationship of the driver to the entity responsible for the participants.

Independent Contractor

If an organization can afford it, using an independent contractor for transportation is the best legal option, since the contract for service shifts liability to the contractor. The independent contractor may be of two types: common or private carrier. A **common carrier** is one that is in the business of transporting goods or persons for hire. A **private carrier**, on the other hand, only hires out to deliver goods or persons in particular cases. With regard to the qualifications of the driver and the condition of the vehicle, a common carrier is typically held to a higher standard of care than a private carrier or a noncommercial driver.

An organization may delegate its duty of safe transportation to third party independent contractors, but the organization must use due diligence to select a contractor with a proven safety record. In most cases, the primary issue for the court is whether the third party is truly an **independent contractor**. This determination is made based on several factors, including who has the right to control the manner in which the work (in this case, the transportation) is conducted, the method of payment, the right to hire and fire employees, the skill required, and who furnishes the tools, equipment, or materials needed to accomplish the work. With respect to transportation, if factors such as the use of specific vehicles, the driver, the route, the intermediate stops, and the manner of driving are all within the control of the transportation company and its employees, then it is likely the relationship is that of an independent contractor (see Chapter 2.12 *Which Parties Are Liable?* and Chapter 2.21 *Defenses Against Negligence*). This is an area fraught with danger, so consultation with an attorney prior to hiring an independent contractor is essential.

Be aware that an organization may not be able to avoid liability if the organization is negligent in its selection of an independent contractor. Therefore, it is always good administrative practice to investigate independent contractors carefully prior to entering into a contract with them. A recent analysis of Division 1 schools revealed that at least 85 used charter bus companies that had one or more deficiencies on federal government safety scores (Lavigne, 2009). The article highlights numerous actual and potential hazards when hiring charter bus companies, and includes suggested questions as well as links to government records to verify company safety records. Additionally, the Federal Motor Carrier Safety Administration (FMCSA) has issued a guide to hiring charter transportation that contains questions to ask and links to other safety information (FMCSA, n.d.). When researching a company for potential hire, secure a **certificate of insurance** verifying the company has sufficient liability insurance for the company and each vehicle, and the company's U.S. Department of Transportation number, which can be used to access the company's latest safety report at www.safer.fmcsa.dot.gov.

Transportation policy became a central theme in the National Transportation Safety Board (NTSB) report regarding the crash of an aircraft transporting members of the Oklahoma State University (OSU) basketball team and other team personnel (NTSB, 2003). Although it was determined that the pilot's spatial disorientations and failure to maintain positive manual control was the major cause of the accident, the NTSB concluded, "OSU did not provide any significant oversight for the accident flight."

OSU policy required charter flights and university airplane flights to be coordinated through the OSU flight department. However, since this specific flight was a donated flight, it was not coordinated through the flight department. Therefore, OSU had no records on file regarding the pilots or the plane as required by its flight department. OSU has since adopted a comprehensive transportation management system in an attempt to ensure necessary oversight. This comprehensive policy provides an outstanding model for transportation issues facing all organizations, and may be accessed at http://www.okstate.com/school-bio/travel-policy.html.

As a result of the OSU accident, the NTSB recommended that collegiate athletic associations review athletic team travel policies and develop a model transportation policy that could be implemented by member schools. In response, the NCAA and the American Council on Education (ACE) produced a transportation manual titled Safety in Student Transportation: A Resource Guide for Colleges and Universities, which contains comprehensive information and recommendations. It is available on the Internet at: http://www.ncaa.org/wps/portal/ncaahome?WCM_GLOBAL_CONTEXT=/ncaa/NCAA/Academics+and+Athletes/Personal+Welfare/Health+and+Safety/Safety+in+Student+Transportation.

Ironically, and tragically, on November 19, 2011, shortly after the 10 year anniversary of the OSU accident, the OSU's women's head basketball coach Kurt Budke and assistant coach Miranda Serna were killed in an airplane crash while on a recruiting trip. The plane was privately owned, and piloted by an 82 year old former Oklahoma State Senator and OSU booster. The University reported that the University travel policy relating to flights did not apply to coaches on recruiting trips, but that the policy would be reviewed once again (Associated Press, 2011). At press time, the NTSB investigation was still ongoing.

Organization-Owned Vehicles

For some organizations or entities, the use of an independent contractor is not a viable option due to the cost involved. Organization-owned vehicles are the most common means of transporting participants, and provide the next best transportation option. Since the organization owns the vehicles, it has the legal responsibility for the safe transportation of the participants. The organization has a duty to see that the vehicles are in safe operating condition and to see that the drivers are properly qualified. In the event of legal action, written policies, checklists, and maintenance records provide documentation that these duties have been fulfilled (see Chapter 4.11 *Risk Management Process* and Chapter 4.22 *Audits in Risk Management*).

Driver. Both the driver and the organization could be liable for the driver's negligence. In order to protect itself, the organization should require that the driver meet established qualifications that may include age, experience, special licenses, training, and verification of driving record. The organization should also use due diligence to determine that the driver complies with its transportation policies.

If an employee is acting in the course and scope of his/her employment when the accident occurs, both the driver and organization will be held liable for the driver's negligence. In *Foster v. Board of Trustees* (1991) (the significant case in this chapter), the Kansas court defined **course and scope of employment** as the employee "performing services for which he has been employed, or when he is doing anything which is reasonably incidental to his employment." However, when the driver commits an *ultra vires* **act** (i.e., an act that is outside the course and scope of employment), the negligence of the driver is not assigned to the organization. Examples of *ultra vires* acts include exceeding the speed limit, running a red light or stop sign, and deviating from the designated route. In *Smith v. Gardner* (1998), the court held that a baseball coach who, after an away game, drove the school van to purchase some tobacco products and decided to sightsee rather than returning to the hotel, was not acting within the course and scope of his employment. It is important to emphasize to drivers that they should not deviate from the scheduled route and itinerary without approval. In *Myricks v. Lynwood Unified School District* (1999), neither the school nor the city (which paid some of the expenses of the traveling summer basketball team) was liable for a driver's negligence. In this case, the driver was not acting within the scope of employment since this was a summer team not affiliated with the school.

Vehicle. Being able to establish the roadworthiness of the vehicle is of utmost importance to the organization. With all organization-owned vehicles, the organization is responsible for maintenance, and failure to maintain the vehicle in a safe condition leaves the organization liable. All vehicles need to be maintained by competent maintenance personnel in accordance with the owner's manual and vehicle specifications. Any vehicle with maintenance problems (e.g., defective lights, worn tires) should not be used until the condition is corrected and documented. Complete documentation of all maintenance should be stored in a safe, accessible manner.

Prior to each trip, each vehicle needs to be inspected by a competent authorized maintenance person. After each trip, a similar inspection should be performed and the driver should report any problems encountered on the trip. Pre-trip and post-trip vehicle inspection forms and checklists need to be developed for this purpose. Emergency equipment (e.g., first aid kit, flares, flashers, spare tires, and jack) should also be included on these forms and in these inspections.

Policies. Prior to the trip, an administrator or another authorized individual must be informed of and authorize travel plans. A trip request form should be utilized which includes the purpose of the trip, the destination, lodging arrangements, route, contact phone numbers, a list of those traveling, the person in charge, and the driver. Irrespective of the mode of travel (e.g., car, van, bus, plane), policies need to be established that address who can travel, maximum distances, traveling at night, disciplinary action, emergency procedures, driver qualifications, maximum driving hours in a 24 hour period, and oversight of the drivers.

Schools. State laws control the right to use a vehicle owned by a school to transport students to activities other than classes. Some states have no restrictions while others limit the use of school buses to providing transportation to and from classes. Other states restrict use depending upon the source of operating funds, which may be a critical factor in the application of governmental immunity.

In the past, state sovereign immunity statues provided liability protection for cities or schools when their employees were negligent. **Sovereign immunity** is the legal theory that a person cannot sue a governmental body without its permission. Now, however, most states have enacted **tort claims acts** that waive sovereign immunity and create liability for governmental entities under certain circumstances. Typically, these statutes make the governmental body liable for injuries caused by the operation of motor vehicles, but limit the amount of financial liability of the governmental institutions. The potential of liability for public colleges and universities, public secondary schools, school boards and districts, and other public agencies such as recreation departments, must be considered in light of these statutes (see Chapter 2.22 *Immunity).*

Privately Owned Vehicles

In some cases, organizations may find it convenient or necessary to use privately owned vehicles for transportation. The vehicles could be owned either by employees or by non-employees (e.g., parents, volunteers, and participants). In either case, liability for negligence is generally retained by the organization.

Before authorizing and approving use of private vehicles, risk management policies should be established to verify that both vehicles and drivers conform to adequate safety standards. These policies should require a physical inspection of the vehicle, review of maintenance records, and current insurance and registration on the vehicle. Policies should also ensure that the driver is properly licensed, has a good driving reputation, has a violation-free driving record, and has no impairments that would preclude driving.

Employee Vehicles. When an employee, as a part of his/her employment, uses a personal vehicle for transporting students or patrons, a **principal-agent relationship** is established. An organization is **vicariously liable** for employee negligence committed within the course and scope of employment. This will hold true even in the situation of an employee driving another employee's vehicle as in the case of *Murray v. Zarger* (1994). Richard Zarger was a volunteer diving coach for Cory Area (Pennsylvania) High School and was compensated a small salary by the school district. While driving Cherese Murray, a member of the diving team, and three others in the head coach's car, Zarger was involved in an accident that resulted in Murray's death. Murray's estate filed suit for damages allegedly caused by the negligence of the school district, the car owner, and Zarger. The school district argued that Zarger was not an employee of the district on the following grounds: they had no control over the manner in which he performed; Zarger was not responsible for the swim team's performance; there was no agreement between Zarger and the school district; Zarger was used for his special diving skills only; and Zarger was an employee of two other companies. In holding that Zarger was an employee of the school district, the court stated that the definition of "employee" in the applicable state statute did not require that an employee be compensated or possess a formal employment contract with the government unit, but only that the person act in the government's interests (see Chapter 2.12 *Which Parties are Liable?).*

In this chapter's significant case, *Foster v. Board of Trustees* (1991), Christopher Foster was a basketball player making a recruiting visit to Butler County Community College. At the request of the head basketball coach, volunteer driver George Johnson picked Foster up at the airport, after which Foster was injured in a collision on the way to the campus. The issue in the case was Johnson's status as either an employee or a volunteer. The court examined the requirements for Johnson to be an employee (even though he was unpaid), found that he was an employee, and that his actions were negligent, thereby making the College vicariously liable for Johnson's negligence.

Use of privately owned vehicles increases the risks to the organization; therefore, the establishment and enforcement of **risk management policies** regarding the driver and the vehicle are essential (see Chapter 4.22 *Audits in Risk Management*). If the employee uses his or her privately owned vehicle as a service to the organization and in accordance with organization policy, most jurisdictions require that the driver exercise reasonable and ordinary care. The employee will be personally liable for negligent operation of the vehicle, in addition to the vicarious liability of the organization.

Non-employee Vehicles. When an organization has a duty to provide transportation and uses a private vehicle provided by someone who is not an employee, a principal-agent relationship is created just as it is when a privately owned employee vehicle is used. The organization is liable for the negligence of the driver. Because an organization has the least control when non-employee vehicles are used, this category creates the greatest risk of liability to the organization. It is imperative that the organization institute and enforce the risk management policies suggested at the beginning of the section, *Privately Owned Vehicles*.

Other Transportation Issues

State Codes. State legislatures enact laws that are related to transportation. However, sometimes it is not clear which part of the Code may apply. At issue in *Barnhart v. Cabrillo Community College* (1999) was whether or not an intercollegiate match was a field trip as defined under Title 5, California Code of Regulations, section 5545. The court of appeals ruled that since school-related athletic activities necessarily include extracurricular sport programs, the trip was a field trip and would fall under the immunity granted in the Code.

Although most states, and the U.S. Congress, have passed volunteer protection statutes providing **immunity** or **limited liability** for volunteers under certain circumstances, virtually all of those statutes contain exceptions for operation of motor vehicles. For example, the federal Volunteer Protection Act (42 U. S. C. § 14501, et. seq.) provides a defense for volunteers meeting the statutory criteria, but excepts from immunity a "volunteer operating a motor vehicle, vessel, aircraft, or other vehicle for which the State requires the operator or the owner of the vehicle, craft, or vessel to (A) possess an operator's license; or (B) maintain insurance." A typical state statute, the Texas Charitable Immunity and Liability Act of 1987 (Texas Civil Practice and Remedies Code § 84.001 et. seq.), creates volunteer liability for "the operation or use of any motor-driven equipment," but limits damages to the extent to which insurance coverage is required and exists, thereby protecting the volunteer who has secured the required insurance. Additional information on state volunteer driver laws may be found on the National Conference of State Legislatures website located at http://www.ncsl.org/issues-research/transportation/information-for-state-volunteer-driver-liability-1.aspx (see Chapter 2.22 *Immunity*). The sport or recreation manager should have the organization's attorney review the state Codes that are applicable to transportation. Knowledge of the Codes is a valuable tool in the policy-making process and can serve to minimize litigation.

Many states are considering banning driving while using electronic communications devices such as cell phones, text messaging, etc. Clearly, a reasonably prudent person would not be doing those things while driving students or participants. The organization should adopt a strict policy that requires leaving the roadway and stopping the vehicle in order to use a cell phone or similar device, except in cases of emergency.

Workers' Compensation. If an individual is injured in an automobile accident while within his/her scope of employment and the business required the employee to be at the place of the accident, workers' compensation may be applicable. In *Bolton v. Tulane University* (1997), Bolton was an assistant basketball coach returning from a recruiting trip, and was a passenger in an automobile driven by another assistant coach. She was injured when the driver fell asleep and the car ended up in a ravine. Tulane provided workers' compensation benefits and paid most of her medical bills, but Bolton sued the University for negligence, seeking additional damages. In deciding the workers' compensation claim, the Court of Appeals held that Bolton was in the course and scope of her employment, and workers' compensation was her exclusive remedy.

Van Accidents. According to the National Highway Traffic Safety Administration (NHTSA), between 1997 and 2006 there were 1,374 15-passenger vans involved in fatal crashes that resulted in 1,090 fatalities to occupants of such vans. Eighty-three percent of people who died in single vehicle rollovers of these vehicles were not wearing safety belts. (NHTSA, 2008a).

Van vs. School Buses. While most states require the use of school buses to transport children to and from school and school-related events, some states do not. Many states have statutes that address whether vans may be used to transport school children to school and extracurricular activities. The prudent sport and recreation manager should be aware of his/her state laws governing such transportation issues. State laws regarding 12 & 15 passenger vans can be found at: http://www.nasdpts.org/documents/vanssurveyfeb04.pdf.

15-Passenger Vans. Recent research conducted by the NHTSA found that the risk of a rollover crash is greatly increased when ten or more individuals ride in a 15-passenger van. The risk of a rollover is increased because the center of gravity of the vehicle is raised when more passengers are transported. Placing any load on the roof also raises the center of gravity and increases the likelihood of a rollover. The result is less resistance to rollover and increased difficulty in steering. The NHTSA identified three major situations that can lead to a rollover in the 15-passenger vans: (1) The van goes off a rural road, striking a ditch, or soft shoulder; (2) the driver is fatigued or driving too fast, and; (3) the driver overcorrects. Further, 80% of people killed in 15-passenger vans were not wearing seat belts, and NHTSA estimates that people wearing seat belts are 75% less likely to be killed in a rollover crash. Organizations should create a policy requiring each person to wear a seat belt, and carefully adhere to the policy. Drivers should check compliance before beginning the trip. Other problems noted were the vans being driven by individuals under 22 years of age (lack of experience) and excessive speed. (NHTSA, n.d.)

On August 10, 2005, Congress passed the Safe, Accountable, Flexible, Efficient Transportation Equity Act: A Legacy for Users (23 U.S.C. § 101). Section 10309, 15-Passenger Van Safety, addresses new safety standards related to the use of 15-passenger vans. The Act defines a 15-passenger van as a vehicle that seats 10 to 14 passengers, not including the driver. The Act prohibits a school or school system from purchasing or leasing a new 15-pasenger van if it will be used significantly by, or on behalf of, the school or school system to transport preprimary, primary, or secondary school students to or from school or an event related to school, unless the 15-passenger van complies with the motor vehicle standards prescribed for school buses and multifunction school activity buses under this title.

Team travel by van has created a problem that does not have an easy solution. Budget restrictions and squad size are major considerations when choosing to use vans or other modes of transportation. If the organization chooses to use a 15-passenger van, Hawes (2000), LaVetter (2005) and McGregor (2000) have made the following policy recommendations that parallel the identified causes of van accidents:

- Eliminate 15-passenger vans, if possible, and travel more frequently by bus
- Eliminate coaches driving any vehicles, and enforce stricter driver qualifications
- Limit the number of passengers in vans to fewer than 10, remove the rear seats from 15-passenger vans, and place passengers and equipment forward of the van's rear axle
- Limit to 300 miles or five hours the number of hours or mileage driven by each driver per day, and avoid travel between midnight and 6 a.m.
- Check the van's tire pressure frequently—and before and after every trip
- Confer with your organization's insurance company or risk-management consultants.
- Schedule competition to permit travel by different teams sharing the same bus.
- Set age limits for the driver, hire outside drivers, and give extensive driver training.
- Require seat belts to be worn at all times
- Stress the importance of adhering to speed limits and the possible need to adjust speed due to weather conditions
- Monitor weather conditions and establish policies that permit the person in charge to decide when to spend the night in a hotel rather than continuing driving in hazardous conditions
- Review vehicle maintenance policies

Policy Recommendations

Every organization should have written travel policies, and should ensure that everyone adheres to them. Prudent administrators should ask and answer the following questions before approving any travel: (a) What is the purpose of the trip, (b) who is travelling, (c) who is in charge, (d) who is allowed to drive, and (e) are emergency procedures in place? The links earlier in this chapter would be a good starting point for developing such a policy. The policy should also require the following documentation: (a) a passenger checklist, (b) a key contact checklist provided to everyone involved in the travel decision, (c) emergency procedures for breakdowns and accidents, (d) accident report forms, if needed, and (e) pre- and post-trip vehicle inspection checklists. (McGregor, 2000).

The NCAA has developed an extensive resource guide "designed for anyone who cares about the safe transportation of college and university students." (NCAA, 2006) It is a comprehensive report, and should be required reading for any sport or recreation manager involved in transporting participants to and from events.

SIGNIFICANT CASE

Christopher Foster was a high school senior basketball player making a recruiting visit to Butler County Community College (BCCC). George Johnson, a volunteer driver acting on behalf of the BCCC coach, picked Foster up at the airport. Returning to the school, Johnson was involved in an accident that killed him, and severely injured Foster. Foster filed suit for injuries claiming negligence by both Johnson and BCCC. The primary issue in the case was whether Johnson was an "employee" of BCCC, thereby creating vicarious liability for the College. Among other legal issues involved in the case are negligence, damages, sufficiency of the evidence, vicarious liability through respondeat superior, comparative negligence, and course and scope of employment.

FOSTER & CLARK V. BOARD OF TRUSTEES OF BUTLER COUNTY COMMUNITY COLLEGE, ET AL.

United States District Court for the District of Kansas
771 F. Supp. 1122, 1991 U.S. Dist. LEXIS 11003

Frank G. Theis, United States District Judge

* * *

This case arose out of a motor vehicle collision occurring at the intersection of Airport/Yoder Road and U.S. Highway 50 in Reno County, Kansas on March 22, 1987. Plaintiff Christopher Foster was a passenger in a car driven by George Johnson. Johnson was travelling south on Airport Road. Plaintiff Gregory Clark was travelling east on Highway 50. Johnson failed to stop at the stop sign on Airport Road and collided with the tractor-trailer rig driven by plaintiff Clark. Johnson died as a result of the injuries he received in the accident. Foster and Clark were injured.

Foster, a native of Ohio, was a high school senior at the time of the accident. He was visiting Kansas on a recruiting visit at the request of defendant Randy Smithson,

the head coach of the BCCC basketball team. Johnson picked Foster up at the Wichita airport at Smithson's request. Smithson had previously taken several other recruits to Hutchinson for the National Junior College Basketball Tournament. Contrary to the instructions given by Smithson, Johnson took Foster to Hutchinson to watch the game. Johnson telephoned Smithson from Hutchinson just prior to the collision. Smithson told Johnson to bring Foster to El Dorado. Johnson was en route to El Dorado when the collision occurred. * * *

At the close of the evidence, the court directed a verdict in favor of the plaintiffs on the issue of respondeat superior, ruling that Johnson was the servant or employee of the BCCC defendants and was acting within the scope of his authority at the time of the accident. On February 27, 1991 the jury returned a verdict finding plaintiff Clark 10% at fault and defendants 90% at fault.

Damages in the amount of $ 2,257,000 were awarded to plaintiff Foster and in the amount of $ 302,000 to plaintiff Clark. After reducing the judgment by Clark's 10% fault, the court entered judgment in the amount of $ 2,031,300 in favor of Foster and $ 271,800 in favor of Clark. These motions for new trial followed.

* * *

The BCCC defendants raise the following issues: (1) the verdict is contrary to the evidence; (2) the amount of damages awarded is so excessive as to appear to have been based on passion and prejudice; (3) the court improperly allowed the jury to consider testimony regarding Johnson's lack of liability insurance coverage and evidence regarding the proof of insurance that must be provided by a student who is operating his own automobile in connection with a school function; (4) the court improperly refused to submit to the jury the questions of whether Johnson was the employee of BCCC and whether Johnson was operating within the scope of his employment at the time of the accident; (5) the court improperly refused to submit the issue of plaintiff Foster's comparative negligence to the jury; (6) the court improperly refused to allow testimony concerning plaintiff Clark's opinion that he considered the intersection where the accident occurred to be a dangerous one. * * *

* * *

* * * It was stipulated that Johnson ran the stop sign at the intersection of Airport Road and Highway 50. This fact alone would have been sufficient to support a finding that Johnson was 100% at fault, notwithstanding the defendants' accident reconstructionist who opined that Clark committed several driving errors. The evidence certainly was sufficient to support a finding that defendants were 90% at fault for the accident. * * * [T]he evidence was sufficient to support the damages awarded. The verdict was not clearly against the weight of the evidence.

* * *

B. Excessiveness of Verdict

* * *

As with all of its functions as trier of fact, the jury has wide discretion in determining the amount of damages that will fairly compensate the aggrieved party. * * *

> Absent an award so excessive as to shock the judicial conscience and to raise an irresistible inference that passion, prejudice, corruption or other improper cause invaded the trial, the jury's determination of the damages is considered inviolate. Such bias, prejudice or passion can be inferred from excessiveness. However, a verdict will not be set aside on this basis unless it is so plainly excessive as to suggest that it was the product of such passion or prejudice on the part of the jury.

* * *

The damage award to Clark is not so excessive as to shock the judicial conscience. The damages in this case included the normal personal injury damage components of past and future medical expenses, lost past and future income, pain and suffering and aggravation of pre-existing condition. The court also instructed the jury on loss of enjoyment of life as a component of the award for pain, suffering, disabilities, and disfigurement. * * *

* * *

C. Evidentiary Rulings

* * *

At trial, plaintiffs introduced evidence that the BCCC defendants were negligent in selecting Johnson as a gratuitous employee. An employer may be liable for injuries to a third person which are a direct result of the incompetence or unfitness of his employee when the employer was negligent in employing the employee or in retaining him in employment when the employer knew or should have known of such incompetence or unfitness. *Plains Resources, Inc. v. Gable,* 235 Kan. 580, 591, 682 P.2d 653 (1984). Johnson was unfit to drive a basketball recruit since he lacked a driver's license and liability insurance and his vehicle was not registered. The BCCC defendants could have discovered Johnson's unfitness for the task had any investigation been conducted. The evidence introduced by the plaintiffs was relevant to show the BCCC defendants' negligence. The evidence of Johnson's lack of liability insurance was relevant to show that the BCCC defendants failed to use due care in selecting Johnson to perform the task of transporting Foster.

* * *

2. BCCC transportation and vehicle policies

In connection with the direct negligence claim and the evidence of Johnson's lack of insurance, the plaintiffs offered evidence of BCCC policies regarding use of college and personal vehicles. The BCCC Policies and Procedures Manual provides in pertinent part:

> *College Vehicle Policy*
> *College vehicles.* All persons, included students, employees, and noncollege personnel, must have a driving record review and clearance. Requests for students and noncollege employees to drive college vehicles must be approved by the Director of Buildings and Grounds. These requests must be in writing and forwarded through the Business Office.
>
> *Personal vehicles.* In cases when a college vehicle has been officially requested and is not available, the person making the request may be reimbursed for mileage if using a personal vehicle. In cases when an instructor or sponsor is not able to drive a college vehicle, a student

with proof of current liability insurance may be permitted to use his/her car and be reimbursed for mileage with prior approval from the Director of Buildings and Grounds.

* * * The BCCC Athletic Policies and Procedures Manual provides that "School transportation must be used whenever possible. Private cars should be used only with permission of the athletic director." * * *

While these policies were not directly applicable since Johnson was not officially a coach, they indicated a general school policy of requiring an inquiry before allowing a teacher or coach to drive a BCCC vehicle and proof of liability insurance before allowing a student to use a personal vehicle for BCCC business. It was undisputed that Smithson did not obtain the permission of the athletic director before arranging for Johnson to transport Foster. This evidence was relevant to plaintiffs' claim that the BCCC defendants were directly negligent in appointing Johnson as a gratuitous employee charged with the duty of transporting Foster.

* * *

D. Directed Verdict on Respondeat Superior

At the close of the evidence, the court directed a verdict on two issues: that Johnson was the servant or employee of BCCC and that Johnson was acting within the scope of his authority at the time of the accident. The BCCC defendants challenge this ruling.

* * *

* * * Under Kansas law, the controlling test in determining the existence of agency, so that the doctrine of respondeat superior would apply, is the right to control the purported employee. *Hendrix,* 203 Kan. at 155; *see also Hughes v. Jones,* 206 Kan. 82, 88, 476 P.2d 588 (1970). When agency relationship is in issue, the party relying on the existence of an agency relationship to establish his claim has the burden of establishing the existence of the relationship by clear and satisfactory evidence. *Highland Lumber Co.,* 219 Kan. at 370.

An employer is not liable for a tortious act committed by his employee, unless the act is done by authority of the employer, either express or implied, or unless the act is done by the employee in the course or within the scope of his employment. *Beggerly v. Walker,* 194 Kan. 61, 64, 397 P.2d 395 (1964). Under Kansas law,

> An employee is acting within the scope of his authority when he is performing services for which he has been employed, or when he is doing anything which is reasonably incidental to his employment. The test is not necessarily whether the specific conduct was expressly authorized or forbidden by the employer, but whether such conduct should have been fairly foreseen from the nature of the employment and the duties relating to it.

Williams v. Community Drive-in Theater, Inc., 214 Kan. 359, 364, 520 P.2d 1296 (1974) (quoting PIK 7.04); *Hollinger v. Jane C. Stormont Hospital and Training School for Nurses,* 2 Kan. App. 2d 302, 311, 578 P.2d 1121 (1978). Whether an act is within the employee's scope of employment ordinarily presents a question to be determined by the jury. *Williams,* 214 Kan. at 365 (quoting 53 Am. Jur. 2d, *Master and Servant* § 427). The liability of the employer for the acts of the employee depends upon whether the employee, when he did the wrong, was acting in the prosecution of the employer's business and within the scope of his authority or whether he had stepped aside from the business and had done an individual wrong. *Hollinger,* 2 Kan. App. 2d at 311.

The determination of whether an employee was acting within the scope of his employment involves a consideration of the individual factual setting of each case, including objective as well as subjective considerations. *Focke v. United States,* 597 F. Supp. 1325, 1339 (D. Kan. 1982). Several factors are relevant to the determination of scope of employment. First, the key consideration in determining whether an employee is acting within the scope of employment is the purpose of the employee's act rather than the method of performance. This calls for consideration of the objective circumstances of the incident as well as the subjective thoughts of the employee. *Id.* at 1340-41. Second, the court must examine whether the employee has express or implied authority to do the acts in question, although in certain situations, an employer may be liable for the acts of the employee, even if the acts are done in excess of the authority conferred. *Id.* at 1341. Third, the determination of whether an employee's acts are incidental to his employment involves a consideration of whether the employee's acts were reasonably foreseeable by the employer. Finally, the time at which the agent commits the alleged wrongful act is a factor to be considered, although it is not accorded great weight. *Id.*

Defendants have not argued that Smithson lacked the authority to hire Johnson to assist in Smithson's recruiting duties. Johnson could be an employee or servant even though no compensation was paid or expected. Whether compensation was paid or not paid is not determinative.

The evidence that Johnson was acting as the employee of Smithson and was acting within the scope of his authority came from the testimony of defendant Smithson. Smithson had the right to control and indeed exercised significant control over Johnson. Smithson testified that he instructed Johnson on what to do that evening. Smithson testified that he instructed Johnson to pick up Foster from the airport, get him something to eat, take him to the motel in El Dorado and await Smithson's return from Hutchinson. Smithson gave Johnson twenty dollars to pay for dinner. Smithson further testified that when Johnson called late that evening from Hutchinson, Smithson told Johnson to bring Foster back to El Dorado as quickly and as safely as possible. Smithson gave Johnson directions on the two routes available from

Hutchinson to El Dorado, via Highway 96 or via Airport Road/Highway 50. Smithson indicated that he used the Airport Road/Highway 50 route. Smithson told Johnson to ask for directions to Airport Road from where Johnson was located.

* * *

Construing the evidence in the light most favorable to the BCCC defendants, the evidence points only one way. There were no conflicts in the evidence. There was no evidence from which a reasonable mind could conclude that Johnson either was not the employee of BCCC or was not acting within the scope of his authority at the time of the collision. There was no evidence upon which

the jury could properly find for the BCCC defendants on the issue of employment and scope. Defendants have pointed to no such evidence in the record.

* * *

IT IS BY THE COURT THEREFORE ORDERED that defendant Pringle's motion for a new trial (Doc. 152) is hereby denied as to plaintiff Clark and is moot as to plaintiff Foster.

IT IS FURTHER ORDERED that defendants Board of Trustees of Butler County Community College, Butler County Community College, and Randy Smithson's motion for a new trial (Doc. 153) is hereby denied as to plaintiff Clark and is moot as to plaintiff Foster.

CASES ON THE SUPPLEMENTAL WEB SITE

Clement v. Griffin (634 So. 2d 412, La.App. 4 Cir. 1994). This court discusses the duty owed by the defendant Community College to (1) maintain the vehicle, (2) select a qualified driver, and (3) properly train the driver. The court also discussed the defendant's vicarious duty to insure the driver properly operated the vehicle. In terms of transportation risk management, this case serves as a model course in "how *not* to do it."

Dixon v. Whitfield, 654 So. 2d 1230 (Fla. Dist. Ct. App., 1st Dist.). This Florida case affirms that schools have "a duty of reasonable care in providing (students) with safe transportation," but also verifies that schools have authority to hire independent contractors to operate the school buses. The defendants were found to be independent contractors rather than employees. By hiring independent contractors, the school avoided liability for the student's death.

Federal Insurance Company v. Executive Coach Luxury Travel, Inc., 944 N.E.2d 215 (2010-Ohio-6300). This case involved the deaths of five members of the Bluffton

University baseball team on a spring break road trip. The issue before the court was whether the driver was covered by the University's insurance policy since he worked for an independent contractor. The Court held that under the terms of the policy, the driver was a covered insured. The case points out the necessity to determine whether or not a driver is covered under the Insured's policy.

Myricks v. Lynwood Unified School District, 87 Cal. Rptr. 2d 734 (Cal. App. 2 Dist. 1999). A girls' summer basketball team made up of players from their high school team, and coached by their high school coach, took an out-of-state trip to play in summer basketball tournaments. After suffering injuries in an accident, team members sued the school as well as the city (which provided some financial support). The court held this was not a school-sponsored activity, so the school was not liable. The court also found that the city was not liable since the city provided only financial support.

QUESTIONS YOU SHOULD BE ABLE TO ANSWER

1. Name numerous specific duties related to providing safe transportation.

2. What are the benefits of using an independent contractor as opposed to other means of transportation?

3. What are the criteria courts use to determine whether a company is an independent contractor?

4. Discuss the relative merits of travelling in organization-owned, employee-owned, or non-employed owned vehicles, buses or 15-passenger vans.

5. Prepare a basic transportation policy for your organization, including specific rules and regulations relating to transporting participants to an activity 200 miles from your normal meeting place.

REFERENCES

Cases

Barnhart v. Cabrillo Community College, 90 Cal. Rptr. 2d 709 (Cal. App. 6 Dist. 1999).
Bolton v. Tulane University of Louisiana, 692 So.2d 1113 (La. App. 4 Cir. 1997).
Foster v. Board of Trustees of Butler County Community College, 771 F. Supp. 1122 (D. Kan. 1991).
Murray v. Zarger, 642 A.2d 575 (Pa. Cmwlth. 1994).
Myricks v. Lynwood Unified School District, 87 Cal. Rptr. 2d 734 (Cal. App. 2 Dist. 1999).
Smith v. Gardner, 998 F. Supp. 708 (S.D. Miss. 1998).

Publications

Associated Press (2011, Nov. 20). Oklahoma State plane crash: travel rules to be examined by University after deaths. *Huffington Post*. Retrieved Feb. 11, 2011 from http://www.huffingtonpost.com/2011/11/21/oklahoma-state-plane-crash-travel-rules_n_1104558.html.

Federal Motor Carrier Safety Administration (n.d.). *Keeping Kids Safe–A guide to hiring charter transportation*. Retrieved February 11, 2012 from http://www.fmcsa.dot.gov/documents/kids/Brochure-Moving-Kids-Safely-Bus-508.pdf.

Hawes, K. (2000, August 28). Warning: Road Risks Ahead. Precautions Reduce Dangers of Van-related Travel. *National Collegiate Athletic Association*.

LaVetter, D. (2005, December 5). Safety Must Drive Decisions in Van Use. *National Collegiate Athletic Association*

Lavigne, P. (2009, March 31). Bus Safety an Issue for Colleges. *ESPN*, retrieved February 11, 2012, from http://sports.espn.go.com/espn/otl/news/story?id=3997988&userid=63b283733d372ce0b01b1146c9fca4d4&messageid=308.

McGregor, I. (2000, March 1). Travel Trouble: Developing Transportation Policies and Procedures. *Athletic Business*, Retrieved March 13, 2009, from http://athleticbusiness.com/articles/article.aspx?articleid=162&zoneid=59.

National Collegiate Athletic Association (2006). Safety in Student Transportation: A Resource Guide for Colleges and Universities. Retrieved February 13, 2012 from http://www.ncaa.org/wps/portal/ncaahome?WCM_GLOBAL_CONTEXT=/ncaa/NCAA/Academics+and+Athletes/Personal+Welfare/Health+and+Safety/Safety+in+Student+Transportation.

National Conference of State Legislatures (2006). Information for State Volunteer Driver Liability Laws. Retrieved Feb. 11, 2012 from http://www.ncsl.org/issues-research/transportation/information-for-state-volunteer-driver-liability-l.aspx.

National Highway Traffic Safety Administration (NHTSA) (2008a). *Fatalities to Occupants of 15-Passenger Vans, 1997–2006*. Retrieved Feb. 11, 2012 from http://www-nrd.nhtsa.dot.gov/Pubs/810947.PDF.

National Highway Traffic Safety Administration (NHTSA) (n.d.) *Reducing the Risk of Rollover Crashes in 15-Passenger Vans*. Retrieved Feb. 11, 2012 from http://riskmanagement.wsu.edu/utils/File.aspx?fileid=4221.

National Transportation Safety Board (NTSB) (January 23, 2003). *Spatial Disorientation Cited in Crash of Airplane Carrying Oklahoma State University Athletes*. Retrieved February 11, 2012 from http://www.ntsb.gov/news/2003/030123a.htm.

Legislation

Safe, Accountable, Flexible, Efficient Transportation Equity Act: A Legacy For Users, 23 U.S.C. § 101 (2008).
Texas Charitable Immunity and Liability Act of 1987, Texas Civil Practice and Remedies Code § 84.001, et. seq. (2007).
Volunteer Protection Act of 1997, 42 U. S. C. § 14501, et. seq. (2009).

2.36 PRODUCTS LIABILITY

Rebecca J. Mowrey | Millersville University of Pennsylvania

Imagine for a moment a local fitness center without equipment; an indoor climbing facility minus a climbing wall or safety harnesses; a track and field team without starting blocks, hurdles, or any jumping or throwing apparatus. Without their equipment the first two businesses would merely be empty buildings, and the track and field team would not be very competitive. These examples make us acutely aware of how dependent the sport and recreation industries are upon specialized products. As recreation and sport professionals we make countless decisions with regard to product selection, purchase, installation, use, and maintenance. Using these products permits our constituents to engage in thrilling recreational, competitive, or sport adventures such as skimming along ocean waves via a sailboard, negotiating challenging descents and turns on a mountain bike, or pursuing personal bests as an amateur or professional athlete.

When no one is injured as a result of product use, there is a tendency to throw caution to the wind and just have fun. However, as soon as injuries or property damages occur and lawsuits are filed, people across the sport and recreation product–chain may be surprised to realize their potential involvement. **Products liability** relates primarily to the negligent action of a manufacturer or seller who produces a defective product; hence the product is unreasonably dangerous to the user. While it is true that most professionals working in sport and recreation are not manufacturing or selling products, claims of products liability may provide recourse against liable parties involved *throughout* the chain of production and distribution of products. Therefore, sport and recreation professionals may be deemed as suppliers, included among those who loan, rent, or assign equipment to others, and can be liable if defective equipment is issued and the supplier should have known about the defect.

A case example that illustrates this point is found in *Everett v. Bucky Warren*, (1978). The court held that the coach, acting as a supplier, negligently selected for and supplied to his team defective and dangerous hockey helmets. In contrast to the decision in *Everett,* more recently in *Fischer v. Olde Towne Tours, LLC* (2011), the court held that the defendant was not in the supply chain and therefore not liable for product defects. While enjoying a cruise of the Panama Canal, Jennifer Fisher and her husband elected to participate in a snorkeling excursion. Transportation to the snorkeling site involved a five mile trip in a two—person inflatable dinghy. During the ride to the snorkeling location a large wave struck the boat and Fisher grabbed the mooring line as instructed, but the line failed. She fell backward, striking her back against a fiberglass bench, sustaining injuries to her lumbar vertebrae which required surgery.

The trial court granted summary judgment to Olde Towne on the negligence claims as the signed liability waiver was in order. The products liability charges failed as a matter of law when the court determined that the tour operator was only an end user of the dinghy. The plaintiff claimed that Olde Towne Tours was liable for the defective condition of the dinghy because it either assembled the dinghy incorrectly or modified it by removing the grab holds. During the trial Olde Towne Tours provided evidence that the dinghy in which Fisher was injured was not equipped with grab holds for passengers but that the dinghy arrived from the manufacturer fully assembled. Furthermore, Old Towne argued that they did not design, manufacture, distribute, test, or assemble the dinghy. If the plaintiff had claimed liability due to Olde Towne Tours providing defective equipment, this case may have had a different outcome.

The contrast between the *Everett* decision in 1978 and the *Fischer* decision in 2011 is worthy of further consideration. Section 20 of the Third Restatement (1997) identifies the scope of liability when one "provides a combination of products and services." In *Fisher* the court held that Old Towne merely furnished services to the public; in this case directions and a mode of transportation, but not products *and* services, thus placing the tour company outside the "chain of distribution". Therefore, while a sport or recreation management professional may be involved in products liability cases as one who selects, purchases, receives, installs, maintains, and uses products; the role of others who only *use* products to provide services may be deemed as being outside the "chain of distribution". Furthermore, sport and recreation managers who do not assemble nor modify equipment may be identified as end users and not responsible for using equipment received in a defective state directly from the manufacturer.

CATEGORIES OF PRODUCT DEFECTS

In this section we will examine the three categories of product defects commonly recognized by the courts and classified by the Restatement (third) of Torts (1997); namely, **design defects, manufacturing defects, and marketing defects**. Manufacturers make many decisions regarding products, including design, material selection, and construction. At each stage of a product's life, the product may fail or be defective, thereby rendering the product to be unreasonably dangerous. We will first examine how things might go wrong with a product from its very inception, the design stage.

Design defects occur in products that cause harm as a result of issues related to the faulty design of a product. Lots of good ideas do not hold up well to the requirements or demands of actual usage. We have an example of a design defect in *Brett v. Hillerich & Bradsby Co.* (2001). The Hillerich and Bradsby Company manufactured baseball bats. Designers working with Hillerich and Bradsby discovered ways to make use of new aluminum materials resulting in improved performance by batters. High school pitcher and plaintiff Jeremy Brett, was seriously injured when hit by a ball coming off of one of these newly designed bats. He alleged that the Air Attack 2, an aluminum composite bat designed by Hillerich & Bradsby Co., had a design defect because it allowed batted balls to reach dangerous speeds, exceeding the reaction time needed for pitchers to protect themselves. The decision in this case was in favor of Brett, resulting in several states banning the use of Air Attack 2 and other similarly designed aluminum bats.

Manufacturing defects refer to production errors that result in flaws to an otherwise defect—free product, design, and manufacturing process. In *Diversified Products Corp. v. Faxon* (1987) Faxon purchased a weight machine manufactured by Diversified Products Corporation. He assembled the machine according to the manufacturer's instructions. While he was performing a standing curl, an eyebolt on the curl bar broke, causing him to fall backward. The eyebolt was a factory-assembled piece of the machine and Faxon had not altered this bar nor tampered with the eyebolt. Faxon's fall resulted in serious injuries to his spine. The court decided in favor of Faxon, finding sufficient evidence to support the plaintiff's claim that the eyebolt was defective while it was still in the possession of Diversified Products Corporation, and that this was a manufacturing defect that the Corporation should have detected prior to selling the machine to Faxon.

Marketing defects occur when the warnings or instructions accompanying a product are inadequate, rendering the product not reasonably safe. Warnings must address both foreseeable misuses of a product (van der Smissen, 1990; *Whitacre v. Halo Optical Products, Inc.,* 1987) as well as dangers inherent in the normal use of the product. In some jurisdictions, even if there is an absence of design and manufacturing defect, failure to warn may stand alone as a cause of action (*Garrett v. Nissen*, 1972; *Pavlides v. Galveston Yacht Basin*, 1984). We see an example of marketing defect in *Sullivan v. Nissen Trampoline Company* (1967). *Sullivan* was using a mini–trampoline called an Aqua Diver. This product consisted of a mini–trampoline that people could bounce on and then dive into a pool or lake. As Sullivan bounced on the Aqua Diver, her foot became caught in the webbing that connected the trampoline to the base. The Nissen Trampoline Company did not provide any warning labels alerting users to this potential risk even though their own pre-market testing had shown this to be a risk.

We see another example of marketing defect in *Dudley Sports Co. v. Schmitt* (1972). Schmitt, a high school student, was simply sweeping the storage room floor where a baseball pitching machine was located. As he was sweeping the floor, the throwing arm of the unplugged and inactive pitching machine suddenly and unexpectedly snapped forward causing severe facial injuries to Schmitt. The court ruled that the manufacturer was negligent in designing the machine without a protective guard around the throwing arm mechanism. The court also concluded that Dudley Sports Co. failed to provide an adequate warning about the specific risks associated with their pitching machines, namely that the machine's throwing arm could be triggered when unplugged. According to the court, the warning label only implied that the machine could be dangerous when in use.

It is not uncommon for plaintiffs to state more than one category of product defect as we see in *Covell v. Bell Sports, Inc.* (2011), which includes allegations of both design defect and marketing defect. Covell was hit by a car while riding his bike to work, and although he was wearing a helmet, the 36 year schoolteacher sustained such severe brain injuries that his parents were appointed his legal guardians. In that capacity they filed suit against the bike helmet manufacturer alleging that the helmet was defectively designed and lacked adequate warnings about the dangers of impact to the helmet.

With the increasing attention directed towards sport and recreation related post-concussive syndrome (PCS), products designed for head protection may be the focus of increasing litigation (theconcussionblog. com). Products designed for protection will also need to keep up with improving athletic performances including speed and strength. We see this illustrated in *Wolf v. Rawlings Sporting Goods Co.* (2010), where the plaintiff's skull was fractured after he was struck in the head by a pitch. Wolf sought damages based upon strict products liability, negligence, and breach of warranty; claiming that the helmet was only made to withstand a sixty-mile-per-hour pitch.

Now that we are familiar with the three categories of defects that might make one liable for harm associated with products, we will examine the three legal causes of action associated with products liability as well as the defenses for each.

Causes of Action and Defenses

In Chapter 2.10 you read about negligence and strict liability. To review, **negligence** is an unintentional tort that injures an individual in person, property, or reputation. **Strict liability** means that a defendant can be held liable without fault. In the context of products liability, strict liability would apply when there is nothing wrong with the design, manufacturing, or warning. You might be wondering how that is possible. Courts have held that some products are just too dangerous to exist. Therefore, if a manufacturer decided to design, manufacture and market such a product, an injured party could claim, under strict liability, that the product could not possibly be made safe and should not have been produced in the first place. **Breach of warranty** occurs when a product fails to fulfill either the expressed or implied warranty.

In Table 2.36.1 you will examine the three causes of action under which recovery for products liability may be sought and the defenses to each cause of action.

TABLE 2.36.1	COMMON CAUSES OF ACTION AND DEFENSES UNDER PRODUCTS LIABILITY LAW	
Negligence	**Strict Liability**	**Breach of Warranty**
A manufacturer, supplier, or seller may be sued for negligence in design, testing, manufacturing, inspecting, packaging, labeling or distribution of a defective product, or for failure to warn (failure to warn users of the non-obvious risks presented by the product, including the dangers of misusing the product).	This cause of action may prevail when a product is deemed to be so inherently and unreasonably dangerous that it cannot truly be made safe; regardless of the amount of care given to the design, construction, labeling, and inspection. For example, a jury may conclude that street luge is inherently dangerous and should not occur, thus finding those who manufacture street luge equipment liable using the theory of strict liability. No defense to strict liability is available if (1) the product is determined to be unreasonably dangerous, (2) a defect existed at the time of the sale, and (3) the product was used properly and was the cause of harm.	When a product fails to perform in a way that is promised (warranted), whether this warranty is expressed or implied, a breach of warranty has occurred. Product liability law is concerned with three types of warranties: express warranty; implied warranty of merchantability; and implied warranty of fitness for a particular purpose (See remainder of chapter for discussion of these three types of warranties).
Defenses to a Negligence Claim Include: No evidence of duty, breach, proximate cause or harm. Specifically: 1. Product defect is unproven. 2. Product defect is not the cause of the harm. 3. Evidence that an adequate warning of non–obvious risk was provided and assumed. 4. The danger/risk were open and obvious. 5. The failure to warn was not the cause of the harm. 6. The actions of the plaintiff contributed to the harm. 7. Reasonable care was used by the manufacturer, supplier, or seller; however, the defect was not detectable via reasonable care.	**Defenses to a Strict Liability Claim Include:** 1. Product was altered following purchase or misused in an unforeseeable manner by the plaintiff. 2. An adequate warning was provided and/or secondary assumption of risk applied to the plaintiff. 3. Wear and tear of the product, due to use and age of the product, was appropriate and predictable. 4. The actions of the plaintiff contributed to the harm. 5. See discussion of the risk–utility balancing test below.	**Defenses to a Breach of Warranty Claim Include:** 1. The product was altered. 2. The product was mis-used. 3. The product was not properly installed. 4. The user failed to properly maintain the product. 5. The actions of the plaintiff contributed to the harm. 6. An adequate warning was provided and/or secondary assumption of risk applied to the plaintiff.

Strict Liability Considerations

Now that we have the basics of products liability covered, we will examine some issues related to strict liability a bit further. Typically only manufacturers and sellers are subject to strict liability for defective products. In *Escola v. Coca-Cola Bottling Co. of Fresno* (1944), Justice Traynor summarizes the burden strict liability places upon manufacturers to resist bringing to market products that are hazardous to life and health.

> Even if there is no negligence, however, public policy demands that responsibility be fixed wherever it will most effectively reduce the hazards to life and health inherent in defective products that reach the market. It is evident that the manufacturer can anticipate some hazards and guard against the recurrence of others, as the public cannot.

So how does one determine if a product is unreasonably dangerous? Without a consistent gauge for measuring or determining what is "reasonable" and "unreasonable," product manufacturers may place themselves in jeopardy of strict liability. One solution may be the use of a **risk-utility balancing test** (Restatement (third) of Torts (1997)) to determine whether or not a product design is unreasonably dangerous. Under this test, a product is considered unreasonably dangerous if the dangers outweigh the social utility of the product. The factors commonly considered in risk-utility balancing are as follows:

1. the gravity of the danger
2. the likelihood of injury
3. the obviousness of the danger
4. the feasibility and expense of an alternate design
5. the common knowledge of consumers
6. the adequacy of warnings
7. the usefulness and desirability of the product as designed

By examining a product against the seven factors of the risk-utility balancing test, those associated with product design and development are better situated to defend against strict liability. For example, if the dangers presented by a product are great but there is high demand from consumers for the product and the dangers and warnings are clear and commonly known, the balancing test may be useful in defending against strict liability. The potential use of this balancing test is perhaps most notable when considering consumers' avid pursuit of extreme sport and recreation activities, and the increasing demand for products to satisfy these pursuits. Similarly, when the risk of using a product is high but the cost of redesigning the product and thereby making it safer is low, a product designer and developer may feel challenged to do so. We will now turn our attention toward special considerations associated with breach of warranty as a cause of action in products liability cases.

Breach of Warranty Considerations and Warranty Liability

There are several issues related to product warranty with which sport and recreation managers should be familiar. The traditional common law rule regarding warranties is that the plaintiff must have entered into a contractual relationship, or **privity of contract**[12], with the defendant to claim breach of warranty as a cause of action. For example, under the privity of contract doctrine, a seller could be liable to the buyer, but the seller would not be liable to others because they were not in privity of contract, or direct contact, with the seller. More recently; however, states are abandoning the privity of contract doctrine, as claims of breach of warranty are now codified and primarily governed by the **Uniform Commercial Code (UCC)**.

The UCC reflects the expanding liability of manufacturers and sellers, including the expectation that the seller, not the consumer, should bear the burden of determining that products are safe and conform to established standards. For example, in Alternative A of the UCC, the version adopted by the most jurisdictions, the seller is liable for the personal injuries to the "buyer, members of the buyer's family, and guests in the buyer's home." Perhaps this expectation for product sellers is broader in scope then what you presumed.

---

[12]"Privity of contract is one of the most basic rules of the common law of contract and one of the defining tests for the validity of any contract. This doctrine essentially determines who is a party to contract and who may rely upon the rights granted under the contract to sue another" (Lim, 2008). The privity of contract doctrine dictates that only persons who are parties to a contract are entitled to take action to enforce it.

Under Alternative A of the UCC, a seller sending athletic equipment home with a purchaser would need to provide guidance regarding where and how it should be stored and secured so siblings or other family members or house guests would not be injured by the equipment. As you can imagine, the increased liability for sellers and manufacturers has resulted in a proliferation of product warnings and warranty conditions.

Under the UCC, implied warranties must accompany products at the time of selling / purchasing. These warranties must include the **implied warranty of merchantability**, promising that a product is "of fair average quality", and the **implied warranty of fitness**, promising that a product is "fit for the ordinary purposes for which such goods are used." (U.C.C. 2-314). More specifically, the implied warranty of fitness addresses the product warranty promise extended to the buyer/user that is relying on the seller's expertise to provide an appropriate product fit for his/her particular purpose. We see this illustrated in *Filler v. Rayex Corp.* (1970), where Filler, a high school baseball coach had purchased sunglasses from the Rayex Corporation based upon their marketing guarantees featuring "instant eye protection." The Rayex advertisements and product packaging specifically identified baseball players as an ideal user group for the Rayex product, as the players would benefit by using these "scientific lenses." Filler lost his right eye when a baseball hit the Rayex lens and it shattered. As explained by the court of appeals "Since they lacked the safety features of plastic or shatterproof glass, the sunglasses were in truth not fit for baseball playing, the particular purpose for which they were sold" (*Filler v. Rayex Corp.*, 1970, p. 338).

Under the UCC, a seller's **express warranty** may be provided in several ways. An express warranty is an oral or written statement of fact, promise, description, or model that a buyer relies upon when purchasing products. As you make a decision about which baseball pitching machine to purchase, you know you are considering the machine that best meets your needs due to the express warranty (product facts; description; photo; model, etc.,). However, you want to know if the height of the pitch can be varied and the seller says "absolutely", but upon delivery you discover that the height cannot be varied. Under the UCC, the court would say that the verbal "absolutely" resulted in an express warranty as this information helped to form the basis of your decision to purchase that particular pitching machine.

Another consideration related to breach of warranty is **misrepresentation of warranty**. This occurs when claims are made, primarily in the marketing or selling phase of a product's life, which are untrue or misleading. When the user's actions are based upon the misrepresentation of warranty and he/she is harmed or property is harmed, the claim to products liability may be misrepresentation of warranty. As an example of misrepresentation of warranty, we will examine *Hauter v. Zogarts* (1975). Louise Hauter purchased a "Golfing Gizmo" for Fred, her 13-year-old son. The Gizmo consisted of a golf ball attached to an elasticized cord that was secured to the ground with metal pegs. Zogarts, the defendant and manufacturer of the Golfing Gizmo, marketed the product as a device that would improve one's swing with this claim: "COMPLETELY SAFE BALL WILL NOT HIT PLAYER." Fred Hauter suffered permanent brain damage after the cord wrapped around his golf club and the ball hit his head with great force. The Hauter's successfully sued, alleging misrepresentation of warranty and breach of expressed and implied liability.

They also successfully sued under strict liability as the court found that the Golfing Gizmo was too dangerous to exist. Although the Hauter case was decided before the Risk—Utility Balancing Test was established, it is easy to see that the Golfing Gizmo would likely fail on all seven factors of the Risk-Utility Balancing Test. In Hauter, the court ruled in favor of the plaintiff on all four causes of action. Regarding the charge of misinformation, the court found that the defendant breached the implied warranty of merchantability as the golf training device, intended for use by novices, would likely injure novice users.

Please note that the marketing on the package encouraged the user to "drive the ball with full power." The combination of this encouragement and the "COMPLETELY SAFE" promotion, according to the court, served to significantly misrepresent the risk to the user. It is virtually impossible to ever claim that a product is "100 percent" anything; "completely safe"; or even "safe" or "foolproof." It is best not to make such claims as part of programs or activities associated with sport or recreation.

In summary, design defects, manufacturing defects, or marketing defects resulting in property damage or personal injury to a user or bystander may lead to products liability for a manufacturer, seller, distributor, or supervisor. The causes of action used by plaintiffs in products liability cases will be negligence, strict liability, and/or breach of warranty. As mentioned earlier in the *Wolf v. Rawlings Sporting Goods Co.*, in some cases the plaintiff will use all of these causes of action.

Although some products are simply too dangerous to exist (such as the previously discussed Golfing Gizmo), other useful and quality products also disappear as a result of products liability claims. Sport and recreation professionals are wise to protect against these products liability cases as cost containment and free enterprise issues, in addition to and secondary to the desire to keep constituents as safe as possible. What is our connection to cost containment and free enterprise? When a manufacturer is successfully sued for design, manufacturing, or marketing defects; that corporation may be hampered financially to the point of bankruptcy, or the corporation may elect to no longer participate in the segment of the industry in which it has been sued. The result of these corporate decisions has a palpable impact upon sport and recreation professionals, resulting in less choice for consumers seeking products, and less competitive pricing. Alternatively, in many cases design improvements are the outcome of products liability cases. For example, sport and recreation management has seen significant design changes in helmets to accommodate growing concerns regarding concussive syndrome.

As you read the following case, consider all that you have learned from reading this chapter. The introduction to the Significant Case provides questions for you to respond to as you read through this design defect case.

SIGNIFICANT CASE

This is an ideal sample case for a products liability chapter as this design defect case involves all three products liability causes of action. This case will provide you with the opportunity to do some critical thinking, problem—solving, and apply some of your knowledge regarding products liability while you read. The questions and suggestions in the remainder of this case introduction will guide you. As you read, make note of the potential liability of different types of defendants, including the manufacturer, retail distributor, and general contractor for the basketball court. What defenses are argued by Cornell University regarding the Institution's duty of care to plaintiff Traub? What issues must the jury consider with regard to what an ordinary person would assume as inherent risks of playing basketball? What is the relevance of Traub's secondary assumption of risk to the case? The court endorsed the use of a risk-utility balancing test, but for what purpose? Lastly, why does the court mention whether or not dunking is a foreseeable use of a basketball hoop?

TRAUB V. CORNELL UNIVERSITY
United States District Court for the Northern District of New York
1998 U.S. Dist. LEXIS 5530

I. Factual Background

A. The Incident
On the date of his accident, Darren—who had been a student at Cornell for approximately ten months—played "pick-up" basketball on the Cornell basketball court. * * * After one or two games, Darren and several other players took turns attempting to dunk a basketball through one of the goals. As Darren descended from his second try, the heel and first joints below the fingertips of his right hand made contact with the rigid rim of the hoop. Darren fell to the macadam surface of the court to the right of the goal. * * * His body landed on top of his wrists.

At this point, he was on his right side with his feet angled to the left.

B. Darren's Prior Basketball Experience
Darren began playing basketball approximately ten years prior to his accident. He received training in basketball from camp counselors and basketball coaches and himself coached five to twelve-year-olds. Darren played at the Cornell court approximately fifteen to twenty times prior to his accident. He had tried to dunk a basketball many times but never succeeded. Darren also never jumped high enough to make contact with the rim and never saw anyone else fall backward after making contact with a rigid rim. He claims that he was unaware of the

danger posed by dunking a basketball into a goal with a rigid rim.

C. The Basketball Court and the Goals

In the mid-1980s Cornell began plans for a construction project that included the basketball court where Darren fell. Cornell's landscape architect specified a particular Burke model as the basketball equipment for the court. Although Burke's model package included backboard, uprights, supports, and fittings, Gared Sports, Inc. ("Gared"), a third-party defendant, actually manufactured the hoops, rims, and goals. The rims of the goals were rigid, that is, they did not give way on contact.

M & B, the general contractor for Cornell's project, acquired the specified goals from Cushman, a sports equipment retailer. M & B constructed the court as specified in Cornell's specifications and installed the goals in accordance with the instructions accompanying them.

After completing the project in fall 1988, Cornell opened the basketball court for recreational use by "members of the Cornell community." Cornell provided no supervision and imposed no policies or guidelines for use of the court. Cornell also did not post any warnings on the court.

* * *

III. Overview of the Parties' Claims

Central to each of plaintiffs' claims is their contention that rigid rims unreasonably increase the risk to a player of attempting to dunk a basketball. According to plaintiffs' experts, when a player's hands come into contact with a rigid rim, the forward momentum of the player's upper body halts while the player's legs continue to swing under the basket. This pendulum-like effect increases the likelihood of an awkward fall. Plaintiffs' experts suggest that a break-away hoop, which gives way on contact, is less likely to cause a player to have an awkward fall.

Defendants claim that they are entitled to summary judgment for several reasons. First, defendant Cornell argues that the Traubs' negligence claim fails because Darren assumed all risks inherent in playing basketball with a rigid hoop. The remaining defendants—Burke, M & B, and Cushman—argue that the Traubs' strict products liability claims should be dismissed because rigid rims are not unreasonably dangerous or defective. These defendants also argue that the negligence counts should be dismissed because (1) any risks presented by a rigid rim to a player attempting to dunk a ball are obvious; (2) Darren Traub assumed the risk of playing basketball with a rigid rim; and (3) the alleged defect was not the proximate cause of Darren's accident. Burke, M & B, and Cushman also contend that I should (1) dismiss the Traubs' express warranty claims because the defendants made no affirmation on which a purchaser relied and (2) dismiss the Traubs' implied warranty claims because there is no proof that the hoop and backboard were unsafe for the ordinary purpose for which they were intended. M & B also separately

argues that it cannot be held liable because (1) it completed the court project in accordance with specifications given to it in Cornell and there were no obvious defects in those specifications and (2) it is not a seller within the meaning of the Uniform Commercial Code or the case law defining strict products liability and negligence.

* * *

Discussion

II. Cornell

The Traubs sued Cornell only on a negligence theory. Cornell urges that it had no duty to Darren because he assumed all ordinary and perceivable risks of playing basketball on a court using a hoop with a rigid rim.

Although assumption of the risk generally is no longer an absolute defense in a negligence action, it sometimes functions like an absolute defense because it eliminates the duty that might otherwise be owed to a plaintiff who assumes the risk of engaging in a particular activity. Participants in an athletic activity consent "to those injury-causing events which are known, apparent or reasonably foreseeable consequences of their participation."

* * *

Cornell contends that Darren clearly assumed the risk of jumping high to dunk a ball because "what goes up must come down." 'The school argues that in light of Darren's years of basketball experience, his prior experience on the Cornell court, and the clear view he had of the hoop, he cannot credibly argue that he was unaware of the risks of dunking or of the fact that the hoop had a rigid rim. However, Darren does not claim he was unaware of the risk of falling when he attempted to dunk or of the fact that the hoop had a rigid rim, but rather that he was unaware of the enhanced risk presented by a rigid rim. See Traub Aff. PP 2-3. According to Dr. Marc A. Rabinoff, a professor of human performance, sport, and leisure studies and one of plaintiffs' experts, the enhanced risk of which Darren complains results from a phenomenon known as "hanging up," which occurs when a player's fingers, hands, and wrists come into contact with a rigid basketball hoop and "'hang up' momentarily on the rim." As the forward motion of the player's hands stops briefly, the legs and body continue in motion and swing under the basketball goal. Consequently, the player has no effective way to get his legs back under his torso, falls with his back angled toward the ground, and has an increased likelihood of serious injury.

* * *

Rabinoff also states that the danger of hanging-up "is not well known to amateur basketball players" * * * The question, then, is whether Darren's testimony that he lacked an appreciation of the danger presented by dunking with a solid rim is adequate to create an issue of fact on assumption of risk. Darren stated that he had never before jumped high enough to "hang up" on the rim and that he had never seen anyone else fall backward or be injured from "hanging up." Defendants argue that this testimony fails to create an issue of fact because "any person beyond the age of majority who moves in a forward direction and leaps into the air toward a stationary object must be deemed to be aware of the risk that his/her body may make contact with the stationary object which may result in halting the forward momentum of the body." Defendants rely on Section 496D, comment d, of the Restatement (Second) of Torts which indicates that "there are some risks as to which no adult will be believed if he says that he did not know or understand them." This comment does not apply to the phenomenon of hanging up. The examples cited in the comment—the risk of being burned by fire, drowning in water, or falling from a height—are all risks that every adult would indeed understand. In contrast, the risk of having one's fall distorted by hanging up on a rigid object is not necessarily one that would be perceived by every adult.

* * *

Therefore, I must deny Cornell's summary judgment motion on Count I.

III. M & B

Plaintiffs allege claims in negligence, express and implied warranty, and strict products liability against M & B. For varying reasons, each claim fails. M & B offers uncontroverted proof that it followed Cornell's specifications in procuring and installing the hoop and rims. Therefore, in order to hold M & B liable in negligence, the Traubs must show that "the defects [in the design were] so glaring and out of the ordinary as to bring home to the contractor that it was doing something which would be likely to cause injury." * * * Plaintiffs do not identify any defect in the specifications that was so glaring that M & B should have refused to construct the court in accordance with the specifications. Therefore, I grant M & B's motion insofar as it requests dismissal of Count X.

M & B also argues that it is entitled to dismissal of the Traubs' express and implied warranty claims because the transfer of the basketball hoops from M & B to Cornell was not a sale within the meaning of the Uniform Commercial Code warranty provisions.

* * *

The Cornell contract provided for the construction of a recreational area and primarily involved excavation, grading, masonry, paving, concrete, installation, and landscaping. The contract also specified, however, that M & B procure and install a specific model Burke basketball goal. The price of the goal was less than one half of one percent of the total contract price. Long estimates that since M & B's incorporation in 1975, the company has installed no more than twelve to twenty-four basketball goals of any type. M & B has never entered into a contract, the sole or primary purpose of which was to furnish a basketball goal.

* * *

In a "mixed" contract involving both goods and services, the Uniform Commercial Code's warranties do not apply if the service-oriented portions of the transaction predominate over the sales transactions. The uncontroverted facts described above establish that the service aspects of M & B's contract with Cornell predominated over the sales aspects. Therefore, Counts XII and XIII of the complaint must be dismissed.

M & B also argues that the Traubs' strict products liability counts must be dismissed because M & B is no more than a casual or occasional seller of basketball goals. * * * a plaintiff cannot hold a seller liable on a strict products liability theory if the seller "is not engaged in the sale of the product in issue as a regular part of its business." (citing Restatement [Second] of Torts § 402 A, comment f). The policy reasons for the distinction between regular and casual sellers are that (1) regular sellers—unlike casual sellers—can exert pressure on manufacturers for improved safety because of their ongoing relationship with the manufacturer; (2) regular sellers "can recover increased costs within their commercial dealings, or through contribution and or indemnification in litigation; "and (3) by marketing certain products as a regular part of their business, regular sellers assume[ ] a special responsibility to the public, which has come to expect them to stand behind their goods."

* * *

A contractor who buys only twelve to twenty-four basketball goals in a twenty year period is not in a good position to exert pressure on manufacturers to increase safety standards. This is especially true where the contractor is bound to buy the goal stated in the specifications. In addition, a contractor who buys equipment mandated by the owner cannot be said to be putting its reputation behind the product purchased. Therefore, the Traubs' strict products liability claims against M & B also must be dismissed.

IV. Cushman and Burke

Plaintiffs seek to hold Burke and Cushman liable on theories of express warranty, implied warranty, negligence and strict products liability.

A. Strict Products Liability

The Traubs' strict products liability claims against Burke and Cushman rest on allegations of defective design, defective manufacture, failure to warn, and failure to recall. Because plaintiffs submitted no evidence the rims were improperly manufactured, that claim must be dismissed. Both the failure to warn and the failure to recall claims assume that the design of the rim presented unreasonable dangers. Defendants thus urge that all three claims should be dismissed because plaintiffs can offer no evidence of defective design.

A plaintiff can hold a manufacturer liable in strict products liability for a design defect regardless of the manufacturer's knowledge of the defect. Strict liability may also be imposed on retailers and distributors. To hold a seller or manufacturer liable for a design defect, the plaintiff must establish that the product was "designed so that it was not reasonably safe and . . . the defective design was a substantial factor in causing plaintiff's injury." The plaintiff has the initial burden of showing that the product "was not reasonably safe because there was a substantial likelihood of harm and it was feasible to design the product in a safer manner." "[A] defectively designed product is one which, at the time it leaves the seller's hands, is in a condition not reasonably contemplated by the ultimate consumer and is unreasonably dangerous for its intended use." The product must be safe for its intended use "as well as an unintended yet reasonably foreseeable use." .2d 115, 348 N.E.2d 571 (1976). Plaintiffs urge that a rigid hoop is not reasonably safe because it is more likely to cause injury in the course of dunking than a break-away hoop. Defendants first contend that plaintiffs have not offered any competent proof that the rigid hoop is more likely to cause injury than a break-away hoop.

Plaintiffs' proof on the issue of design defect is contained in the affidavits of their experts. As noted previously, plaintiffs' experts claim that contact with a rigid rim distorts a player's descent from the basket and makes injury more likely. They also claim that break-away hoops are safer because they soften the direct impact to a player's fingers, hands, and wrists and lessen the possibility of "hanging up" on the rim. * * *

Plaintiffs have also offered competent proof that a safer design existed in the 1980's in the form of a break-away hoop. According to Dr. Roberts, patents on file in the United States Patent and Trademark Office from many years prior to Darren's accident cite improved player safety as a benefit of break-away hoop design. Plaintiffs also offer proof that break-away hoops have been used in indoor competition since the 1960's. Therefore, plaintiffs created issues of fact on both safety and the feasibility of an alternative design that are sufficient to defeat summary judgment on the existence of a defect.

Next, defendants argue that the hoop was in exactly the condition Darren would have anticipated and thus was not defective within the meaning of Robinson, which held that a defective product is one "in a condition not reasonably contemplated by the ultimate consumer." Defendants urge that because Darren was fully aware that the hoop had a rigid rim, he cannot recover in strict products liability. This argument fails because consumer's awareness of the danger of a product is only one factor the jury should consider in determining whether the product is reasonably safe.

Finally, defendants argue—but not with any great spirit—that plaintiffs have not established that dunking is a reasonably foreseeable use of a basketball hoop. Defendants concede "that dunking is a voluntary option attempted by many players of the game." 'Therefore, I must deny the motion for summary judgment on Counts III and XV.

B. Negligence

Counts II and XIV of the complaint are negligence counts against Burke and Cushman. As to Burke, the Traubs allege (1) failure to exercise reasonable care in designing and constructing the hoop and backboard; (2) failure to keep abreast of developments in the field of recreational equipment and to upgrade its design; (3) failure to warn of the dangers of rigid rims and/or to warn against attempting to dunk a basketball into a basketball goal with a rigid rim; (4) failure to advise of the availability of an alternative safer design; and (5) failure to make reasonable efforts to recall, modify, or replace the hoop. Plaintiffs charge that Cushman was negligent in (1) failing to keep abreast of developments in the field of recreational equipment; (2) selling the backboard and hoop to M & B; (3) failing to advise that a safer hoop design was available; (4) failing to warn; and (5) failing to recall, modify, or replace the hoop after the sale. Defendants seek dismissal of the negligence counts arguing that (1) Darren assumed the risk of using the hoops; (2) they had no duty to warn because any risk the hoops presented was obvious; and (3) plaintiffs presented no proof that any alleged defect was a proximate cause of Darren's injuries. For the reasons discussed under Point II, there are issues of fact concerning assumption of the risk. Similar reasons compel the conclusion that there are issues of fact as to whether the dangers of a rigid hoop are so obvious that defendants had no duty to warn. As previously noted, Darren contends that he did not understand that his fall would be distorted by contact with the rigid rim. The issue of whether an injured party knew of the danger presented by the product that injured him generally is for the jury. Defendants' final argument is that plaintiffs have not offered competent proof that any defect in the product caused Darren's injuries. However, plaintiffs' experts supplied competent proof that the rigid rim design contributed to Darren's injuries. Therefore, I must deny defendants' request for dismissal of Counts II and XIV of the complaint.

C. Express Warranties and Implied Warranties

Counts IV and XVI of the second amended complaint allege that Burke and Cushman breached express warranties. N.Y. U.C.C. § 2-313 provides:

> (1) Express warranties by the seller are created as follows:
> (a) Any affirmation of fact or promise made by the seller to the buyer which relates to the goods and becomes part of the basis of the bargain creates an express warranty that the goods shall conform to the affirmation or promise.
> (b) Any description of the goods which is made part of the basis of the bargain creates an express warranty that the goods shall conform to the description.

(c) Any sample or model which is made part of the basis of the bargain creates an express warranty that the whole of the goods shall conform to the sample or model.

Plaintiffs contend that the 1988 Burke Catalog, which represents that its goal is of "slam dunk strength," operated as an express warranty that the goal was safe for dunking. Plaintiffs do not allege that they or any of the defendants read or relied on this catalog's representations. In order to show that a seller made an express warranty through a description in an advertisement, plaintiffs must show that a purchaser relied on that representation and that the representation thus became "part of the basis of the bargain." As plaintiffs conceded at oral argument, their express warranty claims must be dismissed because they cannot show that any purchaser relied on the statement in the Burke catalog.

Plaintiffs also claim that Burke and Cushman breached the implied warranty of merchantability. Section 2-314(c) states that in order to be merchantable, goods must be "fit for the ordinary purposes for which such goods are used. . . ." Although a claim for breach of the implied warranty of merchantability is quite similar to a claim of strict products liability/design defect, there are differences. Most importantly, the plaintiff in an implied warranty case need not establish that the social desirability of a safer design outweighs its cost or that an alternative design is feasible. Instead, the plaintiff can prevail by showing that the "product was not minimally safe for its expected purpose." Id. As noted above, plaintiffs created an issue of fact as to whether dunking is part of the expected purpose of a basketball hoop and as to whether the defendants' design was minimally safe for this purpose. Therefore, I must deny summary judgment on the implied warranty claims against Burke and Cushman.

* * *

It is so ordered.

CASES ON THE SUPPLEMENTAL WEB SITE

Bouillon v. Harry Gill Company (1973 Ill. App. LEXIS 1604). From *Bouillon* we learn about a plaintiff severely injured while pole vaulting. As you read the case, note the cause of action brought against Gill, the athletic equipment manufacturing giant.

Muller v. Jackson Hole Mt. Resort (2006 U.S. App. LEXIS 32098). *Muller* will lead you to consider the role of the service provider and the importance of documenting maintenance in products liability cases. Describe what impact, if any, the risk-utility balancing test has in this case.

Pell v. Victor J. Andrew High School (1984 Ill. App. LEXIS 1712). As you read *Pell*, identify which of the categories of products defects are relevant in this case.

Sanders v. Laurel Highlands River Tours, Inc., (1992 U.S. App. LEXIS 15094). While reading *Sanders*, consider if the UCC applies to this case, and if so, in what ways?

Wissell v. Ohio High School Athletic Association, (1992 Ohio App. LEXIS 904). In *Wissell* we learn about a football player who was rendered a quadriplegic during a high school game. As you read this case, identify the grounds on which the plaintiffs appealed as well as the original products liability causes of action.

QUESTIONS YOU SHOULD BE ABLE TO ANSWER

1. Compare and contrast the three common causes of action in products liability cases.

2. Discuss how manufacturers might use the risk-utility balancing test.

3. Research the Hillerich & Bradsby Company on line and discover what changes they have made to their product line as a result of being named as a defendant in multiple products liability cases.

4. What are the three categories of product defects identified in the Restatement (third) Tort law?

5. What is meant by the Implied Warranty of Fitness?

REFERENCES

Cases
Anthony Pools, Inc. v. Sheehan, 455 A.2d 434 (Md. 1983).
Arnold v. Riddell, Inc., 882 F. Supp. 979 (D. Kan. 1995).
Back v. Wickes Corp., 378 N.E.2d 964 (Mass. 1978).
Bhardwaj v. 24 Hour Fitness, Inc., 2002 Cal. App. Unpub. LEXIS 3288 (Cal. App. 2002).
Brett v. Hillerich & Bradsby Co., 2001 U.S. Dist. LEXIS 26319.
Byrns v. Riddell, Inc., 550 P.2d 1065 (Ariz. 1976).
Covell v. Bell Sports, Inc., 651 F.3d 357; 2011 U.S. App. LEXIS 14252.
Curtis v. Hoosier Racing Tire Corp., 299 F. Supp. 2d 777 (N.D. Ohio 2004).
Diversified Products Corp. v. Faxon, 514 So.2d 1161 (Fla. App. 1987).
Dudley Sports Co. v. Schmitt, 279 N.E.2d 266 (Ind. App. 1972).
Escola v. Coca-Cola Bottling Co. of Fresno, 150 P.2d 436 (1944).
Everett v. Bucky Warren, Inc., 376 Mass. 280, 380 N.E.2d 653 (1978).
Filler v. Rayex Corp., 435 F.2d 336 (1970).
Fisher v. Olde Towne Tours, LLC, 2011 Cal. App. Unpub. LEXIS 5856.
Garrett v. Nissen, 498 P.2d 1359 (N. Mex. 1972).
Gentile v. MacGregor Mfg. Co., 493 A.2d 647 (N.J. Super. L. 1985).
Green v. BDI Pharmaceuticals, 2001 La. App. LEXIS 2390 (La. App. 2001).
Hauter v. Zogarts, 120 Cal. Rptr. 681, 534 P.2d 377 (1975).
Hurley v. Larry's Water Ski School, 762 F.2d 925 (11th Cir. 1985).
   http://theconcussionblog.com
Levey v. Yamaha Motor Corp., 825 A.2d 554 (N.J. Super. 2003).
Mohney v. USA Hockey, Inc., 2001 U.S. App. LEXIS 3584 (6th Cir. 2001)
Mohney v. USA Hockey, Inc., 2005 U.S. App. LEXIS 14373 (6th Cir. 2005).
Pavlides v. Galveston Yacht Basin, 727 F.2d 330 (5th Cir. 1984).
Perton v. Motel Properties, Inc., 497 S.E.2d 29 (Ga. App. 1998).
Rodriguez v. Riddell Sports, Inc., 242 F.3d 567 (5th Cir. 2001).
Traub v. Cornell University, 1998 U.S. Dist. LEXIS 5530 (N.D.N.Y. 1998).
Sullivan v. Nissen Trampoline Company, 1967 Ill. App. LEXIS 938, (1967).
Vantour v. Body Masters Sports Industries, Inc. 147 N. H. 150; 784 A. 2d 1178 (N.H. Supreme C. 2001).
Whitacre v. Halo Optical Products, Inc., 501 So.2d 994 (La. App. 2 Cir. 1987).
Wolf v. Rawlings Sporting Goods Co., 2010 U. S. Dist. 116294.

Publications
Garrett, M. C. (1972). Allowance of punitive damages in products liability claims. *Georgia Law Review, 6*(3), 613–630.
Lim, R. (2008). The Doctrine of Privity of Contract. Http://www.articlealley.com/article_655389_18.html.
Nader, R. (1972). *Unsafe at any speed: The designed-in dangers of the American automobile.* New York: Grossman.
Plant, M. L. (1957). Strict liability of manufacturers for injuries caused by defects in products: An opposing view. *Tennessee Law Review, 24*(7), 938–951.
tulane.baseball.arbitration@gmail.com (The Baseball Arbitration Competition)
van der Smissen, B. (1990). *Legal liability and risk management for public and private entities.* Cincinnati, OH: Anderson Publishing Company.

Legislation
Restatement (Second) of Torts §402A (1965).
Restatement (Third) of Torts §2 and related comments (1997).

2.37 HOSPITALITY AND TOURISM LAW

Sarah J. Young | Indiana University

Imagine for a moment that you are traveling to an exotic island beach resort in the Caribbean where your travel agent booked reservations for you at a four-star hotel right on the beach. Your departure day finds you waiting for a flight delay that extends into hours causing you to miss your connecting flight and arrive one day late for your vacation. Upon check-in at the hotel, you discover they have overbooked and, because you are a day late, have switched your reservation to a three-star hotel two miles inland. The hotel shuttle is involved in a minor traffic accident en route to your new accommodations, causing you to crack your head on the window. Woozy, you finally get to your hotel, only to find that a family of mice has already taken up residence in your room. You inform the front desk that you must have another room (a clean one!) and go to the restaurant for a bite to eat while the hotel straightens out the room situation. At the restaurant, you eat some bad seafood, which resurrects itself at 3 o'clock in the morning. While you lay curled up on your bed watching the television because your stomach hurts, you learn there is a category-four hurricane headed straight for your location, and authorities are mandating evacuation of the island immediately.

Sound like a tourist's worst nightmare? This might lead one to think about the legal duties and responsibilities of travel agents, airlines, hotels, and restaurants to tourists. Although many of the legal concepts and principles discussed in other chapters of this text apply to tourism settings, there are unique legal aspects that arise because of the very nature of tourism. Barth (2009) recognized the interconnectivity of travel and hospitality as one phenomenon that makes legal issues in tourism unique. For example, vacation packages often include transportation, lodging, meals, and recreation activities. When something goes wrong, and the tourist does not receive what was promised, which service provider should be held liable? It is the reliance of one or more service providers on others for quality performance that makes the area of tourism law more complex. Jurisdiction issues, differences in how travel terms are perceived, identity of the actual service provider, weather, civil unrest, and disease are all factors that can create problems for travelers, tourists, and hotel guests, as well as result in litigation. These factors are phenomena over which hotel and restaurant managers, travel agents, and tour operators may or may not have control. Yet, no one in the travel supply chain is immune from legal action. Therefore, what follows is an overview of legal issues unique to managers in the hospitality and travel industries.

FUNDAMENTAL CONCEPTS

Hotels

Dating back to English common law, innkeepers and hotel operators had a duty to receive travelers who registered as guests. Today, common law and statutory law identify hotels, motels, and other establishments providing lodging as places of public accommodation and continue to obligate hotel operators to receive all guests. There are circumstances, however, under which the hotel manager may refuse to register an individual as a guest. Typically, if a person is intoxicated, drunk or disorderly, suffers from an obvious contagious disease, brings property into the hotel that could pose a hazard to other guests (e.g., firearms, explosives, animals), or cannot pay for the price of the room, the manager has the right to refuse accommodation (Jeffries, 1995).

For a person visiting a hotel's property to qualify as a guest, the visit must be for the primary purpose for which the hotel operates—the rental of rooms suitable for overnight stay. The duty owed a guest by a hotel is the same as that owed to an invitee. In other words, the hotel owes a guest a reasonably clean and safe accommodation. An example of this duty is provided in *Grogan v. Gamber Corp.* (2008) where plaintiff was bitten by hundreds of bedbugs while staying at defendant's hotel. Plaintiff claimed defendant had actual notice of bedbugs on the floor on which her room was located, yet failed to take proper steps to check whether her guest room contained the pests. In *Mathias v. Accor Economy Lodging* (2003), an Illinois court granted plaintiffs punitive damages as the bedbug infestation at the hotel was well known among hotel employees, yet they were under strict instructions to rent the rooms. Rather than pay an exterminator's fee or not use the rooms, hotel management preferred to give quick refunds whenever a guest complained about seeing or being bitten by bedbugs. Both of these cases demonstrate the hotel breaching its duty to provide reasonable (i.e., clean and safe) accommodations.

In another example of the hotel's duty to its guests, plaintiff claimed defendant hotel failed to provide adequate security and fire protection after a fire at a Comfort Inn and Suites resulted in the deaths of six guests and severe injuries to 12 additional guests (*Allen v. Greenville Hotel Partners, Inc.*, 2006). The cause of the fire was arson, leading to plaintiff's negligence claim for the hotel installing inadequate sprinklers, leaving the back door to the hotel unlocked, and failing to install surveillance cameras. Additionally, plaintiff claimed the hotel had negligently trained their employees to disengage an active fire alarm until confirming the presence of an actual fire. Not only was this alleged training an obvious violation of fire safety codes, but it created an unnecessary delay in warning guests of the fire danger.

Overbooking

General contract law is enacted every time a potential guest inquires with the hotel as to the availability of a room for a definite period of time at a specified price. Once agreed upon, either verbally or in writing, a breach of this agreement by either the prospective guest or the hotel can result in liability for damages. The hotel reservation, once made and confirmed, constitutes a contract and binds the hotel to provide accommodations as well as the guest to stay there. Yet, many hotels overbook their rooms because of the persistent problem of no-show guests. History and experience prove that a certain percentage of guests will not use their reservations. As a result, some hotels overbook by the expected attrition rate, and then are not able to accommodate all their reservations when the expected no-show guests do actually appear. *Rainbow Travel Services v. Hilton Hotels, Corp.* (1990) showcases a classic example of the liability that can occur from intentional overbooking. Plaintiff was a tour operator who contracted a block of rooms with the Fontainebleau Hilton in Miami, Florida, for University of Oklahoma football fans. When the fans arrived, there were no rooms available at the Hilton because the hotel overbooked their capacity by 15 percent. Upon further investigation, it was discovered that Hilton had a policy regarding overbooking stating that employees should never admit overbooking, but instead refer to factors beyond the hotel's control. The court ruled in favor of plaintiffs because defendants recklessly accepted more reservations than they were able to accommodate.

Protecting Guest Property

Guests bring a variety of personal property with them during their stays on hotel premises. Typically guests bring money, clothing, jewelry, computers, sports equipment, and perhaps, a vehicle. What is the legal responsibility of the hotel to their guests for this personal property? Historically, this responsibility is based on a rule of absolute liability holding the innkeeper liable for any loss of guest property that was "*infra hospitium*, or within the inn" (Garner, 2009, p. 850). This doctrine emanated from the time when not every innkeeper was honest and often was the culprit of missing guest property. There were exceptions, however, to the absolute liability rule. Loss of property because of an act of God (e.g., tornadoes, floods, earthquakes) and loss of property by a public enemy (e.g., terrorists or acts of war) were two exceptions for which the innkeeper was not held liable. A third exception was the negligence of the guest, such as leaving bags unattended in a hotel lobby, sidewalk, hallway, or public area.

Today most states have enacted statutes limiting liability for guest property loss. If a hotel adheres to the statutes it will be liable for the loss only up to an established maximum amount (e.g., $1,000). This is the case even if a guest's property is worth far more than the maximum amount. Although each state's statutes vary in the details, there are common provisions that hotels must generally follow:

1. The hotel must provide a safe available for guest property.
2. The hotel must post notices communicating the availability of safes.
3. The hotel must communicate to guests that their liability for lost or stolen property is limited.
4. The hotel must communicate the maximum recovery amount allowed.

The availability of limited liability provides an incentive for hotel managers to comply with the strict interpretation of these statutes. Without evidence of compliance, the hotel becomes liable under common law for the full amount of the lost or stolen property. Hotels can be held liable beyond the limits of the statute when theft occurs from the safe provided to guests. As illustrated in *Liberty Mutual v. Zurich Insurance* (2010), the hotel guests of a Ritz-Carlton hotel placed jewelry and cash in their guest room wall safe while touring the sites of Chicago. Upon their return they discovered their valuables missing from the safe. Defendants paid the guests $1 million in compensation for their loss.

Within the hospitality industry there are times when a hotel or restaurant manager may be entrusted with a guest's property that is covered under a type of contract law other than the limited liability statute. The theory of bailment is often used by hotels and restaurants for valet parking, coat checks, laundry services, and luggage storage. A **bailment** is defined as the delivery of goods or personal property by one to another with the expectation the property will be returned in the same condition it was received (Garner, 2009). When one hands over possession of his/her personal property for safekeeping by another and the party knowingly has exclusive control over the property, a bailment is established. The individual who gives his/her property to another is known as the **bailor**, whereas the individual who accepts responsibility for the property is known as the **bailee**. Morris, Marshall, and Cournoyer (2008) identified the essential elements of a bailment as personal property, delivery of possession, acceptance of possession by bailee, and a bailment agreement, either implicit or express. Bailments only involve tangible, personal property like cars, clothing, and sports equipment.

The *Arguello v. Sunset Station* (2011) case provides not only an example of a bailment, but also an attempt of the hotel to apply the limited liability statute. Plaintiff left his car keys with the valet at Sunset Station Casino located in Henderson, Nevada, and received a claim ticket. When he was ready to leave the resort property it was discovered his car had been stolen from the valet parking lot. Upon recovering his car the following day in a stripped condition, plaintiff filed a lawsuit against the hotel for breach of a bailment contract. The hotel argued it was shielded by Nevada's limited liability statute and only owed plaintiff a maximum of $750 to which the district court agreed. The appellate court reversed the lower court's ruling by stating the intent of the statute was to limit liability for loss of personal property within a vehicle, not for the vehicle itself and that the hotel had breached the bailment agreement.

Guest Privacy

A registered hotel guest has the right to privacy and peaceful possession of his/her room without disruption from hotel personnel. Morris et al. (2008) identified five exceptions to this right of hotel guests. An innkeeper is authorized to enter a guest's room for normal maintenance, to warn of imminent danger, for nonpayment of the room, when requested to enter by the guest, and upon expiration of the rental period. Unless there is a legal basis for entry, hotel staff and non-guests are not permitted to enter a guest's room at will as illustrated by *United States v. Mitchell* (2008). Police entered the guest room of the defendant who was thought to be running a methamphetamine lab in his room. Police obtained a search warrant *after* arresting both guests in the room on outstanding warrants. Defendant claimed his Fourth Amendment rights were violated as he had not freely and voluntarily consented to police entering his room nor was there evidence of meth or any drugs in his room. The court agreed finding no probable cause for police to enter and search defendant's guest room. However, sometimes guests do engage in illegal activity in their hotel rooms. If evidence of illegal activity is discovered by a hotel employee who is legally in the guest's room, the hotel has an obligation to report their findings to the police. This was the case in *Commonwealth v. Molina* (2011) where hotel security discovered large quantities of marijuana, plastic bags, and a set of scales in a guest's room after responding to complaints of strong odors on a non-smoking floor. Upon return to his room, the guest was arrested for possession and dealing of drugs.

Recreational Facilities

Often hotels provide additional services and facilities such as spas, swimming pools, workout rooms, trails, putting greens, and other specialized facilities for their guests' enjoyment. In most states, the general standard for hotels is to exercise reasonable care in preventing injury to a guest who uses these activity areas. Whether reasonable care is exercised depends on the facts and circumstances in each case. In *Bradshaw v. ITT Sheraton Corporation* (2005), plaintiff sued after she fell off a carpeted transition incline leading to the dance floor.

Summary judgment for the hotel was denied because there were factual questions as to whether defendant failed to exercise reasonable care to protect its guests from harm.

Because they are attractive to guests, especially children, most hotels have aquatics facilities on their property, yet aquatics facilities represent a potential liability to the hotel operator. Most hotels provide signage around the pool area indicating that no lifeguard is on duty and that guests should swim at their own risk (*Yi v. Pleasant Travel Service*, 2011). However, the duty to maintain a reasonably safe pool area for hotel guests is emphasized in *Uddin v. Embassy Suites Hotel* (2005). Here, the hotel was found negligent for a 10-year old girl's drowning because the water was so murky and cloudy that one witness stated she could not see her feet while standing in the pool.

Because hotel guests have access to recreational activity areas does not always mean the area is within the hotel's **sphere of control**. *Fabend v. Rosewood Hotels and Resorts* (2004) illustrates this concept. Plaintiff sued the Rosewood Hotel and the National Park Service (NPS) after he was injured bodysurfing in the Virgin Islands. He claimed the hotel failed to warn him of a dangerous shorebreak condition on the beach, which created a forceful wave driving him into the sand and leaving him a quadriplegic. Although the hotel advertised the white, sandy beaches in their promotional materials, the NPS maintained physical control over all the beaches. Additionally, NPS provided signs and brochures warning visitors of the dangerous conditions of the park. The court ruled that because the beach was not in the hotel's sphere of control, it did not have a legal duty to warn swimmers of the shorebreak danger.

Travel and Tourism

Jurisdiction

Most plaintiffs expect to pursue their filed claim in their local courts, yet when travel is involved, and the defendant resides in a different state, the plaintiff's local court must have jurisdiction over both plaintiff and defendant in order for the claim to move forward. Travel, by its very nature, creates issues that call into question the authority of a court to rule on legal matters. For example, a resident of New York City was injured while on vacation at a hotel casino in Las Vegas. The injured party sued the hotel for negligence, claiming the hotel's employees left a chair in a common pedestrian area, causing her to fall (*Smith v. Circus Circus Casinos, Inc.*, 2003). At issue was in which state, Nevada or New York, must the plaintiff make her claim. **Jurisdiction** is defined as the authority of the court to decide a matter of controversy (Garner, 2009) as well as maintain control over the subject matter and parties to the dispute. In most states, jurisdiction over corporate defendants is determined by the amount and frequency of business defendants conduct in a given state. Generally, "doing business" depends on factors such as the existence of an office in the state, the solicitation of business, the presence of bank accounts or property in the state, and the presence of employees.

The importance of establishing jurisdiction is illustrated in *McCrann v. Riu Hotels* (2010) where plaintiffs fell while horseback riding on a tour arranged by an Aruban enterprise that promoted its services in the defendant's hotel. Because defendant's primary offices were located in Spain and Florida, plaintiffs had to show that their home state of New York had jurisdiction. Because defendant had no bank accounts, property, or employees in New York, plaintiffs were unable to produce evidence showing defendant "engaged in any systematic or continuous business solicitation in New York" (p. 7). The court therefore ruled that a New York court did not have jurisdiction over defendant. For more information regarding jurisdiction, see Chapter 1.10 *The Legal System*.

Internet Sales. The sale of travel and vacation packages via the Internet has not only increased exponentially over the past decade, but also affects the jurisdiction of legal claims. Many courts have adopted a sliding scale analysis categorizing websites as passive to interactive for the purpose of determining whether specific jurisdiction exists (*Zippo Manufacturing, Co. v. Zippo Dot Com*, 1997). A **passive website** containing information about the hotel or travel destination available to the general public, but not providing a way to take reservations, is viewed as an insufficient basis for establishing jurisdiction. In *Cervantes v. Ramparts, Inc.* (2003), a California plaintiff filed suit against the Luxor Hotel located in Las Vegas, Nevada, after he slipped and fell in the hotel's restroom. Plaintiff tried to establish that California courts would have jurisdiction over the defendant because defendant maintained a website accessible in California. The court disagreed, noting the hotel's website was passive and only provided information about the Luxor. On the other end of the scale, an **interactive**

website is generally characterized by information, e-mail communication, detailed descriptions of goods and services, and online sales. *Kaloyeva v. Apple Vacations* (2008) illustrates this type of web site. Plaintiffs, New York residents, sought relief for fraud, negligence, and breach of contract, *inter alia*, from defendant, a representative of Santana Beach Resort and Casino located in the Dominican Republic. Defendant provided to the general public a website on which customers could make reservations. The court ruled that jurisdiction over a defendant could be exercised under two conditions: (1) where the website is used to actively transact business, and (2) where a consumer can exchange information with the host computer. In *Kaloyeva*, Apple Vacations actively solicited business on its website and allowed consumers to enter into legal contracts based upon services advertised, resulting in defendants effectively placing their business and its services into the stream of commerce of the state of New York. However, in a more recent case (*Martino-Valdes v. Renaissance Hotel*, 2011) the court ruled the mere presence of an interactive website, on its own, was not enough to establish general jurisdiction, especially if it was not used to make a reservation.

Forum Non Conveniens. Related to issues of jurisdiction is **forum non conveniens**, which refers to the discretionary power of the court to "divest itself of jurisdiction" when convenience of the parties and justice would be better served if the case was brought forth in another forum (Garner, 2009, p. 726). In determining whether a different venue would be more convenient for the parties involved in a case, the court typically considers three factors provided by an analysis from a 1947 U.S. Supreme Court case (*Gulf Oil Corp. v. Gilbert*).

First, the court must determine whether an alternative forum exists. For example, an Illinois couple was the guest of the Atlantis Hotel in the Bahamas when the husband was injured in a jet ski accident. Plaintiff alleged negligence against the hotel since the jet ski business was on the beach owned and solely controlled by the hotel. The Bahamas was deemed an adequate alternative forum because Bahamian law follows the same basic principles of tort law as does an Illinois court (*Horberg v. Kerzner International Hotels Limited*, 2007).

Secondly, the court must determine the private interest of the litigant including the relative ease of access to sources of proof, availability of compulsory processes to obtain unwilling witnesses' attendance in court, cost of obtaining attendance of witnesses, the possibility of viewing the premises, and any other practical considerations that make the hearing of a case more expedient and less expensive. As an example, the court in *Ellis v. Marriott International* (2011) ruled it was more reasonable and convenient for the court proceedings to be moved from Pennsylvania to Hawaii where plaintiff's injury occurred.

The third and final consideration balances public interest factors such as court congestion, the burden of jury duty on the people of the community who have no relation to the litigation, and the appropriateness of trying a case in a forum familiar with the governing law of the case. A good illustration of how *forum non conveniens* works is found in *Campbell v. Starwood Hotels and Resorts* (2008). A resident of Florida vacationing in the Bahamas was swimming in an area designated as safe by the hotel where he was a registered guest. While swimming, plaintiff was struck by a motorboat operated by a vendor who was contracted by the defendant hotel to provide water sports to hotel guests. Plaintiff sued defendant for a variety of negligence claims in federal district court while defendant moved to dismiss the case on the basis of *forum non conveniens*. After determining the Bahamas was an adequate alternative forum because their laws recognized negligence as a cause of action, the court concluded that private and public interest factors favored the trial taking place in Florida. This decision was supported by the fact that the majority of witnesses were located in the United States and "the hardships associated with obtaining evidence while litigating in the Bahamas forum would be greater" (p. 13) than litigating the case in a Florida district court.

Forum Selection Clauses. Often tourist destinations and common carriers will include a **forum selection clause** in the agreement between agency and tourist citing any litigation must be brought forth in the court where the agency is headquartered. Dickerson (2004) explained that hospitality and travel providers institute forum selection clauses as a way to discourage guests or travelers from prosecuting their legal claims. Historically and traditionally the courts have held firm in the enforcement of forum selection clauses once the terms and conditions of a contract have been reasonably communicated (*Morales v. Royal Caribbean Cruises*, 2006). For example in *Vega v. Norwegian Cruise Lines* (2007), the ticket for plaintiff's (residing in New York) cruise to the Bahamas contained a forum selection clause clearly stating that any legal disputes had to be litigated in the courts of Miami-Dade County, Florida.

The U. S. Supreme Court in *Carnival Cruise Lines, Inc. v. Shute* (1991) also noted the forum selection clause must be deemed fundamentally fair. Similarly, in *Lischinskaya v. Carnival Corporation* (2008), the court ruled the forum selection clause was fair and enforceable, primarily because plaintiff had plenty of time to review her ticket, and the explicitly stated terms contained within.

Although the majority of forum selection clause cases favor defendants, this is not always the case. *Stobaugh v. Norwegian Cruise Line* (1999) provides a good example of when a travel service provider's forum selection clause was deemed fundamentally unfair. Plaintiffs, residents of Texas, had contracted with the cruise line to take a seven-day cruise to Bermuda departing August 31. They received their passenger tickets with all the terms of the agreement, including the forum selection clause, on August 8. A few days before their departure, plaintiffs learned of several tropical storm systems in the Atlantic Ocean. On inquiring with Norwegian about refunds if they decided to cancel on account of the weather, they were told they should proceed with the trip and trust the judgment of the ship's captain. Plaintiffs did as suggested, and defendant's ship sailed into Hurricane Eduardo, which allegedly resulted in physical and emotional injuries to many passengers on board. Plaintiffs filed a class action lawsuit in Texas court against Norwegian Cruise Lines, who asserted their forum selection clause (based in Florida) as a basis to dismiss the case. The court ruled against the cruise line stating that because their forum selection clause was not clearly communicated to passengers until after they paid in full for the cruise, the clause was not fair nor enforceable.

Transportation

Transportation is another major dimension of the travel and tourism industry with airplanes, cruise ships, buses, tour buses, trains, and taxis serving as common carriers. A **common carrier** is one who takes on the responsibility to transport from place to place any person who chooses to employ it for hire (Garner, 2009). A common carrier owes its passengers the highest degree of care with the passenger–carrier relationship continuing until the passenger has had a reasonable opportunity to reach a place of safety. Furthermore, common carriers are vicariously liable for their employees' intentional and negligent torts, even when they are committed outside the scope of employment (*Twardy v. Northwest Airlines, Inc.*, 2001).

Air travel is the method of choice for long-distance travel for many tourists. The contract between an airline and its passengers is known as a **tariff** and outlines the terms to which the passenger agrees when purchasing a ticket. The terms of the tariff affect how passengers are treated and vary among the major carriers. For example, not all airlines have the same policy regarding flight delays and how passengers whose flights are delayed are handled. The terms of handling flight delays are contained in the tariff, or ticket information. On the other hand, federal regulations require all airlines to provide a standard compensation to passengers who are bumped from their flights due to overbooking. Although most passengers accept the airlines' compensation, there are some who choose to claim damages for breach of contract of the tariff. A bumped passenger claiming contract damages may sue for costs of alternate transportation, meals, and compensation for inconvenience caused by the bump. Illustrated in *Stone v. Continental Airlines* (2005), plaintiff and his thirteen-year-old daughter were bumped on Christmas day from their flight from New York City to Telluride, Colorado, for a ski trip. Plaintiff was awarded damages totaling $3,110 for unrecoverable lodging accommodations, lost baggage, and inconvenience of missing the scheduled holiday vacation trip.

For airlines operating international flights, liability for personal injury, damaged or lost baggage, and damages caused by delays is limited by the Warsaw Convention. The **Warsaw Convention** is an international treaty, to which the United States is a party, governing and limiting the liability of air carriers transporting passengers and cargo on international flights. For example, in *Bernardi v. Apple Vacations* (2002) plaintiff originally filed her claim in a Pennsylvania state court for extreme and inhumane conditions suffered by passengers during an international flight. Yet, because the U.S. is a signatory to the convention, not only was defendant's liability limited, but plaintiff's state law claims were preempted by the Warsaw Convention. Applicable only to the actual flight, the Warsaw Convention does not limit the liability of airport security checkpoints for stolen bags, as shown by *Dazo v. Globe Airport Security Services* (2002). The passenger's carry-on bag containing over $100,000 worth of jewelry was stolen as she passed through the metal detector on an international flight connecting in St. Louis, Missouri. The security company attempted to seek shelter from liability through the Warsaw Convention, but the court ruled the limitation on liability did not apply.

Vacations aboard luxury cruise ships have increased in popularity with more than 15 million people participating in cruises in 2010 and an estimated 16 million passengers for 2011 (State of Industry, 2011). Modern-day cruise ships are essentially floating hotels (Barth, 2009; Dickerson, 2004) with amenities including ice-skating rinks, rock-climbing walls, golf simulators, water slides, private pools, spas, and planetariums. As a result, many of the legal issues of guest safety, security, and liability are similar to those faced by land-based hospitality managers. Furthermore, like all common carriers, those operating cruise ships are subject to a wide array of local, state, federal, and international laws. Yet, in addition to these legal principles, cruise ships and their passengers are subject to **maritime laws**, a system of law relating to navigable waters. In *Bird v. Celebrity Cruise Line, Inc.* (2005), plaintiff alleged that she became ill and was diagnosed with bacterial enteritis from food ingested on board the cruise. The district court found in favor of defendant because maritime law governed the case and plaintiff's allegations of implied warranty of merchantability and strict product liability are not recognized causes of action under maritime law. Furthermore, liability waivers used to protect cruise lines from liability for injuries aboard ship are not enforceable. Federal statute 46 App. U.S.C. Appendix §183c states:

> It shall be unlawful for . . . owner of any vessel transporting passengers . . . to insert any . . . provision or limitation purporting, in the event of loss of life or bodily injury arising from the negligence or fault, . . . to relieve such owner . . . from liability. . . . All such provisions or limitations . . . are declared to be against public policy and shall be null and void and of no effect.

Similar to the limits on liability provided for international air travel, the **Athens Convention** limits liability of cruise ships to passengers aboard cruises not touching a U.S. port. Although the United States is not a signatory to the Athens Convention, many of the cruise lines serving U.S. passengers are owned by companies located in countries that do abide by the terms of the convention. For example, in *Henson v. Seabourn Cruise Line Limited, Inc.* (2005), defendant sought limits on liability from negligence claims by the plaintiff. Defendant cruise line was flagged as a vessel of the Bahamas, which is party to the treaty, and the Athens Convention was included as a term in the ticket contract with the plaintiff. The court ruled, however, that because the cruise was scheduled to make several stops at U.S. ports, U.S. federal law prevailed over the liability limitations of the Athens Convention.

Agency Law

Inherent to understanding legal liability in the travel and tourism industry is **agency law**, an area of law governed by a combination of contract law and tort law (Cheeseman, 2013). At the heart of agency law is the principal–agent relationship. A party employing another to act on its behalf is known as the **principal**, whereas the **agent** becomes the party agreeing to act on another's behalf. The **principal–agent relationship** is created when both parties agree that the agent has the authority to represent the principal and can enter into contracts on the principal's behalf. This principal-agent relationship is illustrated in *Belik v. Carlson Travel Group* (2011) where plaintiff embarked on a cruise purchased from defendant Carlson who touted itself as the largest singles cruise operator in the U.S. Plaintiff was seriously injured in a diving accident and sued both the cruise line and Carlson through which he had booked his vacation. Plaintiff claimed that because the actions of the operator mirrored those of an agent for its principal that both defendants were liable. The court agreed when the evidence clearly showed the cruise line acknowledged the defendant would act on its behalf thereby making it an actual agency relationship.

Formation of the agency relationship can occur through an express agreement, an implied agreement, or an apparent agency. The express agreement involves either an oral or written contract, whereas the implied agreement is inferred by the conduct of both parties. An **apparent agent** is one whom the principal allows others to believe is acting as its agent, regardless of whether or not the principal has actually conferred that authority (Garner, 2009, p. 72). This concept is illustrated in *Bridgewater v. Carnival Corp.* (2011) where plaintiff, a ticketed passenger on a Carnival cruise, participated in an excursion involving a watersport. While on the excursion, plaintiff was struck by lightning as she held onto a metal cable on the excursion boat. Plaintiff claimed the excursion operator was an apparent agent of Carnival because at no time did the cruise line company state the excursion operator was not an agent or employed by Carnival. The court ruled that just because Carnival failed to disavow an agency relationship did not mean they had engaged in an agency relationship with the excursion operator.

Travel Agents. Many people making travel plans use the services of a travel agent whose job is to provide customers travel information, organize travel packages, and sell travel services such as airline tickets, cruise vacations, hotel rooms, and excursion trips. Travel agents work on commission from airlines, hotels, tour operators, and other types of travel services, making them legal representatives (agents) of the service provider (principal). Although travel agents are viewed as legal representatives of different travel services, they also have a duty to their customers to act with skill, care, and diligence in rendering the kind of services that can reasonably be expected. Travel agents owe a fiduciary duty to their clients. For example, if an agent had a conflict of interest that would be adverse to the client, the agent must disclose that fact to the client. This was the case in *Krautsack v. Anderson* (2006) where plaintiff booked an African safari with his travel agent. The trip was booked for the dry season, but the trip was marred by extremely heavy rainfall due to El Nino. Plaintiff had checked with his travel agent prior to the trip about the unusual weather conditions, but was advised that the weather information plaintiff had received was incorrect and he should proceed with the trip. What defendant also failed to share with his client was that he had already paid his African suppliers and to cancel the trip at that point would have resulted in him losing any profits from plaintiff's booking.

Travel agents are not insurers or guarantors of customers' travel safety as illustrated in *Abramson v. Ritz-Carlton Hotel* (2010); however, they do have a duty to disclose. When a travel agent has knowledge of safety factors or quality issues, he/she has a duty to inform the customer of those facts. For example, in *Hallman v. Unique Vacations* (2010) plaintiffs claimed negligence against their travel agency after resort hotel personnel providing a scuba diving activity left them stranded on the open ocean for more than two hours. Plaintiffs alleged Unique Vacations "breached its duty to warn of the dangerous operation" (p. 2) as evidence of similar prior occurrences of the hotel leaving divers stranded emerged from discovery.

Likewise, websites providing online users with travel related products and services are viewed as 21st century travel agents. In *Hofer v. Expedia, Inc.* (2007) plaintiff booked her travel and accommodations to Jamaica via the Expedia.com website. Upon arrival at the resort hotel, plaintiff discovered the stairs leading up to the lobby of the hotel were dimly lit and did not have a handrail. During her stay plaintiff lost her balance at the top of those stairs and fell into an adjacent turtle pond, severely cutting her leg on sharp rocks in the pond. Plaintiff alleged Expedia breached its duty to warn her that the resort hotel's stairway was dimly lit and lacked a handrail. The court held that a travel agent cannot be held responsible for conditions at a hotel if the agent exercises no control over the facilities. Although the Expedia.com website contained a promise that their "travel specialists visit thousands of hotels across the globe to ensure our descriptions are accurate and up-to-date" (p. 168), there was no evidence that Expedia exercised any control over the resort property where plaintiff was injured.

When customers rely on the expertise of travel agents for information about third-party suppliers (such as tour operators), the travel agent has a duty to provide accurate information and take reasonable care in investigating these travel suppliers. The role of the travel agent in terms of third-party suppliers is illustrated in *Wolf v. Tico Travel* (2011). Plaintiffs traveled to Costa Rica for a fishing expedition. Defendants booked all the necessary arrangements with a local fishing guide company with which they had planned previous excursions. The fishing guide took plaintiffs out on the ocean to fish even though the Coast Guard had issued a warning that day against doing so due to the turbulent and choppy nature of the seas. The boat capsized, and while one plaintiff was able to swim to shore his travel companion drowned. There was no evidence presented showing that defendant "failed to exercise good faith or reasonable skill, care, or diligence in making travel plans" (p. 14) for plaintiffs. The court ruled that travel agents are not liable for the acts or omissions of independent suppliers of services because they have no control over such entities.

Tour Operators. Tour operators are distinguished from travel agents in that operators are usually in a position to actually provide a travel service, such as excursions, guided tours, and trips. Tour operators are often considered the primary provider of the service, whereas the travel agent is a representative of their services. Tour operators can be held liable for their own negligent actions that result in injuries to tourists. A bicycle tour company could be held liable for selection of a dangerous road for the tour (*Coles v. Jenkins*, 1998). Likewise, a Peruvian tour operator involved in a traffic accident while transporting passengers from the airport could be liable for injuries to the passengers (*Vermeulen v. Worldwide Holidays, Inc.*, 2006). However, like the travel agent, if a tour operator is contracting with another third-party travel supplier, then they are not liable for the negligence of that third-party supplier provided they exercised care in the selection of the supplier. For example, a Missouri-based tour operator was not held liable for a client's negligence claim because they had contracted with a third-party to handle the ground transportation for an Egyptian tour on which plaintiff was a party (*Sachs v. TWA Getaway Vacations, Inc.*, 2000).

When a travel agent accepts the additional role of tour operator, the agent assumes the duties and responsibilities of the principal, or the actual service provider. An Arizona travel agency organized, promoted, sold, and operated student vacation tours to Mazatlan, Mexico, which plaintiff's eighteen-year old-daughter, Molly, had purchased. Part of the tour was a train ride called the party train, from which Molly fell when walking from one train car to another (*Maurer v. Cerkvenik-Anderson Travel*, 1994). The travel agency, relying on its role of agent, claimed it had no duty to control the train to make it safe, nor did it have knowledge of the specific condition causing Molly's death. The court disagreed and ruled that because of defendant's dual role as both agent and principal, the travel agency had a duty to warn of dangers of which they were aware, or should have been aware. In another illustration of a travel agent taking on the role of tour operator, a Chicago independent travel agent made arrangements for a private school's eighth-grade graduation trip to Six Flags near St. Louis, Missouri (*Lewis v. Elsin*, 2002). Additionally, the travel agent agreed to serve as the group's tour guide and accompanied them on the trip. Upon check-in at the hotel where the group was staying overnight, defendant left the group and went out for the evening. While absent from the group, one of the students drowned in the hotel's swimming pool. The travel agent/tour guide was sued because he had neglected his role as tour guide and failed to provide for appropriate supervision of the pool area for the group.

Tour operators can gain some protection by using liability waivers and disclaimers as illustrated in *Brocker v. Norwegian Cruise Line Limited* (2007). Plaintiff, a cruise ship passenger, purchased a ticket for a shore-based deep-sea fishing excursion provided by a third party tour operator. While on the deep-sea fishing boat, plaintiff was injured when he fell through rotten boards on the deck into the boat's engine room. The guest ticket contract entered into by the parties precluded liability for conduct of the third-party tour operator, but was not successful in protecting the cruise line from plaintiff's negligence claim.

SIGNIFICANT CASE

Any entity within the travel supply chain can be sued for a variety of claims. This case illustrates the interconnectivity of the travel industry and how the dependence of one business on another does not necessarily mean liability for damages is shared by all travel service providers.

COLLETTE V. UNIQUE VACATIONS, INC.

State of Massachusetts, Appellate Division, Northern District
2004 Mass. App. Div. 59
2004 Mass. App. Div. LEXIS 19
March 30, 2004, Decided

Opinion By: Judge Greco

The evidence introduced during the trial of this case would have warranted a finding that the plaintiffs' honeymoon at Sandals Resort was ruined by a hurricane. What made this loss the subject of litigation as opposed to merely bad luck was Sandals' Blue Chip Hurricane Guarantee by which Sandals promised a free replacement vacation with round trip airfare if a hurricane interrupted a customer's stay. * * *

After a jury-waived trial, the plaintiffs recovered $3,922.00 on their breach of contract claim against Unique. The trial judge also found that Unique had violated the Consumer Protection Act, G.L.c. 93A, and awarded triple damages to the plaintiffs plus costs and attorney's fees. Unique filed this appeal on the ground *inter alia*, that the evidence was insufficient as a matter of law to warrant the court's findings against it on either the plaintiff's contract claim or their G.L.c. 93A claim* * *

Viewed in the light most favorable to the plaintiffs, the evidence indicated the following: Plaintiffs Heather and Kevin Collette booked their honeymoon trip through the Vacation Outlet at Filene's Basement Store. The accommodation component of that trip was a stay of seven nights to be split between two Sandals resorts in Jamaica at Negril Beach and Montego Bay. One of the main reasons the Collettes picked Sandals was the hurricane guarantee mentioned above, which was set forth in writing in a Sandals' brochure and which they specifically discussed with the Vacation Outlet employee with whom they dealt. The Collettes paid for the accommodations by a check made out to the Vacation Outlet. The Vacation Outlet then, in turn booked the hotel reservations with defendant Unique Vacations, Inc. In so doing, the Vacation Outlet generated a written "Passenger Invoice and Confirmation," which listed Sunburst Holidays as the airline vendor and Unique as the hotel vendor. The Vacation Outlet also forwarded payment to Unique in the amount of the money paid by the Collettes, less Vacation Outlet's commission. The Collettes had no personal dealing with any employee of Unique in planning their honeymoon.

Because of Hurricane Mitch, the Collettes were unable to use many of the facilities at Negril Beach. Three of the four restaurants there were closed, and many resort activities were not available. Moreover, the Collettes were not able to go to the second resort at Montego Bay. During their stay at Sandals, the Collettes had no contact with any employee of Unique to complain about the accommodations or for any other purpose. In fact, the Collettes' only interaction with Unique involved complaints which they made after the trip. After the Vacation Outlet contacted Unique to learn who would be the appropriate person at Sandals to address the Collettes' concerns, the Collettes sent G.L.c. 93A demand letters to Sandals, the Vacation Outlet, and Unique. Sandals and the Vacation Outlet responded, but Unique did not. Sandals' response, however, offered a complimentary stay at its resort but instructed the Collettes to contact Unique to select a date in order to accept its offer.

The Sandals brochure stated that "Sandals Resorts and beaches are represented worldwide by Unique Vacations." Unique is a Florida corporation with its principal place of business in Miami. Its Miami address was listed on the Sandals' brochure. If one were to call the toll free number given in the brochure, one would reach the offices of Unique and would be able to make reservations for any Sandals resort without going through a travel agent such as the Vacation Outlet. There was testimony at trial that Unique provided marketing and reservation services to Sandals and had the exclusive right to use the Sandals name and logo for purposes of taking reservations. No evidence was presented, however, as to who owned the two Sandals Resorts in Jamaica, who owned Unique, who held management positions in the corporations, or who held stock.

In essence, the evidence at trial indicated only that Unique was held out to be the worldwide representative of Sandals and had the exclusive right to use the Sandals name in the booking of reservations. Unique's only connection to the travel arrangements for the Collettes was its acceptance of payment from the Vacation Outlet. There was no evidence of what Unique did with this money. Such evidence would have warranted a finding that Unique was Sandals' agent and, perhaps, that the Collettes knew Unique was Sandals' representative, assuming they read every word in the brochure. However, Unique would not have become a party to any contract made with the Collettes because its principal, Sandals, was disclosed. Moreover, there was no evidence that Unique played any role in formulating or offering the Blue Chip Hurricane Guarantee, that the Collettes dealt directly with Unique in making their decision to go to Sandals, or that they even discussed the Hurricane Guarantee with anyone from Unique.

In these circumstances, the Collettes could have recovered on their breach of contract claim against Unique only if there had been some evidence which indicated that Sandals and Unique were engaged in a joint venture. * * * As noted, there was no evidence in this case that Unique had any role in the control or management of the Sandals resorts, other than to accept bookings. The Collettes' attempt to portray Unique as a Sandals principal is not advanced by their characterization of Unique as a tour operator. First, it is far from clear whether Unique was, in fact, a tour operator, which is defined as a seller of travel services that creates and sells travel packages. In any event, a tour operator is not liable for the negligence of a third part supplier of services which the tour operator does not operate, manage, or control.

* * *

Applying these factors, the evidence in the record before us was insufficient to permit the trial judge to disregard the separate corporate identities of Sandals and Unique. There was no evidence of who owned Sandals and who owned Unique, who ran the two companies, whether Unique did anything other than to take reservations, whether employees of Unique wrote the Sandals brochure or had any say in how the Sandals resorts were run or conversely, whether Sandals actively participated in the day to day operations of Unique. The Collettes could never have been deceived by Unique, never discussed the Guarantee with anyone from Unique, and had no reason to be aware of the mechanics of the reservation process or to be concerned about it. * * *

As the evidence was insufficient to permit a finding of a breach of contract or a G.L.c. 93A violation by Unique, the judgment against the defendant cannot stand. The judgment for the plaintiffs is reversed and vacated. A judgment for the defendant, Unique Vacations, Inc., is to be entered.

CASES ON THE SUPPLEMENTAL WEB SITE

Arguello v. Sunset Station, Inc. (252 P.3d 206, 2011). This case is a good example of a breach of bailment contract as well as a failed attempt of the defendant hotel to apply the Nevada statute of limited liability as a defense for stolen property in the hotel's possession.

Belik v. Carlson Travel Group, Inc. (2011 U.S. Dist. LEXIS 60337). This case illustrates negligence, agency and contract issues. It also provides the reader with a good distinction between actual and apparent agency.

Campbell v. Starwood Hotels & Resorts Worldwide, Inc. (2008 U.S. Dist. LEXIS 75883). The reader should note the consideration of all factors in determining the best court venue for this case (i.e., *forum non conveniens*).

Kaloyeva v. Apple Vacations (866 N.Y.S.2d 488, 2008). The reader should identify how the court applied the test for defendant "doing business" in a State.

Yi v. Pleasant Travel Service, Inc., (2011 U.S. Dist. LEXIS 137924). In this near drowning case, the reader should note how the hotel was not held liable for two reasons: 1) the pool had a "No Lifeguard On Duty" sign, and 2) the pool was viewed as an open and obvious risk.

QUESTIONS YOU SHOULD BE ABLE TO ANSWER

1. What is a hotel's legal responsibility to their guests for guest's personal property?

2. Explain the essential elements that must occur for the theory of bailment to apply.

3. How is jurisdiction determined when one uses the Internet to transact travel arrangements?

4. Explain the factors to consider when a claim of *forum non conveniens* is made.

5. What is the legal duty of travel agents to their clients?

REFERENCES

Cases

Abramson v. The Ritz-Carlton Hotel Company, LLC, 2010 U.S. Dist. LEXIS 107001
Allen v. Greenville Hotel Partners, Inc., 2006 U.S. Dist. LEXIS 1855
Arguello v. Sunset Station, Inc., 252 P.3d 206 (2011)
Belik v. Carlson Travel Group, Inc., 2011 U.S. Dist. LEXIS 60337
Bernardi v. Apple Vacations, 236 F. Supp. 2d 465 (2002)
Bird v. Celebrity Cruise Line, Inc., 428 F.Supp.2d 1275 (2005)
Bradshaw v. ITT Sheraton Corporation, 2005 Mass. Super. LEXIS 331
Bridgewater v. Carnival Corporation, 2011 U.S. Dist. LEXIS 20626
Brocker v. Norwegian Cruise Line Limited, 2007 U.S. Dist. LEXIS 54096
Campbell v. Starwood Hotels & Resorts Worldwide, Inc., 2008 U.S. Dist. LEXIS 75883
Carnival Cruise Lines, Inc. v. Shute, 111 S. Ct. 1522 (1991)
Cervantes v. Ramparts, Inc., 2003 Cal. App. Unpub. LEXIS 1283
Coles v. Jenkins, 34 F.Supp.2d 381 (1998)
Collette v. Unique Vacations, Inc., 2004 Mass. App. Div. LEXIS 19
Commonwealth v. Molina, 948 N.E.2d 402 (2011)
Dazo v. Globe Airport Security Services, 295 F.3d 934 (2002)
Ellis v. Marriott International, 2011 U.S. Dist. LEXIS 145417
Fabend v. Rosewood Hotels and Resorts, L.L.C., 381 F.3d 152 (2004)
Grogan v. Gamber Corporation, 858 N.Y.S.2d 519 (2008)
Gulf Oil Co. v. Gilbert, 67 S. Ct. 839 (1947)
Hallman v. Unique Vacations, Inc., 2010 U.S. Dist. LEXIS 138919
Henson v. Seabourn Cruise Line Limited, Inc., 2005 U.S. Dist. LEXIS 26221
Hofer v. Expedia, Inc., 516 F.Supp.2d 161 (2007)
Horberg v. Kerzner International Hotels Limited, 2007 U.S. Dist. LEXIS 97693
Kaloyeva v. Apple Vacations, 866 N.Y.S.2d 488 (2008)

Krautsack v. Anderson, 861 N.E.2d 633 (2006)

Lewis v. Elsin, 2002 Mo. App. LEXIS 435

Liberty Mutual v. Zurich Insurance Company, 930 N.E.2d 573 (2010)

Lischinskaya v. Carnival Corporation, 865 N.Y.S.2d 334 (2008)

Martino-Valdes v. Renaissance Hotel Management Company LLC, 2011 U.S. Dist. LEXIS 127487

Mathias v. Accor Economy Lodging, Inc., 347 F.3d 672 (2003)

Maurer v. Cerkvenik-Anderson Travel, Inc., 890 P.2d 69 (1994)

McCrann v. Riu Hotels, 2010 U.S. Dist. LEXIS 129194

Morales v. Royal Caribbean Cruises, Ltd., 419 F.Supp. 2d 97 (2006)

Rainbow Travel Services v. Hilton Hotels, Corp., 896 F.2d 1233 (10th Cir. 1990)

Sachs v. TWA Getaway Vacations, Inc., 125 F.Supp.2d 1368 (2000)

Smith v. Circus Circus Casinos, Inc., 304 F.Supp.2d 463 (2003)

Stobaugh v. Norwegian Cruise Line Limited, 5 S.W.3d 232 (1999)

Stone v. Continental Airlines, 804 N.Y.S.2d 652 (2005)

Twardy v. Northwest Airlines, Inc., 2001 U.S. Dist. LEXIS 2112

Uddin v. Embassy Suites Hotel, 848 N.E.2d 519 (2005)

United States of America v. Mitchell, 2008 U.S. Dist. LEXIS 10071

Vega v. Norwegian Cruise Lines, 2007 U.S. Dist. LEXIS 44642

Vermeulen v. Worldwide Holidays, Inc., 2006 Fla. App. LEXIS 1551

Wolf v. Tico Travel, 2011 U.S. Dist. LEXIS 136024

Yi v. Pleasant Travel Service, Inc., 2011 U.S. Dist. LEXIS 137942

Zippo Manufacturing Co. v. Zippo Dot Com, 952 F. Supp. 1119 (1997)

Publications

Barth, S. (2009). *Hospitality law* (3rd ed.). Hoboken, NJ: John Wiley & Sons.

Cheeseman, H. R. (2013). *Business law* (8th ed.). Upper Saddle River, NJ: Prentice Hall.

Garner, B. A. (Ed.) (2009). *Black's law dictionary* (9th ed.). St. Paul, MN: Thomson Reuters.

Morris, K. L., Marshall, A. G., & Cournoyer, N. G. (2008). *Hotel, restaurant, and travel law: A preventive approach* (7th ed.). Clifton Park, NY: Thomson Delmar Learning.

State of industry: Cruise business emerges from recession. (2011, March 15). *Cruise Industry News*. Retrieved February 18, 2012 from http://www.cruiseindustrynews.com/cruise-news/5250-31511-state-of-industry-cruise-business-emerges-from-recession.html

Dickerson, T. A. (2004). Recent development: The cruise passenger's dilemma: Twenty-first-century ships, nineteenth-century rights. *Tulane Maritime Law Journal, 28,* 447–465.

Jeffries, J. P. (1995). *Understanding hospitality law* (3rd ed.). East Lansing, MI: Educational Institute of the American Hotel and Motel Association.

Legislation

46 App. U.S.C. Appendix §183c (2006)

INTENTIONAL TORTS AND CRIMINAL ACTS

3.00

Some actions go beyond the level of the unintentional tort—negligence. Two such actions included in this section are intentional torts and criminal acts. An *intentional tort* is a tort, or wrong, in which the actor possessed intent or purpose to injure. An intentional tort contains three elements: (1) there must be an injury, (2) the act is the proximate cause of an injury, and (3) there must be intent to bring about the injury. Legal action must be instituted by the victim or plaintiff and in civil suits punishment generally takes the form of a monetary award to the victim.

Intentional Torts and Criminal Acts address a number of actions that are a concern for the recreation and sport manager. Section 3.10 *Intentional Tort Applications* addresses several intentional torts that are of particular interest to the recreation or sport manager. They are assault and battery, defamation, invasion of privacy, breach of fiduciary duty, tortious interference with contract, and intentional infliction of emotional distress. The chapter on Defamation is a new chapter by a new author.

Recreation and sport managers are becoming more concerned with the effects of crimes on their programs. *Criminal law* is that body of law made up of state and federal statutes that define certain offenses against persons, against public welfare, and against the government. The punishment for crimes can range from fines to long-term prison sentences, depending upon the nature of the crime. The state must institute the action and there is generally no remuneration to the victim.

Section 3.20 *Sport-Related Criminal Acts* includes two chapters. The chapter Criminal Law and Sport brings a totally new approach to the subject by a new author. Also included in this section is a chapter on hazing—which can be considered a crime or an intentional tort.

3.10

INTENTIONAL TORT APPLICATIONS

3.11 ASSAULT AND BATTERY

Curt Hamakawa | Western New England University

Suppose that you, as a sport or recreation manager, just heard from one of your employees that "There's a fight out front and a guy is bleeding all over the place!" Your first reaction might be to respond quickly to the scene to try to break up the scuffle and render first aid. But after stabilizing the situation and returning to your office, you realize that the physical altercation resulting in injuries might lead to legal liability. Questions swirl through your head: What would be the **cause of action**? Who would be liable; just the aggressor or both combatants? Could you, as the manager, and the organization you work for, be liable as well? Might criminal charges be filed in addition to a civil lawsuit, as a result of the fight? And most importantly, what can you do to minimize risks of harm and legal liability to you and your organization?

Sport and recreation managers must be familiar with actions in **tort** that constitute intentional harms[1], because as the manager in the above example may discover, liability for assault and battery could extend to management as well. **Assault** and **battery** generally involve either the threat of bodily harm or an unlawful touching of another person without justification or excuse. Both are torts as well as crimes (Black's Law Dictionary, 2004) and will be defined in more detail later in this chapter. You may be aware that it is not uncommon in the sport or recreation environment for a person to be harmed as a result of another's intentional conduct, both on and off the "field of play." One need only tune in to the news to learn about the latest and most sensational assault and battery cases involving professional athletes or other celebrity figures. In December, 2011, cross-town basketball rivals Xavier and Cincinnati made the national news following a televised game that featured a bench-clearing brawl. Several players were injured necessitating the game being called with nine seconds remaining. Only after meeting with both teams' coaches and being convinced that the aggressors would be severely disciplined, did the prosecutor decide against filing criminal charges. Another highly publicized incident was the "Malice at the Palace" or "Basketbrawl" that took place on November 19, 2004, at the Palace of Auburn between the NBA Detroit Pistons and Indiana Pacers. Near the end of the highly charged game, Piston forward/center Ben Wallace was fouled by Pacer forward Ron Artest, and after a shove back by Wallace, several players from both teams joined in the fray. After a spectator threw a cup at Artest near the scorer's table, Artest charged the stands and a melee broke out between several spectators and Pacers. In addition to NBA suspensions handed down to players on both teams, five Pacers and seven Pistons fans were criminally charged with assault and battery.

In addition to well-publicized allegations of criminal and/or civil assault and battery involving high-profile athletes (*e.g.,* Vancouver Canuck Todd Bertuzzi's career-ending sucker punch on Colorado Avalanche player Steve Moore in a game during the NHL's 2004 season; NBA's Kobe Bryant's 2003 sexual assault of a 19-year-old woman at a Vail, Colorado, resort; Los Angeles Laker Kermit Washington's infamous punch out of the Houston Rockets' Rudy Tomjanovich in 1977; and Golden State Warrior Latrell Sprewell's choking take down of coach P.J. Carlesimo at a practice in 1997), local media are replete with reports that can and do give rise to liability for assault and battery. Obviously, such liability is not limited to athletes-as-combatants. At a youth football game in September, 2011, in Sarasota, Florida, a referee was attacked by three coaches and tackled by a 14-year-old player, resulting in charges of felony battery. In addition, the offending team and coaches were suspended and expelled from the conference. Thus, recreation and sport managers should be aware that their organizations are not immune from incidents involving participants, parents and other spectators, coaches and officials, security personnel, and anyone else who might find occasion to become engaged in behavior that meets the threshold requirements for assault and battery.

---

[1]Note that while intentional torts and negligence fall within the same family and classification as "civil wrongs," intentional torts are separate and distinct from negligence, which is addressed in Chapter 2.11 *Negligence.*

Although the conduct giving rise to assault and battery can result both in civil lawsuits and criminal charges, this chapter addresses only *civil* assault and battery. It is worth reiterating that in the sport and recreation context, parties to assault and battery could involve athletes, coaches, officials, spectators (including parents), club patrons, and any variety of "innocent" bystanders. Furthermore, while most sport- and recreation-related assaults and batteries never make the national headlines, it should not escape anyone's notice that such incidents occur with regularity. Consequently, sport and recreation managers must be educated about the potential risks posed by the intentional torts of assault and battery, and remain vigilant to these threats by devising measures to prevent or mitigate their occurrence.

FUNDAMENTAL CONCEPTS

While most people know—from their television and movie viewing habits, as well as from media reports—that assault and battery are types of crimes, probably fewer are aware that they also constitute torts, which are *civil* wrongs (Black's Law Dictionary, 2004). Thus, a person's conduct constituting assault and battery is actionable in both criminal and civil law. In other words, an individual who is accused of assault and battery can be charged by the police and prosecuted by the public prosecutor (referred to in the states variously as the district attorney, state's attorney, or prosecuting attorney, and in the federal system as the U.S. attorney) in criminal court, and be subject to criminal punishment (*e.g.*, incarceration, probation, and/or fines), and/or be sued by the injured party for **damages** (*i.e.*, monetary award to the plaintiff) in civil court (see Chapter 2.11 *Negligence*). The reason that a person can be subjected to *both* civil and criminal prosecutions and not run afoul of **constitutional** provisions is because the **Fifth Amendment** prohibition against **double jeopardy**[2] applies only to crimes, and not civil actions. You may recall that O.J. Simpson, who was found **not guilty** by the jury in his criminal trial for the murders of his ex-wife Nicole Brown Simpson and her friend, Ronald Goldman, subsequently was held **liable** for their **wrongful deaths** in the civil trial. In the sport and recreation environment, criminal prosecutions for assault and battery occur far less frequently than civil suits for several reasons.

First, the culture of sport is averse to the idea that someone should be held criminally responsible for causing harm to another person in an organized sporting or recreational activity, where harsh and even violent physical contacts are deemed "part of the game." Second, the **standard of proof** in a criminal case is a much higher burden than in a civil case[3], thus making criminal prosecutions more difficult to win (which in part explains the differing **verdicts** in the O.J. Simpson cases mentioned above). And third, there is a societal reluctance to prosecute—never mind convict—a class of people who pursue the ideal of an active and healthy lifestyle and who are often venerated for their on-field achievements. Assault and battery cases that involve non-competitors (*e.g.*, parents or spectators) or that involve athletes and occur off the field of competition (*e.g.* domestic abuse, bar fights) are entirely situation dependent. Perhaps as many people believe that athletes-as-celebrities receive favorable treatment when it comes to criminal prosecution, as defendant-athletes believe they are unfairly singled out for prosecution *because* they are famous.

Thus, a district attorney's decision to prosecute a criminal defendant on behalf of the public and an aggrieved private party's decision to sue the same person for civil remedies arising out of the same set of facts are based on independent variables. Without a doubt, decisions *not* to prosecute or sue for assault and battery far outnumber decisions to bring legal action. Two prominent examples of havoc in the field of battle that did *not* result in either criminal charges or lawsuits include heavyweight boxer Mike Tyson's biting off part of Evander Holyfield's ear in a 1997 bout, and France's Zinedine Zidane's horrific head butt of Italy's Marco Materazzi near the end of the 2006 World Cup Final. The remainder of this chapter focuses on *civil* assault and battery, while *criminal* assault and battery are addressed elsewhere (see Chapter 3.21, *Sport Related Crimes*).

---

[2] Legal concept that protects an individual from being subjected to prosecution more than once for the same alleged crime.
[3] In a criminal case, the government must prove all the elements of a crime **beyond a reasonable doubt**, while in a civil case, a plaintiff need only prove his/her case by a **preponderance of the evidence**.

Torts of Assault and Battery

While the terms "assault and battery" commonly are used in concert, they are actually separate and distinct torts. Thus, in seeking redress for harms caused by an intentional tort, a **plaintiff's** lawsuit against a **defendant** for assault, battery, or both, will be dictated by the facts and circumstances of the case. By definition, assault and battery are intentional torts, meaning that the **tortfeasor** desired "to bring about [a] result that will invade [the] interests of another" (*Wager v. Pro*, 1979), as distinguished from **negligence,** which is characterized by "inadvertence, thoughtlessness, inattention, and the like" (Black's Law Dictionary, 2004).

Assault

Assault is any willful attempt or threat to inflict injury upon the person of another, when coupled with an apparent present ability to do so and giving the victim reason to fear or expect immediate bodily harm (*State v. Murphy*, 1972). In fact, the Louisiana Criminal Code defines assault as "an attempt to commit a battery, or the intentional placing of another in reasonable apprehension of receiving a battery" (LA-R.S. 14:36). Put another way, assault is an attempt or threat to cause offensive contact with another person, coupled with the victim's reasonable apprehension of immediate bodily harm. Even more succinctly, it is putting someone in fear of receiving a battery (Kinsella, 1996). Thus, the tort of assault can be committed without actually touching, striking, or doing bodily harm to the victim (*State v. Murphy*, 1972). Still, words alone—regardless how insulting, provocative, or threatening—without the requisite elements, do not constitute assault.

Elements of Assault

In order for an assault to occur, the following elements must be present:

- an intentional act by the defendant
- that causes reasonable apprehension on the part of the plaintiff
- of imminent harmful or offensive contact

For example, a coach's statement to a player that he will "ring his bell" if the player messes up the play again would not constitute assault, because mere words unaccompanied by any act to cause apprehension of imminent injury do not satisfy the elemental requirements. However, an ominous approach by a just-fouled pickup basketball player with a clenched fist and cocked arm, accompanied by some unflattering name calling and his threat to "get even" would likely constitute assault if the second player feared that he was about to be struck by the fouled player. Importantly, the tortfeasor must have intended to cause a harmful or offensive contact with the plaintiff (American Law Institute, 2009), and the plaintiff's apprehension of fear cannot be derived from the defendant's **negligent** or **reckless** conduct.

Because assault requires apprehension of harm on the part of the victim, no assault can occur where the victim is not aware that he or she is about to be struck. Thus, for example, a field hockey player who is blindsided and intentionally taken down by an opposing player cannot sue for assault (although she could sue for battery!). Finally, the harmful or offensive contact must be imminent and likely to occur momentarily; as opposed to the more distant threat of a sports bookie to "break your legs" if he does not receive the amount owed him on losing bets within 24 hours of the event's outcome.

Battery

If assault can be characterized in a loose and general way as attempted battery, then the completion of the threat or act culminating in actual physical contact, without consent, is battery. Put another way, battery is the consummation of an assault (*People v. Solak*, 1985). The classic definition of **battery** is the "intentional and wrongful physical contact with a person without his or her consent that entails some injury or offensive touching" (*Mason v. Cohn*, 1981). Prosser and Keeton (1984) stated that the freedom from intentional and unpermitted contacts with an individual's person "extends to any part of the body, or to anything which is attached to it and practically identified with it." Thus, an untoward and unwelcomed contact with a person's clothing, handbag, backpack, or even a held object could be grounds for a suit in battery. Also, a baseball pitcher who intentionally throws a fast ball at a heckling fan in the stands and injures him would be liable for battery even though the pitcher was not in the immediate physical presence of the fan.

Elements of Battery

In order for there to be a battery, the following elements must be present:

- intentional conduct by defendant
- causing harmful or offensive contact to plaintiff
- without consent

As with assault, battery is an intentional tort that requires a willful act on the part of the perpetrator. Unlike assault, however—which has no necessity of physical contact—battery (as the term implies) requires a "battering" or otherwise unwelcome or unpermitted touching. To be sure, there need not be any grievous injury; all that is required is a physical touching, however slight, as the law does not discriminate between degrees of force (*Steele v. State,* 1989). Thus, a jubilant fan who gets caught up in the excitement of his team's victory and spontaneously turns to kiss an unknowing spectator might be liable for battery (provided the gesture was unwelcomed and nonconsensual). The requirement of the tortfeasor's intent for battery applies to the resulting harmful or offensive contact to the victim, and not to the willful commitment to do the act. For example, in a case for battery against a golfer whose tee shot struck a resident who was standing outside her condominium bordering the fairway, the court said that the mere fact that the golfer *intended to hit the ball* was insufficient. What was required for battery was the golfer's intent to cause "an offensive contact with or unconsented touching of, or trauma upon [the plaintiff]" (*Hennessey v. Pyne, 1979*). An important distinction from assault is that battery does not require that the victim be aware of the harmful or offensive contact. There is no requirement that the plaintiff have an apprehension of the impending physical contact for battery to occur.

Consent

Consent, or rather the absence thereof, is an essential element in proving battery, and many cases will hinge on whether the plaintiff could be construed to have given his or her consent to participate in the activity that resulted in the allegation of battery. In a suit for battery brought by a high school basketball player against his coach, a question arose whether the physical contact at a pre-practice altercation involving wrestling techniques was consensual, since the coach disputed the player's assertions that he twice told the coach to release his arm. The coach characterized the incident instead as "playfully antagonistic" (*Goff v. Clarke,* 2003). This, of course, is a question of fact for the jury to determine, but it also raises the issue of consent in the realm of horseplay. One person might be enjoying the jovial, good-natured roughhousing activity, while another person is feeling abused and victimized. In *Clayton v. New Dreamland Roller Skating Rink* (1951), a woman who was skating at a roller skating rink injured her arm in a fall and was taken to the rink's first aid room, where a rink employee proceeded to manipulate the woman's arm. The employee was not a medical doctor and not authorized to perform physical manipulation treatments. Yet in the face of protestations by the woman, he continued to work on the woman's arm by applying traction. Subsequently, the woman was taken to a hospital, where x-rays revealed a fracture. This case reaffirms the rule that, absent consent, even a do-gooder's unwanted physical intervention on the person of another would subject him to liability for assault and battery, regardless of noble intentions.

In a classic case of an injury sustained in the course of a game (*Cunico v. Miller,* 2002), a high school soccer goalie sued an opposing player, her parents, and the opposing player's coach after being kicked by the opposing player. In rejecting the battery claim, the court said that as a matter of law, plaintiff "consented to the inherent risks of soccer from the undisputed fact of her voluntary participation in the soccer game." Such consent negates one of the elements of a battery claim because "the act of stepping onto the field of play may be described as 'consent to the inherent risks of the activity' " (*Ritchie-Gamester v. City of Berkley,* 1999). In another case involving a game-related injury (*Overall v. Kadella,* 1984), the court held that while consent (to bodily contacts that are permitted by the rules of the game) is manifested by a player' participation in a hockey game, an intentional act causing injury that goes beyond what is ordinarily permissible is actionable in tort (see the Supplemental Web Site).

Defenses to Assault and Battery

Since winning a case of assault or battery requires the plaintiff to prove the elements of the tort by a preponderance of the evidence, any defense would be predicated on the **absence of one or more of the requisite elements**. A defendant could also claim self defense or defense of another, in which the alleged assault and/

or battery were justifiable in order to protect oneself or a third party from harm. Thus, in a heated exchange between a baseball manager and umpire who are nose-to-nose with one another, if the manager was readying to spew a wad of spit at the umpire's face, the umpire could raise his arms to protect himself, even if he brushes the manager's face or pushes him away in the process.

Express or Implied Consent

In the sport and recreation context, however, perhaps the most common defense against assault and/or battery is that the alleged victim either expressly or impliedly consented to the harms visited upon him or her. The reason is that where no public interest is implicated, the law does not seek to intervene by protecting against one's own folly (Prosser and Keeton, 1984). In other words, if in undertaking to enter a martial arts competition an athlete consents to any and all physical harms caused by an opponent in the ordinary course of the competition, the consent negates not only the opponent's otherwise wrongful conduct, but also the very existence of the tort. The concept of a person's consent to expose oneself to the inherent risks in sport applies whether the activity is ultimate fighting or table tennis.

For example, in the combative sports of boxing, ultimate fighting, wrestling, karate, judo, taekwondo, and the like, the object of the game is to physically beat or subdue the opposing player/athlete, just as the rules of certain team sports condone blocking, tackling, and body checking, and otherwise encourage harsh physical play. As noted previously, conduct that would readily result in criminal action or civil lawsuits off the field of play is given closer scrutiny within the confines of organized sport, under the guise that the injured participant is deemed to have consented to the contact and attendant risk of harm. Again, a player's consent implies acceptance of the risks inherent in sport, and does not extend to intentional contacts that are not usually and ordinarily a part of the game or activity. In *Esshaki v. Millman* (2009), the Michigan Court of Appeals said that "Even assuming that soccer includes a degree of intentional—and potentially harmful—contact, we conclude that, as a matter of law, a participant's consent to the risks inherent to participating in a soccer match does not include consent to be attacked by a co-participant." Thus in the right circumstances, an aggrieved party might still press for criminal prosecution and/or civil remedies. In *Brokaw v. Winfield-Mt. Union Community School District* (2010), a court found a high school basketball player liable for striking an opposing player in the head with his elbow, and awarded damages of $13,000 for medical expenses, and $10,000 for pain and suffering. (See also Chapter 2.13 *Liability of Sport Participants* and Chapter 3.21 *Criminal Law and Sport* relating to liability for negligent and criminal actions.)

Privilege

Another defense to intentional torts is that of privilege, which is in the realm of excuse or justification. An action that might otherwise result in liability is **privileged** if the defendant acted in furtherance of an interest of such social importance that it is entitled to legal protection, even though the plaintiff suffered harm (Prosser and Keeton, 1984). In essence, the tortfeasor is shielded from liability because circumstances and social policy permit or require it, as in the case of self defense. In the sport and recreation context, a coach or trainer might be entitled to such privilege in demonstrating a skill or technique to a participant.

Immunity

Related, but different, is the concept of **immunity**, which prevents even the initiation of a lawsuit or prosecution. An example of immunity would be the acts of law enforcement personnel acting in their official capacities as peace officers. Thus, police officers who physically accost a criminal suspect in the performance of their duties would be immune from suit or criminal prosecution for assault and battery.

Tort Remedies

Typically, the remedies available to plaintiffs who prevail in suits in tort (including assault and battery) are **damages**, or the award of a sum of money to the plaintiff. **Compensatory damages** (also referred to as **actual damages**) are those which compensate the plaintiff for the injury sustained; the rationale being that such damages would restore the injured party to the position he or she would be in but for the injury (*Northwestern Nat. Cas. Co. v. McNulty*, 1962). In general, if the injury is slight or there is no substantial loss, the damages will be nominal, since the purpose of compensatory damages is not to provide the prevailing party with a windfall. On the other hand, **punitive damages** (also referred to as **exemplary damages**), may be awarded in cases of particularly grievous circumstances where the plaintiff suffered extreme anguish, or to punish the perpetrator for horrific or heinous behavior and to make an example of him (Black's Law Dictionary, 2004), as well as to deter others from engaging in similar conduct in the future. Punitive damages can amount to large sums of money, and are often criticized as a financial windfall by defendants because they reward the plaintiff above and beyond the extent of his or her injuries (see discussion of damages in Chapter 2.11 *Negligence*). It should be noted, however, that punitive damages are less commonly awarded, because courts must first be persuaded that the requisite extenuating circumstances exist to merit this extraordinary remedy.

Plaintiffs can also seek **equitable** relief, which takes the form of an **injunction** or **specific performance**. These are essentially court orders that command or prohibit an act. For example, in the wake of the infamous spectator-infused donnybrook at the Detroit Pistons-Indiana Pacers NBA game in 2004, Pacer Ron Artest obtained a **restraining order** against John Green, the Pistons fan who threw a cup at Artest that fueled the melee in the stands.

Vicarious Liability

Recreation and sport managers should be aware that supervisors and organizations can be held liable for the intentional torts committed by their employees under the employer-employee doctrine of *respondeat superior* (see Chapter 2.12 *Which Parties Are Liable?*). A significant, and practical, reason for naming parties in addition to the actual tortfeasor as defendants in a suit is that oftentimes the perpetrator is **judgment proof**, meaning that he or she does not have the assets with which to satisfy the plaintiff's award for damages. In order to attach liability to the employer, the tort must have been committed by an employee within the course and scope of employment. For example, under this theory, if security personnel at an event or a bouncer at a club wrongfully manhandles a patron resulting in injury, the patron could bring suit against the assailant's employer. On the other hand, if the employee committed an assault and/or battery in a capacity that was unrelated to the performance of his job (*e.g.*, carrying out a personal grudge), then the employer would not be liable to the injured party. Thus, recreation and sport managers should be aware of this potential liability and take steps to ensure that their employees—particularly those employees whose duties contemplate the likelihood of physical contact with others—are properly trained in the appropriate use of force.

Toone v. Adams (1964) involved a suit by a minor league umpire against a baseball manager and his club for injuries sustained in a punch from a fan after a particularly contentious game. The umpire alleged that the manager's on-field protests of the umpire's calls incited the fan to commit the assault. The court, however, concluded that the manager and club were not liable because the manager's conduct was not directly related to the ensuing assault. In this case, the nexus between the manager's antics and fan's violent act was not sufficiently drawn for one to be a natural and proximate result of the other.

In *Godfrey v. Iverson* (2009), nightclub patron Marlin Godfrey was battered by NBA player Allen Iverson's bodyguard and suffered injuries that required hospital emergency room attention. Even though Iverson was not personally involved in the scuffle, he was present and watched the fight from the VIP section of the nightclub. The appellate court said that "negligent supervision arises when an employer knew or should have known that its employee behaved in a dangerous or otherwise incompetent manner, and that the employer, armed with that knowledge, failed to adequately supervise its employee," and upheld the trial court's verdict against Iverson and award of $260,000 for Godfrey. (For other cases involving assault and battery and naming the assailants' employer as an additional defendant under the doctrine of vicarious liability, see *Hackbart v. Cincinnati Bengals* [1979] and *Manning v. Grimsley* [1981] on the Supplemental Web Site.)

For an excellent discussion and to obtain a better understanding of an employer's liability for intentional torts committed by an employee, see *Baumeister v. Plunkett* (1996), where the court held that defendant Humana Hospital was not liable for the assault committed by a nursing supervisor on a nurse technician, because even though the assault occurred during the supervisor's course of employment (*i.e.*, during working hours and at the hospital's premises), the act of violence was neither primarily employment rooted nor reasonably incidental to the performance of the supervisor's duties.

SIGNIFICANT CASE

The following case involves an injury sustained by an age-group football player in practice as a result of his being the subject in a tackling demonstration conducted by a coach. It raises the issue of consent and whether the scope of this consent extends to his participation in direct physical contact with participants beyond his age and experience. Note the court's analysis of assault and battery, and its conclusion that the plaintiff's apprehension of imminent harm—a requisite element of assault—was wanting in this case. Note also the court's admonishment on remand that the plaintiff could pursue its claim for punitive damages. The dissenting opinion that immediately follows the court's opinion is provided to illustrate the nuanced views of the law.

KOFFMAN V. GARNETT

Supreme Court of Virginia
265 Va. 12, 574 S.E.2d 258
Jan. 10, 2003

Opinion by Justice Elizabeth B. Lacy

In this case we consider whether the trial court properly dismissed the plaintiffs' second amended motion for judgment for failure to state causes of action for gross negligence, assault, and battery.

***

In the fall of 2000, Andrew W. Koffman, a 13-year old middle school student at a public school in Botetourt County, began participating on the school's football team. It was Andy's first season playing organized football, and he was positioned as a third-string defensive player. James Garnett was employed by the Botetourt County School Board as an assistant coach for the football team and was responsible for the supervision, training, and instruction of the team's defensive players.

The team lost its first game of the season. Garnett was upset by the defensive players' inadequate tackling in that game and became further displeased by what he perceived as inadequate tackling during the first practice following the loss.

Garnett ordered Andy to hold a football and "stand upright and motionless" so that Garnett could explain the proper tackling technique to the defensive players. Then Garnett, without further warning, thrust his arms around Andy's body, lifted him "off his feet by two feet or more," and "slamm[ed]" him to the ground. Andy weighed 144 pounds, while Garnett weighed approximately 260 pounds. The force of the tackle broke the humerus bone in Andy's left arm. During prior practices, no coach had used physical force to instruct players on rules or techniques of playing football.

In his second amended motion for judgment, Andy, by his father and next friend, Richard Koffman, and Andy's parents, Richard and Rebecca Koffman, individually, (collectively "the Koffmans") alleged that Andy was injured as a result of Garnett's simple and gross negligence and intentional acts of assault and battery. Garnett filed a demurrer and plea of sovereign immunity, asserting that the second amended motion for judgment did not allege sufficient facts to support a lack of consent to the tackling demonstration and, therefore, did not plead causes of action for either gross negligence, assault, or battery. The trial court dismissed the action, finding that Garnett, as a school board employee, was entitled to sovereign immunity for acts of simple negligence and that the facts alleged were insufficient to state causes of action for gross negligence, assault, or battery because the instruction and playing of football are "inherently dangerous and always potentially violent."In this appeal, the Koffmans do not challenge the trial court's ruling on Garnett's plea of sovereign immunity but do assert that they pled sufficient facts in their second amended motion for judgment to sustain their claims of gross negligence, assault, and battery.

***

The disparity in size between Garnett and Andy was obvious to Garnett. Because of his authority as a coach, Garnett must have anticipated that Andy would comply with his instructions to stand in a non-defensive, upright, and motionless position. Under these circumstances, Garnett proceeded to aggressively tackle the much smaller, inexperienced student football player, by lifting him more than two feet from the ground and slamming him into the turf. According to the Koffmans' allegations, no coach had tackled any player previously so there was no reason for Andy to expect to be tackled by Garnett, nor was Andy warned of the impending tackle or of the force Garnett would use.

As the trial court observed, receiving an injury while participating in a tackling demonstration may be part of the sport. The facts alleged in this case, however, go beyond the circumstances of simply being tackled in the course of participating in organized football. Here Garnett's knowledge of his greater size and experience, his instruction implying that Andy was not to take any action to defend himself from the force of a tackle, the force he used during the tackle, and Garnett's previous practice of not personally using force to demonstrate or teach football technique could lead a reasonable person to conclude that, in this instance, Garnett's actions were imprudent and were taken in utter disregard for the safety of the player involved. Because reasonable persons could disagree on this issue, a jury issue was presented, and the trial court erred in holding that, as a matter of law, the second amended motion for judgment was inadequate to state a claim for gross negligence.

***

The trial court held that the second amended motion for judgment was insufficient as a matter of law to establish causes of action for the torts of assault and battery. We begin by identifying the elements of these two independent torts. See Charles E. Friend, Personal Injury Law in Virginia 6.2.1 (2d ed. 1998).

The tort of assault consists of an act intended to cause either harmful or offensive contact with another person or apprehension of such contact, and that creates in that other person's mind a reasonable apprehension of an imminent battery. Restatement (Second) of Torts 21 (1965); Friend 6.3.1 at 226; Fowler V. Harper, et al., The Law of Torts 3.5 at 3:18-:19 (3d ed. Cum. Supp. 2003).

The tort of battery is an unwanted touching which is neither consented to, excused, nor justified. See Washburn v. Klara, 263 Va. 586, 561 S.E.2d 682 (2002); Woodbury v. Courtney, 239 Va. 651, 391 S.E.2d 293 (1990). Although these two torts "go together like ham and eggs," the difference between them is "that between physical contact and the mere apprehension of it. One may exist without the other." W. Page Keeton, Prosser and Keeton on Torts 10 at 46; see also Friend 6.3.

The Koffmans' second amended motion for judgment does not include an allegation that Andy had any apprehension of an immediate battery. This allegation cannot be supplied by inference because any inference of Andy's apprehension is discredited by the affirmative allegations that Andy had no warning of an imminent forceful tackle by Garnett. The Koffmans argue that a reasonable inference of apprehension can be found "in the very short period of time that it took the coach to lift Andy into the air and throw him violently to the ground." At this point, however, the battery alleged by the Koffmans was in progress. Accordingly, we find that the pleadings were insufficient as a matter of law to establish a cause of action for civil assault.

The second amended motion for judgment is sufficient, however, to establish a cause of action for the tort of battery. The Koffmans pled that Andy consented to physical contact with players "of like age and experience" and that neither Andy nor his parents expected or consented to his "participation in aggressive contact tackling by the adult coaches." Further, the Koffmans pled that, in the past, coaches had not tackled players as a method of instruction. Garnett asserts that, by consenting to play football, Andy consented to be tackled, by either other football players or by the coaches. Whether Andy consented to be tackled by Garnett in the manner alleged was a matter of fact. Based on the allegations in the Koffmans' second amended motion for judgment, reasonable persons could disagree on whether Andy gave such consent. Thus, we find that the trial court erred in holding that the Koffmans' second amended motion for judgment was insufficient as a matter of law to establish a claim for battery.

For the above reasons, we will reverse the trial court's judgment that the Koffmans' second amended motion for judgment was insufficient as a matter of law to establish the causes of actions for gross negligence and battery and remand the case for further proceedings consistent with this opinion.*

Reversed and remanded.

JUSTICE KINSER, concurring in part and dissenting in part.

I agree with the majority opinion except with regard to the issue of consent as it pertains to the intentional tort of battery. In my view, the second amended motion for judgment filed by the plaintiffs, Andrew W. Koffman, by his father and next friend, and Richard Koffman and Rebecca Koffman, individually, was insufficient as a matter of law to state a claim for battery.**

Absent fraud, consent is generally a defense to an alleged battery. See Banovitch v. Commonwealth, 196 Va. 210, 219, 83 S.E.2d 369, 375 (1954); Perkins v. Commonwealth, 31 Va. App. 326, 330, 523 S.E.2d 512, 513 (2000); People ex rel. Arvada v. Nissen, 650 P.2d 547, 551 (Colo. 1982); Bergman v. Anderson, 411 N.W.2d 336, 339 (Neb. 1987); Willey v. Carpenter, 23 A. 630, 631 (Vt. 1891); Restatement (Second) of Torts 13, cmt. d (1965). In the context of this case, "[t]aking part in a game manifests a willingness to submit to such bodily contacts or restrictions of liberty as are permitted by its rules or usages." Restatement (Second) of Torts 50, cmt. b (1965), quoted in Thompson v. McNeill, 559 N.E.2d 705, 708 (Ohio 1990); see also Kabella v. Bouschelle, 672 P.2d 290, 292 (N.M. Ct. App. 1983). However, participating in a particular sport "does not manifest consent to contacts which are prohibited by rules or usages of the game if such rules or usages are designed to protect the participants and not merely to secure the better playing of the game as a test of skill." Restatement (Second) of Torts 50, cmt. b (1965) quoted in Thompson, 559 N.E.2d at 708; see also Kabella, 672 P.2d at 292.

The thrust of the plaintiffs' allegations is that they did not consent to "Andy's participation in aggressive contact tackling by the adult coaches" but that they consented only to Andy's engaging "in a contact sport with other children of like age and experience." They further alleged that the coaches had not previously tackled the players when instructing them about the rules and techniques of football.

It is notable, in my opinion, that the plaintiffs admitted in their pleading that Andy's coach was "responsible . . . for the supervision, training and instruction of the defensive players." It cannot be disputed that one responsibility of a football coach is to minimize the possibility that players will sustain "something more than slight injury" while playing the sport. Vendrell v. School District No. 26C, Malheur County, 376 P.2d 406, 413 (Ore. 1962). A football coach cannot be expected "to extract from the game the body clashes that cause bruises, jolts and hard falls." Id. Instead, a coach should ensure that players are able to "withstand the shocks, blows and other rough treatment with which they would meet in actual play" by making certain that players are in "sound physical condition," are issued proper protective equipment, and are "taught and shown how to handle [themselves] while in play." Id. The instruction on how to handle themselves during a game should include demonstrations of proper tackling techniques. Id. By voluntarily participating in football, Andy and his parents necessarily consented to instruction by the coach on such techniques. The alleged battery occurred during that instruction.

The plaintiffs alleged that they were not aware that Andy's coach would use physical force to instruct on the rules and techniques of football since neither he nor the other coaches had done so in the past. Surely, the plaintiffs are not claiming that the scope of their consent changed from day to day depending on the coaches' instruction methods during prior practices. Moreover, they did not allege that they were told that the coaches would not use physical demonstrations to instruct the players.

Additionally, the plaintiffs did not allege that the tackle itself violated any rule or usage of the sport of football. Nor did they plead that Andy could not have been tackled by a larger, physically stronger, and more experienced player either during a game or practice. Tackling and instruction on proper tackling techniques are aspects of the sport of football to which a player consents when making a decision to participate in the sport.

In sum, I conclude that the plaintiffs did not sufficiently plead a claim for battery. We must remember that acts that might give rise to a battery on a city street will not do so in the context of the sport of football. See Thompson, 559 N.E.2d at 707. We must also not blur the lines between gross negligence and battery because the latter is an intentional tort. I agree fully that the plaintiffs alleged sufficient facts to proceed with their claim for gross negligence.

For these reasons, I respectfully concur, in part, and dissent, in part, and would affirm the judgment of the circuit court sustaining the demurrer with regard to the claim for battery.

*Because we have concluded that a cause of action for an intentional tort was sufficiently pled, on remand, the Koffmans may pursue their claim for punitive damages.

**Although the circuit court sustained the demurrer with regard to the alleged battery on the basis that an intention to batter and inflict injury on Andy could not be inferred from the alleged facts, the majority does not address that holding. Since the majority discusses only the issue of consent, I confine my dissent to that question.

CASES ON THE SUPPLEMENTAL WEB SITE

Archibald v. Kemble, 971 A.2d 513 (Pa. Super. 2009), appeal denied, 989 A.2d 914 (Pa. 2010). Note the court's application of the reckless—versus intentional—conduct standard in the situation of an adult, no-check hockey game, where injury was sustained as a result of an illegal check.

Hackbart v. Cincinnati Bengals, Inc., 601 F.2d 516 (10th Cir. 1979), cert. denied, 444 U.S. 931 (1979). Stands for the proposition that even in professional football, a player may be held responsible for injuring an opponent if he acts with reckless disregard for the opponent's safety.

Overall v. Kadella, 361 N.W.2d 352, 138 Mich.App. 351 (1985). Pay heed to the proposition that while a hockey player's participation in a game manifests his consent to bodily contacts that are permitted by the rules of the game, a player is liable for intentional acts resulting in injury that go beyond what is ordinarily permissible.

Manning v. Grimsley, 643 F.2d 20 (First Cir. 1981). Examines the issue of vicarious liability, and how an employer can be held liable for damages for injuries attributable to an employee's assault of a patron.

Regina v. Cey, 48 C.C.C. 3d 480 (Sask. Ct. App. 1989). Consider this Canadian court's guidelines in determining whether an ice hockey player's violent conduct exceeds the bounds of normality.

QUESTIONS YOU SHOULD BE ABLE TO ANSWER

1. What are the elements necessary to prove a case for assault? Battery?

2. Since assault and battery are crimes as well as torts, is it possible for a person to be prosecuted in criminal court and sued in civil court for committing the same acts? Why or why not?

3. How is negligence distinguishable from assault and battery?

4. What are the legal remedies available to a victim of civil assault and battery?

5. In the sport and recreation environment, how can managers insulate themselves and their organizations from liability for assault and battery?

REFERENCES

Cases

Baumeister v. Plunkett, 673 S.2d 994 (La. 1996).
Brokaw v. Winfield-Mt. Union Community School District, 788 N.W.2d 386 (Ia. 2010).
Claytonv. New Dreamland Roller Skating Rink, 82 A.2d 458 (N.J. Super. 1951).
Cunico v. Miller, 2002 WL 339385 (Cal.App. 2 Dist.).
Esshaki v. Millman, 2009 Mich. App. Lexis 582.
Godfrey v. Iverson, No. 07-7151 (D.C. Cir. 2009).
Goff v. Clarke, 302 A.D.2d 725, 755 N.Y.S.2d 493 (NY App.Div. 2003).
Hennessey v. Pyne, 694 A.2d 691 (R.I. 1979).
Mason v. Cohn, 438 N.Y.S.2d 462 (Sup. Ct. 1981).
Northwestern Nat. Cas. Co. v. McNulty, 307 F.2d 432 (5th Cir. 1962).
People v. Solak, 382 NW2d 495 (Mich.App. 1985).
Ritchie-Gamester v. City of Berkeley, 461 Mich. 73, 597 N.W.2d 517 (1999).
State v. Murphy, 500 P.2d 1276 (1972).
Steele v. State, 778 P.2d 929 (Ok.Cr.App. 1989).
Toone v. Adams, 262 N.C. 403, 137 S.E.2d 132 (1964).
Wager v. Pro, 603 F.2d 1005 (D.C. Cir. 1979).

Publications

American Law Institute, (2009), Restatement (Second) of Torts.
FindLaw, http://injury.findlaw.com/assault-and-battery/elements-of-assault.html, accessed March 16, 2009.
Garner, B.A., ed. (2004), Black's Law Dictionary, 8th edition, Thomson West.
http://hoopedia.nba.com/index.php?title=Pacers-Pistons_Brawl, accessed March 15, 2009.
Keeton, W.P., Dobbs, D.B., Keeton, R.E., Owen, D.G. (1984), Prosser and Keeton on Torts, 5th ed., West Publishing Co., St. Paul, MN.
Kinsella, N.S. (1996), "Punishment and Proportionality: The Estoppel Approach," Journal of Libertarian Studies, 12:1.
Legal Information Institute, http://topics.law.cornell.edu/wex/asault, accessed December 17, 2008.
McCarthy, M., "Fan Who Ignited Brawl Forever Banned from Pistons' Homes Games," USA Today, November 17, 2006.

Legislation

LA-R.S. 14:36 (Louisiana Criminal Code), definition of assault.

3.12 DEFAMATION

Anita M. Moorman | University of Louisville

The tort of defamation dates back to early sixteenth-century common law. Defamation law provides recourse for false, insidious, or irresponsible statements that damage an individual's reputation. As defined by *Black's Law Dictionary* (Black, 1990), **defamation** is "that which tends to injure reputation; to diminish the esteem, respect, goodwill or confidence in which the plaintiff is held, or to excite adverse, derogatory or unpleasant feelings or opinions against him" (p. 417).

FUNDAMENTAL CONCEPTS

In the sport industry, defamation claims are raised in a variety of settings that may include statements made by an athletic director about reasons for terminating a coach; statements made by a coach about one of his assistant coaches; statements made by a professional athlete about his agent; statements published by a newspaper about an athlete; statements published on an Internet discussion board about an athlete, coach, or owner of a professional sport team; or statements made during a television sports program comparing an athlete to another person convicted of numerous crimes. All of these examples, depending on the substance and truthfulness of the statements made, could easily form the basis of a defamation action. For example, Mike Price sued Time, Inc. for defamation based upon a Sports Illustrated article which detailed his actions the night he visited a topless bar in Pensacola, Fla., in April 2003, while he was head coach at Alabama. Alabama fired Price a few days before the article was published. Price sued for $20 million, claiming he was defamed and slandered by the story. He acknowledged being heavily intoxicated, but denied allegations of sex at his hotel. The parties ultimately settled for an undisclosed sum without any admission of wrongdoing on the part of Time (Caldwell, 2005).

Elements of a Defamation Claim

The tort of defamation is a state law claim which means each state will define the essential elements of the claim. Most states follow elements very similar to those included in the Restatement (Second) of Torts § 558, which requires the following four elements to establish a defamation claim:

1. a false and defamatory statement of fact,
2. publication to a third party,
3. fault or negligence of the publisher, and
4. damage or actual injury.

The plaintiff bears the burden of proof in a defamation action (Restatement [Second] of Torts). Under common law defamation, the standard for proving negligence or fault varies depending upon whether the person about whom the statement is made is a **public** or **private figure**. For example, in order for a sport celebrity or other public figure, such as Tom Brady of the New England Patriots, to prove negligence or fault (the third element identified above), he would have to demonstrate that the person making the statement did so with actual malice. To show **actual malice**, it must be shown that the speaker knew the statement was false or published it with a total disregard for whether it was true or false. A private person would only have to prove that the statement was published negligently which means that the speaker failed to exercise reasonable care to determine whether the statement was true or false. This is a much lower burden of proof for the private individual. Although private figures are not required to show actual malice in order to recover for defamation, they must prove actual injury. As defined by the Supreme Court in *Gertz v. Robert Welch, Inc.* (1974), actual injury includes "impairment of reputation and standing in the community, personal humiliation, and mental anguish and suffering" (p. 350). The distinction between the burden of proof for public figures as opposed to a private individual, such as spectator or security guard is explained further in the Defamation and the First Amendment section.

Franklin & Rabin (1996, p. 880) also observed that "no liability exists if a third person unexpectedly over-hears a private conversation between plaintiff and defendant." Further, publications that are merely embar-rassing do not qualify as defamatory. Rather, publications must truly reflect "sharp criticism" that damages reputation (Franklin & Rabin, 1996). Regardless, when ascertaining whether a defendant is liable for defama-tion, the entire publication (e.g., title, punctuation, paragraphing, full article) will be considered versus one particular phrase or statement.

Types of Defamation: Slander and Libel

The tort of defamation includes both slander and libel. Defamatory comments made verbally, such as those heard on television, exemplify **slander**. **Libel** is a broader category of communication. Written comments, photographs, and cartoons, such as those appearing in newspapers, on the Internet, and in other written or tangible forms, are examples of libel. A verbal comment is slanderous *per se* (which means inherently defama-tory) and a written comment is libel *per se* if it falls into one of the following categories: (1) accuses the plaintiff of criminal conduct; (2) accuses the plaintiff of having a loathsome disease; (3) accuses the female plaintiff of being unchaste; (4) accuses the plaintiff of misconduct in public office; or (5) injures the plaintiff's profession, business, or trade. If a statement falls into one of these categories, it is presumed as a matter of law that the repu-tation of the individual about whom the false statement was made will be injured. For example, false comments accusing someone of embezzling funds from a community youth sports organization, having sex with an entire lacrosse team, or engaging in illegal student athlete recruiting practices could be construed as slanderous *per se* (Carpenter, 1995). No reasonable person could ever interpret such statements as reflecting positively upon the person about whom they were spoken. As explained by the court in *Romaine v. Kallinger* (1988), if a pub-lished statement is susceptible of one meaning only, and that meaning is defamatory, the statement is libelous as a matter of law. This can be an important distinction since statements that are considered defamatory *per se* do not require the plaintiff to prove special damages because the damage is presumed since the statements are *per se* (inherently) harmful. The Significant Case at the end of the chapter applies these concepts to statements made by an athletic director about a coach. Recall this distinction between defamation and defamation *per se* as you read through that case.

Slander and libel were originally recognized as two distinct types of defamation. Libel, written defamatory statements, was thought to be more damaging because, at the time the distinction arose, few persons could read or write. Therefore, anything which was written would carry a louder ring of purported truth (*Matherson v. Marchello*, 1984). In addition, a written defamation could be disseminated more widely and carried a degree of permanence. For example, newspapers and magazines could be retained for weeks while statements made on television vanished within seconds. Technology now secures media statements in a tangible form and most jurisdictions refer to the two terms (i.e., slander and libel) interchangeably as simply defamation (Pember, 1990).

The growth of Internet-based information and news sources and social media has triggered a new wave of online defamation claims which raise several interesting questions. First, issues of jurisdiction arise since typi-cally a defamation case should be filed in the state in which the defamation occurs (i.e. the statement is made). However, when the statement is made via social media such as Facebook and Twitter, the person making the statement is mobile and the statement itself is disseminated immediately to hundreds and possibly thousands of third parties simultaneously. The first Twitter defamation case brought by a landlord against a tenant mak-ing disparaging remarks about her apartment was dismissed and the judge ruled that a "tweet was nonaction-able as a matter of law" (Bennett, 2010). Since that time however, a more visible case against Courtney Love by a fashion designer resulted in a $430,000 settlement. Love had intended to use the "it's just a tweet defense" which seemed successful in the landlord/tenant case, but the California trial court refused to dismiss the case (Gardner, 2009). Love settled before trial started.

Defamation and the First Amendment

The tort of defamation, as most tort theories, evolved as a matter of state law. However, unlike other torts, the law of defamation has been influenced significantly by First Amendment considerations since the mid-1960s (Franklin & Rabin, 1996). Allowing one person to sue another person because of what that person said or wrote often collides with First Amendment freedom of speech and freedom of the press. Thus, the interests of the state in protecting its citizens from defamatory statements is often weighed against the interests preserved in the First Amendment insuring an open forum for all ideas.

Elaborating on the importance of defamation law to an individual, Justice Stewart said, "The right of a man to the protection of his own reputation from unjustified invasion and wrongful hurt reflects no more than our basic concept of the essential dignity and worth of every human being . . . " (*Rosenblatt v. Baer*, 1966, p. 92). Conversely, critics say defamation law stifles individual commentary which contributes to the marketplace of ideas. As stated earlier, the judicial system attempts to balance the right to preserve one's reputation with individual Constitutional rights.

To promote balance between plaintiff and defendant, Supreme Court decisions have recognized that certain persons enjoy greater protection from damaging statements than do other persons. For example, we have a right to know, ask, and talk about the past financial dealings of our elected officials in a public forum because it may affect their ability to perform and our confidence in them. However, we certainly have no right to know, ask, or talk about the past financial dealings of our next door neighbor or a coworker in a public forum. Simply put, some people, such as a celebrity, professional athlete, or sports broadcaster must tolerate more intrusive or hurtful comments made publicly about them based upon their position or actions in our society. Thus, three categories have emerged from Supreme Court decisions to help correctly balance individual interests against First Amendment rights. These three categories are: public officials, public figures, and private figures.

The Public Official

Defamation law changed drastically in the mid-1960s from earlier sixteenth-century interpretations which considered attacks on public officials as seditious libels that could be treated as criminal (Franklin & Rabin, 1996). The 1964 Supreme Court decision in *New York Times Co. v. Sullivan* (hereinafter "*New York Times*") revolutionized the way the judiciary interpreted and applied defamation law. As stated by Pember (1990), "This is one of the most important First Amendment cases ever decided . . . " (p. 129). In *New York Times*, the Supreme Court prohibited *public officials* from recovering damages for defamatory comments relating to official conduct unless the plaintiff could prove with convincing clarity that the statement was made with *actual malice*. Communication made with **actual malice** was defined by the Court as communication made "with knowledge that it was false or with reckless disregard of whether it was false or not" (*New York Times*, 1964, p. 380).

The Supreme Court believed that the public had a right to know and evaluate for themselves how leaders governed. Further, open debate, although at times caustic and unpleasant, assured the exchange of ideas necessary to bring about political and social change desired by the people (*New York Times*, 1964). Further, the freedom of the people to criticize freely and without actual malice better balances the absolute privilege enjoyed by the public official.

Pember (1990) succinctly defines a **public official** as "someone who works for a government and draws a salary from the public payroll" (p. 133). The Supreme Court also attempted to define the public official. In *Rosenblatt v. Baer* (1966) the Court questioned whether all individuals employed by the state are public officials or just those employed in "high-powered" positions. As stated by Justice Douglas in a concurring opinion, "anyone on the public payroll" qualifies as a public official (p. 89).

It would appear from the above decisions that subsequent court decisions would classify all teachers, coaches, and recreation supervisors as public officials. However, a contrary decision was issued by the Supreme Court of Kentucky in *Warford v. Lexington Herald* in 1980. As decided by this court, an assistant basketball recruiting coach at the University of Pittsburgh was not classified as either a public official or a public or limited-purpose public figure (see the section below dealing with the public figure and limited-purpose public figure).

The Public Figure

In a subsequent landmark case, *Curtis Publishing Co. v. Butts* (1967), the Supreme Court extended the constitutional protection given to statements about public officials in *New York Times* to public figures as well. Celebrities, television personalities, and highly successful business/industry leaders (i.e., public figures) often had as much societal influence as government officials, hence the similar constitutional protection afforded to those communicating about these individuals. Similar to the standard of proof established in *New York Times*, the *Curtis* court stated that individuals falling into the status of a public figure must prove actual malice to recover for damages. The determination of whether a person is a public figure is a matter of law. Public figure status does not depend on the desires of the individual. A plaintiff may not escape public figure status if he voluntarily engages in a course of conduct that invites attention and comment. Indeed, the distinction between public and private figures is based upon two considerations: the plaintiff's access to the media, and the extent to which the plaintiff, by virtue of his position in the community or involvement in a particular matter of public concern, can be said to invite public comment and attention.

As explained by the Supreme Court in *Curtis Publishing Co. v. Butts* (1967), a **public figure** is an individual who has, because of his or her activities, "commanded sufficient continuing public interest" (p. 155). The Supreme Court recognized the Athletic Director of the University of Georgia (Wally Butts), as a public figure. To date, *Butts* is the only Supreme Court case to apply the public figure test to a sports figure; since then many other courts have treated athletic directors, coaches, and athletes as public figures in a variety of settings from professional sports to high school athletics. In *Waldbaum v. Fairchild Publications, Inc.* (1980) the district court observed that "many well-known athletes, entertainers, and other personages endorse commercial products. . . . This phenomenon, regardless of whether it is justified, indicates that famous persons may be able to transfer their recognition and influence from one field to another" (p. 1294). Athletes, like politicians, can sway individual thinking. Consequently, their individual actions are open to public debate and scrutiny.

The *Curtis* court further provided two reasons for its extension of the actual malice standard to public figures as well as public officials. First, the plaintiff–public figure voluntarily "thrusts" himself or herself into the "vortex" of "important public controversies" (*Curtis Publishing Co. v. Butts*, 1967). If society chooses to direct massive public attention to a particular sphere of activity, those who enter that sphere invite such attention and must overcome the *Times* [actual malice] standard (*Chuy v. Philadelphia Eagles Football Club*, 1979, p. 267). Second, like public officials, public figures had "sufficient access to the means of counter argument" via the media. Certainly most, if not all, persons classified as public figures have ready access to the media and public forums in which they can defend themselves or respond to criticism or controversial statements.

The Limited-Purpose Public Person

Persons with instant national recognition and constant national media exposure such as Jay Leno, Peyton Manning, Dick Vitale, and Diane Sawyer are considered all-purpose public figures (Barron & Dienes, 1979). However, the 1974 Supreme Court decision in *Gertz v. Robert Welch, Inc.* introduced the concept of a **limited purpose public person** as ". . . an individual [who] voluntarily injects himself or is drawn into a particular public controversy and thereby becomes a public figure for a limited range of issues" (p. 351). The limited-purpose public figure has instant *local* recognition and constant media coverage on a *local* level. A limited purpose public figure is a person who becomes a public figure for a specific range of issues by being drawn into or voluntarily injecting himself into a specific public controversy.

To determine whether a person is a limited purpose public figure we must examine that person's participation in the controversy from which the alleged defamation arose, and whether he has attained a general notoriety in the community by reason of that participation (*Daubenmire v. Sommers*, 2004). A three-part test is used to make this determination: The court must determine that (1) there is a public controversy; (2) the plaintiff played a sufficiently central role in that controversy; and (3) the alleged defamation was germane to the plaintiff's involvement in the controversy (*Daubenmire v. Sommers*, 2004).

For example, if your community is considering building a multimillion dollar sports stadium, and a local university professor who is an expert in stadium finance appears on a local radio talk show and actively participates in the public debate on the funding initiative, she may qualify as a limited-purpose public figure, even though in any other context she would have most certainly been a private person. Most sport figures (e.g., coaches, athletes, sport broadcasters) tend to be classified as limited-purpose public figures. For example, in *Bell v. the Associated Press* (1984), a wide receiver for the Tampa Bay Buccaneers, whose notorious career includes a litany of misdeeds, was found to be a limited purpose public figure. The court held, "with respect to professional athletes . . . charges of criminal misconduct are a subject of public controversy and those who are the subject of such charges are public figures for that limited purpose."

Further, many jobs "produce at least limited-purpose public figure status by virtue of the associations it entails" (Franklin & Rabin, 1996, p. 991). To recover in a defamation action, a public figure, including a limited purpose public figure, must show by clear and convincing evidence that the statements were made with actual malice, that is, with knowledge that the statements were false or with reckless disregard of whether they were false or not. Sufficient evidence must exist to permit the conclusion that the defendant in fact had serious doubt as to the truth of the statements (*Daubenmire v. Sommers*, 2004).

The Private Figure

The "private figure" classification refers to individual citizens who are not involved in public issues or employed as a public official. Distinguishing between a public versus private figure is a critical issue for a plaintiff. Classification as a private person is important as private figures need only prove that an alleged defamatory statement was negligently made rather than made with actual malice as discussed above. Negligence is the failure to exercise "reasonable care." This is a much lower standard of proof than that required for public officials, public figures, or limited-purpose public figures.

The difficulty comes in ascertaining who qualifies as a "private figure." Defendants allege that private citizens involved in matters of interest to the public constitute limited-purpose public figures and are subject to the actual malice standard of proof required by *New York Times*. According to the Supreme Court's plurality decision in *Rosenbloom v. Metromedia, Inc.* (1971), all publication regarding matters of general interest or public concern should be protected by requiring plaintiffs to prove actual malice. Subsequent courts, concerned about the improper balance between competing interests, repudiated the "public interest" or "subject matter" standard established in the 1971 *Rosenbloom* case.

Two dominant reasons explain why the Court preserved the private person status granting individuals a lower standard of proof. First, it is assumed that private individuals do not have the same ability to access the media as public officials and public figures. Access to the media provides public officials and public figures with an opportunity to refute defamatory statements. The value of media access is illustrated by the Iowa Libel Research Project. According to this research project, almost 75 percent of defamed plaintiffs indicated they would have found adequate recourse if "the news medium would have published or broadcast a correction, retraction or apology" (Pember, 1990). Second, it is said that public figures and public officials relinquish rights when they voluntarily become entangled in an issue of public concern. Private individuals, in comparison, are not attempting to influence society and are not desirous of media attention.

Statements of Fact v. Expressions of Opinion

Early common law protected statements of opinion from defamatory allegations. The Supreme Court affirmed this sentiment in the *Gertz* case in 1974. As stated by the Supreme Court, "Under the First Amendment there is no such thing as a false idea" (*Gertz v. Robert Welch, Inc.*, 1974, p. 339). However, statements based upon false facts, or undisclosed facts, are actionable. In other words, if an opinion is stated, then all the facts that were used in deriving the opinion should be disclosed. This enables an individual to read the facts and then draw his or her own conclusion (i.e., opinion), which may differ from that of the writer or publisher. The decision as to whether a statement constitutes fact or opinion is a question of law for the court to decide.

The Supreme Court in *Milkovich v. Lorain Journal Co.* (1990) further narrowed the protection given to statements of opinion. As explained by the Court, merely prefacing a statement with "In my opinion . . ." does not insulate an individual from defamation liability. More specifically, the Court stated

> "Even if the speaker states the facts upon which he bases his opinion, if those facts are either incorrect or incomplete, or if his assessment of them is erroneous, the statement may still imply a false assertion of fact. Simply couching such statements in terms of opinion does not dispel these implications . . ." (p. 2706).

Statements made or included on websites, discussion boards, and chat rooms all have the potential to raise questions regarding defamation. While most statements in an Internet chat room would be considered statements of opinion, often statements of opinion are cloaked with statements of fact (See *Diebella v. Hopkins* (2002) included in the supplemental Web Site) and as mentioned previously could form the basis of a defamation action when posted to Facebook or Twitter.

In *Stepien v. Franklin* (1988) the Court of Appeals of Ohio held an assortment of disparaging adjectives to be constitutionally protected opinion. The adjectives included the following: "Stupid," "dumb," "buffoon," "nincompoop," "scum," "a cancer," "an obscenity," "gutless liar," "unmitigated liar," "pathological liar," "egomaniac," "nuts," "crazy," "irrational," "suicidal," "lunatic" (p. 1327). As illustrated above, the specific language used by the defendant is overtly injurious. However, the syllabus by the court, justifying its action, stated, "The area of sports is a traditional haven for cajoling, invective, and hyperbole . . ." (p. 1326).

Society commonly accepts rowdy behavior as "part of the game." Even during the 1960s, the era of individual rights, the heckling involved in sport was viewed as commonplace. As explained by the Supreme Court of North Carolina in *Toone v. Adams* (1964), "For present day fans, a goodly part of the sport in a baseball game is goading and denouncing the umpire when they do not concur in his decisions, and most feel that, without one or more rhubarbs, they have not received their money" (p. 136).

The Supreme Court of Ohio (*Scott v. News-Herald*, 1986) concluded that most information conveyed in the sports section of a newspaper is "constitutionally protected." The *Scott* court's decision, although of limited precedential value, is precarious because it suggests that comments about a sport-related figure, regardless of their veracity or the publisher's degree of fault, are constitutionally protected.

Defenses to Defamation Claims

Truth is an absolute defense to all claims of defamation. Even if the actual facts turn out to be different than those contained in the statement, a defense of truthfulness may still apply. The statements do not necessarily have to be completely accurate, only substantively correct or truthful for the Truth defense to shield them. For example, truth would still serve as a viable defense in the situation where a personal trainer was charged with selling $250,000 worth of steroids to players when in actuality he only sold $125,000.

Privilege, a second defense, refers to "a particular and peculiar benefit or advantage enjoyed by a person, company, or class, beyond the common advantages of other citizens" (Black, 1990, p. 1197). Privileged statements made without malice are immune from defamation liability (*Iacco v. Bohannon*, 1976; *Institute of Athletic Motivation v. Univ. of Ill.*, 1982). Common types of privilege include absolute privilege, qualified privilege, and fair comment.

Absolute privilege is enjoyed by those in: (1) a legislative forum (e.g., congressmen, congresswomen, senators, city council members); (2) the judicial forum (e.g., judges, lawyers, plaintiffs, defendants); and (3) administrative and executive branches of government (e.g., presidents, mayors, department heads). Persons occupying these roles have **"absolute" privilege**, i.e., there can be no liability for statements regardless of their falsity or disregard for the truth. This privilege exists to avoid censorship of desired communication that could otherwise possibly benefit society. The media is also protected from liability if during the broadcast or publication of statements during a public debate, defamatory comments are made by individuals who are protected by absolute privilege (Franklin & Rabin, 1996).

Qualified or conditional privilege represents a defense available to other defendants. Similar to absolute privilege, some situations demand the protection of communication to benefit society at large. As explained by Carpenter (1995), **qualified privilege** applies to statements made: (1) without knowledge of falsity, (2) by a person with reason to communicate the statement, and (3) communicated only to a person with a "justifiable interest in knowing." Individual managers often have qualified privilege, for example, when discussing employee behaviors with superiors and when providing employee references.

Fair comment represents a defense commonly used by media defendants. As explained by (Black, 1990), **fair comment** is a "form of qualified privilege applied to news media publications relating to discussion of matters which are of legitimate concern to the community as a whole because they materially affect the interests of all the community" (p. 596). There typically is no liability if the media publishes defamatory information so long as their report represents a fair and accurate summary or restatement of communication available to the public upon which they are relying. The fair comment defense is only appropriate when comments are made without malice and statements are based on true facts (Black, 1990; *Cohen v. Cowles Publishing Co.*, 1954; *Conkwright v. Globe News Publishing Company*, 1965).

Neutral reportage represents another defense similar in concept to fair reporting that is available to media defendants in certain circuits. Based upon the U.S. Court of Appeals landmark decision in *Edwards v. National Audubon Society* (1977), media defendants can publish statements made by responsible or prominent organizations even though the publisher doubts the veracity of the statements.

Damages

Defamation law encompasses two types of damages (*Matherson v. Marchello*, 1984). First, **special damages** reflect "actual pecuniary losses that the plaintiff can prove he or she sustained" as a direct result of the defendant's comments (Franklin & Rabin, 1996, p. 895; *Liberman v. Gelstein*, 1992). Lost wages or the loss of identified business customers, for example, are quantifiable and reflect special damages. Second, **general damages**, on the other hand, reflect nonquantifiable damages such as the presumed damage to one's reputation. Plaintiffs suing for slander must prove special damages unless the cause of action is slander *per se*.

Although an anomaly in tort law, the tort of defamation does not always require proof of damage. For example, in some states, plaintiffs suing for libel are not required to prove special damages (Franklin & Rabin, 1996). Rather, the existence of damage is *presumed* as a result of the publication itself (*Matherson v. Marchello*, 1984).

SIGNIFICANT CASE

The significant case presented below not only outlines the elements of a defamation action very well, but also addresses the concepts of special damages and the defense of qualified privilege. This case is also particularly helpful for current study since the allegedly offending statements were made in connection with employment termination. An increasing number of lawsuits involving wrongful termination and/or discrimination claims also include allegations of defamation. This emphasizes the importance of taking care in discussing employee performance and systematically evaluating employee performance consistent with established policies and practices.

WEISMANN V. RIVERHEAD UNION FREE SCHOOL DISTRICT

Supreme Court of New York, Suffolk County
2010 N.Y. Misc. LEXIS 4592

This is an action brought by the plaintiff Gerald G. Wiesmann (hereinafter Wiesmann) against the defendants Riverhead Union Free School District, William Groth (Athletic Director), Paul Doyle (District Superintendent), W. Brian Stark (member of the Board of Education) and Timothy S. Griffing (member of the Board of Education; hereinafter Griffing). The defendants shall be referred to collectively, hereinafter, as the School District. This action stems from Wiesmann's basic contention that the School District wrongfully terminated him from his employ as the coach of the high school varsity basketball team after the 2005-2006 season (first cause of action) and that the defendant Griffing defamed Wiesmann when, on two separate occasions, Griffing stated to two different individuals that, "Jerry [sic; meaning the plaintiff Gerald Wiesmann] let a player push him during a game and did nothing about it"

***

Turning now to the defamation claim (second cause of action), the School District argues that the actual words uttered are not defamatory and, in any event, were subject to a qualified privilege, were uttered with regard to a single instance and since they were not slanderous per se, the complaint is required to allege special damages, the absence of which requires dismissal.

In reviewing the complaint's defamation claim (second cause of action), the plaintiff Wiesmann alleges, inter alia, as follows:

"9. On or about November 2006 Defendant Griffing, on two occasions maliciously, spoke the following false and defamatory words concerning plaintiff 'Jerry [sic] let a player push him during a game and did nothing about it', in the presence of others including Lori [sic] Downs, and Ziggy Wilenski [sic].

"10. As intended by defendant Griffing these words were understood by those who heard them as to charge the plaintiff with professional incompetence."

At the hearing, Wiesmann provided hearsay testimony to the effect that Ziggy Wilinski, a volunteer assistant with the basketball program at the time in question, told Wiesmann that during the course of an unrelated conversation, Wilinski asked Griffing (a member of the School District's board of education at the pertinent time), why Wiesmann was being given a "hard time" and Griffing responded that he had witnessed a player of Wiesmann's push Wiesmann during a game and that Wiesmann did nothing about it and let the player "get away with it". Wiesmann gave further hearsay testimony at the hearing to the effect that Downs (president of the Parent Teacher Organization at the pertinent time) told Wiesmann that she heard from Griffing that "some kid pushed [Wiesmann] and that [Wiesmann] didn't have the respect of the kids". Wiesmann also testified that there were no other claims of defamation aside from these two incidents.

In order for a statement to be defamatory per se, it must naturally imply disgraceful professional conduct on the part of the subject person in the mind of an intelligent person (43 NY Jur § 70). Where a statement is slanderous per se, special damages need not be alleged in the complaint; if not slanderous per se, then special damages must be alleged (43 NY Jur 2d, Defamation & Privacy § 8.

Here, there is merely a recitation of facts by Griffing that he saw a player push the coach during a game for which the coach took no apparent action. On its face, there is no charge of disgraceful conduct contained in these words. At worse, the statement may be somewhat deprecating but it certainly does not rise to the level of charging "disgraceful" conduct. Also, courts will not strain to find defamation where none exists (see Cohn v Natl. Broadcasting Co., 50 NY2d 885, 408 N.E.2d 672, 430 NYS2d 265 [1980], cert denied 449 US 1022, 101 S. Ct. 590, 66 L. Ed. 2d 484 [1980]).

Nor is there an opinion stated by Griffing based upon the facts he stated he observed. In any event, any stated opinion flowing from such a factual recitation would be pure opinion and not actionable (see e.g. Versaci v Richie, 30 AD3d 648, 815 NYS2d 350 [3d Dept 2006]). In this case, the plaintiff contends that the statement itself gives rise to the implication that Griffing thought that Wiesmann was not fit to be the coach. As such, according to the plaintiff, Griffing was impugning Wiesmann's performance and such a statement would be actionable per se.

Even assuming arguendo that Wiesmann's arguments have merit, a statement impugning one's professional competence is not actionable where it refers to a single instance unless special damages are pleaded. In this case, the purported defamatory remarks attributed to Griffing both refer to the same single instance observed by Griffing during a game. Accordingly, Griffing's remarks are protected by the single instance doctrine unless the complaint contains allegations of special damages (id.). Here, the complaint is utterly devoid of any allegations as to special damages. Moreover, the plaintiff's opposition papers fail to mention any special damages and, indeed, the plaintiff takes the position that the statements made by Griffing are per se slanderous and, thus, need no allegations of special damages. The Court disagrees. The statements at issue are not slanderous on their face and evidence no express statement or opinion as to Wiesmann's professional competence. Moreover, the statements refer to a single instance and are not actionable without allegations of special damages (id.).

In addition, the defendant Griffing is entitled to a qualified privilege for the statements he made because they were made with regard to matters within his professional concern as a member of the board of education, made to others with a corresponding interest in the subject matter (a colleague of the plaintiff's in the basketball program and the president of the Parent Teacher Organization), were expressed in a reasonable manner and for a proper purpose (in response to questions regarding Wiesmann). (See, 43 NY Jur 2d, Defamation & Privacy § 120).

Unless the plaintiff can show malice and falsity, a qualified privilege covers the statements alleged herein (see 43 NY Jur 2d, Defamation & Privacy § 161). Here, the plaintiff has made no showing of malice. As to falsity, his self-serving statement in his purported affidavit in opposition that he was never pushed by a player lacks credibility and the lack of any corroborating affidavits from anyone else present at the game weighs heavily against the plaintiff.

In conclusion, whether the statements made by the defendant Griffing were true or not, they would not be actionable in view of the single instance rule and the qualified privilege, both of which are applicable here. The Court, therefore, finds that the defendants have made a prima facie showing of entitlement to summary judgment dismissing the defamation cause of action and the plaintiff has not met his burden to show the existence of a material issue of fact requiring a trial (see Zuckerman v City of New York, 49 NY2d 557, 404 N.E.2d 718, 427 NYS2d 595 [1980]).

Accordingly, dismissal of the complaint in its entirety as to all defendants pursuant to CPLR 3212 is granted as provided herein.

CASES ON THE SUPPLEMENTAL WEB SITE

Barry v. Time, Inc., 584 F. Supp. 1110 (N.D. Cal. 1984). This case further illustrates the public controversy requirement of *Gertz* in determining whether a person is a limited purpose public figure.

Brewer v. Rogers, 439 S.E.2d 77 (Ga. App. 1993). This case illustrates how the public figure and limited purpose public figure standards were applied to a high school coach. This is a good case to compare to cases involving college and professional coaches.

Bull v. Ball State University, 2011 U.S. Dist. LEXIS 147774 (S.D. Ind. 2011). This case provides a good discussion of defamation under Indiana law and the application of immunity principles when individual state employees make statements in their official capacity as state employees.

Clemens v. McNamee, 615 F.3d 374 (5th Cir. 2011). This case involves Roger Clemens defamation claims against his former trainer. It addresses the jurisdictional issues that are common in defamation claims which will continue to be of greater importance with the rise of defamation claims based on online statements.

Diebella v. Hopkins, 187 F. Supp.2d 192 (S.D.N.Y. 2002). This case outlines the elements of a libel action and addresses how to determine whether a statement is an expression of opinion or fact. This is a good case to compare and contrast with the Significant Case above.

QUESTIONS YOU SHOULD BE ABLE TO ANSWER

1. What is the difference between libel and slander?

2. What makes a statement libel "*per se*" or slander "*per se*"; and why is that designation important?

3. What are the elements of a defamation claim?

4. What is actual malice and why are public figures required to prove actual malice in order to prevail in a defamation case?

5. What are three common defenses to a defamation action?

REFERENCES

Cases
Bell v. the Associated Press, 584 F. Supp. 128 (D.D.C. 1984)
Brooks v. Paige, 773 P.2d 1098 (Colo. App. 1988).
Cepeda v. Cowles Magazines and Broadcasting, Inc., 392 F.2d 417 (9th Cir. 1968).
Chuy v. Philadelphia Eagles Football Club, 595 F.2d 1265 (3rd Cir. 1979).
Cohen v. Cowles Publishing Co., 273 P.2d 893.
Conkwright v. Globe News Publishing Company, 398 S.W. 385 (1965).
Curtis Publishing Co. v. Butts, 388 U.S. 130 (1967).
Daubenmire v. Sommers, 805 N.E.2d 571 (Ohio App. 2004).
Edwards v. National Audubon Society, 556 F.2d 113 (2nd Cir.), *cert. denied*, 434 U.S. 1002 (1977).
Garrison v. Louisiana, 379 U.S. 64 (1964).
Gertz v. Robert Welch, Inc., 418 U.S. 323 (1974).
Gomez v. Murdoch, 475 A.2d 622 (N.J. Super. A.D. 1984).
Hotchner v. Castillo-Puche, 551 F.2d 910 (2nd Cir. 1977).
Iacco v. Bohannon, 245 N.W.2d 791 (Mich. 1976).
Institute of Athletic Motivation v. Univ. of Ill., 170 Cal. Rptr. 411 (Cal. App. 1982).
Liberman v. Gelstein, 605 N.E.2d 344 (1992).
Masson v. New Yorker Magazine, Inc., 960 F.2d 896 (9th Cir. 1991).
Matherson v. Marchello, 473 N.Y.S.2d 998 (1984).
Milkovich v. Lorain Journal Co., 497 U.S. 1 (1990).
Montefusco v. ESPN, Inc., 2002 U.S. App. LEXIS 19740; 30 Media L. Rep. 2311 (3rd Cir. 2002).
New York Times Co. v. Sullivan, 376 U.S. 254 (1964).

Ollman v. Evans, 750 F.2d 970 (D.C. Cir.), *cert. denied,* 471 U.S. 1127 (1985).

Philadelphia Newspapers, Inc. et al. v. Hepps et al., 475 U.S. 767 (1986).

Romaine v. Kallinger, 537 A.2d 284 (1988).

Rosenbloom v. Metromedia, Inc., 403 U.S. 29 (1971).

St. Amant v. Thompson, 390 U.S. 727 (1968).

Stepien v. Franklin, 528 N.E.2d 1324 (Ohio App. 1988).

Toone v. Adams, 137 S.E.2d 132 (1964).

Waldbaum v. Fairchild Publications, Inc., 637 F.2d 1287 (D.C. Cir.), *cert. denied,* 449 U.S. 898 (1980).

Warford v. Lexington Herald, 170 Cal. Rptr. 411 (1990).

Washington v. Smith, 893 F. Supp. 60 (D.D.C. 1995).

Weismann v. Riverhead Union Free School District, 2010 N.Y. Misc. LEXIS 4592 (Sup. Ct. N.Y. 2010).

Wolston v. Reader's Digest Ass'n, 443 U.S. 157 (1979).

Publications

Anderson, D. (1984). Reputation, compensation, and proof. *William & Mary Law Review, 25*(5), 747.

Anderson, D. A. (1991). Is libel law worth reforming? *University of Pennsylvania Law Review, 140*(2), 487–554.

Anderson Publications, Inc. (2002, August). Focus on: Pending litigation. *Legal Issues in Collegiate Athletics, 3*(10), 4.

Barron, J., & Dienes, C. T. (1979). *Handbook of free speech and free press.* Boston: Little, Brown.

Bennett, N.K. (2011, February 8). Did Courtney Love make a good decision to settle her Twitter case. *Connecticut Business Litigation.* Retrieved at http://www.connecticutbusinesslitigation.com/2011/02/articles/technology-1/did-courtney-love-make-a-good-decision-to-settle-her-twitter-case/

Black, H. C. (1990). *Black's law dictionary* (6th ed.). St. Paul, MN: West Publishing Co.

Carpenter, L. J. (1995). *Legal concepts in sport: A primer.* Reston, VA: AAHPERD.

Franklin, M. A., & Rabin, R. L. (1996). *Tort law and alternatives: Cases and materials* (6th ed.). Westbury, NY: The Foundation Press.

Gardner, E. (2009, October 27). Courtney Love loses motion to dismiss Twitter defamation case. *Entertainment and Media Law.* Retrieved at: http://www.entmedialaw.com/defamation/lawsuit/privacy/.

Highlight case. (2002, February). *Legal Issues in Collegiate Athletics, 3*(4), 3.

Mayer, M. F. (1987). *The libel revolution: A new look at defamation and privacy.* Chelsea, MI: BookCrafters.

Pember, D. R. (1990). *Mass media law* (5th ed.). Dubuque, IA: Wm. C. Brown Publishers.

Ransom, E. (1995). The ex-public figure: A libel plaintiff without a class. *Seton Hall Journal of Sport Law, 5*(2), 389–417.

Restatement (Second) of Torts § 558.

Smolla, R. A. (1983). Let the author beware: The rejuvenation of the American law of libel. *University of Pennsylvania Law Review, 132*(1), 1–94.

Soocher, S. (2002, October). Bit parts. *Entertainment Law & Finance, 18*(7), 10.

3.13 OTHER INTENTIONAL TORTS

INVASION OF PRIVACY
BREACH OF FIDUCIARY DUTY
TORTIOUS INTERFERENCE WITH CONTRACT
INTENTIONAL INFLICTION OF EMOTIONAL DISTRESS

Gary Rushing | Minnesota State University, Mankato

Intentional torts are deliberate wrongs done to others that cause harm. This type of tort differs from negligence torts in that lack of due care or engaging in abnormally dangerous activity is immaterial. Liability for intentional torts is predicated on the tortfeasor purposely causing harm to another person or engaging in an activity that is substantially certain to harm another (Restatement of Torts, 1965). Recreation- or sport-related intentional torts can occur on or off the playing field. This chapter discusses four "off field" intentional torts that occasionally occur in sport and recreation settings. They are invasion of privacy, breach of fiduciary duty, tortious interference with contract, and intentional infliction of emotional distress (IIED). Although not an intentional tort, negligent infliction of emotional distress is also included in this chapter as it relates very closely to IIED.

INVASION OF PRIVACY

Privacy, as defined by the courts, is "the right to be left alone; to live one's life as one chooses free from assault, intrusion, or invasion except as they can be justified by the clear needs of the community under a government of law" (*Rosenbloom v. Metromedia, Inc.*, 1971). The legal principles that serve as the bases for privacy protection are found primarily in three sources of the law—the Fourteenth Amendment, the Constitution, and tort law. The Fourteenth Amendment and the Constitution are concerned with the rights claims against any of the various governmental entities. Tort law is devoted to rights claims against a person or persons (Wriggins, 2010). Further, most states recognize the right of privacy either by means of common law case decisions or by applicable statutes and state constitutions (Carper, McKinsey, & West, 2008).

Right of privacy, as found in tort law, involves four distinct theories or ways in which one's privacy can be invaded. Keeton, Dobbs, Keeton, Prosser, and Owen (1984) explained that these theories do not concern one tort, but a complex of four kinds of invasion. They have little in common except that each represents intrusion upon an individual's reasonable expectation "to be let alone," which is at the center of all wrongful invasion suits. The four types of invasion are (1) unreasonable intrusion on the seclusion of another, (2) appropriation of another's name or likeness, (3) unreasonable disclosure of private facts, and (4) publicity that unreasonably places the other in a false light before the public. Because each type of "invasion" is notably different, only one of the torts, not all four, must be proven for a successful claim of invasion of privacy (Franklin, Cardi, & Green, 2008).

Unreasonable Intrusion on Seclusion

The first form or theory is straightforward and concerned with the invasion of one's home or illegally searching someone's personal belongings or documents. Usually, the intrusion takes the form of window peeking, eavesdropping, excessive surveillance, or constant annoyance (Yasser, McCurdy, Goplerud, & Weston, 2011). However, the courts have extended this tort to include eavesdropping by wiretap, unauthorized examining of a bank account, and compulsory blood testing (Cross & Miller, 2009). Although untested in court, it would seem logical to assume that this notion would also include scanning of cellular phones and computer hacking.

In addition to the actual intrusion, any information obtained in these or similar ways that is made public is also invasion of privacy. This is true even if the information obtained is truthful and it serves the public's right to know (Schubert, Smith, & Trentadue, 1986). The requisite question is: Was the intrusion offensive or objectionable to a reasonable person? (Keeton et al., 1984). If so, then it is an illegal invasion of one's privacy.

A court case that illustrates this point is *Bilney v. Evening Star Newspaper Co.* (1979). In this dispute, six members of the University of Maryland basketball team brought action against reporters and newspaper publishers for articles detailing their poor academic standing, thus putting them in danger of being declared ineligible to play. The question was addressed as to how the reporters obtained the academic information they had published. The court determined that they had obtained the information from an anonymous source and that there was no evidence that the defendant news reporters had learned of the players' academic problems from confidential records or by any acts of invasion or intrusion. However, had the information been obtained through wiretaps, computer hacking, or some other offensive manner, the court may have considered this to be invasion of privacy.

Appropriation

The second form of invasion of privacy involves the **unauthorized use of a person's name or likeness** for commercial purposes such as advertising or trade. The protection provided by this law is especially important to sport figures because it gives them some control over the extent to which their name and likeness can be commercially exploited. Without this control, an athlete would lose a significant source of income from commercial endorsements, trading cards, and other enterprises. It is the most common "privacy" complaint of athletes (Byrd, 1988).

Although sport figures can prohibit most unauthorized use of their names and likenesses, courts have upheld unauthorized uses for editorial purposes as well as when reused by publishers or broadcasters for campaigns to increase circulation or broadcasting audiences. According to the Citizen's Media Project (http://www.citmedialaw.org/legal-guide/using-name-or-likeness-another, 2012) when used in this manner, it is considered to be protected incidental use. (For more information on the "incidental use" exception, see Chapter 7.23, *Image Rights*.)

In a classic case that illustrates the salient issues in this area, Joe Namath sued *Sports Illustrated* (*Namath v. Sports Illustrated*, 1975) for the unauthorized use of his photo to promote subscription sales. He contended that this use was commercial and violated his **right to privacy**. Further, because he was in the business of endorsing products and selling the use of his name and likeness, it interfered with his right to profit from such sale. The photograph had originally been used without objection from Namath, in conjunction with a 1969 Super Bowl article. However, because it was reprinted to promote subscription sales, he felt he should be compensated for its use. In siding with *Sports Illustrated*, the court noted that the use of the photo was merely "incidental" advertising because it was used to illustrate the quality and content of the periodical in which it originally appeared.

In a similar invasion of privacy case (*Montana v. San Jose Mercury News, Inc.*, 1995), Joe Montana brought action against the *San Jose Mercury News* for misappropriation of his name, photograph, and likeness. At issue was the reproduction of Montana's photograph that originally appeared in conjunction with a 1990 Super Bowl victory for the San Francisco 49ers. His photo had been reproduced in poster form. Some of the posters were sold for five dollars each, and the rest were donated to charity organizations. The court reached a decision similar to that of the *Namath* case and found in favor of *San Jose Mercury News* for two reasons. First, the original newspaper account and the subsequent photograph constituted matters in the public interest. Second, the posters were sold to advertise the quality and content of its newspaper. They contained no additional information and they did not convey Montana's endorsement.

In another case, *Palmer v. Schonhorn Enterprises, Inc.* (1967), a toy manufacturing company appropriated the names and career profiles of golfers Arnold Palmer, Gary Player, Doug Sanders, and Jack Nicklaus for use in a game. In this situation, the court sided with the plaintiffs because the commercial use of their names and profiles was done without their permission and without compensation.

The appropriation theory of invasion of privacy generated the **right of publicity** cause of legal action (Breaux, 2005; Cozzillio, Levinstein, Dimino & Feldman, 2007; Thorton, 2010). The major difference between the two concepts is that redress in a right of privacy (misappropriation) dispute is based on the mental duress resulting from "not being left alone," whereas the focus of redress in a right of publicity case is the financial loss caused by the appropriation of an individual's identity for commercial exploitation. (See *Doe v. TCI Cablevision*, 110 S.W.3d 363(Mo.2003) on the Supplemental Web Site for an expanded explanation of the differences.)

Celebrities, including athletes, have had a difficult task in demonstrating to the courts that public exposure caused them mental duress in that "they sought such attention and profited from it" (Stapleton & McMurphy, 1999). For this reason, more and more states are adopting the right of publicity, which provides celebrities with stronger legal leverage for preventing the use of their name or image (Stapleton & McMurphy, 1999). (For more information on Right of Publicity, see Chapter 7.23, *Image Rights*.)

Unreasonable Disclosure of Private Facts

A third type of invasion of privacy involves public disclosure of private facts about an individual that an ordinary person would find objectionable. Public disclosure suits are sometimes referred to as embarrassment suits because they arise from objections to publicity of embarrassing private information (Dill, 1992). At the center of this type of suit is the balance between the public's right to know and the extent of the intrusion into one's private life. Although secondary issues must be satisfied to prevail in an embarrassment suit (see Keeton et al., 1984, pp. 856–857), where public figures such as sport personalities are concerned, there are two major issues that the courts will address. They are (1) whether the disclosed information was **truly private** or was it public, and (2) if the disclosed information was **highly offensive** to an ordinary person.

Private v. Public Facts

For a plaintiff to succeed in a public disclosure suit, it must be shown that the disclosed publicity was a situation in which there was a legitimate expectancy of privacy. In other words, the disclosure must have involved truly private matters. What constitutes truly private for the average citizen, in terms of publicity, is different from that of a sport figure. Sports personalities, especially the highly paid athletes, have little privacy protection due to their public figure status. A **public figure** is someone who by "his [or her] accomplishments, fame, or mode of living, or by adopting a profession or calling which gives the public a legitimate interest in his doings, his affairs, and his character, has become a public personage" (Keeton et al., 1984, p. 859). (For an in-depth discussion of public figure status, see Chapter 3.12 *Defamation*.) By way of this notion, the Constitution allows the press to report matters that have become public interest.

The justification for this loss of privacy protection is the result of three considerations about public figures. First, public figures have, to a certain extent, sought publicity and have consented to it. Second, their personalities and affairs have become public and are no longer private business. Third, the press has a right to inform the public about those who have become matters of public interest (Prosser, 1960).

Whether or not college athletes are considered public figures is sometimes at issue. In the previously mentioned case of *Bilney v. Evening Star Newspaper Co.* (1979), because there was no evidence that the defendant news reporters had learned of the players' academic problems through improper methods, the court examined the issue of "public figure" status of the six players. The court reasoned that college basketball is a "big-time" sport and generates a great deal of public interest and excitement throughout the country. The court further stated that the players had "achieved the status of public figures . . . by virtue of their membership on the basketball team (and) . . . having sought . . . the limelight. . . . It's clear at least in this court that college athletes in big time sports are 'public figures'" (p. 574).

As for high school athletes, it remains unclear as to whether or not they would be considered public figures. A leading case on the subject suggests that most high school athletes will not be considered public figures regardless of their notoriety or the public interest (see *Wilson v. Daily Gazette Co.*, 2003). Deem (2006) and Long (2009), however, suggest that courts prefer to find "much publicized" high school athletes to be limited-purpose public figures as opposed to all purpose public figures. (See Chapter 3.12 *Defamation*, for discussion of limited-purpose public figures.)

In addition to the preceding issues dealing with private information, it should be noted that information that has been previously reported, or that has already been made accessible to the public through public records or other documentation, or that is newsworthy is not considered to be purely private in nature and therefore is discloseable (Wong, 2011).

Highly Offensive

Even though some facts may be newsworthy and therefore non-private, they may not be publishable if they can be viewed as highly offensive to the average person. For example, publication of a person's sexual orientation, HIV status, or financial troubles could lead to liability for publication of offensive private facts. However, because community norms vary from jurisdiction to jurisdiction, courts may have mixed decisions regarding what is permissible disclosure. Therefore, where public figures are concerned, even conservative courts will allow most private truthful facts, although embarrassing, to be disclosed unless they are " unredeemably offensive and not even remotely in the 'public interest' " (Dill, 1986, p. 137).

False Light Intrusion

Under this theory, an invasion of privacy occurs when publicity places the plaintiff in a **false light** in the public eye (i.e., a large audience, not just a few individuals). For example, in a sport setting, this could occur if someone in the media uses a photograph or makes a statement about a sport figure that gives a false impression to the public This false impression could emanate in several ways including "misleading descriptions, confusion of the person's identity with another, fictionalization of actual events, or photographs taken out of context" (Bussian & Levine, http://www.floridabar.org/, 2004)

However, for sport figures to prevail in a false light suit, they must not only show that the published information was false, but also that the disclosure was done by one knowing it was false or who had reckless disregard for the truth. This standard was established in *Time, Inc. v. Hill* (1967), which held that the First Amendment protects reports of newsworthy matters.

False light action is different from libel in that the publicity does not have to be defamatory. The depiction in question could be either complimentary or defamatory. Although most false light cases involve unflattering portrayals, the central issue is "being let alone" from the *effects* of a false reputation or false publicity (Samar, 1991). Both false light and libel complaints are permitted in some states; however, other states do not recognize false light claims and permit only libel suits.

An example of false light invasion occurred in the case of *Spahn v. Messner, Inc.* (1967). This case centered on an unauthorized biography written about Warren Spahn, a celebrated pitcher for the Milwaukee Braves. The author used "invented dialogue, and imaginary incidents" which he knew to be false and knew to present an untruthful depiction of Spahn. Spahn objected to this portrayal even though parts of the story were complimentary. The court awarded Spahn $10,000 in damages and enjoined further publication of the book (see the Supplemental Web Site).

BREACH OF FIDUCIARY DUTY

Another intentional tort is breach of fiduciary duty or responsibility. *Black's Law Dictionary* (Black, 1979) defines a **fiduciary** as "[a] person having duty, created by his undertaking, to act primarily for another's benefit in matters connected with this undertaking." As an adjective, it means ". . . relating to or founded upon a trust or confidence" (p. 563). Carper et al. (2008) clarified this by adding that a fiduciary relationship is one involving a person in a position of trust who undertakes to act for the benefit of another. Examples of fiduciary relationships include lawyer–client, parent–child, and coach–athlete.

In the sport setting, the fiduciary relationship that is most troublesome is the association between a professional athlete and his or her agent (Ehrhardt & Rodgers, 1988; Powers, 1994). An agent can be responsible for managing many of the athlete's financial concerns such as tax planning, financial planning, money management, investments, estate planning, income tax preparation, incorporating the client, endorsements, sports medicine consultation, physical health consultation, post-career development, career and personal development and counseling, legal consultation, and insurance matters (Davis, 2006). Because many of these dealings are legally binding to the represented athlete, the law imposes a high obligation of trustworthiness on the agent. If an agent violates this trust and the athlete is harmed as a result, the agent is guilty of tortious conduct and may have to make restitution (Restatement (Second) of Torts #874, 1984, p. 300).

A fiduciary duty requires that the sport agent act with complete honesty in all dealings with athlete–clients. In addition, the agent must avoid any personal **conflicts of interest**. In other words, the interests of the athlete must come before those of the agent. Also, an agent must not represent two adverse parties in the same transaction. For example an agent cannot represent two or more athletes vying for the same endorsement contract nor represent both an athlete and the company with which he is negotiating for a contract. Finally, an agent must not receive hidden compensation or profits from third parties for transacting the player's business and must not take advantage of any business opportunity that rightfully belongs to the athlete (Thornton, 2010). An agent can avoid liability in this area by fully disclosing any possible conflicts of interest or other potentially improper conduct and obtaining the athlete's prior consent to the action.

Detroit Lions, Inc. v. Jerry Argovitz (1984) offers an instructional example of breach of fiduciary duty. In this case, Billy Sims' agent, Jerry Argovitz, engaged in a series of unethical practices with the intent of inducing Sims to sign a contract with the Houston Gamblers of the United States Football League. After the Gamblers made an offer to Sims, Argovitz failed to give the Detroit Lions an opportunity to match the bid. Sims signed with the Gamblers believing theirs to be the best offer. After it was revealed Argovitz was a substantial owner in the Gamblers' franchise and that he had withheld information that might have swayed Sims' decision, the court allowed Sims to rescind his contract and sign with the Detroit Lions. Sims was unaware of the extent of Argovitz's association with the Gamblers. (See the Supplemental Web Site.)

Dominion Sports Services, Inc. v. Bredehoft (2006) illustrates the necessity of having a valid fiduciary relationship established in order to have a successful claim of breach of fiduciary duty. Hockey North America (HNA) started an adult men's novice hockey league in Minnesota. Bradford Bredehof, an independent contractor, was hired as the local administrator of the league. His contract had a restrictive covenant that prohibited him from starting a competing league in the area. After HNA encountered financial difficulties and owed money to many creditors, Dominion Sports Services purchased its assets but retained the HNA league name. As the purchase was being negotiated, Bredehoft met with the players and informed them of HNA's financial problems. This discussion ultimately prompted them to organize their own competing league. Dominion filed suit against Bredehoft and others for breach of contract, breach of fiduciary duty, and tortious interference with contractual relations. The court ruled against HNA on all claims. HNA did not have a valid breach of contract or tortious interference claim against Bredehoft because he did not have a contract with the new management. Dominion's purchase agreement explicitly stated that it would not assume the employment contracts of the former management employees. Without a valid contract, Bredehoft was never an agent of the new HNA, therefore, a breach of fiduciary duty claim could not be upheld.

TORTIOUS INTERFERENCE WITH CONTRACT

Tortious interference with contract involves the intentional inducement of another to breach one's contractual obligations (Gleason, 2008). **Tampering** is an alternate term sometimes used to describe when one team attempts to lure a player who is clearly under contract to another team. It is the equivalent of tortious interference with contract (Epstein, 2002). Because contracts play a vital role in sport, this is a significant area of concern. Inducement to break contracts has been alleged in situations that involve teams competing for talented players (*Cincinnati Bengals v. William Bergey, et al.*, 1974), boxing promoters arguing over promotion rights (*Don King Productions v. James "Buster" Douglas, et al.*, 1990), and agents interfering with a college player's eligibility (Gray, 2006; Woods & Mills, 1988).

There are three elements necessary to prove the existence of a wrongful interference tort:

1. A valid, enforceable contract must exist between two parties.

2. The defendant must have known of the contract's existence.

3. The defendant must have, without justification, knowingly induced either of the two parties from full performance of the contract. This interference must have been done for the purpose of advancing the economic interest of the inducer. It does not matter if the action was done in bad faith or with malice (the intention to harm another); however, bad faith or malice is usually a factor (Cross & Miller, 2009).

Plaintiff has the burden to prove that the defendant knew of the contract's existence and knowingly induced the breach of the contractual relationship. The defendant can refute the charge if it can be shown that the interference was justified or permissible. For example, aggressive marketing and advertising strategies may entice customers to break contracts with competitors but are not unlawful.

In a significant case involving a tortious interference complaint, the Cincinnati Bengals sued Bill Bergey (*Cincinnati Bengals v. William Bergey, et al.*, 1974), their premier linebacker, the Virginia Ambassadors, and the other eleven teams of the newly formed World Football League (WFL). At the heart of this complaint was the claim that the WFL defendants were inducing a breach of contract by Bergey and, unless enjoined, would do the same with other key Bengals players. While under contract with the Bengals, Bergey had negotiated and signed a contract with the Virginia team for his future services. His new contract was to begin when his existing Bengals contract expired. The Bengals felt that his signing of a contract with a different team while under contract with the Bengals would cause him not to perform his current contractual duties with them. The court denied an injunction, primarily because the Bengals failed to show how the negotiations and the subsequent contract signing interfered with the performance of his existing contract.

The case of *Central Sports Army Club v. Arena Association, Inc.* (1997) serves to illustrate another tortious interference cause of action and is instructive in the pertinent elements of a tortious interference situation. (See the Supplemental Web Site.) The central issue in this case was a contract dispute between the Central Sports Army Club (CSKA), a Russian hockey club, and the Detroit Vipers of the International Hockey League (IHL). A 17-year-old Russian hockey player named Sergei Samsonov had originally entered into a one-year contract for the 1996–97 season with CSKA. For several reasons, including not being paid the promised compensation, he decided before the season began to play elsewhere. He retained an agent of Arena Associates, who began to make arrangements for him to play in the United States. This sport agent was working under the assumption that Samsonov did not have a valid contract with CSKA because he was only 17 when he signed the contract, his father had not signed the contract, and CSKA had failed to fulfill the terms of the contract.

Through his agency (Arena Associates), Samsonov's agent was able to obtain a visa and a 1996–97 player contract with the Detroit Vipers hockey team of the IHL. At the time of his signing the new 1996–97 season contract, the owner of the Vipers believed that Samsonov was under no obligation to play for the CSKA. When Samsonov began playing, CSKA filed a lawsuit in the United States claiming among other things that the Detroit Vipers and Samsonov's agents tortiously interfered with their contract with Samsonov. The first and the most pivotal issue in this tortious interference with contract case was whether or not a valid contract existed. Both Russian Civil Code as well as New York and Michigan laws allow a minor to void a contract unless he obtained express written consent of parents. Because Samsonov had signed his first contract when he was a minor and had not obtained his parents' permission, the court ruled that the CSKA contract was not valid. Additionally, even if a valid contract had existed, the plaintiffs failed to show the three necessary elements for tortious interference with contract: (1) that the defendants were aware of the contract between the CSKA and Samsonov, (2) that there had been inducement by the defendants, and (3) that the defendants had improper motive (*Central Sports Army Club v. Arena Association, Inc.*, 1997, p. 190).

INTENTIONAL INFLICTION OF EMOTIONAL DISTRESS

Intentional infliction of emotional distress (IIED) is a relatively recent tort claim for intentional conduct that results in extreme emotional distress (also called mental distress) (Clarkson, Miller, Jentz, & Cross, 2004) and is meant to protect a person's emotional tranquility (Wong, 2011). Although seldom successful due to its rigorous criteria, it has become a fairly common complaint in sport and recreation tort-related lawsuits. In some jurisdictions it is referred to as the tort of "outrage" due to its standard that requires the conduct in question be such that it would cause a reasonable person to respond with outrage (Huffaker, 2001).

Elements of Intentional Infliction of Emotional Distress

In order to prove a claim of IIED, the plaintiff must demonstrate that: (1) the defendant acted *intentionally* or with *reckless* disregard of the probability of causing emotional distress, (2) the defendant's action must have been *extreme* and *outrageous*, and (3) the action must have caused *severe* emotional distress. It should be noted that mere insults, indignities, threats, annoyances, petty oppressions, or other trivialities would not sustain an IIED claim. The conduct in question has to be so *extreme* and *outrageous* "as to go beyond all possible bonds of decency, and to be regarded as atrocious, and utterly intolerable in a civilized community" (Prosser, 1964, pp. 46-47; Rest. 2d Torts, 46). Whether or not the conduct is illegal does not determine whether it meets this standard. Additionally, "The emotional distress must in fact exist, and it must be severe" (Prosser, p. 51; Rest. 2d Torts, 46).

Measuring severe distress poses a problem. Many jurisdictions require that the emotional distress manifest itself in some physical symptom or illness or some documented emotional disturbance. (See this chapter's significant case to examine exactly how the courts apply these criteria.)

Claims of IIED have arisen frequently and in a wide variety of situations in sport and recreation. These claims have included circumstances such as forcing an athlete to do "bear crawls" on hot asphalt for being late to practice (*Gorthy v. Clovis Unified Sch. Dist., 2006*); a swimmer being forced to sit on a hot deck chair (*Kelly v. N. Highlands Recreation & Park Dist., 2006*); failure of an official to inform players in a timely manner of their next game thus causing them to be eliminated from a tournament (*Warren v. United States Specialty Sports Ass'n, 2006*); a high school athlete who was distressed because he failed to make the varsity baseball team (*Cronk v. Suffern Senior High School, 2005*); a Pop Warner football coach who uttered insulting and humiliating remarks to a young player (*PPA v. The Pop Warner Football Team of Shelton, Inc., 2010*); and a mother who embarked on an e-mail campaign against a teacher in which she repeatedly referred to the teacher as a "pedophile" and alleged that the teacher had "abused" her daughter. (See the significant case, *Bojko v. Lima, 2009*.)

For various reasons, the *Bojko* case was the only case of the above-mentioned IIED lawsuits that was successful (the *Pop Warner* case is pending). As mentioned earlier, IIED cases are rarely successful due to the stringent requirements needed to prove *extreme* or *outrageous* conduct and *severe* emotional stress. *Chuy v. Philadelphia Eagles Football Club* (1979), is an oft-cited case that is exemplary in how to satisfy the high standards needed to succeed in an IIED claim. Don Chuy, an Eagles lineman, was subjected to severe emotional distress because a team doctor erroneously reported to the news media that he had a life threatening disease. When Chuy, who had no previous knowledge of the existence of the condition, heard of the statement he reportedly "panicked and his mind just snapped." In court, he was able to show that during a six-month period in which he had anticipated his death, he suffered extreme emotional anguish and torment, he became a mental wreck, lost his marriage, and suffered serious emotional stress. The court held that the doctor's conduct was sufficiently outrageous and stated:

> If you intentionally make a statement the material and probable consequences of which it will be known to the person and cause him or her emotional distress and if the making of that statement is shocking and outrageous and exceeds the bounds of decency with respect to its natural and probable impact, then a case of intentional infliction of emotional distress is made out. (*Chuy v. Philadelphia Eagles Football Club,* 1979, p. 10)

Wong (2011), in referring to the above case, recommended that sport and recreation personnel be very cautious when they are making statements to the media about a participant's playing ability, a coach's employment tenure, or an athlete's injury status.

Negligent Infliction of Emotional Distress

Although *not* an intentional tort, a cause of action that is closely aligned with *IIED* is *negligent infliction of emotional distress*. The obvious difference between the two is that IIED is caused by an intentional act which the defendant knew or should have known would cause severe emotional distress; whereas, NIED is the result of an act that negligently (unintentionally) causes severe emotional distress and resultant damage. In NIED, the plaintiff is relieved of the burden of proving that the defendant intended to cause severe emotional distress.

The requirements for proving NIED vary significantly from state to state, but the requirements typically parallel the four elements necessary to prove negligence (see Chapter 2.11 *Negligence*). To establish a claim for NIED in most states, the plaintiff must demonstrate that: (1) the defendant owed a duty to the plaintiff not to create a foreseeable risk of inflicting emotional distress; it may be a general duty or one created by statute; (2) the defendant breached that duty by engaging in behavior that the defendant should have realized involved an unreasonable risk of causing emotional distress that might result in illness or bodily injury; (3) the plaintiff suffered injury in the form of extreme emotional distress; and (4) the breach of the duty was the proximate cause of the injury (Clinton & McKain, 2005). If these elements can be sustained then NIED has been proven.

In *Turner v. Mandalay Sports Entm't*, LLC (2008), a fan was struck in the face by a foul ball while sitting in an unprotected area near a concession stand. She sued the team for negligence and NIED. The plaintiff was aware of stadium warnings regarding foul balls and that the team was not responsible for resultant injuries. The Supreme Court of Nevada determined that the woman's negligence claim failed to survive summary judgment under the limited duty rule (see Chapter 2.31 *Premises Liability* for a description of the limited duty rule). Because she could not establish that there was a breached duty of care, she was not able to establish her NIED claim either.

SIGNIFICANT CASE

This recent case provides an example of "extreme and outrageous" conduct that resulted in a rare, successful IIED claim by the plaintiff. The case also provides insight into a successful "false light" invasion of privacy claim. Careful reading of the application of the criteria provides bountiful insight into how the courts evaluate both of these intentional torts.

MARY ANNE BOJKO V. LAURIE A. LIMA

Superior Court of Connecticut, Judicial District of Hartford at Hartford
2009 Conn. Super. LEXIS 1359
May 12, 2009, Decided
May 12, 2009, Filed

Overview

The teacher taught and coached swimming at a high school. The student at issue was a swimmer on the team. The student's mother was complimentary of the teacher's performance as a coach until she sent the teacher an e-mail in which she suggested that the teacher obtain some money to pay for a banquet for the swimming team. The teacher did not agree to that request. The mother than embarked on an e-mail campaign against the teacher in which she claimed that the teacher had "abused" her daughter and repeatedly used the term "pedophile." The court held the teacher proved her claim for libel per se as accusing anyone who worked with children of being a pedophile was certainly defamatory on its face. The mother's conduct was extreme and outrageous and caused the teacher severe emotional distress. The mother clearly acted with malice and with an intent to harm the teacher. Moreover, the mother admittedly enjoyed the fact that the false allegations caused distress to the teacher. The court found that the filing of the counterclaim caused the teacher to suffer emotional distress in addition to that caused by the e-mails. Thus, it trebled an award of $ 2,500 for the vexatious suit claim.

Opinion

In this action the plaintiff, Mary Anne Bojko, seeks money damages, punitive damages and injunctive relief against the defendant, Laurie A. Lima, for libel, libel per se, intentional infliction of emotional distress, tortious interference with business relationship, invasion of privacy and vexatious suit. After a trial the court finds the following facts.

The plaintiff comes from a family of teachers and school administrators. She was a high school and college swimmer, softball, and basketball player who graduated from Penny High School in East Hartford in 1983 and from Southern Connecticut State University in 1987. She obtained a Masters degree in Health Education and commenced her teaching career in 1988.

The plaintiff taught and coached at East Hartford High School from 1988 through 1999, and then left and taught in the Windsor school system from 1999 through 2006 when she returned to East Hartford High School where she taught and coached. She coached swimming in 2006. Hope Lima, the daughter of the defendant, was a swimmer on the team. The defendant was by her own admission very involved in the academic lives of her two daughters. Several times, the plaintiff was surprised to find the defendant in the girl's locker room. The defendant was generally pleased with the plaintiff's performance as a coach in 2006.

The plaintiff again coached the swim team in 2007. The defendant was complimentary of the plaintiff's performance as a coach until the end of the season. On October 26, 2007 the defendant sent the plaintiff an e-mail in which she complimented her as a coach and suggested that the plaintiff obtain some money to pay for a banquet for the swimming team. In the memo the defendant acknowledged that she understood that the school had not paid for the banquet in the past.

The plaintiff did not agree to support the defendant's wish that the school should pay for the swimming banquet because East Hartford High School had a policy of providing an all-sports dinner at the end of the athletic season. If a team wanted its own separate banquet, the school left it to the students or their parents to pay for it. The defendant was clearly aware of this policy. Most parents would have accepted the school's policy and the plaintiff's response as reasonable. But the defendant did not. Instead, she sent e-mails to the school's athletic director and principal. When they would not support her position vis-a-vis the banquet, she lashed out at the plaintiff in an e-mail dated November 1, 2007 to the school principal, Matthew Ryan:

> As this is unfolding to me, Bojko told the swimmers more than a few days ago there was to be no banquet, when I explored the reasoning behind this . . .
>
> Bojko has a policy of confidentiality with her swimmers concerning what is swim team business . . . so this woman encouraged our girls to withhold information directly concerning our children from us (their parents)
>
> When an adult ask a minor to keep a secret that is . . . I don't even know what to call it, one step away from a pedifile (sic).
>
> This woman needs to be removed from her position, she is dangerous.
>
> Do what you will, this is my papertrail.
>
> Laurie Lima.

The defendant admitted that she realized that the allegation that the plaintiff was a pedophile was sensitive, so she sent the e-mail only to Mr. Ryan. However, when Mr. Ryan did not respond to her, she published the e-mail "all over the world," to the plaintiffs' fellow teachers and administrators, politicians, including the Mayor of East Hartford, the Attorney General, the Governor of Connecticut and even to students. Thereafter, the defendant embarked on an absolutely unbelievable e-mail campaign against the plaintiff in which she claimed that the plaintiff had "abused" her daughter, repeatedly used

the term "pedophile," demanded that the plaintiff be fired from her coaching position, alleged that the plaintiff was "dangerous" to children, demanded a background check on the plaintiff, demanded an investigation by the State Board of Education and an investigation by the Department of Children and Families.

The defendant's character assassination of the plaintiff was extended to anyone either directly or remotely connected with the plaintiff. This compounded the plaintiff's embarrassment and emotional distress.

The plaintiff hired an attorney, Christopher Stone, to represent her. Mr. Stone demanded a retraction from the defendant. Notwithstanding that the defendant admitted that she had no basis for her claim that the plaintiff was a pedophile, the defendant refused to publish any retraction. Instead, she sent more e-mails in which she linked the plaintiff and the term "pedophile."

One such e-mail was to the Superintendent of Schools, Marion Martinez, amongst other recipients, and stated:

> Subject: I want a copy of the back ground check you did on the former girls swim coach Ms Bojko, In the interest of time, I will pick it up or you can hand deliver it.
>
> You know the swim team facility
>
> The attire is a bathing suit
>
> where the lockers are that my daughter had to undress to put on her bathing suit the place where any female can come and go at will
>
> where the showers are
>
> where my daughters self esteem was beat to a pulp
>
> I asked you for this many months ago Mr. Ryan and you ignored me are you people actually believing I had no right to ask for this.
>
> This is my third request for the background check on this coach.

The defendant admitted that she had never had any evidence that the plaintiff was a pedofile. And while the defendant claimed the plaintiff "emotionally" abused her daughter, neither of the defendant's daughters testified. There was some evidence that her daughters did not agree with their mother's characterizations. In an e-mail to Principal Ryan the defendant's daughter, Rachel, stated:

> I don't want to bother you like my mother does, but I wanted to talk to you because I know you've received emails from her to Mrs. Rell, and theyre about you. I wanted to tell you that I never said that to my mom, because I know you never said

those things to me. I told my mom that she may have misunderstood me (or else she just likes to lie for the hell of it).

In addition to refusing to retract her admittedly baseless e-mails about the plaintiff on December 17, 2007, the defendant also filed a counterclaim against the plaintiff for $ 500,000. During the prejudgment remedy hearing before this court, McWeeny, J., the defendant admitted that she filed the counterclaim only to try to intimidate the plaintiff into withdrawing her action against the defendant and verbally withdrew the counterclaim.

The court finds that there was absolutely no evidence that the plaintiff abused the defendant's children or any other child. Furthermore, there was no evidence that the plaintiff engaged in any improper conduct whatsoever. All the negative allegations in the e-mails were prompted by the defendant's predilection to "lie for the hell of it." These e-mails were sent for the sole purpose of inflicting emotional distress and harm to the plaintiff professionally and personally. Laurie Lima's e-mail attacks on Mary Anne Bojko were singularly malicious, outrageous and evil.

The defendant's numerous e-mails calling for background checks, and investigations into the plaintiff's history with other school systems, and making unsubstantiated claims of child abuse had a negative impact on the plaintiff's emotional and physical well being. The plaintiff loved her job as a teacher and a coach, but the defendant's malicious e-mail tirade literally took the joy out of teaching and coaching for the plaintiff. The plaintiff saw a counselor and required medication for her loss of sleep, anxiety and weight loss caused by the defendant's crusade against her. The plaintiff's bills from the counselor, Dr. Joan Gleason, totaled $ 874. The plaintiff was so distraught over the defendant's baseless, malicious accusations that she also took a leave of absence from teaching.

The plaintiff had intended to continue to coach swimming, but the defendant's conduct caused the plaintiff to resign as coach of the swimming team after the 2007 season. It is reasonable to assume that the plaintiff would have continued to coach swimming for at least 5 years. She earned an extra $ 4,400 per year for coaching. Ms. Lima's conduct caused the plaintiff to lose $ 22,000.

***

In the Third Count the plaintiff alleges **intentional infliction of emotional distress**. [HN4] To establish a claim of intentional infliction of emotional distress, the plaintiff must plead and prove the following four elements: "(1) that the [defendant] intended to inflict emotional distress or that he knew or should have known that emotional distress was the likely result of his conduct; (2) **that the conduct was extreme and outrageous**; (3) that the defendant's conduct was the cause of the plaintiff's distress; and (4) that the emotional distress sustained by the plaintiff was severe." (Internal quotation marks omitted.) *Tracy v. New Milford Public Schools*, 101 Conn. App. 560, 568, 922 A.2d 280, cert. denied, 284 Conn. 910, 931 A.2d 935 (2007).

The evidence shows that the defendant found it "enjoyable" and "hysterical" to send defamatory e-mails

to as many people as possible. She clearly engaged in such conduct to inflict emotional distress on the plaintiff, her conduct was extreme and outrageous and it did cause the plaintiff severe emotional distress. The court finds in favor of the plaintiff, Mary Anne Bojko, against the defendant, Laurie Lima, on the Third Count.

***

In the Fifth Count the plaintiff alleges an invasion of privacy by false light. [HN6] The existence of a cause of action for invasion of privacy has been recognized by the Connecticut Supreme Court. *Venturi v. Savitt, Inc.*, 191 Conn. 588, 591, 468 A.2d 933 (1983); *Goodrich v. Waterbury Republican-American, Inc.*, 188 Conn. 107, 127, 448 A.2d 1317 (1982). In recognizing this cause of action, the Supreme Court adopted the definition and categories of invasion of privacy as set forth in 3 Restatement (Second), Torts 652A: (a) unreasonable intrusion upon the seclusion of another; (b) appropriation of the other's name or likeness; (c) unreasonable publicity given to the other's private life; or (d) publicity that places the other in a false light before the public. *Goodrich v. Waterbury Republican-American, Inc., supra*, 128; see *Venturi v. Savitt, Inc., supra*.

[HN7] In order to establish invasion of privacy by false light, the plaintiff must show "(a) the false light in which the other was placed would be highly offensive to a reasonable person, and (b) the actor had knowledge of or acted in reckless disregard as to the falsity of the publicized matter and the false light in which the other would be placed." 3 Restatement (Second), Torts 652E; see *Goodrich v. Waterbury Republican American, Inc., supra*. The essence of a false light privacy claim is that the matter published concerning the plaintiff (1) is not true; and (2) is such a 'major misrepresentation of his character, history, activities or beliefs that serious offense may reasonably be expected to be taken by a reasonable man in his position.' *Id.*, comment c." *Goodrich v. Waterbury Republican-American, Inc., supra*, 131.

Mary Anne Bojko has proved that the statements made by Laurie Lima that the plaintiff was a pedophile and abused children were untrue and were such a major misrepresentation of Ms. Bojko's character the it was reasonable to expect Ms. Bojko to take serious offense at such statements. The court finds in favor of the plaintiff, Mary Anne Bojko, against the defendant, Laurie Lima, on the Fifth Count.

***

The court awards the plaintiff $ 22,874 for her economic damages. That amount is comprised of her loss of coaching income and her therapist bills. The court further awards the plaintiff damages of $ 25,000 for the emotional distress caused by the defendant's conduct.

***

Judgment is hereby entered in favor of the plaintiff, Mary Anne Bojko, against the defendant, Laurie] Lima, in the total amount of $ 88,374.

By the court,
Aurigemma, J.

CASES ON THE SUPPLEMENTAL WEB SITE

Montana v. San Jose Mercury News (1995 Cal. App. LEXIS 411). Examine the section dealing with *The Posters Reported on Newsworthy Events* and *A Newspaper Has a Constitutional Right to Promote Itself by Reproducing Its News Stories* as the central reasons used to justify appropriation of Montana's image.

Detroit Lions v. Argovitz (1985 U.S. App. LEXIS 14360). Please note that at the core of this Breach of Fiduciary Duty case is the defendant's personal interest in Sims contracting with the Gamblers; conflicting with his fiduciary duty to advance Sims' best interests.

Central Sports Army Club v. Detroit Vipers (1997 U.S. Dist. LEXIS 615). Please note the *No Inducement* and *No awareness of contractual obligations* explanations of

the case. These are key to a "contractual" interference case

Doe v. TCI Cablevision, 110 S.W.3d 363 (Mo.2003). Please note the discussion in the "Head-notes" that addresses the difference between Invasion of Privacy: *Appropriation (right of privacy)* and the *Right of Publicity.* This section provides clarification as to the differences between the two.

Spahn v. Messner, (1964 N.Y. Misc. LEXIS 1711). This is an oft-cited case that illustrates the elements of false light invasion of privacy.

Cases from Other Chapters

See cases related to Right to Publicity in Chapter 7.23 *Image Rights.*

QUESTIONS YOU SHOULD BE ABLE TO ANSWER

1. Compare and contrast defamation with false light invasion of privacy.

2. The four theories of invasion of privacy have one common theme. Name and briefly explain this theme.

3. List and briefly explain the elements necessary to support a claim of *Breach of Fiduciary Duty.*

4. List and briefly explain the necessary elements required to sustain a claim of *Tortious Interference with Contract.*

5. What is the "tort of outrage" and what is the reason for this designation?

REFERENCES
Cases
Bilney v. Evening Star Newspaper Co., 43 Md. App. 560; 406 A.2d. 652 (Md. App. 1979).
Bojko v. Lima, 2009 Conn. Super. LEXIS 1359
Central Sports Army Club v. Arena Association, Inc., 952 F. Supp. 181 (S.D.N.Y. 1997).
Chuy v. Philadelphia Eagles Football Club, U.S. App. LEXIS 16338 (1979).
Cincinnati Bengals v. William Bergey, et al., 453 F. Supp. 129 (1974).
Cronk v. Suffern Senior High School, 2005 N.Y. Misc. LEXIS 2820 (2005).
Davis v. Baylor University, 976 S.W.2d 5 (Mo. App. 1998).
Detroit Lions, Inc. v. Jerry Argovitz, 580 F. Supp. 542 (1984).
Doe v. TCI Cablevision, 110 S.W.3d 363 (Mo.2003)
Dominion Sports Servs. Inc. v. Bredehoft, 2006 Minn. LEXIS 132 (Minn., Mar. 14, 2006).
Don King Productions v. James "Buster" Douglas, et al., 735 F. Supp. 522 (1990).
Gorthy v. Clovis Unified Sch. District, 2006 WL 236939 (E.D. Cal. 2006).
Holt v. Cox Enterprises, 590 F. Supp. 408 (N.D. Ga. 1984).
Kelly v. N. Highlands Recreation & Park Dist., 2006 U.S. Dist. LEXIS 39785 (E.D. Cal. 2006).
Montana v. San Jose Mercury News, Inc., 34 Cal. App.4th 790 (1995).
Namath v. Sports Illustrated, 48 A.D.2d 487; 371 N.Y.S.2d 10 (1975).
Palmer v. Schonhorn Enterprises, Inc., 323 A.2d 458 (1967).
PPA v. The Pop Warner Football Team of Shelton, Inc. 2010 Conn. Super. LEXIS 3122 (2010)

Rosenbloom v. Metromedia, Inc., 403 U.S. 29; 29 L.Ed.2d 296 (1971).
Spahn v. Messner, Inc., 18 N.Y.2d 324; 274 N.Y.S.2d 877; 221 N.E.2d 543; *vacated* 387 U.S. 239; 18 L.Ed.2d 744 (1967).
St. Louis Convention & Visitors Commission v. National Football League, 154 F.3d 851 (8th Cir. 1998).
Time, Inc. v. Hill, 385 U.S. 374 (1967).
Turner v. Mandalay Sports Entm't, LLC, 180 P.3d 1172 (Nevada 2008).
Warren v. United States Specialty Sports Ass'n., Ok Civ. App 78 (Okla. Civ. App. 2006).
Wilson v. Daily Gazette Co., 588 S.E.2d 200 (2003)..

Publications

Berkman Center for Internet & Society at Harvard University. (2012). Retrieved February 9, 2012 from http://www.citmedialaw.org/legal-guide/using-name-or-likeness-another

Berry, R. C., & Wong, G. M. (1993). *Law and business of the sports industries* (2nd ed.). Westport, CT: Praeger Publishers.

Black, H. C. (1979). *Black's law dictionary* (5th ed.). St. Paul, MN: West Publishing Co.

Breaux, P. (2005). *Introduction to sports law and business.* Reno, NV: Bent Tree Press.

Bussian, J. A., & Levine, P. J. *Invasion of Privacy and the Media: The Right "To Be Let Alone".* (2005). Retrieved February 9, 2012 from http://www.floridabar.org/ .

Byrd, L. L. (1988). Privacy rights of entertainers and other celebrities: A need for change. *Entertainment and Sports Law Reporter, 5*(95), 95–116.

Carper, D. L., McKinsey, J. A., & West, B. W. (2008) *Understanding the law* (5th ed.). Mason, OH. Thompson Higher Education.

Clarkson, K. W., Miller, R. L., Jentz, G. A., & Cross, F. B. (2004). *West's business law* (9th ed.). Mason, OH: West Legal Studies in Business. Thompson Learning.

Clinton, M., & McKain, B. (2005). *Intentional infliction of emotional distress. Retrieved* March 23, 2009. from http://www.lawguys.com/Negligent_Infliction_of_Emotional_Distress.htm

Couch, B. (2000). How agent competition and corruption affects sports and the athlete-agent relationship and what can be done to control it. *Seton Hall Journal of Sports, 10,* L 111.

Cozzillio, M. J., Levinstein, M. S., Dimino, M. R., & Feldman, G. (2007). *Sports law: Cases and materials.* Durham, NC: Carolina Academic Press.

Cross, F. B., & Miller, R. L. (2009). *West's legal environment of business.* (7th Ed.). Mason, OH: South-Western Cengage Learning.

Davis, T. (2006). Regulating the athlete-agent industry: Intended and unintended consequences. *Willamette L. Rev. 42,* 781–791.

Deem, J. (2006). Student work: Freedom of the press: Classifying school athletes under the Gertz Public Figure Doctrine. *West Virginia Law Review, 108,* 799–839.

Dill, B. (1986). The journalist's handbook on libel and privacy. New York: The Free Press.

Ehrhardt, C. W., & Rodgers, J. M. (1988). Tightening the defense against offensive sports agents. *Florida State University Law Review, 16,* 634–674.

Epstein, A. (2002). Sports Law. Clifton Park, NY: Delmar Learning: West Legal Studies.

Franklin, M. A., Cardi, W. J., & Green, M. D. (2008) *Torts.* (24th Ed.). Chicago, IL: Thomson/West.

Gleason, J. P. (2008) .Comment: From Russian with love :The legal repercussion of the recruitment and contracting of foreign players in the National Hockey League. *Buffalo Law Review,* 599–654.

Gray, J. (2006). Sports agent's liability after Sparta?. *Va. Sports & Ent. L. J.* 6, 141–162.

Huffaker, M. L. (2001). Recovery for infliction of emotional distress: A comment on the mental anguish accompanying such a claim in Alabama. *Alabama Law Review, 52* ,1003–1043.

Keeton, W. P., Dobbs, D. B., Keeton, R. E., Prosser, W. L., & Owen, D. G. (1984). *Prosser and Keeton on torts* (5th ed.). St. Paul, MN: West Publishing Co.

Long J. G. (2009). High Standards for High School Athletes: Defamation Law and Tomorrow's Stars. *Sports Law. Journal,* 16, 255-275.

Powers, A. (1994). The need to regulate sports agents. *Seton Hall Journal of Sport Law, 4,* 253–274.

Prosser, W. L. (1960). Privacy. *Cal. L. Rev., 48,* 383–398.

Prosser, W. L. (1964). *Handbook of the law of torts.* (3rd ed.). St. Paul, MN: West Publishing Co.

Ramsey, K. (2002, September 4). *Student records open to government.* University Daily Kansan.

Samar, V. J. (1991). *The right to privacy.* Philadelphia: Temple University Press.

Schubert, G., Smith, R. K., & Trentadue, J. C. (1986). *Sports law.* St. Paul, MN: West Publishing Co.

Smolla, R. A (1999). Symposium on: Privacy and the law: The media's intrusion on privacy: Privacy and the first amendment right to gather news. *Geo. Wash. L. Rev., 67,* 1097.

Sobel, S. (1987). The regulation of sports agents: An analytical primer. *Baylor Law Review, 39,* 705–709.

Stapleton, L. L., & McMurphy, M. (1999). The professional athlete's right of publicity. *Marquette Sports Law Journal, 10,* 23–68.

Thornton, P. K. (2010). *Sports law.* Sudbury, MA. Jones and Barlett Publishers, LLC.

Warren, S., & Brandeis, L. (1890). The right to privacy. *Harvard Law Review, 4,* 193.

Weistart, J. C., & Lowell, C. H. (1979). *Law and sports.* Charlottesville, VA: Michie/Bobbs Co.

Wong, G. (2011). *Essentials of sports law.* Denver, Co.: Praeger Publishers.

Woods, R. P., & Mills, M. R. (1988). Tortious interference with an athletic scholarship: A university remedy for the unscrupulous sports agent. *Alabama Law Review*, *40*, 141–180.

Wriggins, J. B. (2010). Constitution day lecture: Constitutional law and tort law: Injury, race, gender, and equal protection. *Maine Law Review. 63, 263–272.*

Yasser, R., McCurdy, J. R., Goplerud, C. P., & Weston, M. A. (2011). *Sport law*: Cases and materials. San Francisco, CA. Matthew/Bender. LexisNexis.

Legislation

Restatement (Third) of the Law of Unfair Competition (1995).

Restatement of Torts, Second, Torts 8A (1965).

Restatement of Torts, Second § 46, com. d

Restatement (Second) of Torts #874, 1984

SPORT-RELATED CRIMES
3.21 CRIMINAL LAW AND SPORT

3.20

Kristi L. Schoepfer Bochicchio | Winthrop University

The intersection of criminal law and sport has increased in recent years. While many lawsuits involving sport and recreation managers and participants are filed in civil courts (see Chapter 2.13, *Liability of Sports Participants, Sports Instructors, and Sports Officials*), sport and recreation managers must be aware of the evolving criminal law landscape. In recent years, many more athletes, coaches, and recreation participants have been charged criminally for acts occurring during an athletic event; in fact, some scholars claim sport violence, and subsequently sport crime, is an "epidemic plaguing our nation" (Harary, 2002). Further, crimes such as hazing, point shaving, and ticket scalping continue to impact sport and recreation managers. While all professionals in the sport and recreation industry hope to avoid sport or recreation related crime, the recent trends mandate that managers have the requisite knowledge to prevent or respond to such a circumstance.

FUNDAMENTAL CONCEPTS

Criminal Law Origins

Federal, state, and local legislative bodies deem certain conduct criminal, meaning the conduct is punishable by fines or imprisonment, or both. **Criminal statutes** define criminal conduct and dictate possible punishments; the statutes are written by legislatures in each jurisdiction to control conduct that is deemed harmful to citizens or to the government. All 50 states and the federal government have criminal statutes, but no jurisdiction is bound by a different jurisdiction's statute or interpretation (Kaplan, et. al., 1996). In virtually all states, criminal law is statutory in origin, meaning that "conduct is not criminally punishable unless it has been proscribed by statute" (Kaplan, et. al., 1996).

Aside from statutory origin, there are other important considerations regarding criminal law. Before criminal law can be considered as it impacts sport and recreation, additional foundations of criminal law must be established. Two of these of specific importance are the distinction between civil law and criminal law and the elements of a crime.

Criminal Law v. Civil Law

The American legal system allows for both civil law cases and criminal law cases; however, the two are quite different. In **civil law**, the plaintiff files a lawsuit against the defendant on his or her own behalf seeking monetary damages, or specific performance, to remedy or compensate for an incurred loss. However, in **criminal law**, the plaintiff is a government representative prosecuting an offense against the state; the victim does not prosecute his or her own case. Although the victim is the person or organization that incurred the harm, criminal law mandates that the government prosecute on behalf of the victim, because all crimes are considered crimes against society. Also distinguishable is the standard of proof required to succeed with the lawsuit (see Chapter 1.10, *The Legal System*). In a civil case, a plaintiff only needs to prove a "**preponderance of the evidence**" to support his or her claim; however, in a criminal case, the government (plaintiff) must prove that the defendant is guilty of the crime "**beyond a reasonable doubt**." The criminal law standard presents a more significant burden; this heightened standard exists because criminal punishments are more severe, and government is "far more willing to tolerate erroneous acquittal than erroneous convictions" (Kaplan, et. al., 1996). Lastly, civil cases are often adjudicated by only a judge, whereas in criminal law, trial by jury is much more common.

Elements of a Crime

For each alleged crime that is committed, the state must prove two things; *actus reus* and *mens rea*. *Actus reus* (guilty act) requires proof that the defendant committed an act in violation of a state or federal statute. An act is defined as "an outward manifestation of behavior or bodily movement, caused by a person's own will and volition" (Model Penal Code § 2.01). ***Mens rea*** (guilty mind) requires proof that the defendant had the intent to commit the act. Intent is defined as committing the act "purposely, knowingly, recklessly or negligently, as the law may require, with respect to each material element of the offense" (Model Penal Code, § 2.02). These required elements are essential in criminal law; determining what the defendant was thinking when the crime was committed, as well as what the defendant intended, will impact the outcome of any criminal case. Also, note that the Model Penal Code provides the standard definitions; however, each state jurisdiction has its own interpretation. Specific state criminal statutes are influenced by the Model Penal Code, but most states include their own variations of these required elements.

Classifications of Crime

Crimes are most often thought of as harmful acts against individuals; however, criminal acts have a much broader scope. Some crimes that are committed are not against a person, but rather against the best interest of society, or the government itself. To best identify the varying crimes that are possible in recreation and sport, crime should be classified as (1) Crimes against Persons; (2) Crimes against Public Welfare; and (3) Crimes against Government (Epstein, 2009).

Crimes Against Persons

This classification is appropriate when the victim is an individual person (or persons). Crimes against persons are most likely to be prosecuted because these crimes typically receive the most investigative resources and perpetrators are often easy to identify (Kaplan, et. al 1996). Athletes, coaches and recreation participants may all potentially commit a crime against a person during an athletic contest; specifically, these crimes may include assault and/or battery, criminal negligence, reckless endangerment or homicide, and hazing.[1]

Assault and Battery

As discussed in Chapter 3.11 *Assault and Battery*, assault and/or battery that occurs as part of an athletic contest is most often remedied in civil courts. Historically, individuals have not been accused of criminal liability for imposing injuries during athletic contests; however, there is a growing trend to prosecute these acts as crimes in many jurisdictions.

Assault is defined as "the threat or use of force on another that causes that person to have a reasonable apprehension of imminent harmful or offensive contact; the act of putting another person in reasonable fear or apprehension of an immediate battery by means of an act amounting to an attempt or threat to commit a battery (Black's, 2009). Further, the Model Penal Code distinguishes between two types of assault: simple assault and aggravated assault; the later involving a more severe degree of harm (Model Penal Code § 211.1). Also, although assault and battery are often thought of as one act, they are in fact two distinguishable crimes. **Battery** is defined as "the use of force against another, resulting in harmful or offensive contact" (Black's, 2009). Most important to note is that each state jurisdiction has its own statute, and specific statutory definitions do vary from state to state.

Criminal Negligence, Recklessness, or Homicide

As discussed in Chapter 2.11, *Negligence*, an individual's conduct can deviate from the reasonable person standard to varying degrees. When conduct is so unreasonable that it transcends the standards required for civil liability, an individual may also face liability for criminal negligence or recklessness. C**riminal negligence** or **recklessness** refer to criminal activity in which the defendant did not intend to commit the crime, but was not careful enough with his or her actions to avoid a crime occurring; in other words, the conduct was

---

[1]Criminal activity among sport spectators is also prevalent; however, recreation and sport managers are best served by discussion of criminal law as it applies to athletes, coaches and recreation participants.

so unreasonable that it may be considered criminal. The difference between negligence and recklessness is a matter of degree; recklessness is the higher level of guilt. In 2009, a high school football coach was charged with reckless homicide for the heat-related death of a student athlete at practice. While the coach was also alleged to be liable in civil court, his actions (or omissions) were so unreasonable that he was charged criminally for his behavior (this case will be discussed more completely later in this chapter).

Many jurisdictions use the Model Penal Code as a directive when creating criminal statutes. The Code defines criminal negligence as "acts committed with such a blatant breach of duty that courts can assume the defendant acted with intent to injure" (§ 2.02). Crimes most commonly committed through criminal negligence or recklessness are involuntary manslaughter (conscious disregard of a substantial and unjustifiable risk that would cause death [Model Penal Code § 210.3]; criminally negligent homicide (inadvertent homicide [Model Penal Code, § 210.4]); and reckless endangerment (conscious disregard for a substantial and unjustifiable risk that endangers another [Model Penal Code § 2.02.2c]). However, the exact terminology and language used to identify and define each crime varies from state to state.

Hazing

Hazing encompasses a broad range of behaviors; the definition of hazing varies significantly from state to state. However, in many jurisdictions, activities that require a subordinate person to endure some type of mental or physical threat will be considered **hazing** and classified as a crime. For a full discussion of hazing, including criminal hazing, see Chapter 3.22, *Hazing*.

Likelihood of Occurrence

Athletes/Recreation Participants. There is no shortage of overtly violent acts in sport. Athletes and participants at all levels of sport experience pressure to win; winning at all costs is a common mentality. This mindset often results in violent acts among athletes, resulting from aggressive play. Many of these potential assaults and batteries would certainly be considered criminal if they occurred away from the game; however, when they happen during a sport contest, they are often considered part of the game. Prosecutorial restraint has likely limited the cases involving recreation participants and athletes as defendants. Even so, there is no shortage of case law citing athletes who were charged criminally for an injury they caused while participating in athletics.[2] For example, in *State v. Forbes* (1975), an NHL player was prosecuted for committing aggravated assault with a hockey stick; in *People v. Freer* (1976), a football player was convicted of assault after punching a ball carrier while tackling him; in *State v. Floyd* (1990), the basketball player was convicted of assault after delivering a hard foul. Similarly, in *State of Washington v. Shelley* (1997), Shelley struck another player during a basketball game and broke his jaw in three places. He was convicted of assault in the second degree (see Supplemental Web Site). In 2001, a basketball player in Texas was sentenced to 5 years in prison for aggravated assault with serious bodily injury (see *State v. Limon*, 2000). In *State v. Guidugli* (2004), a collegiate athlete was convicted of assault for punching an opponent in the eye during an intramural basketball game. More recently, a high school wrestler in Minnesota was convicted of fifth-degree assault and adjudicated delinquent for striking an opponent in the face during a high-school wrestling match (*In the Matter of the Welfare of J.S.I.*, 2009, see Supplemental Web Site). Most notable is the 2009 conviction of Sean Sanders, a recreational softball player found guilty of negligent homicide and third degree assault for punching an opposing player in the head after a contentious recreational softball game. As in common in recreational sport, the game was heated and included trash talking and verbal taunts; however, Sanders assaulted the opposing player from behind as the game concluded (Quinlan, 2009). Sanders served two years in prison before being paroled in 2011.

In addition to the case law, other notable violent acts by athletes are reported regularly. For example, in 2012, the NFL declared that the New Orleans Saints were operating a "bounty system" in which defensive players received payments and other bonuses for deliberately injuring opposing offensive players. The NFL investigation determined that violent hits were directed against specific opposing players, and that the amounts received in return were significant. While there can be no automatic conclusion that players who participated

[2]At the time of publication, the 2012 NFL investigation of the New Orleans Saints bounty program was still developing. While criminal charges against players and/or coaches seem plausible, the available information was insufficient to discuss in this section.

in the "bounty program" committed criminal acts, it can be inferred that the players had both the necessary *actus reus* and *mens rea* required for criminal liability.[3]

When athletes and participants are alleged to have committed a crime during the course of play, an automatic assumption of guilt is inappropriate. In most cases, athletes or participants assert consent of the participant as a defense against criminal liability. Multiple variations of the "consent defense" have been argued by defendant athletes and participants; these will be discussed in a subsequent section of this chapter.

Coaches. In recent years, coaches have increasingly been investigated for, or formally accused of, criminal conduct. For example, in 2009, Mike Leach, the former head coach of Texas Tech football, was investigated for mistreatment of a player whom he allegedly isolated in a dark electrical closet after the player refused to practice with a concussion (Johnson, 2009); in 2010, two Middletown, CT, football coaches were charged with reckless endangerment after a student-athlete collapsed while working out on a hot day (Fitzgerald, 2010); in 2011, former Pennsylvania State University assistant football coach Jerry Sandusky was accused of inappropriate sexual relationships with minors (Viera & Becker, 2011); similarly, Bernie Fine, an assistant basketball coach at Syracuse University was investigated for sexual misconduct with minor ball boys in the same year (Schwarz & Berko, 2011).[4] And, in 2012, police launched a criminal investigation against a high school football coach in Pennsylvania for allowing players to return to play despite having concussions (Toporek, 2012).

Similarly, a notable allegation of criminal conduct by a coach resulted from the heatstroke death of a high school football player in Kentucky. As noted above, in 2009, Jason Stinson, former head football coach at Pleasure Ridge High School in Louisville, KY, was charged with reckless homicide and wanton endangerment for the death of Max Gilpin, a lineman on the team. The charges stemmed from a summer practice, on a day with a heat index of 94 degrees, in which players were required to run sprints up and down the field, after already practicing for three hours. The team sprinted 12 times before Gilpin collapsed (he was the second player to collapse), and witnesses reported that Stinson denied the players water breaks. When Gilpin reached the hospital, he was suffering heat stroke with a body temperature of 107 degrees; Gilpin died three days later (McCann, 2009). The prosecutors in the case attempted to show that Stinson committed reckless homicide, which under Kentucky law is defined as the reckless causing of another person's death. Specifically, prosecutors attempted to demonstrate that Stinson: "(1) failed to perceive a substantial and unjustifiable risk of such a nature and degree that his failure constituted gross deviation from a reasonable standard of care; and (2) his failure resulted in Gilpin's death" (McCann, 2009). Regarding the wanton endangerment charge, prosecutors attempted to show that Stinson manifested an extreme indifference to the value of Gilpin's life. After Stinson pleaded not guilty, and a three week jury trial, Stinson was not convicted of either charge;[5] however, this case caused many coaches to re-examine their conduct, especially when it comes to players who are showing signs of fatigue and injury during practice or in a game. The shift from civil negligence to criminal negligence occurs across a fine line; all recreation and sport administrators should be cognizant of their susceptibility to criminal conduct.

Defenses

As noted, the most common defense used in criminal cases by athletes and others in sport and recreation is the consent defense; in other words, that the victim consented to the harm incurred by virtue of participation in the athletic event. While victim consent is not a defense allowed under traditional criminal law applications, the Model Penal Code creates an exception to this rule specifically for sport (Model Penal Code § 2.11.2(b)). Understandably, athletes and recreation participants must consent to some amount of physical contact, and possible harm, especially in contact sports. Some acts that may be perceived as assault or battery in non-sport settings are acceptable in sport given the nature, and expectation, of vigorous play. The line, however, between what acts are consented to and what acts are beyond consent has been vigorously discussed by the courts. The three approaches taken by the courts regarding the consent defense are: (1) Athletes only consent to those acts

---

[3]At the time of publication, no player or coach has been charged criminally for participation in the bounty program.
[4]Sexual misconduct by coaches has received significant recent attention due to the two high profile cases listed. While all administrators and coaches should be aware of criminal statutes regarding sexual misconduct, this chapter will not focus specifically on this area.
[5]The civil lawsuit filed by Max Gilpin's parents against the Jefferson County Public School District was settled for $1.75M.

within a game that are reasonably foreseeable; (2) Athletes can only consent to those acts which are within the rules of the game; and (3) Athletes consent to any act in-connection to the athletic event.

Reasonably Foreseeable. In *State v. Guidugli* (2004), the court noted that the reasonably foreseeable test was most appropriate in determining whether a victim had consented to a harm incurred in an athletic event; victims can only consent to those harms that are reasonably foreseeable. Relying on *People v. Greer* (1976), *State v. Floyd* (1990), and *State of Washington v. Shelley* (1997), the court reasoned that there is a line between physical aggression that is reasonably foreseeable within the context of game play, and violence that takes place "after play has stopped, or is purely retaliatory, or exceeds in brutality or degree of injury anything that the player might have otherwise agreed to." The issue with this test is determining what actions within an athletic contest are reasonably foreseeable. This determination becomes even more challenging when individual sports are considered. Certainly, the amount of harm that is reasonably foreseeable will vary among sports. Take baseball for example; in *Avila v. Citrus Cmty. Coll. Dist.*, (2006), a civil case, the court decided that pitches thrown at a batter's head are part of the game of baseball. Although determined in a civil case, this could be used to substantiate the consent defense for a pitcher accused criminally for harm to a batter. Similar questions could be asked in each sport. As in civil law, determining reasonable foreseeability requires a case-by-case analysis. The same is true when applying the reasonably foreseeable test to the consent defense in criminal law.

Rules of the Game. While limited in application, this test was also discussed in *State of Washington v. Shelley* (1997). The trial court reasoned that the consent defense was unavailable to the defendant because the defendant's conduct exceeded what is permissible within the rules of basketball; the court stated that "consent is to contact that is contemplated within the rules of the game." However, the appellate court rejected this theory, arguing that fouls outside the rules of the game occur in almost all athletic contests; to hold that an athlete can only consent to actions within the rules of any game is far too narrow an application. Specifically, the court stated that in any athletic contest, "it may be ordinary and expected for minor assaults to occur" outside the rules of the game.

In-Connection Standard. A New York court followed a third approach in *People v. Shacker* (1998) (see Supplemental Web Site). In a hockey game, the defendant skated up behind the victim, who was standing near the goal, and struck the victim on the back of the neck with his hand. The victim's head hit the crossbar, causing a concussion and other minor injuries. The court reasoned the victim had consented to all harms "in-connection" with the hockey game; thus the defendant's assault was excused. While the rules of the game test presented an application that was too narrow, the "in-connection" standard presents one that is too broad; by holding that athletes consent to all harm "in-connection" with an athletic contest, the court gives athletes far too much latitude for permissible sport violence (Standen, 2009).

Crimes against Public Health, Safety, and Welfare
Crimes where there is generally no single victim have been categorized as crimes against public health, safety, and welfare.

Point Shaving
Conspiracy to commit sports bribery is a federal crime [18 U.S.C.S § 224 (2012)]. One example of such a conspiracy is point-shaving. In the past 60 years nearly every bribery-related college betting scandal has involved point-shaving (Gustky, 2001; McCarthy, 2007).[6] **Point-shaving** is defined as deliberately limiting the number of points scored by one's team in an athletic contest, in return for a payment from gamblers to ensure winnings. Typically, point shaving is collaboration among athletes and gamblers to commit criminal sports wagering by manipulating the scores of sporting events. Athletes are bribed to manipulate the scores between teams so that the point margin is less than the point spread estimated by odds makers.

Recently, there have been an alarming number of point shaving allegations. In 2009, the University of Toledo was rocked by such a scandal; six former athletes, three football players and three basketball players,

---

[6]Among the most notable scandals are the 1951 point shaving scandal at City College of New York; a 1979 men's basketball point shaving scheme at Boston College [see *U.S. v. Burke, et. al.*, (1983)]; a 1985 scandal at Tulane University; a 1994 scandal at Arizona State University, in which basketball player Stevin Smith served nearly a year in prison for shaving points in four basketball games; and a 1995 scandal at Northwestern University.

were indicted by federal authorities on charges of conspiracy to commit sports bribery (Gilbert & Silka, 2009). Specifically, the players were accused of regularly discussing point spreads with a local gambler, purposefully manipulating the score of games, and receiving a payoff if the gambler won his bet (White, 2011). Three of the players pleaded guilty, receiving prison sentences for the crime; however, the charges for the other three defendants have not been resolved. In 2011, two University of San Diego (USD) basketball players and a USD assistant basketball coach were indicted for conspiracy to commit sports bribery and operating an illegal sports bookmaking service. The indictment alleged that one of the players took a bribe to influence the outcome of a game and solicited an individual to affect the outcome of USD basketball games. The other player and the assistant coach were alleged to have each solicited an individual to affect the outcome of a college basketball game. As of early 2012, the three defendants have all pleaded not guilty and are awaiting trial. Regardless of the outcome, the examples illustrate the importance of educating student athletes about the potential perils of any conspiracy to commit sports bribery.

Sport Agent Crimes

Athlete agents may be found criminally liable under both state and federal law for inappropriate conduct with respect to student athletes. The Sport Agent Responsibility and Trust Act is a federal law that governs the athlete-agent relationship (15 U.S.C. §7801 et seq. (2012); the Uniform Athlete Agent Act is a model law that has been adopted in 40 states (www.ncaa.org, 2012). While these laws are discussed fully in Chapter 7.40, *Sport Agent Legislation*, it is important to note the recent trend of imposing harsh criminal penalties for illegal athlete agent conduct. Specifically, recent legislation in Texas renders agent misconduct a third degree felony, imposing a possible 10-year prison sentence [Tex. Occ. Code §2051.501 (2012)]; similarly, Arkansas also now considers agent misconduct as a felony offense, raising the maximum fine from $50,000 to $250,000 [A.C.A. §17-16-115 (2012)].

Crimes Against Government

Crimes against government include crimes that are in violation of government statutes. These include crimes such as ticket scalping and gambling.

Ticket Scalping

The resale of event tickets for above face value, also called **ticket scalping** or **ticket resale**, is a criminal activity in many jurisdictions; however, in-person resale and private party transactions occur for almost every sporting event. Further, ticket scalping also occurs in the online market. In 2006, websites such as eBay, StubHub, and RazorGator estimated annual ticket sales of approximately $3 billion; 2012 projections show an increase to $4.5 billion (Kirkman, 2009). The growing ticket resale market must be analyzed in two ways: (1) Statutory Regulation; and (2) Relevant Case law.

Statutory Regulation. According to Dodds, et. al., (2012), there is little consistency among the state laws that regulate ticket resale. Some jurisdictions prescribe specific requirements for resale, some jurisdictions prohibit any form of resale, and some jurisdictions have no prohibitions at all. For example, Rhode Island prohibits resale over face value, except for a service charge up to $3 or 10% over its face value (R. I. Gen Law § 5-22-26; 2011); New York allows resale by registered resellers without percentage over face value restrictions, but prohibits resale on the street within 1,500 feet of a venue with a seating capacity of more than 5,000 (N.Y. Arts & Cult. Aff. § 25.08 and § 25.13; 2011); and, Minnesota allows resale generally, but prohibits use of software to circumvent a ticket security or access control measure (Minn. Stat. 245 § 609. 806; 2011). Regardless of the jurisdiction or statute involved, state level regulation presents many challenges. First, many transactions take place using the Internet, and often across state lines; thus, personal jurisdiction and choice of law concerns arise. Second, enforcement of a statute in cyberspace is virtually impossible. For example, if a reseller in Rhode Island were to use Craigslist.com to post tickets for sale at 25% above face value, accept payment online via PayPal, and ship the buyer the tickets, there is no reasonable method to enforce the statute. For this reason, several states, such as Virginia, have recently modified prior prohibitive legislation and currently allow Internet transactions (Va. Code Ann. § 15. 2-969; 2011).

Relevant Case Law. Many parties, including fans, sport organizations, and ticket brokers, have attempted to control the ticket resale through litigation. Specifically, in *Cavoto v. Chicago National Baseball Club* (1993), a class action group of Cubs fans sued the Chicago Cubs (Cubs) after the team created Wrigley Field Premium Ticket Services (Premium). The class action fans alleged that the Cubs sold choice seat locations at face value to Premium, who then sold them at above face value to fans, allowing the Cubs to capitalize on revenues generated by the secondary market. The lawsuit alleged that this practice violated the Illinois anti-scalping statute. The trial court ruled that the statute did not prohibit the Cubs' parent company from establishing a ticket brokerage entity; thus, the Cubs did not violate the statute. On appeal, this decision was affirmed. In *New England Patriots, L.P. v. Stubhub, Inc.,* (2007) roles were reversed, with the sport organization filing the lawsuit against a resale broker. The New England Patriots sued StubHub, seeking access to the names, addresses, and phone numbers of season ticket holders who resold their tickets on StubHub's website. The Patriots alleged that StubHub was encouraging resale in violation of Massachusetts anti-scalping laws. StubHub countered the claim with allegations that the Patriots were trying to monopolize control of the secondary market for Patriot games; however, court held that StubHub needed to release the names to the Patriots (*See* Supplemental Web Site). Lastly, in *Ticketmaster, L.L.C. v. RMG Technologies, Inc.,* (2007), the ticket broker Ticketmaster filed a complaint against RMG Technologies alleging that RMG produced and sold software that allowed users to circumvent Ticketmaster security and quantity access measures, aiding in mass ticket procurement. The court ruled in favor of Ticketmaster on the grounds of copyright infringement and the Digital Millennium Copyright Act, awarding Ticketmaster over $18 million. Interestingly, since this decision, some jurisdictions, such as Minnesota (as noted above), have amended ticket resale statutes to specifically prohibit use of these software applications.

Gambling

Criminal activities related to gambling have the most relevance for a recreation or sport manager when they potentially impact the integrity of the game, as discussed in the section on point shaving and bribery. Further integrity issues may involve student athlete ineligibility for participating in gambling, or other NCAA rule violations relating to gambling within an athletic department. However, other than these unique concerns, gambling is a crime against government that does not have a direct impact on recreation and sport managers. While the federal and state governments have criminal statutes regulating gambling, violation of such statutes by an individual gambler will likely not impact a sport organization.[7]

SIGNIFICANT CASE

The following case is an example of an athlete's attempt to use the consent defense after being charged criminally as the result of violent acts in a recreational basketball game. Of important note is the philosophical discussion the court provides regarding the appropriateness of charging athletes in criminal court for on-court aggression. While the appellate court applies the reasonably foreseeable test, and finds no legal ground on which to overturn the trial court decision, the appellate court clearly states that prosecuting athletes for criminal conduct in connection with a game is a misapplication of criminal law.

STATE V. GUIDUGLI
Court of Appeals of Ohio
157 Ohio App. 3d 383 (2004)

---

[7]Federal laws that serve to regulate gambling include: Wire Communications Act of 1961; Racketeer-Influenced and Corrupt Organizations Act of 1970; Professional and Amateur Sports Protection Act of 1992; and the Unlawful Internet Gambling Enforcement Act of 2006. Additionally, 49 states have laws that criminalize sports gambling.

Gorman, Judge.

Viewed narrowly, this appeal presents a simple question: whether the trial court erred by convicting the defendant-appellant, Gino Guidugli, of misdemeanor assault, in violation of R.C. 2903.13(A), for his role in a scuffle that broke out between members of opposing teams after a hard foul in a closely contested intramural basketball game at the University of Cincinnati. Viewed broadly, this appeal presents a far more complex social issue involving the wisdom of strictly applying the criminal law to physical altercations that arise within the context of sports contests, especially those contests that are already subject to league regulation and internal discipline—and particularly where the bodily injury to the alleged victim is not serious.

Unfortunately, the larger social question is not directly addressed by the legal issues presented on appeal, which concern only the sufficiency of the evidence and the competency of counsel in presenting Guidugli's unsuccessful claim of self-defense. Although questioning the necessity of prosecuting as a criminal offense what may have been dealt with internally by the University, and the harshness of the sentence imposed by the trial court, we are unable to find any reversible legal error. As a court of law, not of social policy, we affirm.

A Hard Foul Ignites a Fight

On March 9, 2003, Guidugli, the starting quarterback for the University of Cincinnati football team, was playing in an organized student intramural basketball game at the Armory Field House on the University of Cincinnati campus. When Guidugli's teammate protested a foul called by the referee, his teammate and an opposing player exchanged heated words, and the opposing player grabbed his teammate by the shirt. Both benches emptied as players took to the floor.

There was conflicting testimony regarding the nature of the ensuing scuffle. Keith Steineman, the intramural supervisor, described it as a "fracas" involving "pushing and shoving." He stated that supervisors were trained to "let players like work it out themselves so we don't get involved and get hit." Steineman testified, though, that the only punch he saw thrown was that by Guidugli. But one of Guidugli's teammates, Doug Monaghan, testified that the pushing and shoving quickly escalated into a donnybrook. In his words, "fists were flying."

According to Steinman, he witnessed Guidugli enter the fracas, and it was his opinion that Guidugli was, initially at least, "trying to break up [the] scuffle." But he then saw Guidugli knock over one of the opposing players, Levi Harris, and "punch him with a full swing" around the eye. Chris Brunswick, who was acting as scorekeeper, testified that he thought Harris was already on the ground when Guidugli ran onto the court and punched him. Guidugli, however, testified that he was one of the players on the floor and had taken a position along the foul lane, getting ready for the foul shots, when

the fight broke out. He stated that he saw another teammate of his, Kevin Hazel, punch Harris, and that he was pulling someone off Monaghan when he saw a punch coming in his direction out of the corner of his eye. He stated that when he turned around, he recognized the person attempting to throw the punch as Harris and he "just defended himself."

Whatever the degree of the fight, Steineman testified that afterward the teams "worked it out" and order was restored. Guidugli's team was told, apparently by Steineman, that they had forfeited the game and should leave the gym, which they did.

The university police were called after Steineman reported the "group fight" by radio to the main office. Officer Kevin Manz arrived two minutes after being dispatched, but some thirty to forty-five minutes after the incident. Although Guidugli and his team had left, Harris and his team had remained because they had another game. Officer Manz spoke to Harris, who was holding a wet cloth to the area around his left eye. Officer Mainz took photographs of Harris's face. Harris then signed a complaint charging Guidugli with criminal assault. Harris's affidavit accompanying the complaint stated, "As I was walking away I was hit with two punches, one from the side and one from the back. I was unaware who hit me."

The trial court, upon hearing all the various versions of the fight and punch, rejected Guidugli's claim of self-defense, stating that the evidence showed that he had punched Harris in retaliation rather than to protect himself. The court thus convicted Guidugli of misdemeanor assault. After listening to arguments in favor of mitigation made by Guidugli's trial counsel, the court imposed a 180-day jail sentence, which it then suspended in favor of one year's probation with the conditions that Guidugli undergo 60 days of home incarceration using an electronic monitoring unit, and that he participate in any treatment or counseling, including anger management, recommended by the probation department. Further, Guidugli was required to pay a $100 fine and court costs.

On July 3, 2003, Guidugli, represented by new counsel, filed a written motion to mitigate, requesting the court to reconsider its sentence. In his motion, Guidugli asked the court to sentence him to community service only, asserting that the incident that had led to his conviction was an isolated event in which he had allowed his competitive nature to interfere with his better judgment. He claimed that he deeply regretted his behavior and had learned a valuable lesson that would preclude him from ever committing a similar offense. In support of his character, he pointed out that he had been a law-abiding citizen for the first twenty years of his young life and had maintained a grade point average of 3.27 as a business-management major at the University of Cincinnati while maintaining the rigorous schedule of a college athlete. He also pointed out that he had been an active member of CPAWS, a student-athlete group that took part in service projects throughout the greater Cincinnati area, and that he had voluntarily spoken at numerous fundraisers and had traveled to Mississippi Gulf Coast Community College to work as a camp counselor for disadvantaged children. He also observed that the sentence as imposed by the trial court had forced him to cancel plans to attend the Peyton Manning Sports Camp, and that it threatened his participation in certain media events important in garnering awards during the college football season, as well as his presence at a team training camp considered integral in preparation for the first game of the season.

On July 7, 2003, the trial court denied the motion. On August 14, 2003, the trial court granted Guidugli's motion to stay further execution of the sentence pending this appeal.

Other Available Defenses—Sports Violence and the Criminal Law

In mitigation, in other words after the trial court's finding of guilt, defense counsel raised the argument for the first time that such fights were typical of hard fought athletic contests, particularly among young college-aged men eager to test their manhood. As defense counsel pointed out, "You don't have to go any further than Riverfront Stadium to see athletes in altercations." Defense counsel asked that the trial court take into consideration that "this young man [Guidugli], like all the other guys who are out there that night, were competitors and in a game. And the game got a little out of control at a point. And it escalated into this * * *."

This argument brings into focus the larger question alluded to at the outset of this opinion: whether physical altercations arising in sports contests that are already subject to some form of internal regulation and discipline should necessarily result in criminal charges, at least where there are no serious physical injuries as a result. Legal scholars have questioned the strict application of the criminal law to sports contests in which, contrary to real-world norms that generally condemn such behavior, a premium is placed upon physical aggression, intimidation, and enforcement. See, e.g., Clarke, Law and Order on the Courts: The Application of Criminal Liability for Intentional Fouls During Sporting Events (2000), 32 Ariz. St.L.J. 1149; Harary, Aggressive Play or Criminal Assault? An In Depth Look at Sports Violence and Criminal Liability (2002), 25 Colum. J.L. & Arts 197.

"From an early age, athletes are taught to intimidate opponents and to precipitate physical altercations rather than to avoid them. Athletes learn that they need to be tough to get noticed and to excel in higher levels of competition." Clarke, supra, at 1157–1158. "Violence in sports can be attributed to many factors, including: the interplay between competition, frustration, and aggression; the 'game reasoning' or 'sport reasoning' that supplements—or, at times, replaces—ordinary moral reasoning during sporting events; the degree of 'sport socialization' that leads players to perceive sports violence as legitimate; *the sports norm of reciprocity for acts of aggression by opposing players*; and the significance placed upon winning at all costs. It is the confluence of these

factors that create the curious world which is sports— a world in which real world behavioral models have no place." *Id.* at 1155–1156 (emphasis supplied).

Given the unique social dynamic involved in sports, "criminal prosecution of sports participants for conduct that occurs with the playing of the game is rare." *Id.* at 1168, citing Yasser, Mcurdy, and Goperlud, Sports Law (1990) 378. Most prosecutions, not surprisingly, have involved hockey games. See Calvert-Hanson and Dernis, Revisitng Excessive Violence in the Professional Sports Arena: Changes in the Past Twenty Years? (1996), 6 Seton Hall L.Rev. 127, 138. Perhaps saying something about the American competitive nature, prosecutors in the United States have shown far less zeal in punishing sports violence than their Canadian counterparts, who have been observed to use the criminal law much more frequently. See White, Sports Violence as Criminal Assault: Development of the Doctrine by Canadian Courts (1986), 1986 Duke L.J. 1030, 1034.

One stated rational for prosecutorial restraint is the inherent safeguards of league play, with its system of in-game punishment and suspension. As one commentator has written, "It is inevitable that players' passions will at times be aroused, but game officials and coaches are vested with the authority to impose sanctions for misconduct during the game. The penalties imposed by referees or umpires may seem minor when compared to those imposed on perpetrators of the same conduct outside the sport context, but those punishments are quick and certain, and are thought by some criminologists to be more effective in deterring undesirable behavior than the imposition of more severe penalties." Clarke, supra, at 1192.

* * * *

Canadian courts were among the first to establish the implied-consent doctrine of sports in criminal cases, see *Regina v. Green* (Ont. Provincial Ct. 1970), 2 C.C.C.2d 442, and *Regina v. Maki* (Ont. Provincial Ct. 1970), 1 C.C.C.2d 333, but, interestingly, the American Law Institute had earlier adopted the doctrine in its 1962 Official Draft of the Model Penal Code. Section 2.11(2) of the code provides that consent can be an absolute defense to bodily harm if "the conduct and the harm are a reasonably foreseeable hazard of joint participation in a lawful athletic competition or competitive sport * * *."

The Model Penal Code section has no analog in the Ohio Revised Code. As a matter of decisional law, the doctrine, although acknowledged, has found limited application in American courts. See *State v. Floyd* (Iowa App.1990), 466 N.W.2d 919, 922; *People v. Freer* (1976), 86 Misc. 2d 280, 381 N.Y.S.2d 976, 979; and *State v. Shelley* (Wash.App. 1997), 85 Wn. App. 24, 929 P.2d 489, 493. Courts have appeared to draw the line between physical aggression that can be reasonably foreseen within the context of game play, and thus, by inference, consented to by the player, and violence that takes place after play has stopped, or is purely retaliatory, or exceeds in brutality or degree of injury anything that the player might have otherwise agreed to. For example, in *Floyd* the court refused to apply the doctrine to a recreational basketball game in which the defendant assaulted players resting on the sideline during a timeout. In *Freer*, the court held the doctrine inapplicable to a punch thrown by a football player in retaliation for a punch thrown by the complainant in the midst of a game tackle. And in *Shelly* the court refused to allow the doctrine to justify a punch thrown by another recreational basketball player who felt the blow justified after the complainant had scratched him across the face during play.

Our research has not disclosed any Ohio cases involving application of the implied-consent doctrine in a criminal prosecution for sports violence. In *State v. Dunham* (1997), 118 Ohio App. 3d 724, 693 N.E.2d 1175, this court rejected application of the doctrine of mutual consent to a prosecution for felonious assault arising out a street fight. In *Dunham*, we noted that the doctrine of mutual consent arose out of the ancient maxim *volenti non fit injuria* (no legal wrong is done to him who consents) that forms the basis in civil law of the doctrine of assumption of the risk. Notwithstanding the survival of the Roman principle in the area of torts, we nonetheless concluded that, except for professional or amateur boxing exhibitions held pursuant to R.C. 3773.31, "fighting must be held to be illegal in this state because each combatant may be guilty of an assault in law as well as the battery which might follow as a consequence of the exchange of blows or, at least, by the demonstration of the ability to do harm. The fact that street fighters agree to engage in a public brawl to settle old or current differences cannot and does not negate the penal consequences." *Id.* at 729, 693 N.E.2d 1175.

Given its limited application, and our holding in *Dunham*, we cannot say that Guidugli's trial counsel was ineffective for not advancing the doctrine of implied consent as another affirmative defense. As noted, trial counsel appears to have argued the doctrine, in principle at least, during mitigation following the verdict, but not before. Even if we were to assume that the doctrine exists in Ohio, it is unlikely that the trial court would have found the doctrine applicable in this case. To have successfully argued the doctrine, Guidugli would have had to have persuaded the trial court that the punch he threw was a foreseeable part of the game and one to which Harris impliedly consented. Although it is specious to suggest that basketball remains today a non-contact sport, it is quite a stretch to argue that retaliatory punches during a pause in play are to be accepted as the unavoidable cost of playing the sport at the intramural level. It bears emphasis in this regard that the punch, as described by the state's witnesses, was entirely outside the scope of play and did not arise, for example, as a result of a scuffle under the basket or in a fight for a rebound.

Official's Time Out

Finally, we observed earlier that the trial court imposed a 180-day suspended jail sentence, 60 days of home incarceration/electronic monitoring in lieu of the suspended sentence, one year of probation, anger management counseling as recommended by the probation department, a $100 fine, and court costs—all for a minor welt in a basketball game suffered by a complainant who could not leave work to attend the trial. Later, the trial court denied a motion to reconsider its sentence despite several cogent arguments advanced by new counsel. Although the sentence may appear harsh, it has not been challenged on appeal and is not in any case subject to review. Guidugli, as the starting quarterback on the University of Cincinnati football team, can now serve the balance of his sentence before fall practice and the upcoming season begins. As Clarke notes, "Accountability among athletes is avoided by the simple expedient of ignoring anything but the on-court consequences of behavior." Clarke, supra, at 1156. At the very least, it seems, among the lessons learned from this case is that while sports norms may be very different from real-world norms, conduct on the court may still have very serious real-world consequences off the court.

The judgment of the trial court is affirmed.

CASES ON THE SUPPLEMENTAL WEB SITE

In the Matter of the Welfare of J.S.I., 2009 Minn. App. Unpub. LEXIS 140. This case demonstrates that even minors may be adjudicated delinquent if harm inflicted in an athletic contest is considered criminal.

NPS, LLC. v. StubHub, Inc., 22 Mass. L. Rptr 717 (2007). This case illustrates a professional football team's attempt to use anti-scalping laws to limit resale of tickets by a third party vendor.

People of the State of Colorado v. Hall, 999 P.2d 207 (2000). This case details a skier who was acquitted of reckless manslaughter after killing another skier in a skiing accident. While the text provides examples of recreation participants that were found criminally liable, this case details a finding in favor of the defendant.

People of the State of New York v. Shacker, 670 N.Y.S.2d 308 (1998). This case provides discussion of the consent defense and highlights the overly broad "in-connection" theory.

State of Washington v. Shelley, 929 P.2d 489 (1997). This case discusses both the rules of the game test and the reasonably foreseeable test; further, the case offers reasoning for upholding a criminal conviction for conduct stemming from a recreational basketball game.

QUESTIONS YOU SHOULD BE ABLE TO ANSWER

1. Describe the required elements of a crime.

2. What is the primary difference between civil negligence and criminal negligence?

3. What practical advice should you give recreational participants, athletes and coaches regarding potential criminal liability?

4. How would you best educate student athletes regarding the perils of point shaving?

5. How can the state anti-scalping laws benefit a sport organization?

REFERENCES

Cases

Avila v. Citrus Cmty. Coll. Dist., 131 P.3d 383 (2006)
Cavoto v. Chicago National League Ball Club, Inc., 222 Ill.2d 569 (2006)
In the Matter of the Welfare of J.S.I., 2009 Minn. App. Unpub. LEXIS 140
New England Patriots, L.P. v. Stubhub, Inc., 22 Mass. L. Rptr 717 (2007)
People of the State of New York v. Shacker, 670 N.Y.S.2d 308 (1998).
People v. Freer, 381 N.Y.S.2d 976 (1976).
State of Washington v. Shelley, 929 P.2d 489 (1997)
State v. Forbes, No. 63280 Minn. Dist. Ct. (1975)
State v. Floyd, 466N.W.2d 919 (1990).
State v. Guidugli, 157 Ohio App. 3d 383 (2004)
State v. Limon, No. 1999-CR-2892 Dist. Ct. Texas (2000).
Ticketmaster, L.L.C. v. RMG Technologies, Inc., 507 F. Supp. 2d 1096 (2007)
U.S. v. Burke, et. al, 700 F.2d 70 (1983)

Publications

Black, H. C. (1990). Black's Law Dictionary, (6th Ed.) St. Paul: West Publishing Co.
Epstein, A. (2009) *Incorporating the Criminal Law in Sport Studies.* 12 The Sport Journal 3. Available at: http://www.thesportjournal.org/article/incorporating-criminal-law-sport-studies
Fitzgerald, D. (2010). *Friday night rights: Arrest of Middletown coaches evokes lessons of Stinson case.* Available at: http://ctsportslaw.com/2010/07/13/friday-night-rights-arrest-of-middletown-coaches-evokes-lessons-of-stinson-case/
Gilbert, M. & Silka, Z. (2009). *6 former University of Toledo athletes charged in point shaving scheme.* Available at: http://www.toledoblade.com/UT/2009/05/07/6-former-University-of-Toledo-athletes-charged-in-point-shaving-scheme.html
Gustky, E. (2001). *The problem still hasn't been fixed.* Available at: http://articles.latimes.com/2001/mar/30/sports/sp-44540
Harary, C. (2002). *Aggressive play or criminal assault? An in-depth look at sports violence and criminal liability.* 25 Colum. J.L. & Arts 197.
Johnson, G. (2009) *Isolation for concussed athlete scandal get worse.* Available at http://www.subtlebraininjury.com/blog/tag/texas-tech-coach-mike-leach-suspended-for-concussion-isolation-of-adam-james
Kaplan, J. et. al. (1996). *Criminal law: Cases and materials.* Boston, MA. Little, Brown and Company.
Kirkman, C. P. (2009). *Note: Who needs tickets? Examining problems in the growing online ticket resale industry.* Federal Communications Law Journal, 61, 739–763.
McCann, M. (2009). *Kentucky trial of high school coach has wide implications.* Available at : http://sportsillustrated.cnn.com/2009/writers/michael_mccann/08/26/kentucky.coach/index.html
McCarthy, M. (2007). *Point-shaving remains a concern in college athletics.* Available at: http://www.usatoday.com/sports/college/2007-05-08-point-shaving-cover_N.htm
Model Penal Code § 2.01 (2001).
Model Penal Code § 2.02 (2001).
Model Penal Code § 2.02.2(c) (2001).
Model Penal Code § 210.3–4 (2001).
Model Penal Code § 211.1 (2001).
Model Penal Code § 2.11.2(b) (2001).
Quinlan, L. (2009) *Irondequoit man convicted of homicide in softball player's death.* Available at: http://www.mpnnow.com/towns/irondequoit/x1098985647/Irondequoit-man-convicted-of-homicide-in-softball-players-death
Schwarz, M. & Berko, A. (2011). *Syracuse's Bernie Fine placed on leave.* Available at: http://espn.go.com/espn/otl/story/_/id/7248184/syracuse-police-investigating-bernie-fine-molesting-boy-1980s

Standen, J. (2009). *The manly sports: The problematic use of criminal law to regulate sports violence*. 99 J. of Crim. Law & Criminology 3.

Toporek, B. (2012). *Police open investigation into H.S. coach's concussion management*. Available at: http://blogs.edweek.org/edweek/schooled_in_sports/2012/01/police_open_investigation_into_hs_coachs_concussion_management.html

Viera, M & Becker, J. (2011). *Ex-coach denies charges amid new allegations*. Available at: http://www.nytimes.com/2011/11/15/sports/ncaafootball/jack-raykovitz-chief-of-second-mile-resigns-amid-penn-state-scandal.html

White, E. (2007). *Cuomo guilty in point-shaving scheme*. Available at: http://www.foxtoledo.com/dpp/news/local/Cuomo-guilty-in-point-shaving-scheme

Legislation

A.C.A. § 17-16-115 (2012)

Minn. Stat. 245 § 609. 806 (2011)

N.Y. Arts & Cult. Aff. § 25.08 and § 25.13 (2011)

R. I. Gen Law § 5-22-26 (2011)

Tex. Occ. Code § 2051.501 (2012)

Va. Code Ann. § 15. 2-969 (2011)

15 U.S.C. §7801 et seq. (2012)

18 U.S.C.S § 224 (2012)

3.22 HAZING

Ellen J. Staurowsky | Drexel University

On an October day in 1881, seven upper class students assaulted a Bowdoin College freshman in his dorm room as part of a hazing ritual (*Strout v. Packard*, 1884). The case offers a vivid description of escalating events not unfamiliar to us today. There was an invasion of an unsuspecting student's room, a beating, and general mayhem as more than one assailant threw "missiles" at the student. The issue raised in this case was whether a conspiracy existed among Strout's seven attackers and subsequently, who was liable for the harm done to Strout, who suffered, among other things, a serious eye injury after being hit with a thrown object. In ruling that there was not sufficient evidence to determine that a conspiracy existed, and culpability for the injury could be assigned only to the person from whose hand the object had been thrown, the judges of the Supreme Judicial Court of Maine raised considerations that resonate today about what constitutes hazing and who is responsible. Although the rights of the defendants were upheld in this case, there is a palpable sense in reading the opinion that the judges were aware that justice had not been served by so narrow a reading of the defendants' collective contribution to the events that occurred.

Over 125 years later, the practice of hazing endures and with it the attendant questions of accountability and culpability. As a case in point, in November of 2011, Robert Champion, the head drum major for the Florida A & M University (FAMU) Marching 100 band, died following the alleged hazing of several band members in a bus parked in a hotel lot following a football game. Champion suffered multiple blows to the body; the autopsy revealed that he passed away from shock due to excessive bleeding (Schneider, 2012). The FAMU administration initially moved to expel four students who were said to have been connected to the death and dismiss band director, Dr. Julian White. The expulsions and dismissal were reversed several weeks later pending completion of the investigation into the incident (Middleton, 2012). Two months later, no charges had yet been filed. With the investigation underway, the university also announced the creation of an anti-hazing committee charged to develop recommendations to end hazing on the FAMU campus (FAMU, 2012).

Despite the efforts of educators, administrators, public policy makers, and others to create awareness about the negative consequences of hazing and develop prevention programs, much remains unknown about the magnitude and degree of hazing as it occurs in school or professional sport and recreational settings. Conflicting perspectives regarding what constitutes hazing continue to be issues for parents and teachers, school officials and local law enforcement, students and athletes.

Three cases that occurred during the 2011–2012 academic year illustrate this point. Upon learning that members of the Bellaire (Ohio) School District football team had been accused of punching freshman teammates, urinating on them, and engaging in acts too graphic for one local station to mention, Superintendent Tony Scott indicated that an attitude of "boys will be boys" or "kids will be kids" was not acceptable justification for that kind of behavior (Del Rosso, 2012; Staskey, 2012).

In contrast, the boys' ice hockey coaching staff at Howell High School (MI) was fired after pictures surfaced of the team dressed in women's lingerie parading through a bar where their coaches were drinking after an away game. According to news reports, the head coach viewed the incident as one that was "high spirited" and designed as a "rite of passage" for new members of the team. The coach went on to describe the annual "talent show" as one of the team's traditions, akin to the prayer they made at the beginning of a team meal (Banovic, 2012; Thompson, 2012). Some of the parents also saw nothing wrong with the event. As one father said, "I asked and he [my son] said, well dad I want to do it and no one is forcing me to do it. As strange as it was, it was just clean fun" (Banovic, n.p.).

While the coaching staff at Howell was fired because of their tolerance for behavior deemed to be hazing by a school official, an assistant football coach at Milford (MA) High School was dismissed from his position because of his reaction to the alleged hazing of a freshman by members of his team. Upon walking into the locker room and witnessing an incident that the coach found disturbing, he reprimanded the team forcefully, expressing his outrage at times with expletives and, at one point, kicking a trash can. The superintendent deemed the behavior of the team to be "roughhousing" and not hazing, while the behavior of the assistant coach was sufficient grounds for termination (Macdonald, 2011).

It is unclear if the adoption of hazing laws at the state level has served to deter the frequency of such behavior or diminish its magnitude. In February of 2012, numerous accounts of hazing incidents that impacted the lives of athletes, coaches, families, and communities were reported in media sources around the United States. A lawsuit filed by a Munster High School swimmer in the Northern District of Indiana—U.S. District Court alleged school officials allowed him to be hazed because they were aware that a tradition of hazing existed in the program and they failed to prevent it (Schultz, 2012). A Wisconsin Rapids team of male and female wrestlers avoided a trial on disorderly conduct charges for an incident occurring in 2010–2011 after a plea deal was reached by the parties. If convicted of the charges, the wrestlers faced a maximum 90-day jail sentence and $1,000 fine (Staff, 2012).

Hazing incidents have increasingly resulted in one or more of the affected parties leaving the institution or being suspended for a period of time. In Mississippi, two 15-year-old boys transferred from Picayune Memorial High School to another school after suffering verbal abuse and being hospitalized for beatings. Due to Mississippi High School Athletic Association (MHSAA) regulations which prohibit students from switching schools to play sports, the two boys have been deemed ineligible. Despite parental claims that the transfers were made in order to protect the safety of the boys, the MHSAA ruled that they could not determine that a hardship warranting an exception to the transfer rules could be determined (Wall, 2012). In a different scenario, the three-week suspension of long-time Kennedy High School (CA) baseball coach, Manny Alvarado, by school officials after an alleged hazing incident led parents to march outside of the school expressing outrage over the decision based on their belief that hazing between players had not occurred (Sondheimer, 2012).

To complicate the issue further, Crow and MacIntosh (2009) point out that many definitions of hazing begin with an assumption that in order for hazing to occur, students seek membership in groups such as fraternities and sororities. As a threshold matter, definitions that address hazing in fraternities or sororities may not be adequate to address hazing in sport teams. They point out that while hazing may be a part of the process used to become a member of a fraternity, coaches determine membership on athletic teams. Thus, hazing in sport contexts speaks to issues associated with group acceptance and power structure rather than membership *per se*. They conclude that definitions of hazing should be redrafted to acknowledge this distinction.

Whereas individual instances provide rich examples of behavior that falls within the scope of hazing definitions, research findings provide some measures of magnitude. Studies reveal that hazing occurs among students in grades 6 through college at rates ranging from just over 17% to 79% (Allan & Madden, 2008; Campo, Poulos, & Sipple, 2005; Crandall, 2003; Gershel, Katz-Sidlow, Small, & Zandieh, 2003; Hoover, 1999, 2000). The general trends as documented in the research as well as individual instances show that recreation and sport managers must be proactive in their response to hazing by (1) anticipating that hazing will occur on teams and within student organizations; (2) questioning and monitoring the initiation activities of athletes, students, and employees; (3) working within existing organizational structures to formulate anti-hazing policies; (4) developing anti-hazing education programs. They must also be informed about policies that exist within their organizations and be knowledgeable about the local, state, and national laws that apply to hazing.

FUNDAMENTAL CONCEPTS

Definition and Scope

Definitions of hazing range from the succinct to the comprehensive. For example, in the state of Ohio, **hazing** "means doing an act or coercing another, including the victim, to do any act of initiation into any student or other organization that causes or creates a substantial risk of causing mental or physical harm to any person" (Ohio Revised Code 2903.31). In contrast, Florida law defines hazing to mean

> any action or situation which recklessly or intentionally endangers the mental or physical health or safety of a student for the purpose of initiation or admission into or affiliation with any organization operating under the sanction of a postsecondary institution. Such term includes, but is not limited to, any brutality of a physical nature, such as whipping, beating, branding, forced calisthenics, exposure to

the elements, forced consumption of any food, liquor, drug, or other substance, or other forced physical activity which could adversely affect the physical health or safety of the student, and also includes any activity which would subject the student to extreme mental stress, such as sleep deprivation, forced exclusion from social contact, forced conduct which could result in extreme embarrassment, or other forced activity which could adversely affect the mental health or dignity of the student. (Florida State Code 240.1325)

Whereas the statutory definition of hazing is important, so too is the interpretation of the meaning of the term "student organization." In *Duitch v. Canton City Schools* (2004), a freshmen high school student alleged that on "Freshman Friday," he was beaten in a restroom by eight to ten juniors and seniors. Both the trial and appellate courts found that "the actions of the students did not constitute initiation into any student or other organization" and that "the attack was merely due to the appellant's status as a freshman." Initiation into the entire student body rather than into a specific student organization prevented the appellant from finding relief under the existing hazing law in the state of Ohio (see Cases on the Supplemental Web Site).

The Court of Appeals of Ohio in Clermont County reached a similar determination in *Golden v. Milford Exempted Village School District Board of Education* (2011). In *Golden*, the family of a high school basketball player sought relief after their son was wrestled to the ground, punched, and held there while another player exposed his penis, rubbing it on their son's face, and attempting to force it into their son's mouth. Affirming an earlier decision by the trial court granting summary judgment regarding the civil claim of hazing, the Court noted that the reported actions to which Golden's son was subjected did not meet the statutory requirements of hazing under Ohio law because the acts were not designed to initiate their son into the team but to drive him away. The language of the opinion, however, points to Ohio bullying law as an area of relief. As stated in the opinion, ". . . the incident in the vestibule was the culmination of disturbing acts of bullying by T. toward R." (n.p.). (see Cases on Supplemental Web Site).

The vast majority of hazing laws create a link between hazing and student welfare, thus limiting the applicability of the law to manifestations of hazing that may occur in other groups, like professional sport teams or athletic teams sponsored by national sport governing bodies (e.g., U.S. Olympic team). The New York statute reflects consideration for this possibility as seen in the language of the statute, which reads in part, "A person is guilty of hazing in the first degree when, in the course of another person's initiation into or affiliation with any organization . . ." (New York 120.16).

Civil Litigation

This section explores the legal basis on which a hazing victim may establish a cause of action in a civil suit. In a civil case, a hazing victim may be awarded monetary damages. Several challenges exist in establishing who is accountable and can be held liable in hazing cases. First, at the college and university level, negligence hinges on the ability to argue that a special relationship exists between the victim and the institution. In the absence of a **special relationship**, there is no **duty of care**. Second, in determining whether both parties (perpetrator and victim) may bear responsibility for hazing, the mere fact that an athlete agreed to participate on a team, by itself, does not provide a supportable rationale to establish **comparative negligence**. Third, coaches and school administrators may be **immune** from civil liability if their actions fall within the realm of professional discretion. Fourth, **parents** may be held negligent for not exercising appropriate supervision of their children.

Negligence. Within the past twenty years, as the number of hazing cases has risen, victims have increasingly sought redress in the courts alleging negligence on the part of athletes who haze as well as coaches, school administrators, and the institutions they represent.

At one time, college officials under the doctrine of *in loco parentis* could be held liable for hazing because administrators had a duty to care for their students much the same as parents had a duty to care for their children. Changing societal views of college students as young adults rather than dependent children shifted the burden of responsibility for student misbehavior from college officials to students. This does not mean, however, that there is no basis for an institutional or professional duty of care. Under the **landowner-invitee theory**, landlords owe a duty of reasonable care to those who are invited onto their property. Through offers of admission and assessment of fees, a similar relationship exists between institutions of higher education and their students (Crow & Rosner, 2002).

In *Knoll v. Board of Regents of the University of Nebraska* (1999), the Nebraska Supreme Court used this theory to reason that the university had an obligation to take steps to protect a student against reasonably foreseeable acts of hazing, which included abduction from his dorm room on campus, transport to a fraternity house off campus, and harm that accrued as a result of his attempt to escape. The implications of this case point to the necessity for school administrators and employers to acknowledge the history of hazing in athletics and to take proactive measures in the form of anti-hazing policies and education or risk failing in their duty to protect students and other persons associated with their organization (Crow & Rosner, 2002).

In *Siesto v. Bethpage Union Free School District* (1999), the Nassau County Supreme Court (NY) awarded summary judgment to the plaintiff, a member of the football team, who sustained a serious head wound as a result of a hazing incident that occurred in the locker room just a short distance from the coach's office. In dismissing the affirmative defenses of comparative negligence and assumption of risk asserted by the school district, the trial court determined that athletes who voluntarily participate in athletics do not assume the risk of injury resulting from being hazed.

Coach accountability and culpability are receiving increased scrutiny as well. In August of 2008, two baseball coaches from Wilson High School in Western New York were charged with endangering the welfare of a child and failure to prevent alleged sex-related attacks on players during a team bus ride the previous spring (Besecker, 2008). In the spring of 2009, an Anderson County High School softball coach resigned her position after authorizing an event in which upper class players arranged for first year teammates to stand in a hotel swimming pool wearing only one article of clothing, an event that violated the school's rules as well as Florida state law (Fowler, 2009). Also in the spring of 2009, five officials of the Las Vegas City Schools (the superintendent, athletic director, and three coaches) were accused of failing to report sexual assaults that younger players were subjected to during a pre-season football camp prior to the start of the academic year (Medina, 2009).

Immunity is a common defense in hazing cases. Immunity can free educational institutions and their employees from liability for negligence (Crow & Rosner, 2002). In *Caldwell v. Griffin Spalding County Board of Education, et al.* (1998), a first-year football player was attacked, beaten, and knocked unconscious in his dorm room during preseason. In a civil suit brought by the player against school officials, the Georgia Court of Appeals upheld a lower court ruling granting summary dismissal on the grounds that the principal, coach, and school board members were immune from civil liability.

In *Elbaz v. Beverly Hills Unified School District* (2007), a member of the BHUSD soccer team was severely beaten by several teammates while on a trip to play in a summer tournament. Attempting to assert three causes of action for negligence, the Court of Appeals of California upheld a lower court ruling granting a demurrer on the grounds that the school district was immune from liability because the trip to the tournament constituted a "field trip" or "excursion" rather than a "school sponsored activity." Whereas a "school sponsored activity" would have provided a basis for the complaint to proceed, under California law, students participating in "excursions" waive all claims against a school district for injury that occurs during such a trip. Further, according to California law, the beating itself did not fall under the definition of hazing in the California Penal Code because the student was already a member of the team.

Constitutional Rights—Students. Among the many avenues that students have pursued in seeking redress for harms endured as a result of hazing is protection under the First and Fourteenth Amendments. In 1993, a high school football player was accosted by teammates while leaving the showers, forcibly restrained, and bound to a towel rack with athletic tape. His former girlfriend was then led into the locker room to see him hanging there (*Seamons v. Snow*, 2000). Upon Seamon's release from the team because of his refusal to apologize for reporting the incident, he filed suit claiming that his First Amendment rights to free speech had been violated by the coach and the school district (*Seamons v. Snow*, 1994). After the district court granted summary judgment in favor of the defendants in 1998, the appellate court reversed that decision sending the case to trial—asserting for a second time that the coach was not entitled to qualified immunity for suspending Seamons from the team (*Seamons v. Snow*, 2000; see *Significant Case* later in this chapter).

In 2000, the Centennial Area School District (PA) settled a lawsuit brought forward by a former high school wrestler so as to avert a court decision regarding its liability. The wrestler alleged his Fourteenth Amendment right to protection of his own bodily integrity had been violated after the school failed to prevent his hazing, despite knowledge of the activity (*Nice v. Centennial Area School District*, 2000). However, in *Meeker v. Edmunson* (2005), the U.S. Court of Appeals for the Fourth Circuit determined that a wrestling coach who had authorized physical attacks on rookies by other members of his team was not protected by qualified immunity. The court determined that the action of a school official to cause a student to be beaten is contrary to the constitutional rights of a student under the Fourteenth Amendment.

In *Perkins, et al. v. Alamo Heights Independent School District* (2002), two high school cheerleaders were stripped of their eligibility to try out for future teams by school authorities because of their involvement in a party where underage drinking and hazing occurred. They sought an injunction claiming their rights under Title IX and the equal protection clause of the U.S. Constitution had been violated because school officials had not provided an adequate hearing prior to taking action and had engaged in disparate treatment of female students. In rejecting their request, the court determined that the "lengthy history of problematic behavior" exhibited by the team and advance warnings about inappropriate behavior served as adequate notice and concluded that the evidence to show disparate treatment was unpersuasive (see Cases on the Supplemental Web Site).

These cases highlight two issues pertaining to the protection of student rights for coaches and administrators. In the *Seamons v. Snow* case, Coach Snow potentially violated Brian's First Amendment right to free speech by punishing him for breaking the silence that surrounds hazing. In contrast, the Alamo Heights school officials were successful in defending against allegations of failure to provide due process because they had given appropriate notice and acted preemptively to reduce liability prior to the hazing event occurring.

Constitutional Rights—School Officials. School administrators, coaches, and teachers who believed they were wrongly disciplined or dismissed for the manner in which they handled hazing incidents have sometimes asserted that their constitutional rights were violated. In *Cioffi v. Averill Park Central School District* (2006), a high school athletic director appealed the ruling from the U.S. District Court for the Northern District of New York granting summary judgment to the defendants. It was the assertion of the athletic director that the school district's decision to reorganize administrative staffing leading to the abolishment of his position as athletic director was the result of retaliation for complaints he made about the football coach's approach to student health and welfare. In the aftermath of a student filing a criminal charge for sexual assault which allegedly occurred during a football team hazing incident, the athletic director made public comments regarding threats to student safety and potential district liability. In taking issue with the lower court's findings, the U.S. Court of Appeals for the Second Circuit found that statements made by the athletic director about the assault were of public concern and that as an employee, the athletic director's comments should not be deprived of First Amendment protection. Further, the short time between the public statements made by the athletic director and the school district's decision to abolish his position was sufficient to raise a triable issue on causation (see Cases on the Supplemental Web Site).

In contrast to this case, a softball coach at Brewer School Department, challenged the non-renewal of her contract in violation of the Maine Human Rights Act. According to the plaintiff, the superintendent did not rehire her because of her sexual orientation. The school district, in turn, took the position that the plaintiff should not be rehired because of a history of hazing that had developed during the time that she was coaching the team. In the final analysis, the court granted summary judgment in favor of the defendant (*Cookson v. Brewer School Department*, 2007).

Other Civil Charges. School administrators who show deliberate indifference in cases of peer-to-peer harassment may be subject to liability for the resulting damages (*Davis v. Monroe County Board of Education*, 1999). The case of *Snelling & Snelling v. Fall Mountain Regional School District, et al.* (2001) tested this theory. Derek and Joel Snelling, members of the basketball team, claimed they were targets of persistent verbal and physical abuse by teammates, and, on occasion, by the coach. Although the district court granted summary judgment to Fall Mountain dismissing Section 1983 claims made by the plaintiffs that the harassment violated their Fourteenth Amendment rights to substantive due process and equal protection, District Judge Joseph DiClerico also found a pattern of harassment that presented a trial-worthy issue for action under Title IX and raised an issue as to whether the defendants were deliberately indifferent to the treatment of the brothers (*Snelling & Snelling v. Fall Mountain Regional School District, et al.*, 2001).

While many hazing cases focus on the misbehavior of adolescents and young adults and the conduct of school employees, less attention has been directed toward the role that parents or other adults play in fostering a climate that supports hazing. Following the worldwide distribution of videotaped evidence documenting the violent hazing of girls from Glenbrook (IL) North High School, questions were raised regarding the culpability of adults who had supplied alcohol to the underage participants in the event. Although existing Illinois law does not provide for social host liability, in the wake of this incident Illinois lawmakers are considering the adoption of legislation that would allow victims and their families to recover damages from the adults who willfully give, sell, or deliver alcohol to minors (Flock, 2003).

Signaling what may be increasing attempts to hold parents accountable for the behavior of their children, four former coaches at Mepham High School, who lost their sport-related job assignments following a well-publicized football hazing scandal, sued the parents of three of the students involved in the physical and sexual assaults of younger players, seeking $20 million in damages. The attorney for the coaches reasoned that the parents knew or had reason to know that their sons were prone to violence and did not use care to restrain them ("Ex-coaches sue," 2004).

Hazing and Sex Crimes

In September of 2003, at a camp in the Pocono Mountains of Pennsylvania, Mepham High School varsity football players lured younger players into a cabin under the pretense that they would be subjected to some form of mild initiation. From that day forward until the end of camp, the new members of the team were sodomized, beaten, subjected to painful and humiliating treatment, and required to haze other players (Wencelblat, 2004). According to accounts, by the end of camp, the entire team knew what had happened but they all remained silent (Wayne County Grand Jury, 2004). There is strong evidence to suggest that, if not for the fact that two of the victims required medical treatment for their injuries, the incidents would not have been reported. Ultimately, four identified perpetrators were tried as juveniles rather than adult offenders and charged with involuntary deviate sexual intercourse, aggravated assault, and kidnapping (Wencelblat, 2004). Two pleaded guilty to felony charges and began serving time in a juvenile facility, a third pleaded guilty to felony charges and received a sentence of probation, and a fourth pleaded guilty to a misdemeanor charge.

Once notified that hazing had occurred at the camp, Mepham school officials cancelled the 2003 football season, reassigned the head football coach and one of the assistants who were tenured teachers to another school in the district, and elected not to reappoint them to their coaching positions the next year. The former coaches alleged they were improperly reassigned without explanation and denied due process to discuss the reasons for their reassignment (*McElroy & Canestero v. Bellmore-Merrick School District*, 2004). Although McElroy and Canestero were unsuccessful in their suit, this case illustrates the difficulties faced in balancing the interests and rights of students and teachers/coaches. The behavior of the coaches had been the subject of a Wayne County (PA) Grand Jury, who considered whether their conduct during the camp constituted crimes of endangering the welfare of children and recklessly endangering another person. The Grand Jury determined that by legal definition the coaches had not acted criminally, although there was "clear evidence that the coaches displayed a lack of common sense accountability". Given a history of previous hazing incidents in the program and in light of this finding, school administrators would have risked allegations of deliberate indifference if they had not acted in the manner they did. At the same time, Mr. McElroy has asserted that the burden of responsibility should have fallen on the players who committed the crimes because they were bound by Mepham High School's student code of conduct (Jones, 2003).

Given that the Mepham High School case is not an isolated one, it behooves school administrators, coaches, and teachers to be aware of hazing and sex abuse reporting laws within their states. They should also be vigilant for treatment that, if ignored, constitutes endangering the welfare of children.

Criminal Hazing

In contrast to the civil justice system, where hazing victims personally seek relief for the harms done to them, in the criminal justice system, a state entity, such as a county prosecutor, will bring charges against alleged perpetrators for the purpose of determining whether they are guilty or innocent of a criminal act.

Anti-hazing Statutes. The number of states that have adopted anti-hazing statutes has increased dramatically from 25 in 1990 to 44 in 2012. While the number of athletes charged criminally for their participation in hazing activities has increased as well during that span of time, substantial barriers to the enforcement and prosecution of anti-hazing laws remain due to the lack of uniformity in the laws from state to state and the modest penalties that go along with them (Crow & Rosner, 2002; Sussberg, 2003). An analysis of current state statutes, which appears in Table 3.22.1, reveals the following information.

| TABLE 3.22.1 | STATE ANTI-HAZING LAWS |

State	State Hazing Statute	Classification of Crime	Is Failure to Notify a Crime?	Is Anti-hazing Policy Required in Schools?	Is Victim's Willingness a Defense?	Public/Private Status of School; Educational Level
AL	16-1-23	Class C misdemeanor	Yes	No	No	Any school
AK	None					
AZ	15-2301		No	Yes	No	Public
AR	6-5-201	Class B misdemeanor	Yes	No	Yes	Any school
CA	32050-1	Misdemeanor or Felony	No	No	No	Any school
CO	18-9-124	Class 3 misdemeanor	No	No	Yes	Any school
CT	53-23(a)		No	No	No	Higher education
DE	9301-04	Class B misdemeanor	No	Yes	No	Each institution
FL	1006.63	1st degree misdemeanor, 3rd degree felony	No	Yes	No	Postsecondary Public & Private
GA	16-5-61	High and aggravated misdemeanor	No	No	No	Any school
HI	WCHR 0-9			Yes		Statewide system of Public education
ID	18-917	Misdemeanor	No	No	Yes	College or university
IL	720 ILCS 120	Class A misdemeanor, Class 4 felony	No	No	Yes	Any school
IN	IC 35-4-2-2	Class A or B misdemeanor, Class C or D felony	No	No	No	Not restricted to school settings; any person
IO	708.10	Serious or simple misdemeanor	No	No	No	Any school
KS	21-3434	Class B misdemeanor	No	No	Yes	Any social or fraternal organization—not limited to schools
KY	164.375		No	Yes	Yes	State colleges & universities
LA	17:1801		No	Yes	No	Only fraternities in any educational institution receiving state funds: Public elementary & secondary schools
ME	20-AMRS		Yes	Yes	Yes	Public school; postsecondary institution incorporated or chartered by the state
MD	27-268H	Misdemeanor	No	No	No	Any school, college, or university
MA	269-17		Yes	Yes	No	Any student or other person on public or private property Postsecondary schools
MI	7504411	Misdemeanor, Felony	No		No	Educational Institution
MN	127.465 135A-155		No	Yes		Each school board; student or staff hazing; state colleges and universities, private postsecondary

(Continued)

TABLE 3.22.1		**STATE ANTI-HAZING LAWS (CONTINUED)**					
State	**State Hazing Statute**	**Classification of Crime**	**Is Failure to Notify a Crime?**	**Is Anti-hazing Policy Required in Schools?**	**Is Victim's Willingness a Defense?**	**Public/Private Status of School; Educational Level**	
MS	97-3-105	Misdemeanor	No	No	Yes	Not specific to schools; any organization	
MI	578.365	Class A misdemeanor, Class C felony	No	Yes	No	Public or private college or university	
MT	None						
NE	28-311.06	Class II misdemeanor	No	No	No	Postsecondary institution	
NV	200.605	Misdemeanor, Gross misdemeanor	No	No	No	High school, college, or university in the state	
NH	631.7	Class B misdemeanor	Yes	No	No	Any school	
NJ	2c:40-3	4th Degree crime	No	No	No		
NM	None						
NY	120.16	Class A misdemeanor	No	No		Not specific to schools or students	
NC	9:14:35-38	Class 2 misdemeanor	Yes	No		Any school or college	
ND	12.1-17-08	Class A Misdemeanor Class B Misdemeanor	No	No	No	Not limited to schools	
OH	2307.44; 2903.31	Misdemeanor	No	No	No	Any school	
OK	21-1190	Misdemeanor	No	Yes	No	Any school	
OR	163.197	Misdemeanor	No	No		College or university	
PA	5352	3rd Degree misdemeanor	No	Yes	No	Institution of higher education; associate degree or higher	
RI	11-21-1	Misdemeanor	No	No	Yes	Any school	
SC	59-101-200	Misdemeanor	Yes	No	No	Institution of higher learning	
SD	None						
TN	49-7-123		No	Yes	No	Higher education	
TX	37.152	Misdemeanor or Felony	Yes	Yes	No	Any school	
UT	76-5-107.5	Misdemeanor or felony	No	Yes	No (under 21)	High school level	
VT	76		No	Yes	No	All educational institutions	
VA	18.2056	Class I misdemeanor	No	No	Yes	Any school	
WA	28B.10.901	Misdemeanor	Yes	No	No	Any school	
WV	18-2.33	Misdemeanor	No	Yes	No	Public Schools	
WI	948.51	Class A misdemeanor, Class H & G felony	No	No	Yes	School, college & university	
WY	None						

Source: Lexis Nexis Academic Search State Statutes

- Thirty-five of the 45 state codes (77%) classify hazing as a misdemeanor, whereas ten states expressly provide that hazing resulting in serious bodily harm and/or death is classified as a felony. The classification of hazing as a crime does not supersede or change penalties covered by other criminal statutes (see *Classification of Crime* column).
- Nine anti-hazing statutes (20%) specify that it is a crime to fail to report an incident to authorities (see *Is Failure to Notify a Crime?* column).
- Of the existing anti-hazing statutes, nearly 35% (16 of 45) require schools to either develop anti-hazing policies and penalties or devise specific means to educate students, teachers/faculty, and other employees about the state's anti-hazing laws (see *Is Anti-hazing Policy Required in School?* column). However, there is considerable variability with regard to the level and type of school to which statutes apply. For example, 62 percent (28 of 45) include any school or other institution, whether private or public, while two are restricted solely to public schools. Additionally, 11 percent of the codes (5 of 45) pertain solely to higher education institutions (see *Public/Private Status of School; Educational Level* column).
- Sixty-four percent (29 of 45) of the codes provide that implied or express consent on the part of the victim, or a willingness on the part of the person hazed to participate in their own hazing, is not an available defense (see *Is Victim's Willingness a Defense?* column).
- A further limitation is the lack of conformity across hazing laws regarding the mental harm associated with hazing (Sussberg, 2003).

In the state of Utah, school boards have been charged to adopt a policy to prohibit bullying, cyber-bullying, harassment, and hazing under 53A-11a-301. In addition, the Education code (R277-605) provides that "Coaches, assistants and advisors shall act in a manner consistent with Section 53A-11-908 and shall not use foul, abusive, or profane language while engaged in school related activities; nor permit hazing, demeaning, or assaultive behavior, whether consensual or not, including behavior involving physical violence, restraint, improper touching, or inappropriate exposure of body parts not normally exposed in public settings, forced ingestion of any substance, or any act which would constitute a crime against a person or public order under Utah law." The contours of these laws shape a complaint filed by the parents of a teenager who committed suicide, alleging that the on-going harassment, hazing, and bullying their son experienced, the active participation of coaches in fostering a climate that tolerated and encouraged hazing, and the failure of school officials to report and respond to known incidents of bullying, hazing, and harassment against their son constituted negligence which led to the death of their son (*Hancock v. Galbraith, 2012*, see Supplemental Web Site).

Numerous improvements to existing anti-hazing laws have been proposed, including the adoption of a federal anti-hazing statute and the imposition of a duty for school personnel to act on these issues (Edelman, 2004; Sussberg, 2003). Additionally, as Ball (2004) pointed out, the Federal Educational Rights and Privacy Act (FERPA), which prohibits the disclosure of student records, may be in conflict with the Campus Security Act (CSA), which requires colleges and universities to make full reports of crimes committed on their campuses. Given the secretiveness surrounding hazing, the protections afforded students may be contributing to schools maintaining silence when these incidents occur. Some argue that rather than more legislation at the state or federal level, another way to bring uniformity to the system would be for the NCAA to adopt a uniform policy regarding athlete misconduct, with hazing being one of the behaviors included in the policy (Gutshall, 2008).

Whereas the evolution of anti-hazing law reflects a growing awareness that behavior assumed to be harmless may, in fact, be criminal, the definitional issues that remain to be resolved along with the meager penalties associated with hazing deserve consideration. As Table 3.22.2 shows, those convicted of hazing crimes are subject to modest fines that range between $10 and $10,000, imprisonment for as little as ten days to a maximum not to exceed one year, or a combination of both. As the Texas statute reveals, even when death results from hazing, the perpetrator may receive no more than two years in prison.

Bullying Laws

Increasingly, the terms hazing and bullying are appearing together in cases of sport team misconduct. Emblematic of that trend, in November of 2011, two members of the Andover High School boys basketball team were expelled and five students suspended for an unspecified amount of time and barred from playing varsity sports for the remainder of the year after an investigation resulted in a finding that an incident occurring at a summer

TABLE 3.22.2	PENALTIES FOR HAZING			
State	Minimum School Penalty	Fine	Sentence	Both Fine & Sentence
AL[1]				
AK	Expulsion			
AZ[2]				
CA	Suspension Expulsion	$100 to $5,000	Not more than one year	Possible
CT	Appropriate penalty Individual	not more than $1,000		
	Group	not more than $1,500 & suspension for no less than one year		
DE	Class B misdemeanor	$1,150	up to 6 months	Possible
FL		$5,000		
LA	Expulsion	$10 to $100	10 to 30 days	Possible
MD		$ 500	6 months	Possible
MA		$3,000	12 months	Possible
MS		$1000–$2,000	6 months	Possible
MI[3]		$1000 to $10,000		
NE		$10,000		
NC	Expulsion	$500	6 months	Possible
OK		$1500	3 months	Possible
OR		$1,000		
PA	Withhold diploma, other punishment			
RI[4]		$500	30 days to 12 months	Possible
SC	Dismissal, Expulsion			
TX[5]		$500 to $5,000	180 days to 12 months	Possible
VT		$5,000		
WA	forfeit state-funded grants, scholarships, or awards			
WV		$100 to $1,000	9 months	Possible

Source: Lexis Nexis Academic Search State Statutes

[1]In Alabama, state funding for scholarships and awards may be forfeited;
[2]In Arizona, an organization's permission to operate may be revoked and employees face disciplinary action.
[3]In Michigan, a $10,000 penalty in cases where hazing results in death.
[4]In Rhode Island, penalty for school official allowing hazing to go on can receive a monetary penalty between $10 to $100 per year.
[5]According to the Texas statute, "Any other offense under this section which causes the death of another is a misdemeanor punishable by a fine of not less than $5,000 nor more than $10,000, confinement in county jail for not less than one year nor more than two years, or both such fine and confinement." In convictions where the violation did not result in death, the judge may substitute community service for imprisonment.

camp five months previous violated the school's anti-bullying and anti-hazing policies. In this case, it was found that older students on the team forced two younger students to play a sex game that resulted in the loser having to eat a semen-covered cookie (Putnam & Messenger, 2011).

The catalyst for the enactment of anti-bullying legislation in the United States was the 1999 Columbine High School shooting incident. Since that time, "Bullying in schools has become widely viewed as an urgent social, health, and education concern that has moved to the forefront of public debate on school legislation and policy" (Stuart-Cassel, Bell, & Springer, 2011, p. ix). As of the fall of 2011, forty-six states have bullying laws (three of these prohibit bullying but do not define it).

SIGNIFICANT CASE

In this case, the court considered whether a high school football coach was liable for violating a player's free speech rights after dismissing the player from the team for refusing to apologize for reporting to authorities that he had been hazed by his teammates. The court also addressed whether the coach was entitled to qualified immunity.

SEAMONS V. SNOW

206 F.3d 1021 (2000)

High school football player who was assaulted by his teammates brought §1983 action against school district, football coach, and school's principal, alleging that player's free speech rights under First Amendment were violated when he was suspended and later dismissed from football team because he refused to apologize for reporting assault to police and school authorities. After summary judgment was granted for all defendants, 864 F.Supp. 1111, that judgment was reversed and remanded, 84 F.3d 1226. Upon remand, the United States District Court for the District of Utah, Dee V. Benson, J., again granted summary judgment for all defendants, 15 F.Supp.2d 1150. Player appealed. The Court of Appeals, Seymour, Chief Judge, held that: (1) if proven, coach's alleged actions could subject him to liability; (2) school district could be liable for coach's alleged conduct; (3) principal's lack of prior knowledge of or involvement in relevant events precluded his liability; and (4) coach was not entitled to qualified immunity.

Affirmed in part, reversed in part, and remanded.

* * *

Seymour, Chief Judge.

This case arises out of the locker-room assault of a high school football player, Brian Seamons, by several of his teammates. Brian filed this action under 42 U.S.C. § 1983 against the school's football coach and principal, as well as the school district. * * *

In the fall of 1993, Brian Seamons was a student at Sky View High School in Smithfield, Utah, and a member of the school's football team. On Monday, October 11 of that year, Brian was assaulted in the locker room by a group of his teammates. As Brian emerged from the showers, four teammates grabbed him, forcibly restrained him, and then bound him to a towel rack with highly adhesive athletic tape. Another teammate brought a girl Brian had dated into the locker room so that she could see what had been done to him.

Brian and his parents reported this incident to the police and to school authorities, including Myron Benson, Sky View's principal, and Doug Snow, the football coach. Two days after the assault, Brian and his parents met with Principal Benson and Coach Snow to discuss whether Brian would press criminal charges against the team members who assaulted him and whether Coach Snow would take any disciplinary action against them. Coach Snow stated he did not plan to remove any of the assailants from the team. Brian indicated that, in light of this, he would need to think about whether he wanted to remain on the team.

On Friday, October 15, the football team was scheduled to play an away game at Logan High School. That afternoon Brian informed Coach Snow that he wanted to remain on the team, and the two attended the traditional pre-game team-only spaghetti dinner in the school cafeteria. Coach Snow told Principal Benson that Brian was back on the team and everything had been worked out. In the meantime, Brian went home to get his uniform so he could dress for the game. When he returned to the school, Coach Snow asked Brian to meet with the four team captains, two of whom had participated in the assault. The purpose of this meeting, at which the Coach was present, was to allow the boys to clear up any residual hard feelings prior to the game.

During this meeting, a confrontation occurred between Brian and Dan Ward, a captain who had also been one of the assailants, over whether Brian should have to apologize to the team for reporting the assault to the police and school authorities. Specifically, Dan stated that he thought Brian had "betrayed the team" by reporting the assault and that Brian should not be allowed to play with the team until he apologized. Aplt.App., tab 14 at 376, 379. At this point, Coach Snow intervened and told Brian he needed to "forgive and forget and apologize" to the team captains. *Id*. at 359. When Brian refused, Coach Snow told him to "take the weekend and think about this," because without an apology he couldn't play with the team. *Id*. at 326. This ended the meeting.

Brian did not play in the game that night. He went home and told his parents he wasn't allowed to play because he had refused to apologize to the team. Brian's father, Sherwin Seamons, called the principal and angrily told him what had transpired at the meeting. Principal

Benson, surprised to hear that Brian wasn't going to attend the game, drove to Logan High School and discussed the matter with Coach Snow.

The following Tuesday, Brian confronted Coach Snow in school, telling him he wasn't going to apologize to the team and he still wanted to play football. At this point, Coach Snow told Brian that he was "sick of [his] attitude, sick of [his] father's attitude," and that he was off of the team. Aplt.App., tab 15 at 432–33. The following day the remainder of Sky View's football season was canceled.

* * *

A. First Amendment Claim

In ruling on the motion for summary judgment, the district court determined that Coach Snow did not ask Brian to apologize for reporting the assault, and that Brian's ultimate failure to be involved with the football team was unrelated to his speech or refusal to speak. *See Seamons III,* 15 F.Supp.2d at 1155, 1157. Given the conflicting testimony presented at the evidentiary hearing and contained in the depositions, we fail to see how the district court could reach these conclusions without resolving factual disputes—something it cannot do at this stage of the proceedings. *See, e.g., MacLean,* 247 F.Supp. at 190 ("The Court's role in summary judgment proceedings is not to resolve issues of fact, but merely to pinpoint those facts which are not at issue."). We note in particular that the district court devoted a large portion of its opinion to a discussion of the differing accounts of the captains' meeting offered by Brian, Coach Snow, and Dan Ward during the evidentiary hearing. *See Seamons III,* 15 F.Supp.2d at 1156–57.

1. Whether Coach Snow asked Brian to apologize to the team captains

The district court found that Brian was not asked to apologize for reporting the hazing incident. In his deposition and at the evidentiary hearing, Brian testified to the following: during the captains' meeting Dan Ward told him he had betrayed the team by reporting the assault and demanded an apology; when Brian refused, Coach Snow said he would need to "forgive and forget and apologize" in order to remain playing on the team; Coach Snow further stated, "we would need an apology before we let you back on the team." Coach Snow admits to making statements of this nature, although he denies ever directly telling Brian to apologize. If we credit Brian's version, and we must at this stage, there is clearly a disputed issue of fact as to whether Coach Snow asked Brian to apologize to the team captains.

2. The intended scope of this apology

The district court found that, even if Coach Snow used the word "apologize," he was not asking Brian to apologize for reporting the assault. Instead, the court concluded that "[t]he request for an 'apology' was not a demand, or a request, for Brian to say he was wrong for reporting the hazing incident; it was rather a request for a mutual reconciliation among Brian and his teammates to allow the boys to function together as friends and teammates." *Seamons III,* 15 F.Supp.2d at 1157. Brian testified that Coach Snow's statements regarding the apology came in response to a heated discussion between Brian and Dan Ward, wherein Dan insisted that Brian not be allowed to play unless he apologized for reporting the assault. Coach Snow interrupted the exchange and expressed his desire that Brian apologize in order to remain on the team. Coach Snow further stated that the team would need an apology before Brian could return. When these remarks are taken in context, it is reasonable to infer that Coach Snow was telling Brian he could not return to the team unless he apologized for reporting the assault. In any event, that is how Brian interpreted the statement, and a jury could properly do the same. Thus, the intended scope of the apology is also a matter of dispute.

One difficulty presented here is the fact that the scope of the requested apology is dependent in part on Coach Snow's intent in asking for it. The Coach's purpose in making these statements to Brian is not easily ascertained and requires inferences drawn from the Coach's behavior throughout the meeting and the broader controversy. This is precisely why summary judgment is not appropriate at this stage. * * *

3. Whether Brian's failure to apologize was a significant factor in his dismissal from the team

The district court found that Brian had failed to produce facts showing a "legal causal connection between his speech and his ultimate failure to be involved with the football team." *Seamons III,* 15 F.Supp.2d at 1155. We disagree. There are ample facts in the record to indicate that Brian's suspension and dismissal from the football team were directly related to his failure to apologize for reporting the assault.

Brian testified that when Coach Snow told him to "take the weekend and think about it," he understood he was being told not to participate in that night's game. Aplt.App., tab 14 at 337, 350–52. Coach Snow testified that by making this statement he was telling Brian he couldn't participate in that night's game. *Id.* at 402, 405. Presumably, had Brian offered the apology at the captains' meeting he would have been allowed to suit up for the game. He was at school and ready to play on Friday. There was no indication that he didn't want to play or would be prevented from playing in the Logan game. The only thing that happened to alter this situation was the captains' meeting at which Brian was asked, and refused, to apologize. Thus, there is evidence that Brian's refusal to apologize was directly related to the fact that he couldn't play in the Friday game, which was, in effect, a temporary suspension from the team.

A few days later when Brian told Coach Snow he was not going to apologize, he did not think he needed to apologize, and he still wanted to play football, Coach Snow stated that he was "sick of [his] attitude" and took him off the team for good. Aplt.App., tab 15 at 472.

It can clearly be inferred that this final confrontation, which resulted in Brian's dismissal from the team, was a product of Brian's refusal to apologize. * * *

In this case, the record indicates that Coach Snow, and only Coach Snow, was vested by the school district with the authority to make final decisions regarding membership on the Sky View football team. Aplt.App., tab 18 at 434, 436, 492. Because of this delegation of authority, the school district can be held liable for Coach Snow's actions on team membership. *See Pembaur,* 475 U.S. at 483, 106 S.Ct. 1292 ("Authority to make municipal policy . . . may be delegated by an official who possesses such authority . . .") * * *

B. Qualified Immunity

The district court alternatively found that even if the evidence supported a First Amendment claim, defendant officials were entitled to qualified immunity because "Brian has failed to show *any law* sufficiently well established in 1993 to support the proposition" that under the circumstances of the case he is entitled to relief. *Seamons III,* 15 F.Supp.2d at 1159 (emphasis added). "We review the district court's grant of summary judgment based on qualified immunity de novo, applying the same standard used by the district court." *Roberts v. Kling,* 144 F.3d 710, 711 (10th Cir.1998) (per curiam) (citation omitted).

When the case was last before us, we held that Brian's complaint stated a claim that defendants violated clearly established law and that they therefore were not entitled to qualified immunity. *See Seamons II,* 84 F.3d at 1238–39. We went on to note that defendants could reassert their entitlement to qualified immunity at summary judgment, but only if "Brian's allegations in the complaint prove to be unfounded." *Id.* at 1238. The district court's conclusion that the law was not clear in 1993 is inconsistent with our mandate and relevant case law.

* * *

Coach Snow was the person most directly involved with Brian's suspension and dismissal from the football team. It was his responsibility to determine who played on the team and to make disciplinary decisions. He orchestrated the captains' meeting, instructed Brian not to attend the Logan game when Brian refused to apologize, and arguably dismissed Brian from the team when Brian again expressed an unwillingness to apologize. "[A] reasonably competent public official should know the law governing his conduct." *Chapman v. Nichols,* 989 F.2d 393, 397 (10th Cir. 1993) (quotation omitted). A "precise factual correlation between the then-existing law and the case at-hand is not required." *Patrick v. Miller,* 953 F.2d 1240, 1249 (10th Cir. 1992) (quotation omitted). Coach Snow is not entitled to qualified immunity for his actions with respect to Brian's suspension and removal from the Sky View football team.

In the proceedings below, the district court expressed a belief that this case had gone on for too long, spawned an inordinate amount of controversy, and was not significant enough to warrant time in the federal courts. While this sentiment by a busy judge may be understandable, it cannot justify summary disposition in the face of genuine issues of material fact . . . Brian has asked for his day in court. Because he meets the requirements for stating a claim and alleging material facts in dispute, he is entitled to a trial.

CASES ON THE SUPPLEMENTAL WEB SITE

Cioffi v. Averill Park Central School District Board of Education et al. (2006 U.S. App. LEXIS 814). As you read this case, consider whether a school employee loses a right to publicly express concern about the health and safety of students in programs offered in the Averill Park School District.

Duitch v. Canton City Schools (2004) Ohio App. LEXIS 1878). As you read this case, note the court's ruling regarding the term "hazing" as defined by Ohio state law.

Perkins & Phillips v. Alamo Heights Independent School District et al. (204 F. Supp.2d 991). (2002). In this case, were female cheerleaders treated differently than male athletes by being disciplined differently for their involvement in hazing? Was their treatment a violation of Title IX?

The Estate of Jon Thomas Carmichael, By and Through Jon Timothy and Tami Carmichael, Individually and Upon Behalf of His Heirs, Plaintiffs, v. Ronnie Galbraith, et al., Defendants. 2012 U.S. Dist. LEXIS 857. In this case, what would the plaintiffs need to do in order to successfully argue a plausible claim to establish that Joshua Independent School District officials violated Carmichael's rights under the Equal Protection Clause of the Fourteenth Amendment?

QUESTIONS YOU SHOULD BE ABLE TO ANSWER

1. Identify the range of behaviors that may constitute hazing.

2. What does it mean that consent is not a defense in a hazing case?

3. How might an athlete who has been hazed make a negligence claim against a school district or college? What grounds might they seek to establish in order for a negligence claim to be argued?

4. In *Cioffi v. Averill Park School District*, what was the issue related to the athletic director's right to express his concerns regarding the health and safety of athletes?

5. Under what circumstances may parents be held accountable for the actions of their children in hazing cases?

REFERENCES

Cases

Caldwell v. Griffin Spalding County Board of Education et al., 22 Ga. App. 892 (1998).

Cookson v. Brewer School Department et al., 2007 Me. Super. LEXIS 232.

Davis v. Monroe County Board of Education, 526 U.S. 629; 119 S. Ct. 1661; 143 L. Ed.2d 839 (1999).

Duitch v. Canton City Schools, et al., 157 Ohio App. 3d 80; 2004 Ohio 2173; 809 N.E. 2d 62 (2004)

Elbaz v. Beverly Hills Unified School District, 2007 Cal. App. Unpub. LEXIS 4318

Golden v. Milford Exempted Village School District Board of Education, 2011 Ohio 5355; 2011 Ohio App. LEXIS 4384

Knoll v. Board of Regents of the University of Nebraska, 601 N.W.2d 757 (1999).

McElroy and Canestro v. Board of Education of the Bellmore-Merrick Central High School District, 5 Misc. 3d 321; 783 N.S.S.2d 781 (2004).

Meeker v. Edmunson et al.., 415 F. 3d 317 (2005).

Nice v. Centennial Area School District, 98 F. Supp.2d 665 (2000).

Perkins & Phillips v. Alamo Heights Independent School District et al., 204 F. Supp.2d 991 (2002).

Seamons v. Snow, 864 F. Supp. 1111 (D. Utah 1994).

Seamons v. Snow, 206 F.3d 1021 (2000).

Siesto v. Bethpage Union Free School District, QDS: 72701944 (*New York Law Journal*, December 30, 1999).

Snelling & Snelling v. Fall Mountain Regional School District et al., 2001 DNH 57 (2001).

Strout v. Packard, 76 Me. 148 (1884)

The Estate of Jon Thomas Carmichael, by and through Jon Timothy and Tami Carmichael, Individually, and Upon Behalf of His Heirs, Plaintiffs v. Ronnie Galbraith, et al., Defendants, 2012 U.S. Dist. LEXIS 857

Publications

Allen, E. J., & Madden, M. (2008). Hazing in view: College students at risk. Initial findings from the national study of student hazing. Orono, ME: University of Orono. Online. Internet. http://www.umaine.edu/hazingstudy/hazinginview1.htm

Anderson, C. (2009, February 4). Fairhaven parents anquished over decision to file hazing lawsuit. *Southcoast Today.* Online. Internet. http://www.southcoasttoday.com/

Besecker, A. (2008, August 9). New allegations made in Wilson hazing case. *The Buffalo News.*

Banovic, j. (2012, January 12). Three varsity hockey coaches fired from Howell High School after claims of hazing. *ABC News.* Online. Internet. http://www.wxyz.com/dpp/news/region/livingston_county/three-varsity-hockey-coaches-fired-from-howell-high-school-after-claims-of-hazing

Campo, S., Poulos, G., & Sipple, J. W. (2005). Prevalence and profiling: Hazing among college students and points of intervention. *American Journal of Health Behavior, 29* (2), p. 37–149.

Cook, B. (2012, February 6). Parents protest hazing-related suspension of longtime L.A. high school baseball Coach. *Forbes.* Online. Internet. http://www.forbes.com/sites/bobcook/2012/02/06/parents-protest-hazing-related-suspension-of-longtime-l-a-high-school-baseball-coach/

Crow, B., & MacIntosh, E. W. (2009, December). Conceptualizing a meaningful definition of hazing in sport. *European Sport Management Quarterly 9* (4), 433–451.

Crow, B., & Rosner, S. R. (2002, Winter). Institutional and organizational liability for hazing in intercollegiate and professional team sports. *St. John's Law Review*, 76.

Del Rosso, A. (2012, February 15). Hazing investigation underway at Bellaire high school. Online. Internet. http://www.wtov9.com

"Ex-coaches sue over students' behavior." (2004, August 4). *New York Law Journal, 24*, p. 2.

FAMU (2012, February 9). FAMU announces a new anti-hazing committee. Press release. Online. Internet. http://www.famu.edu/index.cfm?a=headlines&p=display&news=2539

Flock, J. (2003, May 22). Two adults charged in violent hazing incident. *CNN.com.* Online. Internet. http://articles.cnn. com/2003-05-21/justice/hazing.charges_1_glenbrook-north-high-school-hazing-school-board?_s=PM:LAW

Gershel, J. C., Katz-Sidlow, R. J., Small, E., & Zandieh, S. (2003). Hazing of suburban middle school and high school athletes. *Society for Adolescent Medicine*, *32* (5), p. 333–335.

Gutshall, B. (2008, Spring). A new uniform: NCAA policy and student-athlete misconduct. *University of Missouri-Kansas City Law Review, 76.*

Hoover, N. O. (principal investigator). National survey: Initiation rites and athletes for NCAA sports teams. Alfred University (August 30, 1999). Online. Internet. www.alfred.edu/news/html/hazing_study.html

Hoover, N. O., & Pollard, N. J. Initiation rites in American high schools: A national survey. Alfred University (2000). Online, Internet. www.alfred.edu/news/html/hazing_study.html

Jones, L. (2003, October 14). Hazing in schools: Allegations highlight the challenge of ensuring safety. *New York Law Journal*, p. 16.

Medina, M. (2009, April 7). Adults charged in Robertson High hazing. KRQU.com. Online. Internet. http://www.krqu.com/

Middleton, B. (2011, December 2). Four FAMU students expelled after band members death. *BET.com.* Online. Internet.http:// www.bet.com/news/national/2011/12/01/four-famu-students-expelled-after-band-member-s-death.htm

Monroe, I. (2012, January 27). Robert Champion death: Hazing or hate crime? *Huffington Post.* Online. Internet. http://www. huffingtonpost.com/irene-monroe/robert-champion-death_b_1232089.html

Putnam, G. M., & Messneger, B. (2011, December 1). Expulsions, suspensions meted out in Ando-ver hazing case. Eagle Tribune. Online. Internet. http://www.eagletribune.com/local/x910011623/ Expulsions-suspensions-meted-out-in-Andover-hazing-case

Report of the Wayne County Investigative Grand Jury pursuant to 42 Pa. C.S. Section 4552 Investigation #4. No. 26-2003 -Crminal Misc. (2004, February 24). Published by *Newsday* on March 10, 2004. Online. Internet. http://www.newsday.com/

Schneider, M. (2012, January 10). FAMU hazing: Robert Champion's family plans to sue owner of bus where student died. *Huffington Post.* Online. Internet. http://www.huffingtonpost.com/2012/01/10/family-to-sue-owner-of-bu_0_n_1196317.html

Schultz, T. A. (2012, February 15). Former Munster swim team member claims in lawsuit he was hazed. *Post Tribune.* Online. Internet. http://posttrib.suntimes.com/news/lake/10643112-418/former-munster-swim-team-member-claims-in-lawsuit-he-was-hazed.html

Sondheimer, E. (2012, February 5). Suspension of Manny Alvarado for hazing riles parents. *Los Angeles Times.* Online. Internet. http://articles.latimes.com/2012/feb/05/sports/la-sp-0206-sondheimer-column-20120206

Staff. (2012, February 14). Plea deal reached Wisconsin Rapids wrestlers' hazing case. *Greenbay Press Gazette.* Online. Internet. http://www.greenbaypressgazette.com/article/20120214/GPG0101/302150009/ Plea-deal-reached-Wisconsin-Rapids-wrestlers-hazing-case

Staskey, S. (2012, February 15). Bellaire school district deals with hazing issues. *Times Leader.* Online. Internet. http://www. timesleaderonline.com.

Stuart-Cassell, V., Bell, A., & Springer, J. F. (2011). *Analysis of state bullying laws and policies.* Report prepared for the U.S. Department of Education Office of Planning, Evaluation and Policy Development Policy and Program Studies Service. Online. Internet. http://www2.ed.gov/rschstat/eval/bullying/state-bullying-laws/state-bullying-laws.pdf

Sussberg, J. (2003). Shattered dreams: Hazing in college athletes. *Cordozo Law Review 24.*

Thompson, P. (2012, January 25). 'It's tradition': High school hockey coach fired for 'hazing' after players paraded through a bar in women's lingerie. *The Daily Mail.* Online. Internet. http://www.dailymail.co.uk/news/article-2091425/Its-tradition-High-school-hockey-coach-fired-hazing-players-paraded-bar-womens-lingerie.html?ito=feeds-newsxm

Wall, J. (2012, February 15). Hazed students not allowed to play sports after switching schools. *Yahoo Sports.* Online. Internet. http://sports.yahoo.com/blogs/highschool-prep-rally/hazed-students-not-allowed-play-sports-switching-schools-160736540.html

Legislation
Florida State Code 240.1325
Minnesota State Code 127.465
Ohio Revised Code 2903.31
New York State Code 120.16

RISK MANAGEMENT

4.00

The primary purpose of a risk management plan is not the avoidance of legal liability. Rather, it is the maintenance of a quality program; that is, one which deals reasonably and fairly with its clients or students and their families. A program that delivers what it says it will deliver, and does so in the context of reasonable management of the risks, is not assured of "safety" or freedom from lawsuits. But generally, if such a level of performance is achieved, legal liability issues are minimized and take care of themselves (Charles R. Gregg. *Staying in the Field and Out of the Courthouse.* 2002)

Many recreation and sport managers erroneously look upon risk management as safety or accident prevention. *Risk management* is much more than just safety or preventing accidents—it is an organized plan by which a recreation or sport business can manage or control both the programmatic risks and the financial risks facing the organization. Risk management involves not only *what to do* to control risks, but also involves *why to do it*—thus a sound risk management program is based upon the fundamental legal concepts discussed in Sections 2.10 *Negligence Theory*, 2.20 *Defenses*, and 2.30 *Recreation and Sport Management Applications.*

Section 4.00 is divided into two major parts. They are Section 4.10 *Risk Management Theory* and 4.20 *Recreation and Sport Management Applications. Risk Management Theory* discusses the fundamental concepts and foundations comprising risk management. Section 4.20 *Recreation and Sport Management Applications* looks more closely at a number of crucial aspects of risk management—standards of practice, risk management audits, crisis management, crowd management, and insurance protection and requirements.

RISK MANAGEMENT THEORY

4.10

4.11 RISK MANAGEMENT PROCESS

Robin Ammon, Jr. I Slippery Rock University

Globally sport has reached epic proportions. Recreation constitutes a growth industry as well. In addition to the parks and recreation field, which is immense, there is growth in the fitness industry, in traditional participant sports, in adventure sports, in extreme sports, and much more. This surge of recreation and sport activity has created a tremendous potential for injuries and financial losses.

Identification of the risks involved in recreation and sport did not become a serious concern until the early 1970s. Even though the concept of risk management had been extensively used by private business for some time, the recreation and sport industries' interest in managing risks only came after sovereign governmental immunity began to erode and litigation related to sport and recreation began to rise (van der Smissen, 1990). The focus of risk management in the business industry is financial. When risk management concepts are applied to the recreation and sport industries, a much broader focus is needed.

Some researchers believe that, while risk management literature suggested the concept was necessary to limit legal liability, risk management for many years was perceived as a hindrance (Sharp, Moorman, and Claussen, 2007). Obviously, in light of the litigious nature of our society, risk management becomes a necessary burden. Therefore, recreation and sport managers must become aware of the potential for injury and loss and must learn to effectively manage the immense risk that exists in their professions. The process of managing and controlling these risks has, over the last two or three decades, resulted in the field of risk management. The purpose of this chapter is to introduce students interested in recreation or sport management to the basics involved in a risk management process.

FUNDAMENTAL CONCEPTS

One of the first definitions of risk management as it applied to sport and recreation was developed in 1993. At that time Ammon defined **risk management** as controlling the financial and personal injury losses from sudden, unforeseen, unusual accidents and intentional torts (Ammon, 1993). Later Wong & Masteralexis (1998) termed it as "a management strategy to maintain greater control over the legal uncertainty that may wreak havoc on a sport business" (p. 90). In 2002, Corbett described risk management as "managing financial and human resources wisely, governing effectively, making decisions soundly and projecting a positive image towards sponsors, government funders and the community" (¶. 4). One of the more recent definitions (Spengler, Anderson, Connaughton & Baker, 2009) defined risk management as a "course of action designed to reduce the risk (probability or likelihood) and loss to sport participants, spectators, employees, management and organizations" (p. 46).

Regardless of the definition the "loss" resulting from the risk can be physical or financial in nature. For example, YMCA administrators must continually attempt to reduce risks that cause physical injury to their members. In addition, financial losses may occur at stadiums or arenas due to incidents such as vandalism, poorly written contracts, stolen equipment, and accidents in the venue's parking lot due to poor lighting. Risk management, however, doesn't seek to eliminate *all* risks, but rather it creates an environment where the inherent and negligence risks within activities and services provided by an organization are minimized without producing a change in the activity itself.

The D.I.M. Process

The **D.I.M. process** was developed as a tool to establish an effective risk management program. When used as an anticipatory technique rather than as a reactionary procedure, the D.I.M. process will assist organizations in decreasing the chance of litigation. This process involves three basic components: (1) *Developing* the risk management plan; (2) I*mplementing* the risk management plan; and (3) M*anaging* the risk management plan. Every organization, no matter the size, should have a current risk management plan. Each plan, however, should be specifically developed for that provider. Every organization will have risks specific to that business. For example, due to the specific risks, a risk management plan that works for a football facility will not be the same as one used at a baseball venue (Ammon, Southall & Nagel, 2010). However, components used in creating this plan will be similar no matter what type of organization. Thus, managers at golf courses, aquatic centers, ski areas, skateboard parks, or park and recreation departments will utilize the same basic principles.

Developing the Risk Management Plan

Developing a risk management plan consists of three separate stages: (1) identifying the risks, (2) classifying the risks, and (3) selecting methods of treatment for the risks.

Identification Stage

The **identification stage** is one of the key aspects of developing a successful risk management program. If the recreation or sport manager wants to control risks in the program, he or she must first identify those risks. Risks are present in all sport and recreation facilities and events including privately or municipally owned buildings, professional or intercollegiate entertainment facilities, and outdoor or indoor recreational settings. Each event or activity is different and has its own unique risks or areas of potential loss. Identifying these risks, therefore, needs to be specific, constant, and ongoing.

An effective step to identify risk is to create categories of risk and then to list risks within each category. There are several approaches that can be used to **categorize risk**.

van der Smissen (1990) categorized risks as (1) public liability caused by negligence in program services, (2) public liability [excluding negligence], (3) business operations, and (4) property exposures. Figure 4.25.1 in Chapter 4.25 *Managing Risk Through Insurance* was developed using this categorization method. By studying the table, one can see the typical risks included in each category.

Recreation and sport managers often focus on bodily injuries resulting from **public liability caused by negligence.** Injuries may include death, quadriplegia or other paralysis, brain damage, loss of limbs, loss of senses, injury to internal organs, strains, sprains, fractures, ligament damage, cuts, punctures, and abrasions. This type of risk typically relates to the activities or a service offered by an organization and often occurs when a member of the organization is negligent in performing his or her duties. However, if risk identification is limited to only those bodily injuries, many financial risks to an organization will be overlooked.

Risks grouped under **public liability (excluding negligence)** include such areas as malpractice by personnel, product liability, intentional torts, employment practices, sexual harassment, and civil liberty violations. Recreation and sport managers should note that the management of risk relating to employment law issues is becoming a great concern to many in the recreation and sport industries (Curtis, 2002). Individuals involved in the human resource operations of an organization must be aware that risks lurk within their purview as well. Typical cases in this category might relate to sexual harassment, discrimination, equal pay disputes, and wrongful termination claims. Tools that can be used to identify risks include **questionnaires** and **discussions and interaction with employees** relating to employment practices. Also, it is helpful to **read the literature** published by professional organizations (e.g., The National Recreation and Park Association) and consult with colleagues regaring potential risks relating to employment practices of which the manager might not be aware.

The risk of child abuse has been well documented in the alleged child molestation incident involving ex-Penn State coach Jerry Sandusky. Apparently there was a failure to have an established policy of reporting child abuse allegations. Incidents such as this illustrate the need for both an established policy and effective channels for reporting child abuse allegations. In addition, the existence of a policy is only worthwhile if employees know the policy and the steps involved to report an incident. A recent study indicated that 48 percent of 7-12 grade student respondents experienced some form of sexual harassment during the 2010–11 school year. An additional 30% were harassed via electronic means (texts, e-mails, Facebook, or other electronic means). The authors mentioned that many of the students who had been harassed through traditional methods were also harassed via cyberspace (AAUW, 2011). Since many sport and recreation participants are children, recreation and sport managers need to pay particular attention to devising strategies to control the risk of child abuse.

Property exposures are financial risks related to the ownership of real and personal property. Loss may occur as a result of fire, natural elements like lightning and floods, vandalism, and theft. Recreation and sport managers should rely on the help of various **professionals** in identifying potential risks related to property exposures. For example, an insurance agent should be contacted to insure that the organization has adequate property insurance. The 2011 spring floods along the Missouri River forced the Sioux City, Iowa, YMCA to relocate across the river to a part of the Tyson Arena. Having flood insurance enabled the YMCA to move back into their original facility once the waters subsided. In addition, a good agent can also help in identifying other risks.

Recreation and sport managers can also be exposed to risks via their organization's **business operations**. These risks are financial risks that result from business interruption, embezzlement and theft, the medical condition of employees, the health of key personnel, and employee accidents and injuries. To identify risks associated with business operations, a recreation or sport manager should examine the organization's operational **policies and procedures** to determine if the policies and procedures expose the organization to loss. Also, the manager can **observe** his or her employees at work to identify any activities that may lead to sickness, accidents, or disability.

The methods used to look for potential risks will vary depending upon the nature and size of the organization or business. Every entity, however, must establish a systematic procedure to assure that a complete risk assessment occurs (van der Smissen, 1990).

Classification Stage

Once the potential risks have been identified, the second stage in developing the plan is to **classify the risk**. The purpose of the classification stage is to determine how often (**frequency**) the risk may occur and the degree (**severity**) of the potential loss arising from the risk. Once the various risks have been identified, the risk manager takes each of the identified risks and evaluates them in terms of frequency and severity. The *frequency* of the risk is dependent on the number of times the risk or loss is likely to occur. The risk manager will view each identified risk and assign a frequency of "high," "medium," or "low." The *severity* of the risk is determined by the intensity of the potential injury and/or the degree of the threat to the financial stability of the organization. It is classified as "catastrophic," "critical," "moderate," or "low." The level of severity and the frequency are determined by the risk manager, based on his/her expertise derived from experience and training.

Spengler et al. (2009) developed similar approaches to categorize the risks. Spengler lists the categorization process as the second step of an "Analysis." "Risk Evaluation" is the step where the identified risks are evaluated by their frequency and severity.

Regardless of the terminology, once the risks have been classified a matrix can be created that allows a consistent approach to the classification process. A matrix gives the risk manager a method by which to classify all identified risks on the basis of frequency and extent of potential loss. Table 4.11.1 is such a matrix with some of the risks from a municipal basketball tournament placed into their proper categories. *All identified risks should be appropriately placed in the matrix, making clear the classification of each risk.* By placing the identified risks in the matrix, the risk manager will have successfully completed the classification stage. However, it should be noted that risk assessment and classification is an ongoing process, always subject to change.

Treatment of Risk

The final stage in developing the risk management plan is to determine a **treatment** for each identified and classified risk. A treatment is a method used to reduce, control, manage, or eliminate financial risks and bodily injuries. There are four basic treatments available to the risk manager. They are avoidance (or elimination) of the risk, transfer of the risk to another party, retention of the risk by the recreation or sport organization, and reduction of the risk (Spengler et al., 2009).

The type of treatment a risk manager uses for the identified and classified risks depends on the nature of the risk and the likelihood of the risk occurring. Although it is sometimes difficult to determine the appropriate treatment, a risk treatment matrix can assist in this process. A risk treatment matrix provides the recreation or sport manager with information that helps in deciding upon the treatment needed for any given risk. The manager, having identified and categorized each risk in Table 4.11.1, should then refer to Table 4.11.2 for the appropriate treatment. *Note: While the contents of Table 4.11.1 vary from activity to activity, the contents of Table 4.11.2, once established by the philosophy and the finances of the organization, remain the same for all activities.*

TABLE 4.11.1	RISK CATEGORY MATRIX			
	Severity of Injury or Financial Impact			
	Catastrophic Loss	Critical Loss	Moderate Loss	Low Loss
High Frequency	None	None	• Fan suffers hip injury when she trips in poorly lighted area in or about premisis. • Player injures knee due to uneven playing surface or wet spot on court	• Spectators evade admission fee • Spectator in bleachers suffers gouge from protruding screw
Medium Frequency	None	None	• Vandalism of arena • Player twists ankle on piece of ice thrown from the bleachers	• Incorrect change given to spectators • Fans suffer nausea from poorly prepared food at concession stands
Low Frequency	• Player breaks neck running into unpadded wall • Armed terrorist group takes hostages during tournament	• Spectator suffers facial laceration during altercation in bleachers • Poor crowd management leads to fight between players and fans	• Youth sustains eye injury during on-the-court promotion • Spectator suffers concussion from player diving into crowd after loose ball due to inadequate buffer zone	• Program seller gives away programs • Players' wallets are stolen fom the locker room

Avoidance/Elimination. This treatment requires that specific activities should not be included within the content of a program (avoidance) or they should be discontinued if they are presently being offered (elimination). Risks should be avoided or eliminated when they could cause a catastrophic or critical loss with medium or high frequency. In other words, the severity of the incident would be great and risk management could not control the frequency. Ideally, a risk manager should identify these risks before the accidents occur and avoid them completely. For example, if a high-risk activity such as cheerleading has a history of causing moderate to severe injuries, the school or athletic program may wish to eliminate the activity if the risks cannot be controlled (*Noffke v Bakke, 2008*).

In most situations, eliminating activities offered by recreation and sport organizations is not an attractive option. Therefore, elimination should not be the first choice for a risk manager. In the previously mentioned cheerleading situation, the decision to eliminate cheerleading might be unnecessary if strict policies regarding cheerleader supervisors, supervision, facility, progression, and approved stunts are implemented. Avoidance or elimination of an activity should only be implemented as a last resort when risk is substantial and likelihood of injury is significant. An example of avoidance occurred about 40 years ago. The use of trampolines was a standard fixture in most physical education programs, but was eliminated from most school districts due to the large number (frequency) of injuries and their severity.

TABLE 4.11.2	RISK TREATMENT MATRIX			
	Severity of Injury or Financial Impact			
	Catastrophic Loss	Critical Loss	Moderate Loss	Low Loss
High Frequency	Avoidance	Avoidance	Transfer & Reduction	Transfer/Retain & Reduction
Medium Frequency	Transfer/Avoidance & Reduction	Transfer/Avoidance & Reduction	Transfer & Reduction	Retain & Reduction
Low Frequency	Transfer & Reduction	Transfer & Reduction	Transfer/Retain & Reduction	Retain & Reduction

Transfer. Transfer is the shifting of the liability or responsibility for loss from the service provider to another party. This risk treatment occurs when two conditions exist: (1) the risk of loss is not substantial enough to warrant the avoidance of the activity, and (2) the risk is greater than the organization can assume on its own.

An important means of transfer is through the purchase of sufficient **insurance** coverage (see also Chapter 4.25 *Managing Risk Through Insurance* and Chapter 4.26 *Workers' Compensation*). Property insurance and personal injury liability insurance are often selected to provide protection from potential risks. It is important to understand that the insurance company will only cover the policyholder up to the limits of the coverage. For example, if a defendant has a $1 million liability policy and loses a $3 million judgment, the insurance company will *only* cover the first $1 million (Kaiser & Robinson, 1999).

Another important means of transfer is by **contract**. Examples of these contracts include liability waivers, indemnification clauses and the use of independent contractors. A **waiver** is a contract by which a person voluntarily gives up the right to sue another party (e.g., the service provider) for its negligence. The signer of the waiver (normally the participant) agrees to accept the risks of harm caused by the negligent actions of the other party. However, a waiver generally does not protect a service provider from liability for gross negligence or reckless misconduct. Waivers signed by parents on behalf of minor participants are likely to be enforced in only a few states (see Chapter 2.23 *Waivers and Releases*).

Indemnification clauses are clauses in a contract that provide for one party to indemnify or reimburse the other for loss. These clauses are generally included in equipment and facility rental contracts. For instance, an organization leasing a facility generally agrees contractually to indemnify the facility owners against any loss or litigation resulting from the event. These clauses, sometimes called **hold harmless agreements**, require the organization to be compensated by the individuals renting the facility if any damage occurs during the event or if someone is injured and files suit against the facility owner. Thus the risks during the event are *transferred* to the outside organization (see also Chapter 2.12 *Which Parties Are Liable?* and Chapter 2.21 *Defenses Against Negligence*).

An **independent contractor** is a person or business that contracts to perform a specific task for a service provider. Independent contractors provide expertise and are generally free to perform tasks as they see fit. The independent contractor is not an ordinary employee of the organization. Some personnel (e.g., team doctors, referees, personal trainers, and aerobic instructors) may function as independent contractors. These individuals are responsible for providing their own unemployment and liability insurance and are generally solely responsible for their negligent actions. Many organizations use independent contractors to provide adventure activities (such as whitewater rafting, scuba, ropes courses, and rock climbing). A landowner is often immune from the contractor's negligence when hiring an independent contractor. The risk is transferred from the landowner to the independent party. However, a landowner is not always shielded from liability. If a landowner hires a contractor to perform an inherently dangerous activity, he or she then is responsible for supervising the actions of the contractor. A landowner must ensure the activity is being performed as safely as possible and that the contractor is taking the appropriate safety measures. This is known as the "inherently dangerous activity exception". It should be noted that a landowner is not liable if a contractor's negligence is unusual in nature. However, a landowner *is* liable when the negligence of the contractor should have been initially considered by the landowner. The inherently dangerous activity exception is illustrated in *Hatch v. V.P. Fair Foundation and Northstar Entertainment* (1999). The plaintiff was injured during a bungee jump operated by the Fair Foundation. Northstar Entertainment, the independent contractor, violated several of its own safety policies including: number of staff present, age of the jump master, and failure to conduct a daily safety inspection. The jump master failed to attach the bungee cord to the crane, resulting in a 170-foot fall and serious injuries to the back, legs, and shoulders of the plaintiff. Due to the inherently dangerous activity exception the jury found that both the Fair Foundation and the contractor were liable and awarded the plaintiff $5 million (see Chapter 2.12 *Which Parties Are Liable?* and Chapter 2.21 *Defenses Against Negligence*).

A combination of these methods of transfer is usually preferable. For example, if the service provider wishes to offer rock climbing and realizes that the risk involved is too great for the organization, the provider may seek to transfer the risk. In this situation, the risk manager would pay an insurance company a premium to cover any physical or financial damages that may occur (Ammon et al., 2010). In addition, the manager can require that participants sign a liability waiver through which the participant releases the provider from liability for negligence. In doing so the provider has endeavored to transfer the risk to the insurance company and the participant. If the risk is substantial, as in rock climbing, and cannot be adequately transferred, the activity should be avoided.

Retention. A third treatment of risks, **retention**, means that the organization keeps the risk and assumes financial responsibility for certain injuries or financial losses that may occur. Retention is often preferred for minor or inexpensive risks. Retaining these risks is often less expensive than buying insurance to cover them.

Sometimes retention is termed **self-insurance**. In essence, the sport or recreation organization is simply paying a premium to itself. But this is not as easy as it sounds. If utilized, the organization must include retention as a line item in the budget and accumulate a reserve or "pool" of revenue to pay for such injuries (Ammon et al., 2010). Looking at the risk treatment matrix (see Table 4.11.2), the risks to be retained are those that have a low potential for loss and occur with low to medium frequency. An organization can accept these risks due to the fact that there is very little chance of incurring substantial financial losses. This, of course, is assuming that once the risk manager decides to keep the risk, proper precautions are taken to decrease the occurrence and/or monetary losses associated with the risk.

Reduction. The fourth treatment, and arguably the most important, is the reduction of risks. Risk reduction is a proactive approach to the management of risks. The objective of reduction is to reduce the chance for injury as well as the chance of litigation The reduction section of the risk management plan establishes a variety of operational practices for reducing the likelihood of loss related to the identified risk. Every risk cannot be eliminated from an activity, but often the frequency and severity can be minimized by the proper maintenance of property and equipment, establishing emergency procedures, providing better training for personnel, and other risk reduction techniques. This should be the focus of any risk management program. For example, when efforts are made to reduce the frequency and severity of losses in a youth soccer league there is less likelihood that losses will occur over a planned retention level. Requiring shin guards, anchoring the soccer goals, and inspecting the soccer field for obstructions or holes are all specific risk reduction techniques.

The primary objective of reduction is for the responsible party to be aware of potential losses (from the identification of risk) and to do something to reduce the potential loss. There are four major tools that the recreation or sport manager can use to reduce risk. The first is to **design a regular systematic inspection program**. A system of inspection must be established, a written record of that inspection must be kept, and a system of follow-up on hazards must be implemented. Inspection of facilities and equipment is a key to reducing loss. An organization is liable for the dangerous maintenance situations about which it knows and for those that it should have known if a proper professional job had been done on inspection (*Felipe v. Sluggers of Miami, Inc. and Sluggers, Inc.*, 2008).

Planned inspection should include machines that have critical parts such as cables on weight machines and maintenance items like chlorine storage for a swimming pool. Individuals knowledgeable about the items they are inspecting must complete these inspections. Also, this type of inspection helps locate newly created risks caused by vandalism, abuse or misuse, and theft. If a hazard is found during inspection, a system for addressing the hazard must be implemented. The system should include the following steps: (1) the hazard must be reported to maintenance personnel; (2) the individual overseeing the area where the hazard is located must be notified; (3) the equipment or area must be taken out of service until the repair is made; (4) once the identified hazard is eliminated, maintenance personnel must inform the manager; and (5) there should be established steps to follow in the event the repair has not been made in a reasonable period of time. (See also Chapter 2.31 *Premises Liability* and Chapter 4.22 *Audits in Risk Management*.)

The second major tool involves **establishing a maintenance program for facilities and equipment**. The maintenance program must be described in an organization's risk management plan and include both preventative and remedial maintenance that occurs on a regular basis. With the exception of slip and falls, the failure to provide proper maintenance is the leading cause of litigation against most sport/entertainment facilities (Ammon et al., 2010).

A third tool involves **training the staff**. Staff should be trained to identify normal wear and tear and general deterioration of equipment, facilities, and other athletic areas that may lead to loss. Employees also need to understand how to conduct activities so that proper care is afforded to participants. The recreation or sport manager should verify that his or her staff knows how to ensure participants have the proper skill level and conditioning for activities, understands proper supervision, and understands how to enact the organization's emergency procedures (see also Chapter 2.34 *Supervision*). For most situations, it is important that the staff know certain information about the individual's ability to participate in the activity safely (van der Smissen, 1990). For example, in an age-group gymnastics program, the skill level and developmental stage of participants must be known to place them in the proper class. An organization must determine what skill and conditioning level is required for participation in the program for each activity or service.

Finally, the fourth tool recreation and sport managers must utilize is **a system under which documents related to program participation may be filed.** They also must be able to retrieve these documents when necessary. Forms that should be filed include parental permission forms, agreements to participate, waivers, membership applications, contracts, inspection checklists, accident report forms, health records, records containing operations information, rules and regulations, copies of employee credentials, and any other program-related document. With the growing threat of litigation, the need to document and to preserve documentation takes on added importance. In 2008, a 19-year-old plaintiff suffered a damaged testicle when a pitching machine delivered a 60 mph baseball when the machine's light indicated it was off. The plaintiff's attorney argued that the defendant did not have a maintenance log, checklist or manuals or any safety policies. The defendants also had prior knowledge that the machine was operable even when the light was off. The jury returned a $1.16 million award to the plaintiff (*Felipe v. Sluggers of Miami, Inc. and Sluggers, Inc.*, 2008).

When a risk manager develops a risk management plan, the most efficient and effective way to decrease the occurrence of various risks is to use reduction techniques such as the above. When a risk manager decides to retain or transfer the risks, he or she must be ready to also incorporate these reduction techniques to insure that each situation is handled in a manner that will reduce the chance of liability. *A crucial concept to remember is that risk reduction should be a risk management treatment any time an activity is offered—in conjunction with transfer or retention.* If the risks are not managed with the use of reduction techniques, more claims will occur and greater costs will be incurred. This will create a drain on funds allotted for retained risks and will eventually cause the insurer to raise the organization's premiums to cover the risks in question. By utilizing reduction techniques to reduce the occurrence of risks, the service provider should be able to keep insurance premiums and budgeted expenses at a minimum. In fact, by managing the risks, it is probable that the number of claims will decrease, which may cause the insurance rates to diminish as well (Ammon et al., 2010).

Implementing the Risk Management Plan

The second component in the D.I.M. process consists of implementing the risk management plan. Each individual in an organization must understand the overall risk management plan and risk reduction strategies and know what his or her role is in implementing the plan. Therefore, it can be said that the effectiveness of the overall plan is in direct proportion to the effectiveness of the communication regarding the plan. If communication about the plan is nonexistent, incomplete, or inadequate, the program will become inoperable and the risks will not be reduced as they should be. Direct interpersonal communication is required to insure the plan functions properly.

A risk manager can supplement oral communication with printed guidelines outlining risk reduction techniques. These guidelines can be inserted in the employee manual during the first orientation. Examples of the items covered in the guidelines include: the organizational layout and operation, personnel and organizational management, rules and regulations of the business, responsibilities of various employees, correct methods of documenting records and reports, and emergency procedures. The manual is sometimes erroneously termed a "safety manual."

Some organizations make the mistake of placing the entire risk management plan into every employee manual. The sheer comprehensiveness of the plan will cause many new hires to avoid reading the manual. Only place the pertinent portions of the overall plan into the specific employee's manual. Employee dedication to the process is a key component for a successful risk management plan.

The utilization of a **sound training program** is another way to ensure communication and the implementation of the risk management plan. An in-service education program can be used to communicate staff responsibilities in relation to the plan and provide an opportunity for individuals to improve their ability to identify various types of risks. In-service educational opportunities allow the risk manager to explain the risk management plan to the organization's employees while stressing the importance of implementing the reduction strategies in it. For risk reduction to be effective, three in-service areas need to be addressed on a regular basis: (1) communication of responsibilities—what is each individual's role in implementing the plan; (2) development of professional judgment and decision making—what standard of care is required of each employee; and (3) credential education/training—the provision of expertise or an increased knowledge base that will lead to an increased ability to make sound judgments. The risk manager must verify that personnel are qualified for their positions and hold the necessary certifications.

Managing the Plan

The final component of the D.I.M. process is to **manage the plan**. The first step in managing the plan is to **designate a risk manager** or the selection of a risk management committee. Sport and recreation organizations may hire a risk manager or assign one person the role of risk manager as part of his or her other duties. Effective risk managers and risk management committee members share many of the same traits. The risk manager must be a highly motivated individual, must be committed to risk management, and must be able to motivate others to believe in the risk management plan. Whichever system is chosen, the responsible party should monitor the risk management plan, implement changes, assist in fostering a genuine risk management attitude among other employees, conduct inspections, review accidents, and supervise in-service training (van der Smissen, 1990).

The second step in managing the plan is to provide the risk manager and committee with the **authority to lead.** This authority should be described in the policy statement of the organization because it provides a foundation for the plan. The policy statement should clearly delineate the responsibilities of the risk manager. The statement should outline and define the authority of the person responsible for administering the plan.

The management staff and ownership of the organization must also endorse and support the idea of risk management. They must be willing to assist the risk manager or risk management committee with verbal and financial support. Various costs are associated with any effective risk management plan—insurance comprising the greatest expense. Due to the society we live in and the potential for terrorism, the cost of some types of insurance have increased ten-fold. Therefore the organization's budget should include a line item devoted specifically for the implementation and continual assessment of the risk management plan. Without upper management's support a risk management plan will not succeed. The risk manager and the risk management committee must be given the freedom to act independently, but within the philosophy of the sport or recreation organization (Ammon et al., 2010).

The third step in managing the plan is to **provide employees with the opportunity for continuous input** into the risk management plan. Including employees, particularly those who have contact with clients, on the risk management committee is a possible source for this input. The continual success of a risk management plan mandates that employees, supervisors, and managers on all levels have the ability to interact with each other. Additionally, anyone whose expertise may improve the quality of the risk management plan should be included in the overall risk management process. The size of the committee depends on the overall goals and size of the organization.

As previously mentioned, risks are constantly changing and shifting due to the variety of activities and programs offered by an organization. The size of the organization, the type of activity being conducted, the age of the participants, the skill level of the participants and the age of any associated venue will cause the risks to vary. The risks will never remain the same so the assessment of these risks needs to be both flexible and constant. As soon as an organization ceases assessing the risks they open themselves up to potential litigation.

Risk management is a necessity for sport and recreation managers today. Even though many risks can be identified, classified, and treated, some hazards will still exist and accidents will occur. It is impossible and unrealistic to expect a risk manager to eliminate all injuries and financial losses. However, by developing an extensive risk management plan, implementing the plan, and bestowing the authority to manage the plan upon a concerned risk manager, recreation and sport managers can diminish a number of dangerous risks.

SIGNIFICANT CASE

The case illustrates the lack of a proper swimming pool risk management plan including appropriate emergency procedures. The defendant argued they had no duty to provide lifeguards at the swimming pool. The defendant also maintained there had been no previous incidents of a similar nature. Therefore the defendant claimed they could not have foreseen that the incident could have occurred. Several key concepts such as the presence of a proper risk management plan, proper supervision and response to emergencies are important to keep in mind while reading the case.

BENITA NORTHINGTON V. GOSPEL VOLUNTEERS INC.

2007 U.S. Dist. LEXIS 14361
February 16, 2007, Decided

I. Introduction

On or about September 24, 2004, Benita Northington filed suit against Gospel Volunteers, Inc., a not for profit corporation as well as the Salvation Army. Plaintiff alleges that Decedent, who was participating in a Salvation Army drug and alcohol rehabilitation program held at Gospel's facility in Hamilton County, New York, Camp-of-the-Woods, was under Gospel's care when he drowned while using the camp's indoor swimming pool on September 28, 2002. Plaintiff contends, among other things, that "knowing that the registrants were fighting drug and/or alcohol addiction problems and might make decisions that were not in their best interests, [Gospel was] responsible for [the] registrants' well-being . . . and were under individual and/or joint duties and obligations to take reasonable steps to protect the registrants from harm" and that Gospel breached its duty "to employ and position lifeguards and/or other life-saving, rescue or water-safety personnel at or around the swimming pool."

On or about August 24, 2006, Gospel moved for summary judgment arguing that (1) "Gospel did not owe a duty to the plaintiffs, statutory or common-law" because, among other things, "Gospel was under no duty to provide a lifeguard at the pool at the time of the incident" and "Decedent signed a release of liability, expressly assuming the risk of injury and negating any duty owed by Gospel" and (2) the Report of Charles D. Alston, dated August 11, 2006 submitted by Plaintiff in opposition to Defendant's motion for summary judgment, is inadmissible because it "is wholly conclusory and based on pure speculation."

On or about September 15, 2006, Plaintiff filed an opposition arguing that: (1) "Defendant Gospel Volunteers owed the decedent statutory duties . . . to have implemented a plan for daily bather supervision . . . and to supervise use of its pool" and "Decedent did not release defendant . . . from the consequences of its own negligent conduct" and (2) the Alston Report should

not be excluded because the conclusions were based on "deposition testimony, the report on the decedent's death, photographs and other factual data relating to Lamar Spruance's death."

***

For the reasons set forth below, Defendant's motion for summary judgment is denied.

II. Background

By a contract, dated March 27, 2002, the Salvation Army leased Camp-of-the-Woods from Gospel in order to conduct a drug and alcohol rehabilitation workshop for the two-day period September 27, 2002 to September 29, 2002. The Contract lists several rules and regulations relating to the camp's facilities, including regulations about the usage of the camp's indoor swimming pool.

Decedent, who "was a registered participant in Salvation Army's drug and alcohol rehabilitation program," was present at Camp-of-the-Woods for the September 27, 2002 to September 29, 2002 program. On September 27, 2002, Decedent signed a "Release of Liability" which states, among other thing, that "I . . . hereby assume any and all risk associated with my/our use of the swimming pool" and that Plaintiff "release[s] Gospel . . . from any and all liability for any injury or death that may result from my use" of the indoor pool. The Release also states that "a minimum of two adults, 18 years of age or older must be present whenever this swimming facility is in use. At least one adult must be on the pool deck."

On the evening of September 28, 2002, "Mr. Spruance was playing volleyball with other members of the group and suffered a cramp in a leg. He then went to the pool to work out the cramp." Marcus Boone, another program participant, was swimming in the shallow end of the pool when Decedent arrived. "While in the pool, Decedent experienced leg cramps and other cramps or physical problems that prevented him from remaining afloat while trying to swim." After hearing Decedent yell for help, "Mr. Boone . . . tried to reach Mr. Spruance while hanging onto a torpedo buoy but could not reach the bottom of the pool." Boone sought help from the camp's front desk, where he immediately alerted a Gospel staff member, Brian Bledsoe, to Decedent's condition. When Bledsoe arrived at the indoor pool facility, he pulled Decedent from the water and then "asked Mr. Boone to return to the front desk and use the emergence [sic] phone located there to dial 911 and report the problem." Decedent was transported to Nathan Littauer Hospital in Gloversville, New York and declared dead on September 29, 2002 at 1:30 a.m.

During discovery, Plaintiff submitted an expert report from Charles D. Alston, an American Red Cross Water Safety Instructor, which identifies certain alleged deficiencies in Gospel's pool management procedures and concluded that "based on the documents provided me in this matter, it is my opinion, based on my experience, training, and education, that Gospel did not adequately safeguard Mr. Lamar Spruance . . . and contributed to this death on September 28, 2002." "As stated in their emergency plan, in the event of an emergency, the front desk is required to notify 911 first; instead Brian Bledsoe (front desk staff) responded and retrieved Mr. Spruance from the pool bottom. After [Bledsoe's] failed attempt to perform CPR, which [he] was not currently qualified to perform, Mr. Bledsoe left the victim to seek qualified help. This action wasted several minutes . . .

***

IV. Analysis

Negligence Claim

Defendant argues, among other things, that "it is undisputed that Gospel was under no statutory duty to provide a lifeguard at the pool at the time of the incident," the "waiver of liability [signed by Decedent] is enforceable," and "decedent voluntarily assumed the risk of injury from swimming." Plaintiff counters that "there are material fact issues as to whether Gospel Volunteers failed to take reasonable actions to safeguard its guests who used

its pool after a prior near drowning incident . . . whether Gospel Volunteers failed to post a warning sign in the pool area that one adult was required to be on the pool deck . . . whether Gospel Volunteers had the required statutory safety equipment at pool side and whether it failed to adequately follow its safety plan." Plaintiff further argues that "the law frowns upon contracts intended to exculpate a party from the consequences of his own negligence," and that Decedent "could not have assumed the risk that Defendant Gospel Volunteers had no viable safety plan."

"[T]he elements of negligence under New York law . . . are . . . (1) the defendant must owe the plaintiff a duty of care; (2) that duty of care must be breached; (3) the plaintiff must suffer an injury; and (4) the defendant's breach must be the proximate cause of the injury."

***

The record before the Court reflects several factual issues which should be reserved for trial, including, among other things, (i) whether Gospel complied with New York Sanitary Code provisions requires that "operators of swimming pools must develop, update and implement a written pool safety plan, consisting of procedures for daily bather supervision, injury prevention; reacting to emergencies, injuries, and other incidents, providing first aid and summoning help"), (ii) whether Gospel employee, Brian Bledsoe, acted properly and timely in calling 911 emergency services upon learning of Decedent's injury and (iii) whether Gospel's alleged failures were the proximate cause of decedent's death,

With respect to Defendant's two principal contentions, (a) a party's compliance with a safety statute does not preclude a finding of negligence, and (b) New York courts have in some circumstances rejected broad exculpatory clauses.

***

V. Conclusion and Order

For the reasons stated above, Defendant's motion for summary judgment is denied.

CASES ON THE SUPPLEMENTAL WEB SITE

Clahassey v C Ami Inc. (2002 Mich. App. LEXIS 1352). The case illustrates the importance of a sound risk management plan. The reader needs to pay attention to how the location of the event and the failure to warn impacted the court's decision.

John Hopkins v. Connecticut Sports Plex. LLC. (2066 Conn. Super. LEXIS 1710). The case illustrates the concept of foreseeability. While reading the case pay

attention to the lack of a proper alcohol management plan, proper numbers of security staff and documentation of prior incidents.

Maisonave v. Newark Bears (2005 N.J. LEXIS 1108). Examine what the NJ Supreme Court decided about the limited duty rule. When did it apply? What was the standard of care in the other sections of the ballpark?

Sciarrotta v. Global Spectrum, et al. (2008 N.J. LEXIS 314). The two aspects of the limited duty rule are discussed. Pay particular attention to the Supreme Courts conclusion pertaining to the pre-game warm-up.

Beglin v. Hartwick College, 2009 N.Y. App. Div. LEXIS 7970. This case illustrates the importance of actual or constructive notice of a dangerous condition.

QUESTIONS YOU SHOULD BE ABLE TO ANSWER

1. Describe the significance of risk management.

2. Explain the DIM Process. What are the steps and how do they relate to each other?

3. Discuss the various types of transfer. Which of them do you believe is used most often?

4. Analyze as many reduction treatments as you can think of. If you were a sport or recreation venue manager which ones would be of the highest priority?

5. Identify two to three risks that a sport or recreation manager would encounter. Classify the risks and then select a treatment for each risk.

REFERENCES

Cases

Hatch v. V.P. Fair Foundation and Northstar Entertainment, 990 S.W.2d 126; 1999 Mo. App. LEXIS 315
Felipe v. Sluggers of Miami, Inc. and Sluggers, Inc., No. 07-18180 CA 22, Miami-Dade County Circuit Court, 11th, FL 2008
Noffke v. Bakke, 748 N.W.2d 195 (2008)

Publications

Ammon, R., Jr. (1993). Risk and game management practices in selected municipal football facilities. (Doctoral dissertation, University of Northern Colorado, 1993). *Dissertation Abstracts International, 54*, 3366A.

Ammon, R., Jr., Southall, R., & Nagel, M. (2010. *Sport facility management: Organizing events and mitigating risks* (2nd ed.) Morgantown, WV: Fitness Information Technology, Inc.

Corbett, R. (2002, August). *Risk management for sport organizations and sport facilities.* Presented at the Sports   Management: Cutting Edge Strategies For Managing Sports as a Business Symposium, Toronto.

AAUW (2011). *Crossing the line: Sexual harassment at school.* Retrieved from http://www.aauw.org/learn/research/upload/ CrossingTheLine.pdf

Curtis, T. (2002, Fall). Still the next big thing: Discrimination lawsuits keep coming in sports as the issue shows no sign of slowing. *SSLASPA Newsletter, 9*(3), 3.

Kaiser, R., & Robinson, K. (1999). Risk management. In B. van der Smissen, M. Moiseichik, V. Hartenburg, & L. Twardzik (Eds.), *Management of park and recreation agencies* (pp. 713–741). Ashburn, VA: NRPA.

Sharp, L. A., Moorman, A. M., & Claussen, C. L. (2007). *Sport law: A managerial approach.* Scottsdale, AZ: Holcomb Hathaway.

Spengler, J. O., Anderson, P. M., Connaughton, D. P., & Baker, T. A. (2009). *Introduction to sport law.* Champaign, IL: Human Kinetics.

van der Smissen, B. (1990). *Legal liability and risk management for public and private entities.* Cincinnati, OH: Anderson Publishing Co.

Wong, G. M., & Masteralexis, L. P. (1998). Legal principles applied to sport management. In L. P. Masteralexis, C. A. Barr, & M. A. Hums (Eds.), *Principles and practice of sport management* (pp. 87–116). Gaithersburg, MD: Aspen Publishers.

RECREATION AND SPORT MANAGEMENT APPLICATIONS
4.21 STANDARDS OF PRACTICE
JoAnn M. Eickhoff-Shemek I University of South Florida, Tampa

In a negligence lawsuit, a **standard of care** will be applied to measure the competence of a professional. If the professional's conduct falls below such a standard, he/she may be liable for injuries or damages resulting from such conduct (Black, 1991). The standard of care can be determined in various ways, but one way is from **standards of practice** developed and published by **professional** and **independent** organizations. This chapter will focus on the legal implications associated with these types of standards, not those dealing with accreditation, licensure, certification, statutes, or those developed by risk management authorities (*e.g.*, some states and municipalities) and insurance companies.

Standards of practice published by professional organizations are commonly referred to as standards, guidelines, recommendations, or position statements. Many professional organizations have published these documents to provide benchmarks of desirable practices for practitioners and managers. In addition to these types of standards, there are "technical physical specifications" (van der Smissen, 2000) published by independent organizations such as the American Society of Testing and Material (ASTM), the Consumer Product Safety Commission (CPSC), and equipment manufacturers. For example, ASTM has published standard specifications for safety signage for fitness equipment/facilities and standard specifications for playground equipment. CPSC has published standard specifications on equipment such as bicycle helmets and on facilities such as spas, hot tubs, and whirlpools. Equipment manufacturers also publish specifications regarding proper use, installation, maintenance, warnings, etc. with regard to the various types of equipment they sell.

Published standards of practice can be entered into evidence (via expert testimony) in a court of law to help determine the standard of care or **duty** that a defendant owes to a plaintiff. Therefore, it is critical for recreation and sport managers to incorporate these standards of practice into their risk management plans.

FUNDAMENTAL CONCEPTS

Potential Legal Impact of Published Standards of Practice

As demonstrated in Figure 4.21.1, published standards of practice can be introduced as evidence via expert testimony to help determine duty. If the defendant's conduct is inconsistent with these standards of practice, it can result in a breach of duty that can then lead to negligence. However, if the defendant's conduct is consistent with the standards of practice, it will be difficult for the plaintiff to prove there was a breach of duty.

Generally, the failure to adhere to published standards of practice can lead to claims of "ordinary" negligence against the defendant(s) as demonstrated in the Significant Case (*Elledge v. Richland/Lexington School District Five*) presented in this chapter. However, "gross" negligence claims also can be made against the defendant, *e.g.*, see *Xu v. Gay* (2003). (See this case on the Supplemental Web Site). In addition to ordinary and gross negligence claims, plaintiffs also might file a "breach of express warranty" claim against the defendant.

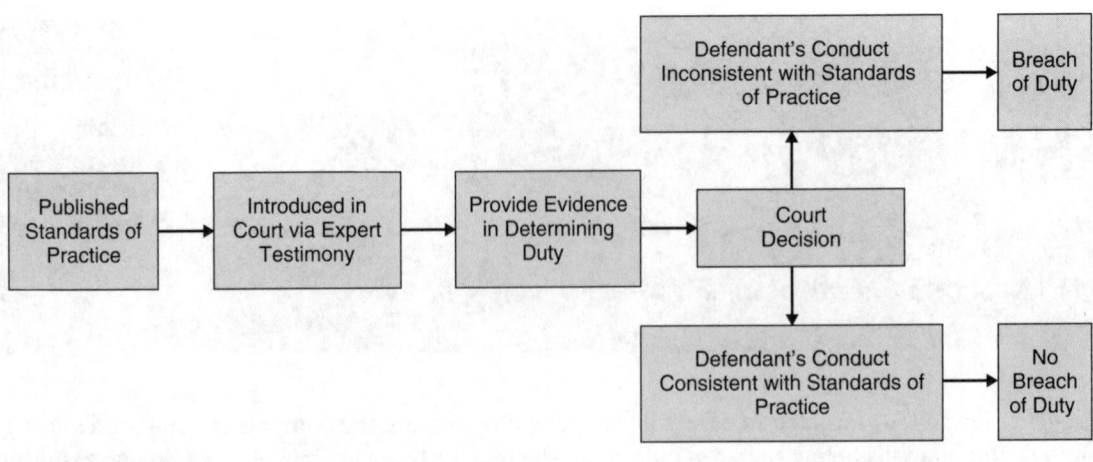

FIGURE 4.21.1 **EXAMPLE OF THE POTENTIAL LEGAL IMPACT OF PUBLISHED STANDARDS OF PRACTICE**

For example, the complaint filed in *Gloria Hicks v. Bally Total Fitness Corp.* not only included a wrongful death action for both ordinary and gross negligence, but also for breach of express warranty (Herbert, 2009a). The wrongful death actions in this 2008 case involved the failure of Bally Total Fitness Corp. to provide appropriate emergency care to Malcolm Hicks when he suffered a sudden cardiac arrest while exercising at the fitness club. Mr. Hicks died several days later in the hospital. In the breach of express warranty claim, the plaintiff claimed that ". . . Bally pledged, agreed and warranted to its members that it would . . . conform to all relevant laws, regulations and published standards . . ." and ". . . would support and abide by guidelines and recommendations of the American College of Sports Medicine . . ." (Herbert, 2009, pp. 4-5).

Standards of Practice Published by Professional Organizations

Following is a list of some of the professional organizations that have published standards of practice for various types of recreation and sport practitioners/managers. By no means is this a comprehensive list.

Exercise/Fitness Professionals

1. American College of Sports Medicine: *ACSM's Health/Fitness Facility Standards and Guidelines*
2. American College of Sports Medicine and American Heart Association Joint Position Statement: *Recommendations for Cardiovascular Screening, Staffing, and Emergency Policies at Health/Fitness Facilities* and *Automated External Defibrillators in Health/Fitness Facilities*
3. International Health, Racquet & Sportsclub Association: *IHRSA Club Membership Standards*

Strength and Conditioning Professionals

National Strength and Conditioning Association: *Strength and Conditioning Professional Standards and Guidelines*

Recreation Professionals

1. National Therapeutic Recreation Society and National Recreation and Park Association: *NTRS Code of Ethics and Interpretive Guidelines*
2. American Therapeutic Recreation Association: *ATRA Standards for the Practice of Therapeutic Recreation*

Physical Educators

American Alliance for Health, Physical Education, Recreation and Dance—National Association for Sport and Physical Education: *Moving into the Future: National Physical Education Standards*

Coaches

American Alliance of Health, Physical Education, Recreation and Dance:—National Association for Sport and Physical Education: Quality Coaches, Quality Sports: *National Standards for Sport Coaches*

Athletic Trainers

Board of Certification (BOC): *BOC Standards of Professional Practice*

The Proliferation of and Inconsistency Among Published Standards of Practice

One of the major purposes for developing and publishing standards of practice is to help standardize the delivery of services. Published standards of practice serve as "benchmarks" of practices that reflect the minimal acceptable level of service owed to participants and that should be universally applied by properly trained and educated professionals (Eickhoff-Shemek, Herbert, & Connaughton, 2009). Most often, these are developed by leaders within a given organization using a consensus and peer-review approach. However, a major challenge for some recreation and sport managers is that there has been a proliferation of such published statements, not to mention the many inconsistencies that exist among them.

This is especially true in the exercise/fitness field. In addition to the three published documents listed above under "exercise/fitness," several other organizations (*e.g.,* Medical Fitness Association, YMCA, Aerobics and Fitness Association of America) have also published standards of practice in recent years. The high number of these published standards of practice has led to many inconsistencies among them. For example, IHRSA's published standards of practice (IHRSA Club Membership Standards, 2005) do not require their clubs to have an Automated External Defibrillator (AED). However, ACSM does require health/fitness facilities to have an AED. ACSM Standard #7 states that "Facilities must have as part of their written emergency response system a public access defibrillation (PAD) program" (Tharrett, McInnis & Peterson, 2007, p. 2).

Not only do these inconsistencies make it difficult for exercise/fitness professionals to know which standards of practice they should follow, but these inconsistencies also allow expert witnesses to select—among the various standards of practice —those that best support their individual opinions. This can lead to differences in court rulings with regard to the establishment of the standard of care owed to participants in exercise and fitness programs. Therefore, given the inconsistencies that exist (discussed next), it is recommended that professionals **"follow those [published standards of practice] that are the most authoritative or safety oriented in their approach, regardless of how they are defined and/or stated . . ."** (Eickhoff-Shemek, Herbert, & Connaughton, 2009, p. 53).

In an attempt to address the many inconsistencies, the National Sanitation Foundation (NSF) International—an independent, non-profit organization—formed a Joint Committee for Health and Fitness Facilities in August, 2009. This committee was made up of industry experts representing various professional organizations (Herbert, 2009b). The intent of this effort was to develop a uniform set of standards that could lead to certification for facilities that met the standards. These standards can be found at: http://standards.nsf.org/apps/group_public/download.php/12743/341i1r16.pdf.

In December 2011, this NSF Joint Committee passed the ballot for a standard for a fitness facility certification so that facility operators can volunteer to have their facility certified by meeting the NSF standards (Goldman, 2011). Before the certification can begin, it has to be approved by the NSF Council of Public Health Consultants. It is too early to know what effect, if any, the NSF standards will have on all of the other current standards published by professional organizations in the exercise/fitness field.

Inconsistencies in Terminology

Certain professional organizations (*e.g.,* ACSM and NSCA) have distinguished, by definition, a standard from a guideline (Tharrett, McInnis, & Peterson, 2007; NSCA, 2009). Both ACSM and NSCA have defined **standards** as requirements and **guidelines** as recommendations. Standards are written as "must" statements and guidelines are written as "should" statements. Other published standards of practice, e.g., *BOC Standards of Professional Practice* use the term "standards" in the title of their publication, but all the standards are written as "should" or "shall" statements, not "must" statements. Another inconsistency in the use of terminology is demonstrated in the ACSM and American Heart Association (AHA) joint position paper titled *Recommendations for Cardiovascular Screening, Staffing, and Emergency Policies at Health/Fitness Facilities* which includes requirements (must statements) and recommendations (should statements), though the title specifically states "recommendations."

Although differences clearly exist in how professional organizations define and use the terms standards and guidelines, does it make a difference to the courts when establishing the standard of care? It probably does not (see *Xu v. Gay* on the Supplemental Web Site). In *Xu*, Ning Yan died from a severe head injury resulting from a fall off a treadmill that had only 2½ feet clearance behind it at the defendant's fitness facility. The expert witness for the plaintiff, Dr. Marc Rabinoff, stated that the industry's standard of care for the safety distance behind treadmills should be a minimum of five feet. Though he did not specify the industry standards he was referring to, he did state that they were voluntary, not mandatory. Interestingly, the court made no distinction with regard to voluntary or mandatory stating that the "defendant's ignorance of and failure to implement these standards . . . establishes a case of ordinary negligence . . ." (p. 171). It appears from this case that even though the expert witness stated in his testimony that the industry standards were voluntary, the court still considered them as evidence of the standard of care that the defendant owed to Yan.

To add more concern with regard to how standards and guidelines are defined, a New York court ruled that the *ACSM's Health/Fitness Facility Standards and Guidelines* could not be applied to help determine the legal duties of the defendants because of a disclaimer included in the third edition of the publication (*Bloom v. ProMaxima Manufacturing Company*, 2009). The disclaimer (which was not included in the first and second editions), states that the standards are not to be used as evidence to determine the standard of care in the event of injuries and subsequent claims or lawsuits.

Two well-known expert witnesses, Harvey Voris and Marc Rabinoff, have often referred to these ACSM standards (as well as the NSCA and ASTM standards) in their expert testimony to communicate with courts as to what is appropriate with regard to facility operation and exercise equipment design and maintenance (Voris and Rabinoff, 2011). They state that, until the ruling in *Bloom*, these standards were never questioned with regard to their legal effect. They also state that "these statements need to be meaningful so they can be relied upon to establish . . . a standard of care especially when adherence to such a standard would prevent incidents from continuing to occur" (p. 21). In addition, they encourage ACSM and other professional organizations not to include damaging disclaimers in their publications because "how can a standard be a standard if the professional organization that writes them does not stand by them?" (p. 21).

The Law and Standards of Practice Continually Change

New issues arise which can potentially change the law as well as published standards of practice. It is important for recreation and sport managers to stay abreast of these changes. For example, in recent years several states have passed legislation that mandate fitness facilities to have an AED (Eickhoff-Shemek, Herbert, & Connaughton, 2009). In addition, several professional organizations have recently revised their published standards of practice to "require" fitness facilities to have an AED versus recommending an AED. Recreation and sport managers also need to stay abreast of new standards that are under development. For example, the ASTM is currently developing a new standard: New Specification for Universal Design of Fitness Equipment for Inclusive Use by Persons with Functional Limitations and Impairments, (ASTM WK 34535, 2011). Finally, it is important for recreation and sport managers to carefully consider both applicable laws and published standards of practice when developing their risk management plans.

Standards of Practice as they Apply to Risk Management

It is essential for recreation and sport managers to incorporate applicable standards of practice into their risk management plan. Managers are ultimately responsible for the development and implementation of the risk management plan. However, all professionals responsible for the program must be involved in various aspects of the risk management process.

Head and Horn (1997) developed a five-step risk management decision-making process: (1) identifying and analyzing exposure to loss, (2) examining alternative risk management techniques, (3) selecting risk management techniques, (4) implementing techniques, and (5) monitoring results. This five-step approach can be adapted into the following four steps with regard to the application of standards of practice (see also Chapter 4.11 *Risk Management Process*)

Step 1. Identifying and Selecting Applicable Standards of Practice

Because there are so many published standards of practice from a variety of organizations, it is challenging for the recreation and sport manager to be aware of all applicable standards and to determine which ones should be selected and incorporated into the risk management plan. A risk management advisory committee (e.g., experts in the field, a knowledgeable lawyer, and an insurance expert) can provide excellent assistance in this step as well as the remaining steps. Because it is almost impossible to know which standards of practice will be introduced into a court of law, it is best to select those that are the most authoritative or safety oriented in their approach.

Step 2. Developing Risk Management Strategies That Reflect Standards of Practice

This step involves writing procedures that describe specific responsibilities or duties that staff members would carry out given a particular situation. For example, all programs should have written emergency procedures that not only reflect published standards of practice, but also describe specific tasks that staff members must perform when someone is hurt.

Once the written procedures are finalized, they should be included in the facility's policy and procedures manual. Policies and procedures from this manual can also be introduced as evidence in determining duty (see *Darling v. Charleston Community Hospital* (1964), where the defendant's own by-laws along with published standards were entered into evidence to determine duty). It is best for the procedures be written clearly and succinctly without too much detail. Too much detail in the written procedures will not allow for a certain amount of flexibility the staff members may need in a particular situation and may make it difficult for the staff to remember everything they are to do.

Step 3. Implementing the Risk Management Plan

Implementation of the risk management plan primarily involves staff training. Staff training will help ensure that staff members carry out the written policies and procedures properly. The policy and procedures manual should be used with initial training for new employees as well as with regular in-service training throughout the year for all employees. In regular in-service training, actual practice of a particular procedure (*e.g.,* emergency procedures) should take place. It is also important to explain to staff members why it is essential that they carry out their duties appropriately from a legal perspective.

Step 4. Evaluating the Risk Management Plan

Evaluation of the risk management plan should be done throughout the year. For example, the recreation and sport manager should regularly supervise staff to be sure they are carrying out their duties appropriately and if they are not, corrective action should take place, which may involve re-training. Evaluation should also occur after each injury to determine if the staff carried out the emergency procedures correctly and to determine if anything could be done to prevent a similar incident in the future. A formal evaluation of the entire risk management plan should be done at least annually. Like the law, standards of practice are not static and can change and evolve over time. Therefore, written procedures will need to be updated periodically to reflect these changes.

The following case demonstrates that courts do allow expert witnesses to introduce published standards of practice as admissible evidence in determining duty in negligence cases. The trial court in this case excluded evidence provided by expert witnesses involving standards of practice published by ASTM and CPSC. The plaintiffs claimed that the trial court erred in excluding this evidence and appealed. The Court of Appeals of South Carolina (Elledge v. Richland/Lexington School District Five, 2000) found that the trial court did err in refusing to admit relevant evidence of the ASTM and CPCS industry standards. Citing a variety of cases to support its decision, the Court of Appeals stated: **"Safety standards promulgated by government or industry organizations in particular are relevant to the standard of care for negligence . . . Courts have become increasingly appreciative of the value of national safety codes and other guidelines issued by governmental and voluntary associations to assist in applying the standard of care in negligence cases . . . A safety code ordinarily represents a consensus of opinion carrying the approval of a significant segment of an industry, and it is not introduced as substantive law but most often as illustrative evidence of safety practices or rules generally prevailing in the industry that provides support for expert testimony concerning the proper standard of care"** *(pp. 477–478). (Emphasis added). The Court of Appeals reversed the trial court's decision and the Supreme Court of South Carolina affirmed the Court of Appeals decision. This is an excellent case to illustrate that not adhering to published standards of practice can lead to charges of negligence.*

ELLEDGE V. RICHLAND/LEXINGTON SCHOOL DISTRICT FIVE

Supreme Court of South Carolina
2002 S.C. LEXIS 235
November 25, 2002, Filed

Opinion: Justice Waller

We granted a petition for a writ of certiorari to review the Court of Appeals' decision in Elledge v. Richland/Lexington Sch. Dist. Five, 341 S.C. 473, 534 S.E.2d 289 (Ct. App. 2000). We affirm.

Facts

On December 9, 1994, nine-year-old Ginger Sierra (Ginger) slipped and fell on a piece of playground equipment at Irmo Elementary School where she attended fourth grade. The playground equipment was a metal monkey bar device which the children walked upon; it extended above the ground approximately two feet. As a result of the fall, Ginger broke her right leg. The growth plate in that leg was significantly damaged, and Ginger eventually underwent surgery in both legs to remove the growth plates. * * *

Ginger and her mother, Christine Elledge (collectively respondents), sued petitioner Richland/Lexington School District Five (the District) for negligence. A jury returned a verdict for the District. On appeal, the Court of Appeals reversed and remanded for a new trial. * * *

At trial, James Shirley, the principal at Irmo Elementary since 1990, testified that shortly after he arrived at the school, he had concerns about the school's playground. He was especially concerned by the lack of a fall surface and by the height of some of the playground equipment. As to the monkey bar which Ginger fell on, Shirley stated that children had been walking on it and this was also a concern. In 1991, Shirley contacted Jim Mosteller who redesigned the playground. As part of the playground renovations, the monkey bar which Ginger fell on was modified by Mosteller. Originally, the monkey bar was higher and had a bench underneath it. As part of the modifications performed in 1991, the height was lowered from about four feet to two feet, and the bench was removed. On the modified monkey bar, students would walk or crawl across it, although there were no hand-held supports on the side. Shirley testified that he knew the children were walking across the apparatus after the modification.

Both of respondents' playground safety experts testified that the monkey bar was, in its original form, designed to develop children's upper body strength. Archibald Hardy stated that this piece of equipment was known as a "pull and slide" and the children were supposed to lie back on the bench underneath the bars and pull themselves along the apparatus. According to Hardy, the original design "definitely wasn't for walking" because the metal rungs were small enough for children's hands and were "fairly slick." The modification to the equipment encouraged children to "run up and jump on top of it;" however, Hardy stated that children "shouldn't have been playing on top of it at all." Hardy, who sold to and installed playground equipment for Irmo Elementary, had visited the playground on several occasions since 1992, and had recommended to Shirley that all the older equipment on the playground be "bulldozed."

Steven Bernheim, respondents' other expert, similarly testified about the equipment and stated that it "was not meant as a climber." According to Bernheim, the equipment was safe as originally designed, but in its modified form, it was unsafe because the narrow bars were originally designed for hands, not feet, and no grit had been placed on the metal bars to prevent slipping.

Bernheim stated generally that the playground at Irmo Elementary did not meet the proper safety standards in the industry. Respondents sought, however, to introduce specific evidence regarding the Consumer Product Safety Commission (CPSC) guidelines for playground safety and the American Society for Testing and Materials (ASTM) standards for playground equipment. The trial court granted the District's motion in limine to exclude this evidence. At trial, respondents argued that this evidence was relevant to establishing the District's common law duty of care. The trial court found the evidence inadmissible because the guidelines were not "binding" on the District and the District had not "adopted" them in any way.

Respondents proffered the following evidence. Bernheim would have testified that in 1994, when Ginger fell, the CPSC guidelines and ASTM standards were in effect and would have applied to "any group . . . utilizing the playground equipment for public use," including a school district. He stated that these guidelines are industry standards and are distributed to schools via superintendents' or principals' meetings. Significantly, Bernheim opined that the District should have had policies and procedures in place for retrofitting existing equipment so that it complied with the guidelines. Furthermore, Bernheim believed the modified monkey bar did not comply with the national guidelines because there were no handrails and no grit on the walking surface. According to Bernheim, because Ginger's injury involved getting caught in an entrapment between the ladder areas, it was the type of injury the guidelines are designed to prevent. While Bernheim acknowledged that the industry standards were guidelines only, he stated they are what the playground equipment industry "stands by."

Respondents also proffered testimony from the District's purchasing coordinator, Joe Tommie. According to Tommie, the District would specify in its bids for purchasing new playground equipment that the equipment must meet the CPSC guidelines and ASTM standards. He stated: "That's normally the standard we use to ensure that we purchase safe equipment."

* * *

On appeal, respondents argued the exclusion of this evidence was prejudicial error. The Court of Appeals agreed. Stating that "evidence of industry standards, customs, and practices is 'often highly probative when defining a standard of care,'" the Court of Appeals held the trial court erred by excluding evidence of the CPSC guidelines and ASTM standards. Elledge, 341 S.C. at 477,

534 S.E.2d at 290-91. * * * The Court of Appeals found the trial court was under "the mistaken belief that the District must have adopted these national protocols before such evidence was admissible. . . . While such proof might be necessary in attempting to establish negligence *per se*, it is not required when the evidence is offered to demonstrate an applicable standard of care." Id. at 478, 534 S.E.2d at 291. As to the District's argument there was no prejudice from any error, the Court of Appeals stated that the "exclusion of this testimony was clearly prejudicial since such evidence would tend to show the District's compliance with industry standards, which directly conflicts with the District's assertion that such standards were never recognized." Id. at 480, 534 S.E.2d at 292.

Issue

Did the Court of Appeals correctly decide that the trial court's exclusion of the CPSC guidelines and ASTM standards evidence was reversible error?

Discussion

The District argues that the trial court correctly excluded the CPSC guidelines and ASTM standards evidence. Specifically, the District maintains respondents failed to establish that these guidelines were accepted and used by school districts in South Carolina to determine the safety of existing playground equipment. In addition, the District contends that even if the trial court erred, the error was not prejudicial. We disagree.

To establish a cause of action in negligence, a plaintiff must prove the following three elements: (1) a duty of care owed by defendant to plaintiff; (2) breach of that duty by a negligent act or omission; and (3) damage proximately resulting from the breach of duty. * * * In our opinion, respondents' proffered evidence was relevant to, and admissible on, the first required element of negligence—the District's duty of care to respondents. * * * We agree with Chief Judge Hearn's observation that the trial court was under "the mistaken belief that the District must have adopted these national protocols before such evidence was admissible." Elledge, 341 S.C. at 478, 534 S.E.2d at 291.

As recognized by the Court of Appeals, the general rule is that evidence of industry safety standards is relevant to establishing the standard of care in a negligence case. See, e.g., McComish v. DeSoi, 42 N.J. 274, 200 A.2d 116, 120-21 (N.J. 1964) (holding that construction safety manuals and codes were properly admitted as objective standards of safe construction); Walheim v. Kirkpatrick, 305 Pa. Super. 590, 451 A.2d 1033, 1034-35 (Pa. Super. 1982) (holding that safety standards regarding the safe design and use of trampolines, including ASTM standards, were admissible on the issue of the defendants' negligence, even though the defendants were unaware of the standards); Stone v. United Eng'g, 197 W.

Va. 347, 475 S.E.2d 439, 453-55 (W.Va. 1996) (no error to admit evidence of safety standards for the design and guarding of conveyors even though the standards had not been imposed by statute and did not have "the force of law"); see generally Daniel E. Feld, Annotation, *Admissibility in Evidence, on Issue of Negligence, of Codes or Standards of Safety Issued or Sponsored by Governmental Body or by Voluntary Association*, 58 A.L.R.3d 148, 154 (1974) (modern trend is to admit safety codes on the issue of negligence). This kind of evidence is admitted not because it has "the force of law," but rather as "illustrative evidence of safety practices or rules generally prevailing in the industry." McComish v. DeSoi, 200 A.2d at 121.

Indeed, the District even acknowledges this is the general rule. Respondents' expert, Bernheim, laid an adequate foundation for the admission of these safety standards when he stated they: (1) were in effect at the time of Ginger's accident, and * * * (2) would have applied to any group using playground equipment for public use, including a school district. Thus, the Court of Appeals correctly held that the trial court erred by excluding evidence of the CPSC guidelines and ASTM standards.

The District, however, argues this evidence was inadmissible because respondents did not show that school districts generally accepted or followed the guidelines with regard to existing playground equipment. * * * We find this argument completely unavailing. Since the evidence showed the District followed the CPSC guidelines when purchasing new playground equipment, and the guidelines are intended for general playground safety which logically includes the maintenance of existing playground equipment, the District's contention that the safety standards somehow did not apply to it on existing equipment is simply untenable. It is clear to us that a public school is exactly the type of entity to which the public playground safety guidelines should, and do, apply. Simply because the District did not utilize the guidelines in 1994 with regard to existing equipment does not mean that it should not have. * * *

We find this evidence is highly probative on the issue of defining the District's duty of care. Rules 401, 402, SCRE (evidence is relevant and admissible if it has any tendency to make the existence of any fact of consequence to the action more or less probable than it would be without the evidence); see also Elledge, 341 S.C. at 477, 534 S.E.2d at 290 ("Evidence of industry standards, customs, and practices is 'often highly probative when defining a standard of care.'") (quoting 57A Am.Jur.2d Negligence § 185 (1999)). Consequently, we hold the trial court abused its discretion by excluding this evidence. * * *

The District further argues that any error made by the trial court did not result in prejudice to respondents. The District contends that the evidence was cumulative to the admitted testimony of respondents' experts and the expert testimony was limited only by excluding specific references to the safety standards. We disagree.

Evidence of objective safety standards is generally offered "in connection with expert testimony which identifies it as illustrative evidence of safety practices or rules generally prevailing in the industry, and as such it provides support for the opinion of the expert concerning the proper standard of care." McComish v. DeSoi, 200 A.2d at 121 (emphasis added); see also Brown v. Clark Equip. Co., 62 Haw. 530, 618 P.2d 267, 276 (Haw. 1980) (evidence of safety codes is "admissible as an alternative to or utilized to buttress expert testimony") (emphasis added).

Respondents sought to introduce evidence of industry standards to identify and establish the duty of care owed by the District to respondents. According to respondents' expert, the modified monkey bar did not comply with the guidelines. According to the District's purchasing coordinator, the District utilized the guidelines to ensure the safety of new equipment purchases. The import of the expert's evidence is clear. Respondents sought to show that the same standards that were used to purchase safe new equipment, should have been used to safely modify and/or maintain the existing equipment.

Furthermore, this type of evidence constitutes an objective standard and as such would have greatly enhanced the opinions offered by respondents' experts. We therefore disagree with the District's argument that the evidence would have been cumulative to the experts' testimony. One of the main purposes of industry standard evidence is to provide support for an expert's opinion on what the applicable standard of care is, and thus, the evidence is not merely cumulative to the expert's testimony. * * *

In addition, we note that the bulk of the experts' testimony went to the element of breach of duty whereas the specific evidence of industry standards was intended to establish the applicable duty of care. In other words, while respondents' experts were allowed to offer their opinions that the equipment did not conform with the industry's guidelines and was not meant to be walked upon, this testimony primarily relates to breach of a duty, not to demonstrating precisely what the objective duty of care was. Since the evidence at issue went to a different element on the negligence cause of action—duty versus breach - clearly the evidence cannot be considered cumulative.

Accordingly, we hold the trial court's error in excluding this evidence prejudiced respondents' case.

Conclusion

The general rule is that evidence of industry safety standards is admissible to establish the standard of care in a negligence case. The evidence of CPSC guidelines and ASTM standards which respondents sought to have admitted in the instant case is exactly the type of evidence contemplated by this general rule. The Court of Appeals correctly held the trial court committed reversible error in excluding the evidence. Therefore, the Court of Appeals' opinion is **AFFIRMED.** * * *

CASES ON THE SUPPLEMENTAL WEB SITE

Bloom v. ProMaxima Manufacturing Company, 669 F.Supp. 2d 321 (2009 W.D.N.Y.). In this case, the court ruled that the *ACSM's Health/Fitness Facility Standards and Guidelines* could not be used as evidence to establish the standard of care because this publication contains a disclaimer that specifically states that the standards should not be used to give rise to a duty of care.

Corrigan v. Musclemakers, Inc. 686 N.Y.S2d 143 (1999 N.Y.App.Div. LEXIS 1954). This case involved a personal fitness trainer's failure to instruct his client on how to safely use the treadmill before using it. The court referred to the operator's manual that included a guideline that states the importance of understanding the treadmill's operation prior to use.

Darling v. Fairfield Medical Center, 142 Ohio App. 3d 682 (2001 Ohio App. LEXIS 3268). This case involved

specifications published in the manufacturer's Owner's Manual regarding proper set up of a treadmill and provision of cautions and warnings. Note the court's rationale for not applying the assumption of risk defense.

Xu v. Gay, 257 Mich. App. 263 (2003 Mich. App. LEXIS 1505). This case involved industry standards regarding the distance (clearance) behind treadmills. Explain why the court ruled that the failure to implement the standards did not establish a case of gross negligence.

L.A. Fitness International v. Mayer, 980 So. 2d 550 (2008 Fla. App. LEXIS 5893). This case involved IHRSA and ACSM standards regarding emergency procedures. Describe why most recreation and sport managers would not agree with the appellate court's ruling in this case.

QUESTIONS YOU SHOULD BE ABLE TO ANSWER

1. Describe the potential legal impact of published standards of practice.

2. Investigate and then develop a list of the standards of practice published by both professional and independent organizations that apply to your specific practice as a recreation and sport manager.

3. Explain what recreation and sport managers should do if they find inconsistencies among the published standards of practice.

4. Describe how published standards of practice can be applied to the four risk management steps. Include the specific actions that recreation and sport managers should take within each step.

5. Using the court's reasoning in the Significant Case (*Elledge*), explain how and why published standards of practice can be relevant to the standard of care.

REFERENCES

Cases

Bloom v. ProMaxima Manufacturing Company, 669 F.Supp. 2d 321 (W.D.N.Y. 2009).
Darling v. Charleston Community Hospital, 200 N.E.2d 149 (Ill. App. Ct. 1964).
Elledge v. Richland/Lexington School District Five, 341 S.C. 473 (S.C. Ct. App. 2000).
Elledge v. Richland/Lexington School District Five, LEXIS 235 (S.C. 2002).
Xu v. Gay, 668 N.W.2d 166 (Mich. App. 2003).

Publications

Black, H. (1991). *Black's law dictionary* (6th ed.). St Paul, MN: West Publishing Company.
Head, G., & Head, S. (1997). *Essentials of risk management* (Vol. I, 3rd ed.). Malvern, PA: Insurance Institute of America.
Eickhoff-Shemek, J., Herbert, D. & Connaughton, P. (2009). *Risk management for health/fitness professionals: Legal issues and strategies.* Baltimore, MD: Lippincott Williams & Wilkins.
Goldman, S. (2011). NSF Joint Committee Passes Standard for Fitness Facility Certification, *Club Industry.com,* December 28, 2011. Available at: http://clubindustry.com/forprofits/nsf-joint-committee-passes-standard-fitness-facility-certification-20111228/
Herbert, D. (2009a). New AED case filed. *The Exercise Standards and Malpractice Reporter,* 23(1), 1, 4–7.

Herbert, D. (2009b). NSF International Continues to Develop Standards for Health/Fitness Facilities. *The Exercise Standards and Malpractice Reporter, 23*(5), 79.

IHRSA Club Membership Standards (2005). In *IHRSA's guide to club membership & conduct.* (3rd. ed.). Boston, MA: International Health, Racquet & Sportsclub Association (IHRSA).

ASTM WK34535 (2011). New Specification for Universal Design of Fitness Equipment for Inclusive Use by Persons with Functional Limitations and Impairments. Available at: http://www.astm.org/DATABASE.CART/WORKITEMS/WK34535.htm

National Strength and Conditioning Association (NSCA): Strength and Conditioning Professional Standards and Guidelines. (2009). *National Strength and Conditioning Journal, 31*(5), 14–38.

Tharret, S., McInnis, K. & Peterson, J. (Eds.) (2007). *ACSM's health/fitness facility standards and guidelines* (3rd ed.). Champaign, IL: Human Kinetics.

van der Smissen, B. (2000). *Standards and how they relate to duty and liability.* Paper presented at the 13th Annual Sport, Physical Education, Recreation and Law Conference, Sponsored by the Society for the Study of the Legal Aspects of Sport and Physical Activity, Albuquerque, NM.

Voris, H.C. & Rabinoff, M. (2011). When is a standard of care not a standard of care? *The Exercise Standards and Malpractice Reporter, 25*(2), 20–21.

4.22 AUDITS IN RISK MANAGEMENT

RISK MANAGEMENT PLAN
LEGAL AUDIT
FACILITY AUDIT

Todd L. Seidler I University of New Mexico

Jury Awards $15,000,000 to Paralyzed Teenager
Catastrophic Injury Leads to $8M Settlement
Pool Drain Cover Case Settled for $30.9 Million
Programs Eliminated: Title IX Lawsuit Follows
Sandusky Scandal Costing PSU Millions
Teen Killed in Soccer Goal Post Accident
7 Die in Basketball Team Van Crash
$19.5M Settlement Reached in Weight Machine Suit
Overloaded Bleachers Collapse Killing One and Injuring Over 200

These are real headlines of actual incidents. Thousands of people are injured each year as a result of watching, volunteering, working, or participating in sport and physical activities. As a result of those injuries, litigation against the sponsoring organization or recreation or sport business often occurs. Due in part to the expansion of programs, an increase in the number of participants, and the proliferation of personal injury lawsuits, risk management has become one of the most important concerns for today's sport or recreation manager. As covered throughout this text, managers of recreation and sport programs have a number of legal duties they are obligated to perform. Management in a recreation or sport organization has a duty to use reasonable care for participant, spectator, and staff safety in providing recreation and sport programs, facilities, and equipment. As discussed in previous chapters, the establishment of a good, effective, formal risk management program has become the expected standard of practice for all sport and recreation programs.

In addition to litigation resulting from physical injury, recreation and sport managers are often faced with a wide variety of other legal actions such as contract disputes, employment issues, Title IX claims, compliance with Occupational Safety and Health Administration (OHSA) regulations, Americans with Disabilities Act (ADA) regulations, and allegations of Constitutional rights violations. As a result of the increase in litigation against recreation and sport organizations, managers of these agencies are increasingly called upon to defend themselves and their organizations from legal challenges. The purpose of this chapter is to present three risk management tools for recreation and sport managers—the **risk management plan**, the **legal audit**, and the **facility audit**. Each of these can be of immense value in protecting against harm to individuals and defending an organization from litigation. Other chapters throughout the text have focused on the risk management process and on many of the legal issues facing today's sport and recreation managers. Throughout this chapter, the reader will be directed to other sections of the text that will expand on the specific topic being discussed.

RISK MANAGEMENT PLAN

According to van der Smissen (1996), "There are two types of risks: the risk of financial loss and the risk of personal injury". She goes on to say, "A **risk management plan** is more than safety checklists! It is the systematic analysis of one's operations for potential risks or risk exposures and then setting forth a plan to reduce such exposures". A good risk management plan analyzes all potential risks that an organization faces and selects the optimal method to treat each.

As described in previous chapters, there are four methods of treating risks once they have been identified. They are (1) risk avoidance or elimination, (2) risk reduction, (3) risk retention, and (4) risk transfer (see also Chapter 4.11 *Risk Management Process*).

It is important to recognize that a risk management plan should be unique and be developed specifically for each particular organization. A youth baseball league will face different risks and have different requirements than a high school athletic department, a college recreation program, or a nonprofit organization sponsoring a large event. All components that are appropriate for a given situation should be included in the risk management plan.

In developing a risk management plan, it is important to understand the concept of developing **layers of protection.** This means that whenever an identified risk cannot be completely eliminated, several strategies should be used to treat the risk. For instance, instead of relying solely on a waiver to transfer the risk to the user, the waiver should be used in conjunction with other methods of treating the risk (e.g., an agreement to participate, special releases from a physician for a pre-existing condition, extra insurance, regular inspections, developing policies for transportation, or special training for personnel). In this way, if the waiver is successfully challenged in court, there are several other methods of protection still in place. The more layers of protection that are in place, the more likely the organization will be able to successfully defend itself in court—or avoid a lawsuit altogether.

The following are the major components of a risk management plan for a typical recreation or sport organization. This is only an outline as many of these concerns are discussed in depth in chapters throughout this text. References to the appropriate chapters will be provided when appropriate. It is also important to note that this is a generic outline and that each organization must develop a plan that is customized for its particular situation. Finally, the reader should realize there is no one best format or outline for a risk management plan. Most formats are acceptable as long as each of the sources of risk is addressed.

Organization Description

It is not always necessary but is usually advantageous to begin with an overview and description of the organization along with its purpose and function. The following information may be useful:

- Organization mission statement, values and/or statement of philosophy
- A description of the services or programs provided
- An overview of the clientele served
- A description of the facilities and spaces that will be utilized
- The organizational structure of the organization—organizational chart
- Financial resources

Personnel

As part of an overall risk management plan, it may be desirable to review or develop policies and procedures for personnel such as might be found in the organization's personnel manual (see also Chapter 4.11 *Risk Management Process*). When discussing ways to avoid employment litigation, Schuler and Jackson (1996) state "One excellent avoidance technique is to undertake a comprehensive audit of all employment procedures, policies, and practices to ensure that all are in accord with the rapidly changing state and federal employment laws." A review of personnel-related policies and procedures should include the following:

- Develop thorough hiring procedures to ensure that employees are qualified to perform the job they are hired to do. This may include required initial and ongoing training for each position. Background checks, both in-state and out-of-state, should be required for all positions that work with children or other susceptible populations. This is a minimum requirement—it is advisable that they be conducted for all employees since responsibilities may change after one is employed.
- Develop complete and accurate job descriptions for all personnel, and describe the essential tasks necessary to do each job including individual responsibilities for safety and risk management. (This is also helpful in fully complying with the ADA.)
- Provide an evaluation and discipline process that allows for accurate and thoroughly written documentation of employee performance and discipline. This may include termination procedures.
- Develop and implement a policy of nondiscrimination in the workplace. Comply with the requirements of federal and state laws that prohibit discrimination on the basis of race, religion, national origin, age, sex, pregnancy, and disability.

- Develop a procedure to field complaints of sexual harassment in the workplace. Be sure it effectively protects the rights of the accused and the accuser. Ensure compliance with government-mandated training requirements regarding the illegality of sexual harassment.
- Review all policies and procedures for possible due process considerations.
- Provide a location for conducting employment interviews that is fully accessible to those with disabilities, pursuant to the ADA.
- Ensure the hiring process is not subject to claims of discrimination because of a narrow applicant pool.
- Develop a policy manual or handbook for using volunteers.
- Update the employee handbook, manual, or policy to ensure compliance with recent changes to state and federal employment laws. Check your employment manual for any provisions that are contrary to state or federal law.
- Post all required notices in the workplace (e.g., "Sexual Harassment is Illegal," state and federal wage and hour laws, state and federal OSHA guidelines, state and federal fair employment laws, privacy laws and the Family and Medical Leave Act).
- Consider if a policy regarding violence in the workplace is appropriate for your situation.
- Ensure compliance with the Immigration and Naturalization Service requirement to complete work authorization (I–9) forms for all employees.

Conduct of Activities

This section of the risk management plan is a description of the programs being offered and the necessary standards for conduct (see also Chapter 2.34 *Supervision*). Issues to consider include:

- **Proper instruction.** Maintain policies ensuring adequate instruction and providing for proper methodology and progression.
- **Warnings and participation forms.** Review or develop all appropriate pre-participation forms: physical exam, waiver, warning, assumption of risk, parental consent, consent for emergency treatment, as well as any other appropriate forms necessary for the activities sponsored by the organization (see also Chapter 2.23 *Waivers and Releases* and Chapter 2.24 *Agreements Related to Inherent Risks*).
- **Mismatch situations.** Review or develop policies to avoid mismatches. (Should prevent mismatches between children and staff /adults as well as mismatches with other participants) (see also Chapter 2.34 *Supervision*).
- **Transportation policy.** If transportation is provided for participants, a thorough policy regarding vehicles, inspections, driver qualifications and training, insurance, maintenance and record keeping is necessary (see also Chapter 2.35 *Transportation*).
- **Hazing policy.** If applicable, a hazing policy should be developed, communicated, and enforced (see also Chapter 3.22 *Hazing*).
- **Rules.** Develop, communicate, and enforce rules that govern behavior of all participants, spectators, staff, and visitors.

General Supervisory Practices

Supervision is almost always an issue when injuries occur in recreation and sport programs and has to be an important aspect of the risk management plan (see also Chapter 2.34 *Supervision*). Some aspects of supervision that need to be addressed are:

- **A supervisory plan.** The plan should outline duties, responsibilities, qualifications, and schedules of supervisors.
- **Management of behavior of participants, spectators, staff, and visitors.** Crowd control can be considered an aspect of behavior management (see also Chapter 4.24 *Crowd Management*).
- **Rules and regulations for supervisors.** Supervisors must understand their duty and be well-trained in how to supervise properly. This may include a policy making it clear that an inappropriate relationship between a staff member and a participant is not allowed.

- **Security and access control.** A secure facility is a must.
- **Emergency care and accident reporting.** Preparedness for emergency care is a part of supervision (see also Chapter 2.33 *Emergency Care*).
- **Protection from foreseeable criminal acts.** The organization has an obligation to be prepared to protect participants, spectators, staff, and visitors from foreseeable criminal acts. There is generally no liability for unforeseeable criminal acts.
- **A plan for unplanned absence of supervisor.** Supervisors should be instructed as to the policy to follow in the event the supervisor unexpectedly has to leave persons in his or her charge.

Facilities

The risk management plan should address the reduction or elimination of foreseeable hazards related to environmental conditions. A **facility audit** is a systematic method of identifying such hazards and risks related to a sport or recreation facility and determining the optimal method of treating each. The audit should cover all facilities, equipment, and all indoor and outdoor spaces. A detailed description of the facility risk audit is provided later in this chapter (see also Chapter 2.31 *Premises Liability*). The audit should address:

- Hazardous conditions
- Equipment
- Facility layout
- Maintenance
- Security

- Health hazards
- Access control
- ADA
- OSHA
- Signage

Crisis Management and Emergency Response Plans

The risk management plan should include a crisis management and/or emergency response plan. It is important to identify the crisis and emergency situations that are likely to occur and develop response plans and procedures for each. This should include all documentation and forms that are to be used. Once developed, regular training and testing of appropriate personnel is necessary to ensure that the plans are carried out as anticipated. The **emergency response plan** should include first-aid plans, reporting procedures (911) and medical services policies (see also Chapter 2.33 *Emergency Care* and Chapter 4.23 *Crisis Management*). Types of emergencies and crisis situations that may be planned for include:

- Serious personal injuries of participants, spectators, staff, visitors
- Weather related emergencies—tornado, hurricane, lightning, flood
- Hazardous material spill
- Civil disturbance

- Bomb or terrorism threat
- Earthquake
- Medical emergencies
- Fire
- Dealing with participants, family members of victims, lawyers, and the media

Insurance Coverage

Make certain the necessary insurance is in place and that it is adequate for foreseeable events (see also Chapter 4.25 *Managing Risk Through Insurance* and Chapter 4.26 *Workers' Compensation*). Every possible situation that can be envisioned should be considered to determine whether all staff, participants, volunteers, administrators and visitors will be adequately protected. Without such coverage, an injured party may feel it necessary to sue in order to pay medical bills and other costs. When evaluating insurance plan coverages, consider:

Organization or Business

- General liability
- Umbrella liability
- Employment practices liability

- Property
- Event
- Motor vehicle

Employee

- Workers' compensation
- Liability protecting employees

Participant

- Basic medical (often required of participant)
- Catastrophic injury

As mentioned previously, this is a generic risk management outline. The needs of each business or organization differ depending upon its goal, the activities offered, its size, whether it's public or private, and many other factors. In some organizations other areas should be included in the risk management plan. Some possible topics to add may be identified during a legal audit.

THE LEGAL AUDIT

A **legal audit** is a formal review of policies that attempts to address all pertinent legal aspects of the organization. A legal audit involves a complete legal checkup of the organization in which all aspects of the operation are examined in order to discover and minimize potential financial threats. Although the line between a risk management plan and a legal audit is often blurred, a legal audit includes more than what is typically thought of as a risk management plan. The legal audit helps ensure the *legal health* of a recreation or sport program and should be done in conjunction with the risk management plan of the organization. The legal audit is typically broken down into a four-step process.

Content of the Legal Audit

A list of the areas that are appropriate to address for the particular organization must be identified. Such a list can sometimes be obtained through legal counsel or from an insurer, but will most likely have to be developed within the organization. The structure of the legal audit covers a number of different categories and will vary somewhat from one organization to another. The legal requirements of a private sport organization may be very different from those of a nonprofit entity. Since some of the categories may not be applicable in certain situations and the number will vary somewhat, it is necessary for the sport or recreation manager to select those that are appropriate for a given situation. Such a comprehensive list of pertinent information helps to create a profile from which one can determine the current and potential *legal health* problems of the entity and to address these problems before they reach crisis proportions. If produced internally, it can be very helpful to develop the audit with the help of legal counsel, financial advisors, insurance specialists, and/or a risk management consultant.

According to Grange and Oliver (1985), some categories that may be included in a legal audit are:

- General information regarding the entity
- Governance/authority of the entity
- Function and purposes of the entity
- Policies related to contracts
- Financial information
- Books and records
- Information regarding property/facilities
- Employee and labor relations
- Personnel policies and records
- Operational licenses
- Records supporting tax-exempt status
- Copyright and/or patent records
- Regulatory requirements
- Compliance with government regulations (e.g., Title IX, ADA)

Fried (1999) also provides a list of issues that should be considered for inclusion:

- Partnership agreements
- Corporate formation procedures
- Tax issues
- Advertising liability
- Contract negotiations and compliance
- Employment issues
- Employer liability
- Dangerous facilities
- Liability for the acts of volunteers
- Product liability
- Criminal law

- First aid and OSHA regulations
- Selling food and licensing/permits
- Government relations
- Zoning issues
- Nuisance from noise
- Insurance
- Facility rental agreements
- Sponsorship contracts
- Real estate issues
- Alcohol-related concerns
- Crowd management
- Copyright, trademark, and patent issues
- Property rights
- Spectator violence
- Drug testing

Selecting the Manager and Committee

Once the list has been established, a qualified staff person must be selected and assigned to manage the legal audit process. It is crucial that a person be selected who is sensitive to detail, who has the ability, and has the perceived authority to secure cooperation of other employees. The logical person may be the business manager if one exists in the organization. With smaller organizations, the athletic director or program administrator may be the best one to manage the process. Proper selection is key to a successful audit.

Once the manager has been chosen, a committee can then be selected to help carry out the audit. The members of the committee should represent the various major areas of the business operation. It is important to note that those selected for a legal audit committee are often different from those selected for a risk management committee.

It is also essential to obtain expert evaluation of the audit by legal, financial, and managerial counsel. For example, an attorney can examine the audit from a legal standpoint, a CPA can inspect it from a financial standpoint, and a manager or someone from upper administration can study it from an operational point of view. Large organizations may have the necessary experts available to help, but others may have to hire outside consultants at this point. Specific examples include bringing in a specialist to study an athletic department's compliance with Title IX, hiring an insurance expert to evaluate the organization's current insurance package, or having an attorney review hiring policies and contracts.

Conducting the Audit

When an appropriate committee has been selected, it is time to conduct the audit. Each committee member is selected to study the policies and procedures specific to his or her area of expertise. Often, two or more will share interest areas and should collaborate on their evaluation. The committee should then come together and discuss each part individually with input from all members. As agreement on one area is achieved, the committee addresses the next item in the audit. Eventually, the committee should come to agreement on all aspects of the audit and prepare recommendations to the upper administration.

Implementing the Audit

For the final step, upper administration should receive copies of the completed legal audit. Typically, those overseeing the organization must then decide whether to act on each recommendation. A careful review of the document will help to sensitize them to areas that require immediate attention as well as those requiring long-range consideration. The more support garnered from these administrators, the stronger and more effective the entire process will be. It is important to note that this is an ongoing process. The audit should be reviewed on a regular basis and it should never be assumed that, because it was done before, it is still adequate.

The legal audit is becoming an essential task of sport and recreation managers and has a direct impact on the legal and financial health of their organizations. Sport and recreation managers must become familiar with the details of legal audits and be able to develop and refine them in order to improve the organization's protection from litigation.

THE FACILITY AUDIT

A **facility audit** is a systematic method of identifying the hazards and risks related to a sport or recreation facility and determining the optimal method of treating each. A claim of unsafe facilities is one of the most common allegations made in lawsuits alleging negligence in recreation or sport programs. Addressing facility liability, Page (1988) called it one of the largest subcategories within the broad spectrum of tort law. When determining the conduct expected of a facility manager, courts have ruled that they be held to a standard of that of a reasonably prudent and careful facility manager. As specified in Chapter 2.31 *Premises Liability*, a facility operator has a general duty to exercise reasonable care for the safety of its patrons. That duty for ordinary care includes the obligation to:

- Inspect regularly for hazards or dangers
- Properly maintain the premises and correct defects
- Warn users, participants, and spectators about hazards or dangers that are not readily apparent
- Warn users, participants, and spectators about the inherent risks of the sport or activity

A facility audit helps to ensure that the above obligations are carried out. If someone is injured in a facility and initiates a lawsuit claiming that the injury was caused by a situation the facility manager should not have allowed to exist, the court will partially base its findings of liability on the concept of foreseeability. Was it foreseeable that the situation in question was likely to cause an injury? If the court determines that a reasonable, prudent facility manager would have recognized a potential danger and acted to reduce or eliminate the hazard and the defendant did not, the chances of being found liable for the injury are greatly enhanced. However, if it is determined that a reasonable, prudent facility manager probably would not have identified the situation as likely to cause an injury, the potential for liability is greatly reduced.

It is the legal obligation of facility managers and program directors to address or treat all foreseeable risks in one way or another in order to reduce each unwanted risk as much as possible. According to Eickhoff-Shemek, Herbert, and Connaughton (2009), "In general, facilities should be properly designed, equipped, and maintained in all program areas if liability is to be controlled at manageable levels. All areas should be regularly checked and kept free of defects and nuisances to minimize the chances of participant injury, illness, or death". Additionally, Wolohan states, (2006) "Establishing a system of inspection, including documenting the dates of inspection, any potential problem areas and all necessary corrective measures, also can help dramatically cut down on a facility's potential liability". The best method of performing the above obligations and ensuring facility safety is through the development of a facility risk audit. This audit consists of a systematic inspection for potential hazards and developing a procedure for dealing with the hazards identified. The facility risk audit is broken down into two major parts: 1) the inspection (comprehensive, periodic, or daily), and 2) risk treatment.

Inspections
Comprehensive Inspections
The **comprehensive inspection** is conducted by one or more staff members who walk throughout the facility trying to identify as many potential risks or hazards as possible. Typically, the larger the organization or facility, the more people will make up an inspection team. It is often advantageous to include inspectors who have different backgrounds or specialties. A maintenance person will look at the facility from a different point of view than will a coach or a security officer. Each will look at the facility from his/her unique perspective and possibly identify different hazards.

It is also desirable and beneficial to have someone from outside the organization come in and inspect. Often, those who work in a facility become used to the environmental conditions they see every day and may not notice a hazard, whereas someone looking at it from a fresh point of view may spot it easily. It is often beneficial for two sport or recreation managers to trade off and inspect each other's facility. When more people are involved in inspections, fewer hazards will be overlooked.

An example of a hazardous condition that should have been identified and treated before someone was injured is illustrated in *Cohen v. Boys & Girls Club of Greater Salem Inc.* (2010) (see the Supplemental Web Site). Dillon

Cohen was playing basketball when he struck an unpadded cement wall only 1½ feet from the end line. He suffered a skull fracture, a C–7 spinous process fracture, and a left clavicle fracture. An initial inspection by a qualified person should have identified the hazardous condition of the gym prior to play so it could be treated before someone was injured. It can also be beneficial to hire a professional risk management consultant to come in and assist in conducting the initial inspection and the development of checklists for daily, periodic, and comprehensive inspections.

In addition to identifying hazardous conditions, other facility issues must be addressed as part of the facility audit. Issues that may expose the organization to legal threats other than lawsuits from injury should be identified and dealt with. Among these are access control, security, compliance with ADA, Title IX and OSHA regulations, and proper signage regarding warnings and rules for facility usage.

The comprehensive inspection should include all interior areas (e.g., gyms, locker rooms, pools, hallways, lobbies, restrooms) as well as all exterior areas (e.g., playgrounds, fields, sidewalks, parking lots, fences). Each inspector should independently tour the entire facility and make a list of potential hazards. All of the individual lists should then be compiled into one comprehensive list of potential hazards. This comprehensive list must then be prioritized. The priority list will establish the order in which the hazards are treated. The more likely a hazard is to cause an injury and the more serious the potential injury, the higher the priority assigned to that hazard. Following completion of the priority list, each hazard must be considered and the best method of treating each determined (see Risk Treatment below). It is important to understand that a thorough comprehensive inspection is not a one-time event and should occur on a regular basis (annually or more often if needed). In between these major inspections, periodic inspections should take place.

Periodic Inspections

After the comprehensive inspection is complete, an ongoing program of inspections should be implemented. In most facilities, it is appropriate to conduct **periodic inspections** on a daily, weekly, biweekly, and/or monthly basis, whatever is called for by the activities and usage of that particular facility. It is common practice to develop several different types of inspection checklists. It is often a good idea to develop checklists that can be used for **daily inspections**. Such an inspection may be done before opening the facility each day and should cover safety items that are likely to occur or change quickly such as checking for standing water or trash on a court, making sure doors are secure, or looking for holes on a softball field. An example of the need for frequent inspections is illustrated in *Zipusch v. LA Workout, Inc.*, 2007 Cal. App. LEXIS 1652 (see Significant Case). Zipusch filed suit for personal injuries sustained when she was injured on a treadmill. She claimed her foot became stuck to a sticky substance on the treadmill, causing her to fall. As part of her claim, she alleged the club's failure to inspect and maintain the exercise equipment resulted in the sticky substance remaining on the treadmill. The Court of Appeal felt that a reasonable argument could be made that inspecting the premises was especially important and the case was remanded to the trial court for further proceedings.

Inspections performed on a less frequent basis, such as weekly or monthly, might include looking for hazards that are less likely to occur or that take time to develop. Examples may include inspections of bleachers for loose bolts, bent or broken supports, damaged footboards or loose railings. Also, frayed cables or worn pulleys on weight machines, improper functioning of treadmills and other cardio equipment, and loose bolts and padding on basketball backboards and rims are examples of hazards that may occur over time. Inspections should occur as often as a reasonable and prudent professional would do in the same or similar circumstances. Facility managers should use their best professional judgment to determine the frequency of the periodic inspections. The more quickly a problem may occur or the greater the usage of the facility, the more often an inspection should be conducted.

In a spectator facility, however, it is often more appropriate to perform an inspection immediately **prior to each event**. The inspection in such a facility may focus on issues of spectator safety such as hazards that may cause a slip or trip and fall, the condition of seats and bleachers and emergency response equipment (e.g., fire extinguishers, alarms, and emergency lighting).

Developing the Checklists

Once the hazards identified through the comprehensive and periodic inspections have been identified, a checklist with which to perform periodic facility inspections on a regular, ongoing basis should be developed. This checklist should be designed for each facility and customized for that particular situation. It is all too common that sport and recreation managers will borrow a checklist from another facility, put their name and logo on it, and use it for their facility. This is not a safe or effective practice. Each facility and situation is unique. Therefore, every checklist should be customized for a given situation. It can be very helpful to study checklists from other facilities and borrow ideas from them, but it is essential that each item be suitable for the situation. It is also important to keep the checklist relatively straightforward and simple. If it is so long and complex that it becomes a major operation to perform, it probably won't be performed correctly, if at all. On the other hand, all items of importance must be included. All checklists should be modified as facility conditions and equipment change. It is important to ensure that checklists are appropriate, complete and up to date.

When developing a facility checklist, the following items should be included in order for it to be as effective as possible:

- Name of the organization
- Inspector's name (printed)
- Date of inspection
- Location of inspection (if needed)
- Inspector's signature
- Problems discovered

Figures 4.22.1 is an example of a daily checklist while Figure 4.22.2 represents how a monthly checklist may appear. When writing the questions for the checklist, it can be very helpful to write them so that if each item is satisfactory, the *Yes* column will be checked (see Figures 4.22.1 and 4.22.2). This way it will be easy to look at each page of the list and see if any checks appear in the *No* column. If none exist, no problems were identified.

Risk Treatment

Once the potential hazards in the facility have been identified and prioritized, one or more **risk treatment** methods are utilized in order to eliminate each risk or at least make it as safe as possible. Chapter 4.11, *Risk Management Process*, provides a good description of treating risks after they have been identified. When treating physical hazards related to facilities or equipment, two methods are typically used:

1. **Risk elimination.** Fix it so that it is no longer a problem.
2. **Risk reduction.** If it cannot be eliminated, make it as safe as possible and identify other methods of treating the remaining hazard.

Deciding on the optimal method(s) of risk treatment will rely on the best professional judgment of the facility and risk managers and staff involved. As each hazard is dealt with, the next one on the list can then be addressed. This does not mean that items with a lower priority on the list must wait until the ones before have been treated. If an item cannot be treated immediately (e.g., waiting on a part for repair), it is important to mark the equipment or area temporarily off limits, and deal with the next hazard on the list. Many situations can be quickly and easily treated and removed from the priority list while others may take some time.

With some hazards it will be obvious how to best remedy the situation. For example, if there is a hole in a soccer field, repair it and determine its source. If it was a one-time incident, the hazard has been eliminated and no more concern is necessary. If, however, the problem is likely to recur, as when the holes are caused by gophers, the cause should be remedied as soon as possible. If it will take some time before it can be fixed permanently, it may be necessary to compensate for it by warning participants of the hazard, using cones to block off the area, posting warning signs, or closing the area until repair is completed.

Another example of risk reduction is illustrated when the sideline of a basketball court is two feet from a concrete block wall, an obvious hazard that must be dealt with. It is probably not possible to completely eliminate the hazard by moving the wall out several more feet. One method to reduce the hazardous situation might be to use floor tape and create a new sideline a few feet inside the current one. It may also be appropriate to warn the participants of the situation and to pad the wall. For a permanent fix, the boundary lines may be moved away from the wall, thereby increasing the buffer zone. The baskets may also have to be moved to match the new lines. Making the basketball court smaller may seem like an extreme measure but it is a totally appropriate way to reduce such a dangerous condition.

Again, for most facility hazards, completely eliminating the dangerous condition is the ideal method of risk treatment. However, when a hazard cannot be completely eliminated, sport and recreation managers must be creative and determine the optimal way to protect everyone involved.

Daily Inspection Checklist

Inspector's Name _____ Kevin Finn _____ Date ___ 9/17/12 _____

Location of Inspection _____ Main Gym _____

Inspector's Signature _____

Instructions for Inspector:

1. Inspect and complete all items.

2. Include comments on all "NO" responses.

3. Fill-out and report problems on completion of inspection.

# POTENTIAL HAZARD	YES	NO	COMMENTS
1. Floor clear of obstacles and debris	X		
2. Floor clear of standing water	X		
3. Floor swept, good traction	X		
4. All standards, mats & goals properly stored	X		
5. All other equipment properly stored	X		
6. Gym rules clearly posted	X		
7. Bleachers secure and in good repair	X		
8. Warning sign on bleachers clearly visible	X		
9. All lights undamaged and working		X	Light over center court is out
10. Emergency procedures clearly posted	X		
11. Emergency telephone accessible	X		
12. Emergency phone numbers and directions to facility are posted by the phone	X		
13. Rims unbroken, straight & in good shape	X		
14. Backboards unbroken & in proper position	X		
15. Wall pads in place	X		
16. Access—Ingress and egress points opened or locked as appropriate		X	N.E. outside door open
17. Supervisor present	X		
18. No unsupervised children present	X		
19. All of participants' equipment properly stored in hallway	X		
20. Other			

FIGURE 4.22.1   **JOE DAILEY RECREATION CENTER**

Monthly Inspection Checklist

Inspector's Name _____ Paul Edwards _____ Date ___ 9/17/12 ___

Location of Inspection _____ Weight Room _____

Inspector's Signature _____

Instructions for Inspector:

1. Inspect and complete all items.

2. Include comments on all "NO" responses.

3. Fill-out and report problems on completion of inspection.

# POTENTIAL HAZARD	YES	NO	COMMENTS
1. Weight machines clean & lubricated	X		
2. Cables, belts and pulleys undamaged		X	Belt on leg curl frayed
3. Benches, seats and back rests secure	X		
4. Proper storage available for weights, bars	X		
5. All other equipment properly stored	X		
6. Weight room rules clearly posted	X		
7. Instruction signs clearly visible		X	Missing on overhead press
8. Warning signs clearly visible	X		
9. Flooring flat and level	X		
10. Emergency procedures clearly posted	X		
11. Emergency telephone accessible	X		
12. Emergency phone numbers and directions to facility are posted by the phone	X		
13. Emergency exits clearly marked	X		
14. Electrical cords out of traffic flow	X		
15. Cardio machines in good working order	X		
16. Proper spacing between machines	X		
17. Other			

FIGURE 4.22.2   JOE DAILEY RECREATION CENTER

Documentation

Documenting and saving everything that relates to organizational legal issues, safety, and risk management is essential to protecting the assets of the organization and is good management practice. If litigation occurs, the court will want to see evidence of what the organization or business has done to protect others from harm. An organized, thorough, consistent method of documenting all efforts to make a program safe and legally sound is an integral part of any risk management program, legal audit, or facility audit. In each of these, documenting all efforts provides good protection for the organization. Keeping good records is essential if one has to demonstrate in court that everything that could be reasonably expected had been done. The old adage, "If it wasn't written down, it didn't happen" is a great one to apply to such programs. It is important to keep copies of all aspects of the risk management plan as well as the factors addressed in the legal audit. Finally, all records should be stored in such a way that they are safe, secure, and easily retrievable. Digitally saving documents on DVDs, external hard drives or using cloud backup is an excellent way to store large amounts of information. Multiple copies can then be stored in different locations to ensure availability in future years.

CONCLUSION

In order for a risk management program to be most effective, it must be valued by the organization. If the employees believe that the upper administration feels that the safety of all participants, spectators and staff is an important aspect of the culture of the organization, they are more likely to take their risk management responsibilities seriously. Administrators should communicate the need for and reward efforts toward making the facility as safe as it can be.

The need for recreation and sport managers to conduct risk management becomes increasingly clear every day. We have both a moral and legal obligation to do our best to both provide safe programs and to protect the assets of the organization. Along with the increased awareness of the necessity to provide risk management programs and legal audits has come a need for help in developing them. Sport and recreation managers often do not have the background and expertise required to develop a risk management plan that will keep injuries to a minimum and provide maximum protection against litigation. This has created an opportunity for those with such expertise to sell their services and help administrators devise appropriate plans, policies, and procedures. There are a number of risk management consultants that provide such a service in the recreation and sport fields and the number is increasing. Many risk management consultants have specialized knowledge in certain areas and have developed great expertise in their area. Examples of such areas include playgrounds, aquatics, strength and conditioning programs, crowd control, the use of waivers, and outdoor adventure programs. Along with specialized knowledge in managing risk for recreation and sport businesses, opportunities are appearing for positions as professional risk managers. More and more, large organizations are recognizing the need to have a person who is knowledgeable in risk management on the staff. Large arenas and stadiums, school districts, and city park and recreation departments are examples of entities that are now hiring professionals with these unique skills. Good risk management is now expected of all recreation and sport organizations.

 # SIGNIFICANT CASE

Yoko Zipusch joined a fitness club called LA Workout in 2004. A couple of months later, while walking on a treadmill, Zipusch claimed that her foot stuck to a sticky substance on the belt of the treadmill, causing her to fall and be injured. Zipusch filed a complaint against LA Workout for general negligence and premises liability alleging a failure to inspect and maintain the exercise equipment. This case provides an interesting discussion on the expectations for frequent inspections in a busy club.

YOKO ZIPUSCH, Plaintiff and Appellant, v. LA WORKOUT, INC., Defendant and Respondent

2007 Cal. App. LEXIS 1652
October 3, 2007, Filed

Procedural Posture

Plaintiff health club member brought an action for negligence and premises liability against defendant health club owner for personal injuries sustained when her foot became stuck to a sticky substance on a treadmill at the club. The owner purchased the club pursuant to bankruptcy proceedings. [LA Workout, Inc., is the predecessor-in-interest of Northridge GG, Inc. Northridge GG, Inc. purchased LA Workout on December 6, 2004, pursuant to bankruptcy proceedings. Northridge defended this action brought by Zipusch.] The Los Angeles County Superior Court, California, granted the owner's motion for summary judgment. The member appealed.

* * *

Facts and Proceedings

Zipusch signed a "Membership Agreement" in October 2004 and thereafter became a member of LA Workout. The double-sided membership agreement contains a readily identifiable assumption of risk provision located at the bottom of the front page which states: "The use of the facility at LA Workout naturally involves the risk of injury to yourself or your guest, whether you or someone else cause [sic] it. As such you understand and voluntarily accept this risk and agree that LA Workout will not be liable for injury, including without limitation, personal, bodily or mental injury, economic loss or damage to you, your spouses [sic], guests, unborn child, or relatives resulting from the negligence or other acts of anyone else using LA Workout. If there is any claim by anyone based on injury loss or damage described here, which involves you or your guest, you agree to (1) defend LA Workout against such claims and pay LA Workout for all expenses relating to the claim and (2) indemnify LA Workout for all liabilities to you, your spouse, guests, relatives, or anyone else, resulting from such claims. The member or guest will defend and indemnify LA Workout for any negligence EXCEPT the sole negligence of the club. This agreement is not effective until you sign and date it. By signing below, you agree to the terms above."

On or about December 10, 2004, Zipusch allegedly sustained injuries when her foot became stuck to a sticky substance on a treadmill at the health club, causing her to lose her balance. Zipusch filed a complaint against LA Workout for general negligence and premises liability alleging its failure to inspect and maintain the exercise equipment resulted in the sticky substance remaining on the treadmill, causing her to lose her balance when her foot became stuck to it.

Northridge answered the complaint and later moved for summary judgment. In the motion, Northridge argued the release provision of the membership agreement exculpated the health club from claims arising during a member's use of the athletic facilities. Circumventing the exact wording of the release, Northridge argued in the health club context parties reasonably contemplate release provisions bar claims arising while exercising. Thus, Northridge appeared to argue, the unambiguous existence of a release exculpates a health club from claims arising while exercising without examining what the release's exact wording actually covers. Additionally, irrespective of the release provision, Northridge argued Zipusch could not raise a triable issue of material fact regarding any alleged negligence on the part of the health club, including its actual or constructive notice of the sticky substance on the treadmill.

Zipusch opposed the motion for summary judgment, arguing the release only barred claims against the health club caused by negligent third party conduct and, alternatively, the release contained an ambiguity which should be construed against the drafter, LA Workout. Either way, Zipusch argued the release did not bar claims against the health club for its own negligence. After addressing the threshold issue of the release, Zipusch presented evidence indicating the health club negligently inspected and maintained its equipment. First, Zipusch stated in her declaration, based on her own observations, 85 minutes had elapsed between the time of the accident and the last time a gym employee had inspected and cleaned the equipment. Zipusch argued a reasonable trier of fact could find the health club negligently inspected and maintained its exercise equipment by inferring the sticky substance was on the treadmill for this time period and concluding it was unreasonable and negligent to not remove the sticky substance during this time period. Additionally, at his deposition, an assistant manager of the health club testified the undersides of treadmill belts are not inspected in the normal course by gym employees monitoring the exercise area throughout the day. Zipusch argued a reasonable trier of fact could find this failure, in combination with the 85-minute gap between inspections, constituted negligence.

The trial court granted summary judgment in favor of Northridge based on the assumption of risk provision of the membership agreement, finding that while the release did not bar all claims arising during use of the health club, it did bar all claims involving third party conduct. The trial court found Zipusch had presented no evidence establishing the sticky substance materialized on the treadmill by non-third-party conduct.

* * *

Yoko Zipusch appeals from a summary judgment entered in favor of Northridge GG, Inc. (Northridge), in her negligence action for personal injuries sustained when her foot became stuck to a sticky substance on a treadmill at a health club owned by Northridge. Zipusch contends the trial court erroneously concluded there were no triable issues of material fact regarding two matters: first, whether the liability release contained in the signed membership agreement exculpated the health club from its own negligence; and second, whether the health club negligently failed to inspect and clean its exercise equipment. On de novo review, we conclude (1) the release is too ambiguous to insulate the health club from liability to Zipusch for its own negligence, and (2) triable issues of material fact exist regarding whether the health club negligently failed to inspect and maintain its exercise equipment.

* * *

Discussion

La Workout/Northridge's Alleged Negligent Inspection and Maintenance of Exercise Equipment is Not an Inherent Risk of Exercising at a Health Club.

Absent a contractual release from liability, Northridge nonetheless can prevail on summary judgment if Zipusch's alleged injury was an inherent risk of exercising at a health club. As our Supreme Court has made clear, "resolution of the question of the defendant's liability in such cases turns on whether the defendant had a legal duty to avoid such conduct or to protect the plaintiff against a particular risk of harm." Rather than examining the "plaintiff's subjective knowledge or appreciation of the potential risk," the inquiry depends upon whether the defendant breached its general duty "to use due care not to increase the risks to a participant over and above those inherent in the sport." "Thus, although a ski resort has no duty to remove moguls from a ski run, it clearly does have a duty to use due care to maintain its tow-ropes in a safe, working condition so as not to expose skiers to an increased risk of harm."

* * *

In determining whether the accident was an inherent risk of exercising at a health club we turn to the record and common sense. Generally, defective or unnecessarily dangerous equipment is not considered an inherent risk of a sport. This is entirely sensible. The main concern animating inherent risk analysis is the potential for chilling vigorous participation and altering the fundamental nature of a particular sport. However, these concerns are not present in lawsuits alleging defective or unnecessarily dangerous equipment where the issue is whether the defendant increased the risk above the inherent risk of the sport.

* * *

Here, Zipusch alleges the health club negligently inspected and maintained its exercise equipment, allowing a risk to remain for an unreasonable amount of time. Despite Northridge's misplaced reliance on *Leon v. Family Fitness Center (#107), Inc.,* we find nothing to support the contention the negligent inspection and maintenance of exercise equipment is an inherent risk of exercising at a health club. Unlike those who run outside on cracked sidewalks speckled with gum, Zipusch and other health club members pay dues in exchange for access to a safe and well-maintained exercise environment. Instead of chilling exercise at a health club, reasonably inspecting and maintaining exercise equipment should have the opposite effect. Further, Northridge acknowledges it already monitors and cleans the exercise facility. Accordingly, we find the negligent inspection and maintenance of exercise equipment is not an inherent risk of exercising at a health club.

* * *

IV. Zipusch has Raised a Triable Issue of Material Fact Regarding Whether La WorkOut/Northridge Negligently Inspected and Maintained its Exercise Equipment.

Given our interpretation of the release provision as set forth above, we find Northridge did not meet its burden on summary judgment of demonstrating Zipusch's causes of action have no merit. But even if Northridge had met its burden, we find Zipusch has raised a triable issue of material fact which precludes summary judgment.

Circumstantial evidence of a property owner's failure to inspect the premises before an accident is sufficient to infer the risk existed long enough for the property owner, in the exercise of due care, to have discovered and removed it. In other words, a property owner's failure to reasonably inspect can be used to infer constructive knowledge of the dangerous condition, providing a causal link between the accident and the time period between inspections. The determination of what constitutes a reasonable time period between inspections will necessarily vary according to the particular circumstances. For instance, "'[a] person operating a grocery and vegetable store in the exercise of ordinary care must exercise a more vigilant outlook than the operator of some other types of business where the danger of things falling to the floor is not so obvious.'" Thus, while a 15- to 30-minute interval between inspections at a busy commercial retail center may lead to an inference of negligence, the same inference might not be found elsewhere.

* * *

Zipusch has raised a triable issue of material fact regarding whether LA Workout negligently inspected and maintained its exercise equipment. In her declaration, Zipusch stated, based on her own observations, no staff member inspected or cleaned the exercise equipment in the 85-minute time period prior to the accident. In the health club context where numerous individuals are engaging in vigorous physical activity, a reasonable argument can be made that inspection of the premises is especially important, and an 85-minute time period between inspections is unreasonably long. Further, an LA Workout employee testified the undersides of the treadmill belts are not routinely inspected. From this evidence a reasonable trier of fact could find the health club negligently inspected and maintained its exercise equipment.

For the foregoing reasons, we conclude the trial court erred in granting Northridge's motion for summary judgment.

The judgment is reversed and the case is remanded to the trial court for further proceedings. Appellant is entitled to recover her costs on appeal.

CASES ON THE SUPPLEMENTAL WEB SITE

Barnhard v. Cybex Intl. 2011 N.Y. App. Div. LEXIS 8264. Plaintiff claimed weight machine was defectively designed and tipped over and severely injured her.

Cohen v. Boys & Girls Club of Greater Salem Inc., 2010 N.H. Super. LEXIS 2. A dangerous condition existed in a gym where there was an inadequate buffer zone and no wall padding.

Flores v. 24 Hour Fitness, 2005 Cal. App. Unpub. LEXIS 207. Example of how a good inspection and

maintenance program would have prevented an injury and lawsuit.

Guerra v. Howard Beach Fitness Center, 2011 N.Y. Misc. LEXIs 3346. A good inspection and maintenance program may have prevented a treadmill injury and lawsuit.

Range v. Abbott Sports Complex, 2005 Neb. LEXIS 36. Interesting discussion as to whether Range Sports Complex had constructive knowledge of a hole in a soccer field.

QUESTIONS YOU SHOULD BE ABLE TO ANSWER

1. When discussing a risk management plan, what is meant by "layers of protection?"

2. What is the difference between a legal audit and a facility audit?

3. What duty and obligations do facility managers owe to patrons using their facilities?

4. Why is it important to document the things that are done for safety and risk management?

5. How do you determine how often a facility inspection should be performed?

REFERENCES

Cases

Barnhard v. Cybex Intl. 2011 N.Y. App. Div. LEXIS 8264
Burkart v. Health & Tennis Corporation of America, Inc. 1987 Tex. App. LEXIS 7544.
Cohen v. Boys & Girls Club of Greater Salem Inc., 2010 N.H. Super. LEXIS 2
Flores v. 24 Hour Fitness, 2005 Cal. App. Unpub. LEXIS 207.
Guerra v. Howard Beach Fitness Center, 2011 N.Y. Misc. LEXIs 3346
Range v. Abbott Sports Complex, 2005 Neb. LEXIS 36
Zipusch v. LA Workout, Inc., 2007 Cal. App. LEXIS 1652.

Publications

Berg, R. (1994). Unsafe. *Athletic Business, 18(4),* 43–46.
Dougherty, N. J. (1993). *Principles of safety in physical education and sport.* Reston, VA: National Assn. for Sport and Physical Education.
Dougherty, N., & Seidler, T. (2007). Viewpoints: Injuries in the buffer zone: A serious risk management problem. *Journal of Physical Education Recreation and Dance, 78(2),* 4–7.
Eickhoff-Shemek, J., Herbert, D. & Connaughton, D. (2009). Risk Management for Health/Fitness Professionals. Philadelphia, PA: Lippincott, Williams & Wilkins.
Fried, G. B. (1999). *Safe at first.* Durham, NC: Carolina Academic Press.

Grange, G. R., & Oliver, N. S. (1985). Head off trouble with a legal audit. *Association Management*. Nov. 103 B 104.

Jewell, D. (1992). *Public assembly facilities* (2nd ed.). Malabar, FL: Krieger Publishing Co.

Kaiser, R., & Robinson, K. (1999). Risk management. In B. van der Smissen, M. Moiseichik, V. Hartenburg, and L. Twardgik (Eds.), *Management of park and recreation agencies* (pp. 713–741). Ashuba, VA: NRPA.

Maloy, B. P. (1993). Legal obligations related to facilities. *Journal of Physical Education, Recreation, and Dance, 64*(2), 28–30, 68.

Schuler, R.S. & Jackson, S.E. (1996). *Human resource management: Positioning for 21st century*. Minneaplois/St. Paul: West Publishing Co.

Seidler, T. (2006). Planning and designing safe facilities. *Journal of Physical Education Recreation and Dance, 77(5), 32–37, 44.*

Seidler, T. (2009). Planning facilities for safety and risk management. in T.H. Sawyer, (Ed.), *Facility planning and design for health, physical activity, recreation and sport.* (12th ed.). Champaign, IL: Sagamore.

van der Smissen, B. (1990). *Liability and risk management for public and private enterprises*. Cincinnati, OH: Anderson Publishing Co.

van der Smissen, B. (1996). Tort liability and risk management. In B. L. Parkhouse (Ed.), *The management of sport: Its foundations and applications* (pp. 164–183). St. Louis, MO: Mosby.

4.23 CRISIS MANAGEMENT

Daniel Connaughton | University of Florida

Thomas A. Baker, III | University of Georgia

> "If you prepare for everything you can think of,
> you will be prepared when the unthinkable happens."
>
> Rudy Giuliali, March 28, 2012
> Speaking about the 9-11 attack

How important is crisis management to the recreation or sport manager? Contrast two situations in which a crisis was reasonably foreseeable—the 1993 University of Wisconsin/Michigan football game, where it was announced in the school paper that the students would charge the field after a Wisconsin victory, and the June, 2000, Atlanta Braves/New York Mets baseball game that was John Rocker's first trip to New York after controversial remarks in a Sports Illustrated article. In each situation, there was the potential for a crisis and the likelihood of serious injury. In the University of Wisconsin situation, newspapers reported that University management increased uniformed security from about 55 to about 65 officers. The increase proved inadequate, resulting in more than 60 injuries. In contrast, the Mets and New York City increased the number of assigned officers from 60 to 560 (plus an unnamed number of plainclothes officers in the stands), the Mets placed a limit of two on the number of beers that could be purchased at one time, and the Mets constructed a chain-link fence to protect Rocker in the bullpen. As a result of the crisis management measures taken, there were no serious incidents, and consequently, the crisis was averted.

The potential for many crisis situations regularly confronts the recreation or sport manager. The athletic director learns that one of his athletes just committed suicide. A fire breaks out in the gymnasium. A set of bleachers collapses injuring dozens of spectators. A coach is accused of sexual abuse (e.g., Jerry Sandusky, Penn State; Bernie Fine, Syracuse University) (Steinbach, 2012). An employee or athlete is arrested and charged with a crime. Each of these situations constitutes a crisis situation. A common mistake that many sport or recreation managers make is thinking that they and their staff will automatically know what to do in the event of a crisis. However, in many crisis situations, there is no plan, and the staff does not know how to properly, quickly, and calmly react.

In recent years, crises have become a regular event for most organizations (Ashby & Diacon, 2000; Choi, Sung & Kim, 2010). According to a survey of intercollegiate athletic administrators, 93 percent of National Collegiate Athletic Association (NCAA) athletic departments experienced a crisis within the period studied (1999–2000), yet fewer than half of the respondents had written plans in place to deal with the crisis. Furthermore, only 22 percent of the athletic directors reported that they provided any crisis management training to their staffs (Syme, 2005). Having an established crisis philosophy and **Crisis Management Plan (CMP)** will prepare an organization in the event of an actual crisis. A comprehensive CMP will address major crisis risks ranging from fires, bleacher collapses, bomb threats, criminal activity, violent acts, litigation against the organization, and major power outages to environmental emergencies such as hurricanes and floods.

On a daily basis, numerous problems, incidents, and issues confront the recreation or sport manager. A medical emergency arises when a serious illness or injury occurs involving a participant, spectator, or staff member. Although such situations are important and may involve the utilization of an emergency medical plan, they typically do not constitute a crisis—unless they are improperly handled. Regular incidents require organizational resources to respond, but they are usually readily manageable, and normal business can still take place while the incident is dealt with. Nevertheless, these types of incidents can quickly escalate into crises if they are not brought under control, if there is significant media coverage, and/or if several resources are required from within, or from outside, the organization. Herman and Oliver (2001) defined a crisis as a sudden situation that threatens an organization's ability to survive: an emergency, a disaster, a catastrophe. A crisis may involve a death or injury, lost access to the use of facilities and/or equipment, disrupted or significantly diminished operations, unprecedented information demands, intense media scrutiny, and irreparable damage to an agency's reputation (p. 6).

Hermann (1972), whose definition is widely accepted in the literature, defined a **crisis** as a situation that incorporates three conditions: (1) a surprise to decision makers, (2) a threat to high-priority goals, and (3) a restricted amount of time available to respond. A crisis situation is generally an unforeseen situation that can be extensive in its scope of disruption and damages to the organization. Although a crisis may strike without warning, others may build over time. For example, the sudden accidental death of an athlete or employee may catch everyone in the organization by surprise. In other cases, the actions, or inactions, of key personnel may cause a crisis to come about slowly. In both examples, staff may claim they "never saw it coming." A crisis may result in extensive organizational damage that typically cannot be corrected very easily or quickly. Crises often threaten the organization's mission and reputation and can have an adverse effect on business, fund-raising, and overall public relations. Outside assistance is often necessary. The organization may even need to be closed for a period of time to reestablish services and repair damage.

In summary, crises have common characteristics. First, they are negative. Second, a crisis can create improper or distorted perceptions. Third, crises are almost always disruptive to the organization. Finally, a crisis typically takes the organization by surprise, and the organization is placed in a reactive mode. Therefore, having a crisis management plan is particularly important for smaller organizations because they often have fewer resources to draw from when a crisis erupts. The purpose of this chapter is to assist the recreation or sport manager in becoming more informed about crisis planning and management.

FUNDAMENTAL CONCEPTS

Crisis management, a subset of risk management, focuses on allowing the organization to achieve its mission under extraordinary circumstances. The primary goal of managing a crisis is public safety. Not addressing public safety can intensify the damage from a crisis (Coombs, 2007). Secondary goals are to prevent the crisis from damaging the organization's (1) ability to achieve its mission and goals, (2) reputation, and/or (3) finances. **Crisis management** is a process intended to prevent or reduce the damage a crisis can cause to an organization and its stakeholders (Coombs, 2007). Having a crisis management plan in place is critical because it facilitates the establishment of a unified organizational philosophy, thereby eliminating the need to decide how to respond and what to do during a crisis situation (Ajango, 2003). How an organization conducts itself during and after a crisis can mitigate the damage and its duration.

Crisis Management Plan

Every organization is at risk of facing a crisis. How and where a crisis occurs can seldom be controlled. What can be controlled is how an organization prepares, reacts, and responds. A key determinant of how well an organization will cope in the midst of a crisis is how well it addressed its crisis management plan (CMP) before the actual crisis occurs. The steps an organization takes months, or even years, prior to a crisis occurring may be as important as its immediate response to a crisis.

The primary goal of planning for crises is to develop comprehensive, written contingency plans based on currently existing resources and operational capabilities that will enable the organization to effectively deal with crises. CMPs cannot be copied from a book or from plans developed by other organizations, but rather must be specifically developed for each and every program. Every program has unique factors that must be considered. However, several basic components should form the foundation of CMPs.

A piece that is commonly missing or overlooked when developing CMPs lies in the relationship between the overall CMP and the organization's core values. Whether an organization wants to set, and present, a tone of open communication, care, and concern or one of quiet toughness, the long-term strategy will be a reflection of the organization's values. If employees at all levels do not agree with, or are not aware of, the philosophy behind the CMP, there is a high probability that the plan will not proceed smoothly once it is put into action. Perhaps one of the worst possible things that can happen to an organization undergoing a crisis is for an unexpected lack of agreement on core philosophies to surface. To avoid this pitfall, an organization should prioritize its intent and objectives regarding its CMP. There should be a stated purpose behind the plan, specifically as it relates to the organization's mission and philosophy. Well before a crisis occurs, CMP decision makers should freely discuss how a post accident investigation would be conducted. Various opinions should be carefully considered. Several other questions should also be carefully considered prior to developing a CMP. Are the needs of victims a priority? Are employees' opinions secondary? Will legal ramifications drive the plan, or is public reputation more of a concern? It is important to discuss these issues and identify the organization's philosophy and goals prior to the onset of a crisis (Ajango, 2003).

Developing the Plan

The initial step in developing and writing a CMP is to **formulate a planning committee** who will begin the process. Awareness is the initial step to preparedness, and a crucial step in crisis planning is identification. Once the organization's philosophy and goals as they relate to managing a crisis are identified, the committee's primary task is to **identify the significant possible risks and crises** that may arise in their organization. The committee should scrutinize the core functions of the organization to identify and, in many cases, reduce or eliminate risks that could cast the organization into crisis mode. Examples of such crises may include an incident or event that would potentially result in serious injury or death, result in litigation, deter customers or otherwise impair income, impair the organization's ability to meet its core operating expenses, render the organization unable to deliver core services, or garner negative publicity and/or media attention resulting in the death of the organization.

Crisis risks can be categorized into avoidable (preventable) and unavoidable (unpreventable). Avoidable crisis risks may include actual or alleged client/participant maltreatment, service or product failure, severe injuries or death, transportation-related mishaps, and criminal conduct. Unavoidable crisis risks may include natural disasters (hurricanes, tornadoes, floods, wildfires, etc.), bomb threats, hazardous material incidents, terrorist attacks, and utility failures (Herman & Oliver, 2001). Although an organization may not be able to prevent these events from occurring, they can identify which ones are inherent to their area and are more likely to strike and then take steps to be as prepared as practically and reasonably possible to cope with the events if they occur.

Once crisis risks are identified, similar to a risk assessment, a crisis assessment is performed. However, instead of broadly focusing on any potential risk, a crisis assessment highlights the risks that would put the organization into crisis mode. Therefore, situations that could severely jeopardize the organization's credibility and/or resources should be the focus. Similar to classifying risks (see Chapter 4.11), potential crises should be individually assigned frequency and severity ratings. A frequency rating estimates how often this crisis may occur. A severity rating is based on how damaging to the organization the crisis would be if it does occur. Looking at the two ratings, an organization can determine its greatest risks (see Table 4.11.1, Risk Category Matrix, in Chapter 4.11, *Risk Management Process*).

The next step is to develop an **action plan for crisis response** for each major crisis risk that may confront the organization. An action plan is a document that details carefully considered courses of action. These alternatives can be selected when a crisis occurs. Herman and Oliver (2001) suggest keeping the format simple and easy to read, using short sentences and bulleted phrases, using flowcharts to indicate responsibilities and actions, including boxes that can be checked when the task is completed, and using tabs for quick access.

When developing such plans, identify all resources that may be needed in each crisis situation. Consider resources in the immediate area. Contact the local/state offices of the Federal Emergency Management Agency (FEMA), U.S. Department of Education, American Red Cross, local hospital, police and fire departments, and emergency medical services. Determine how they respond to crisis and how they may be able to assist your organization (Schirick, 2002).

Developing an action plan answers the crucial question: "What will we do if a crisis occurs?" In some cases, aspects of an organization's action plans may be identical, regardless of the cause, or source, of the crisis. For instance, a uniform step in an action plan may be contacting an insurance broker. In other cases, specific crises may require unique, specific responses. A beginning point for formulating action plans is to revisit the major crisis risks initially identified. The following sections present several components that should be considered as general guidelines when developing action plans.

Personnel Issues. There are two phases to personnel preparation. The first involves actions to be taken by the frontline leader (the person(s) in charge of the activity when the crisis occurs). Personnel should be educated on what immediate steps to follow (e.g., calling 911, activating the CMP). The second phase of personnel preparation involves subsequent actions to take in the crisis situation. The action plan should identify, by job title, those employees who will handle, or actively assist with, the crisis. Specific duties and responsibilities of each responder should be outlined in a simple and very clear format. The action plan should account for personnel trained to render emergency care, communication procedures, an incident reporting system, and a follow-up approach. In addition, personnel should know how to address the ongoing cause of the crisis (e.g., a gunman, terrorist, fire). They should know whom to contact for assistance (see Chapter 2.33, *Emergency Care*).

When developing the action plan and addressing the preceding components, input from various organizational levels and other affected agencies should be solicited. Both managerial and frontline staff should be consulted as well as athletes/participants and outside agencies, including groups such as local EMS, fire and police departments, legal counsel, crisis planning and management consultants, and the organization's insurance company.

Facility Issues. The location of emergency exits and shelters; gas, power, and water shutoff valves; alarm systems; backup power systems; main electrical panels; and fire hoses/extinguishers should be clearly identified. Location(s) for meeting EMS and other authorities (e.g., police, fire, and utility personnel) should be identified. Evacuation procedures should **also be developed.**

Emergency Equipment Issues. Identify the type of equipment available (e.g., public address and communication equipment, firefighting equipment, first aid kits, automated external defibrillators). Identify where each is stored and who will access it.

Communication Issues. Two major aspects of effective communication are necessary. The first involves the **immediate notification of the proper authorities** (e.g., police, medical personnel, mental health personnel). Designate who makes such calls and in what order. It is important to identify and get to know outside experts who will work side by side with your organization in a crisis. During a crisis is not the time to meet these key people. Train staff as to where and how to make emergency communications. The location of telephones and other communication devices should be specified, and emergency phone numbers should be identified.

The second aspect of effective communications involves the need to **quickly communicate with constituencies**. For example, an athletic director may need to communicate with EMS, law enforcement, victims and their families, parents of athletes, school officials and other employees, professionals who can provide crisis counseling and other support, news media, and possibly others following a riot incident at a sporting event. Before the crisis occurs the following should be considered.

- Who will need to be contacted in the event of a crisis?
- What is the best method to communicate? Consider telephone, broadcast fax, news conference, public address system, intercom, pagers, etc.
- What backup system is available if the primary means of communication is compromised?
- Is the list of personnel that would need to be contacted readily available to more than one staff member?
- Who is responsible for making the communication—one person or a group of people? (Herman & Oliver, 2001).

A crucial factor is **communication with the news media.** It is often the adverse publicity, rather than the actual damage from the crisis itself, that severely damages the organization. Therefore, a preassigned, trained spokesperson should contact the media at the earliest possible time. When speaking to these parties, the spokesperson should stick to the basic facts (e.g., type of crisis, which medical facility the victim was transported to, number of victims) and never assign or admit fault. The medical staff that provides care should only furnish medical or fatality information. Questions regarding insurance should be answered by the insurance agent/company. Finally, questions regarding liability should be addressed by the organization's risk management department or legal counsel. The staff should also be instructed not to speak to anyone regarding the incident unless approval has been obtained from the designated spokesperson. All requests for information should be immediately directed to the designated spokesperson. (For more on dealing with the media, see the following section.)

Documentation. Determine when and who completes what reports. Assigned personnel should know how to complete them and to whom they should be sent. Establish policies for filing and retaining reports.

Follow-up Procedures. There are several aspects to the follow-up procedures. First, it is necessary for the media spokesperson to follow up with the media. Depending on the crisis and its impact, there may need to be a follow-up with the victims, their families, classmates, colleagues, teammates, and/or friends, as well as with employees. Finally, it is important that the CMP be evaluated and modified where necessary.

Forming a Crisis Response Team

A small team should be formed to coordinate an organization's response to a crisis. This team needs to be formed and trained *before* a crisis occurs. Proper training will allow the team to react more calmly, effectively, and efficiently. The makeup of the crisis response team will vary depending on a number of factors, including the size of the organization, the nature of the services provided by the organization, the likely sources of crisis in the organization, and the organization's prior experience responding to a crisis. The makeup of the team may include the executive director, department heads, senior staff members, physical plant/building superintendent, board members, legal counsel, and outside advisors.

Practicing the Plan

Although responses to certain crises cannot be easily rehearsed, others can be simulated, practiced, or simply discussed to enhance readiness for an actual crisis and to identify any flaws in the action plans. When feasible, the plan should be tested in conditions as close to real life as possible. When flaws are noticed, the plans should be modified accordingly. Every time an organization conducts a CMP drill, key personnel involved should do a brief review of the exercise. Documentation of the review should be maintained by the organization. In between major drills, in-service training and tabletop exercises keep the strategies and process fresh in the minds of staff (Herman & Oliver, 2001; James, 2008).

Surviving a Crisis

The first step in addressing a crisis is to recognize and acknowledge it may be occurring. Oftentimes, individuals in organizations have different perceptions of when a crisis is at hand. It is important to recognize the signs of a crisis so the CMP has the best chance of working effectively.

Activating the plan

Once a crisis has been recognized, the plan should be followed. According to Herman and Oliver (2001), the team leader should contact the crisis response team and attempt to answer the following questions.

- What has occurred?
- Who has been affected by the events thus far? Who are the known victims?
- What steps have been taken to control the crisis? Who has done what?
- Is the media aware of the crisis? Are we prepared to give a statement?

The crisis response team should discuss and carefully decide what steps need to be taken to:

- Provide and/or arrange care or support for the victims
- Notify key personnel
- Respond to media inquiries
- Brief the staff and key constituents of the organization
- Ensure continued service delivery or coordinate transfer to another provider
- Secure important documents, files, computer backups, etc.
- Ensure that the communication systems are up and operating

Proper Crisis Communication

One of the most important aspects of handling a crisis is communication. How an organization communicates with key constituents, responds to inquiries and criticisms, handles the media, and tells its story may very well determine its survival. A failed communications strategy can be disastrous for any organization. All communication during a crisis should be carefully considered and orchestrated. Whether it is directed to an internal or external audience and whether it is written, visual, or verbal, extra care should be taken when crafting messages. Seymour and Moore (2000) recommended applying the "Five Cs" to crisis communication.

1. **Care.** The public is often very reluctant to forgive a lack of compassion from an organization whose programs or services caused harm. An effective spokesperson is one who can express empathy and care with conviction and sincerity.
2. **Commitment.** The organization's message should clearly indicate that it is committed to investigating the incident and preventing future occurrences.

3. **Consistency.** A clear plan of how the organization will respond and what its spokesperson will say ensures a consistent message.
4. **Coherence.** It is important to be clear, be concise, and stick to the facts.
5. **Clarity.** Because the opportunity to convey a message may be slim and come without warning, it is vital to avoid jargon, technical terms, and other language that may confuse the listener.

Since communication is essential when managing a crisis, it has been recommended that schools with Sport Information Departments include such staff as part of crisis planning and response teams (McKindra, 2009). Sports information professionals are valuable campus assets who can help when communicating with the university community, staff, fans, and the media.

Use of Social Media in Crisis Management

For sport managers, social media can be a tool for managing a crisis or the instrument used to create a crisis that requires management. In order to make proper use of social media and control for problems caused by the medium, it is critical that sport managers stay current in communicative technologies, understand how social media is used, and stay current in communicative advances in technology.

An example of social media's potential use in managing crisis can be found in how it was used to locate earthquake victims in Haiti. On January 12, 2010, the worst earthquake in 200 years, a 7.0 in magnitude, occurred near the Haitian town of Port-au-Prince. The quake collapsed Haiti's communication infrastructure, impeding the rescue efforts of responders. Social media filled in for the traditional means of communication. Responders relied on social media. Twitter was used as a prime resource for communication and relief efforts were organized through both Google and Facebook (Palmer, 2010).

Sport managers have also made use of social media in responding to problems at their events. For example, both college and professional sports have made use of "**tattle texting**", a policy that provides patrons with a phone number that can be used to text complaints concerning unruly fans or other problems with the facility (e.g., being stuck in an elevator) (Reilly, n.d.). Patrons can use this service to text facility managers of problems that are occurring within the venue that require the attention from security officers or other facility personnel. This can help prevent a relatively minor problem from erupting into a major problem or crisis situation.

Social media can also be used by sport managers for crowdsourcing after a crisis (Stephens, 2011). **Crowdsourcing** is the term used to describe the process of distributing tasks to a crowd of people. After a crisis, sport managers could look to posts and pictures on Twitter, Facebook, and other social media forums to identify areas for improvement so as to better handle future crises. As communication technologies continue to advance and expand in use, so will the means for using these technologies to assist sport managers charged with the responsibility of managing crisis.

While social media has the potential to help in managing a crisis, it can also be the instrument used to create a crisis. Social media has been used by sport consumers to say things about the sport organization or sport facility that impact consumption and have the potential for instigating a crisis situation. For example, a person could post unflattering comments on a sports blog, on Yelp.com, or on Facebook about a sport organization that influences consumer opinion concerning the organization. It is important that sport managers understand that statements made on social media can be used to harm an organization's brand. Thus, sport managers should have a strategy for addressing a potential social media crisis. Henry (2010) advises managers to address rather than ignore the problem, utilize contacts in the media to counter the problem, be honest with consumers, and refrain from using "hot" language in any response. Also, managers should assign a point person to handle the matter until it subsides and continue to gauge consumer response by monitoring social media.

Dealing with the News Media

Organizations should educate designated spokespersons who will work with the news media during a crisis situation. This aspect of the CMP should address the following details.

- Who decides what information is released?
- Who speaks for the organization/releases materials to media? Typically one spokesperson should be designated. A central spokesperson provides a singular face for the media with whom the public becomes

familiar. Centralized information also minimizes miscommunication. Backup spokespeople should be designated in the event that the central spokesperson is unavailable or is the subject of the crisis.

- Which members of the news media should be notified in a crisis?
- What are the phone numbers of key media people?
- What are the logistical details including locations where press conferences can be held; phone lines that media can use to call in; backup power supplies; parking area for the media; and what support staff is available to assist.

Preparations for a timely, accurate, and appropriate response must begin at the first sign of a potential crisis involving an organization, whether before or after exposure in the news media. News media will expect and demand an immediate response. If the organization does not provide an immediate response, others will. Others may provide inaccurate information, or may try to use the opportunity to attack the organization. Therefore, crisis managers must have a timely response (Coombs, 2007).

A decision on whether a news conference and/or release would be an appropriate means of conveying information to the news media and public must be made. What means of internal communication will be used if the crisis affects employees and participants should also be determined. At the earliest possible stage, advise staff members of the situation. Give clear instructions regarding handling the media and telephone calls and alert them that they may be called to perform special duties related to the incident. Discuss alternative or additional means of conveying information. This might include such items as letters to parents, clients, or fans, letters to newspaper editors, or consultation with boards. Use of the Internet, websites, and social media can also help to provide a quick response.

Information files should be set up to contain all materials related to the incident. Internet, newspapers and television reports should be scanned daily for related stories. If necessary, arrange for videotaping of any TV coverage. Related material, including clippings, statements, memos, and any other documents should be filed in chronological order. Plan to frequently update employees and administrators on the status of the incident. Conduct a follow-up assessment to determine what did and did not work, and what changes might be made in the future for improved media relations during a crisis.

Guidelines for the Media Contact Person

Several strategies exist that will make dealing with the media as positive as possible. In any crisis, try to find out as much information as possible. That way, you avoid inadvertently saying the wrong thing or sending unintended messages.

The following are seventeen guidelines for dealing with the media.

1. Always return media calls, even if they call repeatedly and/or are hostile. Ignoring them will not make the problem disappear. The more cooperative you appear, the better.
2. Occasionally, a media representative will make a special request. If possible and if it does not violate the CMP, an effort should be made to accommodate reasonable requests.
3. Avoid antagonizing media representatives. A sharp tone at a press conference, during a telephone call, or elsewhere may affect your relationship with that individual and with others who may hear the conversation.
4. Try to remain levelheaded at all times when speaking to the media. Some of their questions may seem hostile or may seem like a personal attack. It must be remembered that they are trying to get as much information as possible on a crisis-oriented story that may have widespread impact to their audiences.
5. Refrain from getting mad or taking it personally when asked tough questions.
6. Always try to have an answer for reporters' questions and always tell the truth. However, never be afraid to say, "I don't know, but I'll find out."
7. Avoid using "no comment." Doing so often makes it appear that you have something to hide.
8. Additionally, stay "on the record" in all interviews. Any comment worth stating should be said "on the record." If you go "off the record," be prepared to hear or read it. Although it is unethical for reporters to report "off the record" comments, anything can, may, and will be done to advance a story.
9. Consider how information you release may affect others. If things you say will result in the media calling other organizations or individuals, call those individuals first to alert them to the information.

10. When speaking to the media, be sure to credit other agencies or individuals assisting with the crisis, including your staff. This enhances relationships and reflects well on you.
11. Try to be proactive with new information. If you acquire new information regarding the crisis advise the media.
12. When communicating with the media and/or the public, accurate information is important. People desire correct information about what occurred and how it may affect them. Due to the time pressure associated with a crisis response, there is a risk of providing inaccurate information. Incorrect statements can make an organization appear incompetent and/or inconsistent (Coombs, 2007). Admit when a mistake has been made and correct it as soon as possible. This is often the first step to reestablishing confidence and credibility with the public and key constituencies.
13. Maintaining a sense of humor is important, but inappropriate humor will work against you.
14. Professional dignity is very important, particularly in unpleasant times.
15. As the crisis progresses, take notes. They can help you remember things and may be useful for later review.
16. If you are on camera, always dress professionally. Casual or mussed clothing may send a signal to viewers that things are out of control.
17. Try to give yourself some downtime and stress reduction. Overwork and little sleep can lead to misstatements and irritability.

Debrief Employees and Others Affected

When a crisis results in serious injuries or death(s), stress and trauma counseling for employees and other victims must be made available (Coombs, 2007). Even when victims survive, there may still be emotions to deal with, particularly for first responders. There may be feelings of guilt; others may recall their initial reaction, panic, or response. Some may wonder if they could have done more (James, 2008).

Critical Incident Stress Management (CISM) is a specific seven-stage group crisis intervention technique that has been adapted and used by rescue, disaster, and health-care groups in different settings, programs, and industries (Everly & Mitchell, 1999). This technique is designed to bring "psychological closure" to groups of victims or witnesses after a traumatic event and ideally is implemented 24 hours after the end of someone's involvement with the event. A professional needs to facilitate the process where each participant describes the event that occurred, their reaction to the event, and its psychological impact. The participant then learns how to manage the related stress (Herman & Oliver, 2001).

Have plans for dealing with emotional and mental health needs of staff, classmates, teammates, or friends and family of the victim(s) (Bacon & Anderson, 2003). Have procedures for communicating with the immediate families of all victims. Some organizations may have psychologists or mental health professionals available for the victims and/or their families, whereas others may refer affected individuals to available, trained professionals. Prior relationships with such trained professionals can be very helpful in these situations.

Evaluate the Response

Once the crisis is over, an evaluation should occur in a timely fashion.

- First, consider and review why the crisis occurred. What, if anything, could have been done to prevent or limit the crisis?
- Next, **how soon was the crisis noticed and how was it handled** should be evaluated. What was done appropriately or inappropriately should be addressed.
- Were others who were involved or affected timely informed?
- How effective was the crisis response team? Were certain skills or talents missing in the makeup of the team?
- How was the action plan followed? Was it effective and useful? What could have been done better?
- Also, **similar scenarios** should be examined. For example, what would you do in a similar situation in the future?

- Does the plan need to be changed? If so, how? Revising CMPs is an ongoing process.
- Finally, **send notes of appreciation** to those who have been of service, outside and inside the organization, including your own staff.

Terrorism and Crisis Management

The tragic events of September 11, 2011, signaled the emergence of terrorism as a foreseeable threat that warrants the attention and diligence of sport and recreation managers. Terrorists tend to select acts designed to destroy critical infrastructure and key assets, cause mass fatalities, weaken the economy, and damage the nation's morale and confidence (Arquilla, Ronfeldt, & Zanini, 1999). Terrorists could accomplish these goals with an effective and impactful attack on a sport facility. In fact, the U.S Department of Homeland Security (DHS) identified sport stadia and events as likely terrorist targets due to their potential for mass casualties, widespread media coverage, and social impact. Sports events occur at set times and set locations, attract large crowds, and involve activities that Americans hold dear; thus, they serve as effective targets for acts of terror. Accordingly, it is imperative that those charged with managing the threat of terrorism at sport events and facilities exercise reasonable care under the circumstances to protect participants and spectators from this foreseeable threat.

Specifically, it is critical that sport managers create, implement, and practice terrorism-specific crisis management plans. These plans should involve safety and security measures aimed at preventing and managing a crisis produced by acts of terror. Studies conducted on terrorism management have found that sport managers charged with managing the risk of terrorism at sport events should: conduct risk assessments; develop emergency response plans; properly train personnel in dealing with terrorism; and implement physical protection, access control, and crisis communication systems (Schwarz, Hall, & Shibli, 2010). Terrorism management strategies must also be coordinated with all first and second responder agencies and organizations on the local, state, and federal levels. This includes law enforcement fire and hazardous material management (hazmat), and emergency medical care (Hall, Fos, Marciani, & Zhang, 2011).

To assist facility and event managers in developing terrorism management plans and coordinating with responding agencies, the DHS has developed the **National Incident Management System** (NIMS). The NIMS provides a systematic, proactive approach to guide those who must manage incidents like acts of terror (National Incident Management System, 2004). It is necessary for sport managers to understand how NIMS operates so that they can develop crisis management plans that comply with NIMS standards, guidelines, and compliance procedures and protocols. Failure to take the proper steps necessary to manage the very realistic threat of terrorism could result in mass casualty and the imposition of legal liability.

Useful Websites for Crisis Management Information and Materials

The *Nonprofit Risk Management Center* has a significant number of references (resources, articles, tutorials, tests, fact sheets, links, etc.) available regarding risk and crisis management. Their website is located at: www.nonprofitrisk.org/

The *U.S. Department of Education* provides many crisis management-related educational materials including but not limited to: Crisis Planning Guide, Practical Information on Crisis Planning, Action Guide for Emergency Management at Institutions of Higher Education, and Tips for Helping Students Recovering from Traumatic Events. Their website is located at: http://www.ed.gov/admins/lead/safety/emergencyplan/index.html

The *International Association of Assembly Managers* (IAAM) provides information, training, and certification on several crisis management issues including but not limited to: crowd management, and venue safety and security. Their website is located at: http://iaam.org/

The *Center for Safe Schools* provides professional development and training, technical assistance, and acts as a resource clearinghouse for materials that address violence prevention and school safety. Their website provides links to a model school crisis management plan, crisis communication guides and toolkit, and other related references. Their website is located at: http://www.safeschools.info/about.

The *Federal Emergency Management Agency* (FEMA) provides information and training on disasters, planning for emergencies, and risk management. Their website is located at: http://www.fema.gov/

SIGNIFICANT CASE

In the Significant Case that follows, the defendants had a CMP that proved to be inadequate. Despite knowing in advance that the students planned to charge the field following a victory, insufficient precautions were taken to prevent the students from charging the field. More than 60 injuries resulted. Newspaper reports revealed that many University officials made potentially damaging statements to the press following the crisis. One official, in an attempt to make the necessary corrections to avoid a duplicate disaster, stated, "We can't ignore any possibility about what could be done to prevent this. We have to sit down and find some answers." Problems that were investigated included overcrowding in the student section, duplicate tickets, students moving from their seats in other sections of the stadium to the student section, use of alcohol inside the stadium, whether students should be assigned to seats instead of general admission, and whether the entire student section should be moved or dispersed (Schultz, 1993). Despite the failure of the crisis management plan to prevent the disaster, no defendant was found liable for his or her actions or inactions due to governmental immunity.

ENEMAN V. RICHTER

Court of Appeals of Wisconsin, District Four
217 Wis. 2d 288; 577 N.W.2d 386
February 5, 1998, Released

OPINION: ROGGENSACK, J. The appellants alleged they suffered personal injuries after a University of Wisconsin football game at Camp Randall Stadium, which injuries they claim resulted from the negligence of David Ward, Patrick Richter, Susan Riseling, Michael Green and David Williams, while the respondents were employed by the State on behalf of the University of Wisconsin. Respondents moved for summary judgment, based on the common law doctrine of public officer immunity. The circuit court concluded there were no material factual disputes and dismissed the appellants' claims. Because we agree that the material facts are not in dispute and that the respondents are entitled to immunity, we affirm.

* * *

Background

This is a consolidated appeal of summary judgments dismissing the claims of the appellants, all of whom are alleged to have suffered personal injuries when they were crushed by persons attempting to come onto the playing field at Camp Randall Stadium after the 1993 Wisconsin/Michigan football game. They assert their injuries would not have occurred if certain gates had not been closed by security personnel at the conclusion of the game and that the closing of the gates constituted negligence. David Ward, Chancellor for the University of Wisconsin-Madison; Patrick Richter, Athletic Director for the University of Wisconsin-Madison; Susan Riseling, Chief

of Police and Security for the University of Wisconsin-Madison; Michael Green, Camp Randall Facilities and Events Coordinator; and David Williams, a University police officer in Riseling's department, were state governmental employees on the date of the appellants' alleged injuries. They filed an answer denying negligence, and based on their status as state governmental employees, they asserted the affirmative defense of discretionary immunity, on which they moved for summary judgment.

Camp Randall Stadium is the site used for football games and other outdoor events at the University of Wisconsin-Madison. The football field is encircled by a chain link fence with a walkway between the fence and the bottom row of bleachers. Ingress and egress of the bleachers varies, depending on the section of the stadium. Sections O and P are at issue in this lawsuit. The lower rows of sections O and P exit to the walkway and then through the home team tunnel. It was also possible for those rows to exit to the field itself, even though security personnel directed spectators not to do so.

Prior to the 1993 football season, access to the field was limited by hand held ropes, which provided no real barrier to a spectator determined to enter the field. In anticipation of the 1993 football season, the University installed metal gates that could be positioned to close off the walkway at the bottom of the bleachers in order to permit the team to exit the field into the tunnel without interference from the spectators. When the walkway was closed off by the gates, sections O and P spectators' means of egress was restricted, until the team had made its way through the tunnel and the gates were opened again.

On October 30, 1993, after the University of Wisconsin's football team defeated the University of Michigan's team at Camp Randall, many of the students in sections O and P attempted to come onto the playing field. However, a few minutes before the game's end, the gates had been closed and latched by security personal. This provided a significant barrier to the spectators' egress onto the field, and it also created a dead end for tunnel egress from sections O and P, at a time when spectators were moving down the bleachers to exit the stadium or to push onto the field. The appellants were crushed against a metal railing and the gates when security personnel were unable to quickly unlatch the gates to open them.

Ward and Richter had no personal responsibility to manage the crowd at the Camp Randall games. On the other hand, Riseling's, Green's and Williams's activities at Camp Randall were arguably within the scope of the Standard Operating Procedures for Camp Randall relating to crowd control. Additionally, prior to the Michigan game, and subsequent to the installation of the gates, Riseling knew that it was possible that the students might try to rush onto the field at the game's end. In response to this potential for congestion in the student sections, she formulated and issued a directive entitled, "POST GAME CROWD TACTICS," whose goal was "to prevent injury to people—officers, band members and fans." The plan outlined a general strategy to follow which, in her judgment, would have prevented injury. Although her plan was implemented by security personnel, it was not successful.

Discussion

* * * It is well established that this court applies the same summary judgment methodology as the circuit court. Smith v. Dodgeville Mut. Ins. Co., 212 Wis. 2d 226, 232, 568 N.W.2d 31, 34 (Ct. App. 1997). We first examine the complaint to determine whether it states a claim, and then we review the answer to determine whether it presents a material issue of fact or law. Id. If we conclude that the complaint and the answer are sufficient to join issue, we examine the moving party's affidavits to determine whether they establish a prima facie case for summary judgment. Id. If they do, we look to the opposing party's affidavits to determine whether there are any material facts in dispute which entitle the opposing party to a trial. Id. at 233, 568 N.W.2d at 34.

Whether immunity lies because of the common law doctrine of public officer immunity is a question of law which we review de novo. Kimps v. Hill, 200 Wis. 2d 1, 8, 546 N.W.2d 151, 155 (1996) (citing K.L. v. Hinickle, 144 Wis. 2d 102, 109, 423 N.W.2d 528, 531 (1988)). A question of law is also presented when we decide whether the safe place

statute applies to this case. Ruppa v. American States Ins. Co., 91 Wis. 2d 628, 639, 284 N.W.2d 318, 322 (1979).

Public Officer Immunity

* * *

Based on the information before us, we assume, without deciding, that there was a compelling and known danger of injury of sufficient magnitude to create a ministerial duty to act for Riseling, as Chief of Police and Security, due to her knowledge of the possibility of a crowd surge onto the field. However, Riseling did not ignore the potential danger. She, with the assistance of others, formulated a plan, the "POST GAME CROWD TACTICS," the goal of which was "to prevent injury to people—officers, band members and fans."

The plan established no specific tasks that were to be performed at a time certain; rather, it made general statements and set general guidelines such as,

We expect that if Wisconsin wins today, especially if it is a close game, there will be an attempt by fans to come onto the field.

> If there is a crowd surge, officers at that point will make the initial decision to move aside and begin pulling back to the goalpost assignment. Lt. Johnson will be observing from the press box and will make decisions on giving the command for all officers to pull back.

There may be times during and after the game when people crowd the fence and put pressure against it. Actively encourage them to move back. If it seems there is danger of the fence breaking (it has in the past) move back to a safe position. * * * Here, the formation of the post-game crowd control plan represented Riseling's judgment about how best to reduce the potential for injury to persons at the game. "A discretionary act is one that involves choice or judgment." Kimps, 200 Wis. 2d at 23, 546 N.W.2d at 161 (citation omitted). Additionally, the implementation of the plan required Riseling, Green and Williams to respond to their assessment of what the crowd's actions required. By its very nature, the way the plan was effected had to change from moment to moment because the plan was responsive to the crowd. Reacting to the crowd also constituted the exercise of discretion. Furthermore, neither the documents nor the testimony contained in any of the portions of the depositions submitted in opposition to respondents' motion for summary judgment established a factual dispute about whether any specific acts were required of any of the respondents. Therefore, we conclude that the decision about what type of a plan to formulate to safely manage the crowd, as well as the implementation of the chosen plan, were discretionary, not ministerial, acts.

4. Non-governmental acts.

* * *

Here, documents provided in support of, and in opposition to, the respondents' motion for summary judgment establish no inconsistency between the actions of those respondents whose job duties took them personally into crowd control management activities, and the University's policy of safe management of the crowd at football games. Rather, they acted in accord with the General Operating Procedures for Camp Randall Stadium. Neither the formulation of the plan nor the implementation of it required highly technical, professional skills, such as a physician's. Therefore, we conclude that the respondents' activities were governmental in nature and we decline to extend the exception to immunity found in Gordon in this context.

* * *

CONCLUSION

Because the appellants have submitted no evidentiary facts from which we could conclude that the respondents had ministerial duties which they failed to perform and because neither the safe place statute nor any other theory of liability put forth by the appellants applies to the respondents, we affirm the summary judgment dismissing appellants' claims against the respondents.

By the Court.—Judgment affirmed.

CASES ON THE SUPPLEMENTAL WEB SITE

Kleinknecht v. Gettysburg College (1993 U.S. App. LEXIS 6609). The reader should pay particular attention to the defendants' response to Kleinknecht's collapse on the field. How could they have been better prepared for such a crisis?

Mogabgab v. Orleans Parish School Board (1970 La. App. LEXIS 5219). Carefully review the coaches' response to this medical emergency. What should they have done differently?

Cater et al. v. City of Cleveland (1998 Ohio LEXIS 2212). Pay special attention to the defendant's lack of proper training and practice in how to call the emergency medical services. How did this affect the outcome of the crisis and lawsuit?

Dibartolomeo v. New Jersey Sports and Exposition Authority (2011, N.J. Super. LEXIS 345). While this case primarily deals with dangerous conditions and premises liability, note how the New Jersey Sports Authority handled crowd management after the manifestation of the dangerous condition. How can sport/recreation managers properly protect patrons from dangerous conditions when the primary means for ingress and egress are not functioning properly?

Maussner v. Atlantic City Country Club (1997 N.J. Super. LEXIS 155). Notice that Court noted the Country Club did not have a written "evacuation plan" for inclement weather nor was it posted anywhere at the Club. How could the Club have been better prepared for lightning? How can sport/recreation managers best plan for the dangers associated with inclement weather?

QUESTIONS YOU SHOULD BE ABLE TO ANSWER

1. Explain what is meant by the term "crisis."

2. Identify several possible crises that could affect a specific local recreation or sport business.

3. Identify and explain the main components of a Crisis Management Plan (CMP).

4. Search for examples of CMPs for recreation or sport management-related organizations/facilities on the Internet. Review them and identify their strengths and weaknesses.

5. Explain several ways you would practice different aspects of a CMP.

REFERENCES

Case

Eneman v. Richter, 577 N.W.2d 386; 1998 Wisc. App.

Publications

Ajango, D. (2003). The ultimate goal in crisis response. In *Recreation & Adventure Program Law Conference Proceedings*. Vail, CO. p. C1–6.

Arquilla, J., Ronfeldt, D., & Zanini, M. (1999). Networks, netwar, and information-age terrorism. In Lesser, I.O., Hoffman, B., Arquilla, J., Ronfeldt, D., & Zanini, M. *Countering the new terrorism* (pp. 39–84). Santa Monica, CA: Rand Corporation.

Ashby, S., & Diacon, S. (2000). Strategic rivalry and crisis management. *Risk Management, 2*(2), 715.

Bacon, V. L. & Anderson, M. K. (2003). Crisis interventions for sport related incidents. *The Sport Journal, 6*(4). Retrieved December 15, 2005 from http://www.thesportjournal.org/2003Journal/Vol6-No4/crisis.asp

Cheley, D. (1997, Spring). *Crisis at camp . . . What do we do now*? Paper presented at American Camping Association Mid-States Conference.

Choi, J. N., Sung, S. Y., & Kim, M. U. (2010). How do groups react to unexpected threats? Crisis management in organizational teams. *Social Behavior and Personality, 36*(6), 805–826.

CNN/Sports Illustrated. (2002, November 24). *That kind of Fiesta. . . . Postgame fires, car damage leads to 45 arrests of OSU fans*. Associated Press. Retrieved March 25, 2009 from http://sportsillustrated.cnn.com/football/college/news/2002/11/23/rowdy_fans_ap

Coombs, W.T. (2007). *Ongoing crisis communication: Planning, managing, and responding* (2nd ed.). Los Angeles: Sage.

Coombs, W.T. (2007, October 30). *Crisis management and communications*. Gainesville, FL: Institute for Public Relations. Retrieved March 20, 2009 from http://www.instituteforpr.org/essential_knowledge/detail/crisis_management_and_communications

Everly, G.S., & Mitchell, J.T. (1999). *Critical incident stress management: CISM, A new era and standard of care in crisis intervention* (2nd ed.). Elliot City, MD: Chevron Publishing.

Hall, S., Fos, P., Marciani, L., & Zhang, L. (2011). Multiple criteria decision making (MCDM) application in evaluating protective security measures for major sport events. *International Journal of Sport Management, 12*, 191–207.

Henry, L. (2010). Surviving a social networking crisis. *PR News*. Retrieved on January 1, 2012 from http://www.prnewsonline.com/prinsiders/Surviving-a-Social-Networking-Crisis_14077.html

Herman, M. L. & Oliver, B. B. (2001). *Vital signs: Anticipating, preventing and surviving a crisis in a nonprofit*. Washington, DC: Nonprofit Risk Management Center.

Hermann, C. F. (1972). *International crises: Insights from behavioral research*. New York: Free Press.

James, M. (2008, October). Sudden death at a fitness center. *Fitness Management*. Retrieved March 20, 2009 from http://fitnessmanagement.com/articles/article.aspx?articleid=2505&zoneid=28

McKindra, L. (2009, August 31). SIDs asked to be in the crisis-management loop. *The NCAA News*. Indianapolis: NCAA.

National Incident Management System. (2004). U.S. Department of Homeland Security. Washington D.C.

Palmer, J. (2010). Social networks and the web offer a lifeline in Haiti. *BBC mobile news*. Retrieved January 1, 2012 from http://news.bbc.co.uk/2/hi/8461240.stm

Reilly, R. (n.d.). Unruly fans, your days are done. Big Brother is watching. *ESPN The Magazine, Life of Reilly*. Retrieved December 28, 2012 from http://sports.espn.go.com/espnmag/story?id=4012452

Seymour, M. & Moore, S. (2000). *Effective crisis management: Worldwide principles and practice*. New York: Cassell.

Schirick, E. (2002, March). Risk management and crisis response are you prepared? *Camping Magazine*. Retrieved March 20, 2009 from http://www.acacamps.org/campmag/rm023risk.php

Schwarz, E. C., Hall, S., & Shibli, S. (2010). *Sport Facility Operations Management: A Global Perspective*. Oxford, United Kingdom: Butterworth-Heinemann.

Schultz, R. (1993, November 1). Richter looks for solutions. *The Capital Times*, p. B1.

Steinbach, P. (2012, February). College coaches on the front lines of crisis management. *Athletic Business*. http://athleticbusiness.com/articles/article.aspx?articleid=3838&zoneid=38

Stephens, K. (2011). How can university emergency managers use social media? *Idisaster 2.0*. Retrieved on December 27, 2011 from http://idisaster.wordpress.com/2011/08/12/how-can-universities-use-social-media-for-emergency-management/

Stoldt, G. C., Miller, L. K., Ayres, T. D., & Comfort, P. G. (2000). Crisis management planning: A necessity for sport managers. *International Journal of Sport Management, 4*, 253–266.

Syme, C. (2005, January 17). Writing about crisis best way to avert one. *The NCAA News Online*. Retrieved March 20, 2009 from http://www.ncaa.org/wps/ncaa?ContentID=5760

USA Today. (2003, January 3). *Hello, Columbus*, p. C13. AP Wire.

U.S. Department of Education. (2009). *Emergency Planning*. Retrieved March 21, 2009 from http://www.ed.gov/admins/lead/safety/emergencyplan/index.html

4.24 CROWD MANAGEMENT

Robin Ammon, Jr. I Slippery Rock University

Nita Unruh I University of Nebraska/Kearney

Recreation, sport, and entertainment events share a number of common factors. Each involves some type of activity. The activity may range from a church-league softball game to the Coachella Valley Music and Arts Festival. All of these events are held in or at some type of venue. The venues take on numerous forms such as stadiums, arenas, swimming pools, golf courses, parks, and ski areas. Each of these events will entail numerous risks that could result in personal and/or financial loss. Examples of these risks include simple slip & falls, vandalism, fights among spectators, or an active shooter. One of the final similarities among these events is that, in most cases, they involve a crowd. A **crowd** is a group of individuals who gather to involve themselves in some specific event. A major element in providing a safe, entertaining, and valuable experience for the consumer is effective crowd management. This chapter will discuss the development of crowd management and modern techniques of effective crowd management.

FUNDAMENTAL CONCEPTS

A facility or event manager has a duty to provide as safe and secure an environment as possible. van der Smissen (1990) classified **crowd management** as part of the duty facility managers owe to their patrons to protect them from unreasonable risk of harm from themselves or other individuals. Others have defined crowd management as a tool to assist facility or event managers in providing a safe and enjoyable environment for their guests by implementing the facility/event policies and procedures. A crowd manager's responsibilities include managing the movement and activities of the crowd/guests, (*e.g.*, searching fans as they enter the facility) assisting with potentially dangerous situations (*e.g.*, preventing exuberant fans from storming the field of play), and aiding guests with specific concerns related to their enjoyment and/or involvement with the event (*e.g.*, investigating a fan's text message pertaining to a potentially dangerous, intoxicated spectator).

Why Is Crowd Management Important?

A facility manager has a legal duty to provide a reasonably safe environment. Failure to meet this duty can result in legal liability for both the facility and the manager provided the incident was foreseeable. If the risk was not foreseeable, there can be no liability.

Foreseeability as defined by Black (2011) is the "The quality of being reasonably anticipatable." (p. 319). If the facility manager fails to foresee a crowd-related incident that would have been foreseen by a reasonable, prudent facility manager, injuries resulting from the incident leave the organization and manager vulnerable to a lawsuit. **Therefore** a prudent facility manager will **need to** anticipate rather than react (see also Chapter 2.11 *Negligence*).

Foreseeability, however, is not as clear as it once was. Due to the litigious nature of our society, individuals at various events *expect* to be kept safe no matter the risk. The plaintiff in *Cohen v Sterling Mets* (2007) was a vendor in the stands at Shea Stadium who was injured by a spectator scrambling for a t-shirt that had been launched into the stands during a between-the-innings promotional give-away. A public address announcement regarding the **giveaway** had been made prior to the promotion and security was present. Nevertheless, the vendor felt he should be compensated for his injuries. In 2010, another situation involving a promotion occurred when a plaintiff sued "Sluggerrr", the mascot of the KC Royals. The mascot had been shooting foiled wrapped hotdogs into the stands when one of them hit the plaintiff in the face. John Coomer, the plaintiff maintained that the Royals were negligent in failing to train the mascot on how to shoot the hotdogs. In both of these situations, the likelihood of injury should have been foreseeable by management.

Fans rushing onto the athletic field at the end of a game have become a common sight—making such incidents foreseeable. For example, after the December, 2011, Oklahoma State-Oklahoma football game, fans rushed the field intending to tear down the goal posts. Approximately 12 fans were injured in the melee (Wire reports, 2011). In an effort to reduce the risks, some universities such as Southern Methodist University purchased collapsible goal posts while others, like the University of Florida, employ both uniformed law enforcement officers and additional outsourced security staff and dogs to keep the fans from rushing the field. A third group, of which The Ohio State University is a member, recognizes the difficulty of trying to prevent tens of thousands of fans from going where they want. The fans are allowed on the field to celebrate if they are so inclined—regardless of the possible consequences.

Dangerous crowd situations are by no means unique to the United States. In March, 2009, a wall collapsed from the pressure of fans pushing each other while attempting to gain entry to a qualifying match for the 2010 World Cup in Abidjan, Ivory Coast. During the ensuing stampede 19 spectators died and 132 were injured. Police firing tear gas to disperse the crowd were blamed for the disaster (Associated Press, 2009). In February, 2012, more than 70 Egyptian soccer fans perished after hundreds of fans rushed the field following a match between two heated rivals. Reports surfaced after the tragedy that riot police had been told not to become involved as a result of previous sectarian violence (Fayed & Perry, 2012).

Sport and recreation managers need to be aware of the impact of trends in society relating to foreseeability and crowd management problems. For example, in 2008, a large crowd of frenzied shoppers at a Long Island, NY, Wal-Mart trampled a security employee to death during the early stages of Black Friday. Wal-Mart executives stated they could not have anticipated such a tragic incident. However, they expected a large number of early shoppers and employed additional outsourced crowd management staff, scheduled extra internal security, and store associates, as well as used barricades to control the early morning shoppers (Neff, 2008).

Whether shopping on Black Friday or attending a major league sports event, the potential for injury to patrons cannot be eliminated. Injuries can arise from interactions among spectators; for example, the beating of Bryan Stow in the Los Angeles Dodgers parking lot after a game against the San Francisco Giants (Wilson, 2011). Another example occurred during a 49ers v. Raiders game, in the fall of 2011. A 26-year old man was severely beaten in a men's restroom and another was shot multiple times in the parking lot at Candlestick Park (Sherbert, 2011). Physical problems with the facility caused by such things as fire and weather can also be a factor. For example, at least five people died at the Indiana State Fair during a Sugarland Concert when the stage blew apart during a summer storm (Usborne, 2011). In light of such incidents, event and facility managers should devise a crowd management plan to reduce the risk of injury resulting from common, foreseeable crowd activity.

Evolution of Crowd Management

An examination of the history of crowd management reveals some type of security measures have always been used at major sport/entertainment events. In the early Roman days, lions and other wild animals took care of anyone attempting to "rush the field". Since those early days providing the appropriate number of trained crowd management personnel has become a more structured endeavor.

Two of the early rock and roll band promoters, Bill Graham on the west coast and Barry Fey in the midwest, are often credited with recognizing the need for adequately trained crowd management staff. They, along with a few other promoters, realized that uniformed law officers were not the best individuals to protect the bands and their fans during the late 1960s and early 1970s. Graham and Fey introduced the concept of using "peer group" security personnel recruited from the same demographics as the concert fans. Not only were the early "peer group" security better able to relate to the crowds, but the **T-shirt security** (as they were called) also received specific training in how to deal with rock and roll fans.

Many sport and recreation managers contract with outside companies to provide the crowd management service for their venues. Contracting or outsourcing crowd management services eliminates the headaches associated with the hiring, firing, training, and scheduling of the crowd management staff and provides necessary expertise. This practice of contracting outside agencies is known as **outsourcing**. At most major sporting events, a shirt or jacket emblazed with a term such as "Event Staff" helps the spectator know that some measure of crowd management is being provided. Some events still use **uniformed** or **off-duty law enforcement** officers, but due to high salaries, improper training, and litigation concerns, using uniformed security for crowd management duties is no longer the industry standard. However, uniformed security is still used to provide security services and to arrest intoxicated or unruly individuals at many events. In addition, because of the heightened concerns since September 11, 2001, more facilities are turning to armed law enforcement officers in addition to the outsourced crowd management staff.

Crowd Management Companies

In 1967, Contemporary Services Corporation (CSC) became the pioneer in peer-group security. CSC has expanded to provide service to various political, sport, and entertainment venues and events, including every Olympics since the 2004 Summer Games in Athens, Greece. Landmark Event Staffing Services is one of the newer crowd management companies whose management brings over 50 years of experience to the industry. Located in northern California, Washington, Wyoming, Colorado, New Mexico, and Pennsylvania, Landmark employees are trained in the latest techniques pertaining to crowd and risk management as well as guest services. The reputation of Landmark has already made its mark by securing clients in the entertainment industry, intercollegiate football and basketball venues, NFL stadiums, and MLB baseball parks across the country. Another company that provides security, primarily on the West Coast, is StaffPro. It services over 3,000 concerts, sporting events, conventions, and special events every year (Contemporary Services, n.d.; Landmark, n.d.; Staff Pro, n.d.).

Crowd Management Since September 11, 2001

The terrorist actions of September 11 have forever affected the way facilities and events are managed. Since that fateful day, a multitude of events have been classified as "National Special Security Events". This classification allows the federal government to take over the control of the security of the event. The Secret Service takes charge and, along with the Federal Emergency Management Agency (FEMA) and the FBI, devises a comprehensive security plan. There have been less than 50 of these occasions since 1998 when President Clinton signed Presidential Decision Directive 62 creating this category of event. World governmental meetings, presidential inaugurations, presidential funerals, political conventions and various sporting events such as the Olympics have made up the bulk of these events.

Even for those events which are not included in this special category, operational costs have increased exponentially because insurers now view these types of events as attractive targets for terrorists. The availability of terrorist insurance will remain limited and the premiums astronomical for an indefinite period. Thus, it is paramount for sport/recreation/entertainment facility operators to recognize their venue's vulnerability and take corrective measures. Guidelines developed and security measures implemented to combat terrorism are effective crowd management techniques under any circumstances.

Changes in Operational Procedures

The U. S. Department of Homeland Security has developed a tool that allows venue security managers the opportunity to assess the vulnerabilities of their public assembly facilities. The Risk Self-Assessment Tool (RSAT) is an online program designed for stadium and other venue managers to integrate along with their **"standard operating procedures"**. The tool helps in minimizing facility risks brought about by facility vulnerabilities. Information is collected from the facility administration and provides options to them to improve the security at their venue. The application prepares two separate reports: "the Self-Assessment Report" and "the Benchmark Report" (DHS, 2009).

Tools such as the RSAT can be implemented and utilized by the sport or recreation manager of any type of venue no matter its size or degree of importance. In addition, the vulnerabilities identified by such tools are not limited to threats posed by potential terrorists. Additional components that need to be included in any facility's self-assessment include topics such as physical security, central monitoring, and evacuation. Some of these measures can be expensive to implement and are more appropriate for large facilities; however, the prudent sport or recreation manager will examine how the concepts can apply to his/her facility.

An effective security system can discourage potential terrorists from attempting an attack. The more secure your facility, the less likely you will be a target. The current security measures must be examined, threat assessment carried out, and associated probabilities identified. Cost should not be the deciding factor but obviously needs to be taken into consideration.

Physical Security Measures

A small vehicle loaded with explosives parked near a facility can cause tremendous damage and multiple deaths (*e.g.*, the Oklahoma City bombing). Thus the parking and delivery policies of the facility should be examined. Security checks along with biometric verification can be utilized. Large concrete planters can be situated to keep trucks (or cars) from parking too close to the venue's walls. Filled with flowers and plants, these barriers need not appear ominous. Small steel posts known as bollards can be anchored in the ground or can pneumatically be raised or lowered to monitor the flow of traffic into sensitive areas.

Technological communication networks, such as **closed circuit television** (CCTV) should be installed around venue access points (e.g., doors, gates, windows). In addition, sensors should also closely monitor access points for the air conditioning, ventilation and water systems. These sensors should be sensitive enough to quickly detect the release of chemical and biological agents. Smaller facilities may not have funding for extensive CCTV or chemical sensors, but they should insure that access points are secure.

No matter the level of preparedness, the facility manager needs to be able to adapt. For example, Hurricane Katrina taught facility managers that telephone service, water, heating/air conditioning, electricity and other essential services may be disrupted for extended periods of time. In addition, if the towers used by cell phones are damaged, a sport/recreation/entertainment facility (e.g., Louisiana Superdome) can have its communication system rendered totally inoperative. The purchase and use of satellite phones may need to be investigated.

Central Monitoring

A control room or command post should be established for the management of facility security, and should be located in a position that can survey the overall event. This is crucial for effective communication. Having the command post in a central location will allow crowd management and law enforcement personnel to view the entire venue, and enable them to utilize binoculars to identify disruptive or intoxicated individuals. In the UK, the command post or control room, by law, must have a view of the stadium interior.

In larger venues, the trend in the United States has been to establish a centralized location that contains a variety of CCTV monitors. This control room is usually situated in a secure location inside the stadium and is manned 24 hours a day, 365 days a year. In addition a game-day command post is located higher up in the venue that provides good lines of sight for representatives of the various command agencies such as law enforcement, emergency medical, facility maintenance, and crowd management. A specific number of staff members should be equipped with multi-channel radios, with each channel designated for specific groups (e.g., channel 1—peer group security; channel 2—housekeeping; channel 3—law enforcement; channel 4—medical services). Staff members from each group may then be contacted by the command post, via radio, to handle various situations quickly and safely.

Evacuation

Response time in an emergency requiring evacuation of the facility is critical. Each facility should have a specific evacuation plan in place for a variety of attack or other emergency scenarios. Electronic signs and emergency lighting are extremely important. Panic can increase the number of deaths as well as spread any contamination resulting from an attack. Most facilities today have devised an evacuation plan but often leave out important components, such as the evacuation of their disabled guests. Sport venues such as the PNC Park, AT & T Park and the Staples Center have all conducted mock evacuation drills to evaluate their current plans. One of the most successful evacuations in history took place at Santiago Bernabeu Stadium (home to Real Madrid, a professional soccer team in Spain). After a bomb scare on December 12, 2004, over 80,000 spectators were evacuated in an amazing eight minutes and 37 seconds. There were no fatalities and only a few minor injuries.

NFL Fan Behavior Policies

Although this section is specific to the National Football League (NFL), many of these concepts and procedures are adaptable to other organizations and venues.

Prior to the 2008 season, the NFL and its 32 teams agreed upon a Fan Code of Conduct. The Code states:

When attending a game, you are required to refrain from the following behaviors: behavior that is unruly, disruptive, or illegal in nature, intoxication or other signs of alcohol impairment that results in irresponsible behavior, foul or abusive language or obscene gestures, interference with the progress of the game (including throwing objects onto the field), failing to follow instructions of stadium personnel, and verbal or physical harassment of opposing team fans (McCarthy, 2008, ¶ 1-3).

Violators of the Code face various penalties that may include ejection and revocation of season tickets if the behavior is judged to be detrimental enough. The league has sent a firm message that they intend to hold season ticket owners responsible for the conduct of anyone using their tickets and occupying their seats (McCarthy, 2008).

The Code requires fans to abstain from behaviors that hamper the enjoyment of other fans or interfere with the product on the field of play ("NFL teams", 2008). With the increased scrutiny on potential alcohol problems inside the facility, some fans try to circumvent the policies by engaging in outlandish behavior outside the stadium while tailgating before the game begins. As a result many stadiums have increased the presence of uniformed police officers throughout their parking lots. In order to prevent problems with tailgaters during games, fans at Soldier Field and at Candlestick Park must either enter the game after kickoff or leave the parking lots (Muret, 2011a).

Additional initiatives have been put in place at numerous stadiums to stop intoxicated spectators from entering the stadium or from driving home drunk after the event. Several stadiums employ crowd management staff to walk among the spectators entering the stadium in the hopes of preventing intoxicated individuals from entering the stadium. Management at MetLife Stadium took another approach by utilizing an "anti-knucklehead" unit. Their task is to find intoxicated and disruptive fans and notify them they are being observed. If the behavior continues the offender may be ejected (Muret, 2011b). Heinz Field management instituted the "Tattle text" program which allows fans to send a text message to the control room if they observe an obnoxious or intoxicated third party. Management also provides a 1–800 number for the same purpose. An alcohol management team is then dispatched to the location to assess the situation and eject the transgressors if deemed necessary. Other facilities offer "designated driver" programs where individuals sign a pledge card not to drink alcohol and oftentimes are rewarded by being provided with free soft drinks during the game. Elsewhere, venues such as Gillette Stadium and Lucas Oil Stadium have implemented "Fan Code of Conduct Awareness" courses. Fans that violate the venue's code of conduct must complete a course including topics such as alcohol abuse and the impact of obscene language (Muret, 2011b). Each of these initiatives demonstrates the intent of the NFL and its teams to curtail alcohol transgressions and to enforce the Code of Conduct.

Criminal Trespass

Fans entering restricted areas may be subject to ejection or criminal charges. It should be noted that the charge for this type of offense varies from misdemeanor to felony, depending on the state. For example, during the summer of 2002 a father and son breached U. S. Cellular Field security, came onto the field, and proceeded to attack the Kansas City Royals' first base coach during a baseball game. This confrontation along with four incidents of field intrusion during the 2004 baseball season at The Great American Ball Park prompted state legislators in Ohio to pass state legislation pertaining to persons who enter any restricted area at a place of public amusement. Section 2911.23 of the Ohio Revised Code states "An owner or lessee of a place of public amusement, an agent of the owner or lessee, or a performer or participant at a place of public amusement may use reasonable force to restrain and remove a person from a restricted portion of the place of public amusement if the person enters or remains on the restricted portion of the place of public amusement and, as a result of that conduct, interrupts or causes the delay of the live performance, sporting event, or other activity taking place at the place of public amusement" (ORC 2911.23, 2006). Violators are charged with criminal trespass, punishable by jail term, fine, or other sentence including community service.

Searches and Resulting Litigation

Outsourced crowd management and security companies play a large role in managing and controlling the public in office buildings, schools, parks, recreation and sport facilities, and concert venues. However, the courts have placed various limitations on the authority of private crowd management companies. Often, any violation of state law will cause a crowd manager to be held to the same civil and criminal liability as any private individual. In addition, the courts have ruled that a search of a person's belongings without their consent will generally be viewed as trespass. Many of the claims of illegal searches allege a violation of privacy rights and rely on the Fourth Amendment's guarantee of freedom from unreasonable searches. In determining if a search is legal, the courts look at three issues: ((1) if the conduct was considered to be state action, (2) if the conduct could be considered a search, and finally (3) if the search was reasonable (see Chapter 6.15 *Search and Seizure/ Right to Privacy*).

With no further incidents since the terrorist attacks on 9/11/2001 many individuals have become less tolerant of increased security measures, especially those pertaining to searches. Three cases illustrate the legal questions regarding pat-down searches and their impact on crowd management policies.

In 2005, the Supreme Court of North Dakota held that a mass pat-down search of spectators at college ice hockey games was unconstitutional (*State of North Dakota v. Seglen*, 2005). Seglen, a minor, was searched by a campus police officer upon entering the ice arena on the campus of the University of North Dakota. A can of beer was found in his possession and he was cited for it. The court ruled that signage in the arena warning of the search did not mean Seglen consented to the search and that a physical "pat-down" search was more intrusive than a limited visual search. Even though the facility was privately owned, the officer conducting the search was found to be acting in an official capacity as a police officer for the University of North Dakota, so the Fourth Amendment applied. The North Dakota state Supreme Court ruled that the search was intrusive and violated Seglen's Fourth Amendment rights.

The next two incidents were a result of the NFL's "limited" pat-down search policy that was put into practice before the 2005 season. As per the new NFL directive, the San Francisco 49ers began searching all fans entering Candlestick Park during the 2005 football season. Mr. and Mrs. Sheehan purchased season tickets and were subjected to pat down searches during each home game during that season. In December, 2005, after the season was completed, the Sheehan's filed suit against the team claiming the 49ers violated their privacy rights. The trial court dismissed the action. The court stated the Sheehans did not have a reasonable expectation of privacy since they were subjected to the pat down searches at every game during the 2005 season. Therefore, they had full notice of the pat down policy, consented to the pat down prior to admittance to the game and never complained. Therefore, the Sheehans had no reasonable expectation of privacy. The Sheehans appealed the decision and the state Court of Appeals dismissed the case (153 Cal. App. 4th 396, 2007 Cal.). In March, 2009, the state Supreme Court restored the case. The court stated they believed the case warranted further review and instructed the 49ers to justify the search policy. The Supreme Court reversed the Court of Appeals decision and remanded the case. It will be interesting to see how the decision of this case impacts the NFL's search policy (*Sheehan*, 2009).

Raymond James Stadium (home of the Tampa Bay Buccaneers) halted their searches after Gordon Johnston, a season ticket holder, sued the Tampa Bay Sports Authority (TSA), the government agency that manages Raymond James Stadium. Similar to the *Seglen* case, Johnston filed suit against the Tampa Bay Sports Authority (TSA) claiming that the pat-downs violated his Fourth Amendment rights. Johnston successfully challenged the NFL policy in two Florida state court decisions and one Federal court. However, in June, 2008, the 11th Circuit Court (U.S. Court of Appeals) ruled that Johnston gave up his right to challenge the searches when he consented to them. The court concluded that Johnston, as well as other fans, knew they were going to be subject to searches before they entered the stadium. Knowing this information, in the judge's opinion, Johnston voluntarily submitted to the search. In January, 2009, the U.S. Supreme Court declined to hear the case (*Johnston v Tampa Sports Authority*, 2008).

Previous 11th Circuit decisions (*Bourgeois v Peters*, 2004) have used the unconstitutional conditions doctrine to nullify consent. In the *Bourgeois* case the 11th Circuit considered the constitutionality of suspicionless, warrantless searches of a group of protestors standing on public land. The court held the suspicionless search was unconstitutional and violated the plaintiff's rights under both the First and Fourth Amendments. In the *Bourgeois* case the government created the policy and performed the search. However, the appellate court recognized several differences between the *Bourgeois* and *Johnston* cases. First, the search utilized in *Bourgeois* prevented people from gathering on public land whereas the plaintiff in *Johnston* had no constitutional right to enter Raymond James Stadium for a Buccaneers football game and since the ticket was a revocable license he could be barred from entering for any reason. Since the entrance policy was imposed by a private party, Johnston was not forced by the government to choose between his constitutional rights and a benefit to which he was entitled. Unlike the City's policy in *Bourgeois* the pat-down policy in *Johnston* was developed and mandated by the NFL Commissioner and applied exclusively to NFL events. The pat-down search was imposed by the NFL and the Buccaneers, who were both classified as private entities, and not a state actor.

Crowd Management Plan

A crowd management plan is an important component of the overall risk management plan of any organization whose activities or events are attended by large numbers of people. The facility manager is either directly or indirectly responsible for both risk management and crowd management. In order for the facility manager to effectively carry out these responsibilities, an effective crowd management plan addressing such issues as capacity of the venue, geographic location, demographics of guests, and type of event must be designed and implemented. In the event of litigation alleging failure to control crowds, courts will look to see if such a plan existed, if it was in writing, how it was implemented, and how it was disseminated to the involved employees. Each employee needs to be aware of his or her role in the plan, even if the role is only a small part of the plan (see also Chapter 4.11 *Risk Management Process*).

Trained and Competent Staff

The first component of a good plan is to have properly trained and competent staff to carry out the policies. Before September 11, 2001, the biggest concern for event managers stemmed from alcohol problems. Now, crowd managers must make their spectators feel safe while at the facility.

Screeners/searchers may be employed as trained staff to identify prohibited items such as bottles, cans, coolers, cameras, weapons, fireworks, umbrellas, or alcoholic beverages. This "search," depending on local statutes, may be a visual screening or a physical "pat-down." In light of the terrorist threat emanating from the tragedies on September 11, 2001, this search has become a much more critical element of the crowd management plan. While a physical pat-down may prove effective at times, some fans still manage to smuggle in dangerous weapons. During the 2011 NFL season one fan managed to bring a "stun gun" into MetLife Stadium during a New York Jets-Dallas Cowboys game. During an altercation emanating from his refusal to stand during the national anthem, the individual used the weapon on several other fans. As a result, the NFL changed their search policy and began using handheld magnetometers (metal detectors or wands) at all 31 stadiums across the country.

The second group of crowd management personnel includes **ticket takers** who collect or scan the tickets of those entering the facility. The main role of the ticket taker is to ensure that everyone entering the event has a valid ticket for that day's event.

Ushers comprise the third wave of crowd management personnel. They should be well versed in the layout of the facility, including locations of first aid stations, pay phones, restrooms, concession stands, authorized smoking areas, and exits. Ushers should also assist the guests in finding their seats. The usher should observe the patrons and call for assistance when necessary to assist injured patrons, remove food and beverage spills, and defuse potential crowd altercations.

The last wave in crowd management is perhaps the most visible—the **peer-group** or **T-shirt security**. Peer group security is trained to handle crowd disturbances such as unruly, disruptive, or intoxicated patrons. These individuals will also assist in protecting the athletes or performers on the floor or field of the facility. Most recreation, sport, and entertainment facilities also require additional peer-group security personnel to fill various crowd management roles backstage and/or in the press box.

To reduce the risk of a lawsuit due to personnel errors, whether outsourced personnel are used or the facility hires its own security personnel, it is paramount for all staff—ticket takers, screeners, ushers, or T-shirt security—to go through an **orientation program**. This orientation should include an understanding of the facility layout, location of first-aid stations, restrooms, telephones, lost and found, emergency exits, and perhaps most important, a clear understanding of their duties and authority (including the legal ramifications of their actions).

Unfortunately some venue managers (or outsourced agencies) have failed to properly screen potential employees. This failure has resulted in the hiring of individuals with a variety of criminal records. These negligent hiring practices have led to the necessity of criminal background checks for all potential employees. These investigations are costly but being proactive is far more important than the expense.

Crisis Management and Emergency Action Plan

The second major component in a crowd management plan is to prepare for crises or emergencies. Being prepared to handle these incidents includes the capacity to respond to two types of situations—a crisis or an individual injury or illness. **Crises** include events such as fire, bleacher collapses, bomb threats, power loss, tornados, and, in today's society, active shooters and terrorist activities. **Emergencies** generally take the form of individual medical problems (e.g., heart attacks, injuries from falls, heat-related illnesses). Crisis management plans and emergency action plans are necessary so minor problems don't become serious ones and serious ones don't become a disaster. Such plans must be designed and implemented by crowd managers, practiced, and documented (see also Chapter 2.33 *Emergency Care* and Chapter 4.23 *Crisis Management*).

Procedure for Handling Disruptive, Unruly, or Intoxicated Patrons

The third component of an effective crowd management plan pertains to dealing with **fan ejections.** Examples of behaviors that could result in an ejection include disruptive or unruly behavior, intoxication, possession of prohibited items, evasion of admission fees, or field intrusion. Plans also need to be in effect for enforcing the venue's policy when a fan behaves in a prohibited manner. For example, in 2010 during a Philadelphia Phillies-St. Louis Cardinals MLB game a 17-year old fan hopped out of the stands onto the field at Citizens Bank Park. He became a YouTube sensation as police officers pursued him across the field. Finally one of the officers used his Taser to subdue the teenager. The YouTube images initiated discussion worldwide regarding the officer's conduct.

Another problem that may necessitate an ejection is third-party assaults. Third-party assaults occur for various reasons, some foreseeable and some not. Foreseeability does not depend on whether the exact incident was foreseeable. The question is whether an incident of that general nature was reasonably foreseeable. However, if there has been a history of violence or disruptive behavior, the courts have held that actions should be taken to prevent such occurrences (*Bishop v. Fair Lanes Georgia Bowling, Inc.*, 1986; *Cassanello v. Luddy*, 1997; *Leger v. Stockton*, 1988).

Well-written policies should be established that address ways to handle disruptive behavior. The language should be clear and concise, stating what actions will not be tolerated and what measures will result. Ejection policies should be printed on tickets and posted for patrons. Policies may differ among athletic event, recreational activity, or concert depending upon the request of the event manager. It is crucial for personnel with ejection authority to be well trained regarding the legal ramifications of their role (e.g., individual liability, understanding of human rights, protection of evidence, excessive force, rules of detention and arrest, and crimes against persons and property). It is also very important that ushers and other staff members who do not have ejection authority receive in-service training regarding their role.

Usually it is best to include a warning before an actual ejection takes place. If an ejection is necessary, it should be carried out swiftly. Handling patrons in this way sends a quick, but firm message to others in the crowd as to what will and will not be tolerated.

Every ejection must be properly documented. This is an extremely crucial step in the ejection process, as it serves to produce a valuable defense for the crowd management employee and facility administration if subsequent litigation ensues. In addition, photographs or video should be utilized as an additional step in the ejection process. This measure accurately portrays the ejected fan's condition and further protects the employees from unnecessary legal harassment. As previously mentioned, closed-circuit televisions (CCTV's) are prevalent in many sport and recreation venues and they can be used to document fights as well as ejections.

Effective Communication Network

An effective communication network is the fourth component of an effective crowd management plan. The network allows the crowd management staff to work efficiently and cooperatively to handle situations as they occur. Representatives from each group (facility management, medical, security, and law enforcement) should have input in the organization of the communication network. Familiarity with the communication network should be a part of the employee orientation and training for each event. Crowd management needs more than a *planning* emphasis; the timely implementation of communication policies is essential. The decisions made in the first two minutes *after* an incident will save lives.

Effective Signage

The fifth component of a crowd management plan is **signage**. Signage is an underutilized tool in risk and crowd management. Signage may be directional or informational in nature and each has its own specific function. **Directional signs** have a number of important uses. Directional signs provide patrons with directions to important locations such as interstate highway entrances and exits, main roadways, and parking areas. Other directional signs serve to indicate the correct entrance gate or portal, as well as directing the patrons to the ticket office.

Informational signs are signs that inform the public. Prohibited items (e.g., cans, bottles, backpacks, weapons, food, recording devices, and cameras) and rules (including ejection policies) are often communicated through such signs. In addition, informational signage helps to provide answers to spectator questions by identifying the location of concession stands, first-aid rooms, telephones, restrooms, smoking areas, and exits.

Implementation and Evaluation of the Plan

As with the risk management plan, the last step in a crowd management plan is the **implementation and evaluation** of the plan. A recreation or sport facility will not benefit from a well-written crowd management plan unless it is effectively implemented during an event. Implementation should start with a review of both the risk and crowd management policies before the event. Event-specific activities, such as half-time promotions, VIP guests on the sideline, or band members coming out into the crowd should be discussed. Each staff member should understand how the activity might affect his or her event responsibilities. After an event, all of the personnel should come together for a debriefing. They should also look into ways to improve the plan. As stated earlier, a crowd management plan should be flexible and allow for change as needed. Without implementation and evaluation, a well-organized crowd management plan becomes ineffective.

SIGNIFICANT CASE

This case is an example of assumption of risk. The plaintiff was an invited guest to the game, but as soon as he set foot onto the playing surface his status changed to that of a trespasser. The change in his status resulted in no duty being owed by the university.

JOSEPH P. MOENING ET AL. V. THE UNIVERSITY OF TOLEDO

Court of Claims of Ohio
2006 Ohio 6471; 2006 Ohio Misc. LEXIS 174

Decision

* * *

Plaintiff was injured on September 20, 2003, during a melee that occurred immediately following the conclusion of a football game held on defendant's premises. A throng of fans and revelers formed on the field and soon thereafter congregated under the goal posts. Plaintiff voluntarily left his seat after the game, climbed over a railing, and proceeded to slide several feet down a concrete wall to gain access to the playing field. Students, spectators, and fans stormed onto the field and climbed onto the north goal posts in an effort to tear them down. Plaintiff witnessed the crowd tear down the north goal posts and carry them out of the stadium. A crowd also surrounded the second or south set of goal posts and began the process of bringing them down as well. There were several persons sitting on or hanging from the crossbar while others were on the ground pulling and twisting at the structure in order to bring it down to ground level. At one point, the crossbar broke free sending parts of the structure along with the persons previously seated on it, hurtling to the ground, trapping plaintiff underneath the pile. Plaintiff was knocked unconscious and suffered injury to his lower back.

Plaintiff claims that his legal status at all times was that of an invitee. Plaintiff insists that he never heard the announcements warning fans to stay off the field. Plaintiff further asserts that defendant is liable for failing to eliminate the risk of harm from the dismantling of the goal posts, either by installing collapsible goal posts or by providing enhanced police presence to control the crowd around the goal posts.

Defendant argues that no duty was owed to plaintiff and that plaintiff's claim should be barred based on the doctrine of primary assumption of the risk. Defendant insists that plaintiff assumed the risk of harm when he joined the revelers and placed himself in the area near the goal posts. In addition, defendant argues that plaintiff's status was that of a trespasser, not an invitee, because he exceeded the scope of his invitation when he left the stands and trespassed onto the playing field. Defendant also maintains that the danger to plaintiff was open and obvious.

In order for plaintiff to prevail upon his claim of negligence, he must prove by a preponderance of the evidence that defendant owed him a duty, that defendant's acts or omissions resulted in a breach of that duty, and that the breach proximately caused his injuries. As stated by the Supreme Court of Ohio, primary assumption of the risk "prevents a plaintiff from establishing the duty element of a negligence case and so entitles a defendant to judgment as a matter of law, [therefore] it is an issue especially amenable to resolution pursuant to a motion for summary judgment. The doctrine is applicable as a defense where "the risk is so obvious that plaintiff must have known and appreciated it." The Supreme Court of Ohio ruled that "when a plaintiff is found to have made a primary assumption of risk in a particular situation, that plaintiff is totally barred from recovery, as a matter of law."

As to plaintiff's privilege or lack thereof to be on the field, the court finds that the issue whether defendant warned fans to stay off the field and the extent to which any person could hear the announcement over the crowd noise is not material to the analysis of this case. Plaintiff's method of arriving on the field, in and of itself, describes a path that was clearly not intended or provided for by defendant. Rather, plaintiff ignored obvious barriers and risked serious harm during each stage of his journey to the field. The court finds that plaintiff was clearly not an invited guest by the time he arrived on the playing field and joined the fracas. Thus, because the duty owed to a licensee and a trespasser is the same, defendant would only owe plaintiff the duty to refrain from wanton or reckless conduct which is likely to injure him.

In the instant case, however, the court finds that plaintiff knowingly and consciously placed himself in close proximity to the goal post with utter disregard for the obvious risk of harm he was exposed to from the actions of an unruly crowd. Plaintiff chose to leave the seating area, climb over a railing, and slide down a concrete wall over six feet high to join the crowd on the field. Therefore, defendant is entitled to assert the defense of primary assumption of the risk and the court finds that defendant owed no duty to plaintiff. Despite the arguments raised by plaintiff at the oral hearing, it is enough that plaintiff voluntarily and knowingly embraced the risk of harm. "To impose primary assumption of the risk, the plaintiff need only consciously expose himself to the known risk, not directly to the exact episode which causes the injury."

Thus, based upon the foregoing analysis and construing the evidence most strongly in plaintiffs' favor, the court finds that there are no genuine issues of material fact and that defendant is entitled to judgment as a matter of law. Accordingly, defendant's motion for summary judgment shall be granted.

An oral hearing was conducted in this case upon defendant's motion for summary judgment. For the reasons set forth in the decision filed concurrently herewith, defendant's motion for summary judgment is GRANTED and judgment is rendered in favor of defendant. Court costs are assessed against plaintiffs. The clerk shall serve upon all parties notice of this judgment and its date of entry upon the journal.

CASES ON THE SUPPLEMENTAL WEB SITE

Bearman v University of Notre Dame (1983 Ind. App. LEXIS 3387). Analyze the court's reasoning about foreseeability. Even though the university may not know the particular danger posed by an intoxicated third party they should have foreseen that some people would become intoxicated and pose a general threat to the safety of other patrons.

Cohen v Sterling Mets (2007 N.Y. Misc. LEXIS 5270). This case provides an excellent example of how the assumption of risk defense is viewed in comparison to the duty a sport venue has to protect employees and spectators. The concept of between-the-innings promotions and the risks they entail is also touched upon.

Heenan v. Comcast Spectacor (2006 Phila. Ct. Com. Pl. LEXIS 138). This case is an excellent example of what can happen if a facility doesn't plan properly or utilize an effective crowd management plan. The operators were aware that the concert would likely be canceled, but they failed to make a timely announcement of the cancellation. In addition, they failed to formulate a plan to properly execute a safe and organized exit from the arena.

Schoneboom v B.B. King Blues Club (2009 N.Y. Misc. LEXIS 3914). This case involves a plaintiff injured during a "mosh pit" incident while watching a concert. The plaintiff claimed that additional security could have prevented the incident. The defendants maintained that the plaintiff assumed the risk of his injury and that additional security could not have prevented his injured knee.

John Hopkins v Connecticut Sports Plex, L.L.C. (2006 Conn. Super. LEXIS 1710). The case illustrates the concept of foreseeability. Several key concepts such as the presence of a proper alcohol management plan, proper numbers of security staff and documentation of prior incidents are important to keep in mind while reading the case.

QUESTIONS YOU SHOULD BE ABLE TO ANSWER

1. Describe three reasons why crowd management is a necessary component of an effective risk management plan.

2. Do an Internet search on Bill Graham and Barry Fey. What were some of the major concerns for the early promoters?

3. Research the NFL's Fan Code of Conduct. Do you believe it will be effective?

4. Analyze the *Seglen*, *Johnston*, and *Sheehan* cases. What are two similarities between the three cases?

5. Identify the components necessary for an effective crowd management plan. How would you implement a crowd management plan?

REFERENCES

Cases

Bishop v. Fair Lanes Georgia Bowling, Inc., 803 F.2d 1548 (11th Cir. 1986).
Bourgeois v Peters 387 F.3rd 1303 (2004 U.S. App.)
Cassanello v. Luddy, 695 A.2d 325 (1997 N.J. Super.)
Cohen v Sterling Mets 840 N.Y.S.2d 527 (2007 N.Y. Misc.)
Leger v. Stockton, 249 Cal. Rptr. 688 (July 25, 1988).
Johnston v Tampa Sports Authority, 530 F.3d 1320 (2008 U.S. App.)
Sheehan v. San Francisco 49ers, Ltd., 201 P.3d 472 (2009 Cal.)
Stark v The Seattle Seahawks, et al., CASE NO. C06-1719JLR (2007 U.S. Dist.)
State of North Dakota v. Seglen, 700 N.W.2d 702 (2005 N.D.)

Publications

Associated Press. (2009, March 30). Ivory Coast soccer fans blame police for deadly stampede that killed 19. *FoxNews.com* Retrieved April 1. 2009 from http://www.foxnews.com/story/0,2933,511555,00.html
Black, H. C. (2011). *Black's Law Dictionary* (6th ed.). St. Paul: West Publishing Co.
Contemporary Services Corporation (n. d). About us. Retrieved from http://www.contemporaryservices.com/pages/about.html.
Criminal Trespass on Place of Public Amusement, Ohio Revised Code § 2911.23 (2006)
DHS. (2009, December 7). Risk Self-Assessment Tool for Stadiums and Arenas. Retrieved from http://www.dhs.gov/files/programs/gc_1259861625248.shtm
Fayed, S. & Perry, T. (2012, February 2). Egyptians Incensed After 74 Die in Soccer Tragedy. *Reuters.com*. Retrieved http://www.reuters.com/article/2012/02/02/us-egypt-soccer-violence-idUSTRE81022D20120202
Landmark Event Staffing Services (n.d.). Home page. Retrieved from https://www.landmarkeventstaff.com/Home_Page.html
McCarthy, M. (2008, August 6). NFL unveils new code of conduct for its fans. *USA Today*. Retrieved from http://www.usatoday.com/sports/football/nfl/2008-08-05-fan-code-of-conduct_N.htm
Muret, D. (2011a, November 21–27). Venue parking lots get more security. *Street & Smith's SportsBusiness Journal 14*(14) 28.
Muret, D. (2011b, November 21–27). Schooling fans on good behavior. *Street & Smith's SportsBusiness Journal 14*(14)25–26, 33.

Neff, J. (2008, December 8). Marketing blamed in Wal-Mart death; Lawsuit says advertising 'specifically' designed to attract large crowds. *Advertising Age.* 23

NFL teams implement fan code of conduct. (2008). NFL.com. Retrieved from http://www.nfl.com/news/story?id=09000d5d809 c28f9&template=without-video&confirm=true.

Sherbert, E. (2011, April). Videos show abusive fans at 49ers and Raiders game, two people shot. *San Francisco Weekly.* http://blogs.sfweekly.com/thesnitch/2011/08/witnesses_sought_in_49ers_shoo.php

Staff Pro. (n. d.). History. Retrieved January 20, 2006 from http://www.staffpro.com/aboutus/history.asp.

Usborne, D. (2011, August). Five killed as 'freak wind' blows down Indianapolis festival stage. *The Independent.* http://www .independent.co.uk/news/world/americas/five-killed-as-freak-wind-blows-down-indianapolis-festival-stage-2337797.html

van der Smissen, B. (1990). *Legal liability and risk management for public and private entities.* Cincinnati, OH: Anderson Publishing Co.

Wilson, S. (2011, May). Bryan Stow lawsuit: Family to sue Dodgers in L.A. Superior Court for slow security response to Stow's beating. *Los Angeles Weekly.* http://blogs.laweekly.com/informer/2011/08/stadium_violence_san_francisco.php

Wire reports. (2011, December 5). At least 12 injured as Oklahoma State fans celebrate. *USA Today,* 4C.

4.25 MANAGING RISK THROUGH INSURANCE[1]
Doyice J. Cotten | Sport Risk Consulting

Insurance is a method by which an individual or business pays a defined expenditure (premium) to protect against the possibility of a large, undetermined future loss or expense. Conducting business without insurance is like rock climbing without a safety line—very risky. Insurance spreads the financial risks and costs of an individual or business among a large group of persons or businesses so that the losses of those few who experience them are shared with the many who do not. In so doing, insurance provides protection against financial catastrophe and is an indispensable risk management technique.

Many persons look at the purchase of insurance and risk management as one and the same. This, however, is not true. Risk management involves the identification of risks, determination of the extent of the risks, and the implementation of one or more control approaches. Control approaches include: (1) elimination of the activity; (2) reduction of risks through operational control; (3) retention (through such techniques as self-insurance, current expensing, and deductibles); (4) transfer by contract (through indemnity agreements, exculpatory clauses, and by requiring insurance by the other party); and (5) purchasing insurance from an insurance company.

Obviously, insurance is but one of many techniques available to help manage risks in a recreation or sport business. The recreation or sport manager should purchase insurance to protect against all risks that could have a significant impact upon the financial integrity of the business, but should not try to insure against every possible risk and potential loss. In addition to protection against property loss, loss of business income, and monetary judgments in lawsuits, insurance also protects the recreation or sport business from legal expenses resulting from litigation.[2] It is usually less expensive to simply pay for minor losses when they occur. A major danger, however, is that failure to meet claim reporting requirements can jeopardize coverage when a seemingly minor injury (a strained knee) eventually reveals itself as a major injury (an ACL tear). It is obviously important that the recreation or sport manager be knowledgeable enough to determine which risks are of such a magnitude as to allow retention by the business, which can be transferred by contract, and which require protection through insurance coverage. The purpose of this chapter is to help the recreation or sport manager become more informed about this aspect of risk management and, subsequently, be able to better protect the business from financial risks.

FUNDAMENTAL CONCEPTS

Understanding the Policy

To become more knowledgeable about insurance and to be better able to protect the recreation or sport business from financial risks, the recreation or sport manager must learn to read and understand an insurance policy. Most can be long and confusing, particularly if one does not know exactly what to look for and does not know the contextual meaning of the terms used. Novick (2000) suggested that the policy should **not** be read like a book or article—from beginning to end. He suggests that the policy be read in the following order for maximum understanding.

---

[1]Special thanks to Denise Brown, Director of Claims for **Fitness Pak,** Chico, CA, for making sure this chapter is up-to-date and accurate.

[2]It is estimated that the average legal expense incurred by an insurance company in taking a suit to trial is approximately $45,000. When the business is insured (and the loss is covered), the insurance company absorbs this cost. When there is no insurance, the business incurs this expense (usually, even if the business wins the lawsuit).

Declarations

This is the section that includes the facts and figures regarding your particular policy. This section includes such items as the name of the insured, address, policy period, coverages, amounts of insurance, the applicable deductibles, and the cost of the policy. If parties other than the corporate entity are covered (e.g., employees, directors), those parties should be named in the declarations section. Careful study of this section can help one to better understand the coverage of the policy.

Endorsements

Look for the endorsements at the end of the policy. **Endorsements** are coverage provisions, added by the carrier, which change the terms of coverage in the main body of the policy. These may broaden or extend coverage in certain instances and may limit or reduce coverage in others. This final section of the policy is an identification of the specific endorsements included with your policy.

The reader should turn to the referenced portion in the main body of the policy and note the endorsement number in the margin beside the coverage language the endorsement is to replace. Do this for each endorsement. Then, when the reader begins to read the main body of the policy, the reader can flip to each endorsement at the appropriate time.

Endorsements may be added when the policy is purchased or at a later date as the needs of the recreation or sport business change. Examples of endorsements might include adding insured persons, coverage of fine art, and peak-season coverage (which increases inventory coverage by 25 percent during the peak season when inventory is higher than usual). A separate Difference in Conditions policy or endorsement might be purchased to protect against earthquake and flood.

Definitions

The key terms of the policy are defined in this section. The reader must understand the terms in this section in order to understand the coverage that is being purchased. Many key words or phrases used in the document are carefully defined. Examine these carefully because many terms have specific meanings in insurance that may differ from the recreation or sport manager's concept of the term. For instance, one might assume that "personal injury" refers to physical injuries of an individual. However, personal injury refers to injuries caused by such acts as slander, libel, false arrest, false imprisonment, humiliation, and invasion of privacy. The reader should refer back to this section when encountering an unfamiliar term.

In *Federal Insurance Company v. Executive Coach Luxury Travel, Inc.* (2010; see the Supplemental Web Site for Chapter 2.35 *Transportation*), definitions proved to be critical in determining if the driver of a bus transporting a team was covered by the policy. The court looked at the definitions of "hire" and "permission" in determining that the incident was covered by the policy.

Contractual Agreement

This part is the actual contractual agreement between the insurance company and the recreation or sport business. The statement of agreement may be quite short. The section simply states that the insurance company agrees to insure the business to the extent indicated in the declarations in exchange for the agreed-upon premium.

The **coverages section** includes a listing of what is being insured in the policy. Following each coverage is a detailed explanation of what is included in the coverage. For example, the building might be listed including any attached structures. The section might state that rental structures away from the main building are not included. This section will also include the perils which the insurance covers (e.g., fire, theft). Additional benefits coverage includes coverage of newly acquired property.

The **exclusions section** of the policy describes what is not covered by the policy. Items that are often excluded from a standard commercial policy include landscaping, buildings under construction, and cash. Some perils that are usually excluded from the standard policy are earthquake; volcanic eruption; water damage from floods, sewers, or surface ground water; power interruption; war; and nuclear hazard. When a coverage is needed by the business that is not listed in the inclusions and is excluded by the exclusions, riders or endorsements adding the coverage to the policy may be purchased.

Houston Wellness Center, Inc., upon filing a claim, discovered the importance of the listed exclusions in a policy when it found that its policy excluded "bodily injury" arising out of the rendering of or failure to render any service (*Houston Wellness Center, Inc. v. York Insurance Company*, 2003; the Significant Case later in the chapter). Careful reading of the policy would probably have led *Houston* to select a different policy or company.

The **conditions section** sets forth the various things the recreation or sport business must do to meet the obligations of the insured. Some of these conditions might include prompt reporting obligations following a loss, giving sworn affirmation of loss, providing an inventory, or provision of receipts.

This section also includes the responsibilities of the insurance company in the event of a claim. Specified here are such things as when cash replacement is mandated, when replacement items may be utilized, procedures to be followed if the insurer and insured fail to agree on the loss, and whether repair is the option of the insurance company.

Determining Necessary Coverage[3]

In reviewing a current insurance policy or when considering the initial purchase of insurance coverage, the recreation or sport business must take four steps to make a wise insurance purchase. First, examine the risks and potential losses that the organization might encounter. Then, establish an effective risk reduction program to reduce the likelihood of the risks occurring. Third, identify the remaining risks and determine which are of a magnitude that can be safely retained by the business and which might be handled by transfer by contract. Finally, the remaining risks that can significantly impact the business should then be covered by an insurance policy that will protect the business from financial loss.

Figure 4.25.1 provides a list of financial risks faced by recreation or sport businesses. Of course, the risks faced vary from one type of business to another, so many of the risks listed in the figure will not apply to a particular business and some businesses may encounter risks that are not listed. Nevertheless, the figure can serve as a guide or checklist in helping the recreation or sport manager make certain the business is properly covered.

Types of Insurance Coverage

There are several types of insurance coverage. Each is designed to offer protection from loss for certain risks. The two types that are most indispensable for a recreation or sport business are property insurance and general liability insurance. Other types of insurance include umbrella liability, liability protection for employees, employment practices liability, motor vehicle, workers' compensation, and event insurance. Each type will be explained below.

Property Insurance

Property insurance is the primary means of protecting the recreation or sport business from loss due to damage or destruction of its facility, the facility contents, and accompanying properties. There are three levels of property coverage offered: basic, broad (or extended coverage), and special form (sometimes referred to as open perils). The **basic coverage** includes protection against a limited number of hazards (e.g., fire, malicious mischief, lightning, explosion, windstorm, aircraft or vehicles, sprinkler leakage, sinkhole collapse, volcanic action, and vandalism). **Broad coverage** includes protection against the exposures listed in basic coverage plus several other exposures (e.g., falling objects, weight of ice, water damage, and smoke). **Special form** coverage includes all losses (e.g., collapse, burglary, and theft) except those that are specifically excluded. The recreation or sport manager should examine the policy carefully to determine what risks are included under each type of

---

[3]Independent contractors in recreation and sport activities (e.g., aerobics instructors, personal trainers, massage therapists) should remember that their operation constitutes a business entity and needs insurance just as larger recreation and sport businesses do. Independent contractors are not generally covered by the insurance of the club at which they work. By way of example, **Fitness Pak** offers liability plans for ACE-certified professionals with coverage ranging from $1 million to $6 million. The policy covers legal expenses and any financial judgments for covered losses (up to the limits of the policy) against the insured. The policy cost ranges from $141 to $316 annually.

coverage, and should realize that even with special form coverage, some property risks are not covered. If the recreation or sport manager feels more coverage is needed, additional endorsements must be purchased. Some exposures that might not be included and might require additional endorsements include theft by employees, vehicles such as golf carts, and boilers. Property insurance also does not include normal wear and tear, cracking, settling, vermin, earthquakes, or floods.

Two endorsements of special importance to many recreation or sport businesses are **extra expense insurance** and **business income insurance**. Extra expense insurance protects the business against certain indirect losses that may occur. For instance, if a health spa is destroyed by fire, some expenses that may be encountered are rental of another building during rebuilding, leasing equipment, and advertising expense. Business income coverage includes loss of income due to the insured peril and continuing expenses such as the salaries of key personnel while the business is closed.

Property Exposures
Fire
Smoke
Natural Elements
 Wind & Tornado Damage
 Flood
 Lightning
 Rain
 Hail
 Earthquake
Debris Removal
Vandalism & Malicious Mischief
Riot
Explosion
Boiler & Machinery
Damage to Signs
Glass Coverage
Damage to Parking Lots & Fences
Damage by Aircraft

Valuable Papers
Electronic Data Processing
Computer Systems
Money & Property
 Theft, Burglary, Disappearance
 Embezzlement & Employee
  Dishonesty
 Off Premises Coverage
 Counterfeit Losses

Moveable Equipment (golf carts,
 mowers, etc.)
Golf Green Coverage
Damage to Property of Others (on your
 premises)

Company Vehicles
 Damage to Vehicle (collision)
 Damage to Vehicle (non-collision:
  theft, vandalism, tree limb)
 Damage to Vehicle (uninsured
  motorist)
 Damage to other Vehicles or Property

Public Liability (Excluding Negligence)
Malpractice by Personnel
Products Liability
Contractual Liability (Including
 Indemnification)
Advertisers Liability
Dram Shop/Host Liquor Liability

Intentional Torts (Personal Injury)
 Defamation
 False Arrest or Imprisonment
 Malicious Prosecution
 Invasion of Privacy
 Wrongful Entry or Eviction
 Assault and Battery

Employment Practices
 Sexual Discrimination
 Racial Discrimination
 Handicap Discrimination
 Age Discrimination
Sexual Harassment
Civil Liberty Violations

Business Operations
Business Interruption
 Loss of Income
 Extra Expenses
Sickness/Accidents/Disability of
 Employees
Health of Key Personnel
Workers' Compensation

Public Liability (Neligence)
Death
Paralysis
Brain Damage
Loss of Limbs
Loss of Senses
Internal Organ Injuries
Infliction of Emotional Stress
Broken Bones
Damaged Ligaments & Tendons
Sprains and Strains
Cuts, Punctures, Abrasions, & Bruises

Vehicles:
 Injury to Other Persons
 Damage to Property of Others
 Damage to non-owned or Leased
  Vehicles

Directors & Officers Liability
Professional Liability
Independent Contractors Liability
Adventure & Tripping Liability
Sponsor Liability
Trip Liability
Event Liability

Watercraft
 Injury to Other Persons
 Damage to Property of Others

Injury to Participant
Catastrophic Injury to Participant
Pollution Liability
Suits by Employees (For Wrongful
 Termination, Breach of Employ-
 ment Contract)

FIGURE 4.25.1 **TYPICAL FINANCIAL RISKS FACED BY RECREATION & SPORT BUSINESSES**

Adapted from van der Smissen, B. (1990). Legal Liability and Risk Management for Public and Private Entities. Cincinnati: Anderson Publishing Company.

The recreation or sport manager has other choices when purchasing property insurance. One is whether to purchase **actual cash value** or **replacement cost** insurance. Replacement cost is usually preferred because it pays the entire cost to replace the property rather than an estimate of the actual current value of the property (which might fall far short of what is needed to replace the item). Most policies have a **coinsurance** clause that requires the recreation or sport business to insure the property to at least 80 percent of the replacement cost or actual cash value, depending upon the form chosen. Failure to coinsure for the amount specified in the policy will result in a significant decrease in benefits in the event of a loss. The amount of the **deductible** is another decision that must be made. The business pays the deductible when a claim is made. For instance, if a storm does $3,000 damage to the building and the business carries a $500 deductible, the business pays the first $500 and the insurance covers the remaining $2,500. The higher the deductible, the lower the cost of the insurance, so a business can save money by carrying a high deductible and retaining that degree of risk.

The recreation or sport manager should determine what exposures are covered by the property insurance, determine from Figure 4.25.1 and a knowledge of the risks of the particular recreation or sport business what property exposures are uncovered, and with the help of the insurance agent, determine the best way to provide the protection needed. Most companies offer packages combining several endorsements at a cost less than purchasing the endorsements individually.

A popular property protection enhancement is **building ordinance coverage**. This coverage protects the entity in the event fire or some other catastrophe destroys all or part of the building and ordinances require additions that were not in the damaged building. For instance, the addition of an elevator to meet ADA requirements might be mandated. With this enhancement, the cost to add an elevator would be covered by the policy.

General Liability Insurance

The purchase of **general liability insurance** protects the recreation or sport business from financial loss in the event a person suffers injury or property loss as a result of the negligence of the business or its employees. The policy is called commercial general liability (CGL). If the business is sued and the loss is covered, CGL will cover the legal costs and any award for damages up to the limit of the policy. The insurance company also has the option of paying a settlement to the plaintiff in order to avoid court expenses and risk of a larger award.

Recreation or sport businesses should and usually do carry general liability insurance with coverage of one million dollars or more. Like property insurance, endorsements may be added to supplement the basic coverage. Some of the common endorsements by businesses include the following. **Errors and omissions** coverage (professional liability or malpractice liability) can protect the business from liability for errors by medical personnel, or, in sport settings, by trainers, therapists, or exercise physiologists. **Cross liability** coverage broadens the policy to protect the business from suits from within the organization. For example, CGL would not protect if an injured volunteer worker sued an employee or if an injured employee sued a director. Cross liability would expand the coverage to include suits other than third-party suits. **Pollution liability** is a coverage often purchased by some recreation or sport businesses (e.g., golf courses). This coverage protects the business if acts by the business result in pollution and damage to neighboring property. For instance, a chemical spill in a stream on a golf course could result in damage to the property of others and subsequent legal action against the business.

There are numerous other exclusions from a CGL policy for which endorsements are available. Some of these are damage to the property of others which is stored on your property (saddle animals, watercraft, golf clubs, etc.), fire damage to adjacent property, advertising, adventure and tripping programs, wrongful dismissal, pollution or contamination of the environment, owned saddle animals, owned watercraft, and human rights violations such as sexual harassment.

Businesses and organization sometimes purchase a **Sports Liability Policy** primarily intended to cover athlete injuries. In *Macaisz v. Fireman's Fund Insurance Company* (2008; case is included in the Supplemental Web Site), an athlete died when a van of Christian Cheerleaders of America, Inc. (CCA) was involved in an accident on the way to an event. CCA had purchased a "Sports General Liability Policy-Occurrence Policy" that consisted of (1) a liability portion insured through Chicago Insurance Company, a subsidiary of Fireman's, and (2) an accident-medical portion insured through Hartford Insurance. CCA also maintained an automobile liability policy with Allstate Insurance. Allstate paid the $150,000 they owed according to the policy. Fireman's Fund contended that "all approved sports activities" did not include injuries caused by automobile accidents. The court held that the policy language was not ambiguous and rejected the claim by Macaisz.

Employment Practices Liability

Employment practices liability provides protection for such claims as (1) wrongful termination, (2) sexual harassment, (3) equal pay violations, and (4) discrimination (racial, sex, age, and disability). Some policies cover any violation of certain state and federal statutes, including antidiscrimination laws, Americans with Disabilities Act (ADA), Age Discrimination in Employment Act (ADEA), and the Equal Pay Act.

When this type of policy first emerged a few years ago, the costs were prohibitive for most small recreation or sport businesses. The policies also required a very large deductible. As this policy became more popular, both premiums and deductibles decreased, but both are currently increasing.[4]

Umbrella Liability

Umbrella liability is a policy that greatly increases the liability protection at a reasonable cost. The policy might increase liability coverage from $1 million to $5 million or more and would come into effect only after the limit of the CGL has been surpassed. This extension of coverage generally applies to the CGL policy, the vehicle coverage, and the workers' compensation insurance.

Liability Protecting Employees

Some recreation or sport businesses not only purchase liability insurance to protect the business, but also purchase insurance to protect employees in the event of legal action. The most common of these is **directors and officers liability** that usually provides general liability protection of $1 million or more for their "wrongful acts." Wrongful acts include error, misstatement, misleading statement, act, omission, and neglect of duty in the person's insured capacity. Coverage generally excludes: actions not within the scope of their duties; breach of contract; fines and penalties; dishonesty, infidelity, or criminal activities; human rights or sexual harassment violations; and failure to maintain adequate insurance.

Employee benefits liability is a type of coverage that is currently very popular, inexpensive, and easy to find. To illustrate the coverage, suppose a club pays for health insurance for its employees, but forgets to add a new employee to the policy. Some time later the person is sick, has a claim, and finds no coverage. Employee benefits liability would cover this oversight. Coverage now is usually on a claims-made basis—meaning claims must be promptly and properly made within the term of the policy. Failure to do so may invalidate coverage.

Some recreation or sport businesses provide **professional** or **malpractice insurance** for some or all employees. The professional insurance is designed to protect the employee from liability for negligence in acts related to giving professional advice or counsel. Suits often name the employee personally because the practice today is to sue all who may be potentially at fault; because the act may be an *ultra vires* act leaving only the employee as vulnerable; and because with governmental entities, the entity may be immune, leaving only the employee. Malpractice insurance applies primarily to persons in legal or health-related areas. Malpractice insurance protects both the individual and the business.

Professional and malpractice insurance can also be purchased by the individual employee. Policies are often available through a professional organization at very reasonable rates. They may also be purchased from one's insurance company, but the charge will be significantly higher. One should be aware that many exclusions exist on the policies.

Motor Vehicle Insurance

The recreation or sport manager must be certain that all business vehicles are adequately covered. Maintain coverage for damage to the business vehicles (collision, comprehensive, and uninsured motorist); damage to other vehicles, property, or persons (liability); and medical coverage for injured parties. Business vehicles should be covered with a commercial automobile policy. One's personal automobile policy generally is inadequate for use with business vehicles.

In automobile insurance, as in property insurance, the amount of the deductible must be decided for both collision (damages to your automobile from the collision with another object) and comprehensive (damage to

---

[4]**Fitness Pak** (club insurance specialists located in Chico, CA) offers a $1 million policy with a **$10,000** deductible suitable for a large, high-end, single-location club for about **$3,500** per year.

your automobile other than from collisions, e.g., vandalism to your auto, tree limb falling on your auto). Once again, the higher the deductible, the smaller the premium.

In some recreation or sport businesses, employees occasionally must drive personal automobiles for business purposes. A **non-owned automobile** endorsement may be purchased to insure the business in such cases. Coverage may also be extended to include volunteers who use their own vehicles. If the organization cannot insure the business use of personal vehicles for employees or volunteers, procedures should be instituted to ensure that the owners of all such vehicles have adequate coverage. (Both non-owned automobile and hired vehicle endorsements can be added to the CGL when there is no need for owned auto coverage.)

Many recreation or sport businesses have occasion to rent or lease vehicles for varying periods of time. The business may purchase a stand-alone policy or an endorsement on the firm's automobile policy that covers **hired vehicles**. This policy can provide both liability protection and coverage for the rental vehicle. Be aware, however, that neither the stand-alone policy nor the endorsement (nor for that matter, insurance purchased from the rental company) will cover the loss or theft of personal property or equipment stored in the vehicle.

In *Federal Insurance Company v. Executive Coach Luxury Travel, Inc.* (2010; see the Supplemental Web Site for Chapter 2.35 *Transportation*), Bluffton University contracted with Executive Coach to transport players to some baseball games. The bus, driven by an employee of Executive Coach, was involved in a serious accident. Federal Insurance, one of Bluffton's insurers, contended that the travel company was an independent contractor and that the driver was not using the bus with the university's permission. The University's insurance policy, however, stated that it covered "anyone else" driving the vehicle. The appellate court ruled that the driver was an "insured" and the case was remanded for further proceedings.

Other desirable endorsements are **uninsured/underinsured motorist coverage**, **bodily injury coverage**, and **property damage**. This coverage applies in the event that the other party has no insurance or the limits of that party's insurance have been reached.

Workers' Compensation

Workers' compensation is a no-fault, statutory-based insurance that provides for compensation to employees who suffer injury in the course of their employment. It is mandated in most states (see Chapter 4.26 *Workers' Compensation*). The worker receives compensation for lost income, both temporary and long term, and medical expenses incurred. The law in each state limits the amount of compensatory income allowed. In most states, all recreation or sport businesses with three or more full-time employees are required to carry workers' compensation insurance coverage.[5] The cost of this insurance varies with the amount of risk involved in that type of business and with the claims record of each individual sport business. The premium is based on a certain number of dollars per hundred of payroll for the business. Representative costs per $100 dollars of payroll might range from $15 for a riding club, $6 for a country club, $2 for a health spa, to less than $1 for a business involving all clerical or desk work.

Injured workers simply file a claim in order to receive compensation for work-related injuries. They neither have to file suit against the employer nor prove negligence or fault on the part of the employer. The employee, however, generally cannot receive compensation for pain and suffering through workers' compensation (see also Chapter 4.26 *Workers' Compensation*).

Event Insurance

Many recreation or sport businesses sponsor or conduct events either on an occasional or a regular basis. For any event, the business should purchase additional liability insurance if the event is not included in the CGL policy of the business. The amount of additional insurance coverage depends upon the event and how much investment is involved and/or whether the business is dependent upon a profit from the event. Also, many parties (e.g., venue, merchandisers, media, sponsors, concessionaires, and competing teams) may need to be named as additional insureds on your policy.

---

[5]In California, the law requires that a business provide workers' compensation coverage even if there is only one employee.

A common event liability policy would include bodily injury, personal injury, and property damage; an incident policy which would cover payment for medical expense for minor injuries (injured files a claim; no suit necessary); and settlement for uncontested claims in exchange for a release.

An important coverage for many events is that for **nonappearance/cancellation of event**. Bases for cancellation are specified and the policy generally includes costs, anticipated revenues, and anticipated profits. For some events, **life or accident coverage of participants** is purchased. Other typical endorsements include **automobiles**, **crime**, **prize indemnity**, **fire** (for damages that may not fall under the CGL), and **media coverage** (e.g., loss of signal, failure of transmission, breach of contract by media).

Requiring Insurance of Other Parties

There are situations when it is important that a recreation or sport business require that other parties have insurance coverage. Some of these situations include (1) when another party or organization rents your facility for some type of event, (2) when a contractor or his workers are on the premises for remodeling, repair, or other work, and (3) when independent contractors make use of your facility.

Certificate of Insurance. It is good policy to require that such groups provide the recreation or sport business with a certificate of insurance. This proof of insurance is a form (called an ACORD form certificate) from the insurance company verifying that the party is covered by liability insurance. If the presence of the party covers a period of time, it may be necessary to require a certificate of insurance again at a later date to insure that coverage is still in force.

Additional Insured Endorsement. Many businesses require that the other party (e.g., building contractor doing renovations on the premises) name the recreation or sport business as an additional insured party on their insurance coverage. Additional insured status is intended to provide coverage when the additional insured has a claim made against it because of the activities of the named insured. The Additional Insured Endorsement is attached with the ACORD form. The form provides details about the coverage, including the insurance company name, the policy number, the dates and limits of coverage, and the name of the agent.

In some circumstances, parties are considered an additional insured without being named on an endorsement. In *Bedford Central School District v. Commercial Union Insurance Company* (2002; case is included on the Supplemental Web Site), Bedford allowed Iona Preparatory School to bring a class to use Bedford's obstacle course. The court found that the insurance policy was ambiguous and ruled against the relying insurance company. The court held that Iona and its students were additional insured and required Commercial Union to reimburse Bedford for its costs.

Event Policy. Recreation and sport businesses that make their facilities available to other groups generally require that the organization or group purchase and show proof of a specified amount of event insurance (see previous section). Health clubs, for instance, often make their club available to groups for a dance, party, or even sleepovers. These provide additional revenue and, at the same time, familiarize a number of potential clients with the club. The club generally requires that the group purchase a 24-hour event policy that can be obtained from a specialty insurance provider. Another example of when a user might be required to purchase event insurance would be when a rock group promoter rents a gymnasium for a rock concert.

Independent Contractors. Most recreation and sport businesses do not provide liability insurance coverage for independent contractors (e.g., physical therapists, massage therapists, and personal trainers in health clubs). It is important that the independent contractor be required to carry liability insurance coverage.

Selecting the Agent and Carrier

Few administrators in recreation or sport management are insurance experts. This fact magnifies the importance of selecting both a good agent and a good carrier.

In selecting the carrier, it is important to select a carrier who specializes in recreation or sport entities similar to yours. Such companies often offer enhancements and riders that non-specialists cannot provide. They know the unique types of problems faced by your type of business. Also, it is important to make certain the company has an A rating and has been in business for a number of years.

When selecting an agent, try to find one who has at least a few recreation or sport clients similar to your entity. The better the agent understands the recreation or sport business, the more helpful the agent can be in recommending important coverages that might be critical to the business and in eliminating, or reducing, unnecessary coverages. Also, make certain the agent works for a company that specializes in recreation or sport entity protection. Select an agent from your region. The agent should walk through your facility and discuss your exposures with you. Finally, do not select an agent who is inexperienced or will not take the time to explain coverages and help you evaluate your needs.

SIGNIFICANT CASE

The York Insurance Company v. Houston Wellness Center, Inc. is a simple case that illustrates one of the most common mistakes made by the purchasers of insurance—failure to examine closely the exclusions in the coverage.

YORK INSURANCE COMPANY V. HOUSTON WELLNESS CENTER, INC.

Court of Appeals of Georgia, Third Division
261 Ga. App. 854; 583 S.E.2d 903; 2003 Ga. App. LEXIS 794
June 20, 2003, Decided

Opinion

BLACKBURN, Presiding Judge.

York Insurance Company ("York") appeals the trial court's denial of its motion for summary judgment, arguing that under the plain language of the policy it issued to Houston Wellness Center, Inc. ("Houston"), it had no duty to indemnify and defend Houston in a bodily injury suit filed against it. Finding that coverage was clearly and unambiguously excluded under the terms of the policy, we reverse the trial court's denial of York's motion.

The standard of review of the trial court's denial of [York's] motion for summary judgment is a de novo review of the evidence to determine whether there is any genuine issue of material fact as to the elements required to establish the causes of action stated in the complaint. To obtain summary judgment, [York] as the moving party must demonstrate that there is no genuine issue of material fact, and that the material evidence, viewed in the light most favorable to the nonmoving party, warrants judgment as a matter of law.

In a single enumeration of error, York contends that the trial court erred in denying its motion for summary judgment, arguing that under the unambiguous terms of the insurance policy which it issued to Houston, it was not required to defend and indemnify Houston in a bodily injury suit filed against it by Anne Vandalinda. Specifically, York argues that Vandalinda's allegations against Houston fit squarely within an exclusion in the policy.

An insurance policy is governed by the ordinary rules of contract construction. The hallmark of contract construction is to ascertain the intention of the parties. O.C.G.A. § 3-2-3. However, when the terms of a written contract are clear and unambiguous, the court is to look to the contract alone to find the parties' intent. Under Georgia law, an insurance company is free to fix the terms of its policies as it sees fit, so long as such terms are not contrary to law, and it is equally free to insure against certain risks while excluding others. An insurer's duty to defend is determined by comparing the allegations of the complaint with the provisions of the policy. (Citations and punctuation omitted.) *Capitol Indem. Corp. v. L. Carter Post 4472 Veterans of Foreign Wars.* n2 * * *

Vandalinda signed up for a three-month membership with Houston, a health and fitness club, in order to get physically fit. In her complaint, Vandalinda alleged that she was given instructions by one of Houston's employees on the use of various exercise machines. At the time of her injury, Vandalinda was using an exercise machine which develops the triceps. Vandalinda tried to release the machine using her arms as she had been instructed to do by Houston's employee. However, the complaint alleges the [*4] machine improperly released from Vandalinda's control "due to improper instructions" given by the employee, and, as a result, Vandalinda experienced pain in her left arm for which surgery was later required.

York issued to Houston a commercial general liability policy which contained the following exclusion: *This insurance does not apply to "bodily injury," "property damage" or "personal and advertising injury" arising out of the rendering of or failure to render any service, treatment, advice or instruction relating to physical fitness, including services or advice in connection with diet, cardio-vascular fitness, body building or physical training programs.* [Italics added]

It is apparent from the allegations of the complaint that Vandalinda's claim against Houston falls within the policy exclusion. Her "bodily injury arose out of the . . . failure" of Houston's employee "to render . . . advice or instruction relating to physical fitness, including . . . advice in connection with . . . body building or physical training programs." Accordingly, coverage for Vandalinda's bodily injury was excluded by the unambiguous language of the policy endorsement.

Where the language of the contract fixing the extent of coverage is unambiguous, as here, and but one reasonable construction is possible, this court must enforce the contract as written. A term in an insurance policy that unambiguously and lawfully limits the insurer's liability may not be extended beyond what is fairly within its plain terms. [York] was entitled to judgment as a matter of law because coverage was excluded for this loss. (Citation omitted.) *Bold Corp. v. Nat. Union Fire Ins. Co. &c.* n3

***

Judgment reversed. Ellington and Phipps, JJ., concur.

CASES ON THE SUPPLEMENTAL WEB SITE

Regan v. Mutual of Omaha Insurance Company, (2007 Ill. App. LEXIS 894). This case involves a swimming injury incurred by a baseball player on a team trip. Examine the wording of the policy restrictions and their interpretation by the court.

Maciasz v. Fireman's Fund Insurance Company and Chicago Insurance Company (988 So. 2d 991; 2008 Ala. LEXIS 11). In this case a client was injured in an automobile accident on the way to camp. The primary issue examined by the court is whether the insurance policy is ambiguous.

Ellison v. Kentucky Farm Bureau Mutual Insurance Company, 2010 Ky. App. Unpub. LEXIS 567. After one spectator assaulted a second spectator, the court ruled that the assaulting spectator's homeowner's insurance policy did not cover damages from the altercation.

Feszchak v. Pawtucket Mutual Insurance Company, 2008 U.S. Dist. LEXIS 29295. The insurance company failed to pay a claim due to an exclusion in the policy. The plaintiff filed suit and won.

Bedford Central School District v. Commercial Union Insurance Company (295 A.D.2d 295; 742 N.Y.S.2d 671; 2002 N.Y. App. Div. LEXIS 5737). A student lost an eye while participating on a challenge course owned by another school. The issue was whether the student was covered as an additional insured. Note the reasons given for the judgment.

QUESTIONS YOU SHOULD BE ABLE TO ANSWER

1. When a recreation or sport manager purchases insurance for a business or entity, what are the steps to take in determining the amount of coverage needed?

2. An independent contractor also needs insurance. Generally, what type of insurance is of most importance to the contractor? Explain why?

3. Explain what is meant by (1) exclusions and (2) conditions.

4. Distinguish between liability insurance and umbrella liability coverage.

5. What should be the major factors in selecting an agent and a carrier?

REFERENCES

Cases

York Insurance Company v. Houston Wellness Center, Inc., 2003 Ga. App. LEXIS 794.

Publications

Brooks, D. (1985). Property Insurance. *Risk management today.* Washington: ICMA.

Castle, G., Cushman, R., and Kensicki, P. (1981). *The business insurance handbook.* Homewood, Ill.: Dow Jones-Irwin.

Corbett, R. (1995). *Insurance in sport and recreation.* Edmonton, Alberta: Centre for Sport and Law.

Dahlgren, S. (2000, April). Covering your assets. *Athletic Business.* p. 59.

Kufahl, S. (2002, August). Business without a safety line? *Club Industry*, p. 18.

Mehr, R., Cammack, E., & Rose, T. (1985). *Principles of insurance.* Homewood, Ill.: Richard D. Irwin, Inc.

Novick, L. B. Murky waters: Insurance basics for nonprofits. Washington, D.C.: *Nonprofit Risk Management Institutes.*

Sundheim, F. (1983). *How to insure a business.* Santa Barbara, Calif: Venture Publications.

van der Smissen, B. (1990). *Legal liability and risk management for public and private entities.* Cincinnati: Anderson Publishing Co.

Wilkinson, D. G., (Ed.). (1988). *The event planning process.* Levine, M. A., Kirke, G., Zitterman, D. B., and Kert, E. Insurance. Willowdale, Ontario, Can.: The Event Management & Marketing Institute.

4.26 WORKERS' COMPENSATION

John T. Wolohan I Syracuse University

Under common law, when an employee was injured on the job, there was a good chance the injuries would go uncompensated due to the doctrines of assumption of risk, contributory negligence, and the fellow servant rule (Larson, 1992). Those injured workers who could overcome the preceding defenses usually faced a series of other problems before they received any compensation for their injuries. First, the injured workers, faced with little or no income, were under enormous financial pressure to settle their claims. The injured worker, therefore, usually received much less than the true value of his or her claim to support themselves and their families. Second, even if the injured employee was able to withstand the financial pressure and could afford to litigate the claim, the employer was often able to use the court system to his or her advantage and delay paying the employee any compensation. Finally, if the injured worker was lucky enough to recover his or her damages, the award was usually reduced by hefty attorney fees (Prosser & Keeton, 1984).

In an effort to protect injured workers and alleviate the injustice of the common law system, states began to enact workers' compensation legislation, modeled after the German and English systems. The first state to enact workers' compensation legislation was Maryland when it passed a cooperative accident fund for miners in 1902 (Larson, 1984). Subsequently, Congress passed legislation covering certain federal employees in 1908. By 1911, twenty-five states had enacted some form of law protecting employees; every state in the country having some form of workers' compensation law by 1949 (Larson, 1984). The **workers' compensation legislation**, which is different in every state, provides benefits, including lost wages, usually one-half to two-thirds of the employee's weekly wages, and medical care to an employee who is injured or killed in the course of employment, regardless of fault. The right of an employee to workers' compensation benefits is based on one simple test: Was the injury work-related? In exchange for this protection, the injured worker agrees to forego any tort claim he or she might have against the employer (Larson, 1992). The workers' compensation system, therefore, acts like a "bargain" between the employer and employee. The employer, in exchange for immunity from lawsuits, provides employees with swift, though limited, compensation for work-related injuries. In return, injured workers are guaranteed compensation for their injuries (Ashbrook, 2008).

Workers' compensation is, therefore, a form of strict liability. It makes no difference whether the injury was caused by the employee's negligence or pure accident; *all the employee has to show is that he or she was injured in the course of employment* (Larson, 1992). As a result, the injured worker receives quick financial assistance with minimal interruption in his or her life.

FUNDAMENTAL CONCEPTS

The basic policy behind the workers' compensation system is that the cost of the product should bear the blood of the worker (Prosser & Keeton, 1984). In other words, the employer is required by the state to compensate the employee through private insurance, state-funded insurance, or self-insurance for any damages suffered by the employee. The employer should treat the cost of workers' compensation insurance as part of the cost of production. These extra costs are then added to the cost of production and passed on to the consumer.

Eligibility Requirement

Although every state has its own workers' compensation laws, there are two basic eligibility requirements that an injured party must satisfy before he or she can recover workers' compensation benefits.

The first requirement is that the person must show that he or she was an employee of the organization. An **employee** is defined as any person in the service of another under any contract of hire. In reviewing the relationship between an individual and a recreation or sport organization to determine if he or she was in fact an employee, the courts use an "economic reality test" (*Coleman v. Western Michigan University*, 1983).

Under the **economic reality test**, the court examines the following factors to determine whether there existed an expressed or implied contract for hire.

1. Does the employer have the right to control or dictate the activities of the proposed employee?
2. Does the employer have the right to discipline or fire the proposed employee?
3. The payment of "wages" and, particularly, the extent to which the proposed employee is dependent upon the payment of wages or other benefits for his daily living expenses; and
4. Whether the task performed by the proposed employee was "an integral part" of the proposed employer's business (*Coleman v. Western Michigan University*, 1983 at 225).

In *Coleman v. Western Michigan University* (1983), the Michigan Court of Appeals, citing the *Rensing v. Indiana State University Board of Trustees* (1983) decision, concluded that scholarship athletes are not employees within the meaning of the workers' compensation statute. In particular, the court found that Coleman could only satisfy the third factor of the "economic reality test," that his scholarship did constitute wages. As far as the other factors, the court found that the university's right to control and discipline Coleman required by the first two factors was substantially limited. In considering the fourth factor, the court held "that the primary function of the defendant university was to provide academic education rather than conduct a football program." The term *integral*, the court held, suggests that the task performed by the employee is essential for the employer to conduct his business. The "integral part" of the university is not football, the court said, but education and research.

The second requirement every employee must meet before he or she can collect workers' compensation is that *the injury suffered by the employee must have occurred in the course of his or her employment.*

Recreation and sport managers need to be conscious of workers' compensation in the following areas: staff employees, volunteers, and scholarship athletes. With staff employees, it is clear that the recreation or sport manager should follow the local laws governing workers' compensation insurance. How volunteers and scholarship athletes are classified is much more difficult. For example, a number of states, including California, Oregon, Minnesota, and Tennessee, allow "volunteers" to be covered under the employer's workers' compensation plan (Wong & Wolohan, 1996).

Workers' Compensation and Small Businesses

As mentioned earlier, workers' compensation is primarily regulated by the individual states, and therefore there is no single cohesive set of rules governing benefits, coverage, or premium computation. There are, however, some things that every business, no matter how big or small, must know.

First, in most states, it does not matter how small your business, if you have employees, you need workers' compensation insurance. As a result, workers' compensation insurance can be a significant expense for many small businesses.

Second, to satisfy the workers' compensation obligations, all an employer has to do is purchase an insurance policy. In most states, these policies can be purchased from an insurance company. There are, however, five states and two U.S. territories (North Dakota, Ohio, Puerto Rico, the U.S. Virgin Islands, Washington, West Virginia, and Wyoming), that require employers to get coverage exclusively through state-operated funds (Priz, 2005). Thirteen states also allow employers the option of purchasing their insurance either with the state fund or private insurance. Those states that offer employers this option are Arizona, California, Colorado, Idaho, Maryland, Michigan, Minnesota, Montana, New York, Oklahoma, Oregon, Pennsylvania, and Utah (Priz, 2005).

Third, it is important to remember that if a business fails to carry workers' compensation insurance and an employee is injured, the employer can be required to not only pay the employee's medical expenses, death benefits, lost wages, and vocational rehabilitation out of pocket, but also be liable for any penalties levied by the state (Priz, 2005).

Independent Contractors

Whether an individual is hired as an independent contractor or an employee may impact the obligation an employer has under each state's workers' compensation law. For example, some states require all workers to be covered under its workers' compensation programs, regardless of whether or not they are employees or independent contractors. Other states only require employees to be covered. As a result, it is important that employers know their state's laws to determine who must be covered and what is required of them to comply (Priz, 2005).

Volunteers

Although covering "volunteers" under your workers' compensation plan may seem like a less-attractive option considering the up-front expense for the organization of paying for workers' compensation insurance, there are a number of important benefits from this option. First, by covering "volunteers" under your workers' compensation plan, if a volunteer is injured, you can save your organization both time and money by avoiding a negligence lawsuit. Second, by covering "volunteers" under your workers' compensation plan, you save your organization from any bad publicity that a lawsuit would generate. Finally, you also protect your volunteers from financial hardship by providing them benefits under workers' compensation (Wong & Wolohan, 1996).

For example, in 1999, a girls' softball umpire in Montana was stepping away from the plate when a player accidentally hit him. When a workers' compensation claim was filed on behalf of the umpire, the investigation revealed that local recreation league umpires and referees had no workers' compensation insurance and possibly no medical coverage at all. Without workers' compensation, recreational league umpires have to rely on their own personal medical insurance. The cost for the league to cover the referees under workers' compensation would have been about $3.08 per referee (Hull, 2000). It is important to note that the decision did not affect officials of school games because they were specifically exempted from the law.

Workers' Compensation and Professional athletes

Satisfying the requirements for workers' compensation is usually not difficult for professional athletes. There is no question that professional athletes are employees of their teams and any injury suffered by an athlete is usually well documented and treated. The hard part, however, is to determine in which jurisdiction the athlete may file his or her claim. For example in *Cincinnati Bengals v. Abdullah* (2010), the Bengals sought an injunction barring six of their former players from seeking or receiving workers' compensation benefits in the State of California. The Bengals alleged that the players' contracts expressly required them to file any compensation claims in Ohio pursuant to Ohio law. In rejecting the Bengals claim, the court ruled that since the dispute arose out of the terms of the contracts between the Bengals and the players, the dispute must go to arbitration. In support of this conclusion, the court noted that both the players' contracts and the NFL's collective bargaining agreement required binding arbitration concerning any dispute between players and their clubs involving the interpretation or application of any provision of their contracts.

The question of jurisdiction is extremely important in workers' compensation cases because the laws differ from state to state. For example, California, which only requires that an athlete has played at least one game within the state to qualify for workers' compensation, is also the only state to allow athletes to file claims for long-term injuries years after their injuries (Schwarz, 2010).

On the other end of the spectrum, a number of states have amended their workers' compensation statutes to exclude professional athletes. In *Tookes v. Florida State University* (Claim No. 266-39-0855), a basketball player at Florida State University suffered a knee injury during the 1981–82 season, which required him to sit out most of the season. As a result of his injury, Tookes filed a workers' compensation claim for lost wages and medical expenses. Tookes argued that he was an employee of the university, due to his athletic scholarship, and therefore entitled to workers' compensation benefits (Wong, 1994).

The Florida Department of Labor and Employment Security and Industrial Claims judge disagreed. The judge determined that there was no employer-employee relationship between Tookes and the university. Significantly, the court noted that even if there was an employer-employee relationship between Tookes and the university, Tookes would still be ineligible for benefits; if Tookes was employed by the university to play basketball, under Florida law he would be considered a professional athlete and therefore a member of a class specifically excluded under the Florida Workers' Compensation Statute (Wong, 1994). Besides Florida, at least five other states—Massachusetts, Missouri, Pennsylvania, Texas and Washington—exclude or limit workers' compensation benefits to professional athletes or have considered amending their state workers' compensation statutes to exclude professional athletes (Wolohan, 1994).

Workers' Compensation and College Athletes

Early court cases involving college athletes generally ruled that the athletes were employees of the university and covered under the school's workers' compensation insurance (*University of Denver v. Nemeth*, 1953 and *Van Horn v. Industrial Accident Commission*, 1963). However, the courts began to change their position in the late 1950's when the Supreme Court of Colorado ruled that Ray Herbert Dennison, who was fatally injured while playing football for Fort Lewis A & M College, was not an employee of the university. In making its decision, the Supreme Court of Colorado held that "it was significant that the college did not receive a direct benefit from the activities, since the college was not in the football business and received no benefit from this field of recreation (*State Compensation Insurance Fund, et al. v. Industrial Commission of Colorado*, 1957). In the 65 years since the Supreme Court of Colorado's decision, courts in almost every jurisdiction have upheld the reasoning behind the decision and have ruled that students are not employees of their schools because the business of the university is education, not athletics.

State Legislation Regarding College Athletes

In affirming the decision of the California Workers' Compensation Appeals Board, the California Court of Appeals in *Graczyk v. Workers' Compensation Appeals Board* (1986), denied workers' compensation benefits to Ricky Graczyk after he sustained head, neck, and spine injuries while playing football for California State University, Fullerton. The Court of Appeals ruled that it was the intent of the state legislature to exclude Graczyk, and all scholarship athletes, from receiving workers' compensation benefits for injuries received on the playing field. The court pointed out that the California State Legislature specifically amended the state's workers' compensation statute to define an "employee" to exclude "any person, other than a regular employee, participating in sports or athletics who receives no compensation for such participation other than the use of athletic equipment, uniforms, transportation, travel, meals, lodging, or other expenses incidental thereto."

The California State Legislature amended the statute further in 1981 when it specifically excluded from the definition of employee "[a]ny student participating as an athlete in amateur sporting events sponsored by any public agency, public or private nonprofit college, university or school, who receives no remuneration for such participation other than the use of athletic equipment, uniforms, transportation, travel, meals, lodging, scholarships, grants in aid, and other expenses" [*Graczyk v. Workers' Compensation Appeals Board*, 1986; West's Ann. Cal. Labor Code § 3353 (k)]. Hawaii, New York, and other states have followed California's example of expressly excluding scholarship athletes from workers' compensation benefits.

Consequences of Additional Coverage

As illustrated by *Rensing v. Indiana State University Board of Trustees* (1983), the issue of whether or not a scholarship athlete is an employee is a difficult one. For example, in most states, workers' compensation insurance rates are determined by actuarial tables that take into account the number of accidents and claims for that particular group of employees. If athletes were suddenly added into the group of school employees, the number of injuries and claims of the group would rise substantially. This would make it difficult, if not impossible, for colleges and universities to find an insurance company willing to insure them. Even if the school could find an insurance company, the increased exposure would require the insurance company to raise rates. Faced with higher insurance rates and/or the potential liability of self-insuring, many schools would be forced to evaluate whether the benefits of having an athletic program justifies the increased cost and exposure.

Other Possible Consequences

Additional Workers' Compensation Claims. If scholarship athletes are considered employees of their school, there could be an increase in the number of workers' compensation claims filed and benefits paid (Wolohan, 1994).

Tax Effect on School. If scholarship athletes were considered employees of their school, there would be some interesting tax questions for both the colleges or universities and the scholarship athletes. For example, does the scholarship athlete now have to pay taxes on the value of the scholarship? Also, will schools now be required to pay FICA and Medicare tax on the student's income? If so, how are the taxes to be paid (Wolohan, 1994)?

Employee Benefits. If scholarship athletes are considered employees of the school, are scholarship athletes eligible for employee benefits? Besides tuition, room, board, and books, are scholarship athletes now going to be eligible for life, medical, and dental insurance? How about the school's employee retirement plan, would scholarship athletes be eligible (Wolohan, 1994)?

Nonscholarship Athletes. Even if scholarship athletes are considered employees of the school, what about athletes who do not receive athletic scholarships? Because these athletes receive no compensation, they have no contractual relationship with the university to compete in athletics. Therefore, the non-scholarship athlete could never be deemed an employee and would never be covered by workers' compensation (Wolohan, 1994).

NCAA Catastrophic Injury Insurance Program. One of the reasons scholarship athletes have sought workers' compensation benefits in the past is to recover out-of-pocket medical expenses. Although most schools will pay the medical expenses of injured athletes, there usually is a limit to their generosity. In fact, it is not uncommon for a school to stop paying an injured athlete's medical and other bills. This is especially true when the injury is permanently disabling, and the injured athlete requires prolonged medical care.

In an effort to alleviate such hardships, and perhaps to prevent future court challenges on the status of scholarship athletes, the NCAA, in August 1991, implemented a Catastrophic Injury Insurance Program. The NCAA's Catastrophic Injury Insurance Plan covers every student who participates in college athletics, student coaches, student managers, student trainers, and cheerleaders who have been catastrophically injured while participating in a covered intercollegiate athletic activity. The policy has a $75,000 deductible and provides benefits in excess of any other valid and collectible insurance up to $20,000,000.

The NCAA's Catastrophic Injury Insurance Program is similar to workers' compensation in that it provides medical, dental, and rehabilitation expenses plus lifetime disability payments to students who are catastrophically injured, regardless of fault. The plan also includes $25,000 if the individual dies within 12 months of the accident.

The NCAA plan is more attractive than workers' compensation in a number of ways. First, scholarship athletes can collect benefits without litigating the issue of whether or not the athlete is an employee of the college or university. Second, the NCAA's plan provides the athlete with benefits immediately, without time delays, litigation costs, and the uncertainties involved in litigation. Finally, another benefit of the NCAA's plan is that it guarantees that catastrophically injured athletes will receive up to $120,000 toward the cost of completing their undergraduate degree. (For more information on the NCAA's Catastrophic Injury Insurance Program go to the NCAA Website: http://www.ncaa.org/wps/wcm/connect/public/NCAA/NCAA+Insurance+Programs/Studen t+Athlete+Insurance+Programs/Catastrophic+Insurance+Program.

SIGNIFICANT CASE

Although maybe not the most recent case, the following case is significant in that it provides the reader with a thorough review of the issues surrounding scholarship athletes who suffer career-ending or life-threatening injuries. In particular, the case analyzes the definitions of "employee" for purposes of the workers' compensation laws.

RENSING V. INDIANA STATE UNIVERSITY BOARD OF TRUSTEES

Supreme Court of Indiana
444 N.E.2d 1170 (1983)

The facts established before the Industrial Board were summarized by the Court of Appeals:

"The undisputed testimony reveals that [Indiana State University Board of Trustees] the Trustees, through

their agent Thomas Harp (the University's Head Football Coach), on February 4, 1974 offered Fred W. Rensing a scholarship or 'educational grant' to play football at the University. In essence, the financial aid agreement, which was renewable each year for a total of four years provided that in return for Rensing's active participation in football competition he would receive free tuition, room, board, laboratory fees, a book allowance, tutoring and a limited number of football tickets per game for family and friends. The 'agreement' provided, inter alia, the aid would continue even if Rensing suffered an injury during supervised play which would make it inadvisable, in the opinion of the doctor-director of the student health service, 'to continue to participate,' although in that event the University would require other assistance to the extent of his ability.

The trustees extended this scholarship to Rensing for the 1974–75 academic year in the form of a 'Tender of Financial Assistance.' Rensing accepted the Trustees' first tender and signed it (as did his parents) on April 29, 1974. At the end of Rensing's first academic year the Trustees extended a second 'Tender of Financial Assistance' for the 1975–76 academic year, which tender was substantially the same as the first and provided the same financial assistance to Rensing for his continued participation in the University's football program. Rensing and his father signed this second tender on June 24, 1975. It is not contested the monetary value of this assistance to Rensing for the 1975–76 academic year was $2,374, and that the 'scholarship' was in effect when Rensing's injuries occurred.

* * *

Rensing testified he suffered a knee injury during his first year (1974–75) of competition which prevented him from actively participating in the football program, during which time he continued to receive his scholarship as well as free treatment for his knee injury. The only requirement imposed by the Trustees (through Coach Harp) upon Rensing was attendance at his classes and reporting daily to the football stadium for free whirlpool and ultrasonic treatments for his injured knee.

* * *

As noted above, the financial aid agreement provided that in the event of an injury of such severity that it prevented continued athletic participation, 'Indiana State University will ask you to assist in the conduct of the athletic program within the limits of your physical capabilities' in order to continue receiving aid. The sole assistance actually asked of Rensing was to entertain prospective football recruits when they visited the University's Terre Haute campus.

During the 1975 football season, Rensing participated on the University's football team. In the spring of 1976 he partook in the team's annual three week spring practice when, on April 24, he was injured while he tackled a teammate during a punting drill.

* * *

The specific injury suffered by Rensing was a fractured dislocation of the cervical spine at the level of 4–5 vertebrae. Rensing's initial treatment consisted of traction and eventually a spinal fusion. During this period he developed pneumonia for which he had to have a tracheostomy. Eventually, Rensing was transferred to the Rehabilitation Department of the Barnes Hospital complex in St. Louis. According to Rensing's doctor at Barnes Hospital, one Franz Steinberg, Rensing's paralysis was caused by the April 24, 1976 football injury leaving him 95–100% disabled." *Rensing v. Indiana State University Board of Trustees*, supra, at pp. 80–82 (footnotes omitted).

Rensing's appeal to the Industrial Board was originally heard by a Hearing Member who found that Rensing had "failed to sustain his burden in establishing the necessary relationship of employer and employee within the meaning of the Indiana Workmen's Compensation Act," and rejected his claim. *Id.* at p. 83. The Full Industrial Board adopted the Hearing Member's findings and decision; then this decision was reversed by the Court of Appeals.

In this petition to transfer, the Trustees argue that there was no contract of hire in this case and that a student who accepts an athletic "grant-in-aid" from the University does not become an "employee" of the University within the definition of "employee" under the Workmen's Compensation Act, Ind. Code § 22-3-6-1(b), (Burns Supp., 1982). On the other hand, Rensing maintains that his agreement to play football in return for financial assistance did amount to a contract of employment.

Here, the facts concerning the injury are undisputed. The contested issue is whether the requisite employer-employee relationship existed between Rensing and the Trustees so as to bring him under the coverage of our Workmen's Compensation Act. Both the Industrial Board and the Court of Appeals correctly noted that the workmen's compensation laws are to be liberally construed. *Prater v. Indiana Briquetting Corp.*, (1969) 253 Ind. 83, 251 N.E. 2d 810. With this proposition as a starting point, the specific facts of this case must be analyzed to determine whether Rensing and the Trustees come within the definitions of "employee" and "employer" found in the statute, and specifically whether there did exist a contract of employment. Ind. Code § 22-3-6-1, supra, defines the terms "employee" and "employer" as follows:

"(a) 'Employer' includes the state and any political subdivision, any municipal corporation within the state, any individual, firm, association or corporation or the receiver or trustee of the same, or the legal representatives of a deceased person, using the services of another for pay."

"(b) The term 'employee' means every person, including a minor, in the service of another, under any contract of hire or apprenticeship, written or implied, except one whose employment is both casual and not in the usual course of the trade, business, occupation or profession of the employer."

The Court of Appeals found that there was enough evidence in the instant case to support a finding that a contract of employment did exist here. We disagree.

It is clear that while a determination of the existence of an employee-employer relationship is a complex matter involving many factors, the primary consideration is that there was an intent that a contract of employment, either express or implied, did exist. In other words, there must be a mutual belief that an employer-employee relationship did exist. *Fox v. Contract Beverage Packers, Inc.*, (1980) Ind. App., 398 N.E. 2d 709, *Gibbs v. Miller*, (1972) 152 Ind. App. 326, 283 N.E. 2d 592. It is evident from the documents which formed the agreement in this case that there was no intent to enter into an employee-employer relationship at the time the parties entered into the agreement.

In this case, the National Collegiate Athletic Association's (NCAA) constitution and bylaws were incorporated by reference into the agreements. A fundamental policy of the NCAA, which is stated in its constitution, is that intercollegiate sports are viewed as part of the educational system and are clearly distinguished from the professional sports business. The NCAA has strict rules against "taking pay" for sports or sporting activities. Any student who does accept pay is ineligible for further play at an NCAA member school in the sport for which he takes pay. Furthermore, an institution cannot, in any way, condition financial aid on a student's ability as an athlete. NCAA Constitution, Sec. 3-1-(a)-(1); Sec. 3-1-(g)-(2). The fundamental concerns behind the policies of the NCAA are that intercollegiate athletics must be maintained as a part of the educational program and student-athletes are integral parts of the institution's student body. An athlete receiving financial aid is still first and foremost a student. All of these NCAA requirements designed to prohibit student-athletes from receiving pay for participation in their sport were incorporated into the financial aid agreements Rensing and his parents signed.

Furthermore, there is evidence that the financial aid which Rensing received was not considered by the parties involved to be pay or income. Rensing was given free tuition, room, board, laboratory fees, and a book allowance. These benefits were not considered to be "pay" by the University or by the NCAA since they did not affect Rensing's or the University's eligibility status under NCAA rules. Rensing did not consider the benefits as income as he did not report them for income tax purposes. The Internal Revenue Service has ruled that scholarship recipients are not taxed on their scholarship proceeds and there is no distinction made between athletic and academic scholarships. Rev. Rul. 77-263, 1977-31 I.R.B. 8.

As far as scholarships are concerned, we find that our Indiana General Assembly clearly has recognized a distinction between the power to award financial aid to students and the power to hire employees since the former power was specifically granted to the Boards of Trustees of state educational institutions with the specific limitation that the award be reasonably related to the educational purposes and objectives of the institution and in the best interests of the institution and the state. Ind. Code § 20-12-1-2(h) (Burns 1975).

Furthermore, we find that Ind. Code § 22-4-6-2 (Burns 1974) is not applicable to scholarship benefits. In that statute, which deals with contributions by employers to unemployment insurance, employers are directed to include "all individuals attending an established school . . . who, in lieu of remuneration for such services, receive either meals, lodging, books, tuition or other education facilities." Here, Rensing was not working at a regular job for the University. The scholarship benefits he received were not given him in lieu of pay for remuneration for his services in playing football any more than academic scholarship benefits were given to other students for their high scores on tests or class assignments. Rather, in both cases, the students received benefits based upon their past demonstrated ability in various areas to enable them to pursue opportunities for higher education as well as to further progress in their own fields of endeavor.

Scholarships are given to students in a wide range of artistic, academic and athletic areas. None of these recipients is covered under Ind. Code § 22-4-6-2, supra, unless the student holds a regular job for the institution in addition to the scholarship. The statute would apply to students who work for the University and perform services not integrally connected with the institution's educational program and for which, if the student were not available, the University would have to hire outsiders, e.g., workers in the laundry, bookstore, etc. Scholarship recipients are considered to be students seeking advanced educational opportunities and are not considered to be professional athletes, musicians or artists employed by the University for their skills in their respective areas.

In addition to finding that the University, the NCAA, the IRS and Rensing, himself, did not consider the scholarship benefits to be income, we also agree with Judge Young's conclusion that Rensing was not "in the service of " the University. As Judge Young stated:

> *"Furthermore, I do not believe that Rensing was 'in the service of' the Trustees. Rensing's participation in football may well have benefited the university in a very general way. That does not mean that Rensing was in the service of the Trustees. If a student wins a Rhodes scholarship or if the debate team wins a national award that undoubtedly benefits the school, but does not mean that the student and the team are in the service of the school. Rensing performed no duties that would place him in the service of the university." Rensing v. Indiana State University, at 90.*

Courts in other jurisdictions have generally found that such individuals as student athletes, student leaders in student government associations and student resident-hall assistants are not "employees" for purposes of workmen's compensation laws unless they are also employed in a university job in addition to receiving scholarship benefits.

All of the above facts show that in this case, Rensing did not receive "pay" for playing football at the University within the meaning of the Workmen's Compensation Act; therefore, an essential element of the employer-employee relationship was missing in addition to the lack of intent. Furthermore, under the applicable rules of the NCAA, Rensing's benefits could not be reduced or withdrawn because of his athletic ability or his contribution to the team's success. Thus, the ordinary employer's right to discharge on the basis of performance was also missing. While there was an agreement between Rensing and the Trustees which established certain obligations for both parties, the agreement was not a contract of employment. Since at least three important factors indicative of an employee-employer relationship are absent in this case, we find it is not necessary to consider other factors which may or may not be present.

We find that the evidence here shows that Rensing enrolled at Indiana State University as a full-time student seeking advanced educational opportunities. He was not considered to be a professional athlete who was being paid for his athletic ability. In fact, the benefits Rensing received were subject to strict regulations by the NCAA which were designed to protect his amateur status. Rensing held no other job with the University and therefore cannot be considered an "employee" of the University within the meaning of the Workmen's Compensation Act.

It is our conclusion of law, under the facts here, including all rules and regulations of the University and the NCAA governing student athletes, that the appellant shall be considered only as a student athlete and not as an employee within the meaning of the Workmen's Compensation Act. Accordingly, we find that there is substantial evidence to support the finding of the Industrial Board that there was no employee-employer relationship between Rensing and the Trustees, and their finding must be upheld.

For all of the foregoing reasons, transfer is granted; the opinion of the Court of Appeals is vacated and the Industrial Board is in all things affirmed.

CASES ON THE SUPPLEMENTAL WEB SITE

Coleman v. Western Michigan University, 125 Mich. App. 35; 336 N.W.2d 224; (1983). This case examines whether college sports are an integral part of business of a university.

Norfolk Admirals and Federal Insurance Company v. Ty A. Jones, 2005 Va. App. LEXIS 443. This case examines whether fighting, when following his coach's instructions, is part of a professional hockey player's job and therefore covered by workers' compensation.

Rudolph v. Miami Dolphins, 447 So. 2d 284 (Fla. App., 1983). This case examines the impact of the Florida Workers' Compensation Act on professional athletes.

Waldrep v. Texas Employers Insurance Association, 21 S.W.3d 692 (Tex. App, 2000). This case reexamines the issue of college athletes and whether they are employees of the schools.

QUESTIONS YOU SHOULD BE ABLE TO ANSWER

1. Are college athletes covered under workers' compensation?

2. How do you determine if an individual is an employee of an organization?

3. What are some of the benefits of the NCAA's Catastrophic Injury Insurance Program?

4. What are the benefits and disadvantages to workers of state enacted workers' compensation programs?

5. What are the benefits and disadvantages to employers of state enacted workers' compensation programs?

REFERENCES

Cases

Cincinnati Bengals v. Khalid Abdullah, et al., 2010 U.S. Dist. LEXIS 54102
Coleman v. Western Michigan Univ., 125 Mich. App. 35, 336 N.W.2d 224 (1983).
Graczyk v. Workers' Compensation Appeals Board, 184 Cal. App.3d 997, 229 Cal. Rptr. 494, 58 A.L.R. 4th 1245, 34 Ed. Law Rep. 523 (Cal. App. 2 Dist., Aug 8, 1986).

Rensing v. Indiana State University Board of Trustees, 437 N.E.2d 78 (1982).
Rensing v. Indiana State University Board of Trustees, 444 N.E.2d 1170 (1983).
State Compensation Fund v. Industrial Commission, 135 Colo. 570, 314 P.2d 288 (1957).
Tookes v. Florida State University, Claim No. 266-39-0855.
University of Denver v. Nemeth, 257 P.2d 423 (1953).
Van Horn v. Industrial Accident Commission, 219 Cal. App. 2d 457, 33 Cal. Rptr. 169 (1963).

Publications

Ashbrook, W. J. (Summer, 2008). Defining "Employee" Within Arizona's Workers' Compensation Statute: An Argument for Inclusion. *Arizona State Law Journal, 40,* 69–712.
Bacon, J. (1997, Oct. 21). Jury: Injured college athlete ineligible for workers' comp. *USA Today.*
Hull, R. (2000, April 26). Referees and umpires cry foul in workers' comp decision. *The Daily Inter Lake.*
Larson, A. (1984). *Workers' Compensation Law.* New York: Matthew Bender & Co.
Larson, A. (1992). *The law of workers' compensation.* New York: Matthew Bender & Co.
NCAA Catastrophic Injury Insurance Policy. http://www.ncaa.org/insurance/catastrophic.html
Priz, E. (2005). *Ultimate guide to workers' compensation insurance.* Irvine, CA: Entrepreneur Press.
Prosser, W. L., & Keeton, W. P. (1984). *The law of torts* (5th ed.). St. Paul, MN: West Publishing Co.
Schwarz, A. (2010, April 7). Teams Dispute Workers' Comp Rights. *New York Times,* p. B10
Stumes, L. (2002a, Feb. 28). Rising premiums create unstable racing industry. *San Francisco Chronicle,* p. C7.
Stumes, L. (2002b, Dec. 22). Trainers, owners get some relief. *San Francisco Chronicle,* p. B15.
Wolohan, J. T. (1993, June). Ruling may have Texas-size impact. *Athletic Business, 17,* 22–23.
Wolohan, J. T. (1994). Scholarship athletes: Are they employees or students of the university? The debate continues. *Journal of Legal Aspects of Sport, 4,* 46–58.
Wong, G. M. (1994). *Essentials of amateur sports law* (2nd ed.). Westport, CT: Praeger Publishing.
Wong, G. M., & Wolohan, J. T. (1996, March). Pitching in. Schools have alternatives in determining volunteers' legal status. *Athletic Business, 20,* 10–14.

CONTRACT LAW 5.00

One of the most fundamental duties performed by sport and recreation administrators is contract negotiations. Therefore, it is important for everyone involved in the sport and recreation business to understand the basics of contract law and contract formation. Once a contract is drafted, the recreation or sport manager must also implement the terms of the contract and must understand the ramifications of failing to meet the contractual obligations. The following section examines the essentials of contract formation, the elements necessary for a legally valid contract what are the legal implications of breaching a contract.

The *Contract Law* section is divided into three parts. The first part reviews the fundamental aspects of all contracts, presents some principles of interpretation used by the courts in deciding contract disputes, discusses the concept of breach of contract and the remedies for breach, refers to provisions that are typically found in all contracts, and familiarizes you with the principles relating to signature authority. The first part is also meant as an introduction to subsequent sections that deal with sport-specific contract law topics in more detail. The second part applies the essential contract elements to employment contracts, and game, event, and sponsorship contracts. The third section looks at alternative dispute resolution methods and their growing role in sport and employment contracts.

CONTRACT ESSENTIALS
Bridget Niland | Daemen College

Contracts are the cornerstone of any business relationship. Since before medieval times, merchants have used contracts to formalize the promises that underlie business transactions (Simpson, 1986). Contract law has greatly evolved since then, but its principle function has remained the same: to provide a framework for the enforcement of promises (Davis, 1996; Hanson, 2006).

Contracts are common throughout the sport and recreation industry (Wong, 2010). Whether working in professional or amateur sports, or in the recreation, health and fitness industry, sport and recreation managers will encounter contracts in their daily tasks (Miller, Comfort & Stoldt, 2001). For example, two contractual agreements govern the day-to-day operations of the National Football League (NFL): the Collective Bargaining Agreement (CBA) between the players and the league and the Standard Player Contract (SPC) between a player and team. Other examples of contracts in the sport and recreation industry include: membership agreements at health and fitness facilities; liability waivers between participants and athletic event operators; scholarship agreements between student-athletes and colleges; vendor contracts between concessions and professional teams; facility lease agreements between club sport teams and school districts; purchase agreements between sports memorabilia collectors; and employment contracts between a coach and a college athletics department.

Contract law is complex. As such, sport and recreation managers should consult a licensed attorney before entering into an agreement (Sharp, 2007). Not dismissing that advice, the important and pervasive role contracts play in the sport and recreation industry makes it imperative for managers to understand the basic principles of contract law. Understanding the basics of contract law will allow sport and recreation managers to make informed decisions and limit the chance of costly lawsuits. This chapter will familiarize sport and recreation managers with the fundamental concepts of contract law and explore how those concepts apply within the industry.

FUNDAMENTAL CONCEPTS

Contract is a formal term to describe a voluntary agreement that imposes duties and benefits upon the parties. It is a promise or a set of promises for which, if breached, the law will provide a remedy (Restatement (Second) Contracts §1). If properly formed, a contract creates a private law between the parties. If a dispute should arise between the parties, the contract is the first resource a court will consider in resolving the matter.

There are three sources of contract law in the United States: common law principles, the Restatement of Contacts and the Uniform Commercial Code. As mentioned in Chapter 1.10, common law is created by previous court decisions involving similar issues. The bulk of the common law of contracts evolved through state, rather than federal, court systems. The Restatement of Contracts is a compilation of contract law principles drafted by judges and legal scholars from throughout the United States. Although it lacks the authority of common law, courts often look to the Restatement for guidance in deciding contractual disputes. The Uniform Commercial Code (U.C.C.) is a set of laws that all states have adopted in whole or in part. Article 2 and of the U.C.C specifically applies to contracts for the sale of goods, and Article 2a applies to the lease of goods, either of which would cover the purchase of game tickets or lease of sporting equipment (Wong, 2010). Louisiana is the only state in the union that has not adopted Article 2 or 2a.

Common law, the Restatement and the U.C.C. all recognize different types of contractual agreements. The most basic distinction is between express or implied contracts. In an **express contract**, the parties clearly state the terms of their agreement, verbally or in writing. The standard player contract common in professional sports is one example of an express contract. **Implied contracts** occur when the conduct indicates that an agreement exists (this is also referred to as a *quasi contract*), yet there is no proof of a formal exchange of promises. For example, an implied contract exists when the parties continue to perform duties of an expired contract (*Athletes Foot Brands, LLC v. Whoohah., Inc*, 2007). There is little legal consequence between the two types of contracts; however, it is easier to prove the existence of a contract that is expressed and in writing (Shubert, Smith & Trentadue, 1986). As such, it is best to formalize all agreements in a written document.

Contract law also classifies contracts by whether they are valid, void or voidable. If a court determines that a contract is **valid**, then it will enforce the contract or grant some other relief to the non-breaching party. A court will not enforce a contract that fails to meet the legal requirements or is contrary to some other rule of law. In such cases, the contract is rendered either **void,** meaning neither party is obligated to perform, or **voidable,** which provides one party the option of canceling the agreement.

Contract Formation

The goal of sport and recreation managers should be to structure business agreements that are valid and enforceable should a dispute arise. To form a valid and enforceable contract the following elements must be present: agreement; consideration; capacity; and legality.

Agreement (Mutual Assent)

The first step in creating a valid and enforceable contract is to confirm that the parties mutually assent to the fundamental terms of the agreement. Mutual assent is simply evidence that the parties had a "meeting of the minds" as to the agreement. Courts will determine mutual assent by considering whether the parties had the same understanding as to the material terms of the agreement starting with the offer and acceptance (Miller, Comfort & Stoldt, 2001).

Offer

An **offer** is a conditional promise from the offeror (the party who makes the offer) to the offeree (the party to whom the offer was made). An offer occurs when one party demonstrates a willingness to enter into an agreement with definite terms that leaves another party in a position to respond (Restatement (Second) Contracts §24). Definite terms include: (1) the parties; (2) the subject matter; (3) the time and place for the subject matter to be performed; and (4) the consideration or price to be paid (Wong, 2002). For example, Sport Agent offers to represent Superstar in endorsement negotiations with a major sneaker company in exchange for Superstar agreeing to pay Sport Agent five percent of the endorsement earnings.

Most offers involve an exchange of promises that create a **bilateral contract**. An example of a bilateral contract within the sport and recreation industry is a scheduling agreement between college football teams, wherein the offeror, Private U, promises to pay the offeree, State U, $100,000 in exchange for State U's promise to play an away contest on Private U's campus. A **unilateral contract,** by contrast, involves the offeror making a promise to the offeree if the offeree takes some specified action. An example of a unilateral contract in recreational sports would be a 5 kilometer road race that offers prize money to the first finisher. The only method of accepting the offer is to win the race. Promising to win the race or even running in the race does not respond to the offer.

Acceptance

In addition to demonstrating a unilateral contract, the 5k road race also highlights the importance of **acceptance** in contract formation. The offeror is not bound and an agreement is not formed until the offeree accepts the offer. Only the offeree can accept the offer from the offeror. An offeree can accept an offer by signature, verbally, through performance (in the case of a unilateral contract) or any other mode permitted by the offeror (Restatement (Second) Contracts §30). Unless the parties agree otherwise, an offer is accepted when it is sent (i.e., mailed, faxed or by email), even if the acceptance is lost in delivery or transmission. This is known as the "mailbox rule."

In limited circumstances, silence by the offeree can be construed as acceptance of the offer. To avoid confusion as to acceptance, sport and recreation managers should formally respond to each offer (Wong, 2010). Failure to do so can lead to ambiguity between the parties and ultimately result in a lawsuit as to whether or not a contract existed. For example, in *Giulani v. Duke University* (2009), the plaintiff, a recruited non-scholarship athlete, sued after he was removed from the team. The suit hinged on whether promises made during the recruitment process and statements contained in institutional manuals created a contract between the school and the student-athlete. In particular, the court was presented with the issue of what constitutes an offer on part of the institution and acceptance by the student-athlete. Similar issues existed in *LoPiccolo v. American University* (2012), where a recruited scholarship wrestling student-athlete attempted to enforce as a contract promises of a four-year athletic scholarship.

The acceptance also must mirror the offer (Restatement (Second) Contracts §58). A **counteroffer,** which alters the terms of the offer, is not acceptance. Rather, it terminates the offeror's offer and creates a new offer. *Brooks v. Paige* (1988) demonstrates the effect of a counteroffer. During contract negotiations, Brooks, a star soccer player, responded to the Denver Avalanche's salary offer by asking for a larger amount. The team declined and Brooks later filed a lawsuit related to the contract negotiations. In reviewing the plaintiff's claims, the Colorado state court held that Brooks' response to the Avalanche's initial offer was a counteroffer that terminated the Avalanche's offer and created a new offer, which the team rejected.

Consideration

In addition to offer and acceptance, an enforceable contract must include consideration. **Consideration** is the exchange of something of value between the parties. It involves each party giving-up something to gain the benefit of the contract. An agreement that lacks this exchange renders the contract unenforceable (Wong, 2010). Agreements that are based on **gifts** are typically dismissed for lack of consideration because there is no mutual exchange of detriment and benefit. One party is merely benefiting from another's generosity.

Because past actions occur prior to the making of a contract and were not intended to induce a promise in exchange, they are also insufficient consideration. In such instances, the offeror is making a promise because the event occurred; he is not making the promise in order to get the event to happen. For example, in *Blackmon v. Iverson* (2003), plaintiff sued basketball star Allen Iverson alleging that the plaintiff was the first to suggest that Iverson use "The Answer" as a nickname and for product merchandising. Iverson later decided to use the term for a line of apparel with Reebok. Iverson then promised to pay the plaintiff twenty-five percent of those earnings. Iverson recanted this promise and plaintiff sued to enforce what he argued was a valid oral contract. In dismissing the claim, the court held that the agreement lacked consideration for two reasons. First, plaintiff's suggestion of the nickname constituted a gift as there was no evidence he sought to be compensated at that time. Second, Iverson's after-the-fact offer to pay the plaintiff a portion of the earnings amounted to **past consideration** between the two parties.

Capacity

Contracts are voluntary agreements. As such, parties to a contract must possess the **capacity** to comprehend its terms and how those terms affect the party's legal interests. Courts will not enforce agreements in which one of the parties is shown to have lacked the capacity to represent his or her interests effectively (Wong, 2010). To void the contract, the party must show that they either lacked sufficient mental capacity, due to age or a medical condition, or were so intoxicated that the party could not understand the nature of the agreement. In either instance, contract law renders the agreement voidable by the impaired party.

For example, as a matter of public policy, "courts have protected minors from improvident and imprudent contractual commitments by declaring that the contract of a minor is voidable at the election of the minor after he attains his majority" *Jones v. Dressel* (1981). Accordingly, with the exception of the necessaries of life (e.g., food, clothes), contracts are unenforceable against the minor, but enforceable against the other party (Sharp, 2007). The process of a minor rescinding a contract to which he or she is a party is known as **disaffirmance**. For example, in *Milicic v. Basketball Marketing Co., Inc.* (2004), the court upheld a professional basketball player's right to rescind an agency agreement he entered into as a minor.

A party can also affirm a contract entered into as a minor by simply continuing to perform his or her contractual duties as an adult. For example, the plaintiff in *Jones v. Dressel* (1981) was seventeen when he signed a contract with a recreation company that ferried skydivers to a parachute jumping site. The contract included an exculpatory agreement protecting the company from liability for accidents during or leading up to sky diving activities. The plaintiff continued to use the company's services in the several months after he turned eighteen. Just before his nineteenth birthday, plaintiff was injured when the company's plane crashed en-route to the jumping site. Plaintiff filed a negligence lawsuit against the sky diving company and its owner. In dismissing the suit, the court held that although a minor at the time he signed the exculpatory agreement, it was nonetheless enforceable because plaintiff continued to use the services of the company to sky dive in the months after his eighteenth birthday.

Legality

Courts will not enforce a contract involving illegal action or a subject matter that violates public policy. For example, a court will not enforce an agreement between an athletic trainer and a professional athlete under which the athletic trainer agreed to inject the athlete with illegal performance enhancing drugs. Courts also will refuse to enforce employment contracts that include overly broad **covenants not to compete**. Also known as non-compete clauses, these provisions attempt to limit the ability of an employee to compete against the employer in the event that the employment is terminated or the employee resigns. Most coaching contracts include some type of non-compete clause. For example, it is common for a team to prohibit a head coach from accepting another head coaching position within the same league, conference or state.

Sport managers, however, must take care in drafting non-compete clauses because courts will not enforce clauses that are geographically broad or extend for an unduly long period of time. Such agreements, courts have reasoned, constitute an unfair restraint of trade. If properly drafted, covenants not to compete can be an effective tool in limiting the coaching carousel described in *Northeastern University v. Brown,* (2004). In that case, Northeastern University (NU) attempted to enforce a non-compete clause against Donald Brown, its head football coach. The coach's contract contained a provision that prohibited him from discussing coaching opportunities at other institutions without first gaining permission from NU's president, a provision included in almost all coaching contracts. When the University of Massachusetts attempted to hire Brown without NU's permission, NU filed a breach of contract lawsuit and sought an injunction to bar the coach from leaving. The court upheld the NU's claims citing that the close proximity of the two institutions greatly increased the likelihood that Northeastern would suffer irreparable harm if the contract was not enforced.

Special Doctrines of Contract Law

Promissory Estoppel

Promissory estoppel is a remedy courts will apply when an agreement lacks the requirements of a contract (i.e., agreement, consideration, capacity and legality), but nonetheless creates some form of detrimental reliance by one or more of the parties. Courts may apply promissory estoppel when plaintiff has shown that the agreement included (1) a promise that reasonably expected reliance, (2) there was reliance on the promise, and (3) an injustice to the party who relied on the promise.

Promissory estoppel is a common claim in breach of contract lawsuits filed by disgruntled student-athletes against college athletic programs. For example, in *Fortay v. University of Miami* (1994), the plaintiff, a highly recruited football student-athlete, sued the university after he failed to secure the starting quarterback position. Fortay claimed that during the recruiting process and again while an enrolled student, two of the university's football coaches promised him the position. After he was passed over for the spot, he filed the suit hoping to recover $10 million in damages (compensatory and punitive) for the broken promise. The case ultimately settled and the terms were not disclosed but it opened the door to similar lawsuits against college coaches who make unreasonable promises during the recruiting process (New York Times, 1996).

Writing and Formality

The **Statue of Frauds** is a legal doctrine that dates back to common law in England. It is designed to prevent fraudulent claims and unkept promises and encourage certain transactions to be reduced to writing (Wong, 2010). Under the doctrine, certain transactions must be in writing to be enforced. Transactions common to the sport and recreation industry and subject to the statute of fraud includes: (1) contracts that cannot be performed within a year; (2) agreements to guarantee another party's debt; (3) agreements for the sale or lease of land and; (4) contracts in which an executor or administrator promises to be personally liable for the debt of an estate. For example, courts have dismissed attempts by student-athletes to enforce a coach's verbal offer of a four- year athletic scholarship because such an agreement could not be performed within a year and thus must be in writing under the statute of frauds (*Shepard v. Loyola Marymount University*, 2002).

Parol Evidence Rule

Parol evidence consists of any oral or written terms outside the four corners of the final contract. It includes earlier versions of a contract or comments or statements made during contract negotiations. *Chuy v. Philadelphia Eagles Football Club* (1977), provides an example of parol evidence and the conflict it creates for courts trying to resolve breach of contract disputes. In that case, the plaintiff, Donald Chuy, a lineman for the Philadelphia Eagles, filed a breach of contract claim against the Eagles after the team released him under a provision in the standard player contract. Chuy argued that his contract with the team was actually a compilation of three separate contracts, one of which would have prevented his dismissal. The court waivered on considering the other contracts noting that the contracts constituted parol evidence.

The dilemma of how to handle parol evidence led courts to develop the parol evidence rule. According to the **Parol Evidence Rule**, if the contract is a complete final statement of the parties agreement (i.e., fully integrated), any prior or contemporaneous oral or written statements that alter, contradict or add new information regarding the agreement are inadmissible in any court proceeding concerning the contract (Restatement (Second) Contracts §213). The rule is intended to address breach of contract disputes in which one or more of the parties' referenced drafts of the contract or statements made in the negotiations process. The rule also covers contracts where it is unclear whether all relevant terms were included. *Vanderbilt University v. DiNardo* (1999), discussed in detail in Chapter 5.21, is a case in which the court had to consider whether to apply the parol evidence rule to bar comments made between a head football coach and an athletic director during contract negotiations. For another example of the parol evidence rule see *Hanlon v. Providence College* (1980).

Breach of Contract

A breach of contract occurs when a party to the agreement fails to perform the duties imposed under the contract. The degree of non-performance dictates the remedy sought by the non-breaching party. A minor breach exists when one party substantially performs most of its duties under the agreement. In such circumstances, the non-breaching party may negotiate with the breaching party as to the remaining duties owed under the contract, or seek damages that resulted from the minor breach. A minor breach does not automatically relieve the non-breaching party from fulfilling its obligations under the contract. A material breach occurs when one party either fails to perform its duties under the contract or its performance was so inferior that it destroys the original intent of the agreement. Under those circumstances, the non-breaching party may immediately rescind the contract and file a lawsuit to recover damages (Wong, 2010). To succeed on a breach of contract claim, the non-breaching party will have to show: (1) there was a valid contract; (2) plaintiff performed as specified by the contract; (3) defendant failed to perform as specified by the contract; and (4) plaintiff suffered an economic loss as a result of the defendant's breach of contract.

Duty to Mitigate

Prior to issuing legal remedies, a court will consider whether the non-breaching party attempted to mitigate its damages. This duty to mitigate requires the non-breaching party to take actions that will reduce the loss incurred by the breach if possible. Basketball legend Michael Jordan's contract with now defunct communication company MCI provides an example of a plaintiff's duty to mitigate. In that case, Jordan attempted to collect compensation for an endorsement contract with MCI despite the company's bankruptcy. The company objected citing that upon learning of MCI's collapse Jordan made no attempts to mitigate his loss of the MCI compensation. The court agreed that Jordan did have an obligation to mitigate damages and required Jordan to submit additional evidence as to why his failure to mitigate should not bar recovery of his lost compensation (*In re Worldcom, Inc.*, 2007).

Defenses to a Breach of Contract Claim

To defeat a breach of contract claim, the breaching party often argues that the agreement lacked one or more elements of an enforceable contract. A defendant also may argue that one or more of the parties was mistaken as to the subject matter of the contract and thus there was no agreement. Mistake defenses are only successful if the breaching party can show that the mistake was a **mutual mistake** and involved the subject matter of the agreement. Generally, courts do not rescind contracts based on a **unilateral mistake** of the breaching party or contracts involving mutual mistakes over the value of the exchange. However, courts may rescind contracts involving **fraud** in either the inception of the contract or in the inducement to sign the contract. Prominent football coach Rich Rodriguez sought such relief in *West Virginia University v. Rodriguez* (2008). Rodriguez was under contract as the school's head football coach when he accepted the same position at the University of Michigan. WVU sued for breach of contract. In an attempt to defeat the institution's claim, Rodriguez argued that the employment contract was unenforceable because he had been fraudulently induced to sign the agreement by WVU's president. The case settled before the court could rule on the merits. Under the terms of the settlement, however, WVU received its damage claim $4 million dollars with payments from Rodriguez and the University of Michigan.

A defendant also may contend that the contract is void because one or more of the parties lacked the authority to bind the organization or athlete to the contract. Employees act as agents of the employer or principal and subject to agency law have actual authority, apparent authority or no authority to bind the organization to a contract. Authority to contract was the focus of *HBCU Pro Football, LLC, v. New Vision Sports Properties, LLC* (2011). In this case, the plaintiff, HBCU Pro Football (HBCU), had entered into a contract with the purported agent of College Sports Television Network, Inc., (CSTV) for the broadcast of athletic contests involving historically black colleges and universities. After games failed to appear on CSTV, as outlined in the contract, HBCU learned that the agent, owner of New Vision Sports Properties (NVSP), had misrepresented his ability to get the athletic contests shown on the CSTV network. HBCU ultimately sued both NVSP and CSTV receiving damages from both entities. Although the dispute resulted in HBCU's favor, the company spent considerable resources on the dispute. To avoid such legal disputes and the associated costs, it is in the best interest of sport and recreation organizations to clearly communicate the authority and limits to authority of its employees in contractual settings (Sharp, 2007). Likewise, prior to entering into an agreement, companies working with a purported agent should confirm that agent's authority.

Remedies for a Breach of Contract

If a court finds that a party has breached a contract, it will grant relief that attempts to place the non-breaching party in the same position as if the contract had been performed (Restatement (Second) Contracts, 1981, §347). There are several types of remedies available to the non-breaching party: legal remedies, equitable remedies and restitution.

Legal Remedies

Legal remedies are most prevalent and result in the court awarding the non-breaching party a monetary award for the damage incurred due to the breach. Monetary damages are distinguished as compensatory, consequential, nominal, punitive or liquidated.

Compensatory Damages

Compensatory damages are awarded to compensate the non-breaching party for the loss of the bargain. Compensatory damages are calculated according to one of three theories. Under an **expectation interest theory,** compensatory damages will reflect the benefit the non-breaching party expected to receive from the contract. An award based on reliance expectation reflects the losses suffered in the non-breaching party's belief that the breaching party would perform. A damage award under this theory could include expenses and investments made by the non-breaching party in anticipation that the breaching party would perform its duties under the contract. The restitution interest focuses on placing the non-breaching party in the condition it was in prior to the formation of the breached contract (Wong, 2010).

Consequential Damages

Consequential damages are awarded where there are foreseeable damages that result from circumstances out of the contract. To recover consequential damages, the non-breaching party must show that the breaching party knew or had reason to know that a breach will cause special damages to the other party. For example, a professional sports team buys computer software that will allow automated ticket purchases. The computer software fails and the team spends $15,000 on temporary employees who process orders over the phone. In this situation, the team may seek to recover the $15,000 paid to the temporary employees.

Nominal Damages

Courts will award nominal damages in situations when a breach of contract occurred but did not result in any significant economic loss. Cases resulting in nominal damages are usually motivated by principle, not money. Nominal damage awards amount to a few dollars. Nominal damages would be an appropriate remedy to a breach of contract claim involving a scheduling dispute in which the non-breaching party was able to secure another opponent and did not suffer any loss in revenue.

Punitive Damages

Punitive damages are awarded to punish a defendant's reprehensible behavior and discourage others from doing the same in the future. Punitive damages are more common in tort lawsuits. Nonetheless, a small number of jurisdictions in the United States allow punitive damages in breach of contract claims involving malicious or oppressive behavior.

Liquidated Damages

Liquidated damages are the only legal remedies not determined by a court or jury. These damages arise from a clause in the contract that specifies the damage award should either party fail to perform its duties under the agreement (Wong, 2010). In order for the clause to be enforced, it must be consistent with the actual harm suffered. Clauses that include a damage amount that far exceeds the actual harm constitute an unenforceable penalty. Liquidated damage provisions are common in professional and college sport employment contracts, as well as contest scheduling agreements. An example of the execution of such a clause is the 2009 football scheduling agreement between the Florida State University (FSU) and West Virginia University. Initially, WVU and FSU had contracted for WVU to play a home game at FSU in September 2012. Shortly after its decision to move a new athletics conference, WVU notified FSU that it would not be honoring the terms of that contract. FSU then announced it intended to enforce its right to $500,000 in liquidated damages under the contract. It further indicated that if WVU refused to honor the liquidated damages clause, FSU would sue for any consequential damages resulting from the breach (sportsillustrated.com, 2012). Another example of the prevalence and use of liquidated damages in sport and recreation law is the 2006 scheduling contract between the University of Buffalo and WVU. The contract between the two schools contained a liquidated damages clause that required the breaching party to pay the non-breaching party $200,000. After the contract was signed, UB was contacted by Auburn University and offered $450,000 to play a game on their campus on the same day as the WVU game. UB accepted Auburn's offer and breached the contract with WVU. As a result, UB was obligated to pay WVU the $200,000 (Thamel, 2006).

Equitable Remedies

There are certain contractual disputes that cannot be adequately remedied by a monetary award. In such cases, court will look to non-monetary judgments referred to as equitable remedies. The most common forms of equitable remedies are specific performance and injunctions.

Specific Performance

Specific performance requires the breaching party to perform its duties under the contract. Courts will award specific performance in cases that are unique, such as the purchase of an autographed jersey or tickets to a particular sporting event. Specific performance may be impossible depending on the terms of the contract. For example, courts rarely order specific performance for a breach of a personal service contracts such as a player's or coach's contract. In addition, plaintiffs seeking specific performance must show that there is no other appropriate legal remedy that will make them whole. A claim for specific performance will fail if requested to merely place a burden or penalty on the breaching party (*Brotherson v. the Professional Basketball Club, LLC*, 2008). In *Brotherson*, the plaintiffs were season ticket holders of the Seattle SuperSonics. They sought to punish the defendant for moving the team to Oklahoma City by requesting that the court enforce all the agreements with ticketholders residing in Seattle. Because the plaintiffs did not truly seek to retain the benefit of specific courts, the court rejected their claims for relief. For an additional example of season ticket holders seeking specific performance in a breach of contract case see *Yocca v. Pittsburgh Steelers, Inc.*, (2004).

Injunction

An injunction is the opposite of specific performance. It is sought when a party wishes to stop another party from acting. Courts will issue an injunction where there is evidence that a party will be irreparably harmed if relief is not granted (Wong, 2010). There have been numerous injunction cases against the NCAA in which a student-athlete seeks to enjoin the NCAA from applying a particular eligibility rule. In the context of a contract dispute involving a player or coach, this type of equitable relief is often referred to as a negative injunction because it is commonly used to block the player or coach from breaching a contract and going to play or work for another sport organization (Johnson, 1989).

Rescission and Restitution

Contracts that are unconscionable or involve illegal or fraudulent conduct, mistake or duress are often rescinded or voided by courts. The act of rescission undoes the contract. It is most often accomplished by ordering restitution, which requires all parties to return the consideration provided and any benefits reaped from the agreement (Sharp, 2007).

For example, rescission and restitution are often at issue in disputes involving health and fitness club memberships (*Robinson v. Lynmar Racquet Club, Inc.*, 1993). In *Robinson,* the plaintiff terminated her fitness club membership still owing two months of dues. The club filed a suit to collect the dues. Arguing that the contract violated the Colorado Consumer Protection Act, plaintiff also filed a lawsuit seeking rescission and restitution. In deciding the dispute, the court noted that the party seeking restitution must be capable of returning the opposite party to the position it occupied prior to entering into the contract. The court ultimately rejected plaintiff's claim noting that she was unable to do this. More specifically, plaintiff could not restore defendant with her use of its facilities and services that she had received over the course of the contract. As such, rescission was not a remedy available to resolve the dispute.

A court made the opposite ruling in *Taylor v. Wake Forest University* (1972). That case involved a scholarship student-athlete who became academically ineligible to play football for the institution. As a result, the institution cancelled his athletic scholarship. In response, the student-athlete filed a breach of contract suit. The court dismissed the student's case noting that he had failed to comply with his contractual obligation to the school and as such the school was entitled to rescind his athletic scholarship.

SIGNIFICANT CASE

The following case discusses the various promises made by both prospective student-athletes and college athletic staff during the recruiting process and once on campus and whether those promises can arise to a contractual relationship. The student alleged breach of contract claims against the university and its head men's golf coach.

ANDREW GIULIANI V. DUKE UNIVERSITY AND ORRIN DANIEL VINCENT

United States District Court for the Middle District of North Carolina
2009 U.S. Dist. LEXIS 44412 (2009)

Opinion

MEMORANDUM OPINION, RECOMMENDATION, AND ORDER

This matter is before the court on the following motions: (1) a motion for judgment on the pleadings filed by Defendants Duke University ("Duke") and Orrin Daniel Vincent III ("Vincent"), (2) a motion to strike elements of Defendants' pleadings filed by Plaintiff Andrew Giuliani, and (3) a motion for status conference filed by Plaintiff. The parties have responded to the motions, and, in this respect, the matter is ripe for disposition. The parties have not consented to the jurisdiction of the magistrate judge, thus the motion for judgment on the pleadings must be dealt with by way of recommendation. For the reasons stated herein,

(1) it will be recommended that Defendants' motion for judgment on the pleadings be granted on the ground that Plaintiff has failed to establish the elements of a breach of contract claim, (2) the motion to strike elements of Defendants' pleadings will be denied as moot, and (3) the motion for status conference will be denied as moot.

I. Factual Background

This case arises from Plaintiff's dismissal from the Duke men's varsity golf team during the spring of 2008. Plaintiff was recruited to play varsity golf at Duke by Head Coach Rod Myers ("Myers"), who was replaced by Vincent after Myers' unexpected death in the spring of 2007. Plaintiff alleges that he was induced to play at Duke over other institutions because of two promises made by Myers: "life-time access to ['state-of-the-art'] training facilities as an alumnus of the Duke Golf Program" and "the opportunity to compete with his teammates to earn spots in the most competitive [golf] tournaments against the most competitive players in the NCAA." Plaintiff accepted the offer to attend Duke and play on the golf team, hoping to achieve his "dream to become a professional golfer after college." He did not sign a letter of intent or receive an athletic scholarship.

Plaintiff tees up his case by alleging that his dismissal from the Duke golf team was a "secret expulsion . . . without notice, without an opportunity to defend himself, and without cause in violation of University-issued policies enacted to protect students from such arbitrary acts." According to Plaintiff, Myers' promises constituted an offer, and Plaintiff's agreement to attend Duke was an acceptance that created a legally binding contract between Plaintiff and Duke. Plaintiff alleges that this contract "is memorialized in several documents that govern the dimensions of the relationship between [Plaintiff] Andrew Giuliani and the University," specifically, "the Duke University Student-Athlete Handbook, Revised May, 2007; the Duke University Athletic Department Policy Manual; the Duke University Student Bulletin; and the 2007–2008 NCAA Division I Manual Constitution and By-Laws." When Vincent dismissed Plaintiff from the golf team and revoked his student-athlete access to Duke's golf facilities, this contract was allegedly breached. According to Plaintiff, "[t]he only University document that is consistent with O. D. Vincent's scheme [to dismiss Plaintiff] is the library's copy of William Goulding's *The Lord of the Flies.*"

II. Standard of Review

In deciding a motion for judgment on the pleadings under FED. R. CIV. P. 12(c), the court should apply the same standard as when ruling on a motion to dismiss for failure to state a claim upon which relief may be granted under FED. R. CIV. P. 12(b)(6). *Burbach Broad. Co. of Del. v. Elkins Radio Corp.*, 278 F.3d 401, 405–06 (4th Cir. 2002). The Fourth Circuit recently reiterated that standard:

> [W]e "take the facts in the light most favorable to the plaintiff," but "we need not accept the legal conclusions drawn from the facts,"

and "we need not accept as true unwarranted inferences, unreasonable conclusions, or arguments." *Eastern Shore Mkts., Inc. v. J.D. Assocs. Ltd. P'ship,* 213 F.3d 175, 180 (4th Cir. 2000). Additionally, the complaint must be dismissed if it does not allege "enough facts to state a claim to relief that is plausible on its face." *Bell Atl. Corp. v. Twombly,* 550 U.S. 544, 127 S.Ct. 1955, 1974, 167 L.Ed.2d 929 (2007) (emphasis added).

* * *

The conclusion that dismissal is appropriate comports with *Twombly*. . . [when the pleadings do not disclose] "enough facts to state a claim to relief that is plausible on its face." *Id.* at 1974. In *Twombly,* the Supreme Court, noting that "a plaintiff's obligation to provide the 'grounds' of his 'entitlement to relief' requires more than labels and conclusions, and a formulaic recitation of the elements of a cause of action will not do," *id.* at 1964–65, upheld the dismissal of a complaint where the plaintiffs did not "nudge [] their claims across the line from conceivable to plausible." *Id.* at 1974.

III. Discussion

* * *

A. Plaintiff's Breach of Contract Claim

Plaintiff contends that all elements for a breach of contract claim were properly alleged. His analysis, however, slices far from the fairway.

"Under North Carolina law, in order to state a claim for breach of contract there must be (1) a valid contract; and (2) breach of the terms of that contract." *Elina Adoption Servs., Inc. v. Carolina Adoption Servs., Inc.,* 2008 U.S. Dist. LEXIS 87745, (M.D.N.C. Aug. 25, 2008). "A valid contract exists when there is an agreement based on a meeting of the minds and sufficient consideration." "Under North Carolina law, an employee handbook or policy manual does not create a legally binding contract between employer and employee unless the terms of the handbook are expressly incorporated into a separate employment contract." *Brewer v. Jefferson-Pilot Standard Life Ins.* Co., 333 F. Supp. 2d 433, 439 (M.D.N.C. 2004) (employee handbooks "do not constitute a contract unless expressly made part of the employment contract").

Plaintiff argues that a valid contract was created when he accepted Duke's offer to play varsity golf. In his complaint, Plaintiff alleges:

> The specific provisions of the Contract that are at issue in this action are annexed to this Complaint as the Duke University Student-Athlete Handbook, Revised May, 2007; the Duke University Athletic Department Policy Manual; the Duke University Student Bulletin; and the 2007–2008 NCAA Division I Manual (Constitution and By-Laws)).

In his brief, however, Plaintiff states that he "is not alleging that the Bulletins themselves are the Contract, but that elements of the Contract are evinced in the documents which contain, among other things, the terms of the agreement . . . ." This attempt to change arguments between the complaint and the brief is like trying to change clubs after hitting the golf ball—Plaintiff is stuck with the club (in this case the argument) that he first picked.

Non-binding student policy manuals are not binding contracts. *See Love v. Duke Univ.*, 776 F. Supp. 1070, 1075 (M.D.N.C. 1991). Therefore, Plaintiff's reliance on four student policy manuals as evidence of a contract is a swing and a miss. Plaintiff argues that Love does not control because it was decided before *Ryan v. Univ. of N.C. Hosps.*, 128 N.C. App. 300, 494 S.E.2d 789 (N.C. Ct. App. 1998). This would be true if Ryan contradicted Love, but it does not. In *Ryan,* a medical resident signed a written employment contract that expressly included by reference a student manual. The *Ryan* court sustained a breach of an "educational contract," but limited its review to "an identifiable contractual promise that the University failed to honor." Thus, *Ryan* did not contradict the basic rule articulated in *Love* that a non-binding student policy manual, without more, is not a binding contract.

Plaintiff also contends that because the *Ryan* court "relied extensively on *Ross v. Creighton Univ.*, 957 F.2d 410 (7th Cir. 1992)," this court should consider the Seventh Circuit's holding. *Ross* serves as a putter, however, where Plaintiff needs a sand wedge to get out of the hazard. In *Ross,* the plaintiff was a scholarship basketball player who was recruited by Creighton University despite its knowledge that he was not educationally prepared for college academics. Plaintiff alleged that Creighton had breached an identifiable promise to provide specific educational services in exchange for his playing basketball. The court addressed the limited question of "whether the University had provided any real access to its academic curriculum at all." *Ross* cautioned, however, against broad application of its holding: "We agree—indeed we emphasize—that courts should not take on the job of supervising the relationship between colleges and student-athletes or creating in effect a new relationship between them." This court, following *Ross's* caution, declines to supervise the relationship between Plaintiff and Duke.

Reliance on the four student policy manuals as binding contracts is also impermissible because they can be unilaterally altered at any time. *See Brooks v. Hackney,* 404 S.E.2d 854, 857 (N.C. 1991) All of the manuals upon which Plaintiff relies have provisions allowing unilateral changes.

Plaintiff has failed to satisfy the first element of a breach of contract claim: existence of a valid contract. Accordingly, Defendants are entitled to a judgment on the pleadings.

* * *

C. Plaintiff's Tortious Interference with a Contract Claim

Plaintiff alleges that Vincent "intentionally, maliciously, fraudulently, and without justification induced the University to cease performance of the Contract." Plaintiff also shanks this claim.

Under North Carolina law, to state a claim for tortious interference with contract, a plaintiff must allege (1) a valid contract between the plaintiff and a third person, conferring upon the plaintiff some contractual right against the third person; (2) defendant's knowledge of the contract; (3) defendant intentionally induced the third person not to perform her contract with the plaintiff; (4) defendant acted without justification and with malice; and (5) plaintiff suffered actual damages. *Peoples Sec. Life Ins. Co. v. Hooks, 322 N.C. 216 (N.C. 1988).* Because there is no valid contract, the first element is not satisfied, and Defendants are entitled to a judgment on the pleadings.

D. Plaintiff's Promissory Estoppel Claim

Plaintiff's promissory estoppel claim, which was not argued in his brief, brings to mind Carl Spackler's analysis from the movie CADDYSHACK (Orion Pictures 1980): "He's on his final hole. He's about 455 yards away, he's gonna hit about a 2 iron, I think." North Carolina does not recognize affirmative claims of promissory estoppel; thus, Defendants are entitled to a judgment on the pleadings. *See Dealers Supply Co. v. Cheil Indus., 348 F. Supp. 2d 579, 587 (M.D.N.C. 2004)*

Plaintiff tries to get around the slow play of his promissory estoppel claim by arguing that he should recover on a quasi or implied contract theory. Although other jurisdictions may hold that the student-university relationship is contractual in nature, *see, e.g., Havlik v. Johnson & Wales Univ.,* 509 F.3d 25, 35 (1st Cir. 2007); *Fellheimer v. Middlebury Coll.,* 869 F. Supp. 238, 242 (D. Vt. 1994); *Babiker v. Ross Univ. Sch. of Med.,* 2000 U.S. Dist. LEXIS 6921, (S.D.N.Y. May 19, 2000), this court must apply the consistent North Carolina precedents of *Brewer, Johnson,* and *Love* that policy manuals are non-binding.

E. Plaintiff's Declaratory Relief Claim

Plaintiff's fifth and final claim for declaratory judgment, which was also not argued in his brief, can be disposed of with a hole-in-one sentence: no valid contract means no declaratory judgment. *See Shelton v. Duke Univ. Health Sys., Inc.,* 633 S.E.2d 113, 117 (N.C. Ct. App. 2006). Accordingly, Defendants are entitled to a judgment on the pleadings.

IV. Conclusion

For the reasons stated herein, Defendants are entitled to a judgment on the pleadings. Therefore, **IT IS RECOMMENDED** that the Defendants' motion for judgment on the pleadings **GRANTED.** Furthermore, the Plaintiff's motion to strike elements of Defendants' pleadings and the Plaintiff's motion for status conference are **DENIED.**

/s/ Wallace W. Dixon
WALLACE W. DIXON
United States Magistrate Judge

CASES ON THE SUPPLEMENTAL WEB SITE

Blackmon v. Iverson, 324 F.Supp.2d 602 (E.D. Pa. 2003). This case looks at the issue of past consideration and whether an individual's promise created a valid contract.

Brotherson v. the Professional Basketball Club, LLC, 2009 U.S. Dist. LEXIS 13912 (W.D. Wash. 2009). This case discusses whether a brochure soliciting season tickets created a contract between the team and the buyers.

Ross v. Creighton University, 957 F.2d 410 (7th Cir. 1992). This case examines what contractual duty colleges have to educate scholarship athletes.

R. J. Hendricks, II, v. Clemson University, 578 S.E.2d 711(S.C. 2003). This case looks at issues involved in forming a valid enforceable contract when a student-athlete transfers from one college to another.

HBCU Pro Football, LLC, v. New Vision Sports Properties, LLC, 2011 U.S. Dist. LEXIS 55976 (D. Md. 2011). This case provides an example of the contractual issues involved in the broadcasting of sport contests, including an agent's authority to contract on behalf of a third party, and the breach of contract claims that can result when such contracts are not fulfilled.

QUESTIONS YOU SHOULD BE ABLE TO ANSWER

1. What are some examples of contracts in the sport and recreation industry?

2. What are the three sources of contract law in the United States?

3. What are the four elements of an enforceable contract?

4. What will the non-breaching party have to show to succeed on a breach of contract claim?

5. What are the different remedies to a breach of contract claim?

REFERENCES

Cases

Athletes Foot Brands, LLC v. Whoohah, Inc, 2007 U.S. Dist. LEXIS 74778 (D. Idaho 2007).
Blackmon v. Iverson, 324 F.Supp.2d 602 (E.D. Pa. 2003).
Brooks v. Paige, 773 P.2d 1098 (Colo. Ct. App. 1988).
Brotherson v. the Professional Basketball Club, LLC, 2009 U.S. Dist. LEXIS 13912 (W.D. Wash. 2009).
Chuy v. Phiadelphia Eagles Football Club, 431 F.Supp. 254 (E.D. Pa. 1977).
Fortay v. University of Miami, 1994 U.S. Dist. LEXIS 1865 (D.N.J. 1994)
Giuliani v. Duke University, 2009 U.S. Dist. LEXIS 44412 (M.D.N.C. 2009)
HBCU Pro Football, LLC, v. New Vision Sports Properties, LLC, 2011 U.S. Dist. LEXIS 55976 (D. Md. 2011). *Hanlon v. Providence College*, 615 F.2d 535 (1st Cir. 1980).
In re Worldcom, Inc., 2007 WL 446735 (Bkrtcy. S.D.N.Y. 2007)
Jones v. Dressel, 623 P.2d 370 (Colo. 1981)
LoPiccolo v. American University, 2012 U.S. Dist. LEXIS 1300 (D.D.C. 2012)
Milicic v. Basketball Marketing Co., Inc., 857 A.2d 689 (Pa. Super. Ct. 2004)
Northeastern University v. Brown, 2004 Mass. Super LEXIS 64 (2004)
Robinson v. Lymar Racquet Club, 851 P.2d 274 (Colo. App. 1993)
Shepard v. Loyola Marymount Univ., 2002 Daily Journal DAR 11545 (Cal. App.2d Dist. 2002)
Vanderbilt University v. DiNardo, 174 F.3d 751 (6th Cir. 1999).
West Virginia University v. Rodriguez, 2008 WL 1739259 (Trial Pleading) (N.D.W.Va. Feb. 1, 2008)
Yocca v. Pittsburgh Steelers Sports, Inc., 854 A.2d 425 (Pa. 2004)

Publications

American Law Institute. (1981). *Restatement (second) of the law of contracts*. St. Paul, MN: American Law Institute.
Berry, R.C., & Wong, G.M. (1994). *The Law and Business of the Sports Industries* (3rd. ed.). Westport, CT: Prager Publishing.
Davis, T. (1997). Balancing Freedom of Contract and Competing Values in Sports. *South Texas Law Review 38*, 1115.
Greenberg, M.J., & Gray, J.T. (1998). *Sports Law Practice* (2nd. ed.). Charlottesville, VA: Lexis Law Publishing.

Hanson, S.M. (2006). Athletic Scholarships as Unconscionable Contracts of Adhesion: Has the NCAA Fouled Out? *Sports Law Journal 13*, 41–77.

Johnson, A.M. (1989). The Argument for Self-Help Specific Performance: Opportunistic Renegotiation of Player Contracts. *Connecticut Law Review 22*, 61.

Miller, L.K, Comfort, P.G., & Stoldt, G.C. (2001). Teaching Perspective: Contracts 101: Basics and Applications, *Journal of Legal Aspects of Sport 11,* 79.

Sports People: Football; Fortay and Miami Settle. (1996, June 25). *New York Times*, p. B6.

Sharp, L. (2007). Contract essentials. In D.J. Cotton & J.T. Wolohan. *Law for recreation and sport managers* (4th ed.). pp. 364–374. Dubuque, IA: Kendall/Hunt Publishing

Shubert, G.W., Smith J.C., & Trentadue, R.K. (1986). *Sport law* (1st ed.). St. Paul, MN: West Publishing

Simpson, A.W.B., (1987). *A History of the Common Law of Contract: The Rise of the Action of Assumpsit* (2d ed.), Oxford: Oxford Publishing

Sports Illustrated. (2012). *Savannah St visit rounds out FSU's 2012 schedule*. Retrieved from http://sportsillustrated.cnn.com/2012/football/ncaa/wires/02/22/2000.ap.fbc.florida.st.schedule.1st.ld.writethru.0649/index.html#ixzz1nGdMA4bC

Thamel, P. (2006, August 23). *In College Football, Big Paydays for Humiliation. New York Times*, p. A1.

Wong, G.M. (2010). *Essentials of Sports Law* (4th ed.), Santa Barbara, CA. ABC-CLIO, LLC.

RECREATION AND SPORT MANAGEMENT APPLICATIONS

5.21   EMPLOYMENT CONTRACTS

Rodney L. Caughron | Northern Illinois University

5.20

Historically, employment contracts in sport and recreation were a matter of a handshake or a simple letter of agreement. With the increased level of compensation—both in salary and outside income—and the tenuous nature of a coach or administrator's position, employment contracts have evolved into complex legal documents. However, no matter how complicated the contracts have become, employment contracts are essentially the same as other contracts in the "real" world. The only difference is that they have the propensity to be broken on a much more frequent basis—often with the assent of both parties. That is why the more specific a contract can be crafted, specifically defining terms and reducing ambiguity, the more both parties will benefit (Yasser, McCurdy, Goplerud, & Weston, 2000).

FUNDAMENTAL CONCEPTS

Sport and recreation has become a big business in the United States. For example, in 2010–11, athletic programs at Division I colleges and universities generated over $6 billion in revenue (Berkowitz & Upton, 2011). With so much money involved in college and professional sports, there is an increased pressure on organizations to win in order to gain a bigger share of the potential revenue and ensure economic viability. As the pressure to win rises, it is only natural that the expectation on the coaches also increases. A perfect illustration of the tenuous nature of today's college coaching is the turnover in jobs that occurs at the end of each college basketball and football season. For example, in the end of the 2011 regular football season, out of the 66 schools that currently play in the big six football conferences (ACC, Big 10, Big 12, Big East, Pac 12 and the SEC), 12 coaches were fired or resigned to accept other jobs (Coaching Changes, (2011).

This continuous coaching carousel has required all parties, the organization, administrators and coaches, to develop specific contractual language to protect themselves and their interest if the contract is eventually breached. The more precise a contract can be crafted, reducing ambiguity and specifically defining the terms, the more both parties will benefit (Greenberg & Smith, 2007, and Yasser, McCurdy, Goplerud, & Weston, 2000). No matter how well the contract is drafted, however, when one party fails to meet its' obligation, or one side wishes to breach the contract, legal issues are sure to arise over what the proper damages should be.

Elements of a Common Contract

Although it is important to note that no two contracts will be alike, there are a number of elements that should be in every sports-related employment contract. These contracts often involve special perks and other common employment benefits as well as salary. For example, in John Calipari's $31.65 million deal with the University of Kentucky, his base pay was listed at just $400,000 per year. The contract, however, was packed with perks beyond his annual salary, including membership to the country club of his choice, two cars, 20 prime "lower-level" season tickets to UK home games, eight tickets for each UK home football game, and incentives for reaching the NCAA Sweet Sixteen and Final Four and a $375,000 bonus for winning the 2012 NCAA title.

While it is important to note that all contracts have most of the same elements, it is also important that each contract be tailored for the particular job. The following are some of the most common elements of a sport-related employment contract.

Duties and Responsibilities
- The contract should state that the employee agrees to devote his/her best effort to full-time performance as the position requires.
- There should be a specific list of responsibilities required to be performed by the employee.
- The contract should also include a general phrase that the employee agrees to perform other duties assigned to him or her, and mutually agreed upon.

Term of Employment
- The length of the contract should be explicit. For example in *Lindsey v. University of Arizona* (1987), the terms of employment were unclear. As a result, when the university breached an oral commitment to extend his contract for three additional years, Lindsey was forced to sue to recover the remainder of the contract. In another case, *Small v. Juniata College* (1997), the court found that Small's employment contract was for a one-year term and that the college personnel manual termination procedures did not affect the status of these one-year appointments.

Rollover Provisions
- Rollover provisions allow the organization to extend an employee's contract for an extra year, with the mutual agreement of the employee and organization. Rollover provisions tend to be one-sided in favor of the employee, exemplified in the statement by *Atlanta Journal-Constitution* reporter Jeff Schultz, "Now a coach can have an iron-clad, no escape contract signed in vampire blood . . . then weasel out of rollover contracts and jump across the street for a raise" (Schultz, 2006). This is especially true when the contract's rollover agreement requires specific terms of notice for terminating the employee, allowing the employee to collect more monetary damages if the contract is terminated by the organization. For example, in *Cherry v. A-P-A Sports, Inc.* (1983), Cherry's contract provided that if his contract was not renewed for an additional two years, he would automatically receive $35,000 in compensation.

Reassignment Clause
- A reassignment clause allows for the removal of the employee from the originally contracted position and reassigned to another position that is consistent with the employee's education and experience. For example, in *Monson v. State of Oregon* (1995), the University of Oregon had included a provision for reassignment, which they exercised, changing his assignment from men's basketball coach to golf coach. The court upheld the reassignment because it was part of the contractual language.
- The issue of reassignment and future loss of income due to the reassignment was addressed in *Smith v. Alanis & Zapata County Independent School District*, (2002). Smith was hired as the head high school football coach and athletic coordinator, but was reassigned midyear in accordance with his contract. Smith claimed that his removal as head coach, although not reducing his current salary per the contract, would have an effect on future income as a head coach. The court concluded that contract law in Texas did not allow compensation for future earning capacity, and therefore, the actions of the school district were within the scope of the employment contract.
- A reassignment clause should be coupled with the avoidance of any language in the contract that gives the employee the right to be in any specific titled position (e.g., head coach).

Compensation Clause
- A compensation clause should include the base salary, terms of pay increases over the time of the contract, fringe benefits, moving and relocation expenses, bonuses, additional retirement benefits, and all other compensation specifically delineated and agreed upon.

Fringe Benefits
- This area can include a myriad of benefits that organizations offer employees and administrators. Some of these fringe benefits may include: complementary cars, travel, loans, moving and housing expenses, and tickets. Many of the benefits are offered to the normal employee, but in many situations the benefits for

the coach or administrator are inflated or outside the normal employees benefits. The type, amount, date the benefit is available, and penalties for termination of contract should be explicitly written out within the contract.

Bonuses and Incentives

- Bonuses and incentives are becoming more important to all employees. They may include signing bonuses, incentives based on team success, and in the case of college and university coaches and administrators, graduation rates of student–athletes. In *White v. National Football League* (2007), when Ashley Lelie did not report to training camp, he was fined by the Denver Broncos $220,000, the player's option bonus according to the team's interpretation of the NFL CBA. The court saw it differently and ruled that the option was earned as soon as it had been awarded and could not be recovered by the team (also see *Grillier* (2009) below).

Sovereign Immunity

- When dealing with various state organizations, depending on the state's sovereign immunity rules, an employee may not be able to sue the state organization, even for an alleged breach of the contract. In *Leach v. Texas Tech University* (2011), Mike Leach, the head football coach at Tech was fired prior to the conclusion of his contract. In dismissing Leach's claim that the university waived its immunity, the court held that the university was still protected under the state's sovereign immunity. In states that still have sovereign immunity, therefore, it is incumbent on employees to include an expressed waiver of that immunity in your employment contract.

Provisions for Outside and/or Supplemental Income

- These sources of income may include radio and television contracts; endorsements; shoe, apparel and equipment contracts; income from speeches and written materials, as well as camps and other sources of supplemental income.
- The organization should include in the contract that it is not legally liable for claims arising from these outside income sources, and that the organization retains all right of final approval for any outside income sources.
- Greenberg and Smith (2007) delineate the non-base income earned by Bruce Pearl, University of Tennessee Head Men's Basketball coach in the 2006–2007 season. Pearl's base salary was $300,000, but with his additional income sources, Pearl's reported income was approximately $1.5 million that season. Pearl was later fired in March 2011 after a series of university and NCAA violations.

Termination Clause

- A termination clause should state that termination may be caused by the death, disability, or criminal conduct. For example, in *Maddox v. University of Tennessee* (1995), the court upheld the dismissal of Maddox, an alcoholic, due to his arrest for drunk driving. Maddox contended that his dismissal was due to his alcoholism, which violated the Americans with Disabilities Act of 1990 (ADA) and the Rehabilitation Act of 1973. The court did not agree, however, finding that the termination was for his criminal act and the subsequent negative publicity. In a similar case, ABC TV terminated an employee after he was arrested for selling cocaine. The plaintiff claimed he was covered under ADA, but the court ruled that his termination was based on the plaintiff's breach of the morals clause in his contract because he lied about the situation (*Nader v. ABC Television*, 2005).
- The contract should also contain a termination for "just cause" clause, so that if the employee violates either the organization's rules, its affiliation rules, civil or criminal laws, moral turpitude, refusal to perform duties, and so forth, the employee can be fired. These may be explicitly expressed or implied in the contract or in the "customs and mores" of the organization or society. For example, in *Deli v. University of Minnesota* (1994), the head women's gymnastics coach and her husband, the assistant coach, were terminated when the gymnasts viewed a videotape of the coach and her husband having sex. The court upheld the dismissal of both of the coaches, based on the indiscretions with the videotape and for other "just cause" reasons. Other examples are *McKenzie v. Wright State University* (1996), and *Farner v. Idaho*

Falls School District, (2000). In *McKenzie v. Wright State University* (1996); the court upheld the dismissal of McKenzie for NCAA rules violations, which were specifically mentioned in her employment contract as cause for termination. The *Farner* case demonstrated how the master contract for high school teachers, when incorporating coaching and extra duties, requires the same "just cause" for termination as the teaching aspect of the contract. To terminate without just cause violates the individual's due process rights. In Nick Saban's (Head Football Coach at the University of Alabama) contract extension, the Termination for Cause section of the contract contained 15 specifically delineated reasons that the coach could be terminated.

- The termination clause should also spell out the due process rights employees have to challenge their termination. This could include a formal hearing within the organization or the use of an arbitrator. For example, in *Stamps Public Schools v. Colvert* (1996), Colvert was able to prove that the school district had violated its own procedures and had not given him his contractually guaranteed due process. Another example involved Rick Neuheisel and the University of Washington. Neuheisel was fired as head football coach six months before the end of his original contract, based on his involvement in an NCAA men's basketball betting pool. In suing the university, Neuheisel claimed that Washington denied him his contractually guaranteed due process and the subsequent hearing. Neuheisel and Washington later settled for a cash payment of $2.5 million (from the NCAA for defamation) and $500,000 in cash and $1.5 million in a forgiven loan from the university (Greenberg & Thomas, 2005).
- Termination without cause allows the organization to fire the employee for any reason. This will usually come with a price, in that the organization will usually have to negotiate a settlement with the employee if a termination occurs. This was not the case in *Frazier v. University of the District of Columbia* (1990), however, where the court found that Frazier was an at-will employee and could be terminated at any time.
- In *O'Brien v. The Ohio State University*, (2007), James O'Brien, the Head Basketball Coach at The Ohio State University (OSU), was terminated by the athletic director for a "material breach" of his coaching contract. O'Brien gave a $6,000 loan to a recruited basketball player's mother in Yugoslavia in early 1999 (although the athlete was ruled a professional and was not able to play for OSU), based on humanitarian reasons and his belief that the athlete was not eligible anyway. O'Brien disclosed the loan to Ohio State, and OSU self-reported the loan as a NCAA violation. When OSU fired O'Brien on June 8, 2004, for a "material breach" of his contract, it referred to the loan as a "for cause" violation his contract. The court, however, concluded that OSU fired O'Brien for a major NCAA violation, prior to an NCAA determination. As a result, OSU was required to pay O'Brien the remainder of his contract, $2,494,972.83.
- In order to solve some of the problems involving in terminating an employee, employment contracts should contain an agreed upon liquidated damages amount, paid to the coach when he or she is fired (Greenberg, 2006).

Buyout Provisions
- A buyout provision allows the employee or institution to terminate the contract on the payment of a specified amount of money. For example, in *Tolis v. Board of Supervisors of Louisiana State University* (1992), the court upheld an oral agreement to buy out Tolis's contract, which the defendants later violated. The court held that the Board of Supervisors must abide by their oral buyout agreement.
- A buyout provision may include a liquidated damages clause. For example, in January 2010, University of Connecticut coach Randy Edsall breached his contract with two years remaining to take the head coaching job at the University of Maryland (Clarke, Yanda, & Prisbell, 2011). In this type of situation, the schools generally allow the coach to breach his contract after paying an agreed on liquidated damage. In Edsall's instance, since he accepted the Maryland job on January 3, 2011, his contract required him to pay the University of Connecticut $400,000 (Football Bowl Subdivision coaches' salaries for 2010).
- Sometime, even when a written contract does not exist, a buyout may be warranted. For example, the University of Oregon gave Athletic Director, Mike Bellotti a $2.3 million buyout when after only nine months on the job he resigned. This type of situation demonstrates how both parties can come to an agreement for everyone to save face and avoid litigation ("Lariviere: Bellotti," 2010).

Arbitration Agreement

- An arbitration agreement is a clause in the contract that stipulates that if any dispute arises from the interpretation of the contract or other factors concerning the contract, the issues will be dealt with through arbitration (see *Miami Dolphins Ltd. v. Williams*, 2005).
- The areas to be arbitrated should be specifically delineated within the contract if arbitration is to be used. A dispute concerning this concept arose in *Grillier v. CSMG Sports, LTD.* (2009). Grillier was initially an independent contractor working as an agent. He and CSMG agreed upon a Consulting Agreement in which compensation and an arbitration clause were included. Subsequent to this agreement, Grillier was then hired as an employee, under an oral agreement. When a new employment contract was offered it did not include an extra compensation or an arbitration clause. Grillier later resigned and demanded payment for "extra compensation" (both during his Consulting Agreement and his employment contract), but disagreed that the dispute should be settled through arbitration, based on that oral employment agreement. The court allowed arbitration to go forward.
- An interesting case challenging the ability of NFL Commissioner Paul Tagliabue to serve as the arbitrator in contract disputes within the NFL involved coaches with the Minnesota Vikings, who after they were fired claimed they were entitled to incentive pay under their contract. The appellants filed suit to remove Tagliabue as the arbitrator in their dispute, but the court stated that nowhere in the Federal Arbitration Act is there an allowance to challenge an arbitrator—biased or not—prior to a decision by the arbitrator (*Alexander, et al. v. Minnesota Vikings Football Club LLC & National Football League*, 2002).

Covenant Not to Compete

- Covenants not to compete are also commonly used in coaching contracts. For example, in the new football coach's contract, the school could include a clause prohibiting the coach from accepting another head coaching position at any school in the same conference for five years after leaving his current school. The purpose of the clause is to protect the competitive advantage of the school, while at the same time not overly restricting the coach's future earning possibilities. If the clause is too restrictive in scope or time (*MacGinnitie v. Hobbs Group*, 2005), courts will refuse to enforce it against the coach. If the non-compete provision of the contract is seen as a legitimate business requirement, the court, as it did in *Aim High Academy, Inc. v. Jessen* (2008), will uphold the provision as long as the provision is limited in scope
- An interesting case dealing with sports agencies and non-compete clauses in employment contracts was *Steinberg Moorad & Dunn, Inc. v. Dunn*, (2005). In reversing a lower court decision, the appeals court ruled that, under California law, non-compete clauses are invalid in contracts. Steinberg, Moorad & Dunn (SMD) had accused Dunn of breach of contract after he left the firm and started his own sports agency firm, taking several of SMD's professional athlete clients with him.

Discussion of Contract Issues

Typically in sports the employee has the advantage in any contractual situation in which the employee unilaterally decides to terminate the contract. If an employee unilaterally terminates his or her contract, thus breaching the conditions of the contract, the sport organization has essentially no remedy to "force" the employee to perform their duties. The reason the courts are unwilling to enforce such contracts is that to compel performance of a contractual duty would constitute a violation of the Thirteenth Amendment's prohibition against involuntary servitude. In addition, the court has stated that it would be unable to monitor the level of coaching performance and enforce proper coaching skills in a coaching contract (Cozzillio & Levinstein, 1997).

Although unable to compel the employee to perform his or her duties, the sport organization may acquire injunctive relief, which prohibits the employee from acquiring similar employment at another sport organization. This was evident in the case of Chuck Fairbanks and the New England Patriots. Fairbanks, who was head coach of the New England Patriots, breached his contract with New England to take the head coaching position with the University of Colorado. To prevent Fairbanks from leaving, the Patriots obtained injunctive relief, prohibiting the University of Colorado from entering into a coaching contract with Fairbanks (*New England Patriots Football Club Inc. v. University of Colorado*, 1979).

In some instances, problems arise between parties of an employment contract based on their personal relationships and friendship. One typical situation is when there is a verbal understanding that in the future a specific employment relationship will be consummated contractually by the two parties, and the agent of the organization does not have the authority to make such an agreement, or due to the fact that it is only an agreement and not yet a contract, the relationship does not transpire. This was the case in *Barnett v. Board of Trustees for State Colleges and Universities A/K/A University of Louisiana System*, (2001). Barnett was originally hired as basketball coach at Northwestern State University in 1994. A plan was formulated by Barnett and the then-university president, which would elevate Barnett to athletic director in 1996. A letter from the president was sent to Barnett confirming the agreement in 1995, pending approval by the university Board of Trustees (Louisiana state law required personnel appointments at the university to be approved by the Board of Trustees). Before Barnett could be appointed to the AD position, a new president took office at the institution, and someone else was hired as AD. Barnett filed suit against the university for breach of contract. The court ruled that no contract existed because all contracts had to be submitted to the Board, and Barnett was aware of this prerequisite from the beginning of the agreement. This case demonstrates the importance of employees knowing the exact procedural requirements for contracts with a particular institution or organization to become valid and actionable. *Meinders v. Dunkerton Community School District*, (2002) is an example of a similar situation at the high school level.

It is interesting to note that even when an employee breaches his or her contract and jumps from one organization to another, in most cases the parties involved eventually agree on a settlement, either financial or, in the case of professional teams, financial and possible trade of draft picks. For example, the New York Jets settled with the New England Patriots to obtain Bill Parcells for a reported $300,000 charitable donation and the Jets' third-and fourth-round draft picks in 1997, their second-round choice in 1998, and their first-round pick in 1999 (Rosenthal, 1997).

Another area where employers need to pay attention is the issue of perquisites that an employee may be entitled to. For example, in *Rodgers v. Georgia Tech Athletic Association*, (1983) (see the supplemental Web Site), Rodgers, the head football coach at Georgia Tech, asked the court to award him the value of the perquisites for the remainder of his terminated contract. In reaching its decision, the court eliminated those perquisites directly related to the function of Rodgers' job as head coach (i.e., a secretary), but awarded Rodgers the value of those items that were regularly provided to him either through the Association or from outside sources (i.e., television and radio revenues). The court also eliminated items that were gifts, and those items that the Association did not have knowledge of or contemplate as part of the contract. Therefore, the *Rodgers* case set a precedent that allows coaches or administrators to recover items that are specifically or tacitly provided for by the sport organization and those items that the coach or administrator and the organization would normally expect to be perquisites under the contract (*Rodgers v. Georgia Tech Athletic Association*, 1983).

Independent Contractors vs. Employee

A growing issue in the sport, fitness, and recreational industries is the hiring of independent contractors to perform duties that were typically performed by employees. Although the use of independent contractors is a good way to reduce costs and an organization's legal liability, not every individual will actually meet the standards of an "independent contractor." The classification of workers has significant implications for the employer in terms of taxes, tort liability, and other forms of employee compensation (Caughron & Fargher, 2004).

Darryll Halcomb Lewis brought to light the importance of this issue when dealing with sports officials. Halcomb Lewis states that if a sports official hurt on the job is considered an independent contractor, two consequences result: (1) the referee is barred from filing a worker's compensation claim, and (2) that absent legislated immunity, the organization hiring the official may be held liable for those injuries (Halcomb Lewis, 1998). This was echoed in *Wadler v. Eastern College Athletic Conference* (2003), in which a claim of Title VII discrimination based on race was dismissed against an athletic conference due to a lack of an employer–employee relationship—essentially recognizing a college baseball umpire as an independent contractor due to the employment relationship he had with the defendants in the case. A recent case, *Yonan v. United States Soccer Federation, Inc.* (2011), enforced the concept that most referees are considered independent contractors and not subject to employment discrimination statutes (in this case the Age Discrimination in Employment Act).

Although no specific test has been adopted universally by all jurisdictions, the Internal Revenue Service has developed a checklist that includes twenty criteria for determining whether someone is an independent contractor or an employee. The status of the individual is dependent on the following (the more reliant the individual is on the employer, the greater likelihood they are an employee):

1. **Instructions.** Level of instruction to accomplish the work, and the level of supervision;
2. **Training.** Initial and ongoing training;
3. **Integration.** Independence of individual within the workplace;
4. **Services rendered personally.** Ability of individual to subcontract;
5. **Hiring, supervising, and paying assistants.** Ability to hire and treat others as employees by the worker;
6. **Continuing relationship.** The relationship is based on a specific period of time or completion of a specific task;
7. **Set hours of work.** Role of the employer in setting the schedule of the individual;
8. **Full-time required.** Role of the employer in setting minimum or full-time work requirement;
9. **Doing work on employer's premises.** The level of on-site supervision and reliance on employer's facilities and equipment;
10. **Order or sequence set.** Level the employer sets the pattern of work by individual;
11. **Oral or written reports.** The amount of paperwork the individual must file with the employer;
12. **Payment by the hour, week, or month.** Method of payment and the inclusion of sick and vacation days;
13. **Payment of business and/or traveling expenses.** Level of compensation employer provides individual to perform work;
14. **Furnishing of tools and materials.** Level of use by individual of employer's equipment;
15. **Significant investment.** Records are kept to identify individual's contribution (e.g., purchase of equipment) to the employer's facilities;
16. **Realization of profit or loss.** The individual is responsible for their own business accounting and insurance;
17. **Working for more than one firm.** Do the customers pay the individual directly, and can the individual contract with other employers in the same business?
18. **Making services available to the public.** Level of independence the individual has in marketing, advertising, and working independent of employer;
19. **Right to discharge.** Level of ability of employer to discipline and fire individual;
20. **Right to terminate.** Can the individual end relationship with employer or are they bound contractually (Internal Revenue Service, pp. 298–299) (see Caughron & Fargher, 2004, for a full explanation of the classification process).

SIGNIFICANT CASE

This case covers a multitude of contractual issues that are important to individuals involved in contract development and negotiations. The most important issue this case brings forward is that when developing a contract, each side must specifically state their expectations concerning elements of the agreement and write them out explicitly. This is illustrated in the reasons given in the contract for a lengthy contract, program stability, as well as the acceptance of liquidated damages, and the inclusion of the extension into the entire scope of the original contract. Lastly, this case shows that the court will recognize conditional acceptance of contracts, even verbal, which determine the enforcement of the contract.

VANDERBILT UNIVERSITY V. DINARDO

United States Court of Appeals for the Sixth Circuit
174 F.3d 751 (6th Cir. 1999)

Opinion: J. Gibson

On December 3, 1990, Vanderbilt University and Gerry DiNardo executed an employment contract hiring DiNardo to be Vanderbilt's head football coach. Section one of the contract provided:

The University hereby agrees to hire Mr. DiNardo for a period of five (5) years from the date hereof with Mr. DiNardo's assurance that he will serve the entire term of this Contract, a long-term commitment by Mr. DiNardo being important to the University's desire for a stable intercollegiate football program. . . .

The contract also contained reciprocal liquidated damage provisions. Vanderbilt agreed to pay DiNardo his remaining salary should Vanderbilt replace him as football coach, and DiNardo agreed to reimburse Vanderbilt should he leave before his contract expired. Section eight of the contract stated:

Mr. DiNardo recognizes that his promise to work for the University for the entire term of this 5-year Contract is of the essence of this Contract to the University. Mr. DiNardo also recognizes that the University is making a highly valuable investment in his continued employment by entering into this Contract and its investment would be lost were he to resign or otherwise terminate his employment. . . . Accordingly, Mr. DiNardo agrees that in the event he resigns or otherwise terminates his employment as Head Football Coach, prior to the expiration of this Contract, and is employed or performing services for a person or institution other than the University, he will pay to the University as liquidated damages an amount equal to his Base Salary (later negotiated as his net salary), . . . multiplied by the number of years (or portion(s) thereof) remaining on the Contract.

* * *

Vanderbilt initially set DiNardo's salary at $100,000 per year. DiNardo received salary increases in 1992, 1993, and 1994. On August 14, 1994, Paul Hoolahan, Vanderbilt's Athletic Director . . . talk(ed) to DiNardo about a contract extension. (DiNardo's original contract would expire on January 5, 1996). Hoolahan offered DiNardo a two-year contract extension. DiNardo told Hoolahan that he wanted to extend his contract, but that he also wanted to discuss the extension with Larry DiNardo, his brother and attorney.

Hoolahan telephoned John Callison, Deputy General Counsel for Vanderbilt, and asked him to prepare a contract extension. Callison drafted an addendum to the original employment contract which provided for a two-year extension of the original contract, specifying a termination date of January 5, 1998. Vanderbilt's Chancellor, Joe B. Wyatt, and Hoolahan signed the Addendum.

On August 17, Hoolahan returned to Bell Buckle with the Addendum. He took it to DiNardo at the practice field where they met in Hoolahan's car. DiNardo stated that Hoolahan did not present him with the complete two-page addendum, but only the second page, which was the signature page. DiNardo asked, "what am I signing?" Hoolahan explained to DiNardo, "it means that your contract as it presently exists will be extended for two years with everything else remaining exactly the same as it existed in the present contract." Before DiNardo signed the Addendum, he told Hoolahan, "Larry needs to see a copy before this thing is finalized." Hoolahan agreed, and DiNardo signed the document. . . .

On August 16, Larry DiNardo had a telephone conversation with Callison. They briefly talked about the contract extension, discussing a salary increase. Larry DiNardo testified that as of that date he did not know that Gerry DiNardo had signed the Addendum, or even that one yet existed.

On August 25, Callison faxed Larry DiNardo "a copy of the draft Addendum to Gerry's contract." Callison wrote on the fax: "let me know if you have any questions." The copy sent was unsigned. Callison and Larry DiNardo had several telephone conversations in late August and September, primarily discussing the television and radio contract. . . .

In November 1994, Louisiana State University contacted Vanderbilt in hopes of speaking with DiNardo about becoming the head football coach for L.S.U. Hoolahan gave DiNardo permission to speak to L.S.U. On December 12, 1994, DiNardo announced that he was accepting the L.S.U. position.

Vanderbilt sent a demand letter to DiNardo seeking payment of liquidated damages under section eight of the contract. Vanderbilt believed that DiNardo was liable for three years of his net salary: one year under the original contract and two years under the Addendum. DiNardo did not respond to Vanderbilt's demand for payment.

Vanderbilt brought this action against DiNardo for breach of contract. DiNardo removed the action to federal court, and both parties filed motions for summary judgement. The district court held that section eight was an enforceable liquidated damages provision, not an unlawful penalty, and that the damages provided under section eight were reasonable. *Vanderbilt University v. DiNardo*, 974 F. Supp. 638, 643 (M.D. Tenn. 1997). The court held that Vanderbilt did not waive its contractual rights under section eight when it granted DiNardo permission to talk to L.S.U. and that the Addendum was enforceable and extended the contract for two years. *Id.* at 643–45. The court entered judgement against DiNardo for $281,886.43. *Id.* at 645. DiNardo appeals.

I.

DiNardo first claims that section eight of the contract is an unenforceable penalty under Tennessee law. DiNardo argues that the provision is not a liquidated damage provision but a "thinly disguised, overly broad non-compete provision," unenforceable under Tennessee law.

* * *

Contracting parties may agree to the payment of liquidated damages in the event of a breach. *See Beasley v. Horrel*, 864 S.W.2d 45, 48 (Tenn. Ct. App. 1993). The term "liquidated damages" refers to an amount by the parties to be just compensation for damages should a breach occur. *See Id*. Court will not enforce such a provision, however, if the stipulated amount constitutes a penalty. *See Id*. A penalty is designed to coerce performance by punishing default. *See Id*. In Tennessee, a provision will be considered one for liquidated damages, rather than a penalty, if it is reasonable in relation to the anticipated damages for breach, measured prospectively at the time the contract was entered into, and not grossly disproportionate to the actual damages. *See Beasley*, 864 S.W.2d at 48; *Kimbrough & Co. v. Schmitt*, 939 S.W.2d 105, 108 (Tenn. Ct. App. 1996). When these conditions are met, particularly the first, the parties probably intended the provision to be for liquidated damages. However, any doubt as to the character of the contract provision will be resolved in favor of finding it a penalty.

* * *

DiNardo contends that there is no evidence that the parties contemplated that the potential damage from DiNardo's resignation would go beyond the cost of hiring a replacement coach. . . .

DiNardo's theory of the parties' intent, however, does not square with the record. The contract language establishes that Vanderbilt wanted the five-year contract because "a long-term commitment" by DiNardo was "important to the University's desire for a stable intercollegiate football program," and that this commitment was of "essence" to the contract. Vanderbilt offered the two-year contract extension to DiNardo well over a year before his original contract expired. Both parties understood that the extension was to provide stability to the program, which helped in recruiting players and retaining assistant coaches. Thus, undisputed evidence, and reasonable inferences there-from, establish that both parties understood and agreed that DiNardo's resignation would result in Vanderbilt suffering damage beyond the cost of hiring a replacement coach.

* * *

The stipulated damages clause is reasonable under the circumstances, and we affirm the district court's conclusion that the liquidated damages clause is enforceable under Tennessee law.

* * *

II.

DiNardo next argues that Vanderbilt waived its right to liquidated damages when it granted DiNardo permission to discuss the coaching position with L.S.U. Under Tennessee law, a party may not recover liquidated damages when it is responsible for or has contributed to the delay or nonperformance alleged as the breach. *See V.L. Nicholson Co. v. Transcom Inv. And Fin. Ltd., Inc.*, 595 S.W.2d 474, 484 (Tenn. 1980).

Vanderbilt did not waive its rights under section eight of the contract by giving DiNardo permission to pursue the L.S.U. position. *See Chattem, Inc. v. Provident Life & Accident Ins. Co.*, 676 S.W.2d 953, 955 (Tenn. 1984) (waiver is the intentional, voluntary relinquishment of a known right). First, Hoolahan's permission was quite circumscribed. Hoolahan gave DiNardo permission to talk to L.S.U. about their coaching position; he did not authorize DiNardo to terminate his contract with Vanderbilt. Second, the employment contract required DiNardo to ask Vanderbilt's athletic director for permission to speak with another school about a coaching position, and Hoolahan testified that granting a coach permission to talk to another school about a position was a "professional courtesy." Thus, the parties certainly contemplated that DiNardo could explore other coaching positions, and indeed even leave Vanderbilt, subject to the terms of the liquidated damages provision. *See Park Place Ctr. Enterprises, Inc. v. Park Place Mall Assoc.*, 836 S.W.2d 113, 116 (Tenn. Ct. App. 1992) ("all provisions of a contract should be construed as in harmony with each other, if such construction can be reasonably made . . ."). Allowing DiNardo to talk to another school did not relinquish Vanderbilt's right to liquidated damages.

* * *

III.

DiNardo claims that the Addendum did not become a binding contract, and therefore, he is only liable for the one year remaining on the original contract, not the three years held by the district court.

A.

DiNardo argues that the Addendum did not extend section eight, or that there is at least a question of fact as to whether the Addendum extended section eight.

. . . When the agreement is unambiguous, the meaning is a question of law, and we should enforce the agreement according to its plain terms. *Richland Country Club, Inc. v. CRC Equities, Inc.*, 832 S.W.2d 554, 557 (Tenn. Ct. App. 1991).

DiNardo argues that the original employment contract explicitly provides that section eight is limited to "the entire term of this five-year contract," and the plain, unambiguous language of the Addendum did not extend section eight. He points out that the Addendum did not change the effective date in section eight, unlike other sections in the contract.

The plain and unambiguous language of the Addendum read in its entirety, however, provides for the wholesale extension of the entire contract. Certain sections were expressly amended to change the original contract expiration date of January 5, 1996, to January 5, 1998, because those sections of the original contract contained the precise expiration date of January 5, 1996. The district court did not err in concluding that the contract language extended all terms of the original contract.

B.

DiNardo also claims that the Addendum never became a binding contract because Larry DiNardo never expressly approved its terms. DiNardo contends that, at the very least, a question of fact exists as to whether the two-year Addendum is an enforceable contract.

* * *

Under Tennessee law, parties may accept terms of a contract and make the contract conditional upon some other event or occurrence. *See Disney v. Henry*, 656 S.W.2d 859, 861 (Tenn. Ct. App. 1983). DiNardo argues that the Addendum is not enforceable because it was contingent on Larry DiNardo's approval.

There is evidence from which a jury could find that Larry DiNardo's failure to object did not amount to acceptance of the Addendum. The parties were primarily negotiating the radio and television contract during the fall of 1994. We cannot say that Larry DiNardo's failure to object by December 12, 1994, constituted an acceptance of the Addendum as a matter of law.

* * *

Accordingly, we affirm the district court's judgement that the contract contained an enforceable liquidated damage provision, and we affirm the portion of the judgement reflecting damages calculated under the original five-year contract. We reverse the district court's judgement concluding that the Addendum was enforceable as a matter of law. We remand for a resolution of the factual issues as to whether Larry DiNardo's approval was a condition precedent to the enforceability of the Addendum and, if so, whether the condition was satisfied by Larry DiNardo's failure to object.

We affirm in part, reverse in part, and remand the case to the district court for further proceedings consistent with this opinion.

CASES ON THE SUPPLEMENTAL WEB SITE

Grillier v. CSMG Sports, Ltd., 2009 U.S. Dist. LEXIS 50476. This case involves moving from one employment status to another and how contract language can affect the outcome of a case.

Leach v. Texas Tech University, 335 S.W.3d 386 (TX App. 7th, 2011). This case is interesting since it brings in the concept of sovereign immunity of a state against breach of contract charges.

Mullen v. Parchment School District, 2007 Mich. App. LEXIS 1704 (Mich. Ct. App. 2007). This case examines the impact of Collective Bargaining Agreement on extra duty coaching contracts.

Rodgers v. Georgia Tech Athletic Association, 303 S.E.2d 467 (Ga. Ct. App. 1983). This case examines the true value of college coaching contracts.

QUESTIONS YOU SHOULD BE ABLE TO ANSWER

1. Why is it important to distinguish between an employee and an independent contractor? And what process is used to make that distinction?

2. Why is it important to include language in a contract that defines the terms of termination of that contract?

3. Why is it important to be very specific in an employment contract when defining the terms of reassignment of the signee?

4. Are verbal employment contracts able to survive judicial scrutiny?

5. Despite the existence of a legally binding contract, why are employers unable to force the contracted employee or independent contractor to complete the agreed upon work required in the contract?

REFERENCES

Cases

Aim High Academy v. Jessen, 2008 R.I. Super. LEXIS 152.

Alexander, et al. v. Minnesota Vikings Football Club LLC & National Football League, 649 N.W.2d 464 (2002).

Barnett v. Board of Trustees for State Colleges and Universities A/K/A University of Louisiana System, 806 So. 2d 184; 2001 La. App. LEXIS 1676 (La. App. 1 Cir, 2001).

Cherry v. A-P-A Sports, Inc., 662 P.2d 200 (Colo. App. 1983).

Deli v. University of Minnesota, 511 N.W.2d 46 (Minn. Ct. App. 1994).

Farner v. Idaho Falls School District, 135 Idaho 337; 17 P.3d 281 (2000).

Frazier v. University of the District of Columbia, 742 F. Supp. 28 (D.D.C. 1990).

Grillier v. CSMG Sports, Ltd., 2009 U.S. Dist. LEXIS 50476.

Leach v. Texas Tech University, 335 S.W.3d 386 (TX App. 7th, 2011).

Lindsey v. University of Arizona, 157 Ariz. 48, 754 P.2d 1152 (Ariz. Ct. App. 1987).

MacGinnitie v. Hobbs Group, LLC, 2005 U.S. App. LEXIS 16853; 18 Fla. L. Weekly Fed. C 832 (11th Cir. 2005).

Maddox v. University of Tennessee, 62 F.3d 843 (6th Cir. 1995).

McKenzie v. Wright State University, 683 N.E.2d 381 (Ohio App. 1996).

Meinders v. Dunkerton Community School District, 645 N.W.2d 632 (IA Sup. 2002).

Miami Dolphins Ltd. v. Williams, 356 F. Supp. 2d 1301 (S.D. Fla. 2005).

Monson v. State of Oregon, 901 P.2d 904 (Or. App. 1995).

Nader v. ABC Television, 2005 U.S. App. LEXIS 19536 (2nd Cir. 2005).

New England Patriots Football Club Inc. v. University of Colorado, 592 F.2d 1196 (1st Cir. 1979).

O'Brien v. The Ohio State University, 2007 Ohio 4833 (Ohio App. 10th, 2007).

Rodgers v. Georgia Tech Athletic Association, 303 S.E.2d 467 (Ga. Ct. App. 1983).

Small v. Juniata College, 547 Pa. 731; 689 A.2d 235 (1997).

Smith v. Alanis & Zapata Independent School District, 2002 Tex. App. Lexis 5437 (TX App, 3rd 2002).

Stamps Public Schools v. Colvert, No. CA95–318 (Ark. Ct. App. 1996).

Steinberg Moorad & Dunn, Inc. v. Dunn, 2005 U.S. App. LEXIS 5162 (9th Cir. 2005).

Tolis v. Board of Supervisors of Louisiana State University, 602 S.2d 99 (La. App. 1992).

Vanderbilt University v. DiNardo, 174 F.3d 751 (6th Cir. 1999).

Wadler v. Eastern College Athletic Conference, 2003 U.S. Dist. LEXIS 14212 (S. Dist, N.Y. 2003).

White v. National Football League, 183 L.R.R.M. (BNA) 2796 (D. Minn. 2007).

Yonan v. United States Soccer Federation, Inc., 2011 U.S. Dist. LEXIS 66383.

Publications

Berkowitz, S. & Upton, J. (2011, June 15). Athletic departments see surge financially in down economy. *USA Today*. Retrieved from http://www.usatoday.com

Caughron, R., & Fargher, J. (2004). Independent contractor and employee status: What every employer in sport and recreation should know. *Journal of Legal Aspects of Sport, 14*(1), 47–61.

Clarke, L., Yanda, S. and Prisbell, E. (January 4, 2011). Terrapins welcome in Edsall. *The Washington Post*, D1.

Cozzillio, M., & Levinstein, M. (1997). *Sport law: Cases and materials*. Durham, NC: Carolina Academic Press.

Football Bowl Subdivision coaches' salaries for 2010 (2010, December 9). Retrieved from http://www.usatoday.com/sports/college/football/2010-coaches-contracts-table.htm

Greenberg, M. (2001, Fall). College coaching contracts revisited: A practical perspective. *Marq. Sports L.Rev., 12*, 153–226.

Greenberg, M. (2006, Fall). Symposium: National Sports Law Institute Board of Advisors: Termination of college coaching contracts: When does Adequate cause to terminate exist and who determines its existence? *Marquette Sports Law Review, 17*, 197–257.

Greenberg, M., & Smith, J. (2007, Fall). A study of Division I assistant football and men's basketball coaches' contracts. *Marquette Sport Law Review, 18*, 25–72.

Greenberg, M., & Thomas, R. (2005, April–June). The Rick Neuheisel case—lessons learned from the "washout" in Washington. *For the Record: The Official Newsletter of the National Sports Law Institute, 16*(2), 6–11.

Halcomb Lewis, D. (1998, Winter). After further review, are sports officials independent contractors? *American Business Law Journal, 35*, 249.

Hunt, M. (2003, June 3). Limbo tune doesn't get coaches dancing. *Milwaukee Journal Sentinel*, p. 01C.

Internal Revenue Service. (n.d.). *Internal Revenue Manual, 4600 Employment tax procedures*, Exhibit 4640–1. Washington, DC: Department of the Treasury, Internal Revenue Service.

Lariviere: Bellotti getting $2.3M buyout. (2010, April, 6). ESPN.com. Retrieved from http://sports.espn.go.com/espn/print?id=5061452&type=story

NCAA president receives 2-year extension. (2005, August 5). *The Associated Press*, Sports News.

Rosenthal, J. (1997, March 7). Parcells case a journey through contract law precedent. *New York Law Journal*.

Schultz, J. (2006, January 13). AD exit strips Hewitt of ally. *The Atlanta Journal-Constitution*, p. 1H.

Yasser, R., McCurdy, J., Goplerud, C., & Weston, M. (2000). *Sports law: Cases and materials* (4th ed). Cincinnati, OH: Anderson Publishing Co.

5.22 GAME, EVENT, AND SPONSORSHIP CONTRACTS

John D. McMillen l California State University, Fresno

Planning, implementing, and managing a sport or recreation game or event is a complex task. Today's sport and recreation manager may be required to arrange everything from hiring an event management firm, to leasing the facility, to securing corporate sponsorships. The instruments that bind all these arrangements together are game, event, and sponsorship contracts.

Understanding the essential components of game, event, and sponsorship contracts is important because these agreements often involve large sums of money as well as legally obligate the sport and recreation manager and host organization to the terms of the agreement. This chapter, therefore, is designed to provide a general overview of the primary contractual issues sport and recreation managers need to be familiar with when working with these kinds of agreements. With foresight and planning, game, event, and sponsorship agreements can help ensure that the game/event runs as planned.

FUNDAMENTAL CONCEPTS

All sport contracts are subject to the same principles as any other agreement. Depending on the game, event, or sponsorship agreement, a variety of parties will enter into contracts to form a mutually beneficial relationship. The legal principles associated with these agreements parallel the requirements of performance or service contracts discussed in Chapter 5.10, *Contract Essentials*. Sport contracts, for example, identify the parties; specify the time, place, and manner of performance; list the obligations of the parties; and set forth provisions in case one party cannot carry out its obligation. The primary difference between game, event, and sponsorship contracts and other types of contracts is the bargained-for subject matter and the parties involved. Because the parties may include corporate sponsors, vendors, concessionaires, officials, insurance brokers, mascots, staff, and television or radio networks, just to name a few, the type of agreement desired will dictate the specific terms and content of the contract. The following contracts are the most common types of agreements sport and recreation managers are likely to encounter during their careers.

Sponsorship Contracts

Sport sponsorship is a multibillion-dollar business and has been a prominent marketing tool since the 1984 Olympic Games (IEG, 2006). Today, sport sponsorship can be found at virtually all levels of sport, from Pop Warner to Professional Sports, and all levels in-between.

Sponsorships come in various forms, such as, stadium naming rights which first appeared in 1971 when Schaefer Brewing Company paid the New England Patriots $150,000 to name the Patriots' Stadium Schaefer Field. Since then, naming rights have become a lucrative revenue generating tool (Mayer, 2005). The New York Mets recently signed a $400 million naming rights deal with Citigroup (Business of Sports Network, 2009).

A sponsorship contract, whether it is between a company and an athlete or a company and a sport or recreation event, is a legal document that binds two or more parties to agreed-upon obligations. Logistically, sponsorship contracts are an agreement whereby corporate sponsors provide financial packages or some in-kind product (e.g., uniforms, equipment, soft drinks) to the game/event in exchange for advertising space or a promise to use the product by the host organization in a manner that is beneficial to the sponsor. The exact terms of these agreements are then drafted into a **sponsorship contract**. These contracts vary in their construction from a relatively simple $1,500 signage arrangement found in many minor league baseball leagues and some college football bowl games (Heller & Hechtman, 2000) to a sophisticated Olympic sponsorship agreement valued well into the millions of dollars.

On the surface, sport sponsorship appears like a win-win proposition for both the sport organization and the corporate sponsor. By attaching their names to sports teams, companies reap publicity at relatively low cost. But, as several companies have discovered recently, there is also an element of risk. For example, a BMW sponsored team sailboat was eliminated from the America's Cup qualifying competition in Valencia, Spain—before the main event even started. The cost of the failed Cup bid was reported at nearly $200 million (Ewing, 2007). Also, after Tiger Woods' sex scandal, many of his prominent sponsors dropped out due to the allegations. Not surprisingly, unexpected financial losses and public relations challenges are now drawing more focus in sponsorship agreements and the specific language of these contracts are under heavy scrutiny.

Fundamental clauses of a sponsorship agreement include the length of the agreement, the rights granted to the host organization and sponsor, form of payment, use of any marks or products, and termination of the agreement. Although sport and recreation managers likely will not draft sponsorship contracts, it often is the manager's duty to secure whatever agreements are necessary to make the game/event run as planned. Modern naming right agreements go beyond the name of the stadium and include the naming rights to entryways, the field, or even restrooms (Mayer, 2005). These agreements may be a separate agreement or part of a larger corporate sponsorship agreement (Mayer, 2005).

Endorsement Contracts

Unlike the professional services contract, the **endorsement contract** does not involve an employer-employee relationship. Rather, it is one of contractor-independent contractor. An endorsement contract is one that grants the sponsor the right to use or license the athlete's name, image, or likeness in connection with advertising the sponsor's products or services. In most professional sports, the leagues prohibit individual players from endorsing alcoholic beverages and tobacco products. For example, the NFL recently established a policy that players may not endorse certain nutritional supplements. Leagues, teams, and players must balance these issues and rights with **appearance contracts** which compensate athletes for appearing at a public function, such as a sports camp or celebrity golf tournament.

Professional Service Contracts

Most professional athletes sign what is known as a **standard player contract** (SPK). Whether the athlete is involved in a league with a players association or not, the contract typically offered to all of the athletes are the same, other than the salary and bonus, although there can be addendums to the SPK. In most cases, newly formed leagues model their contracts after the NFL, MLB, NBA or NHL. Some start-up leagues, however, have taken a newer approach to professional services contracts by establishing minimal salaries for the athletes in that sport and rewarding the team and athlete on a per game basis with incentives. For example, in 2012, Major League Soccer's salary cap allowed teams to pay players as little as $45,000. The maximum a team could pay a player, who did not fall under one of the league's exemptions, was $350,000. This is primary reason the league was able to pay the players so little was the fact that the league owned all of the teams and acted as a single entity rather than each team serving as a franchise for the league.

None of the four primary sports leagues, NFL, MLB, NBA or NHL, are run by a single entity. Instead, each team is a franchise and competes for individual players. The competition for the best players is one of the primary reasons for the escalation of player salaries. For example, Alex Rodriguez of the New York Yankees has the largest sport contract in history. His 10 year contract is for $275,000,000 which is an average of $27,500,000 per year, or $169,753.09 per game (ESPN.com, 2007).

Exclusive and Nonexclusive Rights

One of the most important components of sponsorship agreements is the "exclusivity" clause. Many sponsors demand exclusive sponsorship rights within their product or service category. Nike, for example, would not likely sponsor a sport or recreation event if the event already has a sponsorship agreement with Adidas or Reebok. An exclusive sponsorship contract does not mean, however, that competitors will not attempt to advertise their product at or near the event. *Ambush marketing,* sometimes referred to as *parasite marketing,* is a marketing strategy that attempts to dilute an official sponsor's association with a game/event. In other words, a nonpaying sponsor attempts to affiliate its organization with the event even though it has not paid for the rights to do so.

Ambush marketing occurs in a variety of ways. One common instance is when a non-sponsoring company purchases advertising time before or during an official event, allowing the company to associate itself with a sport or recreation event without having to pay any sponsorship fees. In other instances, a non-sponsor company might use a logo, symbol, or words that are similar to the logo of the official game/event sponsor (e.g., buy our pizza while you are watching the "Big Game"). If these images create a "likelihood of confusion," this could violate the Lanham Act (see Chapter 7.22, *Principles of Trademark Law*). There have also been instances where companies bought advertising rights directly outside the venue sponsored by a competitor company (e.g., if Northwest Airlines advertised on a billboard just outside the United Center in Chicago).

Many companies are creative in their ambush marketing strategies and technically may not violate the law. For example, in *National Hockey League, et al. v. Pepsi-Cola Canada Ltd.*, the National Hockey League alleged that although Pepsi did not have any rights to NHL trademarks, it used "confusingly similar" marks in a contest called the "Diet Pepsi $4,000,000 Pro Hockey Playoff Pool," whereby fans matched information under bottle caps with actual NHL playoff results to become eligible for prizes. The Supreme Court of British Columbia ruled that Pepsi used a sufficient disclaimer stating that it was not an official sponsor of the NHL. In essence, the judge stated that because Pepsi sells soft drinks and the NHL's product is hockey, there can be no confusion in the consumers' minds as to which product belongs to which company (Wong, 2002). Cases such as this stress the importance of an airtight sponsorship agreement.

Legal issues may also arise between two official sponsors of the same event. During the 1994 World Cup, for example, both Sprint and MasterCard were official corporate sponsors. MasterCard secured exclusive rights to all debit and credit cards, whereas Sprint negotiated exclusive local and long-distance telephone rights. As a promotion, however, Sprint created phone cards, and MasterCard sued, alleging that Sprint's cards infringed on its exclusive debit card rights. This case was arbitrated and settled by allowing Sprint to give away, not sell, its existing phone cards (see *MasterCard International v. Sprint Communications Co.*, 1994).

Another aspect to consider in sponsorship agreements is what efforts the host organization will take to preserve and protect the sponsor's rights should ambush marketing occur. No sponsorship agreement can prevent ambush marketing from occurring, but the contract can help the host organization and its official sponsors to better understand what steps are going to be taken to minimize its affects (Moorman & Greenwell, 2005).

In addition, if an athlete endorses a sport or recreation event, the contract should incorporate the clauses discussed within the chapter. For example, the contract should take into consideration any possible league rules and policies surrounding the marketing of its athletes. The NHL, for example, does not permit its players to be involved in any endorsement of alcoholic or tobacco products.

Venue Concerns

Security, concessions, personnel, and facility leases are the primary provisions covered in the venue portion of the sponsorship agreement. If the venue already has permanent corporate signage, this may pose special legal concerns. For example, it is not unusual for a new event to be sponsored by a competitor of the venue's current sponsor (e.g., Visa versus MasterCard). Some organizations, therefore, may even request that no signs be present at or around the local vicinity of the venue, a common requirement of the NCAA at its Final Four basketball tournament. In these instances, the signage must either be covered up or the existing sponsorship contracts renegotiated. It also may be helpful for the host organization to seek a "variance of contract," meaning the original agreement is amended to temporarily suspend the agreement for a specific period of time while the new sport or recreation tenant occupies the venue. Managers, therefore, will need to examine all current venue agreements to determine whether there are a certain number of days or events before a competing company legally can have a presence in the venue. Otherwise, the new venue agreement could violate an existing contract. In other words, venue rights could greatly impact which corporations you can solicit to sponsor an upcoming sport or recreation game/event.

The Olympic Games are considered the pinnacle venue of sport sponsorship. Few events enable companies to reach so many people around the world—even though sponsors are not allowed to put their names on advertisements at Olympic venues. Visa, for example, was one of the 12 TOPS sponsors which paid $866m for a four-year association covering the 2006 Turin Winter Games and the 2008 Beijing Summer Games (Economist.com, 2008).

Option to Renew and Right of First Refusal

Options to renew and the right of first refusal are also important clauses in a sponsorship agreement. The **option to extend or renew** gives sponsors the choice to lengthen the current agreement when the contract expires. The **right of first refusal** allows sponsors to make an offer to retain sponsorship rights for future games/events. In practical terms, the right of refusal also allows sponsors to walk away from negotiations with the option to match any competitor's offer. Depending on the length of the original contract, sport and recreation managers can protect themselves from these clauses by a provision that mandates that a specific time frame be designated by which the sponsor must declare its intention to either continue or dissolve the relationship. Eight months to a year should be sufficient time for sport and recreation managers to secure another sponsor should the corporate sponsor discontinue its involvement.

Intellectual Property Rights

Many athletic associations and professional sport leagues, such as the NFL and NBA, have a small number of "primary" sponsors that guarantee the association or league a set amount of money or product and services in exchange for certain sponsorship rights (Wong, 2002). In other words, the company has the right to use the association's or league's logo while promoting its product. These rights are often seen on television commercials with a phrase similar to, "Southwest Airlines, the official airline of the NFL."

In addition, consumers spend millions of dollars on licensed sport and recreation products each year. From these sales, corporations generate a portion of their revenue from the use of team/corporate sponsor logos, known as trademarks (see Chapter 7.22, *Principles of Trademark Law*). Sport and recreation managers, therefore, must be careful to properly secure and protect the trademarks associated with the game/event (see *Marvel Entertainment Group, Inc. v. The Hawaiian Triathlon Corp.*, 1990).

The agreements that legally allow managers to use corporate logos during the game/event are referred to as **licenses,** or a clause might be written directly into the sponsorship agreement: "Sponsor grants a non-exclusive license to use any trademark or other intellectual property rights in connection with providing the management provisions stated herein" (Heller & Hechtman, 2000). All "works for hire" (see Chapter 7.22, *Principles of Trademark Law*) also should be included into the agreement: "As part of the services provided, all original logos, concepts, designs, mechanicals, and layouts for the event shall be deemed 'works made for hire' and the Sponsor shall be considered the 'author' of such works" (Heller & Hechtman, 2000).

Sport and recreation managers should also recognize that all promotional materials must be examined to determine whether it abides by the appropriate intellectual property laws. Signage, T-shirts, pamphlets, logos, Websites, and other game/event promotional materials cannot infringe on the rights of the trademark, copyright, or patent owner. To avoid excessive delays in the approval process, sport and recreation managers should specify an appropriate turnaround time to view these materials. It is also important to negotiate how long the materials or logos can be used after the game/event has concluded. It may be both a contract and trademark violation to display logos after the time period specified in the contract. For example, if the Orange Bowl requires that FedEx terminate all uses of its Orange Bowl logos on its trucks within 30 days after the bowl game, failure to do so would not only breach the contract but would also violate the Orange Bowl's intellectual property rights.

Finally, managers must be cognizant of potential geographic rights. International sponsors, for example, may seek authority to use trademarks in some or all countries participating in the event, whereas national sponsors in all likelihood will only be interested in using the marks in the host country. These kinds of clauses are popular in larger venues like World Cup Soccer and the Olympic Games. However, the Internet has added a new twist on geographic rights. Because the Internet has no boundaries, all games or events potentially could have national or international appeal. Therefore, the host organization may want to incorporate specific language to protect these territorial rights. One possible solution is to limit the trademark's use to a certain language on the Web page (e.g., English or Spanish) or per event/sport.

Fees and Expenses

Equally important as the actual services to be performed in the sponsorship agreement is the payment of fees and expenses. Management fees for sport and recreation events can run into the hundreds of thousands of dollars depending on the nature and length of the event. Understandably, event management firms seek fair compensation and timely reimbursement for expenses in the agreement, whereas the corporate sponsor is most concerned that the fees correspond to the nature of the services provided. In general, sponsorship agreements must state the specific amount of money or in-kind goods or services and reimbursement of expenses that are to be performed by all parties. Payment schedules and delivery of services should also be expressly defined to avoid any confusion.

In addition, many events now require sponsors to guarantee a certain amount of services and money to market the event. Other possible areas to negotiate include privileges associated with the sponsorship of the game/event, such as tickets, signage, hospitality, and travel. For smaller events, these items often are included as a benefit, but any of these stipulations should be incorporated into the sponsorship agreement to avoid any future misunderstandings.

Media Issues

Depending on the size and commercial draw of the game/event, sport and recreation managers may have to deal with a variety of media contracts, such as cable, satellite, television, radio, and the Internet. Most television contracts include exclusivity and territorial stipulations that then can be licensed to smaller markets or different stations. NBC, for example, obtained the exclusive rights for the 2002 Winter Olympic Games, but then licensed these rights for limited use to the cable network TNT, allowing it to broadcast Olympic coverage that was limited to specific days and certain hours. Whatever the median of technology used, these types of clauses are certain to become even more common with the increasing international demand for U.S. sporting events.

Other Considerations

It is important that host organization clarify in the agreement all the services it will perform. At the same time, managers should seek an agreement whereby the sponsor acknowledges that the nature of the event may make it impossible to list all the services to be rendered. In other words, managers need authority to go beyond the scope of services outlined within the agreement when necessary to successfully perform the duties associated with the event. To protect managers who are required to perform duties or services outside the written agreement, a provision should be included that allows an adjustment in management fees.

Managers also should keep in mind that some sponsors may demand an **approval clause** for other cosponsors. For example, Pepsi may not want to sponsor an event with McDonalds because of its affiliation with Coca-Cola.

Term and **cancellation** clauses are important in case the game/event is cancelled. These clauses not only allow corporate sponsors and sport and recreation managers the ability to commit to the event, but also ensure flexibility if the event is cancelled. The recent assault of hurricanes along the Gulf and Florida coasts are prime examples of why these clauses are necessary. Overall terms of the agreement can be as short as a few weeks or as long as several years, and cancellation provision may be "at-will," which requires no prior notice, or it can require that certain conditions be met before cancellation.

State law governs the **jurisdiction** of the sponsorship contract. Consequently, a contract's effect may vary depending on the laws of a particular state. Therefore, to avoid possible jurisdiction problems, the agreement should specify the state law to be applied should a dispute arise. For example, if the host organization is in Ohio and the corporate sponsor principally is located in California, the contract might state that "Ohio law will govern this agreement."

Confidentiality may be an important component of sponsorship agreements, particularly if one party provides the other with access to proprietary information such as marketing plans, financial information, client lists, and sales information (Heller & Hechtman, 2000). Also, like all other contracts, sponsorship contracts should define any specific conditions that will be considered a breach of contract as well as specify the amount of **damages**, known as "liquidated damages," should a breach occur. All liquidated damages, however, must be reasonable and based on the actual damage or loss incurred by the nonbreaching party. Otherwise, a court may refuse to enforce excessive liquidated damages. Finally, parties may wish to consider **indemnification** provisions. For example, "Sponsor will indemnify and hold harmless Event Management Firm and its shareholders, affiliates, officers, directors, and employees from and against all claims, expenses, suits, and judgments arising from or connected with a breach of this agreement by the Sponsor, any negligent or intentional acts of the Sponsor in connection with the event, or any violation of the intellectual property rights of a third party associated with the use of the Sponsor's trademarks" (Heller & Hechtman, 2000).

Due to increased work stoppages in professional sports, a growing trend is to include a "force majeure" or **work stoppage provision** into the sponsorship contract (Wong, 2002). Although typically associated with facility or event contracts, these clauses are becoming more common in sponsorship agreements and protect against unforeseeable natural or human events that are beyond the control of the parties of the contract and render the contract impossible (Wong, 2002). This provision may protect one or both parties in the event of a work stoppage from things such as a strike or a lockout, such as the 2004-05 National Hockey League work stoppage.

Another trend is to designate **alternative dispute resolution** provisions within contracts to protect the organization in case of a disagreement regarding the terms of the agreement. Because litigation is expensive, arbitration is the preferred method of resolution, as it provides a speedy and relatively inexpensive means to resolve disputes. If possible, the chosen law should be that of the organization's home state because of convenience and knowledge of the applicable law (see Chapter 6.30, *Alternative Dispute Resolution*).

Game and Event Contracts

Game contracts are agreements designed to facilitate a game/contest between two organizations. Because of these agreements' potential impact on present and future game schedules, these contracts should be prepared with care and under the advisement of legal counsel. In general, both game and event contracts will contain many of the same provisions as sponsorship agreements. For example, sport and recreation managers will need to consider intellectual property rights, as well as the location, date, and time of the game, provisions for officials, governing rules, potential television and radio rights, lease agreements, complimentary or paid tickets, travel expenses and other related costs, and any potential termination and breach procedures.

Event contracts are similar to game contracts in design and concept. The term *event*, however, has a dual meaning. It can signify a single sport/recreation event (e.g., the Super Bowl) or a combination of events (e.g., the NCAA basketball tournament). Event contracts are also synonymous with pre- and postevent activities. In other words, event contracts may not only refer to a game contract, but also to individual or combined agreements for the entire operation of an event from the facility lease, concessions, marketing, and corporate sponsorships, to potential radio or television rights. Like game contracts, event contracts should be prepared with care and include the essential components of game contracts, as well as any other clauses specific to the event's operations.

Lease Agreements

To increase revenues, many organizations now lease facilities to third parties for rental fees. The facility lease may directly influence the success and ease in which a game/event operates (see *Houston Oilers v. Harris County Texas, et al.*, 1997). Whereas a facility lease agreement may be as simple or complex as the parties desire, under the Statute of Frauds (see Chapter 6.10, *Contract Essentials*), all leases must be in writing. In addition to routine elements of time, keys, and opening and closing schedules (Clement, 1998), sport and recreation managers should consider using escape clauses, options to renew, assignment rights, maintenance, restrictive covenants, exit clauses, parking, concessions, merchandise revenue, insurance, and indemnification clauses, as well as sponsorship and signage stipulations in the lease portion of the agreement (Miller, 1997).

Personnel

A variety of employees are needed to run a sport or recreation game/event. Hiring and retaining quality professional employees, therefore, is central to all sport and recreation venues. Sport and recreation managers must be cognizant of how to limit liability regarding personnel issues. Managers, for example, often hire officials, police and/or crowd-control personnel, concessionaires, and emergency personnel. Each of these arrangements can be negotiated for a single game/event or an entire season. Because of the potential liability associated with the type of employment relationship between the host organization and the event personnel (e.g., volunteers, interns, at-will employees, and independent contractors), sport and recreation managers should carefully construct the written agreement to clarify the employment relationship (see Chapter 5.21, *Employment Contracts*). For example, an at-will employment relationship easily can be defined by the event contract: "The parties shall be and act as independent contractors and under no circumstances will this agreement or the relationship between the parties be construed to be an agency, partnership, joint venture, or employment agreement" (Heller & Hechtman, 2000). Furthermore, managers should be aware that some personnel may ask to be a "secured" party, meaning that they will be paid first should the event become bankrupt. Typically, secured employees seek 25 percent up front, 50 percent with satisfactory progress, and the remaining 25 percent on the completion of the work (Irwin, Sutton, & McCarthy, 2002).

Drafting Sport and Recreation Contracts

Professional services contracts have numerous common clauses. For example, according to the standard player's contract of the NFLPA, MLBPA NBPA, and NHLPA, all contract provisions already have been established, except for salary and bonuses. Additionally, the players associations have group licensing arrangements in which players are compensated by licensing their names and likenesses in group package deals to trading card companies and video games. Lawyers who draft these contracts try to anticipate every possible scenario. Though most contracts begin as a beneficial relationship between the parties, over time those relationships can quickly change. Therefore, any contract drafter must use the utmost care to ensure that policies and procedures address situations and legal issues that might arise should something go awry.

SIGNIFICANT CASE

TYR and Speedo both design and manufacture high-end swimwear and accessories sold to competitive swimmers. USA Swimming is the national governing body of the sport of swimming in the United States. Speedo also has a sponsorship agreement directly with USA Swimming, and has been the exclusive swimwear equipment sponsor of USA Swimming. TYR contends that Schubert, wielding extraordinary influence in the swimming community as the Olympic and National Team head coach, made false statements in promoting Speedo's products and disparaging TYR's. This case illustrates how even the smallest conflict quickly can turn into a lawsuit and is an example of why a qualified attorney should draft contracts to ensure that all parties and their rights are protected.

TYR SPORT, INC., V. WARNACO SWIMWEAR, INC., ET AL.

United States District Court for the Central District of California
2010 U.S. Dist. LEXIS 27566 (2010)

Background

TYR and Speedo both design and manufacture high-end swimwear and accessories sold to competitive swimmers. USA Swimming is the national governing body ("NGB") of the sport of swimming in the United States, per the Ted Stevens Amateur Sports Act ("Sports Act"), 36 U.S.C. § 220522. In 2006, USA Swimming hired Schubert to be the National and Olympic Team head coach and general manager, though Schubert was and remained a paid spokesperson for Speedo. Speedo also has a sponsorship agreement directly with USA Swimming, and has

been the exclusive swimwear equipment sponsor of USA Swimming since 1984.

TYR alleges that Speedo, USA Swimming, and Schubert formed a combination to make USA Swimming a de facto sales agent for Speedo. Specifically, TYR contends that Schubert, wielding extraordinary influence in the swimming community as the Olympic and National Team head coach, made false statements in promoting Speedo's products and disparaging TYR's.

Much of the controversy centers on the run-up to the 2008 Olympic Games in Beijing. At the time, high-end swimsuit manufacturers were engaged in something of an arms race. Each was attempting to market suits that could significantly reduce the swimming times of elite swimmers. On February 12, 2008, Speedo released its newest suit, the LZR Racer, an upgrade from its previous suit, the Fast Skin Pro ("FS Pro"). TYR, one of Speedo's primary competitors in the American market, was working to develop its own elite racing suit, the Tracer Rise, in time for the run-up to the Beijing Games.

Schubert, a paid spokesman for Speedo and the head coach and general manager of the Olympic and National Swim Teams, touted the advantages of the just-released LZR Racer. Just prior to a swim meet in Manchester, England, Schubert gathered the swimmers on the National Team and encouraged them to wear the LZR Racer, stating that it offered a "2% advantage." Schubert was also quoted in a newspaper and magazine article by a reporter covering the meet that, "[i]f you take [the] best times of world record holders and their new times [in the LZR Racer], the difference is 2 per cent." Schubert was also allegedly quoted as saying that he "would strongly advise [the swimmers] to wear the [Speedo] suit at trials, or they may end up at home watching [the Olympics] on NBC."

Erik Vendt ("Vendt"), an American swimmer who signed an endorsement deal with TYR in 2006, got caught up in the arms race. In late 2007, as he was training to make the U.S. Olympic Team and potentially win a medal in Beijing, Vendt was dissatisfied with the suit TYR had provided. In fall 2007, he made several calls to Schubert, his coach on the National Team and previously at the University of Southern California, to complain about his TYR suit. Schubert recalls telling Vendt to talk to his agent and TYR about his concerns.

In December 2007, Vendt and his agent met with TYR. TYR invited him to test the yet-to-be-released Tracer Rise. He was apparently very happy with it. (Id.) However, two weeks later, he informed TYR that he planned to wear the Speedo FS Pro at a January 2008 meet in Long Beach, California. TYR responded by promptly canceling Vendt's endorsement deal.

By the time of the U.S. Olympic Trials, only one of the TYR-sponsored swimmers present at the Manchester meet, Katie Carroll ("Carroll"), had switched from wearing a TYR suit to Speedo. Several swimmers wore a TYR suit at the Trials and qualified for the Olympic Team. In particular, Matt Grevers won two gold medals, a silver medal, and set a world record in Beijing while wearing the Tracer Rise. Meanwhile, the Speedo-wearing swimmers experienced unparalleled success at the Olympics. All told, 86% of the swimming medals in Beijing, including 91% of the gold medals, were won by swimmers wearing the LZR Racer.

The arms race continued after the Olympics, with other competitors—including Arena, Jaked, and Blue 70—gaining ground on, and sometimes overtaking, the performance of the suits designed by Speedo and TYR. However, Schubert continued his promotion of the Speedo brand, at one point

advising two swimmers on the Junior National Team to wear the LZR Racer because it was "faster" than the TYR and Blue 70 suits they were wearing at the time.

However, everything came to an end in July 2009, when FINA, the sport's international governing body, decided to ban from competitions the high-performance full-body suits, including the LZR Racer and the Tracer Rise, starting on January 1, 2010. USA Swimming, meanwhile, decided to move the deadline for banning the full-body suits in its own competitions up to October 1, 2009. This effectively ended the market for the high-performance swimsuits.

Discussion

The Court considers two summary judgment motions, one brought by Speedo, the other by USA Swimming and Schubert. Because of significant overlap between the motions, the Court treats them here together. The Court considers the challenged claims in turn.

The Defendants contend that TYR's Sherman Act § 1 and Cartwright Act claims fail because they lack evidence of an illegal agreement. Relying on *Monsanto Co. v. Spray-Rite Service Corp.*, 465 U.S. 752, 104 S. Ct. 1464, 79 L. Ed. 2d 775 (1984) and Matsushita, the Defendants argue TYR fails to raise a triable issue of fact as to whether the various agreements between Speedo, USA Swimming, and Schubert are illegal, because those agreements are entirely consistent with legal sponsorship agreements.

The Defendants misapply the holdings of Monsanto and Matsushita. These cases stand for the proposition that, in an antitrust conspiracy case, one cannot reasonably infer a combination or conspiracy solely from conduct that is consistent with independent action, without additional evidence of an actual agreement. See Matsushita, 475 U.S. at 588; Monsanto, 465 U.S. at 763–64. Here, in contrast, there is unquestionably evidence of an agreement between the parties. TYR need not rely on an inference from circumstantial evidence consistent with independent competition.

Finally, the Defendants argue that they are entitled to summary judgment because TYR cannot show a genuine issue of fact as to the relevant geographic market. TYR alleges a market for "high-end competitive swimwear and accessories" in the geographic market of "the entire United States and its territories."

***

The relevant geographic market is the "area of effective competition . . . where buyers can turn for alternate sources of supply." *Morgan, Strand, Wheeler & Biggs v. Radiology, Ltd.*, 924 F.2d 1484, 1490 (9th Cir. 1991) (citation and quotation marks omitted). It can be demonstrated by the existence of certain barriers to entry, or insulation from a larger geographic market, such that supply and demand are inelastic with the larger market. Id. The boundaries of a market can also be shown by "such practical indicia as industry or public recognition of the submarket as a separate economic entity, the product's peculiar characteristics and uses, unique production facilities, distinct customers, distinct prices, sensitivity to price changes, and specialized vendors." *Image Tech. Servs., Inc. v. Eastman Kodak Co.*, 125 F.3d 1195, 1204 (9th Cir. 1997) (quoting *Brown Shoe Co. v. United States*, 370 U.S. 294, 325, 82 S. Ct. 1502, 8 L. Ed. 2d 510 (1962)). Market definition is generally a factual determination left to the jury. *Forsyth v. Humana, Inc.*, 114 F.3d 1467, 1476 (9th Cir. 1997).

TYR has sufficient evidence of the United States as a separate geographic market to overcome summary judgment on the issue. Internal emails and memos at both Speedo and USA Swimming indicate that they consider the United States market as distinct from the international market. (TYR Exs. 37–39.) Steve Furniss ("Furniss"), the Executive Vice President of TYR and who has worked for 34 years in the performance swimwear industry, testified as to numerous barriers to competition: (1) the ability to provide local technical support; (2) on-the-ground customer service networks able to quickly respond to the needs of elite swim teams; (3) relationships with athletes, coaches, and swim directors; (4) cultural differences in suit preferences; (5) differences in the physiology of swimmers from country to country; (6) differences in sizing and labeling requirements; (7) differences in local regulations regarding consumer protections, packaging, and the environment; and (8) differences in currency and pricing.

Accordingly, the Court finds that the Defendants are entitled to summary adjudication on the issue of antitrust coercion, but not on TYR's antitrust theory of antitrust disparagement.

***

TYR's tortious interference with contractual relations claim is predicated on the termination of the endorsement deal between TYR and swimmer Erik Vendt. During his endorsement deal with TYR, Vendt decided to wear a Speedo suit at a swim meet. TYR canceled his endorsement deal in response.

The elements of a tortious interference with contractual relations claim are "(1) a valid contract between plaintiff and a third party; (2) defendant's knowledge of this contract; (3) defendant's intentional acts designed to induce a breach or disruption of the contractual relationship; (4) actual breach or disruption of the contractual relationship; and (5) resulting damage." *Pacific Gas & Elec. Co. v. Bear Stearns & Co.*, 50 Cal.3d 1118, 1126, 270 Cal. Rptr. 1, 791 P.2d 587 (1990).

The Defendants contend that they cannot be liable because (1) TYR, not Vendt, breached the contract, and (2) TYR has not demonstrated an intentional act on the part of any of the Defendants "designed to induce a breach or disruption." The Court need not reach the breach of contract issue, because TYR does not have sufficient evidence to create a triable issue of fact as to whether any of the Defendants intentionally induced Vendt to breach or disrupt his relationship with TYR.

TYR admits that it does not have direct evidence that the Defendants induced Vendt to breach. However, it points to circumstantial evidence that it claims raises a triable issue of fact as to whether Schubert and Stu Isaac ("Isaac"), a Speedo-sponsored swim coach, induced Vendt to terminate his contract with TYR.

Schubert testified that Vendt called him several times in the fall of 2007 to complain about his TYR suits. He also testified that he told Vendt to talk to his agent and communicate his dissatisfaction directly to TYR. Vendt, however, stated in an interrogatory response that he never discussed his TYR suits with Schubert. When pressed at a deposition, he stated that he did not recall discussing TYR suits with Schubert in 2007, but that he may have around March 2008.

TYR contends that a reasonable jury could find that during the calls in fall 2007, Schubert urged Vendt to end his relationship with TYR based on the following facts: (1) Vendt's evasiveness during discovery regarding the calls; (2) Schubert's public comments urging swimmers to use the LZR Racer; (3) that Schubert used money from his discretionary account to pay Vendt after TYR canceled the contract; (4) Schubert's failed negotiations with TYR for an endorsement deal in 2004; and (5) the fact that Vendt claimed to have secured an endorsement deal with Speedo after TYR canceled his deal.

This circumstantial evidence is insufficient to create a triable issue of fact. First, it is undisputed that Vendt initiated the calls to Schubert, not vice versa. This is, of course, not dispositive, but certainly weighs heavily against the notion that Schubert acted to intentionally induce Vendt to switch vendors.

Second, Schubert's public promotion of Speedo products does not establish that he ever urged a swimmer to breach an endorsement deal. It would be unreasonable to infer that Schubert privately urged Vendt to withhold performance of the endorsement deal from his public comments promoting Speedo.

Finally, the remaining evidence is too tenuous to establish a genuine issue of fact. The Court fails to see how Vendt's evasiveness establishes Schubert's intentional tortious conduct, especially given that Schubert himself appears to have been entirely forthcoming about the calls. The actions taken by Schubert and Speedo after the Vendt lost his TYR deal shed little light on their actions before. And Schubert's alleged motive to injure TYR because of the failure to secure a TYR endorsement deal in 2004 is far too tenuous to provide any significant probative value.

TYR also points to a meeting Vendt allegedly had with Isaac, his Speedo-sponsored coach at Club Wolverine. Vendt testified that he had visited Isaac's home several times, but only when Isaac was not there—Vendt's girlfriend at the time was good friends with Isaac's wife. TYR contends that this is inconsistent with Isaac's testimony that Vendt and his girlfriend once came over to cook a turkey for Thanksgiving. However, Isaac's testimony does not, in fact, establish that he was there or met with Vendt at that time. In any case, nothing indicates that swimsuits were ever discussed.

To overcome summary judgment, TYR needs to show more than a scintilla of evidence. But that is all they have here; disconnected bits of circumstantial evidence. Even if those bits are summed, no reasonable jury could find by a preponderance of the evidence that Schubert or Isaac intentionally induced Vendt to breach his contractual relationship with TYR. Therefore, the defendants are entitled to summary judgment on TYR's Sixth claim.

***

Conclusion

For the foregoing reasons, the motions for summary judgment are GRANTED in part and DENIED in part. Speedo is entitled to summary judgment with respect to TYR's Fourth and Sixth Claims, and USA Swimming

and Schubert are entitled to summary judgment on TYR's Sixth Claim. Speedo, USA Swimming and Schubert are entitled to summary adjudication on the remaining claims to the extent they rely on a coercion theory of antitrust liability.

As noted above, the Court concludes that the Defendants failed to carry their initial Celotex burden with respect to TYR's theory of antitrust liability for disparagement. However, the case law imposes a high burden before speech in the marketplace becomes actionable antitrust conduct. Such statements "must have a significant and enduring adverse impact on competition itself in the relevant markets to rise to the level of an antitrust violation." Harcourt Brace, 108 F.3d at 1152. In fact, the Ninth Circuit "insist[s] on a preliminary showing of significant and more-than-temporary harmful effects on competition (and not merely upon a competitor or customer)."

The Court believes that the issue of the requisite preliminary showing should be tested before the matter proceeds to trial.

It is so ordered.

CASES ON THE SUPPLEMENTAL WEB SITE

Anderson v. Gulf Stream Coach, Inc., (2011 U.S. App. LEXIS 22163). This case explores the various remedies available to breach of contract cases.

AT&T v. NASCAR, (2007 U.S. App. LEXIS 19182). This case illustrates how even the smallest conflict quickly can turn into a lawsuit and is an example of why a qualified attorney should draft contracts to ensure that all parties and their rights are protected.

Harmon and Castillo v. Gordon, (2011 U.S. Dist. LEXIS 7848). Study carefully how courts interpret and decide breach of contract claims.

Huverserian v. Catalina Scuba LUV, Inc., (2010 Cal. App. LEXIS 750). This case demonstrates why using competent legal counsel is essential to drafting sport and recreation contract language.

Race Tires America, Inc. v. Hoosier Racing Tire Corp; Direct Motor Sports, Inc., (2010 U.S. App. LEXIS 15233). Read this case to better understand how exclusive contract agreements are useful.

QUESTIONS YOU SHOULD BE ABLE TO ANSWER

1. What is the primary difference between game, event, and sponsorship contracts?

2. Explain the fundamental clauses of a typical sponsorship agreement.

3. What is the name of the agreements that legally allow managers to use corporate logos during a sport or recreation game or event?

4. What clause allows sponsors the choice to lengthen the current agreement when the contract expires?

5. What clause do sponsors often demand to prevent competitors from sponsoring the same event?

REFERENCES

Cases

Houston Oilers v. Harris County Texas, et al., 960 F. Supp 1202 (S.D. Texas 1997).

Marvel Entertainment Group, Inc. v. The Hawaiian Triathlon Corp., 132 F.R.D. 143 (S.D. N.Y 1990).

MasterCard International v. Sprint Communications Co., 23 F.3d 397 (2d. Cir. 1994).

National Football League Properties v. Dallas Cowboys Football Club, 922 F. Supp. 849 (S.D.N.Y. 1996).

National Hockey League, et al. v. Pepsi-Cola Canada Ltd., 42 C.P.R.3d 390 (B.C. 1992).

Publications

Business of Sports Network (2009), *Sports sponsorship meets the recession,* available at: http://www. businessofsportsnetwork.com/index.php?option=com_content&view=article&id=14:hot-button-sports-banking-and-sponsorships-meet-the-recession

Clement, A. (1998). *Law in sport and physical activity* (2nd ed.). Aurora, OH: Sport and Law Press, Inc.

Economist.com (2008), *Sponsorship form: The value of sport to other businesses,* available at: http://www.economist.com/specialreports/displaystory.cfm?story_id=11825607

Ewing, J. (2007). *Sports Sponsorship: A risky game companies love lending their names to winning teams. But what if a team loses, or worse, finds itself embroiled in scandal?* Business Week, available at: http://www.businessweek.com/globalbiz/content/jun2007/gb20070607_140258.htm

ESPN.com (2007). *Rodriguez finalizes $275M deal with Yankees.* ESPN.com, available at: http://sports.espn.go.com/mlb/news/story?id=3153171

Graham, S., Goldblatt, J., & Delpy, L. (1995). *The ultimate guide to sport event management and marketing.* Chicago: Richard D. Irwin.

Heller, J. G., & Hechtman, J. A. (2000). Corporate sponsorships of sports and entertainment events: Considerations in drafting a sponsorship management agreement. *Marq. Sports L. Rev., 11,* 23.

IEG (2006, December 26). IEG sponsorship report. Retrieved March 31, 2007, from http://www.sponsorship.com/iegsr

Irwin, R. L., Sutton W. A., & McCarthy, L. M. (2002). *Sport promotion and sales management.* Champaign, IL: Human Kinetics.

Masteralexis, L. P., Barr, C. A., & Hums, M. A. (1998). *Principles and practice of sport management.* Gaithersburg, MD: Aspen Publishing.

Mayer, F. A. (2005). Stadium financing: Where we are, how we got here, and where we are going. *Vill. Sports & Ent. L. Forum, 12,* 195.

Miller, L. K. (1997). *Sport business management.* Gaithersburg, MD: Aspen Publishing.

Moorman, A. M., & Greenwell, T. C. (2005). Consumer attitudes of deception and the legality of ambush marketing practices. *J. Legal Aspects of Sport, 15,* 183.

Sponsorship Marketing Global 2004, Last viewed June 3, 2009, available at: http://www.sponsorclick.com/docs/en/smg04_highlights.pdf.

Wong, G. M. (2002). *Essentials of amateur sports law* (3rd. ed.). Westport, CT: Greenwood Publishing Group.

5.30 ALTERNATIVE DISPUTE RESOLUTION
ARBITRATION, NEGOTIATION, AND MEDIATION
Rebecca J. Mowrey | Millersville University of Pennsylvania

Imagine; you are competing for a position on the USA Track & Field Olympic Team. This is your dream; your goal; your obsession. For over ten years you and your family and friends have made significant sacrifices and commitments enabling you to get to this elite level of athletic preparation and competition. Then, following a preliminary heat of your event you are notified that due to an eligibility rule violation you have been disqualified from further participation in the meet. With this one statement from a United States Olympic Committee (USOC) official, your dream, and all that you have worked so hard and so long to accomplish, has been crushed.

When you learn more about the alleged violation, you are absolutely certain that there has been a mistake. During the past twelve hours you and your coaches have already appealed the decision through all the USA Track & Field Association options available to you, and in each decision your appeal has been denied by Association officials. With your next preliminary heat scheduled to begin in fewer than six hours, you now turn your appeal efforts toward a group (**panel**) of neutral decision-makers (**arbitrators**) who are knowledgeable about track & field, as well as the USOC and USA Track & Field Association rules and procedures. This is the last level of appeal available to you. The panel has the full authority to listen to all parties, evaluate all evidence presented, and then make a final and in most cases **binding** (not open to further appeal or reversal) decision regarding your eligibility to continue to participate in the USA Olympic Team Trials in Track & Field. You may write the outcome of this imaginary story for yourself; however, it illustrates several of the unique elements of **arbitration,** and why the International Olympic Committee (IOC) and many International Sports Federations and National Governing Bodies representing a myriad of sport and recreation industries, support the use of arbitrators to address the complex disputes that arise during domestic and international events.

With the popularity of televised courtroom dramas such as *Law and Order* you might think of litigation as the only road to resolving legal disputes. In reality, litigation is just one, albeit the most popular, of several avenues that individuals or groups may pursue for legal remedy. However, litigation is not always an appropriate means for resolving a dispute. **Alternative dispute resolution** (ADR) is a blanket term that includes negotiation, mediation, and arbitration, among other options, as alternatives to adjudication of disputes, with mediation and arbitration being the most commonly used of the three (**www.law.cornell.edu/adr.html**). The use of ADR can be voluntarily pursued by the disputing parties or mandated by a contract or waiver (see also Chapter 2.23, *Waivers and Releases*). Recreation and sport managers interested in personnel-related cases and disputes would be well served to develop a working knowledge of all ADR procedures, language, and the benefits of each specific process. It is important to recognize issues and situations where ADR approaches will be more appropriate than the traditional litigation process.

FUNDAMENTAL CONCEPTS

Court adjudication can be a costly and lengthy process. In recognition of this fact, the federal government established the **Administrative Dispute Resolution Act of 1990**, 5 U.S.C.A. 581, which requires all federal agencies to establish policies for the voluntary use of ADR as a "prompt, expert and inexpensive means of resolving disputes as an alternative to litigation in federal courts."

ADR Basics

Generally Assumed *ADR Benefits v. Litigation*

- Reduced costs (i.e., no attorney fees, limited discovery)
- Usually signi`ficantly faster/less time in dispute (i.e., limited pretrial discovery, overscheduled courts)
- "Expert's" decision can be rendered instead of a non-expert jury or judge. ADR panelists frequently specialize in the types of disputes they hear/decide.
- Greater flexibility and creative solutions instead of win/lose.
- Proceedings and outcome can be kept confidential
- ADR is considered to be the best option when there is a desire to maintain or reestablish the relationships in conflict. This could be critical to schools, offices, teams, or organizations.
- Increased satisfaction with the outcome and process

Generally Assumed *ADR Limitations v. Litigation*

- Legal precedent, if desired, is not established through ADR
- Absence of procedural safeguards if an arbitrator makes an error of law or fact
- Limited opportunity for appeal (in most cases appeals are only granted for arbitrator bias, fraud, or decisions rendered which exceed the arbitrator's authority)
- Enforcement of decisions is voluntary unless bound by contract (i.e., CBA)

Arbitration

Arbitration is the most formal of the ADR approaches discussed in this chapter, yet it is much less rigid than traditional litigation. Arbitration differs from negotiation and mediation significantly, as the arbitrator is not concerned with reaching a decision that is agreeable to the disputing parties. In this process a dispute is submitted to a neutral third party or arbitrator who listens to the disputants and considers the submitted evidence and then makes a decision or award.

The **Federal Arbitration Act of 1925,** 9 U.S.C. Section 1 (FAA) established federal law supporting arbitration as an alternative to litigation. The American Bar Association (ABA), the Uniform Law Commissioners (ULC), and the American Arbitration Association (AAA) approved the **Uniform Arbitration Act of 1955** (UAA) to establish procedure and policy standards for arbitration.

Since Congress's passage of the FAA and approval of the UAA, the number and complexity of arbitration cases has grown dramatically. In many of these cases, the FAA and the UAA failed to provide direction regarding substantive issues, and the need to update and modernize these Acts was evident. Specifically, consensus was reached by active arbitrators that revisions were needed to address the following points: (1) the need to modernize outdated provisions, clarify ambiguities under the Act, and codify important case-law developments; (2) the need to give primary consideration to the autonomy of contracting parties, provided their arbitration agreement conforms to basic notions of fundamental fairness because arbitration is a consensual process; (3) the need to maintain the essential character of arbitration as a means of dispute resolution distinct from litigation, particularly in regard to efficiency, timeliness and cost; and (4) because most parties intend arbitral decisions to be final and binding, the need to limit court involvement in the arbitration process unless unfairness or denial of justice produces clear need for such involvement." (www.nccusl.org). To address these concerns, the Revised Uniform Arbitration Act (RUAA) was approved in 2000 by the ULC, the ABA, and the AAA. The RUAA added significant procedural provisions absent from the UAA, including the use of electronic records and documents which was not a consideration in 1955 (www.aaa.org).

It might help you to think of the arbitration process as a simplified trial with limited discovery and relaxed rules regarding evidence (**www.adr.org**). Although organizations may attach unique elements to their **arbitration clause**, most proceedings contain the following five elements.

1. **Demand for arbitration.** A written demand for arbitration identifying the parties, the dispute, and the relief or remedy sought must be submitted to the opposing party. The arbitration request is less formal than writing a complaint in a civil action, but the issues to be arbitrated must be clear.
2. **Response.** The opposing party typically responds in writing, stating whether they agree that the issue is subject to arbitration under the existing contract or other relevant documents.

3. **Selection of arbitration panel.** A single arbitrator or panel with sufficient knowledge of the subject matter is selected. This process might be described in the arbitration clause of a contract or a permanent arbitrator might be designated.
4. **Arbitration hearing.** Although similar to a trial in some respects, namely, the presentation of witnesses, documents, briefs, memoranda, and closing arguments, the process differs from a trial in that written transcripts are only provided if the parties order them, the evidentiary rules are relaxed, and the extent of discovery and cross-examination are often limited (UAA of 1955).
5. **Decision.** After hearing from all parties the arbitrator renders a decision (**www.adr.org**).

The decision of an arbitrator may be disputed and, under the RUAA, be vacated if: (1) the award was procured by corruption, fraud, or undue means; (2) there was evidence of partiality or corruption in the arbitrators; (3) the arbitrators were guilty of misconduct in refusing to postpone the hearing, on sufficient cause shown, or in refusing to hear evidence pertinent and material to the controversy; or of any other misbehavior by which the rights of any party have been prejudiced; or (4) the arbitrators exceeded their powers, or so imperfectly executed them that a mutual, final, and definite award on the subject matter submitted was not made (9 U.S.C. § 11).

The use of arbitration may be mandated in some contracts but be completely voluntary in others. In **voluntary arbitration** situations, the arbitration is mutually agreeable to both parties and may be **binding** or **nonbinding**, as determined in advance by the involved parties or the arbitration agreement. In **mandatory arbitration** situations, the disputing parties are often required to utilize arbitration as their sole method of addressing unresolved grievances according to the arbitration clause of their employment contracts (see Chapter 5.21, *Employment Contracts*), and in these cases the decision is typically binding (**www.adr.org**). Arbitration decisions are not typically subject to any further judicial review or appeal unless there is evidence that the arbitrator committed fraud or some other form of professional misconduct during the proceeding. If this is the case, the Federal Arbitration Act of 1925 provides for an appeal, and for review of the decision by a judge or court. There are two common approaches to determining the number of arbitrators; either the disputing parties agree on one arbitrator or they are each represented by their own arbitrators and a third impartial arbitrator joins them to form an **arbitration panel**. Disputing parties can seek assignment of an arbitrator from several nongovernment organizations, such as the **American Arbitration Association** (AAA), which maintains a registry of qualified arbitrators or "neutrals."

Arbitration agreements now commonly appear in waivers and service contracts, requiring signers to pursue arbitration, not litigation. For example, in *Cronin v. California Fitness* (2005), it was revealed that the two-page contract gym members sign includes an arbitration agreement capping damages for either party at an amount equal to the annual membership fee. Furthermore, the party making the claim must pay the arbitration cost, discovery is restricted, and the arbitration results must be kept confidential.

Negotiation

Negotiation refers to a consensual bargaining process used primarily to resolve disputes and complete transactions such as labor contracts. The intent of the negotiation process is to arrive at an agreement that is acceptable to all involved parties. The negotiators in these situations are attempting to obtain their client's goals and directives, so some concessions or compromises might be made to obtain the client's desired outcomes. You have likely engaged in hundreds of informal negotiations in your lifetime as you agree to trade resources with your friends, such as the use of your car, computer, phone, video games, or your proofreading skills, for something of theirs that you value. There are four basic steps to negotiation: (1) planning how you will approach the other parties, (2) exchanging information and requests, (3) offering and counter-offering concessions and compromises, and (4) reaching an agreement that is mutually acceptable to all parties (**www.adr.org**). Negotiations are typically confidential, so you will rarely have the opportunity to follow the progress of a negotiation unless you are one of the principal parties involved. However, information concerning many agreements in professional sports, including the standard player contracts for selected professional teams, can frequently be accessed electronically through websites.

Mediation

Mediation is a process in which a **neutral mediator** works collaboratively with the opposing parties to identify the areas of conflict and to assist them in reaching a settlement or agreement that is mutually satisfactory (**www.mediate.com**). Mediation is a consensual, nonbinding process, as the **mediators** have no power to impose or force a solution on the parties. The neutrality of the mediator is critical to ensure a sense of fairness while maintaining the integrity of the process. In some cases, the ability of the mediator to offer a different perspective will help resolve the conflict (**www.campus-adr.org**). You may have served unofficially as a mediator while keeping the peace between friends or classmates. If so, you have discovered one of the unique aspects of mediation versus negotiation or arbitration—the goal is to preserve the relationships and to reach an amicable resolution. As a result, mediation is a good choice for disputants who have strategic alliances or common interests that need to be maintained, such as teammates and coworkers (**www.mediate.com**). Another distinction of mediation is the potential to invoke the use of this process as a conflict intervention or conciliation as part of a larger conflict management program. In other words, as a conflict is developing and escalating, disputants might seek the involvement of a mediator before their conflict reaches a point of stalemate. The role of mediation in this manner is particularly effective when dealing with repetitive conflicts between individuals who need or wish to continue their working relationship (**www.adr.org**).

A less common approach for dispute management, but particularly useful when seeking to rebuild community or relationships i.e., team, staff, or inter-agency disputes; the **restorative justice (RJ)** process is focused on addressing the harm and restoring or rebuilding the prior relationship. Although RJ is actually a theory of criminal justice, often times the RJ results outperform the desired affect of traditional mediation approaches. The RJ process, among other restorative outcomes, provides the opportunity for victims and offenders to meet face to face in a mediated forum, and for each party to fully express the impact the event(s) or harm has had upon him /her. Offenders may reflect upon the impact of their decisions and be held accountable for their actions while victims may seek answers and meaningful restitution (www.restorativejustice.org). Restorative justice may be a good companion to criminal proceedings when crimes such as hazing, assault, or sexual harassment occur among those who must find a way to co –exist in the same school, organization, or community.

Collective Bargaining, Labor Disputes, and ADR

Many employee groups, including professional athletic players associations, have a **collective bargaining agreement** (CBA) with their employers. A CBA refers to an agreement between the employer and the labor union or organization that regulates the terms and conditions of employment for all the employees of a single employer. In some labor matters, the CBA may mandate that certain disputes (e.g., differences in interpretation of the CBA, grievances, salary issues) must be resolved through mandatory arbitration or that mediation may be sought by either party (**www.campus-adr.com**). The collective bargaining agreements of the professional sport leagues in the United States provide for grievances to be addressed through an arbitration process. However, every CBA contains specific clauses and procedures regarding how and when arbitration will be used that are unique to that CBA and the related parties. Since 1974, the CBA for Major League Baseball (MLB) has permitted eligible players to file for salary arbitration. From 1974–2009, a total of 487 MLB salary cases have been decided through arbitration (mlb.mlb.org).

When the parties of a CBA agree to enter into arbitration, the issues the arbitrator(s) is to address are clearly communicated. For example, in the *Matter of the Arbitration Between Terrell Owens and the National Football League (NFL) Players Association v. the Philadelphia Eagles and the NFL Management Council* (2005), an arbitrator was asked by the grievants, Terrell Owens and the NFL Players Association, to examine the decision of the Philadelphia Eagles' management to suspend Owens. Specifically, the arbitrator was asked to reach a decision on the following two issues: (1) Was the four-week disciplinary suspension for just cause; if not, what should the remedy be? (2) Was it a violation of the CBA for the Club to exclude the Player from games and practices, following the four-week suspension? The arbitrator's conclusions and decision follow:

> In summary, there is ample room to find that the Club could respond to this Player's actions, suspending him without pay to the limits permitted by the collective bargaining agreement for his behavior in this matter. Thereafter, the Coach properly exercised his inherent discretion to conclude that, on

balance, the team would be better protected and better off by practicing and fielding a team that did not include Mr. Owens. The problem—a continuing one—was almost entirely off-field, and the response properly dealt with that reality. Both responses, the disciplinary and the discretionary, were specifically understood by these parties and fully countenanced as part of this collective bargaining relationship. The disciplinary side of the equation is expressly established in Article VIII. The non-disciplinary response is part of the core and character of a coaches discretion; significantly, but predictably, it is nowhere constrained by the CBA. The finding, therefore, is that the Club has shouldered its burden of providing clear and convincing evidence of the Player's misconduct and, moreover, that the four-week suspension was for just cause. Additionally, there was no violation of the labor agreement inherent in the Club's decision to pay Mr. Owens, but not to permit him to play or practice, due to the nature of his conduct and its destructive and continuing threat to the team.

AWARD
The grievance is denied.
Richard I. Bloch, Esq.
November 23, 2005

ADR Applications in Sport and Recreation

In professional sports almost all contract disputes between the players and / or coaches and teams are resolved through an arbitration process. For example, in 2008 an arbitrator ruled that former Dallas Mavericks coach Don Nelson was entitled to nearly 6.3 million dollars in deferred salary and compensation payments from his time as a coach at Dallas. Mavericks' owner Mark Cuban alleged that Nelson had violated a noncompete clause in his contract when he became head coach of the Golden State Warriors in 2006.

In the context of intercollegiate sports, the NCAA has utilized ADR approaches to resolve disputes in limited cases. In 1991, the NCAA enacted a legislative policy that capped or restricted the earnings or salaries of some coaching staff personnel at NCAA universities and colleges. These restricted-earnings coaches could not be compensated more than $12,000 during the traditional academic year and no more than $4,000 for summer employment (*Law v. NCAA*, 1998). The NCAA's restricted-earnings policy was found to be in violation of federal antitrust law (see Chapter 7.32, *Antitrust Law: Amateur Sport Applications*). The NCAA appealed the decision of the district court and also entered into mediation with the plaintiffs. As a result of the mediation process, a $54.5 million settlement was announced in 1999 (**www.ncaa.org**).

ADR and International Sport Disputes

Disputes in international sport settings raise several unique dilemmas, such as when to follow the legal system of the host country versus that of the athlete's country of residence. Also, most legal systems do not accommodate the need for nearly immediate decisions to remove athletes from further competition or to approve them for continued competition. The arbitration format is ideal for addressing international disputes that are bound by different judicial systems.

Members of the IOC realized the need for effective and efficient conflict resolution and established the Court of Arbitration for Sport (CAS) to address disputes submitted by international athletes, governing bodies, national Olympic committees, and sport federations (**www.tas-cas.org**). Since establishing the CAS, arbitration has been used to bridge the gap between differing legal systems and to reach a speedy decision that is imperative during multiday events such as the Olympics and world championships. The CAS consists of three divisions: the Appeals Arbitration Division, the Ad Hoc Division, and the Ordinary Arbitration Division. Athletes who disagree with the decisions of their sport federation or sport regulation body during non-Olympic times would seek arbitration through the CAS Appeals Arbitration Division. The Ad Hoc Division is charged with resolving disputes that occur during the Olympic Games, whereas the CAS Ordinary Arbitration Division addresses commercial contract disputes (i.e., official vendors and media). The CAS has courts in Lausanne, Switzerland; New York City, New York, USA; and Sydney, Australia. Unless all parties agree to follow another country's form of law, CAS will use Swiss law or the law of the country where the involved sport federation is located (**www.tas-cas.org**). The International Council of Arbitration for Sport (ICAS) was established in 1994 to administer the CAS and to provide a process for arbitration that is neutral and independent of the IOC. The primary responsibilities of the ICAS are to select neutral arbitrators and to protect the rights of all parties (Oschutz, 2002).

Since establishment, CAS has seen a dramatic increase in appeals filed for arbitration, with many cases tied to drug testing issues. In 2006, the Federation Internationale de Football Association (FIFA) requested that the CAS provide a legal opinion regarding the World Anti-Doping Agency's (WADA) World Anti-Doping Code (CODE). FIFA specifically wished to know if the CODE complied with Swiss law, and if FIFA's sanctions related to doping offences was in compliance with the CODE. The CAS determined that the FIFA policies were in compliance with the CODE. This complex case required arbitrators with knowledge of FIFA, Swiss law, and the WADA CODE.

In *United States Anti-Doping Agency v. Floyd Landis*, the CAS Panel upheld the 2007 American Arbitration Association Panel decision, resulting in Landis's disqualification from the 2006 Tour De France and suspending him from competition from January 30, 2007–January 30, 2009. Furthermore, the CAS Panel ordered Landis to pay $100,000 towards the United States Anti-Doping Agency's (USADA) CAS Arbitration costs. At the request of Landis, all court records were made public, and this was the first public anti-doping hearing ever conducted. The Supplemental Web Site includes the American Arbitration Association (AAA) Panel decision, the dissenting opinion of Christopher L. Campbell, a member of the AAA Arbitration Panel, and the CAS Panel decision.

Understandably, the number of CAS appeals usually increases during the years in which the Summer or Winter Olympic Games are held. In February, 2009, the CAS dismissed the appeal of Swedish wrestler Ara Abrahamian regarding the IOC decision to strip the bronze medal from him during the 2008 Summer Olympic Games. The IOC made their decision after Abrahamian dropped his medal on the floor in protest of a penalty call. In their ruling, the CAS stated that "the decision of the IOC Executive Board was not disproportionate in the circumstances."

In a perhaps more complicated Olympic medal dispute, the seven USA relay teammates of Marion Jones challenged the IOC decision to disqualify their 2000 medals due to the fact that Jones failed a drug test. These teammates included the 4x100m team that won the bronze medal, and the 4x400m team which won the gold medal. The teammates argued that at the time of these races there were no explicit rules in place explaining what should happen to the teammates if one or more members of the relay team tested positive for drug doping. The CAS panel agreed with the women and held that their relay results were not to be disqualified in the records nor were their medals or certificates to be forfeited (*Andrea Anderson, LaTasha Colander Clark, Jearl Miles-Clark, Torri Edwards, Chryste Gaines, Monique Hennagan, Passion Richardson v. International Olympic Committee* (2008) CAS, Aug. 30, 2010).

Although many CAS decisions involve an athlete as plaintiff, this Court has also been useful in disputes between governing bodies. In 2011 a dispute occurred between the Bulgarian Boxing Federation (BBF) and the European Boxing Confederation (EUBC). In January 2011 the BBF was selected to host the 2011 European Men Championships. However, at the time of this announcement the BBF was involved in a pending disciplinary investigation by the International Boxing Association (AIBA) that could result in suspension of the BBF. Due to uncertainty regarding the investigation outcomes, the EUBC revoked Bulgaria's hosting rights and awarded the 2011 European Men Championship to Turkey. The BBF appealed this decision to the CAS arguing that the EUBC had no legal grounds for their decision since the outcome of the AIBA investigation was unknown. Two months prior to the start of the 2011 European Men Championships, the Sole Arbitrator for the CAS decided in favor of the BBF; however, in an example of the unique ability of arbitration, the Arbitrator took the reality of the situation into account, including the cost and preparation to host that was already invested by Turkey, and the Arbitrator ruled that Turkey would still host the 2011 European Men Championship (*Bulgarian Boxing Federation v. European Boxing Confederation*, CAS, June 7, 2011). Additional CAS decisions can be found at their Website www.tas-cas.org.

Another growing area of international litigation is concerned with the protection of intellectual property, including Internet and electronic commerce. With the expansion of the Internet, an increasing number of **cybersquatters** have purchased domain names (.org, .com, .net) that potentially infringe on established trademarks (see Chapter 7.22, *Principles of Trademark Law*). This issue is especially important to professional and university athletic teams, sport merchandisers, and sport media, who stand to lose millions of dollars as a result of domestic and global trademark violations (**www.wipo.org**). As mentioned previously, international disputes are troublesome for those seeking traditional litigation as a remedy.

Established in 1994, the **World Intellectual Property Organization (WIPO)** resolves intellectual property disputes through arbitration and mediation (**www.wipo.org**). WIPO arbitration cases frequently resolve disputes regarding web domain name challenges. It is likely that the WIPO will be presented with a growing number of these cases as more companies compete in world-wide markets. For example, Spalding entered the Chinese market in 1995 at which time they completed Chinese trademark registration of the name Spalding. When the Chinese company Zhang Xue Ming registered the domain name spalding-cn.com, the Spalding company disputed the Chinese company's claim to this domain name. The WIPO Arbitration Panel agreed with Spalding and transferred the domain name to Spalding (2010, *SGC Lisco LLC v. Zhang Xue Ming*). Several additional examples of these cases are included on the Supplemental Web Site.

ADR, Sport Specialists, and Violence

The ICAS, AAA, and the professional player associations have already increased the demand for arbitration and negotiation specialists who are knowledgeable about sport. It is likely that the value of mediation will continue to be appreciated in these situations as well (Galton, 1998). Historically, it is common for the professional sport model to influence the intercollegiate, interscholastic, and club sport programs. Jeffrey Schalley (2001) argued that arbitration can be used to eliminate violence in sports. He proposed that language could be added to the CBA arbitration clauses to address "injury compensation resulting from reckless or intentional torts." Would this work as a deterrent? Without a CBA available in amateur sport settings, perhaps an arbitration clause regarding violence will begin to appear in athlete codes of conduct and/or in waivers (see Chapter 2.23, *Waivers and Releases*) and in participation agreements (see Chapter 2.24, *Informed Consents and Agreements to Participate*). As schools, universities, and communities address the growing concerns regarding "bullying," hazing, and conflict among their student athlete populations, the position of ADR sport specialist might become as commonplace as that of team physician.

The Globalization of Sport and the Role of Arbitration

The efforts to establish international and global sport leagues, coupled with the expansion of annual international competition, will result in increased disputes between participants, management, spectators, and other related constituents. U.S. professional sport programs continue to expand the number of contests that are scheduled outside the United States (NBA, NFL). As we have seen with Olympic situations, the arbitration model for addressing disputes between parties representing more than one country is preferable to litigation. The globalization of sport will continue to raise numerous challenges for the sport law community, and ADR procedures provide more flexibility and responsiveness than a common law system. We will likely see arbitration as the model for dispute resolution in the emerging international leagues, as sport federations have already seen the benefits of the Olympic Court of Arbitration.

SIGNIFICANT CASE

*The following case illustrates the ways by which an Arbitrator reaches a decision. This case was selected because it is **NOT** a WADA case. So many of the CAS and AAA sport—related cases are doping—related; however, other sensitive and critical matters are also decided through arbitration such as team selection. You will note that although this is an appeal of a prior decision, the case is much different from Court of Appeal decisions. Note also the timeliness and costs issues addressed by the Arbitrator that are unique to Arbitration cases. Lastly, if you were Mr. Nieto in this AAA case, would you be satisfied that justice had been served?*

In the Matter of the Arbitration between

Re: 77 190 00275 08 JENF
Jamie Nieto
and
USA Track & Field
and
Dustin Jonas Affected Athlete

Award of Arbitrator

THE UNDERSIGNED ARBITRATOR, having been designated by the American Arbitration Association and in accordance with the United States Olympic Committee Bylaws, having been duly sworn, and having duly heard the proofs and allegations of the Parties, and the Affected Athlete do hereby, AWARD, as follows:

1. This is a difficult case involving two outstanding athletes, only one of whom can go to the Olympics. The decision by USA Track and & Field ("USATF"), the national governing body, to select Dustin Jonas over Jamie Nieto has been challenged by Mr. Nieto as being in violation of Section 220522(a)(14) of the Ted Stevens Olympic and Amateur Sports Act (the "Stevens Act") and Section 9.1 of the United States Olympic Committee ("USOC") Bylaws.

2. The issue to be determined is whether, by requiring athletes to achieve the international qualifying standard by the end of the U.S. Olympic Team Trials for Track & Field (the "Olympic Trials") on July 6, 2008, the USATF has impermissibly denied Mr. Nieto the opportunity to participate in the Olympic Games.

3. In light of all the evidence, the Arbitrator determines that USATF's July 6 deadline neither violates the Stevens Act nor otherwise denies Mr. Nieto the opportunity to participate. The arbitrator therefore denies Mr. Nieto's appeal.

Background

4. Under the rules of the International Association of Athletics Federations ("IAAF") for the 2008 Beijing Olympics, a country may send up to three qualified athletes for each individual event, provided that all athletes achieve the "A" qualifying standard set by the IAAF. The 2008 "A" standard for men's high jump is 2.30 meters. For the high jump event and other events, the IAAF rules require that athletes achieve the "A" standard between January 1, 2007, and July 23, 2008.

5. For the high jump event and other events, the USATF athlete selection procedures for the 2008 Olympics (the "USATF Selection Procedures") provided that, if at least three athletes achieved the "A" standard between January 1, 2007 and the end of U.S.

Olympic Team Trials for Track & Field (the "Olympic Trials") on July 6, 2008, then the top three such finishers at the Trials would be nominated to the 2008 U.S. Olympic Team. This represented a departure from the USATF's practice in previous years of letting top finishers at the Trials "chase the standard" following the Olympic Trials until the IAAF deadline.

6. Prior to the Olympic Trials, Mr. Jonas had achieved the "A" standard; Mr. Nieto had not yet achieved the "A" standard.

7. At the Trials, Mr. Nieto tied for second place but failed to achieve the "A" standard of 2.30 meters. Mr. Jonas tied for sixth place.

8. In accordance with its Selection Procedures, USATF nominated to the Team the top three finishers at the Trials who had by the end of the Trials achieved the "A" standard. Mr. Jonas was nominated to the Olympic Team; Mr. Nieto was not.

9. Six days after the Trials, on June 12, 2008, Mr. Nieto achieved the "A" standard in competition at Cork, Ireland, with a jump of 2.30 meters.

10. On July 15, 2008, Mr. Nieto filed a Demand for Arbitration with American Arbitration Association, along with a Statement of Dispute and various exhibits. The Arbitrator's jurisdiction arises from the USOC Olympic Games Code of Conduct and Grievance Procedures.

11. Also on July 15, 2008, David W. Rivkin was selected by the American Arbitration Association to serve as the sole Arbitrator in this case. After receiving certain disclosures from the Arbitrator, the parties agreed to the selection of Mr. Rivkin. On the morning of July 16, 2008, the Arbitrator held a one-hour preliminary hearing by telephone. On July 17, 2008, USATF and Mr. Jonas made submissions to the Arbitrator.

12. On July 18, 2008, the Arbitrator held a seven-hour hearing at the offices of Debevoise & Plimpton LLP in New York, NY. The hearing included Mr. Nieto, Mr. Jonas, USATF, and the parties' legal representatives. Rana Dershowitz and John Ruger of the USOC participated as observers. During the hearing, each of the parties, including Mr. Jonas, was able to present evidence, question witnesses, and make arguments. Each of the athletes made certain statements and was subject to questioning by counsel for all sides.

Decision

13. Mr. Nieto claims that by requiring athletes to achieve the "A" qualifying standard by July 6, 2008, instead of by the IAAF deadline of July 23, 2008, USATF has impermissibility denied him the opportunity to participate in the Olympic Games as provided in Section 9 of the USOC Bylaws. He argues that the USATF Selection Procedures *(i)* lack a rational basis and *(ii)* violate Section 220522(a)(14) of the Stevens Act, which prohibits USATF as a National Governing Body ("NGB") from having "eligibility criteria related to amateur status or participation in the Olympic Games . . . more restrictive than those of the appropriate international sports federation." He seeks an order to USATF to select him for the Olympic Team.

14. Mr. Jonas and USATF have made a motion to dismiss this case. They assert that Mr. Nieto's claim is more properly a facial challenge to the USATF Selection Procedures, and that it therefore must be brought only under Section 220527 of the Stevens Act and Section 10 of the USOC Bylaws. The provisions require a complainant to exhaust remedies within the NGB and within the USOC before demanding arbitration. They also assert that the relief that Mr. Nieto seeks—an order placing him on the Olympics team—is unavailable under these provisions.

15. The issues raised by the motion to dismiss focus on the complicated interplay among the provisions of the Stevens Act and the USOC Bylaws. USATF and Mr. Jonas make compelling arguments that if an athlete believes that procedures adopted by an NGB violate the mandates of the Stevens Act, then they must be challenged, as they can be under Section 220527 of the Stevens Act and Section 10 of the USOC Bylaws, before athletes and others operate under and rely upon them, and that the remedies provided in those documents do not extend to an order changing an NGB's team selection. On the other hand, the Stevens Act and the USOC Bylaws, especially their Section 9, provide important rights to athletes to protect their opportunity to participate.

16. In *Mary C. McConneloug v. USA Cycling*, AAA Case No. 30 190 00750 04 (July 20, 2004), another Olympics eligibility case, I ruled that the NGB could not change the rules on the athletes after the time period for Olympics qualifying had elapsed. Similarly, after athletes had relied upon the USATF Selection Procedures through the Olympics Trials, an athlete has a heavy burden to convince an arbitrator to adopt different rules after the fact. That is particularly so where, as here, the alleged violation of the rule is clear on its face—the "A" standard deadline of July 6, 2008 instead of July 23, 2008—and was known to the athletes well in advance of the final selections, as compared to a situation where the rules may create ambiguities that are not clear until they are finally applied.

17. Nevertheless, I would not want to fashion a rule that all such challenges must be brought under Section 220527 of the Stevens Act or Section 10 of the USOC Bylaws, because that could impose a serious limitation on the rights of athletes to have the opportunity to participate, as provided in Section 9 of the USOC Bylaws. Because I hold below that the USATF Selection Procedures do not violate either the Stevens Act or the USOC Bylaws, I do need to determine in this case where that line should be drawn or finally to decide the motion to dismiss.

18. *First*, Mr. Nieto has not carried his burden of persuasion to show that the USATF rule barring athletes from chasing the "A" qualifying standard after the end of the Trials on July 6, 2008, lacks a rational basis. USATF has submitted evidence of several rationales for the July 6 deadline that Mr. Nieto cannot prove are irrational by a preponderance of evidence.

19. USATF reasonably believed that the practice of chasing the standard after the Olympics Trials had a negative effect on the physical preparedness of athletes chasing the standard, who were forced to peak twice before the Olympic Games, and on the mental and emotional preparedness of athletes who believed that they had made the team but were in danger of being bumped from it by a competitor chasing the standard. It is reasonable for USATF to give athletes a year and a half to meet an international qualifying standard and then to say that all final selections will be made at the end of the Olympics Trials. Such a rule provides an element of certainty to the athletes that is clearly beneficial. It is a cruel irony that part of the reason for the USATF's current, earlier deadline is the disappointment that Mr. Nieto suffered in 2005 when he was bumped off the World Championships team by another athlete who met the international standard only after the national trials. The rationale for the new rule, however, is not diminished by the misfortune of this reversal.

20. Mr. Nieto argued that USATF had not presented evidence that these performance issues affected high jump athletes in particular. However, it is rational for USATF to want to apply a single qualification deadline to athletes in all of its events, except where an event, like the marathon, has clearly different performance issues.

21. USATF also submitted evidence of a logistical rationale for the July 6 deadline. Although it is doubtful that USATF needed to know the composition of its 2008 Olympic Team on July 6 in order to submit names of the athletes to the USOC and to the Beijing Olympics Organizing Committee or to arrange the logistics of getting the athletes, coaches, and

medical professionals to Beijing, it is certain that these logistical preparations take some amount of time. In light of those logistical considerations, it is rational for USATF to chose a deadline some time in advance of the final deadline for submitting names to the Olympics organizers and to choose as that deadline, for the reasons mentioned above, an event like the Olympics Trials.

22. In arguing against the rationale of the USATF Selection Procedures, Mr. Nieto presented powerful evidence that the means by which USATF adopted these procedures were seriously flawed. It appears that members of the Athletes Advisory Committee, like Mr. Nieto, were not properly consulted, and notice of meetings and of the adoption of the procedures was not properly given before their adoption. Evidence of such procedural violations is more important in a case challenging the validity of the procedures before they have been finally implemented, such as in an action under Section 220527 of the Stevens Act or Section 10 of the USOC Bylaws, than in a claim to change the procedures after the fact. However, USATF should be on notice that if it acts in such a manner in the future in adopting, it may face a serious facial challenge under those provisions.

23. *Second*, USATF's July 6 deadline for achieving the "A" qualifying standard does not violate Section 220522(a)(14) of the Stevens Act. The prohibition on NGB eligibility criteria more restrictive than those of the appropriate international sports federation must be understood in context. Violations of Section 220522 result in the suspension of the NGB or even in the revocation of its recognition. Thus, in determining whether a certain requirement, like a time deadline, is an eligibility criterion that is more restrictive than an international standard, one must take into account the seriousness of the sanction. In this context, it seems clear that the drafters of Section 220522(a)(14) intended to cover serious aberrations from the international standard and not aberrations that may be immaterial. For example, USATF could not permissibly have set its "A"

qualifying standard for the high jump at more than 2.30 meters, as that is a critical eligibility criterion.

24. An aberration in the time deadline for achieving that standard, however, must be very material in order to fall within that proscription. A literal reading of this Section would lead to the absurd result that USATF must wait until the end of the day on July 23, the IAAF qualification deadline, to select its team. Because the IAAF qualification deadline is also the deadline for submitting the names of participating athletes, USATF could be unable in this circumstance to submit its names for the Olympic Team on time. On the other hand, it is clear that USATF could not permissibility have set a qualification deadline in, for example, July of 2007, thereby depriving athletes of over half the time allotted by the IAAF to achieve the "A" standard. In this case, limiting athletes' opportunity to meet the "A" standard by about two weeks—or about 3% of the total qualifying window—is not a material aberration that could violate the Stevens Act. This conclusion is reinforced by the rationale reasons for doing so that are described above.

25. Because the USATF Selection Procedures did not materially or unreasonably restrict athletes' opportunities to achieve the "A" qualification standard, they do not violate Section 220522(a)(14) of the Stevens Act.

26. Because the USATF Selection Procedures neither lack a rational basis nor violate the Stevens Act, they do not deny Mr. Nieto an opportunity to participate in the Olympic Games under Section 9 of the USOC Bylaws.

Therefore, I AWARD as follows:

Mr. Nieto's claim is hereby denied.

The administrative fees of the American Arbitration Association totaling $750.00 shall be borne by Mr. Nieto.

This Award is in full settlement of all claims submitted to this Arbitration. All claims not expressly granted herein are hereby, denied.

July 19, 2008
Date

David W. Rivkin

CASES ON THE SUPPLEMENTAL WEB SITE

Blanco v. USADA (Apr. 1, 2011) CAS 2010/A/2185

Queiroz v. Autoridade Antidopagem de Portugal (Mar. 23, 2011) CAS 2010/A/2226

United States—20 September 2007 Arbitration Case 30 190 00847 06 *United States Anti-Doping Agency (USADA) v. Floyd Landis,* Majority Opinion

United States—20 September 2007 Arbitration Case 30 190 00847 06 *USADA v. Floyd Landis,* Dissenting Opinion

Floyd Landis v. USADA (June 30, 2008) CAS 2007/A/1394

QUESTIONS YOU SHOULD BE ABLE TO ANSWER

1. Compare and contrast the common procedures of negotiation, mediation and arbitration.

2. Identify a recently tried sport or recreation case. Identify both the positive and negative arguments for using ADR vs. adjudication procedures to resolve this dispute.

3. Review the five related Chapter 5.13 cases on the Supplemental Web Site. Determine if you agree with the Majority or Dissenting Arbitrators and indicate why.

4. In the Significant Case included in this chapter, point #16 references *Mary C. McConneloug v. USA Cycling*, AAA Case No. 30 190 00750 04 (July 20, 2004), Locate this arbitration case and compare the reasoning in the appeal and decision in *McConneloug v. USA Cycling* to the reasoning the Arbitrator uses in the Significant Case.

5. Arbitration experts have stated that the MLB Salary Arbitration agreement has resulted in significantly higher salaries for players. Is this a direct result of the use of arbitration versus negotiation or other practices? Be prepared to debate the truth of these statements and support your position with facts.

REFERENCES

Cases
Cronin v. California Fitness, 2005 Ohio App.LEXIS 3056.
Law v. NCAA, 134 F.3d 1010 (10th Cir. 1998).
Sprewell v. Golden State Warriors, 266 F.3d 979 (9th Cir. 2001).

Arbitration Proceedings
Administrative Panel Decision Adidas AG v. Zhifang Wu Case No. D2007–0032
Andrea Anderson, LaTasha Colander Clark, Jearl Miles-Clark, Torri Edwards, Chryste Gaines, Monique Hennegan Passion Richardson v. International Olympic Committee (IOC) CAS 2008 / A/ 1545 (July 16, 2010).
Bulgarian Boxing Federation v. European Boxing Confederation, CAS, June 7, 2011.
CAS 2007/A/1394 Floyd Landis v/United States Anti-Doping Agency
Mr. Ross Rebagliati and International Olympic Committee (IOC). (CAS, Ad Hoc Div., Ref: Arb., NAG 2, Final Award; www.tas-cas.org.
SGC Lisco LLC v. Zhang Xue Ming, 2010, WIPO Arbitration and Mediation Center, Case No. D2010–0748
United States—20 September 2007 Arbitration Case 30 190 00847 06 *United States Anti-Doping Agency v. Floyd Landis,* Majority Opinion

Publications
Cozzillio, M., & Levinstein, M. S. (1997). *Sports law cases and materials.* Durham, NC: Carolina Academic Press.
Donegan, F. (1994). Examining the role of arbitration in professional baseball. *Sports Lawyer Journal, 1,* 183.
Galton, E. (1998). Mediation programs for collegiate sports teams. *Dispute Resolution Journal, 53,* 37–39.
Haslip, S. (2001). A consideration of the need for a national dispute resolution system for national sports organizations in Canada. *Marquette Sports Law Review, 11*(2), 245–270.
Katsh, E., & Rifkin, J. (2001). *Online dispute resolution: Resolving conflicts in cyberspace.* San Francisco: Jossey-Bass.
Oschutz, F. (2002). Harmonization of anti-doping code through arbitration: The case law of the court of arbitration for sport. *Marquette Sports Law Review, 12*(2), 675–702.
Schalley, J. (2001). Eliminate violence from sports through arbitration, not the civil courts. *The Sports Lawyers Journal, 8*(1), 181–206.

Websites
www.aaa.org
www.adr.org
www4.law.cornell.edu/cgi-bi...re.law.cornell.edu/topics/adr.html
www.campus-adr.org
www.mediate.com
www.ncaa.org
www.sportslaw.org
www.restorativejustice.org

www.tas-cas.org
www.mediate.com
www.wipo.org

Legislation
Administrative Dispute Resolution Act of 1990, 5 U.S.C.A. 581.
Federal Arbitration Act of 1925, 9 U.S.C.
Revised Uniform Arbitration Act of 2000
Uniform Arbitration Act of 1955.

CONSTITUTIONAL LAW

6.00

United States Constitution provides everyone certain rights and protections. Before the courts can apply those constitutional protections, however, certain threshold questions must be asked. The following section examines the constitutional safeguards of the First, Fourth, Fifth, and Fourteenth Amendments as they apply to freedom of the press, free speech, due process, equal protection, and the right to privacy and how they relate to the sport and recreation industries.

The *Constitutional Law* section is divided into two parts. The first part examines some of the fundamental principles of Constitutional law, including state action, due process, equal protection, and search and seizure. This part also serves as an introduction to the principles of Constitutional law. The second part examines how the issues of due process, equal protection, and search and seizure apply specifically to the sport, health and fitness, and recreation industries.

CONCEPTS

6.11 JUDICIAL REVIEW, STANDING, AND INJUNCTIONS

6.10

Jim Masteralexis | Western New England University

Lisa Pike Masteralexis | University of Massachusetts

Sport and recreation managers make decisions regarding athletic rules and regulations on a daily basis. Although the courts generally take a "hands-off" approach to reviewing decisions by private athletic organizations, in a limited number of situations courts will review the actions of private athletic organizations to ensure that they have applied the rules and regulations properly. The following section examines when a court will review an athletic organization's action, when a plaintiff has standing to challenge a decision by private athletic organizations, and what types of injunctive relief the courts can order to bar the athletic organization from going forward with its decision.

FUNDAMENTAL CONCEPTS

Judicial Review

Scope of Review

As a general rule, the courts have declined to intervene in the internal affairs of private, voluntary organizations that govern professional and amateur sports. The reasoning behind this policy is that membership in the organizations is voluntary and the organizations are self-regulating. The court will, however, review the decisions where one of the following conditions is met:

1. The rule or regulation challenged by the plaintiff exceeds the scope of the athletic association's authority;
2. The rule or regulation challenged by the plaintiff violates an individual's constitutional rights;
3. The rule or regulation challenged by the plaintiff violates an existing law, such as the Sherman Antitrust Act or the Americans with Disabilities Act.;
4. The rule or regulation challenged by the plaintiff is applied in an arbitrary and/or capricious manner;
5. The rule or regulation challenged by the plaintiff violates public policy because it is considered fraudulent or unreasonable;
6. The athletic association breaks one of its own rules.

The harshness of a rule is not by itself grounds for judicial review. Relief is granted only where the plaintiff can prove to the court that one of the preceding conditions has been met. Even where a rule is subject to review, the court's role is limited. A court will not review the merits of the rule, but simply decide whether the application of the rule is invalid on the basis of meeting one of the six conditions listed.

Application. Despite the standards listed earlier, decisions to grant injunctions in cases that appear factually similar may vary. This is due to variations in precedent across jurisdictions or differences in regional standards, such as when a community is given the right to determine standards. An example would be in the distinction between free speech and obscenity. The U.S. Supreme Court has deferred to communities to define obscenity, so what may be considered obscene in Dallas might not be considered obscene in New York City. It may also be due to the application of state laws or state constitutional rights that grant greater protections than federal laws. One area in which this is common is where states have stronger privacy protections than the Fourth Amendment.

Married Students. One area where there has been some variation is when an amateur athletic association has imposed rules barring married students from participation in high school athletics. In one case, *Estay v.*

La Fourche Parish School Board (1969), a married high school student challenged his exclusion from all extra-curricular activities. The Louisiana Court of Appeals held that the school board had the authority to adopt the regulation. The regulation survived equal protection scrutiny because the court found there was a rational relationship between the rule and its stated objective of promoting completion of high school before marriage. Finally, the court held that the rule was not arbitrary and capricious, for it was applied uniformly and impartially against anyone who sought to participate in extracurricular activities, not simply athletics. Eight years later, and in another jurisdiction, the Colorado Court of Appeals ruled for the student-athlete, stating that he possessed a fundamental right to marry and the reasons proffered by the school board did not establish a compelling state interest to justify the violation of the plaintiff's equal protection rights (*Beeson v. Kiowa County School District*, 1977).

Alcohol and Drugs. Jurisdictions also vary when enforcing rules that prohibit the use of alcohol and drugs, often called good conduct rules. If the rules address a legitimate sport-related purpose, courts will often find that they are within the scope of the association's authority. But where the rule is intrusive and broadly attempts to regulate the conduct of a student-athlete during the off-season or conduct unrelated to athletic participation, a court will likely strike it down. In *Braesch v. De Pasquale* (1978), the Supreme Court of Nebraska ruled that a rule prohibiting drinking served a legitimate rational interest by directly affecting the discipline of a student-athlete. The court also ruled that the rule was not arbitrary nor an unreasonable means to attain the legitimate end of deterring alcohol use among student-athletes. On the other hand, in *Bunger v. Iowa High School Athletic Association* (1972), another court struck down a good conduct rule prohibiting the use of alcoholic beverages. During the summer, the plaintiff was riding in a car containing a case of beer. The car was pulled over by the police, and the four minors in the car were issued citations. The plaintiff reported the incident to his athletic program and was suspended in accordance with the state athletic association rule. The Iowa Supreme Court held the rule was invalid on the grounds that it exceeded the scope of the athletic association's authority. The Court based its decision on the fact that the incident was outside the football season, beyond the school year, and did not involve the illegal use of alcohol.

Athletic Associations. Cases involving athletic association rules that infringe on the constitutional right to freedom of expression have also exhibited variation. In *Williams v. Eaton* (1972), a group of fourteen African American football players for the University of Wyoming sought permission from their coach to wear black armbands in their game against Brigham Young University to protest the beliefs of the Mormon Church. The coach dismissed them from the team for violating team rules prohibiting protests. In a court action challenging the rule, the court held that the First Amendment rights of the players to freedom of speech could not be paramount to the rights of others to practice their religion free from a state-supported (University of Wyoming) protest. On the other hand, *Tinker v. Des Moines Independent School District* (1969), held that student-athletes wearing politically motivated black armbands protesting the Vietnam War in a public high school were found to have a constitutionally protected right to freedom of expression.

Standing

Standing is a plaintiff's right to bring a complaint in court. To establish standing, the plaintiff must meet three criteria:

1. The plaintiff bringing the action must have sustained an injury in fact;
2. The interest that the plaintiff seeks to be protected is one for which the court possesses the power to grant a remedy;
3. The plaintiff must have an interest in the outcome of the case.

The question of standing is generally raised by the defense seeking to dismiss a case and not one the court will raise on its own. In other words, as an initial matter, the plaintiff does not possess a burden of proof with regard to standing, but may be forced to show standing if the defendant raises the issue.

Application. The issue of standing was a determinative factor for the Federal Court when they ruled on a **motion to intervene** in the case of *ProBatter Sports, LLC v. Joyner Technologies*. A motion to intervene can be brought by anyone who is not involved in a court case if they have an interest in the case and it would be difficult for that person, or company, to protect their interest unless they were a party in the case. ProBatter was the owner of all the rights to a "unique" baseball video pitching simulator. In May 2005, ProBatter filed suit against Joyner in the Federal District Court for the Northern District of Iowa alleging patent infringement of their "134 Patent" and "154 Patent". In December 2005, ProBatter filed another lawsuit in the Federal District Court for the District of Connecticut against another company, Sports Tutor, alleging patent infringement of two different patents, the "649 Patent" and the "924 Patent". Sports Tutor was the owner of the "Home Plate non-video pitching system". In February 2006, Sports Tutor filed a motion to intervene in the case in Iowa arguing that it had an interest in the subject matter of the case between ProBatter and Joyner and that their ability to protect their business interest would be impeded if they were not represented in the case. ProBatter opposed Sports Tutor's motion to intervene. The Federal Court for the Northern District of Iowa denied Sports Tutor's motion to intervene because the "649 Patent" and the "924 Patent" were not an issue in the Iowa case. In addition, Pro Batter did not make any claims in Iowa concerning Sports Tutor's Home Plate non-video pitching machine. The Iowa Federal Court held that Sports Tutor did not have standing to intervene because they did not sustain an injury in fact and they could adequately protect their interest in the Connecticut case.

Injunctive Relief

Types of Injunctive Relief

There are four types of injunctive relief available: the temporary restraining order, the preliminary injunction, the permanent injunction, and specific performance.

The **temporary restraining order** is generally issued to a plaintiff in an emergency situation, without notice (appearance at hearing) to the defendant, and is usually effective for a maximum of ten days. Before a court will grant the temporary restraining order, a plaintiff must prove that he/she will face irreparable harm and that money damages would be an inadequate remedy.

The **preliminary injunction** is granted to a plaintiff prior to a trial on the merits of a legal action and lasts throughout the trial process of the case. The defendant is given notice to appear at the hearing for the injunction and may argue against the granting of the preliminary injunction. To be awarded a preliminary injunction, the plaintiff must prove:

1. The plaintiff will face a substantial threat of irreparable harm without the preliminary injunction. (Often where money damages would be an inadequate remedy, granting the injunction would provide the only remedy):
2. The balance of the hardships favors the plaintiff;
3. The plaintiff possesses a likelihood of success on the merits of the pending case;
4. Granting the injunction will serve the public interest.

Application. In the case of *Mancuso vs. Massachusetts Interscholastic Athletic Association*, (2009) the plaintiff was an accomplished swimmer. She has attended a private high school her freshmen year, was not a member of the swim team, but instead was a member of a private swim club. At the end of that year she transferred to her local high school and repeated her freshmen year because she had started school a year earlier than her peers. During this second freshman year she swam for her local high school and was considered one of the fastest swimmers in Massachusetts. She swam during her sophomore and junior years as well. Prior to the start of her senior year the MIAA determined that she was ineligible to compete because she has violated the "fifth year student rule" which states that "a student shall be eligible for interscholastic competition no more than 12 consecutive athletic seasons (i.e. four consecutive years) beyond the first completion of grade 8." Mancuso appealed to the MIAA for a waiver but it was denied. After exhausting the MIAA's internal review process, which included hearings before the Eligibility Review Board and the Massachusetts Interscholastic Athletic Council, the denial of the waiver was upheld.

Mancuso brought suit in Superior Court, a trial court, and claimed, in Count 1, that the MIAA's decision was an error and requested that the court vacate the denial of the waiver and allow her to compete. Count 2 and 3 claimed that the MIAA had violated her right to due process and her civil rights and requested an award of compensatory and punitive damages and an award of attorney's fees and costs. The Superior Court granted Mancuso a preliminary injunction and the plaintiff competed for her high school swim team during her senior year.

The case was scheduled for a trial, but prior to trial Mancuso filed a motion for partial judgment on the pleadings with regard to Count 1, which asserted that the MIAA was in error in denying her the waiver. The MIAA responded by filing a motion for summary judgment on all Counts. The Superior Court judge granted Mancuso's motion for partial summary judgment on Count 1 holding that the MIAA's decision to deny the waiver was "arbitrary and capricious" but denied the motion on the other counts.

At trial the Plaintiff was awarded $10,000 by the jury for the MIAA failing to provide Mancuso with due process, but the judge entered judgment notwithstanding the verdict (judgment n.o.v) which nullified the jury award. Mancuso appealed from this judgment and the MIAA cross-appealed from the entry of judgment on Count 1. The Massachusetts Supreme Judicial Court transferred the case on their own initiative from Appeals Court.

The Supreme Judicial Court found for the MIAA on the due process and civil rights claims and held that Mancuso has no property interest in participating in interscholastic athletics and no due process rights under the circumstances. The Court also held that Mancuso failed to establish an equal protection violation. However, the Court ruled that the MIAA's appeal on Count 1 was technically flawed and not properly before them and thus they did not review the decision of the trial judge, regarding Count 1, that the MIAA's denial of the waiver was arbitrary and capricious. In summary, Mancuso prevailed on Count 1, as it was not reversed on appeal, but she was not awarded any damages. This case, although complicated procedurally, illustrated that a preliminary injunction is a powerful tool which can be used to achieve a timely result, before a full trial, e.g. allowing Mancuso to compete for her local high school during her senior year.

A **permanent injunction** requires the plaintiff to prove the same four elements but is awarded as a remedy following a full hearing on the merits of the case. Finally, **specific performance** is a court order that may be available to the victim of a breach of contract. Specific performance requires that a defendant comply with (honor) the contract. Because money is generally an adequate remedy for a contract breach, specific performance is rarely used. The court will grant this remedy in situations where the subject matter is extremely rare. An example in sport where a court may be willing to grant specific performance is with a breach of a contract for the sale of sports memorabilia. There may be only one Honus Wagner baseball card in the world, and money may be an inadequate remedy to replace the card if the seller were to break the contract. In such a case the nonbreaching party might seek an injunction for specific performance because the card is priceless and rare.

Specific performance will not be granted to enforce a contract of a professional athlete. Although there may be only one LeBron James, if he were to break his contract with the Miami Heat, the court would not grant the Heat a specific performance injunction to force James to honor his contract with the club. The reason is that by granting such an injunction, the court would be forcing James to work and would find its order in conflict with the U.S. Constitutional prohibition against slavery. In such cases, however, there is a remedy for professional teams. Courts are willing to grant negative injunctions against athletes who breach their contracts. The effect of the negative injunction is to prohibit the player from playing his or her sport for any other team or event than the plaintiff's. In this way the court is not ordering the athlete to work, but simply prohibiting him/her from playing his/her sport anywhere except for the team possessing the valid and enforceable contract.

Scope. When a plaintiff seeks judicial review of a decision, the plaintiff will also request a temporary restraining order and/or a preliminary injunction to bar the rule from being applied. Injunctive relief is designed to prevent future wrongs, rather than to punish past actions. It is only used to prevent an irreparable injury that is suffered when monetary damages are inadequate to compensate the injured party. An injury is considered irreparable when it involves the risk of physical harm or death; the loss of a special opportunity; or the deprivation of unique, irreplaceable property. For example, a high school senior student-athlete may be granted an injunction to compete in a championship game because he/she may never again have that opportunity.

Application. In *Oliver v. National Collegiate Athletic Association* ("NCAA"), an Ohio state trial court applied both judicial review and injunctions in reversing a ruling of the NCAA. Andrew Oliver was a star high school pitcher in Ohio and in June 2006 the Minnesota Twins ("Twins") drafted him in the seventeenth (17th) round of the amateur baseball draft. Oliver retained the services of attorneys Robert Baratta, and Tim Baratta ("Baratta") to be his sports advisors and attorneys. Oliver had also been offered a full baseball scholarship at Oklahoma State University ("OSU"). At the end of the summer of 2006, Oliver, his father and Baratta met with representatives of the Twins at the Oliver home and the Twins offered Oliver $390,000 to sign with their team. Oliver rejected the offer and decided to attend OSU. In March of 2008 Oliver decided to terminate Baratta and hired the Boras Corporation to be his advisors and attorneys. Baratta sent an invoice for $113,750 to Oliver for legal services. Oliver brought the invoice to the OSU compliance office and to the Boras Corporation and refused to pay the bill.

In May 2008, Baratta mailed and faxed a letter to the NCAA alleging that Oliver violated NCAA rules by virtue of Baratta attending the meeting with the Twins in 2006. As a result of these complaints, OSU investigated Oliver's amateur status and indefinitely suspended him from playing baseball for violating NCAA Bylaw 12.3.1 by allowing Baratta to previously telephone the Twins on his behalf and attending the meeting at the Oliver home.

The relevant NCAA Bylaw, section 12.3.1, states:

> A lawyer may not be present during discussions of a contract offer with a professional organization or have any direct contact (in person, by telephone or by mail) with a professional sports organization on behalf of the individual. A lawyer's presence during such discussions is considered representation by an agent.

On August 18, 2008, Oliver was reinstated to play baseball at OSU when he was granted a temporary restraining Order by the Ohio Court of Common Pleas. However, in October 2008, OSU filed for reinstatement by the NCAA for Oliver, even though the Court had already granted him the reinstatement. The NCAA, in December 2008, suspended Oliver for one (1) year and charged him with a year of eligibility. The NCAA later reduced the penalty to a suspension from 70 percent of the baseball season and with no loss of eligibility. Oliver filed suit in Ohio court requesting that the court review the NCAA decision, declare that it was legally incorrect and requested injunctive relief to order the NCAA to allow him to play.

The Ohio court ruled that the NCAA's decision was arbitrary and capricious because it allows an athlete to retain an attorney but impermissibly limits what the attorney can do by prohibiting him from attending meetings with the professional organization. In addition, the court held that only the Ohio Supreme Court has the authority to regulate the conduct of Ohio attorneys, not the NCAA. The Court ruled that Oliver, a citizen of Ohio, had the right to have an attorney present when he met with the Twins to help him make an important decision. The Court granted Oliver a permanent injunction ordering the NCAA to reinstate his eligibility to play baseball.

After the Ohio Supreme Court's ruling, a trial was scheduled to determine the amount of damages that NCAA would pay Oliver. However, the case was settled prior to the trial and the NCAA paid Oliver $750,000. As part of the settlement, the trial judge vacated the order prohibiting the NCAA from enforcing Section 12.3.1. against Ohio citizens.

SIGNIFICANT CASE

The case that follows provides an excellent example of an appellate court's review of the grounds for granting a preliminary injunction against conduct that is arbitrary and capricious and conduct that violates an organization's own rules. The case also discusses in detail the concept of public interest in the granting of injunctive relief. The case involves an appeal by Indiana High School Athletic Association (IHSAA) of the trial court's issuance of a permanent injunction against the IHSAA's denial of full eligibility and a hardship exception for a student–athlete. The trial court found that the IHSAA's decision was arbitrary and capricious. Upon appeal, the IHSAA asserts that the trial court's findings are clearly erroneous, given the broad discretion afforded to its eligibility decisions.

INDIANA HIGH SCHOOL ATHLETIC ASSOCIATION V. DURHAM

Court of Appeals of Indiana, Fifth District
748 N.E.2d 404 (2001)

In the summer of 1999, Bernard Durham (B.J.) transferred from Park Tudor High School (Park) to North Central High School (North Central). B.J. participated in varsity cross-country and track during his freshman and sophomore years at Park. B.J. had attended private school, either at Park or at St. Richard's School since second grade. B.J. has three brothers who also attended private schools.

During 1998, B.J.'s mother, Joan Durham, and her husband, Tim Durham, separated and initiated divorce proceedings. Tim is not B.J.'s biological father. B.J.'s biological father lives in France and does not contribute to B.J.'s support. * * * [T]he time came to sign 1999–2000 re-enrollment contracts for B.J. and his three brothers in their private schools. At that time, Joan and Tim's divorce was not yet final. Joan decided not to sign the contracts because she could no longer afford the tuition to send her children to private schools. She instead enrolled her sons in the public school system where they resided. B.J. enrolled in North Central. In the fall of 1999, an IHSAA transfer form was completed on behalf of B.J. so that he could continue participating in sports at North Central. Joan indicated on the form that the recent divorce created such a financial burden on her that she could not afford to keep B.J. enrolled at a private school. Joan also provided the IHSAA with financial information and court filings to support the listed reason for B.J.'s transfer.

* * *

Park, as the sending school, also had to offer the reason for B.J.'s transfer. Initially, Park had included in the transfer form that B.J. told coaches, administrators, and other students that "he wanted to go to a better track/c.c. [crosscountry] program and that is why he is leaving." B.J. denied making such statements. However, Park changed its position after speaking with its athletic director who had subsequently learned that B.J.'s family situation prompted the transfer. Park recommended that B.J. be awarded full eligibility to compete in sports at North Central. On August 25, 1999, IHSAA Assistant Commissioner Sandy Searcy granted B.J. only limited eligibility, which prohibited B.J. from competing at the varsity level, and denied B.J. a hardship exception.

The Durhams, through North Central's athletic director, appealed that decision to the IHSAA Executive Committee. The Durhams were led to believe that the question of whether B.J. transferred for athletically motivated reasons would not be an issue discussed at the hearing scheduled before the Executive Committee. A hearing was held, at which B.J., Joan, and the athletic directors from both schools testified. Evidence was presented that B.J. had been running with the junior varsity cross-country team at North Central, and that if he enjoyed full eligibility, B.J. would be one of the school's top runners. Joan testified that B.J. had suffered a great deal as a result of the IHSAA's decision. She relayed that he had problems with anxiety in the past, and that his running had helped him through this difficult time for his family. B.J. testified that he did not want to leave Park, and that he refused to explain why he was leaving when asked about the move at Park. Assistant Commissioner Searcy also testified that she was convinced that the change in the Durham's financial circumstances was permanent and substantial although not beyond their control. Park's athletic director, referring to Park's initial comment on B.J.'s transfer form, stated that the reference was the result of bantering between athletes and coaches due to the rivalry with North Central.

The Executive Committee agreed with Assistant Commissioner Searcy's decision, denying B.J. full eligibility and issuing findings. The Executive Committee concluded that B.J. transferred schools without a change in residence and failed to fit within any of the criteria of the Transfer Rule to gain full eligibility. Further, the Committee determined that B.J. did not meet the necessary conditions to gain full eligibility through the hardship exception to the Transfer Rule. Even though Searcy had testified that there had been a permanent and substantial change in financial circumstances, the IHSAA Executive Committee reasoned that B.J. failed to produce sufficient proof that the reason for transfer was beyond the control of him and his family. The IHSAA also noted that some evidence existed that the transfer may have been motivated by athletic reasons, even though the Durhams did not know that this was an issue before the Executive Committee.

District Court's Order

The Durhams sought a temporary restraining order in court. On September 17, 1999, the trial court granted the temporary restraining order. On September 20, 1999, B.J. filed the complaint asking that the IHSAA's decision be overturned and that a permanent injunction be issued. * * * On October 22, 1999, the court granted the permanent injunction and found that the IHSAA's findings were arbitrary and capricious. * * * The IHSAA appealed.

Discussion

Upon appeal, the IHSAA asserts that the trial court applied the standard of review over its decisions improperly. The IHSAA contends that its rulings are entitled to great deference and should be reversed only if they are willful and unreasonable without consideration of the facts and circumstances in the case. In this case, the IHSAA argues that the trial court merely reweighed the evidence and substituted its own decision. The Durhams insist that this case is moot because the time for the injunction has expired * * *. Alternatively, the Durhams counter that the IHSAA's conduct is not free from judicial review, and the IHSAA violated its own rules in denying B.J. a hardship exception.

I. IHSAA—Background and Rules

The IHSAA is a voluntary association designed to regulate interschool athletic competition. It establishes standards for eligibility, competition, and sportsmanship. For each school year, the IHSAA publishes a manual containing * * * specific rules regarding eligibility. The rule in question in this case is Rule 19, known as the Transfer Rule. The Transfer Rule guides athletic eligibility when a student moves to a new school district. Rule 19-4 provides that a student will be ineligible for 365 days if he or she transfers schools for "primarily athletic reasons." Further, Rule 19–6.2 gives the IHSAA the authority to grant limited eligibility to a student who transfers to another school without a corresponding change of residence by his or her parent(s)/guardian(s). However, if one or more of the criteria under Rule 19–6.1 are met, then a student may enjoy full and immediate eligibility, even without a change of residence by his or her parent(s)/guardian(s).

If none of the criteria in Rule 19–6.1 are met, then a student must fall within the hardship exception to the Transfer Rule to gain full and immediate eligibility. Rule 17.8, entitled "Hardship" grants the authority to set aside any rule, including the Transfer Rule, if certain conditions are met. In particular, Rule 17–8.1 lists these three conditions:

a. Strict enforcement of the Rule in the particular case will not serve to accomplish the purpose of the Rule;

c. The spirit of the Rule has not been violated; and

d. There exists in the particular case circumstances showing an undue hardship that would result from enforcement of the Rule.

Further, among those situations to receive general consideration for a hardship exception is: "a change in financial condition of the student's family may be considered a hardship, however, such conditions or changes in conditions must be permanent, substantial and significantly beyond the control of the student or the student's family." IHSAA Manual, Rule 17–8.4.

When a student moves to a new school district, an investigation and a transfer report must be completed if athletic eligibility at the new school is desired. Included in this report are forms filled out by the sending school, the receiving school, and the student and/or the student's parent(s)/ guardian(s). The report must include the relevant circumstances and documents and recommendations regarding immediate eligibility from both schools.

II. Mootness

Initially, the Durhams assert that the IHSAA's appeal should be denied because the case is moot. The Durhams contend that there are no outstanding issues between the parties because the injunction has been lifted, the issue of attorney fees has been decided, and North Central did not win any State titles with B.J.'s participation. However, the IHSAA replies that the problem with the majority of litigation surrounding eligibility decisions is that the injunction granted by the trial court expires before the matter has been fully litigated and appealed. The IHSAA also contends that the case is not moot because its Restitution Rule, below, allows the IHSAA to make the school forfeit victories, team awards, and funds received from a tournament if it has been determined that an ineligible student athlete has competed for that school.

The Restitution Rule, Rule 17–6 of the IHSAA Bylaws, reads:

If a student is ineligible according to Association Rules but is permitted to participate in interschool competition contrary to Association Rules but in accordance with the terms of a court restraining order or injunction against the student's school and/or the Association and the injunction is subsequently voluntarily vacated, stayed, or reversed or it is finally determined by the court that injunctive relief is not or was not justified, any one or more of the following action(s) against such school in the interest of restitution and fairness to competing schools shall be taken:

a. Require individual or team records and performances achieved during participation by such ineligible student be vacated or stricken;

b. Require team victories be forfeited to opponents;

c. Require team or individual awards earned be returned to the Association; and/or

d. If the school has received or would receive any funds from an Association tournament series in which the ineligible individual has participated, require that the school forfeit its share of net receipts from such competition, and if said receipts have not been distributed, authorize the withholding of such receipts by the Association.

Alternatively, the IHSAA argues that even if the issues have been decided in this case, this court should hear the case because it involves questions of public interest.

An issue becomes moot when it is no longer live and the parties lack a legally cognizable interest in the outcome or when no effective relief can be rendered to the parties. * * * When the principal questions in issue have ceased to be matters of real controversy between the parties, the errors assigned become moot questions and the court will not retain jurisdiction to decide them. * * * An actual controversy must exist at all stages of the appellate review, and if a case becomes moot at any stage, then the case is remanded with instructions to dismiss. The Durhams insist that the IHSAA failed to assert evidence that there is a live controversy. The evidence about how the Restitution Rule may create a live controversy was introduced only through the Appendix to the IHSAA's Reply Brief.

* * *

Regardless of whether we consider the affidavit, an exception to the mootness doctrine applies. The IHSAA relies upon the exception that an otherwise moot case may be decided on the merits if the case involves a question of great public interest. Indiana courts recognize that a moot case can be reviewed under a public interest exception when it involves questions of great public importance. * * * The IHSAA argues that this exception applies to the instant case because the issue involves children and education, matters that are considered of great public concern, and our court has previously held that a challenge to an IHSAA eligibility rule is an issue of substantial public interest. * * * We agree.

While at first glance high school athletics may not seem to be of great public importance, according to the IHSAA, over 160,000 students statewide participate in sports under the IHSAA eligibility rules. Thus, this issue touches many in our state. Further, the issue of eligibility when a student transfers schools has arisen several times and has been the subject of much litigation * * * Also, the specific issue of a student transferring schools after his or her parents' divorce is likely to recur. * * * The public interest exception to the mootness doctrine applies to this case, allowing us to decide the merits.

III. Were the Trial Court's Findings Clearly Erroneous?

A. Our Standard of Review

The IHSAA asserts that the trial court's findings were clearly erroneous. In this case, the trial court issued an injunction to prevent the IHSAA from enforcing its ruling against B.J. When we review an injunction, we apply a deferential standard of review. * * * The grant or denial of an injunction is discretionary, and we will not reverse unless the trial court's action was arbitrary or constituted a clear abuse of discretion.* * *An abuse of discretion occurs when the trial court's decision is clearly against the logic and effect of the facts and circumstances or if the trial court misinterprets the law. *Id.*

* * *

B. Did the Trial Court Fail to Apply the Correct Standard of Review Governing IHSAA Decisions?

The IHSAA argues that the trial court failed to apply the deferential standard of review afforded to its administrative rulings in granting the Durham's request for a permanent injunction. In *Carlberg*, 694 N.E.2d 222, our supreme court delineated how a trial court should review

an administrative ruling made by the IHSAA. Although the IHSAA is a voluntary association, the court held that student challenges to IHSAA decisions are subject to judicial review. *Id.* at 230. The court reasoned that student athletes in public schools do not voluntarily subject themselves to IHSAA rules, and students have no voice in rules and leadership of the IHSAA. *Id.* The court then determined that IHSAA decisions are analogous to government agency decisions and, hence, adopted the "arbitrary and capricious" standard of review used when courts review government agency action. *Id.* at 231. The arbitrary and capricious standard of review is narrow, and a court may not substitute its judgment for the judgment of the IHSAA. *Carlberg*, 694 N.E.2d at 233. "The rule or decision will be found to be arbitrary and capricious 'only where it is willful and unreasonable, without consideration and in disregard of the facts or circumstances in the case, or without some basis which would lead a reasonable and honest person to the same conclusion.' " *Id.* (quoting *Dep't of Natural Res. v. Ind. Coal Council, Inc.*, 542 N.E.2d 1000, 1007 (Ind. 1989), *cert. denied*, 493 U.S. 1078 (1990)).

In particular, the IHSAA takes issue with the trial court's holding that because B.J. met all of the criteria for the hardship exception, the IHSAA erred in denying him one. The IHSAA contends that even if B.J. would have met all of the criteria listed in the Hardship Rule, Rule 17–8.1, he is not entitled to mandatory relief. Rather, the IHSAA maintains that relief under the Hardship Rule is a matter of grace. In other words, the IHSAA has the discretion of whether to grant a hardship exception even if the Durhams proved that (1) strict enforcement of the Transfer Rule will not serve to accomplish the purpose of the Rule, (2) the spirit of the Transfer Rule has not been violated, and (3) an undue hardship would result if the Transfer Rule was enforced

* * *

However, the IHSAA's position leaves its administrative decisions denying a hardship exception free from judicial review of any sort. While the text of the Hardship Rule states that the IHSAA "shall have the authority to set aside the effect of any Rule," the IHSAA's stance that it can deny a hardship exception even when the student meets the listed criteria implies both that it may have no ascertainable standards for granting or denying a hardship and that its hardship determinations are free from judicial review. IHSAA Manual, Rule 17–8.1. If the IHSAA is truly analogous to a governmental agency, then it must also establish standards on which to base its decisions.

Our supreme court in *Carlberg*, established the appropriate standard of review for IHSAA decisions in no uncertain terms. To reiterate, the *Carlberg* court stated that an IHSAA decision is arbitrary and capricious if it is "willful and unreasonable, without consideration and in disregard of the facts or circumstances in the case, or without some basis which would lead a reasonable and honest person to the same conclusion." 694 N.E.2d at 233 (citation omitted). The IHSAA's suggestion that the Hardship Rule is entitled to an increasingly narrow standard of judicial review flies in the face of the *Carlberg* decision. In *Carlberg*, the supreme court upheld the IHSAA's Transfer Rule in part because there are provisions in place to lessen the severity of the rule. *Carlberg*, 694 N.E.2d at 233. The court reasoned that granting immediate and full eligibility either under the listed exceptions to the Transfer Rule or under the Hardship Rule and granting limited eligibility at the junior varsity or freshman level serves to balance the possible harsh effects of the Transfer Rule. *Id.* If we accepted the IHSAA's assertion that its decisions to deny a hardship exception fall under a more stringent standard of review than the arbitrary and capricious standard enunciated in *Carlberg*, then we would be taking away one of the underpinnings of that case.

Thus, we hold that trial courts may determine whether the denial of a hardship exception in a particular case was the result of arbitrary and capricious action by the IHSAA. In this case, the trial court did not fail to give weight to the IHSAA's broad discretion, as the IHSAA alleges. Rather, in rendering its decision that the IHSAA acted arbitrarily and capriciously, the trial court looked at the IHSAA's particular decision with respect to B.J., applied the appropriate standard, and concluded that the IHSAA's conduct rose to the level of willful and unreasonable decision making that was in disregard of the facts and circumstances before it. For this, the trial court was well within its discretion.

C. Were the IHSAA's Findings Clearly Erroneous?

Finally, the IHSAA asserts that even if the trial court used the appropriate standard of review governing its decisions, the trial court's findings were clearly erroneous. The IHSAA asserts that the evidence, as adduced in its written findings, supports its denial of full eligibility and a hardship exception. In particular, the IHSAA asserts that some evidence existed that B.J. transferred for athletically motivated reasons. It points to the bantering about North Central having a better cross-country and track program. The trial court concluded that this was "hearsay within hearsay" and was not substantial evidence. The IHSAA counters that hearsay is admissible during administrative proceedings, and can be found to be substantial evidence of probative value. * * * The IHSAA also contends that the Durhams failed to establish that the purpose of the Transfer Rule would not be served by denying B.J. a hardship exception due to this evidence of "school jumping."

Here, the trial court did not abuse its discretion in holding that the IHSAA's conclusion that there was some evidence supporting that B.J. transferred for athletic reasons was arbitrary and capricious. Although hearsay may be admissible in administrative

proceedings, this evidence of bantering was based upon Park Tudor's mistaken assumption that B.J. was transferring for athletic reasons. As soon as Park Tudor officials learned of the Durhams' circumstances, the transfer report was corrected to reflect that they recommended that B.J. be given full eligibility under a hardship exception. Thus, any evidence of athletic motivation was recanted by Park Tudor. Further, Park Tudor's retraction is against their own interest, as it would seem that Park Tudor would be interested in not having B.J. compete against it due to its rivalry with North Central. Despite this, Park Tudor supported B.J.'s pursuit of a hardship exception.

Additionally, the Durhams were led to believe that athletic motivation would not be an issue in B.J.'s case. It is unfortunate that the IHSAA listed athletic motivation as a reason for transfer even though little or no evidence supports it. This practice was denounced in *Martin*, 731 N.E.2d at 11, which noted that the IHSAA uses the possibility of an athletically-motivated transfer, although admittedly not primarily athletically motivated, as a "poison pill" to keep students from receiving a hardship exception even if there is no substantial evidence to that effect. In the instant case, the trial court recognized this practice and found no evidence in the record to support the IHSAA's conclusion that athletic motivation played a role in B.J.'s transfer. Thus, the trial court's findings with respect to athletic motivation were not clearly erroneous.

Further, the IHSAA argues that B.J. did not establish undue hardship because he failed to show that his family's circumstances were beyond his or his family's control and that he could not afford to attend private school. The IHSAA contends that the trial court merely reweighed the evidence of the family's finances, and that the Durhams still enjoyed a high standard of living. The IHSAA concluded that the decision to send B.J. to North Central was a choice.

Rule 17–8.1, the general section of the Hardship Rule, states that the IHSAA may grant a hardship exception if (1) strict enforcement of the rule in the particular case will not serve to accomplish the purpose of the rule; (2) the spirit of the rule has not been violated; and (3) there exists in the particular case circumstances showing an undue hardship that would result from enforcement of the rule. Thereafter, specific circumstances are listed as candidates for hardship exceptions. One such circumstance that may be considered a hardship is a change in financial condition of the student or a student's family if the change is permanent, substantial, and significantly beyond the control of the athlete or the athlete's family.

The Seventh Circuit Court of Appeals considered this issue in *Crane*, 975 F.2d 1315, and held that the IHSAA's denial of full eligibility was arbitrary and capricious where a student whose parents were divorced had transferred schools after a change in custody. *Crane*, 975 F.2d at

1322. The IHSAA has concluded that the student failed to prove that the move was beyond his control, as the change in custody occurred after Crane had some discipline problems and trouble with his grades in school. The Seventh Circuit, finding that this decision was arbitrary and capricious, reasoned that the IHSAA had ignored the plain language of its rules and instead used "rambling rationalizations" to come to a "pre-ordained result." *Id.* at 1323, 1325. The court noted that the IHSAA changes its interpretation of its rules depending upon the situation before it. *Id.* At 1325. We also addressed this issue in *Avant*, 650 N.E.2d 1164 (Ind. Ct. App. 1995). In *Avant*, we held that the IHSAA's denial of a hardship exception was supported by the evidence. *Id.* at 1169. Avant transferred from a private to a public school, and Avant's enrollment at a private school created a financial hardship on the family. However, the family's financial situation had not changed, and there was also evidence that Avant had disagreements with his basketball coach. Further, the family's financial situation was never listed on the transfer report. Thus, we concluded that the IHSAA's decision to deny Avant a hardship exception was not arbitrary and capricious. *Id.*

Unlike *Avant*, in this case there was a change in the Durhams' family finances due to the divorce, and this change was documented in the transfer report submitted to the IHSAA. This change was caused by something beyond their control, Joan's recent divorce. Included in the specific list of situations receiving consideration for a hardship exception is a substantial and permanent change in financial condition of the student or the student's family significantly beyond the control of the student or the student's family.

With the evidence submitted by Joan in the IHSAA administrative proceedings regarding her recent divorce and family's change in finances, no reasonable and honest person could conclude that the Durhams have not met this specific consideration listed within the Hardship Rule.

The trial court in the case before us found that the IHSAA ignored its own rules and instead interjected a condition of undue hardship not found in its rules that the Durhams prove their poverty before B.J. be given a hardship exception. We agree.

Contrary to IHSAA's assertion, the Hardship Rule does not read that an athlete's family must prove that it is a hardship case. In fact, financial hardship or poverty is not contained within the change in financial condition provision or the Hardship Rule generally. Instead, the "hardship" referred to in the Hardship Rule focuses on the hardship faced by the student athlete if the rule is strictly enforced. In this case, B.J. would face a hardship if he had to run at the junior varsity level because through no fault of his own and without any athletic motivation,

B.J. was forced to transfer schools because of a substantial and permanent change in his family's financial condition. Just as in *Crane*, the IHSAA is attempting to adjust its interpretation of the Hardship Rule to meet the particulars of this case.

Even if we were to read a financial hardship requirement into the Hardship Rule, the Durhams would meet such a condition. The evidence in the record is undisputed that Joan had a significant amount of debt and her income had decreased by sixty-seven percent as a result of the divorce. At first glance, Joan's taxable income of $134,620 may not appear to suggest a family in financial hardship. However, a closer look reveals that Joan's monthly expenses are about equal to her monthly income. Joan's mortgage and utilities total $ 96,000 yearly, and she has many other regular expenses including health care, insurance, and various household expenses. Joan also has no assets that she could access to alleviate her financial burdens. Although Joan may be able to sell her house, she would net very little in proceeds after her mortgage debt was satisfied. Further, Joan would like to keep her children in the family home to avoid more disruption in their lives, in light of the divorce. The IHSAA should not be in the business of second-guessing personal financial decisions, but should accept the circumstances as they are.

Given the evidence in this case, the trial court did not abuse its discretion in overturning the IHSAA's denial of full eligibility and refusal to grant a hardship exception. While it may be true that in other cases, *see IHSAA v. Vasario*, 726 N.E.2d 325, 333 (Ind. Ct. App. 2000) and *Avant*, 650 N.E.2d at 1169, we have recognized the IHSAA's broad discretion in refusing to grant a student a hardship exception, this discretion is not unreviewable and is subject to the arbitrary and capricious standard upon review. The evidence in this case overwhelmingly leads to the conclusion that the reasons the IHSAA created the Transfer Rule, deterrence of athletic recruiting and equality in competition, would not be served by denying B.J. a hardship exception. The trial court did not simply reweigh the evidence and substitute its opinion, but instead found that the IHSAA ignored the facts and circumstances before it in rendering its decision. No reasonable and honest person would have concluded that B.J. should be denied a hardship exception in this case. This case embodies the reason the Hardship Rule was created. Although the IHSAA contends that its decisions are virtually unreviewable, a court does have the discretion to identify arbitrary and capricious conduct. The trial court in this case properly identified arbitrary and capricious action by the IHSAA.

Judgment affirmed.

CASES ON THE SUPPLEMENTAL WEB SITE

ProBatter Sports, LLC. v. Joyner Technologies, 2006 WL 625874 (N.D. Iowa 2006). The courts description of the lack of standing because the cases in Iowa and Connecticut concerned different patents illustrates problems in standing

Oliver v. National Collegiate Athletic Association, Court of Common Pleas, Erie County Ohio, Docket 2008-CV-0762 (February 9, 2009). The courts description and analysis of the rule prohibiting lawyers from being present to negotiate professional contracts for amateur athletes and the unfairness that is creates is instructive.

NFL v. Coors Brewing and NFL Players Incorporated, 1999 U.S. Lexis 32547. The court gives a clear review of the preliminary injunction elements concerning a trademark infringement case concerning the phrase "the official beer of the NFL players".

QUESTIONS YOU SHOULD BE ABLE TO ANSWER

1. What standard will a court use to review a decision of a private voluntary organization such as the NCAA?

2. What standards will the court use to determine if a person has standing to bring an action in court?

3. What are the four types of injunctive relief?

4. When and under what circumstances will a court issue a permanent injunction?

5. What is specific performance?

REFERENCES

Cases

Beeson v. Kiowa County School District, 567 P.2d 801 (Colo. Ct. App. 1977).
Braesch v. De Pasquale, 265 N.W.2d 842 (Neb. Sup. Ct. 1978).
Bunger v. Iowa High School Athletic Association, 197 N.W.2d 555 (Sup. Ct. 1972).
Estay v. La Fourche Parish School Board, 230 So.2d 443 (La. Ct. App. 1969).
Indiana High School Athletic Association, Inc. v. Durham, 748 N.E.2d 404 (2001).
Mancuso vs. Massachusetts Interscholastic Athletic Association, 453 Mass. 116, 900 N.E.2d 518, 2009 Mass. Lexis 15 (2009)
Oliver v. National Collegiate Athletic Association, Court of Common Pleas, Erie County Ohio, Docket 2008-CV-0762 (February 9, 2009).
ProBatter Sports, LLC. v. Joyner Technologies, 2006 WL 625874 (N.D. Iowa 2006).
Tinker v. Des Moines Independent School District, 383 F.2d 988, rev'd 393 U.S. 503 (1969).
Williams v. Eaton, 468 F.2d 1079 (10th Cir. 1972).

6.12 STATE ACTION

John T. Wolohan I Syracuse University

Under American constitutional law the distinction between governmental or state action and no-governmental or private action is a crucial threshold question (Yeasse, McCurdy, Goplerud and Weston, 2011). This distinction is crucial because the United States Constitution is designed to protect an individual's rights and freedoms from the government, not private individuals. As a result, the protections guaranteed in the Constitution and its amendments apply only to the actions of governmental entities. The only exception to this rule is the Thirteenth Amendment's prohibition on slavery, which is designed to control the actions of private individuals. Therefore, the first question we must ask in any case involving actions that limit or interfere with an individual's constitutionally protected rights is whether the complained of actions constitute state action (Rotunda and Nowak, 1999). The courts call this the "**state action**" requirement (Yeasse, McCurdy, Goplerud and Weston, 2011).

In cases where the complained of action is performed by a governmental entity, whether the Federal Government or any other governmental subdivision, including state, city or municipal, such as the police, state action is a given. Where, however, the complained of action is performed by an otherwise private organization, such as a golf course, college conference or professional sports league, the court must consider whether the conduct is fairly attributable to the state, and thus subject to constitutional claims (*Lugar v. Edmondson Oil Co.*,1982).

FUNDAMENTAL CONCEPTS

Determining when private conduct is state action and thus subject to the limitations imposed by the Federal Constitution has long been one of the most difficult issues in constitutional law (Wilde, 2000). To assist the courts in determining whether the alleged wrongdoer has sufficient connection to the states to subject their actions to the constitutional limitations, the United States Supreme Court has developed two basic theories: (1) the **public function theory** and (2) the **nexus or entanglement theory**.

The Public Function Theory

The public function theory requires the courts to consider whether a private actor is performing a function that has been traditionally reserved to the government or that are governmental in nature (Rotunda & Nowak, 1999). If the private actor is engaged in an activity that has been traditionally reserved to government, the court will generally hold their actions to the same constitutional limitations as if the state were performing the action. However, since the state could reasonably engage in almost any activity, the fact that a private actor is engaged in an activity which could be performed by the state will not in itself subject them to the constitutional scrutiny. It is only those activities or duties that are traditionally associated with sovereign governments, and which are operated almost exclusively by government entities that are deemed public functions (Rotunda & Nowak, 1999). To illustrate this point, the Supreme Court in *Jackson v. Metropolitan Edison Co.*, (1974) and *Flagg Brothers v. Brooks*, (1978) held that private activities would only constitute state action under the public function theory if: 1) the activity involved a function that is traditionally been performed exclusively by the state; and 2) the private entity assumption of the function replaces the government's performance of the function (Wilde, 2000).

The Nexus or Entanglement Theory

The nexus/entanglement theory examines the relationship between the state and the private actor and whether the state's involvement or relationship with the private actor is so entangled that it transforms the private conduct into state action and therefore subject to constitutional review (Wilde, 2000). For example, in *Burton v.*

Wilmington Parking Authority (1961), the Supreme Court found that the actions of a private restaurant which leased space in a public parking facility were subject to the equal protection clause of the constitution. It reaching this decision, the court found that even though the restaurant did not receive any direct governmental aid, it had a "symbiotic relationship" with the state because the restaurant benefited from the location and access to city employees, while the city benefited from the rent it received.

In 1982, the Supreme Court limited the scope of the nexus/entanglement theory in three court decisions: *Blum v. Yaresky*, *Rendell-Baker v. Kohn* and *Lugar v. Edmondson Oil Co.* In *Blum*, the Court refused to find such a symbiotic relationship between the government and a privately owned nursing home despite the fact that the state heavily subsidized the operation of nursing home and paid for 90 percent of the patient's medical expenses. The mere receipt of state funds, the court held, did not transform otherwise private acts into state action unless the state exercises coercive power or provides significant encouragement. In *Rendell-Baker v. Kohn,* the court also refused to find state action by a private school, funded primarily from public funds and regulated by public authorities, because its action in dismissing an employee was neither compelled nor influenced by the state. In *Lugar v. Edmondson Oil Co.*, the court found states action when a private party, with the assistance of the country sheriff seized another person of his property without due process. As a result of these three Supreme Court cases, in order to establish the nexus/entanglement theory, the relationship between the private actor and the state must be more than just receiving state funding or being regulated by the state. Now, according to the Supreme Court, in order for the court to find state action there must also be significant joint participation between the state and private actor.

Application to Sport and Recreation Organizations

Because they are controlled by state or local governments, the activities of public schools, universities and their officials are considered state action and subject to constitutional review. What is not so clear, however, is whether the actions of private sports and recreational organizations that govern high school, college, Olympic and professional sports should also be considered state action (Altman, 2010). The following section looks at how the courts currently view these private organizations.

Recreational Clubs and Facilities

While public lands are constitutionally protected, the question of whether a park and amusement area controlled by a private organization is also constitutionally protected often depends on the facts of the case. For example, in *Evans v. Newton* (1966), the Supreme Court held that a park owned by private trustees constituted state action when it allow only white people to use the park. In the decision, the court implied that the operation of the park was an essential municipal function which could not be delegated to private persons so as to avoid constitutional review (Evans, 1966). The court, however, has narrowed the public function theory since *Evans v. Newton.* As a result, the court in *UAW Local #5285 v. Gaston Festivals (1995)* held that the management and promotion of a municipal festival were not functions exercised traditionally and exclusively by the state and therefore the actions of the private organizers were not state action. A notable exception to this rule is *Pitt v. Pine Valley Golf Club* (1988), where membership to the Pine Valley Golf Club was restricted to home-ownership in the Borough of Pine Valley. In finding that the private club's activities constituted state action, the court noted that the club was in essence issuing a zoning ordinance, power traditionally reserved to the state (Altman, 2010).

High School Athletic Associations

As illustrated by *Brentwood v. Tennessee Secondary School Athletic Association,* the significant case below, the majority of courts to consider the issue have held that statewide high school athletic associations are state actors under either the entanglement or public function theory. The following are just some of the states to conclude that their state athletic associations were state actors: *Griffin High School* v. *Illinois High School Assn.,* (1987); *Clark* v. *Arizona Interscholastic Assn.,* (1982); *In re United States ex rel. Missouri State High School Activities Assn.,* (1982); *Louisiana High School Athletic Assn.* v. *St. Augustine High School,* (1968); *Oklahoma High School Athletic Assn.* v. *Bray,* (1963); *Indiana High School Athletic Assn.* v. *Carlberg,* (1997); *Mississippi High Sch. Activities Ass'n* v. *Coleman,* (1994); *Kleczek* v. *Rhode Island Interscholastic League, Inc.,* (1992); *Cmtys. for*

Equity v. Mich. High School Athletic Ass'n, (2006); *Jones v. W. Va. State Bd. of Educ.*, (2005); *Christian Heritage Academy v. Oklahoma Secondary School Activities Ass'n,*(2007); and *Mancuso v. Massachusetts Interscholastic Athletic Ass'n*, (2009); and *Moreland* v. *Western Penn. Interscholastic Athletic League*, (1978).

National Organizations Governing College Athletics

There are three main associations that govern college athletics in the United States. The National Collegiate Athletic Association (NCAA), which is made up of four-year colleges and universities; the National Association of Intercollegiate Athletics (NAIA), which is made up of those four-year colleges and universities that have chosen not to join the NCAA; and the National Junior College Athletic Association NJCAA), which is made up of junior and community colleges. All of these associations are private organizations composed of both public and private schools and membership is voluntary.

Despite the NCAA's status as a private association, up until the mid-1980s courts historically had found that the NCAA's actions constituted state action and were subject to constitutional review. For example in *Buckton v. NCAA* (1973), the court held that in supervising and policing most intercollegiate athletics nationally, the NCAA performed a public function, sovereign in nature, which subjected it to constitutional scrutiny. In *Howard University v. NCAA* (1975), the D.C. Circuit Court ruled that the NCAA's enforcement of its five year competition rule constituted state action due to the influence of state-supported universities in the NCAA.

Following the Supreme Court's 1982 trilogy of state action cases discussed above, the courts began to move away from this position. The first case to find the actions of the NCAA not to be state action or subject to constitutional review was *Arlosoroff v. NCAA*, (1984). In *Arlosoroff v. NCAA,* the Fourth Circuit Court held that the NCAA's regulation of intercollegiate athletics was not a function traditionally reserved to the state. Mere indirect involvement of state government, the court held could no longer convert private actions into state action. In *NCAA v. Tarkanian* (1988), the United States Supreme Court held that the NCAA's conduct, resulting in Tarkanian's two year suspension as basketball coach by the University of Nevada, Las Vegas (UNLV) did not constitute state action. In rejecting Tarkanian's argument that the NCAA acted jointly with UNLV, a state university, to deprive him of his due process right, the court held that the NCAA did not have the power to directly discipline Tarkanian or to mandate UNLV to take any action against him. The university, the court held, retained the power not to comply with or reject any of the NCAA rules. UNLV, the court ruled, voluntarily chose to abide by the NCAA's rules rather than face future penalties. As a result of the court's decision in Tarkanian, the NCAA rules and activities have generally been found not to constitute state action. However, in a case distinguishable from Tarkanian, the Second Circuit Court in *Cohane v. NCAA* (2007) found that that a coach who was dismissed by his school in the hope of placating the NCAA could show that the NCAA was a "willful participant in joint activity with the state" if all the facts alleged in the case were true.

College Conferences

In determining whether intercollegiate athletic conferences are state actors, the courts have generally examined whether the members of the college athletic conference were public or private, if the conference received direct or indirect or tax breaks or concessions from the state, and if the conference members use public facilities (Wilde, 2000). For example, in *Stanley v. Big Eight Conference* (1978), in finding the actions of the conference constituted state action, the court found important the fact that the conference was composed solely of state supported public universities that delegated supervision over intercollegiate athletics to the Big Eight.

As a result of the Supreme Court's decision in *NCAA v. Tarkanian* (1988) the question of whether a college conference is a state action is a little more difficult, especially when the conference is not made up entirely of public institutions. For example in *Hairston v. Pac-10 Conference* (1994), the court held that "on the issue of whether state action is involved, *NCAA v. Tarkanian* is dispositive.

The United States Olympic Committee (USOC)

Even though created by federal statute and the recipient of federal funding, the courts have held that the actions of the USOC do not constitute state action. Two cases that illustrate this point are: *DeFrantz v. USOC*, (1980) and *San Francisco Arts & Athletics, Inc. v. USOC* (1987). In *DeFrantz v. USOC* the court ruled that the USOC's decision to boycott the 1980 Moscow Olympics did not constitute state action because "the USOC is an independent body, and nothing in its chartering statute gives the federal government the right to control that body or its officers. Furthermore, the facts here do not indicate that the federal government was able to exercise any type of 'de facto' control over the USOC" *DeFrantz v. USOC,* (1980). In *San Francisco Arts & Athletics, Inc. v. USOC,* the Supreme Court held that the USOC's refusal to grant SFAA the right to use the word "Olympic" and certain other Olympic symbols did not constitute state action even though the organization was created by federal statute, received federal funds, and was granted the exclusive right to control the word and symbols by the Amateur Sports Act of 1978 because there was no involvement by the government in withholding the permission (Altman, 2010).

Professional Sports Leagues

Since professional sports teams and leagues do not perform a function that has been traditionally reserved to the state, nor are they usually so entwinement with the government that the state is involved in team or league decisions, their actions have historically been found not to constitute state action. Two cases that illustrate this point are: *Long v. NFL* (1994) and *Sheehan v. San Francisco 49ers* (2009). In *Long v. NFL* the court ruled that the mere fact that a city collected an amusement tax on tickets and that it constructed the stadium for a team was not enough to establish state action in a constitutional challenge to the NFL's drug testing policy. In *Sheehan v. San Francisco 49ers* the court analyzed the NFL's mandated pat-down policy on entering NFL facilities and concluded that the action of the NFL and 49ers was private action, not subject to constitutional review (Altman, 2010).

Not all the activities of professional sport reams and leagues are exempt from constitutional review however. For example, in *Ludtke v. Kuhn* (1978), the court ruled that the New York Yankees were sufficiently entwined with government to consider the team's enforcement of the MLB Commissioner's policy of excluding female reporters from the clubhouse state action. The Yankees, the court noted leased the stadium from the city, public funds were used to improve the stadium, the city provide the Yankees with additional police on game days and the city had exercised its power of eminent domain to acquire Yankee Stadium. Likewise, in *Johnston v. Tampa Sports Authority* (2006), the court found that the TSA was a state actor when it implemented the NFL's mandated pat-down policy on entering NFL facilities (Altman, 2010).

SIGNIFICANT CASE

In Brentwood Academy v. Tennessee Secondary School Athletic Association, the United States Supreme Court is asked to consider whether a private state high school athletic association should be considered a state actor. In making its decision, the court examines the relationship between the private association and its public members.

BRENTWOOD ACADEMY V. TENNESSEE SECONDARY SCHOOL ATHLETIC ASSOCIATION

Supreme Court of the United States
531 U.S. 288 (2001)

JUSTICE SOUTER delivered the opinion of the Court.

The issue is whether a statewide association incorporated to regulate interscholastic athletic competition among public and private secondary schools may be regarded as engaging in state action when it enforces a rule against a member school. The association in question here includes most public schools located within the State, acts through their representatives, draws its officers from them, is largely funded by their dues and income received in their stead, and has historically been seen to regulate in lieu of the State Board of Education's exercise of its own authority. We hold that the association's regulatory activity may and should be treated as state action owing to the pervasive entwinement of state school officials in the structure of the association, there being no offsetting reason to see the association's acts in any other way.

Respondent Tennessee Secondary School Athletic Association (Association) is a not-for-profit membership corporation organized to regulate interscholastic sport among the public and private high schools in Tennessee that belong to it. No school is forced to join, but without any other authority actually regulating interscholastic athletics, it enjoys the memberships of almost all the State's public high schools (some 290 of them or 84% of the Association's voting membership), far outnumbering the 55 private schools that belong. A member school's team may play or scrimmage only against the team of another member, absent a dispensation.

The Association's rulemaking arm is its legislative council, while its board of control tends to administration. The voting membership of each of these nine-person committees is limited under the Association's bylaws to high school principals, assistant principals, and superintendents elected by the member schools, and the public school administrators who so serve typically attend meetings during regular school hours. Although the Association's staff members are not paid by the State, they are eligible to join the State's public retirement system for its employees. Member schools pay dues to the Association, though the bulk of its revenue is gate receipts at member teams' football and basketball tournaments, many of them held in public arenas rented by the Association.

The constitution, bylaws, and rules of the Association set standards of school membership and the eligibility of students to play in interscholastic games. Each school, for example, is regulated in awarding financial aid, most coaches must have a Tennessee state teaching license, and players must meet minimum academic standards and hew to limits on student employment. Under the bylaws, "in all matters pertaining to the athletic relations of his school," App. 138, the principal is responsible to the Association, which has the power "to suspend, to fine, or otherwise penalize any member school for the violation of any of the rules of the Association or for other just cause," id. at 100.

Ever since the Association was incorporated in 1925, Tennessee's State Board of Education (State Board) has (to use its own words) acknowledged the corporation's functions "in providing standards, rules and regulations for interscholastic competition in the public schools of Tennessee," id. at 211. More recently, the State Board cited its statutory authority, Tenn. Code Ann. § 49-1-302 (App. 220), when it adopted language expressing the relationship between the Association and the Board. Specifically, in 1972, it went so far as to adopt a rule expressly "designating" the Association as "the organization to supervise and regulate the athletic activities in which the public junior and senior high schools in Tennessee participate on an interscholastic basis." Tennessee State Board of Education, Administrative Rules and Regulations, Rule 0520-1-2-.26 (1972) (later moved to Rule 0520-1-2-.08). The Rule provided that "the authority granted herein shall remain in effect until revoked" and instructed the State Board's chairman to "designate a person or persons to serve in an ex-officio capacity on the [Association's governing bodies]." App. 211. That same year, the State Board specifically approved the Association's rules and regulations, while reserving the right to review future changes. Thus, on several occasions over the next 20 years, the State Board reviewed, approved, or reaffirmed its approval of the recruiting Rule at issue in this case. In 1996, however, the State Board dropped the original Rule 0520-1-2-.08 expressly designating the Association as regulator; it substituted a statement "recognizing the value of participation in interscholastic athletics and the role of [the Association] in coordinating interscholastic athletic competition," while "authorizing the public schools of the state to voluntarily maintain membership in [the Association]." Id. at 220.

The action before us responds to a 1997 regulatory enforcement proceeding brought against petitioner, Brentwood Academy, a private parochial high school member of the Association. The Association's board of control found that Brentwood violated a rule prohibiting "undue influence" in recruiting athletes, when it wrote to incoming students and their parents about spring football practice. The Association accordingly placed Brentwood's athletic program on probation for four years, declared its football and boys' basketball teams ineligible to compete in playoffs for two years, and imposed a $3,000 fine. When these penalties were imposed, all the voting members of the board of control and legislative council were public school administrators.

Brentwood sued the Association and its executive director in federal court under Rev. Stat. § 1979, 42 U.S.C. § 1983, claiming that enforcement of the Rule was state action and a violation of the First and Fourteenth Amendments. The District Court entered summary judgment for Brentwood and enjoined the Association from enforcing the Rule. 13 F. Supp. 2d 670 (MD Tenn. 1998). In holding the Association to be a state actor under § 1983 and the Fourteenth Amendment, the District Court found that the State had delegated authority over high school athletics to the Association, characterized the relationship between the Association and its public school members as symbiotic, and emphasized the predominantly public character of the Association's membership and leadership. The court relied on language in *National Collegiate Athletic Ass'n* v. *Tarkanian*, 488 U.S. 179, 193, n. 13, 102 L. Ed. 2d 469, 109 S. Ct. 454 (1988), suggesting that statewide interscholastic athletic associations are state actors, and on other federal cases in which such organizations had uniformly been held to be acting under color of state law.

The United States Court of Appeals for the Sixth Circuit reversed. 180 F.3d 758 (1999). It recognized that there is no single test to identify state actions and state actors but applied three criteria derived from *Blum* v. *Yaretsky*, 457 U.S. 991, 73 L. Ed. 2d 534, 102 S. Ct. 2777

(1982), *Lugar* v. *Edmondson Oil Co.,* 457 U.S. 922, 73 L. Ed. 2d 482, 102 S. Ct. 2744 (1982), and *Rendell-Baker* v. *Kohn,* 457 U.S. 830, 73 L. Ed. 2d 418, 102 S. Ct. 2764 (1982), and found no state action under any of them. It said the District Court was mistaken in seeing a symbiotic relationship between the State and the Association, it emphasized that the Association was neither engaging in a traditional and exclusive public function nor responding to state compulsion, and it gave short shrift to the language from *Tarkanian* on which the District Court relied.

***

We granted certiorari, 528 U.S. 1153 (2000), to resolve the conflict and now reverse.

II.

A.

Our cases try to plot a line between state action subject to Fourteenth Amendment scrutiny and private conduct (however exceptionable) that is not. *Tarkanian, supra,* 488 U.S. at 191; *Jackson* v. *Metropolitan Edison Co.,* 419 U.S. 345, 349, 42 L. Ed. 2d 477, 95 S. Ct. 449 (1974). The judicial obligation is not only to "'preserve an area of individual freedom by limiting the reach of federal law' and avoid the imposition of responsibility on a State for conduct it could not control," *Tarkanian, supra,* 488 U.S. at 191 (quoting *Lugar, supra,* at 936–937), but also to assure that constitutional standards are invoked "when it can be said that the State is *responsible* for the specific conduct of which the plaintiff complains," *Blum, supra,* at 1004 (emphasis in original). If the Fourteenth Amendment is not to be displaced, therefore, its ambit cannot be a simple line between States and people operating outside formally governmental organizations, and the deed of an ostensibly private organization or individual is to be treated sometimes as if a State had caused it to be performed. Thus, we say that state action may be found if, though only if, there is such a "close nexus between the State and the challenged action" that seemingly private behavior "may be fairly treated as that of the State itself." *Jackson, supra,* at 351.

What is fairly attributable is a matter of normative judgment, and the criteria lack rigid simplicity. From the range of circumstances that could point toward the State behind an individual face, no one fact can function as a necessary condition across the board for finding state action; nor is any set of circumstances absolutely sufficient, for there may be some countervailing reason against attributing activity to the government. See *Tarkanian,* 488 U.S. at 193, 196; *Polk County* v. *Dodson,* 454 U.S. 312, 70 L. Ed. 2d 509, 102 S. Ct. 445 (1981).

Our cases have identified a host of facts that can bear on the fairness of such an attribution. We have, for example, held that a challenged activity may be state action when it results from the State's exercise of "coercive power," *Blum,* 457 U.S. at 1004, when the State provides "significant encouragement, either overt or covert,"

ibid. or when a private actor operates as a "willful participant in joint activity with the State or its agents," *Lugar, supra,* at 941 (internal quotation marks omitted). We have treated a nominally private entity as a state actor when it is controlled by an "agency of the State," *Pennsylvania* v. *Board of Directors of City Trusts of Philadelphia*, 353 U.S. 230, 231, 1 L. Ed. 2d 792, 77 S. Ct. 806 (1957) *(per curiam)*, when it has been delegated a public function by the State, cf., *e.g., West* v. *Atkins, supra,* at 56; *Edmonson* v. *Leesville Concrete Co.,* 500 U.S. 614, 627–628, 114 L. Ed. 2d 660, 111 S. Ct. 2077 (1991), when it is "entwined with governmental policies" or when government is "entwined in [its] management or control," *Evans* v. *Newton,* 382 U.S. 296, 299, 301, 15 L. Ed. 2d 373, 86 S. Ct. 486 (1966).

Amidst such variety, examples may be the best teachers, and examples from our cases are unequivocal in showing that the character of a legal entity is determined neither by its expressly private characterization in statutory law, nor by the failure of the law to acknowledge the entity's inseparability from recognized government officials or agencies. *Lebron* v. *National Railroad Passenger Corporation,* 513 U.S. 374, 130 L. Ed. 2d 902, 115 S. Ct. 961 (1995), held that Amtrak was the Government for constitutional purposes, regardless of its congressional designation as private; it was organized under federal law to attain governmental objectives and was directed and controlled by federal appointees. Pennsylvania v. *Board of Directors of City Trusts of Philadelphia, supra,* held the privately endowed Gerard College to be a state actor and enforcement of its private founder's limitation of admission to whites attributable to the State, because, consistent with the terms of the settlor's gift, the college's board of directors was a state agency established by state law. Ostensibly the converse situation occurred in *Evans* v. *Newton, supra,* which held that private trustees to whom a city had transferred a park were nonetheless state actors barred from enforcing racial segregation, since the park served the public purpose of providing community recreation, and "the municipality remained entwined in [its] management [and] control," id. at 301.

These examples of public entwinement in the management and control of ostensibly separate trusts or corporations foreshadow this case, as this Court itself anticipated in *Tarkanian, supra. Tarkanian* arose when an undoubtedly state actor, the University of Nevada, suspended its basketball coach, Tarkanian, in order to comply with rules and recommendations of the National Collegiate Athletic Association (NCAA). The coach charged the NCAA with state action, arguing that the state university had delegated its own functions to the NCAA, clothing the latter with authority to make and apply the university's rules, the result being joint action making the NCAA a state actor.

To be sure, it is not the strict holding in *Tarkanian* that points to our view of this case, for we found no state action on the part of the NCAA. We could see, on the one hand, that the university had some part in setting the NCAA's rules, and the Supreme Court of Nevada had gone so far as to hold that the NCAA had been delegated the university's traditionally exclusive public authority over personnel. Id. at 190. But on the other side, the NCAA's policies were shaped not by the University of Nevada alone, but by several hundred member institutions, most of them having no connection with Nevada, and exhibiting no color of Nevada law. Id. at 193. Since it was difficult to see the NCAA, not as a collective membership, but as surrogate for the one State, we held the organization's connection with Nevada too insubstantial to ground a state action claim. Id. at 193, 196.

But dictum in *Tarkanian* pointed to a contrary result on facts like ours, with an organization whose member public schools are all within a single State. "The situation would, of course, be different if the [Association's] membership consisted entirely of institutions located within the same State, many of them public institutions created by the same sovereign." Id. at 193, n. 13. To support our surmise, we approvingly cited two cases: *Clark* v. *Arizona Interscholastic Assn.*, 695 F.2d 1126 (CA9 1982), cert. denied, 464 U.S. 818, 78 L. Ed. 2d 90, 104 S. Ct. 79 (1983), a challenge to a state high school athletic association that kept boys from playing on girls' interscholastic volleyball teams in Arizona; and *Louisiana High School Athletic Assn.* v. *St. Augustine High School*, 396 F.2d 224 (CA5 1968), a parochial school's attack on the racially segregated system of interscholastic high school athletics maintained by the athletic association. In each instance, the Court of Appeals treated the athletic association as a state actor.

B.

Just as we foresaw in *Tarkanian*, the "necessarily fact-bound inquiry," *Lugar*, 457 U.S. at 939, leads to the conclusion of state action here. The nominally private character of the Association is overborne by the pervasive entwinement of public institutions and public officials in its composition and workings, and there is no substantial reason to claim unfairness in applying constitutional standards to it.

The Association is not an organization of natural persons acting on their own, but of schools, and of public schools to the extent of 84% of the total. Under the Association's bylaws, each member school is represented by its principal or a faculty member, who has a vote in selecting members of the governing legislative council and board of control from eligible principals, assistant principals and superintendents.

Although the findings and prior opinions in this case include no express conclusion of law that public school officials act within the scope of their duties when they represent their institutions, no other view would be rational, the official nature of their involvement being shown in any number of ways. Interscholastic athletics obviously play an integral part in the public education of Tennessee, where nearly every public high school spends money on competitions among schools. Since a pickup system of interscholastic games would not do, these public teams need some mechanism to produce rules and regulate competition. The mechanism is an organization overwhelmingly composed of public school officials who select representatives (all of them public officials at the time in question here), who in turn adopt and enforce the rules that make the system work. Thus, by giving these jobs to the Association, the 290 public schools of Tennessee belonging to it can sensibly be seen as exercising their own authority to meet their own responsibilities. Unsurprisingly, then, the record indicates that half the council or board meetings documented here were held during official school hours, and that public schools have largely provided for the Association's financial support. A small portion of the Association's revenue comes from membership dues paid by the schools, and the principal part from gate receipts at tournaments among the member schools. Unlike mere public buyers of contract services, whose payments for services rendered do not convert the service providers into public actors, see *Rendell-Baker*, 457 U.S. at 839–843, the schools here obtain membership in the service organization and give up sources of their own income to their collective association. The Association thus exercises the authority of the predominantly public schools to charge for admission to their games; the Association does not receive this money from the schools, but enjoys the schools' moneymaking capacity as its own.

In sum, to the extent of 84% of its membership, the Association is an organization of public schools represented by their officials acting in their official capacity to provide an integral element of secondary public schooling. There would be no recognizable Association, legal or tangible, without the public school officials, who do not merely control but overwhelmingly perform all but the purely ministerial acts by which the Association exists and functions in practical terms. Only the 16% minority of private school memberships prevents this entwinement of the Association and the public school system from being total and their identities totally indistinguishable.

To complement the entwinement of public school officials with the Association from the bottom up, the State of Tennessee has provided for entwinement from top down. State Board members are assigned ex officio to serve as members of the board of control and legislative council, and the Association's ministerial employees are treated as state employees to the extent of being eligible for membership in the state retirement system.

It is, of course, true that the time is long past when the close relationship between the surrogate association and its public members and public officials acting as such was attested frankly. As mentioned, the terms of the State Board's Rule expressly designating the Association as regulator of interscholastic athletics in public schools was deleted in 1996, the year after a Federal

District Court held that the Association was a state actor because its rules were "caused, directed and controlled by the Tennessee Board of Education," *Graham* v. *TSSAA*, 1995 U.S. Dist. LEXIS 3211, No. 1:95- CV-044, 1995 WL 115890, *5 (ED Tenn., Feb. 20, 1995).

But the removal of the designation language from Rule 0520-1-2-.08 affected nothing but words. Today the State Board's member-designees continue to sit on the Association's committees as nonvoting members, and the State continues to welcome Association employees in its retirement scheme. The close relationship is confirmed by the Association's enforcement of the same preamendment rules and regulations reviewed and approved by the State Board (including the recruiting Rule challenged by Brentwood), and by the State Board's continued willingness to allow students to satisfy its physical education requirement by taking part in interscholastic athletics sponsored by the Association. The most one can say on the evidence is that the State Board once freely acknowledged the Association's official character but now does it by winks and nods. The amendment to the Rule in 1996 affected candor but not the "momentum" of the Association's prior involvement with the State Board. *Evans* v. *Newton*, 382 U.S. at 301. The District Court spoke to this point in finding that because of "custom and practice," "the conduct of the parties has not materially changed" since 1996, "the connections between TSSAA and the State [being] still pervasive and entwined." 13 F. Supp. 2d at 681.

The entwinement down from the State Board is therefore unmistakable, just as the entwinement up from the member public schools is overwhelming. Entwinement will support a conclusion that an ostensibly private organization ought to be charged with a public character and judged by constitutional standards; entwinement to the degree shown here requires it.

C.

Entwinement is also the answer to the Association's several arguments offered to persuade us that the facts would not support a finding of state action under various criteria applied in other cases. These arguments are beside the point, simply because the facts justify a conclusion of state action under the criterion of entwinement, a conclusion in no sense unsettled merely because other criteria of state action may not be satisfied by the same facts.

The Association places great stress, for example, on the application of a public function test, as exemplified in *Rendell-Baker* v. *Kohn*, 457 U.S. 830, 73 L. Ed. 2d 418, 102 S. Ct. 2764 (1982). There, an apparently private school provided education for students whose special needs made it difficult for them to finish high school. The record, however, failed to show any tradition of providing public special education to students unable to cope with a regular school, who had historically been cared for (or ignored) according to private choice. It was true

that various public school districts had adopted the practice of referring students to the school and paying their tuition, and no one disputed that providing the instruction aimed at a proper public objective and conferred a public benefit. But we held that the performance of such a public function did not permit a finding of state action on the part of the school unless the function performed was exclusively and traditionally public, as it was not in that case. The Association argues that application of the public function criterion would produce the same result here, and we will assume, *arguendo,* that it would. But this case does not turn on a public function test, any more than *Rendell-Baker* had anything to do with entwinement of public officials in the special school.

For the same reason, it avails the Association nothing to stress that the State neither coerced nor encouraged the actions complained of. "Coercion" and "encouragement" are like "entwinement" in referring to kinds of facts that can justify characterizing an ostensibly private action as public instead. Facts that address any of these criteria are significant, but no one criterion must necessarily be applied. When, therefore, the relevant facts show pervasive entwinement to the point of largely overlapping identity, the implication of state action is not affected by pointing out that the facts might not loom large under a different test.

D.

This is not to say that all of the Association's arguments are rendered beside the point by the public officials' involvement in the Association, for after application of the entwinement criterion, or any other, there is a further potential issue, and the Association raises it. Even facts that suffice to show public action (or, standing alone, would require such a finding) may be outweighed in the name of some value at odds with finding public accountability in the circumstances. In *Polk County*, 454 U.S. at 322, a defense lawyer's actions were deemed private even though she was employed by the county and was acting within the scope of her duty as a public defender. Full-time public employment would be conclusive of state action for some purposes, see *West* v. *Atkins*, 487 U.S. at 50, accord, *Lugar*, 457 U.S. at 935, n. 18, but not when the employee is doing a defense lawyer's primary job; then, the public defender does "not act on behalf of the State; he is the State's adversary." *Polk County*, *supra*, at 323, n. 13. The state-action doctrine does not convert opponents into virtual agents.

The assertion of such a countervailing value is the nub of each of the Association's two remaining arguments, neither of which, however, persuades us. The Association suggests, first, that reversing the judgment here will somehow trigger an epidemic of unprecedented federal litigation. Brief for Respondents 35. Even if that might be counted as a good reason for a *Polk County* decision to call the Association's action private, the record raises no reason for alarm here. Save for the Sixth Circuit, every

Court of Appeals to consider a statewide athletic association like the one here has found it a state actor. This majority view began taking shape even before *Tarkanian*, which cited two such decisions approvingly, see *supra*, at 9, (and this was six years after *Blum*, *Rendell-Baker*, and *Lugar*, on which the Sixth Circuit relied here). No one, however, has pointed to any explosion of § 1983 cases against interscholastic athletic associations in the affected jurisdictions. Not to put too fine a point on it, two District Courts in Tennessee have previously held the Association itself to be a state actor, see *Graham*, 1995 U.S. Dist. LEXIS 3211, 1995 WL 115890, at *5; *Crocker v. Tennessee Secondary School Athletic Assn.*, 735 F. Supp. 753 (MD Tenn. 1990), affirmance order, 908 F.2d 972, 973 (CA6 1990), but there is no evident wave of litigation working its way across the State. A reversal of the judgment here portends nothing more than the harmony of an outlying Circuit with precedent otherwise uniform.

The judgment of the Court of Appeals for the Sixth Circuit is reversed, and the case is remanded for further proceedings consistent with this opinion.

It is so ordered.

CASES ON THE SUPPLEMENTAL WEB SITE

Johnston v. Tampa Sports Authority, 442 F. Supp. 2d 1257 (M.D. Fla., 2006). After reading this case and the Section 7.12 Significant Case, try to determine what teams have relationships with their stadium/host city that might subject their practices to constitutional analysis.

NCAA v. Tarkarnian, 488 U.S. 179 (1988). Most courts and commentators maintain that this case removed any question of whether the NCAA could be considered a state actor. Can you find any support in the opinion or elsewhere for an alternate view?

Stark v. the Seattle Seahawks, 2007 U.S. Dist. LEXIS 45510. The case examines the "pat-down policies" at a professional sport venue and the relationship between teams, leagues, and stadium managers.

Fricano v. Chicago White Sox, 2012 Ill. App. Unpub. LEXIS 278. The case examines the legal status of off-duty police when they are employed as security guards for private organizations.

QUESTIONS YOU SHOULD BE ABLE TO ANSWER

1. What are the two basic tests to determine state action?

2. What happens if the court cannot find that an organization is a state actors?

3. What are the minimum requirements for the Nexus/Entanglement theory?

4. Has there ever been a case in which a sport or recreation organization has been considered to be performing a "public function"?

5. What makes in the outcome in *Johnston* different than the outcome in *Sheehan*?

REFERENCES

Cases

Arlosoroff v. NCAA, 746 F.2d 1019 (4th Cir. 1984).
Blum v. Yaresky, 457 U.S. 991 (1982).
Brentwood v. Tennessee Secondary Sch. Ath. Ass'n, 531 U.S. 288 (2001).
Buckton v. NCAA, 366 F.Supp. 1152 (D. Mass. 1973).
Burton v. Wilmington Parking Authority, 365 U.S. 715 (1961).
Communities for Equity v. Michigan High School Athletic Ass'n, 178 F. Supp. 2d 805 (W.D. Mich. 2001), *aff 'd*, 459 F. 3d 676 (6th Cir. 2006).
Cohane v. NCAA, 215 Fed. Appx. 12 (2nd Cir. 2007), *cert. den.*, 128 S.Ct.641 (2007).
DeFrantz v. USOC, 492 F.Supp. 1181 (D.D.C. 1980).
Edmondson v. Leesville Concrete, 500 U.S. 614 (1991).

Evans v. Newton, 382 U.S. 296 (1966).
Fortin v. Darlington Little League, 514 F.2d 344 (1st Cir. 1975).
Griffin High School v. Illinois High School Association, 822 F.2d 671 (7th Cir. 1987).
Hairston v. PAC-10 Conference, 893 F.Supp 1485 (W.D. Wash. 1994) *aff 'd,* 101 F.3d 1315 (9th Cir. 1996).
Hippopress, LLC v. SMG, 837 A.2d 347 (N.H. 2003).
Howard Univ. v. NCAA, 510 F.2d 21 (D.C. Cir. 1975).
Jackson v. Metropolitan Edison, Co., 419 U.S. 345 (1974).
Jones v. West Virginia State Bd. Of Educ., 622 S.E.2d 289 (W.Va. 2005).
Johnston v. Tampa Sports Authority, 442 F.Supp. 2d 1257 (M.D. Fla 2006).
Johnston v. Tampa Sports Authoirty, 490 F.3d 820 (11th Cir. 2007).
Long v. NFL, 870 F.Supp 101 (N.D. Pa. 1994).
Louisiana High Sch. Ath. Ass'n v. St. Augustine High School, 396 F.2d 224 (5th Cir. 1968).
Ludtke v. Kuhn, 461 F.Supp. 86 (S.D. N.Y. 1978).
Lugar v. Edmondson Oil Co., 457 U.S. 922 (1982).
Mancuso v. Massachusetts Interscholastic Ath. Ass'n. Inc., 900 N.E.2d 518 (Mass. 2009).
Moreland v. West Pennsylvania Interscholastic Ath. League, 572 F.2d 121 (3rd Cir. 1978).
NCAA v. Tarkanian, 488 U.S. 179 (1988).
Oklahoma High Sch. Ass'n v. Bray, 321 F.2d 269 (10th Cir. 1963).
Perkins v. Londonderry Basketball Club, 196 F.3d 13 (1st Cir. 1999).
Pitt v. Pine Valley Golf Club, 695 F.Supp.778 (D. NJ, 1988).
Rendell-Baker v. Kohn, 457 U.S. 830 (1982).
San Francisco Arts & Athletics, Inc. v. USOC, 483 U.S. 522 (1987).
Sheehan v. San Francisco 49ers, Ltd., 2009 Cal. LEXIS 1638 (Ca. 2009).
Stanley v. Big Eight Conference, 463 F.Supp. 920 (W.D. Mo. 1978).
Stark v. The Seattle Seahawks, 2007 U.S. Dist. LEXIS 45510 (W.D.Wash 2007).
Stevens v. New York Racing Ass'n, 665 F.Supp 164 (E.D.N.Y. 1987).
UAW local #5285 v, Gaston Festivals, 43 F3d. 903, (4th Cir. 1995).

Publications

Altman, S. (2010). State Action. In D. J. Cotton & J. T. Wolohan (Eds.), Law for recreation and sport managers (5th Ed.) pp. 428–439. Dubuque, IA: Kendall/Hunt Publishing Co.
Rotunda, R and Nowak,, J. (1999). *Treatise on Constitutional Law: Substance and Procedure (3rd ed.).* St. Paul, MN: West Group
Wilde, T. J. (2000). State action. In D. J. Cotten, J. T. Wolohan & T. J. Wilde (Eds.), Law for recreation and sport managers (2nd Ed.) pp. 415–426. Dubuque, IA: Kendall/Hunt Publishing Co.
Yeasse, R., McCurdy, J., Goplerud, C.P., and Weston, M. (2011). Sport Law Cases and Materials (7th ed.). New Providence, NJ: LexisNexis

6.13 DUE PROCESS

John T. Wolohan | Syracuse University

The Due Process Clause found in the Fifth Amendment of the United States Constitution states that: "No person shall . . . be deprived of life, liberty, or property without due process of law" (United States Constitution, Amendment V). The Due Process requirement was applied to the states in 1868 when the Fourteenth Amendment was passed. Based on the language of the Due Process Clause, it would seem that the due process only referred to the procedures required before any person is deprived of life, liberty or property (Sullivan and Gunther, 2007). However, there are two basic types of due process protected by the courts: Procedural Due Process and Substantive Due Process. **Procedural Due Process** requires that before a governmental entity (State Actor) deprives an individual of his or her "life, liberty or property" interests, that he or she be provided with the proper procedural due process or procedural fairness (Rotunda and Nowak, 1999). The amount of "due process" required, generally depends on the rights being deprived. For example, the more important the right, the more procedural due process that the state is required to provide. **Substantive Due Process** provides individuals with a level of protection against state interference with certain fundamental rights and liberty interests not specifically protected under the constitution, and ensures that these rights cannot be taken without appropriate governmental justification, regardless of the procedures used to do the taking (Rotunda and Nowak, 1999).

FUNDAMENTAL CONCEPTS

To resolve a dispute under the Due Process Clause, the court must answer three questions: (1) is there governmental or state action; (2) does the government's action deprive an individual of "life, liberty or property;" and (3) how much due process was due (Pierce, 2002).

State Actor

As discussed in Section 6.12, *State Action*, before a court can conclude that one's due process rights have been violated, the court must first find that the defendant is a **state actor**. In general, public schools and universities, as well as state high school athletic associations are all considered state actors for constitutional purposes. This means that they must comply with the due process requirements (Schoonmaker, 2010). As we will see, the NCAA, however, is not considered a state actor and therefore is not subject to the same constitutional due process requirements.

Life, Liberty, or Property Interest

In the area of sport and recreation, there is never going to be a case where a state agency has the power to deprive an individual of his or her life. Therefore, all of the sport and recreation cases are going to involve actions that deprived an individual of his or her liberty or property interests (Schoonmaker, 2010).

Liberty Interest

While usually associated with taking away someone's liberty or freedom by sending them to jail, the Supreme Court has always recognized that "liberty" encompasses far more than personal freedom from jail (Pierce, 2002). The Supreme Court has defined liberty interest to include "the right of the individual to contract, to engage in any of the common occupations of life, to acquire useful knowledge, to marry, establish a home and bring up children, enjoy those privileges long recognized . . . as essential to the orderly pursuit of happiness by free men" (*Meyer v. Nebraska*, 1923). These "unenumerated" rights, those rights not explicitly mentioned in the Constitution, are protected under the "liberty" interests under Substantive Due Process (Hawkins, 2006).

Substantive Due Process, therefore, is simply the recognition that no procedure can be just if it is being used to unjustly deprive a person of his basic human liberties. For example, in *Gross v. Lopez* (1975), the Supreme Court held that a public school student who was suspended from school for alleged misconduct without being provided the opportunity to challenge the charge, was deprived of his liberty interest. The liberty interest identified by the court in Gross was the student's interest in his good name and reputation. Any charges of misconduct against the student, the court held, "could seriously damage the student's standing with their fellow pupils and their teachers as well as interfere with later opportunities for higher education and employment" (*Gross v. Lopez*, 1975)

Since the Supreme Court's decision in *Gross v. Lopez* (1975), the court has begun to limit its interpretation of liberty interests. For example, in 1976, only a year after its decision in *Gross v. Lopez*, the Supreme Court in *Paul v. Davis* (1976) held: "that reputation alone, apart from some more tangible interests such as employment," is insufficient "to invoke the . . . protections of the Due Process Clause" (*Paul v. Davis*, 1976). In *Siegert v. Gilley* (1991), the court held that even when the stigmatizing act was undertaken with malice and has the effect of significantly impairing an individual's future employment opportunities, a person still does not have a protectable liberty interest in his or her reputation. This "more tangible interests" requirement has become known as the "**stigma plus**" test (Schoonmaker, 2010). An example of the "stigma plus" test in the sport industry is *Stanley v. Big Eight Conference* (1978). When Jim Stanley was relieved of his duties as head football coach and reassigned to other duties in accordance with his contract at Oklahoma State University, based on the Big Eight Conference's investigation of NCAA rules violations, Stanley sued the Big Eight Conference. In particular, Stanley claimed that he had a liberty interest under the Fourteenth Amendment due process clause "in his good name and reputation for integrity as they bear directly upon his ability to obtain employment as a collegiate football coach in the future" (*Stanley v. Big Eight Conference*, 1978). In ruling that "Stanley passes the stigma plus test required by *Paul v. Davis*," the court held that "Stanley's interest are more accurately termed 'liberty interest' for Stanley has no contractual or statutory entitlement to continued employment . . . now that his contract has been terminated" (*Stanley v. Big Eight Conference*, 1978).

Arbitrary and Capricious. While the courts do not want to get involved in the internal decision making of voluntary state athletic associations, substantive due process also allow the courts to review the internal decision making of a voluntary state athletic associations if they find the rules were applied arbitrary and capricious (Pierce, 2002). Generally, it is not the responsibility of the courts to inquire into the expediency, practicability, or wisdom of the bylaws and regulations of voluntary associations, no matter how seemingly silly, such as hair length (*Long v. Zopp*, 1973). However, if the rule is applied in an arbitrary and capricious, or the case involving mistake, fraud, or collusion, the courts will review the internal decisions regarding rules and regulations of voluntary state athletic associations (Schoonmaker, 2010). In addition to Due Process, the Administrative Procedure Act (APA) also instructs the courts to set aside any agency action that is "arbitrary, capricious, or an abuse of discretion" (Administrative Procedure Act).

Property Interest

Up until 1970, the Supreme Court used the traditional common law definition of property. For example, if an individual owned sometime of value he or she had a property right protected from arbitrary government deprivation without due process (Pierce, 2002). Benefits an individual received from the government, such as a job, unemployment or welfare benefits, were only privileges that the government could take away at any time for any reason (Pierce, 2002). The courts began to move away from this position in 1961 when it adopted the doctrine of unconstitutional conditions in *Cafeteria & Restaurant Workers Union v. McElroy* (1961). Under the doctrine of unconstitutional conditions, a governmental agency could still withhold without government benefits for no reason. It cannot, however, withhold benefits based on an individual's agreement not to exercise his or her constitutional rights, such as free speech.

In *Goldberg v. Kelly* (1970), the Supreme Court held that governmental "benefits are a matter of statutory entitlement for persons qualified to receive them and procedural due process is applicable to their termination" (*Goldberg v. Kelly*, 1970). In 1972, the Supreme Court expanded on its' decision in *Goldberg v. Kelly* (1970), when it held that "to have a property interest in a benefit, a person clearly must have more than an abstract need or desire for it. He must have more than a unilateral expectation of it. He must instead, have a legitimate claim of entitlement" (*Board of Regents v. Roth*, 1972).

High School Sports. Once a state extends the right to an education, students have a constitutionally protected property right in their education, and the State may not withdraw that right absent fundamental fair process (*Goss v. Lopez*, 1975). Since the courts have determined that students, in most cases, have a protected right in a public education, students have argued that they are also "entitled" to the same property interest in participating in sports (Schoonmaker, 2010). However, even if a student has a constitutionally protected right to an education based on mandatory attendance or mandatory physical education requirement, as a general rule, the courts have ruled "that participation in interscholastic sports a privilege, not a right" (*Reid v. Renowa Hills Public Schools,* 2004).

For example, in *Indiana High School Athletic Association v. Carlberg* (1998), Jason Carlberg and his parents sued the Indiana High School Athletic Association (IHSAA) over its' Transfer Rule. The Transfer Rule stated that a student who transfers schools for nonathletic reasons without a change of permanent residence by the student's parents or guardians has only limited athletic eligibility (365 days) following enrollment. After spending his freshman year at one high school, where he swam on the varsity swim team, Carlberg transferred to another high school for academic reasons. While the trial court ruled that enforcement of the Transfer Rule violated Carlberg's constitutional right to substantive due process, the Supreme Court of Indiana ruled that participation in interscholastic sports was not one of the rights or interests protected by substantive due process. While recognizing that the importance of participation in interscholastic sports, the Supreme Court of Indiana held that the right to participate in interscholastic athletics did not rise "to the level of the kinds of fundamental rights and liberties" protected by substantive due process (*Indiana High School Athletic Association v. Carlberg,* 1998). As a result, the court citing its' decision in *Hass v. South Bend Community School Corportation,* (1972) held that "a student has no constitutional right to participate in interscholastic athletics" (*Indiana High School Athletic Association v. Carlberg,* 1998).

In addition to Indiana, the majority of state have also found that participation in interscholastic sports falls outside due process: *Bruce v. S.C. High School League,* (1972) (participation in high school extracurricular activities is a privilege); *Albach v. Odle,* (1976) (interscholastic athletic participation not a constitutionally protected right); *Hamilton v. Tenn. Secondary School Athletic Association,* (1976) (privilege of participation in interscholastic sports is outside due process protections); *Menke v. Ohio High School Athletic Association,* (1981) (holding that student has no fundamental right to participate in high school athletics); *Whipple v. Oregon School Activities Association,* (1981) ("While we think that participation in interscholastic sports is an important part of the educational process, we are not persuaded by plaintiff's argument that it is a liberty or property interest of constitutional proportions"); *Niles v. Univ. Interscholastic League,* (1983) (student's interest in interscholastic activities falls outside of due process rights); *Davenport v. Randolph Co. Board of Education,* (1984) (privilege of participation in sports falls outside due process); *Simkins v. S.D. High School Activities Association,* (1989) (interscholastic participation is mere expectancy); *Zehner v. Central Berkshire Regional School District,* (1995) (taking part in interscholastic athletics was not constitutionally protected claim of entitlement). It should be noted, however, that some jurisdictions have found that participation in interscholastic athletics was a protected right and not a privilege: *Moran v. School District #7, Yellowstone County,* (1972) and *Duffley v. New Hampshire Interscholastic Athletic Association,* (1982).

College Sports. Because college students pay for college, the courts have ruled that "a student's interest in attending a university is a property right protected by due process" (*Abbariao v. Hamline University School of Law,* 1977). With college athletes, students have asserted that they either have a property right because he or she has a property interest in their scholarship or a property right in a future professional career (Schoonmaker, 2010). For example, in *Hall v. University of Minnesota* (1982), Mark Hall asserted that he had been denied his due process right after the university denied him admission into an academic program after three years at the university, thereby causing him to lose his basketball scholarship. In ruling that Hall had a protected property right based on his future opportunity to play professional basketball, the court found that "the interest at stake here, although ostensibly academic, is Hall's ability to obtain a "no cut" contract with the National Basketball Association" (*Hall v. University of Minnesota,* 1982). In support of its' decision, the court noted that Hall had use his college career as a means of entry into professional sports as do many college athletes. The court found that Hall had "put all of his eggs into the basket of professional basketball . . . and that he would suffer a substantial loss if his career objectives were impaired" (*Hall v. University of Minnesota,* 1982). It should be noted, here, that most courts do not like to assign a property right to future events, such as professional athletic careers, because they are too speculative to be protected. In addition, courts generally have not recognized a right of non-scholarship athletes to participate in intercollegiate athletics (*Colorado Seminary v. NCAA*, 1978).

While students have also been successful in arguing that they had a property right in the present economic value in a college athletic scholarship, *Gulf South Conference v. Boyd* (1979), because the NCAA has reduced the length of athletic scholarships from four years to one year renewable scholarships, students do not have the same property interests in their scholarships as Boyd and Hall. In fact, as long as schools follow proper NCAA procedures, scholarships athletes only have a property interest in the current one year scholarship (Schoon-maker, 2010). For example, in *Conrad v. The University of Washington*, (1992), the court upheld the school's dismissal of a football player when it ruled that he did not have a protected interest in his athletic scholarship.

Another case, dealing with due process property right, is *National Collegiate Athletic Association v. Tarkanian*, (1988). Jerry Tarkanian was the head basketball coach and a tenured teacher at UNLV when the NCAA, after conducting an investigation into improper recruiting practices and other violations of rules, proposed a series of sanctions against the university. Included in the sections was a 2-year probation, and a request that the university show cause why additional penalties should not to be imposed, if the university failed to remove the coach completely from the university's intercollegiate athletic program during the probation period (*National Collegiate Athletic Association v. Tarkanian*, 1988). When the president of the university ordered that Tarkanian be suspended for the probation period, Tarkanian brought suit in Nevada state court against the university alleging that he had been deprived of his due process right under the Fourteenth Amendment. While the Supreme Court of Nevada agreed with Tarkanian and held that the NCAA's regulatory activity constituted state action and that the fact finding procedures used by the association had violated the due process clause, the case was eventually overturned by the United States Supreme Court on the grounds that the NCAA was not a state actor, and therefore not subject to the due process clause (*National Collegiate Athletic Association v. Tarkanian*, 1988).

Due Process Analysis

Having established that the government's action deprive an individual of "life, liberty or property," an individual must now show how much **Procedural Due Process** was required. Up until the Supreme Court's decision in *Goldberg v. Kelly* (1970), the court generally held that due process required a hearing, resembling a judicial trial (Pierce, 2002). By 1973, however, the Court had moved from this position and held that a "hearing" is an ambiguous term that could refer to a wide range of decision making procedures (*U.S. v. Florida East Coast Ry*, 1973). While there is no established requirements, generally the amount of due process required will depend on the right being deprived an individual. For example, if the state was attempting to put you in jail for 10 year, the due process required would be high, including the right to a fair trial, the right to present evidence, to view all the evidence, the right to cross examine witnesses, and the right to counsel. If however the property interest being deprived was a $10 parking ticket, the due process required would be much lower and you would not have many of the same due process protection.

In 1976, the Court developed a four part balancing test to determine the extent to procedural due process. The first part of the test, looks at "the private interest that will be affected by the official action; second, the risk of an erroneous deprivation of such interest through the procedures used, third, the probable value, if any, of additional or substitute procedural safeguards; and finally, the Government's interest, including the function involved and the fiscal and administrative burdens that the additional or substitute procedural requirement would entail" (*Mathews v. Eldridge*, 1976, p. 335). For example, in *Gross v. Lopez* (1975), a number of students were suspended for ten days for disruptive behavior. The students sued claiming their due process rights had been violated. In agreeing with the students, the Supreme Court held that a public school student was entitled to a hearing of some kind before he was suspended for 10 days. Absent the hearing, which the court held could be as simple as an informal meeting between a school official and the student in which the student had a chance to tell his side of the story; the Court held that there was too great a chance that the student would be erroneously deprived an important liberty and property interest (*Goss v. Lopez*, 1975). The Court further outlined the procedures that needed to be followed to meet the standard they had established. Specifically, the student must be given oral and written notice of the charges against him and, if he or she denies them, an explanation of the evidence the authorities have and an opportunity to present his side of the story. The court also held that there need be no delay between the time of the notice and the time of the hearing (*Goss v. Lopez*, 1975).

As a result of *Goss v. Lopez*, and the subsequent cases, if a high school or state high school athletic association would like to suspend a student from athletic competition the due process clause requires that the student receive published standards; notice of the specific charges; advance written notice of the time and place of the hearing notice; a hearing (*Kelley v. Metropolitan County Board of Education of Nashville*, 1968); the right to an impartial decision maker (*Butler v. Oak Creek-Franklin School District,* 2001); a written report of the findings of fact and the basis for punishment; and an appeals procedure (*Behagen v. Intercollegiate Conference of Faculty Representatives*, 1972).

SIGNIFICANT CASE

In seeking due process protection, Joscelin Yeo urged the court to protect her reputation as an athlete. In addressing this question, the court examined the plaintiff's potential financial opportunities and the due process she might be owed.

NATIONAL COLLEGIATE ATHLETIC ASSOCIATION V. JOSCELIN YEO

Supreme Court of Texas
171 S.W.3d 863 (2005)

Opinion

Construing the Texas Constitution's guarantee of due course of law,[1] we held twenty years ago in *Spring Branch I.S.D. v. Stamos*, 695 S.W.2d 556, 560–61, 28 Tex. Sup. Ct. J. 554 (Tex. 1985) like "the overwhelming majority of jurisdictions" construing other constitutional guarantees of due process, that "students do not possess a constitutionally protected interest in their participation in extracurricular activities." We have endorsed the rule in *Stamos* twice since. Respondent nevertheless contends that because of her unique situation as "the most decorated athlete in the history of the Republic of Singapore", to disqualify her from participating in an intercollegiate swimming competition would deprive her of protected property and liberty interests in her reputation and existing and future financial opportunities in violation of the Texas Constitution. The lower courts agreed, distinguishing this case from *Stamos*. We conclude that the rule in *Stamos* applies and therefore reverse the judgment of the court of appeals and render judgment that respondent take nothing.

> 1 TEX. CONST. art. I, § 19 ("No citizen of this State shall be deprived of life, liberty, property, privileges or immunities, or in any manner disfranchised, except by the due course of the law of the land.").

When Coach Michael Walker recruited Joscelin Yeo, a high school student in the Republic of Singapore, to enroll at the University of California at Berkeley, she had already achieved fame in her country as a swimmer. At Berkeley, she won numerous All-American awards and was a member of a world-record-setting relay team in 1999.

Before the 2000–2001 school year, Walker left Berkeley for the University of Texas at Austin ("UT-Austin"). He was helping coach the Singapore Olympic team, of which Yeo was a member, and she went with him to UT-Austin. Berkeley and UT-Austin are both members of the National Collegiate Athletic Association ("NCAA"), which prescribes rules for determining the eligibility of student athletes to engage in competition. A member that violates these rules is subject to sanctions. NCAA rules generally prohibit a student who transfers from one four-year member institution to another from participating in intercollegiate athletic competitions for one full academic year, but this restriction may be waived under certain circumstances if the former institution does not object. Berkeley refused to waive the restriction, and thus Yeo was ineligible to compete at UT-Austin for an academic year.

As permitted by NCAA rules, Yeo did not enroll in classes for the fall semester of 2000 in order to compete in the Olympics. In compliance with the one-year restriction, she did not participate in intercollegiate events during that semester or the spring semester, when she was enrolled in classes. UT-Austin mistakenly believed that Yeo's first semester had counted toward satisfying the restriction and that she was free to engage in competition beginning the fall semester of 2001. After Yeo competed in four events, Berkeley complained to the NCAA. UT-Austin confessed its error and agreed that Yeo would sit out the remainder of the semester, but the NCAA required that she not participate in the first four events the following spring, to match the four events in which she had been disqualified. Yeo did not know of UT-Austin's discussions with the NCAA and simply did as UT-Austin told her.

UT-Austin then added three swimming events at the beginning of its spring semester schedule. After Yeo had sat out those events and a fourth one, UT-Austin allowed her to rejoin the swim team, but Berkeley again complained, arguing that the added events could not be used to satisfy the one-year restriction. NCAA staff agreed and on March 6 issued a decision that Yeo not participate in the next three regularly scheduled events, including the 2002 NCAA women's swimming and diving championship on March 22. UT-Austin immediately appealed the staff decision to the NCAA Student-Athlete Reinstatement Committee ("the SARC"), and a telephonic hearing was scheduled for the next day. For the first time, UT-Austin told Yeo of the problem and advised her simply to plea for sympathy. She did, but at the conclusion of the hearing, the SARC upheld the staff decision.

At UT-Austin's suggestion, Yeo then obtained legal counsel, who persuaded Berkeley on March 15 to waive Yeo's one-year restriction, something it had refused to do before. Counsel moved the SARC to reconsider, especially in light of this development, but it refused.

On March 20, Yeo sued UT-Austin and its vice president for institutional relations and legal affairs, Patricia Ohlendorf, to enjoin them from disqualifying her from competing in the championship meet two days later and for a declaration that UT-Austin had denied her procedural due process as guaranteed by the Texas Constitution. That same day, the trial court issued a temporary restraining order granting Yeo the injunctive relief requested. On March 21, the NCAA intervened in the action, but Yeo moved to strike the intervention, and after a hearing later that day, the trial court granted Yeo's motion. The next morning, the NCAA sought mandamus relief from the court of appeals, and UT-Austin appealed from the temporary restraining order. That afternoon, the court of appeals denied the petition for mandamus and dismissed the interlocutory appeal for want of jurisdiction. Yeo competed in the championship meet.

In November 2002, after a trial to the bench, the trial court rendered judgment for Yeo, declaring that UT-Austin had denied Yeo procedural due process guaranteed by the Texas Constitution, thereby depriving her of protected liberty and property interests. The court permanently enjoined UT-Austin from declaring Yeo ineligible in the future without affording her due process and from punishing her for participating in past competitions, including the 2002 women's championship. The trial court also awarded Yeo $ 164,755.50 in attorney fees through an appeal to this Court.

The NCAA appealed from the order striking its intervention, and UT-Austin appealed from the judgment. The court of appeals affirmed. We granted the NCAA's and UT-Austin's petitions for review.

Since the championship meet in March 2002, Yeo has, of course, moved on. When briefs were filed in this case, we were told that Yeo had graduated from UT-Austin, received a Rhodes Scholarship, and ended her college swimming career. But none of the parties argues that the case has become moot, because the injunction prevents the NCAA from imposing retroactive sanctions under its "Restitution Rule". We agree that the case is not moot.

We first consider whether Yeo has an interest protected by due course of law under article I, section 19 of the Texas Constitution. In so doing, we look as usual to cases construing the federal constitutional guarantee of due process as persuasive authority. The parties have not identified any difference between the state and federal guarantees material to the issues in this case.

Yeo does not challenge our holding in *Stamos* that a student has no interest in participating in extracurricular activities that is protected by the Texas Constitution's guarantee of due course of law. Nor does she dispute that under NCAA rules, she was ineligible to participate in the 2002 NCAA women's swimming and diving championship. Yeo argues that she was entitled to notice and a meaningful hearing before NCAA rules were applied to her because of her unique reputation and earning potential. Had she been disqualified from competing in the championship meet, she contends, people would have suspected that it was for her own misconduct and not for UT-Austin's mistakes in attempting to comply with NCAA rules. Yeo acknowledges that the United States Supreme Court has held that reputation alone is not a protected liberty or property interest. But it is the degree of her interests, Yeo contends, and not merely their character, that bring them within constitutional protection. A student-athlete with a lesser reputation or less certain of her earning potential, she concedes, would not have the same rights. The court of appeals agreed:

In connection with the permanent injunction, the trial court made several material findings of fact that are essentially unchallenged: (1) Yeo had already established a world-class reputation and her "good name, outstanding reputation, high standing in her community, her unblemished integrity and honor are particularly important in the Republic of Singapore and in light of her cultural background"; (2) if NCAA rules did not prohibit athletes from accepting professional compensation while competing in NCAA sanctioned events, Yeo "would be immediately eligible to capitalize on her public persona by entering into lucrative endorsement and marketing opportunities as well as being eligible for prize winnings due to her performance as a member of Singapore's national team"; and (3) "UT-Austin represented to [Yeo] at the time she transferred from [Cal-Berkeley] to become a student-athlete at UT-Austin that UT-Austin would not jeopardize or compromise [Yeo's] eligibility to compete on behalf of UT-Austin in NCAA athletic competition."

These findings of fact support Yeo's theory that her athletic reputation, which was established *even before* she began attending Cal-Berkeley and competing under NCAA regulations, constitutes a protected interest for purposes of due course of law. Yeo had competed in two Olympic games before attending college and had been named sportswoman of the year and Olympic flag-bearer for her native country, Singapore. At both the temporary restraining order and permanent injunction hearings, Yeo represented that it was this continuing interest in her athletic and professional reputation that UT-Austin had damaged by its actions.

* * *

Here, Yeo presented testimony from multiple witnesses indicating that she had established a reputation as a world-class athlete in her home country of Singapore *separate and apart from her intercollegiate swimming career*. As a result, much of her reputation had been built outside of the United States and the structure of NCAA intercollegiate athletics. We cannot say that the trial court erred in holding that Yeo had a protected interest under these facts.

UT-Austin, joined by various *amici curiae*, contends that an affirmance in this case will create a protected interest in every intercollegiate student-athlete to participate in athletic events. We reject this argument and note that we reach this decision because of the unique fact pattern with which we are presented. Based upon the largely undisputed findings of fact, Yeo had already established a protected interest in her reputation as an athlete long before she came to this country to swim competitively as a student-athlete under NCAA rules. Our holding that Yeo, under these facts, has a protected interest should not be read as extending that same protection to every other intercollegiate athlete. The determination of whether a student-athlete has a protected interest is necessarily fact-specific, depending on that athlete's specific situation and reputation. Each such case must

be decided on its own merits, in light of the financial realities of contemporary athletic competition. We hold that Yeo's established liberty interest in her reputation as an athlete is entitled to due course of law protection and we affirm the trial court's decision in that regard.

We reject Yeo's argument and the court of appeals' holding. The United States Supreme Court has stated, and we agree, that whether an interest is protected by due process depends not on its *weight* but on its *nature*. Yeo does not take issue with this principle but argues in effect that the weight of an interest can determine its nature. A stellar reputation like hers, Yeo contends and the court of appeals concluded, is categorically different from a more modest reputation. We disagree. The loss of either may be, to its owner, substantial. The court of appeals held that whether a reputation is constitutionally protected must be decided case by case, but it did not suggest a measure for distinguishing one case from another, and neither does Yeo. We see none, which convinces us that the *nature* of one's interest in a good reputation is the same no matter how good the reputation is.

Yeo's claimed interest in future financial opportunities is too speculative for due process protection. There must be an actual legal entitlement. While student-athletes remain amateurs, their future financial opportunities remain expectations.

Yeo argues that her reputation and future financial interests are entitled to constitutional protection under our decision in *University of Texas Medical School v. Than*. There we held that a medical student charged with academic dishonesty had a protected liberty interest in a graduate education. But since *Than* we have refused to accord a student's interest in athletics the same protection. We decline to equate an interest in intercollegiate athletics with an interest in graduate education.

Accordingly, we hold that Yeo has asserted no interests protected by article I, section 19 of the Texas Constitution. The case must therefore be dismissed. While we need not reach the NCAA's arguments that it should have been permitted to intervene, we expressly disapprove the court of appeals' conclusions that the NCAA's interests were not sufficiently implicated to warrant intervention, and that intervention would have unduly complicated the case.

We have twice reminded the lower courts that "judicial intervention in [student athletic disputes] often does more harm than good." As the Fifth Circuit has said, judges are not "super referees". Along the same vein, the United States Supreme Court has observed: "Courts do not and cannot intervene in the resolution of conflicts which arise in the daily operation of school systems and which do not directly and sharply implicate basic constitutional values." We reiterate this counsel to the trial courts and courts of appeals.

The judgment of the court of appeals is reversed, and judgment is rendered that Yeo take nothing.

CASES ON THE SUPPLEMENTAL WEB SITE

Stanley v. Big Eight Conference, 463 F. Supp. 920 (W.D. MO. 1978). The case examines what due process an athletic conference that is investigating a coach must supply to satisfy the coach's due process rights.

Stone v. Kansas State High School Activities Association, 761 P.2d 1255 (Kan. App. 1988). In this case the court holds that high school students do have a constitutionally protected interest in participating in extracurricular activities.

Palmer v. Merluzzi, 868 F.2d 90 (3rd Cir. 1989). This case examines whether a student was adequately notified of

the accusation against him and was provided a meaningful opportunity to argue against his scholastic and athletic suspensions.

Mancuso vs. Massachusetts Interscholastic Athletic Association, 453 Mass. 116; 900 N.E.2d 518 (2009). This case examines whether students have a "legitimate claim of entitlement," to her participation in interscholastic athletics under State law, if the law recognizes a right to an education, which includes physical education.

QUESTIONS YOU SHOULD BE ABLE TO ANSWER

1. The Due Process Clauses are found in what Amendments of the Constitution?

2. The Due Process Clause is designed to protect what?

3. Substantive Due Process protects what right?

4. Procedural Due Process requires the state to provide what?

5. Do students have a protected right to participate in high school sports?

REFERENCES

Cases

Abbariao v. Hamline University School of Law, 258 N.W.2d 108 (Minn.1977)
Albach v. Odle, 531 F.2d 983 (10th Cir. 1976)
Behagen v. Intercollegiate Conference of Faculty Representatives, 346 F. Supp. 602 (D. Minn. 1972).
Board of Regents v. Roth, 408 U.S. 564 (1972).
Bruce v. South Carolina High School League, 189 S.E.2d 817 (S.C. 1972)
Butler v. Oak Creek-Franklin School District, 172 F. Supp. 2d 1102 (E.D. Wis. 2001).
Cafeteria & Restaurant Workers Union v. McElroy 367 U.S. 885 (1961)
Colorado Seminary v. NCAA, 417 F. Supp. 885 (D. Colo. 1976), *aff 'd,* 570 F.2d 320 (10th Cir. 1978).
Conrad v. The University of Washington, 834 P.2d 17 (Wash, 1992)
Davenport v. Randolph Co. Board of Education, 730 F.2d 1395 (11th Cir. 1984)
Duffley v. New Hampshire Interscholastic Athletic Association, 446 A.2d 462 (Sup. Ct. N.H. 1982).
Goldberg v. Kelly, 397 U.S. 254 (1970)
Goss v. Lopez, 419 U.S. 565 (1975).
Gulf South Conference v. Boyd, 369 So. 553 (Sup. Ct. Ala. 1979).
Hall v. University of Minnesota, 530 F. Supp. 104 (D. Minn. 1982).
Hamilton v. Tenn. Secondary School Athletic Association, 552 F.2d 681 (6th Cir. 1976)
Hass v. South Bend Community School Corporation, 289 N.E.2d 495 (Ind. 1972)
Indiana High School Athletic Association v. Carlberg, 694 N.E.2d 222 (Ind. 1998).
Kelley v. Metropolitan County Board of Education of Nashville, 293 F. Supp. 485 (M.D. Tenn. 1968).
Long v. Zopp, 476 F.2d 180 (4th Cir. 1973).
Mathews v. Eldridge, 424 U.S. 319 (1976).
Menke v. Ohio High School Athletic Association, 441 N.E.2d 620 (Ohio Ct. App. 1981)
Meyer v. Nebraska, 262 U.S. 390 (1923).
Moran v. School District #7, Yellowstone County, 350 F. Supp. 1180 (D. Mont. 1972).
National Collegiate Athletic Association v. Tarkanian, 488 U.S. 179 (1988)
National Collegiate Athletic Association v. Yeo, 114 S.W. 3d 584, rev'd 171 S.W. 3d 863 (Tex. 2003).

Niles v. University Interscholastic League, 715 F.2d 1027 (5th Cir. 1983).

Palmer v. Merluzzi, 868 F.2d 90 (3rd Cir. 1989).

Paul v. Davis, 424 U.S. 693 (1976).

Reid v. Renowa Hills Public Schools, 680 N.W.2d 62 (Mich. App. 2004).

Siegert v. Gilley, 500 U.S. 226 (1991)

Simkins v. South Dakota High School Activities Association, 434 N.W.2d 367 (S.D. 1989)

Spring Branch Independent School District, et al. v. Stamos, 695 S.W.2d 556 (Tex. 1985).

Stanley v. Big Eight Conference, 463 F. Supp. 920 (W.D. MO. 1978).

Stone v. Kansas State High School Activities Association, 761 P.2d 1255 (Kan. App. 1988).

U.S. v. Florida East Coast Ry, 410 U.S. 224 (1973).

Whipple v. Oregon School Activities Association, 629 P.2d 384 (Or. Ct. App. 1981)

Zehner v. Central Berkshire Regional School District, 921 F. Supp. 850 (D. Mass. 1996).

Publications

Hawkins, B. (2006). The Glucksberg Renaissance: Substantive Due Process since *Lawrence v. Texas*. *Michigan Law Review* 105, 409.

Pierce, R. (2002). Administrative Law Treatise (4th. Ed.). New York, NY: Aspen Press

Schoonmaker, L. (2010). State action. In D. J. Cotton & J. T. Wolohan (Eds.), Law for recreation and sport managers (5th Ed.) pp. 428–439. Dubuque, IA: Kendall/Hunt Publishing Co.

Sullivan, K. and Gunther, G. (2007). *Constitutional Law* (17th ed.). New York, NY: Foundation Press

Rotunda, R and Nowak, J. (1999). *Treatise on Constitutional Law: Substance and Procedure (3rd ed.).* St. Paul, MN: West Group

Legislation

Administrative Procedure Act, 5 U.S.C. §§ 551 et seq.

United States Constitution, Amendment V

United States Constitution, Amendment XIV

6.14 EQUAL PROTECTION

Sarah K. Fields I The Ohio State University

In 1868, just after the Civil War, Congress enacted the Fourteenth Amendment to the United States Constitution. The Equal Protection Clause of the Fourteenth Amendment decreed that "no state shall … deny to any person within its jurisdiction the equal protection of the laws." According to contemporary debates on the floor of the House of Representatives and the Senate, the Equal Protection Clause was not intended to be applied literally to all people: it was meant to provide some rights to African-American men; those rights were not intended to include the right to vote, to serve on a jury, or to marry white women. The framers of the Fourteenth Amendment clearly never intended that the clause be applied to women of any race. Thus from the first day, the Equal Protection Clause's literal universal inclusion has been limited, and the challenge for the courts over the past century and a half has been to determine what those limitations are and how to apply the Equal Protection Clause both practically and fairly.

Society and the laws constantly distinguish or discriminate between different groups of individuals. Not everyone is treated equally; for example, eight year olds are not allowed legally to drink alcohol, to join the military, or to drive cars. The Equal Protection Clause simply requires that similarly situated people be treated similarly and that the states be able to articulate and justify why they treat one group differently than another group. Over time, the courts have concluded that to determine if the government's classification is legal under the Equal Protection Clause, the test, or standard of review, will vary according to what category of people the classification describes. Today, courts usually use one of three different standards of review: (1) the easiest test to survive is **mere rationality** and most classifications are tested under this standard; (2) a more difficult middle tier, sometimes called **intermediate scrutiny**, applies to gender classifications; and (3) a very difficult to pass test of **strict scrutiny** applies to deprivations of fundamental rights and to classifications which are suspect—race, **alienage** (status of a foreigner legally within the country) and national origin.

The legal reach of equal protection derives from several sources. Although originally the Fourteenth Amendment only applied to the actions of the states, subsequent Supreme Court interpretation has concluded that the federal government must also comply with equal protection, both because it would be irrational to assume that the state governments must provide equal protection but the federal government would not and because the Fifth Amendment includes a "due process" clause. The Supreme Court ruled in *Bolling v. Sharpe* (1954), that the Fifth Amendment's due process clause inferred an equal protection component for the federal government. Equal protection also derives from the Civil Rights Act of 1871 (42 USC § 1983) which prohibits persons acting under color of law from depriving people of "rights, privileges, or immunities secured by the Constitution." This law protects individuals from having a governmental actor infringe upon their constitutional rights, including their right of equal protection. Additionally, every state constitution has some parallel language to the Equal Protection Clause of the Fourteenth Amendment to the U.S. Constitution, and individuals may file suit in state courts under their state Equal Protection Clause.

FUNDAMENTAL CONCEPTS

State Actor

Before a court can conclude that one's equal protection rights have been violated, the court must find that the defendant is a **state actor**. For an extended discussion of state action, what this means, and how to determine who a state actor is, see Section 6.12, *State Action*. In general, however, public schools and universities are considered state actors, as are community parks and recreation organizations. This means that they must comply with equal protection. Although in general, purely private organizations have greater freedom to discriminate between groups and are not usually limited by equal protection, occasionally courts have concluded that some private organizations have been so intertwined with governmental powers (such as using public facilities or acting in lieu of a governmental agency) that they too can be deemed state actors.

Standing

In order for a plaintiff to file a constitutional claim, the plaintiff must have a direct stake in the outcome of the case in order to have *standing*, see Section 6.11, *Judicial Review, Standing, and Injunctions*. Simply having an interest in the outcome of a case or the topic in general does not satisfy the standing requirement.

Purposeful Discrimination

Courts have determined that the Equal Protection Clause only protects individuals from intentional or **purposeful discrimination**. Unintentional discrimination or a **disparate impact**—when one group is more greatly burdened by a classification than another—on one group does not necessarily mean that equal protection has been violated. For example, on average men are taller than women, so if a fire department has a height minimum taller than the average height of women, more women may be excluded than men. This would be a disparate impact, but by itself, it would not be purposeful discrimination; to prove the regulation violated the Equal Protection Clause; a plaintiff would need evidence to indicate the height minimum was intended to exclude women.

Standards Of Review

Lowest Tier Rational Basis Review

The rational basis review or "**mere rationality**" test is the easiest standard of review and many classifications have survived legal challenges because the state actor has been able to establish that *the classification is rationally related to a legitimate governmental interest*. As mentioned in the example in the introduction to this section, eight year old children cannot legally drink alcohol, join the military, or drive because the vast majority of eight year olds are too young to make safe, informed decisions about their choices and drinking, joining the military, or driving could be dangerous to them and to others. The government has a legitimate interest in the safety of its children and its citizens, and the legal limitations placed on children are rationally related to that legitimate interest. This test applies when the classification the state uses is not subject to one of the more difficult standards of review as described later in this section.

Residency Classifications. Sport and recreation have provided a variety of examples of classifications that have been challenged on equal protection grounds. For example, in *Baldwin v. Fish & Game Commission of Montana* (1978), the Supreme Court concluded that the different classification of residents and non-residents of a state, and charging them different fees for hunting licenses, was rationally related to the legitimate state purpose of preserving a finite resource. (This case is available on the accompanying computer disc.) Similarly, the Ninth Circuit Court of Appeals concluded that excluding non-land owners from accessing restricted beaches did not violate the Equal Protection Clause (*Wright v. Incline Village General Improvement District*, 2011).

Classifications of Students Involved in Extracurricular Activities Compared to Other Students. In *Hageman v. Goshen County School* District (2011), a Wyoming school district adopted a policy of random, suspicionless drug and alcohol testing of all students who participated in extracurricular activities. When challenged on equal protection grounds, the courts upheld the policy because the district had a legitimate interest in deterring the use of drugs and alcohol and that the policy was rationally related to that interest (for more information on this topic see Section 6.23, *Drug Testing*). (This case is available on the accompanying computer disc).

Eligibility Rules. A number of eligibility rules have survived equal protection challenges in which mere rationality was the test. A few examples include, a federal district court in New York upholding a school district rule that athletes have tetanus shots prior to participation in outdoor sports. A young man whose family's religious beliefs precluded vaccinations had argued that the rule violated his equal protection rights. The court concluded that the classification was rationally related to the state's legitimate interest in the safety of its students (*Hadley v. Rush Henrietta Center School District*, 2007). In Virginia, a boy's parents chose to have him repeat the third grade because of a learning disability. As a senior in high school, he was one day too old to participate in high school sports because under the state's age eligibility rule. He turned 19 the day before the Virginia High School League rules allowed participation. The court ruled him ineligible because the eligibility rules were rationally related to a legitimate state interest, and he had no fundamental right to compete (*Sisson v. Virginia High School League*, 2010). In another case involving the Virginia High School League, a federal district court upheld the Leagues' transfer rules, allowing immediate eligibility if the students, after their high school closed, attended the local school closest to them. The court concluded that this was not a violation of the students' equal protection rights (*McGee v. Virginia High School League*, 2011).

Not all eligibility rules survive equal protection challenges, however. For example, in Indiana, an appellate court concluded that the state high school athletic association had violated the equal protection rights of a student who had received poor grades and ultimately withdrawn from the eleventh grade because of illness. The school allowed him to repeat the grade, but the athletic association deemed him ineligible. The court concluded that excluding the student, who had not withdrawn from school to gain any kind of athletic competitive advantage, was arbitrary and capricious (*Indiana High School Athletic Ass'n v. Schafer*, 1992).

Intermediate Scrutiny

Quasi-suspect classifications are subject to intermediate scrutiny. Thus far the Supreme Court has consistently found *gender and illegitimacy to be quasi-suspect categories*, but gender is the most relevant quasi-suspect classification for the sport and recreation manager. The Supreme Court created this middle tier of testing in a series of gender discrimination lawsuits in the 1970s. Prior to the 1970s, gender discrimination had been traditionally examined under the mere rationality test and government discrimination against women frequently survived this test. For example, in *State v. Hunter* (1956), a woman convicted of wrestling without a state license appealed her conviction on the grounds that the state law violated her equal protection rights: the state at that time only issued wrestling licenses to men. She lost her case because the Oregon Supreme Court concluded that the classification was rationally related to the state's legitimate interest in protecting public health, morals, and participants' safety.

As the Women's Rights movement of the twentieth century progressed, however, the Supreme Court made it more difficult for local, state and Federal governments to utilize gender classifications. In *Craig v. Boren* (1976), the majority of the Court held that to survive equal protection scrutiny, *a gender classification must be substantially related to an important governmental objective.*

Gender Classifications and Contact Sport. Female athletes have used the Equal Protection Clause to gain the right to try out of contact sports teams such as football in *Force by Force v. Pierce City R-VI School District*, (1983), and wrestling *Adams v. Baker*, (1996). (The *Adams* case is available on the accompanying computer disc.) In each case the courts recognized that other gender discrimination legislation like Title IX would not help the athlete. The enforcement regulations for Title IX, for example, exempt contact sport from the law, and the Equal Protection Clause can be used to close that exemption. For more information see Section 7.11, *Gender Equity: Opportunities to Participate*. In *Force* and *Adams*, the defendant school districts had argued primarily that the state had an important interest in protecting the female athletes from the dangers of co-educational contact sport, in protecting the psyche of the boys' they would compete against, and in maintaining a smoothly run sports program.

The courts rejected the arguments that the state had an important interest in the psyche of only the male athletes and in logistical ease (like needing a separate changing space for the female athlete). Although the courts agreed that the safety of all students was an important state interest, they did not agree that a gender classification was substantially related to that important interest because that classification erroneously presumed that all boys were bigger and stronger than all girls and thus a gender classification failed to have a substantial relationship with the important governmental interest in children's safety. The Equal Protection Clause does not, however, require that a school create a separate female team in a contact sport, only that the school allow females to try out for sports on the contact sport team (*Mansourian v. Board of Regents*, 2011).

In the converse, schoolboys who have filed equal protection lawsuits to gain access to traditionally female sports like field hockey have been much less successful. For example in 1987, a New Jersey state court concluded that the school district's rule barring boys from playing on girls' sports teams did not violate the state version of the Equal Protection Clause. The school had argued that the classification was substantially related to the important governmental interest in redressing past gender discrimination in high school sport. The court agreed, noting that if boys were to play on girls' teams it might result in fewer girls participating (because boys would take their spots on the team) and that some girls might quit sport altogether when faced with a male competitor (*B.C. v. Cumberland Regional School District*).

Gender Discrimination and Scheduling Seasons. In 2006, the Sixth Circuit Court of Appeals ended a long running battle between a group called Communities for Equity and the Michigan High School Athletic Association. The MHSAA had, for years, scheduled many girls' sports in so-called off or non-traditional seasons. For example, although the game of basketball has traditionally been a winter sport, in Michigan, high school girls played in the fall season. Communities for Equity believed this distinction to be a violation of equal protection and filed suit on those grounds. The MHSAA argued that scheduling girls' sport in nontraditional seasons allowed more girls and boys to play sports and also allowed both boys and girls access to the best facilities and practice and competition times without having internal fights for court or game times. The Sixth Court of Appeals affirmed a lower court decision that the distinction was indeed a violation of the Equal Protection Clause because the state failed to establish that the gender classification was substantially related to that important interest. The court particularly condemned the MHSAA for only scheduling girls' teams in the off-seasons, noting that if scheduling was really so challenging and if non-traditional scheduling was really so helpful, the burden could have been borne equally by boys' and girls' teams (2006). Another interesting case involving the scheduling of games based on gender occurred in 2012, when the Seventh Circuit Court of Appeals overturned a district court's dismissal of an equal protection lawsuit against an Indiana school district. The plaintiffs complained that about 95% of boys' high school basketball games were scheduled for primetime nights whereas only 53% of the girls' games were, and they argued that this was a violation of the girls' equal protection rights. The Appellate Court agreed (*Parker v. Franklin County Community School Corp.*, 2012). (This case is available on the accompanying computer disc).

Workplace Discrimination. The Equal Protection Clause has also been used as a cause of action in response to gender discrimination in the sporting workplace. A female reporter was barred from the New York Yankees' locker room in the city-owned and maintained Yankee Stadium. The Yankees and Major League Baseball argued that the state had an important governmental interest in protecting the privacy of its players, in promoting a family atmosphere in the sport, and in complying with traditional standards of decency. Although the court agreed that protecting the players' privacy was an important governmental interest, they did not agree that barring women from the locker room was substantially related to that interest, given that the privacy could be accorded with the use of towels, robes, or other clothing (*Ludtke v. Kuhn*, 1978). For more information on this topic see Section 7.12, *Gender Equity: Coaching and Administration*.

Strict Scrutiny

Fundamental Rights Deprivation. Strict scrutiny is triggered when a state deprives a person of his or her fundamental rights. These fundamental rights include those articulated in the Constitution—freedom of speech and the right to assemble peaceably for example—and also some rights not articulated. The right to vote, to travel, and to privacy have all been established as fundamental rights. Education has been deemed a nonfundamental right and participating in sport has simply been deemed a privilege; therefore, for sport and recreation managers, fundamental rights deprivations are relatively uncommon.

Fundamental rights deprivations, however, can occur. For example, a Texas school district had a rule prohibiting married students from participating in extracurricular activities including sport. The district argued that the rule was intended to help married student succeed in his or her education and marriage as well as to discourage early marriage between students. The court concluded that because the right to marry is fundamental, the district needed to prove that the *classification was necessary to achieve a compelling governmental interest*. The court found the district failed to do this because the district had no evidence that banning married students from extracurricular activities helped married students in any aspect of their lives (*Bell v. Lone Oak Independent School District*, 1974).

Suspect Classifications. Suspect classifications can also trigger strict scrutiny. The Supreme Court has concluded that race, national origin, and alienage are suspect classifications. To survive an equal protection challenge, the state must prove that *the suspect classification is necessary to achieve a compelling governmental interest, and the classification must be the least restrictive means of achieving that interest.* This test is very stringent and very few laws involving suspect classifications have survived the test and been deemed constitutional.

That said, one recreation case did involve what seemed to be racial discrimination. After long operating racially segregated city pools, the city of Jackson, Mississippi, was ordered to desegregate its pools towards the end of the 1960s because segregation violated the Equal Protection Clause. The city, arguing that they could not afford to operate its pools anymore, closed four of the pools and leased the fifth pool to a private organization that limited access to whites only. Several African-American residents sued, arguing that the city had violated their equal protection rights by closing the pools to African-Americans only, as white citizens had the option of joining the private organization. A closely divided Supreme Court concluded that the city could close its pools to avoid racial integration because all citizens, not just African-American ones, were denied access (*Palmer v. Thompson*, 1971) and the city had no obligation to operate pools.

Allegations of racial discrimination, however, are still made. In 2011 in *Boyd v. Feather River Community College District*, African-American members of the football team claimed that they had been cut from the team because of their race after a season of suffering verbal and physical abuse that was racially motivated. A federal district court rejected the defendants' request to dismiss the case, concluding that sufficient evidence of racial discrimination existed.

Sliding Scale Approach

The three-tier level of testing as described above evolved from the traditional two-tier level of testing (mere rationality and strict scrutiny). Some scholars argue that the courts have on occasion engaged in something known as the sliding-scale approach. This approach, championed by the late Supreme Court Justice Thurgood Marshall, maintained that the courts should dispense with the rigid tier system and balance the rights and interests of the individuals and the state in determining the appropriate level of scrutiny.

As a practical matter, courts, including the U.S. Supreme Court, have seemed to tinker with the levels of tests in their analyses. For example, in 1996 in *U.S. v. Virginia*, the Virginia Military Institute (VMI) attempted to justify its male-only admission policy against the federal government's claims that the policy violated the Equal Protection Clause. Writing for a six-person majority, Justice Ruth Bader Ginsberg seemed to rely on the intermediate level of scrutiny, but added that a state actor must have an "exceedingly persuasive" justification for gender segregation, adding that gender classifications would trigger "skeptical scrutiny." The majority found that VMI's male-only admission policy was a violation of the Equal Protection Clause, because the state had failed to provide that exceedingly persuasive justification. In his concurrence Chief Justice William Rehnquist supported in the decision of the majority but did so while clearly articulating the traditional intermediate scrutiny test. Justice Anton Scalia, in his dissent, argued adamantly against Justice Ginsberg's ratcheted-up test for gender classifications.

Relying on the "exceedingly persuasive" language, a federal court allowed an equal protection challenge to a community golf tournament which was limited to men only to go to trial. A woman had been excluded based on her gender, and the community club justified this because they offered the occasional tournament for women only. The court suggested that tradition was not an exceedingly persuasive justification for gender discrimination (*Joyce v. Town of Dennis*, 2010). As a result, the sport and recreation manager should be aware that the tests surrounding equal protection have evolved over time and are likely to continue to do so.

Over and Under-Inclusive

Perhaps the most common reason that courts reject classifications as violating equal protection is because the classification includes more people than it should or, both alternatively and sometimes simultaneously, the classification does not include all the people it should in order to meet the objective of the law. For example in *Sullivan v. University Interscholastic League* (1981), the state athletic association argued that their rule making transfer students ineligible to compete in varsity basketball and football was rationally related to their legitimate interest in discouraging the recruiting of athletes, a practice which undermined the educational experience of a student. The Texas Supreme Court agreed that the state did have a legitimate interest in promoting a

Chapter 6.10 Concepts 445

"level playing field," in emphasizing education over athletics, and in discouraging the recruitment of athletes. The court, however, thought the rule was not rationally related to the interest because it was over-inclusive; the rule applied to all transfer students, even those who transferred for reasons completely unrelated to sport. For example, if a student transferred because a parent got a better job and the family moved, the student was ineligible. (This case is included on the accompanying computer disc.)

For an example of a classification being struck down because it was both over- and under-inclusive, consider the case of a student-athlete who challenged a rule preventing married students from participating in high school sports. The state argued that the rule existed to promote a wholesome high school atmosphere, to discourage married students from discussing sex in the locker room, to reduce drop-out rates, and to encourage married students to focus on their education and marriage. In ruling for the student, the court concluded that the rule was over-inclusive: some married students of good character would do nothing to detract from a wholesome atmosphere and this student in particular had been allowed to play while the case was pending, and his grades improved, he held a part-time job, and he remained married. The court concluded the rule was also under-inclusive because it did not bar the participation of students who engaged in pre-marital sex nor those students who were of poor character (*Indiana High School Athletics Ass'n v. Raike*, 1975).

SIGNIFICANT CASE

Fusato v. Washington Interscholastic Activities Association is an example of one of the most recent cases involving discrimination against someone because of their national origins in sport. Note how the court applied the strict scrutiny test and dismissed the state's arguments justifying their classification.

FUSATO V. WASHINGTON INTERSCHOLASTIC ACTIVITIES ASSOCIATION

Court of Appeals of Washington, Division Three
970 P.2d 774 (Wash. App. 1999)

Tomoe Fusato challenges the Washington Interscholastic Activities Association's (WIAA) residence and transfer rules, which, with few exceptions, forbid students from playing varsity athletics if they did not relocate to a school district with their parents. The superior court reversed the administrative decision against Ms. Fusato and found the WIAA's rules violated the Fourteenth Amendment's Equal Protection Clause. Although the matter is moot, we proceed and decide the trial court did not err taking judicial notice of certain facts. We conclude that although no fundamental right is threatened, the rule of strict scrutiny applies. This is so because the challenged rules discriminatorily impact Ms. Fusato as a member of a suspect class based upon national origin and there is no showing of a compelling state interest being served by these rules. Additionally, the WIAA did not demonstrate that the least restrictive means were used to accomplish the regulatory purposes of their rules. Accordingly, we affirm.

FACTS

Ms. Fusato, a Japanese National, moved from Okinawa to live with her aunt and uncle in Kettle Falls. The purpose of the move was to experience American culture and help ease the biases prevalent against Americans arising from recent criminal conduct on the part of American servicemen. She was told she was ineligible for varsity sports at Kettle Falls High School under WIAA rules.

The WIAA, a nonprofit organization, regulates interscholastic athletics at 385 secondary schools under RCW 28A.600.200. WIAA Rule 18.10.1(A) does not allow transferring students to be immediately eligible for varsity competition unless they transfer with their "entire family unit." Since Ms. Fusato moved without her parents a "hardship" was required for eligibility. Because neither the District 7 Eligibility Committee nor the Executive Board of the WIAA found her case to be a hardship under WIAA Rule 18.22.1, her eligibility was denied.

The Stevens County Superior Court, Judge Stewart, on appeal from the WIAA regulatory process, initially entered a temporary restraining order, permitting Ms. Fusato to play varsity sports pending final hearing. Judge Schroeder reviewed and maintained the temporary order at a continuation hearing. Finally, Judge Baker at the hearing on the merits, held the rules excluded a class of students based on national origin. The court further found the rules have a disparate impact based on this suspect class. The court took judicial notice that "almost every foreign exchange students and/or I-20 VISA students—it's almost unheard of in a high school setting—that such foreign students are here with their parents." The court also took judicial notice that "a typical foreign exchange or I-20 VISA student is unable to ever establish a hardship under the transfer rules."

The trial court concluded there was no compelling state interest in the WIAA residence and transfer rules and, accordingly, found them to be in violation of the Equal Protection Clause in the Fourteenth Amendment of the United States Constitution.

* * *

Analysis: Equal Protection

1. Issue. The issue is whether the trial court erred by using strict scrutiny and deciding the WIAA residence and transfer rules violated the Equal Protection Clause of the Fourteenth Amendment.

2. Standard of Review. Constitutional challenges are reviewed de novo. *See Washam v. Sonntag*, 74 Wn.App. 504, 507, 874 P.2d 188 (1994) (addressing whether statute violates state constitution as issue of law subject to de novo review).

3. Discussion. The challenger of a rule, regulation or statute claiming an equal protection violation may have to meet one of three different legal standards for judging whether a violation exists. *City of Richland v. Michel*, 89 Wn.App. 764, 768–70, 950 P.2d 10 (1998). The choice is based upon the factual context, giving rise to different degrees of scrutiny in ascending order of difficulty of proof: strict, intermediate, or minimum.

One of three standards of review has been employed when analyzing equal protection claims. Strict scrutiny applies when a classification affects a suspect class or threatens a fundamental right. Intermediate or heightened scrutiny, used by this court in limited circumstances, applies when important rights or semisuspect classifications are affected. The most relaxed (minimum) level of scrutiny, commonly referred to as the rational basis or rational relationship test, applies when

a statutory classification does not involve a suspect or semisuspect class and does not threaten a fundamental right.

State v. Manussier, 129 Wn.2d 652, 672–73, 921 P.2d 473 (1996), *cert. denied*, 520 U.S. 1201, 117 S. Ct. 1563, 137 L. Ed. 2d 709 (1997) (citations omitted). It normally follows that the party seeking to uphold the rule, regulation, or statute generally prefers the minimum scrutiny standard, using the rational relationship test.

Deciding the degree or standard of scrutiny is our first task. *Harris v. Department of Labor & Indus.*, 120 Wn.2d 461, 476–77, 843 P.2d 1056 (1993). Here, Ms. Fusato argues for strict scrutiny and defends the trial court's decision while the WIAA argues for the lesser minimum scrutiny standard and use of the rational relationship test. When strict scrutiny is involved, the classification will be upheld if it is shown to be necessary to accomplish a compelling state interest. *Westerman v. Cary*, 125 Wn.2d 277, 294, 892 P.2d 1067 (1994). If the complaining party demonstrates strict scrutiny is the proper test under the facts, then the burden shifts to the party seeking to uphold the rule, regulation, or statute "to show the restrictions serve a compelling state interest and are the least restrictive means for achieving the government objective. If no compelling state interest exists, the restrictions are unconstitutional." *First United Methodist Church v. Hearing Examiner*, 129 Wn.2d 238, 246, 916 P.2d 374 (1996).

If neither a suspect class is involved nor a fundamental right is threatened, the appropriate standard of review is the rational basis test. *Manussier*, 129 Wn.2d at 673. We answer three questions when deciding if the rational relationship test applies.

1. Does the classification apply alike to all members within the designated class?
2. Do reasonable grounds exist to support a distinction between those within and without each class? and
3. Does the class have a "rational relationship" to the purpose of the legislation?

Harris, 120 Wn.2d at 477. Because the trial court agreed with Ms. Fusato that the strict scrutiny test applies here, we examine it first.

Washington courts have recognized there is no fundamental right to engage in interscholastic sports. *Darrin v. Gould*, 85 Wn.2d 859, 873, 540 P.2d 882 (1975). It follows that for Ms. Fusato to prevail, the WIAA residence and transfer rules must discriminate against a suspect class to warrant strict scrutiny review. Suspect classifications include those based on race, national origin, or alienage. U.S. CONST. amend. XIV; *State v. Wallace*, 86 Wn.App. 546, 552, 937 P.2d 200, *review denied*, 133 Wn.2d 1028, 950 P.2d 478 (1997). Ms. Fusato alleges discrimination and disparate impact based on her national origin.

Under the WIAA residence and transfer rules, foreign exchange and I-20 VISA students, persons of identifiable foreign national origins, cannot compete at the varsity level because their parents usually do not accompany them to the United States. Thus, disparate impact based on alienage is present. Therefore, for persons of foreign national origin the sole recourse is to apply for hardship exception under the WIAA rules. WIAA rule 18.22.1 provides:

A. A hardship exists only when some unique circumstances concerning the student's educational, physical or emotional status exist and only when such circumstances are beyond the student's or, where applicable, their family unit' or legal guardian's control.

B. The circumstances must be totally different from those which exist for the majority or even a small minority of students (e.g., usual maturation problems or family situations which do not cause severe and abnormal emotional problems, and academic or athletic deficiencies in a school's curriculum or extra-curricular activities do not constitute a hardship).

C. There must be no reason to believe that the decision and/or the execution of the decision concerning the student's academic status was for athletic purposes.

D. The burden of providing evidence that a hardship exists shall be borne by the student.

E. There shall be a direct, causal relationship between the alleged hardship and the student's inability to meet the specific eligibility rule(s).

The trial court found, and we agree, a typical foreign exchange or I-20 VISA student cannot meet the hardship criteria. While the alleged purpose of the rules is to prevent school "jumping" for athletic purposes and to ensure equal treatment, the practical effect is that some students are severely limited in eligibility based solely on their national origin. Concerning similar residence and transfer rules, the Indiana Supreme Court points out:

> The rules as presently constituted penalize a student-athlete who wishes to transfer for academic or religious reasons or for any number of other legitimate reasons. Surely, denying eligibility to such transferees in no way furthers IHSAA objectives.

Indiana High Sch. Athletic Ass'n v. Carlberg, 694 N.E.2d 222, 238 (Ind. 1997). Similarly, the application of the rules to Ms. Fusato does not further their stated purposes.

However, the United States Supreme Court has repeatedly held that disparate impact, alone, does not violate the Fourteenth Amendment. *See Harris v. McRae*, 448 U.S. 297, 324 n.26, 100 S. Ct. 2671, 65 L. Ed. 2d

784 (1980) (disparate impact based on financial circumstance); *Personnel Admin. v. Feeney*, 442 U.S. 256, 273, 99 S. Ct. 2282, 2293, 60 L. Ed. 2d 870 (1979) (disparate impact based on gender); *Washington v. Davis*, 426 U.S. 229, 96 S. Ct. 2040, 48 L. Ed. 2d 597 (1976) (disparate impact based on race). Specifically, disparate impact of a suspect class does not trigger strict scrutiny unless the party challenging the government action demonstrates an element of purposeful discrimination or intent. *Macias v. Department of Labor & Indus.*, 100 Wn.2d 263, 269–70, 668 P.2d 1278 (1983).

The burden is on the party alleging discrimination to prove the existence of purposeful discrimination. *Batson v. Kentucky*, 476 U.S. 79, 93, 106 S. Ct. 1712, 90 L. Ed. 2d 69 (1986). The court must undertake "a sensitive inquiry into such circumstantial and direct evidence of intent as may be available." *Id.* (citing *Village of Arlington Heights v. Metropolitan Hous. Dev. Corp.*, 429 U.S. 252, 266, 97 S. Ct. 555, 50 L. Ed. 2d 450 (1977)). Circumstantial evidence may suffice to establish purposeful discrimination. *Batson,* 476 U.S. at 93.

During Ms. Fusato's first administrative hearing, one of the committee members stated in response to an allegation that schools were abusing foreign exchange students:

> I don't really think that was the reason. The abusing of the foreign exchange program was not the problem. The problem was that people were bitching and complaining about the fact that we[']re giving them [foreign students] special privileges and these other people are getting turned down[.] [Our] own people within the country, and that's why they changed the rule. I'm sure that's the reason.

For the WIAA to modify its rules to specifically discriminate against foreign exchange or I-20 VISA students in an attempt to make participation fairer for "our students" establishes discriminatory purpose or intent. Thus, strict scrutiny is warranted because we have both discriminatory impact based upon national origin or alienage and discriminatory purpose.

The WIAA now has the heavy burden of proving that it is necessary to discriminate based on national origin to further a compelling interest. It does not seek to meet this burden but argues solely that the rational relationship applies. In view of our rejection of that proposition, our analysis is complete. We decide the strict scrutiny test applies to these facts shifting the burden to the WIAA to show a compelling state interest. We conclude the WIAA has not met its burden to show a compelling state interest was served by the challenged rules. Further, the WIAA has made no effort to demonstrate that the least restrictive regulatory means have been employed to accomplish the stated purposes. Therefore, we hold the challenged residence and transfer rules are invalid under the equal protection clause of the federal constitution and affirm the trial court.

CASES ON THE SUPPLEMENTAL WEB SITE

Adams v. Baker, 919 F. Supp. 1496 (D. Kan. 1996). The reader should note the state's justifications for gender discrimination and how the court characterized them.

Baldwin v. Fish and Game Commission of Montana, 436 U.S. 371 (1978). Examine Montana's arguments for treating resident and non-resident hunters differently.

Hageman v. Goshen County School District, 256 P.3d 487 (Wyo. 2011). Consider how the Wyoming Supreme Court evaluated the school district's argument that all students were treated equally.

Parker v. Franklin County Community School Corp., 2012 U.S. App. LEXIS 1783 (7th Cir. Jan. 31, 2012). Examine the court's discussion of the substantive experiences of game times in light of the equal protection claims.

Sullivan v. University Interscholastic League, 616 S.W.2d 170 (Tex. 1981). Texas recognized the dangers of high schools recruiting strong athletes, but the state's answer is an example of how a statute can be overbroad.

QUESTIONS YOU SHOULD BE ABLE TO ANSWER

1. Why doesn't equal protection require that the Augusta National Golf Club (home of the Masters Tournament) allow women to join the club?

2. What are the three different standards of review for classifications under the Equal Protection Clause? Explain which standard should be used for which classification.

3. What does it mean for a statute to be void for being over- or under-inclusive? How can a statue be both over and under-inclusive simultaneously?

4. In *Fusato v. Washington Interscholastic Activities Association* what evidence did the court have that suggested the discrimination was intentional or purposeful and not simply a matter of disparate impact?

5. Some scholars argue that the middle level of scrutiny for gender classifications should be collapsed into the strict scrutiny category. Explain why you think this is a logical or illogical argument.

REFERENCES

Cases

Adams v. Baker, 919 F. Supp. 1496 (D. Kan. 1996).
Baldwin v. Fish & Game Commission of Montana, 436 U.S. 371 (1978).
Bell v. Lone Oak Independent School District, 507 S.W.2d 636 (Tex. Civ. App. 1974).
B.C. v. Cumberland Regional School District, 531 A.2d 1059 (N.J. Super. 1987).
Bolling v. Sharpe 347 U.S. 497 (1954).
Boyd v. Feather River Community College District, No. 2:11-CV-0231 JAM-EFB, 2011 U.S. Dist. LEXIS 12168 (E.D. Cal. Oct. 20, 2011).
Communities for Equity v. Michigan High School Athletic Ass'n, 178 F. Supp. 2d 805 (W.D. Mich. 2001), *aff 'd,* 459 F. 3d 676 (6th Cir. 2006).
Craig v. Boren, 429 U.S. 190 (1976).
Force by Force v. Pierce City R-VI School District, 570 F. Supp. 2010 (S.W. Mo. 1983).
Hadley v. Rush Henrietta Center School District, No. 05-CV-6331T, 2007 U.S. Dist LEXIS 30586 (W.D. N.Y., April 25, 2007).
Indiana High School Athletics Ass'n v. Raike, 329 N.E.2d 66 (Ind. Ct. App. 1975).
Indiana High School Athletic Ass'n v. Schafer, 598 N.E.2d 540 (Ind. App. 1992).
Joyce v. Town of Dennis, 705 F. Supp. 2d 74 (D. Mass. 2010).
Ludtke v. Kuhn, 461 F. Supp. 86 (S.D. N.Y. 1978).
Mansourian v. Board of Regents, NO. 2:03-cv-2591 FCD EFB, 2011 U.S. Dist. LEXIS 85396 (E.D. Cal. Aug. 3, 2011).
McGee v. Virginia High School League, 801 F. Supp. 2d 526 (W.D. Va. 2011).
Palmer v. Thompson, 403 U.S. 217 (1971).
Parker v. Franklin County Community School Corp., No. 10-3595, 2012 U.S. App. LEXIS 1783 (7th Cir. Jan. 31, 2012).
Hageman v. Goshen County School District, 256 P.3d 487 (Wyo. 2011).

Sisson v. Virginia High School League, No.7:10CV00530, 2010 U.S. Dist. LEXIS 132264 (W.D. Va. Dec. 14, 2010).
State v. Hunter, 300 P.2d 455 (Ore. 1956).
St. Augustine High School v. Louisiana High School Athletic Ass'n., 270 F. Supp. 767 (E.D. La. 1967), *aff 'd.*, 396 F.2d 224 (Fifth Cir. 1968).
Sullivan v. University Interscholastic League, 616 S.W.2d 170 (Tex. 1981).
Wright v. Incline Village General Improvement District, No. 10-16043, 2011 U.S. App. LEXIS 26086 (9th Cir. Dec. 27, 2011).
United States v. Virginia, 518 U.S. 515 (1996).

Publications
Fields, Sarah K. (2005). *Female Gladiators: Gender, Law, and Contact Sport in America*. Champaign, IL: University of Illinois Press.
Karst, Kenneth (1977). Equal Citizenship under the Fourteenth Amendment. *Harvard Law Review 91*, 1–69.
Sullivan, K. M. and Gunther, G. (2010). *Constitutional Law*, 17th ed. Minneapolis: West Publishing.

Legislation
U.S. Constitution, Amend. 5.
U.S. Constitution, Amend. 14 § 1.
42 U.S.C. § 1983.

6.15 SEARCH AND SEIZURE/RIGHT TO PRIVACY

Margaret E. Ciccolella | University of the Pacific

The right of privacy is fundamental to American heritage and to rights guaranteed by the United States Constitution. While the word "privacy" is not found in the United States Constitution, privacy interests are found in the "penumbra" of rights guaranteed throughout the Constitution, e.g., the First, Fourth, Fifth, and Fourteenth Amendments safeguard privacy interests relevant to freedom of expression, substantive due process, equal protection, and search and seizure of one's person and/or personal effects.

The interpretation of the nature and extent of privacy protections have been contested within the context of education and its athletic programs. First Amendment protections dealing with personal conduct and expression have been challenged by considering the authority of the schools to regulate hair length (*Menora v. Illinois High School Assn.*, 1982; *Tinker v. Des Moines Indep. Comm. School District*, 1969), dress (*Dunham v. Pulsifer*, 1970; *Zeller v. Donegal School District*, 1975), on- and off-court/field behavior (*Bunger v. Iowa H.S. Athletic Assn.*, 1972) and marriage/parenthood of student-athletes (*Davis v. Meek*, 1972; *Estay v. LaFourche Parish School Board*, 1969; *Indiana High School Athletic Assn. v. Raike*, 1975; *Perry v. Granada Municipal School District*, 1969). Confidentiality of educational records protected by the Family Educational Rights and Privacy Act, also known as the "Buckley Amendment," has been challenged (*Marmo v. NYC Board of Education*, 1968). The Freedom of Information Act, often used as a basis on which to challenge confidentiality, has been challenged itself (*Arkansas Gazette Co. v. Southern State College*, 1981). Clearly, privacy exceeds Fourth Amendment protections and is addressed throughout the Constitution and in federal statutory law.

However, it is the Fourth Amendment of the United States Constitution that is considered the "heart" of privacy protection and is therefore central to any discussion of the issue. It is the primary purpose of this chapter to focus upon privacy interests of student-athletes as they relate specifically to the Fourth Amendment of the United States Constitution. Perhaps no issue illustrates this better than case law on urinalysis-drug-testing of high school and intercollegiate athletes.

FUNDAMENTAL CONCEPTS

The Fourth Amendment

The Fourth Amendment to the United States Constitution states:

> The right of the people to be secure in their persons, houses, papers, and effects against unreasonable searches and seizures, shall not be violated, and no Warrant shall issue, but upon probable cause, supported by Oath or affirmation, and particularly describing the place to be searched, and the persons or things to be seized. (United States Constitution, Amendment IV)

The Fourth Amendment, made applicable to the states by virtue of the Fourteenth Amendment, guarantees that individuals are protected against ***"arbitrary invasions by governmental officials"*** (*O'Connor v. Ortega*, 1987). Note that only unreasonable searches and seizures are prohibited. Also, in the context of conduct by law enforcement, warrants based upon probable cause are required.

Once a search or seizure is characterized as "unreasonable," it is unconstitutional and therefore is prohibited. In the context of athletics, searches of lockers, personal items, or a person become potentially serious invasions of privacy by the language of the Fourth Amendment. Valid warrants based upon probable cause are rarely the situation in athletics because school searches are not typically under the authority of law enforcement. More commonly, in the context of public school-aged and college-aged athletes, searches and seizures occur under the authority of school officials.

It is important to distinguish constitutionally permissible from constitutionally prohibited conduct as determined by the Fourth Amendment. Fourth Amendment analysis of search and seizure privacy interests must consider three basic issues. First, does the conduct represent state (governmental) action? Second, is the conduct a search? Third, is the search reasonable?

Is There State Action?

The Fourth Amendment protects individuals from invasions of privacy by the government. It does not protect against the conduct of private individuals or organizations. The NCAA is not subject to Fourth Amendment scrutiny because the regulatory functions of the NCAA are considered to represent private and not state action (*Arlosoroff v. NCAA*, 1984). Action or conduct by state, local, or federal officials is state or governmental action for purposes of the Fourth Amendment. For example, public but not private schools are subject to Fourth Amendment standards of review.

Is the Conduct a Search?

Under Fourth Amendment analysis, a search occurs when an expectation of privacy which society is prepared to consider reasonable is infringed (*Schaill v. Tippecanoe County School Corp.*, 1989). The United States Supreme Court has held that the collection and testing of urine constitute a search under the Fourth Amendment (*Skinner v. Railway Labor Executives' Assn.*, 1989). This is especially relevant to athletes subject to mandatory urine testing. In *Skinner,* the Court stated:

> It is not disputed, however, that chemical analysis of urine, like that of blood, can reveal a host of private medical facts about an employee, including whether he or she is epileptic, pregnant, or diabetic. Nor can it be disputed that the process of collecting the sample to be tested, which may in some cases involve visual or aural monitoring of the act of urination, itself implicates privacy interests (*Skinner v. Railway Labor Executives' Assn.*, 1989).

There remains a legitimate expectation of privacy for both the college and public school student that a student's urine is not subject to public scrutiny. The courts continue to hold that the mandatory urine testing of student-athletes constitutes a search and seizure (*University of Colorado v. Derdeyn*, 1993; *O'Halloran v. University of Washington*, 1988; *Vernonia v. Acton*, 1995). This does not mean that mandatory urine testing of students will result in a violation of the Fourth Amendment. In *O'Halloran v. University of Washington* (1988), the constitutionality of drug testing college athletes was upheld even though it was concluded that, "the NCAA's urine testing program is a search for Fourth Amendment analysis." In 1995, the Supreme Court held that mandatory, random urinalysis testing of public school athletes represented a reasonable search under a Fourth Amendment analysis (*Vernonia v. Acton*, 1995). Most recently, the Supreme Court extended this holding to public school students who participate in competitive extramural activities (*Board of Education v. Earls*, 2002).

It is clear that urine testing of student-athletes represents a search. The more crucial question is whether the search is reasonable. Reasonableness, by considering all of the events or the "totality of the circumstances" surrounding a search, will ultimately determine whether a Fourth Amendment violation has occurred.

Is the Conduct a Reasonable Search?

The Fourth Amendment prohibits only unreasonable searches. However, the test of reasonableness under the Fourth Amendment is not capable of precise definition or mechanical application. The Supreme Court consistently asserts what is "reasonable" depends on the context within which a search takes place (*National Treasury Employees Union v. Von Raab*, 1989; *O'Connor v. Ortega*, 1987; *Skinner v. Railway Labor Executives' Assn.*, 1989). In *New Jersey v. T.L.O.* (1985), the proper standard for assessing the legality of a school search by school officials was determined. In this case, school officials searched a student's purse for drugs. *The Supreme Court held that reasonableness of a search involved a two-fold inquiry.* First, *was the search justified at its inception,* e.g., was there reasonable suspicion for the search? Second, *was the search reasonable in its scope,* e.g., were the measures adopted reasonably related to the objectives of the search and not excessively intrusive in light of the age and sex of the student and the nature of the infraction?

In light of the *T.L.O.* holding and in the context of warrantless school searches, it is common for a court to determine reasonableness by a) considering the existence of reasonable suspicion for the search, and b) balancing the degree of intrusion on individual privacy interests against governmental interests in conducting the search.

Reasonable Suspicion. Reasonable suspicion has been defined as "the existence of reasonable circumstances, reports, information, or reasonable direct observation" leading to the belief that illegal drugs have been used (*Horsemen's Benevolent & Protective Assn. v. State Racing Commission*, 1989). The University of Colorado (CU) amended its suspicionless urine testing program by including a rapid eye examination (REE). REE became the basis for a subsequent mandatory urinalysis on the basis that a positive REE test provided reasonable suspicion of drug use. Other physical and behavioral characteristics were also used as a basis for reasonable suspicion including excessive aggressiveness and poor health habits (*University of Colorado v. Derdeyn*, 1993).

New Jersey v. T.L.O. (1985) required individualized suspicion, but because of the facts of that case, the Court was not required to consider whether circumstances could ever exist that could negate the need for individualized suspicion. *Vernonia v. Acton* (1995) may well have provided the circumstances missing in *New Jersey*. See *Significant Case*, below.

Balancing Test. In addition to considering the existence of reasonable suspicion, the courts typically balance the degree of the intrusion on an individual's privacy interests against the government's interests in testing.

Privacy Interests of the Student-Athlete

Privacy interests of athletes have included the following arguments (*Hill v. NCAA*, 1994):

1. There are few activities in our society more personal or private than the passing of urine. Therefore, the visual or aural monitoring of urination implicates privacy interests.
2. Monitored urine collection is embarrassing and degrading thereby violating privacy and dignitary interests protected by the Fourth Amendment.
3. Chemical analysis of urine violates medical confidentiality because it can reveal a host of private medical facts, e.g., epilepsy, pregnancy, diabetes.
4. Urinalysis testing interferes with privacy rights associated with the right to control one's own medical treatment, including the right to choose among legal medications.
5. Urinalysis testing attempts to regulate "off-the-field" personal conduct thereby violating the right to engage in constitutional protections for enormously diverse personal action and belief.

Alternatively, it has been argued that athletes subject to drug testing have diminished expectations of privacy rendering a Fourth Amendment analysis an insufficient basis on which to declare a Constitutional violation. For example, "communal undress" inherent in athletic participation suggests a reduced expectation of privacy. Also, health examinations are fairly routine to participants in vigorous activities. In the context of such examinations, viewing and touching is tolerated among relative strangers that would be firmly rejected in other contexts (*O'Halloran v. University of Washington*, 1988). More recently the Supreme Court of the United States in *Vernonia v. Acton* (1995) has stated:

> Legitimate privacy expectations are even less with regard to student-athletes. School sports are not for the bashful. They require "suiting up" before each practice or event, and showering and changing afterwards. Public school locker rooms, the usual sites for these activities, are not notable for the privacy they afford (*Vernonia v. Acton*, 1995).

Governmental Interests Served by Urine Testing

The other side of the balancing test considers the governmental interests served by urine testing. In the context of urine testing of student-athletes, the government must show a special need because the testing exceeds the normal need for law enforcement and occurs in the absence of a warrant or probable cause. A search unsupported by probable cause can be constitutional, we have said, "when special needs, beyond the normal need for law enforcement, make the warrant and probable-cause requirement impracticable" (*Vernonia v. Acton*, 1995).

Examples of special needs that have been successfully asserted to justify warrantless, mandatory urine testing of the intercollegiate athlete include: 1) providing fair and equitable competition, 2) guarding the health and safety of student-athletes, and 3) deterring drug use by testing (*Hill v. NCAA*, 1994; *O'Halloran v. University of Washington*, 1988). With regard to public school athletes, these needs as well as the role of the school standing *in loco parentis* to the children entrusted to it has recently and successfully been argued to support mandatory, random urinalysis testing of public school athletes (*Vernonia v. Acton*, 1995). The doctrine of *in loco parentis* has no role in higher education. The role of guardian may help distinguish disparate holdings of cases dealing with random, suspicionless drug testing of college as opposed to public school athletes:

"[A] proper educational environment requires close supervision of schoolchildren, as well as the enforcement of rules against conduct that would be perfectly permissible if undertaken by an adult" (*New Jersey v. T.L.O.*, 1985).

"Fourth Amendment rights . . . are different in public schools than elsewhere; the "reasonableness" inquiry cannot disregard the schools' custodial and tutelary responsibility for children . . . So also when the government acts as guardian and tutor the relevant question is whether the search is one that a reasonable guardian and tutor might undertake" (*Vernonia v. Acton*, 1995).

"We therefore find of only marginal relevance holdings by other courts that high school student-athletes have a diminished expectation of privacy under the Fourth Amendment" (*University of Colorado v. Derdeyn*, 1993) [in reference to drug testing of college athletes by the University of Colorado]).

SIGNIFICANT CASE

The case that follows examines the privacy expectations of public school students at the high school level. Compare the that the majority Supreme Court decision, that random, suspicionless urinalysis testing of interscholastic athletes met the requirements of the Fourth Amendment, to the dissent which spoke strongly to the historical requirement of suspicion in safeguarding Fourth Amendment privacy interests.

VERNONIA SCHOOL DISTRICT V. ACTON
United States Supreme Court
115 S. Ct. 2386 (1995)

At that point, District officials began considering a drug-testing program. They held a parent "input night" to discuss the proposed Student Athlete Drug Policy (Policy), and the parents in attendance gave their unanimous approval. The school board approved the Policy for implementation in the fall of 1989. Its expressed purpose is to prevent student athletes from using drugs, to protect their health and safety, and to provide drug users with assistance programs.

In the fall of 1991, respondent James Acton, then a seventh grader, signed up to play football at one of the District's grade schools. He was denied participation, however, because he and his parents refused to sign the testing consent forms. The Actons filed suit, seeking declaratory and injunctive relief from enforcement of the Policy on the grounds that it violated the Fourth and Fourteenth Amendments to the United States Constitution and Article I, § 9, of the Oregon Constitution. After a bench trial, the District Court entered an order denying the claims on the merits and dismissing the action. 796 F. Supp. at 1355. The United States Court of Appeals for the Ninth Circuit reversed, holding that the Policy violated both the Fourth and Fourteenth Amendments and Article I, § 9, of the Oregon Constitution. 23 F.3d 1514 (1994). We granted certiorari.

II.

The Fourth Amendment to the United States Constitution provides that the Federal Government shall not violate "the right of the people to be secure in their persons, houses, papers, and effects, against unreasonable searches and seizures . . . ." We have held that the Four-teenth Amendment extends this constitutional guarantee to searches and seizures by state officers, *Elkins v. United States,* 80 S. Ct. 1437 (1960), including public school officials, *New Jersey v. T. L. O.,* 105 S. Ct. 733 (1985). In *Skinner v. Railway Labor Executives' Assn.,* 109 S. Ct. 1402 (1989), we held that state-compelled collection and testing of urine, such as that required by the Policy, constitutes a "search" subject to the demands of the Fourth Amendment.

As the text of the Fourth Amendment indicates, the ultimate measure of the constitutionality of a governmental search is "reasonableness." At least in a case such as this, where there was no clear practice, either approving or disapproving the type of search at issue, at the time the constitutional provision was enacted, n1 whether a particular search meets the reasonableness standard "'is judged by balancing its intrusion on the individual's Fourth Amendment interests against its promotion of legitimate governmental interests.'" Skinner, supra, at 619. Where a search is undertaken by law enforcement officials to discover evidence of criminal wrongdoing, this Court has said that reasonableness generally requires the obtaining of a judicial warrant, Skinner, supra, at 619. Warrants cannot be issued, of course, without the showing of probable cause required by the Warrant Clause. But a warrant is not required to establish the reasonableness of all government searches; and when a warrant is not required (and the Warrant Clause therefore not applicable), probable cause is not invariably required either. A search unsupported by probable cause can be constitutional, we have said, "when special needs, beyond the normal need for law enforcement, make the warrant and probable-cause requirement impracticable." *Griffin v. Wisconsin,* 107 S. Ct. 3164 (1987).

We have found such "special needs" to exist in the public school context. There, the warrant requirement "would unduly interfere with the maintenance of the swift and informal disciplinary procedures [that are] needed," and "strict adherence to the requirement that searches be based on probable cause" would undercut "the substantial need of teachers and administrators for freedom to maintain order in the schools." T. L. O., 469 U.S. at 340, 341. The school search we approved in T. L. O., while not based on probable cause, was based on individualized suspicion of wrongdoing. As we explicitly acknowledged, however, "'the Fourth Amendment imposes no irreducible requirement of such suspicion.'" Id., at 342, n. 8. We have upheld suspicionless searches and seizures to conduct drug testing of railroad personnel involved in train accidents, see Skinner, supra; to conduct random drug testing of federal customs officers who carry arms or are involved in drug interdiction . . . and to maintain automobile checkpoints looking for illegal immigrants and contraband . . . and drunk drivers.

III.

The first factor to be considered is the nature of the privacy interest upon which the search here at issue intrudes. The Fourth Amendment does not protect all subjective expectations of privacy, but only those that society recognizes as "legitimate." What expectations are legitimate varies, of course, with context, depending, for example, upon whether the individual asserting the privacy interest is at home, at work, in a car, or in a public park. In addition, the legitimacy of certain privacy expectations vis-a-vis the State may depend upon the individual's legal relationship with the State. For example, in Griffin, we held that, although a "probationer's home, like anyone else's, is protected by the Fourth Amendment," the supervisory relationship between probationer and State justifies "a degree of impingement upon [a probationer's] privacy that would not be constitutional if applied to the public at large." 483 U.S. at 873, 875. Central, in our view, to the present case is the fact that the subjects of the Policy are (1) children, who (2) have been committed to the temporary custody of the State as schoolmaster.

Traditionally at common law, and still today, unemancipated minors lack some of the most fundamental rights of self-determination—including even the right of liberty in its narrow sense, i. e., the right to come and go at will. They are subject, even as to their physical freedom, to the control of their parents or guardians . . . When parents place minor children in private schools for their education, the teachers and administrators of those schools stand in loco parentis over the children entrusted to them. In fact, the tutor or schoolmaster is the very prototype of that status . . .

In T. L. O. we rejected the notion that public schools, like private schools, exercise only parental power over their students, which of course is not subject to constitutional constraints. Such a view of things, we said, "is not entirely 'consonant with compulsory education laws,'" and is inconsistent with our prior decisions treating school officials as state actors for purposes of the Due Process and Free Speech Clauses, T. L. O., at 336. But while denying that the State's power over schoolchildren is formally no more than the delegated power of their parents, T. L. O. did not deny, but indeed emphasized, that the nature of that power is custodial and tutelary, permitting a degree of supervision and control that could not be exercised over free adults. "[A] proper educational environment requires close supervision of schoolchildren, as well as the enforcement of rules against conduct that would be perfectly permissible if undertaken by an adult." 469 U.S. at 339. While we do not, of course, suggest that public schools as a general matter have such a degree of control over children as to give rise to a constitutional "duty to protect" . . . we have acknowledged that for many purposes "school authorities act in loco parentis" . . . with the power and indeed the duty to "inculcate the habits and manners of civility. " Id., at 681. Thus, while children assuredly do not "shed their constitutional rights . . . at the schoolhouse gate," *Tinker v. Des Moines Independent Community School Dist.,* 89 S. Ct. 733 (1969), the nature of those rights is what is appropriate for children in school . . .

Fourth Amendment rights, no less than First and Fourteenth Amendment rights, are different in public schools than elsewhere; the "reasonableness" inquiry cannot disregard the schools' custodial and tutelary responsibility for children. For their own good and that of their classmates, public school children are routinely required to submit to various physical examinations, and to be vaccinated against various diseases. Particularly with regard to medical examinations and procedures, therefore, "students within the school environment have a lesser expectation of privacy than members of the population generally."

Legitimate privacy expectations are even less with regard to student athletes. School sports are not for the bashful. They require "suiting up" before each practice or event, and showering and changing afterwards. Public school locker rooms, the usual sites for these activities, are not notable for the privacy they afford. The locker rooms in Vernonia are typical: No individual dressing rooms are provided; shower heads are lined up along a wall, unseparated by any sort of partition or curtain; not even all the toilet stalls have doors. As the United States Court of Appeals for the Seventh Circuit has noted, there is "an element of 'communal undress' inherent in athletic participation," Schaill by *Kross v. Tippecanoe County School Corp.,* 864 F.2d 1309, 1318 (1988).

There is an additional respect in which school athletes have a reduced expectation of privacy. By choosing to "go out for the team," they voluntarily subject themselves to a degree of regulation even higher than that imposed on students generally. In Vernonia's public schools, they must submit to a preseason physical exam (James testified that his included the giving of a urine sample, App. 17), they must acquire adequate insurance coverage or sign an insurance waiver, maintain a minimum grade point average, and comply with any "rules of conduct, dress, training hours and related matters as may be established for each sport by the head coach and athletic director with the principal's approval." Record, Exh. 2, p. 30, P 8. Somewhat like adults who choose to participate in a "closely regulated industry," students who voluntarily participate in school athletics have reason to expect intrusions upon normal rights and privileges, including privacy. See Skinner, 489 U.S. at 627.

IV.

Having considered the scope of the legitimate expectation of privacy at issue here, we turn next to the character of the intrusion that is complained of. We recognized in Skinner that collecting the samples for urinalysis intrudes upon "an excretory function traditionally shielded by great privacy." 489 U.S. at 626. We noted, however, that the degree of intrusion depends upon the manner in which production of the urine sample is monitored. Under the District's Policy, male students produce samples at a urinal along a wall. They remain fully clothed and are only observed from behind, if at all. Female students produce samples in an enclosed stall, with a female monitor standing outside listening only for sounds of tampering. These conditions are nearly identical to those typically encountered in public restrooms, which men, women, and especially school children use daily. Under such conditions, the privacy interests compromised by the process of obtaining the urine sample are in our view negligible.

The other privacy-invasive aspect of urinalysis is, of course, the information it discloses concerning the state of the subject's body, and the materials he has ingested. In this regard it is significant that the tests at issue here look only for drugs, and not for whether the student is, for example, epileptic, pregnant, or diabetic. See id., at 617. Moreover, the drugs for which the samples are screened are standard, and do not vary according to the identity of the student. And finally, the results of the tests are disclosed only to a limited class of school personnel who have a need to know; and they are not turned over to law enforcement authorities or used for any internal disciplinary function.

Respondents argue, however, that the District's Policy is in fact more intrusive than this suggests, because it requires the students, if they are to avoid sanctions for a falsely positive test, to identify in advance prescription medications they are taking. We agree that this raises some cause for concern. In Von Raab, we flagged as one of the salutary features of the Customs Service drug-testing program the fact that employees were not required to disclose medical information unless they tested positive, and, even then, the information was supplied to a licensed physician rather than to the Government employer. See Von Raab, 489 U.S. at 672–673, n. 2. On the other hand, we have never indicated that requiring advance disclosure of medications is per se unreasonable. Indeed, in Skinner we held that it was not "a significant invasion of privacy." 489 U.S. at 626, n. 7. It can be argued that, in Skinner, the disclosure went only to the medical personnel taking the sample, and the Government personnel analyzing it, . . . and that disclosure to teachers and coaches—to persons who personally know the student—is a greater invasion of privacy. Assuming for the sake of argument that both those propositions are true, we do not believe they establish a difference that respondents are entitled to rely on here.

The General Authorization Form that respondents refused to sign, which refusal was the basis for James's exclusion from the sports program, said only (in relevant part): "I . . . authorize the Vernonia School District to conduct a test on a urine specimen which I provide to test for drugs and/or alcohol use. I also authorize the release of information concerning the results of such a test to the Vernonia School District and to the parents and/or guardians of the student." App. 10–11. While the practice of the District seems to have been to have a school official take medication information from the student at the time of the test, see id., at 29, 42, that practice is not set forth in, or required by, the Policy, which says simply: "Student athletes who . . . are or have been taking prescription medication must provide verification (either by a copy of the prescription or by doctor's authorization) prior to being tested." Id., at 8. It may well be that, if and when James was selected for random testing at a time that he was taking medication, the School District would have permitted him to provide the requested information in a confidential manner—for example, in a sealed envelope delivered to the testing lab. Nothing in the Policy contradicts that, and when respondents choose, in effect, to challenge the Policy on its face, we will not assume the worst. Accordingly, we reach the same conclusion as in Skinner: that the invasion of privacy was not significant.

V.

Finally, we turn to consider the nature and immediacy of the governmental concern at issue here, and the efficacy of this means for meeting it. In both Skinner and Von Raab, we characterized the government interest motivating the search as "compelling." Skinner, supra, at 628 (interest in preventing railway accidents); Von Raab, supra, 489 U.S. at 670 (interest in ensuring fitness of customs officials to interdict drugs and handle firearms). Relying on these cases, the District Court held that because the District's program also called for drug testing in the absence of individualized suspicion, the District "must demonstrate a 'compelling need' for the program." 796 F. Supp. at 1363. The Court of Appeals appears to have agreed with this view. See 23 F.3d at 1526. It is a mistake, however, to think that the phrase "compelling state interest," in the Fourth Amendment context, describes a fixed, minimum quantum of governmental concern, so that one can dispose of a case by answering in isolation the question: Is there a compelling state interest here? Rather, the phrase describes an interest that appears important enough to justify the particular search at hand, in light of other factors that show the search to be relatively intrusive upon a genuine expectation of privacy. Whether that relatively high degree of government concern is necessary in this case or not, we think it is met. That the nature of the concern is important—indeed, perhaps compelling—can hardly be doubted. Deterring drug use by our Nation's schoolchildren is at least as important as enhancing efficient enforcement of the Nation's laws against the importation of drugs, which was the governmental concern in Von Raab, supra, at 668, or deterring drug use by engineers and trainmen, which was the governmental

concern in Skinner, supra, at 628. School years are the time when the physical, psychological, and addictive effects of drugs are most severe. "Maturing nervous systems are more critically impaired by intoxicants than mature ones are; childhood losses in learning are lifelong and profound"; "children grow chemically dependent more quickly than adults, and their record of recovery is depressingly poor." . . . And of course the effects of a drug-infested school are visited not just upon the users, but upon the entire student body and faculty, as the educational process is disrupted. In the present case, moreover, the necessity for the State to act is magnified by the fact that this evil is being visited not just upon individuals at large, but upon children for whom it has undertaken a special responsibility of care and direction. Finally, it must not be lost sight of that this program is directed more narrowly to drug use by school athletes, where the risk of immediate physical harm to the drug user or those with whom he is playing his sport is particularly high. Apart from psychological effects, which include impairment of judgment, slow reaction time, and a lessening of the perception of pain, the particular drugs screened by the District's Policy have been demonstrated to pose substantial physical risks to athletes . . .

As for the immediacy of the District's concerns: We are not inclined to question—indeed, we could not possibly find clearly erroneous—the District Court's conclusion that "a large segment of the student body, particularly those involved in interscholastic athletics, was in a state of rebellion," that "disciplinary actions had reached 'epidemic proportions,'" and that "the rebellion was being fueled by alcohol and drug abuse as well as by the student's misperceptions about the drug culture." 796 F. Supp. at 1357. That is an immediate crisis of greater proportions than existed in Skinner, where we upheld the Government's drug-testing program based on findings of drug use by railroad employees nationwide, without proof that a problem existed on the particular railroads whose employees were subject to the test . . .

As to the efficacy of this means for addressing the problem: It seems to us self-evident that a drug problem largely fueled by the "role model" effect of athletes' drug use, and of particular danger to athletes, is effectively addressed by making sure that athletes do not use drugs. Respondents argue that a "less intrusive means to the same end" was available, namely, "drug testing on suspicion of drug use." Brief for Respondents 45–46. We have repeatedly refused to declare that only the "least intrusive" search practicable can be reasonable under the Fourth Amendment. Skinner, supra, at 629, n. 9 (collecting cases). Respondents' alternative entails substantial difficulties—if it is indeed practicable at all. It may be impracticable, for one thing, simply because the parents who are willing to accept random drug testing for athletes are not willing to accept accusatory drug testing for all students, which transforms the process into a badge of shame.

Respondents' proposal brings the risk that teachers will impose testing arbitrarily upon troublesome but not drug-likely students. It generates the expense of defending lawsuits that charge such arbitrary imposition, or that simply demand greater process before accusatory drug testing is imposed. And not least of all, it adds to the ever-expanding diversionary duties of schoolteachers the new function of spotting and bringing to account drug abuse, a task for which they are ill prepared, and which is not readily compatible with their vocation . . .

VI.

Taking into account all the factors we have considered above—the decreased expectation of privacy, the relative unobtrusiveness of the search, and the severity of the need met by the search—we conclude Vernonia's Policy is reasonable and hence constitutional.

We caution against the assumption that suspicionless drug testing will readily pass constitutional muster in other contexts. The most significant element in this case is the first we discussed: that the Policy was undertaken in furtherance of the government's responsibilities, under a public school system, as guardian and tutor of children entrusted to its care. n4 Just as when the government conducts a search in its capacity as employer (a warrantless search of an absent employee's desk to obtain an urgently needed file, for example), the relevant question is whether that intrusion upon privacy is one that a reasonable employer might engage in, see *O'Connor v. Ortega,* 107 S. Ct. 1492 (1987); so also when the government acts as guardian and tutor the relevant question is whether the search is one that a reasonable guardian and tutor might undertake. Given the findings of need made by the District Court, we conclude that in the present case it is.

We may note that the primary guardians of Vernonia's schoolchildren appear to agree. The record shows no objection to this districtwide program by any parents other than the couple before us here—even though, as we have described, a public meeting was held to obtain parents' views. We find insufficient basis to contradict the judgment of Vernonia's parents, its school board, and the District Court, as to what was reasonably in the interest of these children under the circumstances.

The Ninth Circuit held that Vernonia's Policy not only violated the Fourth Amendment, but also, by reason of that violation, contravened Article I, § 9, of the Oregon Constitution. Our conclusion that the former holding was in error means that the latter holding rested on a flawed premise. We therefore vacate the judgment, and remand the case to the Court of Appeals for further proceedings consistent with this opinion.

It is so ordered.

JUSTICE O'CONNOR, with whom JUSTICE STEVENS and JUSTICE SOUTER join, dissenting.

In justifying this result, the Court dispenses with a requirement of individualized suspicion on considered policy grounds . . . Blanket searches, because they can involve "thousands or millions" of searches, "pose a greater threat to liberty" than do suspicion-based ones, which "affect one person at a time," . . .

For most of our constitutional history, mass, suspicionless searches have been generally considered per se unreasonable within the meaning of the Fourth Amendment.

But having misconstrued the fundamental role of the individualized suspicion requirement in Fourth Amendment analysis, the Court never seriously engages the practicality of such a requirement in the instant case. And that failure is crucial because nowhere is it less clear that an individualized suspicion requirement would be ineffectual than in the school context. In most schools, the entire pool of potential search targets—students—is under constant supervision by teachers and administrators and coaches, be it in classrooms, hallways, or locker rooms . . .

The instant case, however, asks whether the Fourth Amendment is even more lenient than that, i.e., whether it is so lenient that students may be deprived of the Fourth Amendment's only remaining, and most basic, categorical protection: its strong preference for an individualized suspicion requirement, with its accompanying antipathy toward personally intrusive, blanket searches of mostly innocent people. It is not at all clear that people in prison lack this categorical protection . . . and we have said "we are not yet ready to hold that the schools and the prisons need be equated for purposes of the Fourth Amendment." Thus, if we are to mean what we often proclaim—that students do not "shed their constitutional rights . . . at the schoolhouse gate" . . . the answer must plainly be no.

By contrast, intrusive, blanket searches of schoolchildren, most of whom are innocent, for evidence of serious wrongdoing are not part of any traditional school function of which I am aware. Indeed, many schools, like many parents, prefer to trust their children unless given reason to do otherwise. As James Acton's father said on the witness stand, "[suspicionless testing] sends a message to children that are trying to be responsible citizens . . . that they have to prove that they're innocent . . ., and I think that kind of sets a bad tone for citizenship." Tr. 9 (Apr. 29, 1992).

I find unpersuasive the Court's reliance on the widespread practice of physical examinations and vaccinations, which are both blanket searches of a sort . . . It might also be noted that physical exams (and of course vaccinations) are not searches for conditions that reflect wrongdoing on the part of the student, and so are wholly nonaccusatory and have no consequences that can be regarded as punitive. These facts may explain the absence of Fourth Amendment challenges to such searches. By contrast, although I agree with the Court that the accusatory nature of the District's testing program is diluted by making it a blanket one, any testing program that searches for conditions plainly reflecting serious wrongdoing can never be made wholly nonaccusatory from the student's perspective, the motives for the program notwithstanding; and for the same reason, the substantial consequences that can flow from a positive test, such as suspension from sports, are invariably—and quite reasonably—understood as punishment. The best proof that the District's testing program is to some extent accusatory can be found in James Acton's own explanation on the witness stand as to why he did not want to submit to drug testing: "Because I feel that they have no reason to think I was taking drugs." Tr. 13 (Apr. 29, 1992). It is hard to think of a manner of explanation that resonates more intensely in our Fourth Amendment tradition than this.

I do not believe that suspicionless drug testing is justified on these facts. But even if I agreed that some such testing were reasonable here, I see two other Fourth Amendment flaws in the District's program. n2 First, and most serious, there is virtually no evidence in the record of a drug problem at the Washington Grade School . . . Second, even as to the high school, I find unreasonable the school's choice of student athletes as the class to subject to suspicionless testing—a choice that appears to have been driven more by a belief in what would pass constitutional muster . . it seems quite obvious that the true driving force behind the District's adoption of its drug testing program was the need to combat the rise in drug-related disorder and disruption in its classrooms and around campus. I mean no criticism of the strength of that interest. On the contrary, where the record demonstrates the existence of such a problem, that interest seems self-evidently compelling . . . The evidence of a drug-related sports injury problem at Vernonia, by contrast, was considerably weaker.

On this record, then, it seems to me that the far more reasonable choice would have been to focus on the class of students found to have violated published school rules against severe disruption in class and around campus, . . . Such a choice would share two of the virtues of a suspicion-based regime: testing dramatically fewer students, tens as against hundreds, and giving students control, through their behavior, over the likelihood that they would be tested. Moreover, there would be a reduced concern for the accusatory nature of the search . . .

It cannot be too often stated that the greatest threats to our constitutional freedoms come in times of crisis. But we must also stay mindful that not all government responses to such times are hysterical overreactions; some crises are quite real, and when they are, they serve precisely as the compelling state interest that we have said may justify a measured intrusion on constitutional rights. The only way for judges to mediate these conflicting impulses is to do what they should do anyway: stay close to the record in each case that appears before them, and make their judgments based on that alone. Having reviewed the record here, I cannot avoid the conclusion that the District's suspicionless policy of testing all student athletes sweeps too broadly, and too imprecisely, to be reasonable under the Fourth Amendment.

CASES ON THE SUPPLEMENTAL WEB SITE

Brannum v. Overton County School Board (2008 Tennessee WESTLAW 06-5931). Middle-school students successfully sued alleging violations of their privacy rights under the Fourth Amendment when video-surveillance cameras were installed in locker rooms.

Hill v. NCAA, 7 Cal.4th 1 (1994). Stanford University student-athletes sued contending that the NCAA's drug testing program violated the right of privacy as explicitly guaranteed under the California Constitution. The Fourth Amendment was not used since a private actor's conduct was at issue. This case meticulously analyzes privacy rights, examines the competing arguments of the NCAA and students, and details the requirements for a privacy cause of action.

Wooten v. Pleasant Hope R-VI School District, 139 F.Supp.2d 835 (2000). High school student sued alleging common law violations of privacy when her coach publicly disclosed her dismissal from the softball team. Public disclosure of private facts and the distinction of false light and defamation are specifically addressed in this case.

QUESTIONS YOU SHOULD BE ABLE TO ANSWER

1. What language in the Fourth Amendment protects against privacy intrusions by government?

2. The Fourth Amendment protects against "unreasonable" searches. Define and give an example of a "search". Describe/explain the analysis used to determine a "reasonable search".

3. On what basis has it been concluded that student-athletes have "diminished expectations of privacy" with regard to a Fourth Amendment analysis?

4. In addition to drug testing, give examples of privacy interests of student-athletes that have been or could be the subject of litigation?

REFERENCES
Cases
Arlosoroff v. NCAA, 746 F.2d 1019 (1984).
Arkansas Gazette Co. v. Southern State College, 620 S.W.2d 258 (1981).
Board of Education v. Earls, 122 S.Ct. 2559.
Bunger v. Iowa H. S. Athletic Assn., 197 N.W.2d 555 (1972).
Davis v. Meek, 344 F. Supp. 298 (1972).
Dunham v. Pulsifer, 312 F. Supp. 41 (1970).
Estay v. LaFourche Parish School Board, 230 So.2d 443 (1969).
Horsemen's Benevolent & Protective Assn. v. State Racing Commission, 532 N.E.2d 644 (1989).
Indiana High School Athletic Assn. v. Raike, 329 N.E.2d 66 (1975).
Marmo v. NYC Board of Education, 289 N.Y.S.2d 51 (1968).
Menora v. Illinois High School Assn., 683 F.2d 1030 (1982).
National Treasury Employees Union v. Von Raab, 109 S.Ct. 1384 (1989).
New Jersey v. T.L.O., 105 S.Ct. 733 (1985).
O'Connor v. Ortega, 107 S.Ct. 1492 (1987).
O'Halloran v. University of Washington, 679 F. Supp. 997 (1988).
Perry v. Granada Municipal School District, 300 F. Supp. 748 (1969).
Schaill v. Tippecanoe County School Corporation, 864 F.2d. 1309 (1989).
Skinner v. Railway Labor Executives' Assn., 109 S.Ct. 1402 (1989).
Tinker v. Des Moines Indep. Comm. School District, 89 S.St. 733 (1969).
University of Colorado v. Derdeyn, 863 P.2d 929 (1993).
Vernonia School District 47J v. Action, 115 S.Ct. 2386 (1995).
Zeller v. Donegal School District, 517 F.2d 600 (1975).

Legislation
United States Constitution, First, Fourth and Fourteenth Amendments.

6.16 FIRST AMENDMENT

John T. Wolohan I Syracuse University

The First Amendment, which establishes the freedom of speech, freedom of the press and freedom of religion, has been called "the indispensable condition of nearly every other form of freedom" (*Palko v. Connecticut*, 1937). As we will discover below, however, even though the First Amendment is one of most litigated Amendments to the United States Constitution it is still considered to be "a work in progress" (Weaver and Lively, 2003). The reasons the First Amendment has kept the Supreme Court so busy is not only because of the continued development of new means of expression, but also the inherent conflicts in the Amendment's language protecting the freedoms of speech, press and religion.

FUNDAMENTAL CONCEPTS

"Congress shall make no law respecting an establishment of religion, or prohibiting the free exercise thereof; or abridging the freedom of speech, or of the press; or the right of the people peaceably to assemble, and to petition the Government for a redress of grievances" (United States Constitution, Amendment I).

While the language of the First Amendment is clear and would seem to leave little room for misinterpretation, the judicial history of the First Amendment illustrate that the freedoms provided under the law are not set in stone. For example, even though the First Amendment grants Freedom of Speech, the government has a legitimate reason to restrict our speech in some instances. Therefore, in evaluation our rights under the First Amendment, the Court must determine whether the enumerated guarantee must give way to some higher governmental priority (Weaver and Lively, 2003).

FREEDOM OF SPEECH

As the Supreme Court found in *United States v. Schwimmer*, (1937), the First Amendment is not designed to protect the "free thought for those who agree with us, but freedom for the thoughts that we hate." Not all speech is entitled First Amendment protection, however. For example, in *Schenck v. United States*, (1919) a case in which the Supreme Court upheld the conviction of anti-war protesters who urged draft eligible men to resist the draft, the court held that words that create a "clear and present danger" will not be protected. To illustrate the point that not all speech is protected under the First Amendment, the court held that even "the most stringent protection of free speech would not protect a man in falsely shouting fire in a theatre and causing a panic" (*Schenck v. United States*, 1919). As a general rule, the Supreme Court has deemed the following categories of speech: defamation, obscenity, fighting words, and words that create a clear and present danger as unprotected expression. If the court determines that the challenged speech or expression falls into one of these unprotected categories, it receives less than full First Amendment protection and the courts will review it using the rational basis test. (See Chapter 6.14 Equal Protection for a discussion of the rational basis test).

If, however, the Court classifies the speech as protected, it is reviewed using a strict scrutiny. For example, political speech and speech critical of governmental policies, is regarded as high value and protected speech and consistent with this classification, the government would have to show that restricting such speech was necessary to achieve a compelling state interest or that the speech presented a clear and present danger. In addition, the Supreme Court has viewed some speech, such as advertising and other commercial speech and sexually explicit, but non-obscene speech, as protected, but not enjoying the full protections of the First Amendment. In these cases of speech, the court uses an intermediate level of scrutiny (Weaver and Lively, 2003). (See Chapter 6.14 *Equal Protection* for a discussion of the strict and intermediate scrutiny tests).

Therefore before the Court can determine whether someone's free speech rights have been deprived, the court must first determine what category the speech falls into: protected or non-protected. Once it determines the category, it can then apply the standard of review, essentially balancing the competing constitutional right of the individual and the state's interest. In weighting these factors the Court also considers the medium that was used, if any, to disseminate expression, since some media, like newspapers, are afforded more First Amendment protection than others (Weaver and Lively, 2003).

Standard of Review

In reviewing freedom of speech cases involving students, the leading case is *Tinker v. Des Moines Independent Community School District*, (1969). In *Tinker*, three students were suspended from public school for wearing black armbands to protest the war in Vietnam. In finding that "students and teachers do not shed their constitutional rights to freedom of speech or expression at the schoolhouse gate" the United States Supreme Court held that the wearing of armbands was entirely divorced from actually or potentially disruptive conduct and as such was closely akin to "pure speech" which is entitled to comprehensive protection under the First Amendment (*Tinker v. Des Moines Independent Community School District*, 1969).

In order for the State, in this case school officials, to justify prohibiting speech or a particular expression of opinion, the court ruled that the action must be based on "something more than a mere desire to avoid the discomfort and unpleasantness that always accompany an unpopular viewpoint" (*Tinker v. Des Moines Independent Community School District*, 1969). If the state cannot show that engaging in the forbidden conduct would "materially and substantially interfere with the requirements of appropriate discipline in the operation of the school," the Supreme Court held that the state cannot prohibit the speech or expression. In *Tinker*, the Court found that the school officials failed to show that they had any reason to anticipate that the students wearing of the armbands would substantially interfere with the work of the school or impinge upon the rights of other students. In fact, the Court found that the action of the school authorities was based on an urgent wish to avoid any controversy which might result from the silent symbol of armbands. Such a prohibition, the Court held was not constitutionally permissible.

While the *Tinker* test is the standard of review most frequently applied to student speech cases, the Supreme Courts has expanded the exemptions provided school officials in free speech cases (Hayes, 2010). For example in *Frederick v. Morse*, (2007) a student was suspended from school after he refused the principal's direction to take down a banner that he unfurled while watching the Olympic Torch Relay pass through town. The viewing of the relay was a school-sanctioned and school-supervised event. The fourteen-foot banner, which the principal regarded as promoting illegal drug use, read "BONG HiTS 4 JESUS" (*Frederick v. Morse*, 2007).

In overturning the Ninth Circuit Court's decision, the Supreme Court held that consistent with the First Amendment a school official may restrict student speech at a school event, when that speech is reasonably viewed as promoting illegal drug use or other illegal activity. In support of this conclusion, the Supreme Court ruled that the "substantial disruption" rule of *Tinker* was not the only basis for restricting student speech. Considering the special characteristics of the school environment and the governmental interest in stopping student drug abuse, the Court held that schools were entitled to take steps to safeguard those entrusted to their care from speech that could reasonably be regarded as encouraging illegal drug use.

Besides the "substantial disruption" and the "encouraging illegal activity" exemptions, the Supreme Court in *Bethel School District No. 403 v. Fraser*, (1986) found another exemption to a student's free speech. In *Fraser*, a high school student delivered a speech, nominating a fellow student for student government office, at an assembly attended by about 600 students. The entire speech referred to the candidate in terms of sexual metaphor, employing such phrases as "he's firm in his pants … his character is firm," "a man who takes his point and pounds it in," and "a man who will go to the very end—even the climax, for each and every one of you." During the speech, some students were observed to react by hooting and yelling, others by making sexually suggestive gestures, and still others appeared to be bewildered and embarrassed. The morning after the assembly, the student was notified that the school considered his speech to have been a violation of the disciplinary rule, that he would be suspended for 3 days, and that his name would be removed from a list of potential graduation speakers (*Bethel School District No. 403 v. Fraser*, 1986). The District Court, holding that the suspension violated the student's First Amendment right, awarded him damages and enjoined the school district from preventing him from speaking at graduation. The Ninth Circuit Court of Appeals affirmed the judgment of the District Court, rejecting the argument that the speech had a disruptive effect on the education process and that the school district had an interest in protecting students from lewd and indecent language in a school-sponsored setting.

In overturning the decision of the lower courts, the United States Supreme Court held that the First Amendment did not prevent the school district from suspending the student for giving the offensively lewd and indecent speech at the assembly. While the Court found that under the First Amendment, the use of an offensive form of expression would be allowable to adults making what the speaker considers a political point, the Supreme Court held that it does not follow that the same latitude must be permitted to children in a public school. In addition, the Supreme Court held that the First Amendment recognizes a state interest in protecting minors from exposure to vulgar and offensive spoken language, as well as limitations on the otherwise absolute interest of the speaker in reaching an unlimited audience where the speech is sexually explicit and the audience may include children.

Freedom of Speech in Athletics. Students' freedom of speech "rights do not embrace merely the classroom hours. When he is in the cafeteria, or on the playing field, or on the campus during the authorized hours, he may express his opinions, even on controversial subjects . . . if he does so without materially and substantially interfere with the requirements of appropriate discipline in the operation of the school and without colliding with the rights of others" (*Tinker v. Des Moines Independent Community School District*, 1969). Although the Court has recognized that students have freedom of speech rights on the "playing field," since most actions taken by an athlete or a group of athletes are generally going to "materially and substantially interfere" with or disrupt the team, and thus, school activities, student athletes tend to have less freedom to speak out or complain about their coaches. For example, in *Pinard v. Clatskanie School District 6J*, (2006), several members of the boys' basketball team alleged that the school violated their First Amendment rights by suspending them in retaliation for speaking out against their coach. The students had signed a petition requesting the removal of the team's head coach.

Using the *Tinker* standard, the Ninth Circuit ruled that the students' petition and complaints against the coach were protected speech because they could not reasonably have led school officials to forecast substantial disruption of or material interference with a school activity. However, even though the students' actions in signing the petition may have been constitutionally protected, the Ninth Circuit held that the students' protect in refusing to board the bus was properly punishable by school officials as unprotected speech; the game boycott substantially disrupted and materially interfered with the operation of the basketball program (*Pinard v. Clatskanie School District 6J*, 2006).

This standard was reaffirmed by the Sixth Circuit Court of Appeals in *Lowery v. Euverard*, (2007). In Lowery, like in Pinard, a group of high school athletes signed a petition that stated "I hate Coach (coach's name) and I don't want to play for him." Although the petition was to be held until after the football season and then given to the principal of school, in order to have the coach replaced, the coach found out about the petition during the season. When he did, the coach interviewed all the players individually to discover who signed the petition. Players who signed the petition but apologized to the coach were allowed to remain on the team; any player who did not apologize to the coach was removed from the team.

In trying to find the proper balance between a student athlete's First Amendment rights and a coach's need to maintain order and discipline, the Sixth Circuit Court of Appeals rejected the students' argument that the petition did not substantially disrupted the team. In ruling that this argument misapplies the *Tinker* standard, the Sixth Circuit held that school officials "were not obligated to wait until the petition substantially disrupted the team before acting, nor are they now required to demonstrate that it was certain that the petition would substantially disrupt the team. Rather, [the Court held,] school officials must show that it was reasonable for them to forecast that the petition would disrupt the team" (*Lowery v. Euverard*, 2008). Based on the circumstances, the Court held that it was reasonable for school officials to believe that the petition would disrupt the team, by eroding the coach's authority and dividing players into opposing camps. As a result, the Sixth Circuit held that the petition was not protected by *Tinker*, and coach did not violate the students' First Amendment rights by removing them from the football team. *Tinker* did not require teachers to surrender control of the classroom to students, and the standard does not require coaches to surrender control of the team to players.

If the protest is not likely to substantially disrupt the team or erode or interfere with the coach's authority, the courts will allow the speech. For example in *Hysaw v. Washburn University of Topeka*, (1987), several black football players on the Washburn team expressed discontent with their scholarships; that promises had not been carried out and that white players on the team were being favored by the coaching staff. To protest, the players boycotted team practices. The Athletic Director responded to the players' boycott by outlining the administration's position. In particular, he pointed out that "missing practice without an excuse from the coaching staff is a violation of disciplinary rules affecting all players and will be treated in the same manner as any player's unexcused absence" (*Hysaw v. Washburn University of Topeka*, 1987). The players were given a chance to apologize and rejoin the team, those players that did not apologize, were removed from the team.

At trail, the school claimed that even if the players were dismissed for protesting racial mistreatment, the dismissal was justified under *Tinker*, because the activity by students "materially and substantially interfered with the requirements of appropriate discipline in the operation of the school" (*Hysaw v. Washburn University of Topeka*, 1987). In particular, the school argued that the boycott severely disrupted the football team and infringed upon the rights of others participating in the football program. In rejecting this argument, the District Court held that since the coach testified that any absence caused by protesting racial mistreatment would be excused, there was no way the protest could be considered disruptive. To do so, the court held, would be to hold that the coaching staff followed a policy—excusing the players to protest—which caused disruption to the team. In addition, the court also rejected the schools argument that the players' actions infringed upon the rights of others participating in the football program. The *Tinker* exception, the court held, is a narrow one. As such, the court was not prepared to hold that players' actions infringed upon the "rights" of the other players. The boycott may have made practice more difficult, the team's morale may have been dampened by the players' actions, and the season's play may have suffered. But the team's "rights" were not infringed upon, at least not under the narrow definition of "rights" spelled out in *Tinker*. The court will not place the interests of participants in a university extracurricular activity above the rights of any citizen to speak out against alleged racial injustice without fear of government retribution.

Freedom of Speech in Recreational Sports. One of the most troubling areas involving freedom of speech is the use of email to criticize coaches and administrators. For example in *Robinson v. Hicks; King; City of Harrisburg,* (2011) the parents of a minor child, sent numerous emails to league officials expressing their disapproval over comments made by the coach and demanded a new coach. As a result of the Robinson's actions, the Harrisburg Youth Soccer Club (HYSC) Board of Directors unanimously voted to suspend the three Robinsons from HYSC for one year because of their alleged inappropriate behavior, such as using profanity and threats with the staff and players. The Robinsons argued that the city's conduct violated their First Amendment right by retaliating against them for speaking out against Hicks and the soccer program.

In ruling against the Robinsons' the Third Circuit Court ruled that to "state a claim for actionable retaliation under the First Amendment, the Robinsons must allege (1) constitutionally protected conduct, (2) retaliatory action sufficient to deter a person of ordinary firmness from exercising his constitutional rights, and (3) a causal link between the constitutionally protected conduct and the retaliatory action" (*Robinson v. Hicks; King; City of Harrisburg,* 2011). In reviewing the facts, the Third Circuit Court ruled that even if the Robinsons' comments to the city youth soccer president were considered constitutionally protected speech and that they were suspended from the soccer team in retaliation, there was insufficient evidence that the league and its president participated in the retaliatory conduct to subject them to liability. Given the history of the parents' aggressive and disruptive behavior, the Third Circuit Court ruled the decision to suspend them from the soccer team would have been the same even without the exercise of their First Amendment rights.

Freedom of the Press

In examining the question of "Freedom of the Press," the courts have generally interpreted the clause as having no significance independent of the speech clause. Therefore, when presented with a First Amendment Freedom of the Press claim, the court will first examine whether the content is protected under the First Amendment. The constitutional inquiry, however is usually more layered when freedom of press rights are involved. The first consideration is the nature of the speech. Is it protected, is it commercial, or is it unprotected. The higher the value of the speech, the more protection it receives and the higher the level of scrutiny applied. Once the court determines the nature of the speech, it must next look at the nature of the medium used. For each medium of expression, newspaper, radio or television broadcast, cablecast or internet, the standard of First Amendment review varies. The print medium has the highest level of First Amendment protection, and broadcasting, because of the scarcity of broadcast frequencies and it's invasive and accessibility to children has the least. The consequence of this analytical framework is that the same expression published without constitutional constraints in print may be the basis for liability in broadcasting" (Weaver and Lively, 2003).

An example of the different standards of review used by the courts, strict scrutiny applied to content in print media and an intermediate standard of review applied to broadcast media is *Zacchini v. Scripps-Howard Broadcasting* (1977). In Zacchini, a television station secretly taped Hugo Zacchini's performance as the "human cannonball" and broadcast the performance on the 11 o'clock newscast. Since each performance occupies some 15 seconds; the entire act was shown on the news program that night, together with favorable commentary. While holding that a "TV station has a privilege to report in its newscasts matters of legitimate public interest which would otherwise be protected by an individual's right of publicity," the Supreme Court found that the free speech privilege afforded respondent under United States Constitution did not extend to broadcasting Zacchini's entire performance (*Zacchini v. Scripps-Howard Broadcasting,* 1977). The Court emphasized that the broadcast of an entire act was categorically different from reporting on an event, in that it posed a substantial threat to the economic value of the performance, and to Zacchini's livelihood. Zacchini's interest, the Supreme Court held that was more like a patent or copyright, interests which were not subject to claims of constitutional privilege (*Zacchini v. Scripps-Howard Broadcasting,* 1977).

The development of the Internet, and its widespread adoption inside the home poses significant challenges to the traditional model of medium specific analysis (Weaver and Lively, 2003). For example in *Layshock v. Hermitage School District,* (2007), the court was asked to determine whether the school district violated a student's First Amendment right when it suspended him for creating and posting a parody profile of the principal on an Internet website at home outside of school hours. The school district claimed the punishment was justified under either the *Tinker* or *Fraser* tests.

In balancing the freedom of expression of a student with the right and responsibility of a public school to maintain an environment conducive to learning, the court found that the mere fact that the internet may be accessed at school does not authorize school officials to become censors of the world-wide web. Public schools are vital institutions, but their reach is not unlimited. Schools have an undoubted right to control conduct within the scope of their activities, but they must share the supervision of children with other, equally vital, institutions such as families, churches, community organizations and the judicial system (*Layshock v. Hermitage School District,* 2007). In the current case, the court found that the school district failed to demonstrate a sufficient causal nexus between the student's conduct and any substantial disruption of school operations. In particular, the court noted that the school district was unable to show that the "buzz" or discussions in school were caused by this particular student's profile as opposed to the reaction of administrators. Accordingly, the School's right to maintain an environment conducive to learning does not trump the student's First Amendment right to freedom of expression.

The Future of the Press. Before leaving this section, it is important to think about "who is the press"? In 1791 when the First Amendment was adopted, there was only print media. In the past 100 years, we added radio, television and Internet. So when you think about who is the press: is it only the traditional print media? Print and broadcast media? What about an ESPN reporter who also blogs for ESPN's website? What about if he blogs on his own site? What if he creates a website criticizing the play calling of his child's youth basketball coach?

Freedom of Religion

As the Supreme Court stated in *Walz v. Tax Commission,* (1970) "we will not tolerate either governmentally established religion or governmental interference with religion. Short of those expressly proscribed governmental acts there is room for play in the joints productive of a benevolent neutrality which will permit religious exercise to exist without sponsorship and without interference." With so much room for play, it is easy to see why the courts have continuously struggled with First Amendment Freedom of Religion cases and the inherent conflict that exist between the **Establishment Clause,** which prohibits Congress or the states from making any law establishing or promoting a religion, and **Free Exercise Clause,** which prohibits Congress or the states from making any law interfering with the free exercise of religion (Brown-Foster, 2010).

The Establishment Clause

"In the words of [Thomas] Jefferson, the clause against establishment of religion by law was intended to erect a wall of separation between Church and State" (*Everson v. Board of Education*, 1947). Since 1971, the Court's primary test for analyzing Establishment Clause cases is the **Lemon Test**, first developed in *Lemon v. Kurtzman*, (1971). Under the Lemon Test, the Court uses a three prong analysis in which: "[First], the statute must have a secular legislative purpose; second, its principal or primary effect must be one that neither advances nor inhibits religion; finally, the statute must not foster an excessive government entanglement with religion" (*Lemon v. Kurtzman*, 1971).

The Lemon Test, however, has been criticized as "simply not providing adequate standards for deciding Establishment Clause cases" (*Wallace v. Jaffree*, 1985). As a result, the Court has begun to focus on whether a law or policy accommodates (constitutionally acceptable), endorses (constitutionally unacceptable) or coerces others conform to (constitutionally unacceptable) religion. For example in *Lee v. Weisman* (1992), the Court developed the **Coercion Test**, which analyzes whether school-sponsored religious activity has a coercive effect on students. The third test developed by the court is the Endorsement Test. The **Endorsement Test** asks whether government policies or practices are religiously neutral (constitutionally acceptable) or convey or communicate a message of endorsement or disapproval of religion (constitutionally unacceptable) (Brown-Foster, 2010).

In reviewing cases involving prayer in public schools, the courts tend to examine whether students felt coerced into participation in religion. For example in *Santa Fe High Independent School District v. Doe* (2000), a student elected as Santa Fe High School's student council chaplain delivered a prayer over the public address system before each home varsity football game. A group of students challenged this practice under the Establishment Clause of the First Amendment. The United States Supreme Court in striking down the policy held that for purposes of analysis under the Federal Constitution's First Amendment, there is a crucial difference between government speech endorsing religion, which the First Amendment's establishment of religion clause forbids; and private speech endorsing religion, which the First Amendment's free speech and free exercise of religion clauses protect. In ruling that the school district's policy endorses religion, the Supreme Court citing *Lee* v. *Weisman*, (1992) held that "at a minimum, the Constitution guarantees that government may not coerce anyone to support or participate in religion or its exercise, or otherwise act in a way which 'establishes a [state] religion or religious faith, or tends to do so" (*Lee v. Weisman*, 1992). By delivering a prayer over the public address system before each home varsity football game, the court found that the school district's conduct amounted to an endorsement of religion. In cases involving state participation in a religious activity, the relevant question is whether an objective observer would perceive the school's practice as a state endorsement of prayer in public schools. Regardless of the listener's support for, or objection to, the message, the Court held that an objective Santa Fe High School student would unquestionably perceive the school's pregame prayer as state approved.

Free Exercise Clause

The "Free Exercise [clause] embraces two concepts—freedom to believe and freedom to act. The first is absolute but, in the nature of things, the second cannot be. The freedom to act must have appropriate definition to preserve the enforcement of that protection [although] the power to regulate must be so exercised as not, in attaining a permissible end, unduly to infringe the protected freedom" of others (*Cantwell v. Connecticut*, 1940). In other words, the state cannot enact any laws that interfere with, by making it illegal or otherwise burdens, an individual's right to exercise his or her religious beliefs unless the general application of the law has a nonreligious purpose. In addition, the state cannot require, or otherwise encourages, a specific religious practice or conduct that may be forbidden by some religious belief (Shiffrin and Choper, 2006). For example, in ruling that the use of controlled substances during religious ceremonies could be prohibited by the state laws, the Supreme Court found that the purpose of the law was nonreligious and of general applicability (*Employment Division, Department of Human Resources of Oregon v. Smith*, (1990)). Laws of general applicability thus can be analogized to content neutral regulation in the freedom of speech context. When such enactments are challenged, and even if they impose a substantial burden upon free exercise interest, the court will review the law under the rational basis test not strict scrutiny (See Chapter 6.14 Equal Protection for a discussion of the tests). The courts will use the strict scrutiny only in those cases where a law is found aimed directly at religion.

For example, in *Borden v. School District of the Township of East Brunswick* (2008), the head football coach at East Brunswick High School had established a tradition where he would lead the team in prayer. Borden decided to change the tradition where he said prayer for the first pre-game dinner of each season. For every game thereafter, he asked everyone to stand and chose a senior to say a prayer. Additionally, Borden asked the players to take a knee in the locker room to discuss game strategy after which he again led the team in prayer. After a complaint was filed against the coach for his practices, the school district directed Borden to stop what he was doing and provided him with guidelines that coincided with previous court rulings that any prayer had to be truly student-initiated. These guidelines also stipulated that any representative of the school district could not participate.

Upset he could no longer engage in the silent act of bowing his head during his team's pre-meal grace and taking a knee with his team during a locker-room prayer, Borden brought suit seeking a declaratory judgment that the East Brunswick School District's policy prohibiting his participation in student-initiated prayer was unconstitutionally overbroad and vague, and violated his First Amendment rights. In upholding the school district's policy, the Third Circuit Court of Appeals held that even Borden's silent acts could be construed as an endorsement of religion (*Borden v. School District of the Township of East Brunswick*, 2008). In support of this conclusion, the Third Circuit Court held that Borden's silent acts violate the Establishment Clause because, when viewing the acts in light of Borden's twenty-three years of prior prayer activities with the East Brunswick High School football team during which he organized, participated in, and even led prayer activities with his team, a reasonable observer would conclude that Borden was endorsing religion in violation of the Establishment Clause (*Borden v. School District of the Township of East Brunswick*, 2008).

SIGNIFICANT CASE

In this case, the court examines whether the students First Amendment Right of Free Speech was violated when the students were punished for non-disruptive speech made outside of the school setting.

T.V. V. SMITH-GREEN COMMUNITY SCHOOL CORPORATION

United States District Court for the Northern District of Indiana
807 F. Supp. 2d 767 (2011)

Here's what the record reveals: during the summer of 2009, T.V. and M.K. were both entering the 10th grade at Churubusco High School, a public high school of approximately 400 students. Both T.V. and M.K. were members of the high school's volleyball team, an extracurricular activity, and M.K. was also a member of the cheerleading squad, also an extracurricular activity, as well as the show choir, which is a cocurricular activity. Cocurricular activities provide for academic credit but also involve activities that take place outside the normal school day.

Try-outs for the volleyball team for the coming year would occur in July. A couple of weeks prior to the tryouts, T.V., M.K. and a number of their friends had sleepovers at M.K.'s house. Prior to the first sleepover, the girls bought phallic-shaped rainbow colored lollipops. During the first sleepover, the girls took a number of photographs of themselves sucking on the lollipops. In one, three girls are pictured and M.K. added the caption "Wanna suck on my cock." In another photograph, a fully-clothed M.K. is sucking on one lollipop while another lollipop is positioned between her legs and a fully-clothed T.V. is pretending to suck on it.

***

T.V. posted most of the pictures on her MySpace or Facebook accounts, where they were accessible to persons she had granted "Friend" status. Some of the photos involving the lollipops were also posted on Photo Bucket, where a password is necessary for viewing. None of the images identify the girls as students at Churubusco High School. Neither T.V. nor M.K. ever brought the images to school either in digital or any other format. In their depositions, both T.V. and M.K. characterized what they did as "just joking around" and disclaimed that the images conveyed any scientific, literary or artistic value or message, but testified that the photos were taken and were shared on the internet because the girls thought what they had done was funny and "wanted to share with [their] friends how funny it was."

Around August 4, a parent brought printouts of the photographs to Steve Darnell, the Superintendent of Smith-Green Community School Corporation. The parent reported that the images were posted on Facebook and Photo Bucket and that the photographs were causing "divisiveness" among the girls on the volleyball teams, because "two camps" had formed—girls that were "in favor . . . of what was going on with the pictures" and "girls that just wanted to have no part in it." Evidently, this woman's daughter did not play volleyball in the fall of 2009. Superintendent Darnell immediately took the pictures to Principal Couch, reported that the photos were "causing a disruption in extracurricular teams," and told him to "follow code with this." . . .

The Churubusco High School Student Handbook for 2008–2009 contains an "EXTRA-CURRICULAR/CO-CURRICULAR CODE OF CONDUCT AND ATHLETIC CODE OF CONDUCT." On page 25, this code provides: The purpose of the "Extra-Curricular Code of Conduct" is to demonstrate to students at Churubusco High School who participate in organized extra-curricular activities that they not only represent themselves, but also represent Churubusco High School, as well. Therefore, those students who choose to participate in extra-curricular activities are expected to demonstrate good conduct at school and outside of school. . . . This code will be in force for the entire year including out of season and during the summer.

Separately, under the heading "EXTRA-CURRICULAR/CO-CURRICULAR ACTIVITIES" on page 24, the Student Handbook states: "If you act in a manner in school or out of school that brings discredit or dishonor upon yourself or your school, you may be removed from extra-curricular activities for all or part of the year."

After confirming the identities of the girls in the images, and discussing the matter with the Athletic Director and the Assistant Principal, within a day of Principal Couch's receipt of the photographs, he informed M.K. and T.V. that they had violated the athletic code and faced suspension from extracurricular and cocurricular activities. At the time, T.V. and M.K. were both participating in volleyball practices and M.K. was attending rehearsals for the show choir. Principal Couch did not discuss the situation with any member of the volleyball coaching staff, other than approaching the volleyball coach to confirm that the girls were playing volleyball and to inform the coach that he needed to speak with the girls because of an extracurricular violation. Principal Couch did not speak with the director of the show choir until after M.K. was suspended, and then simply to advise the teacher of the suspension.

Defendants explain the basis for Principal Couch's decision as his "determination that the photographs were inappropriate, and that by posing for them, and posting them on the internet, the students were reflecting discredit upon the school." In addition, Principal Couch determined that the photographs had the potential for causing disruption of school activities. . . . Against this background, Principal Couch wanted the new 2009–2010 school year "to get off on the right foot," and "needed to do something before this blew up." The conclusion that the photographs represented a violation of the Student Handbook coupled with the anticipation of potential school disruption from the situation served as the basis for the discipline imposed.

Principal Couch informed T.V. and M.K. that they were being suspended from extracurricular and cocurricular activities for a calendar year pursuant to the school's 2008–2009 policy, for bringing discredit on themselves and the school. The portion of the policy cited provided that "If you act in a manner in school or out of school that brings discredit or dishonor upon yourself or your school, you may be removed from extracurricular activities for all or part of the year." It was explained to the girls that, under the policy, they could obtain a reduction of their punishment by making three visits to a counselor and then meeting with the school's Athletic Board to apologize for their actions. When he was contacted by T.V.'s parents, Superintendent Darnell indicated that he supported Couch's decision.

Both T.V. and M.K. opted to visit the counselor, and completed those requirements by August 13, 2009. Subsequently, the girls each appeared separately before the Athletic Board, a panel consisting of Principal Couch, the Athletic Director, the Assistant Principal and the coaches. As a result, the punishment was modified and the girls were excluded from only 25% of their fall extracurricular activities, which meant that T.V. missed six volleyball games and M.K. missed five games and a show choir performance.

Analysis

Is the speech involved nonetheless unprotected?

The parties dispute whether the case involves speech protected by the First Amendment. Defendants contend that, under distinct standards, the photographs constitute both obscenity and child pornography, neither of which is protected by the First Amendment. *United States v. Stevens*, 130 S.Ct. 1577, 1584, 176 L. Ed. 2d 435 (2010). At the May 27th hearing, after being pressed on the point, counsel for defendants conceded that the law on obscenity and child pornography are not applicable here, and with good reason.

Obscene material is not protected by the First Amendment. Smith-Green and Couch initially invoked the three-part test for obscenity set out by the Supreme Court in

Miller. The second part of that test asks whether "the work depicts or describes, in a patently offensive way, sexual conduct specifically defined by the applicable state law." *Id*. at 24. The state law defendants cite to is Indiana's definition of "sexual conduct" in its statutes on child exploitation and possession of child pornography:

"Sexual conduct" means sexual intercourse, deviate sexual conduct, exhibition of the uncovered genitals intended to satisfy or arouse the sexual desires of any person, sadomasochistic abuse, sexual or deviate sexual conduct with an animal, or any fondling or touching of a child by another person or of another person by a child intended to arouse or satisfy the sexual desires of either the child or the other person.

I.C. §35-42-4-4(a). Tacitly acknowledging that the only item in this list that might apply to the photographs here is "deviate sexual conduct," defendants then turn to the definition of that term in I.C. §35-41-1-9: "'Deviate sexual conduct' means an act involving: (1) a sex organ of one person and the mouth or anus of another person; or (2) the penetration of the sex organ or anus of a person by an object."

Although Smith-Green and Couch once blithely asserted that the photographs depict "deviate sexual conduct" within this definition, as necessary to meet the second element of the *Miller* obscenity test, I cannot reach the same conclusion. Not even a single photograph meets the definition of "deviate sexual conduct" because none of them depicts the sex organ, mouth or anus of two people, and none of the images depicts actual penetration. From the plain meaning of the words of the statutory definition, I conclude—consistent with the defendants' concession on the point—that the photographs do not depict "deviate sexual conduct" as defined in Indiana law, and that as a result the photographs do not constitute obscenity under the Supreme Court's criteria in *Miller*.

Neither do the photographs constitute child pornography under either state or federal statutes. Indiana's statutes addressing child pornography refer to images that include, depict or describe "sexual conduct by a child," using the same definition of "sexual conduct" as has been considered and rejected previously with respect to the obscenity analysis. I.C. §35-42-4-4(b) & (c). Defendants, while glossing over the inapplicable Indiana statutory definition of "sexual conduct" as discussed above, also initially argued that M.K. and T.V. have "admitted" that the photographs depicted oral and anal sexual acts. But this is a complete stretch of the girls' deposition testimony. The testimony referred to does not address the statutory definition of the term, and in any event could not do so, as these lay witnesses cannot offer such legal analysis and conclusions.

The federal definition, found at 18 U.S.C. §2256(8), requires a "visual depiction involv[ing] the use of a minor engaging in sexually explicit conduct." The phrase "sexually explicit conduct" has a multi-part definition, from which defendants invoke this portion: "actual or

simulated . . . sexual intercourse, including genital-genital, oral-genital, anal-genital, or oral-anal, whether between persons of the same or opposite sex." §2256(2)(A)(i). With only candy phalluses and toy tridents, the photographs cannot be said to depict simulated oral-genital sexual intercourse or anal-genital sexual intercourse within the meaning of this statute. Instead, the conduct depicted "must have created the realistic impression of an actual sex act to constitute simulated sexual intercourse." *Tilton v. Playboy Entertainment Group, Inc*., 554 F.3d 1371, 1376 (11th Cir. 2009). An act "only constitutes simulated sexual intercourse . . . if it creates the realistic impression of an *actual* sexual act." *Giovani Carandola, Ltd. v. Fox*, 470 F.3d 1074, 1080 (4th Cir. 2006) (emphasis in original). Given this analysis, and defendants' later concession, the students' First Amendment claim is not defeated by a contention that their speech is unprotected obscenity or child pornography.

What free speech standards apply?

Having rejected Smith-Green and Couch's arguments that the photographs are not protected by the First Amendment, I must next determine what constitutional free speech standards apply. Relying upon *Bethel School District No. 403 v. Fraser*, 478 U.S. 675, 106 S. Ct. 3159, 92 L. Ed. 2d 549 (1986), Smith-Green and Couch first argue that the photographs are not entitled to First Amendment protection because they are lewd, vulgar and/or plainly offensive. In *Fraser*, the Supreme Court held that the First Amendment does not prevent school officials from punishing "a vulgar and lewd speech . . . [that] would undermine the school's basic educational mission." *Id*. at 685. The speech being made by the student in *Fraser* was at a school assembly. M.K. and T.V.'s photographs were taken inside the privacy of their own homes and were published to the internet from outside of school. Defendants contend that "it is undisputed that the photographs did in fact make it into the school." While this may be true, it's beside the point. Neither M.K. nor T.V. brought the material into the school environment. Others did.

Fraser cannot be interpreted as broadly as Smith-Green and Couch want. Context matters, as *Fraser* itself notes: "A high school assembly or classroom is no place for a sexually explicit monologue directed towards an unsuspecting audience of teenage students." *Id*. But as Justice Brennan noted in his concurrence, the Court's holding was limited: "If respondent had given the same speech outside of the school environment, he could not have been penalized simply because government officials considered his language to be inappropriate." *Id*. at 688.

Indeed, the Supreme Court itself has noted *Fraser*'s limited scope: … in *Morse v. Frederick*, 551 U.S. 393 (2007), the Supreme Court plainly stated that "[h]ad Fraser delivered the same speech in a public forum outside the school context, it would have been protected," echoing the observation of Justice Brennan in his *Fraser* concurrence. So here Smith-Green and Couch cannot prevail on a characterization of the photographs as lewd and vulgar in reliance on *Fraser* because, simply put, "[t]he School District's argument fails at the outset because *Fraser* does not apply to off-campus speech."

The Tinker standard and its limits.

All of which brings us to *Tinker v. Des Moines Indep. Cmty. Sch. Dist.*, 393 U.S. 503 (1969), where the Supreme Court considered a schools' punishment of students who wore black armbands to school to represent their objections to the Vietnam War and their support for a truce. The case presented a conflict between the rights of the students to free expression and the interest of the school officials in maintaining order in the educational environment. The Court balanced those competing interests by announcing the following standard: school officials can restrict student expression only if the officials can show "that the students' activities would materially and substantially disrupt the work and discipline of the school." *Id*. at 513. The Supreme Court found that there was "no evidence whatever of petitioners' interference, actual or nascent, with the schools' work or of collision with the rights of other students to be secure and to be let alone." *Id*. at 508. Therefore, the suspension of the students for their expression by wearing the armbands was found to violate their First Amendment rights. *Id*. at 514.

Smith-Green and Couch first argue that students have no constitutional right to participate in extracurricular activities, and therefore the discipline imposed upon M.K. and T.V. requires no showing of "substantial disruption."

But *Tinker* itself defeats this argument: The principle of these cases [on student free speech] is not confined to the supervised and ordained discussion which takes place in the classroom . . . A student's rights, therefore, do not embrace merely the classroom hours. When he is in the cafeteria, or on the playing field, or on the campus during the authorized hours, he may express his opinions, even on controversial subjects like the conflict in Vietnam, if he does so without 'materially and substantially interfer(ing) with the requirements of appropriate discipline in the operation of the school' and without colliding with the rights of others. *Tinker*, 393 U.S. at 512–13.

The constitutional right at issue is freedom of expression, not that of participation in extracurricular activities. That there is no constitutional right to participate in athletics or other extracurricular activities may be pertinent to an analysis of other sorts of constitutional claims, such as a Due Process claim, a Privileges and Immunities claim, or an Equal Protection claim, but as *Tinker* itself notes, not to a freedom of expression claim.

What this means is that a student cannot be punished with a ban from extracurricular activities for non-disruptive speech. For example, in a case involving suspension from a high school football team, the Ninth Circuit observed: "In holding that a student's First Amendment rights are 'not confined to the supervised and ordained

discussion which takes place in the classroom,' the Court extended *Tinker*'s principles to school activities broadly defined, including extracurricular activities." *Pinard v. Clatskanie School District 6J*, 467 F.3d 755, 769 (9th Cir. 2006).

***

In the present context, I will also assume without deciding that *Tinker* applies, because even under its contextual narrowing of the right of free speech, I conclude that the school officials violated the First Amendment rights of plaintiffs T.V. and M.K.

Substantial disruption.

Finally then, I arrive at the First Amendment standard to be applied, namely whether in the circumstances present here, Principal Couch reasonably found that the pictures posted on the internet had disrupted, or would materially and substantially disrupt, the work and discipline of the school. I agree with Principal Couch and Smith-Green that a showing of actual disruption is not required for the punishment to pass constitutional muster. School officials are not required to wait and allow a disruption of their school environment to occur before taking action. However, "*Tinker* requires a specific and significant fear of disruption, not just some remote apprehension of disturbance" *Saxe v. State College Area School District*, 240 F.3d 200, 211 (3rd Cir. 2001).

M.K. and T.V. are under the impression that the defendants concede the actual disruption argument, and that the disciplinary decision was made entirely on the basis of potential future disruption. But this isn't the case. The school defendants rely on the assertion that Principal Couch acted in part on the report of the complaining parent that the photographs *had already caused* divisiveness on school teams. The mother who brought the photos to Darnell reported that they were "causing issues" with her daughter and the extracurricular teams. The trouble was further described as "divisiveness" with the girls on the volleyball teams, that is, the girls' division into "two camps"—those "in favor, you know, of what—was going on in the pictures" and those who "just wanted to have no part of it."

***

Comparison of this testimony reflects a discrepancy in the record as to whether actual disruption of school-sponsored student activity was in fact a basis for the imposition of the discipline meted out to M.K. and T.V. But even assuming it was, the actual disruption in this case does not come close to meeting the *Tinker* standard. Here's what *Tinker* says on that point:

> [I]n our system, undifferentiated fear or apprehension of disturbance is not enough to overcome the right to freedom of expression. Any departure from absolute regimentation may cause trouble. Any variation from the majority's opinion

may inspire fear. Any word spoken, in class, in the lunchroom, or on the campus, that deviates from the views of another person may start an argument or cause a disturbance. But our Constitution says we must take this risk. . . . In order for the State in the person of school officials to justify prohibition of a particular expression of opinion, it must be able to show that its action was caused by something more than a mere desire to avoid the discomfort and unpleasantness that always accompanies an unpopular viewpoint. Certainly where there is no finding and no showing that engaging in the forbidden conduct would 'materially and substantially interfere with the requirements of appropriate discipline in the operation of the school,' the prohibition cannot be sustained. Tinker, 393 U.S. at 508–09, quoting Burnside, 363 F.2d at 749.

Defendants' showing of actual disruption is extremely weak. Petty disagreements among players on a team—or participants in clubs for that matter—is utterly routine. This type of unremarkable dissension does not establish disruption with the work or discipline of the team or the school, much less disruption that is "substantial" or "material."

***

Here, school officials cannot point to any *students* creating or experiencing actual disruption *during any school activity*. Instead, the officials merely responded to the complaints of parents (two in all), and the complaints do not appear to have been confirmed with any students or coaches. As was true of the armbands in *Tinker*, the photos in this case could be said, at best, to have "caused discussion outside of the classrooms, but no interference with work and no disorder." *Tinker*, 393 U.S. at 514. Certainly no evidence has been presented of the kind of serious issues enumerated recently by the Seventh Circuit as indicative of substantial disruption: "[s]uch facts might include a decline in students' test scores, an upsurge in truancy, or other symptoms of a sick school." *Zamecnik v. Indian Prairie School District*, 636 F.3d 874, 876 (7th Cir. 2011).

In sum, at most, this case involved two complaints from parents and some petty sniping among a group of 15 and 16 year olds. This can't be what the Supreme Court had in mind when it enunciated the "substantial disruption" standard in *Tinker*. To find otherwise would be to read the word "substantial" out of "substantial disruption."

***

To sum up: no reasonable jury could conclude that the photos of T.V. and M.K. posted on the internet caused a substantial disruption to school activities, or that there was a reasonably foreseeable chance of future substantial disruption. And while the crass foolishness that is the subject of the protected speech in this case makes one long for important substantive expressions like the black armbands of *Tinker*, such a distinction between the worthwhile and the unworthy is exactly what the First Amendment does not permit. With all respect to the important and valuable function of public school authorities, and the considerable deference to their judgment that is so often due, it would be an unseemly and dangerous precedent to allow the state, in the guise of school authorities, to reach into a child's home and control his/her actions there to the same extent that it can control that child when he/she participates in school sponsored activities. Plaintiffs' motion for partial summary judgment will therefore be granted, and defendants' summary judgment motion denied, on the issue whether T.V. and M.K. were punished in violation of their First Amendment rights.

***

CONCLUSION

Today I determine as a matter of law that the punishment imposed on T.V. and M.K. for their out of school expression violated their First Amendment rights. … Finally, I conclude that a Student Handbook provision that authorizes discipline for out of school conduct that brings "dishonor" or "discredit" upon the school or the student is so vague and overbroad as to violate the Constitution. I wish the case involved more important and worthwhile speech on the part of the students, but then of course a school's well-intentioned but unconstitutional punishment of that speech would be all the more regrettable.

CASES ON THE SUPPLEMENTAL WEB SITE

Besig, Cook, and Garda v. The Dolphin Boating and Swimming Club, 683 F.2d 1271 (9th Cir. 1982). In this case the court examines the right to associate, or right not to associate of private clubs.

Borden v. School District of the Township of East Brunswick, 533 F. 3d. 153 (3rd Cir. 2008). This case closely examines personal rights of an employee serving as a state actor with the rights of a school district to enforce

religious freedoms found in the First Amendment to the United States Constitution.

Doe v. Duncanville Independent School District, 70 F.3d 402 (5th Cir. 1995). This case examines the Establishment Clause and whether faculty-lead prayers violated the clause by improperly entangling the school district with religion and signaled an unconstitutional endorsement of religion.

Tinker v. Des Moines Independent Community School District, 393 U.S. 503 (1969). This case examines the free speech rights of high school students in school and when school officials have the right to prevent student speech.

Zacchini v. Scripps-Howard Broadcasting, 433 U.S. 562 (1977). This case compares the First Amendment protections granted television stations in broadcasting news, to an individual's right of publicity and economic value of his performance.

QUESTIONS YOU SHOULD BE ABLE TO ANSWER

1. What standard of review did the Court develop in *Tinker v. Des Moines Independent Community School District*?

2. In addition to the *Tinker* standard, when else can public school officials restrict student speech?

3. Discuss when a public school coach can and cannot be involved in prayer before a game.

4. Explain why there is a conflict between the Establishment Clause and Free Exercise Clause.

5. Discuss why the Courts protect print media differently than broadcast media?

REFERENCES

Cases

Bethel School District No. 403 v. Fraser, 478 U.S. 675 (1986).
Borden v. School District of the Township of East Brunswick, 523 F. 3d 153 (3rd Cir. 2008).
Cantwell v. Connecticut, 310 U.S. 296 (1940).
Doe v. Duncanville Independent School Dist., 70 F.3d 405 (1995).
Employment Division, Department of Human Resources of Oregon v. Smith, 494 U.S. 872 (1990).
Everson v. Board of Education, 330 U.S. 1 (1947).
Frederick v. Morse, 551 U.S. 393 (2007).
Gitlow v. New York, 268 U.S. 652 (1925).
Hysaw v. Washburn University of Topeka, 690 F. Supp. 940 (1987).
Layshock v. Hermitage School District, 496 F. Supp. 2d 587 (2007).
Lee v. Weisman, 505 U.S. 577 (1992).
Lemon v. Kurtzman, 403 U.S. 602 (1971).
Lowery v. Euverard, 497 F.3d 584 (6th Cir. 2007).
Palko v. Connecticut, 302 U.S. 319 (1937).
Pinard v. Clatskanie School District 6J, 446 F.3d 964 (9th Cir. 2006).
Robinson v. Hicks, King and City of Harrisburg, 450 Fed. Appx. 168 (3rd Cir. 2011).
Santa Fe High Independent School District v. Doe, 530 U.S. 290 (2000).
Schenck v. United States, 249 U.S. 47 (1919).
Tinker v. Des Moines Independent Community School District, 393 U.S. 503 (1969).
United States v. Schwimmer, 279 U.S. 644 (1937).
Wallace v. Jaffree, 472 U.S. 38 (1985).
Walz v. Tax Commission of City of New York, 397 U.S. 664 (1970).
Zacchini v. Scripps-Howard Broadcasting, 433 U.S. 562 (1977).

Publications

Brown-Foster, S. (2010). Religious Issues. In D. J. Cotton & J. T. Wolohan (Eds.), Law for Recreation and Sport Managers (5th Ed.) pp. 517–527. Dubuque, IA: Kendall/Hunt Publishing Co.
Hayes, A. (2010). From Armbands to Douchebags: How *Doninger v. Niehoff* Shows the Supreme Court Needs to Address Student Speech in the Cyber Age. *Akron Law Review*, 43, 247–289.
Sullivan, K., and Gunther, G. (2007). *Constitutional Law* (17th ed.). New York, NY: Foundation Press.
Shiffrin, S. and Choper, J. (2006). *The First Amendment: Cases—Comments—Questions* (4th ed.) St. Paul, MN: West Publishing.
Weaver, R. and Lively, D. (2003). *Understanding the First Amendment*. Newark, NJ: LexisNexis

Legislation

United States Constitution, Amendment I.

RECREATION AND SPORT MANAGEMENT APPLICATIONS

6.21 VOLUNTARY ASSOCIATIONS AND ELIGIBILITY ISSUES

Colleen Colles I **Metropolitan State College of Denver**

Jo Williams I **University of Southern Maine**

By definition, a **voluntary association** is, "a group of individuals joined together on the basis of mutual interest or common objectives, especially a business group that is not organized or constituted as a legal entity" (*Random House*, 2012). Accordingly, state high school athletic associations, the National Federation of High Schools (NFHS), the National Collegiate Athletic Association (NCAA), the National Parks and Recreation Association (NPRA) are all examples of voluntary sport and recreation associations (see also section 6.25 Private Clubs).

In reviewing the rules voluntary associations establish for eligibility or the right to participate in the organization, the courts have historically been reluctant to overturn the bylaws, rules, and regulations of these associations unless they violate constitutional law, public policy or were enforced in an **arbitrary or capricious** manner (see *Indiana High School Athletic Association, Inc. v. Watson, 2010* on Supplemental Web Site). By joining voluntary associations, the courts have held that participants agree to follow the rules and regulations of such organizations (Trichka & Sawyer, 1998).

The following section examines the jurisdiction of courts with regard to voluntary associations and some of the specific eligibility requirements enacted by such organizations. In particular, the section will examine the eligibility requirements of both state high school athletic associations and the NCAA.

FUNDAMENTAL CONCEPTS

Voluntary associations get their authority to govern through a combination of federal, state, and local legislation, and in some cases, litigation (Conn, 2003). States often grant school boards the authority to join governing associations, thereby relieving themselves of the oversight, decision making and enforcement. Local schools have significant independence in determining the rules and regulations regarding their participation in interscholastic sports; however, state athletic associations play a significant role by providing state-wide governance for interscholastic athletics (Van Ann, 2011).

Judicial Review

Generally, the courts will not interfere with the internal affairs of a voluntary association. For example in *Rottmann v. Penn Interscholastic Athletics Association (2004), (*see Supplemental Web Site*)* the court held that:

> In the absence of mistake, fraud, collusion or arbitrariness, the decisions of such associations will be accepted by the courts as conclusive. Such associations may adopt reasonable rules which will be deemed valid and binding upon the members of the association unless the rule violates some law or public policy. It is not the responsibility of the federal courts to inquire into the expediency, practicability, or wisdom of those regulations (*Rottmann v. Penn Interscholastic Athletics Association,* 2004).

As noted in *NCAA v. Yeo (2005),* "judicial intervention in [student athletic disputes] often does more harm than good . . ." and "judges are not 'super referees.'" This notion of judicial deference to the associations was highlighted by the court in *NCAA v. Lasege (2001),* when it stated that members of voluntary associations should be free from unwarranted interference from the courts and members should be allowed to "paddle their own canoe."

However, there are exceptions to this non-interference tenet. For example, in *Florida High School Athletic Association v. Marazzito (2005),* the court affirmed that intervention in the internal affairs of a voluntary association may be appropriate under *exceptional circumstances.* Specifically, a court should only intervene under the following two conditions: (1) a substantial property, contract or economic rights will be adversely affected by the association's action and the internal procedures of the association were unfair or inadequate or (2) the association acted maliciously or in bad faith.

The courts have also consistently ruled that the regulations and/or decisions of associations cannot be unreasonable, arbitrary, or capricious. In a case involving a student's request to transfer schools under a hardship exception, the Indiana High School Athletic Association's (IHAA) decision to deny the student-athlete eligibility was deemed arbitrary and capricious because the IHSAA did not take into account that a substantial change to the family's financial condition had occurred and that the change was out of the student's control. Thus, the court determined that the student should have met the requirements for a hardship waiver (*IHAA v. Durham, 2001*). When allegations of "unreasonableness" arise, courts will decide if the rule has a rational relationship to a reasonable goal of the association.

It is important to note that the member schools are considered "voluntary" members of the governing associations, so judicial review is very limited; however, students are not deemed "voluntary" members and are therefore afforded the stricter arbitrary and capricious standard of review. The focus of many lawsuits involving voluntary sport and recreation associations is on the arbitrary and capricious standard and violations of constitutional rights.

Arbitrary and Capricious Standard

In *Indiana High School Athletic Association v. Carlberg (1997),* the Supreme Court of Indiana found that the transfer rule advanced a legitimate goal of the IHSAA, and as enforced against Carlberg was not arbitrary and capricious and therefore did not violate the student's federal right of equal protection. In reaching this decision, two important points were noted by the court. First, the arbitrary and capricious standard of review is narrow and the court cannot substitute its judgment for the judgment of the IHSAA. Second, the court stated "the rule or decision will be found to be arbitrary and capricious only where it is willful and unreasonable, without consideration and in disregard of the facts or circumstances in the case, or without some basis which would lead a reasonable and honest person to the same conclusion" (*Indiana High School Athletic Association v. Carlberg,* 1997).

State or Federal Constitutional Rights

Since high school athletic associations are widely accepted as **state actors**, the decisions of these associations are subject to constitutional review. *(see Section 6.12 State Action).* As state actors, these voluntary associations cannot deny citizens equal protection and/or due process guaranteed by the Federal Constitution. (*See sections 6.13 Due Process and 6.14 Equal Protection*). The **Equal Protection Clause of the Fourteenth Amendment** provides a constitutional method for checking the fairness of the application of the law. If an association cannot demonstrate a connection between the rule and its purpose, then an equal protection violation may have occurred. Thus, voluntary associations must practice due diligence by providing procedural due process whenever disciplinary action is taken.

In Kentucky, the parents of non-public school students alleged violations of their rights under the First and Fourteenth Amendments through the application of Bylaw 13, which places limits on the amount and type of merit based scholarship assistance a student can receive and remain eligible to participate in athletics (see *Seger v. Kentucky High School Athletic Association,* 2011 on Supplemental Web Site.) The appellate court affirmed the decision of the district court to dismiss the federal claims stating that the Bylaw applied to all non-public schools equally. Of interest in this case are the plaintiffs' allegations that the restrictions in Bylaw 13 are discriminatory on the basis of religion and that a strict scrutiny standard should be applied. The court disagreed and ruled that the bylaw does not discriminate based on a "suspect" or "quasi-suspect" classification and thus is subject to review under the rational basis standard.

In *Sisson v. Virginia High School League* (2010), the plaintiff was one day too old under the league's participation rules and was prohibited from participating in varsity athletics. After a failed appeal to the state athletic association, the plaintiff filed action alleging violations of his right to due process and equal protection and requested that a temporary restraining order be granted. The court, which denied the request, based its ruling on the plaintiff's inability to establish the necessary elements for a preliminary injunction: (1) irreparable harm and (2) a likelihood of success based on the merits. A key consideration by the court was the fact that the plaintiff's parents elected to hold him back a year on the recommendation of the school, he was not held back by the school for academic reasons.

It should be noted that while high school athletic associations have been deemed state actors for constitutional purposes, thereby limiting their regulatory authority, the NCAA has not. Therefore, while the actions of state high school associations are subject to Constitutional review, the courts will not review those of the NCAA (see *NCAA v. Tarkanian*, 1988).

High School Privilege

High school eligibility rules are essentially the products of state high school activities/athletics associations. These associations are created to deal with the management of **extracurricular activities**, which by definition are all those activities for students that are sponsored or sanctioned by an educational institution that supplement or complement, but are not a part of, the institution's required academic program or regular curriculum.

It is well-established that students do not have a general constitutional right to participate in athletics (see *Brentwood Academy v. Tennessee Secondary School Athletic Association*, 2001). Participation is voluntary and, more important, a **privilege**. A school board may decide, usually through its participation in the state high school athletics association, the terms under which students may exercise the privilege. When eligibility standards are challenged in the courts, they must in most circumstances withstand only rational basis scrutiny. This means that if the requirements are rationally related to a legitimate purpose of association and not arbitrary, capricious, or unjustly discriminatory, they will be upheld by the courts (*IHSAA v. Watson, 2010*).

Transfer Rules

High school associations create transfer rules to preclude student-athletes from **"jumping"** (enrolling in different school) for reasons pertaining to athletics. There are many legitimate reasons for transfers involving such things as family relocations, employment, divorce, etc., and as such, constitute a basis for exceptions within the rules. Transfer rules appear to be popular targets for legal challenges based upon claims of violations of equal protection, freedom of religion, right to travel, and due process. Yet courts have generally upheld transfer rules under rational judicial scrutiny.

In a recent case, the Supreme Court of Indiana reversed the decision of the lower courts to grant a preliminary injunction to allow Jasmine Watson, a star basketball player, to play sports. The IHSAA ruled that the transfer was primarily based on athletic reasons and undue influence from Watson's mother. The Supreme Court ruled that the lower courts applied an incorrect standard for analyzing the decision of the IHSAA. In denying Watson's eligibility, the Court ruled that the IHSAA did not act arbitrarily or capriciously and stated that the lower court "substituted its own judgment for the IHSAA's" and "improperly discredited virtually all hearsay evidence" (*IHSAA v. Watson*, 2010).

Home-Schooled Student Eligibility

A number of states, including Arizona, Colorado, Florida, Idaho, Iowa, Maine, Michigan, Minnesota, New Hampshire, North Dakota, Oregon, Utah, Vermont and Washington, currently require public schools to allow homeschoolers access to sports. Potential student-athletes must meet specific eligibility requirements. Even though some state legislatures have supported home-schoolers in providing access to the privilege of public school activities, the courts in many states have taken a different position (Batista & Hatfield, 2005). For example, in *Jones v. West Virginia State Board of Education (2005)*, (see Supplemental Web Site), the state Supreme Court overturned a trial court ruling that the West Virginia Secondary School Activities Commission

(WVSSAC) violated a home-schooled student's rights to equal protection and breached its duty to promulgate reasonable rules and regulations. In reversing the decision, the Supreme Court stated that the WVSSAC did not violate the student's rights because the challenged statute pertained to providing educational resources, not athletic resources, to home-schooled students. Athletic competitions and leagues for "homeschoolers" have become more commonplace at the local, regional and national levels.

Redshirting

The practice of delaying or postponing an athlete's competition in order to extend the athlete's career is known as **"redshirting."** For purposes of maximizing athletic success, redshirting is an effective strategy to take advantage of an extra year's growth and maturity and, of course, skill development. High school athletics association rules do not permit the practice of redshirting because it is contrary to the educational mission. Furthermore, redshirting creates unfair competition advantages, possible dangerous mismatches, and unwarranted exclusion of peer student-athletes.

On the other hand, high school athletics associations recognize illness or injury and purely academic determinations of grade level as legitimate reasons for exceptions to rules precluding redshirting and make appropriate allowances. To address potential problems related to redshirting, **rules of longevity** must be invoked. Longevity rules determine the limits for participation in terms of (1) semesters/years allowed to complete competition, and (2) a maximum age beyond which interscholastic competition may not continue. For example, most high school association rules limit a student-athlete to eight consecutive semesters in which to complete interscholastic competition. Similarly, most associations do not permit competition among student-athletes who have reached their nineteenth birthday before beginning his/her senior year. In general, courts have agreed with the rational argument that longevity and redshirting regulations preserve the privilege of interscholastic sports competition, consistent with their educational mission.

Academic Standards

Alternative means of demonstrating academic eligibility for athletic participation in high schools include grade point average (GPA), courses passed in previous and/or current semesters or previous year, percent daily attendance, enrollment in minimum number of classes, enrollment in minimum full-credit courses, GPA or passing grades in current or previous grading periods. Thus, a variety of standards are used by different states to demonstrate academic qualification for athletic participation in high schools.

Intercollegiate Regulations

Individual eligibility rules for intercollegiate competition begin at the specific institution where the student is enrolled. Depending upon the institution's characteristics and mission, specific eligibility standards for representing that institution in intercollegiate athletic competition may be imposed. Such standards must reflect at a minimum the requirements of the conference in which it competes and, further, the association of conferences and institutions in which it holds membership. The largest such association of four-year institutions is the National Collegiate Athletic Association (NCAA). Therefore, this discussion will focus on the eligibility rules and bylaws of the NCAA and various legal challenges of those rules (see www. NCAA.org).

Article 1.3.1 of the *NCAA Manual* (2011–12) declares its basic purpose:

> The competitive athletics programs of member institutions are designed to be a vital part of the educational system. A basic purpose of this Association is to maintain intercollegiate athletics as an integral part of the educational program and the athlete as an integral part of the student body and, by so doing, retain a clear line of demarcation between intercollegiate athletics and professional sports (p. 1).

Thus, the NCAA is a private, voluntary association of four-year institutions that share a common interest in preserving amateur intercollegiate athletics as part of the educational mission.

Academic Regulations

To maintain the educational mission, the NCAA has legislated at the annual conventions of its members explicit rules for qualifying individuals academically for competition on two dimensions: initial and continuing. To meet *initial* qualifications, i.e., to be academically eligible to compete upon matriculation, the student-athlete must currently demonstrate the following (Bylaw 14.3.1.1):

a. Graduation from high school
b. Successful completion of a required core curriculum of 16 approved academic courses in specified subjects
c. Specified minimum GPA in the core curriculum, and
d. Specified minimum SAT or ACT score

Determination of initial eligibility is conducted by the Eligibility Center and includes a review of academic and amateurism standards. If the student satisfactorily meets the standards, the student is deemed a "qualifier" and is academically eligible to participate and receive athletically related financial aid. If the standards are not met, the applicant is restricted from competing (but may practice), may not receive athletically related financial aid, and surrenders one of his or her four years of competition eligibility.

To satisfy **continuing eligibility** requirements, the student-athlete must demonstrate a consistent record of progress toward a degree. To register "satisfactory progress" the student-athlete's academic record at the beginning of the fall semester or quarter of each year in residence must indicate completion of a requisite percent of course requirements in the student-athlete's particular academic program at a requisite percent of the GPA required for graduation at the particular institution.

In addition, the student-athlete must be enrolled full-time (minimum 12 semester credit hours) in order to maintain current athletic eligibility. Dropping below full-time enrollment immediately disqualifies the student for athletic competition.

Amateurism

As stated previously, the NCAA's basic purpose highlights a focus on the amateur status of student athletes and the NCAA Manual (2011–12) consistently refers to the maintenance of a "clear line of demarcation between college athletics and professional sports" (NCAA Manual, 2011–12). Bylaws applied to amateurism contain restrictions on activities that occur prior to and after enrollment. Initial amateur certification is managed by the Eligibility Center and must be retained throughout the student-athlete's enrollment. A significant case challenging the NCAA's authority to regulate eligibility is *Bloom v. NCAA*, 2004 (see Supplemental Web Site). In the case, which highlighted Bloom's amateur status, the court held that the NCAA had not been arbitrary and capricious in enforcing its rules and denying a waiver for Bloom.

Transfer Rules

NCAA rules governing eligibility following transfer from one institution to another are rather complex. The purposes of transfer rules is to preclude recruitment of athletes from one institution to another, and to discourage interruptions of academic progress due to transfers because of reasons pertaining to athletics. The general principle stated in Bylaw 14.5.1 requires a student who transfers to a member institution from any other collegiate institution to complete one full academic year of residence at the certifying institution before being eligible to compete. There are multiple exceptions to this requirement; the most notable being those involving transfers from two-year colleges.

In Jan 2009, the NCAA adopted more stringent rules (bylaw 14.5.4) for athletes transferring from two-year institutions that required increased requirements with regard to math and English credit hours. As the book went to press, the bylaw were being challenged in federal court by a group of junior college football players in the University of California state system who stated that two-year college athletes were unfairly being singled out in a manner that made transfer unduly difficult (Sander, 2011). Another area of note is Bylaw 14.1.9.1 which applies to graduate students. The bylaw allows student athletes that had graduated with remaining eligibility to transfer and play at another institution where they were enrolled in a graduate degree. Critics of this rule suggested that it created "free agency" in college sports (Martin, 2008).

Longevity

The NCAA also is concerned with the problems presented by interminable eligibility and older-than-expected participants. With regard to the former, the NCAA decided four years of intercollegiate competition is the maximum allowed, regardless of where or at how many institutions the competition takes place. Further, the individual student-athlete is permitted five consecutive calendar years from original matriculation to complete four years of eligibility. Thus, an accommodation is possible following a transfer, or even a redshirt year for maturation or injury, etc. In addition, student-athletes may also seek waivers if they undertake military service, serve with religious organizations, or become pregnant.

With regard to age, the membership became alarmed at the infusion of older athletes, particularly foreign athletes with the advantage of seasoning and experience, supplanting the scholarships of younger athletes. So, in 1980 the membership passed "the age rule," Bylaw 14.2.4.5, which credits any organized sports competition in a particular sport in each 12-month period following the athlete's twentieth birthday as a year of NCAA competition eligibility.

The Restitution Rule

Bylaw 19.7 or the Restitution Rule has undergone a series of modifications since it was introduced in 1975. The current bylaw approved in 2010 applies to a "student-athlete who is ineligible under the terms of the constitution, bylaws or other legislation of the Association" and "is permitted to participate in intercollegiate competition contrary to such NCAA legislation but in accordance with the terms of a court restraining order or injunction operative against the institution attended by such student-athlete or against the Association, or both". Subsequently, if the "injunction is voluntarily vacated, stayed or reversed or it is finally determined by the courts that injunctive relief is not or was not justified", the institution must pay restitution to the NCAA. Restitution can range from individual and team records being stricken, to loss of television coverage and ineligibility for future championship play.

The courts have paid little attention to this rule over the years, in part, due to the fact the rule was effective in curtailing claims made by institutions or student-athletes. However, in 2008, *Oliver vs. NCAA* challenged the Restitution Rule. In this case, the plaintiff, a college baseball player, filed an action against the NCAA seeking a permanent injunction in a dispute over the NCAA's bylaws. Relief was granted due to a number of factors including the arbitrary nature of the bylaw which violated the "covenant of good faith and fair dealing. In addition, it was determined that Oliver would have suffered irreparable injury, loss or damage.

SIGNIFICANT CASE

In a case examining the impact of NCAA rules on high school athletes and lawyers, readers should pay particular attention to the court's reasoning regarding the arbitrary nature of the challenged bylaw and the violation of good faith and fair dealing.

ANDREW A. OLIVER V. NATIONAL COLLEGIATE ATHLETIC ASSOCIATION

Court of Common Pleas, Erie County
2009 Ohio 6587; 920 N.E.2d 203; (2009)

***

OPINION

On January 12, 2009, the court convened a bench trial in the above-captioned case. Present at trial were the plaintiff, Andrew Oliver, represented by his attorney, Richard G. Johnson, and the defendant, the National Collegiate Athletic Association, represented by Linda J. Salfrank and Kimberly W. Herlihy. The plaintiff's evidence included direct examination testimony of the plaintiff, Andrew Oliver the plaintiff's father, David Oliver, and

Michael Murman, Richard Karcher, and Marc Esenberg. The defendant, the National Collegiate Athletic Association, presented direct examination of Rachel Newman Baker, John Shukie, Jennifer Henderson, Carol Iwaoka, Kevin Lennon, and Alvin Mathews Jr. In addition to the direct examination above, the evidence also included trial depositions presented for examination and numerous exhibits. This matter was before the court to determine Count Three, which sought a declaratory judgment, and Count Four, which sought a permanent injunction of the plaintiff's amended complaint. After thorough review of all pleadings, the testimony at trial, the depositions, and exhibits entered into evidence, the court grants the relief requested in Counts Three and Four of the plaintiff's first amended complaint.

Facts

The plaintiff, Andrew Oliver, is a resident of Vermilion, Erie County, Ohio. In 2006, the plaintiff graduated from Vermilion High School, where he was the primary pitcher for its baseball team. The plaintiff is currently in his junior year of college at Oklahoma State University ("OSU"). Since August 2006, the plaintiff has pitched for the baseball team at OSU.

The defendant, the National Collegiate Athletic Association ("NCAA"), is an unincorporated business association having its principal place of business in Marion County, Indiana; it has member institutions not only in Oklahoma but also in Ohio. OSU is a member institution of the defendant; the NCAA association regulates the student-athlete activities at OSU.

The plaintiff, in February 2006, retained the services of Robert M. Baratta, Tim Baratta, and Icon Sports Group, d.b.a. Icon Law Group, as his sports advisors and attorneys. In June of the same year, the Minnesota Twins of Major League Baseball drafted the plaintiff in the 17th round of the draft. At the end of the summer, the Minnesota Twins met with the plaintiff and his father at the Oliver family home in Vermilion before the plaintiff left for his freshman year of college. Tim Baratta also attended the meeting, at his own request, at the Oliver home. During the meeting the Minnesota Twins offered the plaintiff $ 390,000 to join their organization. After heeding the advice of his father, the plaintiff rejected the offer and chose to attend OSU in the fall on a full scholarship for which he had already signed a letter of intent in the fall of 2005.

As a result of deciding to go to OSU and accepting amateur status, the plaintiff would not be eligible for the draft again until his junior year of college in June 2009. The plaintiff played his freshman and sophomore years for OSU, and during that period he never received any invoices requesting payment for any services rendered by his advisors. In fact, the plaintiff avers that the advisors provided nothing of value to him.

In March 2008, plaintiff decided to terminate the Barattas and Icon Sports and retain the Boras Corporation. The plaintiff communicated his intentions of termination

to Robert Baratta. At that time, Robert Baratta attempted to reconnect with the plaintiff and his father, but to no avail. In April 2008, the plaintiff received a letter and an invoice from the Barattas for $ 113,750 for legal services. The invoice did not contain any detail of services rendered or time entries. The plaintiff took the invoice to the OSU baseball team coach, the OSU Athletic Compliance Office, and the Boras Corporation. Subsequently, the plaintiff retained attorney Michael Quiat to assist him with the matter. Quiat requested the time records supporting Baratta's invoice. In May, in response to the request, the Barattas sent a letter dated February 8, 2006, and a contract dated February 8, 2006, to Quiat. The letter listed six items of assistance rendered by them on behalf of the plaintiff. The plaintiff has argued that the contract is fictitious and the assistance stated in it was in fact never performed.

On May 19, 2008, the previous attorneys mailed, faxed, and e-mailed a letter to the defendant complaining about the plaintiff and reporting alleged violations by the plaintiff, i.e. the meeting at the Olivers' home that Tim Baratta had attended. As a result of the allegations, OSU and the defendant investigated the alleged violations in relationship to the plaintiff's amateur status. In May 2008, the plaintiff was indefinitely suspended from playing baseball and was informed by OSU staff that he had violated NCAA Bylaw 12.3.1 by (1) allowing his previous attorneys to contact the Minnesota Twins by telephone and (2) by allowing Tim Baratta to be present in his home when a representative from the Minnesota Twins tendered an offer to him.

On August 18, 2008, the plaintiff was reinstated as a result of a temporary restraining order issued by this court. However, in October 2008, OSU filed for reinstatement of the plaintiff with the NCAA even though the temporary restraining order had reinstated the plaintiff. Subsequently, in December 2008, the plaintiff was suspended for one year and charged a year of eligibility by the defendant. The penalty was subsequently reduced to 70 percent of the original suspension and no loss of eligibility for the plaintiff.

Arguments

The plaintiff requests that this court enter a declaratory judgment and injunctive relief enjoining the NCAA Bylaw 12.3.2.1 as unenforceable because the plaintiff retained legal counsel (the Barattas) to represent him and that legal counsel is subject to the exclusive regulation of the Ohio Supreme Court. Therefore, the defendant has no authority to promulgate a rule that would prevent a lawyer from competently representing his client. As such, the plaintiff maintains that, NCAA Bylaw 12.3.2.1 is void because it is against the public policy of the state of Ohio.

Furthermore, the plaintiff argues that NCAA Bylaw 12.3.2.1 is arbitrary and capricious because, it does not impact a player's amateur status but instead limits the player's ability to effectively negotiate a contract that the player or a player's parent could negotiate. In that regard, the plaintiff contends that he was the victim of unethical attorneys who, under the laws of the state of Ohio, had a duty to protect him, but instead the defendant punished him even though he bore no fault. Thus, according to the plaintiff, the defendant should vacate the findings that were the foundation of the plaintiff's suspension and reinstate him immediately with no further punishment.

Finally, the plaintiff requests that this court also enter a declaratory judgment and permanent injunction enjoining the defendant from enforcing NCAA Bylaw 19.7. The plaintiff argues that the bylaw interferes with the Ohio Constitution's delegation of all judicial power to the courts of this state and, consistent with that premise, exists solely to coerce or direct its agents and members to ignore court orders that are binding upon member institutions of the defendant.

Contrarily, the defendant argues that the plaintiff did not overcome the presumption that its bylaws and decisions as a voluntary association are valid. As such, the defendant contends that it has the right to manage its affairs and apply its bylaws, within legal limits, without interference from the judiciary and since the plaintiff has failed to prove that its bylaws are illegal, arbitrary or fraudulent, the defendant's internal affairs are presumptively correct.

The defendant argues that the plaintiff must prove by clear and convincing evidence that any decision made by the defendant was arbitrary or capricious. The defendant also argues that the plaintiff has failed to sustain such proof. The decision made to reinstate the plaintiff's eligibility, even though a penalty was imposed, was based on admitted and objective evidence obtained by the defendant and this court should not substitute its judgment for that of the defendant's.

Furthermore, the defendant argues that it is not in contract with the plaintiff and that such a relationship must be proven in order to support an entry of a permanent injunction. Likewise, the defendant maintains that since there is no underlying contract claim, there can be no independent basis for granting declaratory relief. The defendant argues that it did not owe a contractual duty of good faith and fair dealing since there can be no implied duty where there is no underlying contract. The defendant supports its contention by stating that Oklahoma's law does not allow this court to imply terms in a contract that the parties did not bargain for, nor does it allow the court to disregard the plaintiff's violation.

The defendant also argues that the plaintiff waived any contractual benefits by his prior breaches, namely, violation of NCAA bylaws and concealing his agent relationship. In accordance with this argument, the defendant declares that these prior breaches bar recovery of any equitable relief since the plaintiff has failed to come to court with clean hands. Similarly, the defendant professes that even if the plaintiff had proven liability on a contract claim, the remedy, according to the defendant,

is not immediate reinstatement or revisions to the "agent rule." The defendant states that what the plaintiff is seeking is overreaching and the remedy sought is dramatic and improper.

The defendant further contends that it in no way tortiously interfered with any contract of the plaintiff. Consequently, the evidence cannot support a finding by clear and convincing evidence that the defendant took actions against the plaintiff for the purpose of inducing any party to breach a contractual obligation to the plaintiff. The defendant asserts that the plaintiff has failed to prove any harm which cannot be compensated at law. As such, the defendant argues that a student-athlete has no legally protected interest in participating in intercollegiate athletics nor does he have a protected interest in performing in Major League Baseball.

The defendant also proclaims that the balance of harm militates against the entry of injunctive relief. The defendant contends that its bylaws are rationally related to the NCAA constitution and preserving the amateur model of collegiate athletics and the bylaws, in particular Bylaw 12.3.2.1, help to retain a clear line of demarcation between collegiate and professional sports, which is a goal of its members. Consequently, the defendant argues that striking Bylaw 19.7 leaves the members without a remedy, and it admonishes the court that it should not strike a bylaw simply because the court believes the members of the institution should govern themselves in a different way.

The defendant also argues that the public is not served by judicial intervention in the bylaws and decisions of a private association and the public would not be served because such injunctive relief would violate the United States Constitution's Commerce Clause and First Amendment Right of Association.

Finally, the defendant asserts that injunctive relief is inappropriate in the absence of a necessary and indispensable party. The plaintiff failed to comply with this court's order (to add OSU as an indispensable party) in the December 12, 2008 judgment entry, and the defendant argues that the plaintiff's demand should be denied.

***

II. Breach of Contract

***

To the extent that the plaintiff's claim of arbitrary and capricious action asserts a violation of the duty of good faith and fair dealing that is implied in the contractual relationship between the NCAA and its members, his position as a third-party beneficiary of that contractual relationship affords him standing to pursue his claims. . . . Previously, Ohio law held that not every contract implicates an implied obligation to use good faith and fair dealing. See, *Sammarco v. Anthem Ins. Cos., Inc.* (1998), 131 Ohio App.3d 544, 554–555, 723 N.E.2d 128. There had to be a distinction between written terms and implied promises within a contract. Without explaining the history of the distinctions, the Sixth Appellate District of Ohio, in whose jurisdiction this court lies, holds that the parties to a contract "are bound toward one another by standards of good faith and fair-dealing." *Bolling v. Clevepak Corp.* (1984), 20 Ohio App.3d 113, 121, 20 Ohio B. 146, 484 N.E.2d 1367. Ohio law now supports that good faith is part of a contract claim. ... Furthermore, the court in *Brown v. Otto C. Epp Mem. Hosp.* determined that "good faith is required of every contract," and this court is in agreement with that premise. *Brown* (1987), 41 Ohio App.3d 198, 199, 535 N.E.2d 325. Thus, this court holds that a party can be found to have breached its contract if it fails to act in good faith.

III. Good Faith and Fair Dealing

Even though the obligation of good faith exists in a contractual relationship, this is not an invitation for this court to rewrite the benefit bestowed on the parties. The court agrees with the defendant that this is not a case about whether the court agrees or disagrees with the bylaws in question. Neither is it a case about how the defendant voted at either the 1975 or 2002 membership conventions. However, since this court has determined that the agreement between the defendants has an implied covenant of good faith and fair dealing as it relates to the plaintiff, there must be in fact honesty and reasonableness in the enforcement of the contract. See, *Littlejohn v. Parrish*, 163 Ohio App.3d 456, 2005 Ohio 4850, 839 N.E.2d 49. Therefore, the defendant, and for that matter OSU, was required to deal honestly and reasonably with the plaintiff as a third-party beneficiary regarding their contractual relationship. Surely each party is entitled to the benefit of its bargain. With that stated, if this court determines that Bylaw 12.3.2.1 is void because it is against the public policy of Ohio or because it is arbitrary and capricious, and Bylaw 19.7 interferes with the delegation of judicial power to the courts of this state, then the defendant has not dealt with the plaintiff honestly or reasonably and the defendant has breached the contract.

***

NCAA Bylaw 12.3.2.1.
However, the crux of this case falls under Bylaw 12.3.2, which carves out an exception to the no agent rule by allowing a student-athlete to retain a lawyer (not even the defendant can circumvent an individual's right to counsel). Yet, the exception to the rule, i.e., NCAA Bylaw 12.3.2 which allows legal counsel for student-athletes attempts to limit an attorney's role as to that representation and, in effect, such as in the case here, puts the onus on the student-athlete. See NCAA Bylaw 12.3.2.1.

The status of the no-agent rule, as firmly pointed out in the direct testimony of Kevin Lennon, vice president of membership services, is a prohibition against agents, not lawyers. Therein lies the problem.

It is impossible to allow student-athletes to hire lawyers and attempt to control what that lawyer does for his client by Bylaws 12.3.2 or 12.3.2.1. These rules attempt to say to the student-athlete that he or she can consult with an attorney but that the attorney cannot negotiate a contract with a professional sport's team. This surely does not retain a clear line of demarcation between amateurism and professionalism. The student-athlete will never know what his attorney is doing for him or her, and quite frankly neither will the defendant. The evidence is very clear that this rule is impossible to enforce and as a result is being enforced selectively. Further, as in this case, it allows for exploitation of the student-athlete "by professional and commercial enterprises," in contravention of the positive intentions of the defendant.

Was Barratta's presence in that room a clear indication that the plaintiff, a teenager who had admitted at trial that he was in no position to negotiate a professional contract and whose father testified to the same, was a professional? According to Bylaw 12.3.2.1, the no-agent rule, he was. As such the following issues must be resolved: Is the no-agent rule against the public policy of Ohio? Is it arbitrary? Is it capricious?

***

For a student-athlete to be permitted to have an attorney and then to tell that student-athlete that his attorney cannot be present during the discussion of an offer from a professional organization is akin to a patient hiring a doctor, but the doctor is told by the hospital board and the insurance company that he cannot be present when the patient meets with a surgeon because the conference may improve his patient's decision-making power. Bylaw 12.3.2.1 is unreliable (capricious) and illogical (arbitrary) and indeed stifles what attorneys are trained and retained to do.

***

This court appreciates that a fundamental goal of the member institutions and the defendant is to preserve the clear line of demarcation between amateurism and professionalism. However, to suggest that Bylaw 12.3.2.1 accomplishes that purpose by instructing a student-athlete that his attorney cannot do what he or she was hired to do is simply illogical. An example of a clear line of demarcation between amateurism and professionalism is indeed drawn within the bylaws and is done so in Bylaw 12.02.3: A professional athlete is one who receives any kind of payment, directly or indirectly, for athletics participation except as permitted by the governing legislation of the Association.

If the membership and the NCAA decide that Bylaw 12.02.3 does not accomplish that purpose, so be it. But no entity, other than that one designated by the state, can dictate to an attorney where, what, how, or when he should represent his client. With all due respect, surely that decision should not be determined by the NCAA and its member institutions, no matter what the defendant claims is the purpose of the rule. If the defendant intends to deal with this athlete or any athlete in good faith, the student-athlete should have the opportunity to have the tools present (in this case an attorney) that would allow him to make a wise decision without automatically being deemed a professional, especially when such contractual negotiations can be overwhelming even to those who are skilled in their implementation.

IV. Arbitrary and Capricious

With that stated, the court now addresses the issue of whether Bylaw 19.7 is arbitrary and capricious. Bylaw 19.7 states:

If a student athlete who is ineligible under the terms of the constitution, bylaws or other legislation of the Association is permitted to participate in intercollegiate competition contrary to such NCAA legislation but in accordance with the terms of a court restraining order or injunction operative against the institution attended by such student-athlete or against the Association, or both, and said injunction is voluntarily vacated, stayed or reversed or it is finally determined by the courts that injunctive relief is not or was not justified, the Board of Directors may take any one or more of the following actions against such institution in the interest of restitution and fairness to competing institutions: (a) through (e).

Following the above-mentioned paragraph, subsections (a) through (e) list penalties that impinge on institutions, student-athletes, or team records for following the dictates of a court order that may later be overturned by a higher court. The plaintiff would ask: "How could any entity punish an individual for accessing their right to Court?" The defendant argues that the member institutions agreed that it was improper to allow an institution to reap the benefits of playing a student-athlete who was finally adjudicated to be ineligible. Just because member institutions agree to a rule or bylaw does not mean that the bylaw is sacrosanct or that it is not arbitrary or capricious.

Throughout the history of this country many institutions and entities have agreed to bylaws that were against the notion of a fair judicial process. The regulations must be fair to the people to whom they were meant to serve, especially when it comes to the right of an individual to petition the court system. Courts of appeal have never been without remedies for cases that they overturn as it relates to the parties that are involved. Student-athletes must have their opportunity to access the court system without fear of punitive actions against themselves or the institutions and teams of which they belong. The old adage that you can put lipstick on a pig, but it is still a pig, is quite relevant here. The defendant may entitle Bylaw 19.7 "Restitution" but it is still punitive in its achievement, and it fosters a direct attack on the constitutional right of access to courts.

Bylaw 19.7 takes the rule of law as governed by the courts of this nation and gives it to an unincorporated business association. The bylaw is overreaching. For example, if a court grants a restraining order that permits a student-athlete the right to play, the institution will find itself in a real dilemma. Does the institution allow the student-athlete to play as directed by the court's ruling and in so doing face great harm should the decision be reversed on appeal? Alternatively, does the institution, in fear of Bylaw 19.7, decide that it is safer to disregard the court order and not allow the student-athlete to play, thereby finding itself in contempt of court? Such a bylaw is governed by no fixed standard except that which is self-serving for the defendant. To that extent, it is arbitrary and indeed a violation of the covenant of good faith and fair dealing implicit in its contract with the plaintiff, as the third-party beneficiary.

***

After this court has engaged in a balancing process that was designed to weigh the equities between the parties, the court determines by clear and convincing evidence that the plaintiff would suffer immediate and irreparable injury, loss, or damage if injunctive relief is not granted. If an injunction is not granted, the plaintiff would suffer loss of his college baseball experience, impairment or loss of his future baseball professional career, loss in being available for the upcoming draft because he is less likely to be seen, and ongoing damage to the plaintiff's reputation and baseball career.

In comparison, the defendant's witnesses stated that if relief were granted, it would be confusing as to which institutions would have to follow this court's ruling. Would it be Ohio members, Oklahoma members, all institutions? However, since this court has personam jurisdiction, this argument is not as persuasive as the plaintiff's and the scales of justice have tilted in the plaintiff's favor.

Judgment accordingly.

CASES ON THE SUPPLEMENTAL WEB SITE

Bloom v. National Collegiate Athletics Association, (2004 Colo. App. LEXIS 781). Examine the court's interpretation of the law with regard to voluntary associations and Bloom's amateur status.

Indiana High School Athletic Association v. Waston, (2010 Ind. LEXIS 800). Examine the court's acceptance of hearsay testimony and the conclusion that the transfer was primarily for athletic reasons.

Jones v. West Virginia State Board of Education, (2005 W. Va. LEXIS 96). Readers should review the Supreme Court's discussion of the challenged statute's application to educational and athletic resources.

Rottmann v. Pennsylvania Interscholastic Athletic Association, (2004 U.S. Dist. LEXIS 27506). Readers should

pay particular attention to the court's discussion of vague and overbroad regulations.

Seger v. Kentucky High School Athletic Association, (2011 U.S. App. LEXIS 25799 (6th Cir. 2011). Pay particular attention to the discussion regarding religious discrimination and the appropriate standard of review.

Significant Cases from Other Chapters

Chapter 6.12 State Action - *Brentwood Academy v. Tennessee Secondary School Athletic Association*, 531 U.S. 288 (2001). Note the court's analysis of the Tennessee Secondary School Athletic Association as a state actor and compare it to the Supreme Court's analysis of the NCAA as a state actor in *National Collegiate Athletic Association v. Tarkanian*, (1988 U.S. LEXIS 5613).

QUESTIONS YOU SHOULD BE ABLE TO ANSWER

1. What does it mean to enforce a rule or policy in an arbitrary and capricious manner? Give a specific sport or recreation related example.

2. High school athletic associations generally accepted as state actors. Why?

3. In general, how have the courts ruled with regard to challenges brought against high school transfer rules?

4. In order to be *initially* qualified as eligible to compete in NCAA athletics, what academic achievements must a student-athlete demonstrate?

5. Explain the Restitution Rule and how it applies to NCAA eligibility.

REFERENCES

Cases

Bloom v. National Collegiate Athletics Association, 2004 Colo. App. LEXIS 781.
Brentwood Academy v. Tennessee Secondary School Athletic Association, 531 U.S. 288 (2001).
Communities for Equity v. Michigan High School Athletic Association, 80 F. Supp. 2d. 729 (W.D. Mich. 2000).
Florida High School Athletic Association v. Marazzito, 891 So. 2d 653 (Fl. App. 2005).
Indiana High School Athletic Association v. Carlberg, 694 N.E.2d 222 (Supr. Ct. Ind. 1997).
Indiana High School Athletic Association v. Durham, 748 N.E.2d 404 (Ind. App. 2001).
Indiana High School Athletic Association v. Waston, 2010 Ind. LEXIS 800.
Jones v. West Virginia State Board of Education, 2005 W. Va. LEXIS 96.
National Collegiate Athletic Association v. Lasege, 53 S.W. 3d (Supr. Ct. KY, 2001).
National Collegiate Athletic Association v. Tarkanian, 488 U.S. 179 (1988).
National Collegiate Athletic Association v. Yeo, 171 S.W. 3d 863 (Supr. Ct. Texas 2005).
Rottmann v. Pennsylvania Interscholastic Athletic Association, 2004 U.S. Dist. LEXIS 27506.
Seger v. Kentucky High School Athletic Association, 2011 U.S. App. LEXIS 25799 (6th Cir. 2011).
Sisson v. Virginia High School League, 2010 U.S. Dist. LEXIS 132264.

Publications

Bastista, P.J., & Hatfield, L.C. (2005). Learn at home, play at school: A state-by-state examination of legislation, litigation and athletic association rules governing public school athletic participation by homeschool students, *Journal of Legal Aspects of Sport, 15*(2), p. 213–265

Conn, J. (2003) Voluntary Sport and Recreation Associations. In D.J. Cotton & T.J. Wolohan (Eds.), *Law for Recreation and Sport Managers* (3rd Ed.) pp. 476–482. Dubuque, IA: Kendall/Hunt Publishing Co.

Martin, W. C. (2008). Comment: The Graduate Transfer Rule: Is the NCAA Unnecessarily Hindering Student-athletes from Traversing the Educational Paths they Desire?, *Villanova Sports and Entertainment Law Journal, 15,* p. 103, 106–107.

NCAA Manual (2011–12). Indianapolis: NCAA.

Sander, L. (2011). Junior-College athletes sue NCAA over transfer rules. Retrieved on March 5, 2012 from https://chronicle.com/blogs/players/junior-college-athletes-sue-ncaa-over-transfer-rules/28270

Trichka, R.E., & Sawyer, T.H. (1998). State high school athletic associations' limited participation rules: Transfer, *Journal of Legal Aspects of Sport, 8,* p. 158–59.

Van Ann, B. (2011). Varsity blues: A call to reconfigure the judicial standard for high school athletic association transfer rules. *Columbia Journal of law & the arts, 34*(2), 231–260.

voluntary association. (n.d.). *Dictionary.com Unabridged (v 1.1)*. Retrieved January 18, 2012, from Dictionary.com website: http://dictionary.reference.com/browse/voluntary association

Legislation

United States Constitution, Amendment XIV

6.22 CONDUCT ISSUES

W.S. Miller I University of Wisconsin-Parkside

As most parents, student-athletes and school administrators would likely acknowledge, it is possible that today's student-athlete faces more conduct-related regulations than any student-athletes ever. While players have always faced rules and basic codes of conduct implemented by coaches and schools, today's student-athletes and athletic administrators have to deal with those rules along with a seemingly ever-increasing amount of regulations implemented by the state governments, state high school athletic associations, league, and conferences. Basic team rules authored by coaches are now often accompanied by rules created by the aforementioned governing bodies that cover uniform characteristics, off-campus conduct, grade point averages, grooming, appearance, and student expression which can include regulating what players can or cannot do on their social networking pages.

This growing body of regulation creates three issues. First, there is more opportunity than ever for student-athletes (and their parents in some cases) to commit conduct-related violations which could have a negative impact on their participation in sports. Second, administrators need to be aware of all of these various rules and the potential legal issues that can be created when they attempt to enforce these rules. Third, administrators also need to be aware of new changes in technology that could necessitate more rules or changes in existing rules to ensure that they can achieve the conduct-regulating objectives that they originally implemented.

FUNDAMENTAL CONCEPTS

An important item for athletic administrators to understand is that the individual pieces of this growing body of conduct-related regulation are not always viewed the same in the eyes of the law. This means that understanding the different types of conduct and the legal implications of addressing these potential violations is essential to protect the interests of both the school and the individual administrator. Potential conduct violations which do not have a connection to a student-athlete's constitutional rights are typically much easier to address from an administrative perspective. Schools have consistently been given wide latitude by the courts to articulate policies and create various forms of discipline in an attempt to regulate conduct that does not affect a student's constitutional rights. As discussed later in this chapter, schools and athletic administrators that articulate and follow basic rules regarding the regulation of non-constitutionally implicated conduct by student-athletes have traditionally been given great deference by the legal system.

In contrast, attempts to regulate conduct that have constitutional implications such as restricting a student's freedom of speech or freedom of expression usually create more substantial challenges for athletic administrators in terms of prohibiting or restricting the conduct. As one might suspect, the courts have generally been very reluctant to allow school administrators to restrict the constitutional rights of students. However, over the past 25 years, the United States Supreme Court has articulated several situations in which administrators can restrict the rights of students through a variety of means including the use of student codes and impose discipline for violations of those codes.

As you will see in the next two sections of this chapter, the biggest challenge for athletic administrators can be in trying to identify what types of student conduct create constitutional implications. Most would understand that student codes of conduct or other rules which attempt to restrict one's freedom of speech or expression could create potential constitutional implications. For example, rules that attempted to eliminate or restrict a student's ability to speak about political or controversial issues in either school or non-school settings would obviously fall into that category. However, seemingly harmless attempts by administrators to create a better learning environment for students by creating regulations which prohibit a student from wearing a shirt or piece of apparel to school that features a flag or support for a cancer-related charity can also create constitutional implications. And as noted above, most students, parents and especially their attorneys understand that being able to link conduct-related regulation and discipline with constitutional protections enhances the chances of success for the student-athlete in getting the potential discipline overturned.

Constitutionally Implicated Conduct

The types of cases that feature student conduct issues with constitutional implications have typically fallen into one of two categories: freedom of religion and freedom of expression.

Freedom of Expression

Over the past four decades, the United States Supreme Court has issued four key rulings which address student-related freedom of expression issues in school settings. These cases have established a framework through which athletic administrators are encouraged to view their attempts to regulate student conduct.

The Tinker Cases

In *Tinker v. Des Moines Independent Community School District* (1969), two public high school students were planning to show their objection to the Vietnam War by wearing black armbands to school along with engaging in several other activities. School administrators found out about the plan and adopted a policy stating that students would be asked to remove all armbands and would be suspended if they refused to do so. The students followed through on their protest and wore the black armbands to school. The administration also followed through on its threat and suspended the students for wearing the armbands.

In its ruling, the Supreme Court offered arguably one of its more famous lines and a key principle that administrators need to keep in mind when considering constitutionally-implicated conduct issues. "First Amendment rights applied in light of the special characteristics of the school environment, are available to teachers and students" (*Tinker v. Des Moines Independent Community School District,* 1969). "It can hardly be argued" the court held "that either students or teachers shed their constitutional rights to freedom of speech or expression at the schoolhouse gate" (*Tinker v. Des Moines Independent Community School District,* 1969). The Court went on to note that discomfort, unpleasantness or unsubstantiated fear of a disturbance cause by the student's freedom of expression was not enough for schools to restrict the constitutional rights of students. The court then added that "in the absence of constitutionally valid reasons to regulate their speech, students are entitled to freedom of expression of their views" (*Tinker v. Des Moines Independent Community School District,* 1969). The Court went on to state, however, that student conduct that had the potential to materially and substantially interfere with the operations of the school or the rights of others was not constitutionally protected. One more additional important item for sports administrators to note is that the *Tinker* ruling specifically stated that the playing field was among the places where students could utilize their constitutionally-protected rights of freedom of expression.

In *Bethel School District No. 403 v. Fraser* (1986), the Supreme Court offered more guidance as to how schools can regulate student conduct with regard to freedom of expression issues. Fraser was a high school student invited to deliver a nominating speech for a fellow student running for office to an assembly of approximately 600 high school students. The speech featured large amounts of sexual innuendo that led some members of the audience to become confused in the words of the Court while others began to make gestures which simulated the acts described in the speech. Fraser was suspended by the school for three days and removed from the potential commencement speaker list because of violations of the school's student code of conduct which prohibited the use of obscene language. The Court upheld the suspension stating that it is appropriate for public school officials to regulate the use of vulgar and offensive terms by students as part of the educational process. It then added that the speech in this situation had no political viewpoint unlike the student conduct in *Tinker*.

Two years after *Fraser*, the Court added further *Tinker* clarification in *Hazelwood School District v. Kuhlmeier* (1988). Hazelwood East High School had a student newspaper which was written by a journalism class at the school and overseen by a teacher and school administrators. In an edition scheduled for publication late in the 1982–83 academic year, school officials removed two pages of content from the proposed six-page newspaper because of content that discussed divorce and teen pregnancy issues. A group of students sued the school district claiming their First Amendment rights were violated. The Court upheld the rights of the school district to remove the pages from the newspaper. While acknowledging *Tinker*, the Court stated that the type of speech in this case was different than *Tinker* because of the fact that it was school-sponsored speech. The Court specifically stated in its ruling that, "We hold that educators do not offend the First Amendment by exercising editorial control over the style and content of student speech in school-sponsored expressive activities so long as their actions are reasonable related to legitimate pedagogical concerns."

After nearly two decades of silence on student freedom of expression issues, the final case of the Supreme Court's four major rulings in this area is *Morse v. Frederick* (2007). The Olympic torch relay was passing in front of the high school and school administrators decided to allow students to watch the event as part of a school-sponsored activity. At the relay, Frederick unveiled a 14-foot banner stating "Bong Hits 4 Jesus" in full view of the crowd. The school's principal demanded that he remove the banner stating that it encouraged illegal activity. Frederick was eventually suspended for eight days as allowed for by school board policy. The Court upheld the suspension and included a long discussion on the problems of illegal drug use both in society and schools as part of its reasoning. It went on to discuss the apparent lack of political value in Frederick's banner. It also acknowledged *Tinker's* concern about restricting speech that features unpopular viewpoints. But it added, "the particular concern to prevent student drug abuse at issue here, embodied in established school policy, extends well beyond an abstract desire to avoid controversy" (*Morse v. Frederick*, 2007).

Applying the Tinker Cases

In reviewing the four major freedom of expression cases, a few guidelines for sports administrators dealing with such issues in conduct-related cases become evident. *Tinker* offers substantial protection for student freedom of expression absent any constitutionally-valid reasons for restricting or prohibiting student expression. *Frasor* begins to allow administrators to restrict those rights when the speech is in-school, vulgar and appears to offer no political value. *Hazelwood* gives administrators greater control over school-sponsored forms of speech. Finally, *Morse* allows the restriction of student speech when advocating illegal drug use. Two major challenges confront sport administrators when attempting to regulate student conduct in light of the *Tinker* quartet of decisions. First, while the *Tinker* decisions offer guidelines they do not articulate a firm list of rules for officials to follow when evaluating student conduct. Second, as will be shown throughout this section, there are still a large number of student conduct issues that have constitutional implications under the *Tinker* cases then many school administrators would typically suspect.

Student Expression About Coaches. The guidelines created by the *Tinker* cases regarding schools regulating freedom of expression can be seen in a series of cases involving actions taken by schools against student-athletes who expressed their discontent with their coaches. In *Pinard v. Clatskanie School District 6J* (2006), several members of the boys basketball team signed a petition requesting the removal of the team's head coach. According to the players, administrators gave the team two options upon learning of the petition. The players could play in the game that evening and participate in mediation or they could maintain their call for the coach's removal and skip the bus trip to that evening's game. Most of the players skipped the trip to the game and were subsequently suspended. Citing Tinker, the Ninth Circuit Court of Appeals concluded that the players' petition and subsequent complaints to school administrators about the coach were protected speech. However, the Court of Appeals also found that the players' refusal to board the bus for the team's game was a substantial disruption of school activity as discussed in *Tinker*. As a result, those actions were not constitutionally protected and the suspensions were upheld.

In *Lowery v. Euverard* (2008) a group of high school football players signed a petition stating that they hated the team's head coach and no longer wished to play for him. The coach found out about the petition and later removed any player from the team who did not apologize to the coach. The Sixth Circuit Court of Appeals upheld the player dismissals using many of the *Tinker* quartet precedents stating that the defendants could reasonably believe that the petition would divide the team and erode the authority of the coach. The Court of Appeals went on to add, "Plaintiffs' regular education has not been impeded, and, significantly, they are free to continue their campaign to have the coach fired. What they are not free to do is continue to play football for him while actively working to undermine his authority" (*Lowery v. Euverard*, 2008).

Student Expression through Social Networking. The effects of the *Tinker* quartet can also be seen in how courts view freedom of expression issues in which the student makes the expression through social networking sites outside of the school. The following two cases feature recent court rulings on social networking issues. In light of technological advancements and the growing use of such social network sites, it is highly likely that there will be a growing amount of litigation in this area going forward. In *J.C. v. Beverly Hills Unified School District* (2010), the plaintiff and a group of students made a four-minute video that contained disparaging remarks about a classmate. The video was posted on YouTube and the plaintiff contacted a group of students encouraging them to watch the video, including the student who was the focus of the video. After school officials were made aware of the video, the plaintiffs were eventually suspended for four days in accordance with school policy. In ruling that the suspensions violated the students' First Amendment right of expression, the court stated that while the school had the ability to suspend the student under the principles advanced in the *Tinker* quartet if the facts warranted it, in this case, the facts did not warrant such an action because no reasonable jury could find that the plaintiffs' video would create a reasonably foreseeable risk of substantial disruption. The court went on to state that the school could not point to the discipline itself as a substantial disruption, since that the biggest effects of the video appeared to be that the two students were sent home from school.

In *T.V. v. Smith-Green Community School Corporation* (2011) a group of high school volleyball players took a series of provocative photos during a summer group sleepover. Racy comments were later added to the photos which were subsequently posted on MySpace and Facebook. The photos, while never brought to school, were brought to the attention of school officials by a parent who said that the photos were causing a division within the team. The student-athletes were suspended from the team for one year due to a violation of the school's student-athlete code of conduct. The suspension were later reduced to smaller portions of the team's schedule once the student-athletes underwent counseling and apologized to the school's Athletic Board for their actions. In ruling that the school violated the student's First Amendment rights, the court found that the photos were taken in a non-school setting and published to the internet outside of school eliminating the *Fraser* argument. The court then used the *Tinker* reasoning to determine while students may not have a constitution right to participate in athletics that does not mean that they cannot pursue their constitutionally-guaranteed rights of freedom of expression. The ruling specifically stated, "What this means is that a student cannot be punished with a ban from extracurricular activities for non-disruptive speech." In reviewing the facts of the case, the court found the issue to be minor disagreements among team members and complaints from two parents, both of which did not rise to the level of substantial disruption as called for in *Tinker*.

Student Expression through Apparel. One of the ways that students often express themselves is through the apparel that they choose to wear. While not usually likely thought of as a constitutional issue, the apparel issue is one that has been addressed by a variety of courts through the years. Two recent cases using the *Tinker* reasoning illustrate how courts have looked at the apparel issue. While these cases do not involve student-athletes, they are indicative of the types of issues that sport administrators can face on a daily basis. In *Defoe v. Spiva* (2010) the school developed a code of student conduct that prohibited students from wearing apparel which drew attention to them as opposed to the learning environment and articulated a variety of example of items that were prohibited. The plaintiff wore a t-shirt and a belt buckle featuring the Confederate flag on two separate occasions. He refused to comply with school officials, requests to comply with the dress code and was subsequently suspended. The Sixth Circuit Court of Appeals using the *Tinker* cases upheld the dress code and the suspension stating that it was reasonable for school officials to foresee a substantial disruption at the school which could be caused by the display of the Confederate flag. The Court of Appeals added that it was not a political viewpoint issue as all apparel that could cause a disruption was banned under the code. In *H. v. Easton Area School District* (2011), a Pennsylvania middle school enacted a policy banning students from wearing bracelets that supported breast cancer awareness which featured the word "boobies." Several students refused to remove the bracelets and were subsequently suspended in-school for a day and a half and prohibited from attending an upcoming school dance. In ruling for the plaintiffs, the court held that the word boobies is not lewd or vulgar as defined by *Fraser*. As such, the court ruled that no substantial disruption could be caused or foreseen at the school by the students wearing the bracelets.

Student Expression through Grooming. Another way students can choose to express themselves is through their personal grooming habits. As such, any attempted restrictions on student-athletes such as hair length or whether they can wear a beard or a mustache can also unwittingly create constitutional implications for sport administrators. In *Dunham v. Pulsifer* (1970), the high school had recently enacted a student-athlete code of conduct which included a variety of apparel and grooming requirements. For example, males had to be clean shaven and their hair was to be tapered in the back and on the sides of the head with no hair over the collar. The plaintiffs were three male tennis players who were ranked as the top three players on the team. All three players were prevented from playing in a match by school officials because of violations of the code. In fact six of the top eight players on the team were eventually dismissed from the team because they violated the aforementioned code provisions. While *Tinker* was discussed in the case, the court utilized an Equal Protection Clause analysis to determine that the school singled out these student-athletes. The court then looked at the reasonableness of the regulation in comparison to its intended purpose and stated that it would allow the regulation if it was not arbitrary and had some reasonable connection with a legislative or administrative purpose. Upon analyzing the facts of the case, the court found no evidence that the grooming rule enhanced team performance, reduced team dissension or created discipline. In addition, while the court acknowledged the important role of the coach, stating that "during the actual competition, the coach's instructions must be accepted without question" (*Dunham v. Pulsifer*, 1970). The court went on to state that the "coach's right to regulate the lives of his team members does have limits" (*Dunham v. Pulsifer*, 1970) and overturned the suspensions and reinstated the players to the team.

Freedom of Religion

In terms of regulating student-athlete conduct, there has been very little litigation with regard to religious freedom issues. However, the litigation that has occurred has an obvious constitutional impact. In *Moody v. Cronin* (1980), the plaintiff was suspended from high school for three days for refusing to attend physical education classes. The dispute arose due to a state law that required students to attend physical education classes on a daily basis and the then-relatively recent passage of Title IX which introduced co-ed physical education classes at the school. The student was a member of the United Pentecostal Church whose tenets include a requirement that members wear modest apparel. Moody believed that the attire required for the physical education class did not satisfy that requirement. The court ruled that the plaintiff had deep religious convictions about the attire issue and the State of Illinois could not deny the plaintiff's free exercise of their religious beliefs absent sufficient state interest. In finding that the state failed to show such an interest, the court noted that the state had a variety of alternative educational methods it could have used to achieve its objectives without restricting the religious rights of the plaintiff.

Non-Constitutionally-implicated Conduct

As shown in the previous section, student-athlete conduct that implicates one's constitutional rights such as Freedom of Expression or Freedom of Religion has often been afforded great protection by the courts. In contrast, schools and administrators are given great latitude in regulating, prohibiting and implementing various forms of discipline when non-constitutionally implicated conduct is at the center of the dispute. In litigation surrounding non-constitutional conduct situation, the main issue courts often examine is whether the student-athlete received proper due process from the school and administrators. (see, Section 6.13 Due Process.) The basic concept you should be aware of is that student-athletes need to be given proper notice of the charges against them and be given a proper ability to respond. As discussed in chapter 6.13, *Goss v. Lopez* (1975) is the key case in this area, especially for academic suspensions.

When dealing with athletic suspensions on top of the academic suspension, the case of *Palmer v. Merluzzi* (1989) illustrates how courts often handle these situations. Palmer was a high school football player who was suspended for ten days academically and later given a 60-day athletic suspension after being caught smoking marijuana and drinking at the school's radio station. The plaintiff challenged the fact that he was not given a second notice and hearing for the athletic suspension. The Third Circuit Court of Appeals upheld the suspension stating that the school handbook and Interscholastic Athletic Program warned that students who did not demonstrate good citizenship were subject to suspension. The Court of Appeals then stated that based on the code provisions, the nature of the offense and common sense, Palmer should have known his athletic status was at risk as well. The ruling went on to add, "[W]e believe it would be unduly disruptive of a school's educational process to require one disciplinary process for football players and similarly situated athletes and another disciplinary process for other students" (*Palmer v. Merluzzi*, 1989).

The limited extent to which student-athletes can challenge conduct-related discipline without Constitutional implications can be seen in a series of decisions authored by the courts over the past decade. In *Wooten v. Pleasant Hope R-VI School District* (2000), the plaintiff was dismissed from the team in accordance with the school's student-parent handbook after failing to show up for a game. The plaintiff met with the coach and school officials the following week and was allegedly told at the meeting by the coach that her teammates did not wish to see her reinstated. Wooten later claimed that she found out this statement was not true and requested a hearing from school officials about her dismissal from the team. School officials did not honor her request and a lawsuit was filed on procedural due process grounds. Despite the alleged misstatements of the coach, the court rejected Wooten's claims stating that the meeting gave the plaintiff notice of the charges against her and an opportunity to present her case. In *Mather v. Loveland City School District Board of Education* (2009), the student-athlete and his father signed the school's athletic code of conduct which prohibited alcohol use. Any violation of this provision, the code stated, were to result in the student-athlete being suspended for 40% of the team's scheduled games. Mather was arrested during the summer for underage drinking and possession of alcohol. As a result, the school's athletic director concluded that a violation of the code had occurred and suspended Mather. Mather appealed to the school principal who upheld the suspension. In upholding the suspension, the court ruled that student-athletes in the state were given no statutory right of appeal for suspensions or expulsion from extracurricular activities. The court went on to state "from a policy standpoint, some could find it troubling that a school board can decide to prohibit a student from playing a sport for nearly any reason, and that the student has no legal recourse. But it is not our role to create a right to appeal—the legislature is the only body that may create such a right" (*Mather v. Loveland City School District Board of Education*, 2009).

In *Sala v. Warwick Valley Central School District* (2009), the student-athlete was arrested after marijuana was found in his home. He was initially suspended for the remainder of the season but this penalty would be reduced to four games if the school's code of conduct was followed. While under suspension, Sala was caught driving too fast in a school parking lot. The school's athletic director asked him to slow down and Sala reportedly responded with obscenities. Following the incident, he was dismissed from the team. Sala appealed to the superintendent claiming the athletic director had "antipathy" toward his family. Following the meeting, the superintendent upheld the suspension and a lawsuit was filed. In ruling for the school district, the court stated that Sala met with the coach on multiple occasions and received written notice of the reason for his dismissal. In addition, the court noted that Sala met with the superintendent where he could present his story and then received a letter explaining the basis for the decision and notice of his right to appeal to the school board.

SIGNIFICANT CASE

The following case illustrates how courts often use the principles first articulated in the Tinker case to decide Freedom of Expression lawsuits involving students in a dispute with their coach. As a result, the reader should consider the issues that administrators need to examine when faced with these types of issues.

Pinard v. Clatskanie School District 6J
United States Court of Appeals (Ninth Circuit)
467 F.3d 755 (9th Cir. 2006).

I. Factual and Procedural Background

Plaintiffs are eight former members of the 2000–01 Clatskanie High School varsity boys basketball team in Clatskanie, Oregon. The defendants include the Clatskanie School District, Jeff Baughman (the varsity boys basketball coach), Michael Corley (the high school principal), Lester Wallace (the high school athletic director), and Earl Fisher (the superintendent). Baughman, a teacher at the high school before taking on coaching responsibilities, became the team's head coach for the 2000–01 school year.

Considering the evidence in the light most favorable to the plaintiffs, as we must at this stage of the litigation, *see Bingham v. City of Manhattan Beach*, 341 F.3d 939, 945–46 (9th Cir.2003), Baughman was verbally abusive and highly intimidating. *** Linn explained that the players did not report Baughman's behavior because Baughman made it clear that "anything that happened in the locker room stays in the locker room."

After one particular home game, Baughman told the players that if they wanted him to quit, they should say so, and he would resign. The players apparently took Baughman at his word. On February 12, 2001, several weeks after Baughman's statement, co-captains Jacob Pinard and Christopher Somes called a team meeting at a local restaurant to discuss Baughman's behavior. Before the meeting, one of the plaintiffs typed up a petition requesting that Baughman resign. The petition stated:

> As of February 12, 2001, the Clatskanie Tigers Boys Varsity Basketball Team would like to formally request the immediate resignation of Coach Jeff Baughman. As a team we no longer feel comfortable playing for him as a coach. He has made derogative [sic] remarks, made players uncomfortable playing for him, and is not leading the team in the right direction. We feel that as a team and as individuals we would be better off if we were to finish the season with a replacement coach. We, the undersign [sic], believe this is in the best interest of the team, school, town, and for the players and fans. We would appreciate the full cooperation of all the parties involved.

With the exception of a foreign exchange student, every varsity player attended the meeting, including Baughman's son. No coaches, teachers or parents attended. After discussing the petition, all but one of the players (Baughman's son) signed it. The players also added a type-written note beneath the signatures stating: "[W]e will not be approached individually on this. This was a team decision and we will be addressed as a team."

The following morning, co-captain Somes delivered the petition to Baughman. The coach immediately took it to the high school principal, defendant Corley, who was in a meeting with the superintendent, defendant Fisher. The three defendants met for 10 to 15 minutes, during which time Baughman expressed that he was "confused," "very upset" and "hurt." Although none of these defendants could recall exactly what was discussed during this meeting, Corley remembers recommending that Baughman not resign, and Superintendent Fisher suggested that they meet with the players to "find out the detail" of the petition. Baughman was also concerned because the team was scheduled to play an important away game that evening. Upset by the events of the morning, Baughman asked Corley for permission to take off the remainder of the day, which Corley granted. Corley did not ask Baughman whether he would coach the game that night.

Once home, Baughman called the junior varsity coach, Gary Points, "to inform him of the situation." According to Points, Baughman stated that he "wanted

to know who his back-stabbers were" and wanted "to corner the little sons-of-bitches and not give them an out." When Points asked what Baughman meant, Baughman responded that Corley had given him two options: he could either resign, or decide not to resign and tell the players to either get on the bus and play or if they chose not to board the bus to turn in their uniforms. According to Points, Baughman claimed that Corley and Wallace were advising him to choose the second option.

After Baughman left the school, Corley called a meeting with athletic director Wallace and all of the players who had signed the petition. The players told Corley and Wallace about Baughman's derogatory remarks, stated he was unfair and expressed their discomfort in playing for him. When the players indicated that they would not play on the team if Baughman was going to coach them, Corley and Wallace explained they could not have Baughman immediately removed without an investigation. According to the plaintiffs, Corley and Wallace presented the players with two options: the players could participate in a mediation process with the two of them serving as mediators and board the team bus for the game that evening, or they could adhere to their position and forfeit their privilege to play in the game. The plaintiffs contend that neither Corley nor Wallace advised them that they would be disciplined further for choosing the second option. The meeting ended without the players expressing whether they intended to board the bus.

Later in the day, Baughman informed Corley and Wallace that he was not going to coach the game that evening. Wallace then made arrangements for a substitute coach to replace Baughman. Corley and Wallace did not inform the players of Baughman's decision.

With the exception of Somes, each of the players who had signed the petition chose not to board the bus and did not play in the game. The junior varsity team played in place of the eight missing players along with Somes, Baughman's son and the foreign exchange student, losing the game by more than 50 points. Baughman did not coach the team, and most of the plaintiffs attended the game as spectators. The plaintiffs contend they decided not to board the bus to demonstrate their resolve and sincerity concerning the petition and complaints against Baughman. They also maintain they would not have refused to travel with the team had they known Baughman was not coaching.

The next day, Corley and Wallace met with the plaintiffs, Somes and several of the players' parents. According to two of the parents in attendance, Corley announced that "all of the players *who signed the petition* were permanently suspended from the team" (emphasis added). Corley stated in the district court that he alone decided to suspend the players from the team, but that he did *not* suspend Somes (who had signed the petition but boarded the bus and played in the game). Rather, the suspension applied only to those members of the team "who had refused to board [the] team bus . . . and play basketball that evening." Although the defendants now argue that Corley had authority to suspend the plaintiffs under the school's "Code of Conduct and Appearance for Athletes," it is not clear from the record that the Code played any role in Corley's decision. Indeed, Corley conceded in a deposition that he was unfamiliar with the Code's contents.

***

III. Discussion

The plaintiffs argue that their petition, complaints to Corley and Wallace and decision to take the option of not playing in the away game constitute speech protected by the First Amendment. The defendants agree that the petition standing alone is "pure speech." *See Bartnicki v. Vopper,* 532 U.S. 514, 526–27, 121 S.Ct. 1753, 149 L.Ed.2d 787 (2001) (suggesting that the "delivery of a tape recording," "handbill" or "pamphlet" are forms of "pure speech"). The defendants also agree that the plaintiffs' refusal to board the bus-while itself not "pure speech"-was "inseparable" from the petition. However, the defendants argue that the plaintiffs' entire course of conduct-the petition, complaints against Baughman and the boycott of the game-was not constitutionally protected because it had no political dimension, was not a matter of public concern and materially interfered with the school's basketball program. The defendants further contend that the plaintiffs were suspended not for their petition or complaints against Baughman, but *only* for their refusal to board the bus.

We have long held that students in public schools do not "shed their constitutional rights to freedom of speech or expression at the schoolhouse gate." *See Chandler v. McMinnville Sch. Dist.,* 978 F.2d 524, 527 (9th Cir.1992) (quoting Tinker, 393 U.S. at 506, 89 S.Ct. 733). However, our precedents make equally clear that the First Amendment rights of public school students " 'are not automatically coextensive with the rights of adults in other settings' and must be 'applied in light of the special characteristics of the school environment.' " *LaVine v. Blaine Sch. Dist.,* 257 F.3d 981, 988 (9th Cir.2001) (quoting *Hazelwood Sch. Dist. v. Kuhlmeier,* 484 U.S. 260, 266, 108 S.Ct. 562, 98 L.Ed.2d 592 (1988)). Thus, in the school context, "we have granted educators substantial deference as to what speech is appropriate." *Id.* But "deference does not mean abdication; there are situations where school officials overstep their bounds and violate the Constitution." *Id.* Our task is to determine whether the district court erred in concluding that this case does not present such a situation.

A. Plaintiffs' Speech

This case involves both a petition-a form of "pure speech"-as well as potentially expressive conduct in the form of the plaintiffs' refusal to board the bus. *See, e.g., Tinker,* 393 U.S. at 505–06, 89 S.Ct. 733 (describing the wearing of armbands as akin to "pure speech"); *see also Baldwin v. Redwood City,* 540 F.2d 1360, 1366 (9th Cir.1976) (suggesting that the "element of conduct" in pure speech is "minimal"). Although the defendants concede that the petition "standing alone" is pure speech, they characterize the plaintiffs' petition, complaints against Baughman and refusal to board the bus as both "concerted action" and one "course of conduct," the entirety of which is constitutionally punishable under *Tinker.* We disagree with that view. As we discuss in Section III.C, because the plaintiffs' petition and grievances against Baughman are a form of pure speech, the defendants may not constitutionally punish the plaintiffs just for filing their petition or complaining about Baughman unless they show "facts which might reasonably have led [them] to forecast substantial disruption of or material interference with school activities" *as a result of the petition or complaints. Tinker, 393 U.S. at 514, 89 S.Ct. 733.*

As for the plaintiffs' refusal to board the bus and play in the game, the plaintiffs assume that this conduct falls within the ambit of the First Amendment's protections because it is expressive in nature. *See, e.g., Rumsfeld v. Forum for Academic & Institutional Rights, Inc.,* 547 U.S. 47, 126 S.Ct. 1297, 1310, 164 L.Ed.2d 156 (2006) ("FAIR ") (explaining that the Supreme Court has "extended First Amendment protection only to conduct that is inherently expressive"); *Roulette v. City of Seattle,* 97 F.3d 300, 302-03 (9th Cir.1996) ("The First Amendment protects not only the expression of ideas through printed or spoken words, but also symbolic speech-nonverbal 'activity . . . sufficiently imbued with elements of communication.' " (quoting *Spence v. Washington,* 418 U.S. 405, 409, 94 S.Ct. 2727, 41 L.Ed.2d 842 (1974))). As we explain below, however, we ultimately need not decide whether the plaintiffs' boycott of the game constitutes "inherently expressive" conduct encompassed by the First Amendment, because even if it does the boycott was properly punishable under *Tinker.*

***

C. Applying Tinker

Because the plaintiffs' speech falls within *Chandler's* third category of "all other speech," the defendants must justify their decision to suspend the players permanently by showing "facts which might reasonably have led[them] to forecast substantial disruption of or material interference with school activities." *Tinker,* 393 U.S. at 514, 89 S.Ct. 733. The *Tinker* rule is a "flexible one," *Karp,* 477 F.2d at 174, and in applying it, "we look to the totality of the relevant facts," including not only the plaintiffs' actions, but "all of the circumstances confronting the school officials" at the time. *LaVine*, 257 F.3d at 989. "[U]ndifferentiated fear or apprehension of disturbance is not enough to overcome the right to freedom of expression," and the "mere desire to avoid the discomfort and unpleasantness that always accompany an unpopular viewpoint" cannot justify a school official's decision to punish or prohibit student speech. *Tinker*, 393 U.S. at 508–09, 89 S.Ct. 733.

Applying these guiding principles here, we conclude that the First Amendment protects the players' petition and their complaints to Corley and Wallace during the ensuing meeting. The defendants do not dispute that the petition and meeting neither disrupted school activities nor impinged on the rights of other students, and the record contains no evidence that Corley suspended the plaintiffs out of any such concern. The players handed their petition to Baughman directly at the start of a school day, and after Baughman left the school, they explained their complaint only to Corley and Wallace in a private meeting. These facts closely resemble those reviewed by the Tenth Circuit in *Seamons v. Snow*, 84 F.3d 1226 (10th Cir.1996). *Seamons* held that the First Amendment protected a student athlete's report to school authorities of a physical assault, because the student's speech "was responsibly tailored to the audience of school administrators, coaches, family and participants who needed to know about the incident." *Id.* at 1237–38.

It is also relevant that neither Corley nor Wallace informed the players of Baughman's decision not to coach the team that evening, even though the players had clearly stated that Baughman was the reason they did not want to play. Thus, to the extent that the petition and meeting might have given the school officials a "reason to anticipate" disruption of the game, the totality of the relevant facts reveals that any such expectation would have been unreasonable given Corley's and Wallace's knowledge of Baughman's decision. Had Corley and Wallace told the players that Baughman was not coaching that night-and the record reveals no reason why they could not have-it appears that the players would have boarded the bus.

Finally, assuming without deciding that the plaintiffs' refusal to board the bus constituted expressive conduct encompassed by the First Amendment, we agree with the district court that the plaintiffs' boycott of the game substantially disrupted and materially interfered with a school activity. Comparing the conduct at issue here with the wearing of armbands in *Tinker* demonstrates why the district court's decision was correct.

In holding that the First Amendment protected the students' right to wear a black armband to school to protest the Vietnam War, *Tinker* noted that "the wearing of armbands . . . was entirely divorced from actually or potentially disruptive conduct by those participating in it." 393 U.S. at 505, 89 S.Ct. 733. The Court emphasized that the "school officials banned and sought to punish petitioners for a silent, passive expression of opinion, unaccompanied by any disorder or disturbance on the part of petitioners." *Id.* at 508, 89 S.Ct. 733. It also noted that the district court made "no finding and no showing that engaging in the forbidden conduct would materially and substantially interfere with the requirements of *appropriate discipline in the operation of the school,*" *id.* at 509, 89 S.Ct. 733 (internal quotation marks omitted) (emphasis added), and that there was "no evidence whatever of [the protestors'] interference, actual or nascent, with the *schools' work,*" *id.* at 508, 89 S.Ct. 733 (emphasis added). In holding that a student's First Amendment rights are "not confined to the supervised and ordained discussion which takes place in the classroom," the Court extended *Tinker's* principles to school activities broadly defined, including extracurricular activities:

> When [a student] is in the cafeteria, *or on the playing field,* or on the campus during the authorized hours, he may express his opinions . . . if he does so without materially and substantially interfer(ing) with the requirements of appropriate discipline in the operation of the school. . . . But conduct by the student, *in class or out of it,* which for *any reason*-whether it stems from time, place, or type of behavior-materially disrupts classwork or involves *substantial disorder* or invasion of the rights of others is, of course, not immunized by the constitutional guarantee of freedom of speech. *Id.* at 512–13, 89 S.Ct. 733.

In this case, unlike in *Tinker,* there is undisputed evidence to support the district court's explicit finding that the plaintiffs' refusal to board the bus for the away game "material[ly] disrupt[ed] . . . the operation of the boys' varsity basketball team." As a general matter, school districts spend much time and money scheduling and hosting their extracurricular events-part of the school's educational program-which involve the coordination of multiple school officials, students, parents and often times volunteers, referees and bus drivers. Here, there is no dispute that the plaintiffs constituted all but three members of the varsity team. Similarly, it is undisputed that the boycotted event was a regularly scheduled out of town game against a rival school, part of the school's varsity basketball program, that the varsity team was scheduled to travel to the game on a school bus and that the plaintiffs refused to board the bus only a few hours before the game was scheduled to begin. The last minute boycott of a regularly scheduled game by nearly every member of the team forced the district either to play the game with replacement players or cancel the event. That the school succeeded in obtaining substitute players-albeit of lesser experience and ability-may have mitigated the disruptive effects of the plaintiffs' actions, but it did not eliminate them or render them less than substantial. Either option materially interfered with the school district's operation of a bona fide school activity.

Under these circumstances, the plaintiffs' conduct plainly "interrupted school activities" and "intrude[d] in the school['s] affairs." *Tinker*, 393 U.S. at 514, 89 S.Ct. 733. Thus, even if we viewed the plaintiffs' boycott as symbolic speech within the First Amendment, school officials could permissibly discipline the players for this disruptive conduct. Like Justice Brennan, we recognize that "[t]he vigilant protection of constitutional freedoms is nowhere more vital than in the community of American schools." *Keyishian v. Board of Regents*, 385 U.S. 589, 603, 87 S.Ct. 675, 17 L.Ed.2d 629 (1967) (quoting *Shelton v. Tucker*, 364 U.S. 479, 487, 81 S.Ct. 247, 5 L.Ed.2d 231 (1960). At the same time, we cannot ignore *Tinker's* admonition that the First Amendment is properly read to permit a school district's "reasonable regulation of speech-connected activities in *carefully restricted* circumstances." *Tinker*, 393 U.S. at 513, 89 S.Ct. 733 (emphasis added). Those circumstances were met here.

***

CASES ON THE SUPPLEMENTAL WEB SITE

Bethel School District No. 403 v. Fraser, 478 U.S. 675 (1986). Study how the Supreme Court distinguished Fraser's situation from that seen in the *Tinker* case and the effect this had on the court's analysis in this and future cases.

Hazelwood School District v. Kuhlmeier, 484 U.S. 260 (1988). The reader should study how the Court distinguished the Freedom of Expression rights the students were claiming in this case versus the ones granted in *Tinker*.

Lowery v. Euverard, 497 F.3d 584 (6th Cir. 2008). Examine how the court used a *Tinker* analysis to uphold the dismissals of the players from the football team.

Palmer v. Merluzzi, 868 F.2d 90 (3rd Cir. 1989). Study how the court uses a different analysis when examining non-constitutionally-implicated student-athlete conduct versus constitutionally-implicated conduct.

T.V. v. Smith-Green Community School Corporation, 2011 WL 3501698 (N.D. Ind. 2011). The reader should look at how the Court used the *Tinker* analysis to examine and resolve a social networking dispute involving student-athletes and an athletic code of conduct.

QUESTIONS YOU SHOULD BE ABLE TO ANSWER

1. Why do students try to make constitutional claims when filing lawsuits against schools and school administrators for conduct-related issues?

2. How did the *Fraser*, *Hazelwood* and *Morse* rulings impact how school administrators view Freedom of Expression conduct cases through the *Tinker* analysis?

3. Why did the courts reach different conclusions about the apparel worn by students in the *Defoe* and *Easton Area School District* cases?

4. In your opinion, should cases revolving around issues like grooming and apparel be considered Freedom of Expression issues with constitutional implications?

5. Should school athletic departments be able to discipline student-athletes for any pictures, videos or written content that are posted on social networking sites?

REFERENCES

Cases

Bethel School District No. 403 v. Fraser, 478 U.S. 675 (1986).

Defoe v. Spiva, 625 F.3d 324 (6th Cir. 2010).

Dunham v. Pulsifer, 312 F. Supp. 411 (D. Vermont 1970).

Goss v. Lopez, 419 U.S. 565 (1975).

H. v. Easton Area School District, 2011 WL 1376141 (E.D. Pa.).

Hazelwood School District v. Kuhlmeier, 484 U.S. 260 (1988).

J.C. v. Beverly Hills Unified School District, 711 F. Supp.2d 1094 (D. Calif. 2010).

Lowery v. Euverard, 497 F.3d 584 (6th Cir. 2008).

Mather v. Loveland City School District Board of Education, 908 N.E.2d 1039 (Ohio App. 2009).

Moody v. Cronin, 484 F. Supp. 270 (C.D. Ill. 1979).

Morse v. Frederick, 551 U.S. 393 (2007).

Palmer v. Merluzzi, 868 F.2d 90 (3rd Cir. 1989).

Pinard v. Clatskanie School District 6J, 467 F.3d 755 (9th Cir. 2006).

Sala v. Warwick Valley Central School District, 2009 WL 225493 (S.D.N.Y.)

Tinker v. Des Moines Independent Community School District, 393 U.S. 503 (1969).

T.V. v. Smith-Green Community School Corporation, 2011 WL 3501698 (N.D. Ind. 2011).

Wooten v. Pleasant Hope School District, 139 F.Supp.2d 835 (W.D. Missouri 2000).

Legislation

United States Constitution, Amendment I.

United States Constitution, Amendment XIV.

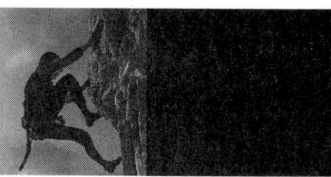

6.23 DRUG TESTING

John T. Wolohan | Syracuse University

On July 10, 2012, if you open the *USA Today* to page 1 of the sports section, you would have read about a district court dismissal of Lance Armstrong's lawsuit attempting to stop the United States Anti-Doping Agency (USADA) from pursuing its' duping case against Armstrong; United States Women's Soccer player Hope Solo receiving a public warning from USADA after she tested positive for a medication prescribed by her personal doctor; and NASCAR driver A.J. Allmendinger's exhausting his last challenge to a failed drug test (*USA Today*, July 10, 2012). Performance-enhancing drugs and recreational drug use are perhaps the greatest threat facing the integrity of sports, as well as the health and safety of today's athletes. In an attempt to protect their sports and athletes from this threat, athletic administrators and organizations from the interscholastic, intercollegiate, Olympic, and professional levels have implementing drug-testing programs.

In their haste to rid sports of performance-enhancing drugs, however, some people have voiced concern that sports and recreational organizations may be violating the privacy rights of the very athletes they are trying to protect. This section examines the various legal principles raised when an institution or organization implements a drug-testing program for athletes.

FUNDAMENTAL CONCEPTS

The main legal areas governing drug testing of athletes are constitutional law and labor law. The law that will govern a particular complaint depends on the individual. For example, drug testing high school or college athletes raises a number of constitutional issues concerning the athlete's right to due process and privacy, as well as protection against illegal search and seizure and self-incrimination. The drug testing of professional athletes will usually be resolved through internal grievance and arbitration systems set up within the league's collective bargaining agreement (CBA). International and Olympic athletes are regulated by the World Anti-Doping Agency (WADA) and the Court of Arbitration for Sport (CAS).

Constitutional Law

The first question to ask whenever a constitutional law issue arises is: "whether they **state action**?" The safeguards of the U.S. Constitution apply only when state action is present. State action is defined as any action taken directly or indirectly by a state, municipal, or federal government. Therefore, before an athlete can claim that a drug-testing program violated his or her constitutional rights, the entity being challenged must be shown to be part of the federal, state, or municipal government. (For more information on state action, see Chapter 6.12, *State Action*).

As discussed in Chapter 6.12, *State Action*, public high schools and colleges are state actors, and students attending these institutions benefit from the protections afforded under the constitution. Private entities, such as the NCAA and professional sports teams, on the other hand, are not subject to constitutional challenges. For example, in *Long v. National Football League* (1994), a NFL player sued the league after he tested positive for anabolic steroids and was suspended pursuant to the league's drug-testing policy. In dismissing his claim, the District Court held that Long failed to show a sufficiently close nexus between the actions of the city and city officials and the decision of the NFL to establish state action based on his suspension. The court concluded that Long was suspended based on independent medical conclusions and the NFL's drug testing policy over which the state had no influence.

Even when the state is involved in the drug testing of professional athletes, the courts have afforded wide latitude to such programs. For example, in *Shoemaker v. Handell* (1986), five jockeys challenged the New Jersey Racing Commission's regulations requiring drug testing of jockeys. The jockeys claimed that this constituted an illegal search and seizure and was a violation of their Fourth Amendment rights. The Court of Appeals, in upholding the regulations, held that the commission's concern for racing integrity warranted the tests and that as long as the commission kept the results confidential, there was no violation of the jockeys' rights.

The Fourth Amendment

Once state action has been established, an organization must meet the safeguards of the Fourth Amendment to the United States Constitution before it can implement a drug-testing program. The Fourth Amendment provides that:

> [T]he right of the people to be secure in their persons, houses, papers and effects, against unreasonable searches and seizures, shall not be violated, and no Warrants shall issue, but upon probable cause, supported by Oath or affirmation, and particularly describing the place to be searched and the persons or things to be seized.

Therefore, before any drug test program can be ruled constitutional under the Fourth Amendment, the "search" or test must be reasonable. To determine whether a drug test satisfies the reasonableness requirement, the court must balance the intrusion of the test on an individual's Fourth Amendment interests against its promotion of legitimate governmental interests. In conducting this balancing test, the court examines the following three factors: legitimate privacy expectation; character of the intrusion and the nature and immediacy of the governmental concern.

The first factor the courts consider is whether the individual has a **legitimate privacy expectation** on which the search intrudes. The Fourth Amendment only protects those expectations of privacy that society recognizes as legitimate. What expectations are legitimate varies depending on whether the individual asserting the privacy interest is at home, at work, in a car, or in a public park. In addition, the legitimacy of certain privacy expectations may depend on the individual's legal relationship with the state. For example, the expectation of privacy by high school students in school is less than college students, members of the general population or even high school students outside the school grounds. The reason high school athletes have a lower privacy expectation to the fact that schools have a custodial and tutelary responsibility for the students. Also affecting the privacy expectations of athletes is the fact that athletes shower and change together before and after each practice or game; therefore, their expectation of privacy is small. As the Supreme Court noted in *Vernonia School District v. Acton* (1995), "high school sports are not for the bashful."

The second factor to be considered is the **character of the intrusion.** In determining the character of the intrusion, the court examines the manner in which the samples are collected and monitored. For example, is the individual required to give a blood test, which courts would find invasive, or a urine sample, which is far less invasive? In *Vernonia School District v. Acton* (1995), the Supreme Court noted that under the school district's testing program, male students produce samples at a urinal along a wall. They remain fully clothed and are only observed from behind, if at all. Female students produce samples in an enclosed stall, with a female monitor standing outside listening only for sounds of tampering. These conditions are nearly identical to those typically encountered in public restrooms, which men, women, and especially schoolchildren use daily. Under such conditions, the Supreme Court held that the privacy interests compromised by the process of obtaining the urine sample are in our view negligible (*Vernonia School District v. Acton*, 1995).

In addition, to the manner in which the samples are collected, the court also considers the type of information being collected by the test, illegal drug and performance-enhancing drugs, and who receives the test results and how the information is used. The test information should only be disclosed to those limited individuals who have a need to know. For example, in *Vernonia School District v. Acton* (1995), the Supreme Court held that it was "significant that the tests at issue here look only for drugs, and not for whether the student is, for example, epileptic, pregnant, or diabetic." Moreover, the Court found that the drugs for which the samples are screened are standard, and do not vary according to the identity of the student. Finally, the Supreme Court noted that the results of the tests are disclosed only to a limited class of school personnel who have a need to know; and they are not turned over to law enforcement authorities or used for any internal disciplinary function (*Vernonia School District v. Acton*, 1995).

The final factor to be considered is the **nature and immediacy of the governmental concern** and the efficacy of the drug test in meeting those concerns. In other words, the court must determine whether the state's interest in conducting the drug test is important enough to justify intruding on an individual's genuine expectation of privacy. For example, in *Vernonia School District v. Acton* (1995), the Supreme Court found that the schools had a compelling state interest in "deterring drug use by our Nation's schoolchildren." Moreover, the court found that the necessity for the State to act is magnified by the fact that this evil is being visited not just upon individuals at large, but upon children for whom it has undertaken a special responsibility of care and direction. Finally, it must not be lost sight of that this program is directed more narrowly to drug use by school athletes, where the risk of immediate physical harm to the drug user or those with whom he is playing his sport is particularly high (*Vernonia School District v. Acton,* 1995).

An example is *Gruenke v. Seip*, (2000), in which a high school swimming coach, who suspected that a member on the team was pregnant, required the athlete to take a pregnancy test. In ruling that under the standard set forth in *Vernonia*, the coach's actions constitute an unreasonable search under the Fourth Amendment, the Third Circuit Court ruled that a school cannot require a student to submit to this intrusion merely to satisfy his curiosity. Even though student athletes have a very limited expectation of privacy, the Third Circuit Court ruled that in order to compel a student to take a pregnancy test, the school must show a legitimate health concern.

The Fourth Amendment also requires that before any search can be conducted there must be **probable cause**. The Supreme Court, however, has recognized that a search unsupported by probable cause can be constitutional when the state has special needs. As the Supreme Court noted in *Vernonia School District v. Acton* (1995), because of the student's age, the state has "special needs" in the public school context. Those same "special needs," however, do not exist at the college, Olympic, or professional levels.

Post–Vernonia Expansions

Since the United States Supreme Court's decision in *Vernonia*, high schools have sought to extend drug testing to more and more students. In 2002, the United States Supreme Court, in *Board of Education v. Earls* (2002), extended the scope of *Vernonia* to include all extracurricular activities. In Earls, the school district instituted a policy that required all students who participated in any competitive extracurricular activities, including band members, choir members, academic team members, and athletic team members, to submit to drug testing. In upholding the policy, the Supreme Court held that the drug-testing policy reasonably served the school district's important interest in detecting and preventing drug use, and the policy did not violate the Fourth Amendment's prohibition against unreasonable searches and seizures.

In *Safford Unified Sch. Dist. # 1 v. Redding* (2009), the United States Supreme Court was asked to determine whether 13-year-old's Fourth Amendment right was violated when she was subjected to a strip search by school officials acting on reasonable suspicion that she had brought forbidden prescription and over-the-counter drugs to school. In holding that the strip search of the student was unreasonable and a violation of the Fourth Amendment, the Supreme Court ruled that in order for a school search to be permissible in its scope, the measures adopted must be reasonably related to the objectives of the search and not excessively intrusive in light of the age and sex of the student and the nature of the infraction. In the Redding case, the court found that the content of the suspicion failed to match the degree of intrusion. In particular, the Supreme Court noted that the school official knew before the search that the pills were only prescription-strength ibuprofen and over-the-counter naproxen, common pain reliever equivalent to two Advil, or one Aleve. In addition, there was no reason to suspect that the drugs were concealed in her bra and underwear.

State High School Athletic Associations. In addition to individual high schools, state high school athletic associations have also started mandatory testing of athletes. In December 2005, New Jersey became the first state to require random steroid testing for athletes on high school teams that qualify for postseason play. The program, which costs $100,000.00 per year, only tests for performance-enhancing drugs in championship tournaments and requires that 60% of the tests come from football, wrestling, track and field, swimming, lacrosse, and baseball. Following New Jersey's example, Illinois, Texas and Florida also started steroid testing programs. After two years and having spent close to $100,000, Florida discontinued its program in 2009. In justifying the decision, Florida officials pointed to the fact that out of the 600 tests it conducted only one athlete tested positive (Popke, 2009). Another state considering dropping its program is Texas. Having spent millions of dollars on its program, and only finding a few athletes that tested positive for steroids, the Texas Legislature has slashed the original $6 million budget to $750,000 in 2012.

Consent Forms

An individual can voluntarily waive his or her Fourth Amendment rights and submit to a drug-testing program. However, even when an individual consents to a drug test, there can be constitutional problems. For example, in *University of Colorado v. Derdeyn* (1993), a group of student-athletes who had signed consent forms challenged the university's mandatory drug testing program. In upholding the students' challenge, the Colorado Supreme Court held that the university failed to show that the students' consent to such testing was voluntary. Absent such voluntary consent, the court concluded that the university's random, suspicionless urinalysis drug-testing program violated the students' constitutional rights.

State Constitutions

It is also important to note that individual state constitutions may afford more liberal protections to citizens with respect to search and seizure when compared to the U.S. Constitution. For example, in *Hill v. NCAA* (1994), Jennifer Hill, a member of the swimming team at Stanford University, challenged the NCAA's drug testing program by arguing that it violated her privacy rights under the California State Constitution. In particular, Hill pointed to the NCAA's procedure for collecting urine samples and the consent form, which asked students to disclose medical and sexual information. In ruling against Hill, the California Supreme Court held that the NCAA's drug-testing policy involving monitoring of urination, testing of urine samples, and inquiry concerning medication did not violate the students' constitutional right to privacy. In holding that the program was consistent with the privacy provisions of the state constitution, the California Supreme Court held that the NCAA's interest in protecting both the health and safety of the athletes and the integrity of the programs outweighed Hill's privacy interests *Hill v. NCAA*, (1994).

Another case involving a state constitutional challenge is *York v. Wahkiakum School District No. 200*, (2008), in which the Supreme Court of Washington ruled that the random and suspicionless drug testing of student athletes violates article I, section 7 of the Washington State Constitution. (See Significant Case)

Due Process

Another theory used by athletes to challenge the constitutionality of drug-testing programs is due process. As discussed in Chapter 6.13, *Due Process*, to establish a violation of due process, an individual must establish that he or she has some type of property or liberty interest that has been adversely affected. Unfortunately, for the student–athletes, it is clear from past court decisions that participation in athletics is not a property right, but is a privilege not protected by Constitutional due process safeguards. For example, in *Brennan v. Board of Trustees* (1997), John Brennan, a student-athlete at the University of Southwestern Louisiana, challenged a positive drug test for anabolic steroids on due process grounds. In the case, Brennan requested and received two administrative appeals in which he contended that the positive test results were "false" due to a combination of factors, including heavy drinking and sexual activity the night before the test and his use of nutritional supplements. Following the unsuccessful appeals, USL complied with the NCAA regulations and suspended Brennan from intercollegiate athletic competition for one year. In rejecting his claim, the court held that Brennan had no liberty or property interest in participating in intercollegiate athletics.

Labor Law

Another legal area governing drug testing is labor law. In professional sports, the conduct of the players is governed by a contract that is negotiated between the league, representing the owners, and the players' association, representing the players. This contract or Collective Bargaining Agreement (CBA) addresses the conditions of the athletes' employment. Because drug-testing programs affect an athlete's condition of employment (if they test positive, they cannot play), it is a mandatory subject of bargaining and must be part of the CBA. (For more information on Labor Relations in Professional Sports, see Chapter 7.33). The first professional sports league to subject its players to drug tests was the National Basketball Players. The program, which only covered street drugs, was adopted in 1983. The NBA added steroids to the list of banned substances in 1999. The first league to test players for steroid use was the NFL in 1987.

One problem with drug testing in professional sports, as demonstrated by the fight over drug testing in Major League Baseball, is the conflict of interest both the union and management have in having a strong testing program. Because the job of the MLB Players Association is to protect the players from anything that might impact their work, which the current drug testing program clearly does, it is in the union's best interest to fight to keep testing out of baseball. As a result of this conflict, it is not surprising that the union only agreed to allow drug testing of players under the threat of Congressional intervention and if baseball could demonstrate that there was a problem. As a result, MLB conducted survey tests in 2003 to gauge the use of steroids among players. If more than 5 percent of the major league players tested had tested positive, the threshold established by the union, MLB could implement a full drug testing program for real in 2004. Even though the 2003 tests were intended to be confidential, and no penalties could be imposed on any players who tested positive, two of the 103 players to test positive in 2003, Alex Rodriguez and Sammy Sosa, have been identified.

The penalties under the current Major League Baseball Drug Testing Policy for a player who tests positive for performance-enhancing substances are: a 50-game suspension for the first offense; 100-game for a second offense; and a permanent suspension from the major or minor leagues for a third. As of 2012, the best known player to be penalized under the program is Manny Ramirez, a 12-time All-Star, who was suspended for 100 games. In addition MLB's drug policy requires drug suspensions to be unpaid.

World Anti-Doping Agency

In 1998, the sport world was rocked by a series of high profile doping scandals. For example, before the 1998 Tour de France a masseur for one of the teams was stopped at the boarder when his car is found to contain more than 400 doping products, including EPO, a drug that increases oxygen in red blood cells. During the race, the police raided a number of the hotel rooms of team members, forcing five teams drop out of the race along with some individuals, including former world champion Luc Leblanc. In addition to the Tour, 1998 also saw four members of the Chinese national swim team test positive before the 1998 world championships and vials of human growth hormone were found in the team's luggage while traveling to the event. Finally, three time gold medal winner, Michelle Smith de Bruin was banned from competition for four years by the International Swimming Federation (FINA) after finding that she had manipulated a drug test by spiking her urine sample with alcohol.

Worried about the impact the drug scandals might have on the future of the Olympic Games, the International Olympic Committee held the First World Conference on Doping in Sport in February 1999 in Lausanne, Switzerland. As a result of the conference, the International Olympic Committee (IOC) and the international sport governing bodies created the Lausanne Declaration on Doping in Sport, which called for the creation of a global anti-doping agency. In November 1999, the World Anti-Doping Agency (WADA) was established to fill this role with temporary headquarters in Lausanne. WADA's headquarters were eventually moved to Montreal, Canada in 2002.

In March 2003, the WADA announced a consolidated drug-control program for all international sports. The World Anti-Doping Code (the Code) was signed by sixty-five sports federations and over fifty nations, including the United States, United Kingdom, Russia, France, Germany, and Australia, and covers all Olympic sports, the federations that govern them, and all their athletes. In developing the Code, WADA sought to create a single list of banned drugs, a uniform system for testing for them, and penalties for violators. Up until the Code was developed, each Olympic sport operated under its own drug program. Since it entered into force on January 1 2004, the Code has led to several significant advances in the global fight against doping in sport, and has brought about harmonization to a system where previously rules had varied, and in some cases did not exist. Additionally, the Code allowed for sanctioning in cases where there was no positive doping test, but there was evidence that an anti-doping rule violation had occurred. For example, Marion Jones won five medals during the 2000 Olympic Games, and even though she passed every drug test she took during the games, she was stripped of her medals after she admitted taking performance-enhancing drugs.

One of the main complaints of the 2003 Code was the inflexibility surrounding violations. The Code held athletes responsible for all positive findings, no matter how the drug got into their bodies. For a first violation under the 2003 Code, an athlete received an automatic 2-year ban from competition; a second violation, and the athlete was banned for life. In an effort to provide some flexibility, the Code was revised as of January 1, 2009. However, the revised 2009 Code also requires athletes to submit to no-notice, out-of-competition tests anytime, anywhere. To do this, every athlete on the national testing register, and any elite athlete in an Olympic or major team sport, must report his or her whereabouts to their national anti-doping organizations for at least one hour a day between the hours of 6 am and 11 pm, seven days a week, three months in advance. Failure of the athlete to be where he or she said they would be counts as a strike. Three strikes in an 18-month period and the athlete is automatically banned from competition. (For more information on the 2009 WADA Code, see: http://www.wada-ama.org/).

Although there have been some calls in Congress and outside the United States to apply the Code to America's professional sports leagues, the leagues and players have resisted those calls. As the Floyd Landis arbitration case illustrates, American individual sport athletes are subject to the WADA Code. During the 2006 Tour de France, Floyd Landis, who would eventually win the race, tested positive for the presence of exogenous testosterone. In his arbitration hearing, the arbitration panel ruled that Landis was stripped of his 2006 Tour de France win and ineligible for competition for two years. In 2008, Landis challenged the penalty imposed by the **United States Anti-Doping Association (USADA)**, the agency in United States responsible for managing the testing and adjudication process of the athletes in the US Olympic and Paralympic Movement. The Court of Arbitration for Sport (CAS), in *Landis v. USADA* (2007), upheld USADA penalty and also required Landis to pay the $100,000 in legal expenses USADA incurred in the arbitration.

Under the WADA Code, for a first offense, athletes are suspended for two years. The ban can be reduced if "an athlete or other Person can establish how a Specified Substance entered his or her body or came into his or her Possession and that such Specified Substance was not intended to enhance the Athlete's sport performance or mask the Use of a performance-enhancing substance, the period of Ineligibility … shall be replaced with the following: At a minimum, a reprimand and no period of Ineligibility from future Events, and at a maximum, two (2) years of Ineligibility" (WADA Code 10.4).

Unhappy that the WADA Code did not include a ban on the next Olympic Games, the IOC enacted Rule 45 which bars any athlete who has received a doping suspension of more than six months from competing in the next Olympic Games. In *USOC v. IOC* (2011), the United States Olympic Committee challenged the rule after 2008 Olympic 400-meter champion, LaShawn Merritt tested positive for a banned substance found in a male-enhancement product. Merritt who completed his suspension in 2011, and would have been eligible to compete in the 2012 London Olympic Games, was ineligible under IOC Rule 45. The USOC, backed by the United States Anti-Doping Agency and anti-doping bodies in Britain, Denmark, Norway, New Zealand, Japan and South Africa, challenged the rule.

In October 2011, the Court of Arbitration for Sport ruled that Rule 45 was "invalid and unenforceable" because it amounts to a second penalty, clearing the way for Merritt and dozens of other athletes around the world to compete in London (*USOC v. IOC*, 2011). As a result, Merritt was allowed to compete in the 2012 Olympics. The IOC said it would push for the rule to be included in a revised WADA code in 2013.

SIGNIFICANT CASE

The following case examines whether the drug testing of student–athletes violates the students state constitutional rights of privacy.

HANS YORK ET AL., V. WAHKIAKUM SCHOOL DISTRICT NO. 200
Supreme Court of Washington
178 P.3d 995 (Wash. 2008)

The question before us is whether random and suspicionless drug testing of student athletes violates article I, section 7 of the Washington State Constitution.

1 Article I, section 7 of the Washington Constitution provides:

No person shall be disturbed in his private affairs, or his home invaded, without authority of law.

Facts

The Wahkiakum School District (school district) requires its student athletes to refrain from using or possessing alcohol or illegal drugs. Beginning in 1994, the school district implemented myriad ways to combat drug and alcohol use among the student population. Nevertheless, drug and alcohol problems persisted. Acting independently of the school district, the Wahkiakum Community Network (community network) began surveying district students. From these surveys, the community network ranked teen substance abuse as the number one problem in Wahkiakum County. As reiterated by the trial court, the community network's surveys showed that in 1998, 40 percent of sophomores reported previously using illegal drugs and 19 percent of sophomores reported illegal drug use within the previous 30 days, while 42 percent of seniors reported previously using illegal drugs and 12.5 percent reported illegal drug use within the previous 30 days. Clerk's Papers (CP) at 484–85 (Undisputed Facts 10(c), (d)). In 2000, 50 percent of student athletes self-identified as drug and/or alcohol users. *Id.*

As a result, the school district decided to implement random drug testing where all student athletes may be tested initially and then subjected to random drug testing during the remainder of the season. The school district formed the Drug and Alcohol Advisory Committee (now the Safe and Drug Free Schools Advisory Committee) to help deal with the student substance abuse problems. CP at 485. The committee evaluated the effectiveness of its previous programs, such as D.A.R.E. (Drug Abuse Resistance Education) and support groups, and contemplated adopting policy 3515, which would require random drug testing of student athletes. The trial court found:

Based upon the evidence of substantial alcohol and drug use among students and pursuant to the School District's statutory authority and responsibility to maintain order and discipline in its schools, to protect the health and safety of its students, and to control, supervise and regulate interschool athletics, the Board of Directors adopted the policy. CP at 486.

As part of the policy, all student athletes must agree to be randomly drug tested as a condition of playing extracurricular sports. The drug testing is done by urinalysis, with the student in an enclosed bathroom stall and a health department employee outside. The sample is then mailed to Comprehensive Toxicology Services in Tacoma, Washington. If the results indicate illegal drug use, then the student is suspended from extracurricular athletic activities; the length of suspension depends on the number of infractions and whether the student tested positive for illegal drugs or alcohol. Also, the school district provides students with drug and alcohol counseling resources. The results are not sent to local law enforcement or included in the student's academic record. And the student is not suspended from school, only from extracurricular sports.

During the 1999–2000 school year, Aaron York and Abraham York played sports and were tested under the policy. And Tristan Schneider was tested under the policy during the 2000–2001 year. The York and Schneider parents brought suit arguing the school district's policy violated the Washington State Constitution. Their motion for a preliminary injunction was denied by superior court Judge Penoyar, and the Court of Appeals dismissed the petition as moot. *See York v. Wahkiakum Sch. Dist. No. 200*, 110 Wn. App. 383, 40 P.3d 1198 (2002). The trial court then held that while the school district's policy "approached the tolerance limit" of our constitution, the policy was nevertheless constitutional and narrowly tailored to reach a compelling government end. CP at 497.

The York and Schneider parents sought and obtained direct review in our court of a summary judgment order and ask us to determine whether the school district's policy 3515 is constitutional.

***

Analysis

We are aware there are strong arguments, policies, and opinions marshaled on both sides of this debate, but we are concerned only with the policy's constitutionality. And while we are loath to disturb the decisions of a local school board, we will not hesitate to intervene when constitutional protections are implicated. . . . No matter the drawbacks or merits of the school district's random drug testing, we cannot let the policy stand if it offends our constitution. Students "do not 'shed their constitutional rights' at the schoolhouse door." *Goss v. Lopez*, 419 U.S. 565, 574, 95 S. Ct. 729, 42 L. Ed. 2d 725 (1975).

The question before us is narrow: Whether Wahkiakum School District's blanket policy requiring student athletes to submit to random drug testing is constitutional. The United States Supreme Court has held such activity does not violate the Fourth Amendment to the federal constitution. *Vernonia Sch. Dist. 47J v. Acton*, 515 U.S. 646, 115 S. Ct. 2386, 132 L. Ed. 2d 564 (1995). But we have never decided whether a suspicionless, random drug search of student athletes violates article I, section 7 of our state constitution. Therefore, we must decide whether our state constitution follows the federal standard or provides more protection to students in the state of Washington.

I. May Wahkiakum School District Perform Suspicionless, Random Drug Tests of Student Athletes?

a. Federal cases concerning public school searches

The school district argues we should follow federal cases and allow suspicionless, random drug testing of its student athletes. Two federal cases are apposite to our consideration. These cases, while helpful, do not control how we interpret our state constitution. *City of Seattle v. Mighty Movers*, 152 Wn.2d 343, 356, 96 P.3d 979 (2004). There are stark differences in the language of the two constitutional protections; unlike the Fourth Amendment, article I, section 7 is not based on a reasonableness standard.

The United States Supreme Court has held public school searches presented a "special need," which allowed a departure from the warrant and probable cause requirements. *New Jersey v. T.L.O.*, 469 U.S. 325, 105 S. Ct. 733, 83 L. Ed. 2d 720 (1985). The *T.L.O.* Court held school teachers and administrators could search students without a warrant if (1) there existed reasonable grounds for suspecting that the search will turn up evidence that the student has violated or is violating either the law or the rules of the school" and (2) the search is "not excessively intrusive in light of the age and sex of the student and the nature of the infraction." *Id*. at 341–42.

Next, in *Acton*, a public school district implemented a random drug testing of school athletes, similar to the one at issue here. *Acton*, 515 U.S. 646. Each student athlete was tested at the beginning of the season, and then each week 10 percent were randomly selected for testing. Most critics of *Acton* are not persuaded the majority's analysis justifies a suspicionless search of the student athletes. But the *Acton* majority claimed individualized suspicion would unduly interfere with the government's goals and might actually make the situation worse. Its reasoning was based primarily on three rationales: (1) individualized suspicion would "transform[ ] the process into a badge of shame," *id*. at 663, where teachers could claim any troublesome student was abusing drugs; (2) teachers and student officials are neither trained nor equipped to spot drug use; and (3) individualized suspicion creates an unnecessary loss of resources in defending claims and lawsuits against arbitrary imposition, when students and parents will inevitably challenge whether reasonable suspicion did indeed exist. *Id*. at 664 ("In many respects, we think, testing based on 'suspicion' of drug use would not be better, but worse.").

But these arguments were unpersuasive several years earlier when the Court applied an individualized suspicion standard to public schools in *T.L.O.* The *Acton* majority never adequately explained why individual suspicion was needed in *T.L.O.* but not in *Acton*. Justice O'Connor spent much of her dissent taking issue with this standard:

[N]owhere is it *less* clear that an individualized suspicion requirement would be ineffectual than in the school

context. In most schools, the entire pool of potential search targets—students—is under constant supervision by teachers and administrators and coaches, be it in classrooms, hallways, or locker rooms. . . .

. . . The great irony of this case is that most (though not all) of the evidence the District introduced to justify its suspicionless drug testing program consisted of first- or second-hand stories of particular, identifiable students acting in ways that plainly gave rise to reasonable suspicion of in-school drug use—and thus that would have justified a drug-related search under our *T.L.O.* decision. *Acton*, 515 U.S. at 678–79 (O'Connor, J., dissenting).

The Wahkiakum School District modeled its policy after the one used by the Vernonia School District. But simply passing muster under the federal constitution does not ensure the survival of the school district's policy under our state constitution. The Fourth Amendment provides for "[t]he right of the people to be secure in their persons, houses, papers, and effects, against unreasonable searches and seizures." U.S. Const. amend. IV. Therefore, a Fourth Amendment analysis hinges on whether a warrantless search is reasonable, and it is possible in some circumstances for a search to be reasonable without a warrant. *See Acton*, 515 U.S. at 652 ("As the text of the Fourth Amendment indicates, the ultimate measure of the constitutionality of a governmental search is 'reasonableness.'"). But our state constitutional analysis hinges on whether a search has "authority of law"—in other words, a warrant. Wash. Const. art. I, § 7.

b. Search and seizure analysis under article I, section 7

Our state constitution provides: "No person shall be disturbed in his private affairs, or his home invaded, without authority of law." Wash. Const. art. I, § 7. It is well established that in some areas, article I, section 7 provides greater protection than its federal counterpart—the Fourth Amendment. *State v. McKinney*, 148 Wn.2d 20, 29, 60 P.3d 46 (2002); *State v. Myrick*, 102 Wn.2d 506, 510, 688 P.2d 151 (1984) ("[T]he unique language of Const. art. 1, § 7 provides greater protection to persons under the Washington Constitution than U.S. Const. amend. 4 provides to persons generally."). When determining whether article I, section 7 provides greater protection in a particular context, we focus on whether the unique characteristics of the constitutional provision and its prior interpretations compel a particular result. *State v. Walker*, 157 Wn.2d 307, 317, 138 P.3d 113 (2006). We look to the constitutional text, historical treatment of the interest at stake, relevant case law and statutes, and the current implications of recognizing or not recognizing an interest. *Id*.

This requires a two-part analysis. First, we must determine whether the state action constitutes a disturbance of one's private affairs. Here that means asking whether requiring a student athlete to provide a urine sample intrudes upon the student's private affairs. Second, if a privacy interest has been disturbed, the second step in our analysis asks whether authority of law justifies the intrusion. The "authority of law" required by article I, section 7 is satisfied by a valid warrant, limited to a few jealously guarded exceptions. Because the Wahkiakum School District had no warrant, if we reach the second prong of the analysis, we must decide whether the school district's activity fits within an exception to the warrant requirement. Relying on federal law, the school district claims there is a "special needs" exception to the warrant requirement that we should adopt. The York and Schneider parents point out we have not adopted such an exception and urge us not to do so here.

II. Suspicionless, Random Drug Testing Disturbs a Student Athlete's Private Affairs

When inquiring about private affairs, we look to "'those privacy interests which citizens of this state have held, and should be entitled to hold, safe from governmental trespass absent a warrant'." *State v. Young*, 123 Wn.2d 173, 181, 867 P.2d 593 (1994) (quoting *Myrick*, 102 Wn.2d at 511). This is an objective analysis.

The private affair we are concerned with today is the State's interference in a student athlete's bodily functions. Specifically, does it intrude upon a privacy interest to require a student athlete to go into a bathroom stall and provide a urine sample, even against that student's protest? Federal courts and our court both agree the answer is an unqualified yes, such action intrudes into one's reasonable expectation of privacy. Indeed, we offer heightened protection for bodily functions compared to the federal courts.

But the school district claims student athletes have a lower expectation of privacy. Certainly, students who choose to play sports are subjected to more regulation. For example, RCW 28A.600.200 provides, "Each school district board of directors is hereby granted and shall exercise the authority to control, supervise and regulate the conduct of interschool athletic activities." And certainly there is generally less privacy in locker rooms than in other parts of a school. But the district does not link regulations and the communal atmosphere of locker rooms with a student's lowered expectation of privacy in terms of being subjected to suspicionless, random drug testing. We do not see how what happens in the locker room or on the field affects a student's privacy in the context of compelling him or her to provide a urine sample. A student athlete has a genuine and fundamental privacy interest in controlling his or her own bodily functions. The urinalysis test is by itself relatively unobtrusive. Nevertheless, a student is still required to provide his or her bodily fluids. Even if done in an enclosed stall, this is a significant intrusion on a student's fundamental right of privacy. *See Robinson*, 102 Wn. App. at 822.

This analysis should in no way contradict what we have previously said about students' privacy interests.

Generally we have recognized students have a lower expectation of privacy because of the nature of the school environment. Courts have held a school official needs some "reasonable" or "individualized" suspicion in order to protect students from arbitrary searches, yet still give officials sufficient leeway to conduct their duties. *T.L.O.*, 469 U.S. at 341; *State v. McKinnon,* 88 Wn.2d 75, 558 P.2d 781 (1977). Our court discussed student searches and student rights under the Fourth Amendment prior to the United States Supreme Court's holding in *T.L.O.* In *McKinnon*, we said: Although a student's right to be free from intrusion is not to be lightly disregarded, for us to hold school officials to the standard of probable cause required of law enforcement officials would create an unreasonable burden upon these school officials. Maintaining discipline in schools oftentimes requires immediate action and cannot await the procurement of a search warrant based on probable cause. We hold that the search of a student's person is reasonable and does not violate his Fourth Amendment rights, if the school official has reasonable grounds to believe the search is necessary in the aid of maintaining school discipline and order. *McKinnon*, 88 Wn.2d at 81. And in *Kuehn*, we also opined in dicta that although a warrant or probable cause might be unnecessary to search a student's backpack, the school nevertheless needed to articulate some reasonable suspicion to justify a search of a student under both the Fourth Amendment and article I, section 7... .

We decided these cases before the United States Supreme Court decided *T.L.O.*, which cited *McKinnon* when it also held reasonable suspicion was necessary to search a student. *T.L.O.*, 469 U.S. at 333 n.2. Nevertheless, in *State v. Brooks*, 43 Wn. App. 560, 568, 718 P.2d 837 (1986), the Court of Appeals analyzed *McKinnon* and *Kuehn* and said, "Accordingly, since the holding in *T.L.O.* is consistent with our Supreme Court's holding in *McKinnon*, we conclude that article 1, section 7 affords students no greater protections from searches by school officials than is guaranteed by the Fourth Amendment." The school district points to this one sentence to say we should adopt whole cloth the federal analysis with regards to both student searches and student drug testing. But *Brooks* did not involve drug testing and was decided before *Acton*. Nor are we bound to the Court of Appeals' broad language.

Because we determine that interfering with a student athlete's bodily functions disturbs one's private affairs, we must address the second prong of the article I, section 7 analysis: does the school district have the necessary authority of law to randomly drug test student athletes?

III. Under Article I, Section 7 There Is No Authority of Law that Allows a School District to Conduct Random Drug Tests

We have long held a warrantless search is per se unreasonable, unless it fits within one of the "'jealously and carefully drawn exceptions.'" *State v. Hendrickson*, 129

Wn.2d 61, 70, 917 P.2d 563 (1996). These exceptions include "exigent circumstances, consent, searches incident to a valid arrest, inventory searches, the plain view doctrine, and *Terry* investigative stops." *Robinson*, 102 Wn. App. at 813. Any exceptions to the warrant requirement must be rooted in the common law. *State v. Ladson*, 138 Wn.2d 343, 979 P.2d 833 (1999); *Robinson*, 102 Wn. App. at 813. And it is always the government's burden to show its random drug testing fits within one of these narrow exceptions. *City of Seattle v. Mesiani*, 110 Wn.2d 454, 457, 755 P.2d 775 (1988). Today the school district asks us to accept an analog to the federal special needs doctrine to justify its drug testing policy. The York and Schneider parents point out we have never formally adopted a special needs exception and therefore claim no exception to the warrant requirement exists here.

***

c. Washington State cases concerning suspicionless searches

Though we have not considered drug testing in public schools, we have a long history of striking down exploratory searches not based on at least reasonable suspicion. *State v. Jorden*, 160 Wn.2d 121, 127, 156 P.3d 893 (2007) ("[T]his court has consistently expressed displeasure with random and suspicionless searches, reasoning that they amount to nothing more than an impermissible fishing expedition."); *Robinson*, 102 Wn. App. at 815 ("Our Supreme Court has thus not been easily persuaded that a search without individualized suspicion can pass constitutional muster."). In *Mesiani*, this court held a random roadblock sobriety checkpoint program initiated by Seattle police was a "highly intrusive" search and violated "the right to not be disturbed in one's private affairs guaranteed by article I, section 7." *Mesiani*, 110 Wn.2d at 458–60. In *Kuehn*, this court held a search of student luggage required by school officials as a condition of participation in a school-sponsored trip to Canada violated both the Fourth Amendment and article I, section 7. 103 Wn.2d at 595. We opined, "[i]n the absence of individualized suspicion of wrongdoing, the search is a general search. '[W]e never authorize general, exploratory searches,'" (alteration in original) and such

searches are "anathema to the Fourth Amendment and Const. art. 1, § 7 protections." *Id.*

The few times we have allowed suspicionless searches, we did so either relying entirely on federal law or in the context of criminal investigations or dealing with prisoners. In *Meacham*, 93 Wn.2d at 738–39, we upheld mandatory blood tests of putative fathers. In *Juveniles A, B, C, D, E*, 121 Wn.2d at 90, we upheld mandatory HIV tests of convicted sexual offenders. In *Olivas*, 122 Wn.2d at 83, we upheld blood tests of convicted felons without individualized suspicion. And recently in *State v. Surge*, 160 Wn.2d 65, 156 P.3d 208 (2007), we held a DNA (deoxyribonucleic acid) sampling of convicted felons did not violate article I, section 7. That case allowed for warrantless testing without individualized suspicion because we asserted such testing did not disturb a reasonable right to privacy. But these cases present far different factual situations from drug testing student athletes. A felon has either already pleaded guilty or been found guilty beyond a reasonable doubt of a serious crime; a student athlete has merely attended school and chosen to play extracurricular sports. Most troubling, however, is that we can conceive of no way to draw a principled line permitting drug testing of only student athletes. If we were to allow random drug testing here, what prevents school districts from either later drug testing students participating in any extracurricular activities, as federal courts now allow, or testing the entire student population?

We cannot countenance random searches of public school student athletes with our article I, section 7 jurisprudence. As stated earlier, we require a warrant except for rare occasions, which we jealously and narrowly guard. We decline to adopt a doctrine similar to the federal special needs exception in the context of randomly drug testing student athletes. In sum, no argument has been presented that would bring the random drug testing within any reasonable interpretation of the constitutionally required "authority of law." *See Mesiani*, 110 Wn.2d at 458.

Accordingly, we hold the school district's policy 3515 is unconstitutional and violates student athletes' rights secured by article I, section 7. Therefore we reverse the superior court. The York and Schneider parents shall recover their costs.

CASES ON THE SUPPLEMENTAL WEB SITE

Board of Education of Independent School District No. 92 of Pottawatomie County v. Earls, 536 U.S. 822 (2002). This case examines whether the state can expand drug testing programs to include all middle and high school students who participate in any extracurricular activity, not just sport.

Doe v. Little Rock School District, 380 F.3d 349 (8th Cir. 2004). This cases examines whether the district's practice of conducting random, suspicionless searches of students and their belongings of randomly selected classrooms by school officials violated the students Fourth Amendment rights.

Hill v. National Collegiate Athletic Association, 865 P.2d 633 (1994). This case examines whether the NCAA drug testing program violates state constitutional protections.

Shoemaker v. Handell, 795 F.2d 1136 (1986). This case examines the state's interest in drug testing jockeys in the horse-racing industry.

Williams v. National Football League, 582 F.3d 863 (8th Cir. 2009). This case examines the rights of professional athletes to challenge positive drug test under state law, instead of the collective bargaining agreement (CBA).

York v. Wahkiakum School District No. 200, 178 P.3d 995 (2008). This case examines whether a school district's policy of random and suspicionless drug test was unconstitutional under Washington State's Constitution.

QUESTIONS YOU SHOULD BE ABLE TO ANSWER

1. What are some of the constitutional protections available to fight an unwanted drug test?

2. Why are NCAA athletes unable to challenge the NCAA drug testing program under the fourth Amendment of the United States Constitution?

3. How does the court determine if a drug test is reasonable under the Fourth Amendment of the United States Constitution?

4. Drug testing of professional team athletes in the Unites States are governed by what?

5. What is WADA? What role does it play in sports?

REFERENCES

Cases

Board of Education of Independent School District No. 92 of Pottawatomie County v. Earls, 536 U.S. 822 (2002).
Brennan v. Board of Trustees, 691 So.2d 324 (1997).
Gruenke v. Seip, 225 F.3d 290 (3rd Cir. 2000).
Hill v. National Collegiate Athletic Association, 865 P.2d 633, 26 Cal. Rptr.2d 834 (1994).
Landis v. USADA, CAS 2007/A/1394
Long v. National Football League, 870 F. Supp. 101 (1994).
Safford Unified Sch. Dist. # 1 v. Redding, 2009 U.S. LEXIS 4735.
Shoemaker v. Handell, 795 F.2d 1136 (1986).
University of Colorado v. Derdeyn, 863 P.2d 929 (Colo. 1993).
USOC v. IOC, CAS 2011/0/2422
Vernonia School District 47J v. Acton, 515 U.S. 646 (1995).

Publications

Popke, M. (2009, April). Drug Wars. *Athletic Business*, p.12.
USA Today, Section C, page 1, July 10, 2012.

Legislation

United States Constitution, Fourth Amendment.

Websites

World Anti-Doping Agency, http://www.wada-ama.org/
New Jersey State Interscholastic Athletic Association Steroid Testing Program,
    http://www.njsiaa.org/NJSIAA/09steroidmemo.pdf.

6.24 PARTICIPANTS WITH DISABILITIES

John T. Wolohan, Terry M. MacDonald | Syracuse University

In the sport and recreation field, the line between lawful refusal to extend eligibility requirements and illegal discrimination against individuals with disabilities is getting clearer all the time. This has especially true since 1990, when the Americans with Disabilities Act (ADA) was originally signed into law and particularly true when the Americans with Disabilities Act Amendment Act (ADAAA) was passed in 2008. Even with the enactment of the ADAAA, individuals with disabilities continue to face a number of obstacles in their effort to participate in sport and recreation programs. This chapter examines some of the many obstacles individuals with disabilities in their fight to participate in sport and recreation activities.

FUNDAMENTAL CONCEPTS

As recently as 1970, children with learning disabilities were denied access to a number of state public school systems because it was thought that their presence would interfere with the learning environment of students without disabilities (Clement, 1988). To remedy this situation, in the early 1970s, Congress began enacting federal legislation designed to increase the opportunities available to individuals with disabilities (Clement, 1988). The first law passed by Congress was the Rehabilitation Act of 1973.

The Rehabilitation Act of 1973

Section 504 of the Rehabilitation Act states that:

> "No otherwise qualified handicapped individual in the United States, . . . shall solely by reason of his handicap, be excluded from participation in, be denied the benefits of, or be subjected to discrimination under any program or activity receiving Federal financial assistance . . ." (29 U.S.C. § 794).

One of the stated intents of the Rehabilitation Act was to provide individuals with disabilities the opportunity to participate in physical education and athletic programs or activities without being discriminated against due to their disability. For an individual to successfully pursue a claim under § 504, he or she must establish four elements:

1. that he or she is an ***individual with a disability*** (Section 504 defines a person with a disability as one who has, one who has a record of having, or one who has been regarded as having a physical or mental impairment that *substantially limits* a major life activity.);
2. that he or she is ***otherwise qualified*** for the athletic activity (The individual with a disability must show that, with reasonable accommodation, he or she can participate);
3. that he or she is being excluded from athletic participation ***solely by reason of*** their disabilities (The person with a disability must demonstrate that he or she is being discriminated against due to his/her disability.); and
4. that the ***school, or institution is receiving federal financial assistance*** (29 U.S.C. 794) (All public schools in the United States would fall in this category since virtually all of the public school systems are recipients of federal funds.)

Because most challenges under § 504 hinge on the determination of the "otherwise qualified" element or the "solely by reason of" element, an examination of the meaning of those two elements is important. The U.S. Supreme Court, in *Southeastern Community College v. Davis* (1979), interpreted the phrase "otherwise qualified" to mean someone who is able to meet all of a program's requirements in spite of his or her disability (*Southeastern Community College v. Davis*, 422 U.S. 397, at 406, 1979). Davis, who has a hearing disability, sought entry into Southeastern Community College's School of Nursing. The Supreme Court, in finding that Davis's hearing disability made it impossible for her to safely complete the nursing program, stated that § 504 of the Rehabilitation Act does not compel an institution to disregard an individual's ability or to make substantial modifications in their programs to accommodate individuals with disabilities. However, the institution must demonstrate that its rules, policies and procedures represent essential elements to the program.

In *Alexander v. Choate* (1985), the Supreme Court addressed what types of modifications would be required under § 504 when it held that although an organization need not be required to make fundamental or substantial modifications to accommodate an individual's disability, *it may be required to make reasonable ones*. Reasonable accommodation may include (1) making facilities used by employees readily accessible to and usable by individuals with disabilities, and (2) job restructuring, part-time or modified work schedules, acquisition or modification of equipment or devices, the provision of readers or interpreters, and similar actions (34 C.F.R. § 104.12. (b)). For example, in *S.S. v. Whitesboro Central School District*, (2012), a student who suffered severe anxiety attacks that would trigger thoughts of drowning. Due to this fear, S.S. requested the accommodation of permitting S.S. to exit the pool for indeterminate periods of time—on unannounced occasions during practices and swim competitions—to calm her nerves, without being kicked off of the team. In rejecting the students § 504 claim the court held that there was nothing the school could do to reasonably accommodate S.S.'s disability. There is no reasonable accommodation that a swim team coach could make for an athlete who is suddenly and sporadically afraid of the water and thus has to exit the pool during practices and competitions. As stated above, one of the essential requirements of swim team members is the ability to enter, and remain in, the pool when required by the coach during practices and competitions. To require otherwise would fundamentally change the nature of the swim team and thus be unreasonable.

The requirement that an individual be excluded *solely by reason of* the disability is met if an individual is being excluded due to their disability. For example, school districts may have policies that require participants to have both of any type of paired organ (e.g., kidneys) for safety reasons. In *Poole v. South Plainfield Board of Education* (1980), the South Plainfield Board of Education denied Richard Poole the right to participate in South Plainfield's interscholastic wrestling program due to the fact that he was born with one kidney. The court concluded that Poole was being excluded from participation in athletics "solely by reason of" the fact he had one kidney.

The issue of whether someone is being excluded "solely by reason of" their disability is more difficult when an individual, due to an illness or learning disability, is over the athletic association's maximum age requirement by the time he or she reaches their senior year in high school. *University Interscholastic League (UIL) and Bailey Marshall v. Buchanan* (1993) is a good illustration of the challenge presented in these cases. In *UIL v. Buchanan* two nineteen-year-old students with diagnosed learning disabilities sought a permanent injunction against the enforcement of UIL's rule requiring all athletes to be under 19 years old. In support of the age requirement, the UIL argued that the age requirement was necessary to ensure the safety of the participating student–athletes and to reduce the competitive advantage of having older participants. The UIL also argued that the age rule did not discriminate against the plaintiffs because of their disability, but was applied equally to all students. Therefore, the plaintiffs were ineligible due to their ages, not their disability.

The Court of Appeals in affirming the trial court's injunction, enjoined UIL from enforcing the age rule against the plaintiffs, held that except for their disability, the students would have turned nineteen after September 1 of their senior year and would have been age-eligible to participate in interscholastic athletics. In determining whether UIL had made reasonable accommodations for the plaintiffs' disabilities, the Court of Appeals examined the waiver mechanism UIL had in place for other eligibility rules. The waiver of the age rule, the Court of Appeals found, would be a reasonable accommodation by UIL to ensure that individuals with disabilities achieve meaningful access. The UIL's "no exception" policy to the age requirement, therefore, had to yield to the reasonable accommodation requirement of § 504 of the Rehabilitation Act.

For other cases challenging high school athletic association eligibility rules, see: *Dennin v. Connecticut Interscholastic Athletic Conference* (1996); *J.M. v. Montana High School Association* (1994); *Johnson v. Florida High School Activities Association* (1995); *Pottgen v. Missouri State High School Athletic Association* (1994); and *Sandison v. Michigan High School Athletic Association* (1995).

Individuals with Disabilities Education Act (IDEA)

In 1973, Congress enacted the *Education for All Handicapped Children Act of 1975*. The purpose of this Education law was to increase the educational opportunity available to school-aged students with disabilities by providing a free appropriate public education in the least restrictive environment emphasizing special education and related services designed to meet their unique needs (20 U.S.C. 1400 (c)). In 1990, the *Education for All Handicapped Children Act* was amended and renamed the **Individuals with Disabilities Education Act (IDEA)**. In 2004, the IDEA was reauthorized as the **Individuals with Disabilities Education Improvement Act (IDEIA)**. The major changes emphasize key requirements in the special education process, increased monitoring of student progress and the use of accommodations outlined in the Individual Education Plan (IEP). Although there was a title change at the time of reauthorization, the current law often continues to be referred to as IDEA. The IDEIA applies to students with diagnosed disabilities from birth to graduation, or a maximum age of 21.

To satisfy the goal of the IDEIA, local educational agencies, together with the student's teachers and parents or guardians, are required to develop a written statement or IEP, outlining achievable educational goals and objectives, reasonable accommodations and related services. Although less specific with regard to athletics than those pursuant to § 504 of the Rehabilitation Act, the regulations adopted under the IDEIA do require each public agency to ensure that a variety of educational programs and services, including physical education, available to students without disabilities are available to those covered under the act. Besides providing educational programs and services, each public agency is also required to provide nonacademic and extracurricular activities and services in such manner as is necessary to afford children with disabilities an equal opportunity for participation in those services and activities (34 C.F.R. § 300.306(a)). For example, in *Lambert v. West Virginia State Board of Education* (1994), a high school basketball player, who has been deaf since birth, won the right to require her school to provide her with a sign language interpreter so that she could compete on the girls' basketball team. In holding that the Board of Education was required to provide a sign language interpreter for the plaintiff, the court found that the assistance of an interpreter was a reasonable accommodation that provided the plaintiff with equal access to extracurricular activities.

Another example of a student–athlete successfully using the IDEIA to gain participation rights is *Crocker v. Tennessee Secondary School Athletic Association* (1992). In *Crocker* the plaintiff transferred from a private school into his local public high school so that he could receive the special education he needed, which was not available in the private school. When the plaintiff attempted to participate in interscholastic athletics at his new school, the TSSAA ruled that he was ineligible. According to TSSAA rules, any student who transfers from one TSSAA member school to another is ineligible to participate in interscholastic sports for 12 months. The plaintiff argued that the TSSAA, by enforcing its transfer rule, was depriving him of his rights guaranteed under the IDEIA. In ruling for Crocker, the Court held that because the plaintiff's transfer was motivated by his disability and not athletics, TSSAA's refusal to waive its transfer rule violated the IDEIA.

Another important issue under IDEIA is whether the student's participation in interscholastic athletics is a related service that should have been incorporated into his or her IEP. The importance of including participation in interscholastic athletics in a student's IEP can be seen in *T.H. v. Montana High School Association* (1992). In *T.H. v. MHSA*, the plaintiff, after being diagnosed as having a learning disability, was provided with an IEP in accordance with the IDEIA. One component of the student's plan was for the student to participate in interscholastic athletics as a motivational tool. Before his senior year, the Montana High School Association ruled T.H. ineligible to compete in interscholastic athletics due to his age. The court, in finding for the plaintiff, held that when participation in interscholastic sports is included as a component of the IEP, the privilege of competing in interscholastic sports is transformed into a federally protected right and entitles the student to a due process hearing. Conversely, when a student's IEP does not include interscholastic athletic participation, the student has no protect right under the IDEIA (*J.M. v. Montana High School Association*, 1996).

Ted Stevens Olympic and Amateur Sports Act

Another piece of legislation impacting the rights of individuals with disabilities is the **Ted Stevens Olympic and Amateur Sports Act**. Originally passed in 1978 and called the Amateur Sports Act (36 U.S.C. §371), the law grants the United States Olympic Committee (USOC) exclusive jurisdiction over amateur athletics in the

United States, including all matters pertaining to United States participation in the Olympic Games, the Paralympic Games, and the Pan-American Games.

In particular, the Amateur Sports Act required the USOC to "encourage and provide assistance to amateur athletic programs and competition for handicapped individuals, including, where feasible, the expansion of opportunities for meaningful participation by handicapped individuals in programs of athletic competition for able-bodied individuals" (36 U.S.C. § 374 (13)). The USOC attempted to accomplish this goal by establishing the Committee on Sport for the Disabled and by financially supporting various other sports organizations, such as Disabled Sports USA and the Wheelchair Sports USA.

In 1998, the Amateur Sports Act was amended and renamed Ted Stevens Olympic and Amateur Sports Act, after the law's sponsor, Senator Ted Stevens of Alaska. The Ted Stevens Olympic and Amateur Sports Act places a greater responsibility on the USOC and its constituent organizations to serve elite athletes with a disability, in particular Paralympic athletes. As a result of the 1998 amendments, the USOC has sought to expand the opportunities available to athletes with disabilities by establishing a Paralympic Division within the USOC, providing increased funding and logistical support for athletes and sporting bodies, recognizing Paralympic athletes as members of the USOC Athletes Advisory Committee and providing other avenues for input from Paralympic athletes.

Not everyone, however, has been satisfied with the funding and support the USOC provides to Paralympic athletes. For example, in *Hollonbeck v. USOC*, (2008) the Tenth Circuit Court of Appeals rejected a lawsuit filed by Scot Hollonbeck, a wheelchair racer who had won multiple medals at three Paralympics, who challenged the USOC's policy of providing Athlete Support Programs only to Olympic team members, to the exclusion of Paralympic team members. In finding that the USOC's policy of excluding Paralympic athletes from Athlete Support Programs was not discriminatory, the court noted that the eligibility requirements that the USOC used to distribute the benefits under its Resource Allocation Policy was that the athlete must be "eligible to represent the United States and . . . intend to compete, if selected, in the next Olympic or Pan American Games." On its face, the court held that such a policy does not contain an explicit requirement of not being disabled. Thus, the court held, the requirement to be an Olympic athlete to be eligible for the Athlete Support Programs is not discriminatory to Paralympic athletes.

The Americans with Disabilities Act (ADA)

The Americans with Disabilities Act (ADA) was signed into law July 26, 1990, extending many of the provisions of Section 504 of Rehabilitation Act to the private sector. The purpose of this civil rights statute is "to provide a clear and comprehensive national mandate for the elimination of discrimination against individuals with disabilities." The ADA focuses on eradicating barriers by requiring entities to consider whether reasonable accommodations could be made to remove any barrier created by a person's disability (Wolohan, 1997a). The ADA defines a "qualified individual with a disability" as any individual with a disability, either physically or mentally, "who, with or without reasonable modifications to rules, policies, or practices, the removal of architectural, communication . . . barriers, or the provision or auxiliary aids and services, meets the essential eligibility requirements for the receipt of services or the participation in programs or activities provided by a public entity" (42 U.S.C. 12115). The ADA is divided into five sections covering the areas of: employment, public services, public services operated by private entities, transportation, and telecommunications. The three sections of which sport and recreational professionals should be aware of are *Title I*, which covers employment; *Title II*, which covers public services; and *Title III*, which covers public accommodations and services operated by private entities.

In 2008, the ADA was reauthorized as the ADA Amendments Act (ADAAA). The major purpose of the ADAAA was to legislatively overturn a series of court decisions that interpreted the ADA in a way that made it difficult to prove that an impairment is a disability. For example, in the original law, a person with a disability was one who had an impairment that "substantially limits" his/her participation in a major life activity. The ADAAA revises the language to describe a person with a disability as one who has an impairment that "significantly restricts" participation, thus broadening the scope of coverage under both the ADA and Section 503 of the Rehabilitation Act and opening the door to a wider range of people with disabling conditions.

Even if an individual is able to meet all the requirements of the ADA, the law still does not require an organization to accommodate a person "*when that individual poses a direct threat to the health or safety of others*" (28 C.F.R. § 36.208). For example, in *Anderson v. Little League Baseball, Inc.* (1992), a youth baseball coach, who was a wheelchair user and had coached Little League Baseball for the previous three years as an on-field coach, sued the league after it adopted a policy prohibiting coaches in wheelchairs from on-field coaching. In support of the policy, the league claimed that the coach posed a direct threat to the health or safety of the athletes and that the policy was intended to protect the players from collisions with the wheelchair. In ruling for the coach, the Court said that the league's policy fell markedly short of the requirements of the ADA. The court found no evidence indicating that the plaintiff posed a direct threat to the health or safety of others.

Another area of concern for sport and recreation administrators around the country, especially after the United States Supreme Court's ruling in *PGA v. Martin* (2001), was what rules are essential to the nature of sport. For example, in *Kuketz v. Petronelli*, (2005), Stephen Kuketz, a nationally ranked wheelchair racquetball player, wanted to join the Brockton Athletic Club men's "A" league so that he could compete against the best able-bodied players available to help prepare for upcoming international wheelchair competitions. Because of his physical limitations, however, Kuketz requested that the club allow him the wheelchair-racquetball-standard two bounces during "A" league play, instead of the one bounce allowable under standard racquetball rules.

Citing safety reasons, the club rejected Kuketz's request (Wolohan, 2005). Disappointed with the decision, Kuketz sued the club claiming the decision violated both federal and state antidiscrimination laws. In evaluating whether the club unlawfully discriminated against Kuketz when it refused to modify its policies and practices, the Supreme Judicial Court of Massachusetts held that the allowance for more than one bounce in racquetball was inconsistent with the fundamental character of the game. As expressly articulated in the rules of racquetball, the court found that the essence of the game of racquetball is the hitting of a moving ball with a racquet before the second bounce. Giving a player in a wheelchair two bounces and a player on foot one bounce in head-to-head competition would alter such an essential aspect of the game that it would be unacceptable, even if it affected all competitors equally. In addition, the court found that unlike golf, the speed at which racquetball is played is important and is one of the factors distinguishing players in different levels. Therefore, if one player were allowed to play the game with two bounces, it would require a change in the strategy, positioning, and movement of the players during the game and would essentially create a new game, with new strategies and new rules.

Title I—Employment

Title I provides that "no covered entity shall discriminate against a qualified individual with a disability because of the disability of such individual in regard to job application procedures, the hiring, advancement, or discharge of employees, employee compensation, job training, and other terms, conditions, and privileges of employment" (42 U.S.C. § 12112). For more information on Title I of the ADA, see Chapter 7.16, *Title I of the Americans with Disabilities Act.*

Title II—Public Services

The section that covers the activities of public entities, such as high school athletic associations, is Title II—Public Services. Title II, which is based on Section 504 of the Rehabilitation Act, provides that "no qualified individual with a disability shall, by reason of such disability, be excluded from participation in or be denied the benefits of the services, programs, or activities of a public entity, or be subjected to discrimination by any such entity" (42 U.S.C. § 12132). In the case of athletic associations, the courts have determined that athletic associations are given oversight authority by public schools of their athletic programs, participation rules, and competition rules, thus giving them a major role in the public service provided. Given this authority, the athletic association often falls within the provision of both Title II of the ADA and Section 504 of the Rehabilitation Act.

In interpreting the meaning of Title II, the Courts used the case history of Section 504 of the Rehabilitation Act. To establish a violation of Title II of the ADA, therefore, an individual must establish the following elements:

1. that he or she is a "qualified individual with a disability";
2. that he or she is "otherwise qualified" for the activity;
3. that he or she is being excluded from athletic participation "solely by reason of" their disabilities; and
4. that he or she is being discriminated against by a public entity.

Once again, it is important to note that as of 2008, the ADAAA has broadened the definition of who is a "qualified individual with a disability" under both the ADA and Section 503 of the Rehabilitation Act and opening the door to a wider range of people with disabling conditions.

Title III—Public Accommodations and Services Operated by Private Entities

The provisions of Title III provide that "no individual shall be discriminated against on the basis of disability in the full and equal enjoyment of the goods, services, facilities, privileges, advantages, or accommodations of any place of public accommodation by any person who owns, leases, or operates a place of public accommodation" (42 U.S.C. § 12182). Places of public accommodation include stadiums, golf courses, gymnasiums, recreational facilities and other places of public gathering. In addition, policies, practices, and procedures of these facilities must ensure equal opportunity for people with disabilities. For example, if a commercial sport facility uses a turnstile for spectators to gain entry, they must be an accessible option to the turnstile for a wheelchair user.

Overall, the ADA and Section 504 are civil rights laws that provide protection from discrimination based on disability. For example, in a consent decree issued in 1998, it was determined that Title III of the ADA applies to the National Collegiate Athletic Association (NCAA), as an organization with some public colleges and universities as members. Consequently, the NCAA has a duty to accommodate student athletes with disabilities and must have a process in place to consider modifications to its policies and procedures on a case-by-case basis.

SIGNIFICANT CASE

The following case raises two interesting questions concerning the application of the Americans with Disabilities Act: first, whether the Act protects access to professional golf tournaments by a qualified entrant with a disability; and second, whether a disabled contestant may be denied the use of a golf cart because it would "fundamentally alter the nature" of the tournaments to allow him to ride when all other contestants must walk.

PGA TOUR V. CASEY MARTIN
United States Supreme Court
532 U.S. 661 (2001)

This case raises two questions concerning the application of the Americans with Disabilities Act . . . to a gifted athlete: first, whether the Act protects access to professional golf tournaments by a qualified entrant with a disability; and second, whether a disabled contestant may be denied the use of a golf cart because it would "fundamentally alter the nature" of the tournament, to allow him to ride when all other contestants must walk.

I.

Petitioner PGA TOUR, Inc., a nonprofit entity formed in 1968, sponsors and cosponsors professional golf tournaments conducted on three annual tours. About 200 golfers participate in the PGA TOUR; about 170 in the NIKE TOUR; and about 100 in the SENIOR PGA TOUR. PGA TOUR and NIKE TOUR tournaments typically are 4-day events, played on courses leased and operated by petitioner. The entire field usually competes in two 18-hole rounds played on Thursday and Friday; those who survive the "cut" play on Saturday and Sunday and receive prize money in amounts determined by their aggregate scores for all four rounds. The revenues generated by television, admissions, concessions, and contributions from cosponsors amount to about $ 300 million a year, much of which is distributed in prize money.

There are various ways of gaining entry into particular tours. For example, a player who wins three NIKE TOUR events in the same year, or is among the top-15 money winners on that tour, earns the right to play in the PGA TOUR. Additionally, a golfer may obtain a spot in an official tournament through successfully competing in "open" qualifying rounds, which are conducted the week before each tournament. Most participants, however, earn playing privileges in the PGA TOUR or NIKE TOUR by way of a three-stage qualifying tournament known as the "Q-School."

Any member of the public may enter the Q-School by paying a $ 3,000 entry fee and submitting two letters of reference from, among others, PGA TOUR or NIKE TOUR members. The $ 3,000 entry fee covers the players' greens fees and the cost of golf carts, which are permitted during the first two stages, but which have been prohibited during the third stage since 1997. Each year, over a thousand contestants compete in the first stage, which consists of four 18-hole rounds at different locations. Approximately half of them make it to the second stage, which also includes 72 holes. Around 168 players survive the second stage and advance to the final one, where they compete over 108 holes. Of those finalists, about a fourth qualify for membership in the PGA TOUR, and the rest gain membership in the NIKE TOUR.

Three sets of rules govern competition in tour events. First, the "Rules of Golf," jointly written by the United States Golf Association (USGA) and the Royal and Ancient Golf Club of Scotland, apply to the game as it is played, not only by millions of amateurs on public courses and in private country clubs throughout the United States and worldwide, but also by the professionals in the tournaments conducted by petitioner, the USGA, the Ladies' Professional Golf Association, and the Senior Women's Golf Association. Those rules do not prohibit the use of golf carts at any time.

Second, the "Conditions of Competition and Local Rules," often described as the "hard card," apply specifically to petitioner's professional tours. The hard cards for the PGA TOUR and NIKE TOUR require players to walk the golf course during tournaments, but not during open qualifying rounds. On the SENIOR PGA TOUR, which is limited to golfers age 50 and older, the contestants may use golf carts. Most seniors, however, prefer to walk.

Third, "Notices to Competitors" are issued for particular tournaments and cover conditions for that specific event. Such a notice may, for example, explain how the Rules of Golf should be applied to a particular water hazard or man-made obstruction. It might also authorize the use of carts to speed up play when there is an unusual distance between one green and the next tee.

The basic Rules of Golf, the hard cards, and the weekly notices apply equally to all players in tour competitions. As one of petitioner's witnesses explained with reference to "the Masters Tournament, which is golf at its very highest level . . . the key is to have everyone tee off on the first hole under exactly the same conditions and all of them be tested over that 72-hole event under the conditions that exist during those four days of the event."

II.

Casey Martin is a talented golfer. As an amateur, he won 17 Oregon Golf Association junior events before he was 15, and won the state championship as a high school senior. He played on the Stanford University golf team that won the 1994 National Collegiate Athletic Association (NCAA) championship. As a professional, Martin qualified for the NIKE TOUR in 1998 and 1999, and based on his 1999 performance, qualified for the PGA TOUR in 2000. In the 1999 season, he entered 24 events, made the cut 13 times, and had 6 top-10 finishes, coming in second twice and third once.

Martin is also an individual with a disability as defined in the Americans with Disabilities Act. Since birth he has been afflicted with Klippel-Trenaunay-Weber Syndrome, a degenerative circulatory disorder that obstructs the flow of blood from his right leg back to his heart. The disease is progressive; it causes severe pain and has atrophied his right leg. During the latter part of his college career, because of the progress of the disease, Martin could no longer walk an 18-hole golf course. Walking not only caused him pain, fatigue, and anxiety, but also created a significant risk of hemorrhaging, developing blood clots, and fracturing his tibia so badly that an amputation might be required. For these reasons, Stanford made written requests to the Pacific 10 Conference and the NCAA to waive for Martin their rules requiring players to walk and carry their own clubs. The requests were granted.

When Martin turned pro and entered petitioner's Q-School, the hard card permitted him to use a cart during his successful progress through the first two stages. He made a request, supported by detailed medical records, for permission to use a golf cart during the third stage. Petitioner refused to review those records or to waive its walking rule for the third stage. Martin therefore filed this action. A preliminary injunction entered by the District Court made it possible for him to use a cart in the final stage of the Q-School and as a competitor in the NIKE TOUR and PGA TOUR. Although not bound by the injunction, and despite its support for petitioner's position in this litigation, the USGA voluntarily granted Martin a similar waiver in events that it sponsors, including the U.S. Open.

Congress enacted the ADA in 1990 to remedy widespread discrimination against disabled individuals. In studying the need for such legislation, Congress found that "historically, society has tended to isolate and segregate individuals with disabilities, and, despite some improvements, such forms of discrimination against individuals with disabilities continue to be a serious and pervasive social problem." . . .

To effectuate its sweeping purpose, the ADA forbids discrimination against disabled individuals in major areas of public life, among them employment (Title I of the Act), public services (Title II), and public accommodations (Title III). At issue now, as a threshold matter, is the applicability of Title III to petitioner's golf tours and qualifying rounds, in particular to petitioner's treatment of a qualified disabled golfer wishing to compete in those events.

Title III of the ADA prescribes, as a "general rule": "No individual shall be discriminated against on the basis of disability in the full and equal enjoyment of the goods, services, facilities, privileges, advantages, or accommodations of any place of public accommodation by any person who owns, leases (or leases to), or operates a place of public accommodation." 42 U.S.C. § 12182(a).

The phrase "public accommodation" is defined in terms of 12 extensive categories, which the legislative history indicates "should be construed liberally" to afford people with disabilities "equal access" to the wide variety of establishments available to the nondisabled.

It seems apparent, from both the general rule and the comprehensive definition of "public accommodation," that petitioner's golf tours and their qualifying rounds fit comfortably within the coverage of Title III, and Martin within its protection. The events occur on "golf courses," a type of place specifically identified by the Act as a public accommodation. § 12181(7)(L). In addition, at all relevant times, petitioner "leases" and "operates" golf courses to conduct its Q-School and tours. § 12182(a). As a lessor and operator of golf courses, then, petitioner must not discriminate against any "individual" in the "full and equal enjoyment of the goods, services, facilities, privileges, advantages, or accommodations" of those courses. *Ibid.* Certainly, among the "privileges" offered by petitioner on the courses are those of competing in the Q-School and playing in the tours; indeed, the former is a privilege for which thousands of individuals from the general public pay, and the latter is one for which they vie. Martin, of course, is one of those individuals. It would therefore appear that Title III of the ADA, by its plain terms, prohibits petitioner from denying Martin equal access to its tours on the basis of his disability. . . .

Petitioner argues otherwise. To be clear about its position, it does not assert (as it did in the District Court) that it is a private club altogether exempt from Title III's coverage. In fact, petitioner admits that its tournaments are conducted at places of public accommodation. Nor does petitioner contend (as it did in both the District Court and the Court of Appeals) that the competitors' area "behind the ropes" is not a public accommodation,

notwithstanding the status of the rest of the golf course. Rather, petitioner reframes the coverage issue by arguing that the competing golfers are not members of the class protected by Title III of the ADA.

According to petitioner, Title III is concerned with discrimination against "clients and customers" seeking to obtain "goods and services" at places of public accommodation, whereas it is Title I that protects persons who work at such places. As the argument goes, petitioner operates not a "golf course" during its tournaments but a "place of exhibition or entertainment," . . . and a professional golfer such as Martin, like an actor in a theater production, is a provider rather than a consumer of the entertainment that petitioner sells to the public. Martin therefore cannot bring a claim under Title III because he is not one of the "'*clients or customers* of the covered public accommodation.'" Rather, Martin's claim of discrimination is "job-related" and could only be brought under Title I—but that Title does not apply because he is an independent contractor (as the District Court found) rather than an employee.

* * *

We need not decide whether petitioner's construction of the statute is correct, because petitioner's argument falters even on its own terms. If Title III's protected class were limited to "clients or customers," it would be entirely appropriate to classify the golfers who pay petitioner $ 3,000 for the chance to compete in the Q-School and, if successful, in the subsequent tour events, as petitioner's clients or customers. In our view, petitioner's tournaments (whether situated at a "golf course" or at a "place of exhibition or entertainment") simultaneously offer at least two "privileges" to the public—that of watching the golf competition and that of competing in it. Although the latter is more difficult and more expensive to obtain than the former, it is nonetheless a privilege that petitioner makes available to members of the general public. In consideration of the entry fee, any golfer with the requisite letters of recommendation acquires the opportunity to qualify for and compete in petitioner's tours. Additionally, any golfer who succeeds in the open qualifying rounds for a tournament may play in the event. That petitioner identifies one set of clients or customers that it serves (spectators at tournaments) does not preclude it from having another set (players in tournaments) against whom it may not discriminate. It would be inconsistent with the literal text of the statute as well as its expansive purpose to read Title III's coverage, even given petitioner's suggested limitation, any less broadly.

* * *

As we have noted, 42 U.S.C. § 12182(a) sets forth Title III's general rule prohibiting public accommodations from discriminating against individuals because of their disabilities. The question whether petitioner has violated that rule depends on a proper construction of the term "discrimination," which is defined by Title III to include: "a failure to make reasonable modifications in policies, practices, or procedures, when such modifications are necessary to afford such goods, services, facilities, privileges, advantages, or accommodations to individuals with disabilities, *unless the entity can demonstrate that making such modifications would fundamentally alter the nature* of such goods, services, facilities, privileges, advantages, or accommodations." § 12182(b)(2)(A)(ii) (emphasis added).

Petitioner does not contest that a golf cart is a reasonable modification that is necessary if Martin is to play in its tournaments. Martin's claim thus differs from one that might be asserted by players with less serious afflictions that make walking the course uncomfortable or difficult, but not beyond their capacity. In such cases, an accommodation might be reasonable but not necessary. In this case, however, the narrow dispute is whether allowing Martin to use a golf cart, despite the walking requirement that applies to the PGA TOUR, the NIKE TOUR, and the third stage of the Q-School, is a modification that would "fundamentally alter the nature" of those events.

In theory, a modification of petitioner's golf tournaments might constitute a fundamental alteration in two different ways. It might alter such an essential aspect of the game of golf that it would be unacceptable even if it affected all competitors equally; changing the diameter of the hole from three to six inches might be such a modification. Alternatively, a less significant change that has only a peripheral impact on the game itself might nevertheless give a disabled player, in addition to access to the competition as required by Title III, an advantage over others and, for that reason, fundamentally alter the character of the competition. We are not persuaded that a waiver of the walking rule for Martin would work a fundamental alteration in either sense.

As an initial matter, we observe that the use of carts is not itself inconsistent with the fundamental character of the game of golf. From early on, the essence of the game has been shot-making—using clubs to cause a ball to progress from the teeing ground to a hole some distance away with as few strokes as possible. That essential aspect of the game is still reflected in the very first of the Rules of Golf, which declares: "The Game of Golf consists in playing a ball from the *teeing ground* into the hole by a *stroke* or successive strokes in accordance with the rules." . . . Over the years, there have been many changes in the players' equipment, in golf course design, in the Rules of Golf, and in the method of transporting clubs from hole to hole. Originally, so few clubs were used that each player could carry them without a bag. Then came golf bags, caddies, carts that were pulled by hand, and eventually motorized carts that carried players as well as clubs. "Golf carts started appearing with increasing regularity on American golf courses in the 1950's. Today they are everywhere. And they are encouraged. For one thing, they often speed up play, and for another, they are great revenue producers." There is nothing in the Rules of Golf that either forbids the use of carts, or penalizes a player for using a cart. That set of rules, as we have observed, is widely accepted in both the amateur and professional golf world as the rules of the game. The walking rule that is contained in petitioner's hard cards, based on an optional condition buried in an appendix to the Rules of Golf, is not an essential attribute of the game itself.

Indeed, the walking rule is not an indispensable feature of tournament golf either. As already mentioned, petitioner permits golf carts to be used in the SENIOR PGA TOUR, the open qualifying events for petitioner's tournaments, the first two stages of the Q-School, and, until 1997, the third stage of the Q-School as well. Moreover, petitioner allows the use of carts during certain tournament rounds in both the PGA TOUR and the NIKE TOUR. . . .

Petitioner, however, distinguishes the game of golf as it is generally played from the game that it sponsors in the PGA TOUR, NIKE TOUR, and (at least recently) the last stage of the Q-School—golf at the "highest level." According to petitioner, "the goal of the highest-level competitive athletics is to assess and compare the performance of different competitors, a task that is meaningful only if the competitors are subject to identical substantive rules." The waiver of any possibly "outcome-affecting" rule for a contestant would violate this principle and therefore, in petitioner's view, fundamentally alter the nature of the highest level athletic event. The walking rule is one such rule, petitioner submits, because its purpose is "to inject the element of fatigue into the skill of shot-making," and thus its effect may be the critical loss of a stroke. As a consequence, the reasonable modification Martin seeks would fundamentally alter the nature of petitioner's highest level tournaments even if he were the only person in the world who has both the talent to compete in those elite events and a disability sufficiently serious that he cannot do so without using a cart.

The force of petitioner's argument is, first of all, mitigated by the fact that golf is a game in which it is impossible to guarantee that all competitors will play under exactly the same conditions or that an individual's ability will be the sole determinant of the outcome. For example, changes in the weather may produce harder greens and more head winds for the tournament leader than for his closest pursuers. … Whether such happenstance events are more or less probable than the likelihood that a golfer afflicted with Klippel-Trenaunay-Weber Syndrome would one day qualify for the NIKE TOUR and PGA TOUR, they at least demonstrate that pure chance may have a greater impact on the outcome of elite golf tournaments than the fatigue resulting from the enforcement of the walking rule.

Further, the factual basis of petitioner's argument is undermined by the District Court's finding that the fatigue from walking during one of petitioner's 4-day tournaments cannot be deemed significant. The District Court credited the testimony of a professor in physiology and expert on fatigue, who calculated the calories expended in walking a golf course (about five miles) to be approximately 500 calories—"nutritionally . . . less than a Big Mac." 994 F. Supp. at 1250. What is more, that energy is expended over a 5-hour period, during which golfers have numerous intervals for rest and refreshment. In fact, the expert concluded, because golf is a low intensity activity, fatigue from the game is primarily a psychological phenomenon in which stress and motivation are the key ingredients. . . .

Moreover, when given the option of using a cart, the majority of golfers in petitioner's tournaments have chosen to walk, often to relieve stress or for other strategic reasons. . . .

Even if we accept the factual predicate for petitioner's argument—that the walking rule is "outcome affecting" because fatigue may adversely affect performance—its legal position is fatally flawed. Petitioner's refusal to consider Martin's personal circumstances in deciding whether to accommodate his disability runs counter to the clear language and purpose of the ADA. As previously stated, the ADA was enacted to eliminate discrimination against "individuals" with disabilities, and to that end Title III of the Act requires without exception that any "policies, practices, or procedures" of a public accommodation be reasonably modified for disabled "individuals" as necessary to afford access unless doing so would fundamentally alter what is offered, § 12182(b)(2)(A)(ii). To comply with this command, an individualized inquiry must be made to determine whether a specific modification for a particular person's disability would be reasonable under the circumstances as well as necessary for that person, and yet at the same time not work a fundamental alteration. . . .

To be sure, the waiver of an essential rule of competition for anyone would fundamentally alter the nature of petitioner's tournaments. As we have demonstrated, however, the walking rule is at best peripheral to the nature of petitioner's athletic events, and thus it might be waived in individual cases without working a fundamental alteration. Therefore, petitioner's claim that all the substantive rules for its "highest-level" competitions are sacrosanct and cannot be modified under any circumstances is effectively a contention that it is exempt from Title III's reasonable modification requirement. But that provision carves out no exemption for elite athletics, and given Title III's coverage not only of places of "exhibition or entertainment" but also of "golf courses," . . . its application to petitioner's tournaments cannot be said to be unintended or unexpected. . . .

Under the ADA's basic requirement that the need of a disabled person be evaluated on an individual basis, we have no doubt that allowing Martin to use a golf cart would not fundamentally alter the nature of petitioner's tournaments. As we have discussed, the purpose of the walking rule is to subject players to fatigue, which in turn may influence the outcome of tournaments. Even if the rule does serve that purpose, it is an uncontested finding of the District Court that Martin "easily endures greater fatigue even with a cart than his able-bodied competitors do by walking." The purpose of the walking rule is therefore not compromised in the slightest by allowing Martin to use a cart. . . . As a result, Martin's request for a waiver of the walking rule should have been granted.

* * *

The judgment of the Court of Appeals is affirmed.

CASES ON THE SUPPLEMENTAL WEB SITE

Poole v. South Plainfield Board of Education, 490 F. Supp. 948 (D. N.J. 1980). The case examines whether school officials have the right to prevent a student from participating in athletics due to a medical condition.

Sandison v. Michigan High School Athletic Association, 64 F.3d 1026 (6th Cir. 1995). In this case, the court ruled that waiving an eligibility requirement was not a reasonable accommodation required under the ADA for high school athletic associations.

Dennin v. Connecticut Interscholastic Athletic Conference, 913 F. Supp. 663 (1996). In this case, the court ruled that waiving an eligibility requirement was a reasonable accommodation required under the ADA for high school athletic associations.

Hoot v. Milan Area Schools, 853. F. Supp 243 (E.D. Mich. 1994). In this case, the court ordered a trial to determine if the student was "otherwise qualified" to participate in his sport which would require a reasonable accommodation to the schools' minimum-credit requirement.

Miller v. Cal. Speedway Corp. 536 F. 3d 1020 (2008). In this case, the plaintiff, an individual with a physical disability, sued the speedway citing violations of Title III of the ADA, related to violation of lines of site for people with disabilities during NASCAR events.

QUESTIONS YOU SHOULD BE ABLE TO ANSWER

1. Under Section 504 of the Rehabilitation Act, what four elements must be established in order to pursue a claim?

2. What has been an acceptable process for a scholastic athlete with a disability to gain access to athletic participation under the IDEA?

3. What are the three sections of the ADA that have greatest applicability to sport and how does the ADA define an individual with a disability who is "other qualified"?

4. Under which titles of the ADA would interscholastic sports cases related to athletic associations, age participation, academic eligibility policies, and paired-organ decisions apply?

5. What are the major obstacles faced by participants with disabilities in gaining access to intercollegiate and professional sport?

REFERENCES

Cases

Alexander v. Choate, 469 U.S. 287 (1985).
Anderson v. Little League Baseball, 794 F. Supp. 342 (1992).
Crocker v. Tennessee Secondary School Athletic Association, 980 F.2d 382 (6th Cir. 1992).
Dennin v. Connecticut Interscholastic Athletic Conference, 913 F. Supp. 663 (1996).
Hollonbeck v. USOC, 513 F.3d 1191 (10th Cir. 2008)
J.M. v. Montana High School Association. 875 P. 2d. 1026 (D. Mont. 1994)
Johnson v. Florida High School Activities Association Inc., 899 F. Supp. 579 (M.D. Fla. 1995).
Kuketz v. Petronelli, 821 N.E.2d 473 (MA. 2005).
Lambert v. West Virginia State Board of Education, 447 S.E.2d 901 (W.Va. 1994).
PGA Tour v. Casey Martin, 532 U.S. 661 (2001).
Poole v. South Plainfield Board of Education, 490 F. Supp. 948 (D. N.J. 1980).
Pottgen v. Missouri State High School Athletic Association, 40 F.3d 926 (8th Cir. 1994).
Sandison v. Michigan High School Athletic Association, 64 F.3d 1026 (6th Cir. 1995).
Southeastern Community College v. Davis, 422 U.S. 397 (1979).
S.S. v. Whitesboro Central School District, 2012 U.S. Dist. LEXIS 11727
T.H. v. Montana High School Association, CV 92-150-BLG-JFB (1992).
University Interscholastic League and Bailey Marshall v. Buchanan, 848 S.W. 2d. 298 (1993).

Publications

Clement, A. (1988). *Law in sport and physical activity.* Dubuque, IA: Brown & Benchmark.
Wolohan, J. (1997a). An ethical and legal dilemma: Participation in sports by HIV infected athletes. *Marq. Sports L.J., 7,* 345.
Wolohan, J. (1997b). Are age restrictions a necessary requirement for participating in interscholastic athletic programs? *UMKC. L. Rev., 66,* 345.
Wolohan, J. (2003, March). The big dance: Administrators must tread carefully when deciding whether to accommodate individuals with disabilities. *Athletic Business,* pp. 20–24.
Wolohan, J. (2005, June). Bounce check: A club is not required to change its racquetball league rules for a wheelchair athlete. *Athletic Business,* pp. 18–22.

Legislation

The Rehabilitation Act of 1973, 29 U.S.C. § 701 *et seq.*
The Individuals with Disabilities Education Act, 20 U.S.C. § 1400 *et seq.*
The Individuals with Disabilities Education Improvement Act, 20 U.S.C. § 1400 *et seq.*
The Amateur Sports Act, 36 U.S.C. § 371–396.
Ted Stevens Olympic and Amateur Sports Act, 36 U.S.C. § 220501–220529.
The Americans with Disabilities Act, 42 U.S.C. § 12101 *et seq.*
The Americans with Disabilities Amendments Act, 42 U.S.C. §12101–12102.

6.25 PRIVATE CLUBS IN SPORT AND RECREATION

Mark Dodds | Suny Cortland

Anne DeMartini | Flagler College

Historically, many groups and organizations, including sport and recreation organizations, have discriminated in their membership criteria against various groups of people based on race, national origin, religion, gender or sexual orientation. For example, in the early 1990's, the PGA Tour and LPGA were forced to create a policy that required a Tour's host country club to have an open membership policy (Lieber, 2003). The policy was necessary due to the media attention and pressure from sponsors when Shoal Creek (Alabama) Country Club, which was hosting the 1990 PGA Championship, did not allow African American as member. The club eventually changed its' policy just prior to hosting the event because of media and social pressure. Media and social pressure, however, are not always enough to force organizations to open up their membership policies. For example in 2003, Martha Burk from the National Council of Women's Organizations protested Augusta National Country Club's male-only membership policy (Lieber, 2003). Even though the protect generated substantial media attention and calls for change, because The Masters golf tournament is a non-PGA co-sponsored event, Augusta National did not have to comply with the PGA rule and the club retained its' male members only policy.

FUNDAMENTAL CONCEPTS

While the discriminatory membership practices of country clubs like Augusta National have been well documented, they are not the only clubs that have discriminatory policies. The purpose of this section, therefore, is to examine the statutory protections as they relate to private sport and recreation clubs, as well as identify the multi factor test used by the courts to identify if a club is truly private. Some of the areas explored include: Freedom of Association; the Civil Rights Act of 1964; the Americans with Disabilities Act; and state anti-discrimination laws.

Freedom of Association

Private clubs, including country clubs or other exclusive sport clubs, are selective by nature. These clubs decide who may join and who to exclude. In most cases, this discrimination is legal, since citizens of the United States enjoy the freedom to associate with persons of their choice, without government intervention or interference (*Roberts v. United States Jaycees*, 1984). Freedom of association also includes the right *not* to associate with certain people. While "Freedom of Association" is not an enumerated right in the Constitution, it has been judicially recognized as one of the rights represented by the concept of liberty (Osborne, 2006). The United States Supreme Court constitution protects the Freedom of Association under the First and Fourteenth Amendments in two distinct ways: expressive association and intimate association (Jolly-Ryan, 2006).

Expressive Association

The First Amendment states that, "Congress shall make no law respecting an establishment of religion, or prohibiting the free exercise thereof; or abridging the freedom of speech, or of the press; or the right of the people peaceably to assemble, and to petition the Government for a redress of grievances" (United States Constitution, Amendment I). Although the Constitution does not directly state that individuals have the right to freely form their own associations, the Supreme Court has interpreted the First Amendment to allow for this based on the right to freedom of expression (Dees, 2010). As a result, citizens of the United States have the protected right to freely form their own associations "in pursuit of a wide variety of political, social, economic, educational, religious, and cultural ends" (*Roberts v. United States Jaycees*, 1984). The freedom of expressive association is characterized by the size of the group, its purpose, its policies, its selectivity, and congeniality (*Roberts v. United States Jaycees,* 1984). The right of freedom of expressive association is fundamental to our Constitution and receives the highest degree of protection. However, this most fundamental freedom is seldom relevant for private golf or country clubs, since generally the purpose of joining these organizations is for recreation, sport, or social opportunities, rather than for engaging in free speech or expression (Jolly-Ryan, 2006).

Intimate Association
Citizens of the United States also have the freedom of intimate association; the constitutional right to enter into and maintain certain intimate human relationships (*Roberts v. United States Jaycees*, 1984). Intimate association originates from the right to privacy implied in the Due Process Clause of the Fourteenth Amendment and is characterized by its relative smallness, high degree of selectivity and seclusion of others. Intimate association cases have generally been used to describe intimate family matters such as marriage, contraception, abortion, family housing, raising children, and homosexuality (Osborne, 2006). The United States Supreme Court, however, has made it clear that some relationships outside of the family may qualify as intimate associations. According to *Roberts v. United States Jaycee* (1984) any relationship between a small group of people that carries "deep attachments and commitments" and forms because an individual shares "distinctly personal aspects of one's life" is protected by intimate association (*Roberts v. United States Jaycees,* 1984).

Balancing Freedom of Association with Anti-Discrimination
Though citizens hold the constitutional rights of expressive and intimate association, the right to associate for expressive purposes is not absolute (*Roberts v. United States Jaycees*, 1984). The government may interfere with expressive association when there is a compelling state interest. For example, the government has a compelling interest in eradicating discrimination, so preventing discrimination is usually enough of a compelling social objective that it may warrant governmental interference in private affairs. Therefore, in determining whether a club's membership policy is discriminatory the state must balance a club member's fundamental rights of association with another person's fundamental right to be free from unlawful discrimination (Osborne, 2006). The legislatively created private club exemptions within many federal anti-discrimination laws display evidence of the attempt to establish this balance.

Anti-discrimination legislation
If an organization is truly private, it will generally be exempt from most federal and state anti-discrimination laws. To determine if a club is private for employment issues, the Equal Employment Opportunity Commission (EEOC), which is charged with enforcing Title VII of the Civil Rights Act of 1964, has established a set of factors for the courts to use. In addition to the EEOC guidelines for Civil Rights cases, the courts can also use the Americans with Disabilities Act and state anti-discrimination to determine if a club fits within the legal designation of a private club.

Civil Rights Act of 1964
The Civil Rights Act of 1964 (Civil Rights Act) was enacted to protect citizens' constitutional rights and prohibit various forms of discrimination in the areas of public accommodations (Title II) and in employment (Title VII) (Dees, 2010).

Title II. Title II of the Civil Rights Act of 1964 prohibits discrimination in places of public accommodation (42 U.S.C. § 2000a). While the law makes it clear that a **place of public accommodation** includes a "sports arena, stadium or other place of exhibition or entertainment" (42 U.S.C. § 201b(3)), due to the freedom of association guarantees found in the United States Constitution, Title II creates an exemption for private clubs (42 U.S.C. 2000a(e)). When addressing whether a club is truly private under Title II, rather than examining one particular issue, the courts use a "factor analysis" approach (Dees, 2010). The following are the relevant factors examined by the court:

1. The genuine selectivity of the group in the admission of its members;
2. The membership's control over the operations of the establishment;

3. The history of the organization;
4. The use of the facilities by nonmembers;
5. The purpose of the club's existence;
6. Whether the club advertises for members;
7. Whether the club is profit or nonprofit;
8. The formalities observed by the club such as bylaws, meetings, etc. (*U.S. v. Lansdowne Swim Club*, 1989).

Out of the eight factors, no one factor controls the determination of public or private status. The courts however have given particular attention to two factors: (1) the club's selectivity with respect to membership, and (2) the use of the club's facilities by nonmembers (Dees, 2010). To determine selectivity, courts examine the number of members of a club, the cost of joining the club, and if the club advertises for members (Osborne, 2006; Jolly-Ryan, 1997). The more exclusive the club, those with fewer members, higher membership fees, stricter standards, and more member control over the selection procedure, the more likely it is to be considered to be private. For example, in *Thornton v. Shaker Ridge Country Club*, (2007) the court found that a country club that advertised for members and had its facilities available to the public was a place of public accommodation under Title II. In another case, *Anderson v. Pass Christian Isles Golf Club, Inc.*, (1974), the court ruled that a golf course that had an arrangement with local hotels to allow hotel guests use of the course was not a private club, but a place of public accommodation.

A genuinely private club, the courts have held, must demonstrate strict exclusivity in its selection processes (Dees, 2010). For example, *Durham v. Red Lake Fishing & Hunting Club, Inc.*, (1987), the court ruled that a private fishing and hunting club that did not have a selective membership application process and allowed public access to its roads was not a private club under the Title II exemption. Historically, the courts have ruled against finding a club private if the club offers too many services to nonmembers or open areas of the club to the public for commercial purposes. For example, *New York v. Ocean Club*, (1984) the court found that the club was a public accommodation and not a private club because membership was extended to a large indefinite segment of the public without any standards of eligibility and without any requirements that might have indicated exclusivity. Additionally, the court noted that club's tennis courts were offered for use by the general public. Finally, any organization or club that receives public benefits will generally be considered a place of public accommodation. For example, in *United States v. Slidell Youth Football Association*, (1974) a non-profit youth football program was not considered a private club because it received public benefits such as rent-free use of the fields, and operating revenue.

Title VII . Title VII of the Civil Rights Act of 1964 deals with discrimination in an employment setting for governmental agencies, labor unions and employers with 15 or more employees (42 U.S.C. § 2000e-2(a)). This law, therefore, applies to all sport and recreation organizations that employee 15 or more people. However, like Title II of the Civil Rights Act, Title VII makes an exception for "**bona fide private membership club.**" To qualify for the exemption, an organization must show both that it is tax-exempt and that it is a "bona fide private membership club." The EEOC's Compliance Manual (2000), defines a "bona fide private membership club" as an organization that:

1. Is a club in the ordinary sense of the word;
2. Is private; and
3. Has meaningful conditions of limited membership.

A "club" is an association of persons for social and recreational purposes or for the promotion of some common purpose who meet periodically. These clubs usually vote in new members who then earn the privilege of using the club property. In determining whether a club is private, the EEOC considers the extent to which the club limits its facilities and services to club members and their guests, the extent to which and/or the manner in which the facilities are controlled or owned by its membership. The EEOC also considers to what extent and in what manner the club publicly advertises to solicit its members and to promote the use of its facilities or services by the general public. Courts address the question as to whether an organization is private on a case-by-case basis; the presence or absence of any one of these factors while important; is not determinative. Finally, to determine whether the requirement of meaningful conditions of limited membership is met, the EEOC considers both the size of the membership, including the existence of any limitations on its size, and membership eligibility requirements (EEOC, 2000).

It is important to note, however, that since under Title VII the clubs are discriminating in the employment practices, unlike Title II where the clubs discriminate in membership issues, the courts are going to analysis Title VII claims different than a Title II claims. For example, in *EEOC v. Chicago Club*, (1996) the court held that a private club's employment decisions are not constitutionally relevant to the individual members' abilities to define their own identities by choosing with whom they wish to associate. For a more in-depth review of the law, see chapter 7.13 Title VII of the Civil Rights Act of 1964.

Americans with Disabilities Act (ADA)

In 1990, Congress passed the **Americans with Disabilities Act (ADA)** (42 U.S.C. § 12101) and in 2008, the **Americans with Disabilities Act Amendment Act (ADAAA)** (42 U.S.C. §12101), to provide a clear and comprehensive national mandate for the elimination of discrimination against individuals with disabilities (42 U.S.C. § 12101 *et seq.*). Under Title III of the ADA, the owners and operators of places of public accommodation must make reasonable accommodations to individuals with disabilities to participate equally in the goods, services, and accommodations provided by the establishment (Thornton, 2011). Title III of the ADA, however, has an exemption for private clubs and religious organizations which states that:

> The provisions … shall not apply to private clubs or establishments exempted from coverage under title II of the Civil Rights Act of 1964 (42 U.S.C. 2000-a(e)) or to religious organizations or entities controlled by religious organizations, including places of worship (42 U.S.C. § 12187).

Therefore, if an entity is exempt under Title II of the 1964 Civil Rights Act, it is also exempt under Title III of the ADA. Likewise, an entity that would fail the test of a private club under Title II would also fail the test under Title III of the ADA (Dees, 2010). An example of the factor analysis used by the courts to determine if a private organization qualifies for an exemption under Title III of the ADA is *Bommarito v. Grosse Pointe Yacht Club*, (2007). In Bommarito, the court was asked to consider whether a yacht club was private and therefore qualified for the exemption under the ADA. In ruling that the club was private, the court examined the extent that the club's facilities or services were limited to club members and their guests; the extent to which the management of the club controls the club and its access; and how the club advertised publicly for new membership or for its services (*Bommarito v. Grosse Pointe Yacht Club*, 2007). In another case, *Staley v. Nat'l Capital Area Council*, (2011) the court ruled that the Boy Scouts, despite the large size of the organization and how it acquired new members, were also a private club for the purposes of the ADA and not required to provide sign language interpreters for deaf members. The court reached this conclusion based on the organizations' selectivity, history and purpose. Those same factors were also considered in *Nicholls v. Holiday Panay Marina*, (2009), when the court held that even though a marina restricted access to tenants-only, it still did not qualify for the private organization exemption under Title III of the ADA. In ruling that the marina had to comply with the ADA and modify the facility to become wheelchair accessible, the court declared that just because the marina "restricted access does not make an accommodation nonpublic" (*Nicholls v. Holiday Panay Marina*, 2009).

State Anti-Discrimination Statutes

In addition to federal law, a number of states have passed anti-discrimination laws that prohibit discrimination based on gender, sexual orientation, race, color, religion and national origin (Kamp, 1998). Since they are state laws, there is no interstate commerce requirement, thus narrowing the private club exemption. Many discriminated plaintiffs, particularly women, have a better chance of succeeding on a state anti-discrimination lawsuit than bringing a federal civil right action (Kamp, 1998).

As of 2009, twenty-one states and Washington DC have enacted statutes prohibiting discrimination on the basis of sexual orientation in employment and/or access to public accommodations. Further, many of the state anti-discrimination statutes are broader in scope than the federal anti-discrimination laws. For example, in *Apilado v. The North American Gay Amateur Athletic Alliance*, (2011), The North American Gay Amateur Athletic Alliance (NAGAAA) disqualified plaintiffs' softball team from the Gay Softball World Series for violating a rule requiring team rosters to hold a maximum of two heterosexual players. The plaintiffs claimed that the NAGAAA was a public accommodation and unlawfully discriminated against them because of their real or perceived sexual orientation. After determining that the NAGAAA met the definition of public accommodation, the court moved on to evaluate if the First Amendment freedom of association protected NAGAAA's ability to exclude someone from membership.

In ruling in favor of the NAGAAA, the court found NAGAAA to be an expressive association since its mission included helping the community and transmitting the value of sportsmanship. In addition, the court concluded the forced inclusion of heterosexual members would diminish NAGAAA's ability to express its message, the "promotion of an athletic, competitive, sportsmanlike gay identity, with a unique set of values, in response to a particular need" (*Apilado v. NAGAAA*, (2011)). Based on these factors, the court determined the plaintiffs did not prove that the state interest in eliminating NAGAAA's exclusionary policies outweighed NAGAAA's associational rights, reasoning "if state public-accommodation statutes truly prohibited discrimination against all groups and in any form, then freedom of association would be toothless" *Apilado v. NAGAAA*, (2011).

SIGNIFICANT CASE

A truly private club does not have to comply with discrimination laws including Title II and Title VII of the Civil Rights Act of 1964 and Title III of the Americans with Disabilities Act. In order to be considered truly private, courts use a multi-factor test. The following case illustrates how a court evaluates a private club using this test.

UNITED STATES OF AMERICA V. LANSDOWNE SWIM CLUB
United States Court of Appeals for the Third Circuit
894 F. 2d 83 (1990)

This appeal is taken from the judgment of the district court, after a non-jury trial, that the Lansdowne Swim Club (LSC) discriminated against blacks on the basis of race or color in violation of Title II of the Civil Rights Act of 1964, 42 U.S.C. §§ 2000a-2000a-6 (1982). LSC challenges the findings of the district court on three grounds: that it is an exempted private club, that it is not a place of public accommodation, and that the United States failed to prove a pattern or practice of racial discrimination. We will affirm the judgment of the district court.

I. Because the district court opinion thoroughly sets forth the facts, *United States v. Lansdowne Swim Club*, 713 F. Supp. 785 (E.D. Pa. 1989), we shall only summarize them here. LSC, a nonprofit corporation organized under the laws of Pennsylvania, is the only group swimming facility in the Borough of the Lansdowne, Pennsylvania. Since its founding in 1957, LSC has granted 1400 full family memberships. Every white applicant has been admitted, although two as limited members only. In that time, however, LSC has had only one non-white member.

The uncontroverted experiences of the following Lansdowne residents are significant. In 1976, the Allisons wrote to LSC requesting an application but LSC did not respond. Dr. Allison is black; his three children are

part-black. In 1977, the Allisons twice again wrote for an application but LSC did not respond. The following year, the Allisons repeated the procedure with similar results. In 1983, the Allisons filed a timely application and otherwise qualified for membership. Nonetheless, they were rejected. Two of the Ryans' adopted children are black. The Ryans then complained to the media and picketed LSC, joined by the Allisons. In 1986, the Iverys, who are black, filed a timely application and otherwise qualified for membership. Nonetheless, they were rejected (as were the Ryans and Allisons who had again applied). ***

II. LSC's first argument is that it is a private club. Under Title II, "a private club or other establishment not in fact open to the public" is exempt from the statute. 42 USC. § 2000a(e). LSC has the burden of proving it is a private club. *See Anderson v. Pass Christian Isles Golf Club, Inc.*, 488 F.2d 855, 857 (5th Cir. 1974). Although the statute does not define "private club", cases construing the provision do offer some guidance. The district court distilled eight factors from the case law as relevant to this determination. Three of which it found dispositive of LSC's public nature: the genuine selectivity of its membership process, e.g., *Tillman v. Wheaton-Haven Recreation Ass'n.*, 410 U.S. 431 (1973), its history, e.g.,

Cornelius v. BPOE, 382 F. Supp. 1182 (D. Conn. 1974), and use of its facilities by nonmembers, *Id*. Appellant disputes these findings.

First, the court concluded that LSC's membership process was not genuinely selective. Essential to this conclusion was the court's finding that "LSC possesses no objective criteria or standards for admission." The court identified four "criteria" for admission to LSC: being interviewed, completing an application, submitting two letters of recommendation and tendering payment of fees. We agree, and LSC apparently concedes, that these criteria were not genuinely selective. Nonetheless, LSC challenges the court's failure to consider membership approval a criterion for admission. We agree with the district court, however, that a formal procedure requiring nothing more than membership approval is insufficient to show genuine electivity. See Tillman, 410 U.S. at 438–39. In addition, LSC stipulated that the only information given to the members prior to the membership vote is the applicants' names, addresses their children's names and ages, and the recommenders' identities. In such a situation, the court was correct to conclude that LSC "provides no information to voting members that is useful in making an informed decision as to whether the applicant and his or her family would be compatible with existing members." Therefore, even if membership approval were considered a fifth criterion, it would not make the process any more genuinely selective in this case.

The district court also found the yields of the membership process indicative of lack of selectivity. Since 1958, LSC has granted full memberships to at least 1400 families while denying them to only two non-black families. LSC contends that emphasizing the few instances of nonblack applicant rejection "misconstrues the significance of selectivity. The crucial question should be whether the members exercised their right to be selective rather than the statistical results of the exercise of that right." As the Court of Appeals for the Fourth Circuit noted a decade ago, formal membership requirements "have little meaning when in fact the club does not follow a selective membership policy." *Wright v. Salisbury Club, Ltd.*, 632 F.2d 309, 312 (4th Cir. 1980) (citing Tillman, 410 U.S. at 438–39). We find the evidence of lack of selectivity convincing.

Second, the court concluded that "the origins of LSC suggest that it was intended to serve as a 'community pool' for families in the area and not as a private club." We believe there was ample evidence to support this finding. A founder of LSC testified that LSC was created as a community pool for the neighborhood children. LSC's stipulations confirm the public nature of the facility: organizers solicited Lansdowne-area residents, conducted public recruitment meetings an accepted every family that applied for membership before opening.

Third, the court concluded that use of the facility by nonmembers "undercut LSC's claim that it is a private club." Among other reasons, the court cited the following factors. LSC hosts several swim meets and diving

meets each year but does not prohibit the general public form attending. LSC also sponsors two to four pool parties each year, for which members and association may sell an unlimited number of tickets to persons who are not members. In addition, LSC's basketball and volleyball courts, located on its parking lot, are open to the public. Finally, LSC permits the local Boys' Club to use its parking lot for an annual Christmas tree sale that is open to the public. Although LSD contends such use is de minimus, we are persuaded otherwise.

III. LSC also contends that it is not a "place of public accommodation" as defined in Title II. Under the statute, a place of public accommodation has two elements: first, it must be one of the statutorily enumerated categories of establishments that serve the public, 42 U.S.C. § 2000a(b); second, its operations must affect commerce, *Id*.

A. The district court concluded that the whole complex, both the recreational areas and the snack bar, was an establishment which served the public. The court began by identifying LSC as a "place of . . . entertainment", one of the categories of covered establishments. "LSC concedes that its swimming and other recreational areas make it an 'establishment'", but maintains that the snack bar is not a covered establishment. The district court held that "bifurcation has no support in the plain language of the Act of the case law interpreting it." Under the facts in the case, we agree. Nonetheless, the court also found the snack bat to be a "facility principally engaged in selling food for consumption on the premises", another category of covered establishments. LSC stipulated that "food for consumption on the premises of the Club is sold" at the snack bar. We believe these findings were sufficient to render the entire facility a covered establishment which serves the public.

B. The district court also concluded that the "affecting commerce" requirement was met. Initially, the court discussed the recreational areas, which it correctly deemed a place of entertainment under § 2000a(b)(3). Under Title II, the operations of a place of entertainment affect commerce if "it customarily presents . . . sources of entertainment which move in commerce". *Id*. § 2000a(c)(3). The court found the slicing board, manufactured in Tesac, and guests from out of state to be sources of entertainment which moved in commerce. See *Scott v. Young*, 421 F.2d 143, 144–45 (4th Cir.) (both recreational apparatus originating out of state and patrons from out of state who entertain other patrons by their activity constitute "sources of entertainment which move in commerce") (relying on *Daniel v. Paul*, 395 U.S. 298, 307–08, 23 L. Ed. 2d 318, 89 S. Ct. 1697 (1969)), *cert. Denied*, 398 U.S. 929, 90 S. Ct. 1820, 26 L. Ed. 2d 91 (1970). Implicitly conceding this, LSC argues that they do not satisfy "the requisite degree of interstate involvement." Nonetheless, the court found both to be "customarily presented:, the sliding board because it is permanently installed, and the out of state guests because the attend regularly and constitute a significant percentage of the guests (13%

in 1986, 8% in 1987). We believe these findings, and the court's consequent finding that operation of the recreational areas affects commerce, are supported by the evidence.

The court then considered the snack bar, which it correctly deemed a facility principally engaged in selling food for consumption on the premises under § 2000a(b)(2). Under Title II, the operations of this category covered establishments affect commerce if "it serves or offers to serves interstate travelers or a substantial portion of the food which it serves . . . has moved in commerce". Id. § 2000a(c)(2). The court found the "affecting commerce" requirement satisfied in three ways. First, it was stipulated that the snack bar serves interstate travelers. Although LSC contends that the statute is meant to cover tourists lured from other states by advertising, the plain language of the statute provides no support for this view. Second, the court found that the snack bar offers to serve all users of the facility, including guests. Third, the court found that a substantial portion of the food served by the snack bar has moved in interstate commerce. The parties stipulated that the syrup in the "Coca-Cola" beverages was produced in Maryland. The court found that many of the purchases at the snack bar were for cold drinks, of which "Coca-Cola" beverages were the most popular. Nonetheless, appellant claims the substantiality test has not been met, citing Daniel v. Paul, 395 U.S. 298, 23 L. Ed. 2d 318, 89 S. Ct. 1697 (1969), in which the Supreme Court found the test met when three of the four foods sold had moved in interstate commerce. Id. at 305. In light of the broad remedial purpose of Title II, we refuse to read the requirement or Daniel so narrowly. These findings are not clearly erroneous.

* * *

CASES ON THE SUPPLEMENTAL WEB SITE

Apilado v. North American Gay Amateur Athletic Alliance, 792 F. Supp. 2d 1151 (W.D. Wash. 2011). This case examines the application of state law to sexual orientation discrimination.

Thornton v. Shaker Ridge Country Club, Inc., 2007 U.S. Dist. LEXIS 94082 (N.D.N.Y. 2007). This case specifically evaluates if a country club is a private club.

EEOC v. Chicago Club, 86 F.3d 1423 (7th Cir. 1996). This case considers a private club and Title VII implications.

Staley v. Nat'l Capital Area Council, Case No. RWT 10cv2768, 2011 U.S. Dist. LEXIS 61986 (D. Md. 2011). This case analyzes the Boy Scouts' selectivity, history and purpose to establish if they are a private club.

United States. v. Slidell Youth Football Ass'n, 387 F. Supp. 474 (E. D. La. 1974). A non-profit football organization was deemed a place of public accommodation and had to face a racial discrimination claim.

QUESTIONS YOU SHOULD BE ABLE TO ANSWER

1. Explain the factors courts examine to determine if a sport and recreational club is truly "private."

2. Research a local club and analyze it to see if it could be considered truly "private"

3. How can public pressure change a discriminatory club's membership policy?

4. Identify the most effective way to eliminate discrimination in private sport and recreation clubs. Justify your answer.

5. If you were to establish your own sport club, would you establish it as a public or private organization?

REFERENCES

Cases
Anderson v. Pass Christian Isles Golf Club, Inc., 488 F.2d 855, 857 (5th Cir. 1974).
Apilado v. The North American Gay Amateur Athletic Alliance, 792 F. Supp. 2d 1151 (W.D. Wash, May 27, 2011).
Bommarito v. Grosse Pointe Yacht Club, 2007 U.S. Dist. LEXIS 21064 (E.D. Mich. 2007).
Cornelius v. BPOE, 382 F. Supp. 1182 (D. Conn. 1974).
Daniel v. Paul, 395 U.S. 298 (1969).

Durham v. Red Lake Fishing & Hunting Club, Inc., 666 F. Supp. 954 (W.D. Tex. 1987).

EEOC v. Chicago Club, 86 F.3d 1423 (7ᵗʰ Cir. 1996).

New York v. Ocean Club, 602 F. Supp. 489 (E.D. N.Y. 1984).

Nicholls v. Holiday Panay Marina, 173 Cal. App. 4th 966, 93 Cal. Rptr. 3d 309 (Cal. App. 2d Dist. 2009).

Roberts v. United States Jaycees, 468 U.S. 609 (1984).

Staley v. Nat'l Capital Area Council, Case No. RWT 10cv2768, 2011 U.S. Dist. LEXIS 61986 (D. Md. 2011).

Thornton v. Shaker Ridge Country Club, Inc. 2007 U.S. Dist. LEXIS 94082 (N.D.N.Y. 2007).

United States v. Lansdowne Swim Club, 894 F.2d 83, 1990 U.S. App. LEXIS 790 (3d Cir. Pa. 1990).

United States. v. Slidell Youth Football Ass'n, 387 F. Supp. 474 (E. D. La. 1974)

Wright v. The Cork Club, 315 F. Supp. 1143 (S.D. Tex. 1970).

Publications

Dees, W. (2010). *Private Clubs in Sport and Recreation.* In D. J. Cotton & J. T. Wolohan (Eds.), Law for Recreation and Sport Managers (5th Ed.) pp. 528–536. Dubuque, IA: Kendall/Hunt Publishing Co.

Jolly-Ryan, J. (1997). Chipping away at discrimination at the country club, *Pepperdine Law Review,* 25, 495–527.

Jolly-Ryan, J. (2006). Teed off about private club discrimination on the taxpayer's dine: Tax exemptions and other government privileges to discriminatory private clubs, *William and Mary Journal of Women and the Law,* 13, 235–272.

Kamp, N. (1998). Gender Discrimination at Private Golf Clubs, *Sports Lawyers Journal,* 5, 94.

Lieber, J. (2003). *Golf's host clubs have open-and-shut policies on discrimination,* Retrieved from http://www.usatoday.com/ sports/golf/2003-04-09-club-policies_x.htm

Osborne, B. (2006). Gender, employment, and sexual harassment issues in the golf industry. *Journal of Legal Aspects of Sport, 16,* 25–84.

Thornton, P. (2011), Sᴘᴏʀᴛꜱ Lᴀᴡ, Jones and Bartlett, Sudbury, MA p. 405.

U.S. Equal Employment Opportunity Commission. (2000). *EEOC Compliance Manual Section 2: Threshold Issues #2IIIB4aii.* Retrieved from http://www.eeoc.gov/policy/docs/threshold.html#2-III-B-4-a-ii

Legislation

United States Constitution Amendment I.

United States Constitution Amendment XIV.

Civil Rights Act of 1964, 42 U.S.C. § 2000a (2000).

Civil Rights Act of 1964, 42 U.S.C. § 2000e (2000).

Civil Rights Act of 1964, 42 USC § 12101

ADA Amendments Act of 2008 (P.L. 110-325), 42 U.S.C. §12101–12102.

The Americans with Disabilities Act, 42 U.S.C. § 12101 *et seq.*

SPORT AND LEGISLATION

7.00

n addition to the federal Constitution, Congress has also enacted a number of laws that affect the sport and recreation industry. The *Sport and Legislation* section examines those laws and the impact they have on the industry. The section is divided into four parts. The first part reviews federal laws as they apply to discrimination in the sport and recreation industry. The section examines such areas as gender equity and race, age, sex, and disability discrimination. The second part examines intellectual property law. In particular, the sections review how important rights of publicity, rights of privacy, copyright, trademark, and patent law are to the sport and recreation industries. The third part examines federal antitrust and labor laws and how they are applied to professional and amateur sports. The final part of the *Sport and Legislation* section examines sport agent legislation. In particular, the section reviews sport agent legislation and the impact of the Uniform Athlete Agent Act of sport agents.

7.10

FEDERAL STATUTES AND DISCRIMINATION

7.11   GENDER EQUITY: OPPORTUNITIES TO PARTICIPATE

Linda Jean Carpenter, Emerita | Brooklyn College

Sport is the laboratory experience through which students may gain skills such as decision-making, risk evaluation, teamwork, leadership, self-appraisal, and personal esteem. These skills are the same skills that allow graduates to successfully use their other academic skills in their adult lives and employment circumstances. As a result, sport's place on campus in the form of intramurals, recreation, athletics, and physical education is defensible, not because of any possible revenue generation or because of fan support, but because of the valuable skills it provides, which are not easily obtained elsewhere in the educational setting. The skills obtained through sport have value to both female and male participants. The legal imperatives for equity found in the Fourteenth Amendment of the United States Constitution and Title IX of the Education Amendments of 1972 (and a variety of similarly worded state legislation) are the two most frequently used tools to judicially increase gender equitable participation in sport. Between the Fourteenth Amendment and Title IX, most circumstances within education are covered. The Fourteenth Amendment requires a state actor; Title IX does not. Title IX requires the presence of federal financial assistance; the Fourteenth Amendment does not. Both cover gender discrimination. Both cover employees and students.

FUNDAMENTAL CONCEPTS

Constitutional Issues

The Equal Protection Clause of the Fourteenth Amendment is the generic protector of equal rights. It guarantees that no **state actor** such as a federal, state, or local governmental agency, or, for example, public school and recreation program, can gratuitously classify people and treat them differently based on those classifications without having a defensible reason.

Levels of Scrutiny

Strict/High: Necessary to Accomplish a Compelling State Interest. The defensible reason required for a state actor to constitutionally treat people differently varies depending on the classification scheme employed. If, for example, a public school (*state actor*) classified its students by race and then treated its African-American students differently, the reason used to defend the constitutionality of such an action would have to withstand the Court's highest level of scrutiny. The school would need to show that its racially based discrimination was *necessary to accomplish a compelling state interest*. It is difficult to imagine a reason for racial discrimination that would meet such a test.

   Mild/Low: Rationally Related to a Legitimate State Interest. As an alternative example, consider the scenario where a public school's (*state actor*) physical education program classified its students by skill level and, as a result, restricted its beginning-level students to a beginning-level course while allowing the more highly skilled students to have access to a variety of advanced electives. The Court would use a lower level of scrutiny to determine if discrimination based on skill level was constitutional. The school would only have to show that its discrimination was *rationally related to a legitimate state interest*. Protecting beginners from the injuries likely to occur if they participated with highly skilled athletes or performed advanced movements for which they were either untrained or unconditioned would appear to be rationally related to the legitimate state interest of protecting the health and safety of the community's schoolchildren.

Intermediate/Midlevel: An Evolving Middle Ground. Most classification schemes are reviewed by the courts using either the strict/high or mild/low levels of scrutiny. Typically only those classifications based on race, alienage, or national origin face strict/high scrutiny. Almost all other classification schemes face only the mild/low level. In the last few decades, however, we have seen the judicial review of classification schemes based on age, gender, and disability elevated from the mild/low level of scrutiny to a reasonably amorphous midlevel of scrutiny.

In its June 1996 decision involving coeducation at Virginia Military Institute (116 S.Ct. 2264) (see the Supplemental Web Site) the Supreme Court elevated the scrutiny applied to *gender* discrimination even higher within this middle ground to a level requiring an exceedingly persuasive justification. Thus if a state actor discriminates on the basis of gender, it will need to show that doing so was considerably more than rationally related to a legitimate state interest, but it will not need to show that it was necessary to accomplish a compelling state interest.

Cases involving gender discrimination in sport and recreation have used the Fourteenth Amendment, but the more prevalently used tool is Title IX. For this reason, and because of the presence of a fuller discussion of constitutional issues elsewhere in this text, the remaining portion of this section dealing with participation issues will focus on Title IX. However, before proceeding to a deeper discussion of Title IX, a brief mention of an issue involving the interrelationship of the Constitution's Fourteenth Amendment and Title IX is appropriate. May the victim of discrimination (in this particularcase, discrimination was in the form of sexual harassment) sue using both Title IX and the Fourteenth Amendment? The Supreme Court answered that question in *Fitzgerald v. Barnstable School Comm.* (see Supplemental Web Site) in the affirmative, when it held that the plaintiff does not have to lose constitutional rights at the school-house door or playground gate. Neither did Congress intend for Title IX to be the solitary mechanism for combating gender-based discrimination in school settings.

Title IX

A Brief History

Title IX was enacted by Congress on June 23, 1972, to prohibit gender discrimination in the nation's education programs. Three basic elements must all exist for Title IX's jurisdiction to be triggered. The elements are:

1. **Gender Discrimination.** Title IX does not protect against discrimination based on race or age; it protects solely against gender discrimination;
2. **Federal Funding.** The receipt of federal funding is required so that the enforcement of Title IX has administrative teeth. If an institution is found to be violating Title IX, its federal funding may be terminated. However, it should be noted, no federal money has ever been removed from a campus due to a Title IX violation;
3. **Education Program.** The definition of this element brought early controversy to the implementation of Title IX. The U.S. Supreme Court's 1984 *Grove City v. Bell* decision resulted in the word *program* being defined as a "subunit" of an institution. As a result of *Grove City*, any subunit that did not receive federal funding would not be obligated to refrain from gender discrimination. Thus college-level athletics and physical education programs, which typically receive no federal funding, were no longer obligated by Title IX to refrain from gender discrimination. In 1988, however, Congress passed the Civil Rights Restoration Act of 1987 over presidential veto saying, in effect, that the Court had misunderstood Congress' intent to have Title IX apply on an institution-wide basis. So, as of 1988, Title IX once again applies to college-level athletics and physical education programs, as well as to all education programs in institutions that receive federal funding.

Title IX Enforcement

There are three main pathways to enforce Title IX. The complainant or plaintiff may select any of the three and need not exhaust, nor even initiate, in-house remedies first. The first method is internal. Each institution under the jurisdiction of Title IX must have a designated Title IX officer. The Title IX officer's job is to educate the faculty, staff, and students about the rights and responsibilities imposed by Title IX and to deal with any Title IX complaints filed in-house.

The second method of enforcement is through the Office for Civil Rights (OCR) of the U.S. Department of Education. Once an administrative complaint is filed with the OCR (legal standing is NOT required in order to file), the OCR investigates and, if violations are found, negotiates a "letter of resolution" with the institution in which the institution agrees to a time frame and a list of changes to be made. The third method involves the filing of a federal lawsuit by someone with legal standing. This method has found increasing favor among plaintiffs since the Supreme Court's unanimous 1992 *Franklin v. Gwinnett County Public Schools* (see the Supplemental Web Site) decision, which made it clear that compensatory and perhaps even punitive damages are available to victims of intentional gender discrimination under Title IX.

Title IX Requirements

When Title IX was enacted in 1972, there was only the one-sentence law saying:

"No person in the United States shall, on the basis of sex, be excluded from participation in, be denied the benefits of, or be subjected to discrimination under any education program or activity receiving Federal financial assistance."

In addition to the one-sentence law, formal regulations were promulgated and ultimately gained the force of law. Even though most Title IX cases and controversies have related to its application to sport, Title IX applies to all of education. However, because of continuing controversy about the details of Title IX's implementation in the area of sport, policy interpretations were adopted in 1979. Policy interpretations do not have the force of law but courts are required to give them significant deference. Policy interpretations are not intended to alter the meaning of the regulations but merely provide a fuller explanation of what compliance with the regulations would look like or how compliance would be evaluated. Another, yet much weaker, source of information about the requirements of Title IX is found in the 1990 *OCR Investigator's Manual*, which provides insight into how the OCR views its own requirements. OCR also has the ability and, some would argue the obligation, to clarify areas of the law that are found to be confusing. Letters of clarification have been issued over the years to explain specific issues that have been the center of controversy such as the applicability of a three pronged test relating to the measurement of the adequacy of opportunities to participate. Letters of clarification do not have the force of law but theoretically simply restate the law. However, some OCR letters of clarification, such as the "Additional Clarification" issued in 2005 concerning the use of surveys to determine interest in participation, exceeded a simple restatement and attempted to alter the law. The 2005 Additional Clarification was rescinded in April, 2010.

Recreation Program Application

Recreation programs are also often under the jurisdiction of Title IX. As long as all three elements (federal money, allegations of sex discrimination, and education program) are met, recreation programs are included in the jurisdiction of Title IX. It would be difficult to conceive of a campus-based recreation program that would not be under Title IX jurisdiction. Nonscholastic, community-based recreation programs need not be operated by the state or federal government to be under the jurisdiction of Title IX. State action is not required to trigger Title IX jurisdiction. The recreation program's primary activity need not be conducting educational programs; it only needs to include an educational component in its programs to be under the jurisdiction of Title IX. If a recreation program is found to be under the jurisdiction of Title IX, offering more activities or more participation opportunities for its male clients, offering those activities in better facilities, or providing a higher quality officiating staff for its male clients, would be examples of potential Title IX violations.

Athletics Application

There are many specific requirements of Title IX relating to coaching, facilities, equipment, travel, and so on. However, since if you are not on the team, you don't need a uniform, coaching and the other items, this section will focus on the legal requirements for participation rather than on the treatment of athletes once they are participating. Title IX's regulations require that "the selection of sports and levels of competition effectively accommodate the interests and abilities of members of both sexes." According to the policy interpretations

(U.S. Department of Education Athletic Guidelines, 1979), an institution has effectively accommodated the interests of its students if it satisfies any ONE of the following three benchmarks:

1. Participation opportunities for male and female students are provided in numbers substantially proportionate to their respective enrollments;
2. The institution can show a history and continuing practice of program expansion demonstrably responsive to the developing interest and abilities of the members of the underrepresented sex;
3. The institution can show that it is fully and effectively meeting the interests and abilities of the underrepresented sex.

Institutions that have maintained their commitment to the legal requirements of gender equity over the years have had no difficulty in meeting either Benchmark 2 or 3 and thus don't even need to address the issue of proportionality found in Benchmark 1. However, institutions that have ignored the requirements of Title IX or that have failed to implement plans to provide equitable athletic participation opportunities for their female students, more than four decades after the passage of Title IX, are now facing a quandary. They have not satisfied Benchmark 2 because they have not expanded their program for their female students. Similarly, if a group of female athletes demonstrates interest and ability sufficient to support the creation of a team in a particular sport in which it would be reasonable to find suitable competition in the school's traditional competitive region, the institution cannot claim that it has satisfied Benchmark 3. That leaves Benchmark 1: proportionality.

For many reasons, including past discrimination, social influences, and the changing enrollment gender balance, very few schools meet Benchmark 1. Typically, the courts have also found such institutions to be in violation of Title IX's requirement to effectively accommodate the interests and abilities of its female (historically underrepresented sex) student-athletes because it is unlikely that Benchmarks 2 or 3 have been met either. Such institutions are therefore at risk of losing their federal funding in addition to being liable for possible compensatory and punitive damages. Consternation and controversy surrounding the measurement of equitable participation has been unabated by the fact that the status of the law and the application of the three-prong test (as found in the 1979 Policy Interpretations and as reiterated unchanged in the form of a 1996 clarification letter from the Office for Civil Rights) has been very straightforward.

One of the three tests of participation, the proportionality prong (Benchmark 1) was created to provide a "safe harbor." In this context "safe harbor" means that a school that can show it has met the proportionality prong will be exempt from creating additional participation opportunities for females, even if there remain significant numbers of females who are denied participation. The school would be granted the "safe harbor" exemption because it is assumed that if its ratio of female athletes mirrors the ratio of females in the student body, gender equity in participation has been met. Reality has demonstrated that schools that have not gradually moved toward compliance over the years or that have left favored teams' budgets and inflated participation numbers unrestrained find that they can meet none of the three prongs in any reasonable way. They cannot rewrite history to meet prong 2, and they cannot claim that they have met the interests and abilities of the underrepresented sex (prong 3) as long as there are sufficient able and interested females wanting to participate Therefore, the only prong over which an institution that has not moved toward compliance over the years has retained any degree of control is the proportionality prong.

Some institutions have manipulated compliance within the proportionality prong in ways that, in effect, reduce participation for males and sometimes even the historically underrepresented females. By canceling men's minor sport teams, the absolute number of male participants is reduced, and the male/female athlete ratio moves closer to the ratio in the student body without having to increase participation opportunities for women. This manipulation is contrary to the spirit of Title IX. Even so, administrators have often defended their decision to cut men's minor sport teams, rather than restrain favored teams, by disingenuously placing the blame on Title IX. The popularity of various sports waxes and wanes even in the absence of Title IX, but those whose sports are cut are understandably frustrated.

Data on both the high school and college levels make it clear that the absolute number of males and females participating as varsity athletes is continuing to expand. The massive increase in women's participation from 16,000 female intercollegiate athletes in 1971 to over 200,000 in 2012 has not come at the cost of men's participation opportunities which are also the highest ever. The same is true for the high school levels where there were 4,494,406 boys and 3,173,549 girls were participating in interscholastic athletics as of 2011.

The number of participation opportunities continues to increase but specific teams at specific schools are sometimes cut.

Manipulation of the proportionality prong by capping men's participation slots or cutting a men's team in order to alter the proportion of female to male athletes without having to increase participation opportunities for females is not an appropriate Title IX compliance technique within the spirit of the law. Although roster manipulation is contrary to the spirit of the law, it is permissible under the law. Frustration born of the manipulation of the proportionality prong most typically arises when a men's team is cut. The frustration is sometimes heightened when the athletic administration blames Title IX for the loss.

However, sometimes the manipulation involves replacing one or more smaller roster women's teams with a single larger roster women's team. Such was the case at Quinnipiac University according to the allegations found in *Biediger v Quinnipiac University* (See Supplemental Web Site). Quinnipiac's women's volleyball team was slated for replacement by a competitive cheer team. Competitive cheer teams carry much larger rosters than volleyball teams thus helping an institution to meet the proportionality prong. The Quinnipiac case involved accusations of dishonest, not merely strategic, manipulation of rosters. In addition the case involved a determination of whether the competitive cheer group met the standards to be considered a 'sport' for Title IX purposes.

Not every activity that involves motion or athleticism fulfills the subjective requirements promulgated by the OCR for the designation, 'sport'. There is a rebuttable presumption that an activity labeled a 'sport' by an intercollegiate athletic association, such as the NCAA, also meets the Title IX 'sport' requirements of OCR if the offering institution is an association member and fulfills the association's requirements for offering the activity as a 'sport'. When the presumption fails to apply or has been rebutted, the OCR may evaluate the particular activity on a case-by-case basis. Among the issues reviewed by the OCR (simplified and condensed for this discussion) are:

1. Are the budget, support services, and coaching staffs provided in a manner consistent with other established sports in the institution's athletics program?
2. Are the participants eligible to receive financial aid and recruited in a manner consistent with established sports at the institution?
3. Are practice opportunities, competitive opportunities (number and length predetermined by a governing athletics organization or group of institutions, defined season) and pre/post season competition available in a manner consistent with established sports at the institution?
4. Is the primary purpose of the activity that of supporting/promoting other athletic activities or to provide intercollegiate or interscholastic competition at varsity levels?
5. Is the selection of participants based on factors related primarily to athletic ability?

Although the Quinnipiac case is likely to be appealed, the currently prevailing decision determined that Quinnipiac's competitive cheer group was not a 'sport' for the purposes of Title IX and thus the group's members could not be counted for the purposes of meeting the proportionality prong. The NCAA is currently discussing whether competitive cheer should be designated as an emerging sport but whatever the NCAA's decision, the NCAA's characterization is not binding on the OCR but simply helps to establish a rebuttable presumption. There are likely to be more institutions desiring to count participants in competitive cheer; large roster women's sports assist an institution in meeting the proportionality prong. Whatever the final determination at a particular institution, it will be interesting to watch the process of determining whether competitive cheer is or is not a sport for the purposes of Title IX.

Opportunities to Participate Free from Harassment

Having the opportunity to participate but facing sexual harassment while participating is not much of an opportunity at all. Sexual harassment invades many areas of human interaction, and the Fourteenth Amendment to a small degree and Titles VII and IX to a larger degree are useful tools with which to combat sexual harassment. Title IX is specifically applicable to sexual harassment of students by both their teachers and coaches. Title VII, on the other hand, applies only in the workplace, and thus does not protect students. See Section 7.14, *Sexual Harassment* for a full discussion of harassment.

Although a relatively old case, the following case is used to illustrate the Title IX guidelines published by the Office for Civil Rights and those requirements needed to come into compliance with the law.

ROBERTS V. COLORADO STATE UNIVERSITY
United States Tenth Circuit Court of Appeals
998 F.2d 824 (10th Cir. 1993)

Current and former members of the Colorado State University's fast pitch softball team sued the university after it announced the discontinuation of the fast pitch softball program. The students, suing as individuals, claimed Title IX violations.

The district court found Title IX violations existed and issued a permanent injunction reinstating the softball program. When, somewhat later, the court held a status conference, the court found the institution had been apparently dragging its feet. Therefore, the court amplified its earlier orders to require defendant to hire a coach promptly, recruit new members for the team, and organize a fall season.

* * *

A

This controversy concerns one subject of the regulations implementing Title IX.34C.F.R.§ 106.41(c) provides:

> *A recipient which operated or sponsors inter-scholastic, intercollegiate, club or intramural athletes shall provide equal athletic opportunity for members of both sexes. In determining whether equal opportunities are available the Director [of the Office for Civil Rights] will consider, among other factors:*
>
> *(1) Whether the selection of sports and levels of competition effectively accommodate the interests and abilities of members of both sexes[.]*

Although § 106.41(c) goes on to list nine other factors that enter into discrimination of equal opportunity in athletics, an institution may violate Title IX simply by failing to accommodate effectively the interests and abilities of student athletes of both sexes.

In 1979, the Department of Health, Education, and Welfare issued a policy interpretation explaining the ways in which institutions may effectively accommodate the interests and abilities of their student athletes.

The Policy Interpretation delineates three general areas in which the OCR will assess compliance with the effective accommodation section of the regulation, as follows:

1. The determination of athletic interests and abilities of students;
2. The selection of sports offered; and
3. The levels of competition available including the opportunity for team competition.

The OCR assesses effective accommodation with respect to opportunities for intercollegiate competition by determining:

1. Whether intercollegiate level participation opportunities for male and female students are provided in numbers substantially proportionate to their respective enrollments; or
2. Where the members of one sex have been and are under represented among intercollegiate athletes, whether the institution can show a history and continuing practice of program expansion which is demonstrably responsive to the developing interest and abilities of the members of that sex; or
3. Where the members of one sex are under represented among intercollegiate athletes, and the institution cannot show a continuing practice of program expansion such as that cited above, whether it can be demonstrated that the interests and abilities of the members of that sex have been fully and effectively accommodated by the present program.

In effect, "substantial proportionality" between athletic participation and undergraduate enrollment provides a safe harbor for recipients under Title IX. In the absence of such gender balance, the institution must show that it has expanded and is continuing to expand opportunities for athletic participation by the under represented gender, or else it must fully and effectively accommodate the interests and abilities among members of the under represented gender.

In addition to assessing whether individuals of both sexes have the opportunity to compete in intercollegiate athletics, the OCR also examines whether the quality of competition provided to male and female athletes equally reflects their abilities. This will depend on whether, program wide, the competitive schedules of men's and women's teams "afford proportionally similar numbers of male and female athletes equivalently advanced competitive opportunities," *Id.*, or "[w]hether the institution can demonstrate a history and continuing practice of upgrading the competitive opportunities available to the historically disadvantaged sex as warranted by developing abilities among the athletes of that sex." However, "[i]nstitutions are not required to upgrade teams to intercollegiate status or otherwise develop intercollegiate sports absent a reasonable expectation that intercollegiate competition in that sport will be available within the institution's normal competitive regions."

B

The district court found that plaintiffs met their burden of showing that defendant could not take shelter in the safe harbor of substantial proportionality. The district court reviewed a substantial quantity of statistical data, and made the undisputed finding that following the termination of the varsity softball program, the disparity between enrollment and athletic participation for women at CSU is 10.5 percent. Defendant maintains that, as a matter of law, a 10.5 percent disparity is substantially proportionate.

The OCR has instructed its Title IX compliance investigators that "[t]here is no set ratio that constitutes 'substantially proportionate' or that, when not met, results in a disparity or a violation." Investigator's Manual at 24. However, in the example immediately preceding this statement, the Manual suggests that substantial proportionality entails a fairly close relationship between athletic participation and undergraduate enrollment. Furthermore, in a Title IX compliance review completed in 1983, the OCR found that CSU's athletic participation opportunities for men and women were not substantially proportionate to their respective enrollments. During the three years that were the subject of that review, the differences between women enrolled and women athletes were 7.5 percent, 12.5 percent, and 12.7 percent. The district court relied on these sources, as well as expert testimony that a 10.5 percent disparity is statistically significant, in concluding that CSU could not meet this first benchmark. *See also Cohen v. Brown University*, 809 F. Supp. 978,991 (D.R.I. 1992) (see Supplemental Web Site) (11.6 percent disparity not substantially proportionate) *aff'd*, 991 F.2d 888 (1st Cir. 1993). Without demarcating further the line between substantial proportionality and disproportionality, we agree with the district court that a 10.5 percent disparity between female athletic participation and female undergraduate enrollment is not substantially proportionate. The fact that many or even most other educational institutions have a greater imbalance than CSU does not require a different holding.

C

The district court also found that defendant could not prove a history and continuing practice of expansion in women's athletics at CSU. Defendant argues that the district court should have given greater weight to its dramatic expansion of women's athletic opportunities during the 1970s. In essence, defendant suggests reading the words "continuing practice" out of this prong of the test. In support of this position, defendant offers anecdotal evidence of enforcement at other institutions, and the OCR's 1983 finding of compliance for CSU, which was contingent upon CSU's fulfilling the provisions of a plan that CSU never met.

Although CSU created a woman's sports program out of nothing in the 1970s, adding eleven sports for women during that decade, the district court found that women's participation opportunities declined steadily during the 1980s. Furthermore, although budget cuts in the last twelve years have affected both men and women athletes at CSU, the district court found that women's participation opportunities declined by 34 percent, whereas men's opportunities declined by only 20 percent. The facts as found by the district court (and largely undisputed by defendant) can logically support no other conclusion than that, since adding women's golf in 1977, CSU has not maintained a practice of program expansion in women's athletics, and indeed has since dropped three women's sports.

We recognize that in times of economic hardship, few schools will be able to satisfy Title IX's effective accommodation requirement by continuing to expand their women's athletics programs. Nonetheless, the ordinary meaning of the word "expansion" may not be twisted to find compliance under their prong when schools have increased the relative percentages of women participating in athletics by making cuts in both men's and women's sports programs. Financially strapped institutions may still comply with Title IX by cutting athletic programs such that men's and women's athletic participation rates become substantially proportionate to their representation in the undergraduate population.

The heart of the controversy is the meaning of the phrase "full and effective accommodation of interests and abilities." Defendant maintains that even if there is interest and ability on the part of women athletes at CSU, the university is obliged to accommodate them only to the extent it accommodates men. Thus, the argument goes, plaintiffs cannot be heard to complain because both women's softball and men's baseball were eliminated in the last round of cuts and there are more disappointed male than female athletes at CSU. The First Circuit rejected this position in *Cohen*, and so do we. "[T]his benchmark sets a high standard; it demands not merely some accommodation, but full and effective accommodation. If there is sufficient interest and ability among members of the statistically under represented gender, not slaked by existing programs, an institution necessarily fails this prong of the test." *Id.* at 898.

Based on the district court's subsidiary findings of fact, we conclude that plaintiffs met the burden of showing that CSU has not accommodated their interest and abilities fully and effectively. Questions of fact under this third prong will be less vexing when plaintiffs seek the reinstatement of an established team rather than the creation of a new one. Here, plaintiffs were members of a successful varsity softball team that played a competitive schedule as recently as the spring of 1992. Although apparently four plaintiffs have transferred and one has been dismissed, seven or eight plaintiffs remain at CSU for at least part of the 1993–94 school year and would be eligible to play on a reinstated team. We agree with the district court that CSU fails the third prong of effective accommodation test.

CASES ON THE SUPPLEMENTAL WEB SITE

Biediger, et al v Quinnipiac University, Case 3:09 – cv621-SRU (2010) This case from the US District Court, District of Connecticut, examines the method of counting participation slots for the purposes of complying with Title IX and also considers whether competitive cheer should or should not be considered a sport for the purposes of Title IX.

Fitzgerald v. arnstable School Committee, 129 S.Ct. 788 (2009). This case examines whether Title IX was the exclusive mechanism for addressing gender discrimination in schools or a substitute for § 1983 suits as a means of enforcing constitutional rights.

Franklin v. Gwinnett County Public Schools, 503 U.S. 60 (1992). This case examines whether Title IX provides a damages for individual students.

United States v. Virginia, 518 U.S. 515 (1996). This case examines Virginia's policy of denying women admission to the Virginia Military Institute, a publicly funded university.

QUESTIONS YOU SHOULD BE ABLE TO ANSWER

1. Does Title IX protect members of discontinued men's teams? Why or why not?

2. Is the lack of money a defense to Title IX?

3. Should failure of Benchmark 1 (proportionality) solely create an irrefutable presumption of either compliance with or violation of Title IX's accommodation/opportunity requirement? If yes, why?If no, why?

4. May a student who has been discriminated against sue using both Title IX and the 14th Amendment as legal theories or must the student select only one theory?

5. Evaluate the recreational sport program at your school or in your community and determine if you think the program is complying with the requirements of Title IX.

REFERENCES

Cases

Biediger, et al v. Quinnipiac University, 728 F. Supp. 2d 62 (2010).
Cohen v. Brown University, 991 F.2d 888 (1st Cir. 1993), 8879 F. Supp. 185 (D. R.I. 1995), cert. denied.
Fitzgerald v. Barnstable School Committee, 555 U.S. 246 (2009).
Franklin v. Gwinnett County Public Schools, 503 U.S. 60 (1992).

Grove City v. Bell, 465 U.S. 555 (1984).

Roberts v. Colorado State University, 814 F. Supp. 1507 (D. Colo.) aff 'd in relevant part sub nom. *Roberts v. Colorado State Bd. of Agric.,* 998 F.2d 824 (10th Cir.), cert. denied, 114 S. Ct. 580 (1993).

United States v. Virginia Military Institute, 116 S.Ct. 2264 (1996).

Publication

U.S. Department of Education.(1979). Athletic Guidelines.

Dear Colleague Letter, September 17, 2008, Office for Civil Rights, US Department of Education. http://www2.ed.gov/about/offices/list/ocr/letters/colleague-20080917.html

Legislation

Title VII: 42 USC sections 2000e –17, plus additions made by the Civil Rights Act of 1991, Pub.L. No. 102–166, 105 Stat 1071 (1991).

Title IX: Education Amendments of 1972, §§ 901–909 as amended, 20 U.S.C.A. §§ 11681–11688. 40 Fed. Reg. 24, 128 (1975) currently appearing at 34 C.F.R. §§ 106 (1992).

U.S. Department of Education Athletic Guidelines; Title IX of the Education Amendments of 1972; A Policy Interpretation; Title IX and Intercollegiate Athletics, 44 Fed. Reg. 71, 413, 71, 423 (1979).

7.12 GENDER EQUITY: COACHING AND ADMINISTRATION

Barbara Osborne | University of North Carolina at Chapel Hill

Although opportunities to participate for girls and women in sport in the United States have increased dramatically over the past 40 years (see Chapter 7.11) leadership and employment opportunities for women have not. In some cases, women's opportunities in sport management have actually decreased. The Institute for Diversity and Ethics in Sport conducts research on discrimination in the sport industry and publishes a "Report Card" annually. The 2011 Racial and Gender Report Card assigned letter grades from A through F for intercollegiate athletics and professional sports leagues. The WNBA earned the highest grade of A, followed by the NBA (A–), intercollegiate sport (B), MLB and MLS (B–), and the NFL (C) for gender policies and employment. The Associated Press once again received an F as 94% of sports editors, 90% of assistant sports editors, 90% of columnists, 89% of reporters and 84% of copy editors are male. While the percentage of sports editors, assistant sports editors and copy editors remained constant from the 2008 data, the percentage of female columnists and reporters declined over this period.

Vivien Acostaand Linda Jean Carpenter have conducted a longitudinal study, "Women in Intercollegiate Sport" since 1977. Although there are more women employed in administrative and coaching positions in intercollegiate athletics than ever before, the number of women as a percentage of total administrators and coaches is not close to the 90% representation in the 1970's when most colleges and universities had separate men's and women's athletics departments. As of 2012, only 20.3% of athletics directors at all NCAA institutions were women, with Division III having the highest percentage of female athletics directors at 33.3%. However, 9.2% of schools have no women employed in athletics administration. Less than half (42.9%) of women's athletics teams have a female head coach. There are more paid assistant coaches in women's college athletics than ever before, and 57.1% of those positions are held by women. Sports medicine and sports information lag woefully behind, with only 30.7% of women employed as head athletics trainers. Athletics communications appears to mirror the professional sports media, as only 9.8% of sports information directors are women, a decrease in representation since 2008(Acosta& Carpenter, 2012). In addition to barriers in employing women in college athletics programs, a gender gap also exists in salaries, with female coaches earning on average only 62% of what male coaches make (Osborne & Yarbrough, 2001).

There are many possible explanations for the decline in women's employment as athletics administrators and coaches. Combining men's and women's athletics programs in the 1970's and 1980's was less of a merger of two departments and more of take-over by the men's athletics department resulting in elimination of female athletics administrators. This transition also resulted in paid positions and improved pay for coaches of women's teams, making positions coaching women more attractive to men. Research indicates the sex of the person making the employment decision matters, and male athletics directors are more likely to hire men (Acosta and Carpenter, 2002). Fewer female coaches and administrators results in fewer role models for female athletes. Lack of interaction with female coaches may have also influenced preference for male coaches by female athletes (Women's Sports Foundation, n.d.). Cultural stereotypes also persist that female coaches are not as qualified, and are softer than male coaches.

A high school coaching case illustrates the sports cultural bias against hiring female coaches. Geraldine Fuhr was the girls' varsity basketball coach at Hazel Park for 10 years, and had also served as the assistant boys varsity basketball coach for 8 years. When the boys' varsity coach announced his retirement, Fuhr and John Barnett, who had been coaching the boys' freshman basketball team for the past two years, were the only two applicants for the position. Both candidates were interviewed by the search committee, and at the end of the process, the Superintendent of Schools informed the search committee that several members of the school board did not want Fuhr as the boys coach and that they had to honor their wishes. The president of the school board announced that he "was very concerned about a female being the head boys' basketball coach in Hazel Park" (*Fuhr v. School District of Hazel Park*, 2004, p. 757). Barnett was hired, and Fuhr was told by the school principal that she did not get the job because of her gender. She sued the school district for sex discrimination under Title VII and the Elliot-Larsen Act, a Michigan civil rights act that prohibits discrimination. A jury held in Fuhr's favor, awarding her $245,000 in present damages and $210,000 in future damages. Subsequently, the district court ordered Hazel Park to hire Fuhr as the boys' varsity basketball coach, and struck the jury's award of future damages, but granted Fuhr attorney's fees. Hazel Park appealed, but the Sixth Circuit affirmed, finding that Hazel Park had intentionally discriminated against Fuhr on the basis of sex by not hiring her as the head boys' basketball coach.

FUNDAMENTAL CONCEPTS

Employment discrimination laws prevent employers, including sport and recreation organizations, from discriminating on the basis of race, sex, religion, country of national origin, disability, and age. These laws seek to prevent bias in all aspects of employment including hiring, work assignment, compensation, promotion, and termination. The United States Equal Employment Opportunity Commission (EEOC) is the federal agency responsible for these laws. This chapter will examine constitutional and statutory protection against employment discrimination based on gender, including the issues of pay equity, pregnancy, and retaliation.

Constitutional Law and Civil Rights Acts

Constitutional law claims for discrimination based on gender may be made under the equal protection clause of the Fourteenth Amendment. Because the proposed Equal Rights Amendment to the United States Constitution was never ratified, sex is nota protected category under the Constitution so the federal courts apply an intermediate scrutiny standard, meaning that the government action must be substantially related to an important government interest (see Chapter 6.14 Equal Protection). Additionally, 42 U.S.C. § 1983 of the Civil Rights Act of 1871 provides for damages when federal constitutional rights are violated. § 1983 claims may also be used to redress deprivation of a right guaranteed by a federal statute.

State Constitutions may also provide heightened protection from discrimination based on sex. For example, the State Constitution of Illinois states in its Bill of Rights that all persons have the right to be free from discrimination on the basis of race, color, creed, national ancestry, and sex. States that include sex as a protected category in the state constitution heighten protection by providing strict scrutiny review by the courts. State civil rights legislation also provides additional protection from gender discrimination. In Michigan, the Elliott-Larsen Civil Rights Act prohibits discriminatory practices on the basis of religion, race, color, national origin, sex, age, height, weight, familial status and marital status in the exercise of civil rights. As protection against discrimination varies from state to state, and federal Constitutional protection is only at an intermediate level, additional federal legislation has been needed to address gender inequity in the workforce.

Equal Pay Act of 1963

An amendment to the Fair Labor Standards Act of 1938 (29 U.S.C.A. §201–219), the Equal Pay Act (EPA) prohibits employers from discriminating on the basis of sex between employees at the same establishment who perform equal work in equivalent positions under similar working conditions. An employee may have a claim for relief under the EPA if the employee proves that the employer pays a higher wage to an employee of the opposite sex for equal work on a job that requires equal skill, effort and responsibility when the job is performed under similar working conditions. Skill is measured as equal based on experience, training, education and ability required in performing the job, effort is the amount or degree of physical or mental exertion required to perform the job successfully, and responsibility is measured by the degree of accountability required with emphasis on the importance of the job obligation. Once the employee has proved differential pay for equal work, the burden then shifts to the employer to justify the wage difference through one of the defenses enumerated in the Act: seniority, merit, quantity or quality of production, and any factor other than the sex of the employee. If the employer offers a justification, the employee has one final opportunity to provide evidence that the employer's defense is pretext and that the real reason for the pay inequity is gender discrimination. The burden of proof standard in an Equal Pay Act claim is very high, making it difficult for an employee to win a claim.

The *Stanley v. University of Southern California* case illustrates this difficulty. In 1993, Marianne Stanley was the successful coach of the USC women's basketball program. As her four-year contract was nearing completion, she began negotiating a new contract with Michael Garrett, Athletics Director at USC. Stanley asked for a contract equal to that of the men's basketball coach at USC. The athletics director agreed that Stanley was worth more, but explained that the athletics department could not afford to pay that type of an increase. The negotiations continued, with the athletics department making offers and Stanley making counter offers. Stanley then retained an attorney to negotiate the terms of a new contract and the athletics director responded by withdrawing a multi-year offer, and instead offered a one-year contract. Stanley asked for additional time to consider the offer, and in the meantime, her current contract expired. On July 15, the AD sent a memo to Stanley withdrawing his offer and informing her that he would be seeking other candidates to fill her position.

On August 5, 1993, Stanley filed a lawsuit in Superior Court for the County of LA claiming that the athletics director and USC had engaged in sex discrimination and retaliation. She argued that she was entitled to be paid a salary that was equal to the salary of the men's basketball coach as the positions required equal skill, effort and responsibility, and is performed under similar working conditions. USC refuted the claim, offering evidence that the men's basketball coach had substantially different qualifications and experience. The men's coach had substantial public relations and revenue generating skills including nine years of marketing experience, Additionally, he had authored two best-selling novels, performed as an actor in a movie, and had appeared on television. USC also refuted that the men's and women's basketball coaching positions are not equivalent positions, as the men's coaching position required substantial public relations and promotional activities related to generating revenue. The university argued that the men's basketball team generated greater attendance, attracted more media interest, inspired larger donations, and produced substantially more revenue than the women's basketball team, which placed greater pressure on the men's basketball coach. The court agreed with the university and found that factors other than gender caused the difference in salary; the appellate court affirmed the decision of the lower court.

It is very difficult for a plaintiff to make a successful Equal Pay Act claim in sports settings. The first hurdle is to establish an equal comparator position. Female athletics administrators, however, are often in a unique position within the athletics department and have no male counterpart in a job that is substantially equal to her own. Coaches may have less difficulty when there are both male and female versions of the same team, but as in the *Stanley* case, courts do not always find that the coach of the men's team and the coach of the women's team in the same sport have substantially equal positions. A coach may choose to compare her position with that of a male coach of another sport, but differences in the number of athletes coached, number of assistant coaches necessary, variety of player positions to train, number of games in a season and other sport-related factors make it easy for the court to conclude that working conditions are not similar.

If the coach or administrator is able to establish an equal comparator, it is still extremely difficult to refute the employer's affirmative defense. Employers are quite successful at establishing that their pay decisions stem from any factor other than sex. Athletics programs have successfully asserted the following justifications for paying male coaches more than comparable female coaches: the men's team produces more revenue than the women's team; the coaching marketplace demands higher salaries for the best coaches; current salary was based on past salary; and the male coach has additional duties. Sex of the athletes coached should not be an acceptable defense, as the sex of the student-athlete is a factor based on sex and not a gender neutral factor (EEOC Guidelines, 1997).

Title VII of Civil Rights Act of 1964

Title VII protects broadly against discrimination on the basis of race, color, religion, country of national origin and sex. Like the Equal Pay Act, Title VII protects against discrimination in compensation. However, the Equal Pay Act is limited to equal pay for equal work, while Title VII offers a victim significantly broader protection.

Victims may make claims for failure to hire or promote, or for improper firing on the basis of sex. Additionally, employers may not discriminate on the basis of sex with respect to the terms, conditions, and privileges of employment beyond pay (See Ch. 7.13 for a thorough examination and analysis of Title VII).

An example of the broader protection provided by Title VII is the case of Kathryn Tomlinson who filed a complaint with the EEOC against the Phoenix Suns. Tomlinson was employed as a member of the "Zoo Crew", an entertainment troupe that shoots T-shirts into the stands, assists with half-time promotions, performs with the team mascot, and participates in community events to promote the Suns. Although Tomlinson and two other female employees performed well as members of the Zoo Crew, the Suns adopted a new hiring policy for the following season, limiting the positions to talented males with athletic ability. Unable to reapply for their former jobs, the women filed a complaint against the Suns and the stadium management team. To resolve the case, the Suns paid over $100,000 to the plaintiffs, and were required to provide training to employees, supervisors, and management prohibiting sex discrimination as well as establishing policies to ensure that sex-restrictive job announcements would not be created in the future.

Title IX Of Education Amendments Of 1972

Although Title IX of the Education Amendments of 1972 is best known for providing opportunities for girls to participate in athletics (see Chapter 7.11), the statute was enacted to address sex discrimination in educational institutions. Inequities also existed for women who were working at educational institutions. In 1972, the majority of women working in education were teaching in elementary and secondary schools. Although there have been increasing opportunities for women employed in education, compared to their male peers, women on average are paid less, hold a lower ranking title, and are not tenured. Title IX is enforced by the Office for Civil Rights (OCR) in the United States Department of Education. Title IX Regulations Sub-part E addresses employment discrimination in educational institutions.

The Title IX Regulations prohibit any educational institution that is a recipient of federal funding from discriminating against an applicant or employee on the basis of sex. It further prohibits discrimination on the basis of sex in hiring, promoting, awarding tenure, demoting, transferring, laying off or terminating an employee. Job classifications, assignments, and training may not be made on the basis of sex either. Rate of pay, or any other form of compensation or benefits may not be related to sex, and the language of the compensation section (§106.54) mirrors the requirements of the Equal Pay Act.

Although Title IX provides a cause of action for coaches who complain of employment discrimination on the basis of sex at federally funded schools, coaches still have difficulty winning these cases in court. Anderson & Osborne (2008) report that only half of Title IX claims of employment discrimination that were litigated and appealed were favorable to the plaintiff coach or administrator. It is also important to note that a Title IX claim of discrimination based on the gender of the athlete coached will be dismissed; the statute only provides protection against discrimination because of the gender of the coach.

Retaliation

One of the most recent developments in the law involves claims for retaliation when coaches have been wrongfully terminated for speaking out against inequities in the men's and women's athletics programs in violation of Title IX. Retaliation occurs when an employee suffers an adverse employment action in response to an action that the employer perceives negatively, such as complaining about unfair treatment to athletes, lack of comparable facilities for practice and/or competition, or other inequitable situations. Neither the plain language of the statute nor the Regulations specifically allows for a claim of retaliation, and the Federal Court of Appeals were split, with some allowing the claim to proceed, and others dismissing the claim for failure to state a recognizable claim. The issue was decided by the Supreme Court in *Jackson v. Birmingham Board of Education* (2005) when it concluded that teachers, coaches, and administrators who complain of sex discrimination on behalf of themselves or others have a right to sue if they are victims of retaliation. Since that decision, there have been a number of lawsuits against colleges and universities across the country, including several in California that have attracted attention because of the large jury awards and settlements.

For example, Fresno State University has been battling complaints about gender discrimination within the athletics program for several years. First, Diane Milutinovich, an athletics administrator, was dismissed from her position for "budget reasons" after she complained about inequities in the men's and women's athletics programs. Then the women's volleyball coach, Lindy Vivas, and women's basketball coach, Stacy Johnson-Klein were fired after questioning administrators and complaining about inequities in facilities, staffing, and employment demands between the men's and women's athletics programs. Fresno State agreed to pay Milutinovich $3.5 million in settlement. Juries in separate trials found that the university intentionally discriminated against the coaches and awarded $5.85 million to Vivas and $19.1 million to Johnson-Klein.

Pregnancy Discrimination Act Of 1978

The fundamental physical difference between men and women is the ability to bear children, and child-bearing as well as child rearing responsibilities have contributed to bias against women in hiring, promotion, and salaries. This physiological difference has historically been used to justify differential treatment between the sexes in a variety of situations. For example, in *Muller v. Oregon*(1908), the Supreme Court upheld an Oregon law that prohibited women from working for more than 10 hours per day because "woman's physical structure and the performance of maternal functions place her at a disadvantage in the struggle for subsistence" (*Muller v. Oregon,* 1908).Although medicine and science have refuted those old-fashioned opinions regarding the proper role of women in society, many people still believe that working mothers are less productive employees who should be paid less because they will have childcare responsibilities that may conflict with work priorities. The Pregnancy Discrimination Act combats that discriminatory reasoning by prohibiting employers from negatively impacting employment or benefits on the basis of pregnancy and childbirth.

Lilly Ledbetter Fair Pay Act Of 2009

The gender wage gap in the United States in 2007 was about 22.2 percent, which translates to women earning about 78 cents for each dollar that a man would earn in the same circumstances. The limitations of the Equal Pay Act, reluctance of women to file lawsuits against their employers, and contrary legal decisions have all contributed to the persistent gender wage gap in the United States. For example, Lilly Ledbetter worked as a supervisor at the Goodyear plant in Gadsden, Alabama for almost twenty years. Just as Ledbetter prepared to retire, she was informed through an anonymous note that she had been paid significantly less than her male peers who were doing the same job. Ledbetter filed suit under Title VII and the trial jury awarded Ledbetter pack pay and damages worth more than $3 million. The case was appealed all the way to the United States Supreme Court which overturned the decision, holding that employees must file wage discrimination complaints within 180 days of the original pay decision, no matter when they became aware of the disparity, so Ledbetter was left with nothing (*Ledbetter v. Goodyear Tire & Rubber Co.,* 2007). This decision significantly restricted the time period in which victims may file claims, severely weakening the statutory protections provided under Title VII.

Unhappy with the precedent that the Supreme Court established in the Ledbetter case, Congress passed the Lilly Ledbetter Fair Pay Act of 2009 which allows victims of pay discrimination to assert their rights under the Equal Pay Act and Title VII for full compensatory and punitive damages. The legislation establishes that an unlawful employment practice occurs each time an individual is paid if that compensation is affected by application of a discriminatory compensation practice or decision. The Act also requires the EEOC to issue regulations and survey pay data that will allow it to improve enforcement of the law. To correct for legal decisions that may have relied on the Supreme Court precedent established in the *Ledbetter v. Goodyear Tire & Rubber Co.* case, the legislation is retroactive to all claims pending on or after May 28, 2007.

This recent Supreme Court decision has expanded the scope of Title IX protection for coaches and administrators who suffer retaliation for speaking out against gender inequity in their athletics programs.

RODERICK JACKSON V. BIRMINGHAM BOARD OF EDUCATION

Supreme Court of the United States
544 U.S. 167 (2005)

Roderick Jackson, a teacher in the Birmingham, Alabama, public schools, brought suit against the Birmingham Board of Education (Board) alleging that the Board retaliated against him because he had complained about sex discrimination in the high school's athletic program. Jackson claimed that the Board's retaliation violated Title IX of the Education Amendments of 1972, Pub L 92–318, 86 Stat 373, as amended, *20 U.S.C. § 1681 et seq.* The District Court dismissed Jackson's complaint on the ground that Title IX does not prohibit retaliation, and the Court of Appeals for the Eleventh Circuit affirmed. *309 F.3d 1333 (2002).* We consider here whether the private right of action implied by Title IX encompasses claims of retaliation. We hold that it does where the funding recipient retaliates against an individual because he has complained about sex discrimination. I

Because Jackson's Title IX claim was dismissed under *Federal Rule of Civil Procedure 12(b)(6)* for failure to state a claim upon which relief can be granted, "we must assume the truth of the material facts as alleged in the complaint." *Summit Health, Ltd. V. Pinhas, 500 U.S. 322, 325, 114 L. Ed. 2d 366, 111 S. Ct. 1842 (1991).*

According to the complaint, Jackson has been an employee of the Birmingham school district for over 10 years. In 1993, the Board hired Jackson to serve as a physical education teacher and girls' basketball coach. Jackson was transferred to EnsleyHigh School in August 1999. At Ensley, he discovered that the girls' team was not receiving equal funding and equal access to athletic equipment and facilities. The lack of adequate funding, equipment, and facilities made it difficult for Jackson to do his job as the team's coach.

In December 2000, Jackson began complaining to his supervisors about the unequal treatment of the girls' basketball team, but to no avail. Jackson's complaints went unanswered, and the school failed to remedy the situation. Instead, Jackson began to receive negative work evaluations and ultimately was removed as the girls' coach in May 2001. Jackson is still employed by the Board as a teacher, but he no longer receives supplemental pay for coaching.

After the Board terminated Jackson's coaching duties, he filed suit in the United States District Court for the Northern District of Alabama. He alleged, among other things, that the Board violated Title IX by retaliating against him for protesting the discrimination against the girls' basketball team. Amended Complaint 2–3, App. 10–11. The Board moved to dismiss on the ground that Title IX's private cause of action does not include claims of retaliation. The District Court granted the motion to dismiss.

The Court of Appeals for the Eleventh Circuit affirmed. *309 F.3d 1333 (2002).* It assumed, for purposes of the appeal, that the Board retaliated against Jackson for complaining about Title IX violations. It then held that Jackson's suit failed to state a claim because Title IX does not provide a private right of action for retaliation, reasoning that "[n]othing in the text indicates any congressional concern with retaliation that might be visited on those who complain of Title IX violations."*Id., at 1344.* Relying on our decision in *Alexander v. Sandoval, 532 U.S. 275, 149 L. Ed. 2d 517, 121 S. Ct. 1511 (2001),* the Court of Appeals also concluded that a Department of Education regulation expressly prohibiting retaliation does not create a private cause of action for retaliation: "Because Congress has not created a right through Title IX to redress harms resulting from retaliation, [the regulation] may not be read to create one either." *309 F.3d, at 1346.* Finally, the court held that, even if Title IX prohibits retaliation, Jackson would not be entitled to relief because he is not within the class of persons protected by the statute.

We granted certiorari, *542 U.S. 903, 159 L. Ed. 2d 266, 124 S. Ct. 2834 (2004),* to resolve a conflict in the Circuits over whether Title IX's private right of action encompasses claims of retaliation for complaints about sex discrimination. Compare *Lowrey v. Texas A & M Univ. System, 117 F.3d 242, 252 (CA5 1997)* ("[T]itle IX affords an implied cause of action for retaliation"); *Preston v. Virginia ex rel. New River Community College, 31 F.3d 203, 206 (CA4 1994)* (same), with the case below, *supra.*

II. A. Title IX prohibits sex discrimination by recipients of federal education funding. The statute provides that "[n]o person in the United States shall, on the basis of sex, be excluded from participation in, be denied the benefits of, or be subjected to discrimination under any education program or activity receiving Federal financial assistance."*20 U.S.C. § 1681(a)*. More than 25 years ago, in *Cannon v. University of Chicago, 441 U.S. 677, 690–693, 60 L. Ed. 2d 560, 99 S. Ct. 1946 (1979)*, we held that Title IX implies a private right of action to enforce its prohibition on intentional sex discrimination. In subsequent cases, we have defined the contours of that right of action. In *Franklin v. Gwinnett County Public Schools, 503 U.S. 60, 117 L. Ed. 2d 208, 112 S. Ct. 1028 (1992)*, we held that it authorizes private parties to seek monetary damages for intentional violations of Title IX. We have also held that the private right of action encompasses intentional sex discrimination in the form of a recipient's deliberate indifference to a teacher's sexual harassment of a student, *Gebser v. Lago Vista Independent School Dist., 524 U.S. 274, 290–291, 141 L. Ed. 2d 277, 118 S. Ct. 1989 (1998)*, or to sexual harassment of a student by another student, *Davis v. Monroe County Bd. of Ed., 526 U.S. 629, 642, 143 L. Ed. 2d 839, 119 S. Ct. 1661 (1999)*.

In all of these cases, we relied on the text of Title IX, which, subject to a list of narrow exceptions not at issue here, broadly prohibits a funding recipient from subjecting any person to "discrimination""on the basis of sex."*20 U.S.C. § 1681*. Retaliation against a person because that person has complained of sex discrimination is another form of intentional sex discrimination encompassed by Title IX's private cause of action. Retaliation is, by definition, an intentional act. It is a form of "discrimination" because the complainant is being subjected to differential treatment. See generally *Olmstead v. L. C., 527 U.S. 581, 614, 144 L. Ed. 2d 540, 119 S. Ct. 2176 (1999)* (Kennedy, J., concurring in judgment) (the "normal definition of discrimination" is "differential treatment"); see also *Newport News Shipbuilding & Dry Dock Co. v. EEOC, 462 U.S. 669, 682, n. 22, 77 L. Ed. 2d 89, 103 S. Ct. 2622 (1983)* (discrimination means "less favorable" treatment). Moreover, retaliation is discrimination "on the basis of sex" because it is an intentional response to the nature of the complaint: an allegation of sex discrimination. We conclude that when a funding recipient retaliates against a person *because* he complains of sex discrimination, this constitutes intentional "discrimination""on the basis of sex," in violation of Title IX.

The Court of Appeals' conclusion that Title IX does not prohibit retaliation because the "statute makes no mention of retaliation," *309 F.3d, at 1344*, ignores the import of our repeated holdings construing "discrimination" under Title IX broadly. Though the statute does not mention sexual harassment, we have held that sexual harassment is intentional discrimination encompassed by Title IX's private right of action. *Franklin, 503 U.S., at 74–7 . . .* Thus, a recipient's deliberate indifference to a teacher's sexual harassment of a student also "violate[s]

Title IX's plain terms." *Davis, supra, at 64 . . .* Likewise, a recipient's deliberate indifference to sexual harassment of a student by another student also squarely constitutes "discrimination""on the basis of sex." *Davis, 526 U.S., at 64 . . .* "Discrimination" is a term that covers a wide range of intentional unequal treatment; by using such a broad term, Congress gave the statute a broad reach. See *North Haven Bd. of Ed. V. Bell, 456 U.S. 512, 521. . . . . .*

Congress certainly could have mentioned retaliation in Title IX expressly, as it did in § 704 of Title VII of the Civil Rights Act of 1964, 78 Stat 257, as amended, 86 Stat 109, *42 U.S.C. § 2000e–3(a)* (providing that it is an "unlawful employment practice" for an employer to retaliate against an employee because he has "opposed any practice made an unlawful employment practice by [Title VII], or because he has made a charge, testified, assisted, or participated in any manner in an investigation, proceeding, or hearing under [Title VII]"). Title VII, however, is a vastly different statute from Title IX, see *Gebser, 524 U.S., at 283–284, 286–28 . . .* and the comparison the Board urges us to draw is therefore of limited use. Title IX's cause of action is implied, while Title VII's is express. See *id., at 283–284. . . .* Title IX is a broadly written general prohibition on discrimination, followed by specific, narrow exceptions to that broad prohibition. See *20 U.S.C. § 1681*. By contrast, Title VII spells out in greater detail the conduct that constitutes discrimination in violation of that statute. See *42 U.S.C. §§ 2000e–2* (giving examples of unlawful employment practices), 2000e–3 (prohibiting "[o]ther unlawful employment practices," including (a) "[d]iscrimination" in the form of retaliation; and (b) the discriminatory practice of "[p]rinting or publication of notices or advertisements indicating prohibited preference . . ."). Because Congress did not list *any* specific discriminatory practices when it wrote Title IX, its failure to mention one such practice does not tell us anything about whether it intended that practice to be covered.

Title IX was enacted in 1972, three years after our decision in *Sullivan v. Little Hunting Park, Inc., 396 U.S. 229 (1969)*. In *Sullivan*, we held that Rev Stat § 1978, *42 U.S.C. § 1982*, which provides that "[a]ll citizens of the United States shall have the same right . . . as is enjoyed by white citizens . . . to inherit, purchase, lease, sell, hold, and convey real and personal property," protected a white man who spoke out against discrimination toward one of his tenants and who suffered retaliation as a result. Sullivan had rented a house to a black man and assigned him a membership share and use rights in a private park. The corporation that owned the park would not approve the assignment to the black lessee. Sullivan protested, and the corporation retaliated against him by expelling him and taking his shares. Sullivan sued the corporation, and we upheld Sullivan's cause of action under *42 U.S.C. § 1982* for "[retaliation] for the advocacy of [the black person's] cause." *396 U.S., at 237*. Thus, in *Sullivan* we interpreted a general prohibition on racial discrimination to cover retaliation against those who advocate the rights of groups protected by that prohibition.

Congress enacted Title IX just three years after *Sullivan* was decided, and accordingly that decision provides a valuable context for understanding the statute. As we recognized in *Cannon*, "it is not only appropriate but also realistic to presume that Congress was thoroughly familiar with *[Sullivan]* and that it expected its enactment [of Title IX] to be interpreted in conformity with [it]." *441 U.S., at 699*. . . . Retaliation for Jackson's advocacy of the rights of the girls' basketball team in this case is "discrimination""on the basis of sex," just as retaliation for advocacy on behalf of a black lessee in *Sullivan* was discrimination on the basis of race.

B. The Board contends that our decision in *Alexander v. Sandoval, 532 U.S. 275 (2001)*, compels a holding that Title IX's private right of action does not encompass retaliation. *Sandoval* involved an interpretation of Title VI of the Civil Rights Act of 1964, 78 Stat 252, as amended, *42 U.S.C. § 2000d et seq.*, which provides in *§ 601* that no person shall, "on the ground of race, color, or national origin, be excluded from participation in, be denied the benefits of, or be subjected to discrimination under any program or activity" covered by Title VI. *42 U.S.C. § 2000d. Section 602 of Title VI* authorizes federal agencies to effectuate the provisions in *§ 601* by enacting regulations. Pursuant to that authority, the Department of Justice promulgated regulations prohibiting funding recipients from adopting policies that had "the effect of subjecting individuals to discrimination because of their race, color, or national origin."*28 C.F.R. § 42.104(b)(2) (1999)*. The *Sandoval* petitioners brought suit to enjoin an English-only policy of the Alabama Department of Public Safety on grounds that it disparately impacted non-English speakers in violation of the regulations. Though we assumed that the regulations themselves were valid, see *532 U.S., at 281*, we rejected the contention that the private right of action to enforce intentional violations of Title VI encompassed suits to enforce the disparate-impact regulations. We did so because "[i]t is clear . . . that the disparate-impact regulations do not simply apply *§ 601*—since they indeed forbid conduct that *§ 601* permits—and therefore clear that the private right of action to enforce *§ 601* does not include a private right to enforce these regulations. "*Id., at 285* . . . Thus, *Sandoval* held that private parties may not invoke Title VI regulations to obtain redress for disparate-impact discrimination because Title VI itself prohibits only intentional discrimination.

The Board cites a Department of Education regulation prohibiting retaliation "against any individual for the purpose of interfering with any right or privilege secured by [Title IX],"*34 C.F.R. § 100.7(e) (2004)* (incorporated by reference by *§ 106.71*), and contends that Jackson, like the petitioners in *Sandoval*, seeks an "impermissible extension of the statute" when he argues that Title IX's private right of action encompasses retaliation. Brief for Respondent 45. This argument, however, entirely misses the point. We do not rely on regulations extending Title IX's protection beyond its statutory limits; indeed, we

do not rely on the Department of Education's regulation at all, because the statute *itself* contains the necessary prohibition. As we explain above . . . the text of Title IX prohibits a funding recipient from retaliating against a person who speaks out against sex discrimination, because such retaliation is intentional "discrimination""on the basis of sex." We reach this result based on the statute's text. In step with *Sandoval*, we hold that Title IX's private right of action encompasses suits for retaliation, because retaliation falls within the statute's prohibition of intentional discrimination on the basis of sex.

C. Nor are we convinced by the Board's argument that, even if Title IX's private right of action encompasses discrimination, Jackson is not entitled to invoke it because he is an "indirect dvers[m]" of sex discrimination. Brief for Respondent 33. The statute is broadly worded; it does not require that the victim of the retaliation must also be the victim of the discrimination that is the subject of the original complaint. If the statute provided instead that "no person shall be subjected to discrimination on the basis of *such individual's* sex," then we would agree with the Board. Cf. *42 U.S.C. § 2000e–2(a)(1)* ("It shall be an unlawful employment practice for an employer . . . to discriminate against any individual . . . because of *such individual's* race, color, religion, sex, or national origin" (emphasis added)). However, Title IX contains no such limitation. Where the retaliation occurs because the complainant speaks out about sex discrimination, the "on the basis of sex" requirement is satisfied. The complainant is himself a victim of discriminatory retaliation, regardless of whether he was the subject of the original complaint. As we explain above . . . this is consistent with *Sullivan*, which formed an important part of the backdrop against which Congress enacted Title IX. *Sullivan* made clear that retaliation claims extend to those who oppose discrimination against others. See *396 U.S., at 237,* (holding that a person may bring suit under *42 U.S.C. § 1982* if he can show that he was "punished for trying to vindicate the rights of minorities").

Congress enacted Title IX not only to prevent the use of federal dollars to support discriminatory practices, but also "to provide individual citizens effective protection against those practices." *Cannon, 441 U.S., at 704* . . . We agree with the United States that this objective "would be difficult, if not impossible, to achieve if persons who complain about sex discrimination did not have effective protection against retaliation." Brief for United States as *Amicus Curiae* 13. If recipients were permitted to retaliate freely, individuals who witness discrimination would be loathe to report it, and all manner of Title IX violations might go unremedied as a result. See *Sullivan, supra, at 237*. . . . .

Reporting incidents of discrimination is integral to Title IX enforcement and would be discouraged if retaliation against those who report went unpunished. Indeed, if retaliation were not prohibited, Title IX's enforcement scheme would unravel. Recall that Congress intended Title IX's private right of action to encompass claims of a recipient's deliberate indifference to sexual harassment.

See generally *Davis, 526 U.S. 629*. Accordingly, if a principal sexually harasses a student, and a teacher complains to the school board but the school board is indifferent, the board would likely be liable for a Title IX violation. See generally *Gebser, 524 U.S. 274*. But if Title IX's private right of action does not encompass retaliation claims, the teacher would have no recourse if he were subsequently fired for speaking out. Without protection from retaliation, individuals who witness discrimination would likely not report it, indifference claims would be short circuited, and the underlying discrimination would go unremedied.

Title IX's enforcement scheme also depends on individual reporting because individuals and agencies may not bring suit under the statute unless the recipient has received "actual notice" of the discrimination. *Id., at 288, 289–290* . . . If recipients were able to avoid such notice by retaliating against all those who dare complain, the statute's enforcement scheme would be subverted. We should not assume that Congress left such a gap in its scheme.

Moreover, teachers and coaches such as Jackson are often in the best position to vindicate the rights of their students because they are better able to identify discrimination and bring it to the attention of administrators. Indeed, sometimes adult employees are "'the only effective dversary[ies]'" of discrimination in schools. See *Sullivan, supra, at 237* . . .

D. The Board is correct in pointing out that, because Title IX was enacted as an exercise of Congress' powers under the Spending Clause, see, *e.g., Davis, supra, at 640*, . . ., "private damages actions are available only where recipients of federal funding had adequate notice that they could be liable for the conduct at issue," *Davis, supra, at 640*. When Congress enacts legislation under its spending power, that legislation is "in the nature of a contract: in return for federal funds, the States agree to comply with federally imposed conditions."*PennhurstStateSchool and Hospital v. Halderman, 451 U.S. 1, 17 (1981)*. As we have recognized, "[t]here can . . . be no knowing acceptance [of the terms of the contract] if a State is unaware of the conditions [imposed by the legislation on its receipt of funds]."*Ibid.*

The Board insists that we should not interpret Title IX to prohibit retaliation because it was not on notice that it could be held liable for retaliating against those who complain of Title IX violations. We disagree. Funding recipients have been on notice that they could be subjected to private suits for intentional sex discrimination under Title IX since 1979, when we decided *Cannon*. *Pennhurst* does not preclude private suits for intentional acts that clearly violate Title IX. *Davis, supra, at 642*.

Indeed, in *Davis*, we held that *Pennhurst* did not pose an obstacle to private suits for damages in cases of a recipient's deliberate indifference to one student's sexual harassment of another, because the deliberate indifference constituted intentional discrimination on the basis of sex. *Davis, supra, at 650* . . . Similarly, we held in *Gebser* that a recipient of federal funding could be held liable for damages under Title IX for deliberate indifference to a teacher's harassment of a student. *524 U.S., at 287–28*. In *Gebser*, as in *Davis*, we acknowledged that federal funding recipients must have notice that they will be held liable for damages. See *Davis, supra, at 642* . . . But we emphasized that "this limitation on private damages actions is not a bar to liability where a funding recipient intentionally violates the statute." *Davis, supra, at 642* . . . Simply put, "*Pennhurst* does not bar a private damages action under Title IX where the funding recipient engages in intentional conduct that violates the clear terms of the statute." *Davis, supra, at 642* . . .

Thus, the Board should have been put on notice by the fact that our cases since *Cannon*, such as *Gebser* and *Davis*, have consistently interpreted Title IX's private cause of action broadly to encompass diverse forms of intentional sex discrimination. Indeed, retaliation presents an even easier case than deliberate indifference. It is easily attributable to the funding recipient, and it is always—by definition—intentional. We therefore conclude that retaliation against individuals because they complain of sex discrimination is "intentional conduct that violates the clear terms of the statute," *Davis, 526 U.S., at 642*, and that Title IX itself therefore supplied sufficient notice to the Board that it could not retaliate against Jackson after he complained of discrimination against the girls' basketball team.

The regulations implementing Title IX clearly prohibit retaliation and have been on the books for nearly 30 years. Cf., *e.g., id., at 643* (holding that Title IX's regulatory scheme "has long provided funding recipients with notice that they may be liable for their failure to respond to the discriminatory acts of certain nonagents"). More importantly, the Courts of Appeals that had considered the question at the time of the conduct at issue in this case all had already interpreted Title IX to cover retaliation. See, *e.g., Lowrey, 117 F.3d, at 252; Preston, 31 F.3d, at 206*. The Board could not have realistically supposed that, given this context, it remained free to retaliate against those who reported sex discrimination. Cf. *Davis, supra, at 644* (stating that the common law of torts "has put schools on notice that they may be held responsible under state law for their failure to protect students from the tortious acts of third parties"). A reasonable school board would realize that institutions covered by Title IX cannot cover up violations of that law by means of discriminatory retaliation.

To prevail on the merits, Jackson will have to prove that the Board retaliated against him *because* he complained of sex discrimination. The amended complaint alleges that the Board retaliated against Jackson for complaining to his supervisor, Ms. Evelyn Baugh, about sex discrimination at EnsleyHigh School. At this stage of the proceedings, "[t]he issue is not whether a plaintiff will ultimately prevail but whether the claimant is entitled to offer evidence to support the claims."*Scheuer v. Rhodes, 416 U.S. 232, 236 (1974)*. Accordingly, the judgment of the Court of Appeals for the Eleventh Circuit is reversed, and the case is remanded for further proceedings consistent with this opinion.

It is so ordered. * * *

CASES ON THE SUPPLEMENTAL WEB SITE

Deli v. University of Minnesota, 863 F. Supp. 958 (D. Minn. 1994) (female coach of women's gymnastics team failed to prove comparator positions of coaches of men's team in Equal Pay Act claim; court also indicated that Title VII and the Equal Pay Act to not prohibit salary discrimination based on the gender of the athletes on the team).

Fuhr v. Sch. Dist. of Hazel Park, 364 F.3d 753 (6th Cir. 2004) (successful employment discrimination case for high school basketball coach).

Medcalf v. Trustees of the Univ. of Pa., 2001 U.S. Dist. LEXIS 10155 E.D. Pa., June 19, 2001 (male coach claimed he was best qualified candidate but did not receive interview because of his sex).

Stanley v. University of Southern California,13 F.3d 1313 (1994) (unsuccessful pay discrimination claims under Equal Pay Act, Title VII and Title IX for women's basketball coach).

Weaver v. The Ohio State University,71 F. Supp.2d 789 (S.D. Ohio 1998).

QUESTIONS YOU SHOULD BE ABLE TO ANSWER

1. What are the limitations of Constitutional protections against discrimination based on sex?

2. Explain the elements of an Equal Pay Act claim and how the burden of proof shifts from plaintiff to defendant and back to plaintiff as a case proceeds.

3. Explain the protection against employment discrimination under Title IX. What are the limitations of this legislation?

4. How does Title IX protect employees from employer retaliation for complaining about gender inequities within athletics programs?

5. How does the Lilly Ledbetter Fair Pay Act improve protection against pay discrimination compared to the Equal Pay Act?

REFERENCES

Cases

Cannon v. University of Chicago, 441 U.S. 677 (1979).
Deli v. University of Minnesota, 863 F. Supp. 958 (D. Minn. 1994).
Fuhr v. Sch. Dist. of Hazel Park, 364 F.3d 753 (6th Cir. 2004).
Grove City College v. Bell, 464 U.S. 555 (1984).
Jackson v. Birmingham Board of Education, 544 U.S. 167 (2005)
Ledbetter v. Goodyear Tire & Rubber Co., 550 U.S. 618 (2007)
Lowrey v. Texas A & M University, 11 F. Supp.2d 895 (S.D. Tex. 1998).
Medcalf v. Trustees of the Univ. of Pa., 2001 U.S. Dist. LEXIS 10155 E.D. Pa., June 19, 2001.
Muller v. Oregon, 208 U.S. 412 (1908)
Stanley v. University of Southern California, 13 F.3d 1313 (9th Cir. 1994).
Stanley v. University of Southern California, 178 F.3d 1069 (9th Cir. 1999).
Weaver v.The Ohio State University, 71 F. Supp.2d 789 (S.D. Ohio 1998).

Publications

Acosta, V., & Carpenter, L.(20112). Women in intercollegiate sport—A longitudinal, National study—Thirty-five year update. Retrieved on February 18, 2012, at http://acostacarpenter.org/AcostaCarpenter2012.pdf
Anderson, P. & Osborne, B. (2008). A Historical Review of Title IX Litigation. *Journal of Legal Aspects of Sport*, 18(1), 127–168.
Osborne, B. & Yarbrough, M.V. (2001). Pay Equity for Coaches and Athletic Administrators: An Element of Title IX? *University of Michigan Journal of Law Reform*, 34(1&2), 231–251.

Press Release (2003 October 9). EEOC Resolves Sex Discrimination Lawsuit Against NBA's Phoenix Suns and Sports Magic for $104,500. Retrieved from the U.S. Equal Employment Opportunity Commission website on April 7, 2009, at http://www.eeoc.gov/oress/10–9–03b.html

Women's Sports Foundation (n.d.). Coaching-Do Female Athletes Prefer Male Coaches?: The Foundation Position. Retrieved May 4, 2009, from http://www.womenssportsfoundation.org/Content/Articles/Issues/Coaching/C/Coaching—Do-Female-Athletes-Prefer-Male-Coaches-The-Foundation-Position.aspx

Legislation

Civil Rights Act of 1987 (Pub. L. No. 100–259, 102 Stat. 28).

EEOC Notice Number 915.002, *Enforcement Guidance on Sex Discrimination in the Compensation of Sports Coaches in Educational Institutions* (Oct. 29, 1997). Retrieved on May 1, 2009, from http://www.eeoc.gov/policy/docs/coaches.html

Elliott-Larsen Civil Rights Act, Mich. C. L. § 37.2101 (2009).

Equal Pay Act of 1963, 29 U.S.C. § 206(d).

Fair Labor Standards Act of 1938, 52 Stat. 1060.

Ill. Const. Art. 1, Sec. 17 (2009).

Lilly Ledbetter Fair Pay Act, 111 P.L. 2 (2009).

Pregnancy Discrimination Act of 1978 (42 U.S.C.A. §2000e(k)).

Title VII of Civil Rights Act of 1964, 42 U.S.C. § 2000 2(a)(1)(2).

Title IX of the Educational Amendments of 1972, 20 U.S.C. § 1681–1688.

7.13 TITLE VII OF THE CIVIL RIGHTS ACT OF 1964

Lisa Pike Masteralexis Stephanie A. Tryce I University of Massachusetts-Amherst

The Civil Rights Act of 1964 is a comprehensive federal law prohibiting discrimination in many settings, including elections, housing, federally funded programs, education, employment, and public facilities and accommodations. Title VII of the Civil Rights Act addresses employment discrimination and is the focal point of the act. It became the first comprehensive federal law prohibiting employment discrimination. Generally, a distinction that is made on the basis of an employee's characteristics (race, gender, religion, national origin)is discriminatory under Title VII.

FUNDAMENTAL CONCEPTS

Scope

Title VII broadly prohibits discrimination in employment. Section 703 (a) states:

> It shall be an unlawful employment practice for an employer—(1) to fail or refuse to hire or to discharge any individual, or otherwise discriminate against any individual with respect to his compensation, terms, conditions, or privileges of employment, because of such individual's race, color, religion, sex, or national origin; or (2) to limit, segregate, or classify his employees or applicants for employment in any way which would deprive or tend to deprive any individual of employment opportunities or otherwise adversely affect his status as an employee, because of such individual's race, color, religion, sex, or national origin [42 U.S.C. §§ 2000e-2(a)].

Title VII applies to employers with fifteen or more employees working at least twenty calendar weeks whose organizations affect interstate commerce. Employers can be individuals, partnerships, joint ventures, corporations, unincorporated associations, and government entities. The definition also includes employment agencies and labor organizations (unions or players associations). Title VII, however, excludes from its definition of employer the U.S. government and some departments of the District of Columbia, Native American tribes, and bona fide membership clubs, such as country clubs.

Graves v. Women's Professional Rodeo Association, Inc. ("WPRA") (1990), provides a clear example that professional associations, which sanction events, will not be considered employers unless they clearly fit the definition of employer. In *Graves*, a male rodeo barrel racer charged that the defendant nonprofit association, which organized female rodeo contestants and sanctioned events, had discriminated against him on the basis of gender when it denied him membership. WPRA was not an "employer" under Title VII because its members were not employees. WPRA did not pay wages, withhold taxes, or pay insurance for members. Furthermore, rules only permitted an opportunity for members to compete for prize money raised by rodeo sponsors, not by the WPRA.

Administration of Title VII

A five-member, presidential-appointed administrative agency, the Equal Employment Opportunity Commission ("EEOC") is charged with the administration of Title VII. The EEOC carries out a number of functions, including investigating charges of employment discrimination. It attempts to conciliate alleged violations. Where the EEOC does not find reasonable cause to go forward with conciliation or where conciliation is not fruitful, the complaining party may proceed with a private Title VII lawsuit. The EEOC may also file suit in federal district court to enforce Title VII, or it may intervene in any private employment discrimination lawsuit. For example, in *EEOC v. National Broadcasting Co., Inc.*, the EEOC sued on behalf of a female applicant for the position of television sports director alleging sex discrimination in violation of Title VII. Further, the EEOC creates guidelines and regulations for the interpretation of Title VII. Although the guidelines and regulations do not possess the full force and effect of law, they are subject to great judicial deference. For example, in *Meritor Savings Bank, FSB v. Vinson* (1986), the U.S. Supreme Court relied on EEOC guidelines to define hostile environment sexual harassment.

Civil Rights Act of 1991

The Civil Rights Act of 1991 established a Glass Ceiling Commission and a Glass Ceiling Initiative through the Department of Labor to examine whether a glass ceiling existed to keep women and minorities underrepresented in management and decision-making positions. Additionally, this Act amended the Civil Rights Act of 1964 to permit jury trials and compensatory and punitive damages in addition to back pay for *all* claims of intentional discrimination under Title VII, not just racial and ethnic discrimination.

Furthermore, the Civil Rights Act of 1991 prohibits "race norming," a practice whereby test scores are adjusted on the basis of race or other Title VII classification. It also adopted the defenses of "business necessity" and "job-related" practices as bases for which an employer can justify an employment practice challenged as discriminatory. Finally, the 1991 Act eliminated challenges to affirmative action consent decrees from individuals who had notice and an opportunity to object when the decree was entered or whose interests were adequately represented by another individual or organization.

Classes Protected under Title VII

Title VII prohibits employment discrimination on the basis of race, color, religion, gender, or national origin in hiring, firing, training, compensating, designating work assignments, promoting, demoting, or any other employment activity. Thus, any employment decision, practice, or policy that segregates individuals and treats them differently on the basis of the preceding classifications violates Title VII.

Race

Although much of the U.S. Civil Rights Movement focused on the treatment of African Americans, Title VII's definition of race is much broader. It is not limited to ethnological races, but protects all classes of people from dissimilar treatment, including, but not limited to Hispanics, Native Americans, and Asian Americans.

Racial discrimination cases involving coaches and athletic directors arose from decisions made in the course of public school desegregation. For example, in *Cross v. Board of Education of Dollarway, Arkansas School District* (1975), the plaintiff, a black high school football coach at a black high school in a segregated school district, was demoted to assistant coach when his school integrated with a white high school. Cross was passed over for the position twice, when white coaches with fewer qualifications were hired. On the second instance, the school superintendent suggested the school board deviate from its policy to promote within to search outside the district for a white coach. The superintendent was of the opinion that the white players would not play for a black coach and the community was not ready for a black head coach and athletic director. The court found the school board's refusal to even consider Cross's application was clear evidence of individual disparate treatment on the basis of his race. As a result Cross was entitled to back pay equal to the difference in the amount he would have received as head coach and that which he did receive as assistant coach. Additionally, the defendant was ordered to promote Cross to the position of head football coach and athletic director or to compensate him at a salary comparable to the position.

In April 2005, a California jury awarded Mike Terpstra, former California State University Stanislaus men's basketball coach, $540,000 in damages in a reverse race discrimination case., Terpstra, a white male, claimed his race was a factor in the university's decision to allow his contract to expire after the 2002–2003 season, because they were interested in replacing him with a black coach. Although Terpstra was ultimately replaced with another white male coach, the jury found that race was a factor in allowing his contract to expire.

An expansion of racial discrimination has come in same-race cases. In *Ross v. Douglas County* (2001), the Eighth Circuit Court of Appeals held that an African-American employee could assert a claim of racial harassment directed toward him by his African-American supervisor's use of racial epithets. The court found that the African-American supervisor's behavior was discriminatory "whatever the motive" and that the supervisor's race "did not alter this." The case, however, does not serve to make clear the distinction between the content of the improper behavior at issue and the motivation for the behavior in the first instance. Juries are likely to have difficulty separating the racially obvert nature of the conduct from whether racial bias was the reason for the harassment in the first place.

Color

An employer's distinction on the basis of skin pigment or the physical characteristics of an applicant or employee's race are discriminatory. For instance, if an employer favors light-skinned African Americans over dark-skinned African Americans, it is treating African Americans differently on the basis of color. Color discrimination often intersects with racial discrimination.

National Origin

In national origin discrimination cases, the focus is on one's ancestry (excluding U.S. territories such as Puerto Rico or the Virgin Islands). Title VII does not prohibit employment discrimination solely on the basis of citizenship. For example, in *Dowling v. United States* (1979), the plaintiff argued that the National Hockey League and the World Hockey Association only hired Canadian referees, and thus, discriminated against him on the basis of his national origin. The court dismissed the claim, stating that Title VII did not bar employment discrimination on the basis of alienage or citizenship. However, the lack of U.S. citizenship may not be used as a method of disguising discrimination that is actually based on race or national origin. An employer may follow a policy of employing only U.S. citizens, but may not give unequal treatment to different noncitizens based on their country of origin.

Sex

Title VII's sex discrimination cases have primarily involved women, but it also applies to men. For example, in *Medcalf v. University of Pennsylvania* (1998), an EEOC investigation found that University of Pennsylvania ("Penn") had discriminated against male applicants when hiring the new women's crew coach. The EEOC found that Penn took extraordinary measures to recruit only female candidates, and that the university failed to interview Andrew Medcalf, its assistant men's rowing coach, even though he was highly recommended.

It is the gender of the employee discriminated against, not the gender of the athletes an employee coaches, which form the basis for Title VII discrimination. The plaintiffs in *Jackson v. Armstrong School District* (1977) lost their Title VII claim because they alleged they were paid less money because they were coaching girls' basketball, rather than alleging that they were discriminated against because they were women. The defendant avoided liability by establishing that men coaching girls' basketball were paid the same amount as the women. The theory of sexual harassment comes from this section of the Act. Liability for sexual harassment was introduced as a legal theory in the late 1970s and continues to evolve, with the most recent decisions focusing on same-sex harassment and employer liability (both are discussed in Section 7.14, *Sexual Harassment*).

Title VII's protection against sex-based discrimination does not include discrimination on the basis of sexual orientation. In 1978 Congress amended Title VII's language "on the basis of sex" to include protection against discrimination on the basis of pregnancy, childbirth, or other related medical conditions (including abortion). Although Title VII does not protect against sexual orientation discrimination in the workplace, twenty-two states have added protection against discrimination on the basis of sexual orientation in their employment discrimination laws. At the same time, and possibly in response to this movement, a number of jurisdictions have sought to prohibit homosexuality in their state and/or local governments. In *Price Waterhouse v. Hopkins* (1989), the U.S. Supreme Court stated that where the employer bases employment decisions on gender stereotyping, a Title VII claim may be sustained. The key in the determination is whether the harassment occurred because of the victim's sex. In *Bibby v. Philadelphia Coca Cola Bottling Co.*, (2001), the Third Circuit of Appeals rejected a plaintiff's claim of unlawful harassment and enumerated three ways to prove where same-sex harassment occurred on account of the victim's sex: "(1) proof that the harasser sexually desires the victim; (2) proof that the harasser displays hostility to the presence of a particular sex in the workplace; and (3) proof that the harasser's conduct was motivated by a belief that the victim failed to conform to the stereotypes of his or her gender" (*Bibby v. Philadelphia Coca Cola Bottling Co.,* 2001),

The scope of Title VII sex discrimination claims now also includes transgender. In *Smith v. City of Salem* (2004), the Sixth Circuit Court of Appeals held that a transsexual has a viable cause of action under Title VII if he is discriminated against because of his failure to conform to sex stereotypes by exhibiting less masculine and more feminine mannerisms and appearance or vice versa. The Sixth Circuit, relying on *Price Waterhouse,* found that "sex" encompasses both the biological differences between men and women, and gender discrimination, which are based on the failure to conform to stereotypical gender norms. Although Title VII does not protect against sexual orientation discrimination, per se, it is possible that the decision in *Salem* could be used by the Lesbian, Gay, Bisexual, Transgender and Questioning ("LBGTQ") community to bring claims under Title VII by asserting that they have been discriminated against for failure to conform to stereotypical gender norms.

Religion

All well-recognized faiths and even those considered unorthodox (provided the court is convinced that the purported belief is sincere and genuinely held, and not simply adopted for an ulterior motive) are protected under Title VII. An employer must make *a reasonable accommodation* to an employee's religious practices and observances, unless it would place an *undue hardship* on the employer. An employer's obligation is simply to make a reasonable accommodation to an employee.

Theories of Liability

Courts applying Title VII have established four theories of liability: individual disparate treatment, systemic disparate treatment, disparate impact, and retaliation.

Individual Disparate Treatment

There are two ways to prove intentional discrimination. The first is through direct evidence of intent from the defendant's statements. In *Morris v. Bianchini, et al.* (1987), the plaintiff and another woman were passed over for promotion to athletic director of the health and fitness club in favor of less qualified males. The reason they were given was that the club sought "a macho, male image" for its athletic director. This statement was used as evidence of intent by the club's management to discriminate against two qualified women in favor of a less qualified candidate on the basis of gender. Another example is *Biver v. Saginaw Township Community Schools, et al.* (1986), in which the plaintiff alleged discrimination in failing to hire her for a boys' or girls' basketball team coaching position. Accepted as evidence of the superintendent's discriminatory intent, the court cited his statement that "hell would freeze over before he would hire a woman for a boys' coaching position" (*Biver v. Saginaw Township Community Schools,* et al., 1986). The superintendent claimed it was not discriminatory, as his policy was to hire men to coach boys and women to coach girls. The plaintiff challenged his credibility by showing many instances in which he had hired men to coach girls.

A second method by which one can prove discrimination is through the use of an *inference*. A plaintiff can establish an inference for the court by comparing how an employer treats similarly situated employees of different protected classes. The model for using an inference to prove discriminatory intent was established in*McDonnell Douglas Corp. v. Green,* (1973). The McDonnell Douglas model is as follows:

"[f]irst, the plaintiff has the burden of proving by the preponderance of the evidence a prima facie case of discrimination. Second, if the plaintiff succeeds in proving the prima facie case the burden shifts to the defendant 'to articulate some legitimate nondiscriminatory reason for the employee's rejection.' Third, should the defendant carry this burden, the plaintiff must then have an opportunity to prove by a preponderance of the evidence that the legitimate reasons offered by the defendant were not its true reasons, but were a pretext for discrimination" (*McDonnell Douglas Corp. v. Green,* 1973).

Under this widely relied upon standard, a ***prima facie case*** is established by the plaintiff showing:

(If applicant)

1. Applicant is a member of a protected class;
2. Applicant applied for a job for which the employer was seeking applicants;
3. Applicant was qualified to perform the job;
4. Applicant was not hired; and
5. Employer continues to seek applicants after rejection.

(If employee)

1. Employee is within the protected class;
2. Employee was performing the task satisfactorily;
3. Employee was discharged or adversely affected by change in working conditions; and
4. Employee's work was assigned to one in a nonminority category.

The burden then shifts to the defendant to rebut the plaintiff's presumption by producing evidence that the plaintiff was rejected and someone else preferred for a ***legitimate, nondiscriminatory reason*** (*Texas Department of Community Affairs v. Burdine*, 1981). The defendant's burden is one of production, not persuasion. For the reason to be legitimate, it must be lawful, clear, and reasonably specific. In other words, when comparing the chosen applicant or employee with the plaintiff, the defendant should elaborate on the criteria necessary for hiring or promotion, the basis for the comparison of the candidates, and that the person hired or promoted, rather than the plaintiff, possessed the qualities the defendant was seeking (*Herman v. National Broadcasting Co., Inc.*, 1984). The defendant need not prove that the chosen employee was a superior candidate, but simply that there were legitimate, nondiscriminatory reasons to justify the employer's decision. It is difficult for a defendant to raise this defense without clear qualification criteria for hiring. For instance, in *Jackson v. World League of American Football* (1994), the court refused to grant summary judgment in a racial discrimination case where the World League of American Football had not set clear qualifications for the position of head football coach. Once the employer provides a legitimate, nondiscriminatory reason for the alleged discrimination, the burden then shifts back to the employee to prove that the legitimate reason is in fact a ***pretext*** for intentional discrimination. A plaintiff may establish evidence of pretext by:

1. providing direct evidence of prejudice toward the plaintiff or members of the protected class;
2. presenting statistical evidence; and
3. presenting comparative evidence that members of a protected class were treated less favorably or members of the majority were treated favorably.

An example of the last point occurred in *Davis v. McCormick* (1995), where a female coach was subject to a more stringent disciplinary policy and her discipline was arguably more severe than any male coach's discipline. The court found that this raised a reasonable inference that the plaintiff's discipline was a pretext for intentional discrimination.

A plaintiff may also present the fact that the legitimate, nondiscriminatory reason was not given to the plaintiff at the time the employment decision was made as evidence that it was an afterthought and, thus, a pretext. For example, in *Baylor v. Jefferson County Board of Education* (1984), a black teacher-coach proved the defendant school board's transfer of him to a teaching-only position was racially motivated. Baylor successfully proved that the defendant's legitimate, nondiscriminatory reason for the job transfer was developed after his hearing and decision to transfer him out of coaching were made.

Finally, failing to comply with the usual hiring procedures may indicate discriminatory actions. For instance, as noted earlier in *Cross* (1975), the school superintendent suggested that the school board deviate from its policy of promoting from within to search outside the district for a white coach. In *Peirick, v. Indiana University-Purdue* (2005), the Court refused to grant summary judgment in a sex discrimination case where the plaintiff offered sufficient evidence that demonstrated "either that a discriminatory reason more likely motivated the employer or that the employer's proffered explanation is unworthy of credence" (*Peirick, v. Indiana University-Purdue*, 2005).

Harassment. The Supreme Court in *Meritor Savings Bank, FSB v. Vinson* (1986), stated that the EEOC "has held and continues to hold that an employer has a duty to maintain a working environment free of harassment based on race, color, religion, sex, [or] national origin . . . and that the duty requires positive action where necessary to eliminate such practices or remedy their effects" (*Meritor Savings Bank, FSB v. Vinson*, 1986). Courts have applied this theory to harassment on the basis of race (*Johnson v. NFL*), religion (*Compston v. Borden, Inc.*, 1976), national origin (*Cariddi v. Kansas City Chiefs Football Club*, 1977), and gender (*Meritor Savings Bank, FSB v. Vinson*, 1986). By far, the application of the harassment theory is most developed for discrimination on the basis of sex. A thorough discussion of sexual harassment is found in Section 7.14, *Sexual Harassment*.

Systemic Disparate Treatment

Under the theory of systemic disparate treatment, plaintiffs challenge broad sweeping employment policies that are discriminatory, such as an employer's policy not to hire women or to segregate employees by race. A plaintiff's initial burden is to "establish by preponderance of the evidence that discrimination is an employer's standard operating procedure—the regular, rather than the unusual practice" (*Lowery v. Circuit City*, 1998, *quoting Teamsters v. United States*, 1977). This creates an inference that hiring or promotion practices were made in furtherance of this discriminatory policy.

When challenging system wide patterns or practices, plaintiffs often rely on statistical evidence bolstered with evidence of individual discriminatory treatment. The statistics will compare the racial, ethnic, or gender balance of the qualified labor population with the population of a workforce that draws employees from that population. In *Teamsters v. United States*(1977), the court stated that statistics showing an imbalance are probative because such imbalance is often a telltale sign of purposeful discrimination. Absent discrimination, it is assumed that over time nondiscriminatory workplace practices will result in a workforce that is representative of a region's general population.

Once a plaintiff establishes a presumption of a discriminatory pattern or practice, the burden then shifts to the employer to demonstrate why an inference of discrimination could not be drawn from the plaintiff's evidence. Here the defendant has two options. First, the defendant can attack the plaintiff's statistical evidence as inaccurate or insignificant. Second, the employer may seek to provide a nondiscriminatory explanation for the apparently discriminatory result. As with individual disparate treatment, once a defendant produces this explanation, the burden will shift to the plaintiff to persuade the court that the defendant's stated explanation is in fact a pretext for discrimination.

Disparate Impact

Disparate impact discrimination exists where a plaintiff is challenging a neutral employment practice, regardless of intent, that has a discriminatory effect on a protected group. This model only applies where the employer has instituted a specific procedure, usually a criterion for employment, which the plaintiff can show has a causal connection with a protected class's imbalance in the workforce (*Pouncy v. Prudential Insurance Co. of America*, 1982).

The prima facie case requires proof that the employment practice or policy has an adverse impact on the protected group to which the employee belongs. This is usually established through statistical evidence documenting the impact of the practice on the protected class. The use of statistical evidence is difficult and the plaintiff's methodology may be attacked as flawed. For instance, in *Wynn v. Columbus Municipal Separate School District* (1988), a female coach used the disparate impact model to challenge her employer's practice of having the head football coach also serve as the athletic director. She argued that the practice had a disparate impact on females, because it was extremely rare that a female would be qualified to be a head football coach. The plaintiff presented statistical evidence from her state, Mississippi. Of the 192 high school athletic directors in the state only 62 were not head football coaches, no women were head football coaches, and just two athletic directors were women. The court found her theory flawed on two grounds. First, the fact that few women in Mississippi were selected to serve as athletic director had little relationship to the issue of whether the defendant, Columbus School District, discriminates against women as athletic director. Second, the plaintiff's statistical evidence is drawn from a pool that includes not only females from the protected class, but a number of nonmembers of that class, namely males who are not qualified as football coach and thus, are denied the athletic director position. The court stated the better approach would be to consider the discriminatory treatment of qualified female coaches in the Columbus schools who had been denied the position of athletic director. Thus, the plaintiff lost on her disparate impact claim, but was successful under her disparate treatment theory.

In addition to attacking statistical evidence, an employer may also rebut the plaintiff's argument by producing evidence that the practice is "job-related." This requires proof that the challenged employment practice is necessary to achieve some legitimate business objective, the practice actually achieves that objective, and there is no reasonable alternative for accomplishing the objective without discriminating. Once the employer establishes the barrier is "job-related," the burden shifts back to the plaintiff to prove that the barrier is a pretext for discrimination, by showing there are other adequate devices that do not discriminate against a protected class.

Retaliation

Title VII provides a cause of action for retaliation in response to a plaintiff's filing of a claim of employment discrimination. Section 704 (a) of Title VII states:

> it shall be an unlawful employment practice for an employer to discriminate against any of his employees
> . . . because [that employee] has opposed any practice made an unlawful employment practice by this
> title or because he has made charge, testified, assisted or participated in any manner in an investigation
> proceeding, or hearing under this title [42 U.S.C. § 2000e-3(a)].

The plaintiff's burden of proof in retaliation claims mirrors that in other Title VII suits. The plaintiff bears the initial burden of establishing a prima facie case of retaliation. To establish the prima facie retaliation case, the plaintiff must show by a preponderance of the evidence that (1) the plaintiff engaged in a statutorily protected activity, (2) adverse action was taken against the plaintiff by the employer subsequent to and contemporaneously with such activity, and (3) a causal link exists between the protected activity and the adverse action (*Jalil v. Advel Corp.*, 1989). Once the plaintiff has established a prima facie case, the defendant may introduce evidence providing legitimate, non-retaliatory reasons for its conduct. If the defendant properly introduces such evidence, the burden shifts back to the plaintiff to show that the defendant's justification is merely pretext for unlawful retaliation. See *Lowery v. Texas A&M University d/b/a Tarleton State University* (1998), where a Lowery, former women's basketball coach, alleged that defendants were liable under Title VII, Title IX, 42 U.S.C. §1983 and the Constitution's First and Fourteenth Amendments for retaliating against her by removing her as Women's Athletics Coordinator in response to comments she made criticizing the university and its officials on gender equity issues.

Additional Defenses

Bona Fide Occupational Qualification

It is not illegal to discriminate on the basis of religion, gender, or national origin if an employer can show the classification is a bona fide occupational qualification (BFOQ). Race and color are never BFOQs. The BFOQ defense requires the employer to prove that members of the excluded class could not safely and effectively perform essential job duties and the employer must have a factual basis for believing that persons in the excluded class could not perform the job. The BFOQ must also be reasonably necessary to the normal operation of the business. An example might be a situation where a boys' overnight recreational program hires only male floor counselors. If the counselors will live in dorms with the boys, the recreation program may prefer males for the comfort of the boy campers and for role modeling. Finally, customer preference cannot be the basis for a BFOQ.

Business Necessity

Business necessity serves as a defense to a disparate impact discrimination claim, where a particular practice causes a protected class to face discrimination. The employer may prove that a particular practice is "job related" and thus a business necessity despite the discriminatory impact of the practice (*Griggs v. Duke Power Co.*, 1971).

Affirmative Action

Affirmative action involves creating policies for giving preference to those underrepresented in the workplace. The policies often possess goals/timetables for increasing percentages of underrepresented workers to rectify past discrimination. The affirmative-action policy may be voluntary or court ordered as a result of a lawsuit. Affirmative action policies often result in discrimination against the overrepresented classes, termed reverse discrimination. It is legal provided:

- The discrimination results from a formal, systematic program;
- The program is temporary, operating only until its goals are reached;
- The program does not completely bar the hiring/promotion of non-minorities;
- The program does not result in the firing of non-minority workers;
- The program does not force the employer to hire/promote unqualified workers.

Where the program is court-ordered, it must be based on actual evidence of discrimination. Where the program is voluntary, it must be based actual evidence of discrimination or evidence that those in underrepresented groups had been underutilized in the past.

Remedies

Section 706(g) provides the following power to remedy employment discrimination under Title VII:

> If the court finds that the respondent has intentionally engaged in or is intentionally engaging in an unlawful employment practice . . . the court may enjoin the respondent from engaging in such unlawful employment practice, and order such affirmative action as may be appropriate, which may include, but is not limited to, reinstatement or hiring of employees with or without back pay . . . or any other equitable relief as the court deems appropriate. . . .

A successful plaintiff most often is awarded back pay. A back pay order requires the defendant to pay all lost wages and benefits that would have been earned were it not for the illegal discrimination. The trial court may grant interest on these wages.

SIGNIFICANT CASE

The following case is an example of a Title VII lawsuit involving a retaliation claim. The employees argued that they were dismissed due to their opposition to the NFL's discriminatory employment practices.

THOMAS V. NATIONAL FOOTBALL LEAGUE PLAYERS ASSOCIATION

U.S. Court of Appeals for the District of Columbia Circuit
131 F.3d 198 (1997)

A principal claim in this case is that the defendant, acting pursuant to "mixed motives," unlawfully retaliated against the plaintiffs in violation of Title VII, 42 U.S.C. § 2000e *et seq.* (1994). The issues on appeal require us to delimit the requirements of *McDonnell Douglas Corp. v. Green*, 411 U.S. 792, (1973), *Texas Dep't of Community Affairs v. Burdine*, 450 U.S. 248 (1981), and *Price Waterhouse v. Hopkins*, 490 U.S. 228 (1989), with respect to a plaintiff's

prima facie case, a defendant's burden of production, and the ultimate burdens of persuasion, in a retaliation/mixed-motives case.

The actions giving rise to this lawsuit occurred when Eugene Upshaw, Executive Director of the National Football League Players Association ("NFLPA"), first laid off, then terminated employees Valerie Thomas and Rita Raymond on the stated grounds that they had been disloyal in criticizing NFLPA staff and policies in an anonymously distributed document and in several legally taped telephone calls. Julie Taylor-Bland (Bland at the time of the events) resigned in the aftermath of the firing of the other two. Before leaving the employ of the NFLPA, Thomas and Bland had suggested to management that NFLPA promotion policy discriminated against African-American women. The three women subsequently sued the NFLPA, charging that the lay-off and discharge of Thomas and Raymond, and the alleged constructive discharge of Bland, came in retaliation to their opposition to discriminatory employment practices, and hence violated Title VII.

After trial, the District Court granted judgment as a matter of law to the NFLPA on the plaintiffs' claim that there existed a pattern and practice of discrimination at the NFLPA. * * * It then found that Thomas had been unlawfully fired, that Raymond had not made out a *prima facie* case of retaliation, and that Bland had not been fired at all. The trial court granted Thomas back pay and prejudgment interest, but declined to reinstate her. *Thomas, et al., v. National Football League Players Ass'n,* 941 F. Supp. 156 (D.D.C. 1996), *reprinted in* J.A. 279. * * *Thomas, et al., v. National Football League Players Ass'n,* No. 91-3332 (D.D.C. Nov. 26, 1996). The NFLPA now appeals the decision adverse to it; Thomas, Raymond, and Bland cross appeal the decisions adverse to them.

We affirm the District Court's judgment on the merits as to Thomas, Raymond, and Bland's claims.

* * *

I. Background

In 1988, Thomas, Raymond, and Bland worked for the NFLPA and belonged to Office and Professional Employees International Union, Local 2 ("Local 2"). After the NFLPA's unsuccessful strike against the owners during the 1987 season, the NFLPA's finances suffered, and Executive Director Upshaw devised a new budget for the NFLPA, which sought to reduce personnel costs through attrition. The board of directors of the NFLPA met during the first week of March 1988, and elected George Martin president and Mike Davis vice president. The board declined to adopt Upshaw's proposed budget, instead demanding a ten percent reduction in personnel costs by layoff.

Thomas, Bland and others complained about promotional opportunities for African-Americans and women in the Local 2 bargaining unit to Martin in an informal meeting. Sometime after March 10, 1988, Martin organized a second meeting, which Thomas and Bland also attended. Similar concerns were raised, and someone present accused Upshaw of racism.

In the weeks that followed, Martin and Davis conducted personal and telephone interviews with staff on a range of employment-related subjects. Interviewees were assured of confidentiality. In their interviews, Thomas and

Bland expressed views on race and sex discrimination at the NFLPA. Davis also interviewed Raymond. Around the same time, Upshaw implemented the NFLPA board's directive to lay off some employees to cut costs. Prior to the lay-offs, Upshaw heard from Davis that Thomas and Raymond had criticized various employees in telephone conversations with Davis, and were suspected of producing and circulating a document harshly critical of the NFLPA. The document was headed and referred to as "What every player should know about the NFLPA." It included, among other allegations, a variety of claims about unfair promotion practices at the NFLPA. It did not include allegations of racial discrimination.

On March 18, 1988, Upshaw laid off six employees, including Thomas and Raymond. At a time proximate to the lay-offs, Martin undertook to investigate the employees' allegations of misconduct at the NFLPA, and asked Upshaw about minority issues at the NFLPA. Martin told Upshaw that Thomas had called him a racist and had complained about promotion of African-Americans and women. Martin and Davis each gave copies of the "What every player should know" memorandum to Upshaw. Davis told Upshaw about his telephone conversations with Thomas and Raymond and that Raymond had mailed him a copy of the memorandum.

On March 23, 1988, Davis gave Upshaw tapes of his telephone conversations with Thomas and Raymond. According to Upshaw's un-contradicted testimony, the conversations included ad hominem attacks on various NFLPA employees, including Upshaw. On the tapes, Raymond promised to send a copy of the "What every player should know" memorandum to Davis. Upshaw concluded that Thomas and Raymond had written the memo.

On April 12, 1988, five of the six employees laid off on March 18 were fired for cause. Upshaw sent each employee an identical letter explaining the firing on the grounds that the employees had libeled and slandered NFLPA personnel, had violated confidentiality, and had shown disloyalty towards and intentionally embarrassed the NFLPA. Upshaw later testified that he fired Thomas and Raymond for what he believed they had said and written about the NFLPA employees. Some weeks later, Bland asked Upshaw about a newly open paralegal/secretary position, and Upshaw told her that he "did not see her in the job"; on May 20, 1988, Bland resigned.

Local 2 pursued grievances against the NFLPA on behalf of Thomas and Raymond. The grievances were appealed to arbitration and an arbitrator ruled that the two had been dismissed without just cause. The arbitrator's award ordered reinstatement, but the NFLPA failed to comply. Thomas, Raymond, and Bland also filed timely charges with the Equal Employment Opportunity Commission ("EEOC"), which issued "no cause" determinations on all their claims. At trial, the District Court dismissed as a matter of law plaintiffs' claim of a pattern and practice of discrimination. It found for Thomas and awarded her back pay, without reinstatement, with prejudgment interest for twenty-one months after her firing, based on expert testimony that estimated the time it should have taken Thomas to find new employment. The District Court found against Raymond, who did not appear at trial. Finally, the District Court found that Bland had not been constructively discharged.

II. Analysis

Burdens of Pleading, Production, and Persuasion Under Title VII.

Title VII makes it unlawful to retaliate against an employee who "has opposed any practice made an unlawful practice" by the statute. 42 U.S.C. § 2000e–3(a).

As in all Title VII cases, the plaintiff must first make out a *prima facie* case of unlawful employment action. *McDonnell Douglas Corp. v. Green,* 411 U.S. 792 (1973). Where retaliation is alleged, a *prima facie* case requires a showing that (1) plaintiff engaged in protected activity, (2) plaintiff was subjected to adverse action by the employer, and (3) there existed a causal link between the adverse action and the protected activity. *Mitchell v. Baldrige,* 759 F.2d 80, 86 (D.C. Cir. 1985). A rebuttable presumption of unlawful discrimination arises when a plaintiff makes out a *prima facie* case. *Texas Dep't of Community Affairs v. Burdine,* 450 U.S. 248, 254 (1981). The defendant may rebut the presumption by asserting a legitimate, non-discriminatory reason for its actions. The defendant's responsibility at this stage has been characterized as a "burden of production," because the ultimate burden of persuasion remains with the plaintiff.

When a defendant satisfies the burden of production, the presumption of discrimination dissolves; however, the plaintiff still has the opportunity to persuade the trier of fact that the defendant's proffered reason was not the actual or sole basis for the disputed action. The plaintiff may aim to prove that a discriminatory motive was the only basis for the employer's action, or the plaintiff may seek to show that the employer was motivated by both permissible and impermissible motives. The plaintiff often will—quite reasonably—argue both alternatives. *See Price Waterhouse v. Hopkins,* 490 U.S. 228, 247 n.12 (Brennan, J.) * * * Where a plaintiff argues that discriminatory motivation constituted the only basis for the employer's action, the plaintiff may persuade the trier of fact of the pretextual nature of the defendant's asserted reason "either directly by persuading the court that a discriminatory reason more likely motivated the employer or indirectly by showing that the employer's proffered explanation is unworthy of credence." *Burdine,* 450 U.S. at 256.

Where, on the other hand, the plaintiff argues that the action resulted from mixed motives, a slightly different model operates. A plaintiff asserting mixed motives must persuade the trier of fact by a preponderance of the evidence that unlawful retaliation constituted a substantial factor in the defendant's action. *Price Waterhouse,* 490 U.S. at 276 (O'Connor, J., concurring); *Id.* at 259 (White, J., concurring). When the plaintiff successfully shows that an unlawful motive was a substantial factor in the employer's action, the defendant may seek to prove in response that it would have taken the contested action even absent the discriminatory motive. If the defendant fails to persuade the trier of fact by a preponderance of the evidence that it would have taken the action even absent the discriminatory motive, the plaintiff will prevail.

This burden on a defendant in a mixed-motives case has been characterized both as an affirmative defense, and as a shifting burden of persuasion. Under *Price Waterhouse* a defendant who is guilty of acting pursuant to an unlawful motive may escape liability by proving that it would have made the same decision in the absence of the unlawful motivation. In short, the ultimate burden of persuasion as to the facts constituting the defense properly falls on the defendant in a mixed-motives case, because the plaintiff has proven that unlawful motivation constituted a substantial factor in the defendant's action.

Appellant's Claims

Meaning and Requirement of Direct Evidence
Appellant NFLPA, the defendant below, argues that, under *Price Waterhouse,* the burden of persuasion shifts to the defendant only where the plaintiff has provided "direct" rather than "inferential" evidence of discriminatory animus. We reject this contention. Under *Price Waterhouse,* the burden of persuasion shifts to the defendant when the plaintiff has shown by a preponderance of "any sufficiently probative direct or indirect evidence" that unlawful discrimination was a substantial factor in the employment decision. *White v. Federal Express Corp.,* 939 F.2d 157, 160 (4th Cir. 1991).

* * *

As this court recently noted, "the distinction between direct and circumstantial evidence has no direct correlation with the strength of [a] plaintiff 's case." *Crawford-El v. Britton*, 93 F.3d 813, 818 (D.C. Cir. 1996) (*en banc*), *cert. granted,* 117 S. Ct. 2451 (U.S. 1997). The purported distinction between "circumstantial" or "inferential" and "direct" evidence urged here does not make logical sense, because the decision to shift the burden of persuasion properly rests upon the strength of the plaintiff 's evidence of discrimination, not the contingent methods by which that evidence is adduced.

* * *

District Court Decision on the Merits
The District Court * * * found that Thomas engaged in protected activity by participating in two conversations with Martin in which she raised the issue of discrimination against women and African-Americans in promotion at the NFLPA, and by distributeding the memo to Martin. The District Court found that the NFLPA fired Thomas

"immediately following" the protected activity, and permissibly concluded that Thomas had made out a prima facie case. Because it did not find evidence that Raymond engaged in protected conduct, the District Court correctly found that Raymond had not made out a *prima facie* case. The District Court further found that Bland was not constructively discharged, because she had not presented evidence of aggravating factors making her work intolerable. Neither of these conclusions was clearly erroneous; the legal framework for both was correct.

The District Court then assessed the evidence that served to refute the NFLPA's claim that it had non-discriminatory reasons sufficient to fire Thomas. It found that the way in which the firing followed Upshaw's learning of Thomas's taped comments; the unusual security measures surrounding the firing; and Upshaw's possession of the memorandum which he believed Thomas had co-authored sufficed to prove that Thomas's firing was motivated "in substantial measure" by her protected activity. This constituted an acceptable finding of mixed motives, and was not clearly erroneous. Although the District Court did not cite *Price Waterhouse,* it correctly concluded that the burden of persuasion had shifted, and that as a result "it was NFLPA's burden to demonstrate that Thomas would have been discharged regardless of her protected activity." In the District Court's view, "the NFLPA failed to sustain that burden" in that it did not successfully separate permissible from impermissible motives in its decision. This conclusion was not clearly erroneous, either, but reflected the fact finder's assessment of the evidence surrounding the firing.

Rejection of Statistical Evidence

The District Court correctly ruled as a matter of law that plaintiffs did not make out a prima facie statistical case of a pattern and practice of discrimination on the part of the NFLPA. The crucial basis for this ruling was that plaintiffs' expert did not consider the relevant qualifications of those passed over or approved for promotion. A *prima facie* case of statistical disparity must include the minimum objective qualifications of the applicants. Here, the expert did not account for minimum qualifications. Indeed, he could not have done so, because Appellees never specifically requested qualification standards from Appellant in discovery. We need not reach the District Court's other reasons for dismissal, because even if the

trial court had found adequate sample size and statistical significance (which it did not), a non-discriminatory, qualifications-based reason for the disparate impact could have existed. * * *

The Relief

The District Court awarded Thomas back pay from the date of her firing to December 1989, by which time, it found, she should have secured employment. The District Court did not abuse its discretion in weighing expert testimony regarding job availability to arrive at this time period.

* * *

The District Court did not abuse its discretion in declining to reinstate Thomas. Although the acrimony of litigation alone probably would not suffice to rule out reinstatement, see *Dickerson v. Deluxe Check Printers, Inc.,* 703 F.2d 276, 281 (8th Cir. 1983), the District Court's denial of reinstatement reflected its own observation that some of Thomas's actions "might well have warranted discharge [as it] reasonably concluded that reinstatement would not serve the interests of justice where the employee engaged in behavior that could conceivably have given rise to a legitimate discharge under other circumstances.

The District Court awarded Thomas prejudgment interest on the back pay. The presumption strongly favors prejudgment interest, but the trial court may disallow interest where attributable to substantial, unexplained delay by the plaintiff. Although Thomas reasonably awaited the EEOC's disposition of her request for a right to sue letter, which was delayed through no fault of her own, the same cannot be said of the three-year period during which Thomas and her co-plaintiffs repeatedly amended their complaint. The District Court must reconsider this issue on remand.

* * *

III. Conclusion

For the foregoing reasons, the judgment of the District Court is affirmed regarding Thomas, Raymond, and Bland.

So ordered.

CASES ON THE SUPPLEMENTAL WEB SITE

Lowrey v. Texas A&M University System, 11 F. Supp. 2d 895 (1998). This case examines whether the university and its' officials discriminated against the coach on the basis of her sex and retaliated against her for complaining about the alleged discrimination.

Peirick v. Indiana University-Purdue University Indianapolis, 2005 U.S. Dist. LEXIS 32479. This case examines whether the university had a legitimate reason for firing an employee.

Wynn v. Columbus Municipal Separate School District, 692 F. Supp. 672 (1988). This case examines whether an applicant was unlawfully discriminated against on the basis of her sex when she was denied the position of Athletic Director.

Medcalf v. University of Pennsylvania, 71 Fe. Appx. 924 2003; U.S. Appl LEXIS 16110. This reverse gender discrimination case examines whether the evidence supported the rejection of the defendant University's proffered reason for hiring a woman over a man.

Nicholas v. Board of Trustees of University of Alabama, 251 Fed Appx. 637; 2007 U.S. App LEXIS 24463. This case examines whether a male assistant coach for the woman's basketball team established a prima facie case of disparate treatment discrimination and retaliation and whether the university established legitimate, nondiscriminatory reasons for its actions.

QUESTIONS YOU SHOULD BE ABLE TO ANSWER

1. What are the classes protected by Title VII?

2. How does a plaintiff put forth the evidence for a Title VII prima facie case, if the plaintiff is an applicant for a job? What if the plaintiff is an employee?

3. What aare the differences between cases based on disparate impact and disparate treatment discrimination under Title VII?

4. What defenses are available to a defendant accused of violating Title VII?

5. What are the remedies available for engaging in intentional unlawful employment practices in violation of Title VII?

REFERENCES

Cases

Baylor v. Jefferson County Board of Education, 733 F.2d 1527 (11th Cir. 1984).
Bianchi v. City of Philadelphia, No. 99-CV-2409, 2002 WL 23942 (E.D. Pa. Jan 2, 2002).
Bibby v. Philadelphia Coca Cola Bottling Co., No. 00-1261 (3d Cir. August 1, 2001).
Biver v. Saginaw Township Community Schools, et al., 805 F.2d 1033 (6th Cir. 1986).
Cariddi v. Kansas City Chiefs Football Club, 568 F. Supp. 87 (8th Cir. 1977).
Compston v. Borden, Inc., 424 F. Supp. 157 (S.D. Ohio 1976).
Cross v. Board of Education of Dollarway, Arkansas School District, 395 F. Supp. 531 (E.D. Ark. 1975).
Davis v. McCormick, 898 F. Supp. 1275 (C.D. Ill. 1995).
Dowling v. United States, 476 F. Supp. 1018 (D. Mass. 1979).
EEOC v. National Broadcasting Co., Inc., 753 F. Supp. 452 (S.D. N.Y. 1990).
Graves v. Women's Professional Rodeo Association, Inc., 907 F.2d 71 (8th Cir. 1990).
Griggs v. Duke Power Co., 401 U.S. 424 (1971).
Herman v. National Broadcasting Co., Inc., 774 F.2d 604 (7th Cir. 1984).
Jackson v. Armstrong School District, 430 F. Supp. 1050 (W.D. Penn. 1977).
Jackson v. World League of American Football, 65 Fair Emp. Prac. Cas. 358 (S.D. N.Y. 1994).
Johnson v. NFL, 1999 U.S. Dist. LEXIS 15983 (S.D.N.Y. October 18, 1999).
Jalil v. Advel Corp., 873 F. 2d 701 (3rd Cir. 1989).
Lowery v. Circuit City, 158 F.3d 742 (1998).
Lowery v. Texas A&M University d/b/a Tarleton State University, 11 F. Supp.2d 895 (1998).
McDonnell Douglas Corp. v. Green, 411 U.S. 792 (1973).
Medcalf v. University of Pennsylvania, 2001 U.S. Dist. Lexis 10155.
Meritor Savings Bank, FSB v. Vinson, 477 U.S. 57 (1986).
Morris v. Bianchini, et al., 43 Fair Emp. Prac. Cases 647 (E.D. Va. 1987).
Peirick v. Indiana University-Purdue, 2005 U.S. Dist. LEXIS 32479.
Pouncy v. Prudential Insurance Co. of America, 668 F.2d 795 (5th Cir. 1982).
Price Waterhouse v. Hopkins, 490 U.S. 228, 250-51 (1989).

Ross v. Douglas County, 244 F.3d 620 (2001).
Smith v. City of Salem, 378 R.3d 566 (6th Cir. 2004).
Teamsters v. United States, 431 U.S. 324 (1977).
Texas Department of Community Affairs v. Burdine, 450 U.S. 248 (1981).
Wynn v. Columbus Municipal Separate School District, 692 F. Supp. 672 (N.D. Miss. 1988).

Publications
Player, M. A. (1988). *Employment discrimination law*. St. Paul, MN: West Publishing Co.
Zimmer, M. J., Sullivan, C. A., & Richards, R. F. (1988). *Cases and materials on employment discrimination*. Boston: Little, Brown, and Co.

Legislation
Title VII of the Civil Rights Act of 1964, 42 U.S.C. § 2000e et seq. (1990).

7.14 SEXUAL HARASSMENT

Barbara Osborne | University of North Carolina at Chapel Hill

With increasing numbers of girls and women participating and working in sports and recreation settings, managers today need to be aware of and prevent sexual harassment. Whether it is a health club owner promising to promote an aerobics instructor in exchange for sexual favors, a coach initiating inappropriate conversations, touching, or engaging in sexual relationships with an athlete at the club, middle school, high school, or collegiate levels, a journalist who is propositioned by a team owner, or an athlete sexually teasing or taunting a peer, sexual harassment is a major problem not only in the sports and recreation industry but in society as a whole.

FUNDAMENTAL CONCEPTS

Sexual Harassment in the Workplace

Although the Civil Rights Act of 1964 was enacted to prevent discrimination on the basis of race, color, religion, sex, or national origin, the Court did not recognize sexual harassment as sex discrimination until *Williams v. Saxbe* in 1976. In that case, the Supreme Court ruled that sexual harassment is a form of sex discrimination actionable under Title VII if the harassment places an artificial barrier on employment. Other ecases, *Barnes v. Costle* (1977) and *Miller v. Bank of America* (1979) narrowly recognized sexual harassment only in situations when the subordinate's employment opportunities were conditioned on entering into a sexual relationship with a superior, commonly described as quid pro quo sexual harassment.

The Equal Employment Opportunity Commission (EEOC) is the administrative agency charged with enforcing Title VII. It was not until 1980 that the EEOC Guidelines first acknowledged sexual harassment as "discrimination because of sex". The Guidelines took a broader approach than the courts and defined sexual harassment as:

> Unwelcome sexual advances, requests for sexual favors, and other verbal or physical conduct of a sexual nature constitute sexual harassment when

1. submission to such conduct is made either explicitly or implicitly a term or condition of an individual's employment
2. submission to or rejection of such conduct by an individual is used as the basis for employment decisions affecting such individual, or
3. such conduct has the purpose or effect of unreasonably interfering with an individual's work performance or creating an intimidating, hostile or offensive working environment.

It is important to note "unwelcome" as a key to the definition of sexual harassment. Conduct is unwelcome if the employee did not solicit or incite it and when the employee regards the conducts as undesirable or offensive. A charging party's claim will fail if the allegedly offensive conduct was "welcome." Table 1 provides a list of behaviors or actions that may be considered harassment given the circumstances.

TABLE 1.	SEXUALLY HARASSING BEHAVIORS

Behavioral

Ogling, leering, staring, gestures, mooning, flashing

Verbal

Request for dates, asking personal questions, lewd comments, dirty or sexual jokes, whistling, catcalling, obscene calls, sexual comments or rumors

Written/Visual

Love letters, poems, obscene letters, cards, notes, posters, pictures, cartoons, graphics, sexual graffiti

Touching

Violation of personal space, patting, rubbing, pinching, bra-snapping, caressing, blocking movement, kissing, groping, grabbing, tackling, hazing

Power

Retaliation, using position to request dates or suggest sexual favors, gender-directed favoritism, disparate treatment, hazing rituals, bullying, intimidation, condescending or patronizing behavior

Threats

Quid pro quo demands, conditioning evaluations or references on sexual favors, retaliation for refusal to comply with requests

Force

Attempted rape or assault, rape, assault, pantsing, stripping, extreme forms of hazing, stalking, sexual abuse, physical abuse, vandalism

The first condition listed in the EEOC definition refers to **quid pro quo** sexual harassment—when an employer conditions an employment benefit on some form of sexual favor. The second condition expands beyond quid pro quo behavior to all **tangible employment actions**, defined as any significant change in employment status, such as hiring, firing, failing to promote, or reassignment. Submitting to sexual advances in order to retain employment is also a tangible employment action, although there is no advancement or demotion in the employee's work status (*Jin v. Metropolitan Life Ins. Co*, 2002). The critical factor is the link between the sexual conduct and the benefit, even if the person demanding the sexual benefit is not the employer. In these cases, the courts uniformly apply strict liability in the same manner that they apply it in racial or religiously motivated cases under Title VII (see Chapter 7.13).

The third condition listed in the EEOC definition of sexual harassment is commonly known as **hostile environment**. The first case recognizing hostile environment sexual harassment was *Meritor Savings Bank, FSB v. Vinson* (1986). The Supreme Court referred to the EEOC guidelines in recognizing that the repeated actions of a supervisor could so contaminate the work environment that it altered the conditions of employment. The Court also expanded the scope of Title VII to include situations that did not result in direct or tangible economic loss. However, the Supreme Court did not define what behavior would constitute a hostile environment, only stating that the harassment must be so severe that it creates an abusive working environment.

Determining whether there is a hostile environment is a three-step approach examining:

1. The totality of the circumstances;
2. Whether a reasonable person in the same or similar circumstance would find the conduct sufficiently severe or pervasive to create an intimidating, hostile or abusive work environment (objective test); and
3. Whether the plaintiff perceived the environment to be hostile or abusive (subjective test).

Totality of the Circumstances. Because sexual attraction may play a role in the day-to-day social exchange between employees, the distinction between invited, uninvited-but-welcome, offensive-but-tolerated, and flatly rejected sexual advances may be difficult to discern. An examination of the totality of the circumstances—the nature of the conduct, the context in which the incidents occurred, the frequency of the conduct, its severity and pervasiveness, whether it was physically threatening or humiliating, whether it was unwelcome, and whether it unreasonably interfered with an employee's work performance—is necessary. Whether there is a repeated pattern of relatively benign behavior or a single incident of gross behavior is not conclusive. The most important analysis is whether the conduct negatively altered the work environment.

Reviewing all the circumstances in determining whether an environment is hostile or abusive also requires both a subjective and an objective test. The **reasonable person (objective test)** requires the plaintiff to prove that the conduct is severe or pervasive enough that a reasonable person would objectively find it hostile or abusive. The **employee's perception (subjective test)** requires that the plaintiff subjectively perceive the environment to be so hostile and abusive that it altered the employment climate. However, in *Harris v. Forklift Systems*, (1993), the Supreme Court established that the plaintiff does not have to prove psychological injury to prove that she was sexually harassed.

Under the EEOC guidelines issued in 1999, an employer is always liable for the actions of a supervisor that result in a tangible effect of employment status of the victim. The employer is liable for harassment by coworkers if the employer knew or should have known of the misconduct, unless it can show that it took immediate and appropriate corrective action. Harassment by non-employees—for example customers, vendors, or club members—are the employer's responsibility under a similar negligence standard, which also takes into account the extent of the employer's control over the harasser.

The Supreme Court and the 1999 Guidance allow for an employer to avoid liability with a two-part **affirmative defense**. The employer bears the burden of proving by a preponderance of the evidence both of these elements:

1. The employer exercised reasonable care to prevent and promptly correct harassment.
2. The employee unreasonably failed to take advantage of any preventive or corrective opportunities provided by the employer or to avoid harm otherwise.

To show reasonable care to prevent and correct harassment, the employer must have established, publicized, and enforced anti-harassment policies and grievance procedures prior to the complaint of harassment. This includes handing out a copy of the policy and complaint procedure to every employee, posting them in central locations, and including them in employee handbooks. The policy and procedures should include a clear explanation of prohibited conduct, an assurance of protection from retaliation for the complainant, a clearly described complaint process, and a promise of confidentiality. The complaint procedure should also provide accessible contact people to receive complaints (although some courts have ruled that reporting to any employee in a supervisory role is sufficient). A prompt, thorough, and impartial investigation should be conducted as soon as the employer learns of a complaint. The employee should be assured that immediate and appropriate corrective measures will be taken, and the employer should initiate intermediate protective measures against further harassment. If it is determined that harassment has occurred, the employer must take immediate corrective/disciplinary action to effectively end the harassment.

The Guidance also established that the employer must show that the employee did not exercise reasonable care by taking advantage of preventive opportunities, complaint procedures, or other ways to avoid harm. A failure to complain in a timely manner about persistent harassment could eliminate the employer's liability. If some, but not all, of the harm could have been avoided by an earlier compliant, damages awarded would likely be reduced.

Once the employer has established both parts of the affirmative defense, the employee has the opportunity to rebut the employer's assertion that the employee unreasonably failed to complain or otherwise avoid harm. The 1999 Guidance lists three explanations that may be reasonable: (1) risk of retaliation, (2) employer-created obstacles in the complaint process or procedures, and (3) belief that the complaint mechanism is not effective.

Although it is illegal to retaliate against an individual for opposing employment practices that discriminate based on sex or for filing a discrimination charge, testifying, or participating in any way in an investigation, proceeding, or litigation under Title VII, research indicates that most employees who fail to report harassment fear retaliation. It is the employer's burden to prove that this fear is unwarranted. One of the easiest ways to satisfy this burden is to have and promote a complaint process that maintains confidentiality and does not punish employees who complain.

State Legislative Protection. State legislation can greatly enhance protection against sexual harassment in the workplace. In *Morehouse v. Berkshire Gas Co.,*(1997) obscenely defaced photos of Morehouse were posted at the Berkshire Gas Company Fall Classic Golf Tournament (one was hung at the first tee, another was affixed to a garbage barrel at the fifth tee and was urinated on, another was attached to the flag at the ninth hole, and at least five more defaced photos were recovered from various other spots). Under *Mass. Gen. Lawsch. 151B, s 4(5)* individuals may be held liable for aiding or abetting discriminatory conduct that is prohibited under state law. Under Title VII, only the employer is liable for the acts of employees under the guidelines previously outlined in Table 1. Massachusetts legislation broadens the application of sexual harassment protection by holding individuals liable for their behavior, as well as others as aiders or abettors. This state legislation also extends the scope of responsibility of the employer, even when the supervisory employees are not acting within the scope of their employment (such as socially golfing at an outing).

Sexual Harassment in the Schools

The other major act of legislation related to sexual harassment is Title IX of the Education Act of 1972. Although it is most often referenced in relation to girls' participation in sport (see Chapter 7.11), Title IX prohibits discrimination on the basis of sex by any educational institution receiving federal funds. Sexual harassment is discrimination based on sex that is prohibited by Title IX because it disrupts and deprives students of equal access to education.

The Office of Civil Rights (OCR) in the U.S. Department of Education is responsible for enforcing Title IX. In the 2001 OCR guidance, sexual harassment is defined as it applies to educational institutions as unwelcome conduct of a sexual nature that rises to a level that denies or limits a student's ability to participate in or benefit from the school's programs.

Because the employment case law under Title VII is more developed, the courts have often referred to Title VII to guide them in Title IX cases. However, the Supreme Court takes a very different approach to institutional liability under Title IX compared to employer liability under Title VII. *Gebser v. Lago Vista Independent School District* (1998) indicates that damages under Title IX are only available when the institution has actual knowledge of the offensive behavior. The Court explicitly rejected the application of agency principles that it applies in Title VII sexual harassment cases. Relying on the "contractual nature" of Title IX, the Court reasoned that Title IX as a Spending Clause statute requires that the institution have actual notice and be deliberately indifferent to the reported behavior before it would be held liable.

For example, in *Davis v. Monroe County Board of Education* (1999), a fifth grader suffered sexual harassment by one of her classmates over several months. Although the victim and her mother repeatedly informed her teachers of the harassment, no one at the school made any effort to separate the two students (who sat next to each other in class) or to discipline the harasser. The Supreme Court concluded that student–student sexual harassment claims under Title IX should be analyzed in the same way as teacher–student sexual harassment. The Court found that schools are responsible for both preventing peer sexual harassment and for handling claims of peer sexual harassment in a prompt and effective manner once an appropriate administrator has actual notice.

The OCR Revised Sexual Harassment Guidance explains the liability of the educational institution under Title IX. If the employee engages in sexual harassment while carrying out responsibilities to provide benefits and services to students, the institution is responsible for the discriminatory conduct, remedying its effects, and preventing future occurrences whether or not it has notice of the harassment. If the employee is acting outside the scope of his or her assigned duties (and sexually harassing behavior is almost always considered outside the scope of the employee's duties), the institution must take prompt and effective action to stop the harassment and prevent its recurrence on notice of the harassment. The institution is considered to have engaged in its own discrimination if it fails to act and allows the student to be subjected to a hostile environment that denies or limits the student's ability to participate in or benefit from the school's program. The institution is responsible for peer or third-party harassment if the institution knew or reasonably should have known of the harassment and failed to take prompt and effective action. This liability is based on the contractual nature of Title IX, which promises an educational environment free from discrimination.

Whether the harasser is an employee or a peer, the victim of sexual harassment bears the burden of proving the following elements:

1. That she is a member of a protected group based on her sex
2. That she was subjected to unwelcome conduct of a sexual nature
3. That the conduct was so severe, pervasive, and objectively offensive that it denied equal access to the school's educational opportunities or benefits
4. That a school official with authority to take corrective action had actual knowledge or notice of the behavior
5. That the school official was deliberately indifferent to the conduct and failed to reasonably respond.

The Supreme Court in *Gebser v. Lago Vista Independent School District* (1998)and *Davis v. Monroe County Board of Education*(1999) did not address the issue of whether a school could raise an affirmative defense by having an effective sexual harassment policy. Schools are required by Title IX regulations to adopt and publish grievance procedures to address sexual discrimination. The procedures do not have to be specific to harassment, but should provide an effective manner for preventing and addressing sexual harassment. The OCR in 2000 reissued the following criteria for evaluating a school's grievance procedure:

1. Notice of policies and procedures must be sent to students, parents (for elementary and secondary students), and employees, including where complaints may be filed.
2. The procedure must actually be applied to complaints alleging harassment.
3. An adequate, reliable, and impartial investigation of the complaints must be conducted, including the opportunities to present witnesses and other evidence.
4. A designated, prompt time frame should be established for the complaint and investigative process.
5. Notice of the outcome of the complaint must be given to the parties involved.
6. An assurance must be made that the school will take corrective measures to eliminate current harassment and similar instances of harassment in the future.

If an educational institution implements these guidelines when developing its sexual harassment policies and procedures, it should function to reduce instances of harassment and provide protection for its students. It may also mitigate liability if a complaint is made to the OCR or a civil suit is filed.

Coach/Athlete Sexual Harassment
Although the liability of the institution is the same when the harasser is a coach and the victim is an athlete as that for teacher/student harassment, there are unique circumstances in the athletics context that merit closer attention. Although the number of female athletes has increased dramatically over the past 40 years, the percentage of female coaches has decreased. This increases the number of men coaching female athletes and also increases the opportunity and possibility of sexual harassment. Male coach/female athlete is not the only context in which sexual harassment occurs, but it is significantly greater than any other combination.

Touching, keeping track of the athlete's life outside athletics, and nicknames are routinely accepted as part of a coach—athlete relationship and could be harmless. However, this conduct should be measured by the unwelcomeness standard: conduct is unwelcome if the athlete did not request or invite it and it is offensive to the victim. The power dynamic in coach–athlete relationships (factors such as power, trust, and control) may affect the ability of a female athlete to freely consent or decline sexual contact, so administrators and coaches must measure whether the conduct is harassing by its impact on the athlete, and not just by the intent of the coach.

Peer Sexual Harassment in Athletics
Complaints of peer harassment are increasing dramatically. A female swimmer from the University of Pittsburgh filed a civil suit seeking reinstatement to the university swim team claiming she was released as a result of her complaints of harassment against a swimmer on the men's team. A former placekicker on the University of Colorado football team publicly alleged that she was sexually harassed by her teammates, which led to her transfer to the University of New Mexico. She stated that she was "treated like a piece of meat" and constantly

called "names that are unrepeatable." The student–athlete indicated she reported the incidents to the coach several times during the season, but the harassment persisted. An educational institution is liable for peer harassment when the harassing conduct is reported and the administration fails to reasonably respond.

Athletics departments may also be held liable under Title IX when a student-athlete (or even a recruit) sexually assaults a student, whether the assault occurred on or off campus. The first case to find that a school may be liable was *Williams v. Board of Regents of the University System of Georgia* (2007). In this case, a female student was allegedly gang raped by three male athletes. The plaintiff claimed that the university was liable under Title IX because the coach, athletics director and university president were aware that the student–athlete who attacked the plaintiff had a history of sexual assaults before he was recruited and admitted to the university. The Eleventh Circuit Court held that given the past history of the recruited student–athlete, the institution had "before the fact notice" and should have made efforts to prevent future harassment from occurring. The Tenth Circuit Court made a similar ruling regarding the alleged rape of female students by football players and recruits at the University of Colorado (see *Simpson v. University of Colorado* in the Supplemental Web Site). These cases, and a series of high profile situations at Yale, Notre Dame, Eastern Michigan, Wake Forest, and several other schools prompted the US Department of Education, Office for Civil Rights to distribute a Dear Colleague Letter addressing Sexual Violence in April 2011. This letter is intended to be a significant guidance document that supplements the 2001 Revised Sexual Harassment Guidance and will be provided deference by the courts.

The 2011 Dear Colleague defines sexual violence as " . . . physical sexual acts perpetrated against a person's will or where a person is incapable of giving consent . . . " (p. 1). OCR requires that a school take "immediate action to eliminate the harassment, prevent its recurrence, and address its effects" when the school knows or reasonably should know about peer harassment that creates a hostile environment (p. 4). This standard is to be applied for victims filing administrative complaints with OCR or for plaintiffs that are requesting injunctive relief. It differs from the precedent established by the Supreme Court in *Davis v. Monroe County Board of Education* (1999) which requires the plaintiff to prove that the school had actual knowledge and was deliberately indifferent in order to be compensated with monetary damages.

SIGNIFICANT CASE

This is the leading case of sexual harassment in the recreation industry. The Supreme Court addressed the conflict of opinions issued by the lower courts and thoroughly explains the new standards for establishing employer liability under Title VII.

BETH ANN FARAGHER V. CITY OF BOCA RATON
United States Supreme Court
524 U.S. 775 (1998)

Between 1985 and 1990, Beth Ann Faragher worked part time and during the summers as an ocean lifeguard for the Marine Safety Section of the Parks and Recreation Department of respondent, the City of Boca Raton, Florida (City). During this period, Faragher's immediate supervisors were Bill Terry, David Silverman, and Robert Gordon. In June 1990, Faragher resigned.

In 1992, Faragher brought an action against Terry, Silverman, and the City, asserting claims under Title VII,

42 U.S.C. § 1983, and Florida law. So far as it concerns the Title VII claim, the complaint alleged that Terry and Silverman created a "sexually hostile atmosphere" at the beach by repeatedly subjecting Faragher and other female lifeguards to "uninvited and offensive touching," by making lewd remarks, and by speaking of women in offensive terms. The complaint contained specific allegations that Terry once said that he would never promote a woman to the rank of lieutenant, and that Silverman had said to Faragher, "Date me or clean the toilets for a year." Asserting that Terry and Silverman were agents of the City, and that their conduct amounted to discrimination in the "terms, conditions, and privileges" of her employment, Faragher sought a judgment against the City for nominal damages, costs, and attorney's fees.

Following a bench trial, the United States District Court for the Southern District of Florida found that throughout Faragher's employment with the City, Terry served as Chief of the Marine Safety Division, with authority to hire new lifeguards, to supervise all aspects of the lifeguards' work assignments, to engage in counseling, to deliver oral reprimands, and to make a record of any such discipline. Silverman was a Marine Safety lieutenant from 1985 until June 1989, when he became a captain. Gordon began the employment period as a lieutenant and at some point was promoted to the position of training captain. In these positions, Silverman and Gordon were responsible for making the lifeguards' daily assignments, and for supervising their work and fitness training.

The lifeguards and supervisors were stationed at the city beach and worked out of the Marine Safety Headquarters, a small one-story building containing an office, a meeting room, and a single, unisex locker room with a shower. Their work routine was structured in a "paramilitary configuration," with a clear chain of command. Lifeguards reported to lieutenants and captains, who reported to Terry. He was supervised by the Recreation Superintendent, who in turn reported to a Director of Parks and Recreation, answerable to the City Manager. The lifeguards had no significant contact with higher city officials like the Recreation Superintendent.

In February 1986, the City adopted a sexual harassment policy, which it stated in a memorandum from the City Manager addressed to all employees. In May 1990, the City revised the policy and reissued a statement of it. Although the City may actually have circulated the memos and statements to some employees, it completely failed to disseminate its policy among employees of the Marine Safety Section, with the result that Terry, Silverman, Gordon, and many lifeguards were unaware of it.

From time to time over the course of Faragher's tenure at the Marine Safety Section, between 4 and 6 of the 40 to 50 lifeguards were women. During that 5-year period, Terry repeatedly touched the bodies of female employees without invitation, would put his arm around Faragher, with his hand on her buttocks, and once made contact with another female lifeguard in a motion of sexual simulation. He made crudely demeaning references to women generally, and once commented disparagingly on Faragher's shape. During a job interview with a woman he hired as a lifeguard, Terry said that the female lifeguards had sex with their male counterparts and asked whether she would do the same.

Silverman behaved in similar ways. He once tackled Faragher and remarked that, but for a physical characteristic he found unattractive, he would readily have had sexual relations with her. Another time, he pantomimed an act of oral sex. Within earshot of the female lifeguards, Silverman made frequent, vulgar references to women and sexual matters, commented on the bodies of female lifeguards and beachgoers, and at least twice told female lifeguards that he would like to engage in sex with them. Faragher did not complain to higher management about Terry or Silverman. Although she spoke of their behavior to Gordon, she did not regard these discussions as formal complaints to a supervisor but as conversations with a person she held in high esteem. Other female lifeguards had similarly informal talks with Gordon, but because Gordon did not feel that it was his place to do so, he did not report these complaints to Terry, his own supervisor, or to any other city official. Gordon responded to the complaints of one lifeguard by saying that "the City just [doesn't] care."

In April 1990, however, two months before Faragher's resignation, Nancy Ewanchew, a former lifeguard, wrote to Richard Bender, the City's Personnel Director, complaining that Terry and Silverman had harassed her and other female lifeguards. Following investigation of this complaint, the City found that Terry and Silverman had behaved improperly, reprimanded them, and required them to choose between a suspension without pay or the forfeiture of annual leave.

On the basis of these findings, the District Court concluded that the conduct of Terry and Silverman was discriminatory harassment sufficiently serious to alter the conditions of Faragher's employment and constitute an abusive working environment. The District Court then ruled that there were three justifications for holding the City liable for the harassment of its supervisory employees. First, the court noted that the harassment was pervasive enough to support an inference that the City had "knowledge, or constructive knowledge" of it. Next, it ruled that the City was liable under traditional agency principles because Terry and Silverman were acting as its agents when they committed the harassing acts. Finally, the court observed that Gordon's knowledge of the harassment, combined with his inaction, "provides a further basis for imputing liability on [sic] the City." The District Court then awarded Faragher one dollar in nominal damages on her *Title VII claim*.

A panel of the Court of Appeals for the Eleventh Circuit reversed the judgment against the City. Although the panel had "no trouble concluding that Terry's and Silverman's conduct . . . was severe and pervasive enough to create an objectively abusive work environment," it overturned the District Court's conclusion that the City was liable. The panel ruled that Terry and Silverman were not acting within the scope of their employment when they engaged in the harassment, that they were not aided in their actions by the agency relationship, and that the City had no constructive knowledge of the harassment by virtue of its pervasiveness or Gordon's actual knowledge. * * *

Since our decision in *Meritor*, Courts of Appeals have struggled to derive manageable standards to govern employer liability for hostile environment harassment perpetrated by supervisory employees. While following our admonition to find guidance in the common law of agency, as embodied in the Restatement, the Courts of Appeals have adopted different approaches. We granted certiorari to address the divergence, and now reverse the judgment of the Eleventh Circuit and remand for entry of judgment in Faragher's favor.

II

A

Under Title VII of the Civil Rights Act of 1964, "it shall be an unlawful employment practice for an employer to fail or refuse to hire or to discharge any individual, or otherwise to discriminate against any individual with respect to his compensation, terms, conditions, or privileges of employment, because of such individual's race, color, religion, sex, or national origin." *42 U.S.C. § 2000e–2*(a)(1). We have repeatedly made clear that although the statute mentions specific employment decisions with immediate consequences, the scope of the prohibition " 'is not limited to "economic" or "tangible" discrimination,' " and that it covers more than " 'terms' and 'conditions' in the narrow contractual sense." Thus, in *Meritor* we held that sexual harassment so "severe or pervasive" as to " 'alter the conditions of [the victim's] employment and create an abusive working environment' " violates *Title VII.*

So, in *Harris*, we explained that in order to be actionable under the statute, a sexually objectionable environment must be both objectively and subjectively offensive, one that a reasonable person would find hostile or abusive, and one that the victim in fact did perceive to be so. We directed courts to determine whether an environment is sufficiently hostile or abusive by "looking at all the circumstances," including the "frequency of the discriminatory conduct; its severity; whether it is physically threatening or humiliating, or a mere offensive utterance; and whether it unreasonably interferes with an employee's work performance." Most recently, we explained that Title VII does not prohibit "genuine but innocuous differences in the ways men and women routinely interact with members of the same sex and of the opposite sex." A recurring point in these opinions is that "simple teasing," offhand comments, and isolated incidents (unless extremely serious) will not amount to discriminatory changes in the "terms and conditions of employment."

These standards for judging hostility are sufficiently demanding to ensure that Title VII does not become a "general civility code." Properly applied, they will filter out complaints attacking "the ordinary tribulations of the workplace, such as the sporadic use of abusive language, gender-related jokes, and occasional teasing." We have made it clear that conduct must be extreme to amount to a change in the terms and conditions of employment, and the Courts of Appeals have heeded this view.

While indicating the substantive contours of the hostile environments forbidden by Title VII, our cases have established few definite rules for determining when an employer will be liable for a discriminatory environment that is otherwise actionably abusive. Given the circumstances of many of the litigated cases, including some that have come to us, it is not surprising that in many of them, the issue has been joined over the sufficiency of the abusive conditions, not the standards for determining an employer's liability for them. There have, for example, been myriad cases in which District Courts and Courts of Appeals have held employers liable on account of actual knowledge by the employer, or high-echelon officials of an employer organization, of sufficiently harassing action by subordinates, which the employer or its informed officers have done nothing to stop. In such instances, the combined knowledge and inaction may be seen as demonstrable negligence, or as the employer's adoption of the offending conduct and its results, quite as if they had been authorized affirmatively as the employer's policy. * * *

Finally, there is nothing remarkable in the fact that claims against employers for discriminatory employment actions with tangible results, like hiring, firing, promotion, compensation, and work assignment, have resulted in employer liability once the discrimination was shown.

A variety of reasons have been invoked for this apparently unanimous rule. Some courts explain . . . that when a supervisor makes such decisions, he "merges" with the employer, and his act becomes that of the employer. Other courts have suggested that vicarious liability is proper because the supervisor acts within the scope of his authority when he makes discriminatory decisions in hiring, firing, promotion, and the like. Others have suggested that vicarious liability is appropriate because the supervisor who discriminates in this manner is aided by the agency relation. Finally, still other courts have endorsed both of the latter two theories.

The soundness of the results in these cases (and their continuing vitality), in light of basic agency principles, was confirmed by this Court's only discussion to date of standards of employer liability, in *Meritor,* which involved a claim of discrimination by a supervisor's sexual harassment of a subordinate over an extended period. In affirming the Court of Appeals' holding that a hostile atmosphere resulting from sex discrimination is actionable under Title VII, we also anticipated proceedings on remand by holding agency principles relevant in assigning employer liability and by rejecting three *per se* rules of liability or immunity. We observed that the very definition of employer in Title VII, as including an "agent," expressed Congress's intent that courts look to traditional principles of the law of agency in devising standards of employer liability in those instances where liability for the actions of a supervisory employee was not otherwise obvious, and although we cautioned that "common-law principles may not be transferable in all their particulars to Title VII," we cited the Restatement § 219–237, with general approval.

We then proceeded to reject two limitations on employer liability, while establishing the rule that some limitation was intended. We held that neither the existence of a company grievance procedure nor the absence of actual notice of the harassment on the part of upper management would be dispositive of such a claim; while either might be relevant to the liability, neither would result automatically in employer immunity. Conversely, we held that Title VII placed some limit on employer responsibility for the creation of a discriminatory environment by a supervisor, and we held that Title VII does not make employers "always automatically liable for sexual harassment by their supervisors," contrary to the view of the Court of Appeals, which had held that "an employer is strictly liable for a hostile environment created by a supervisor's sexual advances, even though the employer neither knew nor reasonably could have known of the alleged misconduct," *477 U.S. at 69–70.*

Meritor's statement of the law is the foundation on which we build today. * * *

B

The Court of Appeals identified, and rejected, three possible grounds drawn from agency law for holding the City vicariously liable for the hostile environment created by the supervisors. It considered whether the two supervisors were acting within the scope of their employment when they engaged in the harassing conduct. The court then enquired whether they were significantly aided by the agency relationship in committing the harassment, and also considered the possibility of imputing Gordon's knowledge of the harassment to the City. Finally, the Court of Appeals ruled out liability for negligence in failing to prevent the harassment. Faragher relies principally on the latter three theories of liability.

I

A "master is subject to liability for the torts of his servants committed while acting in the scope of their employment." Restatement § 219(1). This doctrine has traditionally defined the "scope of employment" as including conduct "of the kind [a servant] is employed to perform," occurring "substantially within the authorized time and space limits," and "actuated, at least in part, by a purpose to serve the master," but as excluding an intentional use of force "unexpectable by the master."

Courts of Appeals have typically held, or assumed, that conduct similar to the subject of this complaint falls outside the scope of employment. In so doing, the courts have emphasized that harassment consisting of unwelcome remarks and touching is motivated solely by individual desires and serves no purpose of the employer. For this reason, courts have likened hostile environment

sexual harassment to the classic "frolic and detour" for which an employer has no vicarious liability.

These cases ostensibly stand in some tension with others arising outside Title VII, where the scope of employment has been defined broadly enough to hold employers vicariously liable for intentional torts that were in no sense inspired by any purpose to serve the employer . . .

The proper analysis here, then, calls not for a mechanical application of indefinite and malleable factors set forth in the Restatement, but rather an enquiry into the reasons that would support a conclusion that harassing behavior ought to be held within the scope of a supervisor's employment, and the reasons for the opposite view. The Restatement itself points to such an approach, as in the commentary that the "ultimate question" in determining the scope of employment is "whether or not it is just that the loss resulting from the servant's acts should be considered as one of the normal risks to be borne by the business in which the servant is employed."

In the case before us, a justification for holding the offensive behavior within the scope of Terry's and Silverman's employment was well put in Judge Barkett's dissent: "[A] pervasively hostile work environment of sexual harassment is never (one would hope) authorized, but the supervisor is clearly charged with maintaining a productive, safe work environment. The supervisor directs and controls the conduct of the employees, and the manner of doing so may inure to the employer's benefit or detriment, including subjecting the employer to Title VII liability." It is by now well recognized that hostile environment sexual harassment by supervisors (and, for that matter, co-employees) is a persistent problem in the workplace. An employer can, in a general sense, reasonably anticipate the possibility of such conduct occurring in its workplace, and one might justify the assignment of the burden of the untoward behavior to the employer as one of the costs of doing business, to be charged to the enterprise rather than the victim.

Two things counsel us to draw the contrary conclusion. First, there is no reason to suppose that Congress wished courts to ignore the traditional distinction between acts falling within the scope and acts amounting to what the older law called frolics or detours from the course of employment. Such a distinction can readily be applied to the spectrum of possible harassing conduct by supervisors, as the following examples show. First, a supervisor might discriminate racially in job assignments in order to placate the prejudice pervasive in the labor force. Instances of this variety of the heckler's veto would be consciously intended to further the employer's interests by preserving peace in the workplace. Next, supervisors might reprimand male employees for workplace failings with banter, but respond to women's shortcomings in harsh or vulgar terms. A third example might be the supervisor who, as here, expresses his sexual interests in ways having no apparent object whatever of serving an interest of the employer. If a line is to be drawn between scope and frolic, it would lie between the first two examples and the third, and it thus makes sense in terms of traditional agency law to analyze the scope issue, in cases like the third example, just as most federal courts addressing that issue have done, classifying the harassment as beyond the scope of employment.

The second reason goes to an even broader unanimity of views among the holdings of District Courts and Courts of Appeals thus far. Those courts have held not only that the sort of harassment at issue here was outside the scope of supervisors' authority, but, by uniformly judging employer liability for co-worker harassment under a negligence standard, they have also implicitly treated such harassment as outside the scope of common employees' duties as well. If, indeed, the cases did not rest, at least implicitly, on the notion that such harassment falls outside the scope of employment, their liability issues would have turned simply on the application of the scope-of-employment rule.

It is quite unlikely that these cases would escape efforts to render them obsolete if we were to hold that supervisors who engage in discriminatory harassment are necessarily acting within the scope of their employment. The rationale for placing harassment within the scope of supervisory authority would be the fairness of requiring the employer to bear the burden of foreseeable social behavior, and the same rationale would apply when the behavior was that of co-employees. The employer generally benefits just as obviously from the work of common employees as from the work of supervisors; they simply have different jobs to do, all aimed at the success of the enterprise. As between an innocent employer and an innocent employee, if we use scope of employment reasoning to require the employer to bear the cost of an actionably hostile workplace created by one class of employees (*i.e.*, supervisors), it could appear just as appropriate to do the same when the environment was created by another class (*i.e.*, co-workers).

The answer to this argument might well be to point out that the scope of supervisory employment may be treated separately by recognizing that supervisors have special authority enhancing their capacity to harass, and that the employer can guard against their misbehavior more easily because their numbers are by definition fewer than the numbers of regular employees. But this answer happens to implicate an entirely separate category of agency law (to be considered in the next section), which imposes vicarious liability on employers for tortious acts committed by use of particular authority conferred as an element of an employee's agency relationship with the employer. Since the virtue of categorical clarity is obvious, it is better to reject reliance on misuse of supervisory authority (without more) as irrelevant to scope-of-employment analysis.

2

The Court of Appeals also rejected vicarious liability on the part of the City insofar as it might rest on the concluding principle set forth in § 219(2)(d) of the Restatement, that an employer "is not subject to liability for the torts of his servants acting outside the scope of their employment unless . . . the servant purported to act or speak on behalf of the principal and there was reliance on apparent authority, or he was aided in accomplishing the tort by the existence of the agency relation." Faragher points to several ways in which the agency relationship aided Terry and Silverman in carrying out their harassment. She argues that in general offending supervisors can abuse their authority to keep subordinates in their presence while they make offensive statements, and that they implicitly threaten to misuse their supervisory powers to deter any resistance or complaint. Thus, she maintains that power conferred on Terry and Silverman by the City enabled them to act for so long without provoking defiance or complaint.

The City, however, contends that § 219(2)(d) has no application here. It argues that the second qualification of the subsection, referring to a servant "aided in accomplishing the tort by the existence of the agency relation," merely "refines" the one preceding it, which holds the employer vicariously liable for its servant's abuse of apparent authority. But this narrow reading is untenable; it would render the second qualification of § 219(2)(d) almost entirely superfluous (and would seem to ask us to shut our eyes to the potential effects of supervisory authority, even when not explicitly invoked). The illustrations accompanying this subsection make clear that it covers not only cases involving the abuse of apparent authority, but also to cases in which tortious conduct is made possible or facilitated by the existence of the actual agency relationship.

We therefore agree with Faragher that in implementing Title VII it makes sense to hold an employer vicariously liable for some tortious conduct of a supervisor made possible by abuse of his supervisory authority, and that the aided-by-agency-relation principle embodied in § 219(2)(d) of the Restatement provides an appropriate starting point for determining liability for the kind of harassment presented here. Several courts, indeed, have noted what Faragher has argued, that there is a sense in which a harassing supervisor is always assisted in his misconduct by the supervisory relationship. The agency relationship affords contact with an employee subjected to a supervisor's sexual harassment, and the victim may well be reluctant to accept the risks of blowing the whistle on a superior. When a person with supervisory authority discriminates in the terms and conditions of subordinates' employment, his actions necessarily draw upon his superior position over the people who report to him, or those under them, whereas an employee generally cannot check a supervisor's abusive conduct the same way that she might deal with abuse from a co-worker.

When a fellow employee harasses, the victim can walk away or tell the offender where to go, but it may be difficult to offer such responses to a supervisor, whose "power to supervise—[which may be] to hire and fire, and to set work schedules and pay rates—does not disappear . . . when he chooses to harass through insults and offensive gestures rather than directly with threats of firing or promises of promotion." Recognition of employer liability when discriminatory misuse of supervisory authority alters the terms and conditions of a victim's employment is underscored by the fact that the employer has a greater opportunity to guard against misconduct by supervisors than by common workers; employers have greater opportunity and incentive to screen them, train them, and monitor their performance.

In sum, there are good reasons for vicarious liability for misuse of supervisory authority. That rationale must, however, satisfy one more condition. We are not entitled to recognize this theory under Title VII unless we can square it with *Meritor's* holding that an employer is not "automatically" liable for harassment by a supervisor who creates the requisite degree of discrimination, and there is obviously some tension between that holding and the position that a supervisor's misconduct aided by supervisory authority subjects the employer to liability vicariously; if the "aid" may be the unspoken suggestion of retaliation by misuse of supervisory authority, the risk of automatic liability is high. To counter it, we think there are two basic alternatives, one being to require proof of some affirmative invocation of that authority by the harassing supervisor, the other to recognize an affirmative defense to liability in some circumstances, even when a supervisor has created the actionable environment.

There is certainly some authority for requiring active or affirmative, as distinct from passive or implicit, misuse of supervisory authority before liability may be imputed. That is the way some courts have viewed the familiar cases holding the employer liable for discriminatory employment action with tangible consequences, like firing and demotion. And we have already noted some examples of liability provided by the Restatement itself, which suggests that an affirmative misuse of power might be required.

But neat examples illustrating the line between the affirmative and merely implicit uses of power are not easy to come by in considering management behavior. Supervisors do not make speeches threatening sanctions whenever they make requests in the legitimate exercise of managerial authority, and yet every subordinate employee knows the sanctions exist; this is the reason that courts have consistently held that acts of supervisors have greater power to alter the environment than acts of co-employees generally. How far from the course of ostensible supervisory behavior would a company officer have to step before his orders would not reasonably be seen as actively using authority? Judgment calls would often be close, the results would often seem disparate even if not demonstrably contradictory, and the temptation to litigate would be hard to resist. We think plaintiffs and defendants alike would be poorly served by an active-use rule.

The other basic alternative to automatic liability would avoid this particular temptation to litigate, but allow an employer to show as an affirmative defense to liability that the employer had exercised reasonable care to avoid harassment and to eliminate it when it might occur, and that the complaining employee had failed to act with like reasonable care to take advantage of the employer's safeguards and otherwise to prevent harm that could have been avoided. This composite defense would, we think, implement the statute sensibly, for reasons that are not hard to fathom.

Although Title VII seeks "to make persons whole for injuries suffered on account of unlawful employment discrimination," its "primary objective," like that of any statute meant to influence primary conduct, is not to provide redress but to avoid harm. As long ago as 1980, the Equal Employment Opportunity Commission (EEOC), charged with the enforcement of Title VII, *42 U.S.C. § 2000e–4*, adopted regulations advising employers to "take all steps necessary to prevent sexual harassment from occurring, such as . . . informing employees of their right to raise and how to raise the issue of harassment," and in 1990 the Commission issued a policy statement enjoining employers to establish a complaint procedure "designed to encourage victims of harassment to come forward [without requiring] a victim to complain first to the offending supervisor." It would therefore implement clear statutory policy and complement the Government's Title VII enforcement efforts to recognize the employer's affirmative obligation to prevent violations and give credit here to employers who make reasonable efforts to discharge their duty. Indeed, a theory of vicarious liability for misuse of supervisory power would be at odds with the statutory policy if it failed to provide employers with some such incentive.

The requirement to show that the employee has failed in a coordinate duty to avoid or mitigate harm reflects an equally obvious policy imported from the general theory of damages, that a victim has a duty "to use such means as are reasonable under the circumstances to avoid or minimize the damages" that result from violations of the statute. An employer may, for example, have provided a proven, effective mechanism for reporting and resolving complaints of sexual harassment, available to the employee without undue risk or expense. If the plaintiff unreasonably failed to avail herself of the employer's preventive or remedial apparatus, she should not recover damages that could have been avoided if she had done so. If the victim could have avoided harm, no liability should be found against the employer who had taken reasonable care, and if damages could reasonably have been mitigated no award against a liable employer should reward a plaintiff for what her own efforts could have avoided.

In order to accommodate the principle of vicarious liability for harm caused by misuse of supervisory authority, as well as Title VII's equally basic policies of encouraging forethought by employers and saving action by objecting employees, we adopt the following holding in this case and in *Burlington Industries, Inc.* v. *Ellerth*, also decided today. An employer is subject to vicarious liability to a victimized employee for an actionable hostile environment created by a supervisor with immediate (or successively higher) authority over the employee. When no tangible employment action is taken, a defending employer may raise an affirmative defense to liability or damages, subject to proof by a preponderance of the evidence, see *Fed. Rule. Civ. Proc. 8(c).* The defense comprises two necessary elements: (a) that the employer exercised reasonable care to prevent and correct promptly any sexually harassing behavior, and (b) that the plaintiff employee unreasonably failed to take advantage of any preventive or corrective opportunities provided by the employer or to avoid harm otherwise. While proof that an employer had promulgated an antiharassment policy with complaint procedure is not necessary in every instance as a matter of law, the need for a stated policy suitable to the employment circumstances may appropriately be addressed in any case when litigating the first element of the defense. And while proof that an employee failed to fulfill the corresponding obligation of reasonable care to avoid harm is not limited to showing an unreasonable failure to use any complaint procedure provided by the employer, a demonstration of such failure will normally suffice to satisfy the employer's burden under the second element of the defense. No affirmative defense is available, however, when the supervisor's harassment culminates in a tangible employment action, such as discharge, demotion, or undesirable reassignment.

Applying these rules here, we believe that the judgment of the Court of Appeals must be reversed. The District Court found that the degree of hostility in the work environment rose to the actionable level and was attributable to Silverman and Terry. It is undisputed that these supervisors "were granted virtually unchecked authority" over their subordinates, "directly controlling and supervising all aspects of [Faragher's] day-to-day activities." It is also clear that Faragher and her colleagues were "completely isolated from the City's higher management." The City did not seek review of these findings.

While the City would have an opportunity to raise an affirmative defense if there were any serious prospect of its presenting one, it appears from the record that any such avenue is closed. The District Court found that the City had entirely failed to disseminate its policy against sexual harassment among the beach employees and that its officials made no attempt to keep track of the conduct of supervisors like Terry and Silverman. The record also makes clear that the City's policy did not include any assurance that the harassing supervisors could be bypassed in registering complaints. Under such circumstances, we hold as a matter of law that the City could not be found to have exercised reasonable care to prevent the supervisors' harassing conduct. Unlike the employer of a small workforce, who might expect that sufficient care to prevent tortious behavior could be exercised informally, those responsible for city operations could not reasonably have thought that precautions against hostile environments in any one of many departments in far-flung locations could be effective without communicating some formal policy against harassment, with a sensible complaint procedure. . . .

III

The judgment of the Court of Appeals for the Eleventh Circuit is reversed, and the case is remanded for reinstatement of the judgment of the District Court.

It is so ordered.

CASES ON SUPPLEMENTAL WEB SITE

Davis v. Monroe County Board of Education, 526 U.S. 629 (1999). This case establishes the standards for institutional liability for peer sexual harassment.

Fitzgerald v. Barnstable School Committee, 129 S. Ct. 788 (2009). The examines whether a complaint of sexual harassment under Title IX preclude a second constitutional claim under § 1983.

Morehouse v. Berkshire Gas Co. 989 F. Supp. 54, 61 (D. Mass. 1997). This case examines a Title VII sexual harassment claim involving harassment of a female employee at a company sponsored golf outing.

Simpson v. Univ. of Colorado, 500 F.3d 1170 (10th Cir. 2007). This case examines the liability of an educational institution for the sexual assault of students at off campus party by recruits and student-athletes.

Williams v. Board of Regents of University System of Georgia, 477 F.3d 1282 (11th Cir. 2007). This case examines the liability of an educational institution for the sexual assault of a student in a dormitory by student-athletes.

QUESTIONS YOU SHOULD BE ABLE TO ANSWER

1. Define sexual harassment under Title VII.

2. Define sexual harassment under Title IX.

3. Explain the similarities and differences between the elements of a plaintiff's complaint and employer or institutional liability under Title VII and Title IX.

4. Explain what an employer must do in order to avoid liability with an affirmative defense.

5. Explain the school's liability for sexual violence under Title IX.

REFERENCES

Cases

Barnes v. Costle, 561 F.2d 983 (D.C. 1977).
Burlington Industries, Inc. v. Ellerth, 524 U.S. 742 (1998).
Davis v. MonroeCounty Board of Education, 119 S.Ct. 1161 (1999).
Faragher v. City of Boca Raton, 524 U.S. 775 (1998).
Gebser v. LagoVistaIndependentSchool District, 524 U.S. 274 (1998).
Harris v. Forklift Systems, Inc., 510 U.S. 17 (1993).
Jin v. Metropolitan Life Ins. Co., 295 F.3d 335 (2nd Cir. 2002).
Meritor Savings Bank, FSB v. Vinson, 477 U.S. 57 (1986).
Miller v. Bank of America, 600 F.2d 211 (9th Cir. 1979).
Morehouse v. Berkshire Gas Co. 989 F. Supp. 54, 61 (D. Mass. 1997).
Simpson v. University of Colorado, 500 F.3d 1170 (10th Cir. 2007).
Williams v. Board of Regents of University System of Georgia, 477 F.3d 1282 (11th Cir. 2007).
Williams v. Saxbe, 1976 413 F.Supp. 654 (DDC 1976).

Legislation

Title VII of the Civil Rights Act, 42 U.S.C. 2000e et seq. (2008).
Title VII Guidelines on Discrimination Because of Sex, 29 C.F.R. 1604.11
EEOC Notice 915.002 (6/18/1999) Enforcement Guidance: Vicarious Employer Liability for Unlawful Harassment by Supervisors.
Title IX of the Education Act of 1974, 20 U.S.C. 1681 (2008).
OCR Notice: Revised Sexual Harassment Guidance: Harassment of Students by School Employees, Other Students, or Third Parties (11/02/2000) 65 Fed. Reg. 213. pp. 66091–66114.
Dear Colleague Letter: Sexual Violence (4/04/2011). Available at http://www2.ed.gov/about/offices/list/ocr/letters/colleague-201104.html

7.15 AGE DISCRIMINATION IN EMPLOYMENT ACT

David Snyder | State University of New York College at Cortland

The Equal Employment Opportunity Commission (EEOC) reported that $95.2 million in damages were awarded in 2011 under the Age Discrimination in Employment Act (ADEA). The $95.2 million figure, which excludes monetary awards from litigation, represents the highest amount recovered from ADEA-related cases in a single year from 1992 to 2011 and breaks down to approximately $119,598 awarded for each claim that was deemed to have "reasonable cause." The total damages derived from ADEA complaints in 2011 almost doubled since 2005, increasing from $51.5 million to $95.2 million (EEOC Website). This data does not include age discrimination actions based on other federal and state laws.

Although not all age discrimination claims involve sport or recreation, these cases appear to clearly be on the rise. With respect to coaches, for example, Ferne Labati, the former coach of the University of Miami's women's basketball team, filed a lawsuit against her former employer alleging age- and gender-based discrimination. Labati, who was sixty years old when she was fired, was replaced by a thirty-seven-year-old. She was inducted into the university's Sports Hall of Fame just eleven months before she was terminated. In 2009, the appellate court upheld the summary judgment ruling by the lower court in favor of the university (*Labati v. University of Miami*, 2009), (See Supplemental Web Site). Another example is Don Moreau, the former baseball coach at Loyola University, New Orleans, who filed an age discrimination lawsuit against the university in 2003. Loyola claimed that Moreau, who had coached baseball at Loyola for twelve years, needed a college degree to be a full-time coach at Loyola. Moreau, who was sixty-five years old at the time he was fired, was replaced by a thirty-three-year-old as head baseball coach.

Coaches are not the only sports figures initiating age discrimination lawsuits. Former NBA star Elgin Baylor sued the Los Angeles Clippers based on age discrimination for firing him from the position he held for twenty-two years as the club's general manager and executive vice president. A jury unanimously sided in favor of the Clippers. Baylor, who was in his seventies when his employment with the team was terminated, had been seeking over $2 million in damages (Los Angeles Times (online edition), March 30, 2011).

In 2009, 73-year old John Vendikos filed a complaint with the EEOC charging that the New York Yankees subjected discriminated against him because of his age when they fired him after twenty-seven years of service as a bartender in the Stadium Club at old Yankee Stadium (Oshlan, 2009). In 2011, Brenda Sniezek, who had served as Community Relations Director for the Kansas City Chiefs for nearly twenty-eight years, was fired at the age of 51. Sniezek alleged that the Chiefs engaged in widespread age discrimination (Thorman, 2011). Popular sport broadcaster Sal Marchiano filed a lawsuit claiming age discrimination against the general manager of WPIX-TV. Marchiano, who was in his sixties when his contract was not renewed, had worked at the station for fourteen years. Marchiano is seeking reinstatement and damages from his former employer (Sandomir, 2010).

Not only are age discrimination lawsuits in sports increasing in number, but the stakes in these cases are often high. In 2000, two former golf coaches at California State University at San Bernardino were initially awarded $1.2 million from a jury as part of an age discrimination case against their former employer. This amount was reduced to $750,000 on appeal. Two years after being fired as a sportscaster by ABC Sports in 1998, former Olympian Donna De Varona filed a $50 million unlawful termination lawsuit against her former employer alleging she was discriminated based on her age and gender. The case was later settled out of court. Former football referee Ben Dreith filed suit against the NFL alleging the league discriminated against him based on his age by refusing to allow him to officiate any playoff games, and by demoting him to line judge during the 1990–91 season. (see the Supplemental Web Site) He also claimed the league retaliated against him for filing his ADEA claim by not renewing his contract. The case reportedly settled for six figures. (Epstein, 2006) These examples, coupled with the legal costs to defend such cases, reflect the financial risk involved with age discrimination litigation.

With people living longer, healthier lives, our workforce is steadily growing older. This demographic shift has often come into direct conflict with the economic reality of reductions in the labor force and other cost-cutting measures. The tension between an aging society and these dynamic market forces, and the growing risk of liability in these cases make it vital for sport and recreation managers to have a clear understanding age discrimination laws.

FUNDAMENTAL CONCEPTS

Federal Legislation

The Age Discrimination in Employment Act of 1967 (ADEA)

The Age Discrimination in Employment Act protects employees and job applicants who are forty years of age or older from employment discrimination based on age. The ADEA, which applies to employers with 20 or more employees, pertains to various terms and conditions of employment, including but not limited to the hiring process, compensation schemes, promotion decisions, job assignments, training opportunities, temporary layoffs, and termination of employment.

Although the ADEA was modeled after Title VII, there are some noteworthy differences between the two statutes. One such distinction is that the definition of what constitutes an "employer" under the ADEA is broader than Title VII. Unlike Title VII, the ADEA does not exclude groups such as religious organizations or Native American tribes, among others, from being characterized as "employer" under the statute. The ADEA specifically defines an "employer" as "a person engaged in an industry affecting commerce who has twenty or more employees for each working day in each of twenty or more calendar weeks in the current or preceding calendar year" (29 U.S.C.A. §630(b)).

There are some limitations to the scope of the ADEA. For example, certain employees that are vital to public safety and welfare, such as police officers, cannot seek protection under the ADEA. Employees under forty years of age cannot seek relief under the ADEA, even if they are subject to discrimination in the workplace based on age.

Enforcement of the ADEA falls under the purview of the Equal Employment Opportunity Commission (EEOC). Code of Federal Regulations contains the procedures for charges made with the EEOC under the ADEA (29 C.F.R. §1625–27). A party alleging age discrimination under the ADEA is generally required to file a claim with the EEOC within 180 days from the date of the challenged conduct (42 U.S.C. §§ 2000e-5(e)(1)). However, that deadline may be extended if the claimant also has a claim under state law. A party who files a charge of age discrimination with the EEOC "may file a civil action at any time after 60 days have elapsed from the filing of the charge with the Commission" (29 C.F.R. §1626.18 (b)).

Until recently, the only way to establish a claim under the ADEA was for the plaintiff to prove that age was the motivating factor for the challenged conduct. One theory of liability under the ADEA is for the plaintiff to prove **disparate treatment** by a direct showing that the employer intentionally discriminated against the plaintiff solely because of the plaintiff's age. Another theory is that the defendant engaged in **systemic disparate treatment** by instituting widespread employment practices that displayed a pattern of discrimination based on age. In 2005, the U.S. Supreme Court substantially expanded the ADEA by also allowing claims based on **disparate impact** in *Smith v. City of Jackson, Mississippi* (2005) (see the Supplemental Web Site), the Court held that an employment practice that discriminates based on age could be considered unlawful under the ADEA, regardless of the discriminatory intent of the employer. Prior to the decision in *City of Jackson*, most federal courts had ruled that such disparate impact claims were not permitted. Now, under the authority of *City of Jackson*, seemingly "neutral" employer practices can be held to violate the ADEA if they result in a disparate impact on older workers. The plaintiff no longer has to establish that the employer intended to discriminate to prevail under the ADEA. Although this represents a significant change in the law, it remains to be seen what impact, if any, this ruling will have on ADEA cases in the future. Although both the ADEA and Title VII now permit claims based on a disparate impact theory, the Supreme Court noted in *City of Jackson* that the scope of the disparate impact theory under the ADEA is narrower than Title VII because under the ADEA, employer conduct is permitted as long as it is based on "reasonable factors" other than age. So even though this case represents a clear expansion of the ADEA, to now include disparate impact cases, the applicability of the disparate impact theory is not as broad under the ADEA as under Title VII.

To establish a prima facie case under the ADEA, the plaintiff must establish the following elements by a preponderance of the evidence:

1. The plaintiff is an employee or applicant for employment with the employer.
2. The employee is a member of the protected class (i.e., forty years old or above).
3. The employer has twenty or more employees.

4. The plaintiff was qualified for the job (if an applicant for employment) or was performing the duties and responsibilities of the job satisfactorily (if an employee).

5. The plaintiff suffered some adverse condition with respect to their employment (e.g., was not hired, was fired).

6. The employer hired someone outside the protected class (for job applicants) or replaced the plaintiff with someone outside the protected class (for employees).

In addition to these theories of liability, it is unlawful to retaliate against someone for filing an age discrimination charge, participating in an investigation, or testifying in a proceeding or lawsuit filed under the ADEA. The ADEA states, "It shall be unlawful for an employer to discriminate against any of his employees or applicants for employment, for an employment agency to discriminate against any individual, or for a labor organization to discriminate against any member thereof or applicant for membership, because such individual, member or applicant for membership has opposed any practice made unlawful by this section, or because such individual, member or applicant for membership has made a charge, testified, assisted, or participated in any manner in an investigation, proceeding, or litigation under this chapter" (29 U.S.C.A. §623(d)). The elements for a retaliation claim under the ADEA are identical to the filing of such a claim under Title VII.

It is also a violation of the ADEA to harass older workers or subject them to a hostile work environment (*Eggleston v. South Bend Community School Corporation*, 1994). Once again, the criteria for a harassment claim under the ADEA and Title VII are the same.

Once the plaintiff is able to establish a prima facie case under the ADEA, the burden than shifts to the employer to establish a defense. One affirmative defense that can be asserted in ADEA cases is that *other reasonable factors besides age* prompted the employer's conduct. Another defense is to prove that a **bona fide occupational qualification (BFOQ)** exists by demonstrating that age is a legitimate factor to consider for the performance of that particular job (e.g., airline pilots, firefighters, police officers) Certain seniority systems may be free from ADEA attack, provided the scheme does not discriminate against older workers.

Assuming the employer is able to provide a legitimate, nondiscriminatory reason for the alleged discrimination, the burden then shifts back to the plaintiff to refute the purported rationale by showing that the justification offered is merely a **pretext** for actual discrimination. Plaintiffs typically attempt to establish pretext by offering evidence of pervasive bias against members of the protected class (older workers in this case) or by introducing into evidence data reflecting inequity or favoritism among certain classes of employees.

If the plaintiff prevails in age discrimination claim under the ADEA, the plaintiff is entitled to back pay for lost wages, injunctive and declaratory relief, and attorney's fees (29 U.S.C. §216(b)). The plaintiff may also receive liquidated damages if the defendant's conduct is found to be willful (29 U.S.C. §626(b)). In addition, the court may, in its discretion, order that the plaintiff be reinstated or promoted or award the plaintiff front pay for loss of future wages. (See Significant Case: *Moore v. The University of Notre Dame*, 1998).

Older Workers Benefit Protection Act (OWBPA)

In 1990, Congress amended the ADEA with the enactment of The Older Workers Benefit Protection Act (OWBPA), which specifically prohibits employers from denying benefits to older workers. However, under the OWBPA, an employer may reduce the benefit plans for older workers provided that the cost of such plans is the same as the cost of providing benefits to younger employees.

The OWBPA is also significant in that it imposes extremely stringent standards for settling a claim under the ADEA. There is no counterpart to these provisions in Title VII, and as a result, it is more difficult to settle an ADEA case. In addition, the OWBPA contains very specific criteria that must be met for an employee to waive rights secured under the ADEA. To be valid, such a waiver must:

1. Be in writing.
2. Be clear and unambiguous.
3. Clearly make reference to ADEA rights or claims.
4. Only apply to current rights and claims. It cannot waive future rights or claims that might arise in the future.
5. Be in exchange for valuable consideration.
6. Contain a clause advising the employee to consult an attorney before signing the waiver.
7. Allow the employee twenty-one days to consider the waiver before it becomes effective.
8. Give the employee at least seven days to revoke the waiver after signing it.

State Legislation

In addition to federal law, most states have some type of law prohibiting age discrimination. Some state statutes provide different or greater protection than the ADEA, and therefore they may provide relief in circumstances where the ADEA does not apply. For example, some states allow age discrimination cases for workers younger than forty years of age. Other states statues extend age discrimination protection to workplaces with fewer than twenty employees. In a few states, age discrimination can be a criminal offense.

In addition, states typically have their own administrative agencies that handle age discrimination claims based on state law, as well as their own deadlines for filing such claims. EEOC refers to such state agencies as **Fair Employment Practices Agencies (FEPAs).** The EEOC and the FEPAs have agreements that are designed to enable the state and federal agencies to work together efficiently and that allow for "dual filing" when a party has a claim based on both state and federal law. The general 180-day deadline for filing an ADEA claim with the EEOC is extended to 300 days if the charge also is covered by a state law. For these reasons, it is important for the sport and recreation manager to be aware of the applicable state laws concerning age discrimination in addition to the pertinent federal legislation.

Alternative Legal Grounds for Relief

In addition to state and federal age discrimination laws, other areas of law may provide the basis for a claim in situations where an individual is discriminated against based on age. However, these are not considered true "age discrimination" cases because the cause of action is not based on a law that prohibits discrimination based on age. For example, Maurice Clarett's lawsuit against the NFL challenged the league rule making players ineligible for the draft until they were three seasons removed from their high school graduations. Although the impact of the league rule was to discriminate against Clarett based on his age, his suit was based on the claim that the league unreasonably restrained free trade in violation of antitrust law.

SIGNIFICANT CASE

One of the more publicized sport-related age discrimination cases involved the termination of Joe Moore as assistant football coach at Notre Dame University. Moore prevailed against Notre Dame on his age discrimination claim at trial and was awarded back pay and liquidated damages by the jury. After the trial, Moore moved to either be reinstated to his former position or awarded front pay in addition to the damages already awarded him by the jury. The portion of the decision dealing with Moore's request for attorney's fees and costs has been omitted.

JOSEPH R. MOORE V. UNIVERSITY OF NOTRE DAME

United States District Court for the Northern District of Indiana
22 F. Supp. 2d 896 (1998)

This cause is before this Court on Plaintiff's Motion for Award of Reinstatement/Front Pay and Plaintiff's Bill of Costs. Plaintiff, Joseph R. Moore (Moore) filed a claim in this Court against The University of Notre Dame (Notre Dame) alleging age discrimination, retaliation, and defamation. Only the age discrimination claim survived summary judgment. The case went to trial in Lafayette on July 9, 1998. On July 15, 1998, after four and one-half hours of deliberation, the Jury found that Notre Dame had violated the Age Discrimination in Employment Act (ADEA) and awarded Moore back pay in the amount of $42,935.28. Additionally, because the jury determined that Notre Dame's violation of ADEA was willful, Plaintiff also was awarded liquidated damages in the additional amount of $42,935.28. Judgment must and now does enter in favor of the plaintiff, Joseph E. Moore and against the defendant, Notre Dame in the amount of $85,870.56. Accordingly, the Court now considers Moore's post-trial motions.

* * *

I. Relief Under the Adea

The remedial scheme for a discriminatory discharge is designed to make a plaintiff who has been the victim of discrimination whole through the use of equitable remedies. See *Albemarle Paper Co. v. Moody*, 422 U.S. 405, 95 S. Ct. 2362, 45 L. Ed. 2d 280 (1975) (discussing equitable remedies for Title VII); *Straka v. Francis*, 867 F. Supp. 767 (N.D. Ill. 1994) (stating that ADEA and Title VII are treated similarly regarding available remedies). When confronted with a violation of the ADEA, a district court is authorized to afford relief by means of reinstatement, back pay, injunctive relief, declaratory judgment, and attorney's fees. 29 U.S.C.§ 626(b); *McKennon v. Nashville Banner Pub'g Co.*, 513 U.S. 352, 357–58, 115 S. Ct. 879, 884, 130 L. Ed. 2d 852 (1995); *see also Lorillard v. Pons*, 434 U.S. 575, 584, 98 S. Ct. 866, 872, 55 L. Ed. 2d 40 (1978). Additionally, in the case of a willful violation of the Act, the ADEA authorizes an award of liquidated damages equal to the back pay award. 29 U.S.C. § 626(b).

* * *

Moore now asks the Court to reinstate him in his former coaching position, or to award five year's front pay in lieu of reinstatement. Notre Dame contends that Moore has received all relief to which he was entitled and therefore asks this Court to deny Moore's Motion for Reinstatement/Front Pay.

A. Reinstatement

Although reinstatement is the preferred remedy in a discrimination case, it is not always appropriate. The factors which should be considered when determining its propriety include, hostility in the past employment relationship and the absence of an available position for the plaintiff. Civil Rights Act of 1964, § 701 et seq., as amended, 42 U.S.C.A. § 2000e *et seq.; McKnight v. General Motors Corp.*, 973 F.2d 1366, 1370 (7th Cir. 1992); *Ward v. Tipton County Sheriff Dept.*, 937 F. Supp. 791 (S.D. Ind.1996). Additionally, under ADEA, when a period for reinstatement is relatively short, such that plaintiff is close to retirement, the strong preference in favor of reinstatement is neutralized by the increased certainty of potential loss of pay permitting consideration of a front pay award. See *McNeil v. Economics Laboratory, Inc.*, 800 F.2d 111, 118 (7th Cir. 1986), *cert. denied*, 481 U.S. 1041, 107 S. Ct. 1983, 95 L. Ed. 2d 823 (1987), overruled on other grounds by *Coston v. Plitt Theatres, Inc.*, 860 F.2d 834 (7th Cir. 1988). See also, *Chace v. Champion Spark Plug Co.*, 732 F. Supp. 605 (D. Md. 1990).

1. Hostility

The decision to reinstate a discriminatorily terminated employee is consigned to the sound discretion of the district court which should not grant reinstatement "where the result would be undue friction and controversy." *McKnight v. General Motors Corp.*, 908 F.2d 104, 115 (7th Cir. 1990); *Wilson v. AM General Corp.*, 979 F. Supp. 800 (N.D. Ind. 1997) (may consider friction that exists between employer and employee unrelated to discrimination). Evidence that hostility developed between the employer and employee during litigation may also be considered, but is not dispositive. *U.S. E.E.O.C. v. Century Broadcasting Corp.*, 957 F.2d 1446 (7th Cir. 1992); *Cassino v. Reichhold Chemicals, Inc.*, 817 F.2d 1338 (9th Cir. 1987).

In the present case, Moore's reinstatement would cause significant friction as well as disruption of the current football program. Moore and Davie, his direct supervisor, are no longer on speaking terms. During trial, sufficient evidence was presented to infer that Moore and Davie would be unable to engage in a workable relationship. Reinstatement in this instance is impracticable. Moreover, even if hostility and undue friction were not a problem, reinstatement is not appropriate in this case.

2. Available Position

The Seventh Circuit has also held that reinstatement can reasonably be denied when "someone else currently occupies the employee's former position." *Century Broadcasting*, 957 F.2d 1446 (quoting *Graefenhain v. Pabst Brewing Co.* 870 F.2d 1198, 1208 (7th Cir. 1989). Other Circuits hold similarly. See e.g., *Ray v. Iuka Special Mun. Separate School Dist.*, 51 F.3d 1246, 1254 (5th Cir. 1995); *Shore v. Federal Express Corp.*, 777 F.2d 1155, 1157–59 (6th Cir. 1985); *Spagnuolo v. Whirlpool Corp.*, 717 F.2d 114, 119–122 (4th Cir. 1983) (holding that reinstatement is not appropriate if it requires bumping or displacing innocent employee in favor of plaintiff). The law is clear. Even if this Court determined that reinstatement is warranted, it is not an appropriate remedy in this case as there is no available position to which Moore could return. Therefore, the Court turns to the more difficult issue of whether front-pay is warranted.

B. Front Pay

Plaintiff is incorrect in stating that "if the Court rejects Moore's request for reinstatement, it must award him front pay." (Pl.'s Mem. at 7) (emphasis added). Front pay is an available remedy under ADEA, however, such an award remains discretionary with court. *Williams v. Pharmacia Opthalmics, Inc.*, 926 F. Supp. 791 (N.D. Ind. 1996), *aff'd*, 137 F.3d 944 (7th Cir. 1997); *Downes v. Volkswagen of America, Inc.*, 41 F.3d 1132, 1141 (7th Cir. 1993); *Tennes v. Commonwealth of Massachusetts Dept. of Revenue*, 944 F.2d 372, 381 (7th Cir. 1991); *Drago v. Aetna Plywood, Inc.*, 1998 U.S. Dist. LEXIS 12249, No.96C2398, 1998 WL 474100 (N.D. Ill. Aug. 3, 1998). The Seventh Circuit has defined front pay as "a lump sum . . . representing the discounted present value of the difference between the earnings (an employee) would have received in his old employment and the earnings he can be expected to receive in his present and future, and by hypothesis, inferior, employment. *Century Broadcasting*, 957 F.2d 1446, 1463 n.18 (quoting *McKnight*, 908 F.2d 104, 116). See also, *Downes*, 41 F.3d 1132, 1141, n. 8. Such a remedy may especially be indicated when the plaintiff has no reasonable prospect of obtaining comparable employment or when the time period for which front pay is to be awarded is relatively short. *Inks v. Healthcare Distributors of Indiana, Inc.*, 901 F. Supp. 1403 (N.D. Ind. 1995). *See e.g., Nelson v. Boatmen's Bancshares, Inc.*, 26 F.3d 796 (8th Cir. 1994) (front pay appropriate when employee is nearing retirement age); *Duke v. Uniroyal, Inc.*, 928 F.2d 1413 (4th Cir. 1991); *Linn v. Andover Newton Theological School, Inc.*, 874 F.2d 1 (1st Cir. 1989); *Stratton v. Department for the Aging for the City of New York*, 922 F. Supp. 857 (S.D. N.Y. 1996) (all holding similarly). The court determines the amount of front pay to award depending on whether:

1. the plaintiff has a reasonable prospect of obtaining comparable employment;
2. the time period for the award is relatively short;
3. the plaintiff intends to work or is physically capable of working; and
4. liquidated damages have been awarded.

Williams, 926 F. Supp. 791, 796 (finding an award of front pay in Title VII context proper and consistent with the 1991 amendments). Front pay is awarded for a reasonable period of time, until a date by which the plaintiff, using reasonable diligence, should have found comparable employment. *Hutchison v. Amateur Electronics Supply, Inc.*, 840 F. Supp. 612 (E.D. Wisc. 1993), *aff'd. in part, rev'd in part*, 42 F.3d 1037 at 1045 (7th Cir. 1994). Moreover, an award must be grounded in available facts, acceptable to a reasonable person and not highly speculative. *Downes*, 41 F.3d at 1142. It cannot be based simply on a plaintiff's own stated intentions with regard to how long he or she would have worked. *Pierce v. Atchison, Topeka & Santa Fe Ry. Co.*, 65 F.3d 562, 574 (7th Cir.1995).

Notre Dame contends that Moore is not entitled to front pay because 1) evidence acquired by Notre Dame after Moore's discharge would have led to his discharge based on legitimate, non-discriminatory reasons, 2) Moore's award of liquidated damages has already made him whole, and 3) Moore has failed to make reasonable efforts to mitigate his damages.

1. Award of Liquidated Damages

The fact that Moore is entitled to damages based on the jury's finding of a wilful violation does not conclusively preclude front pay. Front pay *may be* less appropriate when liquidated damages are awarded. *Id.* (emphasis added); *Hybert v. Hearst Corp.*, 900 F.2d 1050, 1056 (7th Cir. 1990) (liquidated damages are a relevant consideration in determining *whether and how much* front pay to award). Authority clearly states that liquidated damages is *one* factor to be considered in awarding front pay and does not stand for the proposition that front pay and liquidated damages may never be awarded to the same plaintiff. *Century Broadcasting*, 957 F.2d 1446,

1450; *McNeil*, 800 F.2d 111, 118; *Graefenhain*, 870 F.2d 1198, 1,205. Furthermore, an award of front pay, constituting an estimate of what the employee might have earned had he been reinstated at the conclusion of trial is necessarily speculative, this speculative aspect should not deter courts from fashioning awards that accomplish ADEA's goal of making a wronged employee whole. *Selgas v. American Airlines, Inc.*, 104 F.3d 9 (1st Cir. 1997), on remand 977 F. Supp. 100 (D. P.R 1997).

In the present case, Notre Dame argues that Moore's jury award of $42,935.28 and liquidated damages award of $42,935.28 makes him whole and that further compensation would "be a total award greater than the statute contemplates." *Avitia v. Metropolitan Club of Chicago, Inc.*, 49 F.3d 1219, 1232 (7th Cir. 1995). The Court disagrees. Moore's 1996–97 annual salary was $79,552.08. Assuming an annual increase of 4%, his 1997–98 salary would have been $82,734.16 and his 1998–99 salary $86,043.53. In addition to loss of salary, Moore also lost several benefits. It is unlikely he will be able to duplicate the benefits and prestige the Notre Dame position provided him. Moreover, as Moore is at or near retirement age, it is unlikely he will find comparable employment at the salary level he enjoyed while at Notre Dame. *Compare, Stratton*, 922 F. Supp. 857 (S.D. N.Y. 1996) (finding front pay appropriate in ADEA action, where it was clear from evidence presented at trial that employee, who was now 66 years of age, had no reasonable prospect of obtaining positions similar to that she previously held). The evidence showed that Moore had coached at Notre Dame for nine years and intended to continue in that position until retirement. Moore has been unable to replace his Notre Dame position with a comparable one. He is currently earning $46,600 and working three jobs. In this Court's opinion, the jury award has not "made him whole" and front pay may be appropriate.

2. After-Acquired Evidence

Notre Dame also asserts that Moore is not entitled to front pay because Notre Dame Administrators made it clear that had they known of Moore's alleged physical and verbal abuse of players, they would have terminated him immediately. Notre Dame argues that evidence of the alleged abuse was "after acquired" and therefore precludes both front pay and reinstatement.

What sets an after-acquired evidence case apart * * * is that the articulated "legitimate" reason for terminating the employee was non-existent at the time of the adverse decision and could not possibly have motivated the employer to the slightest degree. *DelliSanti v. CNA Ins. Companies*, 88 F.3d 192 (3d Cir. 1996). Furthermore, "Where an employer seeks to rely upon after-acquired evidence of wrongdoing, it must first establish that the wrongdoing was of such severity that the employee in fact would have been terminated on those grounds alone if the employer had known of it at the time of discharge." ADEA, 29 U.S.C. § 621 *et seq.*; *McKennon*, 513 U.S. 352, 115 S.

Ct. 879, 130 L. Ed. 2d 852; *Moos v. Square D Co.*, 72 F.3d 39 (6th Cir. 1995); *Coleman v. Keebler Co.*, 997 F. Supp. 1102 (N.D. Ind. 1998); *Vandeventer v. Wabash Nat. Corp.*, 887 F. Supp. 1178 (N.D. Ind. 1995). It is this Court's opinion that Notre Dames argument fails on both points.

* * *

First, the after-acquired evidence doctrine does not bar front pay to a discharged employee whose alleged wrongdoing was known to the employer at the time of the discharge and was asserted as being a reason for the discharge. *DelliSanti*, 88 F.3d 192, 205. It is this Court's opinion that Defendant's knowledge of Moore's coaching behavior does not fall within the ambit of after-acquired evidence as set forth in *McKennon*. Moore coached football at Notre Dame for nine years. Davie knew of, and in fact argued that Moore's behavior was one of the reasons for his termination. The record is replete with such evidence. (Trial Tr. July 10, 1998 p. 18, 19, 30–38). The jury apparently rejected this argument. Based on its defense at trial, Notre Dame cannot now claim that this "legitimate" reason was non-existent at the time of the adverse decision and could not possibly have motivated it to the slightest degree. *DelliSanti*, 88 F.3d 192, 205–06.

Notre Dame has also failed to establish that Moore's alleged wrongdoing was of such severity that he in fact would have been terminated on those grounds alone. Football is an aggressive sport. Coaching a winning team requires a degree of "killer instinct." Notre Dame's blanket assertion that if certain administrators had known of Moore's alleged abuse of players, Moore would have been immediately fired is insufficient to prove that such would have actually occurred. This assertion is nothing more than an excuse made after the fact. Additionally, this Court will not speculate, like defendant does, as to the reason the jury did not award a large amount of back pay. (Def.'sMem. at 4). An award of back pay less than requested does not necessarily mean the jury concluded Moore would have been terminated for nondiscriminatory reasons and it does not therefore preclude front pay. *See Curtis v. Electronics & Space Corp.*, 113 F.3d 1498, 1504 (8th Cir. 1997); *Downes*, 41 F.3d 1132, 1143–44 (7th Cir. 1994). Accordingly, this Court finds Defendant's after-acquired evidence argument without merit.

3. Failure to Mitigate

Notre Dame finally argues that Moore is not entitled to front pay because he failed to undertake reasonable efforts to mitigate his damages. This Court disagrees. Generally, an ADEA plaintiff satisfies the mitigation of damages requirement that he use "reasonable diligence in attempting to secure employment" by demonstrating his commitment to seeking active employment and by remaining ready, willing and able to work. However, a plaintiff's duty to mitigate his damages is not met by using reasonable diligence to obtain any employment, rather the employment must be comparable employment. *Finch v. Hercules Inc.*, 941 F. Supp. 1395 (D. Del. 1996). The Seventh Circuit has defined "comparable work" as

a position that affords "virtually identical promotional opportunities, compensation, job responsibilities, working conditions and status" as the previous position. *Best v. Shell Oil Co.*, 4 F. Supp. 2d 770 (N.D. Ill. 1998) (quoting *Hutchinson*, 42 F.3d 1037 at 1044). The goal of mitigation is to prevent the plaintiff from remaining idle and doing nothing. Furthermore, an employee is not required to go to heroic lengths in attempting to mitigate his damages, but only to take reasonable steps to do so. *Suggs v. ServiceMaster Educ. Food Management*, 72 F.3d 1228 (6th Cir. 1996); *Ford v. Nicks*, 866 F.2d 865 (6th Cir. 1989). Furthermore, a claimant has no obligation to accept lesser employment . . . or relocate to a new community. *See, e.g., Ford Motor Co. v. E.E.O.C.*, 458 U.S. 219, 231–32, 102 S. Ct. 3057, 3065–66, 73 L. Ed. 2d 721 (1982); *Coleman v. City of Omaha*, 714 F.2d 804, 808 (8th Cir. 1983); *Glass v. IDS Financial Services, Inc.*, 778 F. Supp. 1029 (D. Minn. 1991); *Raimondo v. AMAX, Inc.*, 843 F. Supp. 806 (D. Conn. 1984).

When evaluating the reasonableness and duration of a job search a court may consider the plaintiff's background and individual characteristics. *Rasimas v. Michigan Dep't of Mental Health*, 714 F.2d 614, 624 (6th Cir.1983) (for example, older claimants need not exert same effort as younger claimants); *Sellers v. Delgado College*, 902 F.2d 1189, 1193 (5th Cir. 1990). Moreover, it is the defendant's burden to prove that a plaintiff has failed to discharge his duty. *Smith v. Great American Restaurants, Inc.*, 969 F.2d 430 (7th Cir. 1992); *Padilla v. Metro-North Commuter R.R.*, 92 F.3d 117, 125 (2d Cir. 1996). In the present case, Notre Dame has not met this burden. Moore sought and obtained employment shortly after his discharge. He currently works at three different jobs. The fact that he did not accept a position at Cornell does not indicate a failure to mitigate. That position offered a $40,000 salary, significantly less than Moore's former salary, and involved a tenuous situation where the head coach was seeking other employment. Nor does the fact that Moore did not apply for certain positions mentioned by defendant indicate a failure to mitigate. *Compare Buchholz v. Symons Mfg. Co.*, 445 F. Supp. 706 (E.D. Wis. 1978) (62-year-old salesman, who was discharged in violation of ADEA was not required to relocate for three years of employment until planned retirement as a reasonable effort to mitigate damages). Moore is presently sixty-six years old. The options available to him are not as great as those available to someone younger. Moore has demonstrated his willingness to work, but, the chances of finding "comparable work" as defined by the Seventh Circuit, *supra*, are slim. It is this Court's opinion that Moore used reasonable diligence in attempting to obtain employment.

* * *

3. Summary

The purpose of front pay under the Age Discrimination in Employment Act is to ensure that a person who has been discriminated against on the basis of age is made whole, not to guarantee every claimant who cannot mitigate damages by finding comparable work an annuity to age 70. *Anastasio v. Schering Corp.*, 838 F.2d 701 (3d Cir. 1988). Furthermore, the risk of non-continuity of future employment in a "volatile" must be considered in determining an award of front pay, *Price v. Marshall Erdman & Assoc., Inc.*, 966 F.2d 320, 327 (7th Cir. 1992); 901 F. Supp. 1403, 1408, and the Court has considered this fact.

Defendant's argument that front pay is too speculative when the plaintiff's profession has a high turnover rate (Def.'sMem. at 12) does not preclude a front-pay award. *See Century Broadcasting*, 957 F.2d 1446 (front pay improperly denied on grounds employment in industry was tenuous). In this case, such an award is not "highly speculative." The Court has solid evidence concerning Moore's annual salary and the number of years he hoped to continue his employment. While Moore asserts that five years front pay is warranted, this Court disagrees. The evidence presented at trial establishes that Moore expressed a desire to work two more years and then retire. There was no guarantee that Davie would remain at Notre Dame longer than his current contract or that Moore would indefinitely remain in Davie's employ. The evidence also suggests that Moore and Davie had philosophical differences which may have lead to a parting of the ways. With all evidence considered, the Court finds an award of two years front pay sufficient. The front pay is calculated as follows:

Had Moore remained at Notre Dame his total 1998 salary would have been $84,388.84. Subtracted from this amount is Moore's annual salary from his present employment. Moore testified that he currently earns $1,600 for his services as assistant football coach at Cathedral Preparatory School, $15,000 for his work with the Baltimore Ravens, and $30,000 from his work with Tollgrade Communications. His total current yearly earning amount is therefore $46,600. The difference between Moore's Notre Dame salary and his current salary is $37,788.84 per year. This amount is multiplied by a period of two years and yields a total of $75,577.68. Because the Court is not including an additional amount for lost benefits and is not factoring in any increase for the second year, no discounting of the front pay award is warranted. *See Stratton v. Dep't for the Aging for City of New York*, 132 F.3d 869, 882 (2d Cir. 1997); *see e.g. Gusman v. Unisys corp.*, 986 F.2d 1146, 1147–48 (7th Cir. 1993). Thus, the total front pay award equals $75,577.68 plus post judgment interest.

* * *

Conclusion

For the preceding reasons it is hereby ordered that Plaintiff's Motion for Reinstatement is DENIED. Plaintiff's Motion for Award of Front Pay is GRANTED "in part as modified herein". Plaintiff is awarded front pay in the amount of $75,577.68 plus post-judgment interest.

It is further ordered that Plaintiff's Motion for Costs and Fees is GRANTED. Plaintiff is awarded costs in the total amount of $9,672.45. Plaintiff is also awarded attorney fees and expenses in the total amount of $394,865.74.

Finally, pursuant to jury verdict, the Plaintiff is awarded $42,935.28 in back pay and an additional $42,935.28 in liquidated damages.

IT IS SO ORDERED.

CASES ON THE SUPPLEMENTAL WEB SITE

Dreith v. National Football League, 777 F. Supp, 832 (D. Colo. 1991). This case explores whether the NFL demoted the employee because of his age.

Labati v. University of Miami, 16 So. 3d 886 (Fla. Dist. Ct. App. 3d Dist.,2009). The reader should examine whether the University had any legitimate business justifications for its decision to buy out the coach.

Shreve v. Cornell University, No. 84-CV-918, 1988 U.S. Dist. LEXIS 3109 (N.D.N.Y. 1988). Do you agree with the

court that the individual's age was not a determining factor in the university's employment decision?

Smith v. City of Jackson, Mississippi, 125 S. Ct. 1536 (2005). In this case, the court examines whether granting larger raises to lower echelon employees for the purpose of bringing salaries in line with other similar employees was a decision based on a "reasonable factor other than age."

QUESTIONS YOU SHOULD BE ABLE TO ANSWER

1. What sports-related situations are age discrimination cases likely to arise?

2. Is the ADEA a likely avenue of relief for professional athletes who are banned from participating in their sport because of their age? Give reasons to support your position.

3. What must an aggrieved plaintiff do under the ADEA before filing a federal law suit?

4. Defined and describe some of the main defenses that can be made in ADEA claims.

5. In *Moore v. The University of Notre Dame*, what was meant by "front pay?" Did the court award the plaintiff front pay in this case?

REFERENCES

Cases

Clarett v. National Football League, 306 F. Supp. 2d 379 (S.D.N.Y. 2004), reversed, 369 F.3d 124 (2nd Cir. 2004), cert. denied, 125 S.Ct. 1728 (2005).

Eggleston v. South Bend Community School Corp., 858 F. Supp. 841 (N.D. Ind 1994).

Lane v. Colorado High School Activities Association, No. 96-Z-2143 (Colorado 1996).

Moore v. The University of Notre Dame, 22 F. Supp. 2d 896 (N.D. Ind. 1998).

Legislation

Age Discrimination in Employment Act, 29 U.S.C.A. §§ 621–634.

Age Discrimination Act of 1975, 29 U.S.C.A. §§ 6101–6107.

Publications

Elgin Baylor's lawsuit rejected by Los Angeles County jury, *Los Angeles Times* (online edition), March 30, 2011. Retrieved at http://latimesblogs.latimes.com/sports_blog/2011/03/elgin-baylors-lawsuit-rejected-by-los-angeles-county-jury.html on 2/18/12.

Epstein, A. (2006). ADEA and Sports Law, Journal of Legal Aspects of Sport, 16(2), 177–196. Oshlan, Jeremy. Boo-ze for the Yanks. *New York Post* (online edition). May 26, 2009. Retrieved at http://www.nypost.com/p/news/regional/item_WufDuzcHSLrlkK4jy5nz5N on 2/18/12.

Sandomir, James. Sportscasting Fixture Files Age-Discrimination Lawsuit. New York Times. October 14, 2010, B18.

Thorman, Joel. Chiefs Say Age Discrimination Accusations Are 'Baseless And Ridiculous' Arrowhead Pride, December 7, 2011. Retrieved at http://www.arrowheadpride.com/2011/12/7/2618168/kansas-city-chiefs-age-discrimation on 2/18/12.

Websites

Equal Employment Opportunity Commission (EEOC): www.eeoc.gov

U.S. Department of Labor: www.dol.gov

7.16 TITLE I OF THE AMERICANS WITH DISABILITIES ACT

Mary A. Hums I University of Louisville

What do the following athletes have in common: Magic Johnson (professional basketball), Tamika Catchings, (professional basketball), Natalie Du Toit (Olympic and Paralympic swimming), Oscar Pistorius (Olympic and Paralympic track and field), Marla Runyan (Olympic and Paralympic track and field), and Casey Martin (professional golf)? Each has some type of disability. Johnson is HIV-positive. Catchings is hearing impaired. Du Toit is a single below-the-knee amputee. Pistorius is a double below-the-knee amputee. Runyan is visually impaired. Martin has a circulatory disorder. Yet each has had a successful athletic career.

Events such as the Paralympic Games and the athletes with disabilities who compete in them are becoming more visible every day. But what about other people with disabilities who wish to work as sport and recreation managers in some segment of the sport and recreation industry? What barriers do they face and what kind of legal protections do they have against employment discrimination? In addition to addressing facility issues, the Americans with Disabilities Act (ADA) provides guidelines for employers when dealing with employees with disabilities. These guidelines help ensure equal opportunity for people with disabilities by opening up the definition of who is a "qualified individual" to people of all abilities.

FUNDAMENTAL CONCEPTS

The Americans with Disabilities Act of 1990 (ADA) is not limited to facility accessibility issues, but addresses employment issues as well. It is important to remember that the ADA covers the entire scope of the employment process. Title I of the ADA states "[N]o covered entity shall discriminate against a qualified individual with a disability because of the disability of such individual in regard to job application procedures, the hiring, advancement or discharge of employees, employee compensation, job training, and other terms, conditions, and privileges of employment" [42 U.S.C. 12112(a)]. According to Masteralexis and Wong (2012, p.104), "The sport industry is people intensive, so sport managers must have a working knowledge of how the law affects human resource management, particularly a basic knowledge of labor and employment laws," and this includes The Americans With Disabilities Act. This section focuses primarily on the question of reasonable accommodation. Before examining the ADA's application to sport organizations, some basic definitions must be established.

Employer

According to Title I, § 12111 [sec. 101] (5)(a) of the ADA, the term *employer* means "a person engaged in an industry affecting commerce who has 15 or more employees for each working day in each of 20 or more calendar weeks in the current or preceding calendar year, and any agent of such person." In *Jones v. Southeast Alabama Baseball Umpires Association* (1994), an umpire who wore a prosthetic leg had his request to work an increased number of varsity high school baseball games denied and proceeded to file an ADA claim. The Umpires' Association filed for summary judgment, claiming it did not fall under ADA coverage because it did not employ umpires for more than twenty weeks. Jones was able to show that because the Association assigned umpires during both the school year and for summer youth games, it actually employed umpires for approximately six months, and therefore the Association's request for summary judgment was denied.

Disability

Under the ADA, the term **disability** means (1) a physical or mental impairment that substantially limits one or more of the major life activities of such individual; (2) a record of such impairment; or (3) being regarded as having such an impairment [§ 12103 (Sec. 3)] (2). Although the ADA does not specifically define "major life activities," the Department of Health and Human Services defines it as "functions such as caring for one's self, performing manual tasks, walking, seeing, hearing, speaking, breathing, learning, and working" [45 C.F.R. 84.3(j)(2)(i)(1985)].

Qualified Individual with a Disability

According to Title I, § 12111 [Sec. 101] (8) of the ADA, a "qualified individual with a disability" means: "an individual who, with or without reasonable accommodation, can perform the essential functions of the employment position that such an individual holds or desires." In order to be qualified, a person must still meet certain prerequisites for the position. For example, a teacher who could not pass the required national teachers' examination could be considered not qualified for a teaching position (*Pandazides v. Virginia Board of Education*, 1992). In *Sawhill v. Medical College of Pennsylvania* (1996), the plaintiff, a licensed clinical pathologist, was told his termination was because he did not fit into his department's future plans, but later discovered his termination was related to his disability (clinical depression). The plaintiff alleged termination based on his disability violated the ADA. The defendant's motion to dismiss was denied. The term "qualified individual with a disability" does "not include any employee or applicant who is currently engaging in illegal use of drugs, when the covered entity acts on the basis of such use" (42 U.S.C. 12112(a)). In *Collings v. Longview Fibre Company* (1995), Collings and seven other employees alleged Longview Fibre wrongfully terminated them for their drug addiction disability in violation of the Americans with Disabilities Act. The employees were discharged because of their drug-related misconduct at work and not because of their alleged substance abuse disability. The regulations accompanying the ADA indicate that employers may discharge or deny employment to people illegally using drugs, and the courts have recognized a distinction between termination of employment because of misconduct and termination because of a disability.

Reasonable Accommodation/Undue Hardship

According to the Job Accommodation Network (n.d., p. 1): In relation to the ADA, reasonable accommodation is any modification or adjustment to a job or the work environment that will enable a qualified applicant or employee with a disability to participate in the application process or to perform essential job functions. Reasonable accommodation also includes adjustments to assure that a qualified individual with a disability has rights and privileges in employment equal to those of employees without disabilities.

A reasonable accommodation means making some modifications in the work environment that allows a person with a disability an equal employment opportunity. These accommodations take place in three aspects of employment (Colker & Milani, 2005):

- To ensure equal opportunity in the employment process;
- To enable a qualified individual with a disability to perform the essential functions of a job;
- To enable an employee with a disability to enjoy equal benefits and privileges of employment (p. 20). It is good to ask the following questions when considering reasonable accommodations:
  1. What limitations is the employee experiencing?
  2. How do these limitations affect the employee and the employee's job performance?
  3. What specific job tasks are problematic as a result of these limitations?
  4. What accommodations are available to reduce or eliminate these problems? Are all possible resources being used to determine possible accommodations?
  5. Has the employee with a disability been consulted regarding possible accommodations?
  6. Once accommodations are in place, would it be useful to meet with the employee with a disability to evaluate the effectiveness of the accommodations and to determine whether additional accommodations are needed?
  7. Do supervisory personnel and employees need training regarding disabilities? (Job Accommodation Network, 2011, Accommodating Employees Who Use Wheelchairs section).

To comply with the ADA, employers must make reasonable accommodations for their workers with disabilities. However, employers only need to do so if providing the reasonable accommodation does not result in undue hardship. According to Title I, § 12111 [sec. 101] (9) of the ADA, a "***reasonable accommodation***" may include:

> *Making existing facilities used by employees reasonably accessible to and usable by individuals with disabilities; and Job restructuring, part-time or modified work schedules, reassignment to a vacant position, acquisition or modification of equipment or devices, appropriate adjustment or modifications of examinations, training materials or policies, the provision of qualified readers or interpreters, and other similar accommodations for individuals with disabilities.*

When making reasonable accommodations, employers should consider using the following steps for accommodation (U.S. Department of Labor, 2009):

1. Notify employees
2. Facilitate requests
3. Analyze jobs
4. Identify functional limitations
5. Determine potential accommodations
6. Determine reasonable solutions
7. Make the accommodation
8. Monitor effectiveness

According to Title I, § 12111 [sec. 101] (10)(a) of the ADA, an **undue hardship** is "an action requiring significant difficulty or expense, when considered in light of the factors set forth in subparagraph (b)":

> *(b) In determining whether an accommodation would impose an undue hardship on a covered entity, factors to be considered include:*
>
> *(i) the nature and cost of the accommodation needed under this Act;*
>
> *(ii) the overall financial resources of the facility or facilities involved in the provision of reasonable accommodation; the number of persons employed at such a facility; the effect on expenses and resources, or the impact otherwise of such accommodation upon the operation of the facility;*
>
> *(iii) the overall financial resources of the covered entity; the overall size of the business of the covered entity with respect to the number of its employees; the number, type and location of its facilities; and*
>
> *(iv) the type of operation or operations of the covered entity, including the composition, structure, and functions of the workforce of such entity; the geographic separateness, administrative, or fiscal relationship of the facility or facilities in question to the covered entity.*

The courts have interpreted the meaning of reasonable accommodation and undue hardship differently in different cases (Churchill, 1995). Some reasonable accommodations include working at home for an employee who experiences pain while commuting (*Sargent v. Litton Systems*, 1994); taking a leave of absence for alcoholism treatment (*Schmidt v. Safeway*, 1994); eliminating heavy lifting and strenuous work (*Henchey v. Town of North Greenbush*, 1993); allowing a police officer to carry food, glucose, and an insulin injection kit (*Bombrys v. City of Toledo*, 1993); and transferring an employee to a city where better medical care was available (*Buckingham v. United States*, 1993).

There are instances, however, when the courts have indicated that the requested accommodations were unreasonable or would have resulted in undue hardship. Reasonable accommodation did not require allowing an employee who has unpredictable violent outbursts to remain in the workplace (*Mazzarella v. U.S. Postal Service*, 1993), accommodating frequent or unpredictable absences (*Jackson v. Veteran's Administration*, 1994), or assigning limited tasks that substantially reduce an employee's contribution to the company (*Russell v. Southeastern Pennsylvania Transportation Authority*, 1993).

Accommodations do not have to be expensive according to Hendricks, Batiste, & Hirsch, 2005, Results section):

> One concern of many employers is the perceived cost of accommodating an employee with a disability. A total of 212 employers were able to provide cost information regarding the accommodation(s) made. Of these, half (50.5%) reported the accommodation was made at no cost (e.g., change in work schedule). Another 42.0% said the costs incurred were one-time only in nature, 5.2% said the costs would be incurred on an annual or ongoing basis, and 2.4% reported one-time and annual costs were involved. Of the 42.0% that had a one-time accommodation cost, the median cost reported was $600. Some examples of accommodations and their cost are:

- A timer with an indicator light allowed a medical technician who was deaf to perform laboratory tests. Cost $27.00;
- A groundskeeper who had limited use of one arm was provided a detachable extension arm for a rake. This enabled him to grasp the handle on the extension with the impaired hand and control the rake with the functional arm. Cost $20.00;
- A desk layout was changed from the right to left side to enable a data entry operator who is visually impaired to perform her job. Cost $0;
- A blind receptionist was provided a light probe that allowed her to determine which lines on the switchboard were ringing, on hold, or in use. (A light-probe gives an audible signal when held over an illuminated source.) Cost $50.00 to $100.00;
- A person who had use of only one hand, working in a food service position could perform all tasks except opening cans. She was provided with a one-handed can opener. Cost $35.00 (Job Accommodations Network, 2006, Acquisition or Modification section, ¶ 12)

Providing reasonable accommodations for employees need not be excessively expensive or complicated. Working off EEOC guidance, here are examples of reasonable accommodations:

- Making existing facilities accessible
- Job restructuring
- Reassignment to a vacant position
- Part-time or modified schedules
- Acquiring or modifying equipment
- Changing the physical layout of the work area
- Removing requirements to stand when a job is performed
- Changing tests, training materials, or policies
- Providing readers or interpreters

On the other hand, these are examples of what EEOC says it may view as an unreasonable accommodation:

- Eliminating an essential job function
- Lowering production standards (after reasonable accommodations have been instituted)
- Having to provide personal-use items for daily activities (prosthetics, wheelchairs, hearing aids, etc.)
- Arrangements that conflict with the company's seniority system, regardless of whether it is a product of collective bargaining or simply of management decision (Schleifer, 2007, p. 1).

According to the Job Accommodation Network (2000), a variety of reasonable accommodations can be made for employees with disabilities. A carpentry supervisor who had no functional hearing was required (as part of his job) to order supplies from various vendors. A text telephone used in conjunction with the local relay service allowed the supervisor to make the necessary orders. A maintenance technician restricted from working in extreme temperatures was accommodated with a modified schedule not requiring her to work outside in these conditions. People with low vision who must access information from a computer screen have a variety of accommodation options available. Those who benefit from larger type might find screen magnification software helpful. The creative use of scheduling may be helpful in maximizing an employee's productivity while accommodating potential problems with fatigue related to an illness such as cancer or HIV. The use of flexible scheduling, longer rest breaks, frequent short breaks, part-time work, or self-pacing may be helpful. Allowing an employee to work from home may be another alternative to consider.

Americans with Disabilities Act Amendments Act of 2008

In September of 2008, President George W. Bush signed the Americans with Disabilities Act Amendments of 2008. These Amendments went into law on 1 January 2009. According to the Equal Employment Opportunity Commission (2009, ¶3), the Act retains the ADA's basic definition of "disability" as an impairment that substantially limits one or more major life activities, a record of such an impairment, or being regarded as having such an impairment. However, it changes the way that these statutory terms should be interpreted in several ways. Most significantly, the Act:

- Directs EEOC to revise that portion of its regulations defining the term "substantially limits";
- Expands the definition of "major life activities" by including two non-exhaustive lists:
  (1) The first list includes many activities that the EEOC has recognized (e.g., walking) as well as activities that EEOC has not specifically recognized (e.g., reading, bending, and communicating);
  (2) The second list includes major bodily functions (e.g., "functions of the immune system, normal cell growth, digestive, bowel, bladder, neurological, brain, respiratory, circulatory, endocrine, and reproductive functions");
- States that mitigating measures other than "ordinary eyeglasses or contact lenses" shall not be considered in assessing whether an individual has a disability;
- Clarifies that an impairment that is episodic or in remission is a disability if it would substantially limit a major life activity when active;
- Changes the definition of "regarded as" so that it no longer requires a showing that the employer perceived the individual to be substantially limited in a major life activity, and instead says that an applicant or employee is "regarded as" disabled if he or she is subject to an action prohibited by the ADA (e.g., failure to hire or termination) based on an impairment that is not transitory and minor;
- Provides that individuals covered only under the "regarded as" prong are not entitled to reasonable accommodation.

According to Prosser (n.d.), a number of Supreme Court cases in the 1990s and early 2000s weakened the opportunities for people with disabilities to demonstrate they were entitled to protection under the ADA. The Amendments Act has restored the ADA back to its initial intent. "Under the new amendments, effective January 1, 2009, the determination of whether a person has an impairment that substantially limits a major life activity, a "**disability**" in the legal sense under the ADA, must be made, with a few exceptions, **_without regard_** to the beneficial effects of a mitigating action, such as taking medication" (Prosser, n.d., p. 1). This legislation can help both employees and employers. Employees can more readily establish they have a disability, and employers can more clearly determine if one of their employees is disabled.

In 2006, the United Nations rarified the Convention on the Rights of Persons with Disabilities. The United States is now a signatory to that convention. While it remains to be seen exactly how the Convention will be codified into law in the United States, discussions have now begun regarding its implementation in countries around the world. The Convention deals with access to sport and physical activity for people with disabilities, but also contains language about sport managers United Nations, 2006, p. 22):

(b) To ensure that persons with disabilities have an opportunity to _organize, develop_ and participate in disability-specific sporting and recreational activities and, to this end, encourage the provision, on an equal basis with others, of appropriate instruction, training and resources.

This case offers a good example of the ADA in action. It also involves an illness we do not always think of as being a disability, alcoholism. We usually think of disability in terms of a mobility disability or perhaps a hearing or visual impairment.

MADDOX V. UNIVERSITY OF TENNESSEE
United States Court of Appeals for the Sixth Circuit
62 F.3d 843 (1995)

Opinion: Bailey Brown, Circuit Judge.

The plaintiff-appellant, Robert Maddox, a former assistant football coach at the University of Tennessee, brought suit against the school, its Board of Trustees, and its athletic director, Doug Dickey (collectively "UT"), under § 504 of the Rehabilitation Act of 1973, as amended, 29 U.S.C. § 701, et seq., and the Americans with Disabilities Act of 1990 ("ADA"), 42 U.S.C. § 12101, et seq., alleging discriminatory discharge on the basis of his disability, alcoholism. The district court granted UT's motion for summary judgment, concluding that Maddox was not terminated solely by reason of, or because of, his handicap, but rather, because of a well-publicized incident in which Maddox was arrested for driving under the influence of alcohol. Maddox appealed. We AFFIRM.

I. FACTS
On February 17, 1992, Doug Dickey, acting as UT's athletic director, extended to Maddox an offer of employment as an assistant football coach. The position did not carry tenure and was terminable at will in accordance with the policies of the Personnel Manual. As part of the hiring process, Maddox completed an application. On the line after "Describe any health problems or physical limitations, which . . . would limit your ability to perform the duties of the position for which you are applying," Maddox wrote "None." In response to the question "have you ever been arrested for a criminal offense of any kind?" Maddox replied "No." These responses were not accurate. According to what Maddox alleges in this lawsuit, he suffers from the disability of alcoholism. Also, Maddox was arrested three times before 1992, once for possession of a controlled substance, and twice for driving a motor vehicle under the influence of alcohol. As to the first answer, Maddox claims that it is in fact correct because "it has never affected my coaching ability . . . I never drank on the job." As to the second question, Maddox claims that another university employee, Bill Higdon,

advised him not to include the information concerning his prior arrests on the application.

On May 26, 1992, after Maddox began working at UT, a Knoxville police officer arrested Maddox and charged him with driving under the influence of alcohol and public intoxication. According to newspaper reports, the accuracy of which is not contested, Maddox backed his car across a major public road at a high rate of speed, almost striking another vehicle. When stopped by the officer, Maddox was combative, his pants were unzipped, and he refused to take a breathalyzer. He also lied to the arresting officer, stating that he was unemployed. This incident was highly publicized, and UT was obviously embarrassed by the public exposure surrounding the event.

Maddox entered an alcohol rehabilitation program at a UT hospital after his arrest. UT first placed Maddox on paid administrative leave. In June 1992, however, Dickey and then Head Coach Johnny Majors determined that the allegations were accurate and jointly issued a letter notifying Maddox that his employment was being terminated. They testified that termination was necessary because of: (1) the criminal acts and misconduct of Maddox; (2) the bad publicity surrounding the arrest; and (3) the fact that Maddox was no longer qualified, in their minds, for the responsibilities associated with being an assistant coach. Both Dickey and Majors deny that they were aware that Maddox was an alcoholic or that Maddox's alcoholism played any part in the decision to discharge him. Nevertheless, Maddox brought this action alleging that the termination was discriminatory on the basis of his alcoholism in violation of his rights under the Rehabilitation Act and the ADA. UT responded by filing a motion for summary judgment which the district court granted. The court recognized that, under both statutes, a plaintiff must show that he was fired by reason of his disability. In the court's view, summary judgment was appropriate because Maddox could not establish the existence of a genuine issue of material fact with respect to whether he had been fired by reason of his status as an alcoholic rather than by reason of his criminal misconduct. Maddox now appeals.

1. Standard of Review

Review of a grant of summary judgment is de novo, utilizing the same test used by the district court to determine whether summary judgment is appropriate. A court shall render summary judgment when there is no genuine issue as to any material fact, the moving party is entitled to judgment as a matter of law, and reasonable minds could come to but one conclusion, and that conclusion is adverse to the party against whom the motion is made.

2. Maddox Was Not Terminated Because of His Disability

Maddox raises a number of issues on appeal which he contends show that the district court erred in granting summary judgment to the defendants. Maddox first alleges that the district court erred in analyzing his claim under the Rehabilitation Act. Section 504 of the Act provides, "no otherwise qualified individual with a disability . . . shall, solely by reason of her or his disability, be excluded from the participation in, be denied the benefits of, or be subject to discrimination under any program or activity receiving Federal financial assistance." 29 U.S.C. § 794(a). Thus, in order to establish a violation of the Rehabilitation Act, a plaintiff must show:

(1) The plaintiff is a "handicapped person" under the Act; (2) The plaintiff is "otherwise qualified" for participation in the program; (3) The plaintiff is being excluded from participation in, being denied the benefits of, or being subjected to discrimination under the program solely by reason of his handicap; and (4) The relevant program or activity is receiving Federal financial assistance.

It is not disputed in this case that UT constitutes a program receiving Federal financial assistance under the Act. Likewise, we assume, without deciding, that alcoholics may be "individuals with a disability" for purposes of the Act. . . . Thus, our analysis focuses on whether Maddox is "otherwise qualified" under the Act and whether he was discharged "solely by reason of" his disability. The burden of making these showings rests with Maddox.

In support of its motion for summary judgment, UT contended that both factors weighed in its favor. First, Dickey and Majors contended that they did not even know that Maddox was considered an alcoholic in making both the decision to hire and fire him. Moreover, they contended that Maddox was discharged, not because he was an alcoholic, but because of his criminal conduct and behavior and the significant amount of bad publicity surrounding him and the school. UT alternatively contended that Maddox is nevertheless not "otherwise qualified" to continue in the position of assistant football coach.

The district court granted UT's motion for summary judgment, specifically holding that UT did not discharge Maddox solely by reason of his disability. The court found it beyond dispute that Maddox's discharge resulted from his misconduct rather than his disability of alcoholism. The court noted,

It cannot be denied in this case, Mr. Maddox was charged with . . . [driving while under the influence and public intoxication] which would not be considered socially acceptable by any objective standard. The affidavit testimony of Mr. Dickey and Mr. Majors is clear on the point that it was this specific conduct, not any condition to which it might be related, which provoked the termination of Mr. Maddox's employment.

As a result, the court found it unnecessary to decide the alternative ground of whether Maddox was "otherwise qualified."

Maddox contends that the district court erred in distinguishing between discharge for misconduct and discharge solely by reason of his disability of alcoholism. Maddox claims that he has difficulty operating a motor vehicle while under the influence of alcohol and therefore he characterizes drunk driving as a causally connected manifestation of the disability of alcoholism. Thus, Maddox contends that because alcoholism caused the incident upon which UT claims to have based its decision to discharge him, UT in essence discharged him because of his disability of alcoholism. In support, Maddox relies on *Teahan v. Metro-North Commuter R.R. Co.*, 951 F.2d 511, 516–17 (2d Cir. 1991), cert. denied, 121 L. Ed. 2d 24, 113 S. Ct. 54 (1992), in which the Second Circuit held that a Rehabilitation Act plaintiff can show that he was fired "solely by reason of" his disability, or at least create a genuine issue of material fact, if he can show that he was fired for conduct that is "causally related" to his disability. In *Teahan*, the defendant company discharged the plaintiff because of his excessive absenteeism. The plaintiff responded by claiming that his absenteeism was caused by his alcoholism and therefore protected under the Rehabilitation Act. The district court disagreed and granted summary judgment for the employer because, the court found, Teahan was fired for his absenteeism and not because of his alcoholism. The Second Circuit reversed the district court's grant of summary judgment on appeal, however, rejecting the court's distinction between misconduct (absenteeism), and the disabling condition of alcoholism. The court presumed that Teahan's absenteeism resulted from his alcoholism and held that one's disability should not be distinguished from its consequences in determining whether he was fired "solely by reason" of his disability. *Id.* Thus, Maddox argues that, in the instant case, when UT acted on the basis of the conduct allegedly caused by the alcoholism, it was the same as if UT acted on the basis of alcoholism itself.

We disagree and hold that the district court correctly focused on the distinction between discharging someone for unacceptable misconduct and discharging someone because of the disability. As the district court noted, to hold otherwise, an employer would be forced to accommodate all behavior of an alcoholic which could in any way be related to the alcoholic's use of intoxicating beverages; behavior that would be intolerable if engaged in by a sober employee or, for that matter, an intoxicated but nonalcoholic employee.

Despite Teahan, a number of cases have considered the issue of misconduct as distinct from the status of the disability. In *Taub v. Frank*, 957 F.2d 8 (1st Cir. 1992), the plaintiff Taub, a heroin addict, brought suit against his former employer, the United States Postal Service, alleging discriminatory discharge under the Rehabilitation Act. The Post Office discharged Taub after he was arrested for possession of heroin for distribution. The district court granted the Post Office's motion for summary judgment and Taub appealed. The First Circuit affirmed and held that Taub could not prevail on his Rehabilitation Act claim because his discharge resulted from his misconduct, possession of heroin for distribution, rather than his disability of heroin addiction. The court reasoned that addictionrelated criminal conduct is simply too attenuated to extend the Act's protection to Taub.

The conduct/disability distinction was also recognized by the Fourth Circuit in *Little v. F.B.I.*, 1 F.3d 255 (4th Cir. 1993). In *Little*, the F.B.I. discharged the plaintiff, known by his supervisors to be an alcoholic, after an incident in which he was intoxicated on duty. The district court granted summary judgment in favor of the F.B.I. on the basis that the plaintiff was no longer "otherwise qualified" to serve as an F.B.I. agent. The Fourth Circuit affirmed, noting as an additional basis that the plaintiff 's employment was not terminated because of his handicap. The court noted, "based on no less authority than common sense, it is clear that an employer subject to the . . . [Rehabilitation] Act must be permitted to terminate its employees on account of egregious misconduct, irrespective of whether the employee is handicapped." *Id.*; see also *Landefeld v. Marion Gen. Hosp., Inc.*, 994 F.2d 1178, 1183 (6th Cir. 1993) (Nelson, J., concurring) ("The plaintiff was clearly suspended because of his intolerable conduct, and not solely because of his mental condition.")

Moreover, language within the respective statutes makes clear that such a distinction is warranted. Section 706(8)(c) of the Rehabilitation Act states:

"Individuals with a disability" does not include any individual who is an alcoholic whose current use of alcohol prevents such individual from performing the duties of the job in question or whose employment, by reason of such current alcohol abuse, would constitute a direct threat to property or the safety of others.

Likewise, the ADA specifically provides that an employer may hold an alcoholic employee to the same performance and behavior standards to which the employer holds other employees "even if any unsatisfactory performance is related to the alcoholism of such employee." 42 U.S.C. § 12114(c)(4). These provisions clearly contemplate distinguishing the issue of misconduct from one's status as an alcoholic.

At bottom, we conclude that the analysis of the district court is more in keeping with the purposes and limitations of the respective Acts, and therefore, we decline to adopt the Second Circuit's reasoning in Teahan. Employers subject to the Rehabilitation Act and ADA must be permitted to take appropriate action with respect to an employee on account of egregious or criminal conduct, regardless of whether the employee is disabled. In the instant case, for example, while alcoholism might compel Maddox to drink, it did not compel him to operate a motor vehicle or engage in the other inappropriate conduct reported. Likewise, suppose an alcoholic becomes intoxicated and sexually assaults a coworker? We believe that it strains logic to conclude that such action could be protected under the Rehabilitation Act or the ADA merely because the actor has been diagnosed as an alcoholic and claims that such action was caused by his disability.

3. Pretext

Maddox alternatively contends that even if UT has successfully disclaimed reliance on his disability in making the employment decision, the district court nevertheless erred in determining that Maddox had produced no evidence that the reasons articulated by UT were a pretext for discrimination. A Rehabilitation Act plaintiff may demonstrate pretext by showing that the asserted reasons had no basis in fact, the reasons did not in fact motivate the discharge, or, if they were factors in the decision, they were jointly insufficient to motivate the discharge.

Maddox first alleges that Dickey and Majors knew that Maddox was an alcoholic. Setting aside for a moment the legal significance of this statement, it is not supported factually in the record.

Maddox also claims that he knew of other coaches in the football program who drank alcohol in public and who were arrested for DUI but who were not discharged. This point is also irrelevant. Whether Maddox had such knowledge is immaterial. There is no evidence in the record establishing that Majors or Dickey had knowledge of the public intoxication of any other coach, or failed to reprimand or terminate any coach who they knew to have engaged in such behavior.

Maddox finally contends that UT's conclusion that he is no longer qualified to be an assistant coach at UT is without merit. Maddox claims that his misconduct did not affect his "coaching" responsibilities because an assistant coach's duties are limited to the practice and playing fields, and do not comprise of serving as a counselor or mentor to the players or serving as a representative of the school. Maddox relies on the fact that none of these functions were explained to him in his formal job description.

We first note that this allegation seems more appropriate for determining whether he was "otherwise qualified" rather than whether he was discharged because of his disability. Nevertheless, Maddox's position is simply unrealistic. It is obvious that as a member of the football coaching staff, Maddox would be representing not only the team but also the university. As in the instant case, UT received full media coverage because of this "embarrassing" incident. The school falls out of favor with the public, and the reputation of the football program suffers. Likewise, to argue that football coaches today, with all the emphasis on the misuse of drugs and alcohol by athletes, are not "role models" and "mentors" simply ignores reality.

The district court's grant of summary judgment in favor of the defendants is AFFIRMED.

CASES ON THE SUPPLEMENTAL WEB SITE

McFadden v. Grasmick, 485 F. Supp. 2d 642 (2007). This case examines whether a wheelchair athlete should be allowed to compete with able bodied runners.

PGA Tour v. Martin, 532 U.S. 661 (2001). This case examines whether walking is an essential element in the game of golf.

Bowers v. The National Collegiate Athletic Association, 475 F.3d 524 (3rd Cir. 2007). This case examines the rights of college athletes under the Americans with Disabilities Act of 1990 (ADA) and the Rehabilitation Act of 1973.

QUESTIONS YOU SHOULD BE ABLE TO ANSWER

1. Define reasonable accommodation.
2. Give two examples of how you could make a reasonable accommodation for:
   a. An Assistant Athletic Director with a hearing impairment
   b. A Director of Marketing who is a single below the knee amputee
3. What is meant by a qualified person with a disability?
4. What criteria must a person meet to be a person with a disability? How has the Americans with Disabilities Act Amendments changed this?
5. Which of the following would be classified as an employer? Why or why not?
   a. A Major League Baseball team
   b. A two-week summer basketball camp
   c. A major metropolitan downtown YMCA

REFERENCES

Cases

Bombrys v. City of Toledo, 849 F. Supp. 1210 (N.D. Ohio 1993).
Buckingham v. United States, 998 F.2d 735 (9th Cir. 1993).
Collings v. Longview Fibre Company, 63 F.3d 828 (1995).
Henchey v. Town of North Greenbush, 831 F. Supp. 960 (N.D. N.Y. 1993).
Jackson v. Veterans' Administration, 22 F.3d 277 (11th Cir. 1994).
Jones v. Southeast Alabama Baseball Umpires Association, 864 F. Supp. 1135 (M.D. Ala. 1994).
Mazzarella v. U.S. Postal Service, 849 F. Supp. 89 (D. Mass. 1993).
Pandazides v. Virginia Board of Education, 804 F. Supp. 794 (1992).
Russell v. Southeastern Pennsylvania Transportation Authority, 2 A.D. Cas. [BNA] 1419 (E.D. Pa. 1993).
Sargent v. Litton Systems, 841 F. Supp. 956 (N.D. Cal. 1994).
Sawhill v. Medical College of Pennsylvania, 1996 U.S. Dist. LEXIS 4097.
Schmidt v. Safeway, 864 F. Supp. 991 (D. Ore. 1994).

Publications

Churchill, S. S. (1995, June). Reasonable accommodations in the workplace: A shared responsibility. *Massachusetts Law Review*, 73–83.
Colker, R., & Milani, A. A. (2005).*The law of disability discrimination handbook.*Newark, NJ: Lexis Nexis.

Equal Employment Opportunity Commission. (n.d.). Notice concerning the Americans with Disabilities Act Amendments of 2008. Retrieved from http://www.eeoc.gov/ada/amendments_notice.html

Hendricks, D.J., Batiste, L.C., & Hirsch, A. (2005).Cost and effectiveness of accommodations in the workplace: Preliminary results of a nationwide study. *Disability Studies Quarterly, 25*(4). Retrieved from http://dsq-sds.org/article/view/623/800

Hums, M. A. (1994). AIDS in the sport arena: After Magic Johnson, where do we go from here? *Journal of Legal Aspects of Sport, 4*(1), 59–65.

Hums, M. A., & Wolff, E. A. (2006, January). *Inclusion of athletes with disabilities: Connections and collaborations.* Presented at the Annual NAKPEHE Conference, San Diego, CA.

Job Accommodation Network. (2000). *Home page.* Retrieved from http://www.jan.wvu.edu/

Job Accommodation Network. (n.d.). Frequently asked questions. Retrieved from http://askjan.org/links/faqs.htm#1

Job Accommodation Network. (2006). Technical assistance manual: Title I of the ADA. Retrieved from http://www.jan.wvu.edu/links/ADAtam1.html#III

Job Accommodation Network. (2011). Accommodation and compliance series: Employees who use wheelcahirs. Retrieved from http://www.jan.wvu.edu/media/educators.pdf

Masteralexis, L. P., & Wong, G. (2012). Legal principles applied to sport management. In L.P. Masteralexis, C. A. Barr, & M. A. Hums, *Principles and practice of sport management* (4th ed.) (pp. 85–120). Sudbury, MA: Jones & Bartlett Publishing.

Prosser, A. (n.d.). Americans with Disabilities Act: Big changes in 2009. Retrieved from http://fchr.state.fl.us/fchr/resources/commissioners_speak_out/americans_with_disabilities_act_big_changes_in_2009

Schleifer, J. (2009). Finally . . . . a reasonable explanation of ADA reasonable accommodation.Retrieved from http://hrdailyadvisor.blr.com/archive/2007/07/05/ADA_Americans_with_Disabilities_Act_reasonable_accommodation_undue_hardship_definitions.aspx

United Nations. (2006). *Convention on the Rights of Persons with Disabilities.* New York: Author.

U.S. Department of Labor. (2009). The job accommodation process: Steps to collaborative solutions. Retrieved from http://www.dol.gov/odep/pubs/misc/job.htm

INTELLECTUAL PROPERTY LAW
7.21 COPYRIGHT AND PATENT LAW

Merry Moiseichik I University of Arkansas

7.20

Copyright and patent are both forms of intellectual property. The United States Constitution grants Congress the power to enact laws governing patents and copyrights. Article 1, Section 8 of the Constitution states: "Congress shall have the power . . . to promote the Progress of Science and useful Arts, by securing for limited Times to Authors and Inventors the exclusive Right to their respective Writings and Discoveries." The use and protection of intellectual property is becoming more important to the sport and recreation industry. For example copyright becomes an issue in designs of logos and stadiums, ownership of television and video game rights, and use of music in recreational settings.

FUNDAMENTAL CONCEPTS

Copyright

Congress enacted the United States Copyright Act of 1909 to *protect the work of authors and other creative persons from the unauthorized use of their copyrighted materials and to provide a financial incentive* for artists to produce, thereby increasing the number of creative works available in society. This legislation was completely revised in 1976 to take into account changing technology, and to become more inclusive of the types of medium technology produced. In 1989 the United States became a member of the Berne Convention, where an international copyright treaty was created. This brought new revisions of the Copyright Act in 1990. The act was revised again in 1994, 1999 and 2002 to reflect changing technology and the Internet.

Copyright Protection

The purpose of the copyright law is to protect those who have put time and energy into some creative project. The law is economically motivated, designed to protect the rights of those who produce the many creative endeavors we hear and see daily. A copyright gives the owner of the work the exclusive right to copy, reproduce, distribute, publish, perform, or display the work. There are two fundamental criteria for copyright protection: 1) the work must be original, and 2) it must be in some tangible form that can be reproduced (17 U.S.C. § 102). Registration of a copyright is not required for protection, although no action for infringement can be instituted until the copyright has been registered (17 U.S.C. § 401). The protection exists as soon as the work is fixed in some tangible form, such as on paper, CD, DVD, canvas, and so forth. Copyright protection lasts 70 years beyond the death of the author or for 95 years for anonymous works or works made for hire (17 U.S.C. § 301). The federal government grants registration of a copyright, which provides procedural advantages in enforcing rights under law.

There are eight broad categories of copyright protection, including:

1. literary works;
2. musical works;
3. dramatic works;
4. pantomime and choreographic works;
5. pictorial, graphic, and sculptural works;
6. motion pictures and other audiovisual works;
7. sound recordings; and
8. architectural works (17 U.S.C. § 102).

To appreciate what can be copyrighted, it is instructive to consider what cannot be. "In no case does copyright protection for an original work of authorship extend to any idea, procedure, process, system, method of operation, concept, principle, or discovery, regardless of the form in which it is described, explained, illustrated, or embodied in such work" (17 U.S.C. § 102). Government documents and works in the public domain do not have copyright protection either. Works in the public domain include those with expired copyrights and works where copyright has not been requested (17 U.S.C. § 105).

Works that are not original cannot be considered for copyright (17 U.S.C. § 104). This would include standard works such as calendars, height and weight charts, tape measures, and lists of tables (Talab, 1986). This allows freedom to make use of these articles. The outline of a calendar cannot be copyrighted, but the format and the pictures that go with the calendar can be. This allows recreation or sport programs, for example, to use a common calendar and add their own dimensions including pictures, special events, and any additional information specific to their programs. Similarly, no copyright can be held for blank forms that are used to obtain information (17 U.S.C. § 201). Therefore, agencies can use anyone's accident report form or registration form as long as the forms do not include creative authorship but rather, just request information.

Athletic competitions/games are not copyrightable as they do not fall within "original works of authorship" (*National Basketball Association v. Motorola, Inc.*, 1997). You can, however, copyright the broadcasts, just not the underlying games. To illustrate this point, the Second Circuit Court in *National Basketball Association v. Motorola* (1997) stated that "if the inventor of the T-formation in football had been able to copyright it, the sport might have come to an end instead of prospering. Even where athletic preparation most resembles authorship—figure skating, gymnastics, and, some would uncharitably say, professional wrestling—a performer who conceives and executes a particularly graceful and difficult—or, in the case of wrestling, seemingly painful—acrobatic feat cannot copyright it without impairing the underlying competition in the future" (*National Basketball Association v. Motorola, Inc.*, 1997).

Copyright protection also only extends to works that are the fruits of intellectual labor or those that are significantly creative. Therefore, works where authorship is small, also cannot hold a copyright (17 U.S.C. § 102). This includes slogans, titles, names, variations, typographic ornamentation, lettering, or coloring. If slogans, titles, names, etc., were copyrighted, there would be a loss of freedom to speak. For example, in *Syrus v. Bennett* (2011) the Tenth Circuit Court held Charles Syrus did not have a protected copyright in the phrases "Go Thunder" "Let's Go Thunder" and "Thunder Up" as used by the NBA's Oklahoma City Thunder because adding the team name to a common cheer required "no intellectual labor" (*Syrus v. Bennett*, 2011). These short sayings are protected by the trademark laws (see Chapter 7.22 *Principles of Trademark Law*).

Another thing that is not copyrightable is facts. Research data are facts. Any raw data collected can be used by anyone. In *Feist Publications v. Rural Telephone Service Co.* (1991), Feist Publications published a telephone book. Rural Telephone Service used all the information from Feist book, reorganized it, and published their own book using addresses as the listing. In ruling that Rural Telephone had not infringed the copyright law, the court held that Feist had only published non-copyrightable facts. Rural Telephone used the facts, just in a different way. This issue has come up in area of fantasy sports, where players' game statistics are used. Since the statistics used in these types are merely facts, they are not copyrightable.

Rights of the Copyright Owner

A copyright gives its owner certain rights to the works, including:

1. the right to reproduction;
2. the right to preparation of derivative works including translation from language to language and from one form to another (i.e., from book to movie, from movie to play);
3. the right to public distribution;
4. the public performing rights, which include live renditions that are face to face, on recordings, broadcasts, and retransmissions by cable;
5. the right to the public display, specifically written or art work; and
6. to perform the copyrighted work publicly by means of a digital audio transmission (17 U.S.C. § 106).

This section was strengthened with the passage of the Visual Artists Rights Act of 1990 (VARA, 17 U.S.C. § 106A). Among the rights afforded artists by this law is the right to prevent any intentional distortion, mutilation, or other modification of that work. This allows the artist to control the visual art work until his or her death. In *Phillips v. Pembroke Real Estate* (2003), the city of Boston had granted permission to a developer to build an office building and a convention center in a public sculpture park on Boston Harbor. Phillips, the sculptor, sought an injunction against the manager of the park and sought to prevent the park from moving the sculpture to a different location, from modifying the park and from altering sculptures that he created specifically for the park. Phillips stated that his design was created with the environment in mind and that it would negatively affect the art if it were moved. In rejecting Phillips' argument, the court found that VARA does not protect site specific art and that art can be moved to a different location (*Phillips v. Pembroke Real Estate,* 2006).

Copyright Ownership

Copyright ownership vests initially in the author or creator of the work. However, in the case of a "work made for hire," the owner of the copyright is the employer or person for whom the work was prepared. The Copyright Act provides that "the employer or other person for whom the work was prepared is considered the author for the purpose of this title, and, unless the parties have expressly agreed otherwise in a written instrument signed by them, owns all of the rights comprised in the copyright" (17 U.S.C. § 201(b)). For example, in *Baltimore Orioles v. Major League Baseball Players* (1986), the players claimed ownership in the copyright of televised games. In rejecting the players' claim, the Seventh Circuit Court found that since the players were working for the club, the Orioles owned the copyright, not the players.

Fair Use

An important section of the Copyright Law for users of copyrighted works is the fair use section (17 U.S.C. §107). This section was passed to strike a balance between the copyright monopoly and the greater interest of society (Hohensee, 1988). There are four factors to ascertain fair use: 1) the purpose and the character of use, whether it is for commercial or for nonprofit educational purposes; 2) the nature of the copyrighted work; 3) the amount and substantiality of the material used in comparison with the whole; and 4) the effect of the use on the potential market or value of the work (17 U.S.C. § 107).

Fair use allows for "criticism, comment, news reporting, teaching, scholarship or research." For example, Ted Giannoulas, the creator of the sports mascot, "the Chicken," was sued by the owners of Barney, a purple dinosaur in a children's TV show. The Chicken, as part of a pregame show, beat up on Barney. The owners of Barney said they did not approve of their character being used in that manner and that it negatively affected the small children who loved Barney. In upholding Giannoulas' right to use Barney, the court ruled it was a parody and thus fair use (*Lyons Partnership, L.P. v. Giannoulas,* 1999).

A primary motivator for the passage of the fair use section was the use of copyrighted works for educational purposes. The educational fair use test is based on three rules: 1) brevity (using small parts of the whole); 2) spontaneity (if there is time to request permission, it should be requested); and, 3) cumulative effect (how will it affect the creator). The copying is not allowed when it replaces a book that would be purchased. Consumables are not allowed to be copied under any circumstances. Therefore coloring books, consumable material, cannot be copied for use in after school or day care programs.

Music and Performance

Musical scores that are performed by bands and chorus should be purchased. However, there are guidelines in §110 of the Copyright Act that allow for music and dramatic performances by nonprofit agencies, religious institutions, or educational purposes. Performance of music is legal without paying royalties if it is not for profit and all money goes to charity. Music and dramatic works can be performed in classrooms, for religious assembly, and for transmission to the public, without any purpose of direct or indirect commercial advantage and without payment of any fee or other compensation for the performance to its performers, promoters, or organizers. There can be no direct or indirect admission charged unless the proceeds, after deducting the reasonable costs of producing the performance, are used exclusively for educational, religious, or charitable purposes and not for private financial gain (17 U.S.C. § 110). The 2002 amendments specifically discuss the transmission of these performances. It is not legal to make digital displays of these works unless they are specifically and only for registered students. They also cannot be transmitted or stored where public has access to them for any length of time other than what is absolutely necessary. Section 110 does not include colleges and universities playing their pep music at games or for fraternities and sororities using music at parties, unless the function is to raise money for charity. Licenses must be secured from performance rights agencies.

Public Performance Restrictions

According to the Copyright Act a performance or display is public if it is open to the public or at any place where a substantial number of persons outside a normal circle of a family and its social acquaintances are gathered (17 U.S.C. § 101). For public performances, a license must be obtained. This even includes dormitory public areas. Music is also affected by public performance restrictions. Playing CDs, for example, in a public place is prohibited without a license. If a manager of a fitness center, for example, wants to play background music in the center and people paid to be members, the manager must obtain a license. If that same center has an aerobics instructor who plays CD's during exercises, the center must have a license, especially if there is profit. It is not the responsibility of the aerobics instructor to get the license. It is the responsibility of the center in which the class is being given to get the license, which are not particularly expensive and depend on the size of the facility, the amount of use, and the number of participants in the program. Cases involving copyright infringement for public performances of music include: *Tallyrand Music, Inc. v. Frank Stenko* (1990), involving background music played in a skating rink; *Broadcast Music, Inc. v. Melody Fair Enterprises, Inc.* (1990), involving a club where musical compositions were performed by live artists; *Lorimar Music v. Black Iron Grill Co.* (2010), where a restaurant tried to play karaoke music without a license; and *Broadcast Music Inc. v. Blueberry Hill Family Restaurants, Inc.* (1995), where a restaurant chain operated jukeboxes that patrons played for free. Each of these defendants was found guilty of playing copyrighted music without a license and fined.

Television and Radio Broadcasting

The Copyright Act protects any original works of authorship fixed in any tangible medium, including motion pictures and other audiovisual works. The broadcast, by radio or television, of a live sporting event is eligible for protection. The Act has become a significant source of protection for the major professional sport leagues to combat the unauthorized interception of commercial-free feeds of broadcast signals. For live transmissions "the first fixation is made simultaneously with its transmission, the copyright owner may, either before or after such fixation takes place, institute an action for infringement . . . if . . . the copyright owner (1) serves notice upon the infringer not less than 48 hours before such fixation . . . and (2) makes registration for the work . . . within three months after its first transmission" (17 U.S.C. § 411(b)). For example, in *Live Nation Motor Sports, Inc. v. Davis*, (2007) Live Nation Motor Sports sued Davis for copyright infringement after he transmitted through his website live audio feeds of motor cross events that were being produced live by Live Nation Motor Sports, Inc. for TV. In ruling for Live Nation Motor Sports, the court found that even though the transmission were live and therefore not yet fixed, the broadcast was copyrighted at the time of transmission.

Another issue involving copyright law and television focuses on sport bars that broadcast games that can only be seen through the use of satellite dish antenna systems. The professional sport leagues contend that this piracy of network satellite signals both devalues advertising revenues when patrons at sport bars watch contests commercial free, and affects local ticket sales when a blacked-out game is broadcast in a local sport bar. Under the "home-use" exemption, which is intended to limit the exclusive rights granted copyright owners when the transmission is received by equipment similar to the type "commonly used in private homes" (17 U.S.C. § 110(5)), the sport bars claim that satellite dish equipment is commonly used in private homes and therefore legal. Such arguments, however, have been unsuccessful to date and any sport bar or other public establishments desiring to transmit cable or pay-per-view broadcasts must have a license (*Cablevision Systems Corp. v. 45 Midland Enterprises, Inc.*, (1994); *National Football League v. McBee & Bruno's, Inc.*, (1986); *National Football League v. Rondor*, (1993)).

This "home-use" exemption clause does not include rebroadcasting. It is a copyright infringement, therefore, to tape a copyrighted program and exhibit it at another time in a public setting without explicit permission from the producers. For example, if a sport bar recorded a game for later viewing in their establishment, such a viewing would be a violation of copyright law. The broadcasting rights of time and place are reserved for the broadcasters. On the other hand, it is legal to tape a show for later viewing if it is done in the confines of a home with friends and family. This is considered time shifting and has been held legal in nonpublic settings (*Sony Corp. v. Universal Studios*, 1984).

Internet

The internet is a major issue in copyright infringement as it has made pirating copyrighted material, such as music and movies, easily available to the general public. For example, in *A & M Records, Inc. v. Napster, Inc.*, 2002, Napster created a website that allowed free downloading of music. Although the court eventually shut down Napster, finding the website vicariously libel for copyright infringement since it provided the method for file sharing and should have known copyright infringement was occurring; there continues to be a battle over copyright protection on the internet as more sophisticated software is developed.

In an effort to stop online piracy and protect the TV, music and movie industry, Congress attempted to pass two bills: Stop Online Piracy Act (SOPA) and Protect IP Act (PIPA). When the public however protested that the bills would limit the freedom of the internet, Congress pulled the bills back for further review (Pepitone, 2012). Whether it is the music industry fighting to remove music from the Fair Use section of the Copyright law and prevent the use of music in YouTube videos, short sections in films, or backgrounds in political ads (Henslee, 2009), or internet reporters struggling to blog games, it is clear that the internet will continue to be in the forefront of copyright issues.

Patent

Passed in 1870 and revised the last time in 2002, the goal of United States Patent Law is to "promote the progress of science and the useful arts" (35 U.S.C. § 101). Patent law is designed to advance science and invention. A person can obtain a patent for "any new and useful process, machine, manufacture, or composition of matter, or any new and useful improvement" (35 U.S.C. § 101). A patent is not allowed for laws of nature, natural phenomena, and abstract ideas. Patents, therefore, can be obtained for new sports equipment that would allow the user to hit harder or further or jump higher. Patents can, however, be obtained for designs, such as shoe companies patenting their new designs for shoes.

The invention must be newly created by the filer and useful for the patent to be granted. The purpose of the patent is to allow the holder of the patent to have a monopoly on the way the invention is used for a period of 20 years (35 U.S.C. §154). That includes the right to "exclude others from making, using, offering for sale, or selling" the patented invention. This permits the holder to gain benefits encouraging further advancement.

Originally it was thought that patents were for inventions. As the courts have been more lenient in their interpretation of what could be patented there is lots of controversy. As the courts began allowing patents for business methods and mathematical formulas, doors have opened to a wide variety of patents and sport entrepreneurs have taken advantage of the climate. Dale Miller, for example, patented his grip on the golf club for his putt (Kukkonen, 1998). Nolan Ryan has patented a pitch (Smith, 1999). This trend creates questions as to what else will be patented in the near future. For example, if someone created a new football formation or a new method for moving a soccer ball, this process could be patented. With a patent, the creator would have complete control over who could use it and when. Imagine if the Fosbury Flop in high jump had been patented (Wilson, 1997).

The problem with patenting sport moves is that it would be extremely difficult to enforce. Mr. Miller's grip can only be used by him and others who pay for the right. But, unless he is right there, how will he know a recreation golfer is using it? A second problem with such patents is that they could affect competition. When a player invents a new move that obviously creates an advantage, the playing field is no longer level (Smith, 1999). Loren Weber (2000) sees this to be especially inviting to those in extreme sports. Since the competitors are individuals using specially named moves, the moves would be easy to patent.

SIGNIFICANT CASE

The following case examines the issues surrounding who owns the rights to copyright, the players who provide the entertainment or the owners and producers. The case explains how a game can be a copyrighted work and what constitutes copyright.

BALTIMORE ORIOLES INC. V. M.L.B. PLAYERS ASSOCIATION
United States Court of Appeals for the Seventh Circuit
805 F.2d 663 (1986)

The primary issue involved in this appeal is whether major league baseball clubs own exclusive rights to the televised performances of major league baseball players during major league baseball games.

This appeal arises out of a long-standing dispute between the Major League Baseball Clubs ("Clubs") and the Major League Baseball Players Association ("Players") regarding the ownership of the broadcast rights to the Players' performances during major league baseball games. After decades of negotiation concerning the allocation of revenues from telecasts of the games, the Players in May of 1982 sent letters to the Clubs, and to television and cable companies with which the Clubs had contracted, asserting that the telecasts were being made without the Players' consent and that they misappropriated the Players' property rights in their performances. The mailing of these letters led the parties to move their dispute from the bargaining table to the courtroom.

On June 14, 1982, the Clubs filed an action (entitled *Baltimore Orioles, Inc. v. Major League Baseball Players Association*, No. 82 C 3710) in the United States District Court for the Northern District of Illinois, in which they sought a declaratory judgment "that the telecasts of Major League Baseball games constitute copyrighted 'works made for hire' in which defendant and Major League Baseball players have no rights whatsoever." Baltimore Orioles Complaint. The district court found that the Clubs, not the Players, owned a copyright in the telecasts as works made for hire and that the Clubs' copyright in the telecasts preempted the Players' rights of publicity in their performances.

* * *

Our analysis begins by ascertaining whether the Clubs own a copyright in the telecasts of major league baseball games. In general, copyright in a work "vests initially in the author or authors of the work," 17 U.S.C. § 201(a); however, "in the case of a work made for hire, the employer or other person for whom the work was prepared is considered the author . . . and, unless the parties have expressly agreed otherwise in a written instrument signed by them, owns all of the rights comprised

in the copyright." 17 U.S.C. § 201(b). A work made for hire is defined in pertinent part as "a work prepared by an employee within the scope of his or her employment." 17 U.S.C. § 101. Thus, an employer owns a copyright in a work if (1) the work satisfies the generally applicable requirements for copyrightability set forth in 17 U.S.C. § 102(a), (2) the work was prepared by an employee, (3) the work was prepared within the scope of the employee's employment, and (4) the parties have not expressly agreed otherwise in a signed, written instrument.

* * *

The district court concluded that the telecasts were copyrightable works. We agree. Section 102 sets forth three conditions for copyrightability: first, a work must be fixed in tangible form; second, the work must be an original work of authorship; and third, it must come within the subject matter of copyright. See 17 U.S.C. § 102(a). Although there may have been some question at one time as to whether simultaneously recorded live broadcasts were copyrightable, this is no longer the case. Section 101 expressly provides that "[a] work consisting of sounds, images, or both, that are being transmitted, is 'fixed' . . . if a fixation of the work is being made simultaneously with its transmission." Since the telecasts of the games are videotaped at the same time they are broadcast, the telecasts are fixed in tangible form.

* * *

Moreover, the telecasts are original works of authorship. The requirement of originality actually subsumes two separate conditions, i.e., the work must possess an independent origin and a minimal amount of creativity. * * * It is obvious that the telecasts are independent creations, rather than reproductions of earlier works.

It is important to distinguish among three separate concepts—originality, creativity, and novelty. A work is original if it is the independent creation of its author. A work is creative if it embodies some modest amount of intellectual labor. A work is novel if it differs from existing works in some relevant respect. For a work to be copyrightable, it must be original and creative, but need not be novel. (Thus, in contrast to patent law, a work that is independently produced by two separate authors may be copyrighted by both.)

* * *

As for the telecasts' creativity, courts long have recognized that photographing a person or filming an event involves creative labor. * * * For example, one court held that the Zapruder film of the Kennedy assassination was copyrightable because it embodied many elements of creativity. Among other things, Zapruder selected the kind of camera (movies, not snapshots), the kind of film (color), the kind of lens (telephoto), the area in which the pictures were to be taken, the time they were to be taken, and (after testing several sites) the spot on which the camera would be operated.

The many decisions that must be made during the broadcast of a baseball game concerning camera angles, types of shots, the use of instant replays and split screens, and shot selection similarly supply the creativity required for the copyrightability of the telecasts. * * * ("When a football game is being covered by four television cameras, with a director guiding the activities of the four cameramen and choosing which of their electronic images are sent to the public and in which order, there is little doubt that what the cameramen and the director are doing constitutes 'authorship.'").

The Players argue that their performances are not copyrightable works because they lack sufficient artistic merit. We disagree. Only a modicum of creativity is required for a work to be copyrightable. Contrary to the Players' contentions, aesthetic merit is not necessary for copyrightability. * * * A recording of a performance generally includes creative contributions by both the director and other individuals responsible for recording the performance and by the performers whose performance is captured. * * * Judged by the above standard, the Players' performances possess the modest creativity required for copyrightability. As Justice Holmes once declared, "if . . . [certain works] command the interest of any public, they have a commercial value—it would be bold to say that they have not an aesthetic and educational value—and the taste of any public is not to be treated with contempt." *Bleistein v. Donaldson Lithographing Co.*, 188 U.S. 239, 252, 47 L. Ed. 460, 23 S. Ct. 298 (1903) (holding circus poster copyrightable). Courts thus should not gainsay the copyrightability of a work possessing great commercial value simply because the work's aesthetic or educational value is not readily apparent to a person trained in the law. That the Players' performances possess great commercial value indicates that the works embody the modicum of creativity required for copyrightability.

Moreover, even if the Players' performances were not sufficiently creative, the Players agree that the cameramen and director contribute creative labor to the telecasts. The work that is the subject of copyright is not merely the Players' performances, but rather the telecast of the Players' performances. The creative contribution of the cameramen and director alone suffices for the telecasts to be copyrightable.

Furthermore, the telecasts are audiovisual works, which under § 102 come within the subject matter of copyright. See 17 U.S.C. § 101 (definition of "audiovisual works"); * * * the telecasts are, therefore, copyrightable works.

Section 102(a) provides: Copyright protection subsists . . . in original works of authorship fixed in any tangible medium of expression, now known or later developed, from which they can be perceived, reproduced, or otherwise communicated, either directly or with the aid of a machine or device. Works of authorship include the following categories:

1. literary works;
2. musical works, including any accompanying words;
3. dramatic works, including any accompanying music;
4. pantomimes and choreographic works;
5. pictorial, graphic, and sculptural works;
6. motion pictures and other audiovisual works; and
7. sound recordings. 17 U.S.C. § 102(a). "Audiovisual works" are works that consist of a series of related images which are intrinsically intended to be shown by the use of machines or devices such as projectors, viewers, or electronic equipment, together with accompanying sounds, if any, regardless of the nature of the material objects, such as films or tapes, in which the works are embodied. 17 U.S.C. § 101.

b. Employer-employee relationship

With regard to the relationship between the Clubs and the Players, the district court found, and the Players do not dispute, that the Players are employees of their respective Clubs. We add only that this finding is consistent with the broad construction given to the term "employee" by courts applying the "work made for hire" doctrine. * * * (a person acting under another's direction and supervision is an employee for the purpose of the work made for hire doctrine) * * *.

c. Scope of employment

The district court further found that the scope of the Players' employment encompassed the performance of major league baseball before "live and remote audiences." See Baltimore Orioles, 1985 Copyright L. Dec. at 19,731. On appeal the Players argue that there exist genuine issues of material fact as to whether the performance of baseball for televised audiences is within the scope of the Players' employment. * * * * However, they never claimed that the performance of baseball before televised audiences was not within the scope of their employment. Indeed, the only issue as to which Players argued that there was a genuine issue of material fact concerned the parties' written agreements respecting ownership of the telecasts' copyright. * * * The Players, therefore, failed to preserve this argument.

Moreover, even on appeal, the Players do not identify any evidence that would create a genuine issue of material fact as to the scope of the Players' employment. In contrast to the Players' perfunctory claim that playing baseball for television audiences is not within the scope of their employment, see Appellant's Brief 29, the Clubs brought forth detailed evidence in support of their motion for summary judgment that the scope of the Players' employment encompassed performances before broadcast audiences. Because of the Players' failure to point to any evidence to the contrary, we would not reverse the district court's finding that the performance of baseball before remote audiences is within the Players' scope of employment even if the Players had preserved their contention. * * *

For example, the Clubs adduced evidence that the Players are acutely aware of the fact that major league baseball games are televised, and that the Players understand that television revenues have a bearing on the level of the salaries that they receive.

d. Written agreements

Because the Players are employees and their performances before broadcast audiences are within the scope of their employment, the telecasts of major league baseball games, which consist of the Players' performances, are works made for hire within the meaning of § 201(b). (The parties can change the statutory presumption concerning the ownership of a copyright in a work made for hire, but cannot vary the work's status as a work made for hire). Thus, in the absence of an agreement to the contrary, the Clubs are presumed to own all of the rights encompassed in the telecasts of the games. The district court found that there was no written agreement that the Clubs would not own the copyright to the telecasts, and, therefore, that the copyright was owned by the Clubs.

* * *

The provisions of the three written agreements on which the Players rely to establish a genuine issue of material fact are paragraph 3(c) of the Uniform Player's Contract, paragraph 7 of the Benefit Plan, and article X of the Basic Agreement. First, the Uniform Player's Contract is the standard form contract between individual players and their respective clubs. In 1947, the first year that the Clubs sold network television rights to major league baseball games, the following language was added to the contract:

The Player agrees that his picture may be taken for still photographs, motion pictures or television at such times as the Club may designate and that all rights in such pictures shall belong to the Club and may be used by the Club for publicity purposes in any manner it desires. Uniform Player's Contract 3(c). The language of paragraph 3(c) has remained materially unchanged over the years.

Second, the Benefit Plan sets forth the particulars of the Players' pension fund. First entered into in 1967, the Benefit Plan arose in large part out of the parties' long-standing dispute as to the allocation of national television revenues to the pension fund. In negotiations over the 1969 Benefit Plan, the Players asserted their long-held claim that broadcasts of baseball games without their consent violated their rights of publicity in their performances. The Clubs, however, maintained that the Players had no rights whatsoever in the telecasts. The parties accordingly agreed to the following compromise provision:

The execution of this Agreement shall not be deemed to change any rights or obligations of the Clubs or the Players with respect to the funding of the Plan (except to the extent set forth in other Paragraphs of this Agreement) or with respect to radio and television, as such rights and obligations existed immediately after the execution of the Agreement Re Major League Baseball Players Benefit Plan of January 1, 1967.

Third, the Basic Agreement represents the collective bargaining agreement between the Players and the Clubs. The original Basic Agreement entered into in 1968 provided that grievances would be arbitrated by the Commissioner of Baseball. When the parties entered into the 1970 Basic Agreement, they agreed to arbitration of grievances by a tripartite panel, rather than by the Commissioner; however, the Clubs did not agree to submit to impartial arbitration those disputes concerning the right to broadcast major league baseball games. The parties thus agreed that:

Anything in the Grievance Procedure provided for in the Basic Agreement to the contrary notwithstanding, complaints or disputes as to any rights of the Players or the Clubs with respect to the sale or proceeds of sale of radio or television broadcasting rights in any baseball games by any kind or method of transmission, dissemination or reception shall not be subject to said Grievance Procedure. However, nothing herein or in the Grievance Procedure shall alter or abridge the rights of the parties, or any of them, to resort to a court of law for the resolution of such complaint or dispute. 1970 Basic Agreement art. X. This language has been included verbatim in each Basic Agreement entered into since 1970.

The Players contend that these three provisions create a genuine issue of material fact with respect to the parties' agreements concerning the ownership of the copyright to the telecasts. We disagree. Section 201(b) states that the employer owns the copyright in a work made for hire "unless the parties have expressly agreed otherwise in a written instrument signed by them." The requirement that an agreement altering the presumption that an employer owns the copyright in a work made for hire represents a substantial change in the "work made for hire" doctrine. Under prior law, "such an agreement could be either oral or implied." However, § 201(b) requires that an agreement altering the statutory presumption be both written and express.

* * *

In this case, the parties have not expressly agreed to rebut the statutory presumption that the Clubs own the copyright in the telecasts. Paragraph 3(c) of the Uniform Player's Contract does not declare that the copyright in the telecasts is owned by the Players, rather than by the Clubs. Instead, it merely grants the Clubs the rights to take the Players' pictures for still photographs, motion pictures, and television and to use the pictures for publicity purposes. A limitation on the Clubs' rights to televise the Players' performances perhaps might be implied by the grant of these particular rights; however, even if such an implied limitation were plausible, paragraph 3(c) nowhere contains an express statement that the Clubs do not own the copyright in the telecasts of the Players' performances.

***

Paragraph 7 of the Benefit Plan and Article X of the Basic Agreement similarly do not declare that the Players, rather than the Clubs, own the copyright in the telecasts. The two provisions simply preserved whatever rights in the telecasts that the parties might possess and reserved each party's right to have disputes concerning television rights be resolved in court, rather than by arbitration. They nowhere state that either the Clubs or the Players own the copyright in the telecasts. These provisions thus do not represent an express agreement that the Players own the copyright in the telecasts. If anything, they reflect the parties' express disagreement as to the copyright's ownership.

The Players point to the absence of a provision expressly granting the Clubs the right to televise the games as support for their assertion that they have "reserved" their rights of publicity in their performances. Nonetheless, there is no need for such an express declaration because under § 201(b) the Clubs are presumed to own the copyright in the works produced by their employees unless the parties expressly agree otherwise in a signed, written instrument.

The Players also argue that these three provisions must be read in light of the agreements' collective bargaining history, and that the circumstances surrounding the agreements cannot be determined without a trial. We disagree. Under § 201(b), an agreement altering the statutory presumption that the employer owns the copyright in a work made for hire must be express. This is to say, the parties' agreement must appear on the face of the signed written instrument. Section 201(b) thus bars the use of parol evidence to imply a provision not found within the four corners of the parties' agreement. * * * Moreover, even if extrinsic evidence were admissible to explain an ambiguity in the parties' agreement, the provisions relied upon by the Players are unambiguous with respect to the ownership of the copyright in the telecasts. Since the contractual terms regarding television rights are clear, it is unnecessary to examine the parties' collective bargaining history to ascertain the meaning of the agreements.

The Players rely on labor law cases concerning the construction of collective bargaining agreements. Such cases, however, have no bearing on the consideration in a copyright case of the parties' agreements concerning the ownership of the copyright in a work made for hire. Congress considered incorporating in § 201(b) the "shop right" doctrine of patent law under which the employer would acquire the right to use the employee's work to the extent needed for the purposes of the employer's regular business, but the employee would retain all other rights so long as he or she refrained from authorizing competing uses. Congress rejected this change because it would create uncertainty as to the ownership of the copyright in a work made for hire. * * * In any event, the collective bargaining history behind the parties' agreements similarly reflects a sharp dispute as to the ownership of the television rights to the games. A fortiori, it cannot establish that the parties agreed that the Players would own the copyright in the televised broadcasts.

The Players further assert that the parties' traditional practice of devoting approximately one-third of the revenues derived from nationally televised broadcasts to the Players' pension fund establishes a genuine issue of material fact as to the ownership of the copyright in these telecasts. We disagree. The allocation of revenues from nationally televised broadcasts is determined by the parties' relative bargaining strength and ability. Depending on the Players' bargaining power, they can negotiate a greater or a lesser share of the national telecast revenues. Nevertheless, there is no relationship between the division of revenues from nationally televised broadcasts and the ownership of rights in those telecasts. For example, a motion picture star might negotiate to receive a certain number of "points" from a film's profits; however, that she shares in the film's profits does not mean that she owns some share of the copyright in the film. (Indeed, the producer most likely holds the copyright in the work.) Just as the ownership of points in a film's profits does not represent a proportionate ownership of the copyright in the film, the Players' receipt in the form of pension contributions of a certain fraction of the revenues from nationally televised broadcasts in no way suggests that they own any part of the copyright in the telecasts.

The Players do not claim that they traditionally have received some share of the revenues from locally televised broadcasts. Therefore, even under the Players' analysis, the division of revenues from national broadcasts does not create a genuine issue of material fact as to the ownership of the copyright in local telecasts. Moreover, the Clubs contest the assertion that they traditionally have devoted to the Players' pension fund approximately one-third of the revenues from nationally televised broadcasts. They argue that since it was first entered into in 1967, the Benefit Plan simply has provided for the Clubs to contribute to the pension plan a flat dollar amount from whatever source of revenue they choose, and never has required the Clubs to contribute any amount, let alone one-third, of the national telecast revenues. Nonetheless, as our subsequent discussion indicates, we need not resolve this dispute because it is not material to the ownership of the copyright in the national telecasts.

* * *

We thus conclude that there are no genuine issues of material fact as to the ownership of the copyright in the telecasts, and that the parties did not expressly agree to rebut the statutory presumption that the employer owns the copyright in a work made for hire. We, therefore, hold that the Clubs own the copyright in telecasts of major league baseball games.

* * *

CASES ON THE SUPPLEMENTAL WEB SITE

Baltimore Orioles, Inc. v. M.L.B. Players Assoc, 805 F.2d 663 (1986). This is the continuation of the case as it relates to copyright and pre-emption, right to publicity and master servant.

Incredible Technologies Inc. v. Virtual Technologies Inc, 400 F.3d 1007 (2005). This case examines what one has to prove to succeed in a copyright infringement case.

Lorimar Music A Corp v. Black Iron Grill, 2010 U.S. Dist. LEXIS 76484 (W.D. MO. 2010). This case shows how an infringement case is handled (Note the amount the infringement cost).

Kelley v. Chicago Park District, 635 F.3d 290 (7th Cir. 2011). Note how the elements of copyright are evaluated. Do you agree with the outcome? Explain.

QUESTIONS YOU SHOULD BE ABLE TO ANSWER

1. For what can you get a copyright and what cannot carry a copyright?

2. Explain the difference between public and private and contrast how they are treated differently when playing music or watching videos.

3. What is meant by "fair use" and what rights and privileges does it confer?

4. Many musicians claim that the internet may be the demise of music as a career as musician can no longer make a living through music. Discuss this statement in relation to the copyright law.

5. Look through social media and determine how much of it may be breaking copyright law. Suggest some methods that might be used to curb such infringement.

REFERENCES

Cases

A & M Records, Inc. v. Napster, Inc., 284 F.3d. 1091 (9th Cir. 2002).
Baltimore Orioles v. Major League Baseball Players, 805 F.2d 663 (7th Cir. 1986).
Broadcast Music, Inc. v. Blueberry Hill Family Restaurants, Inc., 899 F. Supp. 474 (N.D. Nev, 1995).
Broadcast Music, Inc. v. Melody Fair Enterprises, Inc., 1990 WL 284743 (W.D. N.Y. 1990).
Cablevision Systems Corp. v. 45 Midland Enterprises, Inc., 858 F. Supp. 42 (S.D. N.Y. 1994).
Feist Publications v. Rural Telephone Service Co., 111 S.Ct. 1282 (1991).
Live Nation Motor Sports, Inc. v. Davis, 81 U.S.P.Q.2d (BNA) 1826 (2007)
Lorimar Music A Corp v. Black Iron Grill, 2010 U.S. Dist. LEXIS 76484 (W.D. MO. 2010)
Lyons Partnership, L.P. v. Giannoulas, 179 F.3d 384 (5th Cir. 1999).
National Basketball Association and NBA Properties, Inc. v. Motorola, Inc., 105 F.3d 841 (2nd Cir., 1997).
National Football League v. McBee & Bruno's, Inc., 792 F.2d 726 (8th Cir. 1986).
National Football League v. Rondor, 840 F. Supp. 1160 (N.D. Oh. 1993).
Phillips v. Pembroke Real Estate, Inc., 459 F.3d 128 (1st Cir. 2006).
SONY Corp. v. Universal Studios, 104 S. Ct. 774 (1984).

Syrus v. Bennett, 455 Fed. Appx. 806 (10th Cir. 2011).
Tallyrand Music Inc. v. Frank Stenko, 1990 WL 169163 (M.D. Pa. 1990).

Publications

Hohensee, J. M. (1988). The Fair Use Doctrine in copyright: A growing concern for judge advocates. *Military Law Review*, 19, 155–197.

Kukkonen, C. A. (1998). Be a good sport and refrain from using my patented putt: Intellectual property protection for sports related movements. *Journal of the Patent and Trademark Office Society*, 80, 808.

Patent Office Reform. Hearing before the Courts, The Internet, and Intellectual Property of the Committee of the Judiciary, House of Representatives, 109th Cong., 1 (2005).

Pepitone, J. (2012, Jan 20) SOPA and PIPA postponed indefinitely after protests. *CNN Money*. Retrieved from http://money.cnn.com/2012/01/20/technology/SOPA_PIPA_postponed/index.htm

Smith, J. A. (1999). It's your move—No it's not! The application of patent law to sports moves. *University of Colorado Law Review*, 70, 1051.

Weber, L. (2000) Something in the way she moves: The case for applying copyright protection to sports moves. *Columbia–VLA Journal of Law and the Arts*, 23, 317.

Wilson, D. C. (1997). The legal ramifications of saving face: An integrated analysis of intellectual property and sport. *Villanova Sports and Entertainment Law Journal*, 4, 227.

Legislation

Copyright Remedy Clarification Act, 104 U.S.C. 2749 (1990).
The 1976 Copyright Act 17 U.S.C. § 101 et seq. (2008).
Patents 35 U.S.C. § 101 et seq. (2008).
Visual Artists Rights Act of 1990, 104 U.S.C. 5128 (1990).

7.22 PRINCIPLES OF TRADEMARK LAW

Paul M. Anderson I National Sports Law Institute of Marquette University Law School

One of the most valuable assets for a recreation or sport organization is its name, logo, or some other defining characteristic that the public will recognize when viewing its products or services. These characteristics help promote the organization and help to sell these products and services. Because such identifying marks are so valuable, competitors will often engage in counterfeiting and other illegal behavior that harms the original organization. A recent study by the Organization for Economic Cooperation and Development (OECD) estimate that the total global economic value of counterfeit and pirated products is as much as $650 billion a year—a value expected to increase to as much as $1.7 trillion by 2015 (Frontier Economics, 2011). In the United States alone the current estimate is between $66 and $100 billion. One of the strongest ways for an organization to protect itself is by seeking trademark protection for its name, logo, or other defining symbols.

FUNDAMENTAL CONCEPTS

The two main purposes of trademark law are to protect the owner of a mark and to prevent others from using the mark in a way that will cause consumer confusion. The Federal Trademark Act of 1946, known as the Lanham Act, governs trademarks, registration, and provides measures to protect from infringement.

Federal Trademark Act of 1946/the Lanham Act

According to the Lanham Act, a **trademark** is any word, name, symbol, or device, or any combination thereof, adopted or used by some entity to identify their goods and distinguish them from those manufactured or sold by others (15 U.S.C §1127). A trademark (1) identifies a seller's goods and distinguishes them from those sold by others, (2) signifies that goods come from one particular source, (3) indicates that products are of a certain quality, and (4) advertises, promotes and assists in selling the particular goods (McCarthy, 1991).

Trademarks can also be categorized by strength. The strongest marks are **arbitrary or fanciful marks** that bear no direct relationship to the product itself, such as "Adidas" for sports apparel, and "Ping" for golf clubs. These marks are inherently distinctive because they serve as an indicator of the source of the goods rather than describing the goods themselves.

Next are **suggestive marks** that hint at the characteristics of the goods or services, but require some consumer imagination to be understood as descriptive. For instance, although some consumers would understand a "Hot Pocket" to be a warm food item, it takes a bit of imagination to understand that the name stands for a meal wrapped in a flaky crust.

Descriptive marks identify a characteristic or quality of a good or service. For example, "SwingAway" is the name of a hitting net with a ball attached on a rope so that the hitter can swing away at the ball and it will come back to the same spot. These marks only receive trademark protection after they obtain "**secondary meaning.**" Secondary meaning is obtained through widespread use and public recognition so that the mark primarily indicates the source of the good or service instead of the good or service itself. For example, in *Board of Supervisors v. Smack Apparel Co.* (2006) several universities sued a company that made apparel using identifiable color schemes from these universities, such as purple and gold for LSU, crimson and cream for the University of Oklahoma, scarlet and gray for the Ohio State University, and cardinal and gold for the University of Southern California. In ruling that such color schemes could receive trademark protection because they had obtained secondary meaning the court found that the defendants had infringed upon the schools' trademarks.

Generic marks receive no trademark protection because they refer to the name or class of the good or service and are so common or descriptive that they are not indicative of the source or sponsorship of the good or service. Some companies who originally adopt distinctive names or logos eventually lose their trademark rights in these same names or logos because they become so well known, such as *Kleenex* for facial tissue and *Jell-O* for gelatin.

The Lanham Act also protects service marks and collective marks. A **service mark** is a mark used in the sale of advertising or services to identify and distinguish the services of one entity from the services of others. Whereas a trademark identifies the source and quality of a product, a service mark identifies the source and quality of an intangible service. The mark "NCAA," as it stands for events and services related to the National Collegiate Athletic Association, is a service mark. A **collective mark** is a trademark or service mark used by the members of a cooperative, association, or other collective organization to indicate membership in that organization. Examples of collective marks in sports include "NBA," "NFL" and "Big East."

Use and Registration

To create ownership rights in a trademark, the trademark owner must be the first to use the mark in trade and make continuous, uninterrupted use from then on. Once the trademark is used, consumers can rely on it to identify and distinguish the owner's particular goods or services from those of others. Federal registration is not required to establish common law trademark rights nor is it required to begin using a trademark. However, with registration, a trademark right extends to the use of the mark across the United States. Federal registration also provides constructive notice to others that the registrant owns the trademark and the right to exclusively use the mark. Every ten years the trademark can be reregistered to provide continuous protection.

Any sport or recreation organization that wants to ensure that its logo, design, or other insignia is not already registered as a trademark can search all federally registered trademarks online at *http://www.uspto. gov/trademarks/index.jsp*. The following is information for the trademark *National Sports Law Institute of Marquette University Law School.*

Word Mark	**NATIONAL SPORTS LAW INSTITUTE** MARQUETTE UNIVERSITY **LAW** SCHOOL
Goods and Services	IC 041. US 100 101 107. G & S: Educational services; namely, conducting educational and international classes, workshops, meetings and seminars in the field of sports law. FIRST USE: 20000531. FIRST USE IN COMMERCE: 20000531
Mark Drawing Code	(3) DESIGN PLUS WORDS, LETTERS, AND/OR NUMBERS
Design Search Code	05.15.02 - Laurel leaves or branches (borders or frames); Wreaths 13.01.02 - Blow torch; Propane torches; Torches; Welding torch 26.01.08 - Circles having letters or numerals as a border; Circles having punctuation as a border; Letters, numerals or punctuation forming or bordering the perimeter of a circle
Serial Number	76133371
Filing Date	September 22, 2000
Published for Opposition	November 6, 2001
Registration Number	2533880
Registration Date	January 29, 2002
Owner	(REGISTRANT) Marquette University CORPORATION WISCONSIN 615 N. 11th Street Room 015 Milwaukee WISCONSIN 53233
Disclaimer	NO CLAIM IS MADE TO THE EXCLUSIVE RIGHT TO USE "SPORTS LAW INSTITUTE" APART FROM THE MARK AS SHOWN
Type of Mark	SERVICE MARK
Distinctiveness	
Limitation Statement	as to "NATIONAL SPORTS LAW INSTITUTE"

Infringement

Even if a recreation or sport organization registers its trademarks, legal disputes may still arise when another organization develops a product that seems to include similar marks. The first organization can then sue the offending organization for trademark infringement.

In order to demonstrate trademark infringement under Section 1114(a) of the Lanham Act, the owner of the trademark must show that she has a protectable property right in the trademark. Use and registration can establish a valid protectable right in a particular trademark. The trademark owner must also show that the other party's use of a similar mark is likely to cause confusion, mistake, or deceive consumers as to who is the true source of the mark. When analyzing potential consumer confusion, the courts focus on the following factors:

1. Strength of the mark,
2. Similarity between the marks,
3. Similarity between the products and marketing channels used to sell them,
4. Likelihood that the trademark owner will expand their use of the mark on future products,
5. Evidence of actual confusion,
6. Defendant's "good faith" intent in adopting the mark,
7. Quality of the defendant's product, and
8. Sophistication of the consumers.

Ohio State University v. Thomas(2010), involved a challenge by the Ohio State University to the use of various federally registered trademarks such as "Buckeyes," "Ohio State," and "OSU," for two electronic magazines, "Buckeye Gameday" and "Ohio State Buckeyes E-Book," as well as a print publication and website, www.buckeyeillustrated.com. In analyzing whether the defendants' use of the word Buckeyes created a likelihood of confusion, the court looked to a combination of the factors listed above, including; strength of the plaintiff's mark, relatedness of the goods or services, similarity of the marks, evidence of actual confusion, marketing channels used,likely degree of purchaser care, intent of the defendant in selecting the mark, and likelihood of expansion of the product lines. Finding that these factors weighed in favor of a likelihood of consumer confusion, the court granted Ohio State's motion for a temporary restraining order and preliminary injunction stopping the plaintiff and his marketing company from infringing upon the university's marks.

Counterfeiting

Another form of trademark infringement is counterfeiting, often known as piracy. The Lanham Act defines a **counterfeit mark** as "a spurious mark that is identical with, or substantially indistinguishable from, a registered mark" (15 U.S.C. § 1127). Counterfeiting is an intentional effort to produce products that reproduce a genuine trademark without a license or permission. Organizations that attempt to counterfeit the trademarks of a recreation or sport management organization are subject to severe criminal and civil penalties.

Dilution

Dilution law protects the distinctive quality and selling power of a trademark, even if consumers are not actually confused by a non-trademark owner's use of the mark. The Federal Trademark Dilution Act of 1995 defines **dilution** as the lessening of the capacity of a famous mark to identify and distinguish goods or services, regardless of either the presence or absence of competition between the parties, or a likelihood of confusion, mistake, or deception. The Trademark Dilution Revision Act of 2006 helped further define the standard for dilution claims emphasizing that in a claim for dilution a trademark owner only needs to show a likelihood of dilution rather than actual dilution.

Recently, the University of Kansas sued an online retailer that was incorporating the school's trademarks on t-shirts that used offensive language and referred to sex and alcohol. Kansas fans complained that these t-shirts reflected negatively on the school's reputation. The court confirmed that a reasonable jury could find that this use of the widely recognized Kansas athletic marks could cause dilution, especially when considered in combination with the fan complaints regarding the negative effect of the t-shirts on the school's reputation (*University of Kansas v. Sinks*, 2008).

Unfair Competition and False Advertising

Unfair competition refers to a broader area of law than trademark infringement. It can involve any activity where one party attempts to deceive or mislead consumers by using the trademarks of another party to give the consumer the mistaken belief that the products of the infringer are actually the products of the true trademark owner. Unfair competition claims can be brought under Section 1125(1)(a) of the Lanham Act, which provides a cause of action for false designation of origin alleging that an infringer has used the trademark rights of another to deceive consumers as to the affiliation, connection, or association of the infringer with the legitimate trademark owner, and Section 1125(1)(b), which provides a cause of action for false advertising alleging that another party has used commercial advertising or promotions to misrepresent the nature, characteristics, quality, or origin of their products.

An example of an unfair competition and false advertising case that involved two well-known football helmet producers is *Riddell, Inc. v. Schutt Sports, Inc.*, (2010). Riddell relied heavily on a certain concussion study in its advertisements, citing various results of the study that concerned concussion rates for players wearing Riddell helmets. Schutt asserted that these advertisements amounted to false advertising and deceptive trade practices. The court, however, noted that Schutt did not have any evidence of actual consumer confusion based on the advertisements. Therefore, it could prevail only if it could show that Riddell's statements were literally false, which they failed to do.

Defenses

Often a recreation and sport organization will fight an infringement claim by arguing that the plaintiff does not have any protectable rights in the trademark, or the defendant's use will not cause consumer confusion. In addition, the organization may claim the trademark has been abandoned, that the doctrine of laches applies, that it is disparaging, that the use was a fair use or parody, or that there has been no infringement due to the presence of certain disclaimers.

Laches

In certain circumstances if trademark owners have neglected to assert their trademark rights in a timely manner, the **doctrine of laches** may limit them from recovery, if such recovery would be prejudicial to the potential infringer. In a case dealing with the University of Pittsburgh, the university was barred from recovery for past infringement when it delayed objecting to the sale of unauthorized clothing and novelty items including its name and mascot for 36 years (*University of Pittsburgh v. Champion Products, Inc.*, 1982). The university, however, was granted an injunction to stop future unauthorized use of its marks.

Abandonment

Although trademark rights can be renewed continuously through registration, a trademark owner must still actively use the mark for it to remain valid. Section 1127 of the Lanham Act defines **abandonment** as discontinued use of a trademark with the intent not to resume such use, or when any act or omission of the owner of a mark causes it to become the generic name for the goods in connection with which it is used. When a defendant asserts abandonment as a defense, the claim is that the mark has fallen into the public domain because of the plaintiff's lack of use and intent not to resume use. An abandoned mark may be claimed and used by the public at large.

Hawaii-Pacific registered the marks "Top Dawg" and Lil Dawg" in the mid-1990s (*Hawaii-Pacific Apparel Group, Inc. v. Cleveland Browns Football Co. LLC*, 2006). In 1999, when Cleveland was awarded a new NFL franchise to replace the franchise that left and became the Baltimore Ravens, NFL Properties attempted to use the mark "Dawg Pound" to associate with the new Cleveland Browns franchise. Hawaii-Pacific contested the NFL's use of the mark claiming that it had abandoned the mark by not using it during the time when Cleveland did not have an NFL franchise. The court disagreed finding that the NFL attempted to protect this mark during this time even though there was no Browns franchise from 1995 to 1999, and that the NFL was the senior user of the mark in the first place.

Fair Use or Parody

Section 1115(b)(4) of the Lanham Act provides that where a trademark is used fairly and in good faith only to describe the goods or services involved, there is no trademark infringement. For example, an artist's renderings of famous University of Alabama football plays containing depictions of players dressed in University uniforms with the University's marks was deemed to be fair use of the marks. The court found that the defendants used their own marks to identify the source of the paintings, which was evidence of good faith and made it clear that the source was the artist and not the University of Alabama (*University of Alabama Board of Trustees. v. New Life Art Inc.*, 2009).

Courts have also held that parody of a trademark is not infringement. In *World Wrestling Federation Entertainment, Inc. v. Big Dog Holdings, Inc.* (2003), the court found that the defendant's use of dog caricatures of WWE wrestlers on novelty items, when used in conjunction with its own registered trademark, dog design logo, and a disclaimer indicating the parody nature, made it clear that the items were spoofs of the WWE and its characters such that there was no likelihood of confusion.

Disparaging Marks

Trademark protection can also be denied if a mark is shown to be immoral, deceptive, scandalous, or disparaging under Section 1052(a) of the Lanham Act. In *Harjo, et al. v. Pro-Football, Inc.* (1999), Native Americans petitioned to cancel the trademark registrations for the marks "Washington Redskins" and "Redskins," both owned by Pro-Football, Inc., the owners of the NFL's Washington Redskins franchise. The Patent and Trademark Office initially granted the petition to cancel the marks. The team then sued for summary judgment to avoid the cancellation of the marks. The district court reversed, finding that the plaintiff presented insufficient evidence that the marks were disparaging to Native Americans and that the claim was barred by the doctrine of laches because there was a twenty-five-year delay in bringing the suit (2003).

Disclaimers

A potential trademark infringer may also argue that a conspicuously placed **disclaimer** alerting consumers that the product or service does not contain certain attributes or features, and that it is not from a certain source organization, absolves it from liability for infringement. In *Heisman Trophy Trust v. Smack Apparel Co.* (2009), the plaintiff alleged trademark infringement regarding various t-shirts produced by Smack Apparel that promoted the candidacy of potential Heisman winners. Smack Apparel claimed that disclaimers it included on each of the t-shirts helped to dispel any consumer confusion that may have existed. The court however rejected this argument and held that where a substantial likelihood of confusion otherwise exists, and the disclaimers are not prominently featured on the products, such disclaimers are of limited value.

Licensing

Merchandisers, manufacturers and sponsors often wish to associate themselves with a recreation or sport organization. One way to do this is through the grant of a license. A **license** is a written document in which the trademark owner grants another entity the right to associate their business and/or product with the name, goodwill, logos, symbols, emblems, and designs of the trademark owner. By paying some form of compensation, the company that receives the license (the licensee) can then use the trademark of the licensor to sell its own products. Problems occur when entities other than the licensee attempt to use the licensor's marks or when the licensor becomes unhappy with the licensee's use of the license.

Professional Sports. Most professional sports leagues have developed profitable licensing programs to capitalize on public demand for sports-related items with team and league affiliations. Each of the four major sports leagues (NFL, NBA, NHL, and MLB) have created separate properties divisions (i.e., NBA Properties) that deal with licensing of league and club trademarks to vendors who manufacture and sell products to consumers. The revenue realized from the sale of such licensed products is then divided among the teams within the league, normally on an equal basis.

The players associations also have formed separate entities that handle licensing issues for athletes (i.e., Players, Inc. for the NFL Players Association and the Players Choice Group Licensing Program for the MLB Players Association). These entities provide marketing and licensing services to companies interested in using the names and likenesses of current and past players. Revenues are normally distributed among the players that make up the association on a pro rata basis.

Some players have even gone so far as to seek trademark protection for their own name and likeness. Michael Jordan owns a trademark for his name for use in the promotion and endorsement of goods and services, clinics, and camps. Major sportswear companies have also recognized the potential value of trademarking a famous athlete's name, as Nike actually owns the name, "LeBron."

The NCAA. The National Collegiate Athletic Association (NCAA) protects the intellectual property of the approximately 75 trademarks and service marks associated with the NCAA and its 89 annual championships through the development of various licensing and marketing programs (www.ncaa.org). However, the NCAA does not monitor individual university marks. Rather, universities are responsible for monitoring their own respective marks.

For instance, the University of Iowa created an extensive licensing and monitoring program for its marks. Approximately 550 companies are licensed through the University of Iowa Trademark and Licensing Program, which offers three different types of nonexclusive license agreements to vendors. All merchandise bearing the University of Iowa trademarks must be approved through this program. The policy lists the three types of available licensing agreements, the purpose of the program, and the standards and restrictions for licensing approval (http://www.hawkeyesports.com/licensing/). In addition, many schools utilize the Collegiate Licensing Company (CLC). Through a complex licensing application process, the CLC aids colleges in protecting their marks and developing their brands and is currently utilized by approximately 200 colleges, universities, bowl games, conferences, the Heisman Trophy, and the NCAA (http://www.clc.com/).

The licensing and monitoring of college and university marks has become a thorny issue program since many high schools use logos and marks either substantially similar, or sometimes even identical, to collegiate marks. As high school athletics have become more high-profile through enhanced media coverage, colleges have been forced to take an increased interest in the logos and trademarks these high schools use for their athletic programs. Recognizing the value of their trademarks, universities are increasingly demanding that high schools stop using these similar or identical logos that have the potential to cause confusion or dilution. In the past, colleges became aware of these high schools often by accident; now however, universities actively protect their marks and search for potential infringers at the high school level.

The Olympics. The International Olympic Committee (IOC) owns the familiar "Olympic Rings" logo and the right to use the mark all over the world. The United States Olympic Committee (USOC) owns the exclusive right to use and license the Olympic marks in the United States and vigorously protects the use of its protected marks and terminology. In addition, unauthorized use of the Olympic name or marks may also be held to violate the Ted Stevens Olympic and Amateur Sports Act.

For example, the USOC sued an operator of a children's summer camp operating under the name, "Camp Olympik" where various Olympic-style athletic events were part of the camp activities. The USOC had previously contacted the defendant, which originally operated under the name "Camp Olympic" and made various uses of the Olympic rings and Olympic torch, to request that they stop using the Olympic words and symbols as they were violating the Amateur Sports Act. In response, the camp changed the name to "Camp Olympik" and slightly altered the logo with the Olympic ring. In agreeing with the USOC, the court found that the changes the camp made were not enough and that a likelihood of confusion still existed (*USOC v. Tobyhanna Camp Corporation*, 2010).

The Internet

In the mid-1990s, as recreation and sport organizations began to promote their products and services on the Internet, many found that someone else had already registered their preferred domain name. These "cybersquatters" attempt to register famous trademarks as domain names in the hopes of selling them to the famous entity for substantial profit.

In the fall of 1999, two measures were established to combat the widespread problem of cybersquatting. The Anti-cybersquatting Consumer Protection Act (ACPA) amended the Lanham Act by creating a specific claim against cybersquatters. The Act outlawed the act of registering, with the bad-faith intent to profit, a domain name that is confusingly similar to a registered or unregistered mark or dilutes a famous mark. The Act allows a court to resolve domain name disputes even when the disputed owner of the name cannot be found or cannot be served in the United States.

A case dealing with a claim under the ACPA involved the NCAA, the Illinois High School Association (IHSA), and the domain name "marchmadness.com." The IHSA began using the phrase "March Madness" to refer to its boys' basketball tournaments in the 1940s. The NCAA's first use was in 1982, when CBS broadcaster Brent Musberger used the phrase to describe the NCAA men's basketball tournament. In the early 1990s both the IHSA and the NCAA claimed exclusive trademark rights to the phrase. After going through some initial litigation, the NCAA and IHSA agreed to work together to protect their rights. In 2000, they formed the March Madness Athletic Association (MMAA), and each retained a license to use the phrase in association with their tournaments. After falsely claiming association with the NCAA, Netfire acquired the domain name "marchmadness.com" in 1996. MMAA sued claiming that Netfire was engaging in cybersquatting in violation of the ACPA. Finding that Netfire acted with bad faith to profit from use of the trademarked phrase, and that the domain name was identical or confusingly similar to the actual trademark, the court upheld the district court determination that Netfirehad violated the ACPA (*March Madness Athletic Association, LLC v. Netfire Inc.*, 2005).

In addition to the ACPA, trademark owners can submit their dispute to a form of alternative dispute resolution. The Uniform Dispute Resolution Process (UDRP) is administered by the Internet Corporation for Assigned Names and Numbers (ICANN). By using the UDRP, a trademark owner must allege that its mark is "identical or confusingly similar" to the mark used by the cybersquatter who has no legitimate rights or interests in the domain name, and that the cybersquatter registered and used the domain name in bad faith. In addition, a UDRP proceeding does not preclude a lawsuit under the ACPA.

In 2011, the PAC-10 Conference filed a complaint with the World Intellectual Property Organization (WIPO) Arbitration and Mediation Center against defendant Lee, challenging registration of the domain names, "pac-12network.com," "pac12network.com," and "pac-12network.org"—names registered following the Pac-10 commissioner's announcement that the conference was looking to expand its membership (*Pac-10 Conference v. Lee*, 2011). The Pac-10 Conference alleged that these domain names were confusingly similar to its trademarks, that Lee had no legitimate interest in the domain names, and that the domain name were registered in bad faith. The arbitration panel agreed and ordered Lee to transfer the domain names to the Pac-10.

Ambush Marketing

With rights fees for events such as the Super Bowl and Olympic Games costing several millions of dollars, official sponsors of these events want to ensure they are the only company given the exposure associated with the particular event. **Ambush marketing** refers to the efforts of companies to weaken or attack a competitor's official association with a sports organization or event by using advertising and promotional campaigns designed to confuse consumers and to misrepresent the official sponsorship of the event. Unfortunately for the official sponsor, these corporations have successfully been able to defend their ambush marketing campaigns with claims of commercial free speech. In addition, most ambush campaigns are short-lived, and courts support the use of disclaimers allowing ambush companies to make limited use of a registered trademark as long as they avoid creating consumer confusion.

Following AT&T's purchase of Cingular Wireless, AT&T wished to replace the Cingular logo on Jeff Burton's NASCAR race car with an AT&T logo. The Cingular logo on the car had been grandfathered in, but NASCAR would not allow a change to the AT&T logo, as it would interfere with Nextel's exclusive sponsorship agreement with NASCAR. Following a U.S. District Court ruling that would have allowed the AT&T logo, NASCAR filed a countersuit against AT&T, alleging among other things, ambush marketing, as the logo on the vehicle would provide an avenue for circumventing Nextel's exclusive sponsorship rights in the NASCAR series.

Regardless of the limited success of ambush marketing claims, sport organizations can minimize the negative effects associated with these tactics by developing a comprehensive anti-ambush marketing plan. As part of this plan, official sponsors should monitor nonsponsor signage and advertisements to ensure that official event names, marks, and logos are not being used.

The following case illustrates how a court will examine likelihood of consumer confusion in a trademark infringement case. Of special note is the court's examination of the similarity of the marks and products and overlap in the geographical markets. The court discussed survey evidence used to demonstrate consumer confusion. The court also noted that even though the Colts did not use the contested mark, they did not abandon it over the intervening period of time.

INDIANAPOLIS COLTS V. METROPOLITAN BALTIMORE FOOTBALL CLUB
United States Court of Appeals for the Seventh Circuit
34 F.3d 410 (7th Cir. 1994)

POSNER, *Chief Judge.* The Indianapolis Colts and the National Football League, to which the Colts belong, brought suit for trademark infringement *(15 U.S.C. §§ 1051et seq.)* against the Canadian Football League's new team in Baltimore, which wants to call itself the "Baltimore CFL Colts." (Four of the Canadian Football League's teams are American.) The plaintiffs obtained a preliminary injunction against the new team's using the name "Colts," or "Baltimore Colts," or "Baltimore CFL Colts," in connection with the playing of professional football, the broadcast of football games, or the sale of merchandise to football fans and other buyers. The ground for the injunction was that consumers of "Baltimore CFL Colts" merchandise are likely to think, mistakenly, that the new Baltimore team is an NFL team related in some fashion to the Indianapolis Colts, formerly the Baltimore Colts. From the order granting the injunction the new team and its owners appealto us under *28 U.S.C. § 1292*(a)(1). Since the injunction was granted, the new team has played its first two games—without a name.

A bit of history is necessary to frame the dispute. In 1952, the National Football League permitted one of its teams, the Dallas Texans, which was bankrupt, to move to Baltimore, where it was renamed the "Baltimore Colts." Under that name it became one of the most illustrious teams in the history of professional football. In 1984, the team's owner, with the permission of the NFL, moved the team to Indianapolis, and it was renamed the "Indianapolis Colts." The move, sudden and secretive, outraged the citizens of Baltimore. The city instituted litigation in a futile effort to get the team back—even tried, unsuccessfully, to get the team back by condemnation under the city's power of eminent domain—and the Colts brought a countersuit that also failed. *Indianapolis Colts v. Mayor & City Council of Baltimore, 733 F.2d 484, 741 F.2d 954 (1984), 775 F.2d 177 (7th Cir. 1985).*

Nine years later, the Canadian Football League granted a franchise for a Baltimore team. Baltimoreans clamored for naming the new team the "Baltimore Colts." And so it was named—until the NFL got wind of the name and threatened legal action. The name was then changed to "Baltimore CFL Colts" and publicity launched, merchandise licensed, and other steps taken in preparation for the commencement of play this summer.

* * *

The Baltimore team wanted to call itself the "Baltimore Colts." To improve its litigating posture (we assume), it has consented to insert "CFL" between "Baltimore" and "Colts." A glance at the merchandise in the record explains why this concession to an outraged NFL has been made so readily. On several of the items "CFL" appears in small or blurred letters. And since the Canadian Football League is not well known in the United States—and "CFL" has none of the instant recognition value of "NFL"—the inclusion of the acronym in the team's name might have little impact on potential buyers even if prominently displayed. Those who know football well know that the new "Baltimore Colts" are a new CFL team wholly unrelated to the old Baltimore Colts; know also that the rules of Canadian football are different from those of American football and that teams don't move from the NFL to the CFL as they might from one conference within the NFL to the other. But those who do *not* know these things—and we shall come shortly to the question whether there are many of these football illiterate—will not be warned off by the letters "CFL." The acronym is a red herring, and the real issue is whether the new Baltimore team can appropriate the name "Baltimore Colts." The entire thrust of the defendants' argument is that it can.

They make a tremendous to-do over the fact that the district judge found that the Indianapolis Colts abandoned the trademark "Baltimore Colts" when they moved to Indianapolis. Well, of course; they were no longer playing football under the name "Baltimore Colts," so could not have used the name as the team's trademark; they could have used it on merchandise but chose not to, until 1991 (another story—and not one we need tell). When a mark is abandoned, it returns to the public domain, and is appropriable anew—in principle. In practice, because "subsequent use of [an] abandoned mark may well evoke a continuing association with the prior use, those who make subsequent use may be required to take reasonable precautions to prevent confusion." 2 McCarthy, *supra*, § 17.01[2], at p. 17–3. This precept is especially important where, as in this case, the former owner of the abandoned mark continues to market the same product or service under a similar name, though we cannot find any previous cases of this kind. No one questions the validity of "Indianapolis Colts" as the trademark of the NFL team that plays out of Indianapolis and was formerly known as the Baltimore Colts. If "Baltimore CFL Colts" is confusingly similar to "Indianapolis Colts" by virtue of the history of the Indianapolis team and the overlapping product and geographical markets served by it and by the new Baltimore team, the latter's use of the abandoned mark would infringe the Indianapolis Colts' new mark. The Colts' abandonment of a mark confusingly similar to their new mark neither broke the continuity of the team in its different locations—it was the same team, merely having a different home base and therefore a different geographical component in its name—nor entitled a third party to pick it up and use it to confuse Colts fans, and other actual or potential consumers of products and services marketed by the Colts or by other National Football League teams, with regard to the identity, sponsorship, or league affiliation of the third party, that is, the new Baltimore team.

* * *

Against this the defendants cite to us with great insistence *Major League Baseball Properties Inc. v. Sed Non Olet Denarius, Ltd., 817 F. Supp. 1103, 1128 (S.D.N.Y. 1993)*, which, over the objection of the Los Angeles Dodgers, allowed a restaurant in Brooklyn to use the name "Brooklyn Dodger" on the ground that "the 'Brooklyn Dodgers' was a non transportable cultural institution separate from the 'Los Angeles Dodgers.' " The defendants in our case argue that the sudden and greatly resented departure of the Baltimore Colts for Indianapolis made the name "Baltimore Colts" available to anyone who would continue the "nontransportable cultural institution" constituted by a football team located in the City of Baltimore. We think this argument very weak, and need not even try to distinguish *Sed Non Olet Denarius* since district court decisions are not authoritative in this or any court of appeals. *Colby v. J.C. Penney Co., 811 F.2d 1119, 1124 (7th Cir. 1987)*. If it were a Supreme Court decision it still would not help the defendants. The "Brooklyn Dodger" was not a baseball team, and there

was no risk of confusion. The case might be relevant if the Indianapolis Colts were arguing not confusion but misappropriation: that they own the goodwill associated with the name "Baltimore Colts" and the new Baltimore team is trying to take it from them. Cf. *Quaker Oats Co. v. Mills Co., 134 F.2d 429, 432 (7th Cir. 1943)*. They did make a claim of misappropriation in the district court, but that court rejected the claim and it has not been renewed on appeal. The only claim in our court is that a significant number of consumers will think the new Baltimore team the successor to, or alter ego of, or even the same team as the Baltimore Colts and therefore the Indianapolis Colts, which is the real successor. No one would think the Brooklyn Dodgers baseball team reincarnated in a restaurant.

* * *

. . . for if everyone *knows* there is no contractual or institutional continuity, no pedigree or line of descent, linking the Baltimore-Indianapolis Colts and the new CFL team that wants to call itself the "Baltimore Colts" (or, grudgingly, the "Baltimore CFL Colts"), then there is no harm, at least no harm for which the Lanham Act provides a remedy, in the new Baltimore team's appropriating the name "Baltimore Colts" to play under and sell merchandise under. If not everyone knows, there is harm. Some people who might otherwise watch the Indianapolis Colts (or some other NFL team, for remember that the NFL, representing all the teams, is a coplaintiff) on television may watch the Baltimore CFL Colts instead, thinking they are the "real" Baltimore Colts, and the NFL will lose revenue. A few (doubtless very few) people who might otherwise buy tickets to an NFL game may buy tickets to a Baltimore CFL Colts game instead. Some people who might otherwise buy merchandise stamped with the name "Indianapolis Colts" or the name of some other NFL team may buy merchandise stamped "Baltimore CFL Colts," thinking it a kin of the NFL's Baltimore Colts in the glory days of Johnny Unitas rather than a newly formed team that plays Canadian football in a Canadian football league. It would be naive to suppose that no consideration of such possibilities occurred to the owners of the new Baltimore team when they were choosing a name, though there is no evidence that it was the dominant or even a major consideration.

Confusion thus is possible, and may even have been desired; but is it likely? There is great variance in consumer competence, and it would be undesirable to impoverish the lexicon of trade names merely to protect the most gullible fringe of the consuming public. The Lanham Act does not cast the net of protection so wide. * * * The legal standard under the Act has been formulated variously, but the various formulations come down to whether it is likely that the challenged mark if permitted to be used by the defendant would cause the plaintiff to lose a substantial number of consumers. Pertinent to this determination is the similarity of the marks and of the parties' products, the knowledge of the average consumer of the product, the overlap in the parties' geographical markets, and the other factors that the cases consider. The aim is to strike a balance between, on the one hand, the interest of the seller of the new product, and of the consuming public, in an arresting, attractive, and informative name that will enable the new product to compete effectively against existing ones, and, on the other hand, the interest of existing sellers, and again of the consuming public, in consumers' being able to know exactly what they are buying without having to incur substantial costs of investigation or inquiry.

To help judges strike the balance, the parties to trademark disputes frequently as here hire professionals in marketing or applied statistics to conduct surveys of consumers. * * *

Both parties presented studies. The defendants' was prepared by Michael Rappeport and is summarized in a perfunctory affidavit by Dr. Rappeport to which the district judge gave little weight. That was a kindness. The heart of Rappeport's study was a survey that consisted of three loaded questions asked in one Baltimore mall.

* * *

The plaintiffs' study, conducted by Jacob Jacoby, was far more substantial and the district judge found it on the whole credible. The 28-page report with its numerous appendices has all the trappings of social scientific rigor. Interviewers showed several hundred consumers in 24 malls scattered around the country shirts and hats licensed by the defendants for sale to consumers. The shirts and hats have "Baltimore CFL Colts" stamped on them. The consumers were asked whether they were football fans, whether they watched football games on television, and whether they ever bought merchandise with a team name on it. Then they were asked, with reference to the "Baltimore CFL Colts" merchandise that they were shown, such questions as whether they knew what sport the team played, what teams it played against, what league the team was in, and whether the team or league needed someone's permission to use this name, and if so whose. If, for example, the respondent answered that the team had to get permission from the Canadian Football League, the interviewer was directed to ask the respondent whether the Canadian Football League had in turn to get permission from someone. There were other questions, none however obviously loaded, and a whole other survey, the purpose of which was to control for "noise," in which another group of mallgoers was asked the identical questions about a hypothetical team unappetizingly named the "Baltimore Horses." The idea

was by comparing the answers of the two groups to see whether the source of confusion was the name "Baltimore Colts" or just the name "Baltimore," in which event the injunction would do no good since no one suggests that the new Baltimore team should be forbidden to use "Baltimore" in its name, provided the following word is not "Colts."

* * *

Jacoby's survey of consumers reactions to the "Baltimore CFL Colts" merchandise found rather astonishing levels of confusion not plausibly attributable to the presence of the name "Baltimore" alone, since "Baltimore Horses" engendered much less. * * * Among self-identified football fans, 64 percent thought that the "Baltimore CFL Colts" was either the old (NFL) Baltimore Colts or the Indianapolis Colts. But perhaps this result is not so astonishing. Although most American football fans have heard of Canadian football, many probably are unfamiliar with the acronym "CFL," and as we remarked earlier it is not a very conspicuous part of the team logo stamped on the merchandise. Among fans who watch football on television, 59 percent displayed the same confusion; and even among those who watch football on cable television, which attracts a more educated audience on average and actually carries CFL games, 58 percent were confused when shown the merchandise. Among the minority not confused about who the "Baltimore CFL Colts" are, a substantial minority, ranging from 21 to 34 percent depending on the precise sub-sample, thought the team somehow sponsored or authorized by the Indianapolis Colts or the National Football League.

* * *

But with all this granted, we cannot say that the district judge committed a clear error (the standard, *Scandia Down Corp. v. Euroquilt, Inc., supra, 772 F.2d at 1427–28*) in crediting the major findings of the Jacoby study and inferring from it and the other evidence in the record that the defendants' use of the name "Baltimore CFL Colts" whether for the team or on merchandise was likely to confuse a substantial number of consumers. This mean[s]—given the defendants' failure to raise any issue concerning the respective irreparable harms from granting or denying the preliminary injunction—that the judge's finding concerning likelihood of confusion required that the injunction issue.

* * *

The defendants make some other arguments but they do not have sufficient merit to warrant discussion. The judgment of the district court granting the preliminary injunction is AFFIRMED.

CASES ON THE SUPPLEMENTAL WEB SITE

Dallas Cowboys Football Club, Ltd. v. America's Team Properties, Inc., 616 F. Supp. 2d 622 (N.D. Tex. 2009). Focuses on how a court examines various factors in order to determine if there is a likelihood of confusion.

National Football League Properties, Inc. v. New York Football Giants, Inc., 637 F. Supp. 507 (D.N.J. 1986).Examines the league's efforts to control its collective trademark rights.

Pro Football, Inc. v. Harjo, 565 F.3d 880 (D.C. Cir. 2009). Examines the application of laches regarding allegedly disparaging team marks.

Abdul-Jabbar v. GMC, 85 F.3d 407 (9th Cir. 1996). Discusses abandonment and fair use defenses to trademark infringement claims.

Board of Supervisors v. Smack Apparel Co., 438 F. Supp. 2d 653 (E.D. La. 2006). Focuses on the application of trademark principles to nontraditional marks as well as defenses such as fair use and laches.

QUESTIONS YOU SHOULD BE ABLE TO ANSWER

1. Explain the functions of a trademark for a recreation and sport management organization.

2. What is the benefit of federally registering your organization's trademarks?

3. What must a trademark owner establish in order to show infringement by another organization?

4. If your recreation or sport management organization is accused of infringing another organization's trademarks, what defenses can you use to show that no infringement took place?

5. As a recreation or sport management organization, why would you want to provide other organization's with a license to use your trademark on their goods or services?

REFERENCES

Cases

Harjo, et al. v. Pro-Football, Inc., 50 U.S.P.Q. 1705 (1999), *rev'd, summary judgment granted in part, summary judgment denied in part*, 68 U.S.P.Q.2d 1225 (2003).
Hawaii-Pacific Apparel Group, Inc. v. Cleveland Browns Football Co. LLC, 418 F. Supp. 2d 501, 509 (S.D.N.Y. 2006).
March Madness Athletic Association, LLC v. Netfire Inc., 120 Fed. Appx.540 (5th Cir. 2005).
Ohio State University v. Thomas, 738 F. Supp. 2d 743 (S.D. Ohio 2010).
Pac-10 Conference v. Lee, WIPO Case No.D2011-0200 (2011) (Sorkin, David, Arb.).
Riddell, Inc. v. Schutt Sports, Inc., 724 F. Supp. 2d 963, 975 (W.D. Wis. 2010).
University of Alabama Board of Trustees. v. New Life Art Inc., 677 F. Supp. 2d 1238 (D. Ala. 2009).
Univesrityof Kansas v. Sinks, 565 F. Supp. 2d 1216 (D. Kan. 2008).
University of Pittsburgh v. Champion Products, Inc., 686 F.2d 1040 (3rd Cir. 1982), *cert. denied* 495 U.S. 1087 (1982).
USOC v. Tobyhanna Camp Corp., 2010 U.S. Dist. LEXIS 117650 (D. Pa. 2010).
World Wrestling Federation Entertainment, Inc. v. Big Dog Holdings, Inc., 280 F. Supp. 2d 413, 440 (D. Pa. 2003).

Publications

Frontier Econimics Ltd., London (2011, February). Estimating the global economic andsocial impacts of counterfeiting andpiracy: A report commissioned by business action to stop counterfeiting and piracy (BASCAP). Retrieved April 28, 2011, from http://www.iccwbo.org/uploadedFiles/BASCAP/Pages/Global%20Impacts%20-%20Final.pdf.
McCarthy, J. T. (1991). *McCarthy's desk encyclopedia of intellectual property*. Washington, DC: BNA Books.

Legislation

The Anti-cybersquatting Consumer Protection Act, 15 U.S.C. § 1125(d) (2012).
The Federal Trademark Act, 15 U.S.C. §§ 1051–1127 (2012).
The Federal Trademark Dilution Act, 15 U.S.C. § 1125(c) (2012).
The Federal Trademark Dilution Revision Act, 15 U.S.C. § 1051 (2012).
Ted Stevens Olympic and Amateur Sports Act, 36 U.S.C. §§ 220501–220529 (2012).

7.23 IMAGE RIGHTS
John T. Wolohan | Syracuse University

The image rights of athletes and other celebrities, if properly managed, can be worth millions of dollars. In fact, for most high profile athletes, endorsing products or lending their name to them has become more lucrative then their professional playing contracts. A good example of the value of an athlete's image is Tiger Woods. In 2009, Tiger Woods earned roughly $100 million more annually in endorsement income, than he did on the golf course. That all changed, however, on November 27, 2009, when Woods crashed his car crash outside his home. Following the crash, a series of news reports linking Woods to numerous extra material affairs came to light. Woods wife eventually divorced him and his public image as a family man was damaged forever. As a result, several sponsors, including Tag Heuer, Accenture, AT&T, Gatorade, Gillette, and *Golf Digest*, valued at around $35 million either stopped featuring him or dropped him outright (Spencer, 2011).

With so much money at stake, it is not surprising that athletes and other celebrities carefully protect the value of their image. The only way to truly protect the value of their image or name, however, is by controlling the use of the image. In the United States there are numerous legal foundations that are available to help athletes and other people control their image rights. However, as we will also see below, the ability to control their image is not absolute.

FUNDAMENTAL CONCEPTS

The term "image rights" has become closely associated with the right of privacy and the right of publicity. Generally, a person's image right relates to his or her name or likeness, such as photograph or other visual representation of the person. Recently, however, the courts have expanded the "traditional meaning of 'name and likeness' to include such things as nicknames, drawings, celebrity look-alikes or by including characteristics such as vocal idiosyncrasies within a more general formulation of identity" (Clay, 1994). For example, in *Motschenbacher v. R.J. Reynolds Tobacco Co.*(1974), R.J. Reynolds produced some television ads utilizing a stock color photograph depicting several racing cars on a race track. Even though the drivers in the cars were not visible in the photo, and the cars had been altered, the numbers were changed, and a spoiler was added on which the company placed their product's name, the Ninth Circuit Court of Appeals still found that the ads violated Motschenbacher's right of publicity. The Ninth Circuit Court reasoned that even though the driver's personal likeness was unrecognizable, his identity could still be inferred by the distinctive decorations on his car (*Motschenbacher v. R.J. Reynolds Tobacco Co.*, 1974).As a way of introducing "image rights,"this chapter examines the legal theories behind image rights and the federal image right protections provided for under trademark and copyright law, as well as the First Amendment to the United States Constitution.

Right of Privacy

"Instantaneous photographs and newspaper enterprise have invaded the sacred precincts of private and domestic life; and numerous mechanical devices threaten to make good the prediction that what is whispered in the closet shall be proclaimed from the roof-tops. For years there has been a feeling that the law must afford some remedy for the unauthorized circulation of portraits of private persons; and the evil of the invasion of privacy by newspapers" (Warren and Brandeis, 1890).

These words are as true today as they were in 1890 when they were first published by Samuel Warren and Louis Brandeis in their article entitled "The Right of Privacy." In the article, Warren and Brandeis argued that the courts should recognize a right of privacy as a way to protect private individuals against the outrageous and unjustifiable infliction of mental distress caused by the press and advertisers. Warren and Brandeis called the new legal theory "the right to privacy" and argued that it should "extend protection to the personal appearance, sayings, acts, and to personal relations, domestic or otherwise"(Warren and Brandeis, 1890).

Not every court was willing to accept Warren and Brandeis' the new theory however. In 1902, the Court of Appeals of New York in *Roberson v. Rochester Folding Box Company* (1902) held that a young woman, whose picture had been used on flour advertisement without her consent could not recover damages based on a violation of her right to privacy. In finding that there was no such right recognized at common law, the court concluded that the injury was of a purely mental character, not physical, and that recognizing such a right would potentially flood the courts in lawsuits. Perhaps most importantly, the court feared that due to the difficulty of determining a private from public figure, recognizing a right of privacy would restrict the First Amendment guarantees of freedom of the press.

As a result of the public storm that followed the court's decision in Roberson, the New York State Legislature responded by amending the New York State Civil Rights Law to establish a statutory right to privacy. For the first time, the new law made it illegal for a person or corporation to use for advertising purposes, or for the purposes of trade, the name, portrait or picture of any living person without having first obtained the written consent of such person (N.Y. Civ. Rights Law, § 50). In addition to making such use illegal, the law also allowed individuals to recover civil damages under tort law, including injunctive relief, compensatory damages, and, if the defendant acted knowingly, exemplary damages (N.Y. Civ. Rights Law, § 51). After New York codified the right of privacy, it was not difficult for most courts in the country to conclude that privates citizens had a legally protected right of privacy either under common law or state statutes. The issue, however, was not so clear for people in the sports and entertainment industry. Even after finding a right of privacy, the courts refused to recognize a celebrity's right of privacy. In support of this position, the court found that since college and professional athletes and celebrities had dedicated their life to the public, they had thereby waived their right of privacy. For example, in *O'Brien v. Pabst Sales Co.* (1941), David O'Brien, a famous American college football player, tried to invoke a right of privacy against a brewery after the beer company used his photograph in uniform on calendars. In rejecting O'Brien's right of privacy argument, the court held that because O'Brien was a famous football player and had completely publicized his name and his pictures he had waived his right of privacy.

The courts started extending the right of privacyto include a "Right of Publicity" in order to protect athletes and other celebrities against commercial misappropriation, and prevent the unjust enrichment of others off a celebrity's reputation. For example, in *Haelan Laboratories v. Topps Chewing Gum, (1953)* Topps, knowing of Haelan's contracts with various professional baseball players, deliberately entered into contracts with the players to use their photograph in connection with the sales of Topps' gum. Haelan's contract with the players provided the company the exclusive right to use the player's photograph in connection with the sales of its' chewing-gum. In addition, the contract also stated that the players agreed not to grant any other gum manufacturer a similar right during the terms of the contract

In rejecting Topps claim that their contracts were valid since the contract between Haelan and the player was no more than a release by the player, which give Haelan the right to use the photographs, the Second Circuit Court of Appeals held that "in addition to and independent of the right of privacy, a man has a right in the publicity value of his photograph, i.e., the right to grant the exclusive privilege of publishing his picture," and that the licensees and assignees of that right could enforce the right against infringing third parties (*Haelan Laboratories v. Topps Chewing Gum, 1953*). It is common knowledge, the court held "that many prominent persons (especially actors and ball-players), far from having their feelings bruised through public exposure of their likenesses, would feel sorely deprived if they no longer received money for authorizing advertisements" (*Haelan Laboratories v. Topps Chewing Gum, 1953*).

Right of Publicity

Since the Second Circuit Court's decision in *Haelan Laboratories v. Topps*, (1953) the right of publicity has been acknowledged in most states either by common law or statute. Although the right of publicity is not uniformly applied by all the states, most states agree with the three goals behind the right's general purpose. "First, the right to publicity recognizes the economic value of an individual's identity. Second, the publicity right is an incentive for creativity, encouraging the production of entertaining and intellectual works. Finally, the right prevents unjust enrichment of those who usurp the identity of another" (*Cardtoons v. MLBPA*, 1993).

Some States have even begun broaden the right of publicity by expanding the "traditional meaning of "name and likeness" to include such things as nicknames, drawings, celebrity look-alikes or by including characteristics such as vocal idiosyncrasies within a more general formulation of identity" (Clay, 1994). For example, in *Palmer v. Schonhorn Enterprises*, (1967) Arnold Palmer, and other well-known professional golfers, sought an injunction to prevent the use of their names and biographical information in conjunction with and as part of a game. Palmer and the other golfers claimed that the use of their names was an invasion of their privacy and an unfair exploitation and commercialization of their names and reputations. Schonhorn claimed that since the information contained in the profiles was readily obtainable public data and available to all, it should not be denied the privilege of reproducing that which is set forth in newspapers, magazine articles and other periodicals.

After acknowledging that Palmer was a celebrity who derived a substantial portion of his earnings from professional golf and the marketability of his name for endorsement purposes, the Superior Court of New Jersey held that there was little doubt that a person was entitled to relief when his name is used without his consent, either to advertise the defendant's product or to enhance the sale of an article. In particular, the court held that "the basic and underlying theory is that a person has the right to enjoy the fruits of his own industry free from unjustified interference" (*Palmer v. Schonhorn Enterprises,*1967). Therefore even though "the publication of biographical data of a well-known figure does not per se constitute an invasion of privacy, the use of that data for the purpose of capitalizing upon the name by using it in connection with a commercial project other than the dissemination of news or articles or biographies does" (*Palmer v. Schonhorn Enterprises*, 1967).

Common Law Misappropriation

In addition to the right of privacy and publicity, the courts in 28 states, including New York, California recognize a common law cause of action for the misappropriation of a person's name, photograph, and likeness for commercial purposes. In order to establish a cause of action for common law misappropriation in these situations, the courts have generally held that an individual must demonstrate four elements:

1. the defendant used the plaintiff's identity;
2. the appropriation of plaintiff's name or likeness provided the defendant some advantage, commercially or otherwise;
3. lack of consent; and
4. resulting injury (*Eastwood v. Superior Court,* 1983).

In determining whether there is a cause of action for common law misappropriation, one of the hardest questions for the court to answer is whether an individual's identity or likeness was even used. For example, in *Newcombe v. Adolf Coors*, (1998) the Ninth Circuit Court of Appeal was asked to determine whether a beer ad featuring an old time baseball game, showing a pitcher in a windup position misappropriated Newcombe's likeness. Newcombe was a former All Star and the only player in Major League Baseball history to ever win the Most Valuable Player Award, the Cy Young Award, and the Rookie of the Year Award. Even though the player's uniforms did not depict an actual team, and the background did not depict an actual stadium, the Ninth Circuit Court ruled that the player's windup was so distinctive that it made the identity of the player readily identifiable as Newcombe.

Another example of state common law and statutory misappropriation is *Dora v. Frontline Video*, (1993). Mickey Dora, a legendary figure in the surfing world, sued the producer of a surfing documentary, seeking damages for the unauthorized use of his name, voice, and likeness in the documentary. The video entitled "The Legends of Malibu" was a documentary that chronicled the events and public personalities at Malibu in the early days of surfing. The program featured footage of famous surfers, including Dora. The program also contained the audio portion of an interview of Dora, which is heard in the background as the viewer sees photographs of him. Dora never consented to the use of his name, photograph, likeness, or voice in the video. Frontline argued that Dora's consent was not required because the program was (1) a sports broadcast, (2) a news account and a publication of matters in the public interest, and (3) truthful, and therefore protected by the Constitution.

Although the Court of Appeals held that both celebrities and non-celebrities have the right to be free from the unauthorized exploitation of their names and likeness, it also noted that not every publication of someone's name or likeness give rise to an appropriation action. In this case, the Court of Appeal held that the public interest in the subject matter of the program gave rise to a constitutional protection against liability. The court also held that the use of Dora's name and likeness by Frontline in the surfing documentary was among those uses exempt from consent under California law, falling under the category of public affairs.

Statutory Protections

In addition to the common law, some states have legislatively recognized the right of publicity / misappropriation via statute. Those states include: Arizona, California, Florida, Illinois,Indiana, Kentucky, Massachusetts, Nebraska, Nevada, New York, Ohio, Oklahoma, Pennsylvania, Rhode Island, Tennessee, Texas, Utah, Virginia, Washington and Wisconsin. It is important to note that these statutes complement rather than codify the common law. The two states that have been most active in protecting the right of publicity of individuals are New York and California.

New York. New York was the first state to enact legislation protecting an individual's right of privacy. New York Civil Rights Law § 50 provides: "A person . . . or corporation that uses for advertising purposes, or for the purposes of trade, the name, portrait or picture of any living person without having first obtained the written consent of such person . . . is guilty of a misdemeanor" (New York Civil Rights Law § 50).

In addition, New York Civil Rights Law § 51 provides: "Any person whose name, portrait or picture is used within this state for advertising purposes or for the purposes of trade without the written consent first obtained . . . may maintain an equitable action . . . against the person . . . or corporation so using [his/her] name, portrait or picture, to prevent and restrain the use thereof; and may also sue and recover damages for any injuries sustained by reason of such use and if the defendant shall have knowingly used such person's name, portrait or picture in such manner as is . . . declared to be unlawful by section fifty of this article, the jury, in its discretion, may award exemplary damages" (New York Civil Rights Law § 51).

California. In 1971, California enacted California Civil Code § 3344(a) which provides that: "any person who knowingly uses another's name, voice, signature, photograph, or likeness in any manner, . . . for purposes of advertising or selling, . . . without such person's prior consent . . . shall be liable for any damages sustained by the person or persons injured as a result thereof" (California Civil Code § 3344).In the statute, California built in an exception. Subdivision (d) of section 3344 states: "[F]or purposes of this section, a use of a name, voice, . . . photograph, or likeness in connection with any news, public affairs, or sports broadcast or account, . . . shall not constitute a use for which consent is required . . ." (California Civil Code § 3344(d)).

An example of the rights available under statutory law is *Ali v. Playgirl,* (1978). In their February 1978 issue, *Playgirl* printed a portrait of a nude black man in the corner of a boxing ring. The man is unmistakably recognizable as Muhammad Ali, former heavyweight boxing champion, and is accompanied by the phrase "the Greatest." In defense of their use, *Playgirl* argued that because Ali was a public figure, he waived his right of privacy and therefore no consent was needed.

In examining Ali's rights under section 51 of the New York Civil Rights Law, the federal District Court held that it was clear that *Playgirl* used Ali's portrait or picture for the purpose of trade within the meaning of § 51 without his consent. Such use, the court held, amounted to a wrongful appropriation of the market value of Ali's likeness. As for *Playgirl*'s argument that the use was privileged, the court ruled that "the privilege of using a public figure's picture in connection with an item of news does not extend to commercialization of his personality" (*Ali v. Playgirl, Inc.*, 1978).

Another example is *John Doe, a/k/a Tony Twist, v. TCI Cablevision*. Tony Twist, a former professional hockey player in the National Hockey League, had a reputation as an enforcer on the ice. The creator of the comic book, *Spawn*, developed a villainous character in the book sharing his name. In trying to determine whether the use of a person's name and identity violated Twist's right to publicity, the Supreme Court of Missouri held that the threshold legal question is whether the use of a person's name and identity is "expressive," in which case it is fully protected, or "commercial," in which case it is generally not protected (*Doe, a/k/a Tony Twist, v. TCI Cablevision*, 2003). For instance, the court went on, "the use of a person's identity in news, entertainment, and creative works for the purpose of communicating information or expressive ideas about that person is protected "expressive" speech. On the other hand, the use of a person's identity for purely commercial purposes, like advertising goods or services or the use of a person's name or likeness on merchandise, is rarely protected (*Doe, a/k/a Tony Twist, v. TCI Cablevision*, 2003).

Intellectual Property Provisions

In addition to state law, federal law can also be an effective tool in defending a person's right of publicity. Federal law is especially important because the right of privacy is only available to individuals, and corporations and partnerships must rely on theories such as trademark law and copyright law to prevent the unauthorized commercial use of their identity.

Federal Trademark Law (The Lanham Act)

The Federal Trademark Act of 1946, also known as the Lanham Act, defines a trademark as "any word, name, symbol, or device, or any combination thereof, adopted or used by a manufacturer or merchant to identify their goods and distinguish them from those manufactured or sold by others" (15 U.S.C. §§ 1051 *et seq*). Although mainly thought of as a means for manufacturers to identify their goods and distinguish them from those manufactured or sold by others, the Lanham Act also protects consumers and competitors from a wide variety of misrepresentations of products and services in commerce, including the unauthorized use of an individual's image rights. Therefore, although narrower in scope than the right of publicity or misappropriation, the federal Trademark Act can be a powerful tool in protecting an athlete's image rights. (See also Chapter 7.22, Principles of Trademark Law).

False Endorsement Claims. Commonly referred to as "false endorsement claims," the Lanham Act bars the unauthorized commercial use of a celebrity's identity to help sell a defendant's goods or services, which is likely to cause confusion among consumers, as to the association, sponsorship, or approval of goods or services by another person (15 U.S.C. § 1125(a)). In deciding whether the unauthorized use of a celebrity's identity is going to cause confusion in the mind of consumers, the courts consider the following factors:

1. the strength of plaintiff's marks and name;
2. relatedness of the goods;
3. similarity of plaintiff's and defendant's marks;
4. evidence of actual confusion;
5. marketing channels used;
6. likely degree of purchaser care (sophistication of the defendant's audience); and
7. defendant's intent in selecting the mark (*Abdul-Jabar v. General Motors,* 1996).

Personal names are not inherently distinctive terms and can only receive trademark protection after they obtain secondary meaning. The rationale behind the requirement that names obtain secondary meaning is that a personal name is not distinctive enough to pinpoint a single source of goods or services (McCarthy, 2004). In order to obtain secondary meaning, the name or mark, must have widespread use and public recognition so that the mark primarily indicates the source of the good or service instead of the good or service itself. For example, in *Hirsch v. S.C. Johnson & Son* (1979) a case involving the use of Hirsch's nickname "Crazylegs" on a shaving gel, the Supreme Court of Wisconsin found that under Trademark law there need be no evidence of prior marketing of a product or service under the nickname Crazylegs. All that was necessary, the court ruled was that Hirsch "show that Crazylegs designated the plaintiff's vocation or occupation as a sports figure and that the use of the name on a shaving gel for women created a likelihood of confusion as a sponsorship"(*Hirsch v. S.C. Johnson & Son,* 1979).

Another example of an athlete using trademark law to prohibit the use of his name is *Abdul-Jabar v. General Motors Corp*(1996). Kareem Abdul-Jabar, who played in the NBA from 1969 to 1989, sued General Motors after they used the name Lew Alcindor in a television commercial without his consent. Born Frederick Lewis Alcindor, Abdul-Jabar used the name Lew Alcindor throughout his college and early professional career, but began using the name Kareem Abdul-Jabar in 1971, after he converted to Islam. The district court, in ruling for General Motors held that Abdul-Jabar had abandoned the name Lew Alcindor and therefore lost his right to protect the name and any other rights associated with its' use. The district court also found that the use of Alcindor's name was protected under the "fair use" doctrine.

In overturning the lower court, the Ninth Circuit Court of Appeals held that there was a genuine issue as to whether the use of Abdul-Jabar old name implied his endorsement or sponsorship. In rejecting General Motors claim that Abdul-Jabar had abandoned the name Lew Alcindor, the Ninth Circuit refused to extend the abandonment theory to cover a person's name. One's birth name, the court held, "is integral part of one's identity; it is not bestowed for commercial purposes, nor is it 'kept alive' through commercial use" (*Abdul-Jabar v. General Motors Corp*,1996). As for General Motors claim that its' use of the name Lew Alcindor was protected under the "fair use" doctrine, which protects the unauthorized use of a trademark when "the mark is used only to describe the goods or services of a party or their geographic origin" (*Abdul-Jabar v. General Motors Corp*,1996). The Ninth Circuit, citing its' decision in *New Kids on the Block v. New America Pub., Inc.,* (1992) ruled that a commercial user is entitled to the nominative fair use defense if it meets three requirements:

1. that the product or service in question must be one not readily identifiable without use of the trademark;
2. that only so much of the mark may be used as is reasonably necessary to identify the product or service; and
3. the user must do nothing that would, in conjunction with the mark, suggest sponsorship or endorsement by the trademark holder.(*New Kids on the Block v. New America Pub., Inc.,*1992)

The district court here found that GMC met the three *New Kids* requirements as a matter of law. We conclude, however, that there was a genuine issue of fact as to the third requirement, implied endorsement or sponsorship. The distinction between this case and *New Kids* is that use of celebrity endorsements in television commercials is so well established by commercial custom that many people may assume that when a celebrity's name is used in a television commercial, the celebrity endorses the product advertised. Likelihood of confusion as to endorsement is therefore a question for the jury. Had GMC limited itself to the "trivia" portion of its ad, the court held that GMC could likely defend the reference to Lew Alcindor as a nominative fair use. "But by using Alcindor's record to make a claim for its car—like the basketball star, the Olds 88 won an "award" three years in a row, and like the star, the car is a "champ" and a "first round pick"—GMC has arguably attempted to "appropriate the cachet of one product for another," if not also to "capitalize on consumer confusion"(*Abdul-Jabar v. General Motors Corp*,1996).

Federal Copyright Act

In addition to the Lanham Act, another piece of federal legislation that can be used to protect an individual's image right is the 1976 Federal Copyright Act (17 U.S.C. § 101 et seq.). The Copyright Act was enacted to protect the creators of all "original works of authorship fixed in any tangible medium of expression" (17 U.S.C. § 102). Included in the list of works that can receive copyright protection are "pictorial, graphic and . . . motion pictures and other audiovisual works" (17 U.S.C. § 102). Once created, the Act gives the owner of the copyrighted work control over how the work is reproduced and distributed.(See also Chapter 7.21, Copyright & Patent Law).

It is important to note, however, that while the Act may give the owner of the copyright exclusive control over the work, (17 U.S.C. § 110) there are some areas where copyright law and image rights clash. For example in *Downing v. Abercrombie & Fitch*, (2001) Abercrombie & Fitch purchased three surfing photos from a photographer to include in an upcoming catalog. One of the photos, taken at the 1965 Makaha International Surfing Championships, was of George Downing. After seeing the catalog, Downing sued Abercrombie & Fitch claiming that the use of the photo violated his publicity rights. Abercrombie & Fitch, however, argued that as the copyright owner, it had the exclusive right to control the reproduction and distribution of the photos. In addition, Abercrombie & Fitch argued that Downing's state law right of privacy claim was preempted by federal copyright law.

In analyzing whether federal copyright law preempts an individual's state law right of privacy claim, the court held that Downing's state law right of privacy was not preempted by the Federal Copyright Act. In support of this position, the Ninth Circuit Court held that while the photograph, as a pictorial work of authorship, was protected under the Copyright Act, Downing's name and his image, which were also used in the photo, were not. "A person's name or likeness is not a work of authorship within the meaning of 17 U.S.C. § 102. This is true notwithstanding the fact that Downing 's name and likeness is embodied in a copyrightable photograph" (*Downing v. Abercrombie & Fitch*, 2001).

Game Data & Statistics. Another issue of concern for the leagues is who owns the player statistics and game data. Under copyright law, facts and statistics are not copyrightable. However, with an estimated 30 million people in the U.S. and Canada playing fantasy sports, generating an estimated $3 billion, it is not surprising that the professional leagues and players associations would want to control the right of others to use the players' profiles and statistics. In *C.B.C. Distribution v. Major League Baseball Advanced Media*, (2007) C.B.C. sought a declaratory judgment against Major League Baseball Advanced Media to establish its right to use, without license, the names of and information about major league baseball players in connection with its fantasy baseball products. Advanced Media counter-claimed, maintaining that CBC's fantasy baseball products violated the players' rights of publicity, and that the players, through their association, had licensed those rights to Advanced Media, the interactive media and Internet company of major league baseball.

In ruling against Major League Baseball Advanced Media, the Eighth Circuit Court found that "the information used in CBC's fantasy baseball games is all readily available in the public domain, and that it would be a strange law that a person would not have a first amendment right to use information that is available to everyone" (*C.B.C. Distribution v. Major League Baseball Advanced Media,* 2007). When balanced against CBC's first amendment rights in offering its fantasy baseball products, the Eighth Circuit ruled the players' rights of publicity was not enforceable.

First Amendment Defenses

Because the intent of the First Amendment is to protect the dual freedoms of speech and the press, the courts will allow the "unauthorized use of an individual's name or likeness" when it is used for the "dissemination of ideas and information" or for other cultural purposes (McCarthy, 2004). However, if an individual's name or likeness is used for commercial purposes, the courts will not protect it. The following are some of the First Amendment defenses involving image rights.

Newsworthiness Doctrine

The newsworthiness doctrine permits the media to use the unauthorized likeness of celebrities or anyone of interest in connection with a news item about the person. The definition of "news" has been given a broad reading and includes matters of public concern and interest. One example of how the doctrine relates to athletes and their image rights is *Montana v. San Jose Mercury News,*(1995). Joe Montana sued the San Jose Mercury News newspaper for reproducing his name, photograph, and likeness in poster form and selling it to the general public without his consent. In ruling that the newspaper had the right to use Montana's image, the California Court of Appeal held that the newspaper accounts of Montana's performance in two Super Bowls and four championships constituted publication of matters in the public interest and was entitled to protection by the First Amendment of the United States Constitution. In particular, the Court of Appeal held that Montana's name and likeness appeared in the posters for the same reason they appeared on the original newspaper pages: because he was a major player in contemporaneous newsworthy sports events and therefore may be republished in another medium, without the person's written consent.

The Incidental Use Exception

The courts have recognized an incidental use exception in cases where a newspaper or magazine has used, for advertising purposes, the image or photo of an athlete or other celebrity previously printed in a story. The advertisements, the courts have held, are simply "incidental" to the original, newsworthy publication. A good example is *Joe Namath v. Sports Illustrated*, (1975). Joe Namath sued Sports Illustrated after the magazine used his photograph in advertisements promoting subscriptions without his consent. The photograph used was originally used in the magazine in conjunction with an article published by Sports Illustrated concerning the 1969 Super Bowl game. In holding that the publication and use of Namath's photo in the advertisements did not violate the law, the court held that the use of the photograph was merely incidental advertising of the magazine. In particular, the court noted that the reproduction was used to illustrate the quality and content of the magazine in which Namath had earlier been properly and fairly depicted and in no way indicated Namath's endorsement of the magazine.

Parody Defense

The First Amendment also allows for the use of parodies under certain circumstances. For example, parodies that use another person's image, when used in a traditionally noncommercial medium such as a newspaper, magazine, television program, book, or movie will likely be granted First Amendment protection. Parodies used in a commercial context, however, will generally not receive First Amendment protection. An example of the parody defense is *Cardtoons, L.C. v. Major League Baseball Players Association*, (1993). Cardtoons, a trading card company, designed "parody" trading cards of active major league baseball players. Cardtoons did not obtain either a license or consent from Major League Baseball Players Association (MLBPA). In ruling for MLBPA, the court stated that the primary purpose behind Cardtoons' parody was commercial. Commercial speech, the Court held, does not receive the same type of Constitutional protection. First Amendment rights end, the court held when Cardtoons preys on the MLBPA's names and likenesses for purely commercial purposes.

Transformative Use Defense

If the challenged work contains significant transformative elements or if the value of the work does not derive primarily from the celebrity's fame, the courts will allow the use under the transformative use defense. The defense "poses what is essentially a balancing test between the First Amendment and the right of publicity" (*Keller v. Electronic Arts*, 2010). To determine whether a work is transformative, the court must first inquire into whether the athlete's likeness is one of the "raw materials" from which an original work is synthesized, or whether the depiction or imitation of the athlete is the very sum and substance of the work in question (*Keller v. Electronic Arts*, 2010). If the court believes that distinctions exist, the First Amendment would bar a right of publicity claims based on appropriation of the plaintiff's identity or likeness; if not, the claims are not barred.

An example of the transformative use defense is *Keller v. Electronic Art*, (2010). Sam Keller a former starting quarterback for the Arizona State University and University of Nebraska football teams sued Electronic Arts, Inc. (EA), the NCAA and the Collegiate Licensing Company (CLC) over the use of his image in EA's video game "NCAA Football"(*Keller v. Electronic Arts*, 2010). Keller alleged that, to make the games realistic, EA designs the virtual football players to resemble their real-life counterparts: they share the same jersey numbers, have similar physical characteristics and come from the same home state. Although EA omits the real-life athletes' names from "NCAA Football," Keller filed suit against EA claiming that its use of his likeness without his consent was in violation of California's statutory and common law rights of publicity.

EA asserted that Keller's right of publicity claim was barred by the First Amendment Transformative Use Defense. In rejecting EA's defense, the court held that EA's depiction of Keller in "NCAA Football" was not sufficiently transformative to bar his California right of publicity claims as a matter of law(*Keller v. Electronic Arts*, 2010). In support of this conclusion, the court noted that in the game, the quarterback for Arizona State University shares many of Keller's characteristics. Further, the game's setting is identical to where the public found Keller during his collegiate career: on the football field. As for EA's assertion that the video game, taken as a whole, contains transformative elements. The court held that such a broad view was not supported by precedent.

At the time this chapter went to press the Keller case was being appealed and was consolidated with a number of other lawsuits involving current and past college athletes against the NCAA and EA in RE: Student-Athlete Name & Likeness Litigation, 763 F. Supp. 2d 1379 (2011).

SIGNIFICANT CASE

Although not a sport case, the Ninth Circuit Court's decision in Vanna White v. Samsung Electronics is important nonetheless because of its expansion of the traditional meaning of "name or likeness" under the Right of Publicity.

VANNA WHITE V. SAMSUNG ELECTRONICS AMERICA
United States Court of Appeals for the Ninth Circuit
971 F.2d 1395 (1992)

Plaintiff Vanna White is the hostess of "Wheel of Fortune," one of the most popular game shows in television history. An estimated forty million people watch the program daily. Capitalizing on the fame which her participation in the show has bestowed on her, White markets her identity to various advertisers.

The dispute in this case arose out of a series of advertisements prepared for Samsung by Deutsch. The series ran in at least half a dozen publications with widespread, and in some cases national, circulation. Each of the advertisements in the series followed the same theme. Each depicted a current item from popular culture and a Samsung electronic product. Each was set in the twenty-first century and conveyed the message that the Samsung product would still be in use by that time. By hypothesizing outrageous future outcomes for the cultural items, the ads created humorous effects. For example, one lampooned current popular notions of an unhealthy diet by depicting a raw steak with the caption: "Revealed to be health food. 2010 A.D." Another depicted irreverent "news"-show host Morton Downey Jr. in front of an American flag with the caption: "Presidential candidate. 2008 A.D."

The advertisement which prompted the current dispute was for Samsung video-cassette recorders (VCRs). The ad depicted a robot, dressed in a wig, gown, and jewelry which Deutsch consciously selected to resemble White's hair and dress. The robot was posed next to a game board which is instantly recognizable as the Wheel of Fortune game show set, in a stance for which White is famous. The caption of the ad read: "Longest-running game show. 2012 A.D." Defendants referred to the ad as the "Vanna White" ad. Unlike the other celebrities used in the campaign, White neither consented to the ads nor was she paid.

Following the circulation of the robot ad, White sued Samsung and Deutsch in federal district court under: (1) California Civil Code § 3344; (2) the California common law right of publicity; and (3) § 43(a) of the Lanham Act, 15 U.S.C. § 1125(a). The district court granted summary judgment against White on each of her claims. White now appeals.

I. Section 3344

White first argues that the district court erred in rejecting her claim under section 3344. Section 3344(a) provides, in pertinent part, that "any person who knowingly uses another's name, voice, signature, photograph, or likeness, in any manner,. . . for purposes of advertising or selling,. . . without such person's prior consent . . . shall be liable for any damages sustained by the person or persons injured as a result thereof."

White argues that the Samsung advertisement used her "likeness" in contravention of section 3344. In *Midler v. Ford Motor Co.*, 849 F.2d 460 (9th Cir. 1988), this court rejected Bette Midler's section 3344 claim concerning a Ford television commercial in which a Midler "sound-alike"

sang a song which Midler had made famous. In rejecting Midler's claim, this court noted that "the defendants did not use Midler's name or anything else whose use is prohibited by the statute. The voice they used was [another person's], not hers. The term 'likeness' refers to a visual image not a vocal imitation." *Id.* at 463.

In this case, Samsung and Deutsch used a robot with mechanical features, and not, for example, a manikin molded to White's precise features. Without deciding for all purposes when a caricature or impressionistic resemblance might become a "likeness," we agree with the district court that the robot at issue here was not White's "likeness" within the meaning of section 3344. Accordingly, we affirm the court's dismissal of White's section 3344 claim.

II. Right of Publicity

White next argues that the district court erred in granting summary judgment to defendants on White's common law right of publicity claim. In *Eastwood v. Superior Court*, 149 Cal. App. 3d 409, 198 Cal. Rptr. 342 (1983), the California court of appeal stated that the common law right of publicity cause of action "may be pleaded by alleging (1) the defendant's use of the plaintiff 's identity; (2) the appropriation of plaintiff 's name or likeness to defendant's advantage, commercially or otherwise; (3) lack of consent; and (4) resulting injury." *Id.* at 417 (citing Prosser, Law of Torts (4th ed. 1971) § 117, pp. 804–807). The district court dismissed White's claim for failure to satisfy Eastwood's second prong, reasoning that defendants had not appropriated White's "name or likeness" with their robot ad. We agree that the robot ad did not make use of White's name or likeness. However, the common law right of publicity is not so confined.

The Eastwood court did not hold that the right of publicity cause of action could be pleaded only by alleging an appropriation of name or likeness. Eastwood involved an unauthorized use of photographs of Clint Eastwood and of his name. Accordingly, the Eastwood court had no occasion to consider the extent beyond the use of name or likeness to which the right of publicity reaches. That court held only that the right of publicity cause of action "may be" pleaded by alleging appropriation of name or likeness, not that the action may be pleaded only in those terms.

The "name or likeness" formulation referred to in Eastwood originated not as an element of the right of publicity cause of action, but as a description of the types of cases in which the cause of action had been recognized. The source of this formulation is Prosser, Privacy, 48 Cal.L.Rev. 383, 401–07 (1960), one of the earliest and most enduring articulations of the common law right of publicity cause of action. In looking at the case law to that point, Prosser recognized that right of publicity cases involved one of two basic factual scenarios: name appropriation, and picture or other likeness appropriation. *Id.* at 401-02, nn.156–57.

Even though Prosser focused on appropriations of name or likeness in discussing the right of publicity, he noted that "it is not impossible that there might be appropriation of the plaintiff 's identity, as by impersonation, without the use of either his name or his likeness, and that this would be an invasion of his right of privacy." *Id.* At 401, n.155. n1 At the time Prosser wrote, he noted however, that "no such case appears to have arisen." *Id.*

Since Prosser's early formulation, the case law has borne out his insight that the right of publicity is not limited to the appropriation of name or likeness. In *Motschenbacher v. R.J. Reynolds Tobacco Co.*, 498 F.2d 821 (9th Cir. 1974), the defendant had used a photograph of the plaintiff 's race car in a television commercial. Although the plaintiff appeared driving the car in the photograph, his features were not visible. Even though the defendant had not appropriated the plaintiff 's name or likeness, this court held that plaintiff 's California right of publicity claim should reach the jury.

In Midler, this court held that, even though the defendants had not used Midler's name or likeness, Midler had stated a claim for violation of her California common law right of publicity because "the defendants . . . for their own profit in selling their product did appropriate part of her identity" by using a Midler sound-alike. *Id.* at 463–64.

In *Carson v. Here's Johnny Portable Toilets, Inc.*, 698 F.2d 831 (6th Cir. 1983), the defendant had marketed portable toilets under the brand name "Here's Johnny"—Johnny Carson's signature "Tonight Show" introduction—without Carson's permission. The district court had dismissed Carson's Michigan common law right of publicity claim because the defendants had not used Carson's "name or likeness." *Id.* at 835. In reversing the district court, the sixth circuit found "the district court's conception of the right of publicity . . . too narrow" and held that the right was implicated because the defendant had appropriated Carson's identity by using, inter alia, the phrase "Here's Johnny." *Id.* at 835–37.

These cases teach not only that the common law right of publicity reaches means of appropriation other than name or likeness, but that the specific means of appropriation are relevant only for determining whether the defendant has in fact appropriated the plaintiff 's identity. The right of publicity does not require that appropriations of identity be accomplished through particular means to be actionable. It is noteworthy that the Midler and Carson defendants not only avoided using the plaintiff 's name or likeness, but they also avoided appropriating the celebrity's voice, signature, and photograph. The photograph in Motschenbacher did include the plaintiff, but because the plaintiff was not visible the driver could have been an actor or dummy and the analysis in the case would have been the same.

Although the defendants in these cases avoided the most obvious means of appropriating the plaintiffs' identities, each of their actions directly implicated the commercial interests which the right of publicity is designed to protect. As the Carson court explained:

the right of publicity has developed to protect the commercial interest of celebrities in their identities. The theory of the right is that a celebrity's identity can be valuable in the promotion of products, and the celebrity has an interest that may be protected from the unauthorized commercial exploitation of that identity. . . . If the celebrity's identity is commercially exploited, there has been an invasion of his right whether or not his "name or likeness" is used. Carson, 698 F.2d at 835.

It is not important how the defendant has appropriated the plaintiff 's identity, but whether the defendant has done so. Motschenbacher, Midler, and Carson teach the impossibility of treating the right of publicity as guarding only against a laundry list of specific means of appropriating identity. A rule which says that the right of publicity can be infringed only through the use of nine different methods of appropriating identity merely challenges the clever advertising strategist to come up with the tenth.

Indeed, if we treated the means of appropriation as dispositive in our analysis of the right of publicity, we would not only weaken the right but effectively eviscerate it. The right would fail to protect those plaintiffs most in need of its protection. Advertisers use celebrities to promote their products. The more popular the celebrity, the greater the number of people who recognize her, and the greater the visibility for the product. The identities of the most popular celebrities are not only the most attractive for advertisers, but also the easiest to evoke without resorting to obvious means such as name, likeness, or voice.

Consider a hypothetical advertisement which depicts a mechanical robot with male features, an AfricanAmerican complexion, and a bald head. The robot is wearing black hightop Air Jordan basketball sneakers, and a red basketball uniform with black trim, baggy shorts, and the number 23 (though not revealing "Bulls" or "Jordan" lettering). The ad depicts the robot dunking a basketball one-handed, stiff-armed, legs extended like open scissors, and tongue hanging out. Now envision that this ad is run on television during professional basketball games. Considered individually, the robot's physical attributes, its dress, and its stance tell us little. Taken together, they lead to the only conclusion that any sports viewer who has registered a discernible pulse in the past five years would reach: the ad is about Michael Jordan.

Viewed separately, the individual aspects of the advertisement in the present case say little. Viewed together, they leave little doubt about the celebrity the ad is meant to depict. The female-shaped robot is wearing a long gown, blond wig, and large jewelry. Vanna White dresses exactly like this at times, but so do many other women. The robot is in the process of turning a block letter on a game-board. Vanna White dresses like this while turning letters on a game-board but perhaps similarly attired Scrabble-playing women do this as well. The robot is standing on what looks to be the Wheel of Fortune game show set. Vanna White dresses like this, turns letters, and does this on the Wheel of Fortune game show. She is the only one. Indeed, defendants themselves referred to their ad as the "Vanna White" ad. We are not surprised.

Television and other media create marketable celebrity identity value. Considerable energy and ingenuity are expended by those who have achieved celebrity value to exploit it for profit. The law protects the celebrity's sole right to exploit this value whether the celebrity has achieved her fame out of rare ability, dumb luck, or a combination thereof. We decline Samsung and Deutch's invitation to permit the evisceration of the common law right of publicity through means as facile as those in this case. Because White has alleged facts showing that Samsung and Deutsch had appropriated her identity, the district court erred by rejecting, on summary judgment, White's common law right of publicity claim.

III. The Lanham Act

White's final argument is that the district court erred in denying her claim under § 43(a) of the Lanham Act, 15 U.S.C. § 1125(a). The version of section 43(a) applicable to this case provides, in pertinent part, that "any person who shall . . . use, in connection with any goods or services . . . any false description or representation . . . shall be liable to a civil action . . . by any person who believes that he is or is likely to be damaged by the use of any such false description or designation." 15 U.S.C. § 1125(a).

To prevail on her Lanham Act claim, White is required to show that in running the robot ad, Samsung and Deutsch created a likelihood of confusion over whether White was endorsing Samsung's VCRs.

This circuit recognizes several different multi-factor tests for determining whether a likelihood of confusion exists. None of these tests is correct to the exclusion of the others. Normally, in reviewing the district court's decision, this court will look to the particular test that the district court used. However, because the district court in this case apparently did not use any of the multi-factor tests in making its likelihood of confusion determination, and because this case involves an appeal from summary judgment and we review de novo the district court's determination, we will look for guidance to the 8-factor test enunciated in *AMF, Inc. v. Sleekcraft Boats*, 599 F.2d 341 (9th Cir. 1979). According to AMF, factors relevant to a likelihood of confusion include:

1. strength of the plaintiff 's mark;
2. relatedness of the goods;
3. similarity of the marks;
4. evidence of actual confusion;
5. marketing channels used;
6. likely degree of purchaser care;
7. defendant's intent in selecting the mark;
8. likelihood of expansion of the product lines.

We turn now to consider White's claim in light of each factor.

In cases involving confusion over endorsement by a celebrity plaintiff, "mark" means the celebrity's persona. The "strength" of the mark refers to the level of recognition the celebrity enjoys among members of society. If Vanna White is unknown to the segment of the public at whom Samsung's robot ad was directed, then that segment could not be confused as to whether she was endorsing Samsung VCRs. Conversely, if White is well-known, this would allow the possibility of a likelihood of confusion. For the purposes of the Sleekcraft test, White's "mark," or celebrity identity, is strong.

In cases concerning confusion over celebrity endorsement, the plaintiff 's "goods" concern the reasons for or source of the plaintiff 's fame. Because White's fame is based on her televised performances, her "goods" are closely related to Samsung's VCRs. Indeed, the ad itself reinforced the relationship by informing its readers that they would be taping the "longest-running game show" on Samsung's VCRs well into the future.

The third factor, "similarity of the marks," both supports and contradicts a finding of likelihood of confusion. On the one hand, all of the aspects of the robot ad identify White; on the other, the figure is quite clearly a robot, not a human. This ambiguity means that we must look to the other factors for resolution.

The fourth factor does not favor White's claim because she has presented no evidence of actual confusion.

Fifth, however, White has appeared in the same stance as the robot from the ad in numerous magazines, including the covers of some. Magazines were used as the marketing channels for the robot ad. This factor cuts toward a likelihood of confusion.

Sixth, consumers are not likely to be particularly careful in determining who endorses VCRs, making confusion as to their endorsement more likely.

Concerning the seventh factor, "defendant's intent," the district court found that, in running the robot ad, the defendants had intended a spoof of the "Wheel of Fortune." The relevant question is whether the defendants "intended to profit by confusing consumers" concerning the endorsement of Samsung VCRs. Toho, 645 F.2d 788 (9th Cir. 1981). We do not disagree that defendants intended to spoof Vanna White and "Wheel of Fortune." That does not preclude, however, the possibility that defendants also intended to confuse consumers regarding endorsement. The robot ad was one of a series of ads run by defendants which followed the same theme. Another ad in the series depicted Morton Downey Jr. as a presidential candidate in the year 2008. Doubtless, defendants intended to spoof presidential elections and Mr. Downey through this ad. Consumers, however, would likely believe, and would be correct in so believing, that Mr. Downey was paid for his permission and was endorsing Samsung products. Looking at the series of advertisements as a whole, a jury could reasonably conclude that beneath the surface humor of the series lay an intent to persuade consumers that celebrity Vanna White, like celebrity Downey, was endorsing Samsung products.

Finally, the eighth factor, "likelihood of expansion of the product lines," does not appear apposite to a celebrity endorsement case such as this.

Application of the Sleekcraft factors to this case indicates that the district court erred in rejecting White's Lanham Act claim at the summary judgment stage. In so concluding, we emphasize two facts, however. First, construing the motion papers in White's favor, as we must, we hold only that White has raised a genuine issue of material fact concerning a likelihood of confusion as to her endorsement. *Cohen v. Paramount Pictures Corp.*, 845 F.2d 851, 852–53 (9th Cir. 1989). Whether White's Lanham Act claim should succeed is a matter for the jury. Second, we stress that we reach this conclusion in light of the peculiar facts of this case. In particular, we note that the robot ad identifies White and was part of a series of ads in which other celebrities participated and were paid for their endorsement of Samsung's products.

IV. The Parody Defense

In defense, defendants cite a number of cases for the proposition that their robot ad constituted protected speech. The only cases they cite which are even remotely relevant to this case are *Hustler Magazine v. Falwell*, 485 U.S. 46, 99 L. Ed. 2d 41, 108 S. Ct. 876 (1988) and *L.L. Bean, Inc. v. Drake Publishers, Inc.*, 811 F.2d 26 (1st Cir. 1987). Those cases involved parodies of advertisements run for the purpose of poking fun at Jerry Falwell and L.L. Bean, respectively. This case involves a true advertisement run for the purpose of selling Samsung VCRs. The ad's spoof of Vanna White and Wheel of Fortune is subservient and only tangentially related to the ad's primary message: "buy Samsung VCRs." Defendants' parody arguments are better addressed to non-commercial parodies. The difference between a "parody" and a "knock-off" is the difference between fun and profit.

V. Conclusion

In remanding this case, we hold only that White has pleaded claims which can go to the jury for its decision.

CASES ON THE SUPPLEMENTAL WEB SITE

Abdul-Jabbar v. General Motors Corp., 85 F.3d 407 (9th Cir 1996). The case examines whether a person retains an interest in their birth name, when he or she adopts another name.

Cardtoons v. Major League Baseball Players Association, 95 F.3d 959 (10th Cir 1996). This case examines the parody defense under the First Amendment and whether it applies to commercial activity.

ETW Corp. v. Jireh Publishing, 332 F.3d 915 (6th Cir 2003). This case examines the fair use defense under the Lanham Act and right of publicity claims

John Doe, a/k/a Tony Twist v. TCI Cablevision, 110 S.W.3d 363 (2003). The case examines whether the use of a fictional character named "Anthony 'Tony Twist' Twistelli" in the Spawn comic book violated Tony Twist's image rights, even though the characters bear no physical resemblance to each other and, aside from the common nickname, are similar only in that each can be characterized as having an "enforcer" or tough-guy persona.

Hirsch v. S. C. Johnson & Son, Inc., 280 N.W.2d 129 (1979). This case examines the unauthorized use of the plaintiff's nickname "Crazy Legs" on a shaving gel for women and whether common law trade name infringement applies.

Namath v. Sports Illustrated, 371 N.Y.S.2d 10 (1975). The case examines whether a magazine can use a photograph, which was originally used by the magazine without objection, in advertisements promoting subscriptions to their magazine.

Newcombe v. Adolf Coors Co., 157 F.3d 686 (9th Cir. 1998). The case examines whether an image in a magazine was the plaintiff and, it so, whether it violated the plaintiff's image rights.

QUESTIONS YOU SHOULD BE ABLE TO ANSWER

1. What are some of the laws available to protect the unauthorized use of your image?

2. Historically, the right of publicity only covered the use of a person's "name or likeness"; however, the courts have now expanded the right to include what else?

3. What are some of the specific uses of a person's image that are protected?

4. What are some of the First Amendment defenses available?

5. What are some of the specific uses of a person's image that are prohibited?

REFERENCES

Cases

Abdul-Jabar v. General Motors Corp., 85 F.3d 407 (9th Cir. 1996).

Ali v. Playgirl, Inc., 447 F.Supp. 723 (1978).

Cardtoons, L.C. v. Major League Baseball Players Association, 838 F. Supp 1501 (N.D. Okla. 1993).

C.B.C. Distribution v. Major League Baseball Advanced Media, 505 F.3d 818 (8th Cir. 2007).

Dora v. Frontline Video, Inc., 15 Cal. App. 4th 536 (1993).

Downing v. Abercrombie & Fitch, 265 F.3d 994 (2001).

Eastwood v. Superior Court, 149 Cal. App. 3d 409, 198 Cal. Rptr. 342 (1983).

Haelan Laboratories, Inc. v. Topps Chewing Gum, Inc., 202 F.2d 866 (2nd. Cir. 1953).

Hirsch v. S.C. Johnson & Son, 280 N.W. 129 (Wis. 1979).

Joe Namath v. Sports Illustrated, 48 A.D.2d 487; 371 N.Y.S.2d 10 (1975).

John Doe, a/k/a Tony Twist, v. TCI Cablevision, 110 S.W.3d 363 (2003).

Keller v. Electronic Arts, 2010 U.S. Dist. LEXIS 10709 (N.D. Cal., Feb. 8, 2010).

Montana v. San Jose Mercury News, 40 Cal. Rptr. 2d 639 (1995).

Motschenbacher v. R.J. Reynolds Tobacco Co., 498 F.2d 821 (1974).

Newcombe v. Adolf Coors Co., 157 F.3d 686 (9th Cir. 1998).

New Kids on the Block v. New America Pub., Inc., 971 F.2d 302, (9th Cir. 1992).

O'Brien v. Pabst Sales Co., 124 F.2d 167 (1941).

Palmer v. Schonhorn Enterprises, 232 A.2d 458 (1967).

RE: Student-Athlete Name & Likeness Litigation, 763 F. Supp. 2d 1379 (2011).

Roberson v Rochester Folding Box Co., 171 N.Y. 538, 64 N.E. 442 (1902).

Publications

Clay, S. (1994). Starstruck: The overextension of celebrity publicity rights in state and federal courts. *Minnesota Law Review,* 79, 485–517.

McCarthy, J. T. (2004). *The rights of publicity and privacy* (3rd ed.). Deerfield IL: Clark Boardman Callaghan.

Prosser, W. (1960). Privacy. *California Law Review, 48,* 383–423.

Spencer, B. (April 4, 2011). *Bill for Pounds 82 Million Tiger's Sex Romps; Loss of Sponsors hit Earnings.* Daily Record, p. 11

Warren, S., & Brandeis, L. (1890). The right of privacy. *Harvard Law Review, 4,* 193–220.

Legislation

California Civil Code § 990.

Federal Copyright Act, 17 U.S.C. § 101 *et seq.*

The Lanham Act, 15 U.S.C. § 1051 *et seq.*

N.Y. Sess. Laws 1903, ch.132 § 1. Amended in 1921, now cited as N.Y. Civ. Rights Law, § 50.

N.Y. Sess. Laws 1903, ch.132 § 2. Amended in 1921, now cited as N.Y. Civ. Rights Law, § 51.

ANTITRUST AND LABOR LAW

7.30

7.31 ANTITRUST LAW: PROFESSIONAL SPORT APPLICATIONS

Lisa Pike Masteralexis I University of Massachusetts-Amherst

Antitrust cases have left an indelible mark on professional sport leagues' structure and labor management relations. No other industry employs such restrictive rules and policies, and thus, the professional sport industry continues to face antitrust challenges. Restraints on free agency and salary spending and restrictions on franchise ownership have exposed leagues to antitrust challenges by players, owners, prospective owners, competitor leagues, cities possessing franchises, cities seeking franchises, and media entities.

FUNDAMENTAL CONCEPTS

Antitrust Law

In 1890, Congress passed the Sherman Antitrust Act to break up business trusts and monopolies. Section 1 of the Act prohibits "every contract, combination . . . or conspiracy in restraint of trade or commerce among the several states [interstate commerce]" (15 U.S.C. §1). Under the statute violators pay three times the damage suffered. Section 2 of the Act makes it a felony, "to monopolize, attempt to monopolize, or combine or conspire . . . to monopolize" (15 U.S.C. § 2).

The Sherman Act's language is vague and thus, it's dependent on judicial interpretation, as to the Act's intent and meaning (Roberts, 1990). As a result, the Supreme Court has adopted three approaches to determine violations of Section 1 of the Act. The first is a "rule of reason" defense that recognizes some restraints are necessary business practices. To evaluate the rule of reason defense, the Court weighs the pro-competitive effects of the rule or practice against the anti-competitive effects. The defense requires an inquiry as to the necessary business practices of the industry, and the defendant must overcome the plaintiff's convictions that the defendant's conduct is unreasonable. The rule of reason is applied frequently in sport due to the numerous, and arguably, necessary rules and restrictions adopted for competitive balance among teams in a league. Such restrictions include player drafts; free agency restrictions; restraints on salary, franchise sale, ownership, and movement; franchise territorial restraints; and revenue sharing, among others, all of which can be justified as necessary for the proper operation of the leagues. Courts will, however, judge such restrictions on their reasonableness, balancing the business necessity against the degree of anticompetitive behavior of the practice.

The second approach is adopted when anticompetitive conduct is deemed **illegal per se**. *Illegal per se* activities are presumed to have no benefit to competition. Use of the *illegal per se* approach is limited and applied in two situations: when the Court is examining agreements between traditional business competitors and when the Court is seeking to avoid a lengthy inquiry into an industry's business operations (Greenberg, 1993). Application of *illegal per se* to professional sport is rare because there usually is some business justification for anti-competitive behavior.

A third approach occurs when the Court focuses on the effect a challenged practice has on consumer welfare (Roberts, 1990). This approach has yet to be applied in professional sport cases. Roberts (1990) has argued the consumer welfare standard may be very important for sport-related antitrust cases and, if applied, would likely limit a plaintiff's success as the plaintiff would be forced to demonstrate that league conduct injures consumer welfare. The success of this approach may vary, for instance, with restrictions in the player market harder to prove under this application than other aspects of the business of professional sport.

Antitrust Law Applied to Baseball

Baseball possesses a unique status in professional sport, as well as in American business, by virtue of its antitrust **exemption**. In *Federal Baseball Club of Baltimore, Inc. v. National League of Professional Baseball Clubs, et al.* (1922), the Supreme Court concluded that baseball was neither interstate nor commerce—two elements necessary for federal antitrust laws to apply. The Supreme Court considered the baseball business to be a local exhibition consisting of personal service contracts with players, rather than commerce. Further, it found the travel of players across state lines was not essential to the baseball business, but purely incidental to the game. Over time the exemption has faced attack and been amended, but, *Federal Baseball* is still controlling. In *Toolson v. New York Yankees* (1953) and *Flood v. Kuhn* (1972), cases challenging the *Federal Baseball* verdict, baseball players contended that the player reserve system violated federal antitrust laws. Under the reserve system, teams could perpetually renewed player contracts, and without a free market in which to sell their services, the players were forced to play with their teams or retire from baseball. In both cases the Supreme Court reaffirmed baseball's exemption by shifting the burden to Congress to create legislation abolishing the exemption. *Flood* also noted that baseball players could use labor relations rather than antitrust law to resolve disputes over the reserve clause (See Supplemental Web Site). Incidentally, the Major League Baseball Players Association used labor arbitration to successfully challenge the player reserve system, ultimately limiting the reserve clause to a one-year renewal favoring the club, ushering in free agency in baseball (*In Re Twelve Clubs Comprising the National League and Twelve Clubs Comprising the American League and Major League Baseball Players Association*, 1975).

In 1998, Congress codified baseball's exemption through the Curt Flood Act (15 U.S.C. § 27). This Act clarified baseball's trilogy of cases by exempting the business of baseball, but not the labor of major baseball players. The Act defines the business of baseball as: the minor leagues and minor league player reserve clause; the amateur draft; franchise expansion, location, or relocation; franchise ownership; marketing and sales of the entertainment product of baseball; and licensed properties.

Antitrust Law Applied to Other Sports

Numerous antitrust suits have been filed by players, owners and prospective owners, and competitors in other sports. *United States v. International Boxing Club* (1955) was the first successful antitrust suit in professional sport. Soon after, football became subject to antitrust law. In *Radovich v. National Football League* (1957), a professional football player challenged a rule that restricted his ability to sign a contract with a team other than the one that held his rights and that blacklisted him from signing as a player-coach with a team affiliated with the NFL. Radovich contended that the blacklist was a group boycott in restraint of trade. The trial and appellate courts dismissed Radovich's claims on the ground that football, like baseball, was exempt from antitrust law. The Supreme Court, however, reversed and held that due to the NFL's radio and television contracts, the NFL was engaged in interstate commerce and subject to the Sherman Act.

Single-Entity Status

In an attempt to gain Section 1 immunity, a number of new leagues have structured themselves as single entities with owners investing in the league rather than in teams. The leagues adopt centralized operations for business and personnel decisions. Centrally administered leagues operated by owner–investors, argue they are a single entity, providing a defense to a league sued on antitrust grounds. The single entity defense is based on a defendant's inability to contract, combine, or conspire in restraint of trade as is required of Section 1. Single-entity status for traditionally organized sports leagues has been rejected by the U.S. Supreme Court (*American Needle v. NFL*, 2010). In *American Needle v. NFL*, the Supreme Court ruled that the NFL was not a single entity because it consisted of distinct businesses with independent centers of decision making that competed and cooperated with one another. This ruling mirrored that in numerous lower court rulings when the NFL had raised the single entity defense (*Sullivan v. NFL*, 1994; *Los Angeles Mem'l Coliseum Comm'n v. NFL*, 1984; *NASL v. NFL*, 1982; *Smith v. Pro Football, Inc.*, 1978; and *Mackey v. NFL*, 1976).

However, Courts of Appeal in *Chicago Professional Sports Limited Partnership (Chicago Bulls) v. National Basketball Association* (1996), *Fraser v. Major League Soccer* (2000)(See Supplemental Web Site), and *Madison Square Garden v. National Hockey League* (2008), have been open to the use of the single entity defense. In *Chicago Bulls*, the Seventh Circuit Court of Appeals suggested the single entity defense should be applied after a case-by-case examination of the sport league activity at issue. *Chicago Bulls* instructed that an analysis be done on the sport league activity at issue on a case-by-case or practice-by-practice basis to determine if it is engaging in single entity or joint venture behavior. Under such an analysis, the court found it possible that the NBA could act as a single entity when imposing league-wide limitations on broadcasting through superstations, yet act as a joint venture when imposing restrictions on player mobility. The Seventh Circuit expressly withheld judgment as to whether the NBA was a single entity and remanded the case to district court for such a finding. The case, however, settled out of court in 1996. In *Madison Square Garden*, the Second Circuit Court of Appeals determined it could not decide if the NHL was a single entity for purposes of its new media policy at the pleading stage. The court favored an examination in line with *Chicago Bulls* that required a factual analysis as to whether new media strategy and practice could be determined centrally, such that competition was barred and individual clubs could be forced to comply with a central management system implementing a standard web page format.

In *Fraser v. Major League Soccer* (2000), the First Circuit Court of Appeals determined that Major League Soccer (MLS) was a hybrid single entity organized as a limited liability company made up of operator-investors who sacrificed local autonomy for centralized operations. MLS owns all the teams in the league, including their intellectual property rights, tickets, and broadcast rights. It sets team schedules, negotiates stadium leases and assumes related liabilities, pays the salaries of league personnel including referees, and supplies certain equipment. *Fraser* makes clear that a sports league can be organized uniquely and avoid antitrust liability provided it is a single entity from its inception, not as a result of restructuring itself to avoid antitrust liability. Although the single-entity defense will not affect the ability to sue leagues under Section 2 of the Sherman Act, it will serve as an exemption of § 1.

Antitrust Challenges by Competitor Leagues

A few Section 2 cases challenge competitor leagues over the practices of established leagues as monopolistic. Only one case, *Philadelphia World Hockey, Inc. v. Philadelphia Hockey Club, Inc.* (1972), was substantially successful for the plaintiff. The World Hockey Association successfully argued that the NHL monopolized the labor pool of talented players through the use of the reserve system. The NHL's reserve system perpetually bound players to a team. The World Hockey Association successfully argued that the system restrained their ability to acquire marquee NHL players.

The two other cases brought by upstart competitors were not as successful. In *American Football League v. National Football League* (1963), the AFL was unable to prove that the NFL, by expanding into Dallas and Minneapolis, two cities the AFL was also considering for expansion, was monopolizing the market for professional football. In *United States Football League v. National Football League* (S.D.N.Y., 1986), a jury found that the NFL had monopolized the market for football in the United States, but only awarded nominal damages.

Antitrust Challenges by Prospective Team Owners and Team Owners

Individual franchise owners have challenged league rules, on the theory that rules diminish competition. Many league rules restrict individual opportunities in favor of the good of the league. Prospective team owners have challenged league ownership restrictions that have kept them from becoming owners. The courts in *Levin v. National Basketball Association* (1974), and *Mid-South Grizzlies v. National Football League* (1983), upheld rules requiring three-fourths approval of league owners for transfer of ownership (*Levin*), and admission to the league (*Mid-South Grizzlies*). The most recent of these challenges, *Piazza v. Major League Baseball* (1993), involved potential owners prevented from purchasing and relocating the San Francisco Giants. The case settled out of court after the *Piazza* court entered a declaratory judgment that the claim should not be dismissed on the basis of baseball's antitrust exemption.

The *Los Angeles Memorial Coliseum and the Los Angeles Raiders v. National Football League*, (1984) is the most celebrated ownership challenge to a restrictive franchise policy. The Raiders' owner Al Davis successfully argued that a three-fourths vote needed to relocate into the Los Angeles market was an unreasonable restraint of trade. At the time, it was highly unusual for an owner to sue co-owners. However, a new breed of owners who have made large investments to purchase teams appear more willing to challenge league policies on antitrust grounds. This represents a major shift away from the "league-think" philosophy championed by former NFL Commissioner Pete Rozelle.

Other lawsuits filed by franchise owners involve challenges to the number of games telecast nationally on a superstation (*Chicago Professional Sports Limited Partnership v. National Basketball Association*, 1996); ownership policies, such as restrictions against public ownership and relocation (*Sullivan v. National Football League*, 1994, *VKK v. National Football League*, 1999); and marketing and revenue sharing (*Dallas Cowboys v. NFL Trust*, 1995).

Antitrust Challenges by Individual Athletes

Suspended athletes have also used antitrust to challenge league actions. In *Molinas v. National Basketball Association* (1961), a NBA player suspended for wagering on games in which he was participating, sued the league when his application for reinstatement was rejected. Molinas argued that expulsion from the league constituted a restrained trade because he had no economic alternative to playing in the NBA. In upholding the suspension, the court held that the restraint was reasonable, as the NBA had a legitimate interest in banning gambling.

Antitrust Exemption for Sport Broadcasting Contracts

In 1961, Congress exempted sports leagues' national television deals from antitrust liability (15 U.S.C. §§ 1291–1294). The statute grants professional leagues an exemption to pool their television rights when negotiating league-wide television packages.

Convergence of Labor and Antitrust Laws

In the early 1900s, employers used the Sherman Act against labor movements, claiming workers organizing boycotts or work stoppages were committing conspiracies in restraint of trade. Employers used injunctions to thwart labor activities and the threat of treble damages to chill the labor movement. In 1914, Congress enacted the Clayton Act to exempt organized labor acting in its own self-interest from antitrust liability. However, the federal courts continued to grant injunctions against labor activity. In response, Congress passed the Norris-La Guardia Act in 1932, often called the Anti-Injunction Act, because it restricted the federal judiciary's power to grant injunctions against labor unions in labor disputes (see Section 7.33, *Labor Law: Professional Sports Applications*). In *Brady v. NFL* (2011), NFL players sought an injunction preventing the league from locking the players out. In rejecting the players' request, the court held that the Norris-LaGuardia and the Clayton Acts barred the federal courts from issuing injunctions in disputes between employers and employees.

During the Term of the Collective Bargaining Agreement

Together, the Clayton and Norris-La Guardia Acts created an antitrust exemption for unions acting in their own self-interest, but did not protect union-management actions, such as entering into collective bargaining agreements (CBAs). CBAs are contracts that contain restrictive provisions and as such could be deemed "contracts, combinations or conspiracies in restraint of trade." The U.S. Supreme Court addressed this issue in a number of non-sport cases and established the non-statutory labor exemption to antitrust law (*Allen Bradley Co. v. Local Union No. 3, International Brotherhood of Electrical Workers*, 1945; *Local Union No. 189, Amalgamated Meat Cutters, and Butcher Workmen of North America, AFLCIO v. Jewel Tea*, 1965; *United Mineworkers of America v. Pennington*, 1965; and *Connell Construction v. Plumbers*, 1975). In balancing the interests of antitrust law against labor law, the court held that the goal of federal labor policy is to bring labor and management together to negotiate a CBA that best suits their needs. Congress, the court held, did not intend for antitrust laws to subvert the goal of achieving labor peace through labor-management relations. The objective of the labor exemption is to protect those mandatory subjects agreed to through good faith bargaining from antitrust scrutiny by a party to the collective agreement. It would not be fair to agree to a restrictive practice, receive concessions in exchange for the agreement, and then turn around and sue a counterpart under antitrust law over the practice (*Brown v. Pro-Football*, 1996)(see Supplemental Web Site). The Supreme Court has established that terms negotiated between labor and management in their collective agreement, which outside a collective agreement would be subject to antitrust law, are in fact exempt from antitrust scrutiny, provided the defendant meets this test:

1. The injured party is a party to the collective bargaining agreement.
2. The subject contested on antitrust grounds is a mandatory subject for bargaining (hours, wages, and other terms and conditions of employment).
3. The collective bargaining agreement was reached through bona fide arms' length bargaining.

Scope of the Labor Exemption

A number of cases address the scope of the labor exemption in the professional sport industry. The league and union are protected from antitrust suits by the labor exemption for suits brought by players not in the league when a collective bargaining agreement with restrictive policies is negotiated (*Wood v. National Basketball Association*, 1987; *Clarett v. National Football League*, 2003). At the time restrictive provisions limit a players' earning capacity, a player is then in the league and must take the burdens of collective bargaining to receive the benefits. The same holds true for suits by former players who may disagree with a union's negotiating decisions and challenge restrictive practices agreed to in negotiation (*Reynolds v. National Football League*, 1978).

Courts have examined practices such as restrictions on free agency, the draft, and salary caps as mandatory subjects. As long as the restriction affects hours, wages, or terms and conditions of employment, the courts have found the provisions to be mandatory subjects of collective bargaining. For example, in *Mackey v. National Football League* (1976), the court found that although the Rozelle Rule, a restriction on free agency that required teams signing free agents to pay compensation to the player's former team, did not directly deal with hours, wages, and terms and conditions of employment, its effect was to depress player salaries (wages), and thus it was deemed a mandatory subject.

Mackey v. National Football League (1976), and *McCourt v. California Sports, Inc.* (1979) highlight the concept of arms length bargaining. In *Mackey*, a number of former and current football players challenged the Rozelle Rule, while owners argued that the labor exemption applied. The court disagreed, finding that there was no bona fide arms length bargaining because the Rozelle Rule remained unchanged from the time it was unilaterally implemented in 1963. Further, there was no evidence that players agreed to the Rozelle Rule as a *quid pro quo* for better pension benefits and the right to individually negotiate their salaries (as was argued by the NFL's defense). In fact, the *Mackey* Court found that there was no direct bargaining on the Rozelle Rule. Contrast *Mackey* with *McCourt*, where the NHL's By-Law 9A, a similar free agent compensation structure, was subject to antitrust attack by Dale McCourt, a player named as compensation. The court found that the labor exemption protected the NHL because the players' association had bargained vigorously against By-Law 9A. The court stated that player benefits were bargained for in connection with the reserve system remaining unchanged, and the inclusion of the free agent compensation clause was not the result of collusion, but of good-faith bargaining.

Duration of the Labor Exemption

The labor exemption continues to protect parties from antitrust scrutiny even after a collective bargaining agreement (CBA) has expired. Collective bargaining agreement provisions survive its expiration because labor law requires parties to maintain the status quo and continue bargaining for a new agreement until impasse. Impasse occurs when there is a total breakdown in negotiations between union and management and often leads to a strike or a lockout. Like the subjects of the CBA, the labor exemption survives the agreement's expiration provided the parties maintain the status quo. If this were not the case, the players' association may have no incentive to bargain and may opt to drag its feet in negotiations until the expiration of the agreement to seek treble damages through an antitrust suit, thereby increasing its leverage in labor negotiations. The duty to maintain the status quo only extends to impasse, and once an employer has bargained in good faith to impasse, they may unilaterally impose changes to the mandatory bargaining subjects without incurring antitrust liability, provided those changes are consistent with the latest proposals made to the union prior to impasse. In *Powell v. NFL* (1989), the court ruled that the labor exemption does not end with impasse and the players association cannot challenge the league on antitrust grounds provided a collective bargaining relationship exists. That result led the players to decertify and forms the basis for the most recent NFLPA and NBPA actions to vote to disclaim or decertify the union in 2011.

In this case, a corporation that designed, manufactured and sold headwear carrying trademarked names and logos of NFL teams brought an antitrust suit against the NFL, its teams, and the competitor, Reebok, that had received exclusive licensing agreement for trademarked headwear and apparel. The case examines whether the NFL's actions are exempt from antitrust scrutiny under the single entity defense.

AMERICAN NEEDLE INC. V. NATIONAL FOOTBALL LEAGUE

United States Supreme Court
130 S.Ct. 2201(2010)
Justice STEVENS delivered the opinion of the Court.

"Every contract, combination in the form of a trust or otherwise, or, conspiracy, in restraint of trade" is made illegal by § 1 of the Sherman Act, as amended, 15 U.S.C. § 1. The question whether an arrangement is a contract, combination, or conspiracy is different from and antecedent to the question whether it unreasonably restrains trade. This case raises that antecedent question about the business of the 32 teams in the National Football League (NFL) and a corporate entity that they formed to manage their intellectual property. We conclude that the NFL's licensing activities constitute concerted action that is not categorically beyond the coverage of § 1. The legality of that concerted action must be judged under the Rule of Reason.

I

Originally organized in 1920, the NFL is an unincorporated association that now includes 32 separately owned professional football teams. Each team has its own name, colors, and logo, and owns related intellectual property. Like each of the other teams in the league, the New Orleans Saints and the Indianapolis Colts, for example, have their own distinctive names, colors, and marks that are well known to millions of sports fans.

Prior to 1963, the teams made their own arrangements for licensing their intellectual property and marketing trademarked items such as caps and jerseys. In 1963, the teams formed National Football League Properties (NFLP) to develop, license, and market their intellectual property. Most, but not all, of the substantial revenues generated by NFLP have either been given to charity or shared equally among the teams. However, the teams are able to and have at times sought to withdraw from this arrangement.

Between 1963 and 2000, NFLP granted nonexclusive licenses to a number of vendors, permitting them to manufacture and sell apparel bearing team insignias.

American Needle, Inc., was one of those licensees. In December 2000, the teams voted to authorize NFLP to grant exclusive licenses, and NFLP granted Reebok International Ltd. an exclusive 10–year license to manufacture and sell trademarked headwear for all 32 teams. It thereafter declined to renew American Needle's nonexclusive license.

American Needle filed this action in the Northern District of Illinois, alleging that the agreements between the NFL, its teams, NFLP, and Reebok violated §§ 1 and 2 of the Sherman Act. In their answer to the complaint, the defendants averred that the teams, NFL, and NFLP were incapable of conspiring within the meaning of § 1 "because they are a single economic enterprise, at least with respect to the conduct challenged." App. 99. After limited discovery, the District Court granted summary judgment on the question "whether, with regard to the facet of their operations respecting exploitation of intellectual property rights, the NFL and its 32 teams are, in the jargon of antitrust law, acting as a single entity." *American Needle, Inc. v. New Orleans La. Saints*, 496 F.Supp.2d 941, 943 (2007). The court concluded "that in that facet of their operations they have so integrated their operations that they should be deemed a single entity rather than joint ventures cooperating for a common purpose." *Ibid.*

The Court of Appeals for the Seventh Circuit affirmed. The panel observed that "in some contexts, a league seems more aptly described as a single entity immune from antitrust scrutiny, while in others a league appears to be a joint venture between independently owned teams that is subject to review under § 1." 538 F.3d, 736, 741 (2008). Relying on Circuit precedent, the court limited its inquiry to the particular conduct at issue, licensing of teams' intellectual property. The panel agreed with petitioner that "when making a single-entity determination, courts must examine whether the conduct in question deprives the marketplace of the independent sources of economic control that competition assumes." *Id*., at 742. The court, however, discounted the significance of potential competition among the teams regarding the use of their intellectual property because the teams "can function only as one source of economic power when collectively producing NFL football." *Id*., at 743. The court noted that football itself can only be carried out jointly. See *ibid*. Moreover, "NFL teams share a vital economic interest in collectively promoting NFL football . . . [to] compet[e] with other forms of entertainment." *Ibid*. "It thus follows," the court found, "that only one source of economic power controls the promotion of NFL football," and "it makes little sense to assert that each individual team has the authority, if not the responsibility, to promote the jointly produced NFL football." *Ibid*. Recognizing that NFL teams have "license[d] their intellectual property collectively" since 1963, the court held that § 1 did not apply. Id., at 744.

We granted certiorari.

II

As the case comes to us, we have only a narrow issue to decide: whether the NFL respondents are capable of engaging in a "contract, combination . . ., or conspiracy" as defined by § 1 of the Sherman Act, 15 U.S.C. § 1, or, as we have sometimes phrased it, whether the alleged activity by the NFL respondents "must be viewed as that of a single enterprise for purposes of § 1." *Copperweld Corp. v. Independence Tube Corp.*, 467 U.S. 752, 771 (1984).

Taken literally, the applicability of § 1 to "every contract, combination . . . or conspiracy" could be understood to cover every conceivable agreement, whether it be a group of competing firms fixing prices or a single firm's chief executive telling her subordinate how to price their company's product.

The meaning of the term "contract, combination . . . or conspiracy" is informed by the " 'basic distinction' " in the Sherman Act " 'between concerted and independent action' " that distinguishes § 1 of the Sherman Act from § 2 *Copperweld*, 467 U.S., at 767. Section 1 applies only to concerted action that restrains trade. Section 2, by contrast, covers both concerted and independent action, but only if that action "monopolize[s]," 15 U.S.C. § 2, or "threatens actual monopolization," *Copperweld*, 467 U.S., at 767 a category that is narrower than restraint of trade. Monopoly power may be equally harmful whether it is the product of joint action or individual action.

Congress used this distinction between concerted and independent action to deter anticompetitive conduct and compensate its victims, without chilling vigorous competition through ordinary business operations. The distinction also avoids judicial scrutiny of routine, internal business decisions.

***

III

We have long held that concerted action under § 1 does not turn simply on whether the parties involved are legally distinct entities. Instead, we have eschewed such formalistic distinctions in favor of a functional consideration of how the parties involved in the alleged anticompetitive conduct actually operate.

As a result, we have repeatedly found instances in which members of a legally single entity violated § 1 when the entity was controlled by a group of competitors and served, in essence, as a vehicle for ongoing concerted activity. . . . We have similarly looked past the form of a legally "single entity" when competitors were part of professional organizations or trade groups. [footnotes and citations omitted].

Conversely, there is not necessarily concerted action simply because more than one legally distinct entity is involved. . . .

The roots of this functional analysis can be found in the very decision that established the intraenterprise conspiracy doctrine. In *United States v. Yellow Cab Co.*, 332 U.S. 218 (1947), we observed that "corporate interrelationships . . . are not determinitive of the applicability of the Sherman Act" because the Act "is aimed at substance rather than form." *Id*., at 227. We nonetheless held that cooperation between legally separate entities was necessarily covered by § 1 because an unreasonable restraint of trade "may result as readily from a conspiracy among those who are affiliated or integrated under common ownership as from a conspiracy among those who are otherwise independent. "*Ibid*.

***

We finally reexamined the intraenterprise conspiracy doctrine in *Copperweld Corp. v. Independence Tube Corp.*, 467 U.S. 752 (1984), and concluded that it was inconsistent with the " 'basic distinction between concerted and independent action.' " *Id*., at 767. Considering it "perfectly plain that an internal agreement to implement a single, unitary firm's policies does not raise the antitrust dangers that § 1 was designed to police," *id*., at 769, we held that a parent corporation and its wholly owned subsidiary "are incapable of conspiring with each other for purposes of § 1 of the Sherman Act," *id*., at 777. We explained that although a parent corporation and its wholly owned subsidiary are "separate" for the purposes of incorporation or formal title, they are controlled by a single center of decisionmaking and they control a single aggregation of economic power. Joint conduct by two such entities does not "depriv[e] the marketplace of independent centers of decisionmaking," *id*., at 769, and as a result, an agreement between them does not constitute a "contract, combination . . . or conspiracy" for the purposes of § 1. . . . [footnotes and citations omitted].

As *Copperweld* exemplifies, "substance, not form, should determine whether a[n] . . . entity is capable of conspiring under § 1." 467 U.S., at 773, n. 21. This inquiry is sometimes described as asking whether the alleged conspirators are a single entity. That is perhaps a misdescription, however, because the question is not whether the defendant is a legally single entity or has a single name; nor is the question whether the parties involved "seem" like one firm or multiple firms in any metaphysical sense. The key is whether the alleged "contract, combination . . ., or conspiracy" is concerted action—that is, whether it joins together separate decisionmakers. The relevant inquiry, therefore, is whether there is a "contract, combination . . . or conspiracy" amongst "separate economic actors pursuing separate economic interests," *id.*, at 769, such that the agreement "deprives the marketplace of independent centers of decision making," *ibid.*, and therefore of "diversity of entrepreneurial interests, *"Fraser v. Major League Soccer, L.L. C.,* 284 F.3d 47, 57 (C.A.1 2002), and thus of actual or potential competition, *see Freeman v. San Diego Assn. of Realtors,* 322 F.3d 1133, 1148–1149 (C.A.9 2003) . . .

Thus, while the president and a vice president of a firm could (and regularly do) act in combination, their joint action generally is not the sort of "combination" that § 1 is intended to cover. Such agreements might be described as "really unilateral behavior flowing from decisions of a single enterprise."*Copperweld,* 467 U.S., at 767. Nor, for this reason, does § 1 cover "internally coordinated conduct of a corporation and one of its unincorporated divisions," *id.,* at 770, because "[a] division within a corporate structure pursues the common interests of the whole, *"ibid.*, and therefore "coordination between a corporation and its division does not represent a sudden joining of two independent sources of economic power previously pursuing separate interests, *"id.,* at 770–771. Nor, for the same reasons, is "the coordinated activity of a parent and its wholly owned subsidiary" covered. See *id.,*at 771. They "have a complete unity of interest" and thus "[w]ith or without a formal 'agreement,' the subsidiary acts for the benefit of the parent, its sole shareholder." *Ibid*.

Because the inquiry is one of competitive reality, it is not determinative that two parties to an alleged § 1 violation are legally distinct entities. Nor, however, is it determinative that two legally distinct entities have organized themselves under a single umbrella or into a structured joint venture. The question is whether the agreement joins together "independent centers of decisionmaking." *Id.*, at 769. If it does, the entities are capable of conspiring under § 1, and the court must decide whether the restraint of trade is an unreasonable and therefore illegal one.

The NFL teams do not possess either the unitary decision making quality or the single aggregation of economic power characteristic of independent action. Each of the teams is a substantial, independently owned, and independently managed business. "[T]heir general corporate actions are guided or determined" by "separate corporate consciousnesses," and "[t]heir objectives are" not "common. "*Copperweld*, 467 U.S., at 771; see also *North American Soccer League v. NFL*, 670 F.2d 1249, 1252 (C.A.2 1982)(discussing ways that "the financial performance of each team, while related to that of the others, does not . . . necessarily rise and fall with that of the others"). The teams compete with one another, not only on the playing field, but to attract fans, for gate receipts and for contracts with managerialand playing personnel.

Directly relevant to this case, the teams compete in the market for intellectual property. To a firm making hats, the Saints and the Colts are two potentially competing suppliers of valuable trademarks. When each NFL team licenses its intellectual property, it is not pursuing the "common interests of the whole" league but is instead pursuing interests of each "corporation itself," *Copperweld*, 467 U.S., at 770;teams are acting as "separate economic actors pursuing separate economic interests," and each team therefore is a potential "independent cente[r] of decision making," *id.*, at 769. Decisions by NFL teams to license their separately owned trademarks collectively and to only one vendor are decisions that "depriv[e] the marketplace of independent centers of decision making," *ibid.*, and therefore of actual or potential competition. See *NCAA,* 468 U.S., at 109, n. 39 (observing a possible § 1 violation if two separately owned companies sold their separate products through a "single selling agent").

In defense, respondents argue that by forming NFLP, they have formed a single entity, akin to a merger, and market their NFL brands through a single outlet. But it is not dispositive that the teams have organized and own a legally separate entity that centralizes the management of their intellectual property. An ongoing§ 1 violation cannot evade § 1 scrutiny simply by giving the ongoing violation a name and label. . . .

The NFL respondents may be similar in some sense to a single enterprise that owns several pieces of intellectual property and licenses them jointly, but they are not similar in the relevant functional sense. Although NFL teams have common interests such as promoting the NFL brand, they are still separate, profit-maximizing entities, and their interests in licensing team trademarks are not necessarily aligned. . . . Common interests in the NFL brand "*partially* unit[e] the economic interests of the parent firms," Broadley, Joint Ventures and Antitrust Policy,

95 Harv. L.Rev. 1521, 1526 (1982) (emphasis added), but the teams still have distinct, potentially competing interests.

It may be, as respondents argue, that NFLP "has served as the 'single driver" of the teams' "promotional vehicle," " 'pursu[ing] the common interests of the whole.' " Brief for NFL Respondents 28 (quoting *Copperweld*, 467 U.S., at 770–771; brackets in original). But illegal restraints often are in the common interests of the parties to the restraint, at the expense of those who are not parties. It is true, as respondents describe, that they have for some time marketed their trademarks jointly. But a history of concerted activity does not immunize conduct from § 1 scrutiny. "Absence of actual competition may simply be a manifestation of the anticompetitive agreement itself. "*Freeman*, 322 F.3d, at 1149.

Respondents argue that nonetheless, as the Court of Appeals held, they constitute a single entity because without their cooperation, there would be no NFL football. It is true that "the clubs that make up a professional sports league are not completely independent economic competitors, as they depend upon a degree of cooperation for economic survival. " *Brown*, 518 U.S., at 248. But the Court of Appeals' reasoning is unpersuasive.

The justification for cooperation is not relevant to whether that cooperation is concerted or independent action. A "contract, combination . . . or conspiracy," § 1, that is necessary or useful to a joint venture is still a "contract, combination . . . or conspiracy" if it "deprives the marketplace of independent centers of decision making," *Copperweld*, 467 U.S., at 769 See *NCAA*, 468 U.S., at 113 ("[J]oint ventures have no immunity from antitrust laws"). Any joint venture involves multiple sources of economic power cooperating to produce a product. And for many such ventures, the participation of others is necessary. But that does not mean that necessity of cooperation transforms concerted action into independent action; a nut and a bolt can only operate together, but an agreement between nut and bolt manufacturers is still subject to § 1 analysis. Nor does it mean that once a group of firms agree to produce a joint product, cooperation amongst those firms must be treated as independent conduct. The mere fact that the teams operate jointly in some sense does not mean that they are immune.[FN7]

FN7. In any event, it simply is not apparent that the alleged conduct was necessary at all. Although two teams are needed to play a football game, not all aspects of elaborate inter league cooperation are necessary to produce a game. Moreover, even if league wide agreements are necessary to produce football, it does not follow that concerted activity in marketing intellectual property is necessary to produce football.

The Court of Appeals carved out a zone of antitrust immunity for conduct arguably related to league operations by reasoning that coordinated team trademark sales are necessary to produce "NFL football," a single NFL brand that competes against other forms of entertainment. But defining the product as "NFL football" puts the cart before the horse: Of course the NFL produces NFL football; but that does not mean that cooperation amongst NFL teams is immune from § 1 scrutiny. Members of any cartel could insist that their cooperation is necessary to produce the "cartel product" and compete with other products.

The question whether NFLP decisions can constitute concerted activity covered by § 1 is closer than whether decisions made directly by the 32 teams are covered by § 1. This is so both because NFLP is a separate corporation with its own management and because the record indicates that most of the revenues generated by NFLP are shared by the teams on an equal basis. Nevertheless we think it clear that for the same reasons the 32 teams' conduct is covered by § 1, NFLP's actions also are subject to § 1, at least with regards to its marketing of property owned by the separate teams. NFLP's licensing decisions are made by the 32 potential competitors, and each of them actually owns its share of the jointly managed assets. Apart from their agreement to cooperate in exploiting those assets, including their decisions as the NFLP, there would be nothing to prevent each of the teams from making its own market decisions relating to purchases of apparel and headwear, to the sale of such items, and to the granting of licenses to use its trademarks.

We generally treat agreements within a single firm as independent action on the presumption that the components of the firm will act to maximize the firm's profits. But in rare cases, that presumption does not hold. Agreements made within a firm can constitute concerted action covered by § 1 when the parties to the agreement act on interests separate from those of the firm itself, and the intrafirm agreements may simply be a formalistic shell for ongoing concerted action [citations and footnotes omitted].

For that reason, decisions by the NFLP regarding the teams' separately owned intellectual property constitute concerted action. Thirty-two teams operating independently through the vehicle of the NFLP are not like the components of a single firm that act to maximize the firm's profits. The teams remain separately controlled, potential competitors with economic interests that are distinct from NFLP's financial well-being. . . . Unlike typical decisions by corporate shareholders, NFLP licensing decisions effectively require the assent of more than a mere majority of shareholders. And each team's decision reflects not only an interest in NFLP's profits but also an interest in the team's individual profits. . . . The 32 teams capture individual economic benefits separate and apart from NFLP profits as a result of the decisions they make for the NFLP. NFLP's decisions thus affect each team's profits from licensing its own intellectual property. "Although the business interests of" the teams "will *often* coincide with those of the" NFLP "as an entity in itself, that commonality of interest exists in every cartel." *Los*

*Angeles Memorial Coliseum Comm'n v. NFL,*726 F.2d 1381, 1389 (C.A.9 1984) (emphasis added). In making the relevant licensing decisions, NFLP is therefore "an instrumentality" of the teams. . . .

If the fact that potential competitors shared in profits or losses from a venture meant that the venture was immune from § 1, then any cartel "could evade the antitrust law simply by creating a 'joint venture' to serve as the exclusive seller of their competing products." *Major League Baseball Properties, Inc. v. Salvino, Inc.*, 542 F.3d 290, 335 (C.A.2 2008) (Sotomayor, J., concurring in judgment). "So long as no agreement," other than one made by the cartelists sitting on the board of the joint venture, "explicitly listed the prices to be charged, the companies could act as monopolies through the 'joint venture.'" *Ibid.* (Indeed, a joint venture with a single management structure is generally a better way to operate a cartel because it decreases the risks of a party to an illegal agreement defecting from that agreement). However, competitors "cannot simply get around" antitrust liability by acting "through a third-party intermediary or 'joint venture'." *Id.*, at 336.

VI

Football teams that need to cooperate are not trapped by antitrust law. "[T]he special characteristics of this industry may provide a justification" for many kinds of agreements. *Brown,* 518 U.S., at 252 (STEVENS, J., dissenting). The fact that NFL teams share an interest in making the entire league successful and profitable, and that they must cooperate in the production and scheduling of games, provides a perfectly sensible justification for making a host of collective decisions. But the conduct at issue in this case is still concerted activity under the Sherman Act that is subject to § 1 analysis.

When "restraints on competition are essential if the product is to be available at all,"*per se* rules of illegality are inapplicable, and instead the restraint must be judged according to the flexible Rule of Reason. *NCAA,* 468 U.S., at 101; see *id.,* at 117 ("Our decision not to apply a *per se* rule to this case rests in large part on our recognition that a certain degree of cooperation is necessary if the type of competition that petitioner and its member institutions seek to market is to be preserved"); . . . In such instances, the agreement is likely to survive the Rule of Reason. See *Broadcast Music, Inc. v. Columbia Broadcasting System, Inc.*, 441 U.S. 1, 23 (1979) ("Joint ventures and other cooperative arrangements are also not usually unlawful . . . where the agreement . . . is necessary to market the product at all"). And depending upon the concerted activity in question, the Rule of Reason may not require a detailed analysis; it "can sometimes be applied in the twinkling of an eye. "*NCAA,* 468 U.S., at 109, n. 39.

Other features of the NFL may also save agreements amongst the teams. We have recognized, for example, "that the interest in maintaining a competitive balance" among "athletic teams is legitimate and important," *NCAA,* 468 U.S., at 117. While that same interest applies to the teams in the NFL, it does not justify treating them as a single entity for § 1 purposes when it comes to the marketing of the teams' individually owned intellectual property. It is, however, unquestionably an interest that may well justify a variety of collective decisions made by the teams. What role it properly plays in applying the Rule of Reason to the allegations in this case is a matter to be considered on remand.

***

Accordingly, the judgment of the Court of Appeals is reversed, and the case is remanded for further proceedings consistent with this opinion.

CASES ON THE SUPPLEMENTAL WEB SITE

Brown, v. Pro Football, Inc., d/b/a Washington Redskins, 518 U.S. 231 (1996). This case examines whether the NFL violated the Sherman Act, when they implemented unilateral changes after the parties had bargained to an impasse.

Flood v. Kuhn, 407 U.S. 258 (1972). This case examines whether the reserve clause in baseball was exempt Federal Antitrust law.

Fraser v. Major League Soccer, L.L.C., 284 F.3d 47 (2002). This case examines whether Major League Soccer was a single entity for antitrust purposes.

Mackey v. National Football League, 543 F. 2d 606 (8th Cir. 1976). This case examines whether a league rule that allows a league's commissioner to require a club acquiring a free agent to compensate the free agent's former club violates antitrust law.

National Basketball Ass'n v. SDC Basketball Club, Inc., 815 F.2d 562 (Cal. 1987). This case considers a franchise's relocation and whether a league can sanction franchise for failing to seek league approval prior to relocation without violating antitrust laws.

QUESTIONS YOU SHOULD BE ABLE TO ANSWER

1. Why is baseball exempt from antitrust law? Why does it continue to be exempt almost 90 years after the original decision granting the exemption by the U.S. Supreme Court?

2. What is the single entity defense and why is it so important to leagues and tours to be declared single entities?

3. Why would professional sports leagues want unions to protect themselves from antitrust challenges?

4. What arguments must a league raise in order to exert the labor exemption defense?

5. Why are sports leagues "magnets" for antitrust litigation?

REFERENCES

Cases

Allen Bradley Co. v. Local Union No. 3, International Brotherhood of Electrical Workers, 325 U.S. 797 (1945).
American Football League v. National Football League, 323 F.2d 124 (4th Cir. 1963).
American Needle v. National Football League, 130 S.Ct. 2201 (2010).
Brady v. National Football League, 644 F. 3d 661 (8th Cir. 2011).
Brown v. Pro-Football, Inc., 518 U.S. 231 (1996).
Chicago Professional Sports Limited Partnership v. National Basketball Association, 95 F.3d 593 (7th Cir. 1996).
Clarett v. National Football League, 306 F.Supp.2d 379 (S.D.N.Y. 2004).
Connell Construction v. Plumbers, 421 U.S. 616 (1975).
Dallas Cowboys v. NFL Trust, 94-C-9426 (N.D. Cal. 1995).
Federal Baseball Club of Baltimore, Inc. v. National League of Professional Baseball Clubs, et al., 259 U.S. 200 (1922).
Flood v. Kuhn, 407 U.S. 258 (1972).
Fraser v. Major League Soccer, 97 F. Supp. 2d 130 (D. Mass. 2000).
Levin v. National Basketball League, 385 F. Supp. 149 (S.D. N.Y. 1974).
Local Union No. 189, Amalgamated Meat Cutters, and Butcher Workmen of North America, AFL-CIO v. Jewel Tea, 381 U.S. 676 (1965).
Los Angeles Memorial Coliseum and the Los Angeles Raiders v. National Football League, 726 F.2d 1381 (9th Cir. 1984).
Mackey v. National Football League, 543 F.2d 606 (8th Cir. 1976).
Madison Square Garden v. National Hockey League, 2008 U.S. Dist. LEXIS 80474 (S.D.N.Y. 2008).
McCourt v. California Sports, Inc., 600 F.2d 1193 (6th Cir. 1979).
Mid-South Grizzlies v. National Football League, 550 F. Supp. 558 (E.D. Pa. 1982), *aff 'd* 720 F.2d 772 (3rd Cir. 1983), *cert. denied*, 467 U.S. 1215 (1984).
Molinas v. National Basketball Association, 190 F. Supp. 241 (S.D. N.Y. 1961).
Philadelphia World Hockey, Inc. v. Philadelphia Hockey Club, Inc., 351 F. Supp. 462 (E.D. Pa. 1972).
Piazza v. Major League Baseball, 831 F. Supp 420 (E.D. Pa. 1993).
Powell v. National Football League, 930 F.2d 1293 (8th Cir. 1989).
Radovich v. National Football League, 352 U.S. 445 (1957).
Reynolds v. National Football League, 584 F.2d 280 (8th Cir. 1978).
Sullivan v. National Football League, 34 F.3d 1091 (1st Cir. 1994).
Toolson v.New York Yankees, 346 U.S. 356 (1953).
United Mineworkers of America v. Pennington, 381 U.S. 657 (1965).
United States v. International Boxing Club, 348 U.S. 236 (1955).
United States Football League v. National Football League, 644 F. Supp. 1040 (S.D. N.Y. 1986).
VKK v. National Football League, 55 F. Supp. 196 (S.D.N.Y. 1999).
Wood v. National Basketball Association, 809 F.2d 954 (2nd Cir. 1987).

Publications

Greenberg, M. J. (1993). *Sports law practice*. Charlottesville, VA: Michie Co.

Roberts, G. (1990). Antitrust issues in professional sports. In G. Uberstine (Ed.), *Law of professional and amateur sports* (pp. 19-1–19-54. Deerfield, IL: Clark Boardman Callaghan.

Legislation

The Clayton Act of 1914, 15 U.S.C. §§ 12–27 (1989).
The Curt Flood Act of 1998, 15 U.S.C. § 27 (1998).
National Labor Relations Act, 29 U.S.C. § 151-69 (1988).
The Sherman Antitrust Act of 1890, 15 U.S.C. § 1, et seq. (1989).

7.32 ANTITRUST LAW: AMATEUR SPORT APPLICATIONS

John T. Wolohan Gina Pauline I Syracuse University

Unlike professional sports organizations, the courts have afforded the NCAA and other amateur athletic organizations plenty of room under the antitrust laws to "retain a clear line of demarcation between intercollegiate athletics and professional sports" (NCAA Manual, 2008–09). Yet, even though the courts have been reluctant to apply the antitrust laws against athlete eligibility requirements and other rules regulating the relationship between member schools, the NCAA and other amateur athletic organizations have faced a number of antitrust lawsuits involving the commercial relationships between member institutions and other organizations. These lawsuits, which range from the unlawful restraint of trade in the television market and the college basketball coaches' market to the unlawful use of their monopoly power to destroy another amateur athletic organization, will all be explored in the following section.

FUNDAMENTAL CONCEPTS

In reviewing Federal Antitrust challenges against the NCAA, the first question the courts must determine is which of the two major sections of the Sherman Act apply. The two sections of the Sherman Act are Section 1 (15 U.S.C. § 1); which prohibits restraints of trade or commerce, and Section 2 (15 U.S.C. § 2), which prohibits monopolies or attempted monopolies. Once the court determines what section of the Sherman Act applies, it must then determine whether the NCAA's rule or policy has a pro-competitive benefit to the consumer (athletes and sports fans) or an anti-competitive effect.

Sherman Antitrust Act

Section 1 of the Sherman Act

Section 1 of the Sherman Act states that "[E]very contract, combination in the form of trust or otherwise, or conspiracy, in restraint of trade or commerce among the several States, or with foreign nations, is hereby declared to be illegal" (15 U.S.C. § 1).

As we will see below, it is important to note, that not every restraint of trade violates the antitrust law. Because nearly every contract that binds the parties to an agreed course of conduct "is a restraint of trade" of some sort, the Supreme Court has limited the restrictions contained in Section 1 to bar only "**unreasonable restraints of trade**" (*NCAA v. Board of Regents of University of Oklahoma*, 1984). Therefore in order to prevail on a Section 1 claim under the Sherman Act, the plaintiff must show that the defendant (1) participated in an agreement that restrained interstate trade or commerce; and (2) that the agreement unreasonably restrained trade in the relevant market.

Establishing a Section 1 Violation

In determining whether a defendant's conduct is an unreasonable restraint of trade, the courts have developed three categories of antitrust analysis: the *per se* rule; the rule of reason analysis; and an abbreviated or "quick look" rule of reason analysis.

Per Se **Rule.** The reasoning behind the *per se* rule is that certain types restraints or agreements, such as price fixing among competitors, resale price maintenance, and market allocations, are almost always antitrust violations, regardless of the intent of the participants or the justifications offered. Once the courts identify something as a *per se* violation, they will refuse to engage in a detailed (and costly) market and effects analysis of conduct. There are only a handful of categories that will trigger the *per se* rule, as such, the courts tend to limit the application of the *per se* rule(Hovenkamp, 2005).

Rule of Reason. Unlike the per se rule,when conducting arule of reason analysis, the court will take a careful look at the type of restraint or agreement and whether it has positive or negative impact on competition in the relevant product market(Hovenkamp, 2005). The focus of the rule of reason inquiry, therefore, is not so much the legal category in which the conduct falls, but rather the actual purpose and effects of the restraint and how it affects competition. Under the rule of reason analysis, the court must perform an economic and legal analysis, not only evaluating the restraint, but also the actual history and purpose behind the restraint and whether it "unreasonably" affects competition.

Since Section 1 only bars "unreasonable restraints of trade," an agreement to restrain trade may still survive scrutiny under Section 1 if the pro-competitive benefits of the restraint reasonably justify the anticompetitive effects. Justifications offered under the rule of reason may be considered only to the extent that they tend to show that, on balance, "the challenged restraint enhances competition" (*NCAA v. Board of Regents of University of Oklahoma*, 1984).

"Quick Look" Rule of Reason. When a practice has obvious anticompetitive effects, almost to the point of deserving per se condemnation, the courts will apply a "quick look" rule of reason analysis which allows the courts to proceed directly to the question of whether the pro-competitive justifications advanced for the restraint outweigh the anticompetitive effects (Hovenkamp, 2005). For example, in *Law v. National Collegiate Athletic Association* (1998), the court, using a quick look rule of reason analysis, found that an "anticompetitive effect is established, even without a determination of the relevant market, where the plaintiff shows that a horizontal agreement to fix prices exists, that the agreement is effective, and that the price set by such agreement is more favorable to the defendant than otherwise would have resulted from operation of market forces"(*Law v. National Collegiate Athletic Association*, 1998).

Section 2 of the Sherman Act

Section 2 of the Sherman Act states that "[E]very person who shall monopolize, attempt to monopolize, or combine or conspire with any other person or persons, to monopolize any part of the trade or commerce among the several States, or with foreign nations, shall be deemed guilty of a felony . . ." (15 U.S.C. 2).

Establishing a Section 2 Violation

Unlike Section 1, which requires that at least two parties combine or conspire in restraint of trade, it is important to note that Section 2 of the Sherman Act can be triggered by a single party acting alone. In order to establish a violation under Section 2, the Supreme Court has identified two elements that must be present: "(1) the possession of monopoly power in the relevant market and (2) the willful acquisition or maintenance of that power as distinguished from growth or development as a consequence of a superior product, business acumen or historical accident" (*United States v. Grinnell Corp.*, 1966) "and has exercised that power" (*Verizon Communications v. Law Office of Curtis v. Trinko*, 2004).

Monopoly power has traditionally been defined as "the power to control market prices or exclude competition" (*United States v. E.I.duPont Nemours & Co.*, 1956). However, in addition to having the ability to control market prices or exclude competition, it is essential that the courts identify the relevant markets adversely affected by the anticompetitive actions. For example, while the NCAA may have a monopoly over college sports, it has very little control over professional sports.

The NCAA and Antitrust Law

The following section looks at just some of the antitrust lawsuits filed against the NCAA. In particular, the cases examine the difficulty the courts have in distinguishing between rules and regulations that are designed to protect the amateur nature of intercollegiate athletes and those that are commercial in nature.

Student-Athletes

In *Banks v. NCAA* (1992), Braxston Banks, while still a college football player, entered his name into the NFL draft. When he was not drafted, Banks sued the NCAA seeking to have his final year of eligibility to play intercollegiate football restored. Banks alleged that the NCAA rule revoking an athlete's eligibility once he or she chooses to enter a professional draft or engages an agent to help him secure a position with a professional team is an illegal restraint in violation of the Sherman Antitrust Act. In rejecting Bank's argument, the Seventh Circuit Court of Appeals held that Bank's failed to allege an anticompetitive effect on a relevant market; at best, the court held, Banks had merely attempted to frame his complaint in antitrust language. Although Banks alleged a restraint on the market of college football players, the complaint failed to explain how the alleged restraint diminished competition in or among the markets.

In *Hairston v. Pacific 10 Conference and NCAA* (1996), the PAC-10 after conducting an eight-month investigation into the allegations of recruiting improprieties levied a number of sanctions against the University of Washington football team. The sanctions included a two-year post-season bowl ban, a one-year television revenue ban, and a two-year probationary period. In an effort to challenge the sanctions a group football players at the university sued the conference alleging that the sanctions violated the Sherman Antitrust Act. In rejecting the players' claim, the Ninth Circuit Court of Appeals held that the players failed to show that the penalties imposed by the PAC-10 constituted an unreasonable restraint of trade.

In *Smith v. NCAA* (1998), Renee Smith sued the NCAA, alleging that the NCAA's enforcement of a bylaw prohibiting her from participating in athletics while enrolled in a graduate program at an institution other than her undergraduate institution violated the Sherman Antitrust Act. The Court of Appeals held that as matter of first impression, the Sherman Act's restraint of trade provision did not apply to NCAA eligibility rules. Even if the Sherman Act was applicable, the court held that the challenged rule was not an unlawful restraint of trade.

In *Agnew v. NCAA* (2012), two former NCAA Division I football players, who had suffered career-ending football injuries and lost their scholarships, sued the NCAA claiming that the NCAA's regulations on the number of scholarships given per team and the prohibition of multi-year scholarships prevented them from obtaining scholarships that covered the entire cost of their college education. These regulations, according Agnew, have an anticompetitive effect on the market for student-athletes, and therefore violate § 1 of the Sherman Act. Although the Seventh Circuit Court of Appeals disagreed with the district court that the former players could not have alleged a relevant cognizable market, the court ultimately concluded that the former players did not sufficiently identify a commercial market, an obvious necessity for Sherman Act violations, and therefore held that the district court's dismissal was justified.

In a case that is still winding its way through the court as this book went to press, Inre NCAA Student-Athlete Name& Likeness Licensing Litigation, a group of former student-athletes who played Division I basketball and football at NCAA member institutions have filed two Antitrust claims against defendants NCAA, Collegiate Licensing Company, and Electronic Arts. In particular, the athletes claim that defendants conspired to restrain trade in violation of Section 1 of the Sherman Act by agreeing to fix at zero the amount of compensation the athletes were allowed to receive under NCAA rules for the use of their names, images, and likenesses in products or media. The second claim accuses the defendants of engaging in a "group boycott" conspiracy by requiring them to sign forms through which student-athletes relinquished for perpetuity all rights pertaining to the use of their images, likenesses, or names. For more information on this case, see Chapter 7.23 Image Rights.

Television

In *NCAA v. Board of Regents of the University of Oklahoma* (1984), the U.S. Supreme Court ruled that the NCAA's plan for televising college football games of member institutions violated the Sherman Antitrust Act. The Supreme Court held that the plan on its face constituted a restraint on the operation of a free market; that the relevant market was college football; and that the restraint was not justified on the basis of procompetitive effect, protecting live attendance, or maintaining competitive balance among amateur athletic teams (See Significant Case).

Women's Athletics

When it was first created, the NCAA only sponsored men's intercollegiate athletic programs. Women's intercollegiate athletic programs were governed by the Association for Intercollegiate Athletics for Women (AIAW), which had 961 member colleges and universities by 1980–81. In 1981, the NCAA began to sponsor women's championships for the first time. Forced to pick between the AIAW and the NCAA, the AIAW suffered a significant drop in membership and participation in its events. As a result of the membership loses, the National Broadcasting Company (NBC) decided not to exercise its exclusive television rights to telecast AIAW championships. In addition, the Eastman Kodak Company and the Broderick Company also sought to withdraw sponsorship of AIAW achievement awards. Because the AIAW's leadership expected these financial hardships only to worsen, it decided to close for business on June 30, 1982.

Claiming that the NCAA unlawfully used its monopoly power in men's college sports to facilitate its entry into women's college sports and to force the AIAW out of existence, the AIAW sued the NCAA. In *Association for Intercollegiate Athletics for Women v. NCAA* (1984), the Court held that the AIAW failed to prove an illegal agreement between the NCAA and NBC to "tie" television rights to the NCAA's newly instituted women's basketball championship to NBC's contract with the NCAA and their men's basketball tournament. The court also held that even if the conduct of the NCAA was avowedly anticompetitive in purpose, the record did not support a finding that its effect on the AIAW was the result of anything but direct competition.

College Coaches

In *Law v. National Collegiate Athletic Association* (1998), the NCAA attempted to reduce the costs of intercollegiate athletics "without disturbing the competitive balance" among member institutions, by limiting the number of coaches on a Division I basketball staff to four members, one head coach, two assistant coaches, and one entry-level coach called a "restricted-earnings" coach. The compensation for the Restricted Earnings Coach (REC) was restricted to a total of $12,000 for the academic year and $4,000 for the summer months or $16,000 per year. Since the NCAA did not dispute that the cost reduction had effectively reduced restricted-earnings coaches' salaries, thereby artificially lowering the price of coaching services, the Tenth Circuit Court of Appeals using a "quick look" rule of reason analysis found that the restricted-earnings coaches' rule was anticompetitive and had no procompetitive rationales and therefore was an unlawful restraint of trade. As a result, the court found the NCAA liable for nearly $22.3 million damages, which when trebled, made the NCAA potentially liable for approximately $67 million. The NCAA eventually settled the case for $54.5 million (Dauner, 2000).

In *Bassett v. NCAA*, (2008), Claude Bassett an assistant football coach for the University of Kentucky filed suit against NCAA, the Southeastern Conference and the University of Kentucky, after he resigned due to allegations of NCAA rules infractions. In rejecting Bassett claim that the actions of the defendants' amounted to a group boycott that prevented him from coaching at any NCAA member school in violation of the Sherman Act, the Sixth Circuit Court found that Bassett's complaint lacked the critical commercial activity component required to permit application of the Sherman Act. The court found that NCAA's rules on recruiting student athletes, specifically those rules prohibiting improper inducements and academic fraud were explicitly non-commercial. Because the rules and the corresponding sanctions were not commercial, the enforcement of the rules could not be commercial. The Sixth Circuit also held that Bassett's complaint failed to allege any antitrust injury because it was devoid of any allegation of the anticompetitive effect of NCAA's enforcement of its non-commercial rules on the coaching market.

SIGNIFICANT CASE

The following antitrust case establishes the precedent that even though the NCAA plays a vital role in protecting and preserving the nature of amateur athletics, when its regulations are purely commercial in nature, it will be held to same antitrust standards as other commercial businesses.

NCAA V. Board of Regents of the University of Oklahoma

United States Supreme Court
468 U.S. 85 (1984)

The University of Oklahoma and the University of Georgia contend that the National Collegiate Athletic Association has unreasonably restrained trade in the televising of college football games. After an extended trial, the District Court found that the NCAA had violated section 1 of the Sherman Act and granted injunctive relief. The Court of Appeals agreed that the statute had been violated but modified the remedy in some respects. We granted certiorari, and now affirm.

I.

The NCAA

Since its inception in 1905, the NCAA has played an important role in the regulation of amateur collegiate sports. It has adopted and promulgated playing rules, standards of amateurism, standards for academic eligibility, regulations concerning recruitment of athletes, and rules governing the size of athletic squads and coaching staffs. In some sports, such as baseball, swimming, basketball, wrestling, and track, it has sponsored and conducted national tournaments. It has not done so in the sport of football, however. With the exception of football, the NCAA has not undertaken any regulation of the televising of athletic events.

The NCAA has approximately 850 voting members. The regular members are classified into separate divisions to reflect differences in size and scope of their athletic programs. Division I includes 276 colleges with major athletic programs; in this group only 187 play intercollegiate football. Divisions II and III include approximately 500 colleges with less extensive athletic programs. Division I has been subdivided into Divisions I-A and I-AA for football.

Some years ago, five major conferences together with major football-playing independent institutions organized the College Football Association (CFA). The original purpose of the CFA was to promote the interests of major football-playing schools within the NCAA structure. The Universities of Oklahoma and Georgia, respondents in this Court, are members of the CFA.

* * *

The Current Plan

The plan adopted in 1981 for the 1982–1985 seasons is at issue in this case. This plan, like each of its predecessors, recites that it is intended to reduce, insofar as possible, the adverse effects of live television upon football game attendance. It provides that "all forms of television of the football games of NCAA member institutions during the Plan control periods shall be in accordance with this Plan." The plan recites that the television committee has awarded rights to negotiate and contract for the telecasting of college football games of members of the NCAA to two "carrying networks."

* * *

In separate agreements with each of the carrying networks, ABC and the Columbia Broadcasting System (CBS), the NCAA granted each the right to telecast the 14 live "exposures" described in the plan, in accordance with the "ground rules" set forth therein. Each of the networks agreed to pay a specified "minimum aggregate compensation to the participating NCAA member institutions" during the 4-year period in an amount that totaled $131,750,000. In essence the agreement authorized each network to negotiate directly with member schools for the right to televise their games. The agreement itself does not describe the method of computing the compensation for each game, but the practice that has developed over the years and that the District Court found would be followed under the current agreement involved the setting of a recommended fee by a representative of the NCAA for different types of telecasts, with national telecasts being the most valuable, regional telecasts being less valuable, and Division II or Division III games commanding a still lower price. The aggregate of all these payments presumably equals the total minimum aggregate compensation set forth in the basic agreement. Except for differences in payment between national and regional telecasts, and with respect to Division II and Division III games, the amount that any team receives does not change with the size of the viewing audience, the number of markets in which the game is telecast, or the particular characteristic of the game or the participating teams. Instead, the "ground rules" provide that the carrying networks make alternate selections of those games they wish to televise, and thereby obtain the exclusive right to submit a bid at an essentially fixed price to the institutions involved. See 546 F.Supp., at 1289-1293.

The plan also contains "appearance requirements" and "appearance limitations" which pertain to each of the 2year periods that the plan is in effect. The basic requirement imposed on each of the two networks is that it must schedule appearances for at least 82 different member institutions during each 2-year period. Under the appearance limitations no member institution is eligible to appear on television more than a total of six times and more than four times nationally, with the appearances to be divided equally between the two carrying networks. See Id., at 1293. The number of exposures specified in the contracts also sets an absolute maximum on the number of games that can be broadcast.

Thus, although the current plan is more elaborate than any of its predecessors, it retains the essential features of each of them. It limits the total amount of televised intercollegiate football and the number of games that any one team may televise. No member is permitted to make any sale of television rights except in accordance with the basic plan.

Background of this Controversy

Beginning in 1979 CFA members began to advocate that colleges with major football programs should have a greater voice in the formulation of football television policy than they had in the NCAA. CFA therefore investigated the possibility of negotiating a television agreement of its own, developed an independent plan, and obtained a contract offer from the National Broadcasting Co. (NBC). This contract, which it signed in August 1981, would have allowed a more liberal number of appearances for each institution, and would have increased the overall revenues realized by CFA members.

In response the NCAA publicly announced that it would take disciplinary action against any CFA member that complied with the CFA-NBC contract. The NCAA made it clear that sanctions would not be limited to the football programs of CFA members, but would apply to other sports as well. On September 8, 1981, respondents commenced this action in the United States District Court for the Western District of Oklahoma and obtained a preliminary injunction preventing the NCAA from initiating disciplinary proceedings or otherwise interfering with CFA's efforts to perform its agreement with NBC. Notwithstanding the entry of the injunction, most CFA members were unwilling to commit themselves to the new contractual arrangement with NBC in the face of the threatened sanctions and therefore the agreement was never consummated. See *Id.*, at 1286–1287.

* * *

II.

There can be no doubt that the challenged practices of the NCAA constitute a "restraint of trade" in the sense that they limit members' freedom to negotiate and enter into their own television contracts. In that sense, however, every contract is a restraint of trade, and as we have repeatedly recognized, the Sherman Act was intended to prohibit only unreasonable restraints of trade.

It is also undeniable that these practices share characteristics of restraints we have previously held unreasonable. The NCAA is an association of schools which compete against each other to attract television revenues, not to mention fans an athletes. As the District Court found, the policies of the NCAA with respect to television rights are ultimately controlled by the vote of member institutions. By participating in an association which prevents member institutions from competing against each other on the basis of price or kind of television rights that can be offered to broadcasters, the NCAA member institutions have created a horizontal restraint—an agreement among competitors on the way in which they will compete with one another. A restraint of this type has often been held to be unreasonable as a matter of law. Because it places a ceiling on the number of games member institutions may televise, the horizontal agreement places an artificial limit on the quantity of televised football that is available to broadcasters and consumers. By restraining the quantity of television rights available for sale, the challenged practices create a limitation on output; our cases have held that such limitations are unreasonable restraints of trade. Moreover, the District Court found that the minimum aggregate price in fact operates to preclude any price negotiation between broadcasters and institutions, thereby constituting horizontal price fixing, perhaps the paradigm of an unreasonable restraint of trade.

Horizontal price fixing and output limitation are ordinarily condemned as a matter of law under an "illegal per se" approach because the probability that these practices are anticompetitive is so high; a per se rule is applied when "the practice facially appears to be one that would always or almost always tend to restrict competition and decrease output." *Broadcast Music, Inc. v. Columbia Broadcasting System, Inc.*, 441 U.S. 1, 19-20 (1979). In such circumstances a restraint is presumed unreasonable without inquiry into the particular market context in which it is found. Nevertheless, we have decided that it would be inappropriate to apply a per se rule to this case. This decision is not based on a lack of judicial experience with this type of arrangement, on the fact that the NCAA is organized as a nonprofit entity, or on our respect for the NCAA's historic role in the preservation and encouragement of intercollegiate amateur athletics. Rather, what is critical is that this case involves an industry in which horizontal restraints on competition are essential if the product is to be available at all.

As Judge Bork has noted: "[Some] activities can only be carried out jointly. Perhaps the leading example is league sports. When a league of professional lacrosse teams is formed, it would be pointless to declare their cooperation illegal on the ground that there are no other professional lacrosse teams." R. Bork, The Antitrust Paradox 278 (1978). What the NCAA and its member institutions market in this case is competition itself—contests between competing institutions. Of course, this would be completely ineffective if there were no rules on which the competitors agreed to create and define the competition to be marketed. A myriad of rules affecting such matters as the size of the field, the number of players on a team, and the extent to which physical violence is to be encouraged or proscribed, all must be agreed upon, and all restrain the manner in which institutions compete. Moreover, the NCAA seeks to market a particular brand of football—college football. The identification of this "product" with an academic tradition differentiates college football from and makes it more popular than professional sports to which it might otherwise be comparable, such as, for example, minor league baseball. In order to preserve the character and quality of the "product," athletes must not be paid, must be required to attend class, and the like. And the integrity of the "product" cannot be preserved except by mutual agreement; if an institution adopted such restrictions unilaterally, its effectiveness as a competitor on the playing field might soon be destroyed. Thus, the NCAA plays a vital role in enabling college football to preserve its character, and as a result enables a product to be marketed which might otherwise be unavailable. In performing this role, its actions widen consumer choice—not only the choices available to sports fans but also those available to athletes—and hence can be viewed as procompetitive.

* * *

Respondents concede that the great majority of the NCAA's regulations enhance competition among member institutions. Thus, despite the fact that this case involves restraints on the ability of member institutions to compete in terms of price and output, a fair evaluation of their competitive character requires consideration of the NCAA's justifications for the restraints.

Our analysis of this case under the Rule of Reason, of course, does not change the ultimate focus of our inquiry. Both per se rules and the Rule of Reason are employed "to form a judgment about the competitive significance of the restraint." *National Society of Professional Engineers v. United States*, 435 U.S. 679, 692 (1978). A conclusion that a restraint of trade is unreasonable may be "based either (1) on the nature or character of the contracts, or (2) on surrounding circumstances giving rise to the inference or presumption that they were intended to restrain trade and enhance prices. Under either branch of the test, the inquiry is confined to a consideration of impact on competitive conditions." Per se rules are invoked when surrounding circumstances make the likelihood of anticompetitive conduct so great as to render unjustified further examination of the challenged conduct. But whether the ultimate finding is the product of a presumption or actual market analysis, the essential inquiry remains the same—whether or not the challenged restraint enhances competition. Under the Sherman Act the criterion to be used in judging the validity of a restraint on trade is its impact on competition.

III.

Because it restrains price and output, the NCAA's television plan has a significant potential for anticompetitive effects. The findings of the District Court indicate that this potential has been realized. The District Court found that if member institutions were free to sell television rights, many more games would be shown on television, and that the NCAA's output restriction has the effect of raising the price the networks pay for television rights. Moreover,

the court found that by fixing a price for television rights to all games, the NCAA creates a price structure that is unresponsive to viewer demand and unrelated to the prices that would prevail in a competitive market. And, of course, since as a practical matter all member institutions need NCAA approval, members have no real choice but to adhere to the NCAA's television controls.

The anticompetitive consequences of this arrangement are apparent. Individual competitors lose their freedom to compete. Price is higher and output lower than they would otherwise be, and both are unresponsive to consumer preference. This latter point is perhaps the most significant, since "Congress designed the Sherman Act as a 'consumer welfare prescription.' " *Reiter v. Sonotone Corp.*, 442 U.S. 330, 343 (1979). A restraint that has the effect of reducing the importance of consumer preference in setting price and output is not consistent with this fundamental goal of anti-trust law. Restrictions on price and output are the paradigmatic examples of restraints of trade that the Sherman Act was intended to prohibit. See *Standard Oil Co. v. United States*, 221 U.S. 1, 52-60 (1911). At the same time, the television plan eliminates competitors from the market, since only those broadcasters able to bid on television rights covering the entire NCAA can compete. Thus, as the District Court found, many telecasts that would occur in a competitive market are foreclosed by the NCAA's plan.

Petitioner argues, however, that its television plan can have no significant anticompetitive effect since the record indicates that it has no market power—no ability to alter the interaction of supply and demand in the market. We must reject this argument for two reasons, one legal, one factual.

As a matter of law, the absence of proof of market power does not justify a naked restriction on price or output. To the contrary, when there is an agreement not to compete in terms of price or output, "no elaborate industry analysis is required to demonstrate the anticompetitive character of such an agreement." Professional Engineers, 435 U.S., at 692. Petitioner does not quarrel with the District Court's finding that price and output are not responsive to demand. Thus the plan is inconsistent with the Sherman Act's command that price and supply be responsive to consumer preference. We have never required proof of market power in such a case. This naked restraint on price and output requires some competitive justification even in the absence of a detailed market analysis.

As a factual matter, it is evident that petitioner does possess market power. The District Court employed the correct test for determining whether college football broadcasts constitute a separate market—whether there are other products that are reasonably substitutable for televised NCAA football games. Petitioner's argument that it cannot obtain competitive prices from broadcasters since advertisers, and hence broadcasters, can switch from college football to other types of programming simply ignores the findings of the District Court. It found that intercollegiate football telecasts generate an audience uniquely attractive to advertisers and that competitors are unable to offer programming that can attract a similar audience. These findings amply support its conclusion that the NCAA possesses market power. Indeed, the District Court's subsidiary finding that advertisers will pay a premium price per viewer to reach audiences watching college football because of their demographic characteristics is vivid evidence of the uniqueness of this product. Moreover, the District Court's market analysis is firmly supported by our decision in *International Boxing Club of New York, Inc. v. United States*, 358 U.S. 242 (1959), that championship boxing events are uniquely attractive to fans and hence constitute a market separate from that for nonchampionship events. See *Id.*, at 249-252. Thus, respondents have demonstrated that there is a separate market for telecasts of college football which "[rests] on generic qualities differentiating" viewers. *Times-Picayune Publishing Co. v. United States*, 345 U.S. 594, 613 (1953). It inexorably follows that if college football broadcasts be defined as a separate market—and we are convinced they are—then the NCAA's complete control over those broadcasts provides a solid basis for the District Court's conclusion that the NCAA possesses market power with respect to those broadcasts. "When a product is controlled by one interest, without substitutes available in the market, there is monopoly power."

Thus, the NCAA television plan on its face constitutes a restraint upon the operation of a free market, and the findings of the District Court establish that it has operated to raise prices and reduce output. Under the Rule of Reason, these hallmarks of anticompetitive behavior place upon petitioner a heavy burden of establishing an affirmative defense which competitively justifies this apparent deviation from the operations of a free market. See Professional Engineers, 435 U.S., at 692–696. We turn now to the NCAA's proffered justifications.

IV.

Relying on Broadcast Music, petitioner argues that its television plan constitutes a cooperative "joint venture" which assists in the marketing of broadcast rights and hence is procompetitive. . . . The essential contribution made by the NCAA's arrangement is to define the number of games that may be televised, to establish the price for each exposure, and to define the basic terms of each contract between the network and a home team. The NCAA does not, however, act as a selling agent for any school or for any conference of schools. The selection of individual games, and the negotiation of particular agreements, are matters left to the networks and the individual schools. Thus, the effect of the network plan is not to eliminate individual sales of broadcasts, since these still occur, albeit subject to fixed prices and output limitations. Unlike Broadcast Music's blanket license covering broadcast rights to a large number of individual compositions, here the same rights are still sold on an individual basis, only in a noncompetitive market.

The District Court did not find that the NCAA's television plan produced any procompetitive efficiencies which enhanced the competitiveness of college football television rights; to the contrary it concluded that NCAA football could be marketed just as effectively without the television plan. There is therefore no predicate in the findings for petitioner's efficiency justification. Indeed, petitioner's argument is refuted by the District Court's finding concerning price and output. If the NCAA's television plan produced procompetitive efficiencies, the plan would increase output and reduce the price of televised games. The District Court's contrary findings accordingly undermine petitioner's position. In light of these findings, it cannot be said that "the agreement on price is necessary to market the product at all." Broadcast Music, 441 U.S., at 23. In Broadcast Music, the availability of a package product that no individual could offer enhanced the total volume of music that was sold. Unlike this case, there was no limit of any kind placed on the volume that might be sold in the entire market and each individual remained free to sell his own music without restraint. Here production has been limited, not enhanced. No individual school is free to televise its own games without restraint. The NCAA's efficiency justification is not supported by the record.

Neither is the NCAA's television plan necessary to enable the NCAA to penetrate the market through an attractive package sale. Since broadcasting rights to college football constitute a unique product for which there is no ready substitute, there is no need for collective action in order to enable the product to compete against its nonexistent competitors. This is borne out by the District Court's finding that the NCAA's television plan reduces the volume of television rights sold.

V.

Throughout the history of its regulation of intercollegiate football telecasts, the NCAA has indicated its concern with protecting live attendance. This concern, it should be noted, is not with protecting live attendance at games which are shown on television; that type of interest is not at issue in this case. Rather, the concern is that fan interest in a televised game may adversely affect ticket sales for games that will not appear on television.

Although the NORC studies in the 1950's provided some support for the thesis that live attendance would suffer if unlimited television were permitted, the District Court found that there was no evidence to support that theory in today's market. Moreover, as the District Court found, the television plan has evolved in a manner inconsistent with its original design to protect gate attendance. Under the current plan, games are shown on television during all hours that college football games are played. The plan simply does not protect live attendance by ensuring that games will not be shown on television at the same time as live events.

There is, however, a more fundamental reason for rejecting this defense. The NCAA's argument that its television plan is necessary to protect live attendance is not based on a desire to maintain the integrity of college football as a distinct and attractive product, but rather on a fear that the product will not prove sufficiently attractive to draw live attendance when faced with competition from televised games. At bottom the NCAA's position is that ticket sales for most college games are unable to compete in a free market. The television plan protects ticket sales by limiting output—just as any monopolist increases revenues by reducing output. By seeking to insulate live ticket sales from the full spectrum of competition because of its assumption that the product itself is insufficiently attractive to consumers, petitioner forwards a justification that is inconsistent with the basic policy of the Sherman Act. "[The] Rule of Reason does not support a defense based on the assumption that competition itself is unreasonable."

VI.

Petitioner argues that the interest in maintaining a competitive balance among amateur athletic teams is legitimate and important and that it justifies the regulations challenged in this case. We agree with the first part of the argument but not the second.

Our decision not to apply a per se rule to this case rests in large part on our recognition that a certain degree of cooperation is necessary if the type of competition that petitioner and its member institutions seek to market is to be preserved. It is reasonable to assume that most of the regulatory controls of the NCAA are justifiable means of fostering competition among amateur athletic teams and therefore procompetitive because they enhance public interest in intercollegiate athletics. The specific restraints on football telecasts that are challenged in this case do not, however, fit into the same mold as do rules defining the conditions of the contest, the eligibility of participants, or the manner in which members of a joint enterprise shall share the responsibilities and the benefits of the total venture.

The NCAA does not claim that its television plan has equalized or is intended to equalize competition within any one league. The plan is nationwide in scope and there is no single league or tournament in which all college football teams compete. There is no evidence of any intent to equalize the strength of teams in Division I-A with those in Division II or Division III, and not even a colorable basis for giving colleges that have no football program at all a voice in the management of the revenues generated by the football programs at other schools. The interest in maintaining a competitive balance that is asserted by the NCAA as a justification for regulating all television of intercollegiate football is not related to any neutral standard or to any readily identifiable group of competitors.

The television plan is not even arguably tailored to serve such an interest. It does not regulate the amount of money that any college may spend on its football program, nor the way in which the colleges may use the revenues that are generated by their football programs, whether derived from the sale of television rights, the sale of tickets, or the sale of concessions or program advertising. The plan simply imposes a restriction on one source of revenue that is more important to some colleges than to others. There is no evidence that this restriction produces any greater measure of equality throughout the NCAA than would a restriction on alumni donations, tuition rates, or any other revenue-producing activity. At the same time, as the District Court found, the NCAA imposes a variety of other restrictions designed to preserve amateurism which are much better tailored to the goal of competitive balance than is the television plan, and which are "clearly sufficient" to preserve competitive balance to the extent it is within the NCAA's power to do so. And much more than speculation supported the District Court's findings on this score. No other NCAA sport employs a similar plan, and in particular the court found that in the most closely analogous sport, college basketball, competitive balance has been maintained without resort to a restrictive television plan. Perhaps the most important reason for rejecting the argument that the interest in competitive balance is served by the television plan is the District Court's unambiguous and well-supported finding that many more games would be televised in a free market than under the NCAA plan. The hypothesis that legitimates the maintenance of competitive balance as a procompetitive justification under the Rule of Reason is that equal competition will maximize consumer demand for the product. The finding that consumption will materially increase if the controls are removed is a compelling demonstration that they do not in fact serve any such legitimate purpose.

VII.

The NCAA plays a critical role in the maintenance of a revered tradition of amateurism in college sports. There can be no question but that it needs ample latitude to play that role, or that the preservation of the student-athlete in higher education adds richness and diversity to intercollegiate athletics and is entirely consistent with the goals of the Sherman Act. But consistent with the Sherman Act, the role of the NCAA must be to preserve a tradition that might otherwise die; rules that restrict output are hardly consistent with this role. Today we hold only that the record supports the District Court's conclusion that by curtailing output and blunting the ability of member institutions to respond to consumer preference, the NCAA has restricted rather than enhanced the place of intercollegiate athletics in the Nation's life. Accordingly, the judgment of the Court of Appeals is Affirmed.

CASES ON THE SUPPLEMENTAL WEB SITE

Agnew v. NCAA, 2012 U.S. App. LEXIS 12256. This case examines whether the NCAA's cap on the number of scholarships given per team and the prohibition of multi-year scholarships violate antitrust law.

Association for Intercollegiate Athletics for Women v. NCAA, 735 F.2d 577 (1984). The case examines whether the NCAA's move into women's athletics violated antitrust law.

Banks v. NCAA, 977 F.2d 1081 (7th Cir. 1992). The case examines the NCAA's rules on player eligibility and whether they restrain the trade of college athletes.

Law v. NCAA, 134 F.3d 1010 (10th Cir. 1998). This case examines the NCAA's rule on the salaries colleges could pay certain coaches and whether the rule violates antitrust law.

McCormack v. National Collegiate Athletic Association, 845 F.2d 1338 (5th Cir. 1988). This case examines whether the NCAA's rules restricting benefits awarded to student athletes violates antitrust law.

Worldwide Basketball & Sport Tours v. NCAA, 388 F.3d 955 (6th Cir. 2004). Compare the district court's use of "quick-look" approach compared to the traditional rule of reason analysis.

QUESTIONS YOU SHOULD BE ABLE TO ANSWER

1. How do courts determine a restraint of trade under a Rule of Reason analysis?

2. What is the significant case concerning women college athletics and antitrust, and what was its impact?

3. How do you define monopoly power?

4. Considering the cases mentioned in the chapter, why do student-athlete eligibility issues often give rise to potential antitrust violations?

5. In evaluating NCAA rules and bylaws, what are some of the things the court look for when considering the reasonableness of the rule?

REFERENCES

Cases

Agnew v. NCAA, 2012 U.S. App. LEXIS 12256.
Association for Intercollegiate Athletics for Women v. NCAA, 735 F.2d 577 (1984).
Banks v. NCAA, 977 F.2d 1081 (7th Cir. 1992).
Hairston v. Pacific 10 Conference, 101 F.3d 1315 (9th Cir. 1996).
Law v. NCAA, 134 F.3d 1010 (10th Cir. 1998).
McCormack, v. National Collegiate Athletic Association, 845 F.2d 1338 (1988).
NCAA v. Board of Regents of the University of Oklahoma, 468 U.S. 85 (1984).
Smith v. NCAA, 139 F.3d 180 (3rd Cir. 1998).
United States v. E.I.duPont Nemours & Co., 351 U.S. 377 (1956).
United States v. Grinnell Corp., 384 U.S. 563 (1966).
Verizon Communications v. Law Office of Curtis v. Trinko, 540 U.S. 398 (2004).
Worldwide Basketball and Sports Tours, Inc. v. NCAA, 388 F.3d 955 (6th Cir. 2004).

Publications

Dauner, J. T. (2000, June 14). Court hears payout arguments from restricted earnings coaches. *The Kansas City Star*, p. D4.
Hovenkamp, H. (2005). Federal Antitrust Policy: The law of Competition and its practice (3rd ed.) St. Paul, MN: West Publishing Group.
Legislation
The Sherman Antitrust Act of 1890, 15 U.S.C.A. § 1 *et seq.*
The Clayton Act of 1914, 15 U.S.C.A. § 12–27.

7.33 LABOR LAW: PROFESSIONAL SPORT APPLICATIONS

Lisa Pike Masteralexis | University Of Massachusetts-Amherst

Labor law has been critical to the U.S. workforce as it created structures for employees to bargain for safe and productive work environments. Labor laws, along with employment laws, delineate what conduct is acceptable in the work environment. Labor laws exist on both state and federal levels. State labor laws apply to public entities, such as a city or state's sports authority or a state university athletic or recreation department. Federal labor laws apply to private employers engaged in a business involving interstate commerce, such as a professional sports league or an arena operated by a facility management company.

The National Labor Relations Act in particular sets forth the parameters of conduct by employers and employees in private-sector unionized workplaces through a process of collective bargaining that allows employees and employers to determine what issues must be resolved in their particular workplace and negotiate a contract for their workplace. As a manager in the sport industry, it is critical that management decisions are made with an eye toward the collective bargaining agreement and its rules, policies, and procedures, lest you find yourself facing a grievance and arbitration process.

FUNDAMENTAL CONCEPTS

Fair Labor Standards Act

The Fair Labor Standards Act (FLSA) establishes minimum hourly wages, overtime wages for work exceeding 40 hours, and child labor protections. The FLSA requires employers keep records on those aspects. There are numerous exemptions from the overtime pay and/or the minimum wage provisions and some from the child labor provisions. Exemptions are narrowly construed against the employer. Consequently, employers and employees should always closely check the exact terms and conditions of an exemption in light of the employee's actual duties before assuming that the exemption might apply to an employee. The burden of proving the exemption rests with the employer. Exemptions likely to apply in the sport industry include those for individuals working in executive or administrative positions and those engaged in commissioned sales for the retail or service industry, of which sports and recreation are a part. In addition, amusement or recreational establishments, "if (1) it does not operate for more than seven months in any calendar year, or (2) during the preceding calendar year, its average receipts for any six months of such year were not more than 33-1/3 per centum of its average receipts for the other six months of such year" [FLSA, 29 USC § 213 (a)(3) (2005)] are also exempt from FLSA wage and overtime provisions.

National Labor Relations Act

The National Labor Relations Act of 1935 (NLRA) applies to private employers. It was enacted to "eliminate . . . or mitigate the causes of certain substantial obstructions to the free flow of commerce . . . by encouraging collective bargaining and by protecting the exercise by workers of full freedom of association, self-organization, and designation of representatives of their own choosing, for the purpose of negotiating the terms and conditions of their employment or other mutual aid or protection" (NLRA, § 151, 2005). The NLRA set forth employee rights to join or assist unions, engage in concerted activity for economic benefits and work protections, and to engage in collective bargaining. It applies to employees and employers in the private sector, drawing distinctions between employees for assignment to bargaining units, such that employees who are in the same bargaining unit need not do the exact same job, but must have common bargaining interests.

Through the NLRA, Congress created the National Labor Relations Board (NLRB) because it believed a specialized agency charged with regulating labor relations was necessary. The two primary activities of the NLRB are to conduct secret ballot union elections for certification and decertification and to prevent and remedy unfair labor practices.

Employee Rights

The NLRA § 7 established three significant employee rights:

1. The right to join or assist unions and the right not to join or assist unions;
2. The right to engage in collective bargaining through representative of own choosing; and
3. The right to engage in concerted activity for one's own mutual aid and protection (29 USCS § 157, 2005).

When employees want to join a union, they must petition the NLRB to conduct a secret ballot election under § 9 of the act to determine whether at least one-third of all employees are interested in conducting an election and whether the group is an appropriate unit to collectively bargain with the employer. The NLRB examines the community of interests of the group to determine if there is enough in common to make bargaining successful. **Community of interests** include: commonality of supervision, work rules, and personnel policies; shared work areas, similarity of job duties and working conditions; similarity of methods for evaluation; similarity in pay and benefits; integration and interdependence of operations; and history, if any, of collective bargaining between the parties (Feldacker, 2000; Gold, 1998).

In *North American Soccer League (NASL) v. NLRB*, (1980), the league challenged the NLRB's certification of all players into a national bargaining unit for purposes of collective bargaining. The NASL argued that employee units at the local team level were the appropriate bargaining unit. The NLRB disagreed, finding that where an employer has assumed sufficient control over the working conditions of employees of its franchisees, the NLRB may require employers to bargain jointly. The court agreed that labor relations were in fact conducted at a league wide level and not delegated to individual teams, and thus, the NLRB's designation was appropriate. If the NASL had successfully limited bargaining to the local level, employers could easily undermine solidarity by trading union supporters. Local units could also undermine the union's strike threat, such that if a team in Boston went on strike, the league could continue to play and give any team playing Boston a bye. By continuing without a franchise, the strike's force would be severely limited. With the shared revenue structures in place in most leagues, the Boston franchise could also still receive a cut of revenues from the league, severely disabling the leverage of the union.

Once a union is designated as an appropriate bargaining unit, elections are held, and a union is certified as the exclusive bargaining representative for employees, granting two important changes for employees. First, management then has a duty to bargain in good faith with the union and second, the union has a duty of fair representation for its employee members.

Duty to Engage in Collective Bargaining. Once a union is in existence, management *must* engage in collective bargaining over mandatory subjects of bargaining or risk being charged with an unfair labor practice under § 8 (a)(5) of the NLRA for failing to bargain in good faith (*NLRB v. Katz*, 1962). Mandatory subjects are hours, wages, and terms and conditions of employment. They are those things "plainly germane to the 'working environment' and not those 'managerial decisions which lie at the core of entrepreneurial control'" (*Ford Motor Co. v. NLRB* at 498, 1979). The result of good faith negotiations is to create a collective bargaining agreement (CBA). Wages are basically anything else that has monetary value including salaries, per diem, bonuses, severance and termination pay, and fringe benefits, such as health care, life or disability insurance. Hours provisions cover anything related to time spent at work. Terms and conditions of employment cover the majority of remaining provisions in one's work life, including job security, seniority, grievance and arbitration provisions, drug-testing provisions, safety concerns, and the like.

There are also permissive subjects for bargaining, over which management is not obligated to negotiate and the union cannot bargain to impasse. An example of a permissive subject is if the National Basketball Players Association wanted its logo to appear in all NBA advertisements. If the NBA refused, the players could not require the NBA to negotiate to an impasse over the issue. An impasse is a stalemate in negotiations that often leads to a strike or a lockout.

Duty of Fair Representation. After certification by the NLRB, a union becomes the exclusive bargaining representative for *all* employees. The duty of fair representation requires that a union represent *all* employees fairly, even those employees who are not union members (*Steele v. Louisville & Nashville Railroad*, 1944). If the union does not represent employees fairly, it commits an unfair labor practice under § 8(b) (1) (A). Fair representation requires that unions must not discriminate or act in an arbitrary or bad faith manner (*Vaca v. Sipes*, 1967). Most duty of fair representation cases challenge decisions to pursue grievances on behalf of employees. In *Peterson v. Kennedy and the NFLPA*, a NFL player sued his union for failing to fairly represent him when it erred in not filing his grievance in a timely manner (1985). The court held that because the union's conduct amounted to no more than negligence, it did not meet the standard required for a duty of fair representation case. The court emphasized that unions are not liable for good faith, nondiscriminatory errors of judgment made in interpreting CBAs, in processing grievances or representing them in the process.

Unfair Labor Practices

Section 8 of the NLRA is the mechanism used to protect § 7 rights as it establishes employer and union unfair labor practices.

Employer Discrimination or Retaliation for Union Activity. It is an unfair labor practice for the employer to interfere with, restrain or coerce employees who are engaged in union activity [NLRA, § 8(a)(1)]. It is also an unfair labor practice to discriminate against employees for engaging in union activities and for support of the union [NLRA, § 8(a)(3)]. Often workplace discipline, demotion, or termination decisions arise from mixed motives—union animus by the employer combined with an employee's poor work performance or misconduct. As a result these cases are often difficult to decide.

Duty to Bargain in Good Faith. Once a union is certified by the NLRB, management and union have a duty to bargain in good faith over hours, wages, and terms and conditions of employment. Either party can negotiate to impasse and decide whether to use their economic weapons of imposing a strike or a lockout. In practice, management may unilaterally implement its last best offer and still fulfill the duty to bargain in good faith (*Brown v. Pro Football*, 1996). Because there is no duty to bargain over permissive subjects, employers can unilaterally impose permissive and "management rights" subjects. Management rights subjects generally encompass managerial decisions that "lie at the core of entrepreneurial control" (*Ford Motor Co. v. NLRB* at 498, 1979). Management need not negotiate management rights, but it may have to negotiate their effect when they impact mandatory subjects for bargaining. For example, management need not negotiate with the union to relocate a sports franchise to a new city, but will have to negotiate with the players' association over the effects of the decision –for instance, how players will cover relocation costs.

Duty to bargain in good faith cases may arise in professional sports when the commissioner attempts to make a new rule that impacts mandatory subjects. For instance, in *National Football League Players Association v. National Labor Relations Board*, the NFLPA argued that the NFL Commissioner's imposition of a rule and corresponding fines for players leaving the bench during fights without negotiating with the union was a refusal to bargain in good faith (1974). Often a conflict arises between the Commissioner's best interest powers and the players' right to negotiate over mandatory subjects. Keep in mind that *NFLPA v. NLRB* does not limit the NFL's ability to impose rules or fines for bench clearing fights, it simply requires that such rules be negotiated with the union.

Taft-Hartley Act of 1947

There is no doubt that the NLRA was pro-labor. A dozen years later the Taft-Hartley Act amended the NLRA to give balance to labor relations by focusing on rights of employers and non-union members.

Collective Bargaining Relationship

The collective bargaining agreement (CBA) is a contract that expresses the final negotiations between management and union over the mandatory subjects of their business. The collective bargaining relationship is an ongoing one; there may be a need for additional negotiations after the CBA is formed that require union and management to continue to discuss or negotiate other issues that affect mandatory subjects. Either side has the right to convince the other side to come back to the bargaining table to discuss or negotiate over a new or current term of employment.

Over the term of the collective bargaining relationship, there is considerable time spent by union and management in the administration of the CBA. An important component of the administration is arbitration; arbitration clauses are common in all labor agreements and create a mechanism for employees and employers to resolve disputes. Arbitration is a less costly, more efficient alternative to the court system, to union striking or to management locking employees out as a means of resolving disagreements. There are two forms of arbitration: rights and interest. Rights arbitration is for disputes over the interpretation or application of the contract. Interest arbitration deals with disputes over the actual terms of contract, such as salary arbitration (*Silverman v. MLBPRC*, 1995). In salary arbitration for example, the contract provision delegates to the arbitrator(s) the power to determine the compensation term for a given player based on a salary dispute between the player and the team.

Despite the quality of negotiating or the clarity of expression in the CBA, disputes are bound to arise during the course of the agreement. Disputes can be lodged through a grievance process negotiated into the CBA. The road to an arbitration case starts with union or management filing a grievance against the other. The contract will set forth a process for resolving the disputes that leads up to a final, binding arbitration hearing. The Steelworkers Trilogy cases (*U.S. Steelworkers v. American Mfg. Co.*, 1960; *U.S. Steelworkers v. Warrior Gulf Co.*, 1960; *U.S. Steelworkers v. Enterprise Corp.*, 1960) established federal policy that an arbitrator's decision should not be the subject of judicial intervention provided that the arbitrator's award is based on the essence of the collective bargaining agreement. Thus, a court cannot substitute its decision for an arbitrator's if it does not agree with the arbitrator's decision. A court can only overturn a decision if the plaintiffs prove the arbitrator has exceeded the scope of the authority granted in the CBA or by the parties or that the arbitrator has decided the grievance in an arbitrary or capricious manner (*MLBPA v. Garvey*, 2001).

A recent issue being addressed through collective bargaining is testing for drugs and/or human growth hormones. Despite Congress' threats to impose uniform policies for these items on professional leagues, policies achieved through collective bargaining will be effective in protecting the rights and obligations of employees and employers. Through a bargaining process an employee's privacy rights, confidentiality of tests, medical concerns, the determination of what to test for and what amounts of those drugs or hormones must be in one's system to be subject to suspension, concerns over "what else" the organization might discover in testing, the role of results and international competition, and the like will be negotiated to develop fair provisions. The bargaining table also provides a forum for the two sides to add educational and rehabilitative components. Further, union and management may negotiate testing policies and procedures in the context of other aspects of their employment relationship, such as disciplinary actions and arbitration provisions.

Professional Sport Labor Relations

The labor movement in professional sports occurred about 30–40 years later than other industries. Despite the NLRA's enactment in 1935, the first decision to enforce union certification in professional sports involved baseball umpires in 1969. In the *American League of Professional Baseball Clubs and the Association of National Baseball League Umpires* (1969), Major League Baseball challenged the NLRB's jurisdiction. MLB argued that because it was exempt from antitrust laws under the 1922 U.S. Supreme Court decision in *Federal Baseball*, then it should likewise be exempt from labor laws. Next, MLB argued that it had an internal system of self-regulation, eliminating the need for NLRB involvement. The NLRB disagreed, arguing that MLB's internal system would put the umpire before the Commissioner for a final resolution of disputes. The NLRB recognized that the system was designed by the employers, who also hire and manage the Commissioner. Without evidence of a neutral third party as the final arbiter, the NLRB noted that this case had the potential to be the beginning of a whole host of employees who might seek NLRB assistance in the future including professional athletes, clubhouse attendants, front office staff, scouts, groundskeepers, and maintenance staff.

Today, virtually all major league teams are unionized workplaces for professional athletes, but not for the other employees envisioned by that umpires case in 1969. The reasons for this are varied, and among them might be (1) there are far fewer white-collar workers in unions, (2) there is high turnover in front office and coaching positions, (3) the competition for jobs might deter people from working together in a union orga-nizing movement, and (4) organizing front office staff or coaches on a national, multiemployer level like the professional athletes is challenging.

Unionized workplaces for professional athlete are unique because the dynamics of the collective bargain-ing relationship make every negotiation a battle. The turnover rate for professional athletes is high due to their short careers. A majority of athletes lack job security, causing players to want to achieve the best deal possible in collective bargaining negotiations. With an average career length hovering around three years and most col-lective bargaining agreements covering three to six-year terms, unions are motivated to negotiate for the best contract possible. Players might conceivably work their entire career under one CBA, whereas in other indus-tries, an employee's career lasts through multiple CBA negotiations, creating more patience in the process. There is a great disparity between players' talent and thus, their need for the union. A superstar will have far different bargaining goals than a bench player. When negotiating for their collective interests, players' unions struggle to keep the superstars and average players equally satisfied. Without the solidarity of all players, a play-ers' association loses its strength.

Players' associations are transnational employee bargaining units that negotiate with a transnational mul-tiemployer bargaining unit. Players associations must constantly spread their message to new members. In spreading the message, the associations face logistical challenges of a large, diverse, geographically expansive bargaining unit. In the high-pressure world of professional team sports, the multiemployer bargaining team also faces challenges by having disparate bargaining priorities, such as large versus small market clubs; cor-porate versus family ownership; ownership stake in one club versus ownership stakes in a more diverse set of sport/entertainment business venture, such as those ownership groups that have cross-ownership in teams, media ventures, and/or facilities. Despite the very contentious labor struggles between owners and players, leagues favor unionized workforces in professional sport for the labor exemption protection from antitrust liability that unions provide. The topic is discussed in greater detail in Section 7.31, *Antitrust Law: Professional Sport Applications.*

SIGNIFICANT CASE

Silverman v. Major League Baseball Player Relations Committee reviews when the National Labor Relations Board (NLRB) can seek a section 10 (j) injunction under National Labor Relations Act as part of unfair labor practice charges filed against baseball owners before NLRB. It also examines whether free agency, reserve issues, and sal-ary arbitration are mandatory subjects of collective bargaining.

SILVERMAN V. MAJOR LEAGUE BASEBALL PLAYER RELATIONS COMMITTEE
United States Court of Appeals for the Second Circuit
67 F. 3d 1054 (1995)

Winter, Circuit Judge:

This is an appeal by the Major League Baseball Player Relations Committee, Inc. ("PRC") and the constituent member clubs of Major League Baseball ("Clubs") from a temporary injunction issued by Judge Sotomayor pursu-ant to section 10(j) of the National Labor Relations Act ("NLRA"), 29 U.S. C. §160(j). The PRC is the collective bargaining representative for the twenty-eight Clubs. The Major League Baseball Players Association is a union that is the exclusive bargaining representative for the forty-man rosters of each major league club. The injunction is based on the district court's conclusion that appellants violated NLRA §§ 8(a)(1) and (5), 29 U.S.C. §§ 158(a)(1) and (5) by unilaterally implementing terms and conditions of employment that differed from those in the last collective agreement. It orders the PRC and the Clubs to: (i) abide by the terms of an expired collective agreement, (ii) rescind any actions taken that are inconsistent with that agreement and (iii) bargain in good faith with the Players Association. *See Silverman v. Major League Baseball Player Relations Comm., Inc.,* 880 F. Supp. 246, 261 (S. D. N.Y. 1995). The injunction is to remain in effect until either (i) the expired agreement is replaced by a new collective bargaining agreement, (ii) the National Labor Relations Board ("NLRB") renders a final disposition of the matters pending before it in the related administrative case, or (iii) the district court finds, upon petition of either of the parties, that an impasse has occurred. We affirm.

BACKGROUND

On January 1, 1990, the most recent collective agreement ("CBA") between appellants and the Players Association became effective. It contained provisions implementing a combination of free agency and a reserve system—that is, a compromise between free competitive bidding for a player's services and an individual club's exclusive rights to those services.

Free agency, in its purest form, is a status in which the rights to a player's athletic services are not owned by a club and may be shopped around by the player in a quest for the most attractive bid. However, for more than a century, Major League Baseball has had a reserve system that to one degree or another affords individual clubs exclusive property rights to the athletic services of certain players. Before the players were organized and a collective bargaining relationship was established, the standard players contract with a club reserved to the club exclusive rights to a player's services and provided for an annual right of renewal of the contract by the club in question. The Clubs interpreted the contract as allowing the club in question to renew all of an individual player's contract, including the right of renewal provision. So interpreted, this provision—known generally as the "reserve clause"—bound a player to one club in perpetuity until traded or released. After the Clubs recognized the Players Association and entered into a collective agreement with it, an arbitrator held in a grievance proceeding that the reserve clause allowed a renewal for only one year rather than a succession of years. *See National & American League Professional Baseball Clubs v. Major League Baseball Players Ass'n,* 66 Lab.Arb. (BNA) 101 (1976) (Seitz, Arb.). Since then, appellants and the Players Association have struggled to accommodate their conflicting interests in the free agency and reserve issues, and a variety of compromises have from time to time been reached. However, relations have been acrimonious, and

several strikes and lockouts have occurred. This appeal itself arises out of a strike that terminated the 1994 season before the playoffs and World Series.

Article XX of the CBA that became effective in 1990 contains a series of provisions that govern free agency and reserve rights. Players with six or more years of major league service are free agents and may seek competing bids in an effort to obtain the best contract, which may of course give exclusive rights to the club for a stipulated number of years. Free agency is guaranteed by an anti-collusion provision, Article XX(F), which prohibits the Clubs from acting in concert with each other with respect to the exercise of rights under Article XX. Article XX(F) thus prevents the Clubs from agreeing either to refuse to bid for the services of free agents or to offer only low bids to them. Article XX(F) also prohibits players from acting in concert with regard to Article XX rights. (citations omitted).

Players with less than six years of service remain under reserve to their individual clubs, although a club may reserve a player only once. Although a minimum annual salary is provided, players with less than three years of major league service must negotiate with their clubs to determine their salary for the coming season. Article XX allows certain reserved players—generally those with more than three but less than six years of service—to demand salary arbitration. Salary arbitration is a mechanism for determining the individual salaries for that group of reserved players if they cannot arrive at an agreement with their clubs. The player and the club each present the arbitrator with a suggested salary figure for a new one-year contract. The arbitrator then inserts either the player's or the club's figure into a blank uniform contract that the parties have already signed. Article VI(F)(12) provides the following with regard to the criteria to be used, and the evidence to be heard, by the arbitrator:

(12) *Criteria.* (a) The Criteria will be the quality of the Player's contribution to his Club during the past season (including but not limited to his overall performance, special qualities of leadership and public appeal), the length and consistency of his career contribution, the record of the Player's past compensation, comparative baseball salaries . . ., the existence of any physical or mental defects on the part of the Player, and the recent performance record of the Club including but not limited to its League standing and attendance as an indication of public acceptance (subject to the exclusion stated in subparagraph (b)(i) below). Any evidence may be submitted which is relevant to the above criteria, and the arbitrator shall assign such weight to the evidence as shall to him appear appropriate under the circumstances. The arbitrator shall, except for a Player with five or more years of Major League service, give particular attention, for comparative salary purposes, to the contracts of Players with Major League service not exceeding one annual service group above the Player's annual service group. This shall not limit the ability of a Player or his representative, because of special accomplishment, to argue the

equal relevance of salaries of Players without regard to service, and the arbitrator shall give whatever weight to such argument as he deems appropriate.

(b) Evidence of the following shall not be admissible:
  (i) The financial position of the Player and the Club;
  (ii) Press comments, testimonials or similar material bearing on the performance of either the Player or the Club, except that recognized annual Player awards for playing excellence shall not be excluded;
  (iii) Offers made by either Player or Club prior to arbitration;
  (iv) The cost to the parties of their representatives, attorneys, etc.;
  (v) Salaries in other sports or occupations.

The CBA expired on December 31, 1993, pursuant to the PRC's notice of termination. Although negotiations for a successor agreement did not get underway until March 1994, the PRC and the Players Association continued to observe the terms of the expired CBA. Prior to the commencement of negotiations, the Clubs and the Players Association had completed individual salary arbitration hearings and had entered into individual player contracts for the 1994 baseball season, which began in April 1994. (citations omitted).

Negotiations for a new collective bargaining agreement continued unsuccessfully. The PRC offered its first formal economic proposal to the Players Association at a meeting on June 14, 1994. It included a "salary cap," a mechanism that establishes a ceiling on the total player salaries paid by each club. The ceiling may allow some flexibility, depending on the details. Generally, the aggregate salaries of each team are determined by an agreed upon formula and must remain above a minimum percentage of industry revenues, also determined by an agreed upon formula, but below a maximum percentage of those revenues. See Wood v. National Basketball Ass'n, 809 F. 2d 954, 957 (2d Cir. 1987). The PRC proposal also eliminated the salary arbitration system and substituted restricted free agency rights for those reserved players previously eligible for salary arbitration. As an alternative to the PRC's proposed salary cap, the Players Association suggested a revenue sharing and luxury "tax" plan that would impose a tax on high-paying clubs. Subsequent proposals reflected disagreement over appropriate tax rates and payroll thresholds above which clubs would be subject to the tax. (citations omitted).

The players struck on August 12, and the 1994 baseball season never resumed. On December 22, 1994, the PRC declared an impasse in negotiations and stated that it intended unilaterally to impose a salary cap and to implement other changes in the terms and conditions of employment, including the elimination of salary arbitration. The Players Association responded with a unilateral ban on players signing individual contracts with the Clubs. (citations omitted).

Thereafter, cross-charges of unfair labor practices were filed with the NLRB by the Players Association and the Clubs. The Players Association alleged that the Clubs had engaged in unfair labor practices by unilaterally implementing the salary cap and other terms because the parties were not at an impasse.

On February 3, 1995, counsel for the PRC notified the NLRB General Counsel that the PRC would revoke the implementation of unilateral changes and restore the status quo ante. The General Counsel indicated that the Players Association charges would be dismissed as a result. Counsel for the PRC informed the General Counsel, however, that the PRC did not believe itself obligated to maintain provisions of the CBA that involved non-mandatory subjects of bargaining. He mentioned salary arbitration in that regard and also suggested that the Clubs might decide to bargain exclusively through the PRC. The NLRB General Counsel declined to offer an advisory opinion on these matters.

Three days later, by memorandum dated February 6, counsel for the PRC notified the Clubs that, until a new collective bargaining agreement was ratified or until further notice, individual clubs had no authority to negotiate contracts with individual players because the PRC was now the Clubs' exclusive bargaining representative. This amounted to an agreement among the Clubs not to hire free agents and thus was a departure from the anti-collusion provision, Article XX(F) of the CBA. It also amounted to an elimination of salary arbitration, because salary arbitration is a method of arriving at a wage for an individual player contract with a club.

The Players Association thereupon filed a new unfair labor practice charge, and the General Counsel issued a complaint alleging, inter alia, that the Clubs and the PRC had violated Sections 8(a)(1) and (5) of the NLRA by unilaterally eliminating, before an impasse had been reached, competitive bidding for the services of free agents, the anti-collusion provision, and salary arbitration for certain reserved players. The NLRB found that these matters were related to wages, hours, and other terms and conditions of employment and were therefore mandatory subjects for collective bargaining. It then authorized its General Counsel to seek an injunction under NLRA § 10(j). On March 27, the NLRB Regional Director filed a petition seeking a temporary injunction restraining the alleged unfair labor practices.

The district court agreed that the NLRB had reasonable cause to conclude that free agency and salary arbitration were mandatory subjects of bargaining and that the Clubs' unilateral actions constituted an unfair labor practice. The district court also concluded that injunctive relief was warranted. This appeal followed.

DISCUSSION

The NLRB is authorized under Section 10(j) of the NLRA to petition for temporary injunctive relief from a district court to enjoin ongoing unfair labor practices. If the court has reasonable cause to believe that an unfair labor practice has occurred and that injunctive relief would be just and proper, it should grant appropriate relief. . . .

We turn now to the merits of the regional director's petition. The petition invokes basic principles of labor law. Section 8(d) of the NLRA mandates that employers and unions bargain in good faith over "wages, hours, and other terms and conditions of employment." These are so-called mandatory subjects of bargaining. Under case law, the parties may propose and bargain over, but may not insist upon, permissive subjects of bargaining. *NLRB v. Wooster Div. of Borg-Warner Corp.*, 356 U.S. 342, 349 (1958). When a collective agreement expires, an employer may not alter terms and conditions of employment involving mandatory subjects until it has bargained to an impasse over new terms. *NLRB v. Katz*, 369 U.S. 736, 741–43 (1962 Thereafter, it may implement the new terms. Generally, when an agreement expires, an employer need not bargain to an impasse over terms and conditions involving permissive subjects but may alter them upon expiration. *Allied Chem. & Alkali Workers v. Pittsburgh Plate Glass Co.*, 404 U.S. 157, 187–88 (1971).

Many of the usual issues that arise in impasse cases are not disputed in the instant matter. The parties agree that the PRC, in directing the Clubs to decline to bargain individually with free agents, unilaterally departed from much of Article XX, which provides for a limited form of free agency and forbids collusive behavior by the Clubs in negotiating with free agents. It is also undisputed that the PRC unilaterally departed from the CBA's provisions with regard to salary arbitration. The PRC does not claim that it had bargained to an impasse over the free agency, the anti-collusion, or the salary arbitration provisions. Finally, it is also agreed that, if those provisions involved mandatory subjects of bargaining, their unilateral abrogation before impasse was a refusal to bargain in good faith.

The PRC and the Clubs argue that the anti-collusion and free agency provisions of the CBA do not involve mandatory subjects of bargaining and are therefore not subject to the *Katz* rule that unilateral implementation of new terms is an unfair labor practice unless the employer has bargained to an impasse over these new terms. The PRC and the Clubs contend that an injunction compelling them to maintain the free agency and anti-collusion provisions undermines their right as a multi-employer group to bargain collectively through an exclusive representative. If so, they would be permissive subjects of bargaining. With regard to salary arbitration, the PRC and the Clubs argue that it is the equivalent of interest arbitration—arbitration of the terms of a new collective agreement—and thus not a mandatory subject of bargaining. (citations omitted).

We are unpersuaded that an injunction compelling the PRC and the Clubs to observe the anti-collusion and free agency provisions of the CBA infringes on their right as a multiemployer group to bargain through an exclusive representative. Free agency and the ban on collusion are one part of a complex method—agreed upon in collective bargaining—by which each major league player's salary is determined under the CBA. They are analogous to the use of seniority, hours of work, merit increases, or piece work to determine salaries in an industrial context. The PRC and the Clubs describe free agency and the ban on collusion as provisions undermining their right to select a joint bargaining representative because those provisions entail individual contracts with clubs. However, the argument ignores the fact that free agency is simply a collectively bargained method of determining individual salaries for one group of players. The anti-collusion provision is not designed to prevent the PRC from representing the Clubs. Rather, that provision guarantees that free agency will be a reality when permitted by the CBA. . .

The question, therefore, is whether the free agency, anti-collusion, and reserve issues are—or there is reasonable cause to believe they are—otherwise mandatory subjects of bargaining. Section 8(d) of the NLRA defines the duty to bargain as "the obligation . . . to meet . . . and confer in good faith with respect to wages, hours, and other terms and conditions of employment. . . ." In *Wood v. National Basketball Ass'n,* , we noted that free agency and reserve issues are "at the center of collective bargaining in much of the professional sports industry," and that "it is precisely because of [free agency's] direct relationship to wages and conditions of employment that [it is] so controversial and so much the focus of bargaining in professional sports." 809 F. 2d 954, 961–62 (2d Cir. 1987).

Wood noted that collective bargaining between professional athletes and leagues raises "numerous problems with little or no precedent in standard industrial relations."*Id*. Such is the case with a free agency and reserve system. For the most part, unionized employees in the industrial sector may leave one employer for another without restriction. The employee may have no bargaining rights with regard to the terms of hire by the new employer, which may be set by a collective agreement, but is nevertheless generally free to go from one unionized job to another.

The professional sports industry has a very different history and very different economic imperatives. Most professional sports leagues have always had some form of what has become known as the reserve system. (citations omitted). . . . Until the arbitration decision in 1976, the reserve system prevented players from offering their services to competing teams. A player's services were thus the property of a single team until he was traded or released. In enforcing a complete reserve system, Major League Baseball was exercising monopsony power—a buyer's monopoly.

However, there are many reasons, apart from maximizing the transfer of revenues from players to clubs, why reserve systems exist within professional sports. Fans might not be interested in games between teams that had entirely new lineups for every contest. Moreover, high quality play may require that individuals practice and play with the same teammates for at least some period of time. Teams may also want to recoup what they regard as training costs invested in players while they gained experience. In antitrust litigation, the leagues perennially argue that some form of reserve system is necessary for competitive balance (citation omitted). Indeed, even in a system of complete free agency, one would expect to see many long-term agreements binding individual players to particular clubs.

There are also reasons, apart from maximizing the transfer of revenues to players, why a union of professional athletes would seek free agency. It is very difficult to set individual salaries in professional sports through collective bargaining. Although unions of professional athletes may bargain for uniform benefits and minimum salaries, they do not usually follow their industrial counterparts and seek relatively fixed salaries by job description, seniority, or other formulae. Players often play positions requiring very different skills. Moreover, the level of performance and value to a team in attracting fans differs radically among players, with star athletes or popular players being far more valuable than sub-par or nondescript players. Usually, therefore, players unions seek some form of free agency as a relatively simple method of setting individual salaries.

Most importantly, however, both the leagues and the players unions view free agency and reserve issues as questions of what share of revenues go to the clubs or to the players. The more restrictive the reserve system is, the greater the clubs' share. The greater the role of free agency, the greater the players' share.

To hold that there is no reasonable cause for the NLRB to conclude that free agency and reserve issues are mandatory subjects of bargaining would be virtually to ignore the history and economic imperatives of collective bargaining in professional sports. A mix of free agency and reserve clauses combined with other provisions is the universal method by which leagues and players unions set individual salaries in professional sports. Free agency for veteran players may thus be combined with a reserve system, as in baseball, or a rookie draft, as in basketball, for newer players. A salary cap may or may not be included. (citations omitted).To hold that any of these items, or others that make up the mix in a particular sport, is merely a permissive subject of bargaining would ignore the reality of collective bargaining in sports.

Indeed, free agency is in many ways nothing but the flip side of the reserve system. A full reserve system does not eliminate individual bargaining between teams and players. It simply limits that bargaining to one team. If free agency were a permissive subject of collective bargaining, then so would be the reserve system.

With regard to salary arbitration, we will assume, but not decide, that if it is a form of interest arbitration, it may be unilaterally eliminated. *See George Koch & Sons, Inc.*, 306 N.L.R.B. 834, 839 (1992)(interest arbitration permissive subject of bargaining). Interest arbitration is a method by which an employer and union reach new agreements by sending disputed issues to an arbitrator rather than settling them through collective bargaining and economic force. (citation omitted). The salary arbitration provisions of the CBA are a method by which salaries for some players who are not eligible for free agency—those with three to six years of major league service—are set. The CBA sets forth criteria by which the arbitrator is to reach a decision. These criteria include the player's performance in the prior year, the length and consistency of career contribution, physical or mental defects, recent performance of the team on the field and at the gate, and salaries of certain comparable players. The CBA also forbids the arbitrator from considering certain facts that might otherwise be relevant. Finally, the CBA requires that the arbitrator pick either the club's suggested salary or the player's.

We decline to analogize Article VI(F) of the CBA to interest arbitration. Salary arbitration provides limited discretion to the arbitrator to set salaries for designated players who are not eligible for free agency. The discretion afforded the arbitrator is arguably less than the discretion afforded arbitrators in grievance arbitration involving disputes arising under an existing collective agreement, which is beyond question a mandatory subject of bargaining. In grievance arbitration, an arbitrator may permissibly imply a term even though the term has no explicit support in the text of the collective agreement. Similarly, a term may be implied from past practices even though somewhat inconsistent with the agreement. (citations omitted). We thus decline to analogize salary arbitration to interest arbitration, and, therefore, we hold that there is reasonable cause to believe that it is a mandatory subject of bargaining.

With regard to whether the granting of relief was "just and proper, we review the district court's determination only for abuse of discretion. We see no such abuse in the present matter. Given the short careers of professional athletes and the deterioration of physical abilities through aging, the irreparable harm requirement has been met. The unilateral elimination of free agency and salary arbitration followed by just three days a promise to restore the status quo. The PRC decided to settle the original unfair labor practice charges while embarking on a course of action based on a fallacious view of the duty to bargain. We see no reason to relieve it of the consequences of that course.

We therefore affirm.

Cases on the Supplemental Web Site

National Football League Players Association v. National Labor Relations Board, 503 F.2d 12 (1974). This case explores the duty to bargain in good faith over mandatory subjects for bargaining.

North American Soccer League v. National Labor Relations Board, 613 F. 2d. 1379 (5th Cir. 1980). This case explores the appropriate bargaining units in professional sports unions and when management has a duty to bargain with players versus its ability to change terms of conditions of employment unilaterally.

Morio v. North American Soccer League, 501 F. Supp. 633 (S.D. N.Y. 1980.) This case explores the parameters duty to bargain collectively with an exclusive bargaining representative in a setting where individual contract negotiations are also present. To avoid undermining a union's authority, management must not bargain with individual employees until an agreement or impasse in bargaining is reached.

Silverman v. Major League Baseball Player Relations Committee, 880 F. Supp. 246 (1995). This case examines the parameters of an employer's ability to impose unilateral changes after impasse and after players have gone on strike.

Palace Sports & Entertainment, Inc. D/B/A/ St. Pete Forum v. National Labor Relations Board, 411 F. 3d 212 (2005). This case explores the concept of an employee's right to organize a union in the workplace. It also examines when an employer may terminate a union leader's employment in the workplace when the firing is allegedly made through mixed motives—alleged anti-union animus toward the employee and alleged employee misconduct.

QUESTIONS YOU SHOULD BE ABLE TO ANSWER

1. What are the mandatory subjects for bargaining? Give an example of each.

2. Why are provisions, such as drug testing, better addressed through collective bargaining than through an Act of Congress?

3. What are employee rights established by the National Labor Relations and the Taft Hartley Acts?

4. What are the unique aspects of professional sports labor relations?

5. What is the difference between rights and interest arbitration?

REFERENCES

Cases

Brown v. Pro Football, Inc., 518 U.S. 231 (1996).
Ford Motor Co. v. NLRB, 441 U.S. 488, 498 (1979).
MLBPA v. Garvey, 532 U.S. 504 (2001).
National Football League Players Association v. National Labor Relations Board, 503 F.2d 12 (1974).
NLRB v. Katz, 369 U.S. 736 (1962).
North American Soccer League v. NLRB, 613 F. 2d. 1379 (5th Cir. 1980).
Peterson v. Kennedy and the NFLPA, 771 F.2d 1244 (1985).
Silverman v. Major League Baseball Player Relations Committee, 880 F. Supp. 246 (1995).
Steele v. Louisville & Nashville Railroad Co., 323 U.S. 192 (1944).
The American League of Professional Baseball Clubs and the Association of National Baseball League Umpires, 180 N.L.R.B. 190 (1969).
U.S. Steelworkers v. American Mfg. Co., 363 U.S. 564 (1960).
U.S. Steelworkers v. Warrior Gulf Co., 363 U.S. 574 (1960).
U.S. Steelworkers v. Enterprise Corp., 363 U.S. 593 (1960).
Vaca v. Sipes, 386 U.S. 171 (1967).

Publications

Feldacker, B. (2000). *Labor guide to labor law* (4th ed.). Upper Saddle River, NJ: Prentice Hall.

Gold, M. E. (1998). *An introduction to labor law* (2nd ed.). Ithaca, NY: ILR Press/Cornell University Press.

Legislation

Fair Labor Standards Act, 29 USCS § 201, et seq. (2005).

Labor Management Relations Act, 29 USCS § 141, et. seq. (2005).

National Labor Relations Act, 29 USCS § 151, et. seq. (2005).

SPORT AGENT LEGISLATION

7.40

John T. Wolohan | Syracuse University

Although the creation of the modern sports agent is usually credited to Boston attorney Bob Woolf in the mid-1960s, individuals have been representing athletes as far back as the 1920s. One of the first sports agents was Charles "Cash & Carry" Pyle, who in 1925 reportedly negotiated a $3,000-per-game contract between Red Grange and the Chicago Bears (Shropshire & Davis, 2008). In truth, however, it was only the rare and special athlete that needed an agent before the 1970s. Before 1976, most professional athletes were bound to their team through a reserve system and were left with few alternatives and little negotiating power. As a result, the only real contract negotiation in these circumstances was a matter of taking what was offered or refusing to play.

Beginning in the mid-1970s, due to court decisions, arbitration, collective bargaining, and in some instances, the emergence of competing professional leagues, players gained greater freedom and bargaining leverage to market their skills to the highest bidder. At this same time, large sums of money were coming into the leagues via increased television and radio rights. These events expanded media coverage,escalating rights fees paid by networks to leagues, and made professional sports more popular and profitable. As a result, team owners had more money to spend, albeit grudgingly, on attracted high quality and high priced players to their teams. With all the millions of dollars coming into professional sports, it became more and more essential for many athletes to seek the help of professional "sports agents" to maximize their salary and other compensation.

FUNDAMENTAL CONCEPTS

Although few would argue that the services of a competent agent can be extremely valuable for a professional athlete, the emergence of the sport agent in professional sports has not been without problems. For example, there is only a limited supply of quality athletes. In the four major sports in America, there are only a total of 3,440 athletes playing at the very top level. At the same time, there are over 1,520 registered agents in those same sports. As a result, there is a lot of competition to secure and sign a client. It should not be all that surprising therefore that agents, and or their employees, are providing college athletes all types of illegal inducements to get the athlete to sign with them. The following section outlines some of the attempts by the state and federal governments and other various organizations to protect college and professional athletes, as well as colleges and universities, from actions of unscrupulous agents.

Sport Agent Legislation

There have been numerous attempts to regulate sport agents, unfortunately, due to a variety of reasons these attempts have mostly failed to stop the unethical, unscrupulous, and illegal conduct of sport agents.

State Legislative Efforts

In 1981, California became the first state to pass legislation regulating sport agents when it enacted the California Athlete Agents Act. Thirty-One (31) years later, the number of states regulating the activities of sport agents has grown to Forty-Three (43). However, instead of protecting the athletes from unethical and unscrupulous agents, the focus of current state sport agent statutes has shifted to addressing the economic damage an unscrupulous agent could cause for a college or university. This current legislative trend is characterized by provisions requiring notice to school and state before and/or after the signing of a representation contract, waiting periods for valid contracts, the creation of causes of action in favor of colleges and universities for agent misconduct resulting in damages, and an abandonment or modification of the onerous registration requirements common in earlier legislative schemes.

Uniform Athlete Agent Act

The most recent attempt by states to regulate the sport agent profession began in 1997, when the National Conference of Commissioners on Uniform State Laws (NCCUSL), at the request of several major universities and the NCAA, appointed a drafting committee to develop a uniform statute for regulating sport agents. The NCCUSL is a national association, which endeavors to promote the uniformity of state laws. As a result of their work, the NCCUSL developed the **Uniform Athlete Agents Act (UAAA)** in the fall of 2000. The stated goal of the UAAA is the protection of student-athletes from unscrupulous agents. To achieve this goal, the UAAA contains a number of important provisions regulating the conduct between athletes and agents. For example, the UAAA requires an agent to provide important information, both professional and criminal in nature. This information enables student-athletes, their parents and family, and university personnel to better evaluate the prospective agent. The UAAA also requires that written notice be provided to institutions when a student-athlete signs an agency contract before their eligibility expires. In addition, the UAAA gives authority to the secretary of state to issue subpoenas that would enable the state to obtain relevant material that ensures compliance with the act. Finally, the UAAA provides for criminal, civil, and administrative penalties with enforcement at the state level (www.ncaa.org, 2012).

In addition, the UAAA also covers such key areas as agent registration requirement; liability insurance; notice to educational institution; a student-athletes' right to cancel, and penalties. Perhaps the most important part of the UAAA is the section allowing an agent's valid certificate of registration from one state to be honored in all other states that have adopted the act. The success of the reciprocal registration process is contingent on states establishing a reasonable fee schedule, including lower registration fees for reciprocal applications and renewals. Thus, more agents are likely to register due to the efficiency of this process, its practical cost-saving implications for the agent, and the benefits of complying with a single set of regulations.

As of 2012, the UAAA had been passed in forty (40) states. In addition, three states have laws dealing with agent behavior on the books that do not conform to the UAAA (see Table 7.40.1). However, some critics argued that the UAAA is more interested in protecting NCAA member institutions, than athletes. For example, the UAAA requires agents and student-athletes to notify the institution within seventy-two hours of the signing of a contract, or before the student-athlete's next scheduled athletics event, whichever occurs first. If a prospective student-athlete has signed a contract, the agent must notify the institution where the agent has reasonable grounds to believe the prospect will enroll. Finally, the act provides institutions with a right of action against the agent or former student–athlete for any damages caused by a violation of this act.

The UAAA has not been the panacea many anticipated, however. Since not every state has passed the Act, there is still a lack of uniformity, which in turn, has had an impact on the number of agents registering with the states. Therefore, it is not surprising that agents prone to abuse have ignored these statutory provisions and continued to conduct business as usual. In addition, differing state requirements have created an administrative nightmare for many honest agents doing business in several states. This, coupled with a perceived lack of enforcement, often encourages the breach of these provisions.

Recently, however, some states have at least made an attempt to control the corruption of sports agents. For example, in 2011, Texas passed a bill that would lead to a felony conviction and up to 10 years in prison for any sports agents or runners who bait college athletes into signing contracts that cause them to lose their eligibility. Under the new bill, prospective agents would have to post a $50,000 bond with the state before signing a student-athlete to a contract. Before a student-athlete's last intercollegiate game, agents would be restricted from directly contacting or providing anything of value from anyone related to the student-athlete, among other limitations. In addition to Texas, Arkansas and Oklahoma also stiffened the penalties for agents who violate state laws governing agent conduct. Under the new Arkansas law, the maximum fine for agents would go up to $250,000 and make violations punishable by up to six years in jail (Arkansas Statute Chapter 16, subchapter 1). In Oklahoma, the fine for a first offense can be up to $250,000 and up to $500,000 for a second offense. In addition to civil damages and penalties the law also imposes criminal penalties ranging up to three years in jail (Oklahoma Statute 70 O.S. § 821).

TABLE 7.40.1	STATES THAT HAVE PASSED THE UAAA, AS OF JULY 2012		
Alabama	Illinois	Nebraska	Rhode Island
Arizona	Indiana	Nevada	South Carolina
Arkansas	Iowa	New Hampshire	South Dakota
Colorado	Kansas	New Mexico	Tennessee
Connecticut	Kentucky	New York	Texas
Delaware	Louisiana	North Carolina	Utah
Florida	Maryland	North Dakota	Washington
Georgia	Minnesota	Oklahoma	West Virginia
Hawaii	Mississippi	Oregon	Wisconsin
Idaho	Missouri	Pennsylvania	Wyoming
States That Have Passed the Non-UAAA Designed to Regulate Athlete Agents			
California	Ohio	Michigan	
States That Have No Existing Laws Regulating Athlete Agents			
Alaska	Massachusetts	New Jersey*	Virginia
Maine	Montana	Vermont	

*As of May 2012, the New Jersey legislature was considering UAAA legislation.
Source: www.ncaa.org, 2012.

National Legislative Efforts

To correct some of the shortcomings of the states' laws,the Unites States Congress passed the **Sports Agent Responsibility and Trust Act (SPARTA)** (15 U.S.C. § 7801 - 7807). Sponsored by Tom Osborne, a Republican from Nebraska and the former football coach at the University of Nebraska, SPARTA was signed into law in 2004. Under SPARTA "it is unlawful for an athlete agent to:

1. directly or indirectly recruit or solicit a student athlete to enter into an agency contract, by
   a. giving any false or misleading information or making a false promises or representation; or
   b. providing anything of value to a student athlete or anyone associated with the student athlete before the student athletes enters into an agency contract, including any consideration in the form of a loan, or acting in the capacity of a guarantor or co-guarantor for any debt;
2. enter into an agency contract with a student athlete without providing the student athlete with a disclosure document described in subsection (b); or
3. predate or postdate an agency contract (15 U.S.C. § 7802a).

As part of the disclosure document that agents are required to give student athletes, the law states that:

"the disclosure document must contain, in close proximity to the signature of the student athlete, or, if the student athlete is under the age of 18, the signature of such student athlete's parent or legal guardian, a conspicuous notice in boldface type stating: 'Warning to student athlete: If you agree orally or in writing to be represented by an agent now or in the future you may lose your eligibility to compete as a student athlete in your sport. Within 72 hours after entering into this contract or before the next athletic event in which you are eligible to participate, whichever occurs first, both you and the agent by whom you are agreeing to be represented must notify the athletic director of the educational institution at which you are enrolled, or other individual responsible for athletic programs at such educational institution, that you have entered into an agency contract" (15 U.S.C. § 7802b3).

SPARTA is enforced by the Federal Trade Commission (FTC). The law, however, also allows the attorney general of any state to bring a civil action against any agent it believes is in violation of the law (15 U.S.C.

§ 7804). Under the law, the state may recover any actual losses and expenses an educational institution may incur as a result of the conduct of the agent (15 U.S.C. § 7805b2).

SPARTA, however, has been criticized. First, some people argue that the limits it places on who can take action if a sport agent does not live up to his or her duties leaves the student athlete with no recourse if the attorney general or the FTC do not want to act on an agents wrongdoing. This point is illustrated by the fact that the FTChas not imposed a single penalty against an agent since the law was passed. Second, like the UAAA, which SPARTA encourages every state to enact, the main goal of SPARTA is to protect colleges and universities by ensuring that student athletes keep their NCAA eligibility. The law, therefore, does nothing to protect professional athletes who no longer have any college eligibility left.

Other Regulatory Efforts

Agent-specific legislation is not the only legal means used to regulate the conduct of athlete agents. Other common law or statutory remedies, although not specifically directed at agents, have been used to attempt to control their abusive conduct. For example, the common law civil remedies of breach of contract, misrepresentation, fraud, deceit, and negligence have been applied in cases of agent misconduct (Shropshire & Davis, 2008). In addition, such organizations as the NCAA, professional sport players' associations, and the American Bar Association can also be used in regulating this relationship between athletes and agents.

The National Collegiate Athletic Association (NCAA)

In the mid-1980s, the NCAA was rocked by one of the largest sports agent abuse cases ever. Norby Walters, a successful agent in the music industry, and his partner Lloyd Bloom signed 58 college football and basketball athletes to postdated contracts. The contracts were dated for after the athlete's eligibility expired. On entering into the contracts, under which the athletes agreed to use Walters as their agent in negotiating professional contracts, Walters provided the students with cash and other perks while they were still in college. When all but two of the students tried signed with new agents and tried to back out of their contracts with Walters, Walters sued the athletes for breach of contract. The federal government eventually got involved in the case and Walters and Bloom were charged with various federal conspiracies and racketeering crimes (*United States v. Norby Walters*, 1993). As a result of the Walters scandal, and other reports of agent abuse, the NCAA has worked with individual states encouraging them to adopt the UAAA as a means of limiting the damage resulting from the impermissible and oftentimes illegal practices of some athlete agents.

Even though the NCAA and its member schools suffer media embarrassment and financial loss every time a new scandal comes to light, as an organization, the NCAA has very little control over agents. The NCAA can only directly punish its members, the colleges and universities, and indirectly the student athletes. For example, under NCAA Bylaw 12.3.1

> "[A]n individual shall be ineligible for participation in an intercollegiate sport if he or she ever has agreed (orally or in writing) to be represented by an agent for the purpose of marketing his or her athletics ability or reputation in that sport. Further, an agency contract not specifically limited in writing to a sport or particular sports shall be deemed applicable to all sports, and the individual shall be ineligible to participate in any sport" (NCAA Manual, 2011–12).

In addition to sports agents, the NCAA Bylaws also prohibits athletes from accepting gift from runner (individuals who befriend student-athletes and frequently distribute impermissible benefits on behalf of sports agents) and financial advisors.

In 2012, the NCAA broadened the of "agent" to include " any individual, agency or organization that represents a prospective student-athlete for compensation in placing the prospective student-athlete in a collegiate institution as a recipient of institutional financial aid shall be considered an agent or organization marketing the individual's athletics ability or reputation (NCAA Bylaw 12.3.3). The goal of the new language is to close a loophole in the NCAA's rules that did not cover the actions of parents, relatives, and friends of student athletes. The "Cam Newton" loophole,which was brought to light in the controversy surrounding former Auburn University star quarterback Cam Newton and the allegations that his father attempted to broker a "pay for play" arrangement with several SEC schools, is designed to prevent parents, relatives, and friends from shopping the athlete around to the highest bidder. Auburn Tigers quarterback Cam Newton throws a pass against the Oregon Ducks during the third quarter their NCAA BCS National Championship college football game in Glendale, Arizona, January 10, 2011. REUTERS/Mike Blake (UNITED STATES - Tags: SPORT FOOTBALL)

The problem with NCAA regulations, however, is that they do not directly apply to sport agents. NCAA rules and regulations are only applicable to the academic institutions in which the athletes are enrolled. The NCAA lacks the authority to penalize agents or athletes once they turn professional. Therefore, an agent can violate NCAA regulations without fear of NCAA sanctions. While the NCAA can revoke the remaining eligibility of student athlete with whom the agent dealt, the real loser in any NCAA sanctions is the academic institution.

Professional Team Sports Players' Associations

The power of the players' associations of the four major sports leagues to regulate sport agents derives from the National Labor Relations Act and other federal labor law. Essentially, the players' associations regulate agents by "requiring their members to hire regulated agents only, and by obtaining the agreement of teams to negotiate with regulated agents only" (Fluhr, 1999). The first professional team sport players' union to initiate a player-agent certification program was the National Football League Players' Association (NFLPA) in 1983. The 1982 collective bargaining agreement between the NFL and NFLPA had reserved the exclusive right for the NFLPA or "its agent" to negotiate individual NFL player contracts. The 1983 program was established to certify agents as "NFLPA Contract Advisors," who, under the program, are required to use a standard representation agreement, comply with certain limits on compensation for contractual negotiations, and attend periodic training seminars. Fines, suspensions, and/or revocations of licenses are among the penalties imposed for noncompliance.

Despite the program's intent to protect athletes from agent incompetence and corruption, several problems still persisted. First, the program, in its original form, did not address the corruption occurring in intercollegiate athletics. Only agents representing current NFL players were covered. Alerted to the potential for agent abuse of athletes who had yet to sign their first NFL contract, the program was amended to prohibit agents from communicating with a college football player who is ineligible to be drafted, including a player who has applied for early eligibility, until his name appears on the NFL's official list of draft-eligible players. Second, the plan was limited in scope. The plan regulated only "contract advisors" of NFL players, and its rules prohibited the charging of excessive fees for only contract negotiation and money-handling services. Agents providing other services could charge excessive fees and effectively evade the plan's restrictions (Dunn, 1988). Third, the plan was devoid of any specific criteria for granting or denying agent certification.

Since 1998, however, the NFLPA, by trying to enforce higher standards, has taken a more active role in policing agents. The union has rolled back the maximum percentage that agents can charge players to negotiate a contract from 4 percent to 3 percent (Freeman, 1998). In 1999, concerned about the quality of the agents representing its players, the NFLPA started testing anyone who registers to become a NFL player's agent. The test covered such areas as the collective bargaining agreement, salary cap issues, and free agency. Any agent who fails the test will not be certified (Freeman, 1998). The NFLPA also requires current agents to pass a testyearly. If the agent fails the exam, his or her certification is suspended until he or she passes the test. Under the CBA, NFL teams are prohibited from engaging in individual contract negotiations with any agent who has not been certified by the NFLPA. If a team does negotiate a contract with a non-certified agent, the Commissioner is obligated to reject the contract and impose a fine of $30,000 upon the Club.

In 1985, the Major League Baseball Players' Association (MLBPA) became the next union to adopt an agent certification plan. The National Basketball Players' Association (NBPA) followed the MLBPA in 1986, when it adopted its agent certification plan. The National Hockey League (NHL), which was the last union to start regulating agents, joined the other major sports leagues in 1996 when it drafted its agent certification program (Couch, 2000). In November 2004, Major League Soccer (MLS) and the MLS Players Union included language in their collective bargaining agreement that allows the union to develop and implement an agent certification program. However, at the present time, no such program exists.

The general scheme in professional sports leagues is that only those agents registered with the unions can negotiate on behalf of the players. The unions also require annual registration and fees, annual attendance at seminars, a disciplinary system including an arbitration provision, and the ban on specific conflict of interest situations. Even with all the safeguards the unions have tried to build into their program, agents are still taking advantage of unsuspecting athletes. For example, in *Hillard and Taylor v. Black,* (2000) two NFL players, Issac Hilliard and Fred Taylor, sued their agent William "Tank" Black to recover over a million dollars. Hilliard and Taylor claimed that Black, who was licensed by the NFLPA as a Contract Advisor, perpetrated two major financial scams. First, Black obtained free stock in a company, which he then sold to Hilliard and some of his other clients for more than $ 1,000,000 dollars and deposited into his personal bank account. Second, Black persuaded Hilliard and Taylor, and other clients to invest approximately $ 8.4 million in a promissory notePonzi schemeby saying that the notes were safe and extremely lucrative. Taylor alone invested $3.4 million in the scheme. Black assured the players that he had no financial interest in the promissory notes; however, he retained 40 percent of the investment returns (*Hillard and Taylor v. Black,* 2000).

The American Bar Association (ABA)

While the ABA's Model Code of Professional Responsibility establishes standards of integrity and conduct for all attorneys, unfortunately, even though many sport agents are attorneys, the code has no effect on agents who are not lawyers. As a result, some commentators have argued that the best way to regulate sport agents would be to require that all agents are licensed attorneys (Evanoff, 2011 and Amoona, 2008). The benefit of such a requirement, they argue would be that athletes who believed they were cheated by an attorney agent would have more of a recourse than simply attempting to have an agent suspended from the league's union. Athletes cannot only sue his or her agent for malpractice, they can also report attorney agents to the state bar, and they could be disbarred for unethical behavior if necessary. The requirement that all agents be licensed to practice law would also protect athletes, by preventing agents who are not licensed to practice law from engaging in the unauthorized practice of law. In addition, requiring a law degree would establish a minimum educational requirement. Currently, there is no educational degree requirement. Finally, rather than taking two to four percentage of a player's contract, attorney agents treat athletes like all other clients and charge them an hourly-fee basis (Amoona, 2008). Tim Duncan, *Shane Battier*, Ray Allen, *Tamika Catchings* and Grant Hill all employ the Williams & Connolly Law Firm to negotiate their contracts. By charging the athletes on an hourly-fee basis rather than a percentage-of-income basis, the firm claims that it can save its athletes hundreds of thousands, if not millions, of dollars over the course of a professional career. For example, when Grant Hill signed his first contract, a six-year, $ 45 million dollar deal with the Detroit Pistons, Hill paid a reported $ 100,000 fee. If Hill would have been represented by an agent, the deal would have cost Hill approximately $ 1.8 million dollars (Amoona, 2008).

Requiring all sports agents to be attorneys does pose a couple of problems however. First, such a requirement would surely be challenged under antitrust law as a restraint of trade. Second, such a requirement would require agents to pass multiple bar exams.

Financial Advisors

In addition to negotiating contracts, a number of agents and their firms act as financial advisor to their clients. In 2002, the National Football League Players Association (NFLPA) became the first sports union to establish regulations governing financial advisor to players. The voluntary program attempts to pre-select and qualify financial advisors for services to NFL players (Yasser, McCurdy, Goplerud & Weston, 2011). To be eligible for the NFLPA's Financial Advisors Program, which is a voluntary program;financial advisors must apply to the NFLPA and submit to annual background checks, developed in conjunction with the Securities and Exchange Commission.

In *Atwater v. The National Football League Players Association*, (2010) several current and former NFL players who had invested with Kirk Wright, a financial advisor approved by the NFLPA sued the NFL and the NFLPA after Wright defrauded the players of around $20 million. The players argued that they would not have invested money with Wright had the NFL and the NFLPA given them accurate information about Wright. More specifically, the players argued that the NFLPA listed Wright with the NFLPA's Financial Advisors Program without first conducting a proper investigation. As for the NFL, Plaintiffs asserted that several Plaintiffs requested, and the NFL provided an inadequate background check on Wright.

In rejecting the players' argument, the Eleventh Circuit Court of Appeals pointed to the disclaimer in the Financial Advisors Program that stated:

"The parties will use best efforts to establish an in-depth, comprehensive Career Planning Program. The purpose of the program will be to help players enhance their career in the NFL and make a smooth transition to a second career. The program will also provide information to players on handling their personal finances, it being understood that players shall be solely responsible for their personal finances" (*Atwater v. The National Football League Players Association,* 2010).

The only recourse for the players therefore was to try and recover their money from Wright. Wright was eventually convicted on 47 counts of mail fraud, securities fraud, and money laundering and faced up to 710 years and $16 million in fines. However, before he could be sentenced, Wright killed himself in prison(Tierney, 2008).

 # SIGNIFICANT CASE

The following case examines the fiduciary duty between an agent to his or her client, and when he or she breaches that duty by failing to disclose material facts that may influence the athlete's contract negotiation.

DETROIT LIONS AND BILLY SIMMS V. JERRY ARGOVITZ
United States Court of Appeals for the Sixth Circuit
767 F.2d 919 (6th Cir. 1985)

This is a cross-appeal from a judgment by which the district court rescinded a contract to play football executed between Billy Sims and the Houston Gamblers, a United States Football League (USFL) franchise. The district court found that the contract resulted from an unconscionable breach of a fiduciary duty by Sim's [Simm's] agent Jerry Argovitz, who was also partial owner of the Houston Gamblers. On this appeal, Argovitz assigns numerous errors in the district court's finding of fact. The Detroit Lions and Sims primarily appeal the district court's denial of two motions to amend their complaints. Upon review of the issues before us, we affirm the district court's rescission of the contract and remand the case for consideration by the district court of two motions to amend the Detroit Lions' and Billy Sims' [Simms'] complaints.

In 1980 the Detroit Lions, a National Football League franchise, drafted Sims and signed him to a four year contract that expired on February 1, 1984. Argovitz entered into an agency agreement with Sims early in 1980 and counseled him on numerous matters. Sims and Argovitz developed a confidential relationship in which, Argovitz testified, Sims looked up to him like a father. Sims sought Argovitz's advice on significant professional, financial, and personal matters.

From April 1982 through June 1983, Argovitz negotiated with the Lions for a renewed contract with Sims. On

May 5, 1983, Argovitz announced at a press conference that his application for what became the Gambler's franchise had been approved. Sims was present at the press conference. The district court found that Argovitz manipulated Sims' contract negotiations with the Lions during the spring of 1983 in light of Argovitz's own interest in the Gamblers. The court also found that Argovitz misrepresented the negotiations with the Lions as not progressing when in fact they were progressing well. Sims received information on the Lions' negotiations only from Argovitz, the court found. During May or June, 1983, Argovitz decided to seek a contract for Sims with the Gamblers. On June 29, 1983, Sims arrived in Houston, believing that the Lions were not negotiating in good faith and were not really interested in his services. On June 30, 1983 the Gamblers offered Sims a $3.5 million, five year contract that included nonmonetary fringe benefits Sims valued greatly. Argovitz told Sims that he thought the Lions would match the Gamblers' financial package and offered to telephone them. Although Sims told Argovitz not to call the Lions, the district court found that to have two teams bidding for a single athlete is "the dream of every agent," and that Argovitz breached his fiduciary duty to Sims by not following the common practice described by both expert witnesses of informing the Lions of the Gamblers' offer. On the afternoon of June 30, while negotiations were proceeding, the Lions' attorney called Argovitz. Argovitz was present at his office, but declined to accept the call. Argovitz attempted to return the call only after 5:00 p.m., when the Lions' attorney had left for the July 4th weekend. The district court found these actions to further breach Argovitz's fiduciary duty towards Sims. Argovitz then left for the holiday weekend. The next day, July 1, 1983, Sims signed an exclusive contract with the Gamblers.

In July 1983, uninformed by anyone of these events, the Lions sent Sims a further offer through Argovitz. On November 12, 1983, at Argovitz's instigation, Sims met with him and reexecuted the Gamblers' contract. Sims also signed a waiver of any claim he might have against Argovitz. Although at this time Argovitz had sold his agency business and no longer represented Sims, Argovitz did not inform Sims' new agent of his intention to have Sims sign a waiver. Nor did Argovitz, despite his fiduciary relationship with Sims, advise Sims to seek independent advice before signing the waiver. On December 16, 1983, Sims executed a second exclusive contract with the Lions for $1 million more than his Gamblers' contract.

On December 18, 1983, the Lions and Sims brought this suit in Michigan state court against Argovitz and the Gamblers seeking rescission of the Gamblers' contract with Sims. After an evidentiary hearing, the district court found that it had subject matter jurisdiction on the basis of complete diversity of citizenship. Argovitz and the Gamblers challenge this finding on the ground that Sims' domicile was Texas, and complete diversity is lacking. A person's domicile determines his citizenship for diversity purposes. *Kaiser v. Loomis,* 391 F.2d 1007, 1009 (6th Cir. 1968). The location of a person's domicile at any given time is a question of intent: what is the fixed location to which he intends to return when he is elsewhere? *Mas v. Perry,* 489 F.2d 1396, 1399 (5th Cir.), cert. denied, 419 U.S. 842 (1974). As such, determination of domicile is primarily a question of fact, that will not be reversed unless clearly erroneous. *Holmes v. Sopuch,* 639 F.2d 431, 434 (8th Cir. 1981) (Per Curiam). See also *Hawes v. Chub Ecuestre El Comandante,* 598 F.2d 698, 702 (1st Cir. 1979). The relevant time at which to determine citizenship and one's intent to remain domiciled in a given state is the time suit is filed. *Napletana v. Hillsdale College,* 385 F.2d 871, 872 (6th Cir. 1967). During the four years preceding this controversy Sims was employed in Michigan, owned and resided in a home there. He also owned a ranch in Hooks, Texas. No evidence emphasized by the appellants establishes a definite and firm conviction in our minds that the district court erred when it found that Sims' domicile was Michigan at the time of this suit. Argovitz and the Gamblers simply ask this court to reweigh the evidence on a cold record.

The district court found that it had personal jurisdiction over Argovitz individually and over the numerous partnerships and corporations that he represented as an agent. Michigan's long arm statutes provide for personal jurisdiction over individuals, partnerships, and corporations that transact business in the state. See M.C.L.A. §§ 600.701, 600.721, 600.725, 600.715. The goal of Michigan's jurisdictional statutes is to reach "the outer limits of personal jurisdiction consistent with due process." *Speckine v. Stanwick International, Inc.,* 503 F. Supp. 1055, 1057 (W.D. Mich. 1980). Due Process requires "certain minimum contacts with [the state] such that the maintenance of the suit does not offend 'traditional notions of fair play and substantial justice.'" *International Shoe Co. v. Washington,* 326 U.S. 310, 316 (1945) (quoting *Milliken v. Meyer,* 311 U.S. 457, 463 (1940)). *UnderHanson v. Denckla,* 357 U.S. 235 (1958), the defendants must have availed themselves of the privilege of conducting business in the forum state. Most recently the Supreme Court has emphasized foreseeability as critical: "the defendant's conduct and connection with the forum State are such that he should reasonably anticipate being hauled into court there." *World-Wide Volkswagen Corp. v. Woodson,* 444 U.S. 286, 297 (1980). Argovitz had conducted business in Michigan for over three years as the agent of Sims, a Michigan citizen. He was acting on behalf of his player representative organizations in doing so. The Houston Gamblers defendants contracted with Billy Sims as an attraction for their football team, which planned to use his contracted services in football games conducted in Michigan under USFL auspices and contracts. The contract between Billy Sims and the Gamblers was negotiated and signed in Texas, but it certainly was to be performed in part in Michigan. The district court was not in error.

The district court granted rescission of the contract between the Gamblers and Sims because it found that Argovitz had breached his fiduciary duty as Sims' agent and confidant. It is uncontested that Argovitz had a personal interest in Sims contracting with the Gamblers, who as a new team in a new football league would greatly benefit from the star attraction of a player of Sims' caliber. Argovitz's self-dealing arose from this conflict with his fiduciary duty to advance Sims' best interests.

As the district court found, under Texas law, where an agent has an interest adverse to that of his principal in a transaction in which he purports to act on behalf of his principal, the transaction is voidable by the principal unless the agent disclosed all material facts within his knowledge that might affect the principal's judgment. *Burleson v. Earnest,* 153 S.W.2d 869, 874–75 (Tex. Civ. App. 1941). This remains true even if the contract is fair. Id. The district court found as a matter of fact that "[a]t no time prior to December 1, 1983, was Sims aware" of all material facts regarding Argovitz's involvement with the Gamblers and Argovitz's failure to pursue Sims' interests in negotiations with the Lions. Argovitz accepts the legal standard as defined by the district court. He maintains that he satisfied his duty of disclosure simply by telling Sims that he was partial owner of the Gamblers and by telling Sims that the Lions would match the financial elements of the Gamblers' offer. A review of the facts as found by the district court reveals that these are but a few of the material disclosures that Argovitz should have made. The district court was not clearly erroneous.

Argovitz maintains that rescission of the contract, an equitable remedy, is improper for a number of reasons having to do with Sims' behavior during 1983. The key to these issues is that the district court found as a matter of fact that Sims was not aware of all material imformation [information] concerning his contract with the Gamblers until at least December 1983. Argovitz and the Gamblers do not point to evidence of behavior by Sims that would render the district court's factual findings clearly erroneous.

The district court denied the Lions' and Sims' motions to amend their complaints without explanation, and in one case without making an explicit ruling. Such action represents an abuse of discretion under *Foman v. Davis*, 371 U.S. 178, 182 (1962). See also *Gootee v. Colt Industries, Inc.*, 712 F.2d 1057, 1065 n.7 (6th Cir. 1983). The district court should reconsider the motions to amend in light of the standards of Foman, which looks to considerations such as undue delay, bad faith, and futility of the amendment. Id. If, on remand, the district court denies leave to amend, it should state its reasons for doing so.

Therefore, the district court's rescission of the contract between Billy Sims and the Houston Gamblers is AFFIRMED. The matter is REMANDED for consideration of the motions to amend the Lions' and Sims' complaints.

CASES ON THE SUPPLEMENTAL WEB SITE

Brown v. Woolf, 554 F.Supp. 1206 (1983). The case looks at the fiduciary relationship between players and their agents.

Hillard and Taylor v. Black, 125 F. Supp. 2d 1071 (2000). The case looks at the fiduciary relationship between players and their agents and the agents' obligation to disclose certain facts.

Smith v. IMG Worldwide, Inc., 2006 U.S. Dist. LEXIS 82566. This case examines the recruitment of athletes, and when what agents can say about another firm or agent.

Steinberg Moorad & Dunn, Inc. v. Dunn, 2002 U.S. Dist. LEXIS 26752. This case examines the fiduciary duty between agents and their firm.

United States of America v. Piggie, 303 F.3d 923 (8th Cir. 2002). The case looks at whether secretly paying high school athletes in violation of NCAA rules and then falsely certifying that they had not previously received payments, was a violation of criminal law.

QUESTIONS YOU SHOULD BE ABLE TO ANSWER

1. What were some of the events that brought about the need for professional sports agents?

2. What was the first state to pass legislation regulating sport agents?

3. What are some of the benefits of the Uniform Athlete Agents Act (UAAA)?

4. What are some of the negatives of the Uniform Athlete Agents Act (UAAA)?

5. What role should the professional sports leagues and their unions play in regulating an agent's relationship with college athletes?

REFERENCES

Cases

Atwater v. The National Football League Players Association, 626 F.3d 1170 (11th Cir., 2010)
Detroit Lions, Inc. v. Argovitz, 580 F.Supp. 542 (1984).
Hillard and Taylor v. Black, 125 F. Supp. 2d 1071 (2000).
United States v. Norby Walters, 997 F.2d 1219 (7th Cir. 1993).

Publications

Amoona, J. (2008). Top Pick: Why A Licensed Attorney Acting as a Sports Agent Is a "Can't Miss" Prospect. Georgetown Journal of Legal Ethics Georgetown Journal of Legal Ethics, 21, 599 – 613.

Couch, B. (2000). How agent competition and corruption affects sports and the athlete-agent relationship and what can be done to control it. *Seton Hall Journal of Sport Law, 10,* 111–137.

Dunn, D. (1988). Regulation of sports agents: Since at first it hasn't succeeded, try federal legislation. *TheHastings Law Journal, 39,* 1031–1078.

Evanoff, C. (2011). Show me the Money: How the Model *Rules of Professional Conduct* Can Deter NCAA Rules Violations Involving Sports Agents & College Athletes. *DePaul Journal of Sports Law & Contemporary Problems*, 8, 63 - 93.

Fluhr, P. (1999). The regulation of sports agents and the quest for uniformity. *Sports Lawyers Journal, 6,*1–25.

Freeman, M. (1998, July 26). Protecting players from their agents: Misconduct leaves N.F.L. Union fearful of incompetence and greed. *The New York Times*, sec. 8, p. 1, col. 1.

NCAA Constitution, Bylaw 12.3 NCAA Manual (2011–12).

Shropshire, K., & Davis, T. (2008). *The business of sport agents* (2nd ed.). Philadelphia, Pa: University of Pennsylvania Press.

Tierney, M. (2008, June 2). *After Financier's Death, Suit against Union Lives On*. The New York Times, p. D 3.

Yasser, R., McCurdy, J., Goplerud P., & Weston, M. (2011). Sports Law: Cases and Materials (7th. Ed.). New Providence, NJ: LexisNexis

Legislation

Sports Agent Responsibility and Trust Act, 15 U.S.C. 7801 *et seq.*
Arkansas Statute Chapter 16, subchapter 1
Oklahoma Statute 70 O.S. 821
Texas Statute Chapter 2051, subchapter A

Websites

http://www.ncaa.org/wps/wcm/connect/public/NCAA/Resources/Uniform+Athlete+Agents+Act+Homepage. Retrieved 7/7/12

CASE INDEX

SUBJECT INDEX